FINE ART

Identification and Price Guide

THIRD EDITION

FINE ART

Identification and Price Guide
THIRD EDITION

SUSAN THERAN

The CONFIDENT COLLECTOR™

AVON BOOKS ◆ NEW YORK

THE CONFIDENT COLLECTOR: FINE ART IDENTIFICATION AND PRICE GUIDE (3rd edition) is an original publication of Avon Books. This edition has never before appeared in book form.

AVON BOOKS, INC.
1350 Avenue of the Americas
New York, New York 10019

Third Edition copyright © 1996 by Auction Index, Inc.
Cover Photograph: The reproduction on the front cover is entitled *October* by James Jacques Joseph Tissot, oil on canvas, courtesy 1995 Sotheby's, Inc.
The *Confident Collector* and its logo are trademarked properties of Avon Books.
Published by arrangement with the author
Library of Congress Catalog Card Number: 96-96187
ISBN: 0-380-78780-6
www.avonbooks.com

First Avon Books Trade Paperback Printing: November 1996

AVON TRADEMARK REG. U.S. PAT. OFF. AND IN OTHER COUNTRIES, MARCA REGISTRADA, HECHO EN U.S.A.

Printed in the U.S.A.

QPM 10 9 8 7 6 5 4 3

*Dedicated
to my mother
Esta Fargotstein*

Acknowledgments

There are due many thanks to the people who have helped this book come into being . . .

- to Lisa Considine, my editor at Avon Books.
- to the art experts who were so generous with their time: Kathryn Carey, Peter Williams, Tony Fusco, and Bob Four, and especially to my friend Dr. Norma Steinberg for her time and knowledge.
- to the many libraries and museums throughout the country that provided their services and information, and most especially to the librarians at the Boston Public Library's Fine Arts Department: Jan Chadbourne, Evelyn Lannon, Kathleen Mesvaros, and Kim Tenney, for their ongoing help and support; and to Eleanor Hernon, reference librarian at the Newton Public Library.
- to Victor Smith of Datatech, without whose programs and expertise this book would not have been possible.
- to Sheldon Fogelman, Esquire, for his, as always, superb advice.
- to my staff, who worked so tirelessly compiling the database and photographs and researching artists: Kristin Dalton, Andrea Des Jardins, Paula Jacoff, Michelle Hartog, and Peggy McDonald.
- to my friends: Maria Danziger for listening to my captions, Eliot Schein for being there in a pinch, and a special thank-you to Alice and Marty Cooper for fifteen years of providing a roof and bed on my trips to New York.
- and most of all, to my daughters, Sally and Rachel.

Auction House Acknowledgments

Special appreciation and thanks to the many auction houses that provide catalogs and prices in a timely manner for the Auction Index database. All of these are listed in Appendix C.

And a special thank-you to the auction houses that so generously provided the photographs and some of the stories behind the captions. They are Sanford Alderfer Auction Center, Altermann & Morris Gallery, James R. Bakker Galleries, Barridoff Galleries, Bider's Auction Gallery, Frank H. Boos Gallery, William Bunch Auction, Butterfield & Butterfield, Caddigan Auctioneers, Christie's New York, Clearing House Auction Galleries, Inc., Dargate Galleries, William Doyle Galleries, Freeman/Fine Arts, Garth's Auctions, Morton M. Goldberg Galleries, Grogan & Company, Hanzel Galleries, Willis Henry Auctions, Leslie Hindman Auctioneers, Illustration House, Inc., James D. Julia, Frank C. Kaminski Co., Louisiana Auction Exchange, Mapes, John Moran Auctioneers, Myers Antiques & Auction Gallery, Neal Auction Company, O'Gallerie Inc., D & J Ritchie Inc., Royal York Auction Gallery, Selkirk's, Skinner's Inc., Sotheby's Inc., Swann Galleries, Kenneth Van Blarcom, Adam A. Weschler & Son, Gustave J. S. White Auctioneers, and Young Fine Arts Gallery.

Table of Contents ────────────────────

FINE ART

Identification and Price Guide

THIRD EDITION

Introduction

When paintings by Picasso, Matisse, and van Gogh sell for millions of dollars, it makes news and draws worldwide attention. The media hype that accompanies mega-sales in the art auction world obscures one vitally important fact—for every million-dollar painting, there are thousands of works by recognized artists that sell for considerably less than $10,000. In fact, in the past fifteen years 40 percent of all the art sold at auction in the United States went for less than $1,000, and 30 percent sold in the $1,000-$5,000 range.

Finding, buying, and collecting art—whether paintings, sculpture, or photographs—has become a compelling interest for thousands of people, and for good reason. They have been caught up in an extraordinary adventure, filled with excitement, learning, the thrill of the chase, possible disappointment, and, very often, success!

Collecting art encompasses everything from an occasional visit to a flea market to a concerted, focused, meticulously prepared search. How you collect depends on you. There are no rules but your own.

The passionate impulse to collect that led to the two volumes of this book, covering the prices of art at auction in America from 1980–1985 and from 1986–1990, remains. An important section has been added with "Works on Paper."

This volume includes prices published in *Leonard's ANNUAL Price Index* from September 1990–August 1995. Sixty percent of the listed artists were not included in the first two volumes because their work was not sold at auction during that time. Conversely, 60 percent of the artists whose sales records appeared in the first two volumes have not sold in the past five years, and are not included here. For complete coverage, you would be wise to peruse both the first and the second editions of this price guide.[1]

The art market keeps changing. It has become more sophisticated and competitive at every level. Now, more than ever, the well-informed buyer has the edge. Good luck as you use this book to find and buy the works you are seeking.

Look Before You Leap

You've probably already taken many of the first steps that culminate in collecting. Most of us begin to develop an interest in fine art by visiting museums. There is no better place to start—the phrase "museum quality"

---

[1] The first edition, *The Official Price Guide to Fine Art*, is out of print but may be obtained from a rare-book dealer. There are limited copies available of the second edition, *The Confident Collector Fine Art Identification and Price Guide*.

denotes the highest standard of workmanship. Museums with extensive collections provide exposure to an encyclopedic variety of styles and artistic media. Smaller museums, especially those with specialized collections, provide an opportunity to study a particular aspect of art in depth.

In every case, museum going will help you develop your own eye for quality. Examine the individual works carefully. Analyze their composition. How does the artist lead you into the work? Are you made to focus on the foreground and then drawn further back? Are you led immediately to a particular point on the canvas? What are the primary lines of composition? How are light and shadow achieved? What did the artist set out to accomplish? Does the painting tell a story? If it is a portrait, does it convey personality? It is the ability of paintings to spark these questions that contributes to their quality. Your ability to respond to them is an indication of your growing understanding of what quality means in art.

At the same time, you will be sharpening your taste and defining your preferences. Is your eye drawn to particular subjects? Do you like still lifes? Landscapes? Animals? Domestic interiors? Abstract shapes? Do you prefer specific color ranges? Do you like looking at pictures of activities you enjoy? What kinds of artistic media attract you? Do you like chalk, pencil, watercolor? Do you like finished paintings, or do you prefer oil sketches? A few leisurely afternoons in a museum will help you make such determinations.

Galleries offer a way of learning about the works of individual artists. Owners are generally knowledgeable and most have chosen to sell art because they love it. Keep in mind, however, that galleries are governed by the realities of the marketplace. Many, but by no means all, are willing to take the time to help educate potential customers and share their often specialized and unique information. Most collectors agree that the very best galleries are the ones which will take the time to educate, confident that their investment in time will ultimately show a return in sales.

Classes, courses, lectures, and workshops offered by museums and historical societies afford additional opportunities to learn. Frequently, individual lectures are planned to coincide with annual or semiannual exhibits and shows. Since smaller institutions often cannot afford to advertise, you will have to call for information or watch local newspaper "calendars" for announcements.

Above all, you must read—art books, magazines, exhibition catalogs, and auction catalogs. When, after conscientious museum going and gallery visits, you determine you are seriously interested in, for example, the Connecticut Impressionists, and want to begin collecting this late-19th- to early-20th-century group, your next stop is the library. Who were the Connecticut Impressionists? In what part of the state did they paint? Who was associated with the movement? By doing your own research, you'll pull together the bits of information gleaned from museum labels and dealers, and begin to assemble a composite body of data. You don't need to be an expert before you begin to buy art—the learning process is continuous. If you're like most collectors, once you've been drawn into a subject, you'll want to learn more and more.

Thorough knowledge and study lay the groundwork for serious collecting. Anyone who builds a valuable collection has worked hard, studying and learning.

Developing Your Taste

The best way to begin is by buying.

Buy what you can afford. Buy in little shops. Buy in junk shops. Buy in antique shops, flea markets, and at low-priced auctions. But buy!

Nothing else shapes your eye so quickly. Nothing sharpens your taste like making a purchase. In making a financial commitment, you make a statement of your likes and dislikes. It is a process subject to constant refinement.

What catches your eye?

Will the first item in your collection be a scene that you recognize, something that evokes a feeling or memory which you want to preserve? For many people, collecting starts with something very specific that is tied to a strong personal interest and then extends and develops. Many real or armchair sailors collect maritime scenes. Gardeners often are drawn to pictures of flowers. Mountain scenes are popular with many collectors.

Discovering what you really like is akin to stripping paint from a piece of old furniture. As you work through to the essence of your taste, you will reveal successive layers of appreciation for different types of work. In the process, you will refine your taste—and you may end up selling some of your early acquisitions.

But begin by buying. Don't be afraid to make mistakes.

In the course of building a collection you will develop a consistent eye. That is, over time you will find everything you buy fits together. Buying will enable you to develop a sureness of taste, and the confidence of your own judgments.

Where to Buy Art

Buying art is somewhat less straightforward than buying a washing machine, but it's more absorbing and more fun. The sheer variety of places in which you can look, and the process of looking, are at once an education and an activity in themselves.

Yard Sales, Garage Sales, and Flea Markets

Yard sales, garage sales, and flea markets are a boon to weekend collectors. Someone we know who has a phenomenal memory for artists' names has been very successful (and very lucky) at turning up pictures that others have cleaned out of their attics. If your personal database is less complete, this book is a reliable substitute.

The first rule for getting to any of these sales is—be early. Most flea markets advertise in the classified section of local newspapers and list their hours. (Some open at dawn.) Often dealers will sell right out of their cars to early arrivals—even before they've had a chance to set up their displays. One word of caution—"early birds" aren't always welcome, particularly at garage sales. But it may be worth the risk of a chilly reception on the chance that you'll catch the proverbial worm.

Brimfield

A little rain, or a lot, doesn't deter an ardent Brimfield goer. These paintings weren't of the highest quality, but there were a lot of them!

At a flea market you'll find most old paintings and drawings in the antiques section. Check a map of the field when you arrive, since some markets divide dealers' merchandise into old and new, and you can waste a great deal of time trudging past racks of bubble gum and shoelaces before you find the right area. But don't overlook the "junk" area. Some of the best buys may be in the section reserved for sellers who have just cleaned out their attics or garages and don't know what they have.

Some flea markets are held regularly, even weekly. Others are occasional—sponsored by service groups, churches, or fraternal organizations.

The queen of the flea markets is held three times a year (May, July, and September) in Brimfield, Massachusetts. Thousands of dealers set up their displays on acres of fields for this event that attracts purchasers not only from the Northeast but from the entire nation and abroad. Some European dealers buy a year's stock of American antiques and paintings at Brimfield.

One veteran Brimfield connoisseur recommends arriving before dawn. The show opens at 5 A.M. and the line begins to form two hours earlier. "Carry a flashlight," she advises, so you can see what's displayed on the tables, and spot the dealers walking around carrying signs that read, "I buy penknives," or "I buy old cameras." Take the time to savor the unique character of this enormous show, which includes the spectacle of pairs of collectors or dealers who race from one display to the next, using walkie-talkies to announce finds to their partners.

Brimfield runs for a week—you may find the very best buys if you're there before first light, but good quality material is on sale all day long. Brimfield is a joy for collectors, and a good place for dealers as well. Many of them save unique pieces to bring to this market, which attracts thousands of sophisticated purchasers.

Atlantique

Searching for art can be fun and tiring! The world's largest indoor antique and collectibles show, advertised as covering over seven acres, is held in Atlantic City each October and March. The Atlantique City megashow houses over 1,200 dealers and has strategically placed computers that help you identify dealers by category. Although there are a large number of toys and collectibles, you can also find prints, paintings, and advertising art. In 1997, Atlantique City will be in the new convention center with more than 2,000 dealers.

Other noteworthy flea markets around the nation include the annual indoor event at the Atlantic City Convention Center conducted each October and March by the Brimfield Associates.

Remingers #1 Antique Market is a Pennsylvania institution. Held every Sunday year-round in Adamstown, this indoor/outdoor spectacular welcomes over 500 dealers each week in its indoor space. In good weather, hundreds more open their stands outdoors. Antiques and collectibles are the mainstay here.

Unbeknownst to most sports fans, the Pasadena Rose Bowl hosts a different sort of competition on the second Sunday of every month. At the Rose Bowl Flea Market and Swap Meet nearly anything is sold and bought by thousands of sellers and shoppers.

Flea markets and garage and yard sales are fun to go to, and great places to buy. They are good sources for watercolors, drawings . . . and fakes. Chances are strong that the painting you find signed "Picasso" isn't the work of Pablo. Even a name-plaque on the frame does not assure that a piece is actually the work of the designated artist. (You might, however, find an original of a more obscure artist.) Some prints, especially chromolithographs, closely resemble paintings. Also, some prints are painted over, closely following the original lines. They are often very difficult to detect. They turn up at places like Brimfield, but they occasionally also turn up at auction, and are sold as "painted by the artist who did the original work for the print."

When you decide to buy at a flea market, yard, or garage sale, examine the condition of the work carefully. Flea market merchandise is sold "as is." Usually it's helpful to ask where the work came from—that is, attic, basement, or Aunt Gertrude. Most sellers know something about what they're selling, and though there won't be a provenance (history) supplied for a picture at a yard sale, there may well be an interesting story attached to it. Some material could be "hot." Several years ago, a painting stolen from a New England historical society surfaced at a church flea market where it was purchased for under $100. The work was recognized when it was brought in for appraisal.

The rule of purchase at yard sales and flea markets is—make an offer. There is usually little science, knowledge, or reason for the price written on the tag. Be ready to negotiate.

One final note.

Don't go to any of these sales expecting to find a lost masterwork. When you buy, buy because you are drawn to the work, because it appeals to you, because it is consistent with the things you like and own, and because you can afford it.

Secondhand, Junk, and Consignment Stores, and Antique Shops

One step up from garage sales and flea markets (and sometimes a very short step indeed) is browser's paradise—secondhand, junk, and consignment shops. With growing numbers of people in the art market, there's more competitive shopping in these stores than before, but there are still finds. Often the owners of these emporia will pick up stray pictures or drawings in the process of acquiring an estate or cleaning out a garage or attic. Art may be almost hidden in many of these stores. Ask if there are any pictures. Look under tables and behind furniture.

Antique stores are another good source. It's hard to be knowledgeable about everything. Store owners may be expert about furniture but unaware of the value of a picture they have bought. They may have purchased a picture in order to acquire an entire estate and be willing to sell at minimal profit to move it, because they specialize in another field.

Wherever you are, look for frames. Good period frames are hard to find.

In fact, there are now auctions just for frames![2] Even if you don't like the picture, the frame may be just what you need for your picture at home.

Dealing with Dealers

A first trip to a big-city gallery can be intimidating. The imposing front entrance and glacial sales staff can combine to keep beginning collectors at a distance. Yet the same people won't hesitate for a second to get out of the car at a country antiques store and ask if there are any pictures in the back room. It's a mistake to assume that a country dealer in a flannel shirt is any less knowledgeable about value and quality than his Madison Avenue or Newbury Street counterpart, or that his prices will be lower. The overhead will be higher in the city, and that will affect prices, but a higher turnover may enable a city gallery to work on a lower profit margin.

Some collectors who are just starting out may hesitate to visit dealers, for they're convinced this is the most expensive way to purchase, or concerned that they'll be pushed into something they really don't want. Others wouldn't begin to look for a work of art without the guidance of a professional.

If, in fact, you end up developing a very serious interest in collecting, you'll become an expert in the area that interests you. When you walk into a tiny up-country store and spot a small dirty canvas that looks promising, you'll have the knowledge you need to examine it carefully and decide if you want to add it to your collection.

Should that happen when you're just starting out and it's a small purchase, go ahead and buy it. As long as the work really appeals to you, there's no such thing as a $150 error. But imagine a different scenario in which the price tag is substantially higher and you really don't know whether the work is fairly priced, or even authentic. (Of course, you'll have this book in hand, and that will give you confidence and credibility if you decide to negotiate the price.) That's a compelling reason for making major purchases from dealers. Until, and even when, you develop your own store of knowledge, they are the professionals.

A good dealer knows an artist's work and style, can authenticate it, and can recognize whether it has been altered. Experienced dealers know a lot about the process of making art, and about the scholarly and technical aspects of art history.

There were, for example, artists who painted the major elements of pictures, and then turned to apprentices to fill in the rest. Works completed during certain periods of an artist's life are worth more than others. There are nuances to a painting which will change its value. If there's a glass in a still life by an artist who didn't usually paint glass, the work is more valuable. If the artist worked in a realistic style during much of his career but later became more impressionistic, the pictures from different periods will have differing values. If, in a particular picture, an artist introduced an element which later became characteristic of his work, the picture will have special

---

[2] Eli Wilner's *Antique American Frames*, published by Avon Books in 1995, is an excellent place to begin your research.

or added value. Some artists chose not to sign their canvases, or signed them on the back so that they didn't disturb the aesthetic balance of the work. This is the type of specialized information for which you will turn to a dealer.

In addition to being a storehouse of knowledge, a dealer can be extremely helpful in locating the kind of work you find most appealing, particularly if your taste is very specialized. Once you've developed a relationship with a dealer, he or she will buy with you in mind and be able to sell to you with a lower markup because there will be a quicker turnover. An ongoing relationship with a reputable dealer is a good way to assure access to quality work. Every serious collector has a good working relationship with at least a few dealers. It's true that you may pay more when you buy from a dealer than you might at an auction, but you're paying for knowledge and time.

Note, too, that most dealers will generally not sell a painting unless it has been cleaned and, if needed, restored by a competent professional restorer. This can save both time and money for a collector.

The key question is, how do you find a dealer with whom you'll be comfortable? There are literally hundreds of galleries, shops, and dealers in most areas. Consult the *Art in America Gallery Guide*, available on newsstands in August and in many libraries. In larger cities you can begin by looking through the Yellow Pages, the gallery listings in newspapers and magazines, weekly calendar supplements, and even guidebooks. In smaller areas where galleries are dispersed, dealers often form regional associations and publish a listing of members and a map showing their locations. These are available in the stores, or at local, state-sponsored tourist information centers.

Galleries may specialize. Visit as many as you can until you find those dealers whose taste is very much like your own, and begin to cultivate a working relationship. Put your name on the mailing list so that you will be invited to previews and kept informed about publications.

Networking and talking with other collectors is essential. Talk to people at auctions. You may get to discover dealers you'd never meet otherwise because they don't generally sell to the public.

Terms

The term *dealer* covers such a broad range of operations that it will be useful to distinguish among the various types who operate at all different levels of the art market. On the very first rung of the ladder are *pickers*, people with a good eye, developed taste, and eternal optimism. They scour flea markets, yard sales, and country auctions, always on the lookout for the underpriced, unrecognized "find." Pickers have established relationships with lawyers representing estates, dealers, galleries, and individual collectors. They buy and sell to their contacts.

Then there are *door knockers*. The name says it all. Door knockers are a variety of picker who go door-to-door in search of old paintings, rugs, and furniture to resell to dealers or through auction houses.

Runners are the matchmakers, the link between dealers, or dealers and collectors. A very few who work the upper end of the market are essentially private dealers who make a handsome commission on costly works of art. Most live a far less glamorous existence, moving individual pieces from one dealer to the next, hoping to make a quick sale and a small profit. *Brokers*

are a more elite version of runners, often relying on a large circle of acquaint-
ances to keep up-to-date about what's for sale and who might be looking.
Brokers never actually own any work (although they may take a piece on
consignment). They direct their energies instead to bringing buyer and seller
together.

Wholesalers don't maintain a retail space, but work directly with galleries
rather than individual collectors.

Collector dealers start as collectors, but become so involved with their interest that they sell parts of their collections in order to "feed their habits" and
upgrade or diversify their holdings.

Strategies

The term *dealer*, as it is usually used, means an individual who owns and
runs a shop or gallery. But the word is so inclusive that it covers everything
from an exquisitely decorated, world-famous gallery which commands instant name recognition to the tiniest, most crowded, backstreet junk store.

But . . . the range of dealers really runs the gamut from part-time entrepre-
neurs who do business out of the trunks of their cars, on up. Some limit
their activities and participate only in shows. Some will see clients only by
appointment.

With this variety, it is clear that no single strategy of dealing with dealers
will work in all situations. What follows is the composite of advice from a
number of dealers, collectors, and personal experience.

On your first visit to a dealer or gallery, you should make your interests
and intentions clear. Establish yourself. Let the owner or salesperson know
why you've come in. Are you there to learn or to buy? Do you know what
you like? (This can be a particularly important question if you're in a major
gallery. Some have enormous inventories, literally hundreds of paintings.
It's no time to start trying to define your taste.)

Are you buying for visual and aesthetic pleasure? Are you buying for
decoration—a blue painting to hang over the sofa? Or are you buying for
investment?

Know what your price range is, and state it, but don't be afraid to look
at things you can't afford. Consider it another step in honing your eye and
developing your own standards of taste by correlating quality and price.

Authenticity

Ask the dealer to show you a painting in a darkened room under a black
light, an uncomplicated ultraviolet light which, when it shines on the canvas,
will reveal inpainting and overpainting. The former is the precise repainting
of a damaged area; the latter, the addition of too much new paint which
alters the appearance of the work. Particularly in an older work, a certain
amount of restoration is acceptable, and perhaps even desirable. A hundred-
year-old painting can show some signs of wear around the edges. A skilled
restorer can repair it, filling in the missing spots, enhancing the painting's
appearance, and increasing its value. Inpainting is an absolute necessity
when a torn or punctured canvas is repaired.

It's when the restorer's skill is abused and a painting is significantly changed from its original form that inpainting becomes a problem. Among the long list of items that can be added to a painting to make it seem more attractive are: parasols, balloons, American flags, baby carriages, little dogs, long white dresses, flowers, pretty women tending gardens or interiors, butterflies, and last, but by no means least, signatures and dates. It is to discover these abuses that a black light is used.

Under a black light, it's easy to detect changes that would otherwise be impossible to see. Paint that is only a few months or years old looks different from paint applied a century ago. Inpainting will fluoresce under a black light. However, some 20th-century pigments will always fluoresce. Surface cracks and other irregularities, changes in composition and color, also become dramatically apparent. Some new techniques, however, do not show up under a black light. If you are buying at auction, some auction houses may give you a "condition" report before the sale.

Thus, if you've found a painting you like, ask to see it under a black light. In fact, a reputable dealer will be eager to show a canvas under a black light and quick to point out any alterations in the surface. If, however, he or she is reluctant to have the painting subjected to such scrutiny, you ought to look for another painting . . . and another dealer. (If you would like to buy your own black light, you can probably find one in a novelty store for less than an art supply store will charge. They're popular with young people because they make fluorescent posters glow.)

If you're looking at paintings in a less formal setting, it may be helpful to carry a magnifying glass so that you can closely examine the surface of the work. With the aid of a lens you can pick out an inscription or signature that would otherwise be difficult to see. You may also be able to tell if a signature or anything else has been added over the varnish that covers the original work.

A final step before making a purchase is to ask to have the picture removed from the frame. If the work is old and hasn't been restored, the canvas shouldn't be taut. The surface of the painting may show some *craquelure*, a web of tiny fine lines caused by the drying out of the canvas. When the canvas is out of the frame, you'll be able to see if the picture has been remounted—if the canvas has been tautened as a result of relining it with another canvas or a board. Ask the dealer why the work was relined. It may not affect the value of the painting, but it's something you should know. At the same time, you can see if the painting has been cropped, or even cut out of a larger work.

Provenance

Depending on the level at which you are buying, a painting may have a written provenance—a life history from the time it left the artist's easel to its arrival at the gallery—which includes the names of previous owners and the dates on which it changed hands. Obviously, the better known and more costly the painting, the likelier and more necessary the provenance. Not surprisingly, a provenance adds to the value of a painting. When *Portrait of Jackie Kennedy Onassis* by René Bouché sold at Sotheby's for $85,000 (est.

$800-$1,000), it was the cachet of a "Jackie O" provenance that caused the price to soar a hundredfold the auction house estimate.

To determine a provenance, you might begin by asking about the painting's history. If the dealer has the estate, he may have the artist's notebook, preliminary sketches for the work (very collectible), or other information. Has the work been in a catalog? Was it included in an exhibit? This may or may not be pertinent to a given work. Quite a number of very fine works have never been shown publicly, and thus, their formal records are short. Because dealers' connections in the art world may give them access to works before any private buyers get to see them, the picture you're looking at may have remained in the hands of a single owner or family and be new to the market. It may, for example, have been the gift of the artist to the grandfather of the present owner, or have some similar history.

A less expensive work may have no written history at all, just the statement of the dealer to the effect that "I bought it from the Smith estate up in Westfield." If you're looking at the work of a relative unknown, this is an acceptable response. The dealer may be able to fill you in on the family that owned the painting, the general nature of the estate, and the artist as well.

Negotiating a Price

While the price that a dealer quotes to you is not necessarily the one you'll end up paying, the issue of price negotiations raises questions, eyebrows, and sometimes tempers.

To negotiate or not to negotiate. Most dealers will insist that they won't. Many buyers will tell you they've tried and sometimes succeeded. If you're embarrassed, don't, but as a general rule of thumb, it's worth a try. Remember that if you can walk away from a potential purchase, there's a far greater chance of getting it at the price you're willing to pay than if you're caught up in the process and dead set on acquiring it.

The possibilities for negotiation depend very much upon the dealer, the gallery, the painting, and the realities of the marketplace. Galleries at prestigious addresses in major cities carry enormous overheads, which are necessarily reflected in the prices of the paintings they sell. There is generally a close relationship between the location and prestige of the gallery, the desirability of the painting, and the readiness of the customer to make an offer and the dealer to accept it. This is complicated by the length of time the picture has been in the dealer's possession, and last, but by no means least, by the percentage which it has been marked up.

In other words, if you want to buy a picture which has been in a gallery for only a week, the dealer is not likely to negotiate. If the picture is still on the wall when you come back six months later, it's much more likely that you'll find some flexibility in the price.

Of course, the whole question of negotiation depends upon whom you are talking to and where. We know one very genteel lady who successfully bargains at Cartier. While small, informal stores which carry a mix of paintings and other things seem to invite bargaining more than others, serious collectors will negotiate anywhere.

Remember, too, that when you question a price, you are at least in part asking why it has been set at a certain level. If it seems especially high, there may be a good reason for it—the work may have some unique quality. Keep in mind as well that some dealers will overprice, expecting to be negotiated down.

Dealers maintain that it is not in their own interest to overprice paintings, since most guarantee that they will take a work back in trade for at least the original price. Most dealers will add that they will not try to outbid an individual collector at auction, since they will later have to resell the painting.

Bear in mind, too, that prices in this *Guide* were achieved at auction, a market that is frequently considered wholesale. It is perfectly reasonable for the dealer who has spent time and money acquiring, and possibly restoring, the work to make a profit on it. Your readiness to make an offer, and the dealer's willingness to be somewhat flexible about pricing, will constitute the negotiation.

Bills of Sale

For major purchases, for purposes of insurance and recordkeeping, it is important to secure a bill of sale. You can be assured of the authenticity of a work of art if the dealer will write out and *sign* the sales slip to read:

"One oil, title, *by* Robert Smith, size, location of signature, and any other significant details."

If the slip reads: "One oil, *signed* Robert Smith," or "One oil, *inscribed* Robert Smith," or "One oil, *attributed to* Robert Smith," then the dealer is not liable should the painting turn out to be a forgery. You can be forceful, or you can be innocent and say that your sister the attorney insisted that you ask for that specific wording, but don't leave the gallery without it.

Methods of Payment

You may find a greater degree of flexibility in price if you can pay cash; however, most people find it more convenient to make major purchases by check.

If you do pay cash, be sure to save your sales slip, since it is the only proof you will have to present to an insurance company in the event of loss.

Some dealers will permit you to pay for a painting in installments, but unless you are a well-established customer, you should not expect to be able to take the work home until it is completely paid for. (However, if you offer to let the dealer keep the painting until you finish paying for it, he may let you take it home.)

Auctions

You don't need a course in assertiveness training to bid at an auction. Neither do you need to sit absolutely still while bidding goes on around you, lest an auctioneer mistake some motion as a hidden signal. Auctions are entertaining to attend, and a good way to purchase art.

Terms

As in all specialized fields, there are specific terms used in auctions which you must understand before you begin. The most important, listed alphabetically, are:

Auction. A sale in which the auctioneer, acting as the agent for sellers (called consignors), offers a series of objects to prospective buyers who bid incrementally. The highest bidder buys the object. The auctioneer always encourages bidding to try to get the highest price, since his payment is generally a percentage of the sale.

Bought-in (sometimes called passed or unsold). If a lot does not achieve its reserve (see page 14,) it is said to be bought-in by the auction house and will be returned to the consignor or be reoffered at a later sale. However, bear in mind that if, on its own momentum, bidding does not reach the reserve, the auction house will bid on behalf of the consignor against bids from the floor. Only if the work still does not reach its reserve is it bought-in. It's not always clear whether there's a reserve on an individual lot. A 1987 New York City law requires the house to announce the disposition of an unsold lot as passed, returned to owner, withdrawn, or bought-in. New York also requires that all lots with a reserve be marked with a black square or dot in the auction catalog.

Buyer's premium. At most auctions, a premium amounting to 10 to 15 percent of the hammer price is added to the cost of each item. Beginning in 1993, the major houses began to charge 15 percent on the first $50,000 and 10 percent thereafter. Most of the smaller auction houses still charge 10 percent, but at some, such as Alderfer's, there is still no buyer's premium. Sales tax is calculated on the total. An auctioneer who adds a buyer's premium will usually indicate this in advertisements or catalogs.

Catalog sale. An auction for which a printed listing of lots is prepared and distributed in advance. Catalogs can be mimeographed lists with brief descriptions or beautifully illustrated, carefully researched, book-length publications.

Consignor. The individual who has asked the auction house to sell a particular piece or pieces.

Estimate. The price range within which an auction house expects to sell a particular lot. The estimate is included in the printed catalog. Reserve is usually two-thirds of the low estimate. For more expensive lots, reserve is often close to the low estimate. At best, an estimate is the auctioneer's best judgment based on the artist's sales history, and on the condition and desirability of the particular piece.

Hammer price (knockdown). The price at which a lot is sold.

Inspection. See "preview."

Left bid (including mail bids). A bid submitted by a prospective buyer who can't attend the auction. These are executed by the auctioneer or a member of his staff during the sale.

Lot. An individual work or group of works offered for sale at one time.

Paddle. A numbered card which may be anything from an imprinted plastic paddle to a paper plate. It is given to bidders when they register and must be held aloft in order to bid.

Passed. If there is no interest from the floor and no bidding on the lot, it is passed over, and the auctioneer goes on to the next.

Preview (exhibition). The period before a sale reserved for the inspection or viewing of items to be auctioned. In larger auction houses, the preview period may be as long as a week. At smaller sales, the preview may be only the day of the sale. Generally, lots cannot be viewed after the sale starts. However, if it is really impossible to schedule a pre-sale inspection, call the auction house in advance and arrange to see the item when you arrive.

Prices realized. A listing of lots sold and the prices achieved. Some auction houses publish these prices and some do not. They may be published with or without the buyer's premium.

Reserve. The lowest price which a consignor will accept for a lot. It is ordinarily used only for high-priced works. The reserve is often two-thirds of the low estimate. At the major houses, the reserve for more expensive paintings is frequently close to the low estimate. If reserve is not reached and the lot is bought-in, the piece may be offered again at a later sale. Reserves are rarely set at country sales, so that sparse attendance, or limited interest, may make it possible to pick up a good buy.

The ring (the pool). An informal agreement among dealers that they will not bid against each other for a specific lot. After the sale they adjourn to the parking lot for a "knockout" in which the lot is sold to one of the dealers in the pool. Each writes down the figure that he or she is ready to pay. The highest bidder ends up with the merchandise, while the others split the difference between the actual purchase price at the auction and the price reached in the post-auction action. Most merchandise sold in this manner leaves the parking lot at the price it should have fetched at the sale. The losers, clearly, are the auction house and the consignor. These activities amount to restraint of trade and are illegal in most states. Curiously, some members of the ring never actually deal in merchandise but manage to make a small living simply by participating. While the ring can be a potent force in controlling prices at an auction, an independent purchaser can beat it. Just set your price and stick to it.

Shill. An individual planted in the crowd by the house or by an individual consignor to bid up the price of a lot. Contracts at most houses forbid the consignor or his agent to bid on the lot he has consigned.

Telephone bid. A bid from someone not attending the auction, who makes advance arrangements with the house to bid actively during the auction. Telephone bidding is generally limited to higher-priced works, and at important auctions there may be a bank of telephones in place for long-distance participation. (Not all telephone bidding is long distance. Some-times, bidders use a pay phone in the auction house so they can bid without being identified.)

Underbidder. The losing bidder.

Withdrawn. A lot removed before the sale begins.

Types of Auctions

Auctions vary widely in the selection, type, and quality of artwork they offer. At country auctions mixed offerings are the rule, and they will include furniture, paintings and drawings, rugs, bric-a-brac, and assorted collecti-bles. A painting sold at a country auction may have been hanging on the same wall for the past hundred years, or it might be the ten-year-old work of a summer painter. That stained work on paper may be an original water-color, or it may have been clipped from a magazine and hung in a five-and-dime-store frame.

Some auctioneers assemble a collection for a sale by combining lots from many different households or sources. Be aware that some dealers will con-sign "hard to sell" merchandise at these sales. Such sales are frequently held in halls and lodges, veterans' posts, or fraternal organizations and may include some paintings and watercolors.

Some paintings are usually put on the block at estate auctions, where the entire contents of a house are sold on site, often on a weekday. Estate auctions bring fresh, new, and thus particularly desirable material to the market.

Catalogs

One advantage of buying a work of art at a large auction house is that a great deal of your work has already been done for you. By the time something appears in an auction house catalog, it has already filtered through the first levels of professional assessment.

An auction house catalog, a listing of lots to be sold at a particular auction, can be anything from a mimeographed list to a splendidly printed and illus-trated volume that looks a great deal like an expensive art book. A catalog can be a source of valuable information, but it should be read in the context in which it is created. An auction house catalog is a sales tool. It can be glamorous and packed with information, but it is compiled to help the house successfully market a product.

Catalogs, while useful art reference tools, are not definitive sources of information. The fact that a work is listed in a catalog does not legitimize it.

Catalogs are not always scholarly works. They may or may not be written by knowledgeable people. They are not infallible and may contain errors in attribution or authentication.

In reading an art auction catalog, it is important to remember that at the major houses, works are generally arranged chronologically, rather than in order of importance. Color illustrations often draw the reader's attention. Whether a lot is illustrated or not, or in black and white or in color, does not indicate importance. Remember that most auction houses charge consignors for illustrations, and charge more for color than black and white.

Auction houses list the title of the painting, if known. Otherwise they give a descriptive title.

A typical catalog description will include the artist's name; the title (in quotation marks or capital letters); whether and where the work is signed; the medium (oil on canvas, oil on board, pencil on paper, etc.); size and condition; and the price estimate. It may also provide information about the provenance of the work, or literature about the artist. (If you buy a picture at an auction, save the catalog, for it becomes part of the provenance.)

The auction house may indicate its confidence in the authenticity of a particular piece in the way it prints the artist's name. For example, if it catalogs a piece by Sir Jacob Epstein, you can be confident that it's by the great 20th-century English sculptor. A little less certainty will shorten the listing to Jacob Epstein. If there's more question, the name may appear as J. Epstein. Dropping a title or abbreviating a first name to an initial usually implies doubt. If the catalog description says "bears signature" or "apocryphal signature," the signature is false. If the catalog says "signature is inscribed," it was written by someone other than the artist. When you read the description, be aware that state laws vary, as does the buyback policy or guarantee. Terminology also varies from house to house. Christie's uses the term "cast from a model by" as its guarantee for bronzes. This term has been picked up by auction houses outside New York State, but does not necessarily mean the same thing.

The same cautions apply to the use of such terms as "school," "school of," "studio of," and "circle of," whether in catalogs or anywhere else. "School of," as in "School of Raphael," is generally applied to the work of students or apprentices who studied with a renowned artist. An individual work by a member of the "school" may actually have been touched in one or two places by the master's brush. "Circle of" covers a broader area—the connection is more tenuous, but the work of art may still be very valuable. "After" means a copy of the work of an artist—perhaps by an art student sitting in a museum—at least a hundred years after the original was completed. "Attributed to" indicates that a work is *most probably* by a particular artist even though it is not signed.

Auction catalogs are compiled and published by the major houses six weeks to a few days before the actual sale. In the United States the art auction market is dominated by two huge New York houses, Sotheby's and Christie's. Together they account for 90 percent of all catalog lots and 95 percent of the dollar total sold annually. Their specialized sales are scheduled in the same seasons each year: major American paintings sales are traditionally early in December and the last week in May; Latin American sales in November and May; etc. Both offer catalogs by subscription, which assures that you are on the auction-house mailing list and will receive its newsletter and notices of forthcoming sales. Most houses also send catalog subscribers lists of the prices realized at sales. Appendix C is a list of the major auction houses. All of them offer some art and sell by catalog or flyer.

Read carefully the "Conditions of Sale" at the front of each catalog, which provides important information on absentee bidding, establishing credit, shipping, insurance, and storage.

Strategy

One basic ground rule covers all purchasing at all auctions:

NEVER BID ON SOMETHING YOU HAVEN'T LOOKED AT FIRST.

Take advantage of the auction preview. Carefully examine the piece you are interested in. Re-examine it just before the sale begins. Sometimes a piece is damaged during the preview.

Inspect carefully. If you've done your reading and research, you'll be aware of the characteristic styles and signatures of the artists you're interested in. Don't be put off by small signs of wear or damage. Don't be afraid to bid on a dirty painting—at least a dirty painting hasn't been damaged by an amateur restorer. Most paintings can be cleaned. Holes can be repaired. Torn canvas can usually be mended. Stains and acid can be removed from paper. Skilled restorers can perform near miracles.

If you've received a catalog in which a piece is described but not illustrated, ask the auction house to send a color photograph or transparency for you to examine. After you've looked at the illustration, know that you're interested enough to buy but can't possibly attend the preview or the sale, and don't want to risk a telephone bid on unseen merchandise, there's still hope. You can arrange with a dealer to bid for you. This method provides a built-in advantage—experience. A firsthand examination by a knowledgeable dealer can help a prospective purchaser decide whether or not to bid. The dealer will preview the painting, check its authenticity, examine its condition, assess its value, and look at the frame. The dealer will then call you from the auction house and discuss overall values, and you will be able to decide whether and how much to bid.

Dealers' commissions will vary for this service. Some charge 5 percent of the purchase price if they bid successfully for you. Some won't charge if they don't get the painting, but others will ask for a flat fee for time and effort. Fees vary and should be negotiated in advance.

Bidding

To bid in an auction you must secure a number by registering and presenting a valid form of identification, usually a driver's license and major credit card, which will enable the auctioneer to accept your check at the end. If you can't establish a line of credit, you will need to leave your merchandise until your check clears.

Bidding strategy is individual. There are as many different strategies as there are bidders. Some people like to be identified as bidders, and others do not. Some prefer to get in early and join the action from the opening bid. Others will follow for a while before jumping in. There's no rule that bidding must begin at the auctioneer's opening figure. However, bidding will occasionally start at that level if the work is very desirable, or if an individual bidder has decided to try to bring action on that particular item to a quick close by getting a psychological jump on others who wanted to start much lower.

Before bidding starts on the lot you are interested in, make sure you know what you think the piece is worth. Keep this *Guide* at hand and remember that there are a number of factors that influence prices. Don't be discouraged by high estimates, for they may be wishful thinking. Write your top price for the lot on your catalog or on a pad of paper. Add 10 percent to give yourself some flexibility and then add another 15 percent for the buyer's premium. If there's a state sales tax, calculate that as well. Be sure that your opening bid is below what you're finally willing to pay. Be alert for symptoms of "auction fever," a potentially dangerous disease in which a purchaser decides to pay whatever is necessary to own a particular work.

Be prepared to exceed your own limit, but only a little. If you've decided that you'll spend $1,250 on a painting, and your last bid of $1,200 was followed by someone else's reluctant $1,300, go ahead to $1,350—you may get what you're after.

If you've left a bid with the auctioneer, make it an odd figure, such as $625, and consider giving instructions that will enable him to up to the next level on your behalf. In this way you have an advantage, since the bidding goes up in round increments.

Don't be reluctant to bid against dealers. Unless a dealer is bidding on behalf of a client, he will have to resell the painting to make a profit, so he must begin by buying at a price he can mark up.

If you were hesitant, pulled out of the bidding, and the item you wanted was bought-in because it didn't reach its reserve, you may still be able to purchase it after the auction. Most auction house contracts empower the auction house to sell the consigned lot at its reserve price for up to sixty days after the sale. After consulting the consignor, the auction house may sell the lot below the reserve price.

How to Sell

Art collectors share certain fantasies. One of the most common follows this scenario: the much-loved, early-20th-century oil painting of a horse that hangs above the mantel, but was inherited from a favorite uncle who lived in a gracious, antique-filled home, turns out to be a very valuable British sporting painting.

That's the fantasy.

The reality is that every age has produced greater and lesser artists, and that our affection for a work does not enhance its value. Art has no absolute financial value. Value is created in the marketplace. Price is influenced by a variety of factors that include the artist's prestige, whether he is currently in vogue or out of fashion, the rarity of his work, the quality of the individual piece, previous auction records, condition, size, and subject matter.

Unpredictable elements may also come into play. If, for example, the auction prices achieved by an individual artist have been inflated by competition between two collectors, and one suddenly withdraws from the market, prices will drop.

While there are many variables that affect art prices, there are still some fundamental guidelines to follow if you want to sell a work of art.

Begin by ascertaining what you're selling. Do you have a provenance (history of ownership) for the work? Where was it bought and when? Is it the work of a listed artist? Is there a sales history? Check Bénézit, Falk, and *Leonard's ANNUAL Price Index*, and, of course, the first two volumes in this series, *The Official Price Guide to Fine Art* and *The Confident Collector Fine Art Identification and Price Guide*.

Review your decision. Are you sure you want to sell? Do you want to keep the work a little longer, or keep it forever to leave to your family?

If you've decided to sell, you should consider the next set of options: you can place the piece at auction, sell it directly to a dealer, or consign it on a commission basis.

Selling at Auction

Selling at auction assures maximum exposure to the largest possible audience. An experienced auction house will publicize a sale effectively, hoping to draw a large crowd of bidders on sale day. This is the most likely way to achieve fair market value for a piece, and the sale price becomes a matter of public record.

Most auction houses will be happy to help sell an estate, though the largest may sell only the best pieces themselves, and contract out the remainder. Sotheby's and Christie's will conduct an on-site sale only if the proceeds are expected to exceed $2-$3 million.

If you are selling only one or two pieces, take a *careful* photograph (of both the front *and* the back if there are marks or labels there). Make an appointment with a local auction house, and bring it to the in-house art specialist. Or you can send a photograph to one of the New York houses. (Before mailing any material, it's a good idea to call ahead and secure the name of the appropriate department head so that you can direct the materials to the right individual. It also provides a name for follow-up.)

The photograph should include the artist's name, signature, the size of the work without the frame, support (canvas, board, paper, etc.), media, and the best provenance you can supply. Working from a photograph, even the instant variety, an expert can usually determine the value of a painting. If you think that you own an especially valuable work, a color transparency made by a professional will cost about $100, and may prove a good investment.

Another approach is to bring the work(s) to an appraisal day, which all auction houses hold, either on their premises or as benefits for museums or historical societies. On these occasions, experts assess the value of work brought in and provide a verbal appraisal for a minimal fee.

In any event, try to get at least three appraisals to help ascertain the value of a work. This will help you safeguard against any unscrupulous appraiser who might set an artificially low value on a work and offer to buy it, only to resell it at its real worth.

One cautionary note—avoid having any restoration done on a work you are consigning to auction. Most paintings sell better before they are restored.

If you think restoration is essential, consult the auction house, and ask for a recommendation. One classic restoration horror story concerns a work by Wifredo Lam which was ruined when the restorer removed all the impasto (paint applied in heavy layers or strokes). The end product looked like a poster.

If you decide to consign to auction, you will be asked to sign a contract with the auction house. There are a number of standard provisions with which you should be familiar.

Auction houses charge the consignor for insurance, shipping, photographs (for catalogs), handling, and the seller's commission. There is a charge, a percentage of the reserve, if the work is bought-in. There is also a withdrawal fee if you change your mind.

Standard commission rates prevail: 20 percent for lots under $2,000, 15 percent for lots between $2,000 and $7,500, and 10 percent for lots above $7,500.

If the fees sound high, they must offset the considerable expenses the house carries—rent, staff, storage, catalog, publicity, overhead, and viewing.

A dealer or appraiser who refers a seller to an auction house may be paid a finder's fee, which is paid by the house out of its commission. The need to pay the fee may limit the house's ability to adjust its commission rates.

But, because flexibility and variability are the rule in the auction world, there is often room to negotiate many of these provisions. If, for example, you agree to the reserve the house suggests, the house in turn may agree to waive the buyback commission. The best rule to remember is to ask every question about costs and procedures that comes to mind. After all, the auction house is there to serve you.

Working with a Dealer

Working with a dealer or a gallery presents two additional options—selling the work directly, or placing it on consignment. The fee in the latter option can range up to 33 percent of the sale price, or it may be a set commission plus the dealer's costs.

There are good reasons to take a work to a dealer, rather than to auction. Going "private" permits exclusivity. The right dealer may know just the right buyer. The right dealer can show only the work you've sold or consigned, and it won't have to compete with other pieces by the same artist. A good dealer is knowledgeable and can act discreetly. The dealer should be willing to agree that the work be shown only to select clients while consigned for an agreed period of time.

If you want to sell a work directly to a dealer, follow the same steps you would take if you wanted to buy. Call your local museum and ask for a reference. Call the Art Dealers Association of America headquarters in New York (212-940-8590) and request a list of members; call the Private Art Dealers Association (PADA), an organization based in New York, at 212-315-4820.

Pick a dealer who specializes in the kind of work you want to sell, and check how long the dealer has been in business. Take the time to check the credentials of any source you use. Try to protect yourself from untrained or self-appointed appraisers.

Trust is essential in this relationship. Some prospective sellers are hesitant about contracting for a commission sale, since it can be difficult to ascertain a final price. If you do choose to work with a dealer, be certain that the conditions of the sale are made explicit in writing at the time that you consign. Ask for a status report within two weeks.

Selling a painting poses some of the same questions as buying—establishing value, creating a working relationship with a sales agent, whether an auction house or a dealer, and investigating the various mechanisms that are needed to achieve a sale. By proceeding thoughtfully and cautiously, you are more likely to achieve the result you hope for.

The Impossible Dream

It happens every year—at least once. The lost work reappears; a locked storage closet opened in a warehouse; a dusty old canvas is brought out of an attic; a masterwork surfaces at a garage sale. It is the stuff that dreams are made of.

The odds against making a major find are overwhelming. However, there is always the possibility of turning up something undervalued or unrecognized. And if you succeed, what then?

The first step is to do your basic research. If the picture is signed, perhaps another work by the same artist is listed in this book, or in some other art price guide. However, the name alone is not enough to authenticate the work, for the signature may have been added. Or the painting may have the wrong attribution inscribed on a plaque on the frame, or on the back of the canvas. Don't believe something just because it's written down.

Next, have the work appraised. Take the picture to an established dealer or auction house. Most auction houses will give a free verbal appraisal. Get a second opinion.

Some museums hold appraisal days. Call for information. On a typical appraisal day, a museum will assemble outside experts, art specialists from auction houses and galleries, who will tell you who, what, and when, but will not set a dollar value. Charges begin at about $25 for a verbal opinion. Some charitable organizations or schools occasionally sponsor appraisal days.

Auction houses offer free verbal estimates, by appointment, at their main galleries. They will supplement the information provided by the museum by appraising the work for its "auction" value. Sotheby's and Christie's maintain offices around the country, and there are numerous smaller houses listed in Appendix C. If you can't bring the work in, mail a photograph to the appropriate department of your favorite auction house and ask for an unofficial appraisal. Auction houses are responsive to these inquiries, and will follow up immediately if they think you've made a find.

Get a second opinion, for an appraisal is a highly subjective process and linked to the constant vagaries of the art market.

For everyone who cherishes the dream of making a find, hope is fed by stories like the one about the William Merritt Chase canvas that was sold at Gustave White's in Newport in 1995.

Find in the Attic

Most auctioneers make appraisals with the hope that they will have a "find" in the attic or under the bed. In the winter of 1995, Michael Corcoran of Gustave White Auctioneers in Newport, Rhode Island, was called for a house appraisal. After looking at the owner's prized possessions he asked, "Do you have anything else? Any paintings, rugs or old furniture?" The owner said there were a couple of old paintings in the attic but they weren't worth much. When Corcoran unrolled one of them out of a plastic bag the first thing he saw was the signature "Wm.M. Chase."

Wm.M. Chase is the signature of William Merritt Chase (1849-1916), a preeminent artist and teacher of the late 19th and early 20th centuries. Chase was born in Indiana and studied at the National Academy of Design in New York and at the Royal Academy in Munich. After returning to the United States in 1878, he settled in New York and began teaching. Chase had an extraordinary career, teaching at the Arts Students League; in his studio; at his summer school in Shinnecock, Long Island, New York; at his own Chase School (est. 1896); and at the Pennsylvania Academy of Fine Art. Georgia O'Keeffe, Charles Sheeler, Rockwell Kent, Edward Hopper, and Marsden Hartley were some of his students. He was not only an influential teacher but an internationally acclaimed painter. Eclectic in his choice of subject matter, Chase painted landscapes, still-lifes, interiors, and portraits.

The painting that Corcoran had discovered in the attic was a portrait of a woman in a white dress on a dark background. The owner thought the subject might have been her husband's aunt. Examination of the oil revealed surface abrasions as a result of the canvas being rolled up for so long, but the face and figure were intact. An unappealing feature was the solid, dark background, nevertheless, the portrait sold for $231,000, much to the delight of the owner. (William Merritt Chase, *Full-length Portrait of Young Woman in White Dress*, oil on canvas, Gustave White Auctioneers, January 25, 1995, $231,000)

Restoration

Great art is undaunted by time, but it can certainly be damaged. Even if it remains unblemished, an oil on canvas which has hung for a century will darken with age; a work on paper may have foxing (chemical impurities), mat stains, or hinge marks; or your oil or drawing may have been harmed by too much attention. In most cases, a skilled conservator can make the painting look as it did when it was new.

You should bring exactly the same criteria to deciding whether to purchase a slightly damaged work of art as to one in pristine condition. If it moves you, and you can afford it, buy. Overlook *small* physical flaws, because they can be repaired. Restorers can accomplish near miracles with canvases that have holes or tears, or even water damage. Stains, mold, and foxing can be removed from paper; fractured sculpture can be mended. If you choose to buy a damaged work and have it restored, you may be getting a bargain and you'll actually come out ahead. Remember, however, that restoration can affect value, and the line between minor and major restoration may be fine where sensitive areas of the painting are concerned. Get the advice of a conservator or knowledgeable dealer before you purchase a work in poor condition.

A word of caution—restoration is a profession, not a hobby. And there *is* a difference between conservation and restoration. The American Institute of Conservators defines a conservator as "a professional devoted to the preservation of cultural properties for the future. A conservator's activities include examination, documentation, treatment, and preventative care supported by research and education." Restoration is defined as "treatment procedures intended to return cultural properties to a known or assumed state after the addition of non-original materials."

Oil on Canvas

Protect your art with preventive measures. Don't touch the surface with anything more than a feather duster, and then only occasionally. Treat all works of art carefully. Avoid extremes of humidity or temperature. Don't hang a painting over a radiator or air conditioner and particularly not over a fireplace or woodstove.

If your canvas needs cleaning, it is not a do-it-yourself job. If you buy a dirty painting and can't afford a professional cleaning, leave it alone until you can have a restorer do the work.

Restoration is a delicate procedure. A restorer has an arsenal of materials and techniques, but the same solvents and materials are available to both highly skilled and inept practitioners. Poor workmanship can do more damage than the ravages of time.

Cleaning a canvas can be as simple as removing old varnish, lightly cleaning the surface, and applying a synthetic varnish that won't discolor.[3] The

---

[3] Restoration can dramatically change the way in which an artist's work is perceived. Subsequent to the cleaning of the Sistine Chapel, art historians have been forced to re-evaluate Michelangelo, long thought to have painted in muted colors. The cleaned ceiling of the chapel revealed amazingly vibrant colors.

Without examining the canvas, I purchased this large 19th-century moonlight scene on an impulse bid for only $302.50 ($275 + 10 percent buyer's premium). What a buy! But a quick examination *after* the sale showed that the painting had prior restoration and had been backed with masonite, probably in the 1950s. Backing a canvas with masonite is an easy way of repairing tears or patches but is not easily reversible. When the painting was brought to Boston restorer Peter Williams, he also pointed out numerous areas of inpainting. The oils used for the inpainting had discolored at a different rate from the original oil and were visible to the naked eye and quite obvious under a black light. A quick dab of

solvent removed some of the yellowed varnish and showed that this dark moonlight scene was really quite a bit brighter. The decision was made to clean and repair the painting. The estimate for the restoring work read "A. Neleson oil on canvas mounted on masonite 24 x 34½ inches (framed and previously restored with repaired holes and discolored over-paint in sky). Signed lower right. Estimate to clean and remove over-paint, clean, and redo inpainting. Rate $40 and $45/hr., 10-14 hours. Total cost of work: NTE (not to exceed $500)." The final bill was $360. And what a difference there was after the discolored areas had been inpainted and the yellowed varnish had been removed!

A quick search of the major art references—Mallet, Fieldings, Havlice, Falk, Bénézit, Vollmer, Thieme-Becker, and the Archives of American Art—yielded no listing for an A. Neleson, and there were no auction records. Even though there is a signature, in most auction catalogues this painting would be listed as American School, 19th century, signed A. Neleson.

To complete the research Suzanne Smeaton, gallery director of Eli Wilner & Co. Period Frames in New York, examined my purchase. According to Suzanne, this is a common 1930s mass-produced frame. The original gold leaf has been overlaid with gold paint and varnish (the iridescent sparkles are a sign of paint); the frame surface and ornamentation are shallow and lack definition. The inner-most liner is most probably original to the painting, but the frame itself is definitely a replacement. There is no intrinsic value to this frame, and it would cost more to repair than it is worth.

This time my buy was not very valuable but a decorative find.

There was a dramatic difference
when the yellowed varnish was removed.

art and science of restoration combine in the decision of which materials to use, in what quantity, and, of the greatest importance, when to stop. Some artists signed their paintings after applying a preliminary coat of varnish. If a restorer fails to detect this, he may remove the signature. Other artists applied alternating layers of paint and varnish to build up a feeling of depth on the canvas. A restorer who doesn't recognize this technique will cause terrible damage.

Relining may be called for if the painting has lost its tautness. Relining is required to restore a punctured or torn canvas. In this process, the work is removed from its stretcher and adhered to another support (board, canvas, fiberglass, etc.). It is important to photograph or preserve in some manner any inscriptions or labels which are on the back prior to mounting. A modern rule of thumb is that restoration should be reversible so that if a better technique is developed, it can be employed.

Sometimes all that is required to restore a work is a bit of inpainting, perhaps to touch up the edges where paint has chipped off at the stretcher line. Flaking or cracking paint requires more concerted attention. A variety of techniques can be used, and most often a painting will require a combination of them to complete the restoration.

Modern art, on the other hand, presents a different challenge to museums and collectors alike. Some artists have used unstable materials that are ephemeral. Chris Ofili, a contemporary British artist, constructs psychedelic glitter abstractions made in part with elephant dung! His works sold recently for $6,000. Many young artists often don't have the money to buy quality materials and costly pigments. Sometimes they don't prime their canvases. When they do start to sell, they may be tempted to invest in sports cars instead of art supplies. The results are awful—cheap paint on bad canvas can require attention in as little as five years.

Proper conservation or restoration is time-consuming and expensive, but worth it. It is better to leave a canvas in the condition in which you bought it than to have the job done poorly.

It must be noted that there is a significant body of opinion that holds that restoration can destroy the value of a work. For clumsy restoration, or restoration that changes the character of the original, that is undoubtedly true. Choosing the right restorer thus becomes vitally important.

Assume that you have purchased an "ancestor portrait" that seems lovely beneath the accumulated dirt, but has a small tear on the left side. How do you go about finding a restorer who will do the job well, but not charge an exorbitant price?

The cost of restoration varies widely, as does the quality. Probably the best source of referrals is a gallery owner, who will share your interest in paying a fair price for quality work. Major museums maintain their own restoration departments, but they will know of outside restorers, who, perhaps, once worked for the museum. Or you can call the American Institute for the Conservation of Historic and Artistic Works (202-452-9545) for a free list of its members.

The price of restoration varies depending on the size of the work and its condition. In 1996, a highly skilled Boston restorer would have charged from $350–$500 to clean, reline, and do minor repairs on a 25 x 30 inch ancestor portrait. More elaborate procedures to deal with flaking, fly spots, fire, or water damage would increase the price two or three times or more. Fire-damaged canvases present a particular problem. In some cases, fire may have damaged only the varnish covering the surface paint. This can be removed and fresh varnish applied. Sometimes fire affects the paint and turns it to a brownish hue which is neither reversible nor restorable.

In requesting an estimate for restoration, you may be asking for the impossible. A complex problem may involve x-raying, testing with a variety of solvents, or other preliminary steps to determine what the best approach will be. Once the preliminary work has been done, a restorer will discuss any unforeseen problems before proceeding. For example, a painting may appear to have a firm surface, but when tested, the paint may show a tendency to lift, indicating that it should be relined. Most restorers will give you a verbal listing of the work they will do, but will charge for a written one.

Works on Paper

Collecting works on paper raises special concerns. Paper is delicate and easily damaged. Whatever media the artists uses—pastel, watercolor, gouache, ink, oil, etc.—can also be damaged by chemical or environmental sources, or by improper handling or framing.

Paper readily absorbs chemicals and moisture from the air. Paper made with wood pulp (since about 1850) has sulfur dioxide deposits which convert to sulfuric acid in the presence of moisture and heat. Once present, sulfuric acid continues to react and break down the paper's cellular structure, causing a brown color to develop. Light can also damage paper through oxidation.

These and other destructive processes accelerate if there is fluctuating heat or humidity. Both mold and insects flourish when the heat and humidity are high—and there are over seventy species of insects that might destroy paper.

As with paper, media are sensitive to their environment and are affected by light, humidity, pollution, or heat. Colors may change or fade. Binding agents in media, such as watercolors or oils, may dry out, causing the media to peel or flake off the paper.

Because of the technical nature of conservation, conservators usually specialize in a particular type of art object. Kathryn Myatt Carey, a paper conservator, has compiled the following checklist for examining a work on paper and answered some of the most frequently asked questions.

Examining a Work on Paper

Always unframe a work to examine it, setting aside the frame, mat, and any inserts or labels. Use a support under the art, and lay it on a clean surface. First, examine the paper. Handmade paper can have laid or chain lines and a watermark or be smoother, as in wove paper. Is there staining or discoloration? Total sheet darkening can be due to exposure to light or acidic materials, adhesives, molds, or oil. Look for insect damage or evidence of surface loss. Are there "flyspecks," or little brown dots, mold damage, or foxing? Paper may be soft or missing in some areas, or it may smell moldy.

Watch out for paper that is brittle to the touch, or that has losses, tears, abrasions, creases, or folds. Evidence of former treatment may include hinges, paper mends, patches, or tapes. Scotch or masking tapes are very hard to remove and usually leave stains. Is the paper "laid down" on a secondary support? Cardboard backings are usually acidic and may be brittle or browned. Because acidic backing can affect the work, they need to be removed, but it can be difficult to do so. Dry mount tissue is the hardest backing to remove, and should be avoided.

Examine the media for rubbing, flaking, losses, or bleeding. Is there fading? Watercolor fades when exposed to light; look for the original color in areas under a previous mat. Graphite pencil and the inks used in lithographs and etchings are usually very stable, but silkscreen inks are on the surface of the paper and are easily rubbed. Ink, gouache, pastel, charcoal, watercolor, and the inks used in some color woodblocks may dissolve in water, and are therefore difficult to clean if there is staining or foxing.

Questions and Answers

What is foxing? Foxing most frequently appears as circular spots on the paper, and is an indication of mold growth. Conservation treatment would include killing of the active mold, washing, deacidification, stain reduction if possible, and slow drying.

How can I tell if paper has been bleached, and what does this do to the paper? If the sheet is brilliant white and smells of chlorine, it probably has been bleached. If the bleach has not been thoroughly rinsed out, it will harm the paper.

What can I do about burn marks from acidic mats? "Burn marks" are caused by browning from acidic mats and can usually be removed or reduced by conservation treatment including washing, deacidification, and slow drying.

What kinds of backings are detrimental? Almost all backings are detrimental and must be removed. If the medium is water-soluble, such as watercolor, the backing must be removed with a scalpel, which can be a painstaking process. If the medium is more permanent, paper that is glued down can often be floated in water to dissolve the adhesive. Glue on the surface of the art must be carefully removed with a cotton swab by a conservator.

What makes the colors on paper fade? Most colors will fade when exposed to light. Conservators use the word "fugitive" to describe the relative fading properties of colors. Keep watercolor, gouache, ink, and pastel in low light or framed with UV-filtering Plexiglas. You may one day want to put UV-filtering film on all your windows.

If you buy a work of art on paper, is there any standard archival procedure one should follow before it is framed? Examine the work and use your best judgment. If you have any questions, have a conservator examine the work of art. Most paper conservators will not charge you to provide a verbal evaluation.

How can I tell if there is inpainting? Inpainting will usually show up with a black light and may also be visible if the work is lit from behind. Too much inpainting is considered "restoration" rather than "conservation."

What special problems can occur with chalk, pastels, or charcoal? All of these media are on the surface of the paper and are easily rubbed. Chalk, pastels, and charcoal should never be framed with Plexiglas; the static charge from the Plexiglas will lift the particles of the media off the surface of the paper.

What special problems can occur with pencil or pen and ink? Pencil does not dissolve in water but can be rubbed away. Inks can be fugitive or subject to color changes.

Are self-adhesive tapes removable? Some self-adhesive tapes can be removed using an organic solvent, but this is not usually a job for an amateur. Staining from tape can be treated only after the tape has been removed.

If the paper is torn, can it be fixed? Yes, conservators mend tears with a patch of Japanese tissue and water-soluble paste applied to the back.

Is water damage reversible? Yes, if the work of art is treated soon after the damage has occurred. Contact your paper conservator as soon as possible!

Are watermarks important? The lack of a watermark may indicate only that a partial sheet was used, but the presence of a watermark can give some clue to the date of the paper and the papermaker. Charles Moise Briquet's four-volume dictionary, *Les filigranes. dictionnaire historique des marques du papier, des leur apparition vers 1282-1600,* published in 1907, is one standard reference source.

Is there anything else you would like to mention? Works of art on paper should not be framed in contact with the glass, because the moisture that collects behind the glass will eventually destroy the paper. Use a mat between the work and the glass, or if the work is floated, use a spacer.

How can I find a paper conservator? Conservators are not licensed or regulated by law. Professional Associates and Fellows of the American Institute for the Conservation of Historic and Artistic Works meet specified levels of peer review and have committed to a mandated Code of Ethics. The AIC has a free referral system (202-452-9545).

Kathryn Myatt Carey is a Professional Associate of the American Institute for Conservation specializing in the conservation of works of art on paper and can be contacted through the AIC.

Art as Investment ————————————

Should you buy art as an investment?

"No!" is the resounding answer of dealers, gallery owners, auction house executives, and investment counselors.

Buy art because it moves you, because it is beautiful, because it appeals to you. Buy quality.

If these are your guidelines, it is quite possible that in ten or twenty years your purchases will be worth substantially more than what you first paid for them. Don't ever buy because you think that a currently underpriced field will come back into demand, or because you've read a glowing review of a popular young painter and you've heard that art is a gilt-edged investment.

Collecting art is an investment in the largest sense. It is an investment in time, in aesthetic pleasure, in developing your own eye and your expertise. If, along the way, your collection appreciates, the increase in value is an added benefit. It should never be a starting point.

Beware of a dealer who suggests a particular painting as a good investment. There's a sales pitch in marketing art, sometimes even a hard sell, and the hope that today's modest purchase will both enhance the living room and help send the children to college can be hard to resist.

"But what about those clever connoisseurs who bought the Impressionists in the 1950s?" you ask. "Haven't they sat smiling while prices for Impressionist works increased forty times and more?"

Indeed they have, but those same people who are fortunate enough to own paintings that now sell for millions made a significant investment when they first purchased, paying prices in the $40,000 range thirty or more years ago. (Note that the same $40,000 invested in an account paying 10 percent interest would have increased to over $1,120,000 in the same time period.)

Remember, too, that while public opinion of the Impressionists has done a complete about-face within a century, time has been less kind to other artists. During the '50s, '60s, and '70s, the paintings of 19th-century academicians William Adolphe Bourguereau and Sir Lawrence AlmaTadema could be bought very inexpensively. Only recently have works by these artists commanded prices similar to what they sold for in the 19th century.

Similarly, 19th-century American painter Thomas Moran was immensely popular during his lifetime, and his works commanded high prices. He was later eclipsed by other artists, and only recently have his works again begun to sell for close to their original prices.

If, despite all these cautions, you are still intent on assembling your collection as an investment tool, you should bear a number of points in mind.

There is usually a strong correlation between cost and investment. Barring the occasional flukes and finds, investment-quality work is expensive. Most works included in museum collections are important examples of an artist's style. A piece in a private collection does not need to be equally representative. In general but not always, a work is more valuable if it is a typical rather than an atypical example. A work that is both decorative and attractive is a safer bet than one that is not. The real trick is to find the museum-quality paintings of the future today.

Studies and drawings done in preparation for major works are more valuable than those done for works that were never completed. Also, any documentation of a painting, especially if the artist has written about it in letters or in a diary, makes the work more valuable. A solid provenance enhances the value of an individual picture. A work that has been part of a major collection has accrued value; similarly, a work that has changed hands frequently, or been hawked around from dealer to dealer, may lose value. A work from a "good" period in the artist's career is more valuable than one produced in a less fertile time.

Where a work is sold can greatly affect its value, for art can be geographically chauvinistic. Scenes of the White Mountains of New Hampshire are popular in New England. Cowboy art is popular in the West. And some subjects do better than others—scenes of dead game are generally not sought after in the United States but are popular in Europe.

In general, pleasant subjects are more sought after than troubling ones: country scenes are more appealing than sickbeds; baskets of fresh flowers are more attractive than those that are withered; bright and colorful pictures are more salable than gloomy and drab ones.

The size and shape of the work are of great importance. Some modern artists have produced canvases of heroic proportion, measuring 10 x 20 feet. Few homes can accommodate such massive works, rendering them difficult to sell. Some dealers consider horizontal pictures easier to sell than

Art as an Investment

There is no sure rule when buying art as an investment. The art market, like any other commodities market, has its ups and downs, its ins and outs. When Andy Warhol died in 1987, he was the quintessential Pop artist. Soon after his death the art market was flooded with Warhol silkscreens, lithographs, paintings, autographed soup cans, and paintings. Fueled by the frenzied buying of speculators, prices for Warhol's works soared. In 1989 a record price for a Warhol work was achieved when *Shot Red Marilyn* sold at Sotheby's for $4.07 million to a Japanese collector. (*Shot Red Marilyn* was created at Warhol's Factory in 1964 when a fan walked in, pulled a gun out of her purse, aimed at a stack of Marilyn Monroe portraits, and shot a hole though the movie star's forehead and the underlying stack of canvases. Warhol had the silkscreens repaired, and they became known as *The Shot Red Marilyns.*)

The art market had been at its height in 1989 when this record price was achieved. In 1994, when the same Japanese collector consigned *Shot Red Marilyn* to Christie's, it carried a conservative estimate of $3–4 million. The price realized was $3.63 million, a strong sale, but when calculated in dollars an 11 percent loss for the investor. And calculated in yen, a 40 percent loss! Buy art because you like it and you want to live with it, NOT as an investment. (Andy Warhol, *Shot Red Marilyn*, synthetic polymer and silkscreen inks on paper, 40 × 40 inches, Christie New York, November 2, 1994, $3.63 million)

vertical ones. The 2 x 3 ratio is thought to be the "ideal" proportion for a painting.

Assembling a collection of older art is a challenge, but the highest risks for the investor/collector are in contemporary art, for it hasn't stood the test of time. Chroniclers of the art market note that only about 5 percent of the artists who have their first one-person shows in major cities in any given year *ever* have another show. Another concern is that, in the curious intersection of art and publicity, some young artists may be heavily promoted by a gallery with a healthy public relations budget and good press contacts. The difference between hype and a consistent display of talent may be difficult to ascertain.

There is, of course, another side to all this caution. Some of today's young artists will be tomorrow's masters, and a collector discerning and lucky enough to find this work will be able to combine aesthetic satisfaction with the pleasure of watching it appreciate.

A collector of contemporary work must be carefully attuned to every turn of the market, attend shows and gallery talks, visit artists' studios, and read the art press. While even the experts make mistakes, if you can buy the artists whom the curators, collectors, gallery owners, and artists themselves are buying, you're closer to the right track, but there are no guarantees. At best, buying contemporary work is a long-term investment, which may take ten years or more to appreciate, if it ever does. Some collectors think that the best time to buy is thirty to forty years after an artist dies, when the sales price for his work hits a low.

One of the few characteristics that art and the traditional financial markets have in common is the tendency to run in cycles, with well-publicized periods of solid growth creating a bandwagon effect of purchases, only to be followed by a sharp decline in prices.

In short, you're more likely to find success as an investor by staying with more conventional financial instruments. Your investment in art belongs in a personal portfolio under "A" for aesthetic and "L" for love.

A Brief Guide to Art Research ─────────

This chapter will not make you a skilled art researcher. It will, however, provide you with basic approaches to art research, the names of the standard sources, and an overall method of developing your knowledge about a school or a movement in painting, or about an individual artist. A selective bibliography appears at the end of this chapter.[4]

---

[4] The approach assumes that you will begin your research in a library. However, it is also advisable to begin to build your own library of art reference books. An inexpensive, pocket-sized handbook, Ralph Mayer's *Dictionary of Art Terms and Techniques*, explains schools, techniques, styles, and art terms. Information is easy to retrieve.

Another very useful book is Lois Swan Jones' *Art Research Methods and Resources: A Guide to Finding Art Information.* This comprehensive guide, geared for more advanced researchers, surveys the basic sources, deals with research methods, and provides practical advice on how to obtain reference material. Of particular value is the inclusion of facsimiles of pages from major reference works and directions for their use. Jones also provides a dictionary of French, German, and Italian art terms.

The Library

General Art Reference Works and Encyclopedias

Where and how you begin to do art research depends very much on what you want to learn. If, fresh from a foray to a museum, you decide to explore a budding interest in flower painting, start at the main branch of your local library.

Inquire at the reference desk for general art sources. The long-awaited thirty-four-volume *Dictionary of Art* is due to be released in the fall of 1996. The other three prime general reference books on the visual arts are *Encyclopedia of World Art*, *McGraw-Hill Dictionary of Art*, and *Praeger Encyclopedia of Art*. Each is well illustrated and geared to the general reader and beginning student. Each contains many articles on artists, periods, styles, terms, museums, and countries. Articles vary in length—from very short ones that define terms to more substantial pieces on individual artists that include bibliographies. The five-volume McGraw-Hill work is especially accessible and readable.

Taking this first step and consulting a general reference book may give you all the information that you need or want to know. Should you require more data, there are various additional sources.

The Card Catalog or OPAC
(On-Line Public Access Catalog)

The card catalog lists every book in a library's collection. Holdings are indexed by author, subject, and title. If you are checking to see if the library owns a specific work, the author and title listings are the place to turn to. If, however, you are pursuing a broader area, track it down in the subject catalog, starting with an inclusive topic, such as "painting," and then working through the subheadings to the one that will lead you to the pertinent titles. Research an artist by looking under his name. (See Appendix D for a detailed explanation of how artists' names are listed.)

The holdings of many libraries are now accessible via the Web, the Telnet, or by modem directly. Various search engines on the Web will give you many of the addresses you need, but if you want to use a Telnet address, you may have to call the library by phone for its site. At some institutions, not all holdings may be searched electronically. The Boston Public Library, founded in 1850, has electronic access only to acquisitions acquired since 1980; all other holdings must be researched manually in the card catalog.

Types of books listed in a card catalog or on-line public access catalog include:

Monographs. Books about an individual artist or artists that provide historical or biographical material and information about his or her more famous works. If you can't find an artist by name, search by subject, such as "still-life paintings." There are also monographs just on frames. A new bibliography of books on frames has been added to this edition.

Oeuvre catalogues. Systematic lists of each work of art in an artist's entire creative output, or the works in a specific medium.

Catalogues raisonnés. Similar to *oeuvre catalogues*, but provide a more complete citation for each work. (An auction catalog may try to give a particular lot added cachet by noting that it has been or will be listed in the *catalogue raisonné.*)

Exhibition catalogs. Document the exhibition of an artist's work at a museum or gallery.

Most public libraries will have some, but not all, of these resources. One time-tested way to find additional titles is to review the bibliography of related books and magazines that is usually found at the end of reference works. Librarians will be able to help you locate the more scholarly materials at an art library or in an adjacent larger city.

General Artist Dictionaries

There are no general dictionaries of artists in English, but there are two outstanding foreign language works that are the basic resources in the field. Many researchers turn first to Emmanuel Bénézit's *Dictionnaire Critique et Documentaire des Peintres, Sculpteurs, Dessinateurs et Graveurs.* Usually called "Bénézit," the ten-volume set, written in French, is an alphabetical listing of names with life dates and other basic information about international artists. It may include the names of cities where they studied and worked, and note any honors or awards given to them. Bénézit also provides facsimiles of some artists' signatures and some sales information. Last revised in 1976, the work retains certain idiosyncrasies. The names of some American and English artists, for example, are altered to the French versions—a Henry may be called an Henri; a Mary, Marie. You may occasionally hear an auctioneer say that an artist is listed in Bénézit—it's nice to know, but it doesn't really confer any value.

Another general reference, in German, is the highly regarded biographical dictionary compiled by Ulrich Thieme and Felix Becker, *Allgemeines Lexikon der bildenden Künstler von der Antike bis zur Gegenwart,* which runs to thirty-seven volumes. Generally preferred by scholars, it is a specialized, alphabetical index that contains material similar to that in Bénézit. At the end of each entry on an individual artist, there is a bibliography from which the data was drawn, with titles in the original language. Thieme-Becker, as it is usually called, was published from 1907 through 1950. Hans Vollmer's *Allgemeines Lexikon der bildenden Künstler des XX Jahrhunderts,* which covers artists born after 1870, is a supplement to Thieme-Becker.

Artist Indexes and General Indexes

An index can best be used as a jumping-off point for further research. Brief entries, listed alphabetically by the artist's last name, provide the complete name, nationality, life dates, and abbreviated notations of books or articles from which the information was compiled. The abbreviations used in a particular index are explained in the introduction to the individual work. These short listings direct you to longer articles and books about the artist in whom you are interested.

The *Artists' Biographies Master Index*, published in 1986, indexes over 257,000 artists from over seventy reference books; it is the most up-to-date index and one of the most comprehensive. Another valuable reference is Patricia Havlice's two-volume *Index to Artistic Biography*, published in 1973; it is a survey of sixty-four different biographical dictionaries exclusive of Thieme-Becker and Bénézit, and thus a valuable source of additional information. A supplement including material in seventy additional sources was published in 1981. Daniel Mallett's *Index of Artists*, first published in 1935, and its supplement, which appeared in 1940, are other good reference tools.

It is especially difficult to find information on little-known 20th-century artists, or on regional or very contemporary artists. The *Biography and Genealogy Master Index* is a guide to more than 725,000 listings in over eighty specialized biographical directories. It includes the names of many individuals who are not listed anywhere else. *The New York Times Index* and *The New York Times Obituaries Index* (last published in 1980) are excellent sources of information about 20th-century artists. The latter, particularly, includes information about regional artists that may not be found elsewhere. The Getty's four-volume *Union List of Artists' Names* and the Witt's *A Checklist of Painters circa 1200-1994* are listings of artist's names, nationalities, and life dates. Though not indexes, the information they provide may direct you to a specialized directory.

Major artists, movements, and periods are the subjects of books; less prominent names may become the special subjects of devoted researchers who publish articles in popular or scholarly periodicals. An index of periodical literature provides easy reference to recent articles on both major and minor artists. There are a number of specialized art indexes. Most libraries subscribe to *Art Index*, a database of over 230 journals that began publishing in 1929. Citations from the *Art Index* (from September 1984 on) are also available via on-line searching or on CD-ROM. (A selective list of art periodicals, tabloids, and newsletters appears in Appendix B.) As comprehensively as they survey periodical literature, none of the indexes includes the highly respected tabloid *The Maine Antique Digest*, to which many avid collectors subscribe—a serious omission.

Specialized Artist Dictionaries and Directories

If you already know the basic facts about an artist's nationality and life dates, you may go directly to a specialized dictionary. Mantle Fielding's *Dictionary of American Painters, Sculptors and Engravers*, first published in 1925 and revised in 1974, is one of the better-known dictionaries, though it is sometimes at variance with other sources and thus less reliable. Peter Falk's *Who Was Who in American Art*, compiled from the original thirty volumes of *American Art Annual, 1898–1933*, and from four volumes of *Who's Who in Art, 1935–1947*, includes biographical data and information about exhibitions, prizes, and membership in artist societies. Chris Pettey's *Dictionary of Women Artists* is international in scope and an excellent source on women artists born before 1900.

Other sources to check are George C. Groce and David H. Wallace's *New York Historical Society's Dictionary of Artists in America, 1565–1860*; William Young's *A Dictionary of American Artists, Sculptors and Engravers*; Peggy and Harold Samuels' *Artists of the American West* and *Contemporary Western Artists*; and Eden Hughes' *Artists in California, 1786–1940*.

Researching contemporary artists is more difficult. Consult *Who's Who in American Art*; the *Art in America Annual Guide to Galleries, Museums and Artists*; *Art Index*; *ARTbibliographies Modern*; the *Index to the Museum of Modern Art Artist Files* and the New York Public Library microfiche, and auction records. Exhibition catalogs can also be helpful. Worldwide Books, specialists in museum and gallery catalogs published from the 1960s to the present, will be going on-line with their database in 1996. Their lists of over 20,000 titles can be searched via the Web at http://www.worldwide.com.

If you are looking for information about a European artist, you will be able to turn to a number of standard texts. The basic biographical references for Italian art are Giulio Bolaffi's *Dizionario Enciclopedico Bolaffi dei Pittori e Degli Incisori Italiani: Dall' XI al XX Sècolo*, published in 1972, and A.M. Comanducci's *Dizionario Illustrato dei Pittori, Disegnatori e Incisori Italiani Moderni e Contemporanei*, last revised in 1962, which covers the 19th and 20th centuries.

Standard biographical references to British art include Christopher Woods' *Dictionary of Victorian Painters*, published in 1971; Grant Waters' *Dictionary of British Artists Working 1900–1950*, 1975; H.L. Mallalieu's *The Dictionary of British Watercolour Artists up to 1920*, 1976; and J. Johnson and A. Greutzner's *Dictionary of British Artists, 1880–1940*, 1976. *The Index to the Times of London* may provide information on lesser-known and more contemporary British artists.

Additional Resources

Additional resources are available to a researcher intent on discovering information about a particular artist. Many are accessible by telephone, greatly easing the research process.

Archives of American Art

The Archives of American Art is a bureau of the Smithsonian Institution which documents the history of the visual arts in America by collecting and preserving original documents, diaries, letters, photographs, oral histories, and other materials.

The main offices of the Archives are in Washington, D.C., and regional offices are located in New York City, Boston, Detroit, San Francisco, and San Marino, California. The Boston Public Library in Boston, and the de Young Museum Library in San Francisco, are depositories for microfilm of the Archives' records. In New York City, San Marino, and Detroit, the regional offices maintain the Archives' microfilm. Interlibrary loans are also available through the Detroit office. Records in the Archives include artists' personal papers, letters, diaries, sketches, photographs, exhibition material, financial information, writings, and lectures. The Archives also contains the records of arts organizations and institutions, and the papers of critics, dealers, collectors, and scholars. In addition, the Archives publishes a newsletter and *The Archives of American Art Journal*. The *Journal* reviews books and exhibitions and publishes a yearly list of master's and doctoral theses on American art. The newsletter, which is available by subscription, publishes a list of important acquisitions. Membership in the Archives, $65 a year, includes a subscription to both the *Journal* and the newsletter.

The Archives is searchable via Telnet or directly by modem (see page 39), but the Archives will also respond to telephone inquiries. Remote electronic access to the Archives will inform you if information on an artist is on microfilm, give you a reel number, and tell you if the information is at the branches or if it is only on hard copy in Washington.

The National Museum of American Art

The Inventory of American Painting Executed Before 1914 was begun as a project to celebrate America's bicentennial in 1976. It is a little-known but invaluable source which now has information on over 22,000 artists and 262,000 paintings, indexed by artist, title, owner/location, and subject matter. The data have been compiled from reports supplied by private collectors, museums, corporate collectors, public art programs, historical societies, and special survey projects. While the information is maintained on computer and the database is constantly updated, it is not absolutely accurate and may contain errors of date or spelling. However, up to twenty pages of information a year will be photocopied free of charge, and nominal charges apply to additional pages.

The Inventory of American Sculpture, another National Museum of American Art project, was begun in 1985. This is a new research database on the location, physical characteristics, and subject matter of outdoor monuments as well as sculpture in over 800 public and private collections. Information on each sculpture includes artist, title, medium, foundry identification, cast number, subject matter, location, and other data. Information on both sources is available by calling 202-357-2941, 1–5 P.M., Monday through Friday. They can be accessed directly through Telnet or by the link with the Smithsonian home page on the Web.

Cyberspace

The same critical evaluation that one should use with books should be used with Web sites. Who is the author? What are his credentials? One researcher defines "Internet wow" as the mistaken belief that because the information is on the Internet, it must be true. Sites on the Web are not regulated, and the degree of scholarship and author attribution varies greatly among disciplines. View the Web as a giant ad book, with over 30,000,000 ads (home pages). The results of a search, via Alta Vista, Yahoo, or some other search engine, may be deceptive. The first hit in a search for Erté is the Art Deco-Erté Museum, but accessing the site reveals the "museum" is the AJ Fine Arts Gallery located in the Mill Basin Deli and Gallery in Brooklyn, New York. Evaluate your sources; most sites are not reliable art-research tools.

More and more auction houses are adding home pages, but their level of sophistication and usefulness varies. One of the menu choices on Sotheby's page is to walk through a simulated auction, well designed and a lot of fun; another option is to download prices from recent sales. Young Fine Arts, in Portsmouth, New Hampshire, was one of the first to provide a catalog, complete with illustrations, via the Web. When you click on the lot number, an image appears; prices are added one to two weeks after a sale. Other houses provide a list of exhibitions or highlights of recent sales. The Internet can be a moving target, and addresses change fairly frequently. Some Internet addresses for auction houses are listed in Appendix C of this book.

There are some commercial sites that are useful and reliable. The trade publications *Maine Antique Digest* and *Antiques and the Arts Weekly* each have home pages that include notices of exhibtions and auctions, book and software reviews, ads, and links to other sites. The *M.A.D.* page also provides links to most auction houses. ArtsLink and Artsite of the Day are two commercial sites that have extensive lists of art museums, exhibitions, art agencies, and other art-related links. However, the Web Museum Paris, one of the most popular sites on the Internet, is authored by Nicolas Pioch, a French computer techie, NOT a noted scholar or authority, and is not an authoritative source. Addresses for reliable commercial sources are:

Maine Antique Digest	http://www.maine.com/mad
Antiques and the Arts Weekly	http://www.thebee.com/aweb/aa.htm
ArtsLink	http://www.artslink.com
Artsite of the Day	http://wwar.world-arts-resources.com

There are professional organizations, universities, and libraries that maintain reliable, informative home pages. ArtSource is a gathering point of resources on art and architecture compiled by art librarians; the Australian National University home page is a site dedicated to information on art and architecture from the Mediterranean basin; the Canadian Heritage Information Network is a government-sponsored list of all arts resources in Canada with schedules and exhibitions; the Cornell University Fine Arts Library has a home page that includes, among other resources, the inventory-catalog of the Biblioteca Ambrosiana.

ArtSource	http://www.uky.edu/Artsource
Australian National University	http://rubens.anu.edu.au
Canadian Heritage Information Network	http://www.chin.gc.ca
Cornell University Fine Arts Library	http://finearts.library.cornell.edu

Telnet is a protocol that connects to libraries and government agencies, reliable reference sources. Your provider may provide a direct connection to Telnet, or you may be able to link through your Netscape or Internet Explorer program. There are many variables and your combination of hardware and software is important; check with your provider or a computer expert if you need help. Internet search engines do not search Telnet sites, so it is best to call your library to obtain its address, or use a Telnet directory.[5] One of the most useful Telnet sites is the Smithsonian Institution page, which houses the Archives of American Art list of artists with their reel numbers, and the database of the Inventory of American Paintings and Sculpture. The various addresses for the Archives are:

> Telnet siris.si.edu
> Web http://www.nmaa.si.edu
> modem 202-357-4304

Sources available through academic libraries may also be available to individual users on a subscription basis. Most of these sources have home pages that provide information about their services. The Artbibliographies Modern database provides bibliographic coverage of articles, books, dissertations, and exhibition catalogs on art and design from the 19th and 20th centuries. The database corresponds to the semiannual publication of the same name. Information is available on the Web via DIALOG; a home page is planned for the fall of 1996. RLIN, the research libraries information network, has two databases: SCIPIO is a database of auction sales catalogs from 1599 to the present, and the RLG Conspectus Online is a tool for comparing and analyzing existing strengths and current collection policies. The Getty Art History Information Program home page gives information about RILA's *Art & Architecture Thesaurus* and the *Union List of Artists' Names*; these databases are available only on CD-ROM or hard copy, but there are free demonstration diskettes.

> RLIN   http://www.rlg.org
> Getty Art History Information Program http://www.ahip.getty.edu/
>   ahip/Text_home.html

Vertical Files

Many libraries maintain files of special material which is not listed in the card catalog, not shelved with books, and which may not be otherwise publicized. Generally filed under specific artists' names, these files preserve "casual" information that is quickly lost and almost impossible to replicate, and may include press releases, exhibition reviews, newspaper and magazine clippings, and obituaries. Librarians generally concentrate on artists working in the region. Historical societies also maintain excellent vertical files. If you can locate an artist's hometown, call the library or museum there and inquire if they have such information and if they will duplicate these

---

[5] Two useful Telnet directories are:
Hytelnet http://library.usask.ca/hytelnet
Yale Guide to Library Catalogs gopher://libgopher.yale.edu

materials. Most will comply and charge only a small fee for the service. These ephemera or vertical files are gold mines of information unavailable anywhere else.

Associations

Many dictionaries will refer to the local or regional associations to which an artist belonged. Many of these groups maintained private archives, another resource of valuable information about individual artists. The *American Art Dictionary* and the *Encyclopedia of Associations* provide the addresses of associations, museums, and art clubs across the nation. The Society of Illustrators may have information on illustrators not found elsewhere. The Guild of Boston Artists, the National Academy of Design in New York, and the National Watercolor Society in Lakewood, California, may all preserve unique resources. Pursue your artist—it's a grown-up treasure hunt.

Price Guides

An artist's sales history is an invaluable record of information. Auction records are frequently the only source of public information about art prices, since those achieved from gallery sales and purchases from estates or personal collections may remain private. More detailed information about the price histories of artists at auction over the past five years is available in the parent publication of this volume, *Leonard's ANNUAL Price Index of Art Auctions*, published annually since 1981 by Auction Index, Inc., Newton, Massachusetts (617-964-2876). *Leonard's Index*, also available on CD-ROM, lists artists alphabetically and includes every original work of art sold at auction at every major and minor auction house in the United States. Updated annually, it provides the most current information, and can be found in many libraries. (Some surprising and prominent names turn up in *Leonard's Index*. The paintings of Red Skelton, Jimi Hendrix, and Winston Churchill—all better known for other endeavors—have all sold at auction.)

Additional price information is available in Richard Hislop's *Annual Art Sales Index*, which is published in England and covers international sales, but excludes all lots under $500 and any artists not listed in Bénézit. Enrique Mayer's *International Auction Records*, translated from the French, is published annually and reports sale results from around the world. Falk's *Art Price Index International* is the newest addition to the field; it reports a large number of sales, but its size can make it cumbersome. *Annuaire Des Cotes*, or *ADEC*, as it is commonly called, is another new guide; verify the prices when using this index.

ArtNet (212-497-9704) is an on-line service that provides information on sale results around the world. The database for ArtNet is the same as for the book *Art Price Index International*. ArtNet's fees begin at $1.25 a minute and there are special package rates: one package is 120 minutes for $90 a month. Be careful; their fees can quickly add up.

A Selective Bibliography

General Art Reference Works and Encyclopedias

Arts in America: A Bibliography. 4 vols. Edited by Bernard Karpel. Washington, D.C., Smithsonian Institution Press, 1979.

The Dictionary of Art. 34 vols. Edited by Jane Turner. New York, Grove Hall Press, 1996.

Encyclopedia of American Art. Edited by Milton Rugoff. New York, E.P. Dutton, 1981.

Encyclopedia of World Art. 15 vols. New York, McGraw-Hill Book Co., 1958.

Jones, Lois Swan. *Art Research Methods and Resources.* 3rd ed. Dubuque, Iowa, Kendall/Hunt Publishing Co., 1990.

Mayer, Ralph. *A Dictionary of Art Terms and Techniques.* New York, Harper and Row Publishers, 1981.

McGraw-Hill Dictionary of Art. 5 vols. Edited by Bernard S. and Shirley D. Meyers. New York, McGraw-Hill Book Co., 1969.

Phaidon Dictionary of Twentieth-Century Art. New York, Phaidon Publishers, 1973.

Praeger Encyclopedia of Art. 5 vols. New York, Praeger Publishers, Inc., 1971.

General Artist Dictionaries

Bénézit, Emmanuel. *Dictionnaire Critique et Documentaire des Peintres, Sculpteurs, Dessinateurs et Graveurs.* 10 vols. 3rd ed. Paris, Grund, 1976.

Thieme, Ulrich, and Becker, Felix. *Allgemeines Lexikon der bildenden Künstler von der Antike bis zur Gegenwart; unter Mitwirkung von 300 Fachgelehrten des In-und Auslandes.* 37 vols. Leipzig, E.A. Seemann, 1907–50; reprint, 37 vols. Leipzig, F. Allmann, 1964.

Vollmer, Hans. *Allgemeines Lexikon der bildenden Künstler des XX Jahrhunderts.* 6 vols. Leipzig, E.A. Seemann, 1953–62.

Artist Indexes and General Indexes

ARTbibliographies Modern. Santa Barbara, California, Clio Press, 1974 +.

Art Index. 1 vol. Edited by Bertrum Deli. New York, H.W. Wilson Co., 1929 +.

Artists' Biographies Master Index, Detroit, Michigan, Gale Research Co., 1986 +.

Biographical Dictionaries Master Index. Detroit, Michigan, Gale Research Co., 1975 +.

Biography and Genealogy Master Index. Detroit, Michigan, Gale Research Co.

A Checklist of Painters c. 1200–1994, Represented in The Witt Library, Courtauld Institute of Art, London. London, England, Mansell Publishing Ltd., 1995.

Freitag, Wolfgang M. *Art Books: A Basic Bibliography of Monographs on Artists.* New York, Garland Publishing, 1985.

Havlice, Patricia Pate. *Index to Artistic Biography.* 2 vols. Metuchen, New Jersey, The Scarecrow Press, Inc., 1973. Suppl. 1981.

Mallett, Daniel Trowbridge. *Mallett's Index of Artists.* New York, R.R. Bowker Co., 1935. Suppl. 1940; reprint, 1948.

Museum of Modern Art Artist Files. Alexandria, Virginia, Chadwyck-Headley, 1993.

New York Times Index. Vol. 1-1913. New York, New York Times Co., 1913 +.

New York Times Obituaries Index, 1858–1968. New York, New York Times Co., 1970. Suppl. 1969–1978, 1980.

Union List of Artists' Names. New York, G.K. Hall & Co., 1994.

Specialized Artist Dictionaries and Directories

Art in America Annual Guide to Galleries, Museums, Artists. Edited by Elizabeth C. Baker. New York, Brant Art Publications, 1986.

Baigell, Matthew. *Dictionary of American Art*. New York, Harper and Row Publishers, 1979.

Catley, Bryan. *Art Deco and Other Figures*. Woodbridge, England, Antique Collectors Club, 1978.

Comanducci, Agostino Mario. *Dizionario Illustrato dei Pittori, Disegnatori e Incisori Italiani Moderni e Contemporanei*. Milan, Italy, Luigi Patuzzi Editore, 1970.

A Dictionary of American Artists, Sculptors and Engravers; From the Beginning Through the Turn of the Twentieth Century. Edited by William Young. Cambridge, Massachusetts, William Young and Co., 1968.

Dictionary of Contemporary American Artists. 4th ed. Edited by Paul Cummings. New York, St. Martin's Press, 1982.

Dizionario Enciclopedico Bolaffi dei Pittori e Degli Incisori Italiani: Dall' XI al XX Sècolo. 11 vols. Turin, Italy, Giulio Bolaffi Editore, 1972–76.

Encyclopedia of New Orleans Artists 1718–1918. New Orleans, The Historic New Orleans Collection, 1987.

Falk, Peter Hastings. *Who Was Who in American Art*. Madison, Connecticut, Sound View Press, 1985.

Fielding, Mantle. *Dictionary of American Painters, Sculptors and Engravers*. Poughkeepsie, New York, Apollo Books, 1983.

Folk Artists Biographical Index. Detroit, Gale Research Co., 1987.

Groce, George C., and Wallace, David H. *The New York Historical Society's Dictionary of Artists in America, 1564 hr –1860*. New Haven and London, Yale University Press, 1957.

Harper, J. Russell. *Early Painters and Engravers in Canada*. Toronto, Canada, University of Toronto Press, 1970.

Houfe, Simon. *The Dictionary of British Book Illustrators and Caricaturists*. Baron Publishing, Woodbridge, England, Antique Collectors Club, 1978.

Hughes, Eden Milton. *Artists in California, 1786-1940*. 2nd ed. San Francisco, Hughes Publishing Co., 1989.

Johnson, J., and Greutzner, A. *Dictionary of British Artists, 1880–1940: An Antique Collectors Club Research Project Listing 41,000 Artists*. Baron Publishing, Woodbridge, England, Antique Collectors Club, 1976.

Kjellberg, Pierre. *Bronzes of the 19th Century, A Dictionary of Sculptors*. Atglen, Pennsylvania, 1994.

Krantz, Les. *American Art Galleries*. New York, Facts on File Publications, 1985.

———. *American Artists*. New York, Facts on File Publications, 1985.

Lester, Patrick. *The Biographical Directory of Native American Painters*. Tulsa, Oklahoma, SIR Publishing, 1995.

MacDonald, Colin S. *A Dictionary of Canadian Artists*. Ottawa, Canada, Canadian Paperbacks, 1972.

Mackay, James. *The Dictionary of Western Sculptors in Bronze*. Woodbridge, England, Antique Collectors Club, 1977.

Mallalieu, H.L. *The Dictionary of British Watercolour Artists up to 1920*. Woodbridge, England, Antique Collectors Club, 1976.

Naylor, Colin, and Genesis, P-Orridge. *Contemporary Artists*. New York, St. Martin's Press, 1977; 2nd ed., 1983.

Pettey, Chris. *Dictionary of Women Artists: An International Dictionary of Women Artists Born Before 1900*. Boston, Massachusetts, G.K. Hall Co., 1985.

Robertson, Jack S. *Twentieth-Century Artists on Art*. New York, G.K. Hall Co., 1996.

Samuels, Peggy, and Samuels, Harold. *Contemporary Western Artists*. New York, Crown Publishing, 1985.

———. *The Illustrated Biographical Encyclopedia of Artists of the American West*. Garden City, New York, Doubleday, 1976.

Tazawa, Yutaka. *Biographical Dictionary of Japanese Art*. New York, Kodansha International, 1981.

Waters, Grant M. *Dictionary of British Artists Working 1900–1950*. Eastbourne, England, Eastbourne Fine Art, 1975.

Westphal, Ruth. *Plein Air Painters of California—The North*. Irvine, California, Westphal Publishing, 1986.

———. *Plein Air Painters of California—The Southland*. Irvine, California, Westphal Publishing, 1982, 1988.

Wood, Christopher. *The Dictionary of Victorian Painters*. 2nd ed. Woodbridge, England, Antique Collectors Club, 1978, 1981.

Association Directories

American Art Directory. 50th ed. New York, R.R. Bowker Co., 1986.

Encyclopedia of Associations. 21st ed. Detroit, Gale Research Co., 1987.

The Official Museum Directory: United States and Canada. 1st issue. Washington, D.C., American Association of Museums, 1971 +.

Period Frame Bibliography

Adair, William. *The Frame in America, 1700–1900*. Washington, D.C., AIA Foundation, 1983.

Brettel, Richard R., and Starling, Steven. *The Art of the Edge: European Frames 1300–1900*. Chicago, The Art Institute of Chicago, 1986.

Burns, Stanley B. *Forgotten Marriage—the Painted Tintype and the Decorated Frame*. Burns Collection Ltd., 1995.

Grimm, Claus. *The Book of Picture Frames*. New York, Abaris Books, 1981.

Heydenryk, Henry. *The Art and History of Frames*. New York, James H. Heinman, Inc., 1963.

In Perfect Harmony, Picture & Frame 1850–1920. University of Washington Press, 1995.

Katlan, Alexander W. *American Artists' Materials Suppliers Directory—Nine-teenth Century.* New Jersey, Noyes Press, 1987.
Newberry, Timothy, Bisacca, George, and Kanter, Larry. *The Italian Renaissance Frame.* New York, Metropolitan Museum of Art, 1990.
Wilner, Eli, with Kaufman, Mervyn. *Antique American Frames Identification and Price Guide.* New York, *The Confident Collector*, Avon Books, 1995.

Price Guides

Annuaire Des Cotes International. Paris, Adec Production, 1988 +.
The Annual Art Sales Index. 1st ed. Edited by Richard Hislop. Weybridge, Surrey, England, Art Sales Index, Ltd., 1969–70 +.
Falk, Peter. *Art Price Index International.* Madison, Connecticut, Sound View Press, 1992.
Leonard's ANNUAL Price Index of Art Auctions. 1 vol. Edited by Susan Theran. Newton, Massachusetts, Auction Index, Inc., 1980 +.
Mayer, Enrique. *International Auction Records: Engravings, Drawings, Water-colors, Paintings, Sculpture.* 1st English ed. Paris, Editions Enrique Mayer, 1967 +.
Theran, Susan. *Fine Art Identification and Price Guide.* New York, *The Confident Collector*, Avon Books, 1992.
———. *The Official Price Guide to Fine Art.* New York, House of Collectibles, 1987.

How to Use This Book ———————————————————

Fine Art Identification and Price Guide is a compilation of prices of fine art sold at auction throughout the United States from September 1990 through August 1995. Prices of fine art are established in the marketplace—at galleries, private sales, and auctions. Only those established at auction are of public record (in most cases governed by state regulations). These are the prices listed in this *Guide.*

The database for this volume consists of 36,239 names. Size limitations have forced us to refine it to 24,397 names, eliminating all artists whose top price was less than $450 at auction during this five-year period. You will find that there are famous artists, especially Old Masters such as Hieronymus Bosch and Vermeer, whose works are extremely rare and who are not listed because their works have not been offered for sale during this period.

By providing data about the *actual prices* realized at auction for the work of thousands of artists, *Fine Art Identification and Price Guide* presents a baseline of information about the art market. Auction prices are sometimes considered to be wholesale and sometimes retail, depending on location and date of sale. This *Guide* will help you assess comparative price data for individual artists and will help you determine whether a particular work is fairly priced, overvalued, or a bargain. The final consideration, however, must be the artistic quality of the painting—condition and other factors being equal.

The price range reflects the low and high prices for a category of work.

Identical prices in "low" and "high" reflect that more than one work by the artist has sold, but at the same price. If only one work by an artist was sold, the price will appear in the high column.

Price ranges are just that. Prices for an artist's work vary for a tremendous variety of reasons, including the importance and quality of the work, its size, and differences in media. Other factors are the desire of competing bidders, condition, subject matter, framing, provenance, attendance, weather, etc. The price ranges in this book reflect these variables.

For the purpose of this *Guide*, fine art is categorized as paintings, drawings, and sculpture. Prints and etchings, while certainly within the category of fine art, are not included, because they are works that exist in multiples. Paintings include oil, tempera, acrylic, casein, and fresco. Drawings include watercolor, pastel, gouache, crayon, pencil, charcoal, pen and ink, and mixed media. Included in the sculpture category are bronzes, marble statuary, bas reliefs, constructions, mobiles, and assemblages. Appendix E provides a complete listing by category.

Indexing in this *Guide* conforms to the *Anglo-American Cataloging Rules* for names, revised in 1979. For reasons of size, we have not cross-indexed artists' names. Appendix D provides a brief summary of the cataloging rules. If there is any doubt, check all the possibilities.

Nationality and life dates are included for all artists where available. When conflicts have arisen as to their validity, we have been diligent in our research and have made informed decisions.

There is sometimes confusion about the authorship of a particular work. John Herring Sr. and his son, John Jr., are frequently confused. We've done our best to sort through all these problems and present accurate prices.

Prices reflect the popularity of a particular artist or style in a certain region, fads, and fashion in art. Above all, they reflect the overall strength of the economy and economic trends. After Black Monday in October 1987, speculators turned to the art market as a safe haven for their dollars, buoying prices for art to false levels. In 1990, the art market retracted as the economy began to recover. A sharp decrease in lots sold for over $10 million made headlines, but the reality was that good art, especially when it was fresh to the market, held its own and even set new records. Contemporary art, which rose sharply in the 1980s, was the most affected by this downturn, as the softening of prices was primarily for those pieces which might have been bought for speculative or investment purposes only. Many feel that this is just a "rightening of the market."

Price is not the only index of value of an individual painting. Price will not tell you if a work is authentic. Nor will it tell you the unique characteristics or rarity of a painting. Note, too, that the price an artist sells for at auction is not necessarily what you will receive if you want to sell.

Finally, don't be discouraged by high prices. If you desire a work by a famous artist, it may be possible to buy a minor example for a reasonable sum. Slight sketches and smaller, less typical examples sell well below the prices of major canvases. The works of lesser-known, undiscovered, or undervalued artists provide many good buying opportunities.

For more specific information on the works of a particular artist, refer to *Leonard's ANNUAL Price Index of Art Auctions*, the parent volume of this *Guide*, which provides more detailed information on titles of works sold, size, auction house, and date of sale.

Artists' Price Ranges

A'BECKET, Maria
American d. 1904
paintings: (L) $258; (H) $1,320

AAGARD, Carl Frederic
Danish 1833-1895
paintings: (H) $10,350

AALTEN, Jacques van
American 20th cent.
paintings: (H) $550

AARONS, George
Russian/American 1896-1980
sculpture: (L) $3,850; (H) $5,500

AARTMANN, Nicolaas
Dutch 1713-1793
drawings: (H) $977

ABADES, E. Martinez
Continental 19th/20th cent.
paintings: (H) $3,300

ABADES, Juan Martinez
Spanish b. 1862
paintings: (L) $8,800; (H) $11,000

ABAKANOWICZ, Magdalena
b. 1930
drawings: (H) $5,500
sculpture: (L) $4,600; (H) $51,750

ABARCA, Raul E.
Argentinean b. 1950
sculpture: (L) $660; (H) $1,100

ABATE, Nicolo dell'
Italian c. 1512-1571
drawings: (L) $22,000; (H) $29,700

ABBATA, G.
drawings: (H) $1,610

ABBATE, Paolo S.
American 1884-1972
sculpture: (H) $770

ABBATT, Agnes Dean
American 1847-1917
drawings: (H) $2,200

ABBEMA, Louise
French 1858-1927
paintings: (L) $1,725; (H) $118,000
drawings: (L) $330; (H) $2,875

ABBETT, Robert
American b. 1926
paintings: (L) $660; (H) $13,200

ABBEY, Edwin Austin
American 1852-1911
paintings: (L) $220; (H) $38,500
drawings: (L) $137; (H) $18,700

ABBOTT, Agnes Anne
American b. 1897
drawings: (L) $22; (H) $1,725

ABBOTT, Dorothy
American contemporary
sculpture: (H) $748

ABBOTT, Lemuel Francis
English 1760-1803
paintings: (L) $3,450; (H) $23,000

ABBOTT, Lena H.
19th/20th cent.
paintings: (H) $522

ABBOTT, Meredith Brooks
American 20th cent.
paintings: (H) $575

ABBOTT, Samuel Nelson
American 1874-1953
paintings: (H) $7,150

ABBOTT, Yarnall
American 1870-1938
paintings: (L) $75; (H) $3,300

ABBRESCIA, Joe
paintings: (H) $2,500

ABDELL, Douglas
American b. 1947
sculpture: (H) $3,163

ABDY, Rowena Meeks
American 1887-c. 1945
paintings: (H) $13,800
drawings: (H) $1,650

ABE, Nobuya
Japanese 1913-1971
drawings: (H) $633

ABEL, Joseph
British 1764-1818
paintings: (H) $660

ABEL-TRUCHET, Louis
French 1857-1918
paintings: (L) $6,613; (H) $21,850

ABELA, Eduardo
Cuban 1892-1966
paintings: (L) $6,900; (H) $27,600
drawings: (L) $1,840; (H) $6,325

ABELARD, Gesner
Haitian b. 1922
paintings: (L) $578; (H) $2,530

ABELES, Sigmund
drawings: (H) $2,530

ABELL, G.
19th cent.
sculpture: (H) $3,850

ABERCROMBIE, Gertrude
American b. 1909
paintings: (L) $1,495; (H) $2,420

ABIL, Charlotte Clarisa
drawings: (L) $11; (H) $963

ABOLTIN, G.
paintings: (H) $1,050

ABRAMOFSY, Israel
Russian/American b. 1888
paintings: (H) $495

ABRAMOVITZ, Albert
American 1879-1963
paintings: (L) $55; (H) $880
drawings: (H) $137

ABRAMS, Lucien
American 1870-1941
paintings: (L) $1,320; (H) $1,760

ABRASSOUT
Continental 19th/20th cent.
paintings: (H) $2,530

ABSOLON, John
English 1815-1895
paintings: (H) $330
drawings: (H) $3,960

ABULARACH, Rodolfo
Guatemalan b. 1934
paintings: (H) $6,600

ACAPPOLI
Italian 19th/20th cent.
drawings: (H) $550

ACCARD, Eugene
French 1824-1888
paintings: (L) $935; (H) $7,700

ACCARDI, Carla
Italian b. 1924
paintings: (L) $6,600; (H) $24,200

ACCONCI, Vito
American b. 1940
paintings: (H) $16,100
drawings: (L) $920; (H) $16,500
sculpture: (H) $12,100

ACERES, T.
Spanish 19th cent.
paintings: (H) $1,540

ACEVES, Gustavo
Mexican b. 1957
drawings: (H) $2,860

ACEVES, T.
Spanish 19th cent.
paintings: (H) $550

ACHEFF, William
American b. 1947
paintings: (L) $550; (H) $31,900
drawings: (H) $1,000

ACHEN, Georg
Danish 1860-1912
paintings: (H) $9,200

ACHENBACH, Andreas
German 1815-1910
paintings: (L) $863; (H) $17,600

ACHENBACH, Anna Thomson
American 20th cent.
paintings: (L) $93; (H) $1,375

ACHENBACH, Oswald
German 1827-1905
paintings: (L) $8,050; (H) $60,500
drawings: (H) $132

ACHILLE, Theodore Emile
Dutch 1851-1904
paintings: (H) $1,540

ACHILLEOS, Chris
drawings: (H) $15,400

ACOSTA LEON, Angel
b. Cuba 1932
paintings: (L) $13,800; (H) $32,200

ADAM, Albrecht
German 1786-1862
paintings: (H) $12,100

ADAM, Benno
German 1812-1892
paintings: (L) $3,520; (H) $10,725

ADAM, Ed.
French ac. 1872-1899
paintings: (H) $2,013

ADAM, Edouard Marie
French 1847-1929
paintings: (H) $8,800

ADAM, Emil
German 1843-1924
paintings: (L) $1,700; (H) $2,990

ADAM, Joseph Donovan
English 1842-1896
paintings: (L) $715; (H) $4,620

ADAM, Julius
German 1826-1874
paintings: (L) $28,600; (H) $29,700

ADAM, Julius
German 1852-1913
paintings: (L) $18,400; (H) $40,700

ADAM, Julius
German 19th cent.
paintings: (L) $20,700; (H) $27,600

ADAM, Marie Edouard
French 1847-1929
paintings: (H) $990

ADAM, Richard Benno
German 1873-1936
paintings: (H) $5,500

ADAM, Robert
Scottish 1728-1792
drawings: (H) $7,475

ADAM, T. Denovan
paintings: (H) $1,045

ADAM, Victor Charles Edouard
French 1868-1938
paintings: (H) $1,540

ADAM, Victor Jean
French 1801-1866
drawings: (H) $495

ADAM, William
American 1846-1931
paintings: (L) $143; (H) $2,875
drawings: (H) $259

ADAMOFF, Helena
Russian b. 1906
paintings: (H) $743

ADAMS, Charles Partridge
American 1858-1942
paintings: (L) $275; (H) $19,550
drawings: (L) $220; (H) $2,750

ADAMS, Douglas
English 1853-1920
paintings: (H) $1,650

ADAMS, Herbert
American 20th cent.
sculpture: (H) $660

ADAMS, J.D.
paintings: (H) $550

ADAMS, J.L.
American
drawings: (L) $350; (H) $600

ADAMS, Jean Crawford
American 20th cent.
paintings: (H) $1,725

ADAMS, John Clayton
British 1840-1906
paintings: (L) $650; (H) $36,800

ADAMS, John Otis
American 1851-1927
paintings: (L) $17,600; (H) $33,000

ADAMS, John Talbot
English 1861-1905
paintings: (H) $825

ADAMS, Lillian
American b. 1899
paintings: (L) $192; (H) $715

ADAMS, Marlin
b. 1949
paintings: (L) $6,600; (H) $13,750

ADAMS, Neal
drawings: (H) $920

ADAMS, Phyllis Kaye
American 20th cent.
paintings: (H) $1,045

ADAMS, Robert
sculpture: (H) $2,090

ADAMS, T.H.
paintings: (H) $880

ADAMS, Walter Burt
American 20th cent.
paintings: (H) $990

ADAMS, Wayman
American 1883-1959
paintings: (L) $1,650; (H) $9,625

ADAMS, Willis A.
American 1854-1932
paintings: (H) $605

ADAMS, Willis Seaver
American 1842-1921
paintings: (L) $3,300; (H) $5,175

ADAMSON, David Comba
British 19th/20th cent.
drawings: (H) $3,450

ADAMSON, Dorothy
British d. 1934
drawings: (H) $3,300

ADAMSON, Harry Curieux
American 20th cent.
paintings: (L) $1,380; (H) $2,970

ADAMSON, Sydney
American ac. 1892-1914
paintings: (L) $2,640; (H) $4,400
drawings: (L) $742; (H) $1,045

ADAN, Louis Emile
French 1839-1937
paintings: (L) $748; (H) $43,125
drawings: (H) $1,045

ADDAMS, Charles
American 1912-1988
drawings: (L) $330; (H) $4,950

ADDISON, Bryon Kent
American b. 1935
sculpture: (L) $577; (H) $660

ADDISON, Robert
American 20th cent.
paintings: (H) $2,420

ADDISON, Williams G.
English b. 1904
drawings: (H) $467

ADEMOLLO, Luigi
Italian 1764-1849
drawings: (H) $1,955

ADICKES, David
American b. 1927
paintings: (L) $192; (H) $1,760

ADKINS, Minnie and Garland
20th cent.
sculpture: (H) $550

ADLER, C.
sculpture: (H) $13,200

ADLER, Edmund
German 1871-1957
paintings: (L) $9,200; (H) $24,150

ADLER, Ellen
American 20th cent.
paintings: (L) $330; (H) $660

ADLER, Jankel
Polish 1895-1949
paintings: (L) $9,775; (H) $11,500
drawings: (L) $230; (H) $33,350

ADLER, Oscar F.
20th cent.
paintings: (L) $660; (H) $880

ADLER, Oscar F., probably
paintings: (H) $1,100

ADLER, Samuel Marcus
American 1898-1979
paintings: (H) $550

ADNET, Francoise
French b. 1924
paintings: (L) $555; (H) $4,884

ADOLPHE, Albert Jean
American 1865-1940
paintings: (L) $88; (H) $2,178

ADRAMS, Bob and Anna
20th cent.
paintings: (H) $13,800

ADRIAENSSEN, Alexander
1587-1661
paintings: (L) $5,462; (H) $6,325

ADRIAN
American 20th cent.
drawings: (L) $220; (H) $5,500

ADRIAN, M.
paintings: (H) $1,430

ADRIANI, Camillo
American 20th cent.
paintings: (L) $275; (H) $2,600

ADRION
paintings: (H) $632

ADRION, Lucien
French 1889-1953
paintings: (L) $1,100; (H) $7,700

AEBERSOLD, Jane Ford
contemporary
sculpture: (H) $1,380

AELST, Willem van
Dutch 1625/26-c. 1683
paintings: (L) $15,400; (H) $82,500

AERNI, Franz Theodor
German 1853-1918
paintings: (H) $5,060

AERTSEN, Pieter
Dutch 1507/08-1575
paintings: (H) $7,700

AESCHBACHER, Arthur
Swiss b. 1923
paintings: (H) $660
drawings: (H) $385

AFFLECK, William
British b. 1869
drawings: (H) $4,125

AFFORTUNATI, Aldo
Italian b. 1906
paintings: (L) $523; (H) $863

AFRICANO, Nicholas
American b. 1948
paintings: (L) $3,300; (H) $15,400
drawings: (H) $660
sculpture: (H) $4,600

AFRO, Afro BASALDELLA
Italian 1912-1976
paintings: (L) $34,500; (H) $154,000
drawings: (L) $1,035; (H) $16,500

AFSARY, Cyrus
American b. 1940
paintings: (L) $2,750; (H) $15,400

AGAM, Yaacov
Israeli b. 1928
paintings: (L) $3,162; (H) $57,750
drawings: (L) $288; (H) $4,140
sculpture: (L) $748; (H) $28,600

AGAR, Charles d'
French 1669-1723
paintings: (H) $6,900

AGAR, Eileen
British b. 1904
drawings: (H) $1,980

AGARD, Charles
paintings: (H) $1,650

AGARD, Charles
French 1866-1950
paintings: (H) $5,175

AGASSE, Jacques Laurent
Swiss 1767-1849
paintings: (L) $4,950; (H) $365,500

AGNEESENS, Edouard Joseph
Alexander
Belgian 1842-1885
paintings: (H) $1,380

AGNESTI
Italian 19th/20th cent.
paintings: (H) $880

AGNEW, J.F.
American 19th cent.
paintings: (H) $715

AGOSTINELLI, Mario
American 20th cent.
paintings: (H) $2,860

AGOSTINI
Italian School 19th cent.
paintings: (H) $605

AGOSTINI, Guido
Italian 19th cent.
paintings: (L) $437; (H) $3,080

AGOSTINI, Peter
American b. 1913
drawings: (L) $770; (H) $1,035

AGOSTINI, Tony
Italian b. 1916
paintings: (L) $137; (H) $2,530

AGOSTINO, Guido
Italian 19th cent.
paintings: (H) $2,200

AGOSTONI
Continental contemporary
paintings: (H) $4,070

AGRASOT Y JUAN, Joaquin
Spanish 1836-1919
paintings: (L) $483; (H) $27,500
drawings: (L) $460; (H) $1,610

AGRESTI, A.
Italian 19th cent.
paintings: (H) $935

AGRESTI, R.
Italian 19th cent.
paintings: (L) $1,380; (H) $4,715

AGRICOLA, Karl Joseph Aloys
German 1779-1852
drawings: (H) $1,150

AGTHE, Curt
German b. 1862
paintings: (H) $5,500

AGUILAR, El Conde de
Spanish 19th cent.
paintings: (H) $3,450

AHEARN, John
American b. 1951
sculpture: (L) $1,380; (H) $9,350

AHIVITTI, F.
paintings: (H) $2,200

AHL, Henry Hammond
American 1869-1953
paintings: (L) $88; (H) $660

AHN, Miriam
American 20th cent.
paintings: (L) $748; (H) $1,210

AHRENDT, William
American 20th cent.
paintings: (H) $1,610

AHRENDTS, Carl Eduard
paintings: (L) $440; (H) $715

AHRENS, H.
paintings: (H) $3,850

AICENY
Continental 20th cent.
paintings: (H) $1,840

AICHELE, P.
French 19th cent.
sculpture: (H) $990

AID, George Charles
American 1872-1938
paintings: (H) $23,000

AIGON, Antonin
sculpture: (H) $863

AIKEN, C.A.
paintings: (H) $484

AIKEN, Henry, Jr.
English 1810-1894
paintings: (H) $8,800

AIKEN, Mary Hoover
American b. 1907
paintings: (L) $385; (H) $495

AIKENHEAD, Steve
contemporary
sculpture: (L) $230; (H) $715

AINSLIE, Maude
paintings: (H) $550

AIRENS, H.
American School 19th cent.
paintings: (H) $2,640

AITKEN, J.
English 19th cent.
paintings: (H) $1,045

AITKEN, James Alfred
Scottish 1846-1897
drawings: (H) $1,045

AITKEN, John E.
British 1881-1957
drawings: (L) $605; (H) $1,375

AITKEN, Robert Ingersoll
American 1878-1949
sculpture: (L) $3,300; (H) $6,900

AIVAZOFFSKI, Ivan
Constantinowitsch
Russian 1817-1900
paintings: (L) $27,500; (H) $134,500
drawings: (L) $880; (H) $880

AIZELIN, Eugene Antoine
French 1821-1902
sculpture: (L) $770; (H) $15,950

AIZENBERG, Roberto
Argentinean b. 1928
paintings: (L) $11,000; (H) $17,600

AIZPIRI, Paul
French b. 1919
paintings: (L) $1,495; (H) $132,000
drawings: (L) $460; (H) $33,000

AJDUKIEWICZ, Sigismund von
Austrian b. 1861
paintings: (L) $1,380; (H) $3,960

AKELEY, Carl Ethan
American 1864-1926
sculpture: (L) $3,850; (H) $5,290

AKEN, Leo van
Belgian 1857-1904
paintings: (H) $1,045

AKERS, Benjamin Paul
American 1825-1861
sculpture: (L) $2,090; (H) $12,650

AKERS, Vivian Milner
American 1886-1966
paintings: (L) $138; (H) $8,800
drawings: (H) $193

AKIMITSU
late 19th cent.
sculpture: (H) $4,312

AKKERINGA, Johannes Evert
Hendrick
Dutch 1864-1942
drawings: (L) $3,960; (H) $5,175

AKKERSDIJK, Jacob
Dutch 1815-1862
paintings: (L) $2,300; (H) $4,400

ALAJALOV, Constantin
Russian/American 1900-1987
drawings: (L) $6,600; (H) $8,250

ALAUX, Alexandre
American 1869-1932
paintings: (L) $220; (H) $495

ALAUX, Jean Pierre
French b. 1925
paintings: (L) $460; (H) $1,045

ALAUX, Marie Fernande
1883-1958
paintings: (L) $605; (H) $715

ALBAN, Vincente
Ecuadoran 18th cent.
paintings: (L) $5,750; (H) $154,000

ALBANI AND STUDIO, Francesco
1578-1660
paintings: (H) $28,750

ALBANO, Salvatore
Italian 19th cent.
sculpture: (L) $1,320; (H) $5,280

ALBEE, Percy
American 1883-1959
drawings: (H) $748

ALBERICI, Augusto
Italian b. 1846
drawings: (H) $2,090

ALBERMANN, Wilhelm
German b. 1835
sculpture: (H) $3,190

ALBEROLA, Jean Michel
b. 1953
paintings: (L) $6,050; (H) $7,475
drawings: (L) $2,640; (H) $5,280

ALBERS, Josef
American 1888-1976
paintings: (L) $523; (H) $286,000
drawings: (L) $3,575; (H) $24,150

ALBERT
paintings: (H) $550

ALBERT
European 20th cent.
paintings: (H) $990

ALBERT, Adolphe
French 19th/20th cent.
paintings: (L) $3,565; (H) $6,050

ALBERT, E. Maxwell
American b. 1890
paintings: (H) $2,530

ALBERT, Ernest
American 1857-1946
paintings: (L) $660; (H) $20,700

ALBERT, Jeannine
French b. 1939
paintings: (L) $920; (H) $1,668

ALBERT, Karl
American b. 1911
paintings: (L) $358; (H) $1,650

ALBERTI, C.
Continental 19th cent.
paintings: (H) $1,100

ALBERTI, Cherubino
Italian 1553-1615
drawings: (H) $1,320

ALBERTI, Giuseppe Vizzotto
Italian 19th cent.
paintings: (H) $3,080

ALBERTI, Henri
French b. 1868
paintings: (H) $1,495

ALBERTINELLI, Mariotto
Italian 1474-1515
paintings: (H) $57,500

ALBERTINELLI, Mariotto, studio of
15th/16th cent.
paintings: (H) $30,250

ALBERTIS, Sebastiano de
Italian 1828-1897
drawings: (H) $1,320

ALBERTOLLI, Giocondo
Italian 1742-1839
drawings: (L) $920; (H) $1,610

ALBINA, Luca
Italian 19th/20th cent.
paintings: (H) $3,025

ALBINSON, Ernest Dewey
American b. 1898
paintings: (H) $1,760
drawings: (L) $88; (H) $550

ALBOTTO, Francesco
Italian 1722-1758
paintings: (L) $23,000; (H) $85,000

ALBRACHT, Willem
Flemish 1861-1922
paintings: (H) $1,650

ALBRICCI, Enrico
Italian 1714-1775
paintings: (H) $18,400

ALBRIGHT, Adam Emory
American 1862-1957
paintings: (L) $440; (H) $35,750
drawings: (H) $546

ALBRIGHT, Gertrude Partington
American 1883-1959
paintings: (H) $1,650

ALBRIGHT, Henry James
American 1887-1951
paintings: (L) $440; (H) $2,750

ALBRIGHT, Ivan Le Lorraine
American 1897-1983
paintings: (L) $302; (H) $1,100
drawings: (L) $770; (H) $2,200

ALBRIGHT, Malvin Marr
American 1897-1983
paintings: (L) $92; (H) $1,265
drawings: (L) $92; (H) $575
sculpture: (L) $460; (H) $863

ALBRO, Maxine
American 1903-1966
paintings: (L) $413; (H) $2,875

ALCANTARA, Antonio
Venezuelan b. 1918
paintings: (H) $1,265

ALCHIMOWICZ, Kasimir
Polish b. 1840
paintings: (H) $11,500

ALCIBAR, Jose de
Mexican 1751-1803
paintings: (L) $16,100; (H) $30,800

ALCIRE
German 19th/20th cent.
paintings: (H) $605

ALCOPLEY
American b. 1910
paintings: (H) $495

ALDE, Yvette
French 1911-1967
paintings: (L) $358; (H) $1,100

ALDELINA
Continental 19th cent.
drawings: (H) $1,725

ALDEN, Cecil
British 1879-1935
drawings: (H) $578

ALDERTON, Henry A.
American 1896-1961
paintings: (H) $990

ALDIN, Cecil Charles Windsor
English 1870-1935
drawings: (L) $4,125; (H) $6,325

ALDINE, Marc
Italian b. 1917
paintings: (L) $2,990; (H) $3,850

ALDINE, Marc, Antoine BOUVARD
French d. 1956
paintings: (L) $1,955; (H) $17,600

ALDRICH, George Ames
American 1872-1941
paintings: (L) $385; (H) $6,613

ALDRIDGE, Frederick James
British 1850-1933
drawings: (L) $248; (H) $467

ALDUNATE, Carmen
b. Chile 1940
paintings: (H) $9,200

ALECHINSKY, Pierre
Belgian b. 1927
paintings: (L) $13,800; (H) $154,000
drawings: (L) $2,640; (H) $17,600

ALEGIANI, *F.***
Italian 19th cent.
paintings: (H) $9,488

ALEGIANI, Francesco
Italian 19th cent.
paintings: (H) $4,950

ALEGRO, J.
sculpture: (H) $605

ALEGRO, L.
late 19th cent.
sculpture: (H) $990

ALEJANDRO, Ramon
b. 1943
paintings: (H) $2,760

ALEXANDER
paintings: (H) $605

ALEXANDER, Clifford Grear
American 1870-1954
paintings: (L) $288; (H) $575

ALEXANDER, F.
French 19th/20th cent.
paintings: (H) $605

ALEXANDER, Francis
American 1800-1880/81
paintings: (L) $345; (H) $770

ALEXANDER, Henry
American 1860-1895
paintings: (H) $12,650

ALEXANDER, John
b. 1945
paintings: (L) $4,600; (H) $12,650

ALEXANDER, John White
American 1856-1915
paintings: (L) $244,500; (H) $266,500
drawings: (L) $165; (H) $1,100

ALEXANDER, Peter
American b. 1939
paintings: (H) $5,750
drawings: (H) $1,320
sculpture: (H) $6

ALEXANDER, Robert
British 19th cent.
paintings: (H) $990

ALEXANDER, Terrance
paintings: (H) $880

ALEXEJEFF, Alexandre
Russian 1811-1878
paintings: (H) $3,450

ALEXI, Johann
Australian late 18th cent.
paintings: (H) $4,312

ALEXIEFF, Alexander I.
Russian b. 1842
paintings: (H) $3,410

ALEXO, C.
Italian 19th cent.
paintings: (H) $715

ALFANO, Vincenzo
Italian b. 1854
sculpture: (H) $2,013

ALFEREZ, Enrique
Mexican b. 1901
paintings: (H) $5,500
drawings: (H) $5,500
sculpture: (L) $578; (H) $8,250

ALFIERI, G.
Continental School 20th cent.
paintings: (H) $4,290

ALFONZO, Carlos
b. Cuba 1950-1991
paintings: (L) $9,200; (H) $40,250
drawings: (L) $3,575; (H) $9,200

ALGARDI, Alessandro
Italian 1595-1654
sculpture: (L) $16,100; (H) $57,500

ALGIE, Jessie
English 20th cent.
paintings: (H) $1,650

ALI, J. Sultan
Indian b. 1920
paintings: (H) $6,325
drawings: (H) $1,150

ALIGNY, H.
French 19th cent.
paintings: (H) $2,760

ALIOTTI, Claude
1925-1989
paintings: (L) $207; (H) $715

ALISON, Henry Y.
British ac. 1913-1939
paintings: (H) $1,210

ALIX, Gabriel
paintings: (H) $715

ALIZONE, H.
French 19th/20th cent.
paintings: (H) $770

ALKEN, Henry Thomas
British 1784-1851
paintings: (L) $5,500; (H) $209,000
drawings: (L) $1,100; (H) $26,400

ALKEN, Samuel, Sr.
British 1756-1815
paintings: (H) $3,575

ALKEN, Samuel Henry, Jr.
British 1810-1894
paintings: (L) $4,600; (H) $42,900

ALLAN, David
British 1744-1796
paintings: (H) $1,760

ALLAN, Georgina
Scottish 19th/20th cent.
paintings: (H) $467

ALLAN, J.B.
American
paintings: (H) $660

ALLAN, Mrs. Charles Beach, S.P.
ALLAN
American b. 1874
paintings: (H) $1,210

ALLAN, Robert Weir
English 1852-1942
paintings: (L) $385; (H) $49,500
drawings: (L) $110; (H) $2,875

ALLAN, Sir William
British 1782-1850
drawings: (H) $550

ALLAN, William
American b. 1936
drawings: (H) $660

ALLAN, William and Bruce Nauman
contemporary
sculpture: (H) $19,550

ALLARD, Charles
French 20th cent.
paintings: (H) $550

ALLEGRAIN, C.G.
sculpture: (H) $1,540

ALLEGRAIN, Christophe Gabriel
sculpture: (L) $2,420; (H) $6,600

ALLEGRAIN, G.C.
sculpture: (H) $605

ALLEGRE, Raymond
French 1857-1933
paintings: (L) $1,430; (H) $3,680

ALLEGRINI, Flaminio
Italian ac. 1625-1635
drawings: (H) $9,350

ALLEGRINI, Francesco
1624-after 1679
drawings: (H) $3,680

ALLEGRINI, Francesco
Italian 1587-1663
drawings: (H) $3,450

ALLEN, Charles Curtis
American 1886-1950
paintings: (L) $55; (H) $2,750
drawings: (L) $330; (H) $880

ALLEN, Courtney
American 1896-1969
paintings: (L) $330; (H) $1,760
drawings: (L) $110; (H) $275
sculpture: (H) $302

ALLEN, Douglas
American 20th cent.
paintings: (L) $825; (H) $1,100
drawings: (L) $247; (H) $247

ALLEN, Edward
paintings: (H) $1,000

ALLEN, Gregory S.
American b. 1884
sculpture: (H) $715

ALLEN, Greta
American b. 1881
paintings: (L) $88; (H) $5,500
drawings: (L) $138; (H) $165

ALLEN, J.E.
American
paintings: (H) $10,285

ALLEN, James
b. 1894
paintings: (H) $6,050

ALLEN, John H.
American 1866-1953
paintings: (L) $55; (H) $2,300

ALLEN, Junius
American 1898-1962
paintings: (L) $1,980; (H) $2,640

ALLEN, Margaret Newton
American b. 1895
sculpture: (H) $5,635

ALLEN, Marion Boyd
American 1862-1941
paintings: (L) $110; (H) $10,725

ALLEN, Robert Weir
British 1852-1942
paintings: (H) $2,420
drawings: (L) $990; (H) $1,610

ALLEN, Thomas
American 1849-1924
paintings: (L) $522; (H) $715

ALLEN, Willard
American 19th/20th cent.
paintings: (H) $880

ALLEYNE, Francis
British 18th/19th cent.
paintings: (H) $3,520

ALLIEVI, Fernando
b. Argentina 1954
drawings: (H) $3,850

ALLIOT, Lucien Charles Edouard
French b. 1877
sculpture: (L) $1,610; (H) $4,620

ALLIS, Arthur S.
American 1904-1973
drawings: (H) $715

ALLIS, C. Harry
American c. 1880-1938
paintings: (L) $220; (H) $2,300
drawings: (L) $40; (H) $187

ALLISON, William
English 19th cent.
paintings: (H) $15,400

ALLMANN
Continental 20th cent.
sculpture: (H) $880

ALLMER, Joseph
paintings: (H) $7,150

ALLOM, Thomas
British 1804-1872
drawings: (H) $5,175

ALLORI, Alessandro, studio of
Italian 16th/17th cent.
paintings: (H) $19,800

ALLORI, Cristofano
1577-1621
paintings: (H) $19,800
drawings: (H) $5,175

ALLOUARD, H.
French 19th cent.
sculpture: (H) $633

ALLOUARD, Henri
French 1844-1929
sculpture: (L) $605; (H) $8,800

ALMA-TADEMA, Anna
British 19th cent.
drawings: (H) $1,150

ALMA-TADEMA, Lady Laura Epps
English 1852-1909
drawings: (H) $4,950

ALMA-TADEMA, Sir Lawrence
English 1836-1912
paintings: (L) $8,250; (H) $2,752,500
drawings: (L) $16,100; (H) $43,700

ALMANZA, Cleofas
Mexican 1850-1915
paintings: (H) $38,500

ALMARAZ, Carlos
Mexican/American 1941-1989
paintings: (L) $1,380; (H) $8,050
drawings: (L) $4,620; (H) $6,900

ALMEIDA, Jose Ferraz de, Jr.
Brazilian 1850-1899
paintings: (H) $16,100

ALMOND, William Douglas
British b. 1866
paintings: (H) $660

ALONSO, Carlos
Argentinean b. 1929
paintings: (L) $3,680; (H) $8,800

ALONSO-PEREZ, Mariano
Spanish 1857-1930
paintings: (H) $16,100

ALONZO, D.
sculpture: (H) $935

ALONZO, Dominique
French aç. 1910-1930
sculpture: (L) $297; (H) $2,420

ALOTT, Robert
French 19th cent.
paintings: (L) $880; (H) $6,900

ALPHONSE, L.V.
American 19th cent.
paintings: (H) $2,090

ALPUY, Julio
b. Uruguay 1919
paintings: (H) $7,700
drawings: (H) $2,475
sculpture: (H) $31,050

ALSHEIM, W.
Continental 19th cent.
paintings: (H) $1,150

ALSINA, Jacques
French 19th/20th cent.
paintings: (L) $880; (H) $7,150

ALSTINE, John van
American b. 1952
sculpture: (H) $1,430

ALSTINE, John van
American b. 1952
sculpture: (L) $1,430; (H) $2,300

ALSTON, Abbey
b. 1864
paintings: (L) $2,750; (H) $2,860

ALT, Franz
Austrian 1821-1914
paintings: (H) $1,955
drawings: (L) $58; (H) $20,900

ALT, Otmar
German b. 1940
paintings: (L) $4,675; (H) $4,888

ALT, Rudolf von
Austrian 1812-1905
drawings: (H) $1,725

ALTEN, Mathias J.
German/American 1871-1938
paintings: (L) $550; (H) $7,475

ALTIERI, E.
Italian 19th/20th cent.
paintings: (H) $1,980

ALTMANN, Alexandre
Russian b. 1885
paintings: (L) $605; (H) $11,500

ALTOMONTE, Martin
1657-1745
paintings: (H) $6,900

ALTOON, John
American 1925-1969
paintings: (L) $935; (H) $5,500
drawings: (L) $633; (H) $2,588

ALTRUI, E.
Italian 19th cent.
paintings: (L) $440; (H) $1,870

ALTSON, Abbey
British ac. 1894-1917
paintings: (L) $2,530; (H) $11,500

ALVAR, Sunol
Spanish b. 1935
paintings: (L) $3,575; (H) $9,075
sculpture: (H) $990

ALVARDI, Carlo
paintings: (H) $7,150

ALVAREZ, Jean
Spanish 19th cent.
paintings: (H) $1,760

ALVAREZ, L.
Spanish 1836-1901
paintings: (H) $55,000

ALVAREZ, Luis Catala
Spanish 1841-1901
paintings: (L) $2,090; (H) $44,000

ALVAREZ, Mabel
American 1891-1985
paintings: (L) $522; (H) $9,775
drawings: (L) $330; (H) $825

ALVAREZ CATALA, Luis
Spanish 1836-1901
paintings: (L) $17,600; (H) $156,500

ALVAREZ-DUMONT, Eugenio
Spanish 1864-1927
paintings: (H) $79,500

ALVERGNE, Adolph Jean
sculpture: (H) $495

ALZIBAR, Jose de
ac. 1730-1806
paintings: (H) $6,900

AMAN, Frederick
American 20th cent.
sculpture: (H) $8,500

AMAN-JEAN, Edmond Francois
French 1860-1935/36
paintings: (L) $2,310; (H) $5,175
drawings: (L) $495; (H) $2,645

AMANDRY, Robert
French b. 1905
sculpture: (H) $4,950

AMANS, Jacques Guillaume Lucien
American 1801-1888
paintings: (H) $6,600

AMAR, Joseph
b. 1954
paintings: (H) $550
sculpture: (L) $2,760; (H) $2,860

AMARAL, Antonio Henrique
b. Brazil 1935
paintings: (L) $3,300; (H) $74,000
drawings: (L) $1,375; (H) $2,475

AMARAL, Olga de
contemporary
sculpture: (H) $4,888

AMAT, Frederic
b. 1952
drawings: (H) $6,325

AMATEIS, Edmond Romulus
American b. 1897
sculpture: (H) $990

AMATI, S.
Italian 20th cent.
paintings: (H) $575

AMATO, Luigi
Italian 20th cent.
paintings: (H) $990

AMATO, Sam
paintings: (H) $518

AMBERG, Wilhelm
German 1822-1899
paintings: (L) $2,750; (H) $6,038

AMBERGER, Gustav A.
German 1831-1896
paintings: (H) $2,070

AMBROGIANI, Pierre
French 1907-1985
paintings: (H) $3,680

AMBROS, Raphael von
Austrian 1845-1895
paintings: (H) $3,450

AMBROSSI, A. d'
French 19th cent.
paintings: (L) $110; (H) $825

AMBUCHI, T.
Italian 19th cent.
sculpture: (H) $3,220

AMEGLIO, Mario
French 1897-1970
paintings: (L) $880; (H) $4,620

AMEN, Irving
American b. 1918
paintings: (L) $110; (H) $715

AMENOFF, Gregory
American b. 1948
paintings: (L) $1,035; (H) $11,000
drawings: (H) $770

AMERLING, Friedrich Ritter von
Austrian 1803-1887
paintings: (L) $1,100; (H) $55,000

AMERONGEN, Friedrich Freiherr von
German b. 1878
paintings: (H) $650

AMES, Ezra
American 1768-1836
paintings: (L) $1,210; (H) $8,800

AMES, Wally
b. 1942
paintings: (L) $193; (H) $825

AMICK, Robert Wesley
American 1879-1969
paintings: (L) $605; (H) $6,600
drawings: (L) $137; (H) $920

AMICO, Peter d'
paintings: (H) $1,380

AMIET, Cuno
Swiss 1868-1961
paintings: (H) $28,600

AMIGONI, Jacopo
Italian 1675-1752
paintings: (L) $4,400; (H) $605,000

AMINO, Leo
American 20th cent.
sculpture: (H) $770

AMISANI, Giuseppe
paintings: (H) $4,600

AMMANN, Eugen
Swiss b. 1882
paintings: (H) $1,595

AMMIRATO, Domenic
Italian b. 1833
paintings: (H) $8,625

AMOROS, A.
Italian 19th cent.
paintings: (H) $2,070

AMOROSI, Antonio
Italian 1660-c. 1736
paintings: (L) $2,185; (H) $4,830

AMOROSI, L.
paintings: (H) $715

AMORSOLO, Fernando
Philippine 1892-1940
paintings: (L) $660; (H) $37,375

AMOS, G.T.
English 19th cent.
paintings: (L) $715; (H) $990

AMSEL, Richard
1947-1985
drawings: (L) $1,430; (H) $11,000

AMYOT, Catherine Engelhart
Danish b. 1845
paintings: (H) $20,700

AMYX, Leon
American b. 1908
paintings: (H) $330
drawings: (L) $110; (H) $660

ANASTASI, William
b. 1933
drawings: (H) $1,650

ANBREINE, J.C.
paintings: (H) $1,320

ANCELET, Emile
French 19th/20th cent.
paintings: (L) $1,650; (H) $1,870

ANCELET, Gabriel Auguste
French 1829-1925
drawings: (L) $3,025; (H) $3,300

ANCELOT, Eugene J.
French 19th cent.
paintings: (H) $550

ANCHER, Michael
Danish 1849-1927
paintings: (H) $690

ANCILLOTI, T.
Italian 19th cent.
sculpture: (H) $1,045

ANCILLOTTI, Torello
Italian 1844-1899
paintings: (H) $1,980

ANDERDONK(?), Ludwig
Continental 19th/20th cent.
paintings: (H) $550

ANDERS, Ernst
German 1845-1911
paintings: (L) $2,530; (H) $20,700

ANDERS, M.
paintings: (H) $880

ANDERSEN, Roy
American b. 1930
paintings: (L) $5,500; (H) $23,100

ANDERSON, Captain J.W.
English ac. 1857-1865
paintings: (H) $4,600

ANDERSON, Carolyn
paintings: (L) $600; (H) $1,650

ANDERSON, Clarence William
American 1891-1972
paintings: (H) $1,430

ANDERSON, Colonel A.A.
paintings: (H) $880

ANDERSON, Dennis
sculpture: (H) $1,320

ANDERSON, Doug
American b. 1954
paintings: (L) $115; (H) $1,045
drawings: (L) $990; (H) $1,320

ANDERSON, Frederic
ac. 1920's
paintings: (H) $9,900

ANDERSON, Frederic A.
b. 1950
paintings: (H) $2,640

ANDERSON, G. Adolph
American b. 1877
paintings: (H) $495

ANDERSON, George Lilly
British 19th cent.
drawings: (L) $1,495; (H) $3,220

ANDERSON, Harry
American b. 1906
drawings: (L) $357; (H) $3,575

ANDERSON, J.W.
paintings: (L) $990; (H) $3,680

ANDERSON, James
1813-1879
paintings: (H) $385
sculpture: (H) $660

ANDERSON, Jeremy
American b. 1921
drawings: (H) $1,320
sculpture: (H) $1,150

ANDERSON, John
American 20th cent.
paintings: (H) $1,760

ANDERSON, John
British 19th cent.
paintings: (H) $1,100

ANDERSON, Karl J.
American 1874-1956
paintings: (L) $1,300; (H) $2,875
drawings: (L) $110; (H) $1,045

ANDERSON, Laurie
American b. 1947
drawings: (H) $2,300

ANDERSON, Lyman M.
American b. 1907
paintings: (H) $1,045

ANDERSON, M.
Swedish 20th cent.
paintings: (H) $522

ANDERSON, Murphy
American b. 1926
drawings: (H) $2,990

ANDERSON, Murphy and Carmine
INFANTINO
American b. 1920's
drawings: (H) $9,900

ANDERSON, Oscar
American 1873-1953
paintings: (L) $110; (H) $935
drawings: (H) $136

ANDERSON, Percy
drawings: (H) $847

ANDERSON, Ronald
American 1886-1926
drawings: (L) $88; (H) $1,760

ANDERSON, Ruth A., Ruth Anderson
TEMPLE
American 1884-1939
paintings: (L) $137; (H) $1,100

ANDERSON, S. B.
British 19th cent.
paintings: (H) $8,050

ANDERSON, Sophie, Mrs. Walter
British 1823-1903
paintings: (L) $1,955; (H) $11,500

ANDERSON, Stephen Warde
b. 1953
paintings: (H) $1,595

ANDERSON, Victor C.
American 1882-1937
paintings: (L) $275; (H) $7,425
drawings: (H) $990

ANDERSON, W.
paintings: (L) $577; (H) $1,210

ANDERSON, W. Livingston
British 19th cent.
paintings: (L) $345; (H) $5,750

ANDERSON, Walter
British ac. 1856-1886
paintings: (L) $9,900; (H) $27,500

ANDERSON, Walter Inglis
American 1903-1965
drawings: (L) $2,420; (H) $2,420

ANDERSON, William
British 1757-1837
paintings: (L) $935; (H) $28,600

ANDERSON, William
British 1856-1893
paintings: (H) $4,400

ANDERSSON, K.
paintings: (H) $550

ANDO, C.
Japanese 19th/20th cent.
paintings: (H) $10,350

ANDOE, Joe
American b. 1955
paintings: (L) $1,265; (H) $11,000

ANDOIREAUX
19th cent.
drawings: (H) $715

ANDRE
French 19th cent.
paintings: (H) $518

ANDRE, Albert
French 1869-1954
paintings: (L) $805; (H) $187,000
drawings: (L) $330; (H) $1,320

ANDRE, Carl
American b. 1935
drawings: (H) $14,850
sculpture: (L) $1,760; (H) $266,500

ANDRE, Charles Hippolyte
French 19th cent.
paintings: (H) $13,200

ANDREA DA FIRENZE, called
Andrea di Bonaiuto
Italian 2nd half 14th cent.
paintings: (L) $176,000; (H) $332,500

ANDREA DI NICCOLO
Italian ac. 1470-1512
paintings: (H) $82,500

ANDREANI, Camillo
Italian 17th cent.
paintings: (H) $2,200

ANDREASI, Ippolito
Italian 1548-1608
drawings: (H) $9,350

ANDREINI, F.
Italian 19th cent.
sculpture: (H) $22,000

ANDREIS, Alex
Belgian 19th/20th cent.
paintings: (H) $770

ANDREIS, Alex
French c. 1830-?
paintings: (L) $4,125; (H) $5,500

ANDREIS, Alex de
Belgian School 19th cent.
paintings: (L) $770; (H) $1,980

ANDREIS, Alex de
British ac. c. 1922
paintings: (L) $660; (H) $12,650

ANDREJEFF, L.
Russian 19th/20th cent.
paintings: (H) $825

ANDREJEVIC, Milet
Yugoslav/American 1925-1989
paintings: (L) $1,725; (H) $2,760

ANDREOLI, Andre
Italian 20th cent.
paintings: (L) $633; (H) $1,100

ANDREONI, G.
Italian 19th cent.
sculpture: (L) $3,300; (H) $34,500

ANDREOTTI, Federico
Italian 1847-1930
paintings: (L) $4,180; (H) $43,700
drawings: (H) $1,650

ANDREU, Mariano
Spanish b. 1888/1901
paintings: (H) $2,200
drawings: (H) $990

ANDREW, G.
19th cent.
paintings: (H) $3,220

ANDREW, Richard
American 1867-1934
paintings: (L) $88; (H) $1,320

ANDREWS, A.
19th cent.
paintings: (H) $2,070

ANDREWS, Ambrose
American ac. 1824-1859
paintings: (L) $1,100; (H) $1,380

ANDREWS, Benny
American b. 1930
paintings: (L) $605; (H) $1,045
drawings: (L) $825; (H) $1,150

ANDREWS, George Henry
English 1816-1898
paintings: (L) $1,045; (H) $6,325

ANDREWS, H.
British 19th cent.
paintings: (H) $2,420

ANDREWS, Helen Francis
American b. 1872
paintings: (L) $165; (H) $550

ANDREWS, Henry
19th cent.
paintings: (H) $9,775

ANDREWS, Henry
British 1794-1868
paintings: (L) $2,750; (H) $5,290

ANDREWS, Henry
British 1816-1868
paintings: (L) $1,870; (H) $3,080

ANDREWS, Henry
British 1816-1898
paintings: (L) $1,650; (H) $8,800

ANDREWS, Henry
British 19th cent.
paintings: (H) $7,475

ANDREWS, Henry
British ac. 1830-1860
paintings: (L) $5,750; (H) $5,750

ANDREWS, J.
British 19th cent.
paintings: (H) $1,540

ANDREWS, Joseph
American 1806-1873
drawings: (H) $3,520

ANDREWS, Marietta Minnigerode
American 1869-1931
paintings: (H) $880

ANDRIAENSSEN, Alexander
Flemish 1587-1661
paintings: (H) $3,738

ANDRIESSEN, Anthonie
Dutch 1746-1813
drawings: (H) $6,900

ANDRIESSEN, Jurriaan
Dutch 1742-1819
drawings: (H) $2,860

ANDRUS, Vera
American 1895-1979
paintings: (L) $27; (H) $1,100
drawings: (L) $22; (H) $330

ANDUJAR, Plutarco
South American 20th cent.
paintings: (H) $660

ANESI, Carlos
Argentinean b. 1965
paintings: (L) $3,850; (H) $19,800

ANESI, Paolo
Italian c. 1700-c. 1761
paintings: (H) $40,250

ANFOSSO, Pierre
French 20th cent.
paintings: (L) $357; (H) $880

ANFREI, Jegorov
Russian 1878-1954
drawings: (H) $550

ANFRIE, Charles
French ac. 1880-1905
sculpture: (L) $495; (H) $2,310

ANGAROLA, Anthony
American 1893-1929
paintings: (H) $1,955

ANGELI, Giuseppe
Italian c. 1709-1798
paintings: (H) $6,900

ANGELICA, Henrietta
Dutch 19th/20th cent.
paintings: (H) $748

ANGELIS, Dominico de
Italian 1852-1904
drawings: (L) $575; (H) $578

ANGELL, Helen Cordelia
English 1847-1884
paintings: (H) $770

ANGELL, Louise M.
American b. 1858
paintings: (H) $1,210

ANGELO, Mary San
American b. 1915
paintings: (L) $330; (H) $550

ANGELVI, C.
Italian 19th/20th cent.
paintings: (H) $715

ANGELVY, G. A.
French late 19th cent.
paintings: (H) $805

ANGERMEYER, Johann Adalbert
German 1674-1740
paintings: (H) $10,450

ANGERS, Pierre Jean David d'
French 1788-1856
sculpture: (H) $1,725

ANGILLIS, Pieter
Flemish 1685-1734
paintings: (H) $18,150

ANGLADA
Continental 19th/20th cent.
paintings: (H) $2,070

ANGLADA-CAMARASA,
Hermengildo
Spanish 1873-1959
paintings: (L) $9,900; (H) $165,000

ANGLADE, Gaston
French 1854-1919
paintings: (L) $920; (H) $9,775

ANGLES, Joaquin
French ac. 1885-1905
sculpture: (H) $2,990

ANGO, Jean Robert
French 18th cent.
drawings: (H) $3,575

ANGO, Jean Robert (?)
ac. 1760
drawings: (H) $7,700

ANGOLO DEL MORO, Battista
Italian 1514-1575
paintings: (H) $33,000

ANGRAND, Charles
French 1854-1926
drawings: (L) $6,325; (H) $11,500

ANGUIANO, Raul
Mexican b. 1915
paintings: (L) $2,875; (H) $20,700
drawings: (L) $920; (H) $6,325

ANGUS, D.
paintings: (H) $1,430

ANIEV
French 20th cent.
sculpture: (H) $660

ANISFELD, Boris
Russian/American 1879-1973
paintings: (L) $748; (H) $770

ANIVITTI, Filippo
Italian 1876-1955
drawings: (L) $715; (H) $1,320

ANKARSTRAND?, G.
19th/20th cent.
paintings: (H) $935

ANNA, Alessandro d'
Italian 1720-1769
drawings: (L) $10,925; (H) $24,150

ANNENKOFF, Georges
Russian 1890/94-1971
drawings: (L) $173; (H) $4,400

ANNES, E.
Continental 19th cent.
paintings: (H) $805

ANNIGONI, Pietro
Italian b. 1900
drawings: (L) $385; (H) $660

ANNISMAN, C. Jacques
paintings: (H) $500

ANNISON, Edward S.
American 19th/20th cent.
paintings: (H) $495

ANQUETIN, Louis
drawings: (H) $9,900

ANRROY, Anton van
Dutch 1870-1949
paintings: (H) $715

ANSDELL, Richard
English 1815-1885
paintings: (L) $385; (H) $209,000

ANSELL, M.D.
English early 20th cent.
paintings: (H) $880

ANSHUTZ, Thomas Pollock
American 1851-1912
paintings: (L) $264; (H) $59,700
drawings: (L) $99; (H) $17,600

ANSON, C.
20th cent.
paintings: (H) $770

ANSON, C.I.
paintings: (H) $1,100

ANTES, Horst
German b. 1936
paintings: (L) $11,000; (H) $51,700
drawings: (L) $1,760; (H) $14,300

ANTEUNIS, Jan
Belgian 20th cent.
sculpture: (H) $3,850

ANTHONIS, Victor
Dutch 19th cent.
paintings: (H) $1,650

ANTHONISSEN, Hendrick van
Dutch c. 1606-1654/60
paintings: (H) $38,500

ANTHONISSEN, Louis Joseph
Belgian 1849-1913
paintings: (L) $11,500; (H) $12,650

ANTHONISZ, Aert
Flemish 1579-1620
paintings: (H) $11,500

ANTHONY, Henry Mark
British 1817-1886
paintings: (H) $1,380

ANTHONY, Jean B.
Belgian b. 1854
paintings: (H) $3,450

ANTIGNA, Alexandre
French 1817-1878
paintings: (L) $1,265; (H) $9,775

ANTOGNINI, Alfredo
20th cent.
paintings: (H) $2,185

ANTOINE, Montas
paintings: (L) $176; (H) $690

ANTOINE, Otto
German 1865-1951
drawings: (L) $230; (H) $920

ANTOLINEZ, Jose
Spanish 1635-1675
paintings: (H) $3,575

ANTONIANI, Pietro
Italian d. 1805
paintings: (H) $48,875

ANTONIO
contemporary
drawings: (H) $825

ANTONIO, Christobal de
Spanish 19th/20th cent.
paintings: (L) $2,300; (H) $4,400

ANTONISSEN, Henricus Josephus
Flemish 1734-1794
paintings: (H) $8,250

ANTRA, A. van
Continental School 19th cent.
paintings: (H) $3,960

ANTROBUS, Edmond G.
English ac. 1876-77
paintings: (L) $88,000; (H) $96,000

ANTUNEZ, Nemesio
Chilean b. 1918
paintings: (L) $4,400; (H) $14,950

ANTWERP, Henry Loos
paintings: (H) $4,400

ANTY, Henry d'
French b. 1910
paintings: (L) $302; (H) $1,540

ANUSZKIEWICZ, Richard
American b. 1930
paintings: (L) $1,495; (H) $7,700

ANVITTI, Filippo
Italian b. 1876
paintings: (H) $3,960

ANZELIN, Eugene
sculpture: (H) $1,210

ANZINGER, Siegfried
Austrian b. 1952
drawings: (H) $2,070

AOUARD, H.A.
sculpture: (H) $3,960

AOVATTI, R.
Italian 19th/20th cent.
paintings: (H) $5,520

AOYAMA, Yoshio
Japanese b. 1894
paintings: (H) $6,050

APOL, Louis
Dutch b. 1850
paintings: (H) $660
drawings: (L) $715; (H) $2,475

APPEL, Charles P.
American b. 1857
paintings: (L) $302; (H) $3,450
drawings: (H) $58

APPEL, Karel
Dutch/American b. 1921
paintings: (L) $2,200; (H) $110,000
drawings: (L) $1,430; (H) $55,000
sculpture: (L) $4,840; (H) $22,000

APPERT, George
French 20th cent.
paintings: (L) $467; (H) $1,100

APPIAN, Adolph
French 1818-1898
paintings: (L) $110; (H) $4,888

APPLEBY, Ernest W.
English exhib. 1885-1907
paintings: (H) $1,430

APPLEBY, John F.
British 19th cent.
paintings: (H) $660

APPLETON, Thomas Gold
American 1812-1884
paintings: (H) $690

APT, Charles
American b. 1933
paintings: (L) $220; (H) $1,980

AQUILARA, Floranio
paintings: (L) $660; (H) $2,200
drawings: (H) $550

ARAGONES, Sergio
drawings: (H) $990

ARAKAWA, Shusaku
Japanese b. 1936
paintings: (L) $9,775; (H) $88,000
drawings: (L) $3,850; (H) $60,500
sculpture: (H) $76,750

ARALICA, Stojan
paintings: (H) $1,380

ARANA, Alfonso
Puerto Rican b. 1927
drawings: (H) $7,150

ARANDA, Jose Jimenez
Spanish 1837-1903
paintings: (H) $3,850

ARANGO, Alejandro
Mexican b. 1950
paintings: (H) $4,600

ARAPOFF, Alexis P.
Russian/American 1904-1948
paintings: (L) $220; (H) $1,840
drawings: (L) $330; (H) $330

ARAUJO, Carlos
b. Brazil 1950
paintings: (L) $12,100; (H) $14,300

ARAUJO Y SANCHEZ, Ceferino
Spanish ac. 1858
paintings: (H) $4,180

ARBANT, Louis
French 19th cent.
paintings: (H) $743

ARBUCKLE, George Franklin
paintings: (H) $2,200

ARCA, Frank Hans Johnston
paintings: (H) $7,975

ARCAMBOT, Pierre
French b. 1914
paintings: (H) $1,320

ARCARD, Louis
French 19th/20th cent.
sculpture: (H) $495

ARCHE, Jorge
b. 1905
paintings: (H) $3,450

ARCHIPENKO, Alexander
Russian/American 1887-1964
paintings: (H) $39,600
drawings: (L) $4,025; (H) $19,550
sculpture: (L) $1,100; (H) $275,000

ARCHULETA, Felipe Benito
1910-1991
sculpture: (H) $5,175

ARCIERI, Charles F.
American b. 1885
paintings: (L) $121; (H) $3,080

ARCURI, Frank
American b. 1946
paintings: (H) $5,500

ARD, Kurt
paintings: (H) $1,650

ARDEMANS, Teodoro
Spanish 1664-1726
drawings: (H) $12,650

ARDEN, George van
American ac. mid. 19th cent.
paintings: (H) $9,900

ARDISSONE, Yolande
French b. 1872
paintings: (L) $385; (H) $2,990

ARDON, Mordecai
Israeli b. 1896
paintings: (H) $35,750

ARDUINO, J.
Spanish 19th cent.
sculpture: (H) $862

ARELLANO
paintings: (L) $79,500; (H) $497,500

ARELLANO
ac. 1690-1720
paintings: (H) $74,000

ARELLANO, Juan de
Spanish 1614-1676
paintings: (L) $165,300; (H) $1,102,500

ARENDS, Jan
Dutch 1738-1805
paintings: (H) $2,970

ARENO, Joseph
American b. 1950
paintings: (L) $990; (H) $3,450
drawings: (H) $1,725

ARGELES, Rafael Escriche
Spanish b. 1894
paintings: (H) $2,300

ARIAS, J**
Spanish 19th cent.
paintings: (H) $880

ARIAS, J.
Spanish 19th cent.
paintings: (H) $523

ARIAS, Miguel
paintings: (H) $4,400

ARIGLIA, G.
paintings: (H) $660

ARIKHA, Avigdor
Israeli b. 1929
paintings: (L) $14,950; (H) $57,500
drawings: (L) $1,320; (H) $5,462

ARIOLLA, Fortunato
American 1827-1872
paintings: (H) $3,300

ARIZA, Gonzalo
Colombian b. 1912
paintings: (L) $12,650; (H) $17,250
drawings: (H) $5,175

ARLDRICH, George Ames
American 1872-1941
paintings: (H) $1,430

ARLES, Henry d', Jean HENRY
French 1734-1784
paintings: (L) $25,300; (H) $189,500

ARMAN
French b. 1928
paintings: (L) $990; (H) $33,000
drawings: (L) $862; (H) $40,250
sculpture: (L) $1,320; (H) $49,500

ARMAND, A.
19th cent.
drawings: (H) $880

ARMAND-DUMARESQ, Edouard
French 1826-1895
paintings: (L) $2,875; (H) $18,700

ARMANS
18th cent.
drawings: (H) $1,035

ARMENISE, Raffaello
Italian 1852-1932
paintings: (L) $805; (H) $1,650

ARMER, Laura Adams
American 1874-1963
paintings: (H) $3,575

ARMET Y PORTANEL, Jose
Spanish 1843-1911
paintings: (H) $4,180

ARMFIELD, Edward
British 19th cent.
paintings: (L) $719; (H) $4,125

ARMFIELD, Edwin
English 19th cent.
paintings: (H) $1,980

ARMFIELD, George
British ac. 1840-1875/80
paintings: (L) $302; (H) $10,350

ARMFIELD, Maxwell Ashby
English 1882-1972
paintings: (L) $3,162; (H) $8,250

ARMFIELD, Stuart
b. 1916
paintings: (L) $2,200; (H) $3,450

ARMIN, Emil
Hungarian/American 1895-1971
paintings: (L) $115; (H) $440
drawings: (L) $143; (H) $990 ·

ARMITAGE, Kenneth
English b. 1916
drawings: (H) $575
sculpture: (L) $38,500; (H) $51,700

ARMITAGE-SMITH, A.
English 20th cent.
drawings: (H) $935

ARMLEDER, John M.
b. Switzerland 1948
paintings: (L) $2,990; (H) $5,750
sculpture: (H) $13,800

ARMOR, C.
paintings: (H) $660

ARMOR, Charles
American 1844-1911
paintings: (L) $110; (H) $990

ARMOUR, George Denholm
Scottish 1864-1949
paintings: (L) $770; (H) $1,610

ARMOUR, Mary Nicol Neill
b. 1902
paintings: (H) $17,600

ARMS, John Taylor
American 1887-1953
drawings: (H) $467

ARMSTEAD, Henry Hugh
British 1828-1905
sculpture: (L) $7,475; (H) $13,200

ARMSTRONG
drawings: (H) $1,430

ARMSTRONG, David Maitland
American 1836-1918
paintings: (L) $4,070; (H) $4,400

ARMSTRONG, Geoffrey
paintings: (H) $577

ARMSTRONG, Rolf
American 1881-1960
paintings: (H) $15,400
drawings: (H) $3,080

ARMSTRONG, William
drawings: (L) $1,320; (H) $3,575

ARMSTRONG, William W.
American 1822-1914
paintings: (H) $4,025

ARNAL, Francois
American b. 1924
paintings: (H) $4,140

ARNALD, George
British 1763-1841
paintings: (H) $3,960

ARNAU, Francisco Pons
Spanish b. 1886
paintings: (H) $27,500

ARNAUD
sculpture: (H) $1,495

ARNAUT, Marcel
French 20th cent.
paintings: (H) $3,300

ARNAUTOFF, Victor M.
Russian/American 1896-1979
paintings: (L) $1,650; (H) $17,600

ARNDT, Franz Gustav
German 1842-1905
paintings: (H) $1,540

ARNDT, Paul Wesley
American b. 1881
paintings: (L) $173; (H) $605

ARNEGGER, A.
paintings: (H) $770

ARNEGGER, Alois
Austrian 1879-1967
paintings: (L) $230; (H) $15,400

ARNEGGER, Gottfried
Austrian b. 1905
paintings: (H) $1,980

ARNEGIER, R.
paintings: (H) $633

ARNESEN, Vilhelm Karl Ferdinand
Danish 1865-1948
paintings: (L) $528; (H) $8,050

ARNESON, Robert
American 1930-1992
drawings: (L) $748; (H) $6,900
sculpture: (L) $1,495; (H) $13,800

ARNETT, Joe Anna
American
paintings: (H) $5,390

ARNHOLT, Waldon Sylvester
American b. 1909
paintings: (L) $412; (H) $460

ARNING, Eddie
American b. 1898
drawings: (L) $920; (H) $1,760

ARNO, Peter
American 1904-1968
drawings: (L) $660; (H) $2,200

ARNOLD
drawings: (H) $467

ARNOLD
American
paintings: (H) $1,650

ARNOLD, Anne
sculpture: (H) $2,310

ARNOLD, Carl Johann
German 1829-1916
paintings: (H) $13,200

ARNOLD, Edward
b. Germany 1824 d. New Orleans
1866
paintings: (L) $4,950; (H) $11,000

ARNOLD, Eliza H.
drawings: (H) $467

ARNOLD, J.
American 20th cent.
paintings: (L) $27; (H) $1,210

ARNOLD, Jay
American 20th cent.
paintings: (H) $550

ARNOLD, Nellie M.
American
paintings: (H) $550

ARNOLD, O.
19th/20th cent.
drawings: (H) $468

ARNOLD, Reginald Edward
British ac. 1791
paintings: (H) $2,645

ARNOLD, Reginald Ernst
English 1853-1938
paintings: (L) $2,200; (H) $2,750

ARNOLD, S.
20th cent.
paintings: (H) $550

ARNOLDI, Charles
American b. 1946
drawings: (L) $978; (H) $6,050
sculpture: (L) $1,725; (H) $7,475

ARNOLDI, P.
Italian 19th cent.
paintings: (H) $550

ARNOLT, Gustav Muss
American 1858-1927
paintings: (H) $1,320

ARNON, Ernie
drawings: (H) $1,568

ARNOSA, Jose Gallegos
Spanish 1859-1917
paintings: (H) $198,000

ARNOUX, B.M.
paintings: (H) $1,540

ARNOUX, Michel
French 1833-1877
paintings: (L) $715; (H) $1,540

ARNTZENIUS, Paul
Dutch 1883-1695
paintings: (H) $2,875

ARNULL, George
British ac. 1825-1838
paintings: (H) $6,900

ARONSON, Boris
drawings: (H) $825

ARP, Jean, or Hans
French 1887-1966
paintings: (L) $1,495; (H) $275,000
drawings: (L) $1,495; (H) $40,250
sculpture: (L) $575; (H) $506,000

ARPA, Jose
Spanish/American b. 1868
paintings: (H) $4,025

ARPAD, Romek
Hungarian b. 1883
paintings: (H) $2,013

ARPARD, Migl de Kasnozy
French b. 1863
paintings: (H) $1,870

ARPEL, K.
sculpture: (H) $2,070

ARRANTS, Shirley
American
drawings: (H) $1,100

ARRIAGA, Juan Antonio
paintings: (H) $5,280

ARRIETA, Jose Agustin
Mexican 1802-1879
paintings: (L) $126,500; (H) $176,000

ARRIETA, Pedro de
Mexican 17th/18th cent.
paintings: (H) $28,600

ARRIGHI, S.
Italian 19th cent.
paintings: (H) $4,620

ARSENIUS, Johann Georg
Swedish 1818-1903
paintings: (H) $5,775

ARSON
Continental 19th/20th cent.
sculpture: (L) $550; (H) $1,650

ARSON, Alphonse Alexandre
French 19th cent.
sculpture: (H) $990

ART, Berthe
Belgian b. 1857
drawings: (H) $4,600

ART & LANGUAGE
drawings: (L) $4,025; (H) $9,775
sculpture: (H) $9,900

ARTAN, Louis
paintings: (H) $575

ARTENS, Peter von
b. Colombia 1937
paintings: (L) $6,900; (H) $13,800

ARTER, H.C.
paintings: (H) $1,980

ARTER, John Charles
American 1860-1923
paintings: (L) $3,575; (H) $4,125

ARTHOIS, Jacques d'
Flemish 1613-1686
paintings: (L) $20,700; (H) $37,375

ARTHURS, Stanley
American 1877-1950
drawings: (H) $660

ARTHURS, Stanley M.
American 1877-1950
paintings: (L) $1,980; (H) $6,050
drawings: (L) $880; (H) $1,430

ARTIGUE, Albert Emile
French 19th cent.
paintings: (L) $368; (H) $6,600

ARTS, Alexis
paintings: (H) $2,860

ARTSCHWAGER, Richard
American b. 1924
paintings: (L) $5,750; (H) $343,500
drawings: (L) $3,575; (H) $20,900
sculpture: (L) $1,540; (H) $203,500

ARTZ, David Adolph
Dutch 1837-1890
paintings: (L) $1,265; (H) $4,888
drawings: (L) $1,150; (H) $4,125

ARTZYBASHEFF, Boris
American 1899-1965
drawings: (H) $825

ARUNDALE, Francis Vyvyan Jago
English 1807-1853
drawings: (H) $2,990

ASADA, Takashi
paintings: (H) $4,400

ASANGER, Jacob
American 1887-1941
paintings: (H) $715

ASAWA, Ruth
b. 1926
sculpture: (H) $2,300

ASCENZI, E.
Italian 19th/20th cent.
paintings: (L) $467; (H) $2,875

ASCENZI, Giuseppe
Italian early 20th cent.
drawings: (H) $1,870

ASCH, Pieter Jansz. van
Dutch 1603-1678
paintings: (L) $5,463; (H) $9,350

ASCH, Pieter Jansz. van
1603-1678
paintings: (H) $12,100

ASCIONE, Aniello
Italian ac. 1680-1708
paintings: (H) $68,500

ASHBAUGH, William E.
American b. 1897
paintings: (L) $110; (H) $517

ASHER, Dan
drawings: (H) $715

ASHLEY, Clifford W.
American 1881-1947
paintings: (H) $1,375
drawings: (H) $770

ASHLEY, Frank
American b. 1920
paintings: (L) $412; (H) $10,350
drawings: (L) $935; (H) $3,300

ASHLEY, James F.
American 20th cent.
paintings: (H) $660

ASHMEAD, Margaret
American 19th/20th cent.
paintings: (H) $633

ASHTON, Ethel V.
American 20th cent.
paintings: (H) $2,750

ASHTON, James
English b. 1830/32
paintings: (H) $660

ASKENAZY, Mischa
American 1888-1961
paintings: (L) $605; (H) $11,000
drawings: (L) $715; (H) $4,675

ASKEVOLD, Anders Monsen
Swedish 1834-1900
paintings: (H) $6,325

ASKEW, John
British 18th/19th cent.
paintings: (H) $6,900

ASOMA, Tadshi
Japanese 20th cent.
paintings: (L) $275; (H) $3,575

ASPELL, Peter
paintings: (L) $403; (H) $1,210

ASPELL, Peter
b. 1918
paintings: (H) $550

ASPETTI, Tiziano, workshop of
sculpture: (H) $17,250

ASPLUND, Tore
American ac. 1938
paintings: (L) $138; (H) $8,800
drawings: (H) $688

ASPREY, M.
19th cent.
paintings: (H) $880

ASSCHE, Henri van
Belgian 1774-1841
paintings: (H) $3,910

ASSE, Genevieve
French b. 1923
paintings: (H) $825

ASSELBERG, Alphonse
Belgian 1839-1916
paintings: (H) $1,610

ASSELIJN, Jan
Dutch 1610-1652
paintings: (H) $25,300

ASSELIN, Maurice
French 1882-1947
paintings: (H) $1,320

ASSERETI, G**vo
18th cent.
paintings: (H) $9,350

ASSETTO, Franco
Italian b. 1911
paintings: (H) $660

ASSUS, Armand Jacques
French b. 1892
drawings: (H) $748

AST, Balthasar van der
Dutch c. 1590-c. 1656
paintings: (L) $71,500; (H) $96,800

ASTE, Joseph d'
Italian 20th cent.
sculpture: (L) $385; (H) $6,325

ASTI, A.
paintings: (H) $770

ASTI, Angelo
French 1847-1903
paintings: (L) $625; (H) $7,700

ASTON, Charles Reginal
British 1832-1908
drawings: (H) $920

ASTRUC, Lawrence
drawings: (H) $660

ASTRUP, Nikolai
Norwegian 1880-1928
drawings: (H) $66,000

ATALAYA, Enrique
Spanish 1851-1914
paintings: (L) $1,840; (H) $6,600

ATAMIAN, Charles Garabed
paintings: (H) $3,450

ATAMIAN, Charles Garabed
Turkish b. 1872
paintings: (H) $12,100

ATHERTON
paintings: (L) $632; (H) $1,100

ATHERTON, C.
paintings: (H) $825

ATHERTON, John
American, d.Canada 1900-1952
paintings: (L) $1,045; (H) $1,650

ATKINS, Arthur
American 1873-1899
paintings: (L) $1,980; (H) $3,300

ATKINS, David
American b. 1910
paintings: (H) $2,640

ATKINS, Emmeline
British 19th cent.
drawings: (H) $920

ATKINS, William H.
American b. 1926
paintings: (L) $3,300; (H) $4,958

ATKINSON, George Mounsey
Wheatley
British b. 1806
paintings: (H) $12,650

ATKINSON, Howard
American 19th/20th cent.
paintings: (L) $110; (H) $805

ATKINSON, Jacob
American 1864-1938
paintings: (H) $19,800

ATKYNS, Edward A.
British 19th cent.
paintings: (H) $1,650

ATL, Dr.
Mexican 1875-1964
paintings: (L) $10,063; (H) $156,500
drawings: (L) $3,163; (H) $38,500

ATL, Dr., Geraldo MURILLO
Mexican 1875-1964
paintings: (L) $34,500; (H) $206,000
drawings: (L) $1,100; (H) $11,000

ATLAN, Jean
French 1913-1960
drawings: (L) $3,575; (H) $16,500

ATSUYOSHI
sculpture: (H) $690

ATTANASIO, Natale
Italian 1845/46-1923
paintings: (L) $2,300; (H) $4,887

ATTENDU, Antoine Ferdinand
French 19th cent.
paintings: (H) $11,000

ATWATER, Lydia J.
American 19th cent.
paintings: (H) $605

ATWOOD, C.
American 20th cent.
paintings: (H) $5,280

ATWOOD, Jesse
American 19th cent.
paintings: (H) $577

ATWOOD, Robert
American b. 1892
paintings: (L) $165; (H) $468

AUBE, Jean Paul
French 19th cent.
sculpture: (H) $1,100

AUBERT
sculpture: (H) $1,925

AUBERT, A.
French 19th cent.
paintings: (H) $2,185

AUBERT, Jean Ernest
French 1824-1906
paintings: (H) $5,463

AUBLET, Albert
French 1851-1938
paintings: (L) $7,975; (H) $387,500

AUBREY, Jean
French ac. 1914-1930
paintings: (H) $12,650

AUBRY, Emile
French 1880-1964
paintings: (L) $5,500; (H) $19,800

AUBRY, Etienne
French 1745-1781
drawings: (H) $21,850

AUDEBERT, Jean Baptiste
French 1759-1800
drawings: (L) $2,415; (H) $8,050

AUDRAN, Gerard
French 1640-1703
drawings: (H) $5,520

AUDUBON, John James
American 1785-1851
paintings: (H) $143,000
drawings: (L) $49,500; (H) $156,500

AUDUBON, John Woodhouse
American 1812-1862
paintings: (L) $31,050; (H) $96,000

AUDY, Jonny
French ac. 1872-1876
drawings: (H) $1,035

AUERBACH, Frank
British b. 1931
paintings: (L) $41,250; (H) $308,000

AUERBACH-LEVY, William
Russian/American 1889-1964
paintings: (L) $385; (H) $2,200
drawings: (L) $110; (H) $660

AUERHAMER
paintings: (H) $460

AUFRAY, Joseph
French b. 1836
paintings: (L) $1,650; (H) $2,200

AUGE, Philippe
French b. 1935
paintings: (L) $275; (H) $3,190

AUGSLEY, S. de
drawings: (H) $715

AUGUSTA, George
American 20th cent.
paintings: (H) $660
drawings: (H) $275

AUGUSTE, Clervaux
paintings: (L) $3,080; (H) $4,950

AUGUSTIN, Francois
French 1867-1893
paintings: (H) $1,320

AUGUSTIN, Ludwig
German 20th cent.
paintings: (H) $1,380

AUMOND, Jean
drawings: (L) $770; (H) $1,100

AUMONIER, James
English 1832-1911
paintings: (L) $460; (H) $1,093
drawings: (H) $2,420

AUMONIER, John
British 1832-1911
paintings: (H) $3,680

AUMONT, Louis Auguste Francois
Danish 1805-1879
paintings: (H) $715

AURELI, Giuseppe
Italian 1858-1929
paintings: (H) $5,750
drawings: (L) $330; (H) $5,750

AURILLI, Rao
sculpture: (H) $495

AUSSANDON, Hippolyte
French b. 1836
paintings: (H) $1,210

AUSSANDON, Joseph Nichols
Hippolyte
French b. 1836
paintings: (L) $1,495; (H) $4,950

AUSTEN, A.
European 19th cent.
paintings: (L) $412; (H) $660

AUSTEN, Alexander
British ac. 1891-1909
paintings: (L) $110; (H) $550

AUSTEN, Alexander
English 19th/20th cent.
paintings: (L) $385; (H) $1,650

AUSTEN, Edward J.
American 1850-1930
paintings: (H) $825

AUSTIN, Charles Percy
American 1883-1948
paintings: (L) $302; (H) $1,540

AUSTIN, Darrel
American b. 1907
paintings: (L) $220; (H) $10,350

AUSTIN, R.S.
American 19th cent.
paintings: (L) $495; (H) $2,990
drawings: (H) $330

AUSTRIAN, Ben
American 1870-1921
paintings: (L) $250; (H) $30,800

AUTERI, L***
American 20th cent.
sculpture: (H) $489

AUTIER
paintings: (H) $550

AUTIO, Rudy
American b. 1926
drawings: (L) $220; (H) $605
sculpture: (L) $4,945; (H) $5,175

AUTIO, Rudy and James LEEDY
American contemporary
sculpture: (H) $6,038

AVATI, James
b. 1912
paintings: (L) $632; (H) $3,300

AVEDISIAN, Edward
American b. 1935/36
paintings: (H) $1,150
drawings: (H) $550

AVENAL, Vidal G.
Spanish 19th/20th cent.
paintings: (H) $6,875

AVENT, Mayna Treanor
American b. 1868
paintings: (L) $160; (H) $1,150

AVERCAMP, Barent
Dutch 1612-1679
paintings: (H) $121,000

AVERCAMP, Hendrick
Dutch 1585-1634/63
drawings: (H) $3,575

AVERY, Frances
American b. 1910
paintings: (H) $5,462

AVERY, March
American 20th cent.
paintings: (H) $522

AVERY, Milton
American 1893-1965
paintings: (L) $920; (H) $352,000
drawings: (L) $1,100; (H) $134,500

AVERY, Sally Michel
American b. 1905
paintings: (L) $605; (H) $825
drawings: (H) $330

AVIAT, Jules Charles
French b. 1844
paintings: (H) $11,500

AVIGNON
drawings: (H) $880

AVILOV, Mikhual Ivanovitch
Russian 1882-1938
paintings: (H) $6,900

AVITABILE, Gennaro
Italian b. 1864
paintings: (L) $2,200; (H) $6,050

AVY, Joseph Marius
French b. 1871
paintings: (H) $4,025
drawings: (H) $1,100

AXENTOWICZ, Theodor
Polish 1859-1938
drawings: (H) $2,875

AYCOCK, Alice
American b. 1946
drawings: (L) $578; (H) $6,600
sculpture: (L) $770; (H) $6,050

AYERS, Dick
American
drawings: (H) $460

AYLWARD, William J.
American 1875-1956
paintings: (L) $742; (H) $6,325
drawings: (L) $495; (H) $1,320

AYRTON, Michael
English 1921-1975
paintings: (L) $1,265; (H) $1,610
drawings: (H) $2,588
sculpture: (L) $3,410; (H) $6,900

AZACETA, Luis Cruz
Cuban b. 1942
paintings: (H) $11,500

AZOMA, Louis
paintings: (H) $462

AZZOLINI, Giovanni Bernardino
Italian 1572-1645
paintings: (H) $34,500

BAADER, L.
French 19th cent.
paintings: (H) $1,650

BAADER, Louis Marie
French 1828-1919
paintings: (H) $24,150

BAAGOE, Carl Erik
Danish 1829-1902
paintings: (L) $550; (H) $550

BABBAGE, F.
British 19th/20th cent.
paintings: (H) $11,500

BABBIDGE, J.C.
paintings: (H) $11,000

BABBIDGE, James Gardner
American 1844-1919
paintings: (L) $3,575; (H) $7,700

BABCOCK, Paul
American 20th cent.
paintings: (H) $467

BABCOCK, William
American 1860-1912
drawings: (L) $138; (H) $1,210

BABCOCK, William P.
American 1826-1899
paintings: (H) $3,450
drawings: (L) $55; (H) $385

BABER, Alice
American b. 1928
paintings: (H) $1,610

BABOULENE, Eugene
French b. 1905
paintings: (L) $3,450; (H) $7,820

BABUREN, Dirck van
Dutch 1570/90-1623/24
paintings: (H) $77,000

BACARISAS, Gustavo
Spanish 19th cent.
paintings: (H) $5,750

BACCI, Edmondo
Italian b. 1913
paintings: (L) $1,320; (H) $10,450
drawings: (H) $6,050

BACERRA, Ralph
contemporary
sculpture: (L) $6,325; (H) $10,925

BACH, Elvira
b. 1951
paintings: (H) $5,175
drawings: (H) $1,265

BACHAND, Robert
paintings: (H) $6,600

BACHARDY, Don
American b. 1934
drawings: (L) $605; (H) $2,185

BACHE, Martha Moffett
American b. 1893
paintings: (H) $1,045

BACHELDER, John Badger
American 1825-1894
paintings: (H) $935
drawings: (H) $10,450

BACHELET, Emile Just
French b. 1892
sculpture: (H) $3,300

BACHELIER, Jean Jacques
French 1724-1806
paintings: (H) $90,500
drawings: (H) $6,900

BACHER, Thomas
American 20th cent.
paintings: (H) $495

BACHERNIA, A.
late 19th cent.
sculpture: (H) $1,100

BACHMAN, Max
American 1862-1921
sculpture: (L) $1,955; (H) $2,680

BACHMANN, Alfred August Felix
German 1863-1956
paintings: (H) $1,980

BACHMANN, Hans
Swiss 1852-1917
paintings: (H) $10,350

BACHMANN, Otto
paintings: (L) $1,402; (H) $2,415

BACHRACH-BAREE, Emmanuel
Austrian b. 1863
paintings: (L) $825; (H) $4,830

BACK, Robert
20th cent.
paintings: (H) $4,600

BACKER, L.
20th cent.
paintings: (H) $1,182

BACKHUYSEN, Ludolf
Dutch 1631-1708
paintings: (L) $3,220; (H) $55,000

BACKSTROM, John
American 20th cent.
paintings: (L) $660; (H) $1,100

BACKUS, Albert E.
American 20th cent.
paintings: (L) $440; (H) $1,650

BACKUS, Standish, Jr.
American b. 1910
drawings: (H) $770

BACLER D'ALBE, Baron Louis Albert
Guillain
1761-1824
paintings: (H) $9,350
drawings: (H) $2,200

BACON, Charles Roswell
American 1868-1913
paintings: (H) $660

BACON, Francis
Irish 1909-1992
paintings: (L) $1,212,500;
(H) $3,850,000

BACON, Henry
American 1839-1912
paintings: (L) $330; (H) $43,700
drawings: (L) $192; (H) $2,415

BACON, I.L.
American 19th/20th cent.
paintings: (L) $1,375; (H) $1,540

BACON, Julia
American d. 1901
drawings: (H) $1,150

BACON, Peggy
American 1895-1987
paintings: (L) $1,320; (H) $3,300
drawings: (L) $201; (H) $1,980

BACQUE, Daniel Joseph
French 1874-1947
sculpture: (H) $9,625

BADCOCK, Mary
English 1799-1863
drawings: (L) $1,650; (H) $1,650

BADEAU, M.E.
Italian 19th/20th cent.
paintings: (H) $522

BADGER, John
American b. 1822
paintings: (H) $550

BADGER, Joseph
American 1708-1765
paintings: (L) $14,950; (H) $30,250

BADGER, Loucilla H.
American
drawings: (H) $715

BADGER, Samuel Finley Morse
American 19th/20th cent.
paintings: (L) $2,200; (H) $12,650

BADIN, C.
paintings: (H) $518

BADONI, M.
sculpture: (H) $1,430

BADOWSKI, Anthoni
Polish 19th cent.
paintings: (H) $3,220

BADUR, Bernard
American 20th cent.
paintings: (H) $2,750

BADURA, Ben
paintings: (L) $400; (H) $2,600

BAECHER, Anthony W.
American ac. 1851-1889
sculpture: (H) $82,250

BAECHLER, Donald
American b. 1956
paintings: (L) $5,175; (H) $55,000
drawings: (L) $935; (H) $52,800

BAEN, Jan de
Dutch 1633-1702
paintings: (L) $3,450; (H) $6,050

BAER, Fritz
German 1850-1919
paintings: (H) $4,950

BAER, George
American b. 1895
paintings: (H) $605

BAER, Jo
American b. 1929
paintings: (L) $3,080; (H) $22,000

BAER, William Jacob
American 1860-1941
paintings: (L) $1,210; (H) $6,325

BAERMANN, Clinton
paintings: (L) $192; (H) $2,200
sculpture: (H) $3,025

BAES, Emile
Belgian 1879-1953
paintings: (L) $7,700; (H) $16,100

BAETS, Marc
Flemish c. 1700
paintings: (H) $4,400

BAGANI, T.
paintings: (L) $660; (H) $990

BAGDATOPOULOS, William Spencer
American b. 1888
drawings: (H) $715

BAGG, Henry Howard
American 1852-1928
paintings: (H) $1,150

BAGLEY, J.M.
paintings: (H) $1,600

BAGLIONE, Giovanni
Italian 1571-1644
paintings: (H) $11,500
drawings: (H) $920

BAHAN, N.
American 20th cent.
paintings: (H) $1,100

BAHAR, Bijan
contemporary
sculpture: (L) $2,475; (H) $3,025

BAHIEU, Jules G.
Belgian 19th cent.
paintings: (L) $1,430; (H) $4,950

BAHIEU, L.
Belgian 19th cent.
paintings: (H) $1,150

BAHILL, C.S.
English 19th/20th cent.
paintings: (H) $1,000

BAHR, E.
German 20th cent.
paintings: (H) $880

BAIERL, Theodor
German 1881-1932
paintings: (L) $2,200; (H) $2,970

BAIL, Franck Antoine
French 1858-1924
paintings: (L) $8,050; (H) $22,000

BAIL, Joseph
French 1862-1921
paintings: (L) $1,870; (H) $22,000

BAILEY, Frederick Victor
British 20th cent.
paintings: (L) $2,875; (H) $17,600

BAILEY, Harry L.
American 1879-1933
paintings: (L) $137; (H) $467

BAILEY, John
American b. 1940
paintings: (L) $220; (H) $522

BAILEY, Ron
sculpture: (H) $1,000

BAILEY, William
American b. 1930
paintings: (L) $8,800; (H) $68,200
drawings: (L) $1,725; (H) $11,000

BAILLIEU, Chretien
French ac. 1830-1895
paintings: (H) $2,090

BAILLIO, R.
French ac. 1790-1810
drawings: (H) $2,475

BAILLY, C.O.
19th cent.
sculpture: (H) $575

BAILLY, Charles E.
1830-1895
sculpture: (H) $605

BAIN, Marcel Adolphe
French b. 1878
paintings: (H) $3,080

BAIRD, C.M.
British 19th cent.
paintings: (H) $690

BAIRD, Nathaniel Hughes John
Scottish 1865-after 1935
paintings: (L) $1,100; (H) $2,875

BAIRD, Victor
English 1857-1924
paintings: (H) $660

BAIRD, William Baptiste
American b. 1847, ac. 1872-1899
paintings: (L) $115; (H) $3,850
drawings: (H) $330

BAIXERAS VERDAGUER, Dionisio
Spanish b. 1862
paintings: (L) $17,250; (H) $25,300

BAIXIONG, Tu
drawings: (H) $900

BAIZE, Wayne
American b. 1943
drawings: (L) $330; (H) $2,000

BAIZERMAN, Saul
American 1889-1957
sculpture: (H) $2,875

BAJ, Enrico
Italian b. 1924
paintings: (L) $1,980; (H) $27,500
drawings: (L) $1,725; (H) $34,100
sculpture: (H) $19,800

BAK, Samuel
b. 1933
paintings: (L) $1,495; (H) $2,990

BAKALOWICZ, Ladislaus
Polish 1833-1904
paintings: (L) $1,210; (H) $25,300

BAKALOWICZ, Stephan
Wladlislawowitsch
Russian b. 1857
paintings: (H) $1,495

BAKER, A.P., Jr.
American 1924-1990
sculpture: (L) $220; (H) $1,375

BAKER, Bryant
American 1881-1970
sculpture: (L) $1,035; (H) $17,600

BAKER, C.F.
paintings: (H) $450

BAKER, Doris Winchell
American 1905-1987
paintings: (L) $880; (H) $935

BAKER, E.
paintings: (H) $1,430

BAKER, Elisha T.
American 1827-1890
paintings: (L) $4,025; (H) $27,500

BAKER, Elizabeth Gowdy
American 1860-1927
drawings: (L) $2,090; (H) $2,090

BAKER, Ernest Hamlin
American 1889-1975
paintings: (L) $165; (H) $1,430
drawings: (H) $2,860

BAKER, F.
19th/20th cent.
paintings: (H) $495

BAKER, George A.
American 1821-1880
paintings: (L) $715; (H) $2,750

BAKER, George H.
American 1878-1943
paintings: (L) $55; (H) $1,150
drawings: (H) $45

BAKER, Howard Russell
American 20th cent.
drawings: (H) $644

BAKER, Joe
American b. 1946
paintings: (H) $4,400

BAKER, Ralph
American 1908-1976
drawings: (L) $248; (H) $660

BAKER, Roger
paintings: (L) $770; (H) $2,860
drawings: (L) $880; (H) $1,540

BAKER, Sarah M.
American 1899-1983
paintings: (L) $192; (H) $825

BAKER, T.E.S.
American 19th/20th cent.
paintings: (H) $1,430

BAKER, Wright
early 20th cent.
paintings: (H) $546

BAKHUYZEN, Gerardina Jacoba van
de Sande
Dutch 1826-1895
paintings: (L) $6,820; (H) $19,800

BAKHUYZEN, Hendrikus van de
Sande
Dutch 1795-1860
paintings: (L) $863; (H) $25,300

BAKKER, Jan
Dutch 1879-1944
paintings: (H) $770

BAKOS, Jozef G.
American 1891-1976
paintings: (H) $4,950
drawings: (H) $3,300

BAKST, Leon
Russian 1866-1924
drawings: (L) $550; (H) $16,500

BALANDE, Gaston
French 1880-1971
paintings: (L) $3,105; (H) $11,550

BALCIAR, Gerald
American b. 1942
sculpture: (L) $850; (H) $4,400

BALDAUGH, Anni
American 1886-1953
paintings: (H) $6,325
drawings: (H) $2,090

BALDERO, Giorgio
Italian 19th cent.
paintings: (L) $330; (H) $1,500

BALDESSARI, John
American b. 1931
paintings: (L) $15,400; (H) $101,750
drawings: (L) $1,840; (H) $33,000

BALDINI, G.
paintings: (H) $880

BALDO
Italian 19th cent.
drawings: (H) $1,650

BALDOCK, James Walsham
British 1822-1898
paintings: (H) $65,750

BALDRIGHI, Giuseppe
Italian 1723-1802
paintings: (H) $42,550

BALDUCCI, Giovanni, IL COSCI
Italian c. 1560-1603
paintings: (L) $23,000; (H) $33,002
drawings: (H) $8,913

BALE, Charles Thomas
English ac. 1868-1875
paintings: (L) $578; (H) $8,250

BALE, T.C.
paintings: (L) $1,208; (H) $1,760

BALEN, Hendrick van
Flemish 1575-1632
paintings: (H) $10,638

BALEN, Hendrik van (the elder) and
Jan BRUEGHEL (younger)
16th/17th cent.
paintings: (H) $60,500

BALESTRIERI, Lionello
Italian 1874-1958
paintings: (L) $3,450; (H) $6,335
drawings: (L) $1,610; (H) $3,300

BALFOUR, Helen J.
American 1857-1925
drawings: (L) $288; (H) $1,870

BALINK, Henry C.
Dutch/American 1882-1963
paintings: (L) $230; (H) $2,750

BALIS, Calvin
American ac. 1817-1856
paintings: (H) $13,750

BALL
paintings: (H) $550

BALL, Alice Worthington
American c. 1929
paintings: (L) $605; (H) $715

BALL, Arthur
British 19th cent.
paintings: (H) $2,200

BALL, L. Clarence
American 1858-1915
paintings: (H) $220
drawings: (H) $522

BALL, Robert
sculpture: (L) $2,750; (H) $3,900

BALL, T.
sculpture: (L) $2,300; (H) $3,220

BALL, Thomas
American 1819-1911
sculpture: (L) $3,850; (H) $12,650

BALL, Thomas Raymond
American 1896-1943
paintings: (H) $880

BALLA, Giacomo
Italian 1871-1958
paintings: (L) $26,400; (H) $74,000
drawings: (L) $39,100; (H) $57,750
sculpture: (L) $1,610; (H) $28,600

BALLAINE, Jerrold
American 20th cent.
paintings: (L) $770; (H) $1,265

BALLAVOINE, Jules Frederic
French ac. 1880-1900
paintings: (L) $660; (H) $17,250

BALLE, G.T.
Continental 19th cent.
paintings: (H) $1,320

BALLEN (?), **de
20th cent.
paintings: (H) $660

BALLESIO, Federico
Italian 19th cent.
paintings: (L) $1,100; (H) $2,760
drawings: (L) $1,265; (H) $18,700

BALLIGUANT
French 19th cent.
paintings: (H) $552

BALLIN, Hugo
American 1879-1956
paintings: (L) $259; (H) $3,163

BALLIN, Robert
French d. 1915
paintings: (H) $605

BALLINGER, Harry
American 1892-1994
paintings: (L) $176; (H) $2,475
drawings: (L) $715; (H) $715

BALLIQUANT
French 19th/20th cent.
paintings: (H) $1,380

BALLIQUANT, N***
French 19th cent.
paintings: (H) $3,335

BALLOWE, Marcia A.
paintings: (L) $1,155; (H) $1,400
drawings: (H) $1,600

BALM, Walter Emerson
1884-1956
paintings: (H) $2,035

BALSADELLA, Mirko
Italian b. 1910
sculpture: (H) $1,725

BALSGAARD, Carl Wilhelm
Danish 1812-1893
paintings: (H) $74,000

BALTHUS, Balthasar KLOSSOWSKI
French b. 1908
paintings: (L) $12,100; (H) $517,000
drawings: (L) $2,200; (H) $57,500

BAMA, James E.
American b. 1926
paintings: (L) $1,320; (H) $12,100
drawings: (H) $2,640

BAMBARTEN, Carl Muller
German 19th cent.
paintings: (H) $1,650

BAMBER, Jim
paintings: (H) $3,520

BAMFYLDE, Copleston Warre
English d. 1791
paintings: (L) $1,980; (H) $3,410

BANCHI, Giorgio
Italian 1789-1853
drawings: (H) $2,475

BANCROFT, Albert Stokes
American 1890-1973
paintings: (L) $275; (H) $825

BANCROFT, Elias
British d. 1924
paintings: (H) $1,725

BANCROFT, Hester
American ac. 1930s
sculpture: (H) $935

BANCROFT, Milton Herbert
American 1867-1947
paintings: (L) $165; (H) $1,430
drawings: (L) $104; (H) $550

BAND, Max
Lithuanian/Am b. 1900
paintings: (L) $330; (H) $2,588

BANDEIRA, Antonio
Brazilian 1922-1967
paintings: (L) $5,175; (H) $43,700
drawings: (L) $1,725; (H) $3,850

BANDINI, Giovanni, workshop of
Italian
sculpture: (H) $55,000

BANDO, Toshio
paintings: (H) $1,093

BANI
paintings: (H) $715

BANIER, E.S.
European 19th cent.
paintings: (H) $522

BANKS, Allen R.
American 20th cent.
paintings: (H) $690

BANKS, Marcia
American 20th cent.
paintings: (H) $1,100

BANKS, Thomas J.
British 19th cent.
paintings: (H) $7,700

BANNARD, Walter Darby
American b. 1931
paintings: (H) $1,840

BANNATYNE, John James
Scottish 1835-1911
paintings: (L) $935; (H) $1,980

BANNISTER, Edward M.
American 1833-1901
paintings: (L) $880; (H) $26,400

BANNISTER, Patti
English/American 20th cent.
paintings: (L) $467; (H) $1,100

BANNISTER, Thaddeus
American b. 1915
paintings: (L) $1,100; (H) $4,950

BANTING, Sir Frederick Grant
Canadian 1891-1941
paintings: (L) $1,100; (H) $5,500

BANTZER, Carl Ludwig Noah
German b. 1857
paintings: (H) $3,575

BANZENMACHER, A.F.
drawings: (H) $495

BAPTISTA DA COSTA, Joao
b. Brazil 1865-1926
paintings: (L) $21,850; (H) $33,000

BAR, Alexandre de
French 1821-1901
paintings: (H) $3,575
drawings: (H) $660

BAR, Bonaventure de
French 1700-1729
paintings: (H) $28,750

BAR, L. Du
French 20th cent.
sculpture: (H) $605

BARA, Leopold
Austrian
paintings: (H) $1,900

BARADUC, Jeanne
French 19th cent.
paintings: (H) $1,320

BARAIZE, E.
Continental School 19th/20th cent.
paintings: (H) $13,225

BARATTA, Carlo Alberto
Italian 1754-1815
drawings: (H) $3,850

BARATTI, Filippo
Italian 19th cent.
paintings: (L) $4,600; (H) $51,750

BARAUSS, Emile
French 1851-1930
paintings: (H) $2,750

BARBAGLIA, Giuseppe
Italian b. 1841
paintings: (H) $9,200

BARBARINI, Emil
Austrian 1855-1930
paintings: (L) $3,740; (H) $7,920

BARBARINI, Ernst
German 20th cent.
paintings: (H) $5,720

BARBARINI, Franz
Austrian 1804-1873
paintings: (H) $6,325

BARBARO, Giovanni
Italian 19th/20th cent.
paintings: (H) $495
drawings: (L) $247; (H) $357

BARBASAN, Mariano
Spanish 1864-1924
paintings: (H) $28,600

BARBEAU, Marcel
drawings: (H) $1,540

BARBELLA, C.
Italian 19th cent.
sculpture: (H) $1,100

BARBELLA, Constantino
Italian 1852-1925
sculpture: (H) $1,093

BARBER, Alfred R.
British ac. 1879-1893
paintings: (H) $5,225

BARBER, Bill
20th cent.
paintings: (H) $715

BARBER, Charles Burton
British 1845-1894
paintings: (L) $1,650; (H) $66,000

BARBER, H.
American
paintings: (H) $726

BARBER, Herb
American 20th cent.
sculpture: (H) $112,500

BARBER, John
American 1898-1965
paintings: (L) $863; (H) $2,200

BARBER, T.S.
British ac. 1891-1899
paintings: (H) $5,462

BARBER, Thomas
English c. 1768-1843
paintings: (H) $20,700

BARBIER, Andre
French 1883-1970
paintings: (H) $2,300
drawings: (H) $83

BARBIER, Georges
French 1882-1932
drawings: (L) $990; (H) $6,050

BARBIER, Joanie
paintings: (H) $500
drawings: (H) $605

BARBIERI, Vittorio
Italian 19th cent.
paintings: (H) $2,200

BARBIERS, Pieter Pietersz.
Dutch 1749-1842
paintings: (H) $19,550

BARBINI, Alfredo
sculpture: (H) $1,840

BARBOSA, Mario
Brazilian 19th cent.
paintings: (H) $2,750

BARBUT-DAVRAY, Luc
French b. 1863
paintings: (H) $1,760

BARBUTO(?)
paintings: (H) $990

BARCELO, Miguel
Spanish b. 1957
paintings: (L) $55,000; (H) $121,000

BARCHUS, Eliza
American 1857-1959
paintings: (L) $412; (H) $5,500

BARCLAY, McClelland
American 1891-1943
paintings: (L) $1,150; (H) $7,700
drawings: (L) $144; (H) $2,750
sculpture: (H) $165

BARD
drawings: (H) $11,000

BARD, James
American 1815-1897
paintings: (L) $8,250; (H) $200,500
drawings: (L) $77,000; (H) $79,500

BARD, James and John
American 19th cent.
paintings: (H) $96,000

BARDELLINI, Pietro
1728-1810
paintings: (H) $18,400

BARDON, Marc
French b. 1891
paintings: (H) $770

BARDONE, Guy
French b. 1927
paintings: (L) $660; (H) $6,600

BARDOT, E.
paintings: (H) $495

BARDOU, Paul Joseph
German 1745-1814
paintings: (H) $4,400

BARDWELL, Thomas
English 1704-d.c. 1780
paintings: (H) $43,700

BARDWELL, Thomas
English ac. c. 1748
paintings: (H) $4,125

BARE, E.
French 19th cent.
paintings: (L) $825; (H) $8,625

BARELLA, Jose Puigdengolas
paintings: (H) $4,950

BARENGER, James, the younger
English 1780-1831
paintings: (L) $3,630; (H) $8,625

BARGER, John
American b. 1953
paintings: (L) $3,300; (H) $5,500

BARGIN, Henri
French 20th cent.
paintings: (H) $1,045

BARGUE, Charles
French 1826-1883
paintings: (L) $55,000; (H) $74,000
drawings: (H) $44,000

BARILE, Xavier J.
American 1891-1981
paintings: (L) $110; (H) $1,035

BARILLOT
sculpture: (H) $550

BARILLOT, E.
sculpture: (H) $770

BARILLOT, Leon
French 1844-1909
paintings: (H) $3,080

BARKER, George
American 1882-1965
paintings: (H) $633
drawings: (H) $330

BARKER, H.
19th cent.
paintings: (H) $690

BARKER, J.
British 19th cent.
paintings: (L) $798; (H) $1,210

BARKER, John
British 1811-1886
paintings: (H) $4,950

BARKER, John
British 1820-1865
paintings: (H) $1,725

BARKER, John
British 19th cent.
paintings: (H) $24,200

BARKER, John
English 19th cent.
paintings: (H) $990

BARKER, John Joseph
British 1824-1904
paintings: (L) $2,530; (H) $11,500

BARKER, Laura
American 20th cent.
paintings: (L) $248; (H) $550

BARKER, Sidney
paintings: (H) $575

BARKER, Thomas
paintings: (H) $550

BARKER, W.H.
19th/20th cent.
paintings: (H) $2,970

BARKER, Wright
British d. 1941
paintings: (L) $1,100; (H) $3,162

BARKER OF BATH, Thomas
British 1769-1847
paintings: (L) $1,150; (H) $5,175

BARKIN, Michael
20th cent.
sculpture: (L) $920; (H) $1,380

BARKLEY, James
b. 1941
drawings: (H) $660

BARKS, Carl
American 20th cent.
paintings: (L) $21,850; (H) $22,000
drawings: (L) $1,100; (H) $112,500

Pure Form

Italian artist Duilio Barnabè (1914-1961) studied at the school of fine arts in Bologna and with Italian still-life painter and etcher Giorgio Morandi. By the 1940s, Barnabè had developed a distinct abstract style. In his paintings, still-lifes and portraits, he attempted to define pure form and create universal abstract symbols. He exhibited in Switzerland in 1949 and achieved international recognition in 1952 with the exhibition of his paintings at the Biennale in Venice. Less abstract in 1959, Barnabè maintained his distillation of elements into geometric shapes, but his portraits became more recognizable. When he was 47 he was killed in an automobile accident on a mountain road in Italy. (Duilio Barnabè, *Man Seated with Pipe*, oil on canvas, 45½ x 35 inches, Butterfield's, October 26, 1994, $2,875)

BARKY
  sculpture: (H) $550

BARLACH, Ernst
  German 1870-1938
  sculpture: (L) $2,200; (H) $63,000

BARLAND, Adam
  British ac. 1843-1885
  paintings: (L) $523; (H) $2,530

BARLETT and HAYWARD
  American 19th cent.
  sculpture: (H) $19,800

BARLOW, John Noble
  Anglo/American 1861-1924
  paintings: (L) $578; (H) $2,300

BARLOW, Myron
  American 1873-1938
  paintings: (L) $440; (H) $13,800

BARNABE, Duilio
  Italian 1914-1961
  paintings: (L) $403; (H) $18,150

BARNARD, A.
  19th cent.
  paintings: (H) $990

BARNARD, Edward Herbert
  American 1855-1909
  paintings: (L) $1,540; (H) $3,300

BARNARD, George
  British 19th cent.
  drawings: (H) $880

BARNES, Archibald Georges
  British b. 1887
  paintings: (L) $825; (H) $7,150

BARNES, E. Paul
  19th/20th cent.
  paintings: (H) $605

BARNES, E.C.
English ac. 1856-1882
paintings: (L) $495; (H) $825

BARNES, Edward Charles
British 19th cent.
paintings: (H) $2,530

BARNES, Ernest Harrison
American 1873-1955
paintings: (L) $55; (H) $3,450

BARNES, Ernie
American 20th cent.
paintings: (H) $1,320

BARNES, Gertrude J.
American b. 1865
paintings: (L) $575; (H) $5,175

BARNES, Lloyd
sculpture: (H) $550

BARNES, Matthew
American 1880-1951
paintings: (L) $467; (H) $1,870

BARNES, Robert
American b. 1934
paintings: (H) $920

BARNES, W.M.
British 19th cent.
paintings: (H) $1,760

BARNET, Will
American b. 1911
paintings: (L) $192; (H) $3,850
drawings: (L) $1,870; (H) $4,313

BARNETT, Bion
American b. 1887
paintings: (H) $660

BARNETT, Herbert
American 1910-1978
paintings: (L) $173; (H) $2,200

BARNETT, Thomas P.
American 1870-1929
paintings: (L) $330; (H) $2,860

BARNETT, William
American 20th cent.
paintings: (L) $121; (H) $825

BARNEY, Frank A.
American b. 1862
paintings: (L) $83; (H) $1,495

BARNEY, J. Stewart
American 1869-1925
paintings: (L) $1,380; (H) $4,600

BARNJUM, Frederick
Canadian ac. 1858-1887
paintings: (H) $3,146

BARNOIN, Henri Alphonse
French 1881-1935
paintings: (L) $770; (H) $12,075
drawings: (L) $330; (H) $605

BARNSLEY, James MacDonald
Canadian 1861-1921/9
paintings: (L) $2,070; (H) $6,900

BAROCCI, Federico, called Fiori da Urbino
Italian 1526/35-1612
drawings: (L) $8,625; (H) $87,750

BARON, Henri Charles Antoine
French 1816-1885
paintings: (L) $1,265; (H) $5,750

BARONE, Antonio
American 1889-1971
paintings: (L) $110; (H) $8,800
drawings: (L) $110; (H) $6,600

BARR, E.
Continental 19th cent.
paintings: (H) $2,200

BARR, George
drawings: (H) $495

BARR, Paul
sculpture: (H) $1,150

BARR, William
American 1867-1933
paintings: (L) $1,320; (H) $1,380

BARRABAND, Jacques
French 1767/68-1809
drawings: (L) $33,000; (H) $33,000

BARRABLE, George Hamilton
British 19th cent.
paintings: (H) $7,475

BARRADAS, Rafael
b. Uruguary 1890-1929
paintings: (L) $37,375; (H) $123,500
drawings: (L) $3,850; (H) $5,980

BARRAIS, Ch.
sculpture: (H) $3,575

BARRALET, John James
American 1747-1815
drawings: (H) $1,320

BARRANTI, P.
Italian 19th cent.
sculpture: (H) $3,080

BARRATT, C.B.
English 19th cent.
paintings: (H) $632

BARRAU, Laureano
Spanish 1864-1957
paintings: (L) $4,312; (H) $51,750

BARRAUD, Francis
British 1856-1924
paintings: (H) $23,100

BARRAUD, Francis
British ac. 1878-1890
paintings: (H) $10,350

BARRAUD, Henry
English 1811-1874
paintings: (L) $1,430; (H) $68,500

BARRAUD, Maurice
Swiss 1889-1954
drawings: (H) $990

BARRAUD, S***
French 19th cent.
paintings: (H) $2,875

BARRAUD, William
English 1810-1850
paintings: (L) $2,310; (H) $66,000

BARRAUD, William and Henry
BARRAUD
British 19th cent.
paintings: (H) $23,000

BARRE, Aristide
French 19th cent.
sculpture: (H) $715

BARRE, Jean Auguste
French 1811-1896
sculpture: (H) $990

BARREDA, Ernesto
Latin American b. France 1927
paintings: (L) $3,450; (H) $17,250
drawings: (H) $2,300

BARREL-BOTTI
American contemporary
paintings: (L) $412; (H) $1,265

BARRELL, George J.R.
19th cent.
drawings: (L) $220; (H) $660

BARRELL, William
paintings: (H) $605

BARRERA, Antonio
Colombian b. 1948
paintings: (L) $6,030; (H) $23,000

BARRERA, Francisco
Spanish ac. 1632-1657
paintings: (H) $46,000

BARRERES, Domingo
American 20th cent.
paintings: (H) $880

BARRET, George, Sr.
British 1732-1784
paintings: (L) $21,850; (H) $255,500
drawings: (H) $6,600

BARRET, Marius Antoine
French b. 1865
paintings: (L) $14,300; (H) $81,700

BARRETT, George, Jr.
English 1767-1842
paintings: (H) $4,675

BARRETT, Jeremiah
Irish d. 1770
paintings: (H) $2,587

BARRETT, Jerry
British 1814-1906
paintings: (H) $3,162

BARRETT, William S.
American 1854-1927
paintings: (L) $220; (H) $2,200

BARRIAS
sculpture: (L) $495; (H) $3,500

BARRIAS, E.
sculpture: (H) $6,600

BARRIAS, Felix
French 1822-1907
paintings: (H) $2,860

BARRIAS, Louis Ernest
French 1841-1905
drawings: (H) $1,092
sculpture: (L) $550; (H) $189,500

BARRICK, Shirley Gordon
American b. 1885
paintings: (L) $132; (H) $770

BARRIER, G.
paintings: (H) $2,750

BARRIER, G.
Scottish/French 20th cent.
paintings: (H) $1,210

BARRIER, Gustave
French 20th cent.
paintings: (H) $1,980

BARRON, Grace
b. 1903
paintings: (H) $495

BARRON, Hugh
c. 1745-1791
paintings: (H) $2,750

BARRON Y CARRILLO, Manuel
Spanish 1814-1884
paintings: (H) $25,300

BARRONE, Antonio
b. 1889
paintings: (H) $715

BARROS, Muidal
Latin American 20th cent.
paintings: (H) $577

BARROW, Julian
paintings: (H) $770

BARROW, W.H.
English ac. c. 1887
paintings: (H) $550

BARRY, John
paintings: (H) $650

BARRY, Robert
b. 1936
drawings: (L) $770; (H) $4,400

BARSANTI, P.
sculpture: (H) $20,900

BARSE, George Randolph, Jr.
American 1861-1938
paintings: (L) $1,870; (H) $17,600
drawings: (H) $1,100

BARSHCH, A.O.
drawings: (H) $3,220

BARSOTTI, Hercules
Brazilian b. 1914
paintings: (H) $7,700

BARSTOW, Montagu
paintings: (H) $9,350

BARSTOW, Susan
American 19th cent.
paintings: (L) $604; (H) $2,090

BARTELS, Hans von
German b. 1856
paintings: (H) $1,650
drawings: (L) $1,320; (H) $6,875

BARTEZAGO, Enrico
Swiss 19th cent.
paintings: (L) $4,313; (H) $28,750

BARTH, Bradi
European 20th cent.
paintings: (H) $2,530

BARTH, Jack
b. 1946
drawings: (H) $2,090

BARTH, Karl
German 1787-1853
drawings: (H) $2,200

BARTH, W.
drawings: (L) $1,035; (H) $1,150

BARTHALOT, Marius
French b. 1861
paintings: (L) $825; (H) $1,495

BARTHE, Richmond
American 1901-1989
sculpture: (H) $2,860

BARTHELEMY, Camille
Belgian 20th cent.
paintings: (H) $990

BARTHELEMY, Gerard
French b. 1927
paintings: (L) $6,325; (H) $10,350

BARTHOLDI, Frederic Auguste
French 1834-1904
sculpture: (L) $990; (H) $13,200

BARTHOLEMEW, Edward S.
American 1822-1858
sculpture: (H) $10,350

BARTHOLOME, Albert
French 1848-1928
sculpture: (L) $690; (H) $4,887

BARTHOLOMEW, Gerard
paintings: (H) $8,050

BARTHOLOMEW, William Newton
American 1822-1898
paintings: (H) $825
drawings: (L) $275; (H) $489

BARTLETT, Carl W.
sculpture: (H) $3,300

BARTLETT, Clarence D.
American b. 1860
paintings: (H) $1,150

BARTLETT, Dana
American 1878/82-1957
paintings: (L) $550; (H) $7,700
drawings: (L) $138; (H) $1,100

BARTLETT, Frederic Clay
American b. 1873
paintings: (L) $1,320; (H) $5,750

BARTLETT, Gray
American 1885-1951
paintings: (L) $230; (H) $5,500

BARTLETT, James W. Bo
American 20th cent.
paintings: (H) $522

BARTLETT, Jennifer
American b. 1941
paintings: (L) $3,850; (H) $176,000
drawings: (L) $2,300; (H) $44,000

BARTLETT, Paul Wayland
American 1865-1925
sculpture: (L) $805; (H) $4,675

BARTLETT, Truman H.
American 1835-1923
sculpture: (H) $5,500

BARTLETT, William H.
British 1858-1932
paintings: (H) $12,075

BARTLETT, William Henry
British 1809-1854
paintings: (L) $110; (H) $1,150

BARTOLENA, Giovanni
paintings: (H) $3,738

BARTOLI, Jacques
French 20th cent.
paintings: (L) $385; (H) $5,720

BARTOLINI, A.
Italian 19th cent.
paintings: (H) $6,325

BARTOLINI, Federico
Italian 19th/20th cent.
drawings: (L) $3,738; (H) $27,600

BARTOLINI, Lorenzo
Italian 1777-1850
sculpture: (H) $29,900

BARTOLINI, P.
Italian early 20th cent.
paintings: (H) $1,035

BARTOLL, William Thompson
American 1817-1857
paintings: (H) $4,313

BARTOLO, Matteo di Giovanni de,
studio of
15th cent.
paintings: (H) $79,750

**BARTOLOMEO DI MESSER
BULGARINI,**
Italian c. 1300/10-1378
paintings: (H) $96,000

BARTOLOMMEO, Fra, Baccio della
Porta
Italian 1472-1517
drawings: (L) $15,400; (H) $27,600

BARTOLOMMEO DI FRUOSINO
Italian 1366/69-1441
paintings: (H) $431,500

BARTOLOMMEO DI GIOVANNI
Italian ac. 1483-1511
paintings: (L) $6,900; (H) $40,250

BARTOLOZZI, Francesco
Italian 1725/27-1815
drawings: (L) $935; (H) $3,080

BARTON, Donald Blagge
American 1903-1990
paintings: (L) $275; (H) $1,540
drawings: (L) $165; (H) $715

BARTON, George
English 19th cent.
drawings: (H) $518

BARTON, Loren R.
American 1893-1975
paintings: (H) $550

BARTON, Rose Maynard
British 1856-1929
drawings: (L) $660; (H) $3,300

BARTON, W.
paintings: (H) $8,800

BARTOO, Catherine
American ac. 1900-1925
paintings: (H) $1,050

BARTTENBACH, H.
paintings: (L) $357; (H) $1,150

BARTTENBACH, Hans
German b. 1908
paintings: (L) $517; (H) $1,760

BARUCCI, Pietro
Italian 1845-1917
paintings: (L) $1,725; (H) $27,600

BARUCHELLO, Gianfranco
Italian b. 1924
drawings: (H) $880

BARVITIUS, Victor
Czechoslovakian 1834-1902
paintings: (L) $1,320; (H) $2,300

BARWICK, John
British ac. 1835-1876
paintings: (L) $1,150; (H) $4,485

BARWOLF, Georges
Belgian 1872-1935
paintings: (H) $5,500

BARYE, Alfred
French 19th cent.
sculpture: (L) $863; (H) $5,750

BARYE, Alfred and Emile GUILLEMIN
French 19th cent.
sculpture: (L) $8,625; (H) $10,350

BARYE, Antoine Louis
French 1795-1875
paintings: (L) $2,875; (H) $37,375
sculpture: (L) $165; (H) $63,000

BARZAGHI, Francesco
Italian 1839-1892
sculpture: (H) $96,000

BARZANTI, L.
Italian 19th/20th cent.
paintings: (H) $1,725

BARZANTI, P.
Italian 19th/20th cent.
sculpture: (L) $550; (H) $6,600

BARZANTI, Paul
Italian early 20th cent.
sculpture: (H) $1,980

BARZANTI, Pietro
Italian 19th cent.
sculpture: (L) $1,320; (H) $33,350

BASCOM, Earl W.
American 20th cent.
sculpture: (L) $1,650; (H) $36,300

BASCOM, Ruth Henshaw
American 1772-1848
drawings: (L) $345; (H) $46,000

BASELITZ, Georg
German b. 1938
paintings: (L) $13,200; (H) $1,100,000
drawings: (L) $4,600; (H) $82,500

BASETTI, A.
Italian 19th cent.
sculpture: (H) $2,730

BASING, Charles
American 1865-1933
paintings: (L) $220; (H) $4,070
drawings: (L) $110; (H) $2,300

BASKE, Yamada
American 20th cent.
paintings: (L) $495; (H) $9,900
drawings: (L) $193; (H) $660

BASKERVILLE, Charles
American b. 1896
paintings: (L) $1,035; (H) $1,955
drawings: (H) $86

BASKIN, Leonard
American b. 1922
paintings: (H) $1,650
drawings: (L) $220; (H) $1,955
sculpture: (L) $132; (H) $7,700

BASLET
19th cent.
sculpture: (H) $1,650

BASOLI, Antonio
1774-1848
drawings: (L) $920; (H) $3,220

BASQUIAT, Jean Michel
American 1960-1988
paintings: (L) $1,093; (H) $294,000
drawings: (L) $1,650; (H) $187,000
sculpture: (L) $22,000; (H) $165,000

BASQUIAT, Jean Michel, and Keith
HARING, Kenny SCHARF
American 20th cent.
sculpture: (H) $9,900

BASSANO, Francesco Giambattista da
Ponte, called Francesco Giambattista
the younger
Italian 1549-1592
paintings: (L) $5,750; (H) $33,000

BASSANO, Francesco da Ponte,
studio of
Italian 16th cent.
paintings: (H) $25,300

BASSANO, Gerolamo
Italian 1566-1621
paintings: (H) $6,325

BASSANO, Jacopo da Ponte
Italian 1510/18-1592
paintings: (L) $1,650; (H) $137,500

BASSANO, Leandro da Ponte, called
Leandro
Italian 1557-1622
paintings: (L) $5,280; (H) $38,500

BASSEK
paintings: (H) $880

BASSEN, Bartholomeus van
Dutch 1590-1652
paintings: (H) $71,500

BASSEPORTE, Madeleine Francoise
French 1701-1780
drawings: (H) $9,775

BASSET
Continental 19th/20th cent.
paintings: (H) $1,045
drawings: (H) $316

BASSFORD
paintings: (L) $110; (H) $880

BASSFORD, Wallace
American b. 1900
paintings: (L) $633; (H) $1,760

BASSI, E.
Italian 19th/20th cent.
drawings: (L) $357; (H) $460

BASTET, Victorien Antoine
French late 19th/early 20th cent
sculpture: (H) $7,700

BASTIANI, Ildebrando
Italian b. 1867
sculpture: (H) $10,350

BASTIEN, Alfred
Belgian 1873-1955
paintings: (L) $4,400; (H) $19,800

BASTIEN-LEPAGE, Jules
French 1848-1884
paintings: (L) $7,475; (H) $706,500
drawings: (H) $4,025

BASTINE
sculpture: (H) $990

BATACCHI, A.
sculpture: (L) $1,840; (H) $3,300

BATCHELDER, John L.
b. 1907
paintings: (H) $1,150

BATCHELLER, Frederick S.
American 1837-1889
paintings: (L) $110; (H) $10,925

BATCHELOR, Clarence D.
1888-1977
paintings: (H) $660
drawings: (H) $99

BATE, Stanley
b. 1903
paintings: (L) $575; (H) $2,090
drawings: (H) $55

BATEMAN, C.W.
American 19th cent.
paintings: (H) $715

BATEMAN, Charles
American b. 1890
paintings: (H) $4,025

BATEMAN, James
British 1893-1959
paintings: (L) $862; (H) $8,250

BATEMAN, Ronald
American contemporary
paintings: (H) $690

BATES, David
American b. 1952
paintings: (L) $650; (H) $17,600

BATES, David
British 1840-1921
paintings: (L) $770; (H) $27,500

BATES, David
British b. 1952
paintings: (H) $13,200

BATES, Dewey
English 1851-1899
paintings: (H) $1,320

BATES, G.
American
paintings: (H) $1,050

BATES, Kenneth
American 1904-1973?
paintings: (L) $165; (H) $990

BATES, Maxwell Bennett
Canadian 1906-1980
paintings: (H) $358
drawings: (H) $1,100

BATES, Sam
20th cent.
drawings: (H) $577

BATHIEU, J.
Belgian 19th cent.
paintings: (H) $990

BATON, Claude
French 20th cent.
paintings: (L) $880; (H) $2,475

BATONI, Pompeo
Italian 1708-1787
paintings: (H) $123,500

BATONI, Pompeo, studio of
18th cent.
paintings: (H) $12,075

BATTAGLIA, C. Pompiani
Italian 19th cent.
paintings: (H) $1,430
drawings: (L) $220; (H) $1,980

BATTAGLIOLI, Francesco
Italian 18th cent.
paintings: (H) $2,475

BATTEM, Gerrit van
Dutch 1636-1684
paintings: (H) $18,400
drawings: (H) $13,200

BATTENBERG, John
American b. 1931
sculpture: (L) $575; (H) $10,450

BATTHYANY, Gyula Graf
Hungarian b. 1888
paintings: (H) $770

BATTIGLIA, E.
Italian early 20th cent.
sculpture: (L) $165; (H) $770

BATTISTA, Giovanni
Italian 1858-1925
paintings: (L) $193; (H) $1,725
drawings: (L) $137; (H) $1,210

BATTLE PLANAS, Juan
Spanish 1911-1966
paintings: (H) $10,350
drawings: (H) $6,600

BAUCHANT, Andre
French 1873-1958
paintings: (L) $5,750; (H) $55,200

BAUDET, ***
paintings: (H) $2,640

BAUDIN, Eugene
French 1843-1907
paintings: (H) $1,725

BAUDISCH, Gudrin
sculpture: (L) $2,070; (H) $4,025

BAUDIT, Amedee
b. Switzerland 1825 d. France 1890
paintings: (L) $3,300; (H) $8,050

BAUDOUIN, Pierre Antoine
French 1723-1769
paintings: (H) $6,050
drawings: (H) $1,760

BAUDRY, Paul
French 1828-1886
paintings: (H) $14,950
drawings: (H) $1,265

BAUDUIN, Roland
French 19th cent.
paintings: (H) $8,625

BAUER, Carl F.
Austrian 1879-1954
paintings: (L) $1,035; (H) $1,760

BAUER, J.
German 20th cent.
paintings: (H) $715

BAUER, Johann Balthasar
German 1811-1883
paintings: (H) $6,600

BAUER, Johann Wilhelm
1607-1641
drawings: (H) $3,105

BAUER, Joseph
German 1820-1904
paintings: (H) $1,035

BAUER, M.
Austrian 19th/20th cent.
sculpture: (H) $1,100

BAUER, Marius A.J.
Dutch 1864-1932
paintings: (H) $2,200
drawings: (H) $605

BAUER, Rudolf
German/American 1889-1953
paintings: (L) $15,400; (H) $66,000
drawings: (L) $2,070; (H) $5,175

BAUER, Sol A.
American b. 1898
sculpture: (H) $935

BAUER, William
American early 20th cent.
paintings: (H) $1,035

BAUER, William C.
American 19th cent.
paintings: (H) $770

BAUERLE, Carl
German 1831-1912
paintings: (H) $90,750

BAUERMEISTER, Mary
German b. 1934
drawings: (L) $805; (H) $1,760
sculpture: (L) $805; (H) $13,200

BAUERNFEIND, Gustave
Austrian 1848-1904
paintings: (H) $46,750

BAUFFE, Victor
Dutch ac. 19th cent.
paintings: (H) $715
drawings: (L) $550; (H) $1,150

BAUGIN, Lubin
French 1612/13-1663
paintings: (H) $26,450

BAUGNIET, Charles
Belgian 1814-1886
paintings: (L) $11,000; (H) $48,300

BAUGNIET, Marcel Louis
b. 1896
drawings: (H) $805

BAUHOFER, L.
Austrian 19th cent.
paintings: (H) $1,980

BAULLOT
sculpture: (H) $2,875

BAUM
paintings: (H) $660

BAUM, Carl
American 1812-1877
paintings: (L) $880; (H) $6,600

BAUM, Paul
German 1859-1932
paintings: (H) $49,500

BAUM, Walter Emerson
American 1884-1956
paintings: (L) $125; (H) $43,700
drawings: (L) $100; (H) $1,450

BAUMANN, Joseph
German 19th cent.
paintings: (H) $1,045

BAUMANN, Karl Herman
American 1911-1984
paintings: (H) $2,035
drawings: (L) $605; (H) $1,100

BAUMEISTER, K.
German 19th cent.
paintings: (H) $715

BAUMEISTER, Willi
German 1889-1955
paintings: (L) $11,500; (H) $88,000

BAUMGARDNER, Wayne
American 20th cent.
sculpture: (H) $523

BAUMGARTNER, Adolf
Austrian 1850-1924
paintings: (L) $978; (H) $1,495

BAUMGARTNER, H.
German 19th cent.
paintings: (L) $690; (H) $4,400

BAUMGARTNER, Johann Wolfgang
Austrian 1712-1761
paintings: (L) $11,000; (H) $12,100

BAUMGARTNER, John Jay
American 1865-1946
drawings: (H) $1,100

BAUMGARTNER, Peter
German 1834-1911
paintings: (L) $11,500; (H) $46,000

BAUMGARTNER, Warren W.
American 1894-1963
paintings: (L) $440; (H) $660
drawings: (L) $110; (H) $1,320

BAUMGARTNER, William
Continental 20th cent.
paintings: (H) $852

BAUMGRAS, Peter
American 1827-1904
paintings: (H) $550

BAUMHOFER, Walter M.
American 1904-1986
paintings: (H) $2,420
drawings: (H) $330

BAUR, H.
paintings: (H) $550

BAUR, Joh.
German 19th cent.
paintings: (H) $1,540

BAUR, Johann Wilhelm
French 1607-1641
drawings: (L) $2,750; (H) $9,200

BAURE, Albert
French d. 1930
paintings: (H) $1,610

BAVAY, M. de
French 19th cent.
paintings: (H) $990

BAWA, Manjit
Indian b. 1941
paintings: (L) $4,312; (H) $11,500
drawings: (L) $690; (H) $1,725

BAXTER, Charles
British 1809-1897
paintings: (H) $935

BAYARD, Emile Antoine
French 1837-1891
paintings: (L) $2,200; (H) $101,500

BAYARD DE LA VINGTRIE, Paul
Armand
French 1846-1900
sculpture: (H) $12,650

BAYER, Herbert
Austrian/American 1900-1985
paintings: (L) $1,725; (H) $8,970
drawings: (L) $920; (H) $1,035

BAYERN, Clara V.
European 18th/19th cent.
paintings: (H) $825

BAYERN, Pilar van
German 1891-1954
paintings: (H) $468

BAYERN, Princess Clara de
1874-1941
paintings: (L) $385; (H) $1,610

BAYES, Gilbert
English 1872-1953
sculpture: (H) $2,750

BAYES, Jessie
English 19th/20th cent.
paintings: (H) $990

BAYLE, Thomas S.
paintings: (H) $1,265

BAYLEY, Josephine
American 19th cent.
paintings: (H) $935

BAYLINSON, Abraham S.
Russian/American 1882-1950
paintings: (L) $110; (H) $550
drawings: (L) $192; (H) $1,320

BAYLISS, Sir Wyke
British 1835-1906
drawings: (H) $920

BAYLISS, Sydney H.
paintings: (H) $825

BAYLOS, Zelma
d. 1950
paintings: (H) $696

BAYNE, Walter McPherson
English ac. 1832-1858
paintings: (L) $385; (H) $1,725

BAYROS, Franz von
1866-1924
drawings: (H) $715

BAZAINE, Jean
French b. 1904
paintings: (L) $5,750; (H) $9,200

BAZANNI, Luigi
Italian 1836-1927
drawings: (H) $4,950

BAZIERE
Continental 19th cent.
drawings: (H) $460

BAZILE, Castera
Haitian 1923-1965
paintings: (L) $5,750; (H) $44,000

BAZIOTES, William
American 1912-1963
paintings: (L) $8,250; (H) $110,000
drawings: (L) $2,310; (H) $30,250

BAZZANI, Luigi
Italian 1836-1926/27
paintings: (L) $5,775; (H) $12,650

BAZZANTI, P.
Italian 19th cent.
sculpture: (L) $1,430; (H) $2,750

Multimedia Works—Where Should They Sell?

In the past the photography market has been viewed as outside the fine arts field, a field unto itself. Recently photographs by artists Cindy Sherman and Barbara Kruger have crossed over to the contemporary auction sales.

Earlier artists of a different generation who worked in a variety of media have not always been easy to define. Few artists were as multidisciplinary as Herbert Bayer (1900-1985). Born in Austria, he began his studies in 1921 at the Bauhaus (1919-1933), the avant-garde German school of architecture and applied arts. Disciples of the Bauhaus believed that craftsmanship and design should be embodied in the industrial arts. This belief that there should be a unity between the arts meant that students worked in a variety of media. Bayer studied painting under Kandinsky as well as learning photography, printmaking, and typography. Walter Gropius, Paul Klee, Lyonel Feininger, Mies van der Rohe, and Laszlo Moholy-Nagy were some of the internationally acclaimed architects and artists who taught and worked at the Bauhaus.

In 1938 Bayer moved to the United States, where he worked for large corporations as an industrial designer and graphic artist. This talented artist also worked in other media—paintings, sculpture, graphic design, photography, and architecture—right up to his death in 1985. The fields on which he had the most impact were graphic design, photography, and typography.

Auction prices for Bayer's paintings are relatively modest. The record price for a Bayer work was at a 1991 Christie's photography sale when his photocollage *In Search of Times Past*, a unique multimedia work that is also the maquette for a well-known photograph, sold for $121,000. Would this same price have been reached if the photocollage had been offered at a contemporary art sale?

Three years later a large liquitex on canvas *Age of Sputnik* was offered at Butterfield's; the price realized was a modest $5,463. (Herbert Bayer, *Age of Sputnik*, liquitex on canvas, 40 x 32 inches, Butterfield's, October 26, 1994, $5,463)

BAZZANTI, Pietro
Italian 19th/20th cent.
sculpture: (H) $57,500

BAZZARO, Leonardo
Italian 1853-1937
paintings: (H) $8,800

BAZZICALUVA, Ercole
Italian 1600-1640
drawings: (H) $1,980

BEACH, Chester
American 1881-1956
sculpture: (L) $460; (H) $17,250

BEACH, Thomas
English 1738-1806
paintings: (L) $748; (H) $7,700

BEACH, Warren
American b. 1914
paintings: (L) $110; (H) $2,070

BEAL, Franz de
English 19th cent.
paintings: (H) $1,210

BEAL, Gifford
American 1879-1956
paintings: (L) $725; (H) $79,500
drawings: (L) $220; (H) $4,950

BEAL, Helen K.
American
drawings: (H) $550

BEAL, Jack
American b. 1931
paintings: (L) $2,640; (H) $16,500
drawings: (H) $115

BEAL, Reynolds
American 1867-1951
paintings: (L) $518; (H) $107,000
drawings: (L) $138; (H) $23,100

BEAL, S.W.
American 19th cent.
paintings: (H) $3,575

BEALE, J.B.
British 19th cent.
paintings: (H) $1,610

BEALE, Mary
English 1632/33-1697/99
paintings: (H) $2,860

BEALES, L.F.
paintings: (L) $575; (H) $1,265

BEALL, Cecil C.
American 1892-1967
paintings: (L) $247; (H) $385
drawings: (L) $523; (H) $880

BEALS, Gertrude
drawings: (L) $220; (H) $935

BEAMAN, Gamaliel Waldo
American 1852-1937
paintings: (L) $460; (H) $2,640

BEAMENT, Thomas Harold
paintings: (H) $1,045

BEAN, Bennett
contemporary
sculpture: (L) $690; (H) $1,840

BEARD, Alice
19th/20th cent.
paintings: (L) $2,200; (H) $2,530

BEARD, Daniel Carter
American 1850-1941
drawings: (L) $550; (H) $1,320

BEARD, James Henry
American 1812/14-1893
paintings: (L) $288; (H) $5,775
drawings: (H) $357

BEARD, William Holbrook
American 1825-1900
paintings: (L) $1,150; (H) $79,500
drawings: (H) $10,350

BEARDEN, Romare
American 1914-1988
paintings: (L) $10,350; (H) $71,250
drawings: (L) $2,420; (H) $43,700
sculpture: (H) $16,100

BEARDSLEY, Aubrey
English 1872-1898
drawings: (H) $2,200

BEARDSLEY LIMNER
American ac. c. 1785-1805
paintings: (H) $57,500

BEARE, George
English ac. 1744-1749
paintings: (H) $19,800

BEATON, Sir Cecil
English 1904-1980
paintings: (H) $2,875
drawings: (L) $440; (H) $5,750

BEATSON, Charles
British ac. 1904
paintings: (H) $2,300

BEATTIE, George
English 19th cent.
paintings: (H) $715

BEATTIE, Lucas
British 19th cent.
paintings: (H) $6,210

BEATTIE-BROWN, William
Scottish 1831-1909
paintings: (H) $1,495

BEATTY, J.W.
American 1850-1924
paintings: (H) $578

BEATTY, John William
Canadian 1869-1941
paintings: (L) $1,430; (H) $2,420

BEAUCE, Pierre de
French 19th cent.
paintings: (H) $688

BEAUCHAMP, Robert
American 20th cent.
paintings: (L) $460; (H) $1,840
drawings: (H) $1,265

BEAUDIN, Andre
French 1895-1980
paintings: (H) $4,025
drawings: (L) $1,760; (H) $2,185

BEAUDUIN, Jean
Belgian 1851-1916
paintings: (L) $385; (H) $8,050

BEAUFILS,
French 19th cent.
sculpture: (H) $8,800

BEAUFORT, Montague
British 19th cent.
paintings: (H) $880

BEAUGUREAU, Francis Henry
American b. 1920
paintings: (L) $3,520; (H) $4,180

BEAULIEU, Anatole Henri de
French 1819-1884
paintings: (L) $495; (H) $8,625

BEAUMONT, Arthur
American 1879-1978
drawings: (L) $302; (H) $605

BEAUMONT, Arthur
American 1881-1942
paintings: (H) $1,430

BEAUMONT, Arthur E.
American 1890-1978
paintings: (L) $605; (H) $1,495
drawings: (L) $275; (H) $6,325

BEAUMONT, Arthur J.
Anglo/American 1877/79-1956
paintings: (L) $863; (H) $1,018

BEAUMONT, Charles Edouard de
French 1812-1888
paintings: (L) $12,650; (H) $93,500
drawings: (H) $977

BEAUMONT, Cyril W., Publisher
drawings: (H) $29,700

BEAUMONT, D.
paintings: (H) $2,200

BEAUMONT, Ernst
American 1871-1933
paintings: (H) $550

BEAUMONT, Thomas Dalton
Continental 19th/20th cent.
paintings: (L) $412; (H) $1,323

BEAUMONT-CASTRIES, Jeanne de
French 19th cent.
sculpture: (H) $1,650

BEAUQUESNE, Wilfrid Constant
French 1847-1913/14
paintings: (L) $1,650; (H) $11,000

BEAUREGARD, C.G.
French 19th cent.
paintings: (H) $522

BEAUREGARD, Charles G.
Canadian 1856-1880
paintings: (L) $495; (H) $2,200

BEAUREGARD, G. Pierre
19th cent.
paintings: (H) $825

BEAUVAIS, Armand
French 1840-1911
paintings: (L) $3,300; (H) $15,400

BEAUVAIS, J**
French 20th cent.
paintings: (H) $2,420

BEAUVERIE, Charles Joseph
French 1839-1924
paintings: (H) $489

China Plates to Portraits

Cecilia Beaux (1855-1942) was a noted portrait painter of the social and intellectual elite at the turn of the century, but after her death her works faded into obscurity. The Feminist Movement and the 1982 opening of the National Museum of Women in the Arts Museum in Washington, D.C., created an interest in works by artists who were female. A renewal of interest in Beaux's works began with a 1974 retrospective at the Pennsylvania Academy of Fine Arts and an exhibition of seventy of her paintings and drawings at the National Portrait Gallery in 1995.

Raised in Philadelphia by her maternal relatives, Cecilia Beaux exhibited talent at an early age. Her grandparents lived in genteel poverty but managed to send Cecilia to a private girls' school and give her painting lessons. She also studied sporadically at the Pennsylvania Academy of Fine Arts but was forbidden to take any classes from the controversial Thomas Eakins because he used nude models. To earn money and gain some independence, she painted portraits of children on china plates. She later called this "the lowest depth I ever reached in commercial art." Eventually she obtained a studio and began painting serious portraits. Her 1883 double portrait of her sister and nephew was exhibited at the Paris Salon of 1887, and in 1888 Cecilia traveled to Paris to study at the Académie Julien. Beaux also spent a summer studying *plein-air* painting at the American art colony in Concarneau. Returning to America in 1889, Beaux established herself as a portrait painter in Philadelphia and later New York. Her subjects included successful businessmen and their wives, professional women, celebrities, and statesmen. Sometimes dismissed as a "mere society painter," she was famous for capturing the essence of the spirit of her sitter. Her sense of color and loose, assured brushstroke gave accurate renderings of the opulent jewels and garments of her subjects.

Beaux's portrait of Alice Davison shows a serious, independent young woman. The sensuous use of color successfully depicts the velvet underside of Alice's hat and the prickliness of the fir tree in the background. Most of Beaux's portraits are set in conventional interiors, and this portrait is unusual for its outdoor setting. When this painting sold in 1992 for $363,000, it established a record price for the artist. (Cecilia Beaux, *Portrait of Alice Davison,* oil on canvas, 66 x 34 inches, Christie New York, December 4, 1992, $363,000)

BEAUX, Cecilia
American 1855-1942
paintings: (L) $4,025; (H) $363,000
drawings: (L) $247; (H) $330

BEAUXGARD, C.G.
19th cent.
paintings: (H) $605

BEAVIS, Richard
English 1824-1896
paintings: (L) $3,220; (H) $5,463

BECCAFUMI, Domenico, called Il Mecarino
Italian c. 1486-1551
paintings: (H) $308,000

BECCARIA, Angelo
Italian 1820-1897
drawings: (H) $2,200

BECHER, Arthur E.
German/American 1877-1941
paintings: (L) $1,870; (H) $8,250
drawings: (H) $104

BECHER, Bernd and Hilla
Germans b. 1930s
paintings: (H) $28,600
drawings: (L) $2,200; (H) $43,700

BECHI, Luigi
Italian 1830-1919
paintings: (L) $2,420; (H) $31,050

BECHTEL, D.B.
American b. 1895
paintings: (L) $550; (H) $2,200

BECHTLE, Robert Alan
American b. 1932
paintings: (L) $4,313; (H) $27,600
drawings: (H) $2,750

BECK, A.R.
American 19th/20th cent.
paintings: (H) $467

BECK, C.C.
drawings: (L) $660; (H) $2,300

BECK, Dunbar D.
American 1902-1986
paintings: (H) $26,400

BECK, E.
German 19th cent.
sculpture: (H) $2,587

BECK, Edmund Philipp
German 20th cent.
sculpture: (H) $990

BECK, Henri van der
French 20th cent.
paintings: (H) $6,325

BECK, J**S**
18th cent.
paintings: (H) $3,738

BECK, Jacob Samuel
German 1715-1778
paintings: (H) $6,050

BECK, John Augustus
American 1831-1915
drawings: (L) $275; (H) $495

BECK, Otto Walter
American b. 1864
drawings: (H) $3,300

BECK, Raphael
American d. 1947
paintings: (H) $770
drawings: (H) $110

BECK, Rick
American
sculpture: (H) $1,265

BECKER, Albert
German 1830-1896
paintings: (L) $1,870; (H) $5,175

BECKER, Carl
German 1862-1926
paintings: (H) $3,450

BECKER, Carl Ludwig Friedrich
German 1820-1900
paintings: (L) $2,200; (H) $17,050

BECKER, Charlotte
American b. 1907
paintings: (L) $935; (H) $1,760

BECKER, E.A.
Austrian 19th cent.
paintings: (H) $660

BECKER, Frederick W.
American 1888-1975
paintings: (L) $275; (H) $715

BECKER, Fredrich
German b. 1808
paintings: (H) $3,410

BECKER, Georges
French b. 1845
paintings: (L) $880; (H) $19,550

BECKER, Jan de
Dutch 19th cent.
paintings: (H) $468

BECKER, Joseph
American 1841-1910
drawings: (H) $633

BECKER, Karl
paintings: (H) $1,045

BECKER, Ludwig Hugo
German 1833-1868
paintings: (H) $8,625

BECKER, Maurice
Russian/American 1889-1975
drawings: (L) $66; (H) $825

BECKER, W.G.
Continental 19th/20th cent.
paintings: (H) $715

BECKER-TEMPLEBURG, Franz
German b. 1876
paintings: (H) $798

BECKETT, Charles E.
1814-1856
paintings: (L) $1,210; (H) $4,290

BECKHOFF, Harry
American 1901-1979
drawings: (L) $357; (H) $2,860

BECKMAN, Ford
paintings: (L) $1,150; (H) $12,650
sculpture: (L) $1,210; (H) $2,070

BECKMAN, William
American 20th cent.
paintings: (H) $8,050

BECKMANN, Ludwig
German 1822-1902
paintings: (H) $935

BECKMANN, Max
American b. Germany 1884, d. 1950
paintings: (L) $200,500; (H) $332,500
drawings: (L) $2,070; (H) $4,600

BECKTEL, D.B.
American
paintings: (H) $880

BECKWITH, Arthur
American 1860-1930
paintings: (L) $357; (H) $990

BECKWITH, Carroll
American 1852-1917
paintings: (L) $1,650; (H) $22,000
drawings: (H) $660

BECKWITH, James Carroll
American 1852-1917
paintings: (L) $1,430; (H) $92,000
drawings: (H) $3,738

BECQUEREL, Andre Vincent
French ac. 1914-1922
sculpture: (L) $3,450; (H) $6,600

BEDA, Francesco
Italian 1840-1900
paintings: (L) $33,350; (H) $288,500

BEDIA, Jose
b. 1959
paintings: (L) $8,625; (H) $13,800
drawings: (H) $8,050

BEDINI, A.
Italian 19th cent.
paintings: (L) $605; (H) $825

BEDINI, Policarpo
Italian 1818-1883
paintings: (H) $2,875

BEEB, E.
20th cent.
paintings: (H) $825

BEECHAM, Gary
contemporary
sculpture: (H) $1,150

BEECHAM, Greg
American 20th cent.
paintings: (L) $165; (H) $3,750
sculpture: (H) $863

BEECHAM, Tom
American 20th cent.
paintings: (L) $578; (H) $1,430
drawings: (H) $385

BEECHER, William Ward
American 20th cent.
paintings: (L) $143; (H) $990

BEECHEY, Sir William
English 1753-1839
paintings: (L) $990; (H) $148,500

BEECHEY, Sir William, studio of
17th/18th cent.
paintings: (L) $2,200; (H) $3,680

BEEHOVA, Mikhail
Russian 20th cent.
paintings: (H) $770

BEEK, Bernard Antoine van
Dutch 1875-1951
paintings: (H) $990

BEEK, Randy van
paintings: (H) $2,860

BEEKHOUT, J.
Dutch 19th cent.
paintings: (H) $495

BEELDMAKER, Adriaen Cornelisz.
c. 1625-1701
paintings: (L) $1,980; (H) $3,520

BEELER, Joe
American b. 1931
paintings: (L) $7,700; (H) $26,400
drawings: (L) $412; (H) $3,190
sculpture: (L) $550; (H) $17,600

BEELER, Tracy
b. 1958
sculpture: (H) $770

BEELT, Cornelis
Dutch 1660-c. 1702
paintings: (H) $25,300

BEER, John
British 1853-1906
drawings: (H) $633

BEER, John
British ac. 1895-1915
paintings: (H) $575

BEER, Wilhelm Amandus
German 1837-1890
paintings: (L) $4,400; (H) $9,775

BEERBOHM, Sir Max
1878-1956
drawings: (H) $4,025

BEERS, Jan van
Belgian 1852-1927
paintings: (L) $3,080; (H) $29,900

BEERS, Marion R.
paintings: (H) $495

BEERSTATEN, Jan Abrahamsz.
Dutch 1622-1666
paintings: (L) $49,500; (H) $63,000

BEESLY, Robert
English School 18th cent.
paintings: (H) $3,080

BEEST, Albertus van
Dutch 1820-1860
drawings: (H) $1,100

BEEST, Sybrand van
Dutch 1610-1674
paintings: (H) $13,200

BEGARAT, Eugene
20th cent.
paintings: (L) $1,150; (H) $2,185

BEGAS, Carl
German 1845-1916
sculpture: (H) $10,350

BEGAY, Harrison
Native American b. 1917
paintings: (L) $440; (H) $2,090
drawings: (L) $60; (H) $1,380

BEGEYN, Abraham Jansz.
Dutch ac. 1655-d. 1697
paintings: (H) $7,150

BEGGS, Helene Warder
American contemporary
paintings: (H) $990

BEGUINE, Michel Leonard
French 1855-1929
sculpture: (H) $1,650

BEHAM, Sebald
German 1500-1550
drawings: (H) $17,250

BEHAR, Ely M.
American b. 1890
paintings: (L) $467; (H) $770

BEHENSKY, Marie
American 20th cent.
paintings: (L) $115; (H) $748

BEHN, Fritz
German b. 1878
sculpture: (H) $4,600

BEHNES, W.
English b. 1824
sculpture: (H) $1,840

BEHRENS, Howard
American contemporary
paintings: (H) $2,090

BEHRENT, Catherine
American 20th cent.
paintings: (H) $787

BEICH
paintings: (H) $978

BEICH, Joachim Franz
German 1665-1748
paintings: (H) $22,000

BEICH, Mary
b. 1915
paintings: (L) $86; (H) $990

BEIGEL, John
American ac. 1855
paintings: (H) $68,500

BEIL, Charles A.
Canadian d. 1976
sculpture: (L) $198; (H) $1,430

BEINASCHI, Giovanni Battista
Italian 1636-1688
drawings: (L) $3,300; (H) $9,350

BEINKE, Fritz
German 1842-1907
paintings: (L) $2,475; (H) $3,220

BEITHAN, Emil
Belgian b. 1878
paintings: (H) $1,540

BEKE, L*** van
17th cent.
paintings: (H) $43,125

BELA, Ivanyi Grunwald
Hungarian
paintings: (H) $1,700

BELANGER, Francois Joseph
French 1744-1818
drawings: (H) $1,430

BELANGER, Louis
French 1736-1816
drawings: (H) $9,900

BELARSKI, Rudolph
1900-1983
paintings: (L) $1,980; (H) $3,410

BELAY, Pierre de
French 1890-1947
paintings: (L) $3,025; (H) $4,950
drawings: (L) $1,610; (H) $7,150

BELCHER, Alan
b. 1957
drawings: (H) $518
sculpture: (L) $1,100; (H) $1,380

BELCHER, Martha Wood
Anglo/American b. 1844
paintings: (H) $1,093

BELICY,
20th cent.
sculpture: (H) $1,380

BELIMBAU, Adolfo
Italian b. 1845
paintings: (L) $357; (H) $29,900

BELIN DE FONTENAY, Jean Baptiste
French 1635-1715/30
paintings: (L) $10,350; (H) $233,500

BELINSKY, G.
paintings: (H) $632

BELKIN, Arnold
Canadian/American b. 1930
paintings: (H) $9,200

BELKNAP, Zedekiah
American 1781-1858
paintings: (L) $1,650; (H) $167,500

BELL, A.D.
British 20th cent.
drawings: (H) $1,045

BELL, Cecil Crosley
American 1906-1970
paintings: (L) $1,045; (H) $11,000

BELL, Charles
American b. 1935
paintings: (L) $23,000; (H) $60,250
drawings: (H) $16,500

BELL, Edward August
American 1862-1953
paintings: (L) $1,210; (H) $18,400

BELL, Enid
American b. 1904
sculpture: (H) $552

BELL, J.C.
British 19th cent.
paintings: (H) $1,955

BELL, James Torrington
British/Canadian 20th cent.
paintings: (H) $605

BELL, John
British 1812-1895
paintings: (H) $14,950
sculpture: (H) $85,000

BELL, John
English 19th cent.
paintings: (L) $1,100; (H) $1,210

BELL, John W.
American 19th cent.
paintings: (L) $110; (H) $990

BELL, Larry
American b. 1939
paintings: (L) $690; (H) $2,070
drawings: (L) $660; (H) $1,980
sculpture: (L) $6,037; (H) $20,900

BELL, Leland
American b. 1922
paintings: (L) $575; (H) $1,150

BELL, Phillip
American b. 1907
paintings: (H) $2,750

BELL, Richard Anning
English 1863-1933
paintings: (L) $489; (H) $1,760
drawings: (L) $550; (H) $990

BELL, Solomon
mid-19th cent.
sculpture: (H) $13,800

BELL-SMITH, Frederic Marlett
Canadian 1846-1923
drawings: (L) $385; (H) $3,575

BELLAGCE, Jacques
ac. 1595-1616
drawings: (H) $4,370

BELLAMY, John Haley
American 1836-1914
sculpture: (H) $90,500

BELLANDI, E.
Italian b. 1842
paintings: (H) $1,320

BELLANGER, Camille Felix
French 1853-1923
paintings: (L) $8,800; (H) $12,100

BELLANGER-ADHEMAR, Paul
French 1868-1925
paintings: (H) $5,500

BELLECOUR, Berne
French 1838-1910
paintings: (H) $2,475

BELLEFLEUR, Leon
paintings: (L) $1,760; (H) $6,050

BELLEI, Gaetano
Italian 1857-1922
paintings: (L) $4,620; (H) $71,500

BELLEL, Jean Joseph Francois
French 1816-1898
paintings: (H) $22,000

BELLENGE, Michel Bruno
French 1726-1793
paintings: (H) $21,850

BELLENOT, Felix
French ac. 1920-1935
paintings: (H) $575

BELLERMANN, Ferdinand
German 1814-1889
paintings: (H) $34,500

BELLEUSE, Albert Ernest Carrier
French 19th cent.
sculpture: (L) $748; (H) $4,400

BELLEVOIS, Jacob Adriaensz.
Dutch 1621-1675
paintings: (H) $22,000

BELLI
Italian 19th cent.
paintings: (H) $1,150

BELLI, A***
paintings: (H) $5,775

BELLI, Giovacchino
Italian 1756-1822
drawings: (H) $1,725

BELLIAS, Richard
French 1921-1974
paintings: (H) $468

BELLING, Rudolf
German b. 1886
sculpture: (H) $14,850

BELLINI, Giovanni, studio of
15th/16th cent.
paintings: (H) $176,000

BELLION, Gabriel Joseph
paintings: (H) $825

BELLIS, Hubert
Belgian 1831-1902
paintings: (L) $1,320; (H) $12,650

BELLMAN, J.J.
British 19th/20th cent.
paintings: (L) $920; (H) $6,325

BELLMER, Hans
German/French 1902-1975
drawings: (L) $633; (H) $26,450
sculpture: (H) $13,800

BELLOC, Jean Baptiste
French ac. 1890-1910
sculpture: (H) $4,950

BELLOLI, Andrei Franzowitsch
Russian d. 1881
paintings: (H) $3,300

BELLON, Camille
French 19th cent.
paintings: (H) $7,475

BELLON, Jean
French b. 1941
paintings: (L) $2,090; (H) $2,640

BELLONI, Giorgio
Italian 1861-1944
paintings: (L) $1,100; (H) $1,980

BELLONI, Jose
Latin American 1882-1965
sculpture: (H) $6,900

BELLOTTI, Pietro
1627-1700
paintings: (H) $4,887

BELLOTTO, Bernardo
Italian 1720/24-1780
paintings: (L) $745,000; (H) $1,322,500

BELLOWS, Albert Fitch
American 1829-1883
paintings: (L) $1,725; (H) $46,200
drawings: (L) $2,530; (H) $23,000

BELLOWS, George
American 1882-1925
paintings: (L) $5,500; (H) $2,862,500
drawings: (L) $302; (H) $12,650

BELLOWS, R.
19th/20th cent.
paintings: (H) $632

BELLOWS, Walter
20th cent.
paintings: (H) $495

BELLUCCI, Antonio
Italian 1654-1726
paintings: (L) $3,575; (H) $28,600

BELLYNCK, Hubert Emile
French b.1859
paintings: (H) $1,375

BELMONT, S.
American b. 1899
paintings: (H) $1,610

BELOFF, Angelina
b. USSR 1905
paintings: (H) $18,700
drawings: (L) $1,540; (H) $7,975

BELSKY, A.
drawings: (L) $2,760; (H) $26,450

BELTRAM-MASSES, Frederic Armand
d. 1949
sculpture: (L) $3,163; (H) $23,000

BELTRAN-MASSES, Frederico
Spanish 1885-1949
paintings: (H) $4,675

BELVEDERE, Andrea
Italian 1652-c.1732
paintings: (H) $17,250

BEMELMANS, Ludwig
Austrian/American 1898-1963
paintings: (L) $518; (H) $4,950
drawings: (L) $38; (H) $3,575

BEMIS, William Otis
American 1819-1893
paintings: (L) $2,145; (H) $3,025

BEN, W.
Continental 19th cent.
paintings: (H) $863

BEN TRE, Howard
American b. 1949
drawings: (L) $132; (H) $5,750
sculpture: (L) $9,200; (H) $10,350

BEN-ZION
Russian/American b. 1897
paintings: (H) $460
drawings: (H) $35

BENARD, Auguste Sebastien
French b. 1810
drawings: (H) $1,840

BENARD, Henri
French 1860-1927
paintings: (H) $2,588

BENARD, Jean Baptiste
ac. 1751-d. after 1798
paintings: (L) $4,400; (H) $25,300

BENASSIT, Louis Emile
French 1833-1902
paintings: (L) $550; (H) $1,980

BENCOMO, Mario
b. 1953
paintings: (H) $2,530

BENCZUR, Gyula Julius de
Hungarian b. 1844
paintings: (H) $5,520

BENDA, Wladislaw T.
American 1873-1948
drawings: (L) $990; (H) $2,090

BENDINER, Alfred
American b. 1899
drawings: (L) $40; (H) $550

BENDIZ, Leopold
German 19th cent.
paintings: (H) $550

BENEDETTO DI BINDO
Italian ac. 1411-1417
paintings: (H) $44,000

BENEDICT, Delmar
20th cent.
sculpture: (L) $440; (H) $4,950

BENEDICTUS, Eduoard
drawings: (H) $1,610

BENEDIKTER, Alois Josef
German 1843-1931
paintings: (L) $165; (H) $3,300

BENEKER, Gerrit A.
American 1882-1934
paintings: (L) $468; (H) $5,750

BENES, Barton
b. 1942
sculpture: (H) $552

BENESSIT, Emanuel
French 19th cent.
paintings: (H) $1,210

BENEZIT, Emmanuel Charles
1887-1975
paintings: (L) $550; (H) $1,760

BENFATTI, Alvise, called Alvise Dal
Friso
Italian 1550-1609
paintings: (H) $16,500

BENGER, Barenger
British 19th cent.
drawings: (H) $495

BENGER, W. Edmund
British 19th cent.
paintings: (H) $690

BENGLIS, Lynda
American b. 1941
paintings: (H) $6,900
sculpture: (L) $345; (H) $22,000

BENGSTON, Billy Al
American b. 1934
paintings: (L) $4,025; (H) $6,050
drawings: (L) $863; (H) $3,025
sculpture: (L) $1,650; (H) $6,210

BENHAM, C.C.
American 19/20th cent.
drawings: (H) $605

BENITES
paintings: (H) $9,775

BENJAMIN, Karl
American 20th cent.
paintings: (H) $1,150

BENJAMIN, Pierre
French
sculpture: (H) $1,092

BENJUMEA, Rafael
Spanish 19th cent.
paintings: (H) $13,800

BENK, Johannes
Austrian b. 1844
sculpture: (H) $1,100

BENLLIURE Y GIL, Jose
Spanish 1855-1919
paintings: (L) $21,850; (H) $222,500

BENLLIURE Y GIL, Juan Antonio
Spanish 19th cent.
paintings: (H) $10,925

BENLLIURE Y GIL, Mariano
Spanish b. 1862
drawings: (H) $15,400

BENLLIURE Y MORALES, E.
sculpture: (H) $1,725

BENLLIURE Y ORTIZ, Jose
Spanish 1884-1916
paintings: (H) $27,500

BENMAN, Waldo G.
paintings: (H) $4,675

BENN, Ben
American 1884-1983
paintings: (L) $220; (H) $3,520
drawings: (L) $55; (H) $1,320

BENNEDSEN, J. Christian
Danish/Swedish 1893-1967
paintings: (H) $1,100

BENNEKER, Gerrit
American 1882-1934
paintings: (H) $14,300

BENNER, Jean
French 1836-1909
paintings: (H) $20,125

BENNETT, Francis I.
American b. 1876
paintings: (H) $3,520

BENNETT, Frank Moss
English 1874-1953
paintings: (L) $345; (H) $23,000

BENNETT, H. Stuart
drawings: (H) $2,588

BENNETT, J. Maynard
American 20th cent.
paintings: (H) $825

BENNETT, Joseph
American b. 1899
paintings: (H) $1,650

BENNETT, T.D.
American late 19th cent.
paintings: (H) $1,540

BENNETT, W.R.
Continental 19th cent.
paintings: (H) $660

BENNETT, William
British b. 1917
paintings: (L) $719; (H) $1,540

BENNETT, William J.
drawings: (H) $1,089

BENNETT-BROWN, Mae
paintings: (L) $110; (H) $495
drawings: (H) $220

BENNINGHAUS, Julius Charles
American b. 1905
paintings: (H) $1,045

BENOIS, Albert
Russian b. 1888
drawings: (H) $517

BENOIS, Alexandre Nikolaevich
Russian 1870-1960
paintings: (H) $990
drawings: (L) $412; (H) $2,200

BENOIS, Nicolai
Russian b. 1901/02
drawings: (H) $2,310

BENOIST-GIRONIERE
sculpture: (H) $1,540

BENOIT, Rigaud
Haitian 20th cent.
paintings: (L) $11,000; (H) $29,700

BENOIT-LEVY, Jules
French b. 1866
paintings: (H) $3,080

BENOLDI, Walter
Italian 19th/20th cent.
paintings: (L) $440; (H) $550

BENSA, Alexander Chevalier de
Austrian 1820-1902
paintings: (H) $6,900

BENSA, Ernesto
Italian 19th cent.
paintings: (L) $550; (H) $550

BENSA, F.
Italian 19th cent.
drawings: (H) $825

BENSELL, George Frederick
American 1837-1879
paintings: (L) $412; (H) $4,400

BENSEN, W.
19th cent.
paintings: (H) $1,610

BENSING, Frank
1893-1983
paintings: (H) $605

BENSO, Giulio
Italian 1601-1668
drawings: (H) $3,680

BENSON, Ambrosius
Flemish 1495-1550
paintings: (L) $123,500; (H) $255,500

BENSON, Eugene
American 1839-1908
paintings: (L) $550; (H) $4,312

BENSON, Frank W.
American 1862-1951
paintings: (L) $880; (H) $4,182,500
drawings: (L) $440; (H) $34,500

BENSON, James
American 20th cent.
paintings: (H) $660

BENSON, John P.
American 1865-1947
paintings: (L) $248; (H) $3,575

BENSON, Nesbit
American ac. c. 1919
drawings: (H) $633

BENSON, Townley
19th/20th cent.
paintings: (L) $55; (H) $660

BENT, Jan van der
1650-1690
paintings: (H) $2,300

BENTHELY, Johanna
paintings: (H) $1,350

BENTHEM-DINSDALE, John
British b. 1927
paintings: (H) $6,900

BENTLEY, Claude
American b. 1915
paintings: (L) $150; (H) $5,500
drawings: (L) $115; (H) $220

BENTLEY, John W.
American 1880-1951
paintings: (L) $220; (H) $10,450

BENTON, Dwight
American b. 1834
paintings: (L) $550; (H) $7,150

BENTON, Fletcher
American b. 1931
paintings: (L) $1,093; (H) $2,090
sculpture: (L) $1,100; (H) $6,900

BENTON, Thomas Hart
American 1889-1975
paintings: (L) $1,100; (H) $308,000
drawings: (L) $198; (H) $140,000
sculpture: (H) $8,913

BENUSSI, Erole
Italian b. 1844
drawings: (L) $770; (H) $1,035

BENVENUTI, Benvenuto
Italian 1881-1959
paintings: (H) $1,725

BENVENUTI, Eugenio
Italian 19th/20th cent.
drawings: (L) $110; (H) $1,725

BENVENUTI, Giovanni Battista, called
L'ORTOLANO
1488-1525
paintings: (H) $63,000

BENVENUTO DI GIOVANNI
Italian 1436-1518
paintings: (H) $93,500

BENVENUTO DI GIOVANNI, and
Girolamo di BENVENUTO
Italian 15th/16th cent.
paintings: (H) $49,500

BENWELL, Joseph Austin
British 19th cent.
drawings: (H) $518

BENYOVSZKY
paintings: (L) $220; (H) $935

BENZONI, Giovanni Maria
Italian 1809-1873
sculpture: (L) $21,850; (H) $176,500

BEOUFF, Pierre le
French 19th cent.
paintings: (H) $2,310

BERANGER, Emmanuel
French 19th cent.
paintings: (H) $14,300

BERANGER, Jean Baptiste Antoine
Emile
French 1814-1883
paintings: (H) $3,300

BERARD, Christian
French 1902-1949
paintings: (L) $17,600; (H) $19,800
drawings: (L) $690; (H) $12,100

BERARD, Desire Honore
French b. 1845
paintings: (H) $9,020

BERARD, Marius Honore
paintings: (H) $880

Carriages and Cars

As a general rule, happy scenes sell better than scenes of disasters; white dresses, balloons, and smiling children also help sell a painting. And carriages are more appealing than cars.

Jean Béraud (1849-1936) was born in St. Petersburg, Russia, of French parents. He studied at the Bonaparte School until 1870 and, after serving in the army, exhibited at the Salon. He was one of the founders of the Société Nationale des Beaux Arts and exhibited there between 1910 and 1929. His works are in numerous French museums. *Sortie du Conservatoire (Leaving the Conservatory)*, a small 12 x 18 inch painting, sold for $184,000 at Doyle's in New York. (Jean Béraud, *Sortie du Conservatoire*, oil on canvas, 12 x 18 inches, Doyle, November 9, 1994, $184,000)

BERAUD, Jean
  French 1849-1936
  paintings: (L) $19,800; (H) $398,500
BERBERIAN, Ovanes
  American 20th cent.
  paintings: (H) $825
BERCHEM, Nicolaes
  Dutch 1620-1683
  paintings: (L) $12,100; (H) $165,000
BERCHERE, Narcisse
  French 1819-1891
  paintings: (L) $2,200; (H) $3,300

BERCHMANS, Emile
  Belgian b. 1867
  paintings: (H) $7,150
  drawings: (H) $2,587
BERCKHEYDE, Gerrit Adriaensz.
  Dutch 1638-1698
  paintings: (L) $9,200; (H) $10,350
BERDANIER, Paul, Sr.
  paintings: (H) $1,100
BERDANIER, Paul F.
  American b. 1879
  paintings: (L) $330; (H) $550

BERDIA, Norberto
Latin American 1900-1984
paintings: (H) $8,625

BEREA, Dimitri
Romanian 1908-1975
paintings: (L) $403; (H) $13,200

BERENTZ, Christian
German 1658-1772
paintings: (H) $55,000

BERG, Anton van den
Dutch
paintings: (H) $1,925

BERG, Fred***
Dutch 19th cent.
paintings: (H) $1,093

BERG, George Louis
American 1868/70-1941
paintings: (L) $495; (H) $1,100

BERG, Karl
sculpture: (H) $3,300

BERG, Louis de
Continental 19th cent.
paintings: (H) $935

BERG, Ralph "Tuffy"
American
sculpture: (L) $2,200; (H) $5,600

BERG, Tom
contemporary
paintings: (H) $1,650

BERG, Travis
sculpture: (H) $715

BERG, Willem van den
Dutch 1866-1970
paintings: (L) $345; (H) $1,430
drawings: (L) $58; (H) $173

BERGAMINI, Francesco
Italian 1815-1883
paintings: (L) $1,500; (H) $16,500

BERGE
American
sculpture: (H) $7,700

BERGE, Edward
American 1876-1924
sculpture: (L) $880; (H) $34,500

BERGE, Edward Henry
American b. 1908/09
sculpture: (L) $1,210; (H) $14,300

BERGEN, Carl von
German b. 1853
paintings: (L) $8,050; (H) $15,525

BERGEN, Claus
German 20th cent.
paintings: (H) $2,310

BERGER
European 19th cent.
paintings: (H) $3,300

BERGER, A.
Continental School 19th cent.
paintings: (H) $518

BERGER, G.
German b. 1917
paintings: (H) $495

BERGER, Hans
Swiss b. 1882
paintings: (H) $3,575

BERGER, Nicholas
American
drawings: (H) $660

BERGER, Ronald
Austrian b. 1943
paintings: (L) $495; (H) $1,870

BERGERET, Denis Pierre
French 1846-1910
paintings: (H) $6,600

BERGERET, Pierre Nolasque
French 1782-1863
paintings: (H) $4,312

BERGERON
sculpture: (H) $1,100

BERGEVIN, Edouard de
French ac. 1896-1928
paintings: (H) $5,750

BERGEY, Earle K.
1901-1952
paintings: (L) $2,860; (H) $3,080

BERGH, Gillis de
Dutch c. 1600-1669
paintings: (H) $55,000

BERGLER, Ettore De Maria
Italian 19th/20th cent.
drawings: (H) $3,220

BERGLER, Joseph
1753-1829
paintings: (H) $6,050

BERGMAN
sculpture: (L) $330; (H) $3,105

BERGMAN, Anna Eva
paintings: (H) $1,320

BERGMAN, Franz, Nam Greb
Austrian 19th/20th cent.
sculpture: (L) $220; (H) $6,325

BERGMANN, George
Continental 19th cent.
paintings: (H) $8,625

BERGMANN, Julius H.
German 1861-1940
paintings: (H) $7,150

BERGNER, Yosl
Israeli b. 1920
paintings: (L) $4,830; (H) $6,325

BERGONZOLI, Giulio
Italian 1822-1868
sculpture: (H) $48,875

BERGUE, Tony Francois de
French b. 1820
paintings: (L) $1,760; (H) $9,900

BERINGUIER, Eugene
French 1874-1949
paintings: (H) $7,150

BERJON, Antoine
French 1754-1843
drawings: (L) $4,620; (H) $9,200

BERK, Henrietta
contemporary
paintings: (L) $880; (H) $1,100

BERKE, Ernest
American b. 1921
paintings: (L) $863; (H) $5,175
sculpture: (L) $165; (H) $4,600

BERKE, Troy
20th cent.
paintings: (H) $880

BERKELEY, Stanley
British d. 1909
paintings: (H) $4,950

BERKES, Antal
Hungarian 1874-1938
paintings: (L) $575; (H) $3,025

BERKEY, John C.
b. 1932
paintings: (L) $605; (H) $2,200

BERKOWITZ, Leon
American 20th cent.
paintings: (L) $2,310; (H) $3,520

BERLANDINA, Jane
American 1898-1962
paintings: (H) $1,840

BERLANT, Anthony
contemporary
sculpture: (H) $1,760

BERLANT, Tony
American b. 1941
paintings: (H) $3,080
sculpture: (L) $3,450; (H) $6,325

BERLINGIER, F.
paintings: (H) $1,650

BERLINGIERI, F***
Italian 19th cent.
paintings: (L) $165; (H) $978

BERMAN, Eugene
Russian/American 1899-1972
paintings: (L) $748; (H) $19,550
drawings: (L) $242; (H) $3,299
sculpture: (H) $2,530

BERMAN, Leonid
Russian 1896/98-1976
paintings: (L) $495; (H) $12,100

BERMAN, Saul
Russian/American b. 1899
paintings: (L) $165; (H) $990

BERMAN, Wallace
American 1926-1976
drawings: (L) $1,150; (H) $3,450

BERMOND, Marguerite
French b. 1911
paintings: (H) $5,750

BERMUDEZ, Cundo
Cuban b. 1914
paintings: (L) $3,300; (H) $343,500
drawings: (L) $1,100; (H) $18,400

BERNADSKY, Gennady
Russian b. 1956
paintings: (H) $825

BERNADSKY, Valentin
Russian b. 1917
paintings: (L) $523; (H) $1,210

BERNARA, L.
French 19th cent.
paintings: (H) $1,100

BERNARD
paintings: (H) $633
drawings: (H) $990

BERNARD, Emile
French 1868-1941
paintings: (L) $1,955; (H) $442,500
drawings: (L) $660; (H) $8,280

BERNARD, Francois
French b. 1814
paintings: (L) $3,520; (H) $5,175
drawings: (H) $715

BERNARD, Jacques Samuel
French 17th cent.
paintings: (H) $14,950

BERNARD, Joseph
French 1864-1933
paintings: (L) $2,200; (H) $11,500

BERNARD, N.T.
19th/20th cent.
paintings: (L) $550; (H) $880

BERNARDI, F.
paintings: (H) $1,265

BERNARDO
Continental 19th cent.
paintings: (H) $550

BERNATH, Sandor
Hungarian/American b. 1892
paintings: (H) $880
drawings: (L) $192; (H) $4,428

BERNDTSON, Gunnar
Swedish 1854-1895
paintings: (H) $19,800

BERNE-BELLECOUR, Emile
French 19th cent.
paintings: (H) $2,300

BERNE-BELLECOUR, Etienne Prosper
French 1838-1910
paintings: (L) $863; (H) $17,600
drawings: (H) $747

BERNE-BELLECOUR, Jean Jacques
French b. 1874
paintings: (L) $1,495; (H) $2,145

BERNEKER, Louis Frederick
American 1872-1937
paintings: (L) $330; (H) $1,840
drawings: (L) $396; (H) $660

BERNHARDT, Sarah Rosine Bernard
French 1844-1923
sculpture: (H) $23,000

BERNI, Antonio
Argentinean 1905-1981
paintings: (L) $6,600; (H) $19,800
drawings: (L) $8,050; (H) $12,100

BERNINGER, Edmund
German b. 1843
paintings: (L) $4,125; (H) $7,700

BERNINGER, John E.
paintings: (L) $150; (H) $1,300

BERNINGHAUS, Charles
American b. 1905
paintings: (L) $1,035; (H) $1,650

BERNINGHAUS, Oscar Edmund
American 1874-1952
paintings: (L) $2,750; (H) $86,250
drawings: (L) $402; (H) $15,525

BERNOUD, E.
French 19th/20th cent.
sculpture: (H) $1,380

BERNSTEIN, Richard
b. 1942
paintings: (H) $1,840

BERNSTEIN, Rick
sculpture: (H) $660

BERNSTEIN, Theresa
American b. 1895
paintings: (L) $259; (H) $26,400
drawings: (L) $100; (H) $935

BERNSTEIN, William
American b. 1945
sculpture: (L) $880; (H) $920

BERONNEAU, Andre
French b. 1905
paintings: (L) $230; (H) $1,540

BEROUD, Louis
French 1852-1930
paintings: (L) $3,335; (H) $55,000

BERRELMANS, Ludwig
Austrian/American 1898-1963
drawings: (H) $880

BERRETTONI, Niccolo
Italian 1637-1682
drawings: (H) $1,430

BERRINGER, Jennifer
American 20th cent.
drawings: (H) $495

BERRIO, Gaspar de
b. Bolivia 18th cent.
paintings: (L) $14,300; (H) $23,100

BERROCAL, Miguel
Spanish b. 1933
sculpture: (L) $286; (H) $30,250

BERRUECO, Luis
paintings: (H) $19,550

BERRY, Louise M.
American 19th cent.
paintings: (H) $805

BERRY, Nathaniel L.
American b. 1859
paintings: (L) $61; (H) $1,540

BERRY, Patrick Vincent
American 1843-1913
paintings: (L) $413; (H) $3,300

BERSTAMM, Leopold Bernard
sculpture: (L) $1,320; (H) $4,125

BERT, Emile
Belgian 1814-1847
paintings: (H) $1,540

BERTAULD, P.
French 19th cent.
paintings: (H) $1,870

BERTELS, George
paintings: (H) $825

BERTHAUD, Paul Francois
French b. 1870
sculpture: (H) $4,675

BERTHELON, Eugene
French 1829-after 1914
paintings: (H) $10,350

BERTHELSEN, Johann
Danish/American 1883-1969
paintings: (L) $550; (H) $6,050
drawings: (L) $880; (H) $920

BERTHOLD, Joachim
sculpture: (H) $1,760

BERTHOT, Jake
American b. 1939
paintings: (L) $1,150; (H) $16,100
drawings: (L) $575; (H) $1,980

BERTHOUD, Blanche
Swiss b. 1864
paintings: (H) $1,725

BERTIER, J.
French School 19th cent.
paintings: (H) $1,725

BERTILLON, Suzanne Marguerite
French ac. 1919-1932
paintings: (L) $3,220; (H) $3,450

BERTIN, Francois Edouard
French 1797-1871
paintings: (H) $2,070

BERTIN, Jean Victor
French 1775-1842
paintings: (L) $2,415; (H) $54,625

BERTIN, Marie
French 19th cent.
paintings: (H) $3,300

BERTIN, Roger
French b. 1915
paintings: (L) $862; (H) $2,875

BERTINI, Giuseppe
Italian 1825-1898
drawings: (L) $863; (H) $1,100

BERTINI, L.
paintings: (H) $578

BERTOIA, Harry
Italian/American 1915-1978
paintings: (H) $460
sculpture: (L) $1,870; (H) $36,300

BERTOIA, Harry and Val BERTOIA
American 20th cent.
sculpture: (H) $825

BERTOIA, Val
American 20th cent.
sculpture: (L) $660; (H) $907

BERTOLI, F.
Italian 19th cent.
paintings: (H) $1,955

BERTOLI, J.
paintings: (H) $1,540

BERTON, Jan George
French 19th/20th cent.
paintings: (H) $715

BERTON, Louis
French 19th cent.
paintings: (L) $2,640; (H) $3,163

Architectural Sculpture

Harry Bertoia (1915-1978) was born in Italy and emigrated to the United States when he was 15 years old. After graduating from a technical high school in Detroit, he entered Cranbrook Academy of Art in Bloomfield Hills, Michigan. Cranbrook Academy during the 1930s was unique: there was no rigid curriculum and no degrees. Studios and shops were accessible at all hours, and teachers and students worked together exchanging ideas. In 1939 Bertoia began teaching metalwork at the academy as well as designing jewelry and making monoprints. Bertoia and his family moved to southern California in 1943

so that he could work with his Cranbrook colleague Charles Eames to design "the perfect chair." Eames was also the director of research and development for the Evans Products Company, a manufacturer of airplane parts, and Bertoia worked in his lab. After the war Bertoia and Eames were lured east by Knoll Associates to design furniture. Florence Schust Knoll, wife of Hans Knoll, had also studied at Cranbrook. Other well-known artists and architects employed at Knoll were Ludwig Mies van der Rohe, Franco Albini, Isamu Noguchi, and Eero Saarinen. Bertoia worked on his sculpture commissions and as a design consultant to Knoll. During the 1950s Bertoia designed a chair made of a web of wires in a diamond design within a metal frame. This popular chair bears his name and is still in wide use. At the same time Bertoia was working on commissions creating architectural sculpture for public buildings. He designed the 70-foot metal screen at the Hanover Trust Company in New York, the reredo (an altarpiece that rises from the ground) for the chapel at M.I.T., the fountain sculpture at the Philadelphia Civic Center, and the sculpture screen at the St. Louis airport. One of his series of sculptures involves a close concentration of metal wires, bound at the base, that spray out. Each sculpture in this series is unique, none are numbered or signed. The five-foot high *Willow Tree* from this series sold at Freeman/ Fine Art in Philadelphia for $20,900. (Harry Bertoia, *Willow Tree*, stainless steel, 62 inches high, base is 12 inches, Freeman/Fine Art, April 14, 1994, $20,900)

BERTONCELLI, G.
paintings: (H) $1,495

BERTONI, A.
Italian 19th cent.
paintings: (L) $880; (H) $1,150

BERTONI, Christine
contemporary
sculpture: (H) $1,380

BERTONI, Mae
American b. 1929
paintings: (H) $880
drawings: (H) $176

BERTOS, Francesco
Italian 17th/18th cent.
sculpture: (H) $13,800

BERTOZZI, M.
Italian 20th cent.
drawings: (H) $825

BERTRAM, Abel
French 1871-1954
paintings: (L) $1,650; (H) $6,900
drawings: (L) $275; (H) $660

BERTRAND, James
French 1823-1887
paintings: (H) $18,150

BERTRAND, Paulin
French 1852-1940
paintings: (L) $2,900; (H) $14,300

BERTRAND, Pierre Philippe
French 1884-1975
paintings: (L) $1,320; (H) $3,850

BERTRAND, S.
French
sculpture: (H) $1,150

BERTUCCI, G.
Italian 19th/20th cent.
paintings: (H) $12,650

BERTY, Paul di
paintings: (H) $550

BERTZY,
Continental 19th cent.
drawings: (H) $2,200

BESAREL, Valentino
Italian 19th cent.
sculpture: (H) $1,725

BESESTI, Antonio
Italian 1865-1938
sculpture: (H) $48,875

BESHARO, Peter "Charlie", BOCHERO
American 1898-1962
paintings: (H) $2,300

BESNARD, Charlotte Gabrielle, nee
Dubray
French 1855-1930
sculpture: (H) $34,500

BESNARD, G.
French 19th cent.
paintings: (H) $605

BESNARD, Paul Albert
French 1849-1934
paintings: (L) $1,265; (H) $5,750
drawings: (L) $1,540; (H) $3,450

BESNARD, Philippe
b. 1885
paintings: (H) $605

BESNUS, Amedee
French 1831-1909
paintings: (H) $1,430

BESS, Forrest
American 1911-1977
paintings: (L) $3,300; (H) $20,900

BESSA, Pancrace
French 1772-1835
drawings: (H) $1,650

BESSE, Raymond
French 1899-1969
paintings: (L) $495; (H) $1,980

BESSEMER, Auriel
American b. 1909
paintings: (H) $687

BESSER, Arne
b. 1935
paintings: (L) $1,265; (H) $2,200

BESSERDICH, Ruffino
sculpture: (H) $605

BESSI, Professor G.
Italian 19th/20th cent.
sculpture: (L) $110; (H) $935

BESSINGER, Frederick
American 1886-1975
paintings: (H) $1,540

BESSIRE, Dale Philip
American 1892-1974
paintings: (L) $450; (H) $1,650

BEST, Arthur W.
American 1865-1935
paintings: (L) $247; (H) $2,300

BEST, H.C.
early 20th cent.
paintings: (H) $518

BEST, Harry Cassie
American 1863-1936
paintings: (L) $230; (H) $3,450

BEST, John
English ac. 1750-1791
paintings: (H) $10,350

BEST, William Robert
English 19th cent.
paintings: (H) $2,200

BETHELL, James
British 19th cent.
paintings: (H) $5,225

BETHERS, Ray
American b. 1902
paintings: (H) $825

BETHKE, Edward J.
drawings: (H) $880

BETHKEL, R.
American 20th cent.
paintings: (H) $863

BETHUNE, Gaston
French 1857-1897
drawings: (H) $483

BETRAND, T.
French 19th cent.
paintings: (H) $1,650

BETSBERG, Ernestine
American 20th cent.
paintings: (H) $1,265
drawings: (H) $605

BETTINGER, Hoyland B.
American 1890-1950
paintings: (L) $132; (H) $1,610

BETTINGER, Paul
paintings: (L) $357; (H) $880

BETTS, Anna Whelan
American 19th/20th cent.
paintings: (H) $6,875

BETTS, Edward H.
b. 1920
paintings: (H) $440
drawings: (L) $495; (H) $935

BETTS, Ethel Franklin
American 19th/20th cent.
paintings: (H) $1,870

BETTS, Grace May
American b. 1885
paintings: (H) $1,380

BETTS, Harold Harrington
American b. 1881
paintings: (L) $110; (H) $990

BETTS, Louis
American 1873-1961
paintings: (L) $220; (H) $6,325

BEUGELINK, Jan
Dutch b. 1811
paintings: (H) $578

BEUL, Frans de
Dutch 1849-1919
paintings: (L) $440; (H) $10,350

BEUL, Henri de
Belgian 1845-1900
paintings: (L) $935; (H) $5,225

BEURONI
19th cent.
paintings: (H) $715

BEUYS, Joseph
German 1921-1986
paintings: (L) $27,500; (H) $41,400
drawings: (L) $880; (H) $288,500
sculpture: (L) $460; (H) $385,000

BEVACQUA, Francesco
paintings: (L) $385; (H) $1,100

BEVEREN, Christian van
Belgian 1809-1850
paintings: (H) $690

BEWLEY, Murray Percival
American 1884-1964
paintings: (L) $770; (H) $17,250

BEYER, Edward
German 1820-1865
paintings: (L) $57,500; (H) $118,000

BEYEREN, Abraham van
Dutch 1620/21-c. 1675/90
paintings: (L) $4,180; (H) $41,800

BEYLE, Pierre Marie
French 1838-1902
paintings: (L) $1,760; (H) $3,300

BEYSCHLAG, Robert
German 1838-1903
paintings: (L) $2,860; (H) $7,700

BEZARD, Jean Louis
French b. 1799
drawings: (H) $1,150

BEZOMBES, Roger
French b. 1913
paintings: (L) $1,150; (H) $3,850

BEZZI, Bartolomeo
Italian 1851-1925
paintings: (L) $4,950; (H) $19,800

BEZZUOLI, Giuseppe
Italian 1784-1855
paintings: (L) $4,125; (H) $4,400

BHATTACHARJEE, Bikash
Indian b. 1940
paintings: (L) $3,162; (H) $10,350
drawings: (H) $3,162

BIAGINI, Alfredo
Italian late 19th/early 20th cent
sculpture: (H) $1,380

BIALA, Janice
Polish/American b. 1903
paintings: (L) $93; (H) $770

BIANCCHINI, E.
Italian 19th cent.
paintings: (H) $719

BIANCHI, Achille
Italian 19th cent.
sculpture: (H) $20,900

BIANCHI, Domenico
b. 1955
drawings: (H) $7,820

BIANCHI, Mose
Italian 1840-1904
paintings: (L) $880; (H) $46,000

BIANCHI, Pietro
Italian ac. 1640-1650
drawings: (H) $2,200

BIANCHINE, Virginie
paintings: (H) $495

BIANCHINI, Antonio
Italian 19th/20th cent.
drawings: (L) $1,320; (H) $1,870

BIANCHINI, Charles
French 1860-1905
paintings: (L) $330; (H) $1,650

BIANCHINI, E.
Italian 19th/20th cent.
paintings: (L) $104; (H) $2,300

BIANCHINI, S.
sculpture: (H) $2,475

BIANCHINI, V.
Italian 19th/20th cent.
paintings: (L) $800; (H) $1,955

BIANCHINI, Victorio
Italian 1797-1880
paintings: (H) $632

BIANCO, Pierreto Bortuluzzi
Italian 1875-1937
drawings: (H) $1,650

BIANCONI, Fulvio
sculpture: (H) $3,575

BIARD, Francois Auguste
French 1798-1882
paintings: (L) $11,500; (H) $134,500

BIARKE, F.
Continental 19th cent.
paintings: (L) $770; (H) $880

BIBIENA, Ferdinando Galli
Italian 1657-1743
drawings: (H) $9,200

BIBIENA, Giuseppe Galli
Italian 1696-1756
drawings: (L) $3,410; (H) $28,600

BICCI, Neri di
Italian 1419-c. 1491
paintings: (H) $97,100

BICKERSTAFF, George
American 1893-1954
paintings: (L) $165; (H) $1,100

BICKERTON, Ashley
b. Barbados 1959
drawings: (H) $1,610
sculpture: (L) $6,325; (H) $82,500

BICKFORD, Sid
drawings: (H) $990

BICKNELL, Albion Harris
American 1837-1915
paintings: (L) $660; (H) $4,950

BICKNELL, Evelyn M.
American 1857-1936
paintings: (H) $1,210
drawings: (L) $193; (H) $440

BICKNELL, Frank Alfred
American 1866-1943
paintings: (L) $330; (H) $7,475
drawings: (L) $82; (H) $137

BIDAU, Eugene
French ac. 1900
paintings: (L) $8,338; (H) $29,900

BIDAULT, Jean Joseph Xavier
French 1758-1846
paintings: (L) $4,025; (H) $16,100

BIDDLE, George
American 1885-1973
paintings: (L) $110; (H) $7,475
drawings: (H) $489

BIDDLE, Joy
20th cent.
paintings: (H) $978

BIDDLE, Laurence
English b. 1888
paintings: (H) $1,380

BIDLO, Mike
American b. 1953
paintings: (L) $2,200; (H) $13,200

BIDNER, Robert
paintings: (H) $1,150

BIE, Cornelis de
Dutch 1621-1654/64
paintings: (L) $4,400; (H) $6,600

BIE, Erasmus de
Flemish 1629-1675
paintings: (H) $2,530

BIEDERMAN, James
b. 1947
paintings: (H) $2,200
drawings: (L) $633; (H) $3,300

BIEDERMANN, Eduard
American
drawings: (H) $2,750

BIEDERMANN-ARENDTS, Hermine
German b. 1855
paintings: (H) $2,070

BIEGAS, Boleslas
Polish 1877-1954
sculpture: (L) $2,070; (H) $14,950

BIEGEL, Peter
British 1913-1988
paintings: (L) $3,738; (H) $19,550
drawings: (L) $605; (H) $6,600

BIEHLE, August
American b. 1885
drawings: (L) $33; (H) $1,320

BIELECKY, Stanley
American 1903-1985
paintings: (H) $1,540

BIELER, Andre Charles
Canadian b. 1906
paintings: (L) $1,320; (H) $2,200

BIELING, Hermann Friedrich
Dutch 1887-1964
paintings: (H) $805

BIENNOURRY, Victor Francois Eloi
French 1823-1893
drawings: (H) $4,125

BIENVETU, Gustave
French 19th/20th cent.
paintings: (L) $5,280; (H) $14,950

BIERHALS, Otto
American b. 1879
paintings: (L) $132; (H) $2,200
drawings: (H) $1,265

BIERSTADT, Albert
German/American 1830-1902
paintings: (L) $1,725; (H) $1,157,500
drawings: (L) $1,100; (H) $12,650

BIESEL, Charles
American 1865-1945
paintings: (L) $165; (H) $715
drawings: (L) $110; (H) $220

BIESSY, Marie Gabriel
French 1854-1935
paintings: (H) $3,850

BIEVRE, Marie de
Belgian b. 1865
paintings: (L) $3,080; (H) $60,500

BIGAUD, Wilson
Haitian b. 1931
paintings: (L) $605; (H) $10,120

BIGELOW, Daniel Folger
American 1823-1910
paintings: (L) $115; (H) $2,090
drawings: (H) $220

BIGG, William Redmore
English 1755-1828
paintings: (H) $1,320

BIGGI, Fauste
Italian 19th cent.
sculpture: (L) $10,350; (H) $17,600

BIGGS, Walter
American 1886-1968
paintings: (L) $2,750; (H) $6,050
drawings: (L) $3,300; (H) $12,100

BIGNOLI, Antonio
Italian b. 1812-1886
paintings: (H) $715

BIGOT, Trophime, or Master of the
Candle
1579-1650
paintings: (L) $18,400; (H) $49,500

BIHET, G.
French 19th cent.
paintings: (L) $1,100; (H) $2,392

BIJLERT, Jan Harmensz van
Dutch c. 1603-1671
paintings: (L) $8,050; (H) $121,000

BILBERS, Johannes Wernardus
Dutch 1811-1890
paintings: (L) $770; (H) $1,210

BILIN
sculpture: (H) $1,540

BILIVERT, Giovanni, studio of
paintings: (H) $5,175

BILL, Carroll M.
American b. 1877
paintings: (H) $660
drawings: (L) $55; (H) $55

BILL, Max
Swiss 1908-1994
paintings: (L) $21,850; (H) $49,500
sculpture: (L) $14,950; (H) $103,700

BILLACOMO?
Italian 20th cent.
paintings: (H) $546

BILLAND, Jules
French 19th/20th cent.
paintings: (H) $1,650

BILLE, Carl
Danish 1815-1898
paintings: (H) $12,100

BILLE, Vilhelm
Dutch 1864-1908
paintings: (H) $1,980

BILLET, Etienne
French b. 1821
paintings: (H) $8,800

BILLET, Pierre
French 1837-1922
paintings: (H) $8,800

BILLMAYER, Kristi
drawings: (L) $350; (H) $935

BILLNEU
Continental 19th/20th cent.
paintings: (H) $9,775

BILLON
20th cent.
paintings: (H) $1,725

BILLON, Charles
Swiss 19th/20th cent.
paintings: (H) $5,500

BILLOTTE, Leon-Joseph
French b. 1815
paintings: (H) $2,090

BILLOTTI, Rene
French 1846-1915
paintings: (H) $2,310

BILLOU, Paul
French b. 1821
paintings: (L) $495; (H) $4,400

BIMBI, Bartolomeo
Italian 1648-c. 1725
paintings: (H) $63,000

BINDER, A.
paintings: (H) $880

BINDER, Jacob
German 19th/20th cent.
paintings: (L) $605; (H) $2,970

BINDER, Tony
Austrian 1868-1944
paintings: (H) $770

BINET, Adolphe Gustave
French 1854-1897
paintings: (L) $2,750; (H) $11,500

BINET, Georges
French 1865-1949
paintings: (H) $3,080

BINET, Victor Jean Baptiste Barthelemy
French 1849-1924
paintings: (L) $4,125; (H) $7,975

BINFORD, Julien
American b. 1908
paintings: (L) $3,300; (H) $5,775

BINGHAM, George Caleb
American 1811-1879
paintings: (L) $4,313; (H) $10,350
drawings: (H) $3,300

BINKS, Reuben Ward
English exhib. 1934
paintings: (L) $2,185; (H) $17,600
drawings: (L) $990; (H) $1,725

BINNING, Bertram Charles
paintings: (H) $2,860

BIOGINI, V.
sculpture: (H) $2,420

BIONDI, Ernesto
Italian 1855-1917
sculpture: (H) $3,105

BIRCH, Craig I.
American
paintings: (H) $1,000

BIRCH, Samuel John Lamorna
English 1869-1955
paintings: (H) $7,475

BIRCH, T.
paintings: (H) $2,530
drawings: (H) $65

BIRCH, Thomas
American 1779-1851
paintings: (L) $1,760; (H) $264,000

BIRCH, William Russell
paintings: (H) $1,210

BIRCHALL, H.G.
British 19th cent.
drawings: (H) $17,250

BIRCHALL, Henry
ac. late 19th cent.
drawings: (H) $1,380

BIRCHALL, William Minshall
American/English b. 1884
paintings: (H) $440
drawings: (L) $110; (H) $1,265

BIRCK, A.
French 19th cent.
drawings: (H) $1,150

BIRD, Edward
1772-1819
paintings: (H) $1,210

BIRD, Issac Faulkner
English
paintings: (L) $550; (H) $1,980

BIRD, John Alexander Harington
British 1846-1936
paintings: (L) $4,600; (H) $43,700

BIRD, Samuel C.
English 19th cent.
paintings: (H) $1,610

BIRDSALL, Amos
American 1865-1938
paintings: (L) $132; (H) $1,375

BIRIUKOVA, Yulia
paintings: (H) $4,620

BIRKHAMMER, Axel
Danish b. 1871
paintings: (L) $1,540; (H) $3,080

BIRKMEYER, Fritz
German 1848-1897
paintings: (H) $3,960

BIRMANN, Peter
Swiss 1758-1844
drawings: (H) $715

BIRMELIN, Robert
American contemporary
paintings: (H) $550

BIRNEY, A.
19th cent.
paintings: (H) $935

BIRNEY, William Verplanck
American 1858-1909
paintings: (L) $207; (H) $8,250
drawings: (H) $633

BIROLLI, Renato
Italian 1906-1959
paintings: (L) $3,080; (H) $6,050

BIRR, Tobey
American
paintings: (H) $700

BIRRADINI, E.
paintings: (H) $495

BIRREN, Joseph Pierre
American 1864-1933
paintings: (L) $495; (H) $4,125

BISBING, Henry Singlewood
American 1849-1919
paintings: (L) $475; (H) $920
drawings: (H) $110

BISCAINO, Bartolommeo
Italian 1632-1657
paintings: (H) $33,000

BISCHOFF, Elmer
American b. 1916
paintings: (L) $14,950; (H) $114,700
drawings: (L) $1,540; (H) $4,675

BISCHOFF, Franz A.
Austrian/American 1864-1929
paintings: (L) $1,100; (H) $71,250
drawings: (L) $1,430; (H) $6,600
sculpture: (L) $10,450; (H) $13,200

BISCHOFF, Friedrich
German 1819-1873
paintings: (H) $30,800

BISCHOFF, Ilse
paintings: (H) $550

BISET, Charles Emanuel
Flemish 1633-1683
paintings: (H) $14,950

BISHOP, Helen
American 20th cent.
paintings: (L) $259; (H) $770

BISHOP, Henry
British 1868-1939
paintings: (H) $1,035

BISHOP, Isabel
American 1902-1988
paintings: (L) $5,750; (H) $11,550
drawings: (L) $546; (H) $3,450

BISHOP, Richard E.
American 1887-1975
paintings: (L) $330; (H) $5,280

BISIGNANO
American 20th cent.
drawings: (H) $1,210

BISLING, O.C.
Swiss School
paintings: (H) $1,375

BISON, Giuseppe Bernardino
Italian 1762-1844
paintings: (H) $5,500
drawings: (L) $770; (H) $33,350

BISPHAM, Henry Collins
American 1841-1882
paintings: (L) $198; (H) $2,300

BISS, Earl
paintings: (L) $935; (H) $1,100

BISSCHOP, Christoffel
Dutch 1828-1904
drawings: (H) $660

BISSCHOPS, Charles Jean
paintings: (H) $13,750

BISSELL, Edgar
American b. 1856
paintings: (L) $440; (H) $880

BISSELL, George Edwin
American 1839-1920
sculpture: (L) $276; (H) $3,080

BISSI, Sergio Cirno
Italian b. 1902
paintings: (L) $1,100; (H) $6,600

BISSIER, Julius
German/Swiss 1893-1965
paintings: (L) $11,000; (H) $33,000
drawings: (L) $6,900; (H) $34,500

BISSIERE, Roger
French 1886/88-1964
drawings: (L) $3,575; (H) $4,400

BISSOLO, Pier Franasco
Italian b.c. 1470, d. 1554
paintings: (H) $6,600

BISSON
French 18th cent.
paintings: (H) $1,980

BISSON, Edouard
French b. 1856
paintings: (L) $1,980; (H) $5,500

BISSON, Frederique Vallet
French 19th/20th cent.
paintings: (H) $5,980

BISSON, Lucienne
French 1884-1964
paintings: (H) $687

BISTTRAM, Emil
Hungarian/American 1895-1976
paintings: (L) $920; (H) $22,000
drawings: (L) $440; (H) $13,800

BITNEY, Bye
paintings: (L) $1,550; (H) $2,500

BITTAR, Pierre
French 20th cent.
paintings: (H) $1,840

BITTER, Ary Jean Leon
French b. 1883
paintings: (H) $990
sculpture: (L) $345; (H) $1,840

BITTER, Karl
1867-1915
sculpture: (L) $935; (H) $5,520

BITTINGER, Charles
American 1879-1970
paintings: (L) $403; (H) $1,430

BIVA, Paul
French b. 1848
paintings: (L) $825; (H) $22,000

BIXBEE, William J.
American 1850-1921
paintings: (L) $220; (H) $3,080
drawings: (L) $165; (H) $385

BIZARD, Jean Baptiste
French 1796-1860
paintings: (H) $4,888

BIZARD, Suzanne
French b. 1873
sculpture: (H) $1,093

BIZET, Andrue
paintings: (H) $660

BJORGE, Ken
sculpture: (L) $495; (H) $4,400

BJULF, Soren Christian
Danish 1890-1958
paintings: (L) $495; (H) $1,100

BJURSTROM, David
American
drawings: (L) $700; (H) $900

BLAAS, Carl von
Austrian 1815-1894
paintings: (H) $5,225
sculpture: (H) $9,200

BLAAS, Eugene von
Austrian 1843-1932
paintings: (L) $2,530; (H) $332,500

BLAAS, Julius von
Austrian 1845-1922
paintings: (L) $2,200; (H) $19,550

BLACK, Andrew
English late 19th cent.
paintings: (H) $1,650

BLACK, Harold
b. 1913
paintings: (L) $2,875; (H) $4,025
drawings: (H) $39

BLACK, LaVerne Nelson
American 1887-1938
paintings: (L) $23,000; (H) $34,500

BLACK, Norman Irving
American/Bermudan b. 1883
paintings: (L) $176; (H) $935

BLACK, Olive Parker
American 1868-1948
paintings: (L) $1,380; (H) $6,050
drawings: (H) $220

BLACK, Paul
American 20th cent.
paintings: (H) $2,750

BLACKADDER, Elizabeth V.
Scottish b. 1931
paintings: (L) $660; (H) $2,475

BLACKBURN, Clarence E.
English 1914-1984
paintings: (H) $1,210

BLACKBURN, Joseph
American ac. 1750-1774
paintings: (H) $22,000

BLACKBURN, Morris
American 1902-1979
paintings: (L) $575; (H) $3,520
drawings: (L) $165; (H) $468

BLACKLOCK, Thomas Bromley
British 1863-1903
paintings: (H) $1,760

BLACKLOCK, William Kay
English b.1872, exhib.1897-1922
paintings: (H) $1,100
drawings: (H) $633

BLACKMAN, Robert
American 20th cent.
paintings: (H) $2,090

BLACKMAN, Walter
American 1847-1928
paintings: (L) $192; (H) $9,900

BLACKOWL, Archie, Mis Ta Moo To
Va, Flying Hawk
Native American b. 1911
paintings: (H) $523
drawings: (L) $187; (H) $880

BLACKTON, James Stuart
paintings: (H) $2,300
drawings: (H) $748

BLADEN, Ronald
contemporary
drawings: (H) $880

BLAEMIS, Eulhimius
Continental 19th/20th cent.
drawings: (H) $2,990

BLAFFERT, P.
20th cent.
paintings: (H) $2,588

BLAGDEN, Allen
American 19th/20th cent.
drawings: (H) $550

BLAINE, Mahlon
1894-1970
drawings: (L) $220; (H) $2,530

BLAINE, Nell
b. 1922
paintings: (L) $121; (H) $4,140

BLAIR, Lee
American b. 1911
drawings: (L) $275; (H) $4,400

BLAIR, Mary
American 1911-1979
drawings: (L) $138; (H) $605

BLAIR, Streeter
American 1888-1966
paintings: (L) $247; (H) $357

BLAIRAT, Marcel
French 19th cent.
drawings: (H) $660

BLAIS, Jean Charles
French b. 1956
paintings: (H) $7,700
drawings: (H) $28,600
sculpture: (H) $2,750

BLAIZE, Candide
French 1795-1885
drawings: (H) $2,200

BLAKE
British 19th cent.
paintings: (H) $605

BLAKE, Buckeye
American
sculpture: (H) $1,400

BLAKE, C.
English 19th cent.
paintings: (H) $522

BLAKE, E.W.
American ac. 1830-1860
paintings: (H) $74,000

BLAKE, Leo B.
American 1887-1976
paintings: (L) $330; (H) $1,725

BLAKE, Nayland
b. 1960
sculpture: (L) $440; (H) $6,600

BLAKE, Peter
b. 1932
drawings: (L) $1,150; (H) $2,300

BLAKELOCK, Ralph Albert
American 1847-1919
paintings: (L) $550; (H) $76,750

BLAKESLEE, Frederick
drawings: (H) $12,100

BLAMPIED, Edmund
English 1886-1966
paintings: (L) $2,990; (H) $7,920
drawings: (H) $920

BLANC, Pierre
Swiss ac. 1920-30s
sculpture: (H) $2,760

BLANCH, Arnold
American 1896-1968
paintings: (L) $440; (H) $3,080
drawings: (L) $165; (H) $200

BLANCH, Lucile
American b. 1895
paintings: (L) $83; (H) $1,840

BLANCHARD, Antoine
paintings: (L) $259; (H) $19,250
drawings: (H) $275

BLANCHARD, Blanche Virginia
American 1866-1959
paintings: (L) $770; (H) $1,210

BLANCHARD, Carol
American 20th cent.
paintings: (H) $495

BLANCHARD, Jacques
French 1861-1942
paintings: (L) $690; (H) $920

BLANCHARD, Maria Gutierriez
Spanish 1881-1932
paintings: (H) $1,610

BLANCHARD, Maurice
French b. 1903
paintings: (H) $690

BLANCHARD, Remy
b. 1958
paintings: (L) $330; (H) $1,100

BLANCHE, Arnold
American 1896-1968
paintings: (H) $546

BLANCHE, Claude
paintings: (H) $605

BLANCHE, Jacques Emile
French 1861-1942
paintings: (L) $3,850; (H) $662,500

BLANCHET, Louis Gabriel
1705-1772
drawings: (H) $3,450

BLANCHI, Pio
Italian b. 1848
drawings: (H) $2,875

BLANCO, Dionisio
Dominican Republic b. 1950
paintings: (L) $3,025; (H) $3,300

BLANCO, Roberto G. de
Continental 20th cent.
paintings: (H) $5,175

BLANCO, Venancio
sculpture: (H) $2,875

BLANDIN, Armand
French 1804-1842
paintings: (H) $2,640

BLANES, Juan Luis
Uruguay 1855-1895
paintings: (H) $21,850

BLANES, Juan Manuel
paintings: (H) $17,250

BLANES VIALE, Pedro
1879-1926
paintings: (L) $13,800; (H) $192,500

BLANEY, Dwight
American 1865-1944
paintings: (L) $55; (H) $770
drawings: (L) $137; (H) $3,740

BLANKE, W.
paintings: (H) $715

BLANQUE, E.
19th/20th cent.
paintings: (H) $1,210

BLANQUET, Lewis
paintings: (H) $800

BLANT, Julien le
French b. 1851
paintings: (H) $18,400

BLARENBERGHE, Henri Desire van
French 1734-1812
drawings: (H) $5,175

BLARENBERGHE, Jacques Willem van
Dutch c. 1679-1742
paintings: (L) $8,525; (H) $27,500

BLARENBERGHE, Louis Nicolas and
Henri Joseph van
18th cent.
paintings: (L) $55,000; (H) $77,000
drawings: (L) $32,200; (H) $103,700

BLARENBERGHE, Louis Nicolas van
French 1716-1794
drawings: (H) $24,200

BLAS, U.
Continental 19th cent.
drawings: (H) $748

BLASCO-FERRER, Eleuterio
sculpture: (H) $575

BLASHFIELD, Edwin Howland
American 1848-1936
paintings: (L) $322; (H) $15,400
drawings: (H) $978

BLASINGAME, Frank Marvin
1903-1967
paintings: (H) $2,588
sculpture: (L) $690; (H) $2,875

BLASKO, Martin
b. Argentina 1920
paintings: (H) $23,000

BLASS, Eugene von
Austrian 1843-1932
paintings: (H) $2,750

BLATAS, Arbit
Lithuanian b. 1908
paintings: (L) $440; (H) $4,370
drawings: (L) $575; (H) $1,495
sculpture: (L) $1,035; (H) $2,090

BLATTER
paintings: (H) $1,320

BLAUVELT, Charles F.
American 1824-1900
paintings: (L) $550; (H) $6,600

BLAY, Miguel
1866-1936
sculpture: (H) $6,900

BLAYNEY, William
American 1917-1986
paintings: (H) $5,463

BLECHEN, Carl
German 1798-1840
paintings: (H) $22,000

BLECKNER, Ross
American b. 1949
paintings: (L) $2,070; (H) $132,000
drawings: (L) $5,750; (H) $11,500

BLEGER, Paul Leon
French 20th cent.
paintings: (H) $3,300

BLENNER, Carle John
American 1864-1952
paintings: (L) $275; (H) $14,950
drawings: (H) $83

BLERIOT, R.
Continental 19th/20th cent.
paintings: (H) $523

BLES, David Joseph
Dutch 1821-1899
paintings: (H) $4,400

BLES, Herri met de, studio of
paintings: (H) $41,975

BLESER, August, Jr.
paintings: (L) $3,190; (H) $3,575
drawings: (H) $2,200

BLEULER, Johann Ludwig
Swiss 1792-1850
drawings: (L) $1,495; (H) $14,300

BLEUMNER, Oscar Florianus
American 1867-1938
paintings: (H) $13,800
drawings: (H) $115

BLEYER, R.
English School 19th/20th cent.
paintings: (H) $825

BLEZER, Joseph Charles de
French ac. 1870-1885
sculpture: (L) $715; (H) $770

BLINKS, Thomas
English 1860-1912
paintings: (L) $3,575; (H) $89,400

BLISS, Lucia Smith Carpenter
American 1828-1912
drawings: (L) $165; (H) $770

BLISS, Rebecca
American c. 1830
drawings: (H) $1,650

BLISS, Robert
American 1925-1981
paintings: (L) $110; (H) $770

BLOCH, Albert
American 1882-1961
paintings: (H) $17,250

BLOCH, Julius T.
American 1888-1966
paintings: (L) $165; (H) $3,300
drawings: (L) $55; (H) $330

BLOCH, Lucienne
American b. 1909
paintings: (H) $5,500

BLOCH, R.
Continental 20th cent.
drawings: (H) $660

BLOEMAERT, Abraham
Dutch c. 1564-1651
paintings: (L) $46,000; (H) $352,000
drawings: (L) $3,450; (H) $18,150

BLOEMAERT, Adriaen
1609-1666
paintings: (H) $7,475

BLOEMAERT, Hendrick
Dutch 1601-1672
paintings: (L) $18,400; (H) $68,500

BLOEMEN, Jan Frans van, called
Orizonte
Flemish 1662-1749
paintings: (L) $13,200; (H) $78,400

BLOEMEN, Norbert van, called
Cefalus
1670-1746
paintings: (H) $8,250

BLOIS, Francois B. de
Canadian/American c. 1829-1913
paintings: (L) $330; (H) $1,100

BLOMMERS, Bernardus Johannes
Dutch 1845-1914
paintings: (L) $5,175; (H) $23,000
drawings: (L) $1,150; (H) $3,740

BLOND, M.
19th cent.
paintings: (H) $605

BLONDAT, Max
French 1879-1926
sculpture: (H) $2,200

BLONDEAU, Paul
French 19th/20th cent.
paintings: (H) $1,980

BLONDEL
French 18th cent.
drawings: (H) $2,070

BLONDEL, Emile
French 1893-1970
paintings: (L) $1,100; (H) $3,850

BLONDEL, Merry Joseph
French 1781-1853
paintings: (H) $184,000

BLONDIN, Charles
French 20th cent.
paintings: (L) $220; (H) $467

BLOODGOOD, Morris Seymour
American 1845-1920
paintings: (L) $110; (H) $1,050

BLOOM, Barbara
b. 1951
sculpture: (L) $1,150; (H) $10,450

BLOOM, Hyman
American b. 1913
paintings: (L) $1,610; (H) $2,860
drawings: (L) $242; (H) $440

BLOOM, John Vincent
American b. 1906
paintings: (H) $605

BLOOM, M.
American 20th cent.
paintings: (H) $660

BLOOMER, Hiram Reynolds
American 1845-1910/11
paintings: (L) $440; (H) $1,100

BLOORE, Ronald Langley
drawings: (H) $2,750

BLOOS, Richard
German 1878-1956
paintings: (H) $17,250

BLOOT, Pieter de
Dutch c. 1602-1658
paintings: (L) $10,350; (H) $18,700

BLOSER, Florence P.
American 1889-1935
paintings: (L) $110; (H) $825

BLOSSOM, Earl
1891-1970
paintings: (H) $880
drawings: (L) $200; (H) $660

BLOWER, David H.
American 1901-1976
paintings: (H) $522
drawings: (L) $715; (H) $825

BLUE EAGLE, Acee, Che Bon Ah Bu
La, Laughing Boy
Native American 1910-1959
drawings: (L) $303; (H) $2,090

BLUEMNER, Oscar F.
German/American 1867-1938
paintings: (L) $165; (H) $27,600
drawings: (L) $44; (H) $25,300

BLUHM, H. Faber
British ac. 1875-1881
paintings: (H) $18,400

BLUHM, Norman
American b. 1920
paintings: (L) $1,725; (H) $24,200
drawings: (L) $345; (H) $7,700

BLUHM, Oscar
German 19th/20th cent.
drawings: (H) $2,090

BLUM
American 19th cent.
drawings: (H) $935

BLUM, Jerome
American 1884-1956
paintings: (L) $193; (H) $18,700

BLUM, Ludwig
1891-1975
paintings: (H) $2,875

BLUM, Maurice
French b. 1832
paintings: (L) $1,840; (H) $3,520

BLUM, Motke
b. 1925
paintings: (H) $2,875

BLUM, O.
American 19th cent.
drawings: (H) $715

BLUM, Robert Frederick
American 1857-1903
paintings: (H) $9,900
drawings: (L) $190; (H) $77,000

BLUMAND, Rose
French b. 1930
paintings: (H) $1,200

BLUME, Edmund
German b. 1844
paintings: (H) $770

BLUME, Peter
American b. 1906
drawings: (L) $184; (H) $2,750

BLUMENSCHEIN, Ernest L.
American 1874-1960
paintings: (L) $1,430; (H) $88,000

BLUMENSCHEIN, Helen Green
American b. 1909
drawings: (H) $2,200

BLUNT, John S.
American 1798-1835
paintings: (L) $8,250; (H) $25,300

BLYTH, Benjamin, possibly by
American 1740-after 1781
paintings: (H) $522

BLYTH, E.
British 19th cent.
paintings: (H) $1,540

BLYTHE, David Gilmour
American 1815-1865
paintings: (L) $1,210; (H) $38,500

BOARDMAN, William G.
American 1815-1895
paintings: (L) $440; (H) $2,760

BOBAK, Bruno Joseph
paintings: (L) $99; (H) $2,860
drawings: (H) $1,760

BOBAK, Molly Joan Lamb
Canadian b. 1922
paintings: (L) $1,705; (H) $3,960

BOBBE, Harry
paintings: (H) $605

BOBBIN, Tim
British 1708-1786
paintings: (L) $5,750; (H) $15,525

BOCARIC, Spiro
1878-1941
paintings: (H) $11,500

BOCCHER(?), E.
drawings: (H) $2,090

BOCCHERINI
American 20th cent.
paintings: (H) $1,870

BOCCIONI, Umberto
Italian 1882-1916
drawings: (H) $170,500

BOCHETTI, B.
sculpture: (H) $4,125

BOCHMANN, Gregor von, the elder
German 1850-1930
paintings: (H) $3,190

BOCHNER, H.
German 20th cent.
paintings: (H) $495

BOCHNER, M.K.
German 19th cent.
paintings: (H) $550

BOCHNER, Mel
American b. 1940
paintings: (L) $3,850; (H) $9,900
drawings: (L) $990; (H) $15,400

BOCK, Charles Peter
German/American b. 1872
paintings: (L) $330; (H) $550

BOCKHORST, Johann
1604-1668
paintings: (H) $8,050

BODDINGTON, Edwin Henry
English 1836-c. 1905
paintings: (L) $935; (H) $7,475

BODDINGTON, Henry John
English 1811-1865
paintings: (L) $770; (H) $18,400

BODDINGTON, Thomas F.
British 19th cent.
paintings: (H) $550

BODDY, William J.
drawings: (L) $375; (H) $600

BODE, Wilhelm
German 1830-1893
paintings: (H) $6,038

BODEMAN, Willem
Dutch 1806-1880
paintings: (L) $8,050; (H) $16,500

BODENMULLER, Friedrich
German b. 1845
paintings: (L) $2,750; (H) $6,325

BODICHON, Eugene
French 19th cent.
drawings: (H) $1,955

BODILY, Sheryl L.
American
paintings: (L) $450; (H) $770

BODINI, Floriano
Italian b. 1933
sculpture: (L) $2,588; (H) $4,025

BODKIN
drawings: (H) $1,430

BODLEY, Josselin
British 20th cent.
paintings: (H) $550

BODMER, Karl
Swiss 1809-1893
paintings: (L) $5,500; (H) $27,600
drawings: (L) $192; (H) $17,250

BODO, Bela Ference
Hungarian 20th cent.
paintings: (H) $825

BODO, Sandor
Hungarian b. 1920
paintings: (L) $1,035; (H) $2,300

BODWELL, A.V.
20th cent.
paintings: (L) $275; (H) $500

BOE, Franz Didrik
Norwegian 1820-1891
paintings: (H) $12,650

BOEH
English late 19th cent.
paintings: (H) $990

BOEHM, Adolph
German b. 1844
paintings: (L) $863; (H) $2,530

BOEHM, E.
Austrian b. 1830
paintings: (H) $7,700

BOEHM, Edouard
Austrian b. 1830
paintings: (L) $1,035; (H) $3,300

BOEHM, Sir Joseph Edgar
English 1834-1890
sculpture: (L) $8,050; (H) $17,600

BOEHME, Hazel Fetterley
American 1900-1941
paintings: (H) $468

BOEHNER, Margaret Huntington
American 20th cent.
paintings: (H) $605

BOEL, John Henry
British 19th/20th cent.
paintings: (L) $374; (H) $575

BOELEMA DE STOMME, Maerten
Dutch d. after 1664
paintings: (H) $35,650

BOELLE
French 19th cent.
paintings: (H) $1,760

BOELTZIG
sculpture: (H) $550

BOERS, Marianne
American b. 1945
drawings: (H) $460

BOERS, Sebastian Theodoros Voorn
Dutch 1828-1893
paintings: (H) $2,750

BOESE, Henry
American b. 1824, ac. 1844-1860
paintings: (L) $575; (H) $4,025

BOESE, J.
German 19th/20th cent.
sculpture: (H) $1,870

BOESEN, Johannes
Danish 1847-1916
paintings: (H) $2,750

BOETHING, Marjory A.
American 1891-1972
paintings: (H) $660

BOETTI, Alighiero
Italian b. 1940
paintings: (L) $3,162; (H) $15,400
drawings: (L) $2,420; (H) $9,200
sculpture: (H) $9,350

BOFILL, Antoine
Spanish ac. 1900-1925
sculpture: (L) $550; (H) $1,320

BOFILL, Josef
Spanish 20th cent.
sculpture: (H) $1,100

BOGAERT, Hendrik
1626/7-c. 1672
paintings: (H) $13,200

BOGART, George H.
paintings: (L) $440; (H) $525

BOGART, Waldo L.
American 19th/20th cent.
paintings: (H) $605

BOGATSKY
Russian 19th cent.
paintings: (H) $1,760

BOGDANI, Jacob
Hungarian 1600-1724
paintings: (L) $16,500; (H) $211,500

BOGDANOVE, Abraham J.
1887-1946
paintings: (L) $3,500; (H) $5,720

BOGDANOVICH, Borislav
contemporary
paintings: (H) $1,650

BOGERT, George Hirst
American 1864-1944
paintings: (L) $192; (H) $4,620

BOGGIO, Emilio
Venezuelan/French 1857-1920
paintings: (L) $2,300; (H) $27,600
drawings: (H) $550

BOGGS, Frank Myers
American/French 1855-1926
paintings: (L) $863; (H) $37,375
drawings: (L) $220; (H) $6,600

BOGH, Carl Henrik
Danish 1827-1893
paintings: (L) $1,210; (H) $13,200

BOGHOSIAN, Varujan
American b. 1926
sculpture: (L) $4,025; (H) $26,400

BOGLEY, S.D.
British 19th cent.
paintings: (H) $800

BOGMAN, Hermanus A., Jr.
Dutch b. 1890
paintings: (H) $1,650

BOGMAN, Hermanus Charles
Christian
Dutch 1861-1921
paintings: (H) $1,210

BOGOJEVIC, H.
Yugoslavian 20th cent.
paintings: (H) $467

BOGOMAZOV, Alexander K.
Russian 1880-1939
paintings: (L) $357; (H) $385
drawings: (H) $660

—**BOGUET,** Nicolas Didier
French 1755-1839
paintings: (H) $107,000

BOHATSCH, Erwin
b. 1951
paintings: (H) $3,520

BOHLAND, Gus
paintings: (H) $3,300

BOHLER, Joseph
American
drawings: (L) $400; (H) $2,100

BOHM, Auguste
German 19th cent.
paintings: (H) $1,870

BOHM, C. Curry
American b. 1894
paintings: (H) $385
drawings: (L) $440; (H) $1,210

BOHM, Francois
Flemish/Belgian 19th cent.
paintings: (H) $990

BOHM, Max
American 1868-1923
paintings: (L) $990; (H) $5,720

BOHM, Pal
Hungarian 1839-1905
paintings: (L) $5,775; (H) $6,380

BOHMEN, Karl
German 19th/20th cent.
paintings: (H) $2,200

BOHN, German von
German 1812-1899
paintings: (H) $3,738

BOHNENBERGER, L.
paintings: (H) $632

BOHROD, Aaron
American 1907-1992
paintings: (L) $518; (H) $23,000
drawings: (L) $44; (H) $4,025

American Tobacco Company

Aaron Bohrod (1907-1992) was born in Chicago and studied at the Chicago Art Institute and at the Art Students League in New York. John Sloan, one of the founders of the Ashcan School, was his teacher at the ASL, and soon Bohrod was painting in a Social Realist manner. Bohrod returned to Chicago in the 1930s and began to paint gritty urban scenes of Chicago life. His popular lithographs of the 1930s and 1940s depicted urban genre subjects and realist farm scenes. His works were widely exhibited, and from 1941 to 1942 he was invited to be an artist-in-residence at Southern Illinois University. In the early 1940s the American Tobacco Company commissioned a group of prominent American regional artists to paint works depicting the tobacco industry. Among those who participated were Thomas Hart Benton, John Steuart Curry, Peter Hurd, Fletcher Martin, and Aaron Bohrod. Bohrod's composition was titled *Unstringing Tobacco Leaves*. Bohrod spent from 1942 till the end of the World War II as an artist-correspondent for *Life* magazine covering the Pacific and Normandy invasions. In the 1950s he began painting *trompe l'oeil* (to fool the eye) still lifes.

In the spring of 1995, the American Tobacco Company deaccessioned eight of their tobacco paintings and placed them for sale at Christie's. Bohrod's painting of a father and son working together to remove tobacco from a drying rack realized $23,000, an auction record for the artist. The previous high for a similar size oil by Bohrod had been $7,700. (Aaron Bohrod, *Unstringing Tobacco Leaves*, oil on masonite, 24 x 29 inches, Christie New York, May 24, 1995, $23,000)

BOHUNEK, R.
20th cent.
paintings: (H) $460

BOICHARD, Georges Lucien
French 19th cent.
paintings: (H) $3,575

BOILAUGES, Fernand
paintings: (H) $605

BOILLE, Luigi
b. 1926
paintings: (L) $1,870; (H) $2,200

BOILLY, Julien Leopold
French 1796-1874
paintings: (H) $63,000
drawings: (H) $1,320

BOILLY, Louis Leopold
French 1761-1845
paintings: (L) $3,450; (H) $937,500
drawings: (L) $2,875; (H) $40,250

BOIS, F.B. de
American 19th cent.
paintings: (H) $660

BOISROND, Francois
French b. 1959
paintings: (L) $308; (H) $3,850
drawings: (H) $1,210

BOISSEAU, A.
paintings: (H) $467

BOISSELIER, Felix
French 1776-1811
paintings: (L) $44,000; (H) $189,500

BOISSIEU, Jean Jacques de
French 1736-1810
paintings: (H) $17,250
drawings: (L) $275; (H) $3,680

BOIT, Edward Darley
American 1840-1915/16
paintings: (L) $2,200; (H) $7,150
drawings: (L) $460; (H) $11,000

BOITARD, Francois
1670-1715
drawings: (L) $1,210; (H) $4,313

BOIZES, Francisco
Spanish 1898-1972
paintings: (H) $2,200

BOIZOT, Antoine Honore Louis
d. 1817
paintings: (H) $4,500

BOIZOT, Simon Louis
French 1743-1809
sculpture: (H) $104,500

BOK, Hannes
paintings: (H) $2,587
drawings: (L) $460; (H) $3,162

BOKS, Evert Jan
Dutch 1838-1914
paintings: (L) $1,980; (H) $11,500

BOL, Ferdinand
Dutch 1616-1680
drawings: (L) $8,800; (H) $11,500

BOL, Hans
Dutch 1534-1593
drawings: (L) $29,900; (H) $51,750

BOLAND, Charles
Continental 19th/20th cent.
paintings: (H) $3,300

BOLANDE, Jennifer
b. 1957
drawings: (L) $437; (H) $575

BOLDINI, Giovanni
Italian 1842-1931
paintings: (L) $46,000; (H) $607,500
drawings: (L) $3,850; (H) $90,500

BOLDRINI, Leonardo
ac. 1452-1493
paintings: (H) $11,500

BOLE, Comtesse Jeanne
French ac. 1870-1883
paintings: (L) $2,300; (H) $2,750

BOLEGARD, Joseph
paintings: (H) $1,045

BOLINGER, Truman
American b. 1944
sculpture: (L) $990; (H) $3,910

BOLINI, F.
Italian 19th cent.
paintings: (H) $633

BOLLAND, Brian
drawings: (H) $2,530

BOLLENDONK, Walter
American 1897-1977
paintings: (L) $110; (H) $1,155

BOLLERA, E.
American 20th cent.
paintings: (H) $460

BOLLES, Enoch
American 20th cent.
paintings: (L) $700; (H) $5,500

BOLOGNE, F.
French 20th cent.
paintings: (H) $863

BOLOGNE, Jean de
Belgian c. 1580-1664
sculpture: (L) $880; (H) $1,500

BOLOTOWSKY, Ilya
Russian/American 1907-1981
paintings: (L) $3,220; (H) $12,650
drawings: (L) $77; (H) $4,675
sculpture: (L) $2,200; (H) $16,500

BOLT, Ronald William
paintings: (H) $2,420

BOLTANSKI, Christian
French b. 1944
drawings: (L) $9,350; (H) $13,200
sculpture: (L) $4,600; (H) $82,500

BOLTBY, J.
British mid-19th cent.
paintings: (H) $5,750

BOLTON, George Henry
American 1833-1905
drawings: (H) $715

BOLTON, Hale William
American 1885-1930
paintings: (H) $1,210

BOLTON, Molly R.
American 1880-1933
paintings: (H) $550

BOMBLED, Louis Charles
French 1862-1927
paintings: (L) $1,155; (H) $3,300

BOMBOIS, Camille
French 1883-1970?
paintings: (L) $1,380; (H) $93,500

BOMMEL, Elias Pieter van
Dutch 1819-1890
paintings: (L) $3,220; (H) $11,500

BOMMELS, Peter
b. 1951
paintings: (H) $1,955

BOMPARD, Maurice
French 1857-1936
paintings: (L) $1,100; (H) $3,575
drawings: (H) $690

BOMPIANI, Augusto
Italian 1852-1930
drawings: (L) $58; (H) $2,420

BOMPIANI, Roberto
Italian 1821-1908
paintings: (L) $2,640; (H) $20,700

BOMPIANI-BATTAGLIA, Clelia
Italian 1846/47-1927
drawings: (L) $1,980; (H) $5,170

BONA, Bona Tibertelli de PISIS
b. 1926
paintings: (H) $3,482

BONAMICI, Louis
French 19th/20th cent.
paintings: (H) $660

BONANE, E.
19th cent.
paintings: (H) $1,210

BONAVIA, Carlo
Italian ac. 1740-1756
paintings: (L) $36,800; (H) $85,000

BOND, Herbert
paintings: (H) $1,150

BOND, M.F.
paintings: (H) $863

BOND, Mary
drawings: (H) $650

BOND, R.H.
English 19th cent.
paintings: (L) $1,650; (H) $2,090

BOND, W** H**
English ac. 1896-1907
paintings: (H) $1,100

BOND, William Joseph Julius Caesar
English 1833-1926
paintings: (L) $357; (H) $4,400

BONDI
American
paintings: (H) $460

BONDOIN, Hariette
American 19th/20th cent.
paintings: (H) $935

BONDT, Jan de
ac. mid 17th cent.
paintings: (H) $12,100

BONELLI, James
American b. 1916
paintings: (H) $1,650

BONELLI, S.
paintings: (H) $990

BONETTI, Alphonse
Italian 19th cent.
paintings: (H) $2,588

BONEVARDI, Marcelo
Argentinean b. 1929
paintings: (L) $1,650; (H) $5,500
drawings: (L) $3,162; (H) $8,800
sculpture: (L) $1,150; (H) $19,800

BONFIELD, George R.
American 1802-1898
paintings: (H) $605

BONFIELD, William van de Velde
American 19th cent.
paintings: (L) $550; (H) $2,415

BONFIGLI, Benedetto .
Italian ac. 1445-1496
paintings: (H) $77,000

BONFILS, Gaston
French 19th cent.
paintings: (L) $550; (H) $3,960

BONFOY, Seth
American 19th cent.
paintings: (H) $990

BONGART, Sergei
Russian/American 1918-1985
paintings: (L) $575; (H) $7,700
drawings: (L) $550; (H) $990

BONGHI, A.M.
sculpture: (H) $1,430

BONHEUR, Auguste
French 1824-1884
paintings: (L) $3,190; (H) $9,350

BONHEUR, Isidore Jules
French 1827-1901
paintings: (H) $3,850
sculpture: (L) $518; (H) $76,200

BONHEUR, Rosa
French 1822-1899
paintings: (L) $1,760; (H) $134,500
drawings: (L) $2,760; (H) $12,100
sculpture: (L) $880; (H) $2,185

BONHORST, A.
paintings: (H) $467

BONI, E.
Italian 19th cent.
drawings: (L) $605; (H) $1,045

BONI, Michele GIOVANNI, called
GIAMBONO
1420-1462
paintings: (H) $165,000

BONIFAZI, Adriano
Italian 19th cent.
paintings: (L) $1,155; (H) $2,760

BONIFAZIO VERONESE, Bonifazio
de' Pitati
Italian c. 1487-1553
paintings: (L) $28,600; (H) $71,500

BONINGTON, Richard Parkes
English 1801-1828
paintings: (H) $3,575

BONITO, Giuseppe
Italian 1707-1789
paintings: (H) $748,000

BONKGER, A.M.
Russian 19th/20th cent.
sculpture: (H) $920

BONNAL, Felicie Palade
French 19th cent.
paintings: (H) $7,150

BONNAR, James King
American 1885-1961
paintings: (L) $137; (H) $3,300
drawings: (L) $330; (H) $715

BONNARD, Pierre
French 1867-1947
paintings: (L) $46,000; (H) $3,190,000
drawings: (L) $863; (H) $26,400
sculpture: (L) $4,312; (H) $26,400

BONNAT, Leon
French 1834-1922
paintings: (L) $853; (H) $123,500

BONNECHOSE, R.
Continental 19th/20th cent.
paintings: (L) $440; (H) $1,100

BONNEFOND, Claude
French 1796-1860
paintings: (L) $1,725; (H) $3,850

BONNEH, Schmuel
Israeli 20th cent.
paintings: (H) $660

BONNET, Francois
French 1811-1894
paintings: (H) $3,680

BONNICE, G.
Continental 19th cent.
paintings: (H) $8,050

BONNY, G.
English 19th cent.
paintings: (H) $920

BONONE, Carlo
1569-1632
drawings: (H) $977

BONSALL, Elizabeth Fearne
1861-1956
paintings: (H) $1,100

BONTECOU, Lee
American b. 1931
drawings: (H) $3,220
sculpture: (L) $6,050; (H) $46,000

BONVAL, A.
19th cent.
paintings: (H) $660

BONVIN, Francois
French 1817-1887
paintings: (L) $2,300; (H) $12,100
drawings: (L) $1,610; (H) $24,150

BOOG, A.J. de
Continental School 19th cent.
paintings: (H) $1,955

BOOG, Carle Michel
American b. 1877
paintings: (H) $3,850
drawings: (L) $302; (H) $1,980

BOOG, M. de
19th/20th cent.
paintings: (H) $1,210

BOOGAARD, Willem Jacobus
Dutch 1842-1887
paintings: (L) $2,200; (H) $4,400

BOOKBINDER, Jack
American 1911-1993
paintings: (L) $286; (H) $1,210
drawings: (H) $55

BOOL, Charles A.
English 19th cent.
drawings: (H) $495

BOOM, Karel
Belgian 1858-1939
paintings: (H) $770

BOOMER, Bob
sculpture: (H) $2,700

BOON, C.
paintings: (H) $1,430

BOONE, Daniel
c. 1630-c. 1700
paintings: (H) $3,162

BOONEN, Arnold
Dutch 1669-1729
paintings: (H) $5,500

BOOTAY, Edward
paintings: (H) $550

BOOTH, Franklin
American 1874-1943/48
paintings: (H) $385
drawings: (L) $88; (H) $4,950

BOOTH, Herb
American b. 1942
drawings: (L) $440; (H) $4,950

BOOTH, S.L.
Continental 19th/20th cent.
paintings: (H) $483

BORCEJAR, M.
Russian
sculpture: (H) $495

BORCHAND, Edmund
French 1848-1922
paintings: (L) $1,035; (H) $3,300

BORCHT, van der
paintings: (H) $1,870

BORCKELOO, Nicholaas van, called Il
Borculo
Dutch 17th cent.
drawings: (H) $5,500

BORDENAVE, Pierre
French 1900-1969
paintings: (H) $1,100

BORDENCHERXXX, J.
Continental School 19th cent.
paintings: (H) $1,650

BORDES, Leonard
1898-1969
paintings: (H) $1,100

BORDIGNON, Noe
Italian 1841-1920
paintings: (H) $57,500

BORDIGNON, Toni
Italian b. 1921
paintings: (H) $715

BORDNER, Jacob
drawings: (H) $750

BORDONE, Paris
Italian 1500-1571
paintings: (H) $132,000

BORDUAS, Paul Emile
Canadian 1905-1960
paintings: (L) $52,800; (H) $198,000

BOREGAR, V.
paintings: (H) $825

BOREIN, Edward
American 1872-1943
paintings: (L) $2,530; (H) $9,900
drawings: (L) $385; (H) $52,250

BOREL, Anna
French b. 1869
paintings: (H) $770

BORELLI, Arthur
American ac. 1930s
paintings: (H) $550

BOREN, James
American 1921-1990
paintings: (L) $4,400; (H) $33,000
drawings: (L) $288; (H) $8,800

BORENSTEIN, Sam
Canadian 1908-1969
paintings: (L) $575; (H) $2,587
drawings: (H) $1,840

BORENTI, P.
Italian 19th/20th cent.
sculpture: (H) $518

BORES, Francisco
Spanish 1898-1972
paintings: (L) $6,050; (H) $35,200
drawings: (L) $2,185; (H) $3,300

BORG, Carl Oscar
American 1879-1947
paintings: (L) $1,430; (H) $44,000
drawings: (L) $275; (H) $9,350

BORGELLA, Frederic
French 19th cent.
paintings: (H) $1,150
drawings: (H) $715

BORGELLI, S.
Italian 19th/20th cent.
paintings: (H) $715

BORGES, Jacobo
Venezuelan b. 1931
paintings: (L) $19,800; (H) $25,300
drawings: (L) $1,650; (H) $4,620

BORGLUM, John Gutzon
American 1867-1941
paintings: (H) $3,163
sculpture: (L) $345; (H) $165,000

BORGLUM, Solon
American 1868-1922
sculpture: (L) $880; (H) $90,500

BORGONI, Mario
Italian 19th cent.
paintings: (H) $10,350

BORGORD, Martin
American 1869-1935
paintings: (H) $935

BORIE, Adolphe
American 1877-1934
paintings: (L) $125; (H) $5,500

BORING, Wayne
drawings: (L) $460; (H) $1,870

BORIONE, Bernard Louis
French exhib. 1911-1920
paintings: (L) $2,070; (H) $4,400
drawings: (L) $1,210; (H) $1,320

BORISOV, Mick
Russian/American 20th cent.
paintings: (H) $715

BORJESON, G.
Swedish 19th/20th cent.
paintings: (H) $522

BORKER, K.V.
Continental 20th cent.
paintings: (H) $522

BORNSTEIN, Eli
sculpture: (H) $5,750

BOROFSKY, Jonathan
American b. 1942
paintings: (L) $6,900; (H) $71,500
drawings: (L) $1,380; (H) $27,500
sculpture: (L) $12,100; (H) $46,000

BORONDA, Lester
1886-1951
paintings: (L) $39; (H) $688

BOROVIKOVSKY, Vladimir Lukitsch
Russian 1757-1825
paintings: (H) $40,250

BORRANI, Odoardo
Italian 1834-1905
paintings: (H) $23,000

BORRAS Y MOMPO, Vincente
Spanish b. 1837
paintings: (H) $74,000

BORRER, J.B.
British 19th cent.
paintings: (H) $633

BORSELEN, Jan Willem van
Dutch 1825-1892
drawings: (H) $605

BORSTEL, R.A.
Australian ac. 1914-1918
paintings: (H) $1,840

BORTIGNONI, Giuseppe
Italian 1778-1860
paintings: (L) $900; (H) $1,650

BORTOLUZZI, Millo
Italian 1868-1933
paintings: (H) $1,540
drawings: (H) $990

BOS, F.
Continental 19th cent.
paintings: (H) $1,320

BOS, Georges van den
Belgian b. 1859
paintings: (L) $2,090; (H) $19,800

BOS, Henk, Hendrik
Dutch b. 1901
paintings: (L) $330; (H) $1,430
drawings: (H) $198

BOS, M.
paintings: (H) $1,100

BOSA, Louis
Italian/American 1905-1981
paintings: (L) $275; (H) $1,540
drawings: (L) $86; (H) $2,255

BOSBOOM, Johannes
Dutch 1817-1891
drawings: (L) $715; (H) $1,430

BOSCH, Edouard van den
paintings: (H) $1,265

BOSCH, Ernst
German b. 1834
paintings: (L) $6,037; (H) $27,500

BOSCH, Paulus van den
c. 1615-after 1655
paintings: (H) $31,050

BOSCH, T. Du
paintings: (H) $495

BOSCHETTI, B.
sculpture: (L) $1,870; (H) $8,625

BOSCHETTO, Giuseppe
Italian b. 1841
paintings: (H) $7,150

BOSCHI, Fabrizio
1570-1642
drawings: (H) $8,625

BOSCOLI, Andrea
Italian c. 1550/60-1606
paintings: (H) $41,250

BOSER
sculpture: (H) $880

BOSHAMER, Jan Hendrik
Dutch b. 1775
paintings: (H) $11,500

BOSHAMER, Johannes Willem
Dutch 1802-1852
paintings: (H) $3,450

BOSHIER, Derek
contemporary
paintings: (H) $2,750

BOSIO, Baron Joseph
French 1768-1845
sculpture: (H) $27,600

BOSKERCK, Robert Ward van
American 1855-1932
paintings: (L) $700; (H) $5,500
drawings: (H) $715

BOSLEY, Frederick Andrew
American 1881-1941
paintings: (L) $1,725; (H) $24,200
drawings: (H) $575

BOSMAN, Paul
American b. 1929
drawings: (H) $7,425

BOSMAN, Paul
S. African 20th cent.
drawings: (H) $2,300

BOSMAN, Richard
American b. 1944
paintings: (L) $2,875; (H) $6,600

BOSS
paintings: (H) $522

BOSS, Henry Wolcott
American
paintings: (H) $1,100

BOSS, Homer
1882-1956
paintings: (H) $8,140

BOSSCHAERT, Ambrosius, I
Flemish 1573-1621
paintings: (H) $1,432,500

BOSSCHAERT, Jan Baptiste
Flemish 1667-1746
paintings: (L) $990; (H) $11,000

BOSSCHE, Balthasar van den
Flemish 1681-1715
paintings: (H) $2,750

BOSSHARDT, Caspar
German 1823-1887
paintings: (H) $743

BOSSOLI, Carlo
Italian 1815-1884
drawings: (L) $495; (H) $12,100

BOSSUET, Francois Antoine
Belgian 1800-1889
paintings: (L) $6,900; (H) $37,375

BOSTON, Frederick James
American 1855-1932
paintings: (L) $330; (H) $1,870

BOSTON, Joseph H.
American 1901-1954
paintings: (L) $110; (H) $1,265

BOSWORTH, Amy
British 19th cent.
paintings: (H) $6,325

BOSWORTH, Winifred
American b. 1885
paintings: (H) $805
drawings: (H) $66

BOTELLO
Puerto Rican contemporary
paintings: (H) $2,860

BOTELLO, Angel
Spanish 1913-1986
paintings: (L) $1,150; (H) $27,600
drawings: (L) $862; (H) $3,300

BOTERO, Fernando
Colombian b. 1932
paintings: (L) $25,300; (H) $1,540,000
drawings: (L) $8,140; (H) $170,500
sculpture: (L) $22,000; (H) $321,500

BOTH, Andries
Dutch 1611/12-1641
paintings: (H) $330,000

BOTH, Jan
Dutch c. 1618-1652
paintings: (H) $57,500

BOTHWELL, Dorr
American b. 1902
paintings: (H) $3,575

BOTKE, Cornelius
Dutch/American 1887-1954
paintings: (L) $880; (H) $8,050
drawings: (H) $880

BOTKE, Jessie Arms
American 1883-1971
paintings: (L) $385; (H) $51,750
drawings: (L) $412; (H) $4,400

BOTKIN, Henry Albert
American 1896-1983
paintings: (L) $110; (H) $862
drawings: (H) $345

BOTO, Martha
sculpture: (H) $550

BOTT, Emil
American 19th cent.
paintings: (H) $17,600

BOTT, W.
paintings: (L) $220; (H) $578

BOTTEE, Isoris
sculpture: (H) $880

BOTTESINI, A.
Italian 19th/20th cent.
paintings: (H) $880

BOTTEX, Jean Baptiste
paintings: (L) $495; (H) $3,630

BOTTICELLI, Sandro, Alessandro
FILIPEPI
Florentine 1445-1510
paintings: (H) $440,000

BOTTICELLI, Sandro, studio of
16th/17th cent.
paintings: (L) $63,000; (H) $167,500

Latin American Art

Sales of Latin American art are held at Christie's and Sotheby's twice a year, traditionally in November and May. Artists who are of Latin American origin or who painted in Latin America are included in these sales. The subject matter and type of art varies from Spanish Colonial to Surrealist to Abstract Expressionism.

Fernando Botero (b. 1932) is from Medellín, Colombia. His first one-man show was in Bogotá in 1951, and the following year he sailed for Madrid to continue his studies at the Real Academia de Bellas Artes de San Fernando. He studied in the traditional manner, copying the works of Goya and Velázquez. (In his later works he made a specialty of painting parodies of works by Old Masters.) Botero spent some time studying in Florence, and in 1955 he returned to Bogotá where he had another one-man show. His work was not well reviewed and he began selling tires and doing magazine layout but continued with his art. His first exposure in the United States was at the 1956 group show, Gulf-Caribbean Art Exhibition, at the Museum of Fine Arts in Houston. Numerous exhibitions followed, and his first solo show in the United States was at the Pan American Union in Washington. In 1961 the Museum of Modern Art in New York bought *Mona Lisa, Age Twelve.* Botero has an international reputation and lives in New York and Paris, but his work is included in sales of Latin American art. His signature style, in both his paintings and bronzes, are large, rounded, voluptuous figures of men, women, and children.

The record price for a Botero bronze was the $462,000 paid for *Man with a Cane* at Sotheby's in November 1989. At Sotheby's November 1994 sale of Latin American art, Botero's bronze relief, executed in 1992, realized $123,500. (Fernando Botero, *Relief (Pareja) Bronze,* bronze with black patina, 24¾ x 18⅞ inches, Sotheby New York, November 16, 1994, $123,500)

BOTTICELLI, Sandro, workshop of
15th/16th cent.
paintings: (H) $231,000

BOTTINI, Georges.
French 1874-1907
drawings: (H) $3,575

BOTTORF, Edna A.
paintings: (H) $650

BOTTS, A.E.
paintings: (H) $550

BOTTSCHILD, Samuel
1640-1707
drawings: (H) $880

BOUCART, Gaston H.
French 1878-1962
paintings: (L) $1,840; (H) $2,750

BOUCHARD, Louis Henri
sculpture: (H) $5,750

BOUCHARD, Paul Louis
French 1853-1937
paintings: (H) $40,250
drawings: (H) $660

BOUCHARD, Pierre Francois
French 1831-1889
paintings: (L) $13,200; (H) $13,800

BOUCHARDON, Edme
French 1698-1762
drawings: (L) $5,750; (H) $14,950

BOUCHE, Carl de
German b. 1845
paintings: (H) $605

BOUCHE, Louis A.
American 1896-1969
paintings: (L) $345; (H) $4,600
drawings: (L) $330; (H) $440

BOUCHENE, Dimitri
Russian/French b. 1898
paintings: (H) $935
drawings: (L) $1,210; (H) $7,700

BOUCHER, Alfred
French 1850-1934
sculpture: (L) $1,870; (H) $101,500

BOUCHER, Francois
French 1703-1770
paintings: (L) $387,500; (H) $800,000
drawings: (L) $1,725; (H) $82,500

BOUCHER, Francois, and studio
French 1703-1770
paintings: (L) $77,000; (H) $330,000

BOUCHET, Jules Frederic
French 1799-1860
drawings: (H) $4,675

BOUCHONVILLE, Andre
19th/20th cent.
paintings: (H) $825

BOUCHOR, Joseph Felix
French 1853-1937
paintings: (L) $322; (H) $2,300

BOUCHOT, Francois
French 1800-1842
drawings: (H) $17,600

BOUCKHORST, Jan Philipsz van
Dutch 1588-1631
drawings: (L) $1,320; (H) $11,000

BOUDAT, Louis
American
paintings: (H) $15,400

BOUDET, Pierre
French b. 1925
paintings: (L) $575; (H) $4,950

BOUDIN, Eugene
French 1824-1898
paintings: (L) $2,750; (H) $715,000
drawings: (L) $264; (H) $187,300

BOUDRY, Alois
Belgian 1851-1938
paintings: (L) $1,100; (H) $2,200

BOUDRY, J.S.
paintings: (H) $4,125

BOUEL, Louis Francois Numance
French 19th cent.
paintings: (L) $3,575; (H) $8,800

BOUGEREAU, Gardner E.J.
American 1837-1922
paintings: (H) $2,750

BOUGH, Samuel
Scottish 1822-1878
paintings: (L) $880; (H) $5,225
drawings: (H) $575

BOUGHTON, George Henry
Anglo/American 1833-1905
paintings: (L) $385; (H) $22,000
drawings: (L) $660; (H) $2,090

BOUGUEREAU, Elizabeth Jane
Gardner
American 1851-1922
paintings: (L) $715; (H) $3,410
drawings: (H) $16,675

BOUGUEREAU, William Adolphe
French 1825-1905
paintings: (L) $6,325; (H) $690,000
drawings: (L) $935; (H) $14,950

BOUHIN, A.
19th/20th cent.
paintings: (H) $880

BOUILLIER, Amable
French b. 1867
paintings: (H) $2,750

BOUILLON, Jacques
French 20th cent.
paintings: (H) $605

BOULANGER, Gustave
French 1824-1888
paintings: (L) $26,700; (H) $43,700
drawings: (L) $990; (H) $1,840

BOULANGER, Louis
French 1806-1867
paintings: (H) $17,250
drawings: (H) $165

BOULARD, Auguste
French 1825-1897
paintings: (L) $1,150; (H) $1,210

BOULARD, Emile
French 1861-1943
paintings: (H) $8,525

BOULARD, Theodore
French 20th cent.
paintings: (H) $3,850

BOULAYE, Paul de la
French b. 1902
paintings: (H) $1,725

BOULET, Cyprien Eugene
French 1877-1927
paintings: (L) $2,070; (H) $2,750

BOULIARD, Marie Genevieve
French 1772-1819
paintings: (H) $51,750

BOULIER, Lucien
French 1882-1963
paintings: (L) $110; (H) $4,255

BOULOGNE, Louis de, the younger
French 1654-1733
drawings: (L) $1,540; (H) $6,900

BOULOGNE, Madeleine de
French 1646-1710
paintings: (H) $134,500

BOULT, F. Cecil
British 19th cent.
paintings: (H) $3,080

BOULTBEE, John
English ac. 1775-1788
paintings: (H) $11,500

BOULTON, Joseph Lorkowski
American b. 1896
sculpture: (L) $121; (H) $660

BOUNDEY, Burton
American 1879-1962
paintings: (L) $660; (H) $7,150

BOUQUET, Andre
French b. 1897
paintings: (L) $611; (H) $920

BOUQUET, Michel
French 1807-1890
paintings: (H) $920
drawings: (H) $1,150

BOURAINE, Marcel
French ac. 1918-1935
sculpture: (L) $633; (H) $26,450

BOURBON-LEBLANC, Louis Gabriel
French 1813-1902
paintings: (H) $40,250

BOURCE, Henri Jacques
Belgian 1826-1899
paintings: (H) $2,300

BOURDELLE, Emile Antoine
French 1861-1929
drawings: (L) $173; (H) $330
sculpture: (L) $2,200; (H) $176,000

BOURDELLE, Pierre
French ?-1966
drawings: (H) $1,760

BOURDILLON, Frank Wright
British 19th cent.
paintings: (H) $4,675

BOURDON, Charles
French 19th cent.
paintings: (H) $1,100

Salon Painter

Beginning in 1667, the French Royal Academy of Painting and Sculpture held an annual exhibition in the Salon d'Apollon in the Louvre. Artists who painted in the officially sanctioned Academic style of art and exhibited in this show were called "Salon painters." In 1881 the government withdrew its official support, and the Société des Artistes Fransais, a committee of 90 artists elected by those who had previously exhibited, was formed to take responsibility for the show. William Adolphe Bouguereau (1825-1905) was a teacher at the Academy and a member of the committee of the Salon. The committee, which served as a jury, was hostile to new and creative artists such as Manet and the Impressionists. (These more independent artists formed their own groups: the Salon d'Automme, the Salon de la Nationale, the Salon des Indépendants, and the forerunner of them all, the 1863 Salon des Refusés.) Bouguereau was at the height of his popularity in the late 19th century. As a teacher at the Academie he enjoyed the favor of state patronage and broad public acclaim. His subject matter was mostly allegorical, mythical, and religious subjects and was painted in a realist, almost photographic, manner with a glossy smoothness and attention to detail. During the mid-20th century the works of Bouguereau and other Salon painters fell out of favor and could be purchased for very little. The last ten to fifteen years have seen a resurgence in the appreciation of their works and a corresponding escalation in value. *Portrait of a Young Girl with Flowers*, a sentimental portrait of a Parisian waif, was consigned to the Royal York Auction Gallery in Pittsburgh, Pennsylvania. The portrait, from the Kerr Estate, realized $105,000. (William Adolphe Bouguereau, *Portrait of a Young Girl with Flowers*, oil on canvas, 34½ x 21 inches, Royal York, February 17, 1995, $105,000)

BOURDON, Sebastian
French 1616-1671
paintings: (H) $247,500

BOURET, Eutrope
French 1833-1906
sculpture: (L) $242; (H) $2,970

BOURGAIN, Gaston
French d. 1921
drawings: (H) $978

BOURGEOIS, Charles Arthur
French 1838-1886
sculpture: (L) $1,980; (H) $12,100

BOURGEOIS, Eugene
French 1855-1909
paintings: (H) $550

BOURGEOIS, Louise
American b. 1911
drawings: (L) $4,400; (H) $14,300
sculpture: (L) $6,900; (H) $200,500

BOURGEOIS, Max
French 19th cent.
sculpture: (H) $4,400

BOURGES, Pauline Elise Leonide
French 1838-1910
paintings: (H) $1,100

BOURGOGNE, Pierre
French 1838-1904
paintings: (L) $4,400; (H) $34,100

BOURGOIN, Marie Desire
French 1839-1912
drawings: (H) $5,750

BOURGUEREAU, William Adolphe
French 1825-1905
drawings: (H) $4,675

BOURLARD, Antoine Joseph
Flemish 1826-1899
paintings: (H) $4,620

BOURNE, Gertrude B.
American 1867-1962
drawings: (L) $825; (H) $1,540

BOURNE, J.
American 19th cent.
paintings: (H) $880

BOURNE, Jean Baptiste C.
French ac. 1815-1900
paintings: (H) $2,200

BOUSQUET
sculpture: (H) $935

BOUSQUET, Charles
French 1856-1946
paintings: (H) $46,000

BOUT, Peeter
Flemish 1658-1702/19
paintings: (L) $3,575; (H) $151,000

BOUT, Pieter and Adriaen Frans
BOUDEWIJNS
17th/18th cent.
paintings: (L) $3,450; (H) $11,000

BOUTELLE, De Witt Clinton
American 1817/20-1884
paintings: (L) $660; (H) $9,200

BOUTER, Cornelis
Dutch 1888-1966
paintings: (L) $1,265; (H) $5,775

BOUTET DE MONVEL, Bernard
French 1884-1949
paintings: (H) $1,495

BOUTIBONNE, Charles Edouard
Hungarian 1816-1897
paintings: (L) $13,200; (H) $57,500

BOUTIGNY, Paul Emile
French 1854-1929
paintings: (L) $1,650; (H) $3,575

BOUTS, Aelbrecht
Dutch after 1451-1549
paintings: (L) $222,500; (H) $310,500

BOUTTATS, Frederik
Flemish ac. 1612-1661
paintings: (H) $112,500

BOUTTATS, Johann Baptiste
Flemish ac. 1706-1735
paintings: (L) $4,370; (H) $5,750

BOUVAL, Maurice
French d. c.1920
sculpture: (L) $489; (H) $20,700

BOUVARD, J***
French 19th cent.
paintings: (H) $4,888

BOUVARD, Noel
20th cent.
paintings: (H) $862

BOUVE, Rosamond Smith
American early 20th cent.
paintings: (L) $413; (H) $8,250

BOUVIER, M.
Continental School 19th/20th cent.
paintings: (H) $1,150

BOUYSSOU, Jacques
French b. 1926
paintings: (L) $230; (H) $5,280

BOVAM, Sam
American 19th cent.
paintings: (H) $1,210

BOVERIE, L.
Belgian ac. 1888
drawings: (L) $863; (H) $1,485

BOVKUN, Vladimir
paintings: (H) $1,100

BOWDOIN, Harriette
American d. 1947/48
paintings: (H) $825

BOWEN, Howard
British 20th cent.
paintings: (H) $1,380

BOWEN, J.
drawings: (H) $853

BOWEN, John T.
American 1801-1856
drawings: (H) $3,300

BOWEN, P.T.
American ac. c. 1836
paintings: (H) $990

BOWER
drawings: (L) $110; (H) $550

BOWER, Alexander
American 1875-1952
paintings: (L) $187; (H) $13,200
drawings: (L) $110; (H) $546

BOWER, J.
drawings: (H) $3,163

BOWER, J.
American ac. c. 1870-1900
drawings: (H) $2,090

BOWER, J.S.
American ac. c. 1850
drawings: (L) $110; (H) $968

BOWERS, Frank Taylor
1875-1932
paintings: (H) $1,540

BOWERS, George Newell
1849-1909
paintings: (L) $220; (H) $3,220

BOWES, David
b. 1947
paintings: (L) $1,870; (H) $2,530
drawings: (H) $978

BOWES, Hy
19th cent.
paintings: (H) $770

BOWIE, Frank Louville
American 1857-1936
paintings: (L) $88; (H) $605
drawings: (L) $82; (H) $110

BOWKETT, Jane Maria
English ac. 1860-1885
paintings: (L) $1,955; (H) $2,200

BOWLER, Joseph
American b. 1928
paintings: (L) $385; (H) $1,210
drawings: (H) $2,860

BOWMAN, A.J.
paintings: (H) $605

BOWYER, Alan
paintings: (H) $550

BOX, Henry
British 19th cent.
drawings: (H) $1,100

BOXER, Stanley
American b. 1926
paintings: (L) $2,475; (H) $3,300
drawings: (L) $55; (H) $418

BOYCE, Thomas Nicholas
British 19th cent.
drawings: (H) $522

BOYD, J. Rutherford
American 1884-1951
paintings: (L) $660; (H) $17,250
drawings: (L) $138; (H) $23,100

BOYD, Jeanie L.
French 20th cent.
paintings: (H) $715

BOYD, Wm.
British 20th cent.
paintings: (H) $467

BOYDEN, Dwight Frederick
American 1860-1933
paintings: (H) $3,190

BOYER, Emile
French 19th cent.
sculpture: (L) $552; (H) $1,955

BOYER, Rodney
20th cent.
sculpture: (H) $977

BOYER-BRETON, Marthe Marie
Louise
French 19th cent.
paintings: (H) $52,250

BOYES, N.
English 19th/20th cent.
drawings: (H) $605

BOYLE, Charles Wellington
American 1861-1925
paintings: (L) $220; (H) $9,350

BOYLE, F.
American 19th cent.
paintings: (H) $1,150

BOYLE, George A.
English 19th cent.
paintings: (L) $522; (H) $770

BOYLE, John J.
American 1852-1917
sculpture: (H) $18,975

BOYLE, Martin
drawings: (H) $550

BOYLE, Neil
paintings: (H) $1,100

BOYLES, N.
sculpture: (H) $1,430

BOYNTON, Ray
American 1883-1951
paintings: (L) $250; (H) $3,300

BOYS, Thomas Shotter
British 1803-1874
drawings: (H) $977

BOZE, Joseph
1744/45-1826
paintings: (H) $1,430

BOZZALLA, Giuseppe
Italian 1874-1958
paintings: (H) $3,080

BOZZANI, Lucien
Italian 19th cent.
drawings: (H) $825

BRAAKMAN, Anthonie
Dutch 19th cent.
paintings: (H) $6,900

BRABAZON, Hercules
English 1821-1906
drawings: (L) $55; (H) $1,760

BRACEY, Arthur
paintings: (L) $345; (H) $660

BRACHO Y MURILLO, Jose
Spanish 19th cent.
paintings: (H) $3,960

BRACK, Emil
German 1860-1905
paintings: (L) $20,700; (H) $50,600

BRACKEN, Clio Hinton
American 1870-1925
sculpture: (L) $1,650; (H) $3,450

BRACKER, M. Leone
American 1885-1937
drawings: (L) $55; (H) $880

BRACKETT, Arthur Loring
paintings: (H) $1,210

BRACKETT, Sidney Lawrence
American 1852-1910
paintings: (L) $110; (H) $1,760

BRACKETT, Walter M.
American 1823-1919
paintings: (L) $2,200; (H) $9,900

BRACKETT, Ward
b. 1914
paintings: (H) $467

BRACKMAN, Robert
American 1898-1980
paintings: (L) $110; (H) $28,600
drawings: (L) $605; (H) $3,300

BRACONY, Leopold
Italian 19th/20th cent.
sculpture: (H) $17,250

BRACQUEMOND, Felix
French 1833-1914
drawings: (H) $3,450

BRACY, Arthur
paintings: (L) $275; (H) $660

BRADBURY, Bennett
American 20th cent.
paintings: (L) $248; (H) $1,870

BRADBURY, Gibeon
American 1833-1904
paintings: (L) $2,310; (H) $3,410
drawings: (H) $1,320

BRADER, Ferdinand A.
drawings: (L) $3,850; (H) $9,460

BRADFIELD, Elizabeth Palmer
American 20th cent.
sculpture: (H) $467

BRADFIELD, Virginia Palmer
drawings: (H) $880

BRADFORD, William
American 1823-1892
paintings: (L) $330; (H) $55,000
drawings: (L) $137; (H) $1,540

BRADISH, Alvah
American 1806-1901
paintings: (H) $9,350

BRADLEY, Anne Carey
American b. 1884
paintings: (L) $39; (H) $4,180
drawings: (L) $55; (H) $743

BRADLEY, John
American ac. c. 1831-1847
paintings: (H) $5,775

BRADLEY, L.
American 19th cent.
paintings: (H) $1,265

BRADLEY, Susan H.
American 1851-1929
paintings: (H) $550
drawings: (L) $165; (H) $357

BRADLEY, William
British 1801-1857
paintings: (L) $935; (H) $20,900

BRADNER, Karl C.
American b. 1898
paintings: (H) $660

BRADSHAW, Eva Theresa
Canadian/American 19th/20th cent.
paintings: (L) $575; (H) $770

BRADSHAW, George F.
Irish d. 1887
paintings: (H) $908

BRADSTREET, J.E.
paintings: (L) $28; (H) $1,650

BRADSTREET, Julia E.
American 19th cent.
paintings: (L) $165; (H) $1,100

BRADWAY, Florence Doll
American b. 1897
paintings: (H) $467

BRADY, Bruce
sculpture: (L) $83; (H) $1,100

BRADY, Larry Vern
paintings: (H) $1,210

BRADY, Mary
American ac. 1880-1913
paintings: (H) $880

BRADY, Robert David
American b. 1946
sculpture: (L) $2,070; (H) $3,738

BRAEKELEER, Adrien Ferdinand de
Belgian 1818-1904
paintings: (L) $1,093; (H) $26,400

BRAEKELEER, Henri de
British 1840-1888
paintings: (H) $10,450

BRAGG, Charles
American b. 1931
paintings: (L) $880; (H) $880
sculpture: (L) $715; (H) $1,650

BRAGNAVAL, L.
19th cent.
paintings: (H) $1,760

BRAILOWSKI, Runina and Leopold
Russian 19th/20th cent.
paintings: (H) $495

BRAITH, Anton
German 1836-1905
paintings: (H) $770

BRAKEN, Julia M.
American 1871-1942
sculpture: (H) $1,320

BRAKENBURG, Richard
Dutch 1650-1702
paintings: (H) $4,070

BRALEY, Clarence
American 19th/20th cent.
paintings: (L) $248; (H) $1,035
drawings: (L) $39; (H) $165

BRAMER, Leonard
Dutch 1596-1674
paintings: (H) $44,850
drawings: (H) $1,035

BRAMHALL
American late 19th cent.
paintings: (L) $1,495; (H) $1,760

Among the Ice Floes

William Bradford (1823-1892) is best known for his grandiose paintings of the Arctic. After he finished his schooling, his first job was running his father's wholesale clothing business, but after it failed Bradford began to study painting under Dutch marine artist Albert van Beest in the whaling town of New Bedford, Massachusetts. It was common in the 19th century for owners or captains of ships to commission a ship's portrait, and these were Bradford's first paintings. From 1861 to 1867, Bradford made annual trips to Labrador and became celebrated both in America and England for his Arctic paintings and photographs. Many of his later paintings are based on his photographs. Spectacular paintings of natural scenery (Hudson River School) were in vogue and Bradford's paintings of the Arctic were very popular. He exhibited frequently at the National Academy of Art in New York and at the Royal Academy in London. In 1875 he made news when he sold a painting to Queen Victoria. During the 1870s and 1880s Bradford painted a large number of oils that are looser than his earlier works. He produced many good paintings during this period, but he was so productive that the quality can be uneven. In his late sixties (1879-1882) he spent time in California and painted Yosemite, the Mariposa valley, and the Sierra Nevada mountains. Occasional lectures about his visits to the polar regions, illustrated with lantern projections of transparencies based on his photographs, enhanced his reputation. Bradford died in New York City in April 1892. This painting of *Ship in Harbor* realized $24,000 at Kaminski's Auction Galleries in Massachusetts. (William Bradford, *Ship in Harbor*, Kaminski, oil on canvas, 20 x 32 inches, November 25, 1994, $24,000)

Primordial Simplicity

The sculpture of Constantin Brancusi (1876-1957) is as popular today as it was 50 years ago. A 1995 retrospective of Brancusi's works, co-organized and exhibited by the Philadelphia Museum of Art and the Pompidou Center in Paris, drew record crowds.

Brancusi was born in rural Romania. As a young boy he wandered the countryside, working as a shepherd and doing odd jobs. When he was 18, Brancusi was apprenticed to a cabinetmaker. He left in 1898 to study on a scholarship at the School of Fine Art in Bucharest. In 1903 Brancusi set off for Paris. Legend has it that he walked most of the way from Bucharest to Paris. He enrolled at the École des Beaux-Arts, a traditional art school, and his works during his first years in Paris are reminiscent of Rodin with their classic naturalism. Brancusi first exhibited at the 1906 Société Nationale des Beaux-Arts; Rodin saw his work and was impressed, offering him a job, but Brancusi left after one month, saying, "Nothing grows beneath great trees." In the *Sleeping Head* series of 1906 and *The Kiss (Le Baiser)* sculptures of 1908, Brancusi's personal style began to emerge. Forms were stripped of all superfluous detail and reduced to a natural simplicity.

Brancusi's sculptures are in limestone, marble, bronze, base metal, and wood, and he often combined several materials, sometimes placing a sleek, stainless steel piece on a rough wooden base. Brancusi exhibited in New York at the famous 1913 Armory show and had his first one-man show in the United States at Alfred Stieglitz's Gallery 291 in 1914. One of his most important Amerian patrons was Walter Arensberg, who donated 22 Brancusi sculptures to the Philadelphia Museum of Art in 1950. Brancusi died in 1957 and bequeathed his studio and its contents to the French nation. The Pompidou Center will open a replica of his studio in a building adjacent to the Center in 1997.

The first *Kiss* was carved in stone, a gravestone for a friend in the Montparnasse Cemetery. This version of *The Kiss,* offered at Christie's in November 1994, is a plaster cast, one of an edition of eight, executed before 1910 by the artist from that original stone. The provenance is impeccable: the first owner had purchased it from the artist before 1913, and the second owner had purchased it at Parke-Bernet Galleries in 1949. The price realized was $882,500. (Constantin Brancusi, *The Kiss,* plaster, height 11 inches, width 10¼ inches, depth 8½ inches, Christie New York, November 9, 1994, $882,500)

BRAMLEY, Frank
British 1857-1915
paintings: (L) $880; (H) $2,300

BRAMTOT, Alfred Henri
French 1852-1894
paintings: (H) $11,000

BRAN, Vicente Malender
European 20th cent.
paintings: (L) $660; (H) $715

BRANCACCIO, Carlo
Italian 1861-1920
paintings: (L) $1,650; (H) $46,750

BRANCHARD, Emile Pierre
American 1881-1938
paintings: (L) $192; (H) $1,430

BRANCUSI, Constantin
Romanian 1876-1957
sculpture: (L) $85,000; (H) $882,500

BRANDANI, Enrico
Italian b. 1914
paintings: (L) $330; (H) $2,310

BRANDAO-GIONO, Wilson
paintings: (H) $2,860

BRANDBURY, Bennett
20th cent.
paintings: (H) $770

BRANDEIS, Antonietta
b. Bohemia 1849 d. 1920
paintings: (L) $1,725; (H) $33,000

BRANDEL, A.
sculpture: (H) $2,475

BRANDES
German 19th cent.
paintings: (H) $660

BRANDES, Willy
German b. 1876
paintings: (H) $770

BRANDI, Domenico
Italian 1683-1736
paintings: (H) $4,600

BRANDI, Giacinto
Italian 1623-1691
paintings: (H) $9,900

BRANDIFF, George
American 1890-1936
paintings: (H) $3,163

BRANDIS, August von
German 1862-1947
paintings: (H) $4,600

BRANDNER, Karl C.
American 1898-1961
paintings: (L) $33; (H) $2,090
drawings: (H) $198

BRANDRIFF, George Kennedy
American 1890-1936
paintings: (L) $1,870; (H) $14,300

BRANDT
paintings: (H) $750

BRANDT, Carl L.
1831-1905
paintings: (H) $3,300

BRANDT, E.
American 20th cent.
paintings: (H) $467

BRANDT, Edgar
1880-1960
drawings: (L) $253; (H) $4,600
sculpture: (H) $2,587

BRANDT, Heidi
American School 20th cent.
drawings: (H) $660

BRANDT, J.
paintings: (H) $880

BRANDT, Joseph van
Polish 1841-1928
paintings: (L) $1,540; (H) $27,600

BRANDT, Otto
English 1828-1892
paintings: (L) $467; (H) $880

BRANDT, Rex
American b. 1914
drawings: (L) $825; (H) $2,750

BRANDT, Warren
American b. 1918
paintings: (L) $440; (H) $715

BRANDTNER, Fritz
German 1896-1969
paintings: (L) $1,485; (H) $28,600
drawings: (L) $1,100; (H) $6,325
sculpture: (H) $1,650

BRANDYETH, Courtenay
American 20th cent.
paintings: (H) $1,155

BRANGWYN, Sir Frank
British 1867-1956
paintings: (L) $1,725; (H) $26,400
drawings: (L) $522; (H) $2,530

BRANNER, Martin
1888-1970
drawings: (L) $440; (H) $495

BRANSOM, Paul
1886-1979
drawings: (L) $110; (H) $3,850

BRANSON, Lloyd
American 1861-1925
paintings: (H) $990

BRANTZ, A. de
19th cent.
paintings: (H) $12,100

BRAQUAVAL, Louis
French 1854-1919
paintings: (L) $2,300; (H) $2,640

BRAQUE, Georges
French 1882-1963
paintings: (L) $1,725; (H) $7,700,000
drawings: (L) $2,875; (H) $1,542,500
sculpture: (L) $3,105; (H) $57,200

BRASCASSAT, Jacques Raymond
French 1804-1867
paintings: (L) $2,310; (H) $3,450

BRASEN, Mans Ole
Danish 1849-1930
paintings: (H) $1,650

BRASHER, Rex
1869-1960
drawings: (L) $660; (H) $1,320

BRASILIER, Andre
French b. 1929
paintings: (L) $9,200; (H) $121,000
sculpture: (H) $4,485

BRASSEUR, G.
paintings: (H) $850

BRAUER, Erik
drawings: (L) $3,850; (H) $3,850

BRAUGHT, Ross
paintings: (H) $1,760

BRAULLE, J.T.
Continental School 19th cent.
paintings: (H) $2,300

BRAULT
sculpture: (H) $1,840

BRAULT, G.
French 19th cent.
paintings: (H) $495

BRAUN, Ludwig
German 1836-1916
drawings: (H) $1,100

BRAUN, Maurice
American 1877-1941
paintings: (L) $1,210; (H) $55,000
drawings: (L) $303; (H) $825

BRAUN, S.
paintings: (L) $385; (H) $632

BRAUNER, Victor
Romanian 1903-1966
paintings: (L) $15,400; (H) $222,500
drawings: (L) $1,650; (H) $352,000

**BRAUNER, Victor and Jacques
HEROLD, Yves TANGUY,**
20th cent.
drawings: (L) $19,550; (H) $24,150

BRAUNTUCH, Troy
American b. 1954
drawings: (L) $288; (H) $6,930

BRAVO, Claudio
Chilean b. 1936
paintings: (L) $13,800; (H) $495,000
drawings: (L) $1,725; (H) $96,000
sculpture: (L) $19,550; (H) $28,600

BRAY, Alan
paintings: (L) $2,990; (H) $3,220

BRAY, Arnold
American 1892-1972
paintings: (L) $495; (H) $1,540

BRAY, Arnold
American 1892-1972
paintings: (H) $495

BRAY, Jim
American contemporary
drawings: (H) $660

BRAY, Salomon de
Dutch 1597-1664
paintings: (H) $29,900

BRAYER, Yves
French 1907-1990
paintings: (L) $6,325; (H) $19,800
drawings: (H) $3,335

BREADY, Joseph H.
American 20th cent.
paintings: (H) $2,860

BREAKELL, Mary Louise
British ac. 1879-1912
paintings: (H) $660

BREAKSPEARE, William A.
English 1855/56-1914
paintings: (H) $1,210

BREANSKI, Alfred Fontville de
British 1877-1945
paintings: (L) $805; (H) $6,050
drawings: (H) $330

BREANSKI, Alfred de, Sr.
English 1852-1928
paintings: (L) $2,415; (H) $34,100
drawings: (H) $495

BREANSKI, Gustave de
British c. 1856-1898
paintings: (L) $770; (H) $2,530

BREBIETTE, Pierre
French 1598-1650
drawings: (H) $19,800

BRECH, Dwayne
paintings: (H) $850

BRECHER, Samuel
Austrian/American 1897-1982
paintings: (L) $248; (H) $770
drawings: (H) $825

BRECHERET, Victor
Brazilian 1894-1955
sculpture: (H) $4,025

BRECK, John Leslie
American 1861-1899
paintings: (L) $29,900; (H) $126,500

BRECKENRIDGE, Hugh Henry
American 1870-1937
paintings: (L) $715; (H) $71,500
drawings: (L) $1,100; (H) $1,320

BREDAEL, A.L.
American 19th cent.
paintings: (H) $2,090

BREDAEL, Joseph van
Flemish 1688-1739
paintings: (L) $35,650; (H) $60,500

BREDAEL, Pieter van
1629-1719
paintings: (H) $16,500

BREDAERT, B**
Dutch 19th/20th cent.
paintings: (H) $798

BREDIN, Christine
American 19th/20th cent.
paintings: (H) $715

BREDIN, Rae Sloan
American 1881-1933
paintings: (L) $4,950; (H) $9,775
drawings: (H) $165

BREDOW, Gustave Adolf
German b. 1875
paintings: (H) $5,175

BREDSDORFF, H.H.
paintings: (H) $1,320

BREDT, Ferdinand Max
German 1860-1921
paintings: (H) $1,045

BREE, *J*** van de
ac. 1670s
paintings: (H) $4,255

BREEDEN, W.L.
sculpture: (H) $977

BREEDVELD, Hendrik
Dutch b. 1918
paintings: (L) $440; (H) $1,650

BREEN, Adam van
ac. 1611-1636
paintings: (H) $79,500

BREEN, Marguerite
1885-1964
paintings: (H) $3,080
drawings: (H) $137

BREENBERGH, Bartholomeus
Dutch 1599/1600-1663
paintings: (L) $63,000; (H) $440,000

BREGENZER, Gustav
Continental 19th cent.
paintings: (H) $1,210

BREHAM, Paul Henri
French 1850-1933
paintings: (H) $2,420

BREHM, George
American b. 1878
paintings: (H) $1,540

BREHMER, K.P.
contemporary
sculpture: (H) $1,650

BREININ, Raymond
Russian/American b. 1910
drawings: (H) $2,420

BREITBACH, Carl
German 1833-1904
paintings: (L) $1,100; (H) $2,420

BREITENSTEIN, Ernst
Swiss 1857-1920
paintings: (H) $6,325

BREITNER, Georg Hendrik
Dutch 1857-1923
paintings: (L) $2,200; (H) $112,500

BREITNER, J.
Continental 19th/20th cent.
sculpture: (H) $805

BREIVIK, Bard
contemporary
sculpture: (H) $12,100

BREKELENKAM, Quiringh Gerritsz.
van
c. 1620-1688
paintings: (L) $6,900; (H) $17,600

BRELY, August de la
French 1838-1906
paintings: (H) $16,500

BREMER, A.
paintings: (H) $825

BREMER, Ann Millay
American 1868-1923
paintings: (L) $495; (H) $605

BREMONT(?), Horose
paintings: (H) $6,325

BRENDEKILDE, Hans A.
Danish 1857-1920
paintings: (L) $5,500; (H) $10,450

BRENNEMAN, George W.
American 1856-1906
paintings: (H) $4,830

BRENNER, Carl
American 1850-1920
paintings: (L) $550; (H) $1,610

BRENNER, Carl Christian
American 1838-1888
paintings: (L) $1,540; (H) $6,050

BRENNER, Victor David
Russian/American 1871-1924
sculpture: (L) $138; (H) $2,640

BRENNERMAN, George W.
American 1856-1906
paintings: (H) $1,540

BRENT, Adalie Margules
American 1920-1992
paintings: (H) $1,045

BRENTANO, Al
paintings: (H) $2,860

BRENTEL, Friedrich
French 1580-1651
drawings: (L) $2,185; (H) $151,000

BRERETON, Earl M.
paintings: (H) $690

BRERETON, J.
British 18th/19th cent.
paintings: (H) $10,560

BRESCHI, Karen
American b. 1941
sculpture: (H) $1,840

BRESDIN, Rudolphe
French 1822-1885
paintings: (H) $247
drawings: (L) $55; (H) $5,175

BRESSAN, V.
paintings: (H) $605

BRESSANIN, Vittorio
Italian b. 1860
paintings: (H) $1,430

BRESSIN, F.
  French 19th cent.
  paintings: (H) $2,420

BRESSLER, Emile Alois Lucien
  Swiss 1886-1966
  paintings: (H) $2,875

BREST, Germain Fabius
  French 1823-1900
  paintings: (H) $107,000

BRET-CHARBONNIER, Claudia
  French 1863-1951
  paintings: (H) $12,650

BRETLAND, Thomas
  English 1802-1874
  paintings: (L) $3,300; (H) $14,950

BRETLAND, Thomas W. and Joseph
  Paul PETTITT
  British 19th cent.
  paintings: (H) $1,700

BRETON
  French 19th/20th cent.
  paintings: (H) $660

BRETON, Charles
  sculpture: (H) $1,540

BRETON, Constant le
  French b. 1895
  paintings: (L) $1,100; (H) $1,380

BRETON, Emile Adelard
  British 1831-1902
  paintings: (L) $495; (H) $1,100

BRETON, Jules Adolphe
  French 1827-1906
  paintings: (L) $5,500; (H) $110,000
  drawings: (L) $357; (H) $2,760

BRETON, Paul Eugene
  French 1868-1933
  sculpture: (L) $3,300; (H) $13,200

BRETON, W.L.
  American
  drawings: (H) $7,475

BRETT, Harold M.
  American 1880-1955
  paintings: (L) $660; (H) $4,730
  drawings: (L) $121; (H) $247

BRETT, John
  English 1830-1902
  drawings: (H) $467

BRETZ, Mary
  American 19th cent.
  paintings: (H) $577

BREU, Max
  German 20th cent.
  paintings: (L) $1,650; (H) $1,980

BREUER, Henry Joseph
  American 1860-1932
  paintings: (L) $385; (H) $23,000

BREUGHEL, Jan, the younger
  Flemish 1601-1678
  paintings: (H) $1,100,000

BREUL, Harold G.
  American b. 1889
  drawings: (L) $440; (H) $575

BREUL, Hugo
  American 1854-1910
  paintings: (L) $83; (H) $880
  drawings: (L) $330; (H) $825

BREVANNES, Maurice
  French 20th cent.
  paintings: (H) $550

BREVOORT, James Renwick
  American 1832-1918
  paintings: (L) $1,320; (H) $9,900
  drawings: (H) $403

BREWER, Adrian Louis
  American 1891-1956
  paintings: (L) $385; (H) $1,430

BREWER, Edwin
  American 20th cent.
  paintings: (H) $460

BREWER, J. Alphege
  English ac. 1909-1938
  drawings: (H) $805

BREWER, Nicholas Richard
  American 1857-1949
  paintings: (L) $468; (H) $4,400

BREWERTON, George Douglas
  American 1820-1901
  paintings: (L) $660; (H) $3,300
  drawings: (L) $330; (H) $2,640

BREWSTER, Amanda
  American b. 1859
  paintings: (H) $3,080

BREWSTER, Anna Richards
  American 1870-1952
  paintings: (L) $110; (H) $2,990
  drawings: (H) $605

BREWSTER, John
paintings: (H) $4,400

BREWSTER, John, Jr.
American 1766-1854
paintings: (L) $23,100; (H) $85,000
drawings: (H) $4,887

BREWTNALL, Edward Frederick
British 1846-1902
paintings: (L) $3,450; (H) $3,850
drawings: (L) $2,750; (H) $4,400

BREYDEL, Karel
Flemish 1678-1733
paintings: (L) $4,600; (H) $7,150

BRIANCHON, Maurice
French 1899-1979
paintings: (L) $5,175; (H) $77,000
drawings: (L) $1,650; (H) $46,750

BRIAND, ***C.
Continental 19th cent.
paintings: (H) $2,875

BRIANTE, Ezelino
Italian 1901-1970
paintings: (L) $220; (H) $2,013

BRIATA, Georges
paintings: (H) $2,070

BRIAUDEAU, P.C.J.
French 1869-1944
paintings: (L) $1,210; (H) $1,870

BRICARD, G.
French 19th/20th cent.
paintings: (H) $1,320

BRICE, William
American b. 1921
paintings: (H) $1,725
drawings: (H) $990

BRICHER, Alfred Thompson
American 1837-1908
paintings: (L) $770; (H) $79,500
drawings: (L) $173; (H) $30,800

BRICKDALE, Eleanor Fortescue
English 1871-1945
drawings: (H) $17,250

BRICKNELL, William Henry Warren
American b. 1860
paintings: (H) $14,300

BRIDE, B*** de
18th cent.
paintings: (H) $3,850

BRIDGEHOUSE, Robert
British 19th cent.
paintings: (L) $2,310; (H) $3,220

BRIDGES, Fidelia
American 1834-1923
drawings: (L) $66; (H) $3,960

BRIDGMAN, Frederick Arthur
American 1847-1928
paintings: (L) $467; (H) $198,000
drawings: (L) $58; (H) $201

BRIERLY, Sir Oswald Walter
British 1817-1894
drawings: (L) $440; (H) $2,415

BRIET, Arthur
Dutch 1867-1939
drawings: (H) $2,300

BRIEVA, Manuel Villegas
Spanish 19th cent.
paintings: (H) $10,925

BRIGANTE, Nicholas P.
American 1895-1989
paintings: (L) $192; (H) $2,970
drawings: (L) $550; (H) $1,650

BRIGAUD, Florentin
French 20th cent.
sculpture: (H) $12,100

BRIGDEN, Frederick Henry
paintings: (H) $1,320
drawings: (L) $1,045; (H) $1,210

BRIGGLE, A. van
American 20th cent.
paintings: (H) $1,430

BRIGGS, Austin
American 1909-1973
paintings: (H) $605
drawings: (L) $440; (H) $935

BRIGGS, C.W.
American 19th cent.
paintings: (H) $2,200

BRIGGS, Lucius A.
American 1852-1931
drawings: (L) $330; (H) $863

BRIGGS, W.D.
paintings: (H) $715

BRIGGS, Warren C.
American 1867-1903
paintings: (H) $770

BRIGHT, F.A.
paintings: (H) $1,155

BRIGHT, Harry
British ac. 1867-1892
drawings: (H) $1,265

BRIGHT, Henry
English 1814-1873
paintings: (L) $825; (H) $7,150
drawings: (L) $248; (H) $1,265

BRIGHTLY, J.H.
American
paintings: (H) $4,400

BRIGLIA, Giovanni Francesco
Italian 1737-1794
paintings: (H) $41,400

BRIL, Paul
Flemish 1554-1626
paintings: (H) $268,500

BRILLOUIN, Louis Georges
French 1817-1893
paintings: (L) $880; (H) $3,162

BRINA, Francesco del
c. 1540-1585/6
paintings: (H) $49,500

BRINANT, Jules Ruinart de
French 1838-1898
paintings: (H) $14,300

BRINDESI, Olympio
American 1897-1965
sculpture: (L) $440; (H) $2,588

BRINGHURST, Robert Porter
American 1855-1925
sculpture: (H) $3,520

BRINK, Guido
sculpture: (H) $495

BRINKMANN, A.
paintings: (H) $518

BRINLEY, Daniel Putnam
American 1879-1963
paintings: (H) $690

BRION, Gustave
French 1824-1877
paintings: (L) $5,750; (H) $63,000
drawings: (H) $1,150

BRIONES, Fernando
Spanish b. 1905
paintings: (H) $550

BRISCOE, Arthur
English 1873-1943
paintings: (H) $748
drawings: (H) $345

BRISCOE, Franklin D.
American 1844-1903
paintings: (L) $220; (H) $11,500

BRISPOT, Henri
French 1846-1928
paintings: (L) $4,888; (H) $13,800

BRISSAUD, Pierre
French b. 1885
drawings: (L) $154; (H) $550

BRISSET, Emile
French d. 1904
paintings: (L) $880; (H) $24,150

BRISSOT, Franck
English School 19th cent.
paintings: (H) $2,200

BRISSOT DE WARVILLE, Felix
Saturnin
French 1818-1892
paintings: (L) $880; (H) $9,200
drawings: (L) $1,320; (H) $2,200

BRISTOL, John Bunyan
American 1826-1909
paintings: (L) $550; (H) $4,620
drawings: (L) $220; (H) $440

BRISTOW, Edmund
English 1787-1876
paintings: (L) $1,045; (H) $13,800

BRITCHER, A.T.
paintings: (H) $19,800
drawings: (H) $4,400

BRITO, Maria
paintings: (H) $4,830

BRITTAIN, Miller Gore
drawings: (L) $1,320; (H) $1,320

BRITTAN, Charles E.
English ac. 1860-1890
drawings: (H) $880

BRIULLOV, Karl Pavlovich
Russian 1799-1852
drawings: (H) $660

BROADBENT, J.H.
English 19th cent.
paintings: (H) $880

BROADHEAD, W. Smithson
British 19th cent.
paintings: (L) $9,200; (H) $18,700

BROCH, A.
paintings: (H) $1,650

BROCHART, Constant Joseph
French 1816-1899
paintings: (L) $1,540; (H) $1,980
drawings: (H) $1,100

BROCHET, Francois
French 2nd half 20th cent.
paintings: (L) $110; (H) $522
sculpture: (H) $1,320

BROCK, C.E.
1870-1938
drawings: (H) $1,430

BROCK, Richard H.
British 19th/20th cent.
paintings: (H) $2,420

BROCK, Sir Thomas
English 1847-1922
sculpture: (L) $1,955; (H) $68,500

BROCKELSBURY, Horace
British 1866-1929
paintings: (H) $1,610

BROCKHURST, Gerald Leslie
British 1890-1978
drawings: (L) $385; (H) $5,225

BROCKMAN, Ann
American 1899-1943
paintings: (L) $55; (H) $825
drawings: (L) $77; (H) $385

BROCKMAN, Robert
American 20th cent.
paintings: (H) $2,300

BRODERS
19th/20th cent.
paintings: (L) $330; (H) $495

BRODERSON, Morris
American b. 1928
paintings: (H) $1,430
drawings: (L) $275; (H) $288

BRODEUR, Clarence
American b. 1905
paintings: (L) $330; (H) $935

BRODIE, Gandy
American 1924-1975
paintings: (L) $287; (H) $2,640

BROE, Vern
American 20th cent.
paintings: (L) $385; (H) $1,320

BROECK, Clemence van den
Belgian b. 1843
paintings: (H) $4,600

BROECK, Elias van den
Dutch 1650-1708
paintings: (H) $17,250

BROEDELET, Andre
Dutch 1872-1936
paintings: (H) $2,750

BROERS, Gaspar
1682-1716
paintings: (L) $8,250; (H) $8,250

BROGE, Alfred
Danish 1870-1955
paintings: (H) $3,520

BROKMAN, Henry
European 19th/20th cent.
paintings: (H) $770

BROMLEY, Frank C.
American 1860-1890
paintings: (L) $495; (H) $1,320

BROMLEY, John Mallord
British 19th/20th cent.
drawings: (H) $1,725

BROMLEY, William
British 19th cent.
paintings: (L) $1,760; (H) $4,600

BRONKHORST, Johannes
1587-1617
drawings: (H) $13,200

BRONKHORST, Johannes
1648-1727
paintings: (H) $935
drawings: (L) $5,750; (H) $6,900

BRONSCHOHL, L.
paintings: (H) $935

BRONSON, Clark
American b. 1939
sculpture: (L) $220; (H) $6,325

BRONSTEIN, L.
sculpture: (H) $1,100

BRONWELL, Alexander
American contemporary
paintings: (H) $1,320

BRONZINO, Agnolo di Cosimo di
Mariano
paintings: (L) $5,225; (H) $7,700

BRONZINO, Alessandro Allori
Italian 1535-1607
paintings: (L) $42,550; (H) $51,750

BRONZINO, and Studio
Italian 1503-1572
paintings: (H) $11,500

BROODTHAERS, Marcel
Belgian 1924-1976
paintings: (H) $11,500
sculpture: (L) $14,000; (H) $101,750

BROOK, Alexander
American 1898-1980
paintings: (L) $495; (H) $2,420
drawings: (L) $104; (H) $1,100

BROOK, Caroline W.
British ac. 1877-1888
paintings: (H) $1,980

BROOKE, E. Adveno
British 19th cent.
paintings: (H) $5,225

BROOKE, Richard Norris
American 1847-1920
paintings: (L) $2,475; (H) $5,500

BROOKER, Harry
English ac. 1876-1902
paintings: (L) $8,050; (H) $27,600

BROOKES, Samuel Marsden
American 1816-1892
paintings: (L) $2,070; (H) $12,650

BROOKS, Allan
Canadian 1869-1946
drawings: (L) $303; (H) $1,430

BROOKS, Cora S.
American 20th cent.
paintings: (H) $4,600

BROOKS, Henry Howard
American 1898-1981
paintings: (L) $220; (H) $880
drawings: (L) $88; (H) $110

BROOKS, James
American 1906-1992
paintings: (L) $1,320; (H) $27,500
drawings: (L) $2,200; (H) $9,900

BROOKS, Kim
drawings: (H) $1,100

BROOKS, Mary Mason
drawings: (H) $880

BROOKS, Nicholas Alden
American ac. 1880-1904
paintings: (L) $330; (H) $38,500

BROOKS, Richard Edwin
American 1865-1919
sculpture: (H) $9,350

BROOKS, Romaine
American
paintings: (H) $3,850

BROOKS, W.W.
English ac. 1838-1870
paintings: (H) $1,320

BROOME, William
English 1838-1892
paintings: (H) $1,210

BROOTA, Rameshwa
Indain b. 1941
paintings: (L) $4,887; (H) $6,325

BROQUET, Esperance Leon
French 1869-1936
paintings: (H) $2,200

BROTAT, Joan
Spanish b. 1923
paintings: (H) $920

BROTHERS HILDEBRANDT
b. 1939
paintings: (H) $7,700

BROUGIER, Adolph M.
American 1870-1926
paintings: (H) $550

BROUSSE, Faubede
French ac. 19th cent.
sculpture: (H) $2,875

BROUWER, Gien
Dutch 20th cent.
paintings: (H) $660

BROUWER, P.M.
Dutch 1819-1886
paintings: (H) $1,210

BROWERE, Albertis
American 1814-1887
paintings: (L) $8,250; (H) $13,800

BROWN, A.F.
19th cent.
paintings: (H) $605

BROWN, Abigail Keyes
American b. 1891
paintings: (H) $880

BROWN, Alexander Kellock
Scottish 1849-1922
paintings: (L) $247; (H) $1,155

BROWN, Amy Difley, O'TOOLE
American 20th cent.
paintings: (L) $165; (H) $660

BROWN, Anna Wood
American 19th/20th cent.
paintings: (L) $880; (H) $2,750

BROWN, Arthur W.
American 1881-1966
drawings: (H) $605

BROWN, Benjamin Chambers
American 1865-1942
paintings: (L) $1,430; (H) $28,600
drawings: (L) $440; (H) $1,540

BROWN, Beverly
American 20th cent.
drawings: (H) $550

BROWN, Byron
American 1907-1961
paintings: (L) $1,320; (H) $1,955

BROWN, C.
19th cent.
paintings: (H) $3,738

BROWN, C. Emerson
b. 1869
paintings: (H) $1,155

BROWN, Carlyle
American 1919/20-1964
paintings: (L) $81; (H) $1,650

BROWN, Carol
American 20th cent.
drawings: (H) $605

BROWN, Christopher
American b. 1951
paintings: (H) $2,750

BROWN, Clinton
American 20th cent.
paintings: (L) $880; (H) $1,430

BROWN, David
ac. 1792-1797
paintings: (H) $8,625

BROWN, Ethel Pennewill
American ac. c. 1925
drawings: (H) $460

BROWN, Florence Bradshaw
paintings: (H) $1,760

BROWN, Frank A.
American b. 1876
paintings: (L) $522; (H) $605
drawings: (L) $55; (H) $82

BROWN, Fred
19th cent.
paintings: (L) $825; (H) $990

BROWN, George Elmer
American 1871-1946
paintings: (L) $70; (H) $1,750

BROWN, George Henry Allen
English b. 1862
drawings: (L) $58; (H) $660

BROWN, George Loring
American 1814-1889
paintings: (L) $605; (H) $12,100
drawings: (L) $138; (H) $990

BROWN, George Lunell
British 19th cent.
paintings: (H) $1,725

BROWN, Grace Evelyn
American b. 1873
paintings: (H) $715

BROWN, H.
paintings: (L) $55; (H) $990
drawings: (H) $17

BROWN, Harley
American b. 1939
drawings: (L) $550; (H) $5,500
sculpture: (H) $1,980

BROWN, Harrison B.
American 1831-1915
paintings: (L) $132; (H) $20,350
drawings: (L) $715; (H) $719

BROWN, Henry Kirke
American 1814-1886
sculpture: (H) $3,080

BROWN, Herbert
American 20th cent.
paintings: (L) $577; (H) $577

BROWN, Horace
American b. 1876
paintings: (L) $110; (H) $1,320

BROWN, Howard V.
American b. 1878
paintings: (H) $605

BROWN, J.
American
paintings: (L) $388; (H) $24,150

BROWN, J. McGibbon
paintings: (L) $137; (H) $468
drawings: (L) $88; (H) $303

BROWN, J. Randolph
American b. 1861
paintings: (H) $165
drawings: (L) $302; (H) $550

BROWN, J.W.
British 1842-1928
paintings: (L) $121; (H) $550

BROWN, James
American b. 1951
paintings: (L) $863; (H) $52,800
drawings: (L) $115; (H) $26,400
sculpture: (L) $2,070; (H) $13,800

BROWN, James Francis
American 1862-1935
paintings: (L) $525; (H) $990

BROWN, Joan
American 1938-1991
paintings: (L) $1,870; (H) $35,650
drawings: (L) $230; (H) $25,300

BROWN, Joe
American 1909-1985
sculpture: (L) $400; (H) $8,250

BROWN, John Appleton
American 1844-1902
paintings: (L) $575; (H) $13,800
drawings: (L) $1,320; (H) $5,750

BROWN, John George
Anglo/American 1831-1913
paintings: (L) $1,045; (H) $297,000
drawings: (L) $403; (H) $1,870

BROWN, John Lewis
French 1829-1890
paintings: (L) $2,200; (H) $24,150
drawings: (L) $440; (H) $14,375

BROWN, Laurus Costello
paintings: (H) $550

BROWN, Louis H.
American 20th cent.
paintings: (H) $495

BROWN, M. Lamont
19th/20th cent.
paintings: (H) $495

BROWN, M.A.
paintings: (H) $2,475

BROWN, Maggi
paintings: (L) $550; (H) $3,080
drawings: (L) $605; (H) $1,430

BROWN, Mather
American, b. London 1761/62-1831
paintings: (H) $3,300

BROWN, Maynard
British 19th cent.
paintings: (H) $1,650

BROWN, N.K.
sculpture: (H) $715

BROWN, Norman A.
b. 1933
paintings: (H) $1,210

BROWN, Paul
American 1893-1958
drawings: (L) $165; (H) $6,900

BROWN, R. Alston
b. 1878
paintings: (H) $1,210

BROWN, Reynold
American 1917-1991
drawings: (L) $2,530; (H) $26,400

BROWN, Robert
19th/20th cent.
paintings: (H) $880

BROWN, R. Woodley
British 19th cent.
paintings: (H) $522

BROWN, Roger
American b. 1941
paintings: (L) $575; (H) $18,700
drawings: (H) $935

BROWN, Roy H.
American 1879-1956
paintings: (L) $330; (H) $6,600
drawings: (L) $110; (H) $920

BROWN, T. Bryant
British 19th/20th cent.
paintings: (H) $3,450

BROWN, Thomas Austen
British 1859-1924
paintings: (H) $770

BROWN, W.
19th/20th cent.
paintings: (L) $302; (H) $935

BROWN, Walter Francis
American 1853-1929
paintings: (L) $165; (H) $1,980
drawings: (H) $110

BROWN, William Beattie
British 1831-1909
paintings: (H) $3,850

BROWN, William Marshall
English 1863-1936
paintings: (L) $990; (H) $6,325

BROWN, William Mason
American 1828-1898
paintings: (L) $2,185; (H) $42,550

BROWN, William Theophilus
American b. 1919
paintings: (L) $2,200; (H) $7,700
drawings: (L) $248; (H) $2,200

BROWN, Woodley
English 19th cent.
paintings: (H) $660

BROWNE
American 19th cent.
paintings: (H) $880

BROWNE, Belmore
American 1880-1954
paintings: (L) $2,750; (H) $3,465

BROWNE, Byron
American 1907-1961
paintings: (L) $495; (H) $17,250
drawings: (L) $690; (H) $1,980

BROWNE, Carlan A.
American 19th cent.
paintings: (H) $880

BROWNE, Charles Francis
American 1859-1920
paintings: (L) $275; (H) $3,738

BROWNE, Edward
British 19th cent.
paintings: (H) $3,850

BROWNE, George Byron
American 1907-1961
paintings: (L) $1,380; (H) $1,495
drawings: (H) $1,150

BROWNE, George Elmer
American 1871-1946
paintings: (L) $110; (H) $7,590
drawings: (L) $110; (H) $605

BROWNE, Gordon Frederick
British b. 1858
drawings: (H) $690

BROWNE, Henriette
French 1829-1901
paintings: (L) $2,200; (H) $6,900

BROWNE, Joseph
18th cent.
paintings: (H) $6,900

BROWNE, Margaret Fitzhugh
American 1884-1972
paintings: (L) $55; (H) $2,090

BROWNE, Matilda
American 1869-1953
paintings: (L) $187; (H) $30,800
drawings: (L) $200; (H) $1,650

BROWNE, R.F.
paintings: (H) $880

BROWNE, William
paintings: (H) $19,800

BROWNELL, Charles de Wolfe
American 1822-1909
paintings: (L) $110; (H) $1,100

BROWNELL, Peleg Franklin
American/Canadian 1857-1946
paintings: (L) $431; (H) $8,800
drawings: (H) $880

BROWNING, Robert Barrett
British b. 1846
paintings: (H) $33,000

BROWNLIE, J. Miller
19th/20th cent.
paintings: (H) $1,100

BROWNLOW, George Washington
English exhib. 1858-1875
paintings: (L) $2,530; (H) $5,500

BROWNSCOMBE, Jennie Augusta
American 1850-1936
paintings: (L) $1,650; (H) $3,300
drawings: (L) $990; (H) $1,540

BROZIK, Wencelas von Vacslaw
Czechoslovakian 1851-1901
paintings: (L) $288; (H) $13,200

BRUANDET, Lazare
French 1755-1804
drawings: (H) $1,320

BRUCE, Edward
American 1879-1943
paintings: (L) $1,380; (H) $3,300

BRUCE, Patrick Henry
American 1881-1936
paintings: (H) $29,700

BRUCE, William
19th/20th cent.
paintings: (H) $770

BRUCHON, Emile
French ac. c. 1855
sculpture: (H) $495

BRUCK, Lajos
Hungarian 1846-1910
paintings: (L) $3,960; (H) $10,450

BRUCKMAN
German 19th/20th cent.
paintings: (H) $550

BRUCKMAN, Lodewyk
American b. Holland 1903
paintings: (L) $248; (H) $1,980

BRUCKNER
paintings: (H) $495

BRUDEL, Ernst
German 19th cent.
paintings: (H) $1,210

BRUEGHEL, Abraham
1631-1697
paintings: (H) $57,500

BRUEGHEL, Abraham
Flemish 1631-1690
paintings: (H) $79,500

BRUEGHEL, Henry Ferdinand
17th cent.
paintings: (H) $24,150

BRUEGHEL, Jan, the elder
Flemish 1568-1625
paintings: (L) $85,000; (H) $209,000

BRUEGHEL, Jan, the younger
Flemish 1601-1678
paintings: (L) $123,500; (H) $772,500

BRUEGHEL, Jan and Hendrik van
BALEN, the elder
16th/17th cent.
paintings: (H) $332,500

BRUEGHEL, Pieter, III
Flemish b. 1589
paintings: (H) $79,500

BRUEGHEL, Pieter, the younger
Flemish c. 1564-1637/38
paintings: (L) $68,500; (H) $1,045,000

BRUESTLE, Bertram
American b. 1902
paintings: (L) $165; (H) $935
drawings: (L) $60; (H) $192

BRUESTLE, George M.
American 1871/72-1939
paintings: (L) $220; (H) $4,140

BRUGADA Y PANIZA, Ricardo
Spanish b. 1867
paintings: (H) $3,680

BRUGAIROLLES, Victor
French 1869-1936
paintings: (L) $495; (H) $52,900

BRUGGHEN, Guillaume Anne van der
Dutch 1811-1891
paintings: (H) $770

BRUGNER, Colestin
German 19th cent.
paintings: (L) $660; (H) $2,990

BRUGNOLI, Emmanuele
Italian 1859-1944
drawings: (L) $165; (H) $1,320

BRUGO, Giuseppe
Italian 19th/20th cent.
paintings: (H) $10,450
drawings: (H) $460

BRULLE, Faure de
sculpture: (H) $1,430

BRULS, Louis Joseph
German 1803-1882
paintings: (H) $19,800

BRUMBACK, Louise Upton
American 1872-1929
drawings: (H) $715

BRUMENT, Albert
French 19th/20th cent.
paintings: (H) $880

BRUN, Edme Gustave Frederic
French 1817-1881
paintings: (H) $4,600

BRUN, Edouard
French 1860-1935
drawings: (H) $690

BRUN, Guillaume Charles
French 1825-1908
paintings: (L) $11,000; (H) $28,750

BRUN-BUISSON, G.
French 19th/20th cent.
drawings: (H) $1,650

BRUNDEL
French ac. 1920s
sculpture: (H) $3,738

BRUNE, Pierre
French 1887-1956
paintings: (H) $660

BRUNEL DE NEUVILLE, Alfred
Arthur
French ac. 1879-1907
paintings: (L) $1,540; (H) $9,775

BRUNELLESCHI, Umberto
Italian b. 1879; ac. 1907-1930
drawings: (L) $633; (H) $2,420

BRUNERY, Francois
Italian b. 1845, ac. 1898-1909
paintings: (L) $4,025; (H) $75,100

BRUNERY, Marcel
French 20th cent.
paintings: (L) $5,500; (H) $49,500

BRUNETTIN, Alfred
American contemporary
sculpture: (H) $852

BRUNHOFF, Laurent de
American 20th cent.
paintings: (H) $1,725

BRUNIN, Leon De Meutter
Belgian b. 1861
paintings: (H) $2,185

BRUNN, A. Le
paintings: (H) $770

BRUNNER, F. Sands
American b. 1886
paintings: (H) $8,800

BRUNNER, Ferdinand
Austrian b. 1870
paintings: (H) $10,350

BRUNNER, Hattie K.
American
paintings: (L) $1,495; (H) $2,300
drawings: (L) $700; (H) $11,500

BRUNNER, Josef
German 1826-1893
paintings: (H) $2,310

BRUNNING, William Allen
British 19th cent.
paintings: (H) $2,200

BRUNONI, Serge
paintings: (L) $2,640; (H) $4,400

BRUNT, Henry van
American 1832-1903
drawings: (H) $3,163

BRUNT, James R. van
drawings: (H) $1,035

BRUSASORCI, Felice
1539/40-1605
drawings: (H) $4,025

BRUSASORZI, Domenico del Riccio
Italian 1516-1567
drawings: (H) $28,600

BRUSH, Christine Chaplin
American 19th cent.
drawings: (H) $495

BRUSH, George de Forest
American 1855-1941
paintings: (L) $316; (H) $376,500
drawings: (L) $316; (H) $1,100

BRUTON, Margaret
American 1894-1983
paintings: (L) $303; (H) $1,430
drawings: (L) $440; (H) $935

BRUTY, C.
sculpture: (H) $468

BRUYCKER, Jules de
Dutch 1870-1945
paintings: (H) $770

BRUYN, Abraham de
Dutch 1540-1587
paintings: (H) $12,075

BRUYNESTEYN
Dutch 20th cent.
paintings: (L) $518; (H) $518

BRUYNSTEIN, Bernardus Johannes
Antonius
Dutch 1830-1920
paintings: (H) $550

BRYANT, Annie Nanna B. Matthews
1870-1933
sculpture: (L) $633; (H) $2,530

BRYANT, Everett Lloyd
American 1864-1945
paintings: (L) $137; (H) $2,200

BRYANT, Henry
English 19th cent.
paintings: (H) $715

BRYANT, Maude Drein
1880-1946
paintings: (H) $6,900

BRYANT, Wallace
American 19th/20th cent.
paintings: (H) $522

BRYERS, Duane
American b. 1911
paintings: (L) $550; (H) $5,500

BRYMNER, William
1855-1925
paintings: (L) $3,080; (H) $26,400
drawings: (H) $935

BRYSON, Tonneson
19th cent.
drawings: (H) $489

BUCCI
18th cent.
paintings: (H) $6,050

BUCHANAN, Georges F.
Scottish ac. 1849-1864
paintings: (L) $1,100; (H) $1,320

BUCHE, Josef
Austrian 1848-1917
paintings: (L) $248; (H) $6,600

BUCHHEISTER, Carl
drawings: (H) $6,050

BUCHHOLZ, Erich
German b. 1891
paintings: (L) $33,000; (H) $33,000

BUCHHOLZ, Karl
German 1849-1889
paintings: (H) $633

BUCHNER, George
German 1858-1914
paintings: (L) $715; (H) $1,100

BUCHNER, Johann Georg
German 1815-1857
paintings: (H) $2,760

BUCHTA, Anthony
American b. 1890
paintings: (L) $196; (H) $550
drawings: (H) $275

BUCHTGER, R.
Russian b. 1862
paintings: (H) $575

BUCK, Adam
Irish 1759-1883
drawings: (L) $1,093; (H) $2,300

BUCK, Claude
American 1890-1974
paintings: (L) $110; (H) $9,900
drawings: (L) $248; (H) $385

BUCK, Crosby
American 20th cent.
paintings: (H) $880

BUCK, Leslie Binner
American b. 1907
paintings: (L) $330; (H) $825

BUCK, William Henry
Norwegian/American 1840-1888
paintings: (L) $4,950; (H) $30,800

BUCKLAND, August P.
American 1879-1927
paintings: (H) $468

BUCKLER, Charles E.
American b. 1869
paintings: (L) $330; (H) $990

BUCKLER, E.
20th cent.
paintings: (H) $660

BUCKLER, William
English 19th cent.
drawings: (H) $550

BUCKLEY, Charles F.
English ac. 1841-1869
drawings: (H) $1,540

BUCKLEY, John M.
American 1891-1958
paintings: (H) $770

BUCKLEY, Stephen
British b. 1944
paintings: (H) $1,650
sculpture: (H) $880

BUDD, Charles J.
American 1859-1926
drawings: (L) $632; (H) $1,320

BUDELOT, Philippe
French ac. 1793-1841
paintings: (H) $3,450

Bayou Country

New Orleans artist William Henry Buck (1840-1888), was a Southerner born in Norway. He emigrated to the United States as a young man and settled in Boston, where he studied painting. In 1860 he moved to New Orleans. Buck supported himself with commercial ventures in the cotton market, working as a clerk, broker, and cotton weigher, but continued to paint. His works won many awards. When he was forty he left the cotton business to devote himself full-time to his art. To make ends meet, he also worked as a paintings restorer and as a *Scherenschnitte* artist. (*Scherenschnitte* is a German word that means "the art of paper-cutting with scissors.") Soon Buck was the leading landscape painter in Louisiana and traveled through the state painting scenes of the Teche and Attakapas regions. *Two Black Women on the Road to Covington* is a quintessential Buck landscape. Estimated to sell for $25,000, the landscape sold for $30,800 at Neal's. (William Henry Buck, *Two Black Women on the Road to Covington*, oil on canvas, 18 x 30 inches, Neal's, December 9, 1994, $30,800)

BUDENAARDE, Peter
American
drawings: (H) $26,450

BUDINGTON, Jonathan
American 1779-1823?
paintings: (H) $40,250

BUDTZ-MOLLER, Carl
Danish 1882-1953
paintings: (H) $1,320

BUEB, Franz
20th cent.
drawings: (H) $825

BUEHLER, Lytton Briggs
American b. 1888
paintings: (H) $880

BUEHR, Karl Albert
German/American 1866-1952
paintings: (L) $690; (H) $90,500

BUEL, Hubert
American 1915-1984
drawings: (L) $220; (H) $770

BUELL, Alfred
b. 1910
paintings: (L) $880; (H) $2,750

BUELL, Marjorie Henderson
drawings: (L) $468; (H) $2,070

BUENO, G. del
Spanish 19th cent.
paintings: (H) $805

BUENO, Xavier
Spanish/Italian 1915-1979
paintings: (L) $3,680; (H) $8,625
drawings: (L) $5,750; (H) $6,600

BUERGERNISS, Carl
American 1877-1956
paintings: (L) $55; (H) $1,320
drawings: (H) $66

BUESTLE, Bertram
b. 1902
paintings: (H) $550

BUFANO, Beniamino
sculpture: (L) $110; (H) $880

BUFF, Conrad
Swiss/American 1886-1975
paintings: (L) $550; (H) $11,000

BUFFET, Bernard
French b. 1928
paintings: (L) $6,050; (H) $550,000
drawings: (L) $2,200; (H) $68,200

BUG, Lilas
paintings: (H) $4,600

BUGATTI, Rembrandt
b. Italy 1883 d. Paris 1916
sculpture: (L) $6,900; (H) $143,000

BUGGIANI, Paolo
paintings: (H) $805

BUGIARDINI, Giuliano
Italian 1475-1554
paintings: (H) $418,000

BUGZESTER, Max
20th cent.
paintings: (H) $660

BUHLER, Augustus
American 1853-1920
paintings: (L) $193; (H) $4,400
drawings: (H) $880

BUHLER, Zuber
Swiss 19th cent.
paintings: (H) $4,400

BUHLMAYER, F***
German 19th cent.
paintings: (H) $2,875

BUHNEN, C.A.
American 19th/20th cent.
paintings: (H) $690

BUHOT, C.
19th cent.
sculpture: (H) $9,570

BUHOT, Felix Hilaire
French 1847-1898
drawings: (H) $2,420

BUHOT, Louis Charles Hippolyte
French 19th cent.
sculpture: (H) $2,200

BUIZARD, A.
Continental 19th cent.
drawings: (H) $4,950

BUKHOVSKY, Alexandre
drawings: (L) $1,093; (H) $4,313

BUKOVAC, Vlacho
Croatian 1855-1923
paintings: (L) $4,400; (H) $5,750

BULAND, Jean Eugene
French 1852-1927
paintings: (H) $9,775

BULFIELD, Joseph
British 19th cent.
paintings: (L) $468; (H) $633

BULIO
sculpture: (H) $6,325

BULL, Charles Livingston
American 1874-1932
paintings: (H) $805
drawings: (L) $110; (H) $1,320

BULL, William H.
American 1861-1940
paintings: (L) $1,840; (H) $5,225

BULLET, S.
paintings: (H) $605

BULLOCK, H.S.
paintings: (H) $770

BULMAN, Orville
American 20th cent.
paintings: (L) $374; (H) $2,300

BULMER, Lionel
paintings: (H) $2,750

BULTMAN, Fritz
drawings: (H) $1,980

BUNABAS
Continental 19th cent.
paintings: (H) $880

BUNCE, Louis Demott
American b. 1907
paintings: (H) $460

BUNCE, William Gedney
American 1840-1916
paintings: (L) $248; (H) $2,415
drawings: (H) $121

BUNDEL, Willem van den
Dutch 1575-1653/55
paintings: (L) $11,500; (H) $23,000

BUNDSHUH, Chas. M.
paintings: (H) $1,725

BUNDY, Edgar
English 1862-1922
paintings: (L) $1,100; (H) $3,738

BUNDY, Gilbert
American 1911-1955
drawings: (H) $605

BUNDY, Horace
American 1814-1883
paintings: (L) $1,100; (H) $5,775

BUNDY, John E.
American 1853-1933
paintings: (L) $880; (H) $4,400
drawings: (L) $460; (H) $660

BUNKER, Dennis Miller
American 1861-1890
paintings: (L) $29,900; (H) $67,100
drawings: (H) $2,875

BUNKER, Ida May
American 20th cent.
paintings: (H) $467

BUNN, George
British ac. 1897-1898
paintings: (L) $385; (H) $935

BUNN, Kenneth
American b. 1938
sculpture: (L) $330; (H) $3,850

BUNNELL, Charles
American 1897-1968
paintings: (L) $230; (H) $1,380

BUNNER, Andrew Fisher
American 1841-1897
paintings: (L) $468; (H) $7,762
drawings: (L) $330; (H) $805

BUNOL, Laureano Barrau
Spanish 1863-1950
paintings: (H) $60,500

BUONACCORSI, Piero, called Perino
del Vaga
Italian 1501-1547
drawings: (L) $3,850; (H) $104,500

BUONGIORNO, Donatus
Italian/American b. 1865
paintings: (L) $137; (H) $2,530
drawings: (H) $165

BUONO, Leon Giuseppe
Italian b. 1888
paintings: (L) $977; (H) $1,870

BUONO, Marco del and Apollonio di
GIOVANNI
1402-1489 and 1415/7-1465
paintings: (H) $39,600

BURAVENINI, S.
paintings: (H) $1,840

BURBANK, Elbridge Ayer
American 1858-1949
paintings: (L) $358; (H) $3,850

BURCH
English 19th cent.
paintings: (H) $1,100

BURCH, Jacques Hippolyte van der
French c. 1786-1856
paintings: (H) $4,887

BURCHFIELD, Charles E.
American 1893-1967
paintings: (L) $715; (H) $88,000
drawings: (L) $110; (H) $222,500

BURCKHARDT, Hans
Swiss 1904-1994
drawings: (H) $605

BURD, Clara Miller
American ac. 1900-1930
drawings: (H) $2,860

BURDEN, Chris
American b. 1946
drawings: (L) $4,312; (H) $12,650
sculpture: (L) $13,200; (H) $22,000

BURDEN, Scott
American b. 1939
sculpture: (H) $143,000

BURDICK, Horace R.
American 1844-1942
paintings: (L) $137; (H) $605
drawings: (L) $55; (H) $220

BUREAU, Leon
French late 19th/20th cent.
sculpture: (H) $880

BURELL, J.
British 19th cent.
paintings: (H) $7,475

BUREN, Daniel
French b. 1938
paintings: (L) $12,100; (H) $25,300

BURGADE, Louis
French 19th cent.
paintings: (H) $825

BURGARILKO, J.
German 19th cent.
paintings: (H) $770

BURGDORFF, Ferdinand
American 1883-1975
paintings: (L) $220; (H) $2,750
drawings: (H) $660

BURGER, Carl
paintings: (H) $1,540

BURGER, Josef
German 1887-1966
paintings: (H) $8,625

BURGERS, Hendricus Jacobus
Dutch 1834-1899
paintings: (H) $2,090

BURGESS, Arthur James
Australian 1879-1957
paintings: (H) $4,125

BURGESS, Captain
drawings: (H) $2,090

BURGESS, Emma Ruth
American b.c. 1882
paintings: (L) $165; (H) $990

BURGESS, George H.
English/American 1831-1905
drawings: (H) $500

BURGESS, John Bagnold
English 1830-1897
paintings: (L) $14,950; (H) $16,100

BURGH, Hendrik van der
Dutch 1769-1858
paintings: (H) $3,300

BURGHART, A.
Dutch 19th cent.
paintings: (H) $3,300

BURGIN, Victor
drawings: (L) $1,210; (H) $1,725

BURGOS, Carl
drawings: (H) $3,300

BURGSTALLER
sculpture: (H) $1,150

BURK, George
paintings: (H) $518

BURKE, Ainslee
American 20th cent.
paintings: (H) $2,475

BURKE, Brenda
American contemporary
paintings: (L) $935; (H) $2,255

BURKE, Dr. Edgar
paintings: (L) $550; (H) $2,970
drawings: (L) $550; (H) $550

BURKEL, Heinrich
German 1802-1869
paintings: (L) $41,250; (H) $93,500

BURKHALTER, Willi
b. 1903
paintings: (H) $1,150

BURKHARD, Henri
French b. 1892
paintings: (L) $83; (H) $660

BURKHARDT
paintings: (H) $1,045

BURKHARDT, Emerson C.
American 1905-1969
paintings: (L) $226; (H) $8,250
drawings: (L) $385; (H) $385

BURKHARDT, Fritz
German 1900-1983
paintings: (H) $575

BURKHARDT, Hans Gustav
Swiss/American 1904-1994
paintings: (H) $1,045
drawings: (L) $1,380; (H) $2,070

BURLANDO, Leopoldo
Italian b. 1841
paintings: (H) $5,060

BURLE MARX, Roberto
Brazilian 1909-1982
paintings: (L) $9,200; (H) $10,925

Son of an Innkeeper

Heinrich Burkel (1802-1869) was the son of a German innkeeper. Burkel choose the life of an artist over that of a tavern owner and studied at the Academy of Munich under Kobell. He is well-known for his landscapes and rural scenes of peasants with their sheep and cattle. *Peasants Traveling the Hills Above Rome* is typical of his style and subject matter. Consigned to William Bunch's auction in Westchester, Pennsylvania, the oil fetched $60,500. (Heinrich Burkel, *Peasants Traveling the Hills Above Rome*, oil on canvas, 19 x 28 inches, Bunch, January 25, 1995, $60,500.)

BURLEIGH, Sydney R.
American 1853-1931
paintings: (L) $1,320; (H) $2,300
drawings: (L) $99; (H) $1,100

BURLIN, Paul Harry
American 1886-1969
paintings: (L) $230; (H) $1,320

BURLINGAME, Charles Albert
American 1860-1930
paintings: (H) $715

BURLINGAME, Dennis
b. 1901
paintings: (L) $4,950; (H) $6,900
drawings: (H) $330

BURLIUK, David
Russian/American 1882-1967
paintings: (L) $165; (H) $22,000
drawings: (L) $50; (H) $1,610

BURMAKIN, Vladimir
Russian b. 1938
paintings: (H) $825

BURMANN, Fritz
paintings: (H) $5,500

BURMESTER, Georg
paintings: (H) $2,200

BURN, Gerald Maurice
British b. 1862
paintings: (H) $1,840

BURNE, Maurice K.
paintings: (H) $825

BURNE-JONES, Sir Edward Coley
English 1833-1898
paintings: (L) $85,000; (H) $165,000
drawings: (L) $4,312; (H) $79,500

BURNETT, Calvin
American b. 1921
paintings: (L) $440; (H) $3,740

BURNEY, Edward Francis
1760-1848
drawings: (H) $1,320

BURNHAM, Anita Willets
American b. 1880
paintings: (L) $55; (H) $1,100

BURNHAM, G.W.
paintings: (H) $2,090

BURNHAM, Ruth W.
American ac. 1920s-1940s
paintings: (H) $715

BURNLEY, Jack
drawings: (L) $1,150; (H) $1,650

BURNS, I.S.
paintings: (H) $1,430

BURNS, James
American 19th cent.
paintings: (H) $4,180

BURNS, James B.
paintings: (H) $880

BURNS, Mark
American b. 1950
sculpture: (H) $3,850

BURNS, Maurice K.
20th cent.
paintings: (L) $385; (H) $1,980

BURNS, Paul C.
1910-1990
drawings: (L) $523; (H) $1,650

BURNS, Robert
British 1869-1941
paintings: (L) $523; (H) $660
drawings: (L) $920; (H) $1,380

BURNSIDE, Cameron
American 1887-1952
paintings: (L) $330; (H) $935
drawings: (L) $110; (H) $275

BURPEE, William Partridge
American 1846-1940
paintings: (L) $3,190; (H) $9,200
drawings: (L) $259; (H) $1,650

BURR, Alexander Hohenlohe
British 1837-1899
paintings: (H) $2,300

BURR, George Brainard
American 1876-1939
paintings: (L) $230; (H) $10,350

BURR, George Elbert
American 1859-1939
drawings: (L) $1,210; (H) $1,650

BURR, John
Scottish/English 1831/36-1893/94
paintings: (L) $440; (H) $2,200

BURR, William Henry
ac. 1841-1859
paintings: (H) $880

BURRELL, A.M.
American ac. c. 1849
paintings: (H) $1,150

BURRELL, Alfred Ray
American 1877-1952
paintings: (H) $550

BURRELL, James
British 19th cent.
paintings: (H) $5,520

BURRI, Alberto
Italian b. 1915
paintings: (H) $11,000

BURRIDGE, Walter Wilcox
American b. 1857
paintings: (H) $748

BURRINI, Antonio, studio of
paintings: (H) $1,870

BURROUGHS, Edith Woodman
American 1871-1916
sculpture: (H) $8,800

BURROUGHS, John Coleman
drawings: (H) $1,150

BURT, Charles Thomas
English 1823-1902
paintings: (H) $1,650

BURT, James
American ac. 1835-1849
paintings: (H) $4,400

BURTON, Arthur Gibbes
American b. 1883
paintings: (L) $1,210; (H) $1,540
drawings: (L) $55; (H) $165

BURTON, Charles
American ac. 1820-1832
drawings: (H) $2,875

BURTON, H.D.
paintings: (H) $1,100

BURTON, J.
English 19th cent.
paintings: (L) $413; (H) $550

BURTON, Marjorie de Krafft
American b. 1886
paintings: (L) $230; (H) $1,265
drawings: (L) $460; (H) $633

BURTON, Richmond
b. 1960
paintings: (L) $1,725; (H) $18,400

BURTON, Samuel Chatwood
American b. 1881
drawings: (H) $715

BURTON, Scott
American 1939-1989
sculpture: (L) $6,050; (H) $143,000

BURTON, Sir Richard Francis
drawings: (H) $4,313

BURWELL, Vernon
b. 1916
sculpture: (L) $2,300; (H) $4,887

BURY, Pol
Belgian b. 1922
sculpture: (L) $2,875; (H) $28,750

BUSA, Peter
American b. 1914
paintings: (L) $660; (H) $3,960

BUSCH, Hans
American
paintings: (H) $578

BUSCH, J.A.H.
Dutch 19th cent.
paintings: (L) $1,100; (H) $2,200

BUSCH, Peter Johan Valdemar
Danish b. 1861
paintings: (H) $1,210

BUSCH, Wilhelm
German 1832-1908
paintings: (L) $5,720; (H) $7,700

BUSH, E.
Continental 19th cent.
paintings: (H) $575

BUSH, Jack
Canadian 1903/09-1977
paintings: (L) $880; (H) $30,250
drawings: (L) $3,740; (H) $6,050

BUSH, Norton
American 1834-1894
paintings: (L) $100; (H) $51,750

BUSHMILLER, Ernest
b. 1905
drawings: (L) $187; (H) $495

BUSHTON, J.
American 19th/20th cent.
paintings: (H) $518

BUSIRI, Giovanni Battista
Italian c. 1698-1757
drawings: (L) $8,050; (H) $16,675

BUSQUETS, Jean
French 20th cent.
paintings: (L) $275; (H) $687

BUSSCHE, Joseph Emanuel van den
Belgian 1837-1908
paintings: (H) $18,400

BUSSCHOP, Abraham
1670-1731
paintings: (H) $140,000

BUSSE, Jacques
French b. 1922
paintings: (H) $495

BUSSI, Renato
Italian 20th cent.
paintings: (H) $715

BUSSON, Charles
French 1822-1908
paintings: (H) $5,390

BUSSON, Georges
French 1859-1933
drawings: (L) $1,725; (H) $1,955

BUSTOS, Hermenegildo
Mexican 1832-1907
paintings: (L) $9,900; (H) $22,000

BUSTROV, Alexander Kirovich
Russian b. 1956
paintings: (H) $550

BUTCHER, Laura Page
American 20th cent.
paintings: (H) $1,485

BUTENSKY, J.
sculpture: (H) $1,980

BUTENSKY, Jules Leon
b. 1871
sculpture: (H) $1,380

BUTEUX, Francois Charles
c. 1732-after 1788
drawings: (H) $1,380

BUTHAUD, Rene
French b. 1886
drawings: (L) $1,650; (H) $8,250
sculpture: (H) $18,400

BUTHE, Michael
German b. 1944
paintings: (H) $4,950

BUTINONE, Bernardino
Italian c. 1450-c. 1507
paintings: (H) $200,500

BUTLER
19th/20th cent.
paintings: (H) $990

BUTLER, Charles Ernest
British 1864-c. 1918
paintings: (L) $220; (H) $57,500

BUTLER, Edward B.
American 1853-1928
paintings: (L) $495; (H) $1,320

BUTLER, Fray Guillermo
Argentinean 1880-1961
paintings: (L) $6,900; (H) $7,475

BUTLER, Howard Russell
American 1856-1934
paintings: (L) $330; (H) $16,100
drawings: (L) $66; (H) $357

BUTLER, Joseph, or Buttler
Swiss 1822-1885
paintings: (L) $1,650; (H) $7,700

BUTLER, Mary
American 1865-1946
paintings: (L) $110; (H) $1,540

BUTLER, Philip A.
American 19th/20th cent.
paintings: (L) $330; (H) $880

BUTLER, Reg
English 1913-1981
drawings: (L) $1,725; (H) $3,450
sculpture: (L) $690; (H) $46,200

BUTLER, Rozel Oertle
American 20th cent.
paintings: (L) $616; (H) $3,025

BUTLER, Theodore Earl
American 1876-1937
paintings: (L) $3,737; (H) $37,950
drawings: (H) $12,650

BUTMAN, Frederick A.
American 1820-1871
paintings: (L) $385; (H) $6,050

BUTTER, Tom
American b. 1952
sculpture: (L) $154; (H) $1,760

BUTTERFIELD, Charles
American 1893-1967
drawings: (H) $880

BUTTERFIELD, Deborah
American b. 1949
sculpture: (L) $17,250; (H) $55,200

BUTTERSACK, Bernhard
paintings: (H) $3,575

BUTTERSWORTH, James E.
American 1817-1894
paintings: (L) $2,420; (H) $187,000

BUTTERSWORTH, Thomas
English ac. 1797-1830
paintings: (L) $1,332; (H) $17,600

BUTTERWORTH, B.F.
paintings: (H) $605

BUTTING, Edwin
British 19th cent.
paintings: (H) $550

BUTTNER, Georg Heinrich
German 1799-1879
paintings: (L) $4,070; (H) $5,750

BUTTNER, Werner
German b. 1954
paintings: (L) $3,450; (H) $7,150

BUTTON, Albert Prentice
American b. 1872
paintings: (L) $275; (H) $3,738
drawings: (L) $77; (H) $522

BUTTS, John
c. 1728-1765
paintings: (H) $14,950

BUXTON, R.M.
20th cent.
sculpture: (H) $460

BUYS, Jacobus
1724-1801
drawings: (H) $1,265

BUZIO, Lydia
American b. 1948
sculpture: (L) $3,163; (H) $4,025

BUZZI, Achille
Italian 19th cent.
paintings: (L) $220; (H) $4,675
drawings: (L) $330; (H) $2,090

BYARS, James Lee
American b. 1932
sculpture: (L) $12,650; (H) $40,250

BYAZZ
paintings: (H) $770

BYE, Ranulph
drawings: (L) $130; (H) $600

BYGRAVE, William
American 19th cent.
paintings: (H) $9,020

BYLANDT, Alfred Edouard van
Dutch 1829-1890
paintings: (L) $412; (H) $7,480

BYLES, William Hounsom
British ac. 1890-1916
paintings: (H) $6,050

BYNG, Robert
British 18th cent.
drawings: (H) $920

BYRD, Frederick
American ac. 1840s
paintings: (H) $550

BYRNE, Bob
drawings: (H) $650

BYRON, Bourmond
Haitian b. 1923
paintings: (L) $220; (H) $1,430

BYRON, Michael
b. 1954
paintings: (L) $22; (H) $2,200
drawings: (H) $1,265
sculpture: (L) $66; (H) $460

BYRUM, Ruthven Holmes
American 1896-1960
paintings: (L) $220; (H) $1,375

CABADA, Havier
contemporary
paintings: (L) $770; (H) $1,540

CABAILLOT, Louis Simon, called
LASSALLE
French b. 1810
paintings: (L) $330; (H) $5,980

CABAILLOT-LASSALLE, Camille
Leopold
French b. 1839
paintings: (H) $5,750

CABALLERO, Jorge Mantilla
paintings: (H) $4,125

CABALLERO, Jose
Spanish 1916-1991
paintings: (H) $6,900

CABALLERO, Luis
Columbian b. 1943
paintings: (L) $16,500; (H) $34,500
drawings: (L) $2,750; (H) $18,400

CABANEL, Alexandre
French 1823-1889
paintings: (L) $1,430; (H) $440,000
drawings: (H) $1,650

CABET, R.
paintings: (H) $797

CABIE, Louis Alexandre
French 1853-1939
paintings: (L) $1,150; (H) $1,650
drawings: (L) $220; (H) $275

CABLE, Laura A.
19th cent.
paintings: (L) $5,463; (H) $8,525

CABOT, Channing
American 1868-1932
paintings: (H) $863

CABOT, Edward Clarke
American 1818-1901
drawings: (L) $110; (H) $522

CABRE, Manuel
Venezuelan b. Spain 1890
paintings: (L) $21,850; (H) $22,000

CABRERA, Miguel
Mexican 1695-1768
paintings: (L) $12,650; (H) $79,500

CACCIARELLI, V***
Italian 19th cent.
drawings: (H) $2,750

CACCIARELLI, V.
Italian 20th cent.
drawings: (H) $4,945

CACCIARELLI, Victor
Italian 19th cent.
drawings: (H) $550

CACERES, Ruiz de
Spanish 19th cent.
paintings: (L) $3,520; (H) $5,060

CACHOUD, Francois Charles
French 1866-1943
paintings: (L) $920; (H) $11,000

CADELL, Francois Campbell Boileau
British b. 1883
paintings: (H) $203,500

CADENASSO, Giuseppe
Italian/American 1858-1918
paintings: (L) $1,650; (H) $13,200
drawings: (L) $1,320; (H) $3,575

CADES, Giuseppe
Italian 1750-1799
drawings: (L) $4,950; (H) $24,150

CADMUS, Paul
American b. 1904
paintings: (L) $1,265; (H) $35,200
drawings: (L) $770; (H) $9,775

CADORET, Michel
French 1912-1985
paintings: (H) $1,430

CADY, Fred
American 1885-1960
paintings: (H) $1,320

CADY, Harrison
American 1877-1970
paintings: (L) $546; (H) $51,750
drawings: (L) $88; (H) $6,325

CADY, Henry N.
American b. 1849
paintings: (L) $412; (H) $2,200
drawings: (L) $55; (H) $770

CAESAR, Doris
American 1892-1971
paintings: (H) $137
sculpture: (L) $357; (H) $6,325

CAFFE, Nino
Italian 1909-1975
paintings: (L) $1,150; (H) $10,450

CAFFERTY, James H.
American 1819-1869
paintings: (L) $660; (H) $825

CAFFI, Cavaliere Ippolito
Italian 1809-1866
paintings: (L) $28,600; (H) $57,500

CAFFI, Margherita
Italian ac. 1660-1700
paintings: (H) $18,700

CAFFIERI, Hector
British 1847-1932
paintings: (L) $5,750; (H) $10,350
drawings: (L) $1,650; (H) $3,190

CAFFYN, Walter Wallor
English ac. 1876-1898; d. 1898
paintings: (L) $247; (H) $8,085

CAGE, John
American 1912-1992
paintings: (H) $6,325
drawings: (H) $2,185
sculpture: (H) $11,500

CAGNACCI, Guido
Italian 1601-1663
paintings: (H) $198,000

CAGNEY, James
American 1899-1986
paintings: (L) $495; (H) $3,740
drawings: (L) $770; (H) $2,420

CAGNIART, Emile
French 1851-1911
paintings: (L) $2,185; (H) $9,200

CAGNONI, Amerino
Italian b. 1853
paintings: (H) $8,800

CAHEN, Oscar
paintings: (H) $1,350

CAHILL, Richard S.
British 19th cent.
paintings: (H) $1,380

CAHILL, William
American 1878-1924
paintings: (H) $6,050

CAHOON, Charles D.
American 1861-1951
paintings: (L) $385; (H) $4,950

CAHOON, Martha
American b. 1905
paintings: (L) $275; (H) $6,900
drawings: (H) $110

CAHOON, Ralph
American 1910-1982
paintings: (L) $1,210; (H) $77,000
drawings: (H) $193

Illustrator and Cartoonist

Harrison Cady (1877-1970) was an illustrator, cartoonist, and author. His father, an ardent naturalist and owner of a general store with a 1,500 book library, taught his son a love of books and nature. Cady was a self-taught artist, and in 1895 he set off from Gardner, Massachusetts, to New York to seek his fortune. His first sale was a set of decorative initial letters for *Truth Magazine*; his next job was illustrating a Mother Goose book. Anthropomorphic animals have always been popular with children, and in 1913 Cady began illustrating Thornton Burgess's *Bedtime Stories of Peter Rabbit*. The Burgess books, *The Adventures of Jerry Muskrat*, *The Adventures of Old Mr. Toad*, and Peter Cottontail, Reddy Fox, and Sammy Jay are children's classics. Cady was an author and illustrator of his own children's books: *Animal Alphabet*, *Johnny Funny-Bunny's Picnic Party*, and many others. Much in demand, he also illustrated articles and drew cartoons for the *Saturday Evening Post*, *Life*, *Ladies' Home Journal*, and the *Sunday Herald Tribune*. Harrison was a printmaker and worked in pen and ink, oils, and watercolor. In 1920 Cady and his wife bought a summer home in Rockport, a small town on Cape Ann, Massachusetts, and a mecca for many artists. His painting of an Essex shipyard, a town on Cape Ann, realized $4,312 when it sold at Skinner's in Bolton, Massachusetts. (Harrison Cady, *Essex Shipyard*, oil with ink and crayon on masonite, 25 x 30 inches, Skinner, September 9, 1994, $4,312)

CAHOURS, Henry Maurice
b. 1889
paintings: (H) $4,400

CAILLE, Leon Emile
French 1836-1907
paintings: (L) $495; (H) $10,925

CAILLEBOTTE, Gustave
French 1848-1894
paintings: (H) $715,000
drawings: (H) $39,600

CAIMI, A.
paintings: (H) $450

CAIN, Georges Jules Auguste
French 1856-1919
paintings: (L) $23,000; (H) $30,800

CAIN, Peter
b. 1959
paintings: (H) $10,350

CAIRO, Francesco del
Italian 1598-1674
paintings: (H) $25,300

CAIRONI, Luigi
Italian 19th cent.
paintings: (H) $2,750

CAJONI, A.
American 20th cent.
paintings: (H) $468

CALA Y MOYA, Jose de
Spanish b. 1850
paintings: (H) $13,225

CALAME, Alexandre
Swiss 1810-1864
paintings: (L) $2,185; (H) $17,600

CALAME, Jean Baptiste Arthur
Swiss 1843-1919
paintings: (L) $1,000; (H) $1,500

CALAWAY, Loren
b. 1950
sculpture: (H) $1,650

CALBET, Antoine
French 1860-1944
paintings: (H) $6,050
drawings: (H) $3,080

CALDER, Alexander
American 1898-1976
paintings: (L) $2,760; (H) $96,000
drawings: (L) $805; (H) $33,350
sculpture: (L) $1,100; (H) $1,817,500

CALDER, Alexander Milne
American 1846-1923
sculpture: (H) $7,150

CALDERINI, Marco
Italian b. 1850
paintings: (H) $74,800

CALDERON, Charles Clement
French 19th/20th cent.
paintings: (L) $743; (H) $6,050

CALDERON, Philip Hermogenes
French 1833-1898
paintings: (L) $935; (H) $22,000

CALDERON, William Frank
British 1865-1943
paintings: (L) $7,700; (H) $24,200

CALDWELL, Edmund
British 1852-1930
paintings: (H) $7,150

CALE, George Viscont
English 19th cent.
paintings: (H) $4,400

CALEB, Uncle
American
paintings: (H) $990

CALES, Pierre
French 1870-1961
paintings: (L) $880; (H) $880

CALGERO, Jean
Italian b. 1922
paintings: (H) $550

CALHOUN, T.
British 19th cent.
paintings: (H) $575

CALIARI, Carlo, called Carletto
Italian 1570-1596
paintings: (H) $23,000

CALIFANO, Eugene
American b. 1893
paintings: (L) $523; (H) $1,045

CALIFANO, Giovanni
Italian b. 1864
paintings: (H) $1,320

CALIFANO, John
Italian/American 1864-1924
paintings: (L) $358; (H) $8,625

CALIFANO, John Edmund
American 1862-1946
paintings: (L) $1,100; (H) $4,675

CALIGA, Issac Henry
American 1857-1960
paintings: (L) $880; (H) $49,450

CALIGO, Domenico
Italian 19th cent.
paintings: (H) $2,420

CALISCH, Moritz
Dutch 1819-1870
paintings: (H) $1,100

CALISTRO, M.
paintings: (H) $770

CALIXTO DE JESUS, Benedito
paintings: (H) $13,200

CALKEN, S.
English 19th cent.
paintings: (H) $546

CALL, Jan van, the elder
Dutch 1656-1706
drawings: (H) $16,500

CALLCOTT, Charles
British 19th cent.
drawings: (H) $550

CALLCOTT, Sir Augustus Wall
English 1779-1844
paintings: (L) $1,150; (H) $4,025

CALLE, Paul
American b. 1928
paintings: (L) $1,045; (H) $22,000
drawings: (L) $6,050; (H) $14,300

CALLE, Sophie
b. 1953
drawings: (L) $6,900; (H) $13,800

CALLERY, Mary
sculpture: (H) $1,210

CALLET, Antoine Francois
French 1741-1823
drawings: (H) $20,700

CALLIANO, Antonio Raffael
Italian 1785-1824
paintings: (H) $24,200

CALLIAS, Horace de
French d. 1921
paintings: (H) $6,900

CALLIYANNIS, Manolis
paintings: (H) $1,035

CALLOT, Jacques
French 1592-1635
drawings: (L) $14,950; (H) $23,100

CALLOW, E.
British 19th cent.
paintings: (H) $1,650

CALLOW, George D.
English exhib. 1858-1873
paintings: (H) $1,265

CALLOW, John
English 1822-1878
paintings: (L) $1,320; (H) $6,325

CALLOW, William
English 1812-1908
drawings: (L) $230; (H) $1,760

CALOGERO, Jean
Italian b. 1922
paintings: (L) $33; (H) $3,565

CALOGIRO
paintings: (L) $440; (H) $770

CALON, Achille Augustin
French d. 1904
paintings: (H) $1,610

CALONI, K.
sculpture: (H) $1,870

CALOT, H.
sculpture: (L) $550; (H) $605

CALS, Adolphe Felix
French 1810-1880
paintings: (H) $9,200

CALVERT, Denys, called Dionisio
FIAMMINGO
c. 1540-1619
paintings: (L) $7,150; (H) $57,500
drawings: (H) $4,400

CALVERT, Frederick
Irish/English ac. 1815, d. 1845?
paintings: (L) $1,100; (H) $1,540

CALVERT, Henry
English ac. 1826-1854
paintings: (L) $880; (H) $4,025

CALVERT, Louis
19th cent.
paintings: (H) $805

CALVERT, S.W.
paintings: (L) $467; (H) $633

CALVES, Leon Georges
French b. 1848
paintings: (L) $880; (H) $1,320

CALVES, Marie
French b. 1883
paintings: (H) $517

CALVI, Ercole
Italian 1824-1900
paintings: (H) $6,710

CALVI, Paolo
Italian ac. 1830-1866
paintings: (H) $1,760

CALVI, Pietro
Italian 1833-1884
sculpture: (L) $4,950; (H) $107,000

CALVO, Maria del Carmen
20th cent.
paintings: (L) $4,025; (H) $5,175

CALVO-LANTARON, Leandro
Spanish 19th cent.
paintings: (H) $2,750

CALYO, Nicolino
Italian/American 1799-1884
paintings: (L) $605; (H) $3,850
drawings: (H) $1,017

CALZADA MASTER
Early 16th century
paintings: (H) $9,900

CAMACHO, Jorge
b. Cuba 1934
paintings: (L) $2,990; (H) $11,500
drawings: (H) $518

CAMARENA, Jorge Gonzalez
Mexican b. 1908
paintings: (H) $17,250

CAMARGO, Sergio
sculpture: (H) $4,950

CAMARROQUE, Charles
French 19th cent.
paintings: (H) $7,425

CAMBELLO, G.***
paintings: (H) $550

CAMBI, A.
Italian 19th cent.
sculpture: (L) $660; (H) $3,850

CAMBIASO, Luca
Italian 1527-1585
paintings: (L) $20,700; (H) $22,000
drawings: (L) $1,725; (H) $16,100

CAMBIER, Guy
French b. 1923
paintings: (L) $440; (H) $4,675

CAMBOS, Jean Jules
French 1828-1917
sculpture: (L) $2,200; (H) $4,313

CAMERARIUS, Adam
ac. 1650-1689
paintings: (H) $10,450

CAMERON, Duncan
Scottish ac. 1871-1900
paintings: (L) $880; (H) $1,650

CAMERON, H.
British 19th cent.
paintings: (H) $3,025

CAMERON, Robert Hartly
American b. 1909
paintings: (L) $977; (H) $2,090

CAMERON, Sir David Young
English 1865-1945
paintings: (L) $660; (H) $1,380
drawings: (L) $489; (H) $748

CAMFIELD, George
paintings: (H) $1,430

CAMINADE, Alexandre Francois
French 1789-1862
paintings: (H) $16,500

CAMINO, Giuseppe
Italian 1818-1890
paintings: (L) $6,600; (H) $22,000

CAMMEN, Emile van der
Dutch 20th cent.
drawings: (H) $1,980

CAMMIULLI, E.
Italian 19th cent.
sculpture: (H) $990

CAMOIN, Charles
French 1879-1965
paintings: (L) $2,300; (H) $77,300
drawings: (L) $2,645; (H) $5,175

CAMOS, H.
19th cent.
paintings: (H) $660

CAMPAGNA, Girolamo, workshop of
Venetian 16th cent.
sculpture: (H) $5,750

CAMPAGNE
sculpture: (L) $345; (H) $2,750

CAMPAGNO, Tomas
Spanish b. 1857
paintings: (H) $1,980

CAMPAGNOLA, Domenico
Italian 1484-1550/80
drawings: (L) $1,430; (H) $8,625

CAMPAIOLA, T.
sculpture: (H) $1,210

CAMPANELLA, Vito
paintings: (H) $4,025

CAMPBELL, Blendon
American b. 1872
paintings: (L) $220; (H) $880
sculpture: (H) $368

CAMPBELL, C. Hay
British 19th/20th cent.
paintings: (H) $990

CAMPBELL, George F.
English 19th/20th cent.
paintings: (H) $1,540

CAMPBELL, Hugh
paintings: (L) $75; (H) $500

CAMPBELL, Lang
American 20th cent.
drawings: (L) $248; (H) $770

CAMPBELL, Laurence
American 20th cent.
paintings: (L) $1,870; (H) $3,300

CAMPBELL, Orville
American contemporary
paintings: (H) $1,045

CAMPBELL, Scott
Scottish/American b. 1930
paintings: (H) $495

CAMPBELL, Stephen
British b. 1946
paintings: (L) $3,163; (H) $15,400

CAMPECHE, Jose
Puerto Rican 1751-1809
paintings: (H) $288,500

CAMPENY Y SANTAMARIA, Jose
Spanish b. 1865
sculpture: (H) $2,300

CAMPHAUSEN, Wilhelm
German 1815-1885
paintings: (H) $26,400
drawings: (H) $495

CAMPI, Bernardino
Italian 1522-1591
paintings: (H) $134,500

CAMPI, Giulio
c. 1502-1572
drawings: (L) $1,840; (H) $2,300

CAMPIDOGLIO, Michelangelo di
Italian 1610-1670
paintings: (H) $59,700

CAMPIGLI, Massimo
Italian 1895-1971
paintings: (L) $37,375; (H) $385,000
drawings: (L) $1,610; (H) $6,050

CAMPIO, H.
Italian 19th cent.
paintings: (H) $3,740

CAMPION, George B.
British 1796-1870
drawings: (L) $357; (H) $6,050

CAMPO, A.D.
paintings: (H) $8,525

CAMPO, Frederico del
Peruvian 19th cent.
paintings: (L) $3,300; (H) $68,200
drawings: (H) $3,450

CAMPOLMI, S.
Italian 19th cent.
paintings: (H) $12,650

CAMPOREALE, Sergio
b. Argentina 1937
paintings: (L) $5,175; (H) $8,337
drawings: (L) $1,150; (H) $10,450

CAMPRIANI, Alceste
Italian 1848-1933
paintings: (L) $5,175; (H) $20,700

CAMPUZANO, Ricardo Gomez
paintings: (H) $1,725

CAMRADT, Johannes Ludvig
Danish 1779-1849
paintings: (L) $2,875; (H) $15,400

CAMRAGNE, Daniel
Continental contemporary
sculpture: (H) $748

CAMUS, Blanche
French 19th/20th cent.
paintings: (H) $1,955

CAMUS, George
French 19th/20th cent.
paintings: (H) $1,650

CAMUS, H.E.
paintings: (H) $920

CAMUS, Jean Marie
French 1877-1955
sculpture: (H) $1,540

CANA, Louis Emile
b. 1845
sculpture: (L) $460; (H) $1,610

CANADE, Vincent
American b. 1879
paintings: (L) $165; (H) $450

CANAL, ***von
Dutch 19th cent.
paintings: (H) $3,410

CANALETTO, Antonio Canal studio of
18th cent.
paintings: (L) $93,500; (H) $126,500

CANALETTO, Giovanni Antonio
CANALE
Italian 1697-1768
paintings: (L) $86,000; (H) $2,642,500
drawings: (H) $14,950

CANALS, Miguel, studio of
paintings: (H) $1,540

CANAS, Benjamin
Brazilian b. 1933
drawings: (L) $1,980; (H) $7,100

CANCIO, Carlos
Puerto Rican b. 1961
paintings: (H) $5,750

CANDBERG
Swedish 20th cent.
paintings: (H) $495

CANDELL, Victor
American 1903-1977
paintings: (H) $880

CANDELLE, L.
19th cent.
drawings: (H) $1,650

CANDIDA, G**
Italian 18th/19th cent.
paintings: (H) $2,760

CANE, Ella du
English 19th cent.
drawings: (H) $495

CANE, Louis
b. 1943
paintings: (L) $345; (H) $1,495
drawings: (H) $825

CANELLA, Carlo
Italian 19th cent.
paintings: (H) $8,050

CANELLA, Giuseppe
Italian 1788-1847
paintings: (L) $9,350; (H) $68,500

CANET, Marcel
French b. 1875
paintings: (H) $825

CANEVARI, Carlo
Italian b. 1926
paintings: (L) $137; (H) $990
drawings: (H) $137

CANFIELD, Jane
American b. 1897
sculpture: (H) $825

CANIFF, Milton
American 1907-1988
paintings: (H) $2,300
drawings: (L) $357; (H) $2,200

CANJURA, Noe
French 1924-1973
paintings: (L) $176; (H) $1,840

CANN, Sidney
British 19th cent.
paintings: (H) $468

CANNAUT, Micheline
French 20th cent.
paintings: (L) $165; (H) $550

CANNELLA, Pizzi
b. 1955
drawings: (H) $2,200

CANNICCI, Nicolo
Italian 1846-1906
paintings: (L) $7,475; (H) $27,600

CANNON, Henry W.
20th cent.
paintings: (H) $990

CANNON, Kevin
contemporary
sculpture: (L) $1,380; (H) $1,725

CANONE, C.
paintings: (H) $1,045

CANOVA, Giacomo
Italian 1851-1894
paintings: (H) $4,125

CANOVAS, Fernando
b. 1960
paintings: (H) $8,912

CANTA, Johannes Antonius
Dutch 1816-1888
paintings: (H) $1,150

CANTAGALLINA, Remigio
Italian 1582-1630
drawings: (H) $6,600

CANTANI, Luigi
Italian 18th cent.
drawings: (H) $770

CANTANIO
Belgian 19th cent.
paintings: (H) $1,150

CANTARINI, Simone, called IL
PESARESE
Italian 1612-1648
paintings: (L) $25,300; (H) $37,400
drawings: (H) $4,140

CANTINEAU, C.
19th cent.
paintings: (H) $935

CANTON, Gustav Jakob
German 1813-1885
paintings: (L) $2,200; (H) $8,800

CANTU, Federico
b. Mexico 1908 d. 1989
paintings: (L) $1,265; (H) $30,800
drawings: (L) $920; (H) $4,400

CANTWELL, James
American 1856-1926
paintings: (L) $1,265; (H) $2,530

CANTY, Bill
paintings: (H) $2,750

CANU, Yvonne
French b. 1921
paintings: (L) $1,380; (H) $11,550
drawings: (H) $1,320

CANUTI, Domenico Maria
Italian 1620-1684
drawings: (H) $522

CANZIANI, Estella
British b. 1887
drawings: (H) $1,610

CAP, Constant Aime Marie
Belgian 1838-1890
paintings: (L) $3,795; (H) $68,500

CAPARN, Thos. J.
drawings: (L) $200; (H) $2,600

CAPEINICK, Jean
Belgian 1838-1890
paintings: (L) $6,900; (H) $29,900

CAPELLAN, Tony
paintings: (H) $2,750

CAPOBIANCHI, Vincente
Italian 19th cent.
paintings: (H) $1,100

CAPOCCI, E.
Italian 19th cent.
paintings: (H) $825

CAPOGROSSI, Giuseppe
Italian 1900-1972
paintings: (H) $7,975

CAPON, Georges Emil
French 1890-1980
paintings: (L) $978; (H) $4,312

CAPONE, Gaetano
Italian 1845-1920/24
paintings: (L) $220; (H) $2,420
drawings: (L) $431; (H) $1,980

CAPORAEL, Suzanne
American b. 1946
paintings: (H) $3,450

CAPP, Al
American 1909-1979
paintings: (H) $375
drawings: (L) $550; (H) $4,312

CAPPELLO, Carmelo
Italian b. 1912
sculpture: (L) $770; (H) $1,380

CAPPENOLLE, E. van
Continental 19th cent.
paintings: (H) $35,750

CAPPULETTI, Jose Manuel
Spanish 20th cent.
paintings: (H) $990

CAPRILE, Vincenzo
Italian 1856-1936
paintings: (L) $1,035; (H) $6,900

CAPRON, Jean Pierre
French b. 1921
paintings: (L) $385; (H) $880

CAPUANO, Francesco
Italian b. 1854
paintings: (H) $1,045

CAPULETTI, Jose Manuel
Spanish b. 1925
paintings: (L) $275; (H) $5,500

CAPUTO, Ulisse
Italian 1872-1948
paintings: (L) $3,738; (H) $20,700

CARABAIN, Jacques
Belgian 1834-1892
paintings: (L) $11,000; (H) $33,350

CARAUD, Joseph
French 1821-1905
paintings: (L) $8,050; (H) $31,050

CARAUD, R.
French 19th cent.
paintings: (H) $8,250

CARAVACQUE, Francois
late 17th cent.
sculpture: (H) $16,500

CARBALLO Y SEGURA, Bernabe
Spanish 19th/20th cent.
paintings: (H) $880

CARBEE, Scott Clifton
American 1860-1946
paintings: (L) $1,150; (H) $12,650

CARBONE, Giovanni Bernardo
Italian 1616-1683
paintings: (H) $13,800

CARBONEL, Miguel
Spanish/American 20th cent.
sculpture: (H) $1,380

CARBONELL, Manuel
sculpture: (L) $550; (H) $7,150

CARBONELL, Santiago
b. Spain 1960
paintings: (L) $30,800; (H) $51,750

CARBONERO, Jose Moreno
Spanish b. 1860
paintings: (L) $11,000; (H) $22,000

CARBONERO, M.
Spanish 19th cent.
paintings: (H) $2,300

CARCANO, Filippo
Italian 1840-1910
paintings: (H) $23,100

CARDENAS, Agustin
Cuban b. 1927
sculpture: (L) $5,500; (H) $30,800

CARDENAS, Juan
b. Colombia 1939
paintings: (L) $14,950; (H) $20,900
drawings: (H) $9,200

CARDENAS, Santiago
Colombian b. 1937
paintings: (L) $4,400; (H) $7,700

CARDI, Lodovico, called IL CIGOLI
studio of
16th/17th cent.
paintings: (H) $14,300

CARDI, Lodovico, called Il Cigoli
Italian 1559-1613
drawings: (L) $4,600; (H) $63,800

CARDON, Claude
English ac. 1892-1915
paintings: (L) $3,450; (H) $4,290

CARDONA, Jose
early 20th cent.
sculpture: (L) $550; (H) $880

CARDONA Y TIO, Juan
Spanish 1877-1958
paintings: (L) $7,475; (H) $10,350

CARDONS, Jose
sculpture: (H) $805

CARDUCCI, Adolfo
Italian 1901-1983
paintings: (L) $431; (H) $1,210

CAREEENEN, Jean Phillipe Robert,
called Jean Raine
Belgian b. 1927
paintings: (H) $660

CARELLI, A***
Neapolitan 19th cent.
drawings: (H) $1,980

CARELLI, C.
paintings: (L) $4,950; (H) $12,375

CARELLI, Conrad H. R.
British b. 1869
drawings: (H) $2,530

CARELLI, Consalve
Italian 1818-1900
paintings: (L) $1,725; (H) $22,000
drawings: (L) $805; (H) $5,390

CARELLI, G.
paintings: (L) $3,850; (H) $5,060

CARELLI, Gabriel
Italian 1821-1900
drawings: (L) $250; (H) $880

CARELLI, Giuseppe
Italian 1858-1921
paintings: (L) $605; (H) $11,000

CARELLI, Gonsalvo
Italian 1818-1900
drawings: (H) $6,600

CARELLI?, Guiseppe
Italian 1858-1921
paintings: (H) $3,410

CARESME, Antoine Philippe
1734-1796
drawings: (H) $6,325

CAREW, F.
English 19th cent.
sculpture: (H) $1,870

CAREY, C.P.
paintings: (H) $4,400

CAREY, H***
American 19th/20th cent.
paintings: (H) $1,150

CAREY, James L.
paintings: (H) $1,438

CAREY, William Joseph
Irish 1859-1937
drawings: (H) $495

CARGILL, G.
English 19th cent.
paintings: (H) $605

CARGNEL, Antonio
Italian 20th cent.
paintings: (L) $165; (H) $825

CARGNELL, V. Antonio
Italian 1872-1931
paintings: (H) $2,750

CARIANI, Giovanni, called Giovanni
De'BUSI
Italian 1485/90-after 1547
paintings: (H) $63,800

CARIANI, Varaldo J.
paintings: (L) $990; (H) $4,950

CARIGIET, Alois
1902-1985
drawings: (H) $1,320

CARILLI, G.
Italian 19th cent.
paintings: (H) $6,600
drawings: (H) $385

CARINI, T.
Italian 19th cent.
paintings: (H) $880

CARLANDI, Onorato
Italian 1848-1939
paintings: (L) $4,025; (H) $7,700
drawings: (L) $880; (H) $3,190

CARLES, Arthur B.
American 1880/82-1952
paintings: (L) $1,092; (H) $18,700
drawings: (L) $132; (H) $1,705

CARLEVARIJS, Luca
Italian 1663-1727
paintings: (H) $60,500
drawings: (H) $9,200

CARLIER, Emile Joseph Nestor
French 1849-1927
sculpture: (L) $2,200; (H) $2,530

CARLIER, Max
Belgian 19th/20th cent.
paintings: (L) $3,850; (H) $25,300

CARLIER, Modeste
Belgian 1820-1878
paintings: (L) $1,650; (H) $27,500

CARLIERI, Alberto
Italian 1672-c. 1720
paintings: (L) $13,200; (H) $18,400

CARLIN, James
American b. Ireland 1910
paintings: (L) $138; (H) $1,840
drawings: (L) $38; (H) $880

CARLIN, John
American 1813-1891
paintings: (L) $1,100; (H) $34,500

CARLING, H.
American 20th cent.
paintings: (H) $920

CARLISLE, Harold I.
American b. 1904
paintings: (L) $330; (H) $660

CARLISLE, Mary Helen
American d. 1925
drawings: (H) $690

CARLO, Chiostri
Italian 19th cent.
paintings: (L) $920; (H) $1,540

CARLO, R.
19th/20th cent.
paintings: (L) $1,150; (H) $1,208

CARLOS, Ernest Stafford
British 1883-1917
paintings: (L) $990; (H) $1,035

CARLSEN, Dines
American 1901-1966
paintings: (L) $330; (H) $26,450
drawings: (H) $275

CARLSEN, E.
American 20th cent.
paintings: (H) $605

CARLSEN, Soren Emil
Danish/American 1853-1932
paintings: (L) $302; (H) $60,500
drawings: (L) $110; (H) $1,870

CARLSON, George
American b. 1940
sculpture: (L) $690; (H) $29,900

CARLSON, John Fabian
Swedish/American 1875-1945
paintings: (L) $440; (H) $22,000
drawings: (L) $220; (H) $1,650

CARLSON, Ken
American b. 1940
paintings: (L) $5,500; (H) $7,150

CARLSON, William
American b. 1950
sculpture: (L) $1,380; (H) $3,300

CARLU, Jean
French b. 1900
drawings: (H) $1,100

CARMAGNOLLE, Adolphe
American 19th cent.
paintings: (H) $3,220

CARME, Felix
French 19th cent.
paintings: (H) $1,150

CARMICHAEL, Franklin
Canadian 1890-1945
paintings: (H) $11,000
drawings: (L) $8,800; (H) $27,500

CARMICHAEL, Herbert
British 1856-1935
paintings: (H) $495

CARMICHAEL, James Wilson
British 1800-1868
paintings: (L) $1,380; (H) $24,200

CARMIENCKE, Johann Hermann
b. Germany 1810 d. U.S. 1867
paintings: (L) $1,100; (H) $20,350
drawings: (H) $522

CARMONTELLE, Louis Carrogis de
French 1717-1806
drawings: (L) $8,800; (H) $60,500

CARNEO, Antonio
Italian ac. 1640-1680
paintings: (L) $13,800; (H) $29,900

CARNIER, E.
French 19th cent.
sculpture: (H) $550

CARNIER, H.
French 19th/20th cent.
paintings: (L) $440; (H) $1,155

CARNWATH, Squeak
American b. 1947
paintings: (H) $1,870
drawings: (H) $920

CARO, Anthony
English b. 1924
sculpture: (L) $1,380; (H) $42,550

CARO-DELVAILLE, Henry
French 1876-1926
drawings: (H) $1,150

CAROLE
paintings: (H) $1,265

CAROLIS, Jacopo de
ac. 14th/15th cent.
paintings: (H) $77,000

CAROLL (?), E.
paintings: (H) $1,380

CAROLSFELD, Julius Schnorr von
German 1794-1872
drawings: (H) $4,025

CAROLUS, Jean
Belgian ac. 1867-1872
paintings: (L) $6,600; (H) $9,200

Canadian Nationalist Painter

Recognition for Emily Carr (1871-1945) came late in life. A native of Victoria, British Columbia, she studied briefly at the San Francisco School of Art when she was only 19. Returning home, she set up a studio in a renovated barn, where she painted and taught art. By 1902 she had saved enough money to study in England, but her 18 months abroad were spent recovering from a sudden illness. Returning to Canada she went back to teaching and painting. Indian motifs, especially totem poles, became a dominant theme after a trip to Alaska in 1907. By 1910 she had once again saved enough money to study in Europe. Her travels in France introduced her to the work of the Fauves (Matisse, Rouault, Vlaminck, Derain, Dufy), a group of painters who used vivid non-naturalistic colors. Carr

adopted their blazing colors and began using a bolder brushstroke. After two years she returned home, but her work was not well-received. She was too avant-garde for Canada. Discouraged and in economic need, she built a boarding house on inherited land and earned a living by raising dogs, hooking rugs, making Indian pottery, running her boarding house, and only occasionally painting. Then in 1927 her fortunes underwent a fairytale-like reversal. Because of her subject matter and the fact that she worked in a remote part of the country, Carr was included in a National Gallery exhibit of regional and native art in Ottawa. During a side trip to Toronto, she met with members of the famous Group of Seven, the acknowledged leaders of Canadian nationalist art. The group, most importantly Lawren Harris, greeted her work with great enthusiasm and encouraged her to start painting again. Carr began painting dramatic pictures of lush Canadian forests and Indian motifs with oil on paper as her medium. After she was diagnosed with a heart condition, she began to write. Carr wrote three autobiographical books and her collection of short stories won the Governor General's literary award. In 1990 a major retrospective of 180 of her paintings and drawings was held at the National Gallery of Art.

An auction record was set for Emily Carr in 1987 when an oil painting sold for $297,000 at a Toronto auction house. *Cape Mudge Totem Poles*, a somber watercolor executed circa 1912, sold at Weschler's for $16,500 in 1995. The grey and brown tones were contributing factors for this relatively low price. (Emily Carr, *Cape Mudge Totem Poles*, watercolor on paper, 22 x 15 inches, Weschler, March 4, 1995, $16,500)

CAROLUS-DURAN, Charles Emile
Auguste
French 1838-1917
paintings: (L) $3,680; (H) $5,500
drawings: (H) $1,100

CARON
French 20th cent.
paintings: (H) $495

CARON, Alexandre Auguste
French 1857-1932
sculpture: (H) $2,875

CARON, Gregory
paintings: (H) $550

CARON, J.
Continental 19th/20th cent.
paintings: (H) $575

CARON, Paul Archibald
drawings: (H) $1,320

CARONI, Emmanuelle
Italian early 19th cent.
sculpture: (H) $5,405

CAROSELLI, Angelo
Italian 1585-1653
paintings: (H) $18,700

CAROSELLI, M.
paintings: (L) $403; (H) $1,495

CAROSI, Alberto
Italian 20th cent.
paintings: (H) $880

CAROT
paintings: (H) $1,430

CARPACCIO, Vittore
Italian c. 1465-1525
paintings: (H) $77,000

CARPANTIER, J.
French 18th cent.
paintings: (H) $3,450

CARPEAUX, Jean Baptiste
French 1827-1875
paintings: (L) $10,350; (H) $38,500
drawings: (L) $575; (H) $4,025
sculpture: (L) $1,380; (H) $90,500

CARPENTE, Pierre
ac. 18th cent.
drawings: (H) $1,100

CARPENTER, Earl
b. 1931
paintings: (H) $7,150

CARPENTER, Francis Bicknell
American 1830-1900
paintings: (H) $633

CARPENTER, Fred G.
American 1882-1965
paintings: (L) $230; (H) $1,100

CARPENTER, G.E.
paintings: (H) $575

CARPENTER, Margaret Sarah
English 1793-1872
paintings: (L) $11,500; (H) $23,000

CARPENTER, Mildred Bailey
American 1894-1985
drawings: (L) $316; (H) $1,540

CARPENTER, Percy
British ac. 1841-1858
paintings: (H) $4,370

CARPENTERO, Henri Joseph
Gommarus
Belgian 1820-1874
paintings: (L) $1,265; (H) $6,613

CARPENTIER, Evariste
Belgian 1845-1922
paintings: (L) $2,300; (H) $17,600

CARPI, Girolamo da
1501-1556
paintings: (H) $299,500
drawings: (H) $2,990

CARPINO, Ralph
20th cent.
paintings: (H) $1,380

CARPIONI, Giulio
Italian 1611-1674
paintings: (L) $6,037; (H) $27,600
drawings: (H) $3,080

CARR, Emily
Canadian 1871-1945
paintings: (L) $18,700; (H) $99,000
drawings: (L) $2,420; (H) $19,800

CARR, Henry
British 1894-1970
paintings: (H) $1,100

CARR, Lyell
1857-1912
paintings: (L) $660; (H) $3,450

CARR, Samuel S.
American 1837-1908
paintings: (L) $688; (H) $24,200

CARRA, Carlo
Italian 1881-1966
paintings: (H) $49,500
drawings: (L) $28,600; (H) $211,500

CARRACCI, Agostino
Italian 1557-1602
drawings: (H) $60,500

CARRACCI, Annibale
Italian c. 1560-1609
paintings: (H) $2,202,500
drawings: (L) $1,980; (H) $28,750

CARRACCI, Lodovico
Italian 1555-1619
paintings: (L) $25,300; (H) $71,500

CARRARA, Biggi Fausto
Italian 19th cent.
sculpture: (H) $805

CARRENO, Mario
Cuban/American b. 1913
paintings: (L) $4,600; (H) $354,500
drawings: (L) $3,300; (H) $44,000

CARRERE, F. Ouillon
sculpture: (L) $805; (H) $1,925

CARRICI
sculpture: (H) $4,400

CARRICK, Beverly
American 20th cent.
paintings: (H) $715

CARRICK, John Mulcaster
English ac. 1854-1878
paintings: (H) $49,500

CARRIER, Eugene
French 1849-1906
paintings: (L) $2,090; (H) $8,800

CARRIER-BELLEUSE, Albert Ernest
French 1824-1887
drawings: (H) $9,900
sculpture: (L) $550; (H) $165,000

CARRIER-BELLEUSE, Louis Robert
French 1848-1913
paintings: (L) $5,500; (H) $43,125
drawings: (H) $11,000
sculpture: (H) $3,162

CARRIER-BELLEUSE, Pierre
French 1851-1932/33
paintings: (L) $4,600; (H) $55,000
drawings: (L) $8,800; (H) $19,550

CARRIERA, Rosalba
Italian 1675-1757
drawings: (L) $20,700; (H) $51,750

CARRIERE, Alphonse
French b. 1808
paintings: (L) $2,875; (H) $17,250

CARRIERE, Eugene
French 1849-1906
paintings: (L) $2,070; (H) $31,900

CARRIGAN, William
American 1868-1939
paintings: (L) $605; (H) $1,210

CARRILLO, Lilia
b. Mexico 1929
paintings: (L) $17,250; (H) $27,600

CARRINGTON, Leonora
English b. 1917
paintings: (L) $10,350; (H) $440,000
drawings: (L) $2,200; (H) $145,500
sculpture: (L) $4,950; (H) $299,500

CARRINO, David
b. 1959
drawings: (L) $115; (H) $920

CARROL, J.C.
paintings: (L) $330; (H) $1,150

CARROLL, John
American 1892-1959
paintings: (L) $440; (H) $5,225
drawings: (L) $99; (H) $143

CARROLL, Lawrence
Australian b. 1954
paintings: (H) $7,700
sculpture: (L) $2,530; (H) $11,500

CARROLL, W.J.
British 19th/20th cent.
paintings: (L) $385; (H) $1,155
drawings: (H) $495

CARROLL, Will
American 20th cent.
paintings: (H) $690

CARROTHERS, Grace Neville
American 20th cent.
paintings: (H) $467

CARRUCI, Jacopo de
Italian 1493-1558
paintings: (H) $27,500

CARSE, Alexander
British 19th cent.
paintings: (H) $4,400

CARSTEN, Christian
sculpture: (H) $1,725

CARSTENSEN, A.
Danish b. 1844
paintings: (H) $770

CARTE, Antoine
Belgian 1886-1954
paintings: (H) $42,900

CARTER, Carol
American contemporary
drawings: (H) $460

CARTER, Charles H.
American 20th cent.
paintings: (H) $489

CARTER, Clarence Holbrook
American b. 1904
paintings: (L) $440; (H) $6,500
drawings: (L) $660; (H) $4,070

CARTER, Dennis Malone
American 1827-1881
paintings: (L) $1,430; (H) $9,900

CARTER, F.A.
American 20th cent.
paintings: (H) $1,045

CARTER, Gary
American b. 1939
paintings: (L) $1,610; (H) $17,600
drawings: (L) $275; (H) $300
sculpture: (L) $3,575; (H) $8,910

CARTER, H.M.
American 20th cent.
paintings: (H) $605

CARTER, Howard
British 1874-1939
drawings: (H) $550

CARTER, Pruett
American 1891-1955
paintings: (L) $625; (H) $10,450
drawings: (H) $715

CARTER, Richard Harry
British 1839-1911
drawings: (H) $2,300

CARTER, William Sylvester
American b. 1909
drawings: (L) $165; (H) $605

CARTIER
paintings: (H) $660

CARTIER, F.
French 19th cent.
sculpture: (H) $1,980

CARTIER, Thomas Francois
French 1879-1943
sculpture: (L) $357; (H) $2,300

CARTIER, Victor Emile
French 1811-1866
paintings: (H) $2,530

CARTLEDGE, William, Ned
b. 1916
sculpture: (H) $687

CARTON, Norman
paintings: (L) $357; (H) $550

CARTWRIGHT, Isabel Branson
American b. 1885
paintings: (L) $1,870; (H) $3,520

CARUSO, Bruno
b. 1927
paintings: (H) $825

CARUSO, Enrico
Italian 1873-1921
drawings: (H) $990

CARVIN, Louis Albert
sculpture: (H) $660

CARY, William de la Montagne
American 1840-1922
paintings: (L) $1,045; (H) $5,750

CARZAIN, Alexandre
French d. 1909
paintings: (H) $770

CARZOU, Jean
French b. 1907
paintings: (L) $550; (H) $5,520
drawings: (L) $1,210; (H) $3,740

CASA
Italian 19th cent.
drawings: (H) $460

CASA, G.
Italian 19th cent.
paintings: (H) $2,750

CASAGEMAS, Carlos
1881-1901
drawings: (H) $1,380

CASALI, Andrea
Italian 1720/24-after 1783
paintings: (L) $20,900; (H) $30,800

CASANODAY, Arcadio
Spanish 19th cent.
paintings: (H) $10,350

CASANOVA, Francesco Giuseppe
Italian 1727-1802
paintings: (L) $17,250; (H) $18,400
drawings: (L) $2,860; (H) $6,050

CASANOVA Y ESTORACH
paintings: (H) $2,750

CASANOVAS, Enrique
Spanish 19th cent.
paintings: (H) $6,600

CASAS, Ramon
Spanish b. 1866
paintings: (H) $12,650
drawings: (H) $9,200

CASCELLA, Andrea
sculpture: (H) $1,760

CASCELLA, Michele
Italian 1892-1989
paintings: (L) $4,025; (H) $17,600
drawings: (L) $1,955; (H) $3,738

CASCELLA, Pietro
Italian b. 1921
sculpture: (H) $1,150

CASCIARO, Giuseppe
Italian 1863-1945
paintings: (L) $3,335; (H) $7,700
drawings: (L) $1,980; (H) $1,980

CASE, Edmund E.
American 1844-1919
paintings: (H) $633

CASE, Frank E.
American 20th cent.
paintings: (L) $247; (H) $715

CASE, Richard
b. 1913
paintings: (H) $1,870

CASEARO, Guido
Italian 19th/20th cent.
paintings: (H) $770

CASENTINO, Jacopo del
ac. 1339; d. 1349/58
paintings: (L) $46,200; (H) $426,000

CASER, Ettore
Italian/American 1880-1944
paintings: (L) $247; (H) $2,760

CASEY, Edward F.
b. 1897
paintings: (H) $660

CASEY, Richard
drawings: (L) $138; (H) $468

CASH, Herbert
19th/20th cent.
paintings: (H) $495

CASH, Sydney
sculpture: (H) $6,600

CASHWAN, Samuel Adolph
Russian/American b. 1900
sculpture: (H) $1,035

CASILEAR, John William
American 1811-1893
paintings: (L) $770; (H) $24,200
drawings: (L) $115; (H) $2,365

CASIMIR, Laurent
Haitian b. 1924/28
paintings: (L) $220; (H) $660

CASINI, Domenico and Valore,
studio of
Italian 17th cent.
paintings: (H) $6,900

CASISSA, Nicola
Italian d. 1731
paintings: (L) $24,150; (H) $40,250

CASNELLI, Victor
American 1867/78-1961
drawings: (L) $577; (H) $2,750

CASORATI, Felice
Italian 1886-1963
paintings: (H) $63,250

CASORATI, V.P. de
Italian 19th cent.
paintings: (H) $7,700

CASS, E.G.
American 19th cent.
paintings: (H) $550

CASS, George Nelson
American 1831-1882
paintings: (L) $825; (H) $3,520
drawings: (H) $385

CASSANA, Giovanni Agostino
1658-c. 1720
paintings: (H) $9,900

CASSANDRE, Adolphe MOURON
French 1901-1968
drawings: (H) $7,700

CASSANOVA, R.
European 19th cent.
paintings: (H) $825

CASSARD, Pierre Leon
French 19th/20th cent.
paintings: (L) $3,450; (H) $10,350

CASSATT, Mary
American 1844-1926
paintings: (L) $46,000; (H) $81,400
drawings: (L) $220; (H) $2,530,000

CASSELL, F.W.
Continental 19th cent.
paintings: (H) $880

CASSELLI, Henry
American b. 1946
paintings: (H) $330
drawings: (L) $468; (H) $5,500

CASSIDY, Ira Diamond Gerald
American 1879-1934
paintings: (L) $288; (H) $2,750
drawings: (L) $247; (H) $8,140

CASSIERS, Henry
Belgian 1858-1944
drawings: (L) $495; (H) $605

CASSIGNEUL, Jean Pierre
French b. 1935
paintings: (L) $9,350; (H) $143,000
drawings: (L) $9,900; (H) $9,900

CASSINARI, Bruno
Italian b. 1912
paintings: (H) $29,900

CASSON, Alfred Joseph
Canadian 1898-1992
paintings: (L) $5,500; (H) $123,200
drawings: (L) $2,420; (H) $16,500

CASTA, Joachim
French b. 1888
sculpture: (H) $14,300

CASTAGNETO, Giovanni
b. Brazil 1851-1900
paintings: (H) $8,800

CASTAGNETTO
Continental School 19th cent.
paintings: (H) $990

CASTAGNINO, Juan Carlos
Argentinean b. 1908
paintings: (H) $17,250

CASTAGNOLA, Gabriele
Italian 1828-1883
paintings: (L) $2,090; (H) $9,900

CASTAIGNE, Carlos
Argentinean 19th/20th cent.
paintings: (H) $550

CASTAIGNE, J. Andre
French 1860-1930
paintings: (L) $495; (H) $2,750
drawings: (H) $660

CASTAN, Pierre Jean Edmond
French b. 1817
paintings: (L) $2,750; (H) $15,400

CASTANEDA, Alfredo
Mexican b. 1938
paintings: (L) $6,325; (H) $132,000
drawings: (L) $2,530; (H) $40,250

CASTANEDA, Felipe
b. Mexico 1933
sculpture: (L) $4,600; (H) $19,550

CASTEELS, Pauwel
17th cent.
paintings: (H) $7,762

CASTEELS, Pieter
1684-1749
paintings: (L) $12,100; (H) $41,800

CASTEGNARO, Felice
Italian b. 1872
paintings: (H) $1,870

CASTEL, Anthony
Continental School 19th cent.
paintings: (H) $5,520

CASTEL, Moishe
Israeli 1909-1992
paintings: (L) $4,830; (H) $25,300

CASTELEIN, Ernest
British 20th cent.
paintings: (H) $880

CASTELL, Anton
German 1810-1867
paintings: (H) $4,025

CASTELLANOS, Carlos Alberto
1881-1945
paintings: (L) $3,738; (H) $11,500

CASTELLI, A.
drawings: (H) $925

CASTELLI, Luciano
Italian/Swiss b. 1951
paintings: (L) $3,025; (H) $13,200

CASTELLO, Battista, called Il
Genovese
Italian c. 1545-1639
paintings: (H) $71,500
drawings: (H) $12,650

CASTELLO, Francesco da
b. 1540
paintings: (H) $25,300

CASTELLO, Valerio
Italian 1624-1659
paintings: (H) $11,500

CASTELLON, Federico
Spanish/American 1914-1971
paintings: (L) $1,870; (H) $8,140
drawings: (L) $138; (H) $2,640

CASTELLUCCI, E.
Italian 19th cent.
sculpture: (H) $770

CASTELUCHO, Claudio
Spanish 1870-1927
paintings: (H) $8,800

CASTENEDA, Alfredo
Mexican b. 1938
drawings: (H) $5,980

CASTENEDA, Felipe
Mexican b. 1933
sculpture: (L) $5,462; (H) $6,600

CASTEX-DEGRANGE, Adolphe Louis
French b. 1840
paintings: (L) $13,800; (H) $17,600

CASTIGLIONE, Francesco
Italian d. 1716
paintings: (H) $8,625

CASTIGLIONE, Giovanni Benedetto
Italian 1616-1665
paintings: (L) $13,800; (H) $16,500
drawings: (H) $8,050

CASTIGLIONE, Giuseppe
Italian 1829-1908
paintings: (L) $2,200; (H) $28,750

CASTILLO, Jorge
Spanish b. 1933
paintings: (L) $1,840; (H) $24,200
drawings: (H) $1,840

CASTILLO Y SAAVEDRA, Antonio
del
Spanish 1616-1668
paintings: (H) $90,500
drawings: (H) $2,200

CASTLE, Wendell
American b. 1932
sculpture: (L) $2,875; (H) $85,250

CASTLE-KEITH, W.
American 20th cent.
paintings: (H) $660

CASTLEDEN, George F.
American 1869-1945
paintings: (L) $247; (H) $1,045

CASTOLDI, B.
paintings: (H) $990

CASTRES, Edouard
Swiss 1838-1902
paintings: (L) $4,400; (H) $6,325

CASTRO, Bernardo Simonet
Spanish b. 1914
paintings: (L) $660; (H) $3,740

CASTRO, Gabriel Henriques de
Dutch 1808-1853
paintings: (H) $1,540

CASTRO, Humberto
paintings: (H) $8,800

CASTRO, M.
paintings: (H) $550

CASTRO Y VELASCO, Antonio
Aclisclo Don Palomino de
1655-1726
paintings: (H) $17,600

CASWALL, Anna Maria
British ac. 1870-1874
paintings: (H) $715

CATALA, Luis Alvarez
Spanish 1836-1901
paintings: (L) $9,900; (H) $104,500
drawings: (H) $1,980

CATALAN, Ramos
Chilean 20th cent.
paintings: (L) $110; (H) $1,380

CATANO, F.
Italian 19th cent.
paintings: (H) $1,100
drawings: (L) $192; (H) $357

CATENA, Vincenzo di BIAGIO
Italian ac. 1506-1531
paintings: (H) $206,000

CATHCART, A.
paintings: (H) $770

CATHELIN, Bernard
French b. 1920
paintings: (L) $3,450; (H) $32,200

CATHELL, Edna S.
American b. 1867
paintings: (H) $1,045

CATHROW, Anne
British 19th cent.
paintings: (H) $1,650

CATLIN, George
American 1796-1872
paintings: (L) $115; (H) $20,700
drawings: (L) $1,320; (H) $27,500

CATS, Jacob
Dutch 1741-1799
drawings: (L) $10,350; (H) $32,200

CATTAN, G.
English 19th cent.
paintings: (H) $523

CATTANEO, Amanzio
Italian b. 1828
paintings: (L) $2,200; (H) $2,990

CATTI, Michele
Italian b. 1855
paintings: (L) $495; (H) $3,300

CATTIER, Armand Pierre
French 1830-1892
sculpture: (H) $660

CATTON, George
paintings: (H) $880

CAUCHOIS, Eugene Henri
French 1850-1911
paintings: (L) $1,100; (H) $30,800

CAUER, R.
sculpture: (H) $1,320

CAULA, Sigismondo
1637-after 1713
drawings: (H) $4,950

CAULAERT, J.D. van
Dutch ac. 1920-1940
paintings: (L) $247; (H) $9,200

CAULDWELL, Leslie Giffen
American 1861-1941
drawings: (H) $550

CAULLERY, Louis de
Flemish 16th/17th cent.
paintings: (H) $66,000

CAUSSE, Cadet Julien
French ac. 1890-1914
sculpture: (L) $2,760; (H) $19,550

CAUSSE, Julien
French 19th cent.
sculpture: (H) $19,550

CAVAILLES, Jules
French 1901-1977
paintings: (L) $2,760; (H) $19,800

CAVALERI, Lodovico
Italian 1867-1942
paintings: (H) $2,200

CAVALIER D'ARPINO, Giuseppe
CESARI
Italian 1560/68-1640
paintings: (L) $37,400; (H) $82,250
drawings: (L) $6,613; (H) $71,500

CAVALIERE, Alik
20th cent.
sculpture: (L) $990; (H) $1,725

CAVALIERI, Luigi
Italian 19th cent.
paintings: (H) $4,400

CAVALLINO, Bernardo
Italian 1616-1656/58
paintings: (H) $36,800

CAVALLON, Giorgio
American b. 1904
paintings: (L) $6,875; (H) $79,200
drawings: (H) $4,600

CAVALLUCCI, Antonio
Italian 1752-1795
paintings: (H) $40,250

CAVANAUGH, Robert M.
American
sculpture: (H) $750

CAVE, Jules Cyrille
French b. 1859
paintings: (H) $29,700

CAVEDONE, Giacomo
Italian 1577-1660
paintings: (H) $7,150
drawings: (L) $3,850; (H) $16,100

CAVIEDES, Hipolito Hidalgo de
Spanish b. 1902
paintings: (L) $715; (H) $935
drawings: (L) $330; (H) $1,210

CAVIOLI
sculpture: (H) $2,070

CAWL, Edith
19th cent.
paintings: (H) $715

CAWTHORN, Christopher
paintings: (L) $23; (H) $1,093

CAWTHORNE, Neil
English b. 1936
paintings: (L) $1,320; (H) $8,050

CAZES, Romain
French 1810-1881
drawings: (H) $57,750

CAZIN, Jean Charles
French 1841-1901
paintings: (L) $275; (H) $28,600
drawings: (H) $440

CECCARELLI, Naddo
Italian ac. 1330-1350
paintings: (H) $178,500

CECCHI, Adriano
Italian b. 1850
paintings: (L) $880; (H) $5,250
drawings: (H) $1,650

CECCOBELLI, Bruno
Italian b. 1952
paintings: (H) $11,000
drawings: (L) $2,750; (H) $9,900
sculpture: (L) $4,025; (H) $4,180

CECCONI, Alberto
Italian b. 1897
paintings: (H) $2,090

CECCONI, Eugenio
Italian 1842-1903
paintings: (H) $2,530

CECCONI, Lorenzo
Italian b. 1867
paintings: (H) $22,000

CECIONI, Adriano
Italian 1838-1886
sculpture: (L) $825; (H) $5,280

CEDER, O.
paintings: (H) $715

CEDERBERG, S.
19th cent.
paintings: (L) $990; (H) $1,045

CEDERQUIST, John
contemporary
sculpture: (H) $4,600

CEDERSTROM, Baron Ture Nikolaus
de
Swedish 1843-1924
paintings: (L) $3,680; (H) $11,500

CEDOR, Dieudonne
Haitian b. 1925
paintings: (L) $1,650; (H) $5,750

CEDRO, A.
paintings: (L) $1,540; (H) $5,280

CEFALY, Andre
Italian 20th cent.
paintings: (H) $880

CEI, Cipriano
Italian 1864-1922
paintings: (H) $1,650

CELEBRANO, Francesco
Italian 1729-1814
paintings: (H) $11,500

CELENTANO, Daniel Ralph
American 1902-1980
paintings: (L) $288; (H) $11,500

CELESTI, Andrea
Italian 1637-1706
paintings: (H) $8,250

CELIS, Perez
Argentinean b. 1939
paintings: (L) $3,300; (H) $8,800

CELMINS, Vija
American b. Latvia 1939
drawings: (H) $23,000

CELOMMI, Pasquale
Italian 1851-1928
paintings: (H) $8,250

CELOMMI, Raffaello
Italian b. 1883
paintings: (L) $1,320; (H) $5,500

CELONI, A.
Continental 19th cent.
paintings: (L) $1,650; (H) $3,080

CELOS, Julien
Belgian b. 1884
paintings: (H) $1,705
drawings: (H) $495

CEMIN, Saint Clair
American b. 1951
drawings: (L) $550; (H) $1,725
sculpture: (L) $978; (H) $20,900

CENT
paintings: (H) $1,000

CENTURION, Emilio
Argentinean 1894-1970
paintings: (H) $16,500

CERAMANO, Charles Ferdinand
Belgian 1829-1909
paintings: (L) $1,650; (H) $8,250

CERCONE, Ettore
Italian 1850-1896
paintings: (H) $1,955

CERIA, Edmond
French 1884-1955
paintings: (L) $660; (H) $1,035

CERIBELLI, Cesar
b. 1841
sculpture: (L) $978; (H) $5,175

CERIEZ, Theodore
Belgian 1832-1904
paintings: (H) $9,200

CERINO, Antonio
American 1889-1983
paintings: (H) $8,360

CERRA, Mirta
drawings: (H) $2,300

CERRI, Vincenzo
Italian 1857-1903
sculpture: (H) $151,000

CERRITO, Egidio
Argentinean b. 1918
paintings: (H) $495

CERRONE, Eduardo
Italian b. 1928
paintings: (L) $412; (H) $1,430

CERUTI, Giacomo, called Il
PITOCCHETTO
Italian 1698-1767
paintings: (H) $10,925

CESAR, Cesar BALDACCINI
French b. 1921
drawings: (H) $13,200
sculpture: (L) $28,600; (H) $77,000

CESARINI, Pier Luigi
Italian b. 1933
paintings: (H) $1,870

CESENA, Linda
American 20th cent.
drawings: (H) $468

CESI, Bartolomeo
Italian 1583-1649
drawings: (H) $24,200

CEULEN, Cornelis Janson van,
studio of
Dutch 17th cent.
paintings: (H) $6,900

CEZANNE, Paul
French 1839-1906
paintings: (L) $376,500; (H) $28,602,500
drawings: (L) $990; (H) $772,500

CHAB, Victor
b. Argentina 1930
paintings: (H) $13,200

CHABAL, Pierre Adrien, called
CHABAL-DUSSURGEY
French 1819-1902
paintings: (H) $16,500

CHABANIAN, Arsene
Turkish 1864-1949
paintings: (H) $770

CHABAS, Maurice
French 1862-1947
paintings: (H) $40,250

CHABAS, Paul
French 1869-1934/37
paintings: (L) $880; (H) $3,220
drawings: (H) $2,750

CHABAUD, Auguste
French 1882-1955
paintings: (L) $5,225; (H) $10,450

CHABOD, Emile Delphes
French 19th cent.
paintings: (H) $15,400

CHABOT, Joseph
American 20th cent.
paintings: (H) $550

CHABRIER, Francois
French b. 1916
paintings: (L) $4,025; (H) $10,350

CHABRIER, George
French 19th cent.
paintings: (L) $259; (H) $2,860

CHABRY, Leonce
French 1832-1883
paintings: (H) $1,955

CHACON, F.
paintings: (H) $1,320

CHADBOURN, Alfred
paintings: (L) $604; (H) $1,380

CHADEAYNE, Robert O.
American 1897-1981
paintings: (L) $110; (H) $825
drawings: (H) $400

CHADWICK, Lynn
English b. 1914
drawings: (L) $1,430; (H) $2,200
sculpture: (L) $3,565; (H) $93,500

CHADWICK, William
American 1879-1962
paintings: (L) $115; (H) $93,500

CHAFFEE, Olive Holbert
20th cent.
paintings: (L) $248; (H) $1,320

CHAFFIN
British 19th cent.
paintings: (H) $460

CHAGALL, Marc
Russian/French 1887-1985
paintings: (L) $440; (H) $5,500,000
drawings: (L) $1,100; (H) $662,500
sculpture: (H) $5,750

CHAGNIOT, Jean Alfred
French b. 1905
paintings: (L) $385; (H) $990

CHAHINE, Edgar
French 1874-1947
drawings: (H) $4,400

CHAIGNEAU, Paul
French 19th/20th cent.
paintings: (H) $1,955

CHAILLOUX, Robert
French b. 1913
paintings: (L) $825; (H) $1,760

CHAINBOURG, Louis Nicholas
French 1831-1851
paintings: (H) $1,725

CHAKRAVATEE, Jayashree
Indian b. 1956
drawings: (H) $805

CHALE, Gertrudis
b. 1910
drawings: (L) $1,650; (H) $3,450

CHALEE, Pop, Blue Flower
1908-1993
drawings: (L) $1,760; (H) $2,070

CHALEYE, Jean
French 1878-1960
paintings: (L) $605; (H) $1,380

CHALFANT, Jefferson David
American 1856-1931
paintings: (H) $308
drawings: (L) $18,400; (H) $26,450

CHALIAPIN, Boris
Russian/American 1902-1979
paintings: (H) $518

CHALKER, James
drawings: (H) $8,050

CHALLE, Charles Michel Ange
French 1718-1778
drawings: (L) $3,575; (H) $11,000

CHALLENGER, J.D.
b. 1951
paintings: (H) $4,950

CHALMERS, Hector
British 19th/20th cent.
paintings: (H) $1,540

CHALMLEY, L.
paintings: (H) $770

CHALON, Henry Bernard
English 1770-1849
paintings: (L) $2,860; (H) $51,750

CHALON, Louis
French b. 1866
drawings: (H) $4,313
sculpture: (L) $1,045; (H) $14,850

CHAMAILLARD, Ernest Ponthier de
French 1862-1930
paintings: (H) $4,400

CHAMANT, Joseph
1699-1768
drawings: (H) $3,450

CHAMBARD, Louis Leopold
French 1811-1895
sculpture: (L) $2,185; (H) $3,163

CHAMBERLAIN, Elwynn
American b. 1928
paintings: (H) $12,650

CHAMBERLAIN, Frank Tolles
American 1873-1961
paintings: (L) $715; (H) $6,050
sculpture: (H) $3,410

CHAMBERLAIN, John
American b. 1927
paintings: (L) $2,300; (H) $9,200
drawings: (H) $77,300
sculpture: (L) $5,175; (H) $365,500

CHAMBERLAIN, Narcisse
American 20th cent.
paintings: (H) $1,430

CHAMBERLAIN, Norman Stiles
American 1887-1961
paintings: (L) $935; (H) $4,675

CHAMBERLAIN, Samuel
American 1895-1975
drawings: (L) $39; (H) $4,730

CHAMBERS
paintings: (H) $825

CHAMBERS, C. Bosseron
American b. 1883
paintings: (L) $550; (H) $4,600
drawings: (H) $220

CHAMBERS, Charles Edward
American 1883-1941
paintings: (L) $550; (H) $3,300

CHAMBERS, George
paintings: (L) $275; (H) $800

CHAMBERS, George
British 19th cent.
paintings: (H) $1,760

CHAMBERS, George W.
American 19th cent.
paintings: (H) $467

CHAMBERS, Richard Edward Elliot
Irish/American 1863-1944
drawings: (L) $66; (H) $3,850

CHAMBERS, Thomas
American c. 1808-1866
paintings: (L) $2,760; (H) $34,500

CHAMBORD, Fernand Maximilien de
French 1840-1899
paintings: (H) $3,163

CHAMP
British 19th cent.
paintings: (H) $1,150

CHAMP-RENAUD, Therese de
French ac. 1885-1895
paintings: (L) $3,738; (H) $8,050

CHAMPAGNE, Horace
b. 1937
drawings: (L) $2,200; (H) $5,500

CHAMPAIGNE, Jean Baptiste de
French 1631-1681
paintings: (L) $27,600; (H) $29,900

CHAMPAIGNE, Phillippe de
French 1602-1624
paintings: (L) $2,860; (H) $77,300

CHAMPEAUX DE LA BOULAYE,
Octave de
French 1827-1903
paintings: (H) $3,450

CHAMPIGNCIELLE
sculpture: (H) $1,100

CHAMPION, Theo
German 1887-1952
paintings: (H) $2,200

CHAMPLAIN, Duane
1889-1964
sculpture: (H) $4,370

CHAMPLIN, Ada Belle
American 1875-1950
paintings: (L) $880; (H) $1,320

CHAMPMAN, Charles Shepard
American 1879-1962
paintings: (H) $2,310

CHAMPNEY, Benjamin
American 1817-1907
paintings: (L) $330; (H) $26,400
drawings: (L) $242; (H) $1,100

CHAMPNEY, E.G.
19th/20th cent.
paintings: (H) $1,035

CHAMPNEY, James Wells
American 1843-1903
paintings: (L) $275; (H) $43,700
drawings: (L) $110; (H) $2,970

CHANCELLOR, H.S.
Irish ac. 1896-1907
paintings: (H) $715

CHANCRIN, Rene
paintings: (H) $1,380

CHANDLER
drawings: (L) $28; (H) $575

CHANDLER, Emma
drawings: (H) $920

CHANDLER, John
paintings: (L) $575; (H) $575

CHANDLER, Joseph Goodhue
American 1813-1880
paintings: (L) $1,430; (H) $34,500
drawings: (H) $357

CHANDLER, Winthrop
American 1747-1790
paintings: (L) $17,250; (H) $596,500

CHANEY, Lester Joseph
American b. Hungary 1907
paintings: (L) $55; (H) $1,035
drawings: (H) $330

CHANILINSKI, H.T.
paintings: (H) $1,045

CHANLER, Robert Winthrop
American 1872-1930
drawings: (H) $770

CHANN, George
American b. 1913
paintings: (H) $715

CHANTEAU, A.
drawings: (H) $495

CHANTRON, Alexandre Jacques
French 1842-1918
paintings: (H) $9,775

CHAPELAIN-MIDY, Roger
paintings: (L) $1,870; (H) $8,800

CHAPERON, Eugene
French b. 1857
paintings: (L) $3,300; (H) $51,750

CHAPIN, Bryant
American 1859-1927
paintings: (L) $115; (H) $10,925
drawings: (H) $357

CHAPIN, C.H.
American c. 1830-after 1874
paintings: (L) $316; (H) $2,990
drawings: (L) $715; (H) $2,200

CHAPIN, Francis
American 1899-1965
paintings: (L) $207; (H) $2,420
drawings: (L) $55; (H) $550

CHAPIN, Henry Michael Antoine
French 1833-1891
sculpture: (H) $1,430

CHAPIN, James Ormsbee
American 1887-1975
paintings: (L) $288; (H) $17,250
drawings: (H) $4,950

CHAPLAIN, Jules Clement
French 1839-1909
drawings: (H) $1,650

CHAPLIN, Arthur
French b. 1869
paintings: (L) $2,200; (H) $25,300

CHAPLIN, Charles
French 1825-1891
paintings: (L) $1,210; (H) $222,500

CHAPMAN, C.W.
American 19th cent.
paintings: (H) $2,310

CHAPMAN, Carlton T.
American 1860-1925/26
paintings: (L) $193; (H) $7,475
drawings: (L) $99; (H) $1,100

CHAPMAN, Charles Shepard
American 1879-1962
paintings: (L) $55; (H) $1,840

CHAPMAN, Conrad Wise
Italian/American 1842-1910
paintings: (L) $7,700; (H) $101,500
drawings: (L) $10,450; (H) $10,450

CHAPMAN, Frederic A.
American 1818-1891
paintings: (H) $55,000

CHAPMAN, J.
drawings: (H) $950

CHAPMAN, John Gadsby
American 1808-1889/90
paintings: (L) $990; (H) $17,825

CHAPMAN, John Linton
American 1839-1905
paintings: (L) $1,540; (H) $28,600
drawings: (L) $137; (H) $192

CHAPMAN, John Watkins
British 19th cent.
paintings: (H) $1,725

CHAPMAN, Laurena
American
drawings: (H) $13,800

CHAPMAN, Manville
paintings: (H) $4,025

CHAPMAN, William Ernest
American 1864-1945
paintings: (L) $275; (H) $2,090

CHAPOVAL, Youla
1919-1951
paintings: (H) $5,750

CHAPPEL, Alonzo
American 1828-1887
drawings: (H) $550

CHAPPEL, Alonzo
American 1828-1887
paintings: (H) $7,475

CHAPPELL, Reuben
English 1870-1940
paintings: (H) $3,565

CHAPU, Henri Michel Antoine
French 1833-1891
sculpture: (L) $374; (H) $8,625

CHAPUIS, H.
French 19th cent.
paintings: (H) $1,980

CHARAVEL, Paul
1877-1961
paintings: (H) $2,990

CHARBOT
French 19th c.
paintings: (H) $1,980

CHARCHOUNE, Serge
Russian 1888-1975
paintings: (H) $2,310
drawings: (L) $1,210; (H) $1,540

CHARD, Daniel
paintings: (H) $1,760

CHARDIET, Jose
contemporary
sculpture: (H) $4,025

CHARDIN, Gabriel Gervais
French 1814-1907
paintings: (H) $748

CHARDIN, Jean Baptiste Simeon
French 1699-1779
paintings: (L) $825; (H) $2,200,000

CHARION, Pierre
French 19th/20th cent.
paintings: (H) $3,737

CHARLAMOFF, Alexei Alexeiewitsch
Russian b. 1842/49
paintings: (L) $9,200; (H) $85,000
drawings: (L) $2,300; (H) $3,450

CHARLAP, Peter
contemporary
paintings: (H) $1,210

CHARLEMONT, Eduard
Austrian 1848-1906
paintings: (L) $2,875; (H) $26,450

CHARLEMONT, Hugo
Austrian 1850-1939
paintings: (L) $2,200; (H) $6,900
drawings: (H) $3,163

CHARLES, James
English 1851-1906
paintings: (L) $770; (H) $2,640

CHARLES, W.W.
paintings: (H) $550

CHARLES-BITTE, Emile
French 19th cent.
paintings: (L) $3,162; (H) $3,450

CHARLESTON, Elizabeth
American 20th cent.
paintings: (H) $2,090

CHARLESWORTH, Sarah
b. 1944
drawings: (H) $1,035

CHARLET, Emile
Belgian b. 1851
paintings: (L) $522; (H) $8,050

CHARLET, Frantz
Belgian 1862-1928
paintings: (L) $1,045; (H) $206,000

CHARLET, Nicholas Toussaint
French 1792-1845
paintings: (H) $550
drawings: (H) $2,200

CHARLIER, E.
French 19th cent.
paintings: (L) $1,610; (H) $1,610

CHARLIER, Jacques
ac. 18th cent.
drawings: (H) $2,530

CHARLOT, Jean
French 1898-1979
paintings: (L) $990; (H) $20,900
drawings: (L) $495; (H) $4,125

CHARLOT, Raymond
French 19th cent.
paintings: (H) $1,100

CHARLTON, John
English 1849-1910
paintings: (H) $6,900

CHARMAN, Jessie
American b. 1895
drawings: (L) $27; (H) $715

CHARMAN, Rodney
paintings: (H) $550

CHARMY, Emilie
French 1877-1974
paintings: (H) $715

CHARNAY, Armand
French 1844-1916
paintings: (H) $25,300

CHAROL, D.
sculpture: (H) $18,700

CHARPENTIER, Felix Maurice
French 1858-1924
sculpture: (L) $880; (H) $4,950

CHARPENTIER, Francois
French 19th/20th cent.
sculpture: (H) $2,530

CHARPENTIER, Georges
b. 1937
sculpture: (H) $1,840

CHARPENTIER, Georges
French 19th cent.
paintings: (L) $357; (H) $14,300

CHARPIN, Albert
French 1842-1924
paintings: (L) $715; (H) $1,045

CHARRAY, Edouard
French 19th/20th cent.
paintings: (H) $1,320

CHARRETON, Victor Leon Jean Pierre
French 1864-1936
paintings: (L) $8,050; (H) $49,500

CHARTON, Ernesto
b. France 1815 d. 1877
paintings: (H) $46,200

CHARTRAN, Theobold
French 1849-1907
paintings: (H) $2,300

CHARTRAND, Augusto
Cuban ac. c. 1850-1899
paintings: (L) $4,025; (H) $28,750

CHARTRAND, Esteban
Cuban 1824-1884
paintings: (L) $4,620; (H) $64,100

CHASE, Adelaide Cole
American 1868-1944
paintings: (L) $770; (H) $5,175
drawings: (L) $748; (H) $1,595

CHASE, Edmund E.
American 1840-1919
paintings: (H) $715

CHASE, Edward Leigh
1884-1965
drawings: (H) $1,210

CHASE, Frank Swift
American 1886-1958
paintings: (L) $316; (H) $4,950

CHASE, Gertrude
American 20th cent.
paintings: (H) $990

CHASE, Henry, called Harry
American 1853-1889
paintings: (L) $193; (H) $11,000

CHASE, Louisa
American b. Panama 1951
paintings: (L) $825; (H) $8,050

CHASE, Powell
British ac. 1893-1908
paintings: (H) $605

CHASE, Susan Miller
American 20th cent.
paintings: (L) $385; (H) $3,575
drawings: (H) $467

CHASE, William Merritt
American 1849-1916
paintings: (L) $3,080; (H) $2,422,500
drawings: (L) $1,150; (H) $3,962,500

CHASE, William Merritt and Irving R.
WILES
American 19th cent.
paintings: (H) $28,750

CHASHNIK, Ilya Grigorevich
Russian 1902-1929
drawings: (H) $20,700

CHASSERIAU, Theodore
French 1819-1856
paintings: (H) $275,000

CHASTAIN
paintings: (H) $605

CHAT, A.A.
American ac. 1890-1910
paintings: (H) $2,750

CHATAUD, Marc Alfred
French b. 1833
paintings: (H) $3,575

CHATEAUX, R***
French 19th cent.
paintings: (H) $4,400

CHATEIGNON, Ernest
French ac. 19th cent.
paintings: (L) $1,870; (H) $4,840

CHATELAIN, James
American b. 1947
paintings: (L) $550; (H) $880

CHATELET, Claude Louis
French 1753-1794/95
drawings: (L) $1,955; (H) $10,350

CHATFORD, Chester H.
American
paintings: (H) $660

CHATHAM, Russell
b. 1940
drawings: (H) $880

CHATILLON, Charles de
1777-1844
paintings: (H) $7,150

CHATTERTON, Clarence K.
American 1880-1973
paintings: (L) $522; (H) $11,500
drawings: (L) $495; (H) $3,300

CHAUD (?), R.
sculpture: (H) $29,000

CHAUDET, Antoine Denis
sculpture: (H) $1,035

CHAUVEAU, Marguerite
American 19th cent.
paintings: (H) $550

CHAUVEL, Georges
French 1886-1962
sculpture: (L) $1,320; (H) $3,450

CHAVES, J.
paintings: (H) $1,320

CHAVES Y ORTIZ, Jose
German 19th cent.
paintings: (H) $9,075

CHAVET, Victor Joseph
French b. 1822
paintings: (L) $2,100; (H) $8,625

CHAVEZ, Eduardo
b. 1917
paintings: (H) $700

CHAVEZ, Gerardo
b. Peru 1937
paintings: (H) $5,280
drawings: (H) $6,900

CHAVEZ, Lorenzo
drawings: (L) $880; (H) $1,700

CHAVEZ MORADO, Jose
b. Mexico 1909
paintings: (L) $9,900; (H) $18,400

CHAVEZ Y ARTIZ, Jose de
Spanish 1839-1903
paintings: (H) $4,025

CHE, Chuang
paintings: (H) $920
drawings: (H) $1,430

CHECA Y SANZ, Ulpiano
Spanish 1860-1916
paintings: (L) $11,500; (H) $173,000

CHECA(?)
sculpture: (H) $1,320

CHEE, Robert
Native American 1928-1971
drawings: (L) $55; (H) $1,100

CHEEK, C.R.
American
paintings: (H) $1,350

CHEERE, John
sculpture: (H) $4,025

CHEEVER, W.H.
paintings: (H) $495

CHELAZZI, Tito
Italian 1834-1892
paintings: (H) $1,540

CHELMINSKI, Jan van
Polish 1851-1925
paintings: (L) $920; (H) $18,400
drawings: (H) $1,540

CHEMETOV, Boris
1908-1982
paintings: (L) $1,980; (H) $4,600

CHEMIAKIN, Mikhail
Russian b. 1943
paintings: (H) $2,200
drawings: (L) $770; (H) $2,640

CHEMIELINSKI, Wladyslaw
Polish b. 1895
paintings: (L) $412; (H) $5,750

CHEMIN, Joseph Victor
French 1825-1901
sculpture: (L) $385; (H) $2,200

CHEN, Hilo
American b. China 1942
paintings: (L) $978; (H) $7,475

CHENEY
paintings: (H) $770

CHENEY, Harold W.
American
paintings: (L) $110; (H) $550

CHENEY, Mary
paintings: (H) $1,430

CHENEY, Russell
American 1881-1945
paintings: (L) $275; (H) $2,090

CHENOWITH, Jane
paintings: (H) $550

CHEONG, Hung
Japanese
paintings: (H) $550

CHERC
sculpture: (H) $1,760

CHEREPOV, George
American 20th cent.
paintings: (H) $825

CHERET, Gustave Joseph
French 1838-1894
sculpture: (H) $2,070

CHERET, Jules
French 1836-1932
paintings: (L) $2,750; (H) $24,150
drawings: (L) $373; (H) $2,875

CHERICI, Professor M.
sculpture: (H) $825

CHERKES, Constantine
American b. 1919
paintings: (H) $1,870

CHERNEY, Marvin
American 1925-1967
paintings: (L) $83; (H) $1,980
drawings: (L) $65; (H) $110

CHERRY, Emma R.
paintings: (H) $3,520

CHERRY, Kathryn
American 1880-1931
paintings: (L) $1,045; (H) $4,025

CHERRY, Kerry
American b. 1880
paintings: (H) $633

CHERUBINI, Carlo
Italian b. 1897
paintings: (L) $1,100; (H) $1,980

CHERY, Jean Rene
paintings: (H) $715

CHESNEY, Clara Mac
American 1860-1928
paintings: (H) $825

CHESTER, George
paintings: (H) $1,980

CHESTNUT, Billy Dohlman
American 20th cent.
drawings: (H) $2,090

CHETCUTI, John
1900-1976
paintings: (H) $55
drawings: (L) $88; (H) $742

CHEVALIER, Peter
b. 1953
paintings: (L) $1,265; (H) $6,600

CHEVIOT, Lilian
English exhib. 1894-1911
paintings: (H) $17,250

CHEVRE, Paul
sculpture: (H) $1,650

CHEW, Richard
American 20th cent.
paintings: (L) $1,555; (H) $3,080

CHHABDA, Bal
Indian b. 1923
paintings: (H) $3,162

CHHABDA, Jeet
Indian contemporary
drawings: (L) $690; (H) $1,150

CHI, Chen
Chinese/American b. 1912
drawings: (L) $330; (H) $8,800

CHIA, Sandro
Italian b. 1946
paintings: (L) $9,900; (H) $101,500
drawings: (L) $1,265; (H) $43,125
sculpture: (L) $21,850; (H) $121,000

CHIALIVA, Luigi
Swiss/Italian 1842-1914
paintings: (L) $23,000; (H) $25,300

CHIAPORY, Bernard Charles
French ac. 1851-1859
drawings: (L) $4,840; (H) $6,600

CHIAPPARELLI, P.
sculpture: (H) $1,540

CHIARI, Giuseppe
Italian 1654-1727
paintings: (H) $22,000

CHICHESTER, Cecil
American b. 1891
paintings: (L) $110; (H) $2,645

CHIDSEY, Jane
American 20th cent.
paintings: (H) $143
drawings: (H) $495

CHIERICI, Gaetano
Italian 1838-1920
paintings: (L) $17,250; (H) $242,000

CHIFFLART, Nicolas Francois
French 1825-1901
paintings: (H) $4,025
drawings: (H) $1,610

CHIGOT, Eugene Henri Alexandre
French 1860-1927
paintings: (H) $7,475

CHIH, Ching Er
Chinese 1913-1972
drawings: (H) $1,540

CHIHULY, Dale
American b. 1941
sculpture: (L) $660; (H) $48,875

CHILD, J. Theo
paintings: (H) $2,750

CHILDE, Elias
paintings: (H) $660

CHILDE, J.W.
English 19th cent.
drawings: (H) $1,430

CHILLIDA, Eduardo
Spanish b. 1924
drawings: (L) $7,150; (H) $14,300
sculpture: (L) $37,950; (H) $253,000

CHILONE, Vincenzo
Italian 1758-1839
paintings: (H) $74,000

CHILVERS, Thomas H.
American 19th cent.
paintings: (H) $1,725

CHIMLINSKY
paintings: (H) $748

CHINNERY, George
British 1748-1847
paintings: (L) $5,170; (H) $115,500
drawings: (L) $1,265; (H) $3,080

CHINTREUIL, Antoine
French 1814/16-1873
paintings: (L) $2,070; (H) $11,500

Home Page on the Web

Glass blowing is an old European craft, but the American art glass movement, glass sculpture as an art form, is a 20th-century phenomenon. The concept that an individual could blow glass alone and that glass could be a valid material for the artist was new to this country. Previously all art glass in the United States had been produced in factories. The renaissance of glass blowing began with the 1962 glass workshop led by Harvey Littleton (b. 1921) at the Toledo Museum of Art. Littleton was also a teacher at the University of Wisconsin, and from 1964 to 1967 he had a glass studio in Madison. One of Littleton's students was Dale Chihuly (b. 1941). Chihuly had been born in Tacoma, Washington, and after working and studying interior design in Seattle, he began to work with Littleton in Wisconsin. He received a master of science degree in sculpture from the University of Wisconsin and a fine arts degree from the Rhode Island School of Design. He continued his studies in Europe and studied glass blowing in Murano, Italy, at the Venini Fabrica. A Fulbright fellowship, the first to be awarded to an American glass artist, allowed him to continue his studies abroad. Chihuly returned to the Seattle area, where he founded the Pilchuck Glass School and opened a studio. The studio is large, 25,000 square feet, room enough to accommodate his team of collaborators, gaffers, and assistants. Chihuly has relied upon his assistants since a 1976 automobile accident blinded him in one eye and left him with no depth perception. In 1986 he had a one-man show at the Louvre, a rare achievement for an American artist. During the late 1980s and 1990s Chihuly began to create large-scale installations. In February 1996 a series of Chihuly's installations was exhibited at the Baltimore Museum of Art, and in the fall of 1996 Chihuly is planning a large-scale installation over the canals of Venice. The name Chihuly is synonymous with the art-glass movement. His works are in the White House and featured at the Smithsonian. He even has a home page on the web (http://www.chihuly.com). His works appear frequently at auction, either in the rare art glass catalog or in sales of 20th century decorative works of art. Most of Chihuly's works offered at auction are individual pieces that realize from $2,000 to $18,000. The record auction price for a work by Chihuly was the $48,875 paid for an installation in February 1991. *Ikebana*, a blown-glass flower in a vase, realized $13,800 when it sold at Sotheby's in March 1995. (Dale Chihuly, *Ikebana*, blown glass, height 38⅞ inches, Sotheby New York, March 18, 1995, $13,800)

CHIPARUS, Demetre H.
Romanian 1888-1950
sculpture: (L) $605; (H) $151,000

CHIRIACKA, Ernest
American b. 1920
paintings: (L) $302; (H) $4,950

CHIRICO, Giacomo de
Italian 1845-1884
paintings: (H) $33,000

CHIRICO, Giorgio de
Italian 1888-1978
paintings: (L) $19,800; (H) $2,420,000
drawings: (L) $7,187; (H) $107,000
sculpture: (L) $13,200; (H) $115,500

CHIRICO, L.
Italian 19th cent.
paintings: (H) $16,500

CHITTENDEN, Alice B.
American 1860-1934
paintings: (L) $440; (H) $16,500
drawings: (H) $110

CHIU, Teng Hiok
Chinese/American b. 1903
paintings: (L) $110; (H) $770

CHIURAZZI, Professor
Italian 19th cent.
sculpture: (H) $43,125

CHIVERS, H.C.
British 19th/20th cent.
paintings: (L) $495; (H) $880

CHLEWBOWSKI, Stanislaus von
Polish 1835-1884
paintings: (L) $9,900; (H) $46,000

CHMIELINSKI, Jean
paintings: (H) $1,210

CHOCARNE-MOREAU, Paul Charles
French 1855-1931
paintings: (L) $5,463; (H) $85,000

CHODOWIECKI, Daniel Nicolas
Polish/German 1726-1801
drawings: (H) $12,075

CHOFFARD, Pierre Phillipe
1730-1809
drawings: (H) $715

CHOHIN, F.
sculpture: (H) $2,310

CHOMAS, M. de
French 19th cent.
sculpture: (H) $4,290

CHOMENKO, Mary
American 20th cent.
sculpture: (H) $4,675

CHONG NETO, Manuel
paintings: (H) $4,950

CHOPIN, C.
paintings: (H) $1,650

CHOPIN, F.
19th/20th cent.
sculpture: (H) $935

CHOPPING, Richard
20th cent.
paintings: (H) $2,300

CHOQUET, Rene
French 19th/20th cent.
paintings: (H) $1,100

CHOUBRAC, Alfred
French 1853-1902
paintings: (H) $11,000

CHOUINARD, Nelbert Murphy
American 1879-1969
paintings: (L) $374; (H) $605

CHOUKHAIEFF, Vassili Ivanovitch
paintings: (H) $8,050

CHOULTSE, Ivan F.
Russian ac. 1880-1920
paintings: (L) $575; (H) $17,250

CHOWDHURY, Jogen
Indian b. 1939
drawings: (L) $1,265; (H) $4,600

CHRETIEN, Eugene Ernest
French late 19th cent.
sculpture: (L) $2,090; (H) $2,990

CHRETIEN, Rene Louis
French 1867-1942
paintings: (H) $1,210

CHRIST, Pieter Casper
Dutch b. 1822
paintings: (H) $1,430

CHRISTENBERRY, William
American contemporary
sculpture: (L) $4,125; (H) $4,675

CHRISTENSEN, Anthonore
Danish 1849-1926
paintings: (H) $28,750

CHRISTENSEN, Dan
American b. 1942
paintings: (L) $575; (H) $6,600

CHRISTENSEN, Florence
American 19th/20th cent.
paintings: (H) $2,640

CHRISTENSEN, Ted
American b. 1911
paintings: (L) $99; (H) $1,265

CHRISTIAN
Spain
paintings: (H) $550

CHRISTIAN-HOWARD, Anthony
20th cent.
paintings: (L) $330; (H) $2,300

CHRISTIANSEN, Nils Hans
Danish 1876-1903
paintings: (L) $358; (H) $2,475

CHRISTIANSEN, Rasmus
Danish 1863-1940
paintings: (H) $1,540

CHRISTIE, James Elder
British 1847-1914
paintings: (L) $920; (H) $1,100
drawings: (H) $1,210

CHRISTIE, Keith
20th cent.
sculpture: (H) $1,210

CHRISTIE, Reid
paintings: (L) $3,300; (H) $3,500

CHRISTIE, Robert E., Bob
paintings: (H) $2,090

CHRISTMAN, Reid
American 20th cent.
paintings: (H) $2,200

CHRISTMAS, Ernst William
American 1856-1918
paintings: (H) $1,045

CHRISTO
Bulgarian/American b. 1935
paintings: (L) $770; (H) $55,000
drawings: (L) $5,750; (H) $220,000
sculpture: (L) $920; (H) $68,500

CHRISTOPHE
sculpture: (L) $605; (H) $1,760

CHRISTY, F. Earl
b. 1883
drawings: (L) $1,495; (H) $3,850

CHRISTY, Howard Chandler
American 1873-1952
paintings: (L) $110; (H) $46,750
drawings: (L) $330; (H) $20,900

CHRYSSA
Greek/American b. 1933
drawings: (H) $990
sculpture: (H) $11,000

CHRYSTIE, Margaret H.
American b. 1895
paintings: (H) $495

CHUCK JONES PRODUCTIONS
drawings: (H) $1,380

CHUMLEY, John
American 1928-1984
paintings: (H) $1,980
drawings: (H) $5,463

CHUMPREY, J. Wills
19th/20th cent.
drawings: (H) $523

CHUN, Lau
Hawaiian contemporary
paintings: (H) $880

CHUNG, He
Chinese mid 19th cent.
paintings: (H) $7,700

CHURCH, F.J.
American 19th/20th cent.
drawings: (H) $2,750

CHURCH, Frederic Edwin
American 1826-1900
paintings: (L) $660; (H) $159,500

CHURCH, Frederick Stuart
American 1842-1924
paintings: (L) $550; (H) $13,800
drawings: (L) $66; (H) $2,860

CHURCHILL, William Worcester
American 1858-1926
paintings: (L) $880; (H) $32,200

CHUTEAU, Jacqueline
paintings: (L) $288; (H) $690

CHWALA, Adolf
Czechoslovakian 1836-1900
paintings: (L) $1,100; (H) $5,500

CHYUSI, Shokaken
sculpture: (H) $17,250

CIAMPANTI, Ansano
early 16th cent.
paintings: (H) $38,500

CIAN, Fernand
early 20th cent.
sculpture: (H) $1,760

CIAPPA, Carlo
Italian 19th cent.
paintings: (L) $403; (H) $3,080

CIAPPA, F.A.
Italian 19th cent.
paintings: (H) $3,300

CIAPPA, J.
ac. c. 1900
paintings: (H) $660

CIAPPA, V.
Italian 19th cent.
paintings: (L) $33; (H) $660

CIARDI, Beppe
Italian 1875-1932
paintings: (L) $1,540; (H) $71,500

CIARDI, Emma
Italian 1879-1933
paintings: (L) $1,380; (H) $60,250

CIARDI, Guglielmo
Italian 1842-1917
paintings: (L) $13,200; (H) $90,500

CIARLO, Franco
b. 1939
paintings: (H) $2,070

CICERI, Eugene
French 1813-1890
paintings: (L) $1,150; (H) $5,520
drawings: (L) $1,320; (H) $5,175

CIENFUEGOS, Gonzalo
b. 1949
paintings: (L) $13,800; (H) $14,950

CIGNAROLI, Gianbettino
Italian 1706-1770
paintings: (L) $33,000; (H) $66,000

CIKOVSKY, Nicolai
Russian/American 1894-1984
paintings: (L) $165; (H) $2,530
drawings: (L) $200; (H) $522

CILFONE, Gianni
American b. 1908
paintings: (L) $66; (H) $1,210

CILLETI, M.
Italian 20th cent.
paintings: (H) $880

CIMA, Luiga
Italian 1860-1938
paintings: (H) $10,350

CIMA DA CONEGLIANO, Giovanni
Battista
15th/16th cent.
paintings: (H) $33,000

CIMAROLI, Giambattista, and studio
18th cent.
paintings: (H) $33,000

CIMAROLI, Gianbattista
Italian ac. c. 1700-1753
paintings: (L) $112,500; (H) $319,000

CIMIOTTI, Gustave
American 1875-after 1929
paintings: (L) $121; (H) $1,955

CINA, Theodore van
20th cent.
paintings: (H) $605

CIOBION
sculpture: (H) $1,705

CIOCI, Antonio
d. 1792
paintings: (H) $167,500

CIOFFI
paintings: (H) $495

CIPOLLA, Fabio
Italian b. 1854
paintings: (L) $1,540; (H) $16,100
drawings: (H) $3,575

CIPPER, Giacomo Francesco, called Il
Todeschini
Italian c. 1670-1738
paintings: (H) $11,500

CIPRIANA, Giovanni-Pinotti
French early 20th cent.
sculpture: (H) $1,100

CIPRIANI
sculpture: (H) $483

CIPRIANI, A.
Italian 19th cent.
sculpture: (L) $990; (H) $170,500

CIPRIANI, C.
Italian 19th cent.
sculpture: (L) $495; (H) $920

CIPRIANI, C.
Italian 19th/20th cent.
sculpture: (H) $495

CIPRIANI, Giovanni Battista
Italian 1727-1785/90
drawings: (L) $385; (H) $2,760

CIPRIANI, Nazzareno
Italian b. 1843
paintings: (L) $990; (H) $11,500
drawings: (H) $2,875

CIRIELLO, Averardo
drawings: (H) $2,070

CIRINO, Antonio
American 1889-1983
paintings: (L) $358; (H) $9,900
drawings: (L) $165; (H) $522

CIRY, Michel
French b. 1919
paintings: (L) $1,380; (H) $1,495
drawings: (H) $1,650

CITRON, Minna
American b. 1896
paintings: (L) $716; (H) $2,300

CITTADINI, Pier Francesco
1616-1681
paintings: (H) $46,000

CLAD, ***
paintings: (L) $550; (H) $935

CLAEISSINS, Anthonie
Flemish c. 1536-1613
paintings: (H) $71,500

CLAES, Constant Guillaume
Belgian 1826-1905
paintings: (L) $1,760; (H) $6,050

CLAESSENS, Jacob, called Jacob van
UTRECHT
Dutch 1480-after 1530
paintings: (H) $123,500

CLAESZ, Anthonie, I
Dutch 1592-1635
drawings: (H) $2,420

CLAESZ, Pieter
Dutch 1597-1661
paintings: (L) $46,200; (H) $770,000

CLAGHORN, Joseph C.
American 1869-1947
paintings: (L) $27; (H) $1,150
drawings: (L) $253; (H) $1,495

CLAGHORN, V.C.
drawings: (H) $1,495

CLAGUE, Richard
American 1812-1873
paintings: (L) $3,025; (H) $77,000

CLAIR, Charles H.
French 1860-1930
paintings: (L) $963; (H) $1,760

CLAIR, Gordon Saint
American 1885-1966
paintings: (L) $230; (H) $1,840

CLAIRIN, Georges Jules Victor
French 1843-1919
paintings: (L) $13,200; (H) $107,000
drawings: (H) $1,870

CLAIRIN, Pierre Eugene
French 1897-1980
paintings: (H) $990

CLAITON, F.
19th cent.
paintings: (H) $605

CLAPHAM, James T.
English 19th cent.
drawings: (H) $935

CLAPMAN, Mark
American b. 1950
paintings: (L) $4,950; (H) $6,600

CLAPP, Clinton W.
American b. 1831
paintings: (L) $220; (H) $880

CLAPP, William Henry
American 1879-1954
paintings: (L) $798; (H) $22,000

CLAPSADDLE, Jerry
American contemporary
paintings: (H) $660

CLARA, Juan
Spanish 1875/78-1958
sculpture: (L) $605; (H) $2,530

CLARE, C.
British 19th cent.
paintings: (H) $550

CLARE, Edward
British 19th cent.
paintings: (H) $935

CLARE, George
English ac. c. 1860-1900
paintings: (L) $825; (H) $8,625

CLARE, Oliver
British c. 1853-1927
paintings: (L) $825; (H) $20,700

CLARE, Vincent
British c. 1855-1925/30
paintings: (L) $800; (H) $6,600
drawings: (H) $1,540

CLARENBACH, Max
German 1880-1952
paintings: (H) $6,325

CLARK, A.
paintings: (L) $66; (H) $550

CLARK, Albert
paintings: (H) $1,760

CLARK, Allan
American 1896/98-1950
sculpture: (L) $1,600; (H) $33,000

CLARK, Alson Skinner
American 1876-1949
paintings: (L) $825; (H) $41,400
drawings: (H) $4,400

CLARK, Benton H.
American 1895/1900-1964
paintings: (L) $192; (H) $14,300
drawings: (H) $825

CLARK, C. Myron
American 1858-1923
paintings: (L) $220; (H) $2,420
drawings: (L) $99; (H) $275

CLARK, Christopher Lee
American b. 1903
paintings: (H) $550
drawings: (L) $88; (H) $325

CLARK, Claude L.
British 19th/20th cent.
paintings: (H) $2,200

CLARK, Dane
American 20th cent.
paintings: (H) $1,980

CLARK, Dixon
British 19th/20th cent.
paintings: (H) $1,100

CLARK, Eliot Candee
American 1883-1980
paintings: (L) $105; (H) $3,163
drawings: (L) $90; (H) $330

CLARK, Frederick Albert
paintings: (H) $1,760

CLARK, Frederick H.
American 1862-1947
paintings: (L) $192; (H) $1,300
drawings: (H) $852

CLARK, George Merrit
American d. 1904
paintings: (H) $3,080

CLARK, Gordon Matta
American 20th cent.
drawings: (H) $805

CLARK, J.A.
paintings: (H) $660

CLARK, J.J.
British 19th cent.
paintings: (H) $1,210

CLARK, James
British 1858-1943
paintings: (L) $2,420; (H) $17,050

CLARK, James
British 1884-1909
paintings: (H) $3,960

CLARK, Lillian Gertrude
paintings: (H) $467

CLARK, Lockfort
19th/20th cent.
paintings: (H) $605

CLARK, Martin E.
paintings: (H) $1,210

CLARK, Matt
American 1903-1972
paintings: (H) $1,100
drawings: (L) $440; (H) $825

CLARK, Octavius T.
British 1850-1921
paintings: (L) $302; (H) $1,018

CLARK, Paraskeva Plistik
paintings: (H) $3,300
drawings: (L) $1,980; (H) $2,200

CLARK, Rances
American 20th cent.
paintings: (H) $1,045

CLARK, Roland
American 1874-1957
paintings: (L) $880; (H) $5,225
drawings: (L) $275; (H) $3,850

CLARK, S.
British 19th cent.
paintings: (H) $3,575

CLARK, S. Joseph
British 19th cent.
paintings: (L) $1,320; (H) $2,185

CLARK, Sally
American b. 1883
sculpture: (L) $825; (H) $5,225

CLARK, W.
British 19th cent.
paintings: (H) $6,050

CLARK, Walter
American 1848-1917
paintings: (L) $330; (H) $2,875
drawings: (H) $110
sculpture: (H) $2,070

CLARK, Walter Appleton
American 1876-1906
paintings: (H) $742

CLARK, William
paintings: (H) $7,700

CLARK, William
British 19th cent.
paintings: (H) $4,370

CLARK, William Albert
British 19th/20th cent.
paintings: (H) $2,200

CLARKE, A.
paintings: (H) $495
sculpture: (H) $495

CLARKE, Allan
American 1896-1950
sculpture: (H) $1,870

CLARKE, Bob
drawings: (L) $99; (H) $715

CLARKE, C.
19th cent.
paintings: (H) $2,200

CLARKE, James
paintings: (H) $1,800

CLARKE, John Clem
American b. 1937
paintings: (L) $880; (H) $8,800

CLARKE, Thomas Shields
American 1860-1920
paintings: (L) $138; (H) $660

CLARY, Jean Eugene
French 1856-1930
paintings: (H) $1,320

CLARY-BAROUX, Adolphe
1865-1933
paintings: (H) $2,200

CLAUDE
paintings: (L) $192; (H) $2,420

CLAUDE, Eugene
French 1841-1923
paintings: (L) $3,450; (H) $28,750

CLAUDE, Jean Maxime
French 1824-1904
drawings: (L) $77; (H) $805

CLAUDEL, Camille
French 1864-1943
sculpture: (L) $12,650; (H) $151,000

CLAUDOT, Jean Baptiste Charles,
called CLAUDOT DE NANCY
1733-1805
paintings: (H) $8,625

CLAUS, Emile
Belgian 1849-1924
paintings: (L) $55,000; (H) $159,500
drawings: (H) $2,070

CLAUS, May Austin
American b. 1882
paintings: (L) $413; (H) $2,200

CLAUS, William A.J.
paintings: (L) $110; (H) $660

CLAUSADES, Pierre de
French 1910-1976
paintings: (L) $425; (H) $880

CLAUSADES, Pierre de
French 20th cent.
paintings: (H) $800

CLAUSELL, Joaquin
Mexican 1866-1935
paintings: (L) $6,900; (H) $332,500

CLAUSEN, Franciska
Danish b. 1899
drawings: (H) $1,650

CLAVE, Antoni
French, b. Spain 1913
paintings: (L) $4,950; (H) $165,000
drawings: (L) $748; (H) $137,500
sculpture: (H) $4,600

CLAVE, Pelegrin
Spain 1811-1880
drawings: (L) $14,950; (H) $27,600

CLAVEAU, Antoine
American ac. 1854-1872
paintings: (H) $18,400
drawings: (H) $1,380

CLAVER, Francois
French b. 1918
paintings: (L) $412; (H) $660

CLAVIERE, Bernard de
French 20th cent.
paintings: (L) $935; (H) $3,025

CLAWSON, W.R.
American 19th/20th cent.
paintings: (L) $27; (H) $675

CLAY, Elizabeth Campbell Fisher
American 1871-1959
paintings: (L) $110; (H) $3,450

CLAY, Mary F.R.
American d. 1939
paintings: (H) $825

CLAY, Pierre Jean
Belgian 1819-1900
paintings: (H) $4,675

CLAYES, Alice des
paintings: (H) $2,200

CLAYES, Berthe des
paintings: (H) $1,100

CLAYK, J.
paintings: (H) $990

CLAYS, Paul Jean
Belgian 1819-1900
paintings: (L) $990; (H) $16,100
drawings: (L) $345; (H) $3,680

CLAYTON, Alexander
b. 1906
paintings: (H) $2,860

CLAYTON, Harold
British 1896-1979
paintings: (L) $3,850; (H) $10,637

CLEAR, G.
paintings: (L) $715; (H) $1,100

CLEARY, Manon
20th cent.
paintings: (H) $2,300

CLEARY, Shirley
drawings: (L) $440; (H) $1,500

CLEAVES, Helen E.
American b. 1878
paintings: (H) $546

CLEEF, Hendrick van, III
1525-1589
drawings: (H) $10,450

CLEENEWERCK, Henry
Belgian 1818-1901
paintings: (L) $2,200; (H) $40,250

CLEGG AND GUTTMAN
contemporary
drawings: (L) $1,650; (H) $5,500

CLEMENCIN, Francois Andre
French b. 1878
sculpture: (L) $1,150; (H) $1,760

CLEMENS, Paul
American b. 1911
paintings: (L) $1,495; (H) $6,325
drawings: (L) $1,150; (H) $4,400

CLEMENT, H.
paintings: (H) $880

CLEMENT, Joseph M.
1894-1956
drawings: (L) $440; (H) $522

CLEMENT, M.
French 19th cent.
paintings: (H) $862

CLEMENT, Serge
paintings: (H) $920

CLEMENT-SERVEAU
French 1886-1972
paintings: (L) $1,320; (H) $3,850

CLEMENTE, Francesco
Italian b. 1952
paintings: (L) $1,265; (H) $266,500
drawings: (L) $1,380; (H) $343,500
sculpture: (H) $25,300

CLEMENTS, George Henry
American 1854-1935
paintings: (L) $165; (H) $660
drawings: (L) $440; (H) $522

CLEMENTS, Grace
American 1905-1969
paintings: (H) $5,500

CLEMENTS, Henry
English 19th cent.
paintings: (H) $633

CLEMINSON, R.
English 19th cent.
paintings: (H) $1,210

CLEMINSON, Robert
English ac. 1865-1868
paintings: (L) $1,320; (H) $4,125
drawings: (H) $467

CLENNAM, R.
19th cent.
paintings: (L) $880; (H) $880

CLERICI, Fabrizio
Italian b. 1913
paintings: (H) $5,750

CLERISSEAU, Charles Louis
French 1721-1820
drawings: (L) $3,565; (H) $47,300

CLERK, John M.
paintings: (H) $13,200

CLERMONT-GALLERANDE,
Adhemar Louis Vicomte de
French d. 1895
paintings: (H) $9,775

CLESINGER, J.
sculpture: (H) $1,650

CLESINGER, Jean Baptiste
French 1814-1883
sculpture: (L) $1,100; (H) $343,500

CLESSE, Louis
1889-1961
paintings: (L) $604; (H) $1,840

CLEVANOT, Ph.
French 19th cent.
paintings: (H) $880

CLEVE, Corneille van
French 1644/45-1735
sculpture: (H) $29,900

CLEVE, Joos van
ac. from 1511-d. 1540/1
paintings: (H) $387,500

CLEVE, Marten van, I
Flemish 1527-1581
paintings: (H) $23,000

CLEVELEY, J.
paintings: (H) $7,975

CLEVELEY, John, the elder
British ac. 1747-1777
paintings: (H) $552,500

CLIFTON, F.C.
American 19th/20th cent.
paintings: (L) $303; (H) $825

CLIFTON, John S.
British ac. 1852-1869
paintings: (H) $25,300

CLIME, Winfield Scott
American 1881-1958
paintings: (L) $115; (H) $4,400
drawings: (L) $138; (H) $385

CLIMER, Emiline Jones
paintings: (L) $325; (H) $2,000

CLINEDINST, Benjamin West
American 1859-1931
paintings: (H) $6,050
drawings: (L) $28; (H) $1,210

CLINEDINST, May Spear
American 1887-1960
paintings: (L) $110; (H) $1,430

CLINT, Alfred
English 1807-1883
paintings: (L) $1,210; (H) $2,750

CLOAR, Carroll
American 1913-1994
paintings: (L) $6,325; (H) $32,200

CLODION, Claude MICHEL
French 1738-1814
sculpture: (L) $1,320; (H) $176,000

CLONNEY, James Goodwyn
American 1812-1867
paintings: (H) $85,000
drawings: (H) $14,950

CLOSE, Chuck
American b. 1940
paintings: (H) $231,000
drawings: (L) $4,830; (H) $93,500

CLOSSON, William Baxter
American 1848-1926
paintings: (L) $192; (H) $1,430
drawings: (H) $220

CLOUET, Francois
French c. 1522-1572
paintings: (H) $475,500

CLOUGH, Arthur
American 20th cent.
drawings: (H) $935

CLOUGH, George L.
American 1824-1901
paintings: (L) $330; (H) $7,150

CLOUTIER, Albert
1902-1965
paintings: (L) $715; (H) $1,375

CLOWES, Daniel
English ac. 1790-1835
paintings: (H) $4,600

CLUNIE, Robert
American 1895-1984
paintings: (L) $3,025; (H) $4,888

CLUSMANN, William
American 1859-1928
paintings: (L) $110; (H) $2,530
drawings: (L) $77; (H) $880

CLYMER, James
b. 1893
paintings: (H) $990

CLYMER, John Ford
American 1907-1989
paintings: (L) $330; (H) $77,000
drawings: (H) $495

COALE, Griffith Baily
American 1890-1950
paintings: (H) $2,860
drawings: (H) $165

COARDING, Gerald
American 20th cent.
paintings: (H) $3,300

COATES, Edmund C.
American 1816-1871
paintings: (L) $690; (H) $19,550

COATES, George James
British 1869-1930
paintings: (H) $770

COBARRUBIAS, Miguel
Mexican-American 1904-1957
drawings: (H) $2,090

COBBE, Bernard
British 19th cent.
paintings: (H) $2,310

COBBETT, Edward John
English 1815-1899
paintings: (L) $660; (H) $9,350

COBELLE, Charles
French b. 1908
paintings: (L) $110; (H) $2,750
drawings: (L) $88; (H) $1,100

COBO, Chema
b. 1952
paintings: (L) $5,082; (H) $6,600
drawings: (H) $4,400

COBURN, Frank
American 1862-1938
paintings: (L) $303; (H) $17,600

COCCAPANI, Sigismondo
1583-1642
paintings: (H) $19,800

COCCORANTE, Leonardo
Italian 1700-1750
paintings: (L) $19,800; (H) $82,500

COCHIN, Charles Nicolas, the younger
French 1715-1790
drawings: (L) $5,225; (H) $7,150

COCHRAN, Allen D.
American 1888-1971
paintings: (L) $192; (H) $1,760
drawings: (H) $500

COCHRANE, Josephine G.
19th/20th cent.
paintings: (L) $770; (H) $1,100

COCK, Cesar de
Flemish 1823-1904
paintings: (L) $1,840; (H) $15,400

COCK, Matthijs
c. 1509-before 1548
drawings: (H) $41,250

COCTEAU, Jean
French 1889-1963
paintings: (H) $2,860
drawings: (L) $797; (H) $4,025
sculpture: (L) $1,610; (H) $3,163

CODARO, V.
Italian 19th cent.
paintings: (H) $14,300

CODAZZI, Viviano
Italian 1603-1672
paintings: (L) $13,750; (H) $28,600

CODAZZI, Viviano and Domenico
GARGIULIO (Micco Spadaro)
17th cent.
paintings: (L) $38,500; (H) $44,000

CODAZZI, Viviano and Michelangelo
CERQUOZZI
17th cent.
paintings: (H) $132,000

CODDE, Pieter Jacobsz.
Dutch 1599-1678
paintings: (L) $10,925; (H) $132,000

CODINA Y LANGLIN, Victoriano
Spanish 1844-1911
paintings: (L) $3,960; (H) $8,250 .
drawings: (H) $495

CODMAN, Charles
American 1800-1842
paintings: (L) $1,380; (H) $15,400

CODMAN, Edwin E.
American 19th/20th cent.
sculpture: (L) $352; (H) $506

CODMAN, John Amory
American 1824-1886
paintings: (L) $1,840; (H) $2,070

COE, David R.
sculpture: (H) $495

COE, Ethel Louise
American 1880-1938
paintings: (L) $22; (H) $1,540

COE, Sue
paintings: (H) $4,600

COE, Theodore Demerest
American b. 1866
paintings: (L) $460; (H) $1,150

COECKE VAN AELST, Pieter, I
Flemish 1502-1550
paintings: (H) $13,200

COEDES, Louis Eugene
French 1810-1906
paintings: (H) $18,700

COELLO, Alonso Sanchez, studio of
16th cent.
paintings: (L) $26,450; (H) $40,250

COEN, Eleanor
paintings: (H) $660

COENE, Jean Baptiste
Flemish b. 1805
paintings: (L) $1,870; (H) $5,500

COESSIN DE LA FOSSE, Charles
Alexandre
French b. 1829
paintings: (H) $5,500

COEVILLERIE, Henry Dele
19th cent.
paintings: (H) $805

COEYLAS, Henri
French 19th/20th cent.
paintings: (H) $2,200

COFFA, Andre
Italian 19th cent.
paintings: (H) $4,600

COFFERMANS, Marcellus
Flemish 1535?-after 1575
paintings: (L) $6,900; (H) $36,300

COFFIN, Elizabeth R.
American 1850-1930
paintings: (L) $330; (H) $1,100

COFFIN, William Anderson
American 1855-1925/26
paintings: (L) $475; (H) $2,750

COFFIN, William Haskell
American 1878-1941
paintings: (L) $88; (H) $3,575
drawings: (H) $880

COGDELL, John Stevens
American 1778-1847
paintings: (H) $10,725

COGGESHALL, John I.
American 1856-1927
paintings: (L) $275; (H) $3,080
drawings: (H) $110

COGGESHALL-WILSON, J.
British 19th/20th cent.
paintings: (H) $3,300

COGNE, Francois
1829-1883
sculpture: (H) $4,950

COGOLLO, Heriberto
b. 1945
paintings: (H) $37,375
drawings: (H) $3,025

COHEN, Carol
contemporary
sculpture: (L) $2,300; (H) $3,163

COHEN, Frederick E.
Canadian ac. 1837-1855
paintings: (L) $605; (H) $2,200

COHEN, Isaac Michael
Australian 20th cent.
paintings: (H) $742

COHEN, Katherine M.
1859-1914
sculpture: (H) $4,313

COHEN, Larry
American 20th cent.
paintings: (H) $2,070

COHEN, Lois
American 20th cent.
paintings: (H) $2,200

COHEN, Nessa
1855-1915
sculpture: (H) $3,450

COHN, Harold
American 1908-1982
paintings: (L) $742; (H) $2,200
drawings: (L) $50; (H) $770

COHN, Max Arthur
American b. 1904
paintings: (L) $1,610; (H) $3,520

COHN, Michael
sculpture: (H) $3,300

COIGNARD, James
French b. 1925
paintings: (L) $1,250; (H) $17,600
drawings: (H) $3,850

COIGNARD, Louis and Louis
BOULANGER
French 19th cent.
paintings: (H) $1,760

COIGNET, Jules Louis Philippe
French 1798-1860
paintings: (H) $4,370

COINCHON, Jacques Antoine
Theodore
French 1814-1881
sculpture: (H) $1,495

COINS, Raymond
b. 1904
sculpture: (L) $2,200; (H) $2,695

COL, Jan David
Belgian 1822-1900
paintings: (H) $3,850

COLACI, Salvatore
Italian/American 20th cent.
paintings: (L) $825; (H) $1,870

COLACICCO, Salvatore
paintings: (L) $330; (H) $3,575

COLAHAN, Colin
paintings: (L) $1,320; (H) $5,500

COLAN, Gene
drawings: (H) $2,070

COLAO, Rudy
paintings: (H) $495

COLBURN, Francis Peabody
American b. 1909
paintings: (L) $165; (H) $605

COLBY, George Ernest
American b. 1859
drawings: (L) $55; (H) $468

COLCORD, H.
paintings: (L) $715; (H) $1,045

COLE, Alphaeus
American b. 1876
paintings: (L) $99; (H) $1,300

COLE, Charles Octavius
American b. 1814
paintings: (L) $3,220; (H) $13,750

COLE, Emily
American 1843-1913
drawings: (H) $552

COLE, George
British 1810-1883
paintings: (L) $1,100; (H) $36,800

COLE, George T.
American 1874-1937
paintings: (H) $495

COLE, George Vicat
English 1833-1893
paintings: (L) $1,380; (H) $49,500

COLE, James
paintings: (H) $6,325

COLE, Joseph Foxcroft
Anglo/American 1837-1892
paintings: (L) $412; (H) $2,310
drawings: (H) $176

COLE, Joseph Greenleaf
American 1806-1958
paintings: (L) $1,540; (H) $2,200

COLE, Lyman Emerson
paintings: (L) $231; (H) $12,100

COLE, Solomon
English 19th cent.
paintings: (H) $1,705

COLE, Thomas
American 1801-1848
paintings: (L) $82; (H) $431,500
drawings: (L) $467; (H) $2,875

COLE, Thomas Casilear
American 1888-1976
paintings: (L) $863; (H) $1,210

COLEMAN, Charles Caryl
American 1840-1928
paintings: (L) $770; (H) $14,950
drawings: (L) $460; (H) $3,300

COLEMAN, Enrico
Italian 1846-1911
drawings: (L) $2,200; (H) $16,500

COLEMAN, Francesco
Italian b. 1851
paintings: (H) $6,900
drawings: (H) $1,320

COLEMAN, G.
paintings: (H) $1,320

COLEMAN, Glenn O.
American 1884/87-1932
paintings: (L) $4,140; (H) $6,600
drawings: (H) $1,380

COLEMAN, Harvey B.
American 1884-1959
paintings: (L) $385; (H) $522

COLEMAN, Henry Enrico
drawings: (H) $920

COLEMAN, J.
paintings: (H) $1,680

COLEMAN, Loring W.
American 1918-1988
paintings: (L) $400; (H) $978
drawings: (L) $144; (H) $201

COLEMAN, Marion
American d. c. 1925
paintings: (H) $3,025

COLEMAN, Mary Darter
American 1894-1956
paintings: (L) $83; (H) $1,265
drawings: (H) $77

COLEMAN, Michael
American b. 1946
paintings: (L) $1,650; (H) $22,550
drawings: (L) $2,990; (H) $5,720

COLEMAN, Ralph P.
1892-1968
paintings: (L) $1,760; (H) $2,750

COLEMAN, Samuel
American 1832-1920
paintings: (H) $550

COLEMAN, Sherman T.
American b. 1920
paintings: (H) $7,700
sculpture: (L) $1,650; (H) $2,200

COLEMAN, William Stephen
English 1829/30-1904
paintings: (H) $6,050
drawings: (H) $1,650

COLEMAN-COOKE, Miranda
British 20th cent.
paintings: (H) $460

COLES, Stephanie Kirschen
contemporary
drawings: (L) $468; (H) $770

COLESCOTT, Robert
American b. 1925
drawings: (H) $880

COLETTI, Joseph
American 1898-1973
sculpture: (H) $6,600

COLFER, John Thomas
American 20th cent.
paintings: (H) $660

COLGATE, C.
American 19th cent.
paintings: (L) $440; (H) $633

COLIN, G.
French late 19th cent.
sculpture: (H) $518

COLIN, Georges
sculpture: (H) $1,380

COLIN, Gustave
French 1828-1910/19
paintings: (H) $1,840

COLIN, Paul
French 1892-1985
drawings: (H) $1,100

COLINET, Claire Jeanne Roberte
French ac. 1929
sculpture: (L) $220; (H) $46,000

COLKETT, Samuel David
English 1800/06-1863
paintings: (L) $2,750; (H) $3,737

COLL, Joseph Clement
American 1881-1921
drawings: (H) $2,750

COLLA, Ettora
contemporary
sculpture: (H) $16,500

COLLAZO, Guillermo
paintings: (H) $5,175

COLLE, ** de
Italian 19th/20th cent.
drawings: (H) $1,320

COLLET, Edouard Louis
French b. 1876
sculpture: (L) $1,540; (H) $4,180

COLLETT, K**
English 19th/20th cent.
paintings: (H) $633

COLLI, Antonio
paintings: (L) $121; (H) $748

COLLIER, Alan Caswell
paintings: (L) $2,200; (H) $4,180

COLLIER, Evert
Dutch ac. 1662, d. 1702/03
paintings: (L) $12,100; (H) $46,750

COLLIER, H.H.
British 19th cent.
paintings: (H) $690

COLLIER, John
English 1850-1934
paintings: (H) $15,400

COLLIGNON
ac. c. 1762
paintings: (H) $7,700

COLLIN, Benjamin
American 1896-1979
paintings: (H) $825

COLLIN, Celia
paintings: (L) $900; (H) $900

COLLIN, L.
American
drawings: (H) $517

COLLIN, Raphael
French 1850-1916
paintings: (L) $1,375; (H) $8,800

COLLINA, Alberto
Italian 19th/20th cent.
drawings: (H) $690

COLLINS, Bruce D.
paintings: (L) $110; (H) $495
drawings: (H) $55

COLLINS, Charles
English 1851-1921
paintings: (L) $1,150; (H) $2,990

COLLINS, Earl
American 20th cent.
paintings: (L) $825; (H) $2,310

COLLINS, G.B.
20th cent.
paintings: (H) $575

COLLINS, Hugh
British 19th cent.
paintings: (L) $748; (H) $8,250

COLLINS, J.
paintings: (H) $660

COLLINS, John, of Manchester
American
paintings: (H) $1,650

COLLINS, John W.
b. 1897
paintings: (L) $460; (H) $605

COLLINS, Kreigh
American 1908-1974
paintings: (H) $550
drawings: (H) $22

COLLINS, L.H.
paintings: (H) $467

COLLINS, R.E.
paintings: (H) $1,320

COLLINS, T.
English 19th cent.
paintings: (H) $770

COLLINS, W.
British 19th cent.
paintings: (H) $935

COLLINS, William
British 1788-1847
paintings: (L) $825; (H) $5,060

COLLINS, William M.
paintings: (H) $2,090

COLLMAN, Daniel
British 20th cent.
paintings: (H) $1,870

COLLOMB, Paul
French b. 1921
paintings: (L) $192; (H) $3,520

COLLOT, Jacques
Italian School 17th cent.
paintings: (H) $20,700

COLLUM, Wendell
paintings: (H) $2,200

COLLVER, Ethel Blanchard
American 1875-1955
paintings: (H) $3,410

COLLYER, Margaret
British 19th cent.
paintings: (H) $1,265

COLMAN, Roi Clarkson
American 1884-1945
paintings: (L) $550; (H) $4,400

COLMAN, Samuel
American 1832-1920
paintings: (L) $412; (H) $13,200
drawings: (L) $192; (H) $7,475

COLOGERO, Jean
Italian b. 1926
paintings: (H) $495

COLOGNA, A.
20th cent.
paintings: (H) $605

COLOMANUS
Hungarian b. 1925
paintings: (H) $518

COLOMANUS, J.
Continental 20th cent.
paintings: (H) $550

COLOMBO, A.
Italian 19th/20th cent.
paintings: (H) $2,760

COLOMBO, Grang
French
sculpture: (L) $550; (H) $2,530

COLOMBO, K.R.
Italian ac. early 20th cent.
sculpture: (H) $2,013

COLOMBO, Renzo
Italian d. 1885
sculpture: (L) $2,310; (H) $3,450

COLOMBO, V.
Italian 19th cent.
drawings: (L) $660; (H) $1,320

COLSON
French 19th cent.
paintings: (H) $3,850

COLSON, Greg
b. 1956
sculpture: (H) $2,760

COLT, James
American 20th cent.
paintings: (L) $440; (H) $467

COLT, Morgan
paintings: (H) $3,500

COLUCCI, Gio
Italian 20th cent.
paintings: (L) $330; (H) $2,200
drawings: (L) $88; (H) $748

COLUMBO, R.
sculpture: (H) $825

COLUMBO, Virgilio
Italian 19th cent.
paintings: (L) $220; (H) $660
drawings: (L) $259; (H) $935

COLUNGA, Alejandro
b. Mexico 1948
paintings: (L) $4,400; (H) $32,200
drawings: (L) $3,575; (H) $20,700

COLVIN, J.M.
American 19th cent.
paintings: (H) $460

COLYER, Vincent
American 1825-1888
drawings: (H) $920

COMAN, Charlotte Buell
American 1833-1924
paintings: (L) $220; (H) $1,540
drawings: (H) $517

COMBA, Pierre
French 1860-1934
drawings: (H) $770

COMBAS, Robert
French b. 1957
paintings: (L) $8,250; (H) $28,600
drawings: (H) $2,640

COMELERA, P.
sculpture: (H) $1,210

COMERRE, Leon Francois
French 1850-1916
paintings: (L) $2,640; (H) $99,000

COMERRE-PATON, Jacqueline
French b. 1859
paintings: (H) $8,250

COMFORT, Charles Fraser
paintings: (H) $2,420

COMMERE, Jean Yves
1920-1986
paintings: (L) $633; (H) $3,910

COMOLERA, Paul
French 1818-c. 1897
sculpture: (L) $440; (H) $3,300

COMP, Norm
paintings: (H) $990

COMPERA, Alexis
American 1856-1906
paintings: (L) $350; (H) $1,210

COMPRIS, Maurice
American 1885-1939
paintings: (L) $2,530; (H) $2,970

COMPTE-CALIX, Francois Claudius
French 1813-1880
paintings: (L) $1,870; (H) $7,700
drawings: (L) $575; (H) $770

COMPTON, Edward Harrison
British 1881-1960?
paintings: (L) $605; (H) $6,050
drawings: (L) $495; (H) $8,050

COMPTON, Edward Theodore
English 1849-1921
paintings: (L) $880; (H) $7,475
drawings: (H) $2,875

COMPTON, T. C.
British 19th cent.
paintings: (H) $770

COMTRI, C.
sculpture: (H) $660

CONANT, Alban Jasper
American 1821-1915
paintings: (L) $1,540; (H) $4,830

CONANT, Lucy Scarborough
American 1867-1921
paintings: (H) $715
drawings: (H) $316

CONANT, Marjorie, Mrs. Bush-Brown
American b. 1885
paintings: (H) $990

CONCA, Sebastiano
Italian c. 1676/80-1764
paintings: (L) $23,000; (H) $39,600

CONCHA, Jerry
contemporary
paintings: (H) $1,100

CONCONI, Luigi
Italian 1852-1917
paintings: (H) $30,800

COND'AMIN, Joseph Henri
French 1847-1917
paintings: (H) $6,900

CONDAMY, Charles Fernand de
French ac. 1878-1882
paintings: (H) $3,162
drawings: (L) $368; (H) $2,750

CONDO, George
American b. 1957
paintings: (L) $805; (H) $66,000
drawings: (L) $920; (H) $46,200

CONDY, N.
paintings: (H) $605

CONDY, Nicholas Matthew
British 1816-1851
paintings: (H) $1,725

CONE, Marvin D.
American 1891-1964
paintings: (L) $6,600; (H) $17,600

CONEL, S.N.
paintings: (H) $495

CONELY, William Brewster
American 1830-1911
paintings: (L) $460; (H) $2,640

CONEYE, Stefan
sculpture: (H) $990

CONFORTINI, Jacopo
1602-1672
drawings: (L) $6,900; (H) $10,350

CONGDON, Anne Ramsdell
American 1873-1958
paintings: (L) $1,760; (H) $6,050

CONGDON, Thomas Raphael
American 1862-1917
paintings: (L) $1,495; (H) $1,650
drawings: (H) $935

CONINCK, David de
Flemish c. 1636-c. 1699
paintings: (L) $11,500; (H) $68,500

CONKLIN, Roy
paintings: (L) $715; (H) $880

CONKLING, Mabel
American b. 1871
sculpture: (H) $7,700

CONLEY, Phillip
Irish/American 20th cent.
paintings: (H) $605

CONLON, M.E.
paintings: (H) $7,475

CONLUNGA, Alejandro
b. Mexico 1948
drawings: (H) $9,200

CONN, Russ
American 20th cent.
paintings: (H) $58
drawings: (H) $748

CONNAWAY, Jay Hall
American 1893-1970
paintings: (L) $385; (H) $4,600

CONNELL, Bunny
American contemporary
sculpture: (H) $690

CONNELL, Edwin D.
American b. 1859
paintings: (L) $950; (H) $1,540

CONNELLY, Chuck
American b. 1956?
paintings: (L) $690; (H) $4,950
drawings: (H) $660

CONNER, Bruce
American b. 1933
sculpture: (H) $12,650

CONNER, John Anthony
American 1892-1971
paintings: (L) $165; (H) $1,650

CONNER, John Ramsey
American 1869-1952
paintings: (L) $93; (H) $5,225
drawings: (H) $325

CONNER, Paul
American 1881-1968
paintings: (L) $275; (H) $1,045
drawings: (H) $220

CONNOLEY, Jerry
paintings: (H) $578

CONNOLLY, Howard
drawings: (H) $1,430

CONNOR, J. Stanley
American b. 1860
sculpture: (L) $5,225; (H) $5,500

CONNOWAY, Jay Hall
American 1893-1970
paintings: (L) $908; (H) $1,320

CONRAD, Dan
American 19th cent.
paintings: (H) $550

CONRADES, Alfred Charles
French 19th cent.
drawings: (H) $863

CONRADI, H.
European 19th cent.
paintings: (H) $1,210

CONREY, Lee F.
b. 1883
drawings: (H) $770

CONSAGRA, Pietro
Italian b. 1920
sculpture: (L) $4,313; (H) $18,700

CONSTABLE, John
English 1776-1837
paintings: (H) $1,100
drawings: (H) $1,210

CONSTABLE, William
American 1783-1861
drawings: (L) $192; (H) $550

CONSTANT, Benjamin
French 1845-1902
paintings: (L) $1,045; (H) $68,500

CONSTANT, Maurice Joseph
French 1892-1970
sculpture: (L) $121; (H) $770

CONSTANTIN, Abraham
Swiss 1785-1855
drawings: (H) $1,150

CONSTANTIN, Auguste Aristide
Fernand
French 1824-1895
drawings: (H) $605

CONSTANTIN, Jean Antoine
French 1756-1844
drawings: (L) $1,045; (H) $1,045

CONSTANTIN, S**
Italian 19th cent.
paintings: (H) $550

CONSTANTINE, George
American School 20th cent.
paintings: (H) $715

CONSTANTINI, Castore
Italian 19th cent.
drawings: (H) $1,092

CONSTANTINI, Giuseppe
Italian 1850-1894
paintings: (H) $5,500

CONSUEGRA, Hugo
Cuban b. 1929
paintings: (L) $1,610; (H) $1,725

CONTE, Guillermo
Mexico b. 1940
paintings: (H) $19,550
drawings: (L) $6,900; (H) $16,100

CONTE, Meiffren
French c. 1630-1705
paintings: (H) $145,500

CONTE, Pino
Italian 20th cent.
sculpture: (L) $209; (H) $715

CONTENT, Dan
American b. 1902
paintings: (L) $880; (H) $5,500
drawings: (H) $2,090

CONTI, Bernardino dei
Italian 1450-1525
paintings: (H) $68,500

CONTI, Cosimo
Italian 1825-1893
paintings: (H) $1,980

CONTI, Gino
American b. 1900
paintings: (L) $110; (H) $770

CONTI, Tito
Italian 1842-1924
paintings: (L) $1,100; (H) $40,250

CONTWAY, Jay
American
paintings: (H) $990
sculpture: (L) $1,100; (H) $3,190

CONTWAY, Ross
American
sculpture: (H) $700

CONWAY, Fred E.
American 1900-1972
paintings: (L) $231; (H) $1,725
drawings: (L) $81; (H) $776

CONWAY, John Severinus
American b. 1852
drawings: (H) $4,400

CONWAY, Marie
American
paintings: (H) $632

CONY, E.R.
paintings: (L) $920; (H) $1,760

COOK, Arthur
American 20th cent.
drawings: (L) $121; (H) $467

COOK, Gordon
American 1927-1985
paintings: (L) $2,200; (H) $4,950
drawings: (L) $1,320; (H) $1,870

COOK, Herbert Moxon
British 1844-1920
drawings: (H) $3,163

COOK, Howard
American 1901-1980
paintings: (H) $715
drawings: (L) $440; (H) $3,025

COOK, Howard Norton
American 1901-1980
paintings: (H) $715
drawings: (H) $440

COOK, John A.
American 1870-1936
drawings: (L) $38; (H) $550

COOK, May Elizabeth
1881-1951
sculpture: (H) $8,625

COOK, Otis
American b. 1900
paintings: (L) $248; (H) $3,300

COOKE, C.A.
paintings: (H) $770

COOKE, Edward William
English 1811-1880
paintings: (L) $14,950; (H) $51,750
drawings: (H) $990

COOKESLEY, Margaret Murray
British d. 1927
paintings: (L) $3,738; (H) $11,500

COOLE, Brian
American 20th cent.
paintings: (L) $660; (H) $4,180

COOLEY, Benjamin
1821-1899
paintings: (L) $1,540; (H) $9,900

COOLEY, J.
British 18th cent.
paintings: (H) $891

COOLIDGE, Cassius Marcellus
American 1844-1934
paintings: (L) $1,100; (H) $17,600

COOLIDGE, Mary Rosamond
American b. 1888
paintings: (L) $88; (H) $770

COOMANS, Diana
Continental 19th cent.
paintings: (H) $4,400

COOMANS, Heva
Belgian 19th cent.
paintings: (L) $8,050; (H) $13,200

COOMANS, Pierre Olivier Joseph
Belgian 1816-1889
paintings: (L) $1,955; (H) $29,900

COOMBS, Catherine
contemporary
paintings: (L) $275; (H) $1,045

COOMBS, Delbert Dana
American 1850-1938
paintings: (L) $275; (H) $11,000

COOPER, Abraham
British 1787-1868
paintings: (L) $935; (H) $18,700

COOPER, Alexander Davis
American 1837-1888
paintings: (H) $2,090

COOPER, Alfred Heaton
British 1864-1929
paintings: (H) $14,950

COOPER, Astley David Montague
American 1856-1924
paintings: (L) $248; (H) $10,450

COOPER, Colin Campbell
American 1856-1937
paintings: (L) $100; (H) $129,000
drawings: (L) $275; (H) $10,450

COOPER, Edwin
British 1785-1833
drawings: (H) $3,960

COOPER, Emma Lampert
American 1860-1920
paintings: (L) $231; (H) $7,475
drawings: (H) $173

COOPER, Frederick Charles
British ac. 1844-1868
drawings: (H) $770

COOPER, Gerald
British 20th cent.
paintings: (L) $6,440; (H) $46,000

COOPER, Henry
English 19th cent.
paintings: (L) $403; (H) $1,760

COOPER, J.D.
paintings: (H) $3,300

COOPER, Margaret M.
American b. 1874
paintings: (L) $165; (H) $550

COOPER, P.
English 19th cent.
paintings: (H) $2,420

COOPER, R.B.
American 20th cent.
paintings: (H) $1,100

COOPER, Rita
Dutch 20th cent.
paintings: (H) $1,210

COOPER, Robert
drawings: (H) $2,700

COOPER, Thomas Sidney
English 1803-1902
paintings: (L) $1,100; (H) $20,700

COOPER, Thomas Sidney and
Frederick Richard LEE
British 18th/19th cent.
paintings: (H) $43,700

COOPER, Virginia S.
American 1875-1940
paintings: (H) $770

COOPER, W. Savage
British ac. 1880-1926
paintings: (H) $40,250

COOPER, William Heaton
English b. 1903
paintings: (L) $550; (H) $605

COOPER, William Henry
English b. 1858
paintings: (H) $660

COOPER, William Sidney
English ac. 1871-1923
paintings: (L) $990; (H) $9,200

COOSEMANS, Alexander
Flemish baptized 1627, d. 1689
paintings: (L) $35,200; (H) $71,250

COPE, Alban
drawings: (H) $1,265

COPE, Charles West
English 1811-1890
paintings: (H) $4,290

COPE, George
American 1855-1929
paintings: (L) $1,550; (H) $209,000

COPE, Gordon Nicholson
American 1906-1970
paintings: (L) $715; (H) $3,575

COPE, Leslie
Anglo/American b. 1913
paintings: (L) $495; (H) $715

COPELAND, Alfred Bryant
American 1840-1909
paintings: (L) $288; (H) $14,300

COPELAND, Charles
American 1858-1945
drawings: (L) $825; (H) $1,155

COPELAND, E.F.
American
paintings: (H) $1,210

COPLEY, John Singleton
American 1737-1815
paintings: (L) $16,675; (H) $90,500
drawings: (L) $1,725; (H) $34,500

COPLEY, William
American b. 1919
paintings: (L) $2,185; (H) $23,100
drawings: (L) $1,870; (H) $4,180
sculpture: (H) $3,450

COPPEDGE, Fern Isabel
American 1883/88-1951
paintings: (L) $1,000; (H) $29,000
drawings: (L) $460; (H) $1,650

COPPENOLLE, Jacques van
French 1878-1915
paintings: (L) $460; (H) $1,650

COPPER, William
sculpture: (H) $1,870

COPPERMAN, Mildred Tuner
American 20th cent.
paintings: (H) $4,180

COPPI, S.
Italian School 20th cent.
drawings: (H) $550

COPPIMI
paintings: (H) $1,210

COPPIN, John S.
Canadian/American 1904-1986
paintings: (L) $209; (H) $3,300
drawings: (H) $22
sculpture: (H) $302

COPPING, Harold
British 1863-1932
drawings: (H) $605

COPPINI, C.
Italian 19th cent.
paintings: (H) $770

COPPINI, Eliseo Fausto
Italian b. 1870
paintings: (H) $3,220

COPPOCK, Barbara
drawings: (H) $800

COPPOLA
Italian 19th cent.
drawings: (H) $2,070

COPPOLA, Antonio
Italian b. 1839
paintings: (H) $495

COQUES, Gonzales
Flemish 1614-1684
paintings: (H) $23,100

CORAY, Sharon Teal
American
paintings: (H) $550

CORBAUX, Fanny or Louise
CORBAUX
English 19th cent.
drawings: (H) $770

CORBELLINI
paintings: (L) $220; (H) $935
drawings: (L) $88; (H) $121

CORBELLINI, Luigi
Italian 1901-1968
paintings: (L) $385; (H) $2,750

CORBET
sculpture: (H) $880

CORBINO, Jon
Italian/American 1905-1964
paintings: (L) $632; (H) $6,050
drawings: (L) $330; (H) $990

CORBIT, George Cecil
American 1892-1944
paintings: (H) $8,250

CORCHON Y DIAQUE, Federico
Spanish 19th cent.
paintings: (H) $49,500
drawings: (H) $5,500

CORCORAN, Annette
American b. 1930
sculpture: (H) $1,380

CORCORAN, John
paintings: (H) $1,650

CORCOS, Vittorio
Italian 1859-1933
paintings: (L) $6,600; (H) $49,500

CORCUERA, Francisco
b. 1944
paintings: (L) $23,000; (H) $25,300

CORDEY, Frederick
1854-1911
paintings: (H) $2,200

CORDIER, Charles Henri Joseph
French 1827-1905
sculpture: (L) $23,100; (H) $82,500

CORDIER, Charles Pierre Modeste
French 1848-1909
paintings: (H) $18,400

CORDOVA, Helen de
paintings: (H) $575

CORDREY, Earl
1902-1977
drawings: (H) $935

CORDREY, John
British c. 1765-1825
paintings: (L) $715; (H) $5,750

CORELLI, Augusto
Italian 1853-1910
drawings: (L) $1,380; (H) $1,840

CORELLI, Conrad H.R.
British b. 1869, ac. 1880-1935
paintings: (H) $357
drawings: (L) $247; (H) $495

CORELLI, G.
Italian 19th cent.
paintings: (H) $550

CORENZIO, Belisario
c. 1560-1643
drawings: (H) $12,650

COREY, Bernard
20th cent.
paintings: (L) $165; (H) $1,210

CORINTH, Lovis
German 1858-1925
paintings: (L) $880; (H) $71,500
drawings: (L) $495; (H) $4,400

CORLEY, Philip A.
Irish b. 1944
paintings: (L) $440; (H) $2,420

CORMIER, Joseph J. Emmanuel,
Joseph J. Emmanuel DESCOMPS
French 1869-1952
sculpture: (L) $920; (H) $8,800

CORMON, Fernand Anne Piestre
French 1854-1924
paintings: (H) $4,025

CORN, T.
paintings: (H) $550

CORNE, Michele Felice
American b. Italy 1752-1832
paintings: (L) $16,675; (H) $96,000

CORNEILLE, Cornelis van Beverloo
Dutch b. 1922
paintings: (H) $3,300
drawings: (L) $330; (H) $9,350

CORNEILLE, Michel, the elder
1642-1708
paintings: (H) $5,500
drawings: (H) $6,600

CORNEILLE DE LYON, called
Corneille de la Haye
Flemish 1500?-1574/75
paintings: (L) $36,600; (H) $90,500

CORNEJO, Francisco
American d. 1963
paintings: (H) $690

CORNELISZ, Cornelis, called Cornelis
van Haarlem
Dutch 1562-1638
paintings: (H) $44,000

CORNELISZ, B.
ac. c. 1655
paintings: (H) $25,300

CORNELISZ VAN OOSTSANEN,
Jacob
c. 1470-1533
paintings: (H) $607,500

CORNELIUS, Peter
German 1783-1867
drawings: (H) $1,320

CORNELIUS, Philip
contemporary
sculpture: (L) $690; (H) $690

CORNELL, Joseph
American 1903-1972
paintings: (L) $8,050; (H) $52,250
drawings: (L) $3,300; (H) $19,800
sculpture: (L) $13,800; (H) $189,500

CORNER, Thomas C.
American 1865-1938
paintings: (L) $715; (H) $4,950

CORNET, Alphonse
French 1814-1874
paintings: (H) $2,640

CORNILLIET, Jules
French 1830-1886
paintings: (H) $1,035

CORNISH, William Permeanus
English 19th/20th cent.
drawings: (H) $5,500

CORNOYER, Paul
American 1864-1923
paintings: (L) $55; (H) $88,000
drawings: (H) $1,495

CORNU, Charles Vital
French 1853-1927
sculpture: (L) $4,830; (H) $5,775

CORNU, Pierre
French b. 1895
paintings: (L) $1,035; (H) $1,320

CORNWALL, G. Fowler
paintings: (H) $660

CORNWELL, Dean
American 1892-1960
paintings: (L) $660; (H) $26,400
drawings: (L) $1,650; (H) $2,200

CORNWELL, Marie
paintings: (H) $825

CORONADO, J***
Continental 19th cent.
paintings: (H) $2,200

CORONEL, Pedro
Mexican b. 1923
paintings: (L) $7,150; (H) $107,000

CORONEL, Rafael
Mexican b. 1932
paintings: (L) $4,400; (H) $167,500
drawings: (L) $2,750; (H) $4,400

COROT, Jean Baptiste Camille
French 1796-1875
paintings: (L) $2,200; (H) $1,432,500
drawings: (L) $138; (H) $4,400

CORPORA, Antonio
Tunisian b. 1909
paintings: (L) $5,500; (H) $7,700

CORREA, Benito Rebolledo
Chilean 1880-1964
paintings: (L) $1,495; (H) $5,500

CORREA, Juan de
ac. 1674-1739
paintings: (L) $27,500; (H) $51,750

CORREA, Rafael
Chilean ac. c. 1889-1930
paintings: (L) $1,610; (H) $2,875

CORREGGIO, Antonio Allegri
Italian 1489/94-1534
paintings: (L) $2,875; (H) $5,225
drawings: (L) $17,250; (H) $181,500
sculpture: (H) $748

CORREGGIO, Max
German 1854-1908
paintings: (H) $11,500

CORRENS, Josef Cornelius
Flemish 1814-1907
paintings: (H) $748

CORRODI, Arnoldo
Italian 1846-1874
paintings: (H) $27,600

CORRODI, Hermann David Salomon
Italian 1844-1905
paintings: (L) $1,430; (H) $233,500
drawings: (H) $853

CORRODI, Salomon
Swiss 1810-1892
drawings: (L) $3,300; (H) $8,250

CORRUTI, Domenico Maria
Italian 1620-1684
drawings: (H) $825

CORSI, Nicolas de
Italian b. 1882
paintings: (H) $3,300

CORSINI, Raffaele
Italian 19th cent.
drawings: (L) $935; (H) $10,450

CORT, Henrick Frans de
1742-1810
drawings: (H) $3,850

CORTAZZO, Oreste
Italian b. 1830
paintings: (L) $1,380; (H) $96,000

CORTE, Juan de la
Spanish 1597-1660
paintings: (H) $79,200

CORTES, Andre
Spanish 1815-1880
paintings: (H) $1,840

CORTES, Antonio
Spanish 1827-1908
paintings: (L) $165; (H) $575

CORTES, Edouard Leon
French 1882-1969
paintings: (L) $2,415; (H) $57,500
drawings: (L) $2,760; (H) $21,850

CORTESE, Federico
Italian 1829-1913
paintings: (H) $2,300

CORTESE, Guglielmo
1628-1679
drawings: (H) $1,650

CORTEZ, Jenness
American b. 1944
paintings: (L) $690; (H) $9,200

CORTI, Constantino
Italian 19th cent.
sculpture: (H) $660

CORTONA, Pietro Berrettini, called
Pietro da, studio of
drawings: (H) $4,140

CORTOR, Eldezer
American 20th cent.
paintings: (H) $687

CORTOT, Jean Pierre
French 19th cent.
sculpture: (H) $825

CORVI, Domenico
1721-1803
drawings: (H) $2,750

CORWIN, Charles Abel
American 1857-1938
paintings: (L) $440; (H) $7,475

CORY, Kate
American 1861-1958
paintings: (L) $193; (H) $825

CORZAS, Francisco
Mexican 1936-1983
paintings: (L) $13,200; (H) $140,000
drawings: (L) $1,870; (H) $5,750

COSAN, L.
paintings: (H) $748

COSENZA, Giuseppe
Italian b. 1847
paintings: (L) $4,400; (H) $8,250

COSGROVE, Stanley Morel
Canadian b. 1911
paintings: (L) $4,400; (H) $13,200

COSILETO, T.
Italian 19th cent.
paintings: (H) $1,610

COSSAAR, Cornelius Johannis
Dutch b. 1874
paintings: (L) $259; (H) $2,090

COSSHE, R.
paintings: (H) $935

COSSMANN, Herman Maurice
French 1821-1890
paintings: (L) $1,320; (H) $9,775

COSSON, Marcel
French 1878-1956
paintings: (L) $770; (H) $18,700

COSTA, B.
Italian 19th cent.
paintings: (H) $1,540

COSTA, Damian de
paintings: (H) $605

COSTA, Emanuele
Italian b. 1875
paintings: (L) $990; (H) $4,888

COSTA, Giuseppe
Italian 1852-1912
paintings: (H) $1,320

COSTA, Joachim
French b. 1888
sculpture: (H) $29,700

COSTA, L.
Italian 19th cent.
paintings: (H) $1,840

COSTA, Lorenzo, II called
MANTOVANO
1537-1583
paintings: (H) $29,900

COSTA, Luigi da
Italian 19th cent.
paintings: (H) $4,125
drawings: (H) $495

COSTA, Olga
Mexican b. 1913
paintings: (L) $3,300; (H) $60,500

COSTA, Oreste
Italian b. 1851
paintings: (L) $1,955; (H) $14,300

COSTA, S. di
Italian 19th cent.
drawings: (H) $495

COSTA and CONTI
paintings: (H) $2,640

COSTANTINI, Castore
Italian 19th cent.
drawings: (H) $605

COSTANTINI, Giuseppe
Italian b. 1850
paintings: (L) $5,175; (H) $13,750
drawings: (H) $1,210

COSTANTINI, Virgil
Italian b. 1882
paintings: (L) $8,625; (H) $107,000

COSTER, Adam de
Flemish c. 1586-1643
paintings: (L) $9,900; (H) $418,000

COSTIGAN, John E.
American 1888-1972
paintings: (L) $495; (H) $31,050
drawings: (L) $400; (H) $2,475

COSTIGAN, Thomas
American
drawings: (H) $935

COSTOR, Ellzier
drawings: (H) $500

COSWAY, Richard
British 1742-1821
drawings: (H) $1,725

COT, J.
English 19th cent.
paintings: (H) $770

COT, Pierre Auguste
French 1837-1883
paintings: (H) $1,980

COTANDA, Vicente Nicolau
Spanish 1852-1899
paintings: (H) $3,850

COTARD-DUPRE, Therese Marthe
Francoise
French b. 1877
paintings: (L) $10,350; (H) $28,750

COTES, Francis
English 1725/26-1770
paintings: (L) $1,760; (H) $40,250
drawings: (H) $2,200

COTMAN, John S.
English 1782-1842
paintings: (H) $990

COTTAVOZ, Andre
paintings: (L) $2,760; (H) $6,325

COTTET, Charles
French 1863-1925
paintings: (L) $825; (H) $19,550

COTTINGHAM, Robert
American b. 1935
paintings: (L) $16,500; (H) $46,200
drawings: (L) $4,600; (H) $11,000

COTTON, John W.
American 1868-1931
paintings: (L) $550; (H) $1,150

COTTON, William Henry
American 1880-1958
drawings: (H) $825

COUBERT, H.
French 19th cent.
paintings: (H) $1,925

COUBINE, Otakar
paintings: (H) $3,025

COUBINE, Othon
Czechoslovakian 1883-1969
paintings: (L) $1,100; (H) $6,038

COUDER, Gustave Emile
French d. 1903
paintings: (H) $29,900
drawings: (H) $6,900

COUDER, Jean Alexandre Remy
French 1808-1879
paintings: (H) $5,175

COUDRAY, Georges Charles
French ac. 1883-1903
sculpture: (L) $825; (H) $4,313

COUILLERIE, Henry Dele
American
paintings: (H) $495

COULDERY, Horatio H.
British 1832-1893
paintings: (L) $2,310; (H) $4,675

COULON, George David
French/American 1822-1904
paintings: (L) $248; (H) $12,100
drawings: (H) $853

COULON, George Joseph Amede
American 1854-1922
drawings: (L) $1,100; (H) $1,100

COULON, Marie Paoline Casbergue
1831-1914
drawings: (H) $825

COULON, Mary Elizabeth Emma
1859-1928
drawings: (H) $660

COULSON, John
Continental 20th cent.
paintings: (H) $2,530

COULTER, Mary J.
American 1880-1966
paintings: (L) $2,475; (H) $9,775

COULTER, William Alexander
American 1849-1936
paintings: (L) $1,650; (H) $18,700
drawings: (L) $2,875; (H) $3,163

COUMONT, Charles
Flemish ac. 1842
paintings: (H) $3,450

COUNE
German 20th cent.
paintings: (L) $173; (H) $770

COUPER, J.S.
American b. 1867
paintings: (H) $1,150

COUPER, William
American 1853-1942
paintings: (H) $220
sculpture: (L) $1,650; (H) $96,000

COURANT, Maurice Francois Auguste
French 1847-1925
paintings: (L) $1,100; (H) $2,200

COURBET, Gustave
French 1819-1877
paintings: (L) $17,600; (H) $1,540,000

COURBET, Gustave, and workshop
French 19th cent.
paintings: (H) $16,500

COURBET, Gustave, studio of
paintings: (H) $2,530

COURBET, Gustave and Cherubin
PATA
French 19th cent.
paintings: (L) $9,200; (H) $28,750

COURBET, Gustave and Marcel
ORDINAIRE
French 19th cent.
paintings: (L) $27,500; (H) $30,800

COURCHE, Felix
French b. 1863
paintings: (H) $660

COURT, Elizabeth van
American 20th cent.
paintings: (L) $66; (H) $770

COURT, Lee W.
American 1903-1992
paintings: (L) $460; (H) $604

COURTANS, Herman
Belgian 1884-1956
paintings: (H) $1,375

COURTAT, Louis
French d. 1909
paintings: (H) $9,350

COURTEN, Angelo de
Italian b. 1848
paintings: (L) $6,900; (H) $18,400
drawings: (H) $770

COURTENS, Franz
paintings: (H) $3,850

COURTENS, Hermann
Belgian 1884-1956
paintings: (H) $11,000

COURTER, Franklin C.
paintings: (H) $715

COURTIER, Pierre le
French 19th cent.
sculpture: (H) $2,200

COURTOIS, Georg
French 20th cent.
paintings: (H) $550

COURTOIS, Guillaume and Abraham
BRUEGHEL
17th cent.
paintings: (H) $242,000

COURTOIS, Gustave Claude Etienne
French 1853-1923
paintings: (L) $1,725; (H) $5,175

COURTOIS, Jacques, called Il
Bourguignon
French 1621-1676
paintings: (L) $3,737; (H) $21,850

COURTOIS, Jacques, called Le
Bourguignon
French 1621-1676
drawings: (H) $32,200

COURTRIGHT, Robert
American b. 1926
drawings: (L) $165; (H) $1,650
sculpture: (H) $330

COUSE, Eanger Irving
American 1866-1936
paintings: (L) $1,380; (H) $244,500
drawings: (H) $2,750

COUSE, William Percy
American b. 1898
paintings: (H) $5,225

COUSIN, Charles
French 19th/20th cent.
paintings: (L) $1,150; (H) $1,650

COUSINS, Jn.
paintings: (H) $2,300

COUSTURIER, Lucie
1876-1925
paintings: (H) $4,370

COUTAN, Jules Felix
French 1848-1939
sculpture: (H) $2,860

COUTAUD, Lucien
French 1904-1977
paintings: (L) $5,225; (H) $5,463
drawings: (L) $358; (H) $1,650

COUTTS, Alice Gray
American 1880-1973
paintings: (L) $1,540; (H) $4,125

COUTTS, Gordon
Scottish/American 1868/80-1937
paintings: (L) $495; (H) $27,500

COUTURE, Thomas
French 1815-1879
paintings: (L) $7,475; (H) $54,625
drawings: (H) $115

COUTURIER, Philibert Leon
French 1823-1901
paintings: (L) $715; (H) $3,850

COUVER, Jan van
Dutch 1836-1909
paintings: (L) $1,760; (H) $3,960

COVARRUBIAS, Miguel
Mexican 1904-1957
paintings: (L) $9,200; (H) $50,600
drawings: (L) $275; (H) $23,000

COVELLI, G.
paintings: (H) $605

COVENTRY, C.C.
English ac. 1802-1819
paintings: (L) $440; (H) $467

COVENTRY, Robert McGowan
British 1855-1914
paintings: (H) $3,300

COVERT, John
American 1882-1960
paintings: (H) $2,185

COVEY, Trevor
paintings: (L) $385; (H) $550

COVEYN, Reynier
1636-after 1667
paintings: (H) $13,800

COVINO, Frank
20th cent.
paintings: (H) $825

COWAN, John P.
b. 1920
drawings: (H) $6,050

COWARD, Sir Noel
English 1899-1973
paintings: (L) $880; (H) $3,850

COWELL, Cyril
ac. 1920s
drawings: (H) $770

COWIESON, Agnes B.
British 19th/20th cent.
paintings: (H) $660

COWLES, Fleur
drawings: (H) $2,475

COWLES, Russell
American 1887-1975/79
paintings: (L) $192; (H) $2,750

COWPER, Frank Cadogan
British 1877-1958
paintings: (H) $37,400

COX
British 19th c.
paintings: (H) $10,450

COX, Albert Scott
American 1863-1920
paintings: (L) $138; (H) $1,760
drawings: (H) $193

COX, Allyn
American 1896-1982
paintings: (L) $165; (H) $1,150
drawings: (H) $440

COX, Charles Hudson
American 1829-1901
paintings: (H) $550

COX, David
British 1783-1859
paintings: (L) $605; (H) $3,850
drawings: (L) $192; (H) $230

COX, Jan
Dutch/American 1919-1980
paintings: (L) $770; (H) $990

COX, Jimmy, guest artist at NAWA
b. 1960
paintings: (H) $715

COX, Kenyon
American 1856-1917/19
paintings: (H) $16,500
drawings: (L) $16; (H) $4,400

COX, Tim
American b. 1957
paintings: (H) $7,150

COXIE, Michiel
1499-1592
paintings: (H) $23,000

COYLE, Terance
b. 1925
paintings: (H) $1,265

COYNE, Sallie E.
sculpture: (H) $4,370

COYPEL, Antoine
French 1661-1722
drawings: (H) $11,000

COYPEL, Charles Antoine
French 1694-1752
drawings: (H) $7,700

COYPEL, Noel
French 1628-1707
paintings: (H) $525,000
drawings: (H) $10,350

COYSEVOX, Antoine, workshop of
late 17th cent.
sculpture: (H) $550,000

COZZENS, Frederick Schiller
American 1846-1928
paintings: (H) $1,331
drawings: (L) $220; (H) $4,945

COZZOLINO, F.
Italian 19th cent.
drawings: (L) $1,485; (H) $1,540

COZZOLINO, Peter
American 20th cent.
sculpture: (L) $1,650; (H) $2,200

CRABEELS, Florent Nicolas
Belgian 1829-1896
paintings: (H) $36,300

CRABETH, Wouter Pietersz.
Dutch c. 1595-1644
paintings: (L) $11,000; (H) $44,000

CRAESBEECK, Joos van
Flemish c. 1606-1654/61
paintings: (L) $2,300; (H) $4,620

CRAFFT, R.B.
ac. c. 1836-1866
paintings: (H) $1,150

CRAFT, Kinuko
b. 1940
paintings: (H) $715

CRAFTY, Victor
French 1840-1906
drawings: (H) $2,420

CRAGG, Tony
English b. 1949
sculpture: (L) $5,750; (H) $104,500

CRAIG
American 1849-1924
paintings: (H) $1,980
drawings: (H) $143

CRAIG, Anderson
paintings: (H) $1,725

CRAIG, Charles
American 1846-1931
paintings: (L) $302; (H) $8,800
drawings: (L) $2,200; (H) $8,250

CRAIG, Frank
British 1874-1918
paintings: (L) $660; (H) $5,500
drawings: (H) $770

CRAIG, Henry Robertson
Irish 1916-1984
paintings: (L) $467; (H) $6,875

CRAIG, Isaac Eugene
American b. 1830
paintings: (L) $1,430; (H) $1,870

CRAIG, James Humbert
British d. 1944
paintings: (H) $1,430

CRAIG, James Stevenson
British 19th cent.
paintings: (H) $3,300

CRAIG, Johnny
paintings: (H) $1,760
drawings: (L) $1,265; (H) $1,495

CRAIG, Thomas Bigelow
American 1849-1924
paintings: (L) $412; (H) $5,225
drawings: (L) $66; (H) $3,300

CRAIG, William
American 1829-1875
paintings: (L) $935; (H) $8,050
drawings: (H) $172

CRAIG, William Marshall
English ac. 1788-1828
drawings: (H) $1,870

CRAM, Allen Gilbert
American 1886-1947
paintings: (L) $770; (H) $3,575

CRAM, Bessie
20th cent.
paintings: (H) $660

CRAM, E.G.
American 20th cent.
paintings: (L) $220; (H) $605

CRAM, Edith T.
American b. 1873
paintings: (H) $1,430

CRAMER, Ernest
20th cent.
paintings: (L) $220; (H) $550

CRAMER, Konrad
German/American 1888-1965
paintings: (L) $275; (H) $5,462
drawings: (L) $920; (H) $935

CRANACH, Lucas, the elder
German 1472-1553
paintings: (L) $27,600; (H) $398,500

CRANACH, Lucas, the elder studio of
15th/16th cent.
paintings: (L) $9,900; (H) $46,200

CRANACH, Lucas, the younger
German 1515-1586
paintings: (H) $40,700

CRANCH, Christopher P.
American 1813-1892
paintings: (L) $852; (H) $2,200

CRANDALL, William E.
American
drawings: (H) $3,190

CRANDELL, Bradshaw
American 1896-1966
paintings: (L) $115; (H) $3,575
drawings: (L) $770; (H) $3,300

CRANE, Bruce
American 1857-1937
paintings: (L) $743; (H) $23,100
drawings: (H) $605

CRANE, Frederick
American 1847-1915
paintings: (H) $1,320

CRANE, H.
British 19th/20th cent.
paintings: (H) $605

CRANE, Robert Bruce, or Bruce
American 1857-1937
paintings: (L) $302; (H) $30,800
drawings: (L) $55; (H) $990

CRANE, Stanley W.
American b. 1905
paintings: (L) $319; (H) $825
drawings: (H) $330

CRANE, Walter
English 1845-1915
paintings: (L) $18,400; (H) $22,000
drawings: (L) . $275; (H) $1,650

CRANESTONE, L.
American ac. 1845-1867
drawings: (H) $880

CRANKSHAW, C.E.
19th/20th cent.
paintings: (H) $825

CRANO, Felix de
French 19th cent.
paintings: (H) $1,760

CRANS, J.
paintings: (H) $715

CRANSTOUN, James Hall
British 1821-1907
paintings: (H) $2,070

CRANT, Mary
American 19th cent.
sculpture: (H) $770

CRARY, Robert Fulton
American 19th cent.
paintings: (H) $1,100

CRASH
20th cent.
paintings: (H) $7,475

CRATZ, Benjamin Arthur
American 1886-1952
paintings: (L) $403; (H) $770

CRAVEN, E.
American 20th cent.
paintings: (H) $1,045

CRAVEN, Edgar Malin
American
paintings: (L) $440; (H) $770

CRAWFORD, Annie
paintings: (H) $460
drawings: (H) $288

CRAWFORD, John
American ac. mid-19th cent.
paintings: (H) $8,800

CRAWFORD, Josephine
American 1878-1952
paintings: (H) $1,540

CRAWFORD, Kathy
drawings: (L) $605; (H) $2,970

CRAWFORD, McKinnon
19th/20th cent.
paintings: (H) $495

CRAWFORD, R.S.
American
sculpture: (L) $288; (H) $633

CRAWFORD, Ralston
American 1906-1977
paintings: (L) $8,250; (H) $24,200
drawings: (H) $6,600

CRAWFORD, Robert C.
British 19th cent.
paintings: (L) $805; (H) $3,450

CRAWFORD, Thomas
American 1813-1857
sculpture: (L) $6,600; (H) $27,600

CRAWFORD, Will
1869-1944
paintings: (L) $605; (H) $880
drawings: (L) $192; (H) $1,870

CRAWLEY, Ida
American b. 1867
paintings: (H) $1,093

CRAWTON, R.C.
paintings: (H) $825

CREDI, Lorenzo di, called Lorenzo
d'ODERIGO
1459-1537
paintings: (H) $1,212,500

CREECY, Herbert
American 20th cent.
paintings: (H) $880

CREGAN, Martin
c. 1788-1870
paintings: (H) $1,725

CREIFELDS, Richard
American 1853-1939
paintings: (L) $176; (H) $1,650

CREIXAMS, Pierre
paintings: (H) $3,960

CREMERS, Paul
Belgian 19th cent.
paintings: (H) $10,925

CREMONINI, Leonardo
Italian b. 1925
paintings: (L) $7,187; (H) $44,000
drawings: (L) $1,100; (H) $1,150

CREO, Cristoforo
Italian 20th cent.
paintings: (H) $990

CRESCITO, F.
Italian 19th cent.
drawings: (H) $605

CRESPI, Daniele
Italian 1598-1630
drawings: (H) $15,400

CRESPI, Enrico
Italian 1854-1929
paintings: (L) $660; (H) $6,900

CRESPI, Giovanni Battista, called
CERANO
c. 1575-1633
paintings: (H) $8,625

CRESPI, Giuseppe Maria, called Lo
SPAGNUOLO
Italian 1665-1747
paintings: (L) $48,875; (H) $431,500
drawings: (H) $16,100

CRESSEY, Bert
1883-1944
paintings: (L) $495; (H) $1,725

CRESSEY, Meta
1882-1964
paintings: (H) $1,725

CRESSEY, Susan
d. 1942
paintings: (H) $2,420

CRESSWELL, William Nichol
Canadian 1822-1888
paintings: (L) $1,540; (H) $2,300

CRESWICK, Thomas
English 1811-1869
paintings: (L) $1,093; (H) $25,300
drawings: (L) $88; (H) $495

CRETAN, Veneto
17th cent.
paintings: (H) $1,320

CRETI, Donato
Italian 1671-1749
paintings: (H) $11,000
drawings: (L) $2,875; (H) $6,600

CREVIER, Frank R.
drawings: (L) $288; (H) $863

CREWS, Monte
American early 20th cent.
paintings: (H) $605

CRIBBS, Keke
contemporary
sculpture: (H) $2,588

CRILEY, Theodore Morrow
American 1880-1930
paintings: (L) $748; (H) $6,600

CRIPPA, Roberto
Italian 1912-1972
paintings: (H) $5,500

CRISCUOLO, P.
Italian 19th cent.
paintings: (H) $2,070

CRISP, G.
British 19th/20th cent.
paintings: (L) $412; (H) $2,090

CRISPE, Sara M.
Continental School 19th cent.
paintings: (L) $4,600; (H) $4,950

CRISS, Francis
Anglo/American 1901-1973
paintings: (L) $3,680; (H) $23,100

CRITE, Allan Rohan
American b. 1910
paintings: (L) $990; (H) $8,800
drawings: (L) $165; (H) $517
sculpture: (H) $288

CRIVELLI, Angelo Maria, called Il
Crivellone
Italian d. 1730/60
paintings: (L) $12,075; (H) $63,250

CROAK
paintings: (H) $1,320

CROATTO, Bruno
1875-1948
paintings: (L) $1,540; (H) $2,420

CROCHEPIERRE, Andre Antoine
French b. 1860
paintings: (L) $1,495; (H) $9,350

CROCKER, Charles
American 1877-1959
paintings: (H) $880

CROCKER, David B.
paintings: (H) $2,200

CROCKER, John Denison
American 1823-1879
paintings: (L) $660; (H) $4,180

CROCKER, Marion E.
paintings: (H) $1,100
drawings: (H) $220

CROCKER, Martha
American b. 1883
paintings: (H) $460

CROCKETT, Linda, Hanzel
paintings: (H) $550

CROCKFORD, Duncan Mackinnon
Canadian 1920-1991
paintings: (L) $1,870; (H) $5,060

CROCKWELL, Douglass
1904-1968
paintings: (L) $715; (H) $6,050

CROEGAERT, Georges
Belgian 1848-1923
paintings: (L) $110; (H) $23,000

CROFT, Arthur
English ac. 1865-1893
paintings: (L) $110; (H) $800
drawings: (L) $165; (H) $1,265

CROFTS, Ernest
British 1847-1911
paintings: (L) $316; (H) $3,080

CROFUT, Robert
b. 1951
paintings: (H) $605

CROISILLIOT, Jean Etienne
French ac. 1836-1848
drawings: (H) $770

CROISY
sculpture: (H) $1,380

CROLIN, David
contemporary
drawings: (H) $2,475

CROME, John Berney
British 1794-1842
paintings: (L) $1,100; (H) $1,320

CROME, Vivian
British ac. 1858-1883
paintings: (L) $467; (H) $550

CROME, William Henry
English 1806-1873
paintings: (H) $770

CROMPTON, C.C.
British 1870-1945
drawings: (H) $770

CROMPTON, Cecilia
English 1864-1926
paintings: (H) $501

CROMPTON, James Shaw
English 1853-1916
drawings: (H) $825

CROMWELL, Joane
American 1889-1966
paintings: (L) $165; (H) $1,045

CROOK, Don
paintings: (L) $495; (H) $6,930

CROOKER, Abby
drawings: (L) $1,320; (H) $9,075

CROOS, Anthonie Jansz. van der
Dutch 1606-1662
paintings: (L) $1,955; (H) $7,700

CROOS, Jacob van der
Dutch ac. 1690-d. before 1700
paintings: (L) $11,500; (H) $14,950

CROOS, Pieter van der
Dutch b. c. 1610
paintings: (L) $3,850; (H) $11,500

CROPSEY, Jasper Francis
American 1823-1900
paintings: (L) $2,990; (H) $1,003,500
drawings: (L) $460; (H) $34,100

CROSBY, A.M.
American 20th cent.
paintings: (H) $1,870

CROSBY, Raymond Moreau
American 1877-1945
drawings: (L) $55; (H) $518

CROSBY, William
paintings: (H) $4,125

CROSLAND, Enoch
English 19th cent.
paintings: (L) $316; (H) $2,750

CROSS, Henri Edmond
French 1856-1910
paintings: (L) $330; (H) $442,500
drawings: (L) $460; (H) $14,850

CROSS, Henry H.
American 1837-1918
paintings: (L) $220; (H) $11,500

CROSS, Jay
American 1889-1950
paintings: (H) $468

CROSS, John
English 1819-1861
paintings: (H) $825

CROSS, Roy
American 20th cent.
paintings: (H) $1,760
drawings: (H) $880

CROSS, Watson, Jr.
American b. 1918
paintings: (H) $165
drawings: (H) $990

CROSSE, Richard
paintings: (H) $3,850

CROSSMAN, Lizze
drawings: (H) $1,495

CROUAN, Julie
French late 19th cent.
paintings: (H) $4,600

CROUCH, Don
American b. 1940
sculpture: (H) $4,400

CROW, Nancy
contemporary
sculpture: (L) $2,875; (H) $3,738

CROWE, Eyre
English 1824-1910
paintings: (H) $3,960

CROWELL, A. Elmer
sculpture: (H) $7,040

CROWELL, Lucius
American 1911-1988
paintings: (L) $440; (H) $660

CROWELL, Nicholas
paintings: (H) $1,705

CROWLEY, Don
b. 1926
drawings: (H) $1,100

CROWLEY, Nicholas Joseph
1813-1857
paintings: (L) $7,700; (H) $9,350

CROWNINSHIELD, Frederic
American 1845-1918
paintings: (L) $770; (H) $1,045

CROWTHER, Henry
British 19th/20th cent.
paintings: (H) $770

CROWTHER, Robert W.
American b. 1902
paintings: (H) $880
drawings: (H) $193

CROZIER, William
b. 1933
sculpture: (H) $3,680

CRUICKSHANK, William
British 1848-1922
paintings: (H) $660
drawings: (L) $440; (H) $660

CRUIKSHANK, George
English 1792-1878
paintings: (H) $4,675
drawings: (L) $137; (H) $715

CRUIKSHANK, Isaac
British 1756-1816
drawings: (H) $660

CRUIKSHANK, Isaac Robert
British 1789-1856
drawings: (L) $550; (H) $690

CRUIKSHANK, William
Scottish/Canadian 1844/49-1922
paintings: (H) $1,380
drawings: (L) $629; (H) $847

CRUISE, Aluyk Boyd
American 1860-1898
drawings: (H) $2,090

CRUISE, Boyd
American 1909-1988
drawings: (L) $495; (H) $16,500

CRUISE, L.J.
paintings: (H) $900

CRULL, Ford
American contemporary
paintings: (H) $518

CRUMB, R. and Harvey PEKAR
drawings: (H) $2,750

CRUMB, Robert
drawings: (L) $1,100; (H) $6,600
sculpture: (H) $5,750

CRUZ, Emil
sculpture: (H) $880

CRUZ-DIEZ, Carlos
Venezuelan b. 1923
paintings: (H) $6,050
drawings: (L) $4,025; (H) $4,400
sculpture: (L) $9,900; (H) $19,550

CSADEK
Continental 19th cent.
sculpture: (H) $1,610

CSAKY, Joseph
Hungarian/French 1888-1971
paintings: (H) $1,045
sculpture: (L) $9,200; (H) $46,000

CSERNUS, Tibor
b. 1927
paintings: (H) $23,000

CSOT
Hungarian contemporary
paintings: (L) $77; (H) $605

CUARTAS, Gregorio
b. Colombia 1938
paintings: (H) $4,400

CUBELLS Y RUIZ, Enrique Martinez
Spanish 1874-1917
paintings: (L) $25,300; (H) $77,000

CUBLEY, Henry Hadfield
British 19th cent.
paintings: (L) $259; (H) $935

CUCCHI, Enzo
Italian b. 1950
paintings: (L) $19,550; (H) $110,000
drawings: (L) $3,450; (H) $73,700
sculpture: (H) $79,200

CUCUEL, Edward
American 1875/79-1951
paintings: (L) $660; (H) $29,700
drawings: (L) $412; (H) $2,587

CUENCA, Arturo
Cuban b. 1955
paintings: (H) $6,900

CUEVAS, Jose Luis
Mexican b. 1933/34
drawings: (L) $468; (H) $9,200

CUGAT, Delia
Argentinean b. 1930
paintings: (L) $4,887; (H) $13,200

CUGAT, Xavier
Spanish 1898-1990
paintings: (L) $220; (H) $460
drawings: (H) $225

CUIXART, Modesto
contemporary
drawings: (H) $3,300

CULLEN, Maurice Galbraith
Canadian 1866-1934
paintings: (L) $5,280; (H) $88,000
drawings: (L) $1,540; (H) $15,400

CULLIN, Isaac
British 19th cent.
paintings: (L) $28,750; (H) $60,250

CULVER, Charles
American 1908-1967
paintings: (L) $121; (H) $935
drawings: (L) $121; (H) $3,105

CULVERHOUSE, Johann Mongels
Dutch b. 1820, ac. 1859-1891
paintings: (L) $230; (H) $14,850

CUMBERWORTH, Charles
French 1811-1852
sculpture: (L) $1,870; (H) $2,200

CUMING, Beatrice
1903-1975
paintings: (H) $495

CUMING, Frederick
American 1865-1949
paintings: (H) $805

CUMING, Frederick
English 20th cent.
paintings: (H) $1,650

CUMMING, Arthur
American 1847-1913
paintings: (L) $550; (H) $990
drawings: (L) $138; (H) $990

CUMMING, Contance Frederica
Gordon
Australian 19th cent.
drawings: (L) $690; (H) $2,530

CUMMINGS, Arthur
American 19th cent.
paintings: (H) $550

CUMMINGS, C.W.
American mid-19th cent.
drawings: (H) $3,520

CUMMINGS, E.E.
drawings: (L) $143; (H) $1,210

CUNAEUS, Conradyn
Dutch 1828-1895
paintings: (L) $1,650; (H) $11,213

CUNDELL, Charles
British 1890-1971
paintings: (H) $990

CUNDELL, Nora L.M.
British 1889-1971
paintings: (H) $495

CUNDIN, Jose Maria
American contemporary
paintings: (L) $330; (H) $1,540

CUNEO, Jose
b. Uruguay 1898
paintings: (L) $8,050; (H) $41,250

CUNEO, Rinaldo
American 1877-1939
paintings: (L) $825; (H) $10,450

CUNEO, Terence
British b. 1907
paintings: (L) $7,187; (H) $7,187

CUNNINGHAM, Earl
1893-1977
paintings: (L) $29,900; (H) $37,375

CUNNINGHAM, Fern
paintings: (H) $935

CUNNINGHAM, Robert M.
b. 1924
paintings: (H) $495

CUPRIEN, Frank W.
American 1871-1948
paintings: (L) $660; (H) $7,475

CURILLON, Pierre
French 19th/20th cent.
sculpture: (H) $460

CURLE (---?), E.
German 19th cent.
paintings: (H) $907

CURRADI, Francesco
1570-1661
drawings: (H) $5,280

CURRAN, Charles Courtney
American 1861-1942
paintings: (L) $550; (H) $112,500
drawings: (L) $2,300; (H) $2,990

CURRIE, Sidney
British ac. 1892-1930
paintings: (L) $715; (H) $2,185

CURRIER, Anne
contemporary
sculpture: (L) $550; (H) $1,045

CURRIER, Cyrus Bates
American 1868-1946
paintings: (L) $110; (H) $605

CURRIER, Edward Wilson
American 1857-1918
paintings: (H) $690
drawings: (H) $303

CURRIER, George H.
American 20th cent.
paintings: (H) $1,210

CURRIER, J. Frank
American 1843-1909
paintings: (L) $1,155; (H) $6,050
drawings: (L) $357; (H) $1,035

CURRIER, Nathaniel K.
American 1813-1888
paintings: (H) $495

CURRIER, Walter Barron
American 1879-1934
paintings: (L) $165; (H) $605

CURRY, John Steuart
American 1897-1946
paintings: (L) $1,045; (H) $162,000
drawings: (L) $770; (H) $15,400

CURRY, Robert F.
American b. 1872
paintings: (L) $55; (H) $825

CURSHIN, Christopher
American 19th/20th cent.
paintings: (H) $460

CURTER, J.
20th cent.
paintings: (H) $575

CURTIS, Calvin
American 1822-1893
paintings: (L) $605; (H) $2,970

CURTIS, David
American 20th cent.
paintings: (L) $330; (H) $1,210

CURTIS, George
American 1826-1892
paintings: (L) $1,900; (H) $5,750

CURTIS, George
American d. 1926
paintings: (H) $1,650

CURTIS, Ida Maynard
American 1860-1959
paintings: (H) $1,210

Cragsmoor Art Colony

Success came early to Charles Courtney Curran (1861-1942). He exhibited at the National Academy of Design when he was 23, and within five years he had won the Third Hallgarten Prize for most "meritorious painting in oil" from the academy. Curran was born in Kentucky and raised in Sandusky, Ohio. He studied briefly at the Cincinnati School of Design and then at the National Academy of Design in New York. In 1889 he traveled to Paris and studied for two years at the Académie Julien. Although he studied at a formal academic school, he was in Paris at the height of Impressionism. After Europe, Curran returned to New York City. In 1903 he was a guest at the Cragsmoor Art Colony in the Hudson River valley where Edward Lamson Henry had built a house about 1884. Charmed by the resort, Curran built a second home there and by 1910 he was dividing his time between the city and country. Curran became a leader of the colony and he and his wife edited its student publication. Some of Curran's best paintings are his sweeping vistas of Cragsmoor and his portraits of lovely women. In his early portraits he frequently painted women surrounded by flowers; at Cragsmoor his portraits were often set against bright sunlight with a blue sky and on top of a hill or mountain. *Among the Hollyhocks*, undated, is most likely an early work. Consigned to James Julia's Auctions in Fairfield, Maine, it sold for $27,500. (Charles Courtney Curran, *Among the Hollyhocks*, oil on canvas, 18 x 22 inches, Julia, August 25, 1994, $27,500)

CURTIS, Jenny C.
  paintings: (H) $2,970

CURTIS, L.B.
  paintings: (H) $1,155

CURTIS, Leland
  American b. 1897
  paintings: (L) $715; (H) $3,850
  drawings: (L) $880; (H) $1,210

CURTIS, N.C.
  paintings: (H) $675

CURTIS, Philip Campbell
  American b. 1907
  paintings: (H) $1,980

CURTIS, Ralph Wormsley
  Anglo/American 1854-1922
  paintings: (L) $550; (H) $1,650

CURTIS, Sidney W.
  American 19th/20th century
  paintings: (H) $605

CURTIS, William Fuller
  American b. 1873
  paintings: (L) $193; (H) $1,100
  drawings: (L) $66; (H) $247
  sculpture: (H) $4,400

CURTS, T***
  American 20th cent.
  sculpture: (H) $1,035

CURZON, Paul Alfred de
French 1820-1895
paintings: (L) $8,250; (H) $9,200

CUSACHS Y CUSACHS, Jose
Spanish 1851-1908
paintings: (L) $25,300; (H) $38,500

CUSI Y FERRET, Manuel
Spanish b. 1857
paintings: (L) $3,680; (H) $17,600

CUSTER, Edward L.
American 1837-1880
paintings: (L) $825; (H) $2,200

CUSTIS, Eleanor Parke
American 1897-1983
paintings: (L) $2,640; (H) $2,750
drawings: (L) $83; (H) $3,575

CUSTODIO, G.
paintings: (L) $440; (H) $660

CUTBERT, Albert
French early 19th cent.
drawings: (H) $495

CUTLER, Carl Gordon
American 1873-1945
paintings: (H) $660

CUTLER, Cecil
drawings: (H) $518

CUTLER, Thomas
American 20th cent.
drawings: (L) $385; (H) $605

CUTRONE, Ronnie
American b. 1948
paintings: (L) $3,850; (H) $4,400
drawings: (H) $550

CUYLENBORCH, Abraham van
Dutch ac. c.1620-1658
paintings: (L) $7,150; (H) $8,250

CUYP, Aelbert
Dutch 1620-1691
paintings: (L) $2,640; (H) $40,700

CUYP, Benjamin Gerritsz.
Dutch 1612-1652
paintings: (L) $15,400; (H) $24,200

CYGNE, E.J., Jose Fernandez
American b. 1929
paintings: (L) $44; (H) $990

CYNDO, Jose Rico
Spanish b. 1864
paintings: (H) $2,530

CZEREPAK, Alfred
American 1928-1986
paintings: (L) $110; (H) $467
drawings: (H) $165
sculpture: (H) $407

CZERNOTZKY, Ernest
Hungarian 1845-1905
paintings: (H) $1,320

CZERNY, Ludwig
Austrian 1821-1889
paintings: (H) $550

CZOBEL, Bela Adalbert
Hungarian 1883-1974
paintings: (H) $805

D'AGOSTINO, Vincent
American b. 1898
paintings: (H) $1,210

D'AGUILAR, M.
paintings: (H) $550

D'AINECY, Henri, Compte de
MONTPEZAT
French 1817-1859
paintings: (H) $6,325

D'AIRE, Paul
French ac. 1890-1910
sculpture: (H) $1,430

D'AMICO, Oskar
contemporary
paintings: (L) $660; (H) $770

D'ANCONA
paintings: (H) $1,760

D'ANGELO, R.A.
sculpture: (L) $633; (H) $805

D'ARCANGELO, Alan
American b. 1930
paintings: (L) $460; (H) $19,800
drawings: (H) $1,035

D'ARCEVIA, Bruno
paintings: (L) $550; (H) $770

D'ASCENZO, Nicola
Italian/American 1871-1954
paintings: (L) $400; (H) $1,350
drawings: (L) $27; (H) $690

D'AURIA, V***
Continental 19th/20th cent.
paintings: (H) $1,380

D'AVINO
paintings: (H) $3,025

D'EPINAY, Charles Adrien Prosper
French b. 1836
sculpture: (H) $3,450

D'ESPIC, Christian
paintings: (H) $5,775

D'LEON, Omar
Nicaraguan b. 1929
paintings: (L) $2,200; (H) $2,750

DA COSTA, Joao Batista
1865-1926
paintings: (H) $18,400

DA COSTA, John
British 1867-1931
paintings: (L) $18,400; (H) $74,000

DA COSTA, S.
drawings: (H) $605

DA RIOS, Luigi
Italian 1844-1892
drawings: (H) $5,750

DAALHOFF, Henri van
Dutch 1867-1953
paintings: (H) $1,320

DABO, Leon
American 1868-1960
paintings: (L) $385; (H) $18,400

DABO, Theodore Scott
American b. 1877
paintings: (L) $275; (H) $3,025

DABOS, Laurent
1761-1835
paintings: (H) $3,080

DABOUR, John
American b. 1837
drawings: (H) $747

DABOURR
paintings: (H) $1,210

DABUDIE, Henri
French 19th cent.
paintings: (H) $1,800

DACOSTA, Milton
Brazilian b. 1915
paintings: (H) $34,500

DADD, Frank
British 1851-1929
drawings: (H) $1,980

DADD, Richard
drawings: (H) $632

DADO, Miodrag DJURIC
b. 1933
paintings: (H) $6,600

DAEL, Jan Frans van
Flemish 1764-1840
paintings: (H) $46,200
drawings: (H) $8,250

DAELE, Casimir van den
Belgian 1818-1880
paintings: (H) $4,620

DAGIU, Francesco, called Il Capella
Italian 1714-1784
paintings: (L) $19,800; (H) $52,800

DAGNAC-RIVIERE, Charles Henri
Gaston
French 1864-1945
paintings: (H) $1,265

DAGNAN-BOUVERET, Pascal
Adolphe
French 1852-1929
paintings: (L) $1,650; (H) $19,550

DAHL, Hans
Norwegian 1849-1937
paintings: (L) $3,220; (H) $18,700

DAHL, Johan Christian Clausen
Norwegian 1788-1857
paintings: (H) $37,375

DAHL, Michael
1656-1743
paintings: (L) $4,400; (H) $6,600

DAHL, von
Dutch b. 1919
paintings: (H) $1,650

DAHLAGER, Jules
20th cent.
paintings: (L) $330; (H) $1,955

DAHLBERG, H. Clay
American b. 1946
sculpture: (L) $3,410; (H) $4,950

DAHLGREEN, Charles W.
American 1864-1955
paintings: (L) $522; (H) $2,420

DAHLGREN, Carl Christian
Danish/American 1841-1920?
paintings: (L) $299; (H) $4,600
drawings: (H) $633

DAHN, Walter
German b. 1954
paintings: (L) $1,380; (H) $19,800
drawings: (L) $1,300; (H) $3,450

DAHN, Walter and Jiri Georg
DOKOUPIL
b. 1950s
paintings: (H) $6,325

DAIL, Van
paintings: (H) $2,300

DAILEY, Dan
American b. 1947
sculpture: (L) $5,280; (H) $8,625

DAILLON, Horace
sculpture: (H) $2,090

DAILY, Mark
b. 1935
paintings: (H) $1,980

DAINAILLE, Alexander Joseph and
Eugene Joseph VERBOECKHOVEN
paintings: (H) $11,550

DAINGERFIELD, Elliott
American 1859-1932
paintings: (L) $805; (H) $7,150

DAINI, Augusto
Italian 19th cent.
paintings: (L) $2,530; (H) $4,313
drawings: (H) $495

DAINI, Hugo
Italian b. 1919
sculpture: (H) $6,600

DAKE, Carel Lodewijk
Dutch 1857-1918
paintings: (H) $1,045

DAKEN, Sidney Tilden
American 1876-1935
paintings: (L) $302; (H) $523

DAKIN, Joseph
British 19th/20th cent.
paintings: (H) $935

DALBERG, G***
German 19th cent.
paintings: (H) $5,463

DALBONO, Edouardo
Italian 1843-1915
paintings: (L) $3,025; (H) $20,700

DALBY, David
British b. 1790
paintings: (L) $4,600; (H) $14,375

DALBY, John
British 1826-1853
paintings: (L) $3,450; (H) $42,550

DALE, Z.
American 20th cent.
paintings: (H) $660

DALEE, Justus
American ac. c. 1833-1841
drawings: (L) $5,775; (H) $28,750

DALENS, Dirck, I
Dutch 1600-1677
paintings: (L) $14,950; (H) $23,100

DALEY, William
sculpture: (L) $2,530; (H) $2,750

DALI, Louis
French 20th cent.
paintings: (L) $110; (H) $1,100

DALI, Salvador
Spanish 1904-1989
paintings: (L) $18,400; (H) $3,522,500
drawings: (L) $1,150; (H) $299,500
sculpture: (L) $345; (H) $104,500

DALLIN, Cyrus Edwin
American 1861-1944
sculpture: (L) $550; (H) $57,500

DALLONI, Emma Segur
French 1890-1968
drawings: (H) $852

DALMAU, Emilio Poy
Spanish 1876-1933
paintings: (L) $3,220; (H) $3,300

DALMBERT, Daniel
French b. 1918
paintings: (H) $660

DALOU, Aime Jules
French 1838-1902
sculpture: (L) $288; (H) $156,500

DALTON, S.
paintings: (H) $747

DALTON, T.J.
paintings: (H) $467

DALWOOD, Hubert
1924-1976
sculpture: (H) $1,150

DAM, Pieter van
Dutch 20th cent.
paintings: (H) $550

DAM, Vu Cao
American b. 1908
paintings: (L) $220; (H) $990

DAMARTIN, Jose Miralles
Spanish b. 1851
paintings: (H) $19,800

DAMBLANS, Eugene
Uruguayan b. 1865
paintings: (H) $1,650

DAMBOURGEZ, Edouard Jean
French 1844-1890
paintings: (L) $3,740; (H) $4,140

DAMERON, Emile Charles
French 1848-1908
paintings: (L) $575; (H) $12,100

DAMIAN, Horia
Romanian b. 1922
paintings: (L) $990; (H) $3,300

DAMIANI, Jorge
Italian b. 1931
paintings: (H) $9,775

DAMMAN, Benjamin Louis Auguste
French b. 1835
paintings: (H) $575

DAMME, E. van
paintings: (H) $523

DAMME, F.A.A.
paintings: (H) $880

DAMME, Roger van
paintings: (H) $2,750

DAMME, S.J.
European 20th cent.
paintings: (H) $577

DAMME-SYLVA, Emile van
Belgian 1853-1935
paintings: (L) $1,320; (H) $2,875

DAMOYE, Pierre Emmanuel
French 1847-1916
paintings: (L) $483; (H) $26,400
drawings: (H) $345

DAMRON, J.C.
paintings: (L) $935; (H) $1,870

DAMRON, J.C.
1903-1989
drawings: (L) $88; (H) $1,210

DAMROW, Charles
American b. 1916
paintings: (L) $288; (H) $2,200

DAMSCHROEDER, Jan Jac Matthys
German 1825-1905
paintings: (L) $990; (H) $3,850

DANA, Charles Edmund
American 1843-1924
drawings: (L) $258; (H) $1,955

DANA, Charles Grafton
1843-1926
paintings: (L) $440; (H) $605

DANA, Edmund T.
American 19th cent.
paintings: (H) $2,750

DANBOURGEZ, Edouard Jean
French 1844-1890
paintings: (H) $3,220

DANBY, Ken
Canadian b. 1940
drawings: (L) $3,080; (H) $4,950

DANBY, Thomas
British
paintings: (H) $1,210

DANCE, Nathaniel
English 1734-1811
paintings: (L) $495; (H) $1,100

DANCER, Monna Jackson
American
paintings: (H) $1,600

DANDINI, Cesare
Italian 1595-1658
paintings: (L) $14,300; (H) $74,000

DANDINI, Ottavino
Italian d. 1750
paintings: (H) $1,540

DANDINI, Pietro
Italian 1646-1712
paintings: (H) $16,100
drawings: (L) $575; (H) $2,070

DANDRE-BARDON, Michel Francois
French 1700-1778/83
drawings: (H) $8,625

DANGER, Henri Camille
French 1857-after 1937
paintings: (H) $35,650

DANGON, Jeanne
French b. 1873
paintings: (H) $2,200

DANHAUSER, Joseph
Austrian 1805-1845
drawings: (H) $4,125

DANIDONI, S.
Italian 19th cent.
drawings: (H) $1,540

DANIEL, William Swift
American 1865-1933
drawings: (H) $880

DANIELE DA VOLTERRA
c. 1509-1566
drawings: (H) $16,100

DANIELL, Thomas
English 1749-1840
drawings: (L) $489; (H) $2,640

DANIELL, William
British 1769-1837
paintings: (H) $13,800
drawings: (H) $247

DANIELS, Andries, or DANEELS
Flemish b. 1580, ac. 1599-1602
paintings: (H) $68,500

DANIELS, Dan
American
sculpture: (H) $1,650

DANIELS, F.H.
American 20th cent.
paintings: (L) $55; (H) $1,072

DANIELS, William
British 1813-1880
paintings: (H) $1,265

DANKMEYER, Charles
Dutch 1861-1923
paintings: (L) $550; (H) $1,500

DANLOUX, Henri Pierre
French 1753-1809
paintings: (L) $1,650; (H) $6,050

DANN, Frode Nielsen
American b. 1892
paintings: (H) $825

DANNASH, H.
drawings: (H) $460

DANNAT, William Turner
American 1853-1929
paintings: (H) $9,430

DANNENBERG, Alice
French b. 1861
paintings: (L) $9,625; (H) $11,500

DANNEQUIN, Alfred Joseph
French d. 1890
paintings: (H) $1,035

DANNER, Sara Kolb
American 1894-1969
paintings: (L) $248; (H) $4,400
drawings: (L) $220; (H) $770

DANSAERT, Leon Marie Constant
Belgian 1830-1909
paintings: (L) $5,750; (H) $7,150

DANSET, George
French 20th cent.
paintings: (H) $489

DANTAN, Antoine Laurent
French 1798-1878
sculpture: (H) $1,815

DANTAN, Edouard Joseph
French 1848-1897
paintings: (H) $211,500

DANTON, Ferdinand, Jr.
American 1849-1908
paintings: (H) $1,210

DAPHNIS, Nassos
American b. 1914
paintings: (L) $1,380; (H) $5,500
drawings: (L) $440; (H) $3,520

DAPRA, R.
Continental 20th cent.
paintings: (H) $522

DARAGON, Charles Joseph Laurent
French 1883-1904
sculpture: (H) $2,100

DARBOVEN, Hanne
b. Germany 1941
drawings: (L) $7,475; (H) $12,650

DARBY, Henry F.
American b. 1831
paintings: (H) $825

DARCH-LEWIS, Edmond
American 1835-1910
drawings: (L) $440; (H) $550

DARCOVICH, Michael
American 20th cent.
paintings: (H) $2,310

DARCY, Jaques
French
drawings: (L) $1,210; (H) $3,025

DAREGLAS, Andre Henri
French 1828-1903
paintings: (H) $2,090

DARGE, Fred
American b. 1900
paintings: (H) $2,420

DARGELAS, Andre Henri
French 1828-1906
paintings: (L) $4,313; (H) $7,700

DARGENT, Jean Edouard
French 1824-1889
paintings: (H) $6,380

DARGER, Henry
American 1892-1973
drawings: (H) $10,350

DARIEN, Henri Gaston
French 1864-1926
paintings: (H) $11,500

DARIEN, Henry
French 19th cent.
paintings: (H) $54,050

DARIO, Ales
drawings: (H) $1,540

DARLEY, Felix Octavius Carr
American 1822-1888
paintings: (L) $403; (H) $3,850
drawings: (L) $247; (H) $9,200

DARLEY, Jane Cooper Sully
American 1807-1877
paintings: (H) $11,550

DARLING, Wilder M.
American 1856-1933
paintings: (L) $220; (H) $522
drawings: (L) $88; (H) $220

DARLING, William S.
Hungarian/American 1882-1963
paintings: (L) $412; (H) $4,025

DARMANIN, Jose Miralles
Spanish b. 1851
paintings: (H) $7,700

DARNAUT, Hugo
Austrian 1851-1937
drawings: (H) $5,175

DARRAH, Ann Sophia Towne
American 1819-1881
paintings: (L) $259; (H) $2,750

DARRIEUX, Charles Rene
French 1879-1958
paintings: (H) $3,960

DARSONT, Joh.
sculpture: (H) $1,100

DARSOW, Johannes
German late 19th/20th cent.
sculpture: (H) $990

DASBURG, Andrew Michael
American 1887-1979
paintings: (L) $2,750; (H) $46,200
drawings: (L) $1,100; (H) $17,600

DASH, Robert
American b. 1932
paintings: (H) $3,740

DASSON, Henry
sculpture: (H) $550

DAUBIGNY, Charles Francois
French 1817-1878
paintings: (L) $1,610; (H) $354,500
drawings: (H) $3,740

DAUBIGNY, Karl Pierre
French 1846-1886
paintings: (L) $575; (H) $17,600

DAUCHOT, Gabriel
French b. 1927
paintings: (L) $403; (H) $8,250

DAUFIN, Jacques
paintings: (L) $412; (H) $4,950

DAUGHERTY, James
American 1889-1974
paintings: (L) $1,150; (H) $16,500
drawings: (L) $55; (H) $770

DAUGHTERS, Robert
American b. 1929
paintings: (L) $2,200; (H) $3,410

DAUMENG, Henri Bouchet
French 19th cent.
paintings: (H) $1,650

DAUMIER, Honore
French 1808-1879
paintings: (L) $101,500; (H) $132,000
drawings: (L) $1,100; (H) $640,500
sculpture: (L) $3,080; (H) $57,500

DAUMIER, Jean
French b. 1919
paintings: (L) $523; (H) $575

DAUMILLER, A.
French 20th cent.
sculpture: (H) $1,045

DAUZATS, Adrien
French 1804-1868
paintings: (L) $13,800; (H) $19,800
drawings: (L) $3,025; (H) $9,200

DAVE, Vinod
Indian b. 1948
paintings: (L) $2,300; (H) $4,025
drawings: (L) $1,150; (H) $3,450

DAVENPORT, Carlson
American 1908-1972
paintings: (H) $8,525

DAVENPORT, Henry
American b. 1882
paintings: (L) $345; (H) $8,800
drawings: (L) $201; (H) $690

DAVENPORT, Rebecca
American b. 1943
paintings: (H) $1,430

DAVENPORT, William Slocum
American b. 1868
paintings: (L) $55; (H) $990

DAVEY, Randall
American 1887-1964
paintings: (L) $495; (H) $10,925
drawings: (L) $413; (H) $4,125

DAVID, Giovanni
Italian 1743-1790
drawings: (H) $2,860

DAVID, Gustave
French 1824-1891
drawings: (H) $460

DAVID, Hermine
French 1886-1971
paintings: (H) $4,620
drawings: (H) $357

DAVID, Jacques Louis
French 1748-1825
drawings: (H) $28,750

DAVID, L.
sculpture: (H) $715

DAVID, Michael
b. 1954
paintings: (L) $1,840; (H) $7,920
drawings: (H) $2,530
sculpture: (H) $1,150

DAVID, Pierre Jean, called David
d'Angers
French 1788-1856
sculpture: (L) $880; (H) $2,090

DAVID, Stanley S.
American 1847-1898
paintings: (L) $14,950; (H) $14,950

DAVIDSON, Alexander
Scottish/English 1838-1887
paintings: (H) $3,190

DAVIDSON, Charles Grant
English 1820/24-1902
paintings: (L) $330; (H) $4,070
drawings: (L) $110; (H) $385

DAVIDSON, Clara D.
American 1874-1962
paintings: (L) $495; (H) $4,025

DAVIDSON, J.O.
paintings: (H) $2,530

DAVIDSON, Jo
American 1883-1952
sculpture: (L) $200; (H) $6,900

DAVIDSON, Julian O.
American 1853-1894
drawings: (L) $110; (H) $1,430

DAVIDSON, Morris
American 1898-1979
paintings: (H) $468
drawings: (H) $248

DAVIE, Alan
English b. 1920
paintings: (L) $4,025; (H) $6,050
drawings: (L) $1,610; (H) $3,738

DAVIES
paintings: (H) $550

DAVIES, A.B.
drawings: (H) $523

DAVIES, Albert Webster
American 1889-1967
paintings: (L) $770; (H) $2,875

DAVIES, Alfred
British 19th cent.
paintings: (H) $660

DAVIES, Arthur B.
American 1862-1928
paintings: (L) $66; (H) $12,100
drawings: (L) $22; (H) $4,675
sculpture: (L) $550; (H) $1,035

DAVIES, B.W.
paintings: (H) $862

DAVIES, Harold Christopher
American 1891-1976
paintings: (L) $1,650; (H) $1,680

DAVIES, James Hey
British 1848-1901
paintings: (H) $1,100

DAVIES, John
British b. 1946
sculpture: (H) $5,500

DAVIES, Kenneth Southworth
American b. 1925
paintings: (L) $550; (H) $6,050
drawings: (H) $138

DAVIES, Norman Prescott
British 19th cent.
paintings: (L) $3,450; (H) $7,700

DAVIES, William
British 1826-1901
paintings: (L) $990; (H) $2,420

DAVILA, Fernando
Colombian b. 1953
paintings: (H) $10,450

DAVILA, Jose Antonio
b. New York 1935
paintings: (L) $3,025; (H) $9,200

DAVIS, Alexander Jackson
American 1803-1892
drawings: (L) $4,887; (H) $9,200

DAVIS, Arthur Alfred
British 19th cent.
paintings: (L) $1,210; (H) $6,325

DAVIS, Arthur Edward
British b. 1893
paintings: (H) $23,000

DAVIS, B.
paintings: (L) $990; (H) $2,990

DAVIS, Brad
American b. 1942
drawings: (L) $805; (H) $3,450

DAVIS, C.H.
paintings: (L) $1,100; (H) $1,540

DAVIS, Charles Harold
American 1856-1933
paintings: (L) $138; (H) $24,200
drawings: (L) $110; (H) $330

DAVIS, Charles Henry
American 1845-1921
drawings: (H) $660

DAVIS, Cornelia Cassady
American 1870-1920
paintings: (H) $3,575

DAVIS, F.
English 19th cent.
drawings: (H) $770

DAVIS, Floyd M.
1896-1966
drawings: (L) $77; (H) $2,200

DAVIS, Gene
American b. 1920
paintings: (L) $2,750; (H) $8,800
drawings: (L) $690; (H) $880

DAVIS, Gladys Rockmore
American 1901-1967
paintings: (L) $55; (H) $6,613
drawings: (L) $220; (H) $275

DAVIS, H.B.
paintings: (H) $797

DAVIS, Henry William Banks
English 1833-1914
paintings: (L) $2,200; (H) $7,425

DAVIS, J. Moor
paintings: (H) $688

DAVIS, J.A., Jane Anthony
American 1821-1855
paintings: (H) $14,375
drawings: (L) $770; (H) $7,475

DAVIS, Jack
American contemporary
drawings: (L) $440; (H) $11,000

DAVIS, Jim
drawings: (L) $402; (H) $747

DAVIS, Joseph E.
drawings: (H) $1,610

DAVIS, Joseph H.
American ac. c. 1832-1838
drawings: (L) $5,175; (H) $90,500

DAVIS, Leonard Moore
American 1864-1938
paintings: (L) $330; (H) $3,450

Left Hand Painter

The itinerant painters, called limners, traveled early 19th-century America, trading room and board and a small fee in exchange for a portrait. Joseph H. Davis (active circa 1832-38) was a limner in rural New Hampshire and Maine during the first half of the 19th century. His watercolors on paper were popular, a compromise between the inexpensive blank-faced silhouettes of the profile-cutter and more costly oil portraits.

Davis's style is distinctive: the subject is always in profile and each portrait is personalized with details of clothing, furnishings, accessories, and sometimes the family's pet cat or dog. These personalized details are unique to each household, not a stereotyped formula as might have been the case in other limner's works. One consistent element that helps identify his paintings are the carpets painted slightly tilted for a full view of a detailed geometric design in dazzling colors. Davis's approach to his work was to first make a rough outline in pencil, trace over it in ink, and then fill it in with watercolor. Below each picture in elegant calligraphy is the name of the sitter and the date of the painting. There is usually not a signature, although one of his paintings is signed "Left Hand Painter."

Joseph H. Davis should not be confused with J.A. Davis (Jane Anthony Davis, 1822-1855) a Rhode Island and Connecticut homemaker who painted numerous watercolor portraits of her friends and relatives. Neither artist signed their works, and both used a calligraphic script at the bottom of the picture to identify the sitter. J.A. Davis, however, painted her sitters full face and bust length, and the mood of her paintings is more somber then that of J.H. Davis. (Joseph H. Davis, *Portrait of William B. Chamberlain*, watercolor on paper, 10¾ x 7½ inches, Caddigan, September 16, 1995, $8,250)

DAVIS, Louis
American 20th cent.
paintings: (H) $660

DAVIS, Paul
drawings: (H) $495

DAVIS, Rebecca
American
drawings: (H) $20,700

DAVIS, Richard
b. 1947
paintings: (H) $6,050

DAVIS, Richard Barrett
English 1782-1854
paintings: (L) $1,495; (H) $2,530

DAVIS, Rita Hicks
b. 1956
paintings: (L) $330; (H) $715

DAVIS, Roger
American 1898-1935
paintings: (H) $825

DAVIS, Ron
American b. 1937
paintings: (H) $1,320
drawings: (L) $2,875; (H) $4,400
sculpture: (H) $660

DAVIS, Stan
American b. 1942
paintings: (L) $2,090; (H) $19,800

DAVIS, Stark
American b. 1885
paintings: (L) $770; (H) $4,125
drawings: (H) $330

DAVIS, Stuart
American 1894-1964
paintings: (L) $20,900; (H) $275,000
drawings: (L) $1,320; (H) $148,500

DAVIS, Ulysses
1913-1984
sculpture: (H) $10,350

DAVIS, Val
paintings: (H) $1,540

DAVIS, Vestie E.
American 1903-1978
paintings: (L) $715; (H) $2,875

DAVIS, W.H.
British 19th Cent.
paintings: (H) $880

DAVIS, W.J.
British 19th cent.
paintings: (H) $468

DAVIS, Warren B.
American 1865-1928
paintings: (L) $165; (H) $10,925
drawings: (H) $220

DAVIS, Wayne Lambert
b. 1904
paintings: (L) $165; (H) $220
drawings: (H) $575

DAVIS, William Henry
English ac. 1803-1849
paintings: (H) $4,600
drawings: (H) $66

DAVIS, William Moore
American 1829-1920
paintings: (H) $2,090

DAVIS, William R.
American 20th cent.
paintings: (L) $440; (H) $3,300

DAVIS, William Steeple
American 1884-1961
drawings: (H) $460

DAVIS, Wm. M.
American 19th cent.
paintings: (H) $1,210

DAVISON, Wilfred P.
American 19th/20th cent.
paintings: (L) $259; (H) $770

DAVISSON, Homer Gordon
American b. 1866
paintings: (L) $605; (H) $1,430

DAVMILLER, A.
sculpture: (H) $1,320

DAVOL, Joseph
American 1864-1923
paintings: (L) $230; (H) $935

DAVOUST, Leon Louis
French ac. 1877-1890
drawings: (H) $2,300

DAWBARN, Joseph Yelverton
English exhib. 1887-1933
paintings: (H) $1,045
drawings: (H) $1,100

DAWES, Edwin M.
American 1872-1934/45
paintings: (L) $605; (H) $1,210

DAWSON, Arthur
Anglo/American 1859-1922
paintings: (L) $1,430; (H) $1,980
drawings: (H) $275

DAWSON, George Walter
American 1870-1938
drawings: (L) $308; (H) $1,265

DAWSON, Henry Thomas
British 1811-1878
paintings: (H) $1,150
drawings: (H) $532

DAWSON, Manierre
American 1887-1969
paintings: (L) $5,500; (H) $14,300

DAWSON, Montague
English 1895-1973
paintings: (L) $2,750; (H) $134,500
drawings: (L) $1,725; (H) $22,000

DAWSON-WATSON, Dawson
Anglo/American 1864-1939
paintings: (L) $275; (H) $6,600
drawings: (H) $275

DAY, ***
ac. 18th/19th cent.
paintings: (H) $6,600

DAY, Francis
American 1863-1942
paintings: (H) $2,875
drawings: (H) $192

DAY, James Francis
1863-1942
paintings: (L) $7,700; (H) $8,800

DAY, James Francis
American 1863-1942
paintings: (L) $7,700; (H) $8,800
drawings: (H) $2,640

DAY, John
American b. 1932
paintings: (L) $303; (H) $715

DAY, Larry
American 20th cent.
paintings: (L) $330; (H) $605
drawings: (H) $247

DAY, Maurice
American 1892-1983
drawings: (H) $550

DAYES, Edward
English 1761/63-1804
drawings: (L) $1,035; (H) $7,975

DAYEZ, Georges
French 1907-1990
paintings: (L) $2,750; (H) $6,050
drawings: (H) $3,300

DAYTON, Lillian
American 20th cent.
paintings: (H) $605

DE, Biren
Indian b. 1926
paintings: (L) $1,150; (H) $6,325

DE ANDREA, John
American b. 1941
sculpture: (L) $19,550; (H) $85,000

DE BECK, Billy
drawings: (H) $1,100

DE BLEZERD
sculpture: (H) $522

DE BOTTON, Jean
French 1898-1978
paintings: (L) $550; (H) $1,100

DE CALLATAY, Xavier
American b. 1932
paintings: (H) $4,400

DE CAMP, Joseph Rodefer
American 1858-1923
paintings: (L) $440; (H) $55,200
drawings: (H) $13,800

DE CAMP, Ralph Earl
American 1858-1936
paintings: (L) $440; (H) $2,588

DE CANUE
French 20th cent.
paintings: (H) $495

DE CRANO, Felix F.
American, b. France d. 1908
paintings: (L) $374; (H) $770

DE CREEFT, Jose
Spanish/American 1884-1982
drawings: (L) $115; (H) $880
sculpture: (L) $1,100; (H) $6,600

DE DECJER, Thomas A.
American b. 1951
paintings: (L) $450; (H) $2,300

DE DIEGO, Julio
Spanish/American 1900-1979
paintings: (H) $468

The Ten

The Ten is the name given to a group of American painters: Childe Hassam, J. Alden Wier, John Twachtman, Thomas Dewing, Edmund Tarbell, Frank W. Benson, Joseph De Camp, Willard L. Metcalf, E. E. Simmons, and Robert Reid. After Twachtman died William Merritt Chase took his place. Dissatisfied with the exhibitions of the National Academy of Design and Society of American Artists the group organized their own exhibition in New York in 1898. Although their styles differed, they are considered a branch of American Impressionism and exhibited together for the next 20 years.

Joseph Rodefer De Camp (1858-1923) had a more subdued palette and traditional approach than the other members of the group. Born in Cincinnati, he studied at the Cincinnati School of Design and in Munich, where he studied at the Royal Academy and with Frank Duveneck. He eventually settled in Boston and by 1883 was teaching in an academic tradition at the Museum School. His first works were landscapes, but his paintings of family and friends were such a success that he soon became one of America's foremost portrait painters. De Camp's *Portrait of a Young Girl*, estimated at $10,000 to $15,000, sold for $18,700 at Bakker's in Cambridge, Massachusetts. (Joseph Rodefer De Camp, *Portrait of a Young Girl*, oil on canvas, 24 x 20 inches, Bakker, September 17, 1994, $18,700)

DE ERDELY, Francis
Hungarian/American 1904-1959
paintings: (L) $605; (H) $13,800
drawings: (L) $82; (H) $825

DE FOREST, Lockwood
American 1850-1932
paintings: (L) $495; (H) $7,150
drawings: (L) $192; (H) $825

DE FOREST, Roy
American b. 1930
paintings: (L) $4,180; (H) $23,000
drawings: (L) $1,045; (H) $18,400

DE HAAS, Mauritz Frederik Hendrik
Dutch/American 1832-1895
paintings: (L) $660; (H) $55,000
drawings: (L) $1,265; (H) $5,500

DE HAAS, William Frederick
1830-1880
paintings: (L) $770; (H) $4,025

DE HAVEN, Franklin
American 1856-1934
paintings: (L) $39; (H) $5,500
drawings: (H) $165

DE KOONING, Elaine
American b. 1920
paintings: (L) $805; (H) $8,050
drawings: (L) $431; (H) $1,100

DE KOONING, Willem
American b. 1904
paintings: (L) $22,000; (H) $8,800,000
drawings: (L) $4,312; (H) $695,500
sculpture: (L) $134,500; (H) $365,500

DE LA MARIA
paintings: (L) $3,300; (H) $3,630

DE LA SERNA, Ismael Gonzalez
1897-1968
paintings: (H) $4,830

DE LATOIX, Gaspard
American ac. late 19th cent.
paintings: (H) $8,800
drawings: (L) $1,760; (H) $6,050

DE LEON, Omar
paintings: (H) $2,200

DE LETTE, G.
Italian 19th cent.
drawings: (H) $770

DE LONGPRE, Paul
French/American 1855-1911
paintings: (L) $1,650; (H) $8,250
drawings: (L) $715; (H) $8,050

DE LONGPRE, Raoul M.
American 19th/20th cent.
paintings: (H) $3,080
drawings: (L) $440; (H) $8,800

DE LORT, Charles
paintings: (H) $3,250

DE LOTTO
sculpture: (H) $5,500

DE LUCE, Percival
American 1874-1914
paintings: (H) $1,100

DE LUE, Donald
American b. 1900
sculpture: (L) $1,045; (H) $6,050

DE LYRA, George
paintings: (L) $719; (H) $1,150
drawings: (H) $1,610

DE MARIA, Walter
American b. 1935
drawings: (H) $8,800

DE MARTELLY, John Stockton
American
paintings: (H) $1,495

DE MARTINI, Joseph
American b. 1896
paintings: (L) $1,100; (H) $1,540

DE NAGY, Ernest
American 1906-1944
paintings: (L) $165; (H) $990

DE NEUVILLE, Bruno
French 19th cent.
paintings: (H) $990

DE NIRO, Robert
American 1922-1993
paintings: (L) $110; (H) $3,163
drawings: (L) $165; (H) $805

DE NITTIS, **
Italian 19th cent.
paintings: (H) $3,300

DE PENNE, Charles Olivier
French 1831-1897
paintings: (L) $4,400; (H) $8,050

Abstract Expressionist

CONTEMP. 11/94

Willem De Kooning (b. 1904), an American citizen, was born in Holland. His first schooling in the arts was at the Rotterdam Academy of Fine Art and Techniques. De Kooning emigrated to the United States in 1926, hoping to find work as a commercial artist, but his first jobs were as a house painter and carpenter. A year spent on the Federal Arts Project in 1935 (until they barred aliens) convinced him he was an artist, and an early friendship with Arshile Gorky drew him into the circle of artists who would later become Abstract Expressionists. De Kooning worked vigorously at his art, but it was not until after his first one-man show in 1948 that he began exhibiting actively. His works during the late 1940s were explicitly nonfigurative, like his Abstract Expressionist colleagues, although he retained suggestions of figure fragments such as a torso or a shoulder. De Kooning's *Woman Paintings*, from 1950 to 1955, were controversial; he had reintroduced figures into his works, archetypes of womanhood painted with gestural strokes that critic Harold Rosenberg called "action painting." In this series De Kooning's figures are organized as a collage of body fragments: eyes, breasts, mouth, and nose. *Monumental Woman*, a charcoal study for this series, was a gift to Harold Rosenberg. The dedication reads "To Harold, Happy Birthday, 1954, From Bill." Forty years later, Rosenberg's gift sold for $695,500 at Sotheby's. (Willem De Kooning, *Monumental Woman*, charcoal on paper, 28 x 22 inches, Sotheby New York, November 11, 1994, $695,500)

DE PONTE, D. Gaspar Augusta
Spanish 18th cent.
paintings: (H) $880

DE RIBCOWSKI, Dey
American 1880-1936
paintings: (L) $288; (H) $3,300

DE ROSNY
sculpture: (H) $1,100

DE SHAZO
American 20th cent.
paintings: (H) $1,045

DE SILVA, Dyer
American 20th cent.
paintings: (H) $495

DE SIMONE
drawings: (H) $3,080

DE SIMONE
Italian 19th cent.
drawings: (H) $1,210

DE SMET
Belgian 19th cent.
paintings: (H) $5,060

DE TROY, Francois
1645-1730
drawings: (H) $4,950

DE VAERE, Jean Antoine "John"
Flemish School
sculpture: (H) $4,400

DE VALIRA, C.
Continental 19th cent.
paintings: (H) $3,080

DE VANNES, Albert
American 1881-1962
paintings: (H) $660

DE VIEN, A.
ac. 1861
paintings: (H) $23,000

DE VILLENEUVE, Boulard
French 1884-1971
paintings: (H) $863

DE VOLL, Frank Usher
American 1873-1941
paintings: (L) $1,650; (H) $4,400

DE VOS, Vincent
Belgian 1829-1875
paintings: (H) $3,220

DE YONG, Joe
American 1894-1975
drawings: (L) $302; (H) $1,650

DE ZAVINGFRIE
sculpture: (H) $525

DEACHMAN, Nelly
American b. 1895
paintings: (H) $633

DEACON, Richard
British b. 1949
drawings: (H) $2,185
sculpture: (H) $16,100

DEAKIN, Edwin
American 1838-1923
paintings: (L) $825; (H) $85,000
drawings: (H) $550

DEAN, Walter Lofthouse
American 1854-1912
paintings: (L) $88; (H) $3,575
drawings: (H) $935

DEANE, Charles
English ac. 1815-1855
drawings: (H) $660

DEANE, William Wood
British 1825-1873
paintings: (H) $8,250

DEARMAN, John
English d. 1857
paintings: (H) $1,650

DEARTH, Henry Golden
American 1864-1918
paintings: (L) $440; (H) $4,600

DEAS, Charles
American 1818-1867
paintings: (H) $310,500
drawings: (H) $357

DEATON, Norman (Neal)
sculpture: (H) $1,650

DEAVY, E.J.
American 20th cent.
paintings: (H) $468

DEBAT-PONSAN, Edouard Bernard
French 1847-1913
paintings: (L) $5,750; (H) $10,350
drawings: (H) $220

DEBAY, Auguste Hyacinth
French 1804-1865
sculpture: (L) $1,840; (H) $22,000

King of the Flowers

Paul De Longpre (1855-1911) grew up in the French countryside with little formal education. He was a natural artist and by age 12 was working in Paris painting flowers on fans. An accomplished watercolorist, he was soon earning enough to support a family and married when he was only 18. By the time he was 21, he was the father of two children *and* had exhibited his first flower painting at the Paris Salon. For six months of each year De Longpre worked in Paris painting fans, and the remainder of the year he lived in the country where he painted floral still lifes. A bank failure in 1890 plunged his family into poverty, and the De Longpres emigrated to New York. Paul De Longpre struggled for five years to reestablish himself. In 1896 he had his first exhibition in the United States. It was a great success, and for the next four years he exhibited regularly in Boston, Chicago, and Philadelphia.

His reputation established, and free from worries, De Longpre and his wife and three daughters moved in 1900 to Hollywood, California. (Raoul De Longpre, another flower painter, is not his son, as is commonly thought but may be a cousin.) The De Longpres purchased three acres of land and built a palatial Mission-Moorish house. An amateur horticulturist as well as an artist, De Longpre designed extensive gardens that soon became a tourist attraction. Special trolleys and tours were organized to view the home and gardens, and magazines reported that De Longpre had planted over 4,000 rosebushes. He was quoted as saying "Never paint a poor specimen of a flower" and his gardeners toiled to produce the best possible flowers. Prints of his paintings were given away with Sunday supplements, and Paul De Longpre, nicknamed "Le Roi des Fleurs" (King of the Flowers), became a wildly popular painter, drawing thousands to his exhibitions.

De Longpre's paintings are highly decorative and are as popular today as they were a century ago. This watercolor of *Violets in a Glass Vase* realized $3,738 when it sold at Butterfield's in June 1995. (Paul De Longpre, *Violets in a Glass Vase*, watercolor on paper, 12 x 18 inches, Butterfield's, June 15, 1995, $3,738)

DEBAY, Jean Baptiste Joseph
French 1779-1863
sculpture: (L) $2,530; (H) $9,200

DEBECK, Billy
1890-1942
drawings: (H) $1,540

DEBERITZ, Per
Norwegian 1880-1945
paintings: (H) $8,800

DEBEUL, Henri
paintings: (H) $7,150

DEBICKI, Stanislaw
Polish 1866-1924
paintings: (H) $495

DEBLOIS, Francois B.
Canadian/American c. 1829-1913
paintings: (L) $230; (H) $1,540

DEBRE, Olivier
French b. 1920
paintings: (L) $2,640; (H) $27,600

DEBRY, Sophie Victoire
French ac. 1920s
sculpture: (H) $2,310

DEBUCOURT, Philibert Louis
French 1755-1832
paintings: (H) $20,900

DEBUEL, L.
European 19th cent.
paintings: (H) $715

DEBUT, Jean Didier
French 1824-1893
sculpture: (L) $633; (H) $1,955

DEBUT, Marcel
French b. 1865
sculpture: (L) $403; (H) $3,680

DECAEN, Alfred Charles Ferdinand
French b. 1820
paintings: (L) $13,800; (H) $42,550

DECAMPS, Albert
French 1862-1908
paintings: (L) $2,200; (H) $4,600

DECAMPS, Alexandre Gabriel
French 1803-1860
paintings: (L) $330; (H) $9,900
drawings: (L) $920; (H) $3,450

DECAMPS, Maurice
French b. 1892
paintings: (H) $3,080

DECHAMPS, Louis
French 19th cent.
paintings: (H) $1,870

DECHAR, Peter
American b. 1942
paintings: (L) $440; (H) $2,860

DECHARD, Paul
drawings: (H) $3,220

DECKER, Cornelis Gerritsz.
Dutch c. 1623-1678
paintings: (H) $12,075

DECKER, Joseph
German/American 1853-1924
paintings: (H) $25,300

DECKER, Robert M.
American b. 1847
paintings: (L) $1,210; (H) $2,090

DECONENE, Henri
Belgian 1798-1866
paintings: (H) $5,462

DECORCHEMONT, Francois Emile
French 1880-1971
paintings: (H) $2,420

DECOSTER, Marc
French 19th cent.
paintings: (H) $6,900

DEDINA, Jean
Czechoslovakian b. 1870
drawings: (H) $6,600

DEED, William J., Jr.
paintings: (H) $715

DEEN, I.J.
paintings: (L) $50; (H) $825
drawings: (H) $125

DEERDELY, Francis
Hungarian/American • 1904-1959
paintings: (H) $2,310
drawings: (H) $230

DEERING, Roger
American 19th/20th cent.
paintings: (L) $110; (H) $900

DEFAUT
Continental 19th cent.
paintings: (H) $990

DEFAUX, Alexandre
French 1826-1900
paintings: (L) $403; (H) $5,750

DEFAUX, J.
Continental 19th cent.
paintings: (H) $2,200

DEFFNER, Ludwig
German 19th/20th cent.
paintings: (H) $690

DEFOREST, Edward
Continental 19th cent.
paintings: (H) $748

DEFOREST, Henry J.
Canadian 1860-1924
paintings: (H) $1,980

DEFOREST, Julie Morrow
19th/20th cent.
paintings: (H) $935

DEFRANCE, Henriette
French 19th cent.
paintings: (H) $6,050

DEFRANCE, Leonard
Flemish 1735-1805
paintings: (H) $12,650

DEFREES, T.
19th cent.
paintings: (L) $440; (H) $2,300

DEFREGGER, Franz von
German 1835-1921
paintings: (L) $4,600; (H) $115,500
drawings: (H) $1,100

DEFREYN, Charles
Belgian 1851-1930
paintings: (H) $1,430

DEGAS, Edgar
French 1834-1917
paintings: (L) $35,650; (H) $7,150,000
drawings: (L) $4,675; (H) $7,042,500
sculpture: (L) $11,500; (H) $354,500

DEGLER, A.E.
American ac. 1879-1880
drawings: (L) $27; (H) $578

DEGLUME, Henri
paintings: (H) $1,265

DEGOTTEX, Jean
French 1918-1988
paintings: (H) $34,100

DEGOUVE DE NUNCQUES, William
Belgian 1867-1935
drawings: (H) $2,300

DEGROFSI, A.
Italian 19th cent.
drawings: (L) $385; (H) $1,320

DEGROOT, Nanno
paintings: (H) $1,760

DEGROSSI, Adelchi
drawings: (L) $575; (H) $1,210

DEHAUSSY, Jules Jean Baptiste
French 1812-1891
paintings: (H) $880

DEHESGHUES, Leon
French 1852-1910
paintings: (H) $30,250

DEHN, Adolf
American 1895-1968
paintings: (L) $517; (H) $3,300
drawings: (L) $165; (H) $14,950

DEHNER, Dorothy
American b. 1901/13
drawings: (H) $345
sculpture: (L) $193; (H) $8,337

DEHOSPODAR, Stephen
American 1902-1959
paintings: (H) $770

DEHOY, Charles
Belgian 1872-1940
paintings: (H) $990

DEIKE, Clara
American 20th cent.
paintings: (L) $880; (H) $3,025
drawings: (H) $4,950

DEIKER, Carl Friedrich
German 1836-1892
paintings: (L) $770; (H) $3,575

DEIKER, Johannes Christian
German 1822-1895
paintings: (H) $7,700

DEL BONO, Dorothy E.
paintings: (H) $2,200

DEL MAZO, Juan Baustista Martinez
c. 1612-1667
paintings: (H) $5,500

DEL MUE, Maurice A.
American, b. Paris 1875-1955
paintings: (L) $605; (H) $1,265

DEL PRETE, Juan
Argentinean 1898-1987
paintings: (H) $6,900

DEL RIO, Jose Lapayese
b. 1926
paintings: (H) $1,650

DEL RIOS
paintings: (H) $880

DEL SOLE, Antonia Maria
paintings: (H) $2,640

DELABORDE, Henri
French 1811-1899
paintings: (H) $31,050

DELABRIERE, Paul Edouard
French 1829-1912
sculpture: (L) $522; (H) $1,980

DELACHAUX, Leon
Swiss 1850-1919
paintings: (L) $2,200; (H) $7,150

DELACROIX, Auguste
French 1809-1868
paintings: (L) $1,650; (H) $2,475
drawings: (H) $978

DELACROIX, Eugene
French 1798-1863
paintings: (L) $1,045; (H) $189,500
drawings: (L) $2,185; (H) $176,000

DELACROIX, Henri Eugene
French 1845-1930
paintings: (H) $17,250

DELACROIX, Michel
b. 1933
paintings: (H) $1,150
drawings: (H) $1,100

DELACROIX-GARNIER, Pauline
French 1863-1912
paintings: (H) $8,250

DELAFONTAINE, Pierre Maximilien
French 1774-1860
drawings: (H) $2,420

DELAFOSSE, Jean Charles
1734-1789
drawings: (H) $3,220

DELAGE, Pierre
English School 1883-1956
paintings: (H) $2,109

DELAGRANGE, Leon Noel
French 1872-1910
sculpture: (L) $1,100; (H) $2,200

DELAHAYE, Ernest Emile
French 19th cent.
paintings: (H) $1,870

DELAHAYE, Ernest Jean
French b. 1855
paintings: (H) $13,200

DELAHOGUE, Alexis Auguste
French 1867-c.1930
paintings: (H) $2,200

DELAMAIN, Paul
French 1821-1882
paintings: (H) $4,025
drawings: (L) $247; (H) $660

DELAMARRE, Theodore
French 19th cent.
paintings: (H) $550

DELANCE, Paul Louis
French 1848-1924
paintings: (L) $412; (H) $17,600

DELANCE-FEURGARD, Julie
French 1859-1892
paintings: (H) $8,050

DELANEY, Jules
paintings: (H) $880

DELANGSDORFF, Amilear
drawings: (H) $605

DELANO, Gerard Curtis
American 1890-1972
paintings: (H) $3,738
drawings: (L) $1,250; (H) $2,090

DELANO, William Adams
American 19th/20th cent.
drawings: (H) $2,200

DELANOY, Hippolyte Pierre
French 1849-1899
paintings: (L) $2,200; (H) $2,990

DELAP, Tony
American b. 1927
paintings: (H) $4,888
sculpture: (H) $2,300

DELAPLANCHE, Eugene
French 1836-1891
sculpture: (L) $550; (H) $165,000

DELAPORT, Eugene
French ac. 1917
paintings: (H) $1,725

DELAPORTE, Maurice Eugene
French b. 1878
paintings: (H) $2,300

DELAPP, Terry
American b. 1934
paintings: (L) $1,980; (H) $4,600

DELAROCHE, Paul
French 1797-1856
paintings: (L) $3,575; (H) $431,500
drawings: (L) $715; (H) $2,750

DELARUE
paintings: (H) $1,870

DELARUE, Louis Felix
1720/31-1765
drawings: (H) $495

DELARUE, Lucien
French b. 1925
paintings: (L) $748; (H) $935

DELASSEUR, H.
sculpture: (H) $4,950

DELATTRE, Henri
French 1801-1876
paintings: (H) $2,090

DELAUNAY, Emile
French 19th/20th cent.
paintings: (H) $1,100

DELAUNAY, Jules Elie
French 1828-1891
paintings: (L) $7,475; (H) $8,050
drawings: (L) $440; (H) $11,500

DELAUNAY, Robert
French 1885-1941
paintings: (L) $34,500; (H) $5,170,000
drawings: (L) $13,200; (H) $154,000

DELAUNAY, Sonia
Russian/French 1885/86-1979
paintings: (H) $81,700
drawings: (L) $863; (H) $39,600

DELAUNEY, Jules
French d. 1906
paintings: (H) $1,100

DELAVAL, Pierre Louis
French b. 1790
paintings: (H) $1,760

DELAVALLEE, Henri
French b. 1887
paintings: (H) $1,540

DELAVILLE, Louis
French 1763-1841
sculpture: (H) $10,350

DELBOS, Julius
American 1879-1970
paintings: (L) $88; (H) $2,875
drawings: (L) $88; (H) $660

DELCOUR, P.
French 19th cent.
paintings: (L) $688; (H) $1,320

DELDEN, Jan Wessel van
Dutch 1820-1848
paintings: (H) $495

DELEN, Dirck van
Dutch 1605-1671
paintings: (L) $10,925; (H) $233,500

DELESSARD, Auguste Joseph
1827- after 1891
paintings: (H) $1,870

DELFAU, Andre
drawings: (L) $385; (H) $715

DELFF, Willem Jacobsz
1580-1638
paintings: (H) $7,700

DELFGAAVW, Gerard J.
Dutch 19th cent.
paintings: (L) $440; (H) $1,320

DELFS, Moritz
German 1823-1906
paintings: (H) $2,070

DELFT, H.
American early 20th cent.
paintings: (H) $770

DELFT, Soloman
Flemish 19th cent.
paintings: (H) $1,093

DELGADO, M. Olbiol
Spanish ?
paintings: (H) $1,100

DELHOGUE, Alexis Aguste
French 1867-1930
paintings: (H) $2,750

DELHOMME, Leon Alexandre
French early 20th cent.
sculpture: (L) $1,320; (H) $2,530

DELIN, Charles
Dutch 1756-1818
paintings: (L) $4,125; (H) $4,400

DELINCOURT, Charles
Continental 19th cent.
paintings: (H) $8,800

DELISI, Lesa
American
paintings: (L) $495; (H) $700

DELISIO, A.
Italian 19th/20th cent.
drawings: (H) $495

DELISLE, Roseline
Canadian b. 1952
sculpture: (H) $2,070

DELL, G.
British 19th cent.
paintings: (H) $8,050

DELL, Juan
American 20th cent.
sculpture: (H) $770

DELL PUBLICATIONS
drawings: (H) $1,725

DELL'ACQUA, Cesare
Italian 1821-1904
paintings: (L) $1,430; (H) $17,600
drawings: (H) $1,150

DELLA BELLA, Stefano
Italian 1610-1660
drawings: (L) $1,840; (H) $10,175

DELLA ROCCA, J.
Italian 19th cent.
paintings: (H) $518

DELLENBAUGH, Frederick Samuel
1853-1935
paintings: (H) $3,850

DELLEPIANE, Davide
French 19th cent.
paintings: (H) $34,500

DELLORCO, Chris
paintings: (H) $1,150

DELMOTTE, Marcel
French 1901-1984
paintings: (L) $1,100; (H) $4,180

DELOBBE, Emile Victor Augustin
French 19th cent.
paintings: (H) $9,200

DELOBBE, Francois Alfred
French 1835-1920
paintings: (L) $1,320; (H) $24,200

DELOBRE, Emile
French 1873-1956
paintings: (L) $3,575; (H) $7,475

DELOOPER, William
American b. 1932
paintings: (H) $5,225

DELOOSE, Basile
Dutch 1809-1889
paintings: (H) $4,537

DELOOSE, Emile
paintings: (H) $5,720

DELORE, Jean
paintings: (H) $460

DELORME, Anton
French 19th cent.
paintings: (H) $575

DELORME, Raphael
French 1885-1962
paintings: (H) $20,700

DELORT, Charles Edouard Edmond
French 1841-1895
paintings: (L) $2,530; (H) $42,550

DELORT?, Charles Edouard
French 1841-1895
paintings: (H) $1,760

DELOUR, P.
Continental School 19th cent.
paintings: (H) $690

DELPY, Hippolyte Camille
French 1842-1910
paintings: (L) $1,650; (H) $79,500

DELPY, Jacques Henry
French 1877-1957
paintings: (L) $990; (H) $17,250

DELUCE, Percival
paintings: (H) $1,485

DELUE, Donald
American b. 1897
sculpture: (L) $4,025; (H) $4,025

DELVAUX, Paul
Belgian b. 1897
paintings: (L) $552,500; (H) $1,375,000
drawings: (L) $13,200; (H) $60,500

DELVILLE, Jean
Belgian 1867-1953
paintings: (H) $2,070

DELYEN, Jean Francois
French c. 1684-1761
paintings: (H) $44,000

DEMACHY, Pierre Antoine
French 1723-1807
paintings: (L) $48,300; (H) $61,900

DEMAHI, J.
Continental School 19th cent.
paintings: (H) $495

DEMAINE, Harry
American 1880-1952
paintings: (H) $495

DEMANET, Victor Joseph Ghislain
Belgian 1895-1964
sculpture: (L) $2,185; (H) $2,415

DEMAREST, Margaret van Wagoner
American 1810-1877
paintings: (H) $13,200

DEMARIA, Nicola
Italian b. 1954
paintings: (L) $25,300; (H) $38,500
drawings: (H) $16,500
sculpture: (H) $2,990

DEMARLE
French 19th cent.
paintings: (H) $687

DEMARNE, Jean Louis
French 1744/54-1829
paintings: (L) $7,150; (H) $23,000

DEMEAUX, Marie
American 19th cent.
paintings: (H) $825

DEMEL, F.
Austrian 19th cent.
paintings: (H) $2,530

DEMERS, Joe
1910-1984
paintings: (H) $1,760
drawings: (H) $1,980

DEMESTER
Continental 20th cent.
paintings: (L) $468; (H) $495

DEMETROPOULOS, Charles
American 1912-1976
drawings: (L) $165; (H) $1,760

DEMING, Adelaide
American 1864-1956
paintings: (H) $715

DEMING, Edwin Willard
American 1860-1942
paintings: (L) $184; (H) $5,500
drawings: (L) $275; (H) $1,870
sculpture: (L) $690; (H) $6,600

DEMING, R.A.
19th/20th cent.
paintings: (H) $518

DEMONT-BRETON, Virginie
French 1859-1935
paintings: (L) $1,150; (H) $28,600

DEMONTREUIL
18th/19th cent.
sculpture: (H) $2,530

DEMOTT, John
b. 1954
paintings: (L) $7,150; (H) $8,800

DEMOUSSEY
drawings: (H) $1,650

DEMSKI, J.
Continental 19th cent.
paintings: (H) $1,430

DEMUTH, Anni von
Austrian b. 1866
paintings: (H) $3,080

DEMUTH, Charles
American 1883-1935
paintings: (L) $110,000; (H) $825,000
drawings: (L) $1,320; (H) $181,500

DENARDE, M.
paintings: (H) $575

DENARIE, J. Paul, called J. SORLAIN
French 1859-1942
paintings: (L) $690; (H) $3,450

DENBERG, Willhelm van
1886-1970
paintings: (H) $990

DENCKER, August
French 19th/20th cent.
paintings: (H) $1,100

DENECHEAU, Seraphim
French 1831-1912
sculpture: (H) $9,200

DENEUX, Garbiel Charles
French b. 1856
paintings: (H) $35,750

DENIS, Claudius
French b. 1878
paintings: (H) $3,105

DENIS, H.
Continental 19th cent.
paintings: (H) $7,700

DENIS, Jose
Spanish 1843-1917
paintings: (L) $3,300; (H) $4,600

DENIS, Louise
Belgian 19th cent.
paintings: (H) $4,180

DENIS, Maurice
French 1870-1943
paintings: (L) $6,820; (H) $156,500
drawings: (L) $38; (H) $5,175

DENISON LIMNER, CIRCA 1790,
Joseph Steward
American 1753-1822
paintings: (H) $63,000

DENMAN, Herbert
American 1855-1903
paintings: (L) $2,420; (H) $17,600

DENNER, Balthasar
German 1685-1749
paintings: (H) $10,925

DENNIS, Curt
sculpture: (H) $2,310

DENNIS, Morgan
American 20th cent.
paintings: (H) $660

DENNIS, Roger Wilson
American b. 1902
paintings: (L) $220; (H) $2,530

DENNY, Gideon Jacques
American 1830-1886
paintings: (L) $2,875; (H) $3,025

DENT, Troy
American 20th cent.
paintings: (H) $1,540

DENTON, Troy
American 20th cent.
paintings: (H) $748

DEPERO, Fortunato
Italian 1892-1960
paintings: (L) $3,850; (H) $55,000
drawings: (L) $4,950; (H) $5,750

DEPERTHES, Jacques
French b. 1936
paintings: (H) $1,150

DEPLECHIN, Eugene
sculpture: (H) $935

DER VEER, Mary van
American b. 1865
paintings: (L) $550; (H) $770

DERAIN, Andre
French 1880-1954
paintings: (L) $3,300; (H) $2,642,500
drawings: (L) $330; (H) $30,800
sculpture: (L) $3,163; (H) $28,600

DERBECQ, Germaine
French 20th cent.
paintings: (H) $10,062

DERBY, Perly
American 1823-1896
paintings: (H) $468

DERCUM, Elizabeth
American 20th cent.
paintings: (H) $920

DERGONOV, Dmitri V.
Russian b. 1961
paintings: (H) $825

DERI, A***
paintings: (H) $1,980

DERILLON, A.
French School 19th/20th cent.
paintings: (H) $935

DEROME, Albert Thomas
American 1885-1959
paintings: (L) $248; (H) $4,675
drawings: (L) $633; (H) $1,760

DEROSE, Anthony L.
American 1803-1836
paintings: (L) $1,100; (H) $2,420

DERRICK, William Rowell
American 1858-1941
paintings: (L) $805; (H) $2,200
drawings: (L) $440; (H) $605

DERUJINSKY, Gleb
Russian/American 1888-1975
sculpture: (L) $1,100; (H) $4,510

DERUTH, Jan
American b. 1922
paintings: (L) $110; (H) $690

DERVAL, G.
French 19th cent.
paintings: (H) $2,750

DESATNICK, Mike
American b. 1943
paintings: (L) $1,375; (H) $4,950

DESAVARY, Charles Paul
French 1837-1885
paintings: (H) $13,225

DESAXE, A.
paintings: (H) $550

DESBOIS, Jules
French 1851-1935
sculpture: (H) $2,185

DESBORDES-JONAS, Louise Alexandra
French 19th cent.
paintings: (H) $5,225

DESBOUTIN, Marcellin Gilbert
French 1823-1902
paintings: (H) $1,980

DESCAMPS, Guillaume Desire Joseph
French 1779-1858
drawings: (H) $990

DESCAMPS, J.A.
19th cent.
paintings: (H) $1,375

DESCH, Auguste Theodore
French b. 1877
paintings: (H) $10,350

DESCH, Frank H.
1873-1934
drawings: (H) $1,045

DESCHAMPS, Gabriel
French b. 1919
paintings: (L) $575; (H) $2,875

DESCHAMPS, Louis
paintings: (H) $3,450

DESCOMPS, Jean Bernard
sculpture: (H) $805

DESCUBES, A***
British or French 19th/20th cent.
drawings: (L) $2,750; (H) $8,250

DESCUBES, A.
drawings: (L) $440; (H) $550

DESEGLISE, Claudine
French 20th cent.
paintings: (H) $660

DESEINE, Claude Andre
French late 18th cent.
sculpture: (H) $2,640

DESEINE, Louis Pierre
French 1749-1822
sculpture: (H) $2,300

DESFLACHES
Continental 19th cent.
paintings: (H) $14,300

DESFONTAINES, F.B.
European 19th cent.
paintings: (H) $1,540

DESFRICHES, Aignan Thomas
1715-1800
drawings: (H) $3,450

DESGOFFE, Blaise Alexandre
French 1830-1901
paintings: (L) $3,450; (H) $19,550

DESHAYES, Charles Felix Edouard
French 1831-1895
paintings: (L) $440; (H) $3,300

DESHAYES, Eugene F.A.
French 19th/20th cent.
paintings: (L) $990; (H) $12,650

DESHAYES, Fredric Leon
French b. 1883
paintings: (H) $1,100

DESHAYES, Jean Baptiste Henri, called de Colleville
French 1729-1765
paintings: (L) $46,000; (H) $200,500

DESIMONE, Tomaso
Italian ac. 1851-1907
paintings: (H) $2,588

DESIR, G.
Haitian 20th cent.
paintings: (H) $550

DESIRE-LUCAS, Louis Marie
French 1869-1949
paintings: (H) $2,310

DESLIENS, Cecile and Marie
French 19th cent.
paintings: (L) $1,650; (H) $10,350

DESMAREES, Georg, studio of
18th cent.
paintings: (H) $1,980

DESMOULINS, Amedee Auguste
French 19th cent.
drawings: (H) $1,980

DESNOS, Ferdinand
French 1901-1958
paintings: (H) $1,725

DESNOS, Louise Adelaide
French b. 1807
paintings: (H) $5,463

DESNOYER, Francois
1894-1972
paintings: (H) $3,450
drawings: (H) $880

DESORIA, Jean Baptiste Francois
French 1758-1832
paintings: (H) $2,645

DESOTO, Enrico
drawings: (L) $460; (H) $805

DESOTO, Raphael
1904-1987
paintings: (H) $3,850

DESOTO, Raphael
American
paintings: (L) $920; (H) $1,150

DESPEAUX, Howard
American 20th cent.
paintings: (H) $1,650

DESPIAU, Charles
French 1874-1946
paintings: (H) $12,650
drawings: (L) $440; (H) $770
sculpture: (L) $2,300; (H) $18,700

DESPORTES, Alexandre Francois
French 1661-1743
paintings: (L) $93,500; (H) $937,500

DESPORTES, Claude Francois
French 1695-1774
paintings: (H) $4,675

DESPREZ, Louis Jean
French 1743-1804
drawings: (L) $1,210; (H) $37,950

DESROUSSEAUX, Henri Alphonse
Louis Laurent
French 1862-1906
paintings: (H) $9,430

DESSAR, Louis Paul
American 1867-1952
paintings: (L) $220; (H) $6,050

DESSART, Danielle
drawings: (L) $935; (H) $1,870

DESSOULAVY, Thomas
British ac. 1829-48
paintings: (H) $22,000

DESTAEBLER, Stephen
American 20th cent.
sculpture: (H) $2,750

DESTOT, Etienne
French 1864-1918
sculpture: (H) $4,600

DESTOUCHES, Johanna von
German 1869-1956
paintings: (L) $2,300; (H) $3,450

DESUBLEO, Michele, called Michele
Fiammingo
Flemish 1601-1676
paintings: (H) $50,600

DESVARREUX, Raymond
French 1876-1963
paintings: (L) $660; (H) $4,370

DESVARREUX-LARPENTEUR, James
American b. 1847
paintings: (L) $514; (H) $3,105

DESVERGNES, Charles
French 19th cent.
sculpture: (H) $825

DETAILLE, Jean Baptiste Edouard
French 1848-1912
paintings: (L) $1,540; (H) $48,875
drawings: (L) $193; (H) $8,800

DETERELLE
French 19th cent.
paintings: (H) $467

DETHLOFF, Peter H.
American 1869-1934
paintings: (H) $715

DETMOLD, Edward Julian
English 1883-1957
paintings: (H) $1,380
drawings: (H) $2,200

DETRIER, Pierre Louis
French 1822-1897
sculpture: (L) $1,870; (H) $2,090

DETROVEN
American 20th cent.
paintings: (H) $633

DETROY, Leon
paintings: (L) $1,320; (H) $3,080

DETTI, Cesare Auguste
Italian 1847-1914
paintings: (L) $1,380; (H) $51,750
drawings: (L) $288; (H) $3,737

DETTMER, A.
paintings: (H) $467

DETTMERS, Julius
Dutch 19th cent.
paintings: (H) $2,875

DETURCK, Henri
French 1858-1898
paintings: (H) $6,325

DETWILLER, Frederick K.
American 1882-1953
paintings: (L) $50; (H) $805
drawings: (H) $550

DEUBERG, Anton von
paintings: (H) $2,200

DEULLY, Eugene
French b. 1860
paintings: (L) $357; (H) $27,500

DEURZEN, James van
American
sculpture: (H) $863

DEUTSCH, Boris
Russian/American 1895-1978
paintings: (L) $4,025; (H) $6,325
drawings: (H) $248

DEUTSCH, David
American b. 1943
drawings: (H) $5,500

DEUTSCH, Ludwig
Austrian b. 1855
paintings: (H) $1,760

DEVAMBEZ, Andre
French 1867-1943
paintings: (L) $1,320; (H) $4,600

DEVAULX
sculpture: (H) $770

DEVE, Eugene
French 1826-1887
paintings: (H) $3,737

DEVEDEUX, Louis
French 1820-1874
paintings: (H) $7,700

DEVENTER, Johann van
Dutch 19th/20th cent.
paintings: (H) $632

DEVENTER, Willem Antoine van
Dutch 1824-1893
paintings: (H) $7,820

DEVERIA, Achille Jacque Marie
French 1800-1857
paintings: (H) $863

DEVERIA, Eugene Francois Marie
Joseph
French 1808-1865
paintings: (H) $11,500

DEVICH, John
American 19th cent.
paintings: (H) $950

DEVIEUX, Henri
French 1839-1898
paintings: (L) $1,870; (H) $3,300

DEVINE, Bernard
American b. 1884
paintings: (H) $3,220

DEVINEY, Jesse
American 1883-1941
paintings: (L) $220; (H) $660

DEVIS, Anthony
English 1729-1816
drawings: (L) $286; (H) $523

DEVIS, Arthur
English 1711-1787
paintings: (H) $19,800

DEVIS, Arthur William
English 1763-1822
paintings: (H) $11,000

DEVOLL, Frederick Usher
American 1873-1941
paintings: (H) $1,100
drawings: (H) $1,650

DEVORE, Richard
contemporary
sculpture: (H) $6,900

DEVOTO, John
French 1719-1796
drawings: (H) $495

DEVRIENT, Wilheim
German b. 1799
paintings: (H) $4,400

DEVRIEZ, Philippe
Polish ac. 1918-1935
sculpture: (L) $1,540; (H) $19,550

DEWASNE, Jean
French b. 1921
paintings: (L) $4,400; (H) $5,060

DEWEVER, Auguste
sculpture: (H) $825

DEWEY, Charles Melville
American 1849-1937
paintings: (L) $488; (H) $13,800
drawings: (H) $165

DEWEY, E.H.
American 1850-1939
paintings: (H) $1,650

DEWEY, W.M.
Continental 19th cent.
paintings: (H) $460

DEWHURST, Wynford
British b. 1864
paintings: (H) $1,980

DEWIME
paintings: (H) $1,150

DEWING, R.A.
American 19th cent.
paintings: (H) $460

DEWING, Thomas Wilmer
American 1851-1938
paintings: (L) $7,700; (H) $143,000
drawings: (L) $518; (H) $8,250

DEWOLF, Wallace Leroy
American 1854-1930
paintings: (L) $330; (H) $660

DEWS, John Steven
British b. 1949
paintings: (L) $2,875; (H) $68,500

DEXTER, Henry
American 1806-1876
sculpture: (H) $1,650

DEY, John William
1912-1978
paintings: (L) $1,650; (H) $2,310

DEYROLLE, Theophile Louis
French 1844-1923
paintings: (L) $4,400; (H) $31,900

DEZIRE, Henri
French 1878-1965
paintings: (L) $1,100; (H) $1,380

DHUPERRIO, D.
sculpture: (H) $1,155

DI BENEDETTO, Steve
b. 1958
paintings: (L) $253; (H) $3,300

DI BENEDETTO, Steve
b. 1958
paintings: (H) $690

DI CAVALCANTI, Emiliano
Brazilian 1897-1976
paintings: (L) $14,950; (H) $118,000
drawings: (L) $2,090; (H) $29,700

DI DONNA, Porfirio
American 1942-1986
paintings: (L) $990; (H) $1,210

DI MANTEGAZZA, Roberti
Italian 19th/20th cent.
drawings: (H) $715

DI ROSA, Herve
20th cent.
paintings: (H) $3,080

DI SCOVOTO
paintings: (H) $2,970

DI SUVERO, Mark
American b. 1933
paintings: (H) $1,650
drawings: (L) $431; (H) $4,125
sculpture: (L) $1,150; (H) $470,000

DIAGO, Roberto
b. Cuba 1920-1957
drawings: (L) $1,380; (H) $14,950

DIAMOND, Jessica
b. 1957
paintings: (L) $253; (H) $920

DIAMOND, Stuart
b. 1942
paintings: (H) $1,150
drawings: (H) $357
sculpture: (H) $575

DIAQUE, L.C.
European 19th cent.
paintings: (L) $330; (H) $495

DIAQUE, Ricardo
Spanish 19th cent.
paintings: (H) $4,600

DIAZ, Huertas Angel
Spanish 19th cent.
paintings: (H) $935

DIAZ, Jose
paintings: (H) $577

DIAZ, N.
paintings: (H) $2,300

DIAZ DE LA PENA, Narcisse Virgile
French 1807-1876
paintings: (L) $575; (H) $37,375
drawings: (H) $1,725

DIAZ GONZALEZ, Jore
Mexican 20th cent.
sculpture: (H) $468

DIBBETS, Jan
Dutch b. 1941
paintings: (L) $8,050; (H) $68,500
drawings: (L) $3,850; (H) $8,800

DIBDIN, Thomas Colman
English 1810-1893
drawings: (L) $660; (H) $1,210

DICIERVO, Jorge
b. 1947
paintings: (H) $5,500

DICK, Sir William Reid
British 1879-1961
sculpture: (H) $2,990

DICKEY, Dan
American 1910-1961
paintings: (H) $3,300

DICKINS, Asbury
paintings: (H) $1,980

DICKINSON, Edwin
American 1891-1978
paintings: (L) $638; (H) $29,900

DICKINSON, Preston
American 1891-1930
paintings: (L) $3,300; (H) $28,750
drawings: (L) $7,700; (H) $11,550

DICKINSON, Sidney Edward
American 1890-1980
paintings: (H) $4,140
drawings: (H) $10

DICKMAN, Charles
American 1863-1943
paintings: (H) $2,750

DICKSEE, John Robert
British 1817-1905
paintings: (L) $690; (H) $1,725

DICKSEE, Sir Frank
British 1853-1928
paintings: (H) $800,000
drawings: (H) $440

DICKSEE, Thomas Francis
British 1819-1895
paintings: (L) $10,925; (H) $27,500

DICKSON, Jane
b. 1952
drawings: (L) $207; (H) $483

DICKSON, William
American 19th/20th cent.
paintings: (H) $1,430

DICKSON, William
English ac. 1881-1904
paintings: (H) $1,870

DIDAY, Francois
Swiss 1802-1877
drawings: (H) $660

DIDIER, Jules
French 1831-1892
paintings: (H) $17,250

DIDIER-POUGET, William
French 1864-1959
paintings: (L) $1,725; (H) $24,150

DIEBENKORN, Richard
American 1922-1993
paintings: (L) $34,500; (H) $662,500
drawings: (L) $4,950; (H) $195,000

DIEBOLT
paintings: (H) $522

DIEBSCHLAG, Hans
German contemporary
paintings: (H) $1,210

DIEDERICH, Hunt
drawings: (H) $550

DIEDERICH, Wilhelm Hunt
Hungarian/American 1884-1953
sculpture: (L) $330; (H) $8,800

DIEDRICKSON, Theodore
American 19th/20th cent.
paintings: (H) $10,925

DIEFFENBACH, Anton
German b. 1831
paintings: (L) $880; (H) $8,050

DIEGHEM, A*** van
Dutch 19th cent.
paintings: (H) $2,300

DIEGHEM, Jacob van
Dutch 19th cent.
paintings: (L) $880; (H) $4,025

DIEGO, Angel
19th cent.
drawings: (H) $550

DIEHL
paintings: (H) $715

DIEHL, Arthur Vidal
American 1870-1929
paintings: (L) $193; (H) $4,180
drawings: (L) $330; (H) $908

DIEHL, C.
19th cent.
paintings: (H) $805

DIEHL, Dorothy
b. 1876
paintings: (H) $523

DIELMAN, F.
drawings: (H) $660

DIELMAN, Frederick
German/American 1847/48-1935
paintings: (L) $1,150; (H) $11,500
drawings: (L) $92; (H) $6,612

DIELMANN, Jacob Friedrich
Furchtegott
German 1809-1885
drawings: (H) $1,150

DIEM, Peter Karl
German/American 1890-1956
paintings: (H) $2,420

DIEMBERG(?), A.
paintings: (H) $2,200

DIEMER, Michael Zeno
German 1867-1939
paintings: (H) $2,750

DIEN, Achille
French 19th/20th cent.
paintings: (H) $4,313

DIEPENBEECK, Abraham van
Flemish 1596-1675
paintings: (H) $11,000

DIES, A.
paintings: (H) $977

DIEST, Adriaen van
Dutch 1655-1704
paintings: (H) $20,700

DIEST, Willem van
before 1610-after 1633
paintings: (H) $16,100

DIETERLE, Marie
French 1856-1935
paintings: (L) $2,760; (H) $13,750

DIETLER, Johann Friedrich
Swiss 1804-1874
paintings: (H) $1,760
drawings: (H) $920

DIETRICH, Adelheid
German b. 1827
paintings: (L) $14,850; (H) $65,750

DIETRICH, Adolph
Swiss 1877-1957
paintings: (H) $1,100

DIETRICH, Carl
paintings: (H) $725

DIETRICH, Christian Wilhelm Ernst
German 1712-1774
paintings: (L) $1,610; (H) $44,850

DIETZE, Carl
Dutch 20th cent.
paintings: (L) $880; (H) $920

DIETZSCH, Johan Jakob
German 1713-1776
drawings: (H) $18,400

DIETZSCH, Johann Christoph
1710-1769
drawings: (L) $2,300; (H) $4,025

DIETZSCH, Margaretha Barbara
1726-1795
drawings: (L) $5,750; (H) $13,800

DIEUDONNE, Emannuel de
French 19th cent.
paintings: (L) $5,750; (H) $13,800

DIEUDONNE, Eugene Paul
French b. 1825
paintings: (H) $8,800

DIEUDONNE, Jules A.
French/American 19th cent.
paintings: (L) $440; (H) $2,200

DIEZ, Wilhelm von
German 1839-1907
paintings: (H) $2,300

DIEZLER, Jakob
German ac. 1826-1850
paintings: (L) $12,100; (H) $15,525

DIEZMANN, F.
drawings: (L) $1,150; (H) $1,150

DIGEMMA, Joseph P.
American b. 1910
paintings: (L) $440; (H) $1,035

DIGHTON, Richard
British 1785-1880
drawings: (L) $440; (H) $770

DIGNIMONT, Andre
French 1891-1965
drawings: (L) $550; (H) $1,495

DIKE, Phil
American 1906-1990
paintings: (L) $1,045; (H) $19,800
drawings: (L) $825; (H) $3,300

DIKES, M.
paintings: (H) $1,430

DIL, Ludwig
German 1848-1940
paintings: (L) $990; (H) $2,860
drawings: (H) $2,530

DILBY, Mrs. B.H.
19th cent.
paintings: (H) $2,415

DILIGENT, Raphael Louis Charles
French early 20th cent.
sculpture: (H) $2,070

DILL, Laddie John
American b. 1943
paintings: (L) $550; (H) $4,400
drawings: (L) $575; (H) $5,500

DILL, Ludwig
German 1848-1940
paintings: (L) $2,310; (H) $4,312

DILL, Otto
German 1884-1957
paintings: (L) $12,650; (H) $23,000

DILLENS, Hendrick Joseph
Belgian 1812-1972
paintings: (H) $4,830

DILLENS, Hendrik Alexander
Belgian 1821-1877
paintings: (H) $3,680

DILLER, Burgoyne
American 1906-1965
paintings: (H) $79,500
drawings: (L) $3,850; (H) $13,200

DILLEY
English 20th cent.
paintings: (H) $990

DILLINGHAM, Rick
contemporary
sculpture: (L) $2,300; (H) $3,450

DILLON, Gerard
paintings: (H) $11,000

DILLON, Julia McEntee
American 1834-1919
paintings: (L) $660; (H) $715
drawings: (H) $247

DILLON, Martin
American 20th cent.
paintings: (H) $495

DIMONDSTEIN, Morton
American 20th cent.
sculpture: (H) $1,100

DINARD, E.
French 19th cent.
paintings: (H) $690

DINCKEL, George W.
American b. 1890
paintings: (L) $247; (H) $1,045
drawings: (L) $88; (H) $330

DINE, Jim
American b. 1935
paintings: (L) $1,100; (H) $192,500
drawings: (L) $1,380; (H) $145,500
sculpture: (L) $660; (H) $159,500

DINEEN, Tom
American contemporary
drawings: (L) $522; (H) $660

DINET, Etienne
French 1861-1929
paintings: (H) $44,000

DING, Henri Marius
French 19th cent.
sculpture: (H) $2,640

DINGLE, John Adrian Darley
paintings: (H) $2,860

DINGLI, Edward Caruana
Maltese b. 1876
paintings: (H) $2,588

DINNERSTEIN, Harvey
paintings: (H) $3,410
drawings: (L) $440; (H) $1,045

DIODATI, Francisco Paolo
Italian b. 1864
paintings: (H) $1,840

DIOMEDE, Miguel
1902-1974
paintings: (H) $2,185

DIOS, Richard
American 19th cent.
drawings: (H) $1,150

DIRISO
paintings: (H) $1,320

DIRIT, Harry
20th cent.
paintings: (L) $1,840; (H) $3,737

DIRK, Nathaniel
American 1895-1961
drawings: (L) $220; (H) $550

DIRKS, Rudolph
1877-1968
drawings: (H) $660

DISCART, Jean
French 19th cent.
paintings: (H) $55,200

DISCEPOLI, Giovanni Battista, called
Zoppo da Lugano
1590-1660
paintings: (H) $7,150

DISLER, Martin
b. 1949
paintings: (L) $1,100; (H) $17,600
drawings: (L) $978; (H) $4,675

DISNEY, Walt
American 1901-1966
drawings: (L) $330; (H) $38,500

DITKO, Steve
American b. 1927
drawings: (L) $1,725; (H) $24,200

DIULGHEROFF, Nicholay
Italian 1901-1982
drawings: (H) $2,090

DIVERIA, Achille
French 1800-1857
drawings: (H) $495

DIVITA, Frank
American b. 1949
paintings: (H) $12,100
sculpture: (H) $8,250

DIX, Otto
German 1891-1969
paintings: (H) $11,000
drawings: (L) $1,210; (H) $101,500

DIXEY, Frederick C.
British ac. 1877-1920
drawings: (L) $110; (H) $880

DIXON, Anna
English d. 1959
paintings: (H) $1,760

DIXON, Charles Edward
English 1872-1934
paintings: (L) $1,045; (H) $2,420
drawings: (L) $230; (H) $1,760

DIXON, Charley
British 19th cent.
drawings: (H) $660

DIXON, Francis Stilwell
American 1879-1967
paintings: (L) $132; (H) $1,210

DIXON, Gertrude Nellie
British ac. 1900-1932
paintings: (H) $690

DIXON, Marie R.
American 19th cent.
paintings: (H) $1,840

DIXON, Maynard
American 1875-1946
paintings: (L) $605; (H) $121,000
drawings: (L) $550; (H) $10,450

DIZIANI, Antonio
Italian 1737-1797
paintings: (L) $40,700; (H) $44,000

DIZIANI, Gaspare
Italian 1689-1767
paintings: (L) $715; (H) $110,000
drawings: (L) $660; (H) $6,900

DJANIRA, Djanira Gomez PEREIRA
paintings: (L) $575; (H) $5,175

DJENYEEF, I.A.
Russian 19th/20th cent.
paintings: (H) $14,950

DO, Giovanni
Italian d. 1656
paintings: (H) $17,250

DOANE, Henry W.
American b. 1905
drawings: (H) $880

DOBASHI, Jun
Japanese/French b. 1917
paintings: (H) $1,380
drawings: (H) $920

DOBBIN, John
English 1815-1888
drawings: (H) $550

DOBBS, John Barnes
American b. 1931
paintings: (L) $330; (H) $715

DOBKIN, Alexander
Italian/American 1908-1975
paintings: (L) $55; (H) $525

DOBOUJINSKY, Mistislav
Russian 1875-1957
drawings: (L) $770; (H) $11,000

DOBROTKA, Edward
American 20th cent.
paintings: (L) $66; (H) $4,950
drawings: (L) $33; (H) $1,650

DOBROWSKY, Josef
Australian
drawings: (H) $1,155

DOBSON, Charles Thomas
British 1817-1898
paintings: (H) $8,800

DOBSON, Henry John
English 1858-1928
paintings: (H) $770

DOCHARTY, James
British 1829-1878
paintings: (L) $633; (H) $1,430

DOCKREE, Mark Edwin
British 19th cent.
paintings: (H) $3,080

DODD, Louis
British 19th cent.
paintings: (L) $1,150; (H) $8,625

DODD, Louise Richardson
paintings: (H) $1,438

DODD, Robert
English 1748-1816
paintings: (H) $6,900

DODDS, Peggy
American
paintings: (L) $330; (H) $2,700

DODDS, Robert Elihu
American b. 1903
drawings: (H) $715

DODGE, Joseph Jeffers
American b. 1917
paintings: (H) $880

DODGE, William De Leftwich
American 1867-1935
paintings: (L) $440; (H) $18,700
drawings: (L) $132; (H) $495

DODSLEY, Anne
British 19th cent.
paintings: (H) $1,783

DOEMING, John Carl
American 20th cent.
paintings: (L) $440; (H) $797

DOESBURG, Theo van
Dutch 1883-1931
drawings: (H) $60,500

DOGARTH, Erich Josef
Austrian b. 1927
paintings: (L) $495; (H) $1,430

DOGHERTY, Felix
American 19th cent.
drawings: (H) $1,495

DOHANOS, Stevan
American 1907-1994
paintings: (L) $805; (H) $28,750
drawings: (L) $303; (H) $6,380

DOHLMANN, Augusta Johanne
Henriette
Danish 1847-1914
paintings: (H) $10,450

DOIGNEAU, Edouard Edmond
French b. 1865
drawings: (H) $2,990

DOKOUPIL, Jiri Georg
b. Czech. 1954
paintings: (L) $2,530; (H) $45,100
drawings: (H) $4,620
sculpture: (L) $2,875; (H) $18,700

DOLCI, Carlo
Italian 1616-1686
paintings: (L) $178,500; (H) $398,500

DOLE, William
American 1917-1983
drawings: (L) $690; (H) $2,300

DOLEMAN, Ruth
19th/20th cent.
drawings: (H) $483

DOLICE, Leon
American 1892-1960
paintings: (L) $495; (H) $660
drawings: (L) $60; (H) $770

DOLINSKY, Nathan
American b. 1890
paintings: (L) $522; (H) $1,980

DOLL, Anton
German 1826-1887
paintings: (L) $7,200; (H) $21,850
drawings: (H) $2,200

DOLLAND, W. Anstey
British ac. 1879-1889
drawings: (H) $2,990

DOLLMAN, John Charles
English 1851-1934
paintings: (L) $1,495; (H) $1,610
drawings: (H) $2,090

DOLLOND, W. Anstey
British ac. 1879-1889
drawings: (L) $1,725; (H) $1,980

DOLPH, John Henry
American 1835-1903
paintings: (L) $468; (H) $9,775

DOLWICK, William
1909-1993
drawings: (H) $2,200

DOMBA, R.
Italian 19th cent.
paintings: (L) $1,150; (H) $2,645

DOMBROWSKY, E.
paintings: (H) $690

DOMELA, Cesar
Dutch b. 1900
drawings: (H) $1,495

DOMELA, Jan
American 1894-1973
paintings: (L) $330; (H) $2,090

DOMENECH, Luis
sculpture: (L) $1,210; (H) $1,320

DOMENICHINO, Domenico
ZAMPIERI
Italian 1581-1641
paintings: (H) $7,700
drawings: (L) $4,830; (H) $8,525

DOMENICHINO, studio of
Italian 17th cent.
paintings: (H) $17,250

DOMENICO DI MICHELINO
Italian 1417-1491
paintings: (H) $88,000

DOMENICO DI MICHELINO,
Domenico di FRANCESCO
1417-1491
paintings: (L) $44,000; (H) $68,500

DOMERGUE, Jean Gabriel
French 1889-1962
paintings: (L) $1,265; (H) $60,500

DOMICENT, Martin
Flemish b. 1823
paintings: (H) $990

DOMINGO, Roberto y Fallola
Spanish 1883-1956
drawings: (L) $431; (H) $1,725

DOMINGO Y FALLOLA, Roberto
Spanish 1867-1956
paintings: (H) $2,530
drawings: (H) $920

DOMINGO Y MARQUES, Francisco
Spanish 1842-1920
paintings: (L) $1,100; (H) $49,500
drawings: (L) $2,310; (H) $6,600

DOMINGUEZ, Nelson
Cuba b. 1947
paintings: (L) $5,175; (H) $6,325

DOMINGUEZ, Oscar
Spanish 1906-1958
paintings: (L) $7,700; (H) $36,800
drawings: (L) $1,725; (H) $20,700

DOMINICI, A*** de
Italian 19th/20th cent.
paintings: (H) $4,600

DOMINICIS, Achille de
Italian 19th cent.
paintings: (H) $4,400
drawings: (H) $460

DOMINIQUE, John A.
American b. 1893
paintings: (L) $248; (H) $3,300

DOMMERSEN, Pieter Christian
Dutch 1834-1908
paintings: (L) $1,955; (H) $7,475

DOMMERSEN, W.R.
British 19th cent.
paintings: (H) $3,450

DOMMERSEN, William Raymond
Dutch d. 1927
paintings: (L) $935; (H) $3,300

DOMMERSHUIZEN, Charles
Russian 19th cent.
paintings: (H) $2,200

DOMMERSHUIZEN, Cornelis
Christian
Dutch 1842-1928
paintings: (L) $1,760; (H) $17,600

DOMMERSON, W.R.
English 19th cent.
paintings: (L) $1,650; (H) $6,600

DOMMERSON, William
Dutch d. 1927
paintings: (L) $1,375; (H) $4,600

DOMOND, Wilmino
paintings: (H) $2,200

DOMOTO, Hisao
Japanese b. 1928
paintings: (L) $5,750; (H) $82,500
drawings: (H) $2,300

DOMPE, Hernan
sculpture: (L) $8,050; (H) $12,100

DONA, Lydia
b. 1955
paintings: (L) $1,100; (H) $5,520
drawings: (H) $330

DONADONI, Stefano
Italian 1844-1911
drawings: (L) $440; (H) $1,320

DONAGHY, John
American 1838-1931
paintings: (L) $605; (H) $3,680

DONALD, John Milne
British 1819-1858
paintings: (H) $3,850

DONAT, Friederich Reginald
Belgian 1830-1907
paintings: (L) $1,210; (H) $4,400

DONAT, M.
Continental 19th cent.
paintings: (H) $495

DONATI
Italian 20th cent.
paintings: (H) $460

DONATI, Enrico
Italian/American b. 1909
paintings: (L) $978; (H) $12,650
drawings: (H) $6,050
sculpture: (H) $2,750

DONATI, Lazzaro
Italian b. 1926
paintings: (L) $173; (H) $2,200
drawings: (H) $575

DONATI, Marina
French b. 1936
sculpture: (H) $633

DONCK, G. van
Flemish before 1610-c. 1640
paintings: (H) $20,700

DONDUCCI, Giovanni Andrea, called
Il Mastelletta
1575-1655
paintings: (H) $9,350

DONELSON, Earl
American 20th cent.
paintings: (L) $440; (H) $550
drawings: (H) $38

DONER, Michele Oka
American b. 1945
sculpture: (L) $660; (H) $1,265

DONGEN, Dionys van
1748-1819
paintings: (H) $6,900

DONGEN, Kees van
Dutch/French 1877-1968
paintings: (L) $9,350; (H) $965,000
drawings: (L) $1,760; (H) $123,500

DONICK, Hendrick von
Dutch 1780-1845
paintings: (H) $1,265

DONNELLY, Thomas
American b. 1893
paintings: (H) $1,210

DONOGHUE, John
American 1853-1903
sculpture: (H) $825

DONOHO, Gaines Ruger
American 1857-1916
paintings: (L) $1,210; (H) $4,400
drawings: (H) $440

DONOHOE, Annie
American 19th cent.
paintings: (H) $1,430

DONOHUE, E.
American 19th cent.
paintings: (H) $1,540

DONOSO, Jose Jiminez
Spanish 1628-1690
paintings: (H) $21,850

DOOD, Louis
English 1748-1816
paintings: (H) $2,645

DOOMER, Lambert
Dutch c. 1623-1700
drawings: (H) $25,300

DOPH, John Henry
1835-1903
paintings: (H) $4,025

DORAZIO, Piero
Italian b. 1927
paintings: (L) $7,150; (H) $12,650
drawings: (L) $660; (H) $3,220
sculpture: (H) $11,000

DORCE, Jacques
paintings: (H) $2,300

DORE, Gustave
French 1832-1883
paintings: (L) $4,400; (H) $77,000
drawings: (L) $770; (H) $40,250
sculpture: (L) $2,760; (H) $34,500

DORE, Schmidt Felling
sculpture: (H) $660

DOREN, R. van
drawings: (H) $880

DORET, E.
Continental School 19th cent.
paintings: (H) $5,225

DORET, Louis
Swiss 18th/19th cent.
paintings: (H) $2,750

DORIAN, C.S.
19th cent.
paintings: (L) $71; (H) $935

DORIES, L.
French 19th cent.
paintings: (H) $8,800

DORING, Adolf S.
American 19th cent.
drawings: (H) $483

DORION, Charles S.
paintings: (L) $330; (H) $1,760

DORN, Carl
German b. 1837
sculpture: (H) $50,600

DORN, J.
paintings: (H) $1,100

DORNA, A.F.
Continental 19th/20th cent.
paintings: (H) $880

DORNBERGER, Karl Johannes
Andreas
Norwegian 1864-1940
paintings: (H) $1,100

DORNE, Albert
American 1904-1965
drawings: (L) $825; (H) $2,750

DORNE, Martin van
Flemish 1736-1808
paintings: (H) $25,300

DORSET, Gerald
paintings: (H) $3,025

DORSEY, William
American 20th cent.
paintings: (L) $248; (H) $4,600

DORVAL, Jacques
French late 19th cent.
sculpture: (H) $1,380

DORVALL, James M.
Scottish
drawings: (H) $1,925

DOSAMANTES, Francisco
b. Mexico 1911
paintings: (L) $1,150; (H) $6,325

DOSKOW, Israel
American b. 1881
paintings: (L) $110; (H) $577
drawings: (H) $137

DOSS, Galen W.
American 1873-1957
paintings: (H) $660

DOSSO DOSSI, Giovanni de LUTERO
Italian 1479-1542
paintings: (L) $31,625; (H) $200,500

DOSTER, Charles
American 20th cent.
paintings: (H) $880

DOTY, Janet
20th cent.
paintings: (H) $1,045

DOTY, John
19th/20th cent.
paintings: (H) $495

DOU, Gerard
Dutch 1613-1675
paintings: (H) $605

DOU, Gerard, studio of
17th cent.
paintings: (H) $14,300

DOUCET, Henri Lucien
French 1856-1895
paintings: (L) $2,760; (H) $20,700

DOUGHERTY, James
American 1886-1974
paintings: (H) $1,650

DOUGHERTY, Parke Custis
American b. 1867
paintings: (L) $440; (H) $6,600

DOUGHERTY, Paul
American 1877-1947
paintings: (L) $385; (H) $13,200
drawings: (L) $333; (H) $385

DOUGHTY, Thomas
American 1793-1856
paintings: (L) $1,540; (H) $46,000
drawings: (H) $4,400

DOUGLAS, B.
Canadian 19th cent.
paintings: (H) $522

DOUGLAS, Edward Algernon Stuart
English 19th cent.
paintings: (L) $3,300; (H) $16,500

DOUGLAS, Edwin
British 1848-1914
paintings: (L) $5,775; (H) $7,700

DOUGLAS, Haldane
American 1893-1980
paintings: (L) $495; (H) $935

DOUGLAS, James
British 19th cent.
paintings: (H) $2,875

DOUGLAS, John
American 19th cent.
paintings: (H) $550

DOUGLAS, R.
paintings: (L) $425; (H) $550

DOUGLAS, Robert
American 20th cent.
paintings: (H) $687
drawings: (L) $110; (H) $242

DOUGLAS, Walter
American b. 1868
paintings: (L) $99; (H) $2,310

DOUKAS, Jean
Greek b. 1840
paintings: (H) $715

DOUSA, Henry
American 1820-c. 1885
paintings: (H) $28,750

DOUST, Jan van
Continental School 19th/20th cent.
paintings: (H) $5,500

DOUST, William H.
British 19th cent.
paintings: (H) $605

DOUTCHEER
American 20th cent.
paintings: (H) $1,155

DOUTRELEAU, Pierre
French 20th cent.
paintings: (L) $715; (H) $1,650

DOUVEN, Jan Frans
Dutch 1656-1727
paintings: (H) $24,200

DOUW, Simon Johannes van
Flemish ac. 1630-1677
paintings: (L) $4,600; (H) $25,300

DOUZETTE, Louis
German 1834-1924
paintings: (H) $2,475

DOVE, Arthur Garfield
American 1880-1946
paintings: (L) $8,050; (H) $242,000
drawings: (L) $2,530; (H) $11,500

DOVERA, Achille
Italian 1838-1895
drawings: (H) $880

DOW, Arthur Wesley
American 1857-1922
paintings: (L) $3,450; (H) $30,800

DOW, Jane Margaret
American b. 1946
drawings: (H) $660

DOWD, Robert
American b. 1937
paintings: (L) $2,750; (H) $12,650
drawings: (L) $110; (H) $1,760

DOWDY, David
sculpture: (H) $880

DOWLING, Michael
American 20th cent.
paintings: (H) $990

DOWLING, W.
paintings: (H) $5,225

DOWNES, Rackstraw
English b. 1939
paintings: (H) $14,300

DOWNEY
English 19th/20th cent.
paintings: (H) $990

DOWNIE, John Patrick
English 1854-1940
paintings: (H) $1,320

DOWNING, M.
American(?)
drawings: (H) $495

DOWNMAN, John
British 1750-1824
paintings: (L) $275; (H) $2,640
drawings: (H) $1,100

DOWNS, Albert
American ac. 1878
paintings: (L) $1,210; (H) $3,163

DOX, C.E.
paintings: (H) $525

DOYEN, Eugene
French 19th cent.
paintings: (H) $805

DOYEN, G.F.
French 18th cent.
drawings: (H) $770

DOYEN, Gustave
French b. 1837
paintings: (H) $13,200

DOYLE, Alexander
American 1857-1922
sculpture: (H) $9,350

DOYLE, Charles Altamont
English 1832-1893
drawings: (H) $1,150

DOYLE, Sam (Uncle Sam)
American 1906-1985
paintings: (H) $8,625

DOYLE, W.M.S.
American 1769-1828
drawings: (H) $17,250

DOYLE-JONES, Francis William
British 1873-1938
sculpture: (H) $3,450

DOZINCHOWSKI, T.
Polish/Russian 19th cent.
drawings: (H) $495

DRABKIN, Stella
American b. 1906
paintings: (L) $385; (H) $2,970

DRAEGERT, Joe
American b. 1945
drawings: (H) $523

DRAGO, Antonio del
ac. late 18th cent.
drawings: (H) $3,300

DRAHONET, Alexandre Jean Dubois
French 1791-1834
paintings: (H) $51,750

DRAMARD, Georges de
French 1839-1900
paintings: (H) $3,025

DRAPER, Francis
American ac. c. 1910
paintings: (H) $460

DRAPER, George O.
American 20th cent.
paintings: (H) $517

DRAPER, Herbert James
British 1864-1920
paintings: (H) $27,500

DRAPER, William Franklin
American b. 1912
paintings: (H) $1,430

DRATHMANN, Christopher
German 1856-1931
paintings: (H) $1,320

Campbell Soup's Kids

Viola Grace Gebbie Wiederseim Drayton, popularly known as Grace Drayton (1877-1936) is best known for creating the Campbell Soup Kids and the Dolly Dingle paper dolls. Drayton grew up in an affluent artistic home in a Philadelphia suburb. Her two older sisters were artists, and her father was the publisher of an art book company. Grace married her first husband, Theodore Wiederseim, when she was 22. Her first drawings, illustrations of sophisticated ladies, appeared in *Booklover's Magazine* and are signed G.G. Wiederseim. Mr. Wiederseim was a salesman for the Keterlinus Lithographic Manufacturing Co., and in 1904 Grace drew doodles to accompany her husband's advertising campaign. Her roly-poly large-eyed children with no necks and no ears were a success. She signed a contract with the Joseph Campbell Company, and the Campbell Soup Kids were born. They appeared on streetcar signs all over the country, and the manufacture of Campbell's kids dolls in 1911 increased their recognition factor. Grace's association with Campbell lasted for the next 15-20 years. The date is unclear, for other artists—Roy Williams, Corrine Pauli, and Dorothy Jones—began to draw "the kids." Their styles are similar but there is a distinct difference. The name Campbell Soup Kids belonged to the company; Grace began drawing roly-poly kids, "Drayton designs," for greeting cards, embroidery, pottery, cast-iron banks, bookends, and paperweights, and she collaborated with her sister Margaret G. Hays on a series of children's books. In 1911 she divorced Mr. Wiederseim, and later that year married W. Heywood Drayton, a wealthy and socially prominent Philadelphian. Grace Drayton continued working during her second marriage and created the Dolly Dingle dolls that appeared in the *Ladies' Home Journal*. Her marriage to Drayton ended in 1923, and she settled in New York. By 1934 Campbell had phased out "the kids," the country was in a depression, and Drayton was out of work. She died in 1936 when she was 58. Campbell brought back the kids, in patriotic attire, during World War II, and forty years later, when nostalgia swept the country, they became more popular than ever. Most of the artwork for the Campbell Soup Kids is owned by the Campbell Soup Company and maintained in its archives in its Camden, New Jersey, headquarters. When the 1910 *Young Girl with Life Preserver* was offered at auction at Illustration House in New York City, the catalogue noted that this was the only drawing, to their knowledge, in private hands. The final price was $2,530. (Grace Drayton, *Young Girl with Life Preserver, 1910*, ink and watercolor, 7½ x 6¼ inches, Illustration House, November 5, 1994, $2,530)

DRAVER, Orrin
paintings: (L) $440; (H) $1,650

DRAYTON, Grace
American 1877-1936
drawings: (L) $210; (H) $2,530

DREIER, Katherine Sophie
American 1877-1952
paintings: (L) $690; (H) $6,900

DREIFOOS, Byron G.
b. 1890
paintings: (H) $770

DREILING, Frederik Hendrik Cornelis
Dutch 1805-1853
paintings: (H) $1,035

DREIN, Maude
American 19th/20th cent.
paintings: (H) $863

DREIR, Virgo P.
American 1892-1972
paintings: (H) $495

DRESCHER, Heinrich
Austrian 19th cent.
paintings: (H) $2,530

DRESSLER, A.
19th cent.
sculpture: (H) $1,320

DRESSLER, Edward James
American 1859-1907
paintings: (L) $770; (H) $2,760
drawings: (H) $29

DREUX, Alfred de
French 1810-1860
paintings: (L) $6,900; (H) $387,500

DREVIN, Alexander
Russian 1889-1938
paintings: (H) $1,150

DREVITSON, Neil
American b. 1944
paintings: (H) $345
drawings: (L) $259; (H) $863

DREW, Clement
American 1806/08-1889
paintings: (L) $550; (H) $7,700

DREW, George W.
American b. 1875
paintings: (L) $165; (H) $2,090

DREW, John
paintings: (H) $990

DREW-BEAR, Jessie
paintings: (H) $450

DREWES, Werner
German/American b. 1899
paintings: (L) $275; (H) $12,650
drawings: (L) $247; (H) $1,870

DREWS, Kaj Jeppe
Danish 1884-1964
paintings: (H) $660

DREYFUS, Bernard
b. Nicaragua 1940
paintings: (L) $4,675; (H) $9,200

DRIEL, F** V**
20th cent.
paintings: (H) $688

DRIESTEN, A.J. van
Continental 19th/20th cent.
drawings: (H) $1,320

DRIGGS, Elsie
American 1898-1992
paintings: (H) $500
drawings: (L) $10; (H) $978

DRIGGS(?), W.W.
paintings: (H) $1,092

DRINKARD, David
American b. 1943
paintings: (L) $220; (H) $8,800
drawings: (L) $220; (H) $1,760

DRISCOLE, H.A.
American 20th cent.
paintings: (H) $578

DRISKELL, Eleanore Johnson
American 20th cent.
paintings: (H) $2,750

DRISSLER
German 19th/20th cent.
sculpture: (H) $2,640

DRIVIER, Leon
sculpture: (H) $6,325

DROGKAMP, Charles
American 20th cent.
paintings: (H) $1,210

DROLLING, Martin
German 1752-1817
paintings: (H) $85,000
drawings: (L) $1,870; (H) $4,400

DROMIK, Richard
French b. 1953
paintings: (H) $1,320

DROOCHSLOOT, Joost Cornelisz.
Dutch 1586-1666
paintings: (L) $25,300; (H) $85,800

DROUAIS, Francois Hubert
French 1727-1775
paintings: (L) $1,840; (H) $7,700

DROUAIS, Francois Hubert, studio of
paintings: (H) $5,500

DROUAIS, Jean Germain
drawings: (H) $3,575

DROUOT
late 19th cent.
sculpture: (H) $3,080

DROUOT, Edouard
French 1859-1945
sculpture: (L) $550; (H) $5,500

DROWN, William Staples
American d. 1915
paintings: (L) $137; (H) $1,650
drawings: (L) $66; (H) $1,045

DRUCKER, Mort
American
drawings: (L) $935; (H) $9,350

DRUET, Antoine
French b. 1857
paintings: (L) $19,550; (H) $44,000

DRUMAUX, Angelina
paintings: (H) $2,415

DRUMMOND
paintings: (L) $60; (H) $660 .
drawings: (L) $110; (H) $220

DRUMMOND, Arthur
British 1871-1951
paintings: (L) $3,850; (H) $4,400

DRUMMOND, J.
Scottish 19th cent.
paintings: (L) $1,540; (H) $8,800

DRUMMOND, Samuel
British 19th cent.
paintings: (H) $920

DRURY, Alfred
English 1856-1944
sculpture: (H) $2,750

DRYANDER, Johann Friedrich
1756-1812
paintings: (H) $3,300

DRYDEN, Helen
American b. 1887
drawings: (L) $115; (H) $5,775

DRYER, Moira
1957-1992
paintings: (L) $1,540; (H) $9,200

DRYER, Roy
drawings: (H) $660

DRYSDALE, Alexander John
American 1870-1934
paintings: (L) $121; (H) $10,725
drawings: (L) $165; (H) $3,575

DU BOIS
paintings: (H) $495

DU BOIS, Guy Pene
American 1884-1958
paintings: (L) $978; (H) $99,000
drawings: (L) $248; (H) $22,000

DU GARDIER, Raoul
French b. 1871
drawings: (H) $1,100

DU MONT
French 19th cent.
paintings: (H) $1,035

DU PAVILLON, Isidore Pean
French 1790-1856
paintings: (H) $2,090

DU PUIGAUDEAU, Fernand
French 1864 or 1866-1930
paintings: (H) $28,750

DUBBELS, Hendrik Jabobsz.
Dutch 1621-1676
paintings: (L) $29,900; (H) $266,500

DUBE, Louis Theodore
b. 1861
paintings: (H) $3,220

DUBE, Mattie
American b. 1861
paintings: (H) $1,650

DUBERT, J.J.
European 19th cent.
paintings: (H) $3,450

DUBOIS
paintings: (L) $402; (H) $550

DUBOIS, Albert
German/American b. c. 1831
paintings: (L) $3,162; (H) $17,250

DUBOIS, Charles Edward
American 1847-1885
paintings: (L) $316; (H) $1,210

DUBOIS, E.
French 19th cent.
sculpture: (H) $3,960

DUBOIS, Ernest Henri
French 1863-1931
sculpture: (H) $5,175

DUBOIS, Henri Pierre Hippolyte
French 1837-1909
paintings: (H) $46,000

DUBOIS, N.
paintings: (H) $935

DUBOIS, Paul
French 1829-1905
paintings: (H) $990
sculpture: (L) $660; (H) $21,850

DUBOIS-PILLET, Albert
French 1845-1890
paintings: (H) $9,200

DUBORD, Jean Pierre
French b. 1949
paintings: (L) $880; (H) $2,760

DUBOS, Angele
French b. 1844
paintings: (H) $14,950

DUBOST, Antoine
French 1769-1825
paintings: (H) $79,500

DUBOVSKI, Nicolav N.
Russian 1859-1918
paintings: (H) $2,640

DUBOY, Paul
French late 19th cent.
sculpture: (H) $2,185

DUBREUIL, Victor
American late 19th cent.
paintings: (L) $385; (H) $3,300

DUBROWSKY, Josef
Austrian 1889-1962
drawings: (L) $330; (H) $1,320

DUBUCAND, Alfred
French 1828-1894
sculpture: (L) $440; (H) $19,550

DUBUFE, Edouard Marie Guillaume
French 1853-1909
paintings: (H) $4,830

DUBUFFE, Edouard Louis
French 1820-1883
paintings: (L) $3,300; (H) $8,800

DUBUFFET, Jean
French 1901-1985
paintings: (L) $25,300; (H) $2,640,000
drawings: (L) $2,587; (H) $495,000
sculpture: (L) $33,000; (H) $233,500

DUBUIS, George S.
American 19th/20th cent.
paintings: (H) $4,950

DUBUISSON, Alexandre
French 1805-1870
paintings: (L) $7,700; (H) $23,000

DUCAIRE-ROQUE, Maryse
French 20th cent.
paintings: (L) $219; (H) $3,850

DUCALE, F.
Italian 19th/20th cent.
paintings: (H) $2,145

DUCASSE, G.E.
Haitian b. 1917
paintings: (H) $605

DUCASSE, Gervais Emmanuel
Haitian b. 1903
drawings: (L) $715; (H) $1,265

DUCASSE, Gervais Emmanuel and
Gabriel ALIX
paintings: (H) $1,380

DUCASSE, Gervais Emmanuel and
Wilbur PAUL
drawings: (H) $1,150

DUCHAMP, Marcel
French 1887-1968
drawings: (L) $9,775; (H) $19,800
sculpture: (L) $2,640; (H) $148,500

DUCHAMP, Suzanne
French 1889-1963
paintings: (L) $605; (H) $2,860
drawings: (H) $1,760

DUCHAMP-VILLON, Raymond
French 1876-1918
drawings: (H) $1,150
sculpture: (H) $20,700

DUCHATEL, Frederikus Jacobus
Dutch b. 1856
drawings: (L) $825; (H) $1,650

DUCHOISELLE
French 19th cent.
sculpture: (L) $500; (H) $31,050

DUCK, Jacob
Dutch c. 1600-after 1660
paintings: (L) $21,850; (H) $233,500

DUCKHARDT, R.
American 20th cent.
paintings: (L) $440; (H) $467

DUCKWORTH, Ruth
British b. Germany 1919
sculpture: (L) $440; (H) $1,725

DUCLAUX, Jean Antoine
French 1783-1868
paintings: (H) $11,500

DUCLOS, Adolphe
French b. 1865
paintings: (H) $1,540

DUCQ, Joseph Francois
1762-1829
paintings: (H) $222,500

DUCROS, Abraham Louis Rodolphe
Swiss 1748-1810
drawings: (H) $552

DUDASH, C. Michael
paintings: (H) $935

DUDGEON, Thomas
English 19th cent.
paintings: (L) $495; (H) $1,430

DUDLEY, Arthur
British ac. 1890-1907
drawings: (H) $1,320

DUDLEY, Charles
paintings: (L) $440; (H) $935

DUDLEY, Frank V.
American 1868-1957
paintings: (L) $220; (H) $3,520

DUDLEY, June
American b. 1940
paintings: (L) $750; (H) $3,520

DUDLY, J.
drawings: (H) $2,860

DUDLY, T.
drawings: (H) $2,200

DUE, O.L. la
paintings: (H) $4,200

DUER, Douglas
American 1887-1964
paintings: (H) $1,045

DUERINCKX, Adrien Paul Francois
Belgian b. 1888
paintings: (H) $1,540

DUESSEL, Henry A.
American 19th cent.
paintings: (L) $33; (H) $1,320

DUEZ, Ernest Agne
French 1843-1896
paintings: (H) $40,700

DUFAIS, P.
Continental 19th cent.
paintings: (L) $275; (H) $495

DUFAU, Clementine Helen
paintings: (H) $1,380

DUFEU, Edouard Jacques
French 1840-1900
paintings: (L) $230; (H) $4,600

DUFF, John
American b. 1943
drawings: (H) $1,210
sculpture: (L) $3,575; (H) $13,200

DUFFAUT, Prefete
Haitian b. 1923
paintings: (L) $550; (H) $5,720

DUFFIELD, William
British 1816-1863
paintings: (L) $1,650; (H) $4,025

DUFFY, Aileen Plaskett
paintings: (H) $700

DUFNER, Edward
American 1871/72-1957
paintings: (L) $825; (H) $57,200
drawings: (L) $660; (H) $8,800

DUFOUR, Bernard
paintings: (L) $1,100; (H) $1,840

DUFOUR, Camille
French b. 1841
paintings: (H) $1,650

DUFOUR, P.
Continental 19th/20th cent.
paintings: (H) $4,180

DUFRAT, Alfred and Pierre TERRE
French 20th cent.
drawings: (H) $14,950

DUFRENOY, Georges
French 1870-1942
paintings: (H) $1,150

DUFRESNE, Charles
French 1876-1938
paintings: (L) $2,070; (H) $3,850
drawings: (L) $1,380; (H) $3,105

DUFTAS, Robert
20th cent.
paintings: (L) $495; (H) $660
drawings: (H) $3,850

DUFY, Jean
French 1888-1964
paintings: (L) $1,650; (H) $52,800
drawings: (L) $575; (H) $25,300

DUFY, Raoul
French 1877-1953
paintings: (L) $275; (H) $852,500
drawings: (L) $550; (H) $319,000
sculpture: (H) $24,200

DUGHET, Gaspard, called Gaspard
Poussin
French 1615-1675
paintings: (L) $9,350; (H) $16,100

DUGMORE, Arthur Radclyffe
American 1870-1955
paintings: (H) $3,080

DUGMORE, Edward
American b. 1915
drawings: (H) $1,093

DUILLO, Elaine
b. 1928
paintings: (L) $192; (H) $495

DUJARDIN, Karel
Dutch c. 1622-1678
paintings: (H) $34,500

DUKE, Alfred
British 20th cent.
paintings: (L) $523; (H) $6,710

DUKE, S.P.
American 20th cent.
paintings: (H) $522

DUKE Y FERRER, Salvatore
20th cent.
paintings: (L) $1,100; (H) $1,725

DULAC, Edmund
French/English 1882-1953
drawings: (L) $920; (H) $46,000

DULL, John
American b. 1859
paintings: (L) $220; (H) $3,520
drawings: (L) $85; (H) $900

DULUARD, Hippolyte Francois Leon
French b. 1871
paintings: (L) $4,600; (H) $6,325

DUMAIGE, Etienne Henri
French 1830-1888
paintings: (H) $2,990
sculpture: (L) $578; (H) $9,200

DUMAS, Pierre Henri
French 1886-1967
paintings: (L) $6,050; (H) $8,625

DUMESNIL, Marie
French b. 1850
paintings: (H) $1,210

DUMM, Edwina
1893-1991
drawings: (H) $880

DUMMER, Joseph Owen
American 1844-1935
drawings: (H) $743

DUMOND, Frank Vincent
American 1865-1951
paintings: (L) $605; (H) $7,475
drawings: (H) $825

DUMOND, Frederick Melville
American 1867-1927
paintings: (L) $978; (H) $4,840

DUMONT
French 19th cent.
paintings: (L) $1,650; (H) $5,750

DUMONT, ***
French 19th cent.
paintings: (H) $2,090

DUMONT, B.
French School 19th/20th cent.
paintings: (H) $1,320

DUMONT, Edme
French 19th cent.
sculpture: (H) $4,400

DUMONT, Eugenio Alvarez
Spanish 1864-1927
paintings: (H) $71,250

DUMONT, Francis
paintings: (H) $1,210

DUMONT, Francois
Belgian 19th cent.
paintings: (H) $863

DUMONT, Francois
French 18th/19th cent.
paintings: (H) $2,200

DUMONT, Henri
French 19th cent.
paintings: (H) $4,400

DUMONT, Henri Julien
French b. 1859
paintings: (H) $71,250

DUMONT, P.
French 19th cent.
paintings: (L) $1,093; (H) $1,495

DUMONT, Pierre
French 1884-1936
paintings: (L) $3,300; (H) $8,800

DUMONT, R.
Continental 19th cent.
paintings: (H) $3,740

DUNACH, J.
sculpture: (H) $748

DUNBAR, Harold C.
American 1882-1953
paintings: (L) $44; (H) $1,045
drawings: (L) $93; (H) $330

DUNBAR, P.
20th cent.
paintings: (H) $990

DUNBAR, Patrick
19th/20th cent.
paintings: (H) $495

DUNCAN, Audrey
paintings: (H) $2,475

DUNCAN, Charles Stafford
1892-1952
paintings: (L) $220; (H) $4,600

DUNCAN, Darwin
American b. 1905
paintings: (L) $303; (H) $660

DUNCAN, Edward
English 1803-1882
paintings: (H) $1,430
drawings: (H) $489

DUNCAN, Frederick
British 19th/20th cent.
paintings: (L) $110; (H) $990

DUNCAN, John
1866-1945
drawings: (H) $1,760

DUNCAN, John A.S.
drawings: (L) $137; (H) $660

DUNCAN, Robert
American b. 1952
paintings: (H) $22,000

DUNCAN, Scott
paintings: (L) $550; (H) $880

DUNCANSON, Robert S.
American 1817/22-1872
paintings: (L) $3,300; (H) $48,300

DUNET, Alfred
1889-1939
paintings: (H) $1,725

DUNHAM, Carroll
American b. 1949
paintings: (L) $12,100; (H) $46,200
drawings: (L) $575; (H) $41,250

DUNHAM, Gregory
American 20th cent.
drawings: (H) $495

DUNINGTON, A.
English exhib. 1885
paintings: (L) $825; (H) $1,100

DUNLAP, Helena
American 1876-1955
paintings: (L) $1,725; (H) $4,125
drawings: (H) $330

DUNLAY, Thomas R.
American
paintings: (L) $605; (H) $935

DUNLOP, Ronald Ossory
British 1894-1973
paintings: (L) $165; (H) $863

DUNN, Harvey T.
American 1884-1952
paintings: (L) $440; (H) $36,800

DUNNING, Lois
American 19th cent.
drawings: (H) $2,200

DUNNING, Robert Spear
American 1829-1905
paintings: (L) $330; (H) $65,750

DUNNINGTON, A.
English exhib. 1885
paintings: (H) $825

DUNOYER, Pierre
b. 1949
paintings: (L) $8,250; (H) $19,800

DUNOYER DE SEGONZAC, Andre
French 1884-1974
paintings: (L) $2,750; (H) $57,750
drawings: (L) $137; (H) $59,700

DUNSMORE, John Ward
American 1856-1945
paintings: (L) $495; (H) $1,760

DUNSTAN, Barnard
drawings: (H) $2,200

DUNTON, W. Herbert
American 1878-1936
paintings: (L) $9,900; (H) $38,500

DUPAIN, Edmond Louis
French b. 1847
paintings: (L) $2,200; (H) $9,350

DUPAS, Jean
French 1882-1964
paintings: (L) $8,050; (H) $255,500
drawings: (L) $1,870; (H) $16,100
sculpture: (H) $2,070

DUPLESSIS, C. Michel H.
18th cent.
paintings: (L) $12,650; (H) $15,400

DUPOIS, Louis C.G.
French 19th cent.
paintings: (H) $770

DUPONT, Gainsborough
English c. 1754-1797
paintings: (L) $2,750; (H) $3,910

DUPONT, Jean Luc
paintings: (H) $468

DUPONT, Louis Richard Francois
1734-1765
paintings: (H) $23,000

DUPONT, W.F.
American 19th cent.
paintings: (H) $575

DUPONT-WATTEAU, Francois
Leonard
French 1765-1821
drawings: (H) $715

DUPRAT, Albert Ferdinand
Italian b. 1882
paintings: (H) $1,650

DUPRAY, Henri Louis
French 1841-1909
paintings: (L) $1,955; (H) $5,060

DUPRE, Giovanni
Italian 1817-1882
sculpture: (L) $3,740; (H) $18,400

DUPRE, Jules
French 1811-1889
paintings: (L) $935; (H) $93,500
drawings: (H) $358

DUPRE, Julien
French 1851-1910
paintings: (L) $1,495; (H) $398,500

DUPRE, L.
paintings: (L) $161; (H) $1,650

DUPRE, Leon Victor
French 1816-1879
paintings: (L) $770; (H) $12,100

DUPRE, Louis
French 1789-1837
drawings: (H) $8,800

DUPRESSOIR, Charles
French 1848-1928
paintings: (H) $8,050

DUPUE
American
drawings: (H) $17,250

DUPUIS, David
20th cent.
drawings: (H) $2,760

DUPUIS, Pierre
French 1610-1682
paintings: (H) $110,000

DUPUY, Paul Michel
French 1869-1949
paintings: (L) $9,200; (H) $23,000

DURA, Alberto
paintings: (L) $6,900; (H) $9,200

DURA, G***
Italian 19th cent.
drawings: (H) $2,200

DURA, G.
Italian 19th cent.
paintings: (H) $1,870
drawings: (H) $1,540

DURAN, A.
American ac. 1886-1900
paintings: (H) $20,900

DURAN, C**
Spanish 19th cent.
paintings: (H) $2,875

DURAN, Carolus
French 1837-1917
paintings: (L) $3,300; (H) $10,101

DURAN, Robert
paintings: (H) $880

DURAND, Alex
British 19th/20th cent.
paintings: (H) $6,325

DURAND, Asher B.
American 1796-1886
paintings: (L) $7,040; (H) $24,200
drawings: (L) $1,650; (H) $4,600

DURAND, C.
paintings: (L) $495; (H) $2,640

DURAND, Carolus Charles
French 1838-1917
paintings: (H) $2,090

DURAND, Elias W.
American ac. 1846-1857
paintings: (L) $275; (H) $1,045

DURAND, F.
sculpture: (H) $770

DURAND, Jean Francois
1731-1778
drawings: (H) $13,800

DURAND, Louis
Swiss 1817-1890
paintings: (H) $1,150

DURAND-BRAGER, Jean Baptiste Henri
French 1814-1879
paintings: (H) $1,495

DURANT, Charles
paintings: (H) $4,125

DURANT, John
paintings: (H) $660

DURANTI, Fortunato
1787-1851
drawings: (H) $1,650

DURBAN, Arne
Swedish 1912-1993
sculpture: (L) $1,610; (H) $8,625

DURCK, Friedrich
German 1809-1884
paintings: (H) $460

DURDEN, James
20th cent.
paintings: (H) $825

DUREAU, George
American b. 1930
paintings: (L) $440; (H) $1,650
drawings: (L) $193; (H) $1,760

DUREL, Gaston
French 1879-1954
paintings: (H) $880

DURENNE, Antoine
19th cent.
sculpture: (H) $6,900

DURENNE, Eugene Antoine
French 1860-1944
paintings: (L) $5,060; (H) $5,500

DURET, Francisque Joseph
French 1804-1865
sculpture: (L) $110; (H) $1,870

DUREVIL, Michel
paintings: (L) $550; (H) $825

DURFEE, Bradford V.
paintings: (H) $3,080

DURIEUX, Rene Auguste
French 1892-1982
paintings: (H) $715

DURIG, Rolf
Swiss 1926-1985
paintings: (L) $330; (H) $935

DUROSEAU, Joseph
sculpture: (L) $715; (H) $935

DURRIE, George Henry
American 1820-1863
paintings: (L) $2,200; (H) $165,000

DURRIE, John, Jr.
1818-1898
paintings: (L) $468; (H) $9,775

DURST, August
French b. 1842
paintings: (H) $7,763

DURSTON, Arthur
Anglo/American 1897-1938
paintings: (L) $330; (H) $6,325

DURWOOD, Bernard
American 1817-1902
paintings: (H) $660

DUSART, Cornelis
Dutch 1660-1704
paintings: (L) $9,900; (H) $22,000
drawings: (H) $25,300

DUSATTI, Walter
Italian b. 1930
paintings: (H) $1,093

DUSEN, A. van
Dutch 19th cent.
paintings: (L) $880; (H) $2,760

DUSHAY
paintings: (H) $1,725

DUSILLION, Jean Baptiste
1748-1788
drawings: (H) $1,840

DUSSART, Gustave
French 1875-1952
sculpture: (H) $862

DUSSAUX, Jean Marie
French ac. 1770s
paintings: (H) $48,875

DUSSIEUX, Louise Stephanie
French 19th cent.
paintings: (H) $3,910

DUTY, Claudius
French b. 1833
paintings: (H) $880

DUVAL, Constant
French b. 1877
paintings: (L) $468; (H) $660

DUVAL, Jean
Belgian 19th cent.
paintings: (H) $7,475

DUVAL-CARRIE, Edouard
paintings: (H) $2,760

DUVALL, Etienne
French 1824-1914
paintings: (H) $550

DUVALL, Fannie Eliza
American 1861-1934
paintings: (L) $770; (H) $3,575
drawings: (L) $518; (H) $690

DUVANNES
American 20th cent.
paintings: (H) $489

DUVENECK, Frank
American 1848-1919
paintings: (L) $1,210; (H) $145,500
drawings: (L) $220; (H) $5,500

DUVERGER, P.
French 18th cent.
drawings: (H) $770

DUVERGER, Theophile Emmanuel
French b. 1821
paintings: (L) $1,100; (H) $16,100

DUVERGNE, Paul
French 19th cent.
paintings: (H) $1,650

DUVIEUX, Henri
French ac. 1880-1882
paintings: (L) $770; (H) $7,700

DUVOISINE, D'ap Roger
paintings: (H) $770

DUXA, Karl
Austrian 1871-1937
paintings: (L) $165; (H) $1,150

DVORAK, Franz
Bohemian/Czech b. 1862
paintings: (L) $4,400; (H) $79,500

DWYER, Anna
American
drawings: (H) $600

DWYER, Meredith Willson
20th cent.
paintings: (H) $522

DWYER, Nancy
American b. 1954
paintings: (L) $115; (H) $4,950
sculpture: (L) $4,025; (H) $7,700

DYBSKY, Evgeni
contemporary
paintings: (H) $4,400

DYCE, William
Scottish 1806-1864
paintings: (H) $2,200

DYCK, Paul
drawings: (H) $715

DYCK, Philip van
Dutch 1683-1753
paintings: (H) $33,000

DYCK, Sir Anthony van
Flemish 1599-1641
paintings: (H) $3,450

DYCK, Sir Anthony van, studio of
paintings: (L) $6,325; (H) $107,000

DYE, Charlie
American 1906-1972/73
paintings: (L) $19,800; (H) $45,100

DYE, Clarkson
American 1869-1955
paintings: (L) $440; (H) $1,100

DYE, J.C.
sculpture: (H) $2,310

DYER, Carlos
American b. 1917
paintings: (L) $990; (H) $1,100

DYER, Charles Gifford
American 1840-1912
paintings: (H) $3,850

DYER, Clara L.
ac. 1893-after 1913
paintings: (H) $495

DYER, Hezekiah Anthony
American 1872-1943
paintings: (L) $413; (H) $495
drawings: (L) $110; (H) $1,430

DYER, Nancy
American b. 1903
drawings: (L) $27; (H) $715

DYER, Uriah
American mid 19th cent.
paintings: (H) $30,800

DYF, Marcel
French 1899-1985
paintings: (L) $1,155; (H) $19,800
drawings: (H) $2,200

DYK, Philip van
Dutch 1680-1753
paintings: (H) $4,025

DYKE, Phil
American b. 1906
drawings: (H) $1,045

DYKE, Samuel P.
American ac. 1856-1869
paintings: (L) $575; (H) $1,760

DYKMAN, Charles K.
Dutch 19th cent.
paintings: (L) $1,210; (H) $1,980

DYLAN, Bob
drawings: (H) $1,100

DYSSELHOF, G. Willem
Dutch 20th cent.
paintings: (H) $2,970

DZIGURSKI, Alex
Yugoslav/American b. 1911
paintings: (L) $495; (H) $4,025

DZUBAS, Friedel
German/American 1915-1994
paintings: (L) $3,450; (H) $27,500
drawings: (L) $460; (H) $2,090

EAKINS, Thomas
American 1844-1916
paintings: (L) $16,500; (H) $90,500
drawings: (H) $2,090

EAMES, G.
English 19th/20th cent.
paintings: (H) $550

EARDMAN, W.
paintings: (H) $2,013

EARHART, John Franklin
American b. 1853
paintings: (L) $220; (H) $880

EARL, Frank Elim
French 20th cent.
paintings: (H) $575

EARL, George
English 19th cent.
paintings: (H) $11,000

EARL, Jack
American b. 1934
sculpture: (L) $4,180; (H) $4,313

EARL, James
American 1761-1796
paintings: (H) $9,200

EARL, Maude
b. England 1848 d. N.Y. 1943
paintings: (L) $495; (H) $15,400
drawings: (H) $275

EARL, Percy
British ac. 1900-1930
paintings: (H) $7,975
drawings: (H) $4,025

EARL, R.E.W.
American 1785/88-1838
paintings: (H) $1,980

EARL, T. Percy
British 1909-1930
paintings: (H) $6,325

EARL, Thomas P.
British ac. 1900-1935
paintings: (H) $7,150

EARLE, Augustus
drawings: (H) $2,415

EARLE, Eyvind
American b. 1916
drawings: (H) $2,090

EARLE, Lawrence Carmichael
American 1845-1921
paintings: (L) $358; (H) $6,900
drawings: (L) $288; (H) $303

EARLE, Ralph
American 1751-1801
paintings: (L) $19,550; (H) $129,000

EARLEY, Mary
American b. 1900
paintings: (H) $1,320

EARLY, Miles J.
American b. 1886
paintings: (L) $33; (H) $805

EARNIST, Florence Reinhold
American 20th cent.
paintings: (H) $550

EARP, Henry
English 1831-1914
paintings: (H) $495
drawings: (H) $201

EASON, T.
English 19th cent.
drawings: (L) $467; (H) $522

EAST, Alfred
English 1849-1913
paintings: (H) $2,420

EAST, Barbara
drawings: (L) $1,600; (H) $2,200

EAST, H.
English 19th cent.
paintings: (L) $935; (H) $2,875

EAST, Sir Alfred
English 1849-1913
paintings: (L) $1,210; (H) $6,050
drawings: (H) $1,320

EASTLAKE, C.
paintings: (L) $150; (H) $805

EASTMAN, Frank Samuel
British 1878-1964
drawings: (L) $345; (H) $575

EASTMAN, Ruth
drawings: (H) $1,760

EASTMAN, Seth
American 1808-1875
drawings: (L) $5,500; (H) $11,500

EASTMAN, William Joseph
American 1888-1956
paintings: (L) $220; (H) $605
drawings: (L) $77; (H) $385

EASTON, E.
American 20th cent.
paintings: (H) $990

EATON, Charles Harry
American 1850-1901
paintings: (L) $990; (H) $17,250

EATON, Charles Warren
American 1857-1937
paintings: (L) $253; (H) $6,050
drawings: (L) $385; (H) $5,520

EATON, Dorothy
American b. 1893
paintings: (L) $165; (H) $1,980

EATON, Elliott
drawings: (L) $750; (H) $1,320

EATON, Joseph Oriel
paintings: (H) $3,750

EATON, Valoy
American 1850-1901
paintings: (L) $115; (H) $3,300

EATON, William Bradley
American 1836-1896
paintings: (H) $968

EBERHARD, Heinrich
paintings: (L) $2,530; (H) $4,400

EBERL, Francois Zdenek
1887-1963
paintings: (L) $460; (H) $484

EBERLE, Abastenia St. Leger
American 1878-1942
sculpture: (L) $660; (H) $52,900

EBERLE, Adolf
German 1843-1914
paintings: (L) $29,700; (H) $41,800

EBERLE, Otto
20th cent.
paintings: (H) $660

EBERLEIN, Gustav Heinrich
German late 19th/early 20th cent.
sculpture: (H) $8,800

EBERT, Anton
Czechoslovakian 1845-1896
paintings: (L) $2,640; (H) $9,900

EBERT, Carl
German 1821-1885
paintings: (L) $4,025; (H) $25,300

EBERT, Carl
German 1835-1885
paintings: (H) $1,375

EBERT, Charles H.
American 1873-1959
paintings: (L) $165; (H) $6,600
drawings: (H) $275

EBERT, Mary Roberts
American 1873-1956
paintings: (H) $9,900

EBERTS, Ken
paintings: (H) $6,875
drawings: (H) $2,640

EBNER, Lajos Deak
Hungarian 1850-1934
paintings: (L) $660; (H) $3,630

EBY, Kerr
American 1889-1946
drawings: (H) $550

ECHLIMANN, Y.
American contemporary
paintings: (H) $2,200

ECHTLER, Adolf
German 1843-1914
paintings: (L) $14,950; (H) $34,500

ECK, Ernest
Austrian 1879-1941
paintings: (H) $3,575

ECK, Jacques
French 1812-1887
paintings: (H) $3,300

ECKARDT, C.
paintings: (H) $3,080

ECKARDT, Christian
Danish 1832-1914
paintings: (L) $230; (H) $1,540

ECKART, Charles
American b. 1935
paintings: (H) $805

ECKART, Christian
b. 1959
paintings: (L) $3,220; (H) $22,000

ECKENBRECHER, Themistocles von
German 1842-1921
paintings: (L) $467; (H) $7,150

ECKERSBERG, Christoffer Wilhelm
Danish 1783-1853
paintings: (H) $66,000

ECKERSBERG, Hansine Kern
Danish 19th cent.
paintings: (H) $6,600

ECKHARDT, Edris
American b. 1907
sculpture: (L) $49; (H) $2,588

ECKHARDT, H.W.
19th/20th cent.
paintings: (H) $863

EDDIE, Charles Earnest Shepherd
American b. 1905
paintings: (H) $770

EDDIS, Eden Upton
British 1812-1901
paintings: (H) $5,500

EDDY, Don
American b. 1944
paintings: (L) $7,475; (H) $17,250

EDDY, Henry Stephens
American 1878-1944
paintings: (L) $440; (H) $880

EDDY, W.
paintings: (L) $523; (H) $2,860

EDELFELT, Albert Gustaf Aristides
Finnish 1854-1905
paintings: (L) $11,000; (H) $57,500

EDELMANN, Charles Auguste
French b. 1879
paintings: (H) $467

EDES, Jonathan Welch
American b. 1751
paintings: (H) $151,000

EDGAR, Mrs. C.H.
paintings: (H) $467

EDGAR, William
American ac. 1870-1918
paintings: (H) $3,300

EDGECOMBE, Hedrick V.
Canadian 19th cent.
paintings: (H) $1,380

EDLICH, Stephen
American b. 1944
paintings: (H) $575
drawings: (H) $5,175

EDLINGER, L.
German 19th cent.
paintings: (H) $1,208

EDMISTON, Marla
paintings: (L) $1,100; (H) $3,000

EDMONDS, Francis William
American 1806-1863
paintings: (L) $1,150; (H) $57,500

EDMONDSON, Edward
19th cent.
paintings: (H) $1,100

EDMONDSON, William John
American 1868-1951/66
paintings: (L) $330; (H) $1,320

EDMUNDS, J.
paintings: (H) $15,400

EDMUNDS, J.
British 19th cent.
paintings: (H) $1,980

EDOUARD, Albert
French b. 1845
paintings: (H) $1,540

EDOUART, Auguste
drawings: (H) $2,990

EDOUART, Augustin Amanat
Constance Fidele
French 1789-1861
drawings: (L) $1,540; (H) $1,870

EDRIDGE, Henry
English 1769-1821
drawings: (H) $550

EDSBERG, Knud
Danish b. 1911
paintings: (H) $935

EDUARDO, Jorge
Brazilian b. 1936
paintings: (L) $2,475; (H) $8,800

EDWARDS, Emmet
b. 1906
drawings: (H) $690

EDWARDS, G.
paintings: (H) $550

EDWARDS, George Wharton
American 1869-1950
paintings: (L) $138; (H) $13,750
drawings: (L) $55; (H) $748

EDWARDS, Howard Arden
American 1884-1953
paintings: (L) $330; (H) $990

EDWARDS, J.
British 19th cent.
paintings: (H) $460

EDWARDS, Kathleen
paintings: (H) $632

EDWARDS, Lionel
English 1877-1966
paintings: (L) $412; (H) $23,000
drawings: (L) $2,420; (H) $13,800

EDWARDS, Lionel L.
American 1874-1954
paintings: (L) $115; (H) $605

EDWARDS, Marjorie
paintings: (H) $550

EDWARDS, Stanley
ac. 1930s
paintings: (H) $1,150

EDWARDS, Steven Dee
sculpture: (L) $1,150; (H) $1,650

EDWARDS, W.D.
paintings: (H) $550

EDZARD, Dietz
German 1893-1963
paintings: (L) $690; (H) $31,050

EECKHOUT, Gerbrand van den
Dutch 1621-1674
paintings: (H) $79,500
drawings: (H) $365,500

EECKHOUT, Jakob Joseph
Flemish 1793-1861
paintings: (L) $15,950; (H) $40,250

EECKHOUT, Victor
Flemish 1821-1879
drawings: (H) $863

EERELMAN, Otto
Dutch 1839-1926
paintings: (L) $3,300; (H) $3,737

EERTVELT, Andries van
Flemish 1590-1652
paintings: (H) $189,500

EFTIMIADI, Froso
20th cent.
sculpture: (H) $2,090

EGAN, Eloise
American 1874-1967
paintings: (L) $28; (H) $1,650

EGAN, Eloise
American 20th cent.
paintings: (H) $1,650

EGELI, Cedric B.
American 20th cent.
paintings: (H) $880

EGERTON, Daniel Thomas
British ac. 1824, d. 1842
paintings: (L) $57,500; (H) $165,000
drawings: (L) $10,350; (H) $24,150

EGGELING, Viking
German 1880-1925
drawings: (H) $1,870

EGGENHOFER, Nick
American 1897-1985
paintings: (L) $3,025; (H) $28,600
drawings: (L) $247; (H) $6,050
sculpture: (L) $1,870; (H) $1,980

EGGER, Hans
Swiss b. 1908
paintings: (H) $1,100

EGGERS, Peter
Scandinavian 19th/20th cent.
paintings: (H) $935

EGGERT, Sigmund
German 1839-1896
paintings: (L) $1,650; (H) $8,050

EGGINTON, Frank
British 1908-1989
paintings: (H) $460
drawings: (L) $550; (H) $2,070

EGGLESTON, Benjamin
American 1867-1937
paintings: (L) $110; (H) $1,955

EGGLESTON, Edward Mason
b. 1885
paintings: (H) $880

EGLAU, Max
German/American b. 1825
paintings: (L) $303; (H) $2,310

EGNER, Marie
Austrian 1850-1940
paintings: (L) $17,250; (H) $26,400

EGUSQUIZA
Spanish
paintings: (H) $3,410

EGUSQUIZA, Rogelio de
Spanish 1845-1915
paintings: (L) $11,500; (H) $35,750

EHLINGER, M.
American 20th cent.
paintings: (H) $935

EHNINGER, John W.
American 1827-1889
paintings: (L) $259; (H) $9,900

EHNLE, Adrionus J.
Dutch 1819-1863
drawings: (H) $468

EHRENBERG, Frederick
d. 1910
paintings: (H) $660

EHRENFEST-SCHRODER, Anny
German b. 1908
sculpture: (H) $9,900

EHRHARDT, Karl Ludwig Adolf
German 1813-1899
paintings: (H) $5,175

EICHENS, Friedrich Eduard
Dutch 1804-1877
drawings: (H) $20,900

EICHHOLTZ, Jacob
American 1776-1842
paintings: (L) $3,300; (H) $5,175

EICHHORN, Peter
German 1877-1960
paintings: (H) $522

EICHHORST, Franz
German 1885-1948
paintings: (H) $2,990

EICHINGER, E.
German 19th cent.
paintings: (L) $880; (H) $1,210

EICHINGER, Erwin
Austrian 19th cent.
paintings: (L) $575; (H) $1,980

EICHINGER, O.
Austrian b. 1905
paintings: (L) $604; (H) $690

EICHINGER, Otto
Austrian b. 1922
paintings: (L) $1,380; (H) $9,200

EICHINGER, Otto
German 20th cent.
paintings: (L) $495; (H) $495

EICHINGER, Ulrich
Austrian 20th cent.
paintings: (L) $1,650; (H) $6,325

EICHLER, Theodor Karl
Austrian b. 1868
sculpture: (H) $1,320

EICKE, Edna
paintings: (H) $1,375

EICKELBERG, William Hendrik
Dutch 1845-1920
paintings: (L) $3,025; (H) $8,970

EIDENBERGER, Josef
Austrian b. 1899
paintings: (H) $1,495

EIGHTS, James
American 1798-1882
drawings: (L) $1,093; (H) $2,070

EIKER, Becky
sculpture: (L) $350; (H) $2,800

EILERS, Conrad
German 1845-1914
paintings: (H) $660

EILERSEN, Eiler Rasmussen
Danish 1827-1912
paintings: (H) $1,035

EILSHEMIUS, Louis Michel
American 1864-1942
paintings: (L) $55; (H) $3,850
drawings: (L) $61; (H) $825

EINBERGER, Andreas
Austrian b. 1878
paintings: (H) $3,450

EINSIEDLER
sculpture: (H) $460

EISCH, Erwin
German b. 1927
sculpture: (L) $935; (H) $2,300

EISELE, C.
paintings: (H) $1,100

EISELE, Charles Christian Carl
American 19th/20th cent.
paintings: (L) $880; (H) $2,300

EISEN, Charles Dominique Joseph
French 1720-1778
drawings: (L) $1,100; (H) $4,140

EISEN, Francois
Flemish c. 1695-after 1778
paintings: (L) $3,850; (H) $8,800

EISEN, Louis
18th cent.
paintings: (H) $3,680

EISENBERGER, L.
sculpture: (H) $690

EISENDIECK, Suzanne
German b. 1908
paintings: (L) $325; (H) $5,060

EISENHOWER, Dwight D.
American 1890-1969
paintings: (H) $6,600

EISENHUT, Ferencz Franz
Hungarian 1857-1903
paintings: (H) $107,000
drawings: (H) $192

EISENLOHR, E.G.
American 1872/73-1961
paintings: (H) $1,210
drawings: (H) $1,210

EISENSCHITZ, Willy
German 1889-1974
paintings: (L) $1,840; (H) $6,600

EISERMANN, Richard
German 19th cent.
paintings: (H) $1,870

EISNER, E.
Continental School 19th/20th cent.
paintings: (H) $1,100

EISNER, Will
drawings: (L) $3,300; (H) $5,500

EKBLAD, F.
American School 19th cent.
paintings: (H) $2,200

EKSERGIAN, Carnig
Armenian/American 1855-1931
paintings: (L) $5,225; (H) $20,350

EL BARON DE CATLLA
Spanish 19th cent.
paintings: (H) $2,420

ELDER, Bill
drawings: (H) $4,950

ELDER, Will and Harvey KURTZMAN
drawings: (H) $3,300

ELDRED, Lemuel D.
American 1848-1921
paintings: (L) $288; (H) $5,500
drawings: (H) $385

ELDRIDGE, E. C.
19th cent.
paintings: (H) $12,650

ELDRIDGE, J.
paintings: (H) $1,610

ELGOOD, George Samuel
English 1851-1943
drawings: (L) $2,860; (H) $3,300

ELIAS, Annette
paintings: (H) $660

ELIS, Joseph
British 19th cent.
paintings: (H) $2,760

ELISCHER
sculpture: (H) $1,150

ELK, Ger van
Dutch b. 1944
paintings: (H) $6,900
drawings: (H) $3,300

ELKINS, Henry Arthur
American 1847-1884
paintings: (L) $440; (H) $10,350

ELLEBY, William A.
British 19th cent.
paintings: (H) $660

ELLENSHAW, Peter
American b. 1931
paintings: (L) $1,540; (H) $3,850

ELLIGER, Ottmar, II
German 1666-1732/35
paintings: (H) $3,520

ELLIGER, Ottmar, the younger
Dutch 1666-1732
paintings: (H) $29,900

ELLINGER, David
American 20th cent.
paintings: (L) $700; (H) $8,750
drawings: (L) $150; (H) $2,300

ELLIOT, Captain Thomas
British ac. 1790-1800
paintings: (H) $33,000

ELLIOT, Charles Loring
American 1812-1868
paintings: (H) $4,400

ELLIOT, John
b. England 1858 d. 1925
paintings: (H) $3,220

ELLIOTT, Freeman
drawings: (H) $770

ELLIOTT, John
American 1859-1925
paintings: (H) $1,320

ELLIOTT, Martha Beggs van
American 1892-1987
paintings: (H) $825

ELLIS, A.
American ac. c. 1830
paintings: (H) $118,000

ELLIS, Dean
drawings: (H) $715

ELLIS, Doan
American 20th cent.
paintings: (H) $990

ELLIS, Edwin
British 1841-1895
paintings: (H) $8,050

ELLIS, Fremont F.
American 1897-1985
paintings: (L) $358; (H) $27,500
drawings: (H) $550

ELLIS, Gerald
European 20th cent.
paintings: (L) $523; (H) $1,045

ELLIS, Harry
paintings: (H) $975

ELLIS, Joseph Francis
English 1783-1848
paintings: (H) $1,045

ELLIS, Maude Martin
paintings: (H) $742

ELLIS, Stephen
American b. 1951
paintings: (H) $4,400

ELLIS, Tristam J.
British 1844-1922
drawings: (L) $165; (H) $2,530

ELLIS, W.E.
English 19th cent.
paintings: (H) $825

ELLIS, William
paintings: (H) $1,320

ELLISON, Robert
paintings: (H) $460

ELLRICK, A.J.M.
paintings: (H) $3,300

ELLRICK, A.M.
paintings: (H) $660

ELLSWORTH, Clarence
American 1885-1961
paintings: (L) $690; (H) $4,888
drawings: (H) $110

ELLSWORTH, James Sanford
American 1802-1874?
drawings: (L) $4,888; (H) $6,050

ELMER, Edwin Romanzo
American 1850-1923
drawings: (H) $605

ELMES, William
American 19th cent.
paintings: (H) $7,820

ELMORE, Alfred
British 1815-1881
paintings: (H) $6,050

ELOUIS, Jean Pierre Henri
American 1755-1840
paintings: (H) $88,000

ELOZUA, Raymon
American b. 1947
sculpture: (L) $1,725; (H) $3,300

ELSASSER, Friedrich August
German 1810-1845
paintings: (H) $4,025

ELSEN, Alfred
Belgian 1850-1900
paintings: (H) $4,400

ELSHEIMER, Adam
German 1574/78-1610/20
paintings: (H) $365,500

ELSHEMIUS, Louis
paintings: (L) $495; (H) $1,320

ELSHOECT, Jean Jacques Marie Carl
Vital
French 1797-1856
sculpture: (H) $2,750

ELSLEY, Arthur John
English b. 1861; ac. 1903
paintings: (L) $43,700; (H) $176,000

ELTONHEAD, Frank
paintings: (H) $525

ELUCHANS, Alejandro
paintings: (H) $1,870

ELVGREN, Gil
20th cent.
paintings: (L) $5,225; (H) $15,400

ELWELL, D. Jerome
American 1847/57-1912
paintings: (L) $330; (H) $1,100
drawings: (L) $88; (H) $302

ELWELL, Robert Farrington
American 1874-1962
paintings: (L) $275; (H) $11,550
sculpture: (H) $2,588

ELWELL, William S.
paintings: (H) $690

ELY, Sir Peter
British 1618-1680
paintings: (H) $2,875

EMANUEL, Frank Lewis
English 1865-1948
paintings: (L) $1,210; (H) $1,265
drawings: (H) $88

EMBRY, Norris
American 1921-1981
drawings: (L) $330; (H) $977

EMBURY, Aymar, II
paintings: (H) $1,100

EMERSON, Charles Chase
American 1874-1922
paintings: (L) $275; (H) $7,425
drawings: (L) $66; (H) $660

EMERSON, Edith
American 1888-1981
paintings: (L) $77; (H) $522
drawings: (L) $86; (H) $275

EMERSON, J.
paintings: (L) $550; (H) $1,100

EMERSON, W.C.
Anglo/American 19th/20th cent.
paintings: (L) $248; (H) $770
drawings: (H) $165

EMERY, James
American 1819-1899
paintings: (L) $963; (H) $2,860

EMERY, John
English 1777-1822
drawings: (H) $522

EMERY, Leslie
American b. 1912
paintings: (H) $495

EMIOT, Pierre Paul
French c. 1920
paintings: (H) $2,200

EMMERSON (?),
drawings: (H) $517

EMMET, Lydia Field
American 1866-1952
paintings: (L) $7,187; (H) $29,900
drawings: (L) $2,415; (H) $11,000

EMMONS, Dorothy Stanley
American b. 1891
paintings: (L) $247; (H) $1,760

EMMONS, T.F.
paintings: (H) $1,430

EMMS, John
English 1843-1912
paintings: (L) $483; (H) $27,500

EMMS, John and BRITISH SCHOOL
British 1841-1912
paintings: (H) $6,900

EMORY, Ella
American ac. c. 1878
paintings: (L) $18,400; (H) $52,900

EMPERAIRE, Achille
French 1829-1898
drawings: (H) $3,105

EMPI, Maurice
b. 1932
drawings: (H) $1,610

ENDARA CROW, Gonzalo
b. Ecuador 1936
paintings: (L) $6,600; (H) $24,200

ENDE, Edgar
paintings: (H) $3,300

ENDE, Hans am
German 1864-1918
paintings: (H) $3,630

ENDER, Eduard
German 1822-1883
paintings: (L) $1,840; (H) $29,900

ENDER, Thomas
Austrian 1793-1875
drawings: (H) $8,338

ENDLICH, F.W.H.
Dutch 1880-1965
paintings: (H) $1,320

ENFIELD, Henry
English b. 1849
paintings: (H) $577

ENGARD, Robert Oliver
American b. 1915
drawings: (H) $1,760

ENGEL, Johann Friedrich
German b. 1844
paintings: (L) $2,200; (H) $3,520

ENGEL, Jules
American b. 1915
paintings: (H) $2,070
drawings: (L) $805; (H) $1,820

ENGEL, Otto Heinrich
German 1866-1949
paintings: (H) $2,990

ENGELEN, Antoine Francois Louis van
Belgian 19th cent.
paintings: (H) $9,200

ENGELEN, Piet van
Belgian 1863-1924
paintings: (H) $715

ENGELHARDT, Edna Palmer
American 20th cent.
paintings: (L) $523; (H) $3,520

ENGELHARDT, George
German 1823-1883
paintings: (L) $2,200; (H) $6,600

ENGLE, F.
paintings: (H) $1,320

ENGLEHART, John J.
American 1867-1915
paintings: (L) $247; (H) $2,475

ENGLISH, Frank F.
American 1854-1922
paintings: (H) $357
drawings: (L) $330; (H) $6,050

ENGLISH, P.
paintings: (L) $495; (H) $825

ENGLISH, Thomas
drawings: (H) $500

ENGSTROM, Leander
Swedish 1886-1927
paintings: (H) $8,580

ENGUERRAND GOURGUE, Jacques
b. 1930
paintings: (H) $2,415

ENJOLRAS, Delphin
French 1857-1945
paintings: (L) $6,325; (H) $25,300
drawings: (L) $9,775; (H) $23,000

ENMAN, Thomas
American 20th cent.
paintings: (L) $413; (H) $770

ENNEKING, John Joseph
American 1841-1916
paintings: (L) $220; (H) $66,000
drawings: (H) $2,090

ENNEKING, Joseph Eliot
American 1881-1942
paintings: (L) $330; (H) $9,775

ENNIS, George Pearse
American 1884-1936
paintings: (L) $880; (H) $1,650
drawings: (L) $550; (H) $798

ENRICH
paintings: (H) $1,980

ENRIGHT, J.J.
b. 1905
paintings: (H) $550

ENRIGHT, Maginel Wright
American 1881-1966
drawings: (H) $2,420

ENRIGHT, Richard D.
American 20th cent.
paintings: (H) $1,320

ENRIQUES, Nicolas
Mexican ac. 1730-1780
paintings: (L) $1,210; (H) $101,500

ENRIQUEZ, Carlos
b. Cuba, 1900-1957
paintings: (L) $8,625; (H) $68,750
drawings: (L) $3,300; (H) $9,200

ENSER, John F.
American b. 1898
paintings: (L) $55; (H) $715

ENSOR, James
Belgian 1860-1949
drawings: (L) $1,430; (H) $13,800

ENSRUD, Wayne
drawings: (H) $660

ENTE, Lily Lena
American 1905-1985
sculpture: (H) $660

ENTRAYGUES, Charles Bertrand d'
French b. 1851
paintings: (L) $3,740; (H) $6,325

ENWRIGHT, J.J.
American b. 1905
paintings: (L) $132; (H) $1,100

EPINAY, Etienne Prosper d'
French 1830-1914
sculpture: (L) $1,093; (H) $24,150

EPISCOPIUS, Johannes, Jan da
BISSCHOP
Dutch 1628-1671
drawings: (H) $10,925

EPP, Rudolf
German 1834-1910
paintings: (L) $863; (H) $63,000
drawings: (H) $690

EPPENS, William H.
American 19th/20th cent.
paintings: (H) $633

EPPLE, Emil
German b. 1877
sculpture: (H) $2,750

EPSTEIN, Henri
Polish 1892-1944
paintings: (L) $690; (H) $3,630

EPSTEIN, Jehudo
Polish 1870-1946
paintings: (H) $9,350

EPSTEIN, Sir Jacob
English 1880-1959
paintings: (H) $1,650
drawings: (L) $550; (H) $8,800
sculpture: (L) $115; (H) $9,900

ERBE, Joan
American 20th cent.
paintings: (L) $144; (H) $1,760

ERBE, Karl August Robert
German 1844-1903
drawings: (H) $1,150

Never Refuse Money

The early works of fashion designer Erté (1892-1990) were exquisite, delicate drawings of beautiful young men and women wearing elegant, sensuous clothes and costumes. Erté, born Romain de Tirtoff, was the son of Russian aristocrats. Emigrating to France in 1912 to study costume design, he quickly established himself as a costume and fashion designer, illustrator, lithographer, and graphic designer. (The name Erté derives from the French pronunciation of his initials, R.T.) *Harper's Bazaar*, the American fashion magazine, placed him under contract, and as he became more well-known, he designed extravagant costumes and stage sets for the Folies Bergères in Paris and George White's Scandals in New York. He was also a set and costume designer for the opera and the theater and briefly for Hollywood. In the 1970s, when he was in his eighties, Erté began to release lithographed sets of his works based on themes such as numbers, alphabets, and seasons. In 1980, in association with a marketing firm, he released authorized numbered bronzes "after" his drawings. The "after" indicates that the bronzes were not executed by Erté but by an unidentified craftsman. Marketed as investment art, 144 different statues were issued. A 1987 *New York Times* interview with Erté quoted him as saying he had lived his life by the advice "Never refuse money," and he added, "I never did."

This bronze of *Madame Butterfly*, "after" Erté's design for the opera, was completed in January 1990 shortly before his death. The edition size was 500 plus 12 artist's proofs and 2 *hors commerce*.

Erté's death in 1990 coincided with the decline of the art market, and prices for his bronzes and lithographs took a sharp downturn, a reflection of the state of the art market and the works in his name in these media. Although Erté sculptures are listed as being valued at $35,000 in consumer publications, it was recently reported that many galleries are selling them for only $3,000. In 1994, this statue of *Madame Butterfly* realized $4,240 at O'Gallerie in Oregon. A month earlier in New York at Christie's East another *Madame Butterfly* fetched $2,760. (Erté, *Madame Butterfly*, bronze, 18½ inches high, O'Gallerie, July 11, 1994, $4,250)

ERCOLA
paintings: (H) $690

ERDMANN, Otto
German 1834-1905
paintings: (L) $4,675; (H) $20,900

ERFMANN, Ferdinand
paintings: (H) $3,850

ERHARDT, Georg Friedrich
German 1825-1881
paintings: (H) $990

ERHARDY, Joseph
American B. 1928
drawings: (H) $88
sculpture: (L) $440; (H) $880

ERICHSEN, Thorvald
Norwegian 1868-1939
paintings: (L) $17,600; (H) $19,800

ERICKSON, Carl, Eric
1891-1958
drawings: (H) $1,100

ERICSON, David
Swedish/American 1870/73-1946
paintings: (L) $330; (H) $7,475

ERIKSEN, Edvard
Danish b. 1876
sculpture: (H) $3,300

ERISTOFF-KAZAK, Princess Marie
Russian 19th/20th cent.
paintings: (H) $5,750

ERLACH, Gertrud von
Swedish b. 1861
paintings: (H) $495

ERLANGER, Baron Rodolphe d'
German 19th/20th cent.
paintings: (H) $467

ERLEMANN, Gunther
German b. 1923
paintings: (L) $330; (H) $495

ERNI, Hans
Swiss b. 1909
paintings: (L) $2,760; (H) $4,950
drawings: (L) $121; (H) $5,500

ERNST, Jimmy
German/American b. 1921
paintings: (L) $978; (H) $10,450
drawings: (L) $440; (H) $3,850
sculpture: (H) $605

ERNST, Max
German/French 1891-1976
paintings: (L) $16,675; (H) $962,500
drawings: (L) $3,115; (H) $706,500
sculpture: (L) $1,100; (H) $1,210,000

ERNST, Max and MAN RAY
19th/20th cent.
sculpture: (H) $6,325

ERNST, Max and Marie Berthe
AURENCHE
paintings: (H) $184,000

ERNST, Rudolf
Austrian 1854-1920
paintings: (L) $4,400; (H) $107,000
drawings: (L) $7,590; (H) $37,375

EROLI, Erulo
Italian 1854-1916
paintings: (L) $33,350; (H) $79,500
drawings: (H) $3,850

ERPIKUM, Leon Vuilleminot
French 19th cent.
paintings: (H) $990

ERRO
Icelandic b. 1932
paintings: (H) $6,900

ERSCHUUR, J.V.
19th/20th cent.
paintings: (H) $715

ERTE, Romain de TIRTOFF
Russian/French 1892-1990
drawings: (L) $248; (H) $35,650
sculpture: (L) $275; (H) $6,050

ERTZ, Bruno
American b. 1873
paintings: (H) $978
drawings: (L) $66; (H) $127

ERTZ, Edward
American b. 1862
paintings: (H) $715

ES, Jacob Floppens van
Flemish ac. 1617-1666
paintings: (H) $43,125

ES, Jacob van
Flemish c. 1596-1666
paintings: (H) $77,000

ESCAZENA, Jose
Spanish 1800-1858
paintings: (L) $1,380; (H) $6,900

ESCHBACH, Paul Andre Jean
American 1881-1961
paintings: (H) $770

ESCHER, Maurits Cornelius
sculpture: (H) $1,100

ESCHERICH, M.
20th cent.
paintings: (H) $633

ESCOBAR, Vicente
paintings: (H) $3,300

ESCOBEDO LAZO, Eberto
b. Cuba 1910
paintings: (L) $4,950; (H) $7,150

ESCRICHE, Rafael Argeles
Spanish b. 1894
paintings: (H) $8,050

ESCUDIER, Charles Jean Auguste
French b. 1848
paintings: (L) $2,070; (H) $14,950

ESHERICK, Wharton
American 1887-1980
sculpture: (L) $9,200; (H) $28,750

ESNER, Arthur L.
American b. 1902
paintings: (H) $1,320

ESPAGNAT, Georges d'
French 1870-1950
paintings: (L) $5,500; (H) $154,000

ESPARZA, Angel
drawings: (L) $633; (H) $748

ESPINOZA, P. d'
Spanish 19th cent.
paintings: (H) $2,070

ESPOVITO, G.A.
drawings: (H) $550

ESPOY, Angel
American 1869-1962
paintings: (L) $440; (H) $5,500

ESPOY, Angel de Service
American 1879-1963
paintings: (H) $990

ESPRONCEDA, A.E.Y.
Spanish 19th cent.
paintings: (H) $605

ESSEN, Johannes Cornelis van
Dutch 1854-1936
paintings: (L) $110; (H) $778
drawings: (H) $2,185

ESTE, Florence
American 19th/20th cent.
paintings: (H) $1,430

ESTE, N. d'
Continental 19th cent.
paintings: (H) $9,900

ESTEN
paintings: (H) $1,210

ESTES, Richard
American b. 1936
paintings: (L) $18,400; (H) $464,500
drawings: (H) $805

ESTEVE, Maurice
French b. 1904
paintings: (H) $8,050
drawings: (L) $1,725; (H) $23,000

ESTEY, A. Genevieve
American ac. c. 1924
paintings: (H) $460

ESTOCK, Stephen
American 20th cent.
paintings: (H) $715

ESTOPINAN, Roberto
b. Cuba 1920
drawings: (H) $1,925
sculpture: (H) $2,750

ESTORACH, Antonio Salvador
Casanova
Spanish 1847-1896
paintings: (H) $8,800

ETCHETO, Jean Francois Marie
Spanish 19th cent.
sculpture: (H) $1,320

ETCHEVERRY, Denis
French 1867-1919
paintings: (L) $1,650; (H) $2,860

ETCHEVERRY, Hubert Denis
French b. 1867
paintings: (L) $165; (H) $4,400

ETIENNE, Charles
French 19th/20th cent.
paintings: (L) $193; (H) $770

ETNIER, Stephen
American 1903-1984
paintings: (L) $440; (H) $4,400

ETROG, Sorel
American b. 1933
sculpture: (L) $605; (H) $12,100

ETTING, Emlen
American 1905-1992
paintings: (L) $110; (H) $4,950
drawings: (H) $176

ETTINGER, Churchill
American 1903-1985
paintings: (H) $880

ETTORE, L.
Italian 19th cent.
drawings: (L) $330; (H) $742

ETTRIK
German 19th cent.
paintings: (H) $1,100

ETTY, William
English 1787-1849
paintings: (L) $1,150; (H) $10,350
drawings: (H) $1,430

EUBANKS, Tony
American b. 1939
paintings: (L) $4,840; (H) $9,900

EUGEN, Prins
Swedish 1865-1947
drawings: (H) $8,800

EURICH, Richard
English b. 1903
paintings: (H) $2,200

EUSTACE, Philippe
French 19th/20th cent.
paintings: (H) $6,900

EVALUARDJUK, Henry
b. 1923
sculpture: (H) $1,100

EVAN, Joseph
American ac. 1857-1898
paintings: (H) $18,700

EVANS
paintings: (H) $7,700

EVANS, B.R.
drawings: (H) $1,840

EVANS, Bruce
paintings: (H) $2,530

EVANS, De Scott
American 1847-1898
paintings: (L) $3,300; (H) $18,400
drawings: (H) $522

EVANS, Donald
American 1946-1977
drawings: (L) $4,125; (H) $6,600

EVANS, G.
English 19th cent.
paintings: (H) $1,540

EVANS, J.
drawings: (H) $1,100

EVANS, J.
American ac. c. 1827-1834
drawings: (L) $3,300; (H) $7,425

EVANS, James Guy
American ac. 1838-1860
paintings: (H) $9,900
drawings: (H) $6,050

EVANS, Jessie Benton
American 1866-1954
paintings: (L) $77; (H) $770
drawings: (H) $302

EVANS, Joseph
American 1857-1898
paintings: (H) $1,155

EVANS, Lucile
American 1894-1993
paintings: (L) $275; (H) $660

EVANS, Minnie, nee Jones
American 1892-1987
paintings: (H) $495
drawings: (L) $3,450; (H) $8,050

EVANS, Nancy Chenault
American
paintings: (H) $550

EVANS, Paul
American 20th cent.
sculpture: (H) $1,100

EVANS, Ray, Jr.
American b. 1887
paintings: (H) $495

EVANTE, R.
paintings: (H) $1,725

EVE, Jean
French 1900-1968
paintings: (L) $1,380; (H) $8,050

EVERAARS, A.M.
Dutch 20th cent.
paintings: (H) $1,150

EVERDINGEN, Allart van
Dutch c. 1621-1675
paintings: (H) $159,500
drawings: (H) $4,600

EVEREN, Jan van
American 20th cent.
paintings: (H) $3,850

EVEREN, Jay van
American 1875-1947
paintings: (L) $137; (H) $880

EVERETT, Walter H.
American 1880-1946
paintings: (L) $2,420; (H) $2,640

EVERGOOD, Philip
American 1901-1973
paintings: (L) $805; (H) $63,000
drawings: (L) $275; (H) $5,500

EVERS, Ivar Elis
American b. 1866
paintings: (H) $1,045

EVERSEN, Adrianus
Dutch 1818-1897
paintings: (L) $1,815; (H) $107,000

EVERSEN, Johannes Hendrik
Dutch b. 1906
paintings: (H) $1,760

EVERSHED, Thomas
1817-1890
drawings: (L) $2,300; (H) $2,300

EVISON, Charles
paintings: (H) $748

EVRARD, Adele
Flemish 1792-1889
paintings: (H) $2,310

EVRARD, Victor
French 1807-1877
sculpture: (L) $605; (H) $2,640

EWALD, V.
German 19th/20th cent.
paintings: (H) $770

EWART, Peter
paintings: (L) $687; (H) $1,375

EWART, Peter
Canadian b. 1918
paintings: (L) $330; (H) $1,485

EWING, G.
Continental 19th/20th cent.
drawings: (H) $2,420

EXNER, R.
paintings: (H) $715

EXNER, R.
English mid-19th cent.
paintings: (H) $2,475

EXTER, Alexandra
Russian 1884-1949
paintings: (H) $8,050
drawings: (L) $1,320; (H) $3,450

EXUME
Haitian 20th cent.
paintings: (H) $495

EXUME, R.
Haitian 20th cent.
paintings: (H) $1,430

EYBERGEN, Hans
Dutch 19th cent.
paintings: (H) $1,980

EYBL, Franz
Austrian 1806-1880
paintings: (L) $1,100; (H) $1,650

EYCK, V.
19th cent.
paintings: (H) $1,430

EYCKEN, Charles van den, Jr.
Belgian 1859-1923
paintings: (L) $1,495; (H) $13,200

EYDEN, W.A.
paintings: (H) $385
drawings: (H) $1,045

EYDEN, William Arnold, Jr.
American b. 1893
paintings: (L) $440; (H) $1,208
sculpture: (H) $55

EYDSEN, Robert van
Dutch 1810-1890
paintings: (H) $1,430

EYRE, Edward
British ac. 1771-1786
paintings: (H) $1,725

EYRE, Ivan Kenneth
Canadian b. 1935
paintings: (H) $37,400

EYRE, Louisa
American 1872-1953
sculpture: (L) $230; (H) $805

EYSDEN, Robert van
Dutch 1810-1890
paintings: (H) $880

EYTELL, Carl A.
1862-1925
paintings: (L) $660; (H) $1,210

EZDORF, Christian
German 1801-1851
paintings: (H) $8,250

EZEKIEL, Moses Jacob
American 1844-1917
sculpture: (L) $990; (H) $2,860

FABBI, Fabio
Italian 1861-1946
paintings: (L) $1,840; (H) $37,375
drawings: (L) $880; (H) $3,146

FABBRI, Laurina
Italian 19th cent.
paintings: (H) $1,540

FABER, W.C.
American 19th/20th cent.
paintings: (H) $577

FABER DU FAUR, Otto von
German 1828-1901
paintings: (H) $28,750

FABERT, Jean
paintings: (L) $345; (H) $605

FABIEN, Louis
French b. 1924
paintings: (L) $330; (H) $3,080

FABRE, Auguste Victor
French 1882-1939
paintings: (H) $1,980

FABRES Y COSTA, Antonio
Spanish 1854-1936
paintings: (L) $13,200; (H) $23,000
drawings: (H) $1,380

FABRI-CANTI, Jose
French 20th cent.
paintings: (H) $990

FABRICATORE, Nic
Italian 19th/20th cent.
paintings: (H) $978

FABRIS, Pietro
Italian 18th cent.
paintings: (L) $242,000; (H) $495,000

FABRO, Luciano
Italian b. 1936
sculpture: (H) $74,000

FABRON, Luigi
Italian 1865-1907
paintings: (L) $880; (H) $1,100

FABRY, Emile
Belgian 1865-1966
paintings: (H) $9,200

FACCHINETTI, Carlo
Italian b. 1870
drawings: (H) $550

FACCINI, Pietro
Italian 1560-1602
paintings: (H) $33,000
drawings: (H) $3,080

FACCIOLA, G.
Italian 19th cent.
drawings: (H) $748

FACCIOLI, Silvio
Italian 19th cent.
paintings: (L) $1,870; (H) $2,090

FACHINETTI, Carlo
Italian b. 1870
paintings: (L) $6,900; (H) $13,750

FADER, Fernando
Argentinean 1882-1935
paintings: (L) $22,000; (H) $28,600

FAED, John
British 1819/20-1902
paintings: (H) $4,180
drawings: (H) $660

FAED, Thomas
Scottish 1826-1900
paintings: (L) $990; (H) $29,900
drawings: (H) $863

FAFARD, Joseph Yvon
Canadian b. 1942
sculpture: (L) $3,520; (H) $6,050

FAGAN, Betty Maude Christian
French 19th cent.
paintings: (H) $2,090

FAGERBERG, Carl Vilhelm
Swedish 1878-1948
sculpture: (H) $2,200

FAGNANI, Giuseppe
1819-1873
paintings: (H) $1,380

FAHNESTOCK, Wallace Weir
American b. 1877
paintings: (L) $220; (H) $825

FAHRBACH, Carl Ludwig
German 1835-1902
paintings: (L) $518; (H) $1,380

FAILLOT, Edme Nicolas
French 1810-1849
sculpture: (H) $550

FAINAS, Domion
paintings: (H) $978

FAIRCHILD, Elizabeth Nelson
exhib. 1945
paintings: (L) $345; (H) $660

FAIRFAX, Frank
English 19th cent.
paintings: (H) $880

FAIRLESS, Thomas Ker
English 1825-1853
paintings: (H) $468

FAIRMAN, Frances C.
British 1836-1923
drawings: (H) $880

FAIRMAN, G.
Continental 19th cent.
paintings: (H) $3,300

FAIRMAN, George
American 1859-1926
paintings: (H) $3,740

FAIRMAN, James
Scottish/American 1826-1904
paintings: (L) $660; (H) $27,600

FAIVRE, Antoine Jean Etienne
French 1830-1905
paintings: (L) $5,175; (H) $7,700

FAIVRE, Ferdinand
French 1860-1937
sculpture: (H) $16,100

FAIVRE, Justin
American b. 1902
paintings: (L) $495; (H) $3,025
drawings: (L) $192; (H) $1,100

FAJON, Rose Jeanne
French b. 1789
paintings: (H) $3,575

FALARDEAU, Antoine Sebastian
Canadian 1822-1889
paintings: (H) $2,750

FALARDIARE, A.L.
19th cent.
paintings: (H) $862

FALCIATORE, Filippo
Italian ac. 1747-1754
paintings: (H) $165,000

FALCONE, Aniello, called Oracolo
delle Battaglie
Italian 1600-1658
paintings: (L) $27,500; (H) $77,000

FALCONER, Ian
contemporary
paintings: (H) $4,400

FALCONER, John M.
1820-1903
paintings: (H) $1,870

FALCONET, Etienne M.
French 1716-1791
sculpture: (L) $770; (H) $2,420

FALCONET?
sculpture: (H) $4,125

FALDA, Antonio
Italian 19th cent.
drawings: (H) $1,100

FALDI, Arturo
Italian 1856-1911
paintings: (H) $19,550

FALENS, Carel van
Dutch 1683-1733
paintings: (L) $13,200; (H) $13,800

FALERO, Emilio
b. Cuba 1947
paintings: (H) $978

FALERO, Luis Riccardo
Spanish 1851-1896
paintings: (L) $1,045; (H) $32,200

FALGUIERE, Jean Alexandre Joseph
French 1831-1900
drawings: (L) $2,070; (H) $2,300
sculpture: (L) $880; (H) $63,000

FALGUIRE, J.
20th cent.
paintings: (H) $660

FALK, Hans
Swiss b. 1918
paintings: (H) $1,725

FALK, Max
English 19th cent.
paintings: (H) $1,210

FALKE, Gisela
Austrian b. 1900
paintings: (L) $248; (H) $2,760

FALKENSTEIN, Claire
American 20th cent.
sculpture: (H) $575

FALLER, Louis Clement
French 1819-1901
paintings: (H) $1,320

FALLIO, P.
Italian 19th cent.
sculpture: (H) $1,045

FALTER, John Philip
American 1910-1982
paintings: (L) $121; (H) $18,700
drawings: (H) $88

FANCHER, Louis
1884-1944
drawings: (H) $660

FANELLI, Francesco
Italian 1590/95-1661
sculpture: (L) $74,000; (H) $442,500

FANFANI, Enrico
Italian 19th cent.
paintings: (L) $687; (H) $17,250

FANGOR, Wojciech
American b. 1922
paintings: (L) $403; (H) $3,300

FANTACCHIOTTI, Cesare
Italian 1844-1922
sculpture: (L) $9,200; (H) $34,100

FANTIN-LATOUR, Henri
French 1836-1904
paintings: (L) $9,200; (H) $1,540,000
drawings: (L) $665; (H) $3,850

FANTIN-LATOUR, Theodore
French 1805-1872
drawings: (H) $6,900

FANTIN-LATOUR, Victoria, nee
DUBOURG
French 1840-1926
paintings: (L) $4,025; (H) $40,250
drawings: (H) $4,250

FANTINI, Philippe
French 19th cent.
paintings: (H) $28,750

FANTONI, Marcello
sculpture: (H) $6,325

FARASYN, Edgard
Belgian 1858-1938
paintings: (L) $805; (H) $1,610

FARASYN, L.
Belgian 1822-1899
paintings: (L) $1,430; (H) $5,060

FARBER, Manny
American 20th cent.
paintings: (L) $495; (H) $6,600

FARE, Felix
European 19th cent.
paintings: (H) $880

FARENGHI, G.
Italian 19th cent.
drawings: (H) $7,425

FARGIULLO, C.
Continental School 19th cent.
drawings: (H) $1,760

FARINATI, Paolo
Italian 1524-1606
paintings: (H) $121,000
drawings: (L) $7,762; (H) $72,600

FARIS, Edgar F.
American 1881-1945
paintings: (H) $550

FARLEY, Richard Blossom
American 1875-1951?
paintings: (L) $935; (H) $6,050

FARMER, Don
American
drawings: (L) $275; (H) $750

FARNDON, Walter
American 1876-1964
paintings: (L) $550; (H) $7,700

FARNHAM, Ammi Merchant
American 1846-1922
paintings: (L) $385; (H) $3,025

FARNHAM, Sally James
American 1876-1943
sculpture: (L) $715; (H) $16,500

FARNSWORTH, Alfred V.
American 1858-1908
drawings: (L) $440; (H) $3,163

FARNSWORTH, Jerry
American b. 1895
paintings: (L) $385; (H) $5,500

FARNSWORTH, L.
sculpture: (H) $2,475

FARNSWORTH, Shirley
American 20th cent.
sculpture: (H) $1,320

FARNUM, Herbert Cyrus
American b. 1866
paintings: (L) $247; (H) $968

FARNY, Henry F.
American 1847-1916
paintings: (L) $12,650; (H) $508,500
drawings: (L) $5,500; (H) $222,500
sculpture: (H) $10,350

FARQUHAR, J.M.
American School early 20th cent.
drawings: (H) $522

FARQUHARSON, David
British 1829/40-1907
paintings: (L) $2,090; (H) $3,300

FARQUHARSON, Joseph
Scottish 1846-1935
paintings: (L) $5,170; (H) $25,300

FARR, Charles
contemporary
paintings: (H) $1,430

FARR, Ellen B.
American 1840-1907
paintings: (L) $440; (H) $1,840

FARRE, Henri
French/American 1871-1934
paintings: (L) $1,870; (H) $5,720
drawings: (H) $1,725
sculpture: (H) $825

FARRELMAN, H.
drawings: (H) $880

FARRER, Henry
American 1843-1903
paintings: (H) $20,900
drawings: (L) $5; (H) $14,950

FARRER, Thomas Charles
American 1840-1891
paintings: (H) $805
drawings: (L) $385; (H) $1,320

FARRIER, Robert
British 1796-1879
paintings: (H) $3,300

FARRIO, G.
Italian 19th/20th cent.
paintings: (H) $495

FARROW, Al
American b. 1943
sculpture: (H) $4,400

FARRY, P.
French 19th/20th cent.
paintings: (H) $2,420

FARSKY, Oldrich
American 19th/20th cent.
paintings: (L) $297; (H) $687

FARSKY, Otto
American 19th/20th cent.
paintings: (L) $138; (H) $1,650

FARTHORN, A. de
Dutch 20th cent.
paintings: (H) $2,200

FARUFFINI, Federico
Italian 1831-1869
paintings: (H) $2,860

FASANELLA, Ralph
American b. 1914
paintings: (H) $37,375

FASINI, Alexandre
Russian 20th cent.
paintings: (H) $1,495

FASSETT, E.S.
paintings: (H) $1,650

FASSETT, Truman E.
American b. 1885
paintings: (L) $489; (H) $690

FASSNACHT, Joseph
German
sculpture: (H) $880

FATH, Richard
French 20th cent.
sculpture: (H) $2,300

FATORI
sculpture: (H) $3,450

FATTORI, Giovanni
Italian 1825-1908
paintings: (H) $57,500
drawings: (L) $1,045; (H) $4,600

FAUGINET, Jacques-Auguste
French 1809-1847
sculpture: (H) $8,625

FAULCONNER
drawings: (H) $550

FAULKNER, Charles
British ac. 1890-1900
paintings: (H) $12,100

FAULKNER, Frank
American b. 1946
paintings: (L) $3,300; (H) $3,450

FAULKNER, John
Irish 1803-1888
drawings: (L) $345; (H) $2,415

FAULKNER, John
Irish 1848-1890
paintings: (H) $1,430

FAURE, Elisabeth
French 1906-1964
paintings: (H) $88,000

FAURE, J.
paintings: (H) $34,100

FAURE DE BROUSSE, Vincent Desire
French b. 19th cent.
sculpture: (H) $3,450

FAUST, Biggi
sculpture: (H) $6,325

FAUST, Victoria
drawings: (L) $385; (H) $1,540

FAUTRIER, Jean
French 1898-1964
drawings: (H) $7,150

FAUVELET, Jean Baptiste
French 1819-1883
paintings: (H) $4,888

FAVAI, Gennaro
Italian 1879-1958
paintings: (L) $275; (H) $7,700

FAVARD, L.
French 19th/20th cent.
paintings: (H) $2,475

FAVE, Paul
French 20th cent.
paintings: (H) $3,300

FAVELLE, R.
Dutch 19th cent.
paintings: (H) $2,300

FAVRE, H.
French 19th/20th cent.
paintings: (H) $880

FAVRE, M.
sculpture: (H) $748

FAVRE, Maurice
French ac. 1895-1915
sculpture: (L) $748; (H) $3,737

FAVRETTO, Giacomo
Italian 1849-1887
paintings: (L) $2,640; (H) $7,150
drawings: (H) $605

FAWCETT, Robert
Anglo/American 1903-1967
drawings: (L) $715; (H) $935

FAXTON, H.
19th cent.
paintings: (H) $2,200

FAY
drawings: (H) $2,300

FAY, Arlene Hooker
paintings: (L) $1,200; (H) $3,190
drawings: (L) $1,200; (H) $3,800

FAY, Clark
American ac. c. 1927-1934
paintings: (H) $1,495

FAY, Claudius B.
American 20th cent.
paintings: (H) $633

FAY, D.R.
American
drawings: (H) $550

FAY, Joe
American b. 1950
drawings: (L) $690; (H) $690

FAY, Joseph
German 1813-1875
paintings: (H) $2,530

FAY, Ludwig Benno
German 1859-1906
paintings: (L) $11,000; (H) $16,100

FAYARD, A.
Continental School 19th cent.
paintings: (H) $1,650

FAYARD, R.
French 19th/20th cent.
paintings: (L) $1,430; (H) $4,400

FAYRAL
sculpture: (H) $633

FAYSASH, Julius
American b. 1904
paintings: (L) $275; (H) $3,190
drawings: (L) $33; (H) $110

Dirty Canvases

If a dirty painting with yellowed varnish is consigned to auction, most experts will advise to "leave it alone." There are several reasons for this advice: The mystery of what might be beneath the grime and yellowed varnish can be very enticing; cleaning a canvas and restoration can be very personal, and most collectors and dealers prefer to go to their own trusted conservator; and once the mystery is gone, reality must be faced: the stain cannot be removed or the revealed signature really *is* that of an unknown.

When this large oil on canvas was consigned to Ken Van Blarcom in the spring of 1995, the canvas needed cleaning and the signature was almost indistinguishable. The name Faure was an educated guess, but it was an unlisted name, so the painting carried a relatively low estimate of $4,000 to $6,000. The painting was advertised in all the trade publications, but since it was without a "name," it was not expected to bring in over $10,000. However, the strong architectural detail and the quality of the painting drew spirited bidding, and the final price was $34,100 to a European dealer. (J. Faure, *The Basilica*, oil on canvas, 29 x 44 inches, Van Blarcom, March 26, 1995, $34,100)

FAZZINI, Pericle
  Italian 1913-1987
  sculpture: (L) $575; (H) $10,925
FEARNLEY, Alan
  paintings: (L) $3,080; (H) $4,620
FEBRES, A.
  Italian 19th/20th cent.
  drawings: (H) $978

FEBVRE, Edouard
  paintings: (H) $3,740
FECE, M. Putti
  sculpture: (H) $1,540
FECHIN, Nicolai
  Russian/American 1881-1955
  paintings: (L) $2,990; (H) $143,000
  drawings: (H) $7,150

FECHT, van der
Dutch 19th cent.
paintings: (H) $3,080

FEDDEN, A. Romilly
British 1875-1939
drawings: (L) $322; (H) $920

FEDDERS, Julius
Russian 1838-1909
paintings: (H) $3,300

FEDELER, Carl
German 1837-1897
paintings: (L) $770; (H) $3,680

FEDERICO, Cavalier Michele
Italian b. 1884
paintings: (L) $288; (H) $2,750

FEDERIGHI, Christine
contemporary
sculpture: (L) $575; (H) $2,185

FEDERLE, Helmut
b. 1944
paintings: (L) $16,500; (H) $55,000
drawings: (L) $1,035; (H) $1,150

FEDI, Pio
Italian 1816-1892
sculpture: (H) $6,900

FEDOSHEUKO, E.
Continental 19th/20th cent.
paintings: (H) $1,430

FEELEY, Paul
American 1910-1966
paintings: (L) $8,250; (H) $13,800

FEHR, Friedrich
German b. 1862
paintings: (H) $2,640

FEININGER, Lyonel
German/American 1871-1956
paintings: (L) $14,950; (H) $1,542,500
drawings: (L) $3,025; (H) $71,500
sculpture: (H) $7,700

FEININGER, Theodore Lux
American b. 1910
paintings: (L) $1,650; (H) $2,750

FEITELSON, Lorser
American 1898-1978
paintings: (L) $4,025; (H) $23,000
drawings: (H) $385

FEITO, Luis
Spanish b. 1929
paintings: (L) $1,840; (H) $6,900

FELBER, Carl
Swiss 1880-1932
paintings: (H) $1,210

FELDHUTTER, Ferdinand
German 1842-1898
paintings: (L) $198; (H) $2,420

FELDSTEIN, Al
paintings: (L) $4,125; (H) $4,888
drawings: (L) $1,955; (H) $5,463

FELGENTREFF, Paul
German 1854-1933
paintings: (L) $2,200; (H) $3,025

FELGUEREZ, Manuel
Mexico b. 1929
paintings: (H) $13,800
drawings: (H) $16,500
sculpture: (L) $2,300; (H) $7,475

FELICE, Giordano
Italian b. 1880
paintings: (H) $1,210

FELICI, Augusto
Italian late 19th cent.
sculpture: (H) $2,640

FELIX, Franz
American b. 1892
paintings: (H) $1,045

FELIX, Karl Eugene
Austrian 1837-1906
paintings: (L) $220; (H) $1,650

FELIX-MASSEAU, Pierre
French 1869-1937
sculpture: (H) $495

FELLING, Schmidt
sculpture: (H) $495

FELLNER, Frank
American b. 1886
drawings: (H) $715

FELLOWS, Fred
American b. 1934
paintings: (L) $2,200; (H) $12,650
sculpture: (L) $2,875; (H) $16,500

FELU, Charles Francois
Belgian 1830-1900
paintings: (L) $2,420; (H) $3,220

FENETTI, F.M.
Italian/American 19th/20th cent.
paintings: (L) $1,045; (H) $2,760

FENG ZIKAI, Feng TZU-K'AI
Chinese 1898-1975
drawings: (H) $23,000

FENIMORE, T.J.
paintings: (H) $1,100

FENN, George
British 1810-1871
paintings: (H) $6,325

FENN, Harry
American 1845-1911
paintings: (H) $1,100
drawings: (L) $138; (H) $2,875

FENO, Gabriel Marc Louis
French b. 1903
paintings: (H) $550

FENOSA, Apelles
1899-1989
sculpture: (L) $1,150; (H) $6,325

FENSON, R.
English 19th/20th cent.
paintings: (L) $440; (H) $920

FENSON, Robert
British 19th/20th cent.
paintings: (H) $1,265

FENSON, Robin
English 19th/20th cent.
paintings: (L) $440; (H) $1,320

FENTON, Beatrice
American 1887-1983
sculpture: (L) $3,450; (H) $88,000

FENTON, Hallie Champlin
American 1880-1935
paintings: (H) $550

FENZONI, Ferrau
Italian 1562-1645
paintings: (H) $8,050

FERARI, L.
Italian 19th/20th cent.
sculpture: (H) $748

FERAT, Serge
Russian 1881-1958
paintings: (H) $3,220
drawings: (L) $575; (H) $3,575

FERBER, Herbert
American b. 1906
sculpture: (L) $2,415; (H) $5,280

FERERA, F.
Continental 19th cent.
paintings: (H) $770

FERG, Franz de Paula
Austrian 1689-1740
paintings: (L) $8,825; (H) $82,500

FERGOLA
Italian 19th cent.
paintings: (H) $3,220

FERGUSON, Elizabeth
American 1884-1925
paintings: (L) $374; (H) $825

FERGUSON, Henry A.
American 1842-1911
paintings: (L) $770; (H) $22,000

FERGUSON, Kenneth
American b. 1938
sculpture: (L) $345; (H) $3,450

FERGUSON, Nancy Maybin
1872-1967
paintings: (L) $192; (H) $3,080

FERGUSON, W.J.
English 19th cent.
drawings: (H) $920

FERGUSON, William Gowe
British 1632- c. 1695
paintings: (H) $6,900

FERGUSON, William J.
British 19th cent.
paintings: (H) $1,725

FERINI, A.
Italian 19th/20th cent.
paintings: (H) $770

FERNAND, Pierre and Abelard
GESNER
paintings: (H) $8,800

FERNAND-DUBOIS, Emile
French 19th cent.
sculpture: (H) $1,650

FERNANDEZ, Aristides
Cuban 1904-1934
paintings: (H) $17,600
drawings: (L) $17,250; (H) $20,900

FERNANDEZ, Augustin
b. Cuba 1928
paintings: (L) $2,300; (H) $20,700
drawings: (H) $660

FERNANDEZ LEDESMA, Gabriel
b. Mexico 1900-1983
paintings: (L) $3,520; (H) $25,300

FERNANDEZ Y JIMENEZ, Federico
Spanish b. 1841
paintings: (H) $6,325

FERNANDEZ Y RODRIGUEZ, Silvio
Spanish b. 1850
paintings: (H) $4,950

FERNE, Hortense
American 1885-1976
paintings: (L) $412; (H) $7,150
drawings: (L) $137; (H) $165

FERNELEY, Claude Lorraine
English 1822-1891/92
paintings: (L) $935; (H) $6,600

FERNELEY, John, Jr.
English c. 1815-1862
paintings: (L) $5,750; (H) $48,875

FERNELEY, John E., Sr.
English 1781/82-1860
paintings: (L) $2,300; (H) $154,000

FERNELEY, Sarah
British 1812-1903
paintings: (H) $1,380

FERON, A****
Continental 19th cent.
drawings: (H) $1,380

FERON, Julien Hippolyte
French b. 1864
paintings: (H) $11,000

FERON, William
Swiss 1858-1894
paintings: (H) $10,350

FERRAGUTI, Arnaldo
Italian 1862-1925
paintings: (H) $5,175
drawings: (H) $1,980

FERRAND, E.J.
sculpture: (L) $660; (H) $1,100

FERRANDIZ Y BADENES, Bernardo
Spanish 1835-c. 1890
paintings: (H) $5,750

FERRANINI
drawings: (L) $687; (H) $1,980

FERRANTI, Carlo
Italian 19th cent.
paintings: (L) $1,760; (H) $3,850
drawings: (H) $1,650

FERRARA, Jackie
American b. 1929
sculpture: (H) $18,700

FERRARA, Joe
paintings: (L) $1,700; (H) $4,800

FERRARETTO
drawings: (H) $460

FERRARI, Arturo
Italian 1861-1932
drawings: (H) $1,155

FERRARI, C.A.
Italian 19th/20th cent.
paintings: (H) $12,650

FERRARI, Carlo
Italian ac. c. 1900
drawings: (H) $1,610

FERRARI, Defendente
Italian c. 1490-after 1535
paintings: (H) $156,500

FERRARI, Francesco
1634-1708
drawings: (H) $1,610

FERRARI, Gaetano
Italian ac. 19th cent.
sculpture: (H) $1,495

FERRARI, Giovani Battista
Italian 1829-1906
paintings: (H) $495

FERRARI, Giuseppe
Italian 1843-1905
paintings: (H) $14,950

FERRARI, Lorenzo de
Italian 1680-1744
drawings: (H) $1,495

FERRARI, P.B.
drawings: (H) $1,725

FERRARINI, Pier Guiseppe
Italian 1852-1887
paintings: (H) $9,775

FERRARIS, Arthur von
Hungarian b. 1856
paintings: (H) $27,500

FERRAT, Charles and Jean FERRAT
French late 19th cent.
sculpture: (H) $2,990

FERRE, Georges
French ac. 1885-1890
paintings: (H) $10,925

FERREN, John
American 1905-1970
paintings: (L) $220; (H) $3,300
drawings: (L) $275; (H) $5,775
sculpture: (L) $345; (H) $2,875

FERRER, Joaquin
b. 1929
paintings: (L) $1,100; (H) $5,175

FERRI
sculpture: (H) $935

FERRI, Ciro
Italian 1634-1689
paintings: (H) $18,400

FERRI, Domenico
Italian 1797-1869
paintings: (L) $18,400; (H) $20,700

FERRIER, Gabriel Joseph Marie
Augustin
French 1847-1914
paintings: (H) $55,200

FERRIGNO, Antonio
Italian b. 1863
paintings: (L) $2,420; (H) $4,950

FERRIN, R.
paintings: (H) $495

FERRIS, Edythe
American b. 1897
paintings: (L) $55; (H) $525
drawings: (H) $45

FERRIS, Jean Leon Gerome
American 1863-1930
paintings: (L) $467; (H) $3,850
drawings: (L) $110; (H) $990

FERRIS, S.J.
drawings: (H) $2,300

FERRO, Gabriel
French b. 1903
paintings: (L) $121; (H) $660

FERRONI, Alberto
paintings: (H) $495

FERRONI, Egisto
Italian 1835-1912
paintings: (L) $1,210; (H) $17,600

FERRONI, Gian Franco
Italian b. 1927
paintings: (L) $990; (H) $1,980

FERRY, H.
American 20th cent.
paintings: (H) $1,150

FERRY, Isabelle H.
American d. 1937
paintings: (L) $110; (H) $1,870
drawings: (L) $110; (H) $330

FERRY, J.
paintings: (H) $575

FERRY, John Georges
French 1851-1926
drawings: (H) $523

FERTIG, David
American contemporary
paintings: (H) $863

FERVILLE-SUAN, Charles Georges
late 19th cent.
sculpture: (L) $3,300; (H) $5,175

FERY, John
Hungarian/American 1865-1934
paintings: (L) $303; (H) $2,800
drawings: (L) $990; (H) $1,760

FETHEROLF
20th cent.
paintings: (H) $1,955

FETHERSTONHAUGH, Olive Jane
Graham
American b. 1896
drawings: (H) $1,045

FETTE, Heinr.
German 1802-1872
paintings: (H) $1,980

FETTI, Domenico
1588/89-1623
drawings: (H) $3,450

FETTING, Rainer
German/American b. 1949
paintings: (L) $10,350; (H) $29,900
drawings: (H) $1,380

FEUBURE, Karl Friedrich le
German 1805-1885
paintings: (H) $825

FEUCHERE, Jean-Jacques
French 1807-1852
sculpture: (L) $1,540; (H) $8,625

FEUCHTER, Louis J.
American 1885-1957
paintings: (L) $192; (H) $1,725
drawings: (L) $55; (H) $2,475

FEUDEL, Arthur
American b. 1857
paintings: (L) $55; (H) $1,100
drawings: (L) $82; (H) $863

FEUDEL, Constantin
German b. 1860
paintings: (H) $2,750

FEUERMAN, Carole Jean
American b. 1945
sculpture: (L) $6,600; (H) $14,300

FEUERSTEIN, Martin
paintings: (H) $990

FEUILLATRE, Jean
French 1870-1916
paintings: (H) $495

FEVAL
French 19th cent.
paintings: (H) $1,380

FEVRE, R.
20th cent.
paintings: (H) $963

FEYEN, Jacques Eugene
French 1815-1908
paintings: (L) $522; (H) $11,500

FEYEN-PERRIN, Francois Nicolas
Augustin
French 1826-1888
paintings: (L) $1,150; (H) $6,600

FEYERABEND, Johann Rudolff
Swiss 1779-1814
drawings: (H) $1,430

FIALA, C.
Austrian
sculpture: (H) $2,300

FIANCAILLES
sculpture: (H) $633

FIASCHI, E.
sculpture: (H) $550

FIASCHI, P.E.
Italian 19th/20th cent.
sculpture: (L) $1,760; (H) $4,675

FIASELLA, Domenico
Italian 1589-1669
paintings: (H) $148,500

FICHEFET, Georges
Belgian b. 1864
paintings: (H) $46,000

FICHEL, Benjamin Eugene
French 1826-1895
paintings: (L) $1,210; (H) $3,738
drawings: (H) $6,900

FICHLER, Gotfried
paintings: (H) $1,320

FICHOT, E.
Continental 18th/19th cent.
drawings: (H) $1,265

FICHT, Otto C.
American 19th cent.
paintings: (H) $550

FIDANI, Orazio
Italian c. 1610-after 1656
paintings: (H) $10,925

FIDLER, Anton
Austrian 19th cent.
paintings: (H) $2,750

FIDLER, Harry
British d. 1935
paintings: (L) $2,750; (H) $5,750

FIEDLER
b. 1946
paintings: (H) $495

FIEDLER, W.
ac. 19th cent.
drawings: (H) $660

FIELD, Edward Loyal
American 1856-1914
paintings: (L) $660; (H) $2,750

FIELD, Erastus Salisbury
American 1805/07-1900
paintings: (L) $6,050; (H) $33,000
drawings: (H) $700

FIELD, Hamilton Easter
American 1873-1922
paintings: (H) $1,150

FIELDING, Anthony Vandyke Copley
English 1787-1855
paintings: (L) $2,750; (H) $3,850
drawings: (H) $495

FIENE, Ernest
German/American 1894-1965
paintings: (L) $193; (H) $20,700
drawings: (L) $133; (H) $3,575

FIENE, Paul
American 1899-1949
sculpture: (L) $1,760; (H) $3,850

FIERAVINO, Francesco, IL MALTESE
Italian b. c. 1640; ac. 1650-1680
paintings: (L) $26,400; (H) $43,700

FIEVEE, Adolphe Joseph Louis
French 19th cent.
paintings: (H) $9,200

FIGARI, Pedro
Uruguayan 1861-1938
paintings: (L) $4,600; (H) $79,500

FILDES, Sir Samuel Luke
English 1843/44-1927
paintings: (H) $26,400

FILIP, Konrad
German b. 1874
paintings: (L) $5,500; (H) $34,500

FILIPPELLI, Cafiero
Italian b. 1889
paintings: (H) $2,200

FILLA, Emil
Czechoslovakian 1882-1953
paintings: (H) $107,000

FILLEAU, Emery A.
American 19th cent.
paintings: (H) $4,400

FILLERUP, Mel
American b. 1924
paintings: (L) $58; (H) $1,650

FILLERUP, Peter
American b. 1953
paintings: (H) $2,530

FILLIARD, Ernest
French 1868-1933
drawings: (L) $715; (H) $3,335

FILLIPPANI, L.
Italian 20th cent.
paintings: (H) $577

FILLON, Arthur
French 1900-1974
paintings: (L) $1,320; (H) $3,025
drawings: (H) $345

FILMUS, Tully
Russian/American b. 1908
paintings: (L) $770; (H) $4,675
drawings: (H) $825

FILOSA, Giovanni Battista
Italian 1850-1935
paintings: (H) $10,450
drawings: (L) $495; (H) $3,850

FILOSINI, C.
Italian 19th cent.
paintings: (H) $2,200

FINART, Noel Dieudonne
French 1797-1852
paintings: (H) $12,650
drawings: (H) $460

FINCH, E.E.
American ac. c. 1833-1850
paintings: (H) $3,300

FINCH, Ruby Devol
American 1804-1866
drawings: (H) $11,500

FINCK, Hazel
American 1894-1977
paintings: (L) $2,860; (H) $22,000

FINE, Lou
drawings: (H) $1,100

FINE, Perle
20th cent.
drawings: (H) $575

FINELLI, Edoardo
Italian 19th cent.
paintings: (H) $12,650

FINET, M.
French 19th cent.
paintings: (H) $1,265

FINI, Leonor
Italian b. 1908
drawings: (L) $825; (H) $2,090

FINK, Aaron
American b. 1955
paintings: (L) $1,210; (H) $1,380
drawings: (H) $460

FINLAY, Virgil
paintings: (L) $690; (H) $8,050
drawings: (L) $287; (H) $4,675

FINNE, Henrik
Norwegian 1898-1992
paintings: (H) $2,760

FINSTER, Reverend Howard
American b. 1916
paintings: (L) $77; (H) $6,325
drawings: (H) $605
sculpture: (H) $385

FIORE, Jacobello del
Italian 1370/85-1429/39
paintings: (H) $77,000

FIORE, Peter M.
paintings: (L) $99; (H) $880

FIORENDINO, S.
drawings: (H) $550

FIORI
Italian 19th/20th cent.
drawings: (H) $805

FIORVANTI, Vincenzo
Italian 20th cent.
paintings: (H) $495

FIOT, Maximilien
French 1886-1953
sculpture: (L) $1,540; (H) $5,750

FIRFIRES, Nicholas S.
American b. 1917
paintings: (H) $2,300

FIRLE, Walther
German 1859-1929
paintings: (H) $4,140

FIRMIN, Claude
French 1864-1944
paintings: (H) $13,750

FIRMIN-GIRARD, Marie Francois
French 1838-1921
paintings: (L) $5,500; (H) $60,500

FIRTH, **
paintings: (H) $450

FISCHBACH, August
Austrian 1828-1860
paintings: (H) $3,680

FISCHBECK, Ludwig
German b. 1866
paintings: (L) $88; (H) $2,090

FISCHER
drawings: (H) $2,415

FISCHER, Anton Otto
American 1882-1962
paintings: (L) $330; (H) $6,325
drawings: (H) $220

FISCHER, August
Danish 1854-1921
paintings: (H) $1,980

FISCHER, Carl Holger
Danish 20th cent.
paintings: (L) $825; (H) $1,100

FISCHER, Ernst Albert
German b. 1853
paintings: (H) $1,150

FISCHER, Ernst Georg
paintings: (H) $3,850

FISCHER, Hans
Swiss 1909-1958
paintings: (H) $550

FISCHER, L.
American 20th cent.
paintings: (H) $687

FISCHER, Ludwig
Austrian 1825-1893
paintings: (L) $330; (H) $715

FISCHER, Ludwig Hans
German 1848-1915
paintings: (H) $2,530
drawings: (H) $1,760

FISCHER, Mark
American 20th cent.
paintings: (H) $1,320

FISCHER, Paul
Danish 1860-1934
paintings: (L) $10,925; (H) $34,500

FISCHER, R.M.
b. 1947
sculpture: (L) $715; (H) $3,080

FISCHL, Eric
American b. 1948
paintings: (L) $12,100; (H) $286,000
drawings: (L) $1,380; (H) $82,500

FISCHL, Peter and David WEISS
contemporary
drawings: (H) $2,300
sculpture: (L) $3,680; (H) $8,050

FISH, George G.
1822-1906
drawings: (H) $1,320

FISH, George G.
American 1849-1880
paintings: (H) $1,452

FISH, H.A.
paintings: (L) $440; (H) $2,310

FISH, Janet
American b. 1938
paintings: (L) $2,200; (H) $44,000
drawings: (L) $5,175; (H) $13,200

FISHER
American 20th cent.
paintings: (H) $550

FISHER, Albert
American 20th cent.
paintings: (H) $550

FISHER, Alvan
Canadian 1792-1863.
paintings: (L) $3,025; (H) $22,000

FISHER, Anna S.
American 1873-1942
paintings: (L) $1,100; (H) $4,950

FISHER, Bud
American 1885-1954
drawings: (L) $330; (H) $770

FISHER, Bud and Al SMITH
18th/19th cent.
drawings: (H) $880

FISHER, Charles
British ac. c. 1881-1890
paintings: (L) $660; (H) $1,430

FISHER, D.A.
American 1867-1940
paintings: (L) $88; (H) $1,155
drawings: (H) $28

FISHER, E.J.
American 19th cent.
paintings: (H) $7,150

FISHER, Ellen Thayer
American 1847-1911
drawings: (L) $92; (H) $518

FISHER, G. Macaulay
Scottish 19th cent.
paintings: (H) $550

FISHER, Harrison
American 1875-1934
paintings: (L) $525; (H) $3,300
drawings: (L) $143; (H) $14,850

FISHER, Horace
British d. 1893
paintings: (H) $2,200

FISHER, Hugo Antoine
American c. 1850/67-1916
paintings: (L) $1,155; (H) $7,700
drawings: (L) $220; (H) $3,450

FISHER, Hugo Melville
American 1876/78-1946
paintings: (L) $55; (H) $1,760
drawings: (H) $522

FISHER, Joel
b. 1947
sculpture: (H) $6,900

FISHER, Joshua
British b. 1859
drawings: (H) $920

FISHER, Leonard Everett
American b. 1924
paintings: (L) $3,575; (H) $9,775
drawings: (H) $220

FISHER, Mark
Anglo/American 1841-1923
paintings: (H) $688

FISHER, Rowland
English 1885-1969
paintings: (L) $275; (H) $467

FISHER, Stanley
American 20th cent.
drawings: (H) $1,100

FISHER, Vernon
American b. 1943
paintings: (L) $6,900; (H) $11,000
drawings: (L) $2,300; (H) $8,050
sculpture: (H) $15,400

FISHER, William Mark
Anglo/American 1841-1923
paintings: (L) $440; (H) $9,200

FISHER-CLAY, Elizabeth Campbell
1871-1959
paintings: (H) $880

FISHKIN, Judy
20th cent.
drawings: (H) $978

FISHMAN, Louise
b. 1939
paintings: (H) $12,650
drawings: (L) $715; (H) $1,100

FISKE
sculpture: (H) $3,738

FISKE, Gertrude
American 1879-1961
paintings: (L) $220; (H) $12,650
drawings: (H) $5,175

FISKE, J.W.
American 19th cent.
sculpture: (H) $38,500

FISKE, Pamela B.
American 19th cent.
drawings: (H) $2,750

FITALCY, C.
paintings: (H) $495

FITCH, A.U.
paintings: (H) $1,495

FITE, Harvey
American 1903-1976
sculpture: (H) $1,035

FITLER, William Crothers
American 1857-1915
paintings: (L) $412; (H) $3,680
drawings: (L) $138; (H) $1,100

FITTKE, A.
paintings: (H) $1,485

FITZ, William
English ac. 1876-1889
paintings: (H) $990

FITZGERALD, Boylan
b. 1909
paintings: (H) $632

FITZGERALD, Gerald
American 20th cent.
drawings: (L) $1,980; (H) $3,850

FITZGERALD, Harrington
American 1847-1930
paintings: (L) $88; (H) $2,415

FITZGERALD, Lionel Lemoine
Canadian 1890-1956
paintings: (L) $6,600; (H) $11,000
drawings: (L) $385; (H) $1,320

FITZGERALD, M.
British 19th cent.
paintings: (H) $1,265

FITZMARSHALL, John
British 1859-1932
paintings: (H) $1,540

FITZPATRICK, Arthur
British 19th cent.
paintings: (L) $863; (H) $1,650
drawings: (H) $330

FITZSIMMONS, Arthur J.
American b. 1909
paintings: (H) $522

FIX-MASSEAU, Pierre Felix
French 1869-1937
paintings: (H) $2,200
sculpture: (L) $2,875; (H) $5,750

FIZELLE, Rah
Australian 1891-1962
drawings: (H) $495

FJAESTAD, Gustaf Adolf Christensen
Swedish 1868-1948
paintings: (H) $5,463

FLACK, Audrey
American b. 1931
paintings: (H) $253,000

FLAGG, H. Peabody
American 1859-1937
paintings: (L) $165; (H) $825
drawings: (L) $92; (H) $742

FLAGG, James Montgomery
American 1877-1960
paintings: (L) $275; (H) $16,100
drawings: (L) $100; (H) $7,150

FLAHERTY, J. Thorp
paintings: (H) $1,265

FLAMENG, Francois
French 1856-1923
paintings: (L) $5,175; (H) $156,500
drawings: (H) $6,050

FLAMM, Albert
German 1823-1906
paintings: (H) $10,925

FLANAGAN, Barry
English b. 1941
paintings: (H) $6,900
sculpture: (L) $3,025; (H) $110,000

FLAND, F.J.
sculpture: (H) $1,100

FLANDRIN, Hippolyte Jean
French 1809-1864
drawings: (H) $4,675

FLANDRIN, Jules
French 1871-1947
paintings: (H) $3,680

FLANNAGAN, John Bernard
American 1897/98-1942
drawings: (H) $770
sculpture: (L) $660; (H) $22,000

FLANNIGAN, Lucy Agnes
American ac. c. 1900
drawings: (H) $523

FLASHER, Bruno
20th cent.
paintings: (H) $715

FLATTERS, Richard Edmond
German 1822-1876
paintings: (H) $5,750

FLATTMAN, Alan
American contemporary
paintings: (H) $880

FLAUBERT, Paul
paintings: (H) $2,090

FLAURENT,
French 19th c.
paintings: (H) $2,475

FLAVELLE, Geoff H.
American 19th/20th cent.
paintings: (H) $1,155
drawings: (L) $82; (H) $489

FLAVIN, Dan
American b. 1933
drawings: (L) $5,175; (H) $19,550
sculpture: (L) $17,250; (H) $170,500

FLECHEAU, George
French 20th cent.
paintings: (L) $440; (H) $660

FLECHEMULLER, Jacques
b. 1945
paintings: (H) $1,650

FLECK, Joseph
American 1893-1977
paintings: (L) $1,380; (H) $6,613
drawings: (H) $165

FLEGEL, Georg
German 1563-1638
paintings: (H) $253,000

FLEISCHBEIN, Francois
American c. 1804-1862
paintings: (L) $1,100; (H) $5,405

FLEISCHER, Otto
German 20th cent.
paintings: (H) $715

FLEISCHMANN, Adolf Richard
German/American 1892-1969
paintings: (L) $13,200; (H) $15,950
drawings: (H) $4,400

FLEMING, A.M.
American
paintings: (H) $550

FLEMING, Alexander
Canadian 20th cent.
paintings: (H) $1,485

FLEMING, Ray Frost
American b. 1936
paintings: (H) $920

FLERS, Camille
French 1802-1868
paintings: (H) $2,070

FLESCH, Joanne L.
American
drawings: (H) $450

FLETCHER, Aaron Dean
American 1817-1902
paintings: (H) $1,760

FLETCHER, Calvin
American 1882-1963
paintings: (H) $1,495

FLETCHER, Edwin
British 1857-1945
paintings: (L) $345; (H) $1,265
drawings: (H) $440

FLETCHER, Fred J.
Anglo/Am. School 19th cent.
drawings: (H) $1,210

FLETCHER, H.
English 19th cent.
paintings: (H) $522

FLETCHER, Mrs. Stuart
British 19th cent.
paintings: (H) $605

FLEURY, A. de
French 20th cent.
paintings: (L) $220; (H) $770

FLEURY, Albert Francois
American 1848-1925
paintings: (H) $17,600

FLEURY, Fanny Laurent
French b. 1848
paintings: (L) $8,800; (H) $21,850

FLEURY, Francois Antoine Leon
French 1804-1858
paintings: (L) $1,600; (H) $5,225

FLEURY, James Vivien de
English 19th cent.
paintings: (L) $77; (H) $4,647

FLEURY, L.
French 19th cent.
paintings: (H) $1,495

FLIACCINI
sculpture: (H) $11,000

FLIEHER, Karl
Austrian 1881-1958
paintings: (H) $605
drawings: (L) $495; (H) $2,990

FLINCK, Govaert
Dutch 1615/16-1660
paintings: (L) $96,000; (H) $112,500

FLINT, Sir William Russell
British 1880-1969
paintings: (H) $27,600
drawings: (L) $1,100; (H) $156,500

FLIPART, Giuseppe
1721-1797
paintings: (H) $8,250

FLOCH, Joseph
American/Austrian 1895-1977
paintings: (L) $550; (H) $7,475
drawings: (H) $1,150

FLOHERTY, John, Jr.
b. 1907
drawings: (H) $770

FLOING, Wilfred O.
paintings: (H) $1,100

FLOR-DAVID
1891-1958
paintings: (H) $863

FLORA, F.
sculpture: (H) $4,830

FLORENTIN
Continental early 20th cent.
paintings: (H) $1,760

FLORES, Leonardo
b. Peru 17th cent.
paintings: (H) $15,400

FLOREY, Benjamin
drawings: (H) $650

FLORIDO, Enrique
Spanish 19th cent.
paintings: (H) $10,925

FLORIO, Salvatore Erseny
American b. 1890
sculpture: (H) $1,400

FLORIS, Frans
1519/20-1570
paintings: (L) $49,500; (H) $195,000

FLOROT, Gustave
French 20th cent.
paintings: (H) $1,210

FLORSHEIM, Richard
American 1916-1976/79
paintings: (L) $115; (H) $550

FLORY, Arthur
American 1914-1972
paintings: (L) $275; (H) $468

FLOUEST, Joseph Marie
French ac. 1789-1791
drawings: (H) $35,200

FLOUTIER, Louis
French 20th cent.
paintings: (H) $495

FLOYD, Donald H.
British d. 1940
paintings: (H) $1,725

FLUMIANI, Ugo
Italian 1876-1938
paintings: (L) $1,320; (H) $1,430

FLYNN, Dianne
British 20th cent.
paintings: (L) $1,380; (H) $3,738

FOCARDI, Ruggero
Italian 1864-1934
paintings: (H) $990

FOCHT, Frederic
French b. 1879
sculpture: (L) $6,325; (H) $11,000

FOERSTER, C.A.
paintings: (H) $11,550

FOERSTER, Emil
1822-1906
paintings: (H) $1,100

FOETIN, P.
paintings: (H) $900

FOGARTH
paintings: (H) $990

FOGARTY, Thomas
American 1873-1938
paintings: (H) $13,200
drawings: (L) $77; (H) $935

FOGG, P.
paintings: (H) $522

FOGGINI, Giovanni Battista
1652-1725
drawings: (H) $4,370

FOLCHI, Paolo
Italian 19th cent.
paintings: (H) $6,037

FOLEY, Sir John Henry
Irish 1818-1874
paintings: (H) $303
sculpture: (L) $1,320; (H) $6,900

FOLGER, James Walter
American 1851-1918
paintings: (L) $523; (H) $2,860
drawings: (H) $1,100
sculpture: (L) $770; (H) $1,210

FOLINGSBY, George Frederick
Irish 1828-1891
paintings: (H) $2,070

FOLINSBEE, John Fulton
American 1892-1972
paintings: (L) $225; (H) $32,200
drawings: (L) $100; (H) $475

FOLLETT, Foster O.
American b. 1872
paintings: (L) $920; (H) $1,380

FOLON, Jean Michel
French b. 1934
drawings: (L) $1,120; (H) $2,875

FOLSOM, Henry
American 1792-1814
paintings: (L) $9,775; (H) $68,500

FOLTA, L.
European 19th cent.
paintings: (H) $770

FOLVA, L.
paintings: (H) $495

FOMINA, I. I.
drawings: (L) $920; (H) $6,325

FON, Jade
American 1911-1983
drawings: (L) $935; (H) $1,650

FONCECA, S.
drawings: (H) $625

FONDA, Harry Stuart
American 1863-1942/43
paintings: (H) $1,100

FONG, C.H.
paintings: (H) $2,750

FONG, Lai
Chinese ac. 1860-1880
paintings: (L) $1,650; (H) $8,250

FONSECA, Gonzalo
b. Uruguay 1922
paintings: (L) $9,200; (H) $11,000
sculpture: (L) $30,800; (H) $107,000

FONSECA, Reynaldo
b. Brazil 1925
paintings: (L) $4,675; (H) $13,800
drawings: (H) $7,130

FONT, Constantin
French b. 1890
paintings: (L) $660; (H) $3,450

FONT, P.
French 19th cent.
paintings: (H) $4,887

FONTAINE, E. Joseph
American 20th cent.
paintings: (L) $715; (H) $2,640

FONTAINE, Gustave
French 19th cent.
paintings: (H) $2,200

FONTAINE, Philippe
French 19th/20th cent.
paintings: (H) $1,265

FONTAINE, Pierre Francois Leonard
1762-1853
drawings: (H) $18,700

FONTAINE, Victor
Belgian 1837-1884
paintings: (H) $2,185

FONTANA, C.
Italian 19th cent.
paintings: (H) $2,875

FONTANA, Lavinia
Italian 1552-1614
paintings: (H) $99,000

FONTANA, Lucio
Italian 1899-1968
paintings: (L) $71,500; (H) $165,000
drawings: (L) $5,750; (H) $93,500
sculpture: (L) $6,600; (H) $38,500

FONTANA, Prospero
Italian 1512-1597
paintings: (H) $46,200
drawings: (L) $1,760; (H) $2,200

FONTANA, Roberto
Italian 1844-1907
paintings: (L) $495; (H) $6,325

FONTANAROSA, Lucien
French 1912-1975
paintings: (L) $495; (H) $1,210

FONTE, P.
European 19th cent.
paintings: (H) $852

FONTEBASSO, Francesco
Italian 1709-1769
paintings: (L) $90,500; (H) $140,000
drawings: (L) $4,600; (H) $28,750

FONTENAY, Andre
French b. 1913
paintings: (L) $522; (H) $1,100

FONTS (?), Paul
paintings: (H) $1,100

FOOTE, Jim
paintings: (H) $1,000

FOOTE, Mary Hallock
American 1847-1938
paintings: (H) $2,200
drawings: (H) $2,860

FOOTE, Will Howe
American 1874-1965
paintings: (L) $220; (H) $23,000

FOPPIANI, Gustavo
Italian 20th cent.
paintings: (L) $1,093; (H) $3,025

FORAIN, Jean Louis
French 1852-1931
paintings: (L) $22; (H) $360,000
drawings: (L) $184; (H) $20,700

FORBES, Alexander
English d. 1839
paintings: (H) $3,575

FORBES, Charles Stuart
American 1856-1926
paintings: (L) $605; (H) $1,100
drawings: (L) $110; (H) $165

FORBES, Edwin
American 1839-1895
paintings: (H) $660

FORBES, Elizabeth Adela Stanhope
b. Canada 1859 d. England 1912
drawings: (L) $6,325; (H) $35,750

FORBES, Helen
American 1891-1945
paintings: (L) $660; (H) $4,125
drawings: (L) $330; (H) $605

FORBES, John Colin
Canadian 1846-1925
paintings: (L) $220; (H) $8,250

FORBES, Kenneth Keith
paintings: (L) $2,640; (H) $4,400

FORBES, Leyton
English 19th/20th cent.
drawings: (L) $55; (H) $550

FORBES, Stanhope Alexander
Irish 1857-1948
paintings: (L) $863; (H) $19,800

FORCELLA, N.
Italian 19th cent.
paintings: (L) $10,350; (H) $14,950

FORD, Dale
American
sculpture: (L) $1,540; (H) $1,540

FORD, Elise
American 20th cent.
paintings: (L) $825; (H) $1,150

FORD, Henry Chapman
American 1828-1894
paintings: (L) $880; (H) $32,200

FORD, Henry Justic
French 1860-1941
drawings: (H) $2,300

FORD, Henry O.
American 19th/20th cent.
paintings: (H) $1,093

FORD, Lauren
American b. 1891
paintings: (H) $935

FORD, Ruth van Sickle
American 1897-1980
paintings: (L) $403; (H) $2,070
drawings: (L) $66; (H) $605

FOREAU, Henri
French 1866-1938/40
drawings: (L) $220; (H) $495

FORESTIER, Henri Joseph de
French 1787-1868
paintings: (H) $44,000

FORESTIER, R.
English 19th cent.
paintings: (H) $1,540

FORG, Gunther
German b. 1952
paintings: (L) $7,150; (H) $35,200
drawings: (L) $5,175; (H) $22,000
sculpture: (L) $8,800; (H) $19,800

FORMIS, Achille B.
Italian 1832-1906
paintings: (H) $44,000

FORMOZOV, Valerian
Russian b. 1921
paintings: (L) $99; (H) $1,210

FORNARI, E.
Italian 19th cent.
paintings: (H) $7,475

FORNER, Walter
paintings: (H) $715

FORRESTALL, Thomas de Vany
paintings: (H) $3,960

FORRY, B.
American 20th cent.
paintings: (H) $467

FORSBERG, Jim
paintings: (H) $2,860

FORST, A.
English 20th cent.
drawings: (H) $660

FORSTER
paintings: (H) $1,380

FORSTER, D.K.
American 19th/20th cent.
paintings: (H) $578

FORSTER, George
American ac. c. 1850-90
paintings: (L) $3,680; (H) $32,200

FORSTER, John Wycliffe Lowes
paintings: (H) $2,860

FORSTER, Mary
British 1853-1885
drawings: (H) $1,100

FORSTNER, Leopold
Continental 19th cent.
paintings: (H) $18,700

FORSYTH, William
American 1854-1935
paintings: (L) $1,980; (H) $8,800

FORSYTHE, (Victor) Clyde
American 1885-1962
paintings: (L) $220; (H) $2,875

FORTE, David
paintings: (H) $467

FORTE, Vicente
Argentinean b. 1912
paintings: (L) $770; (H) $908

FORTENAY, Andre
contemporary
paintings: (H) $1,100

FORTESCUE, William Banks
British 1850-1924
paintings: (H) $9,775

FORTESCUE-BRICKDALE, Eleanor
British 1871-1945
drawings: (H) $8,800

FORTESS, Karl
American 1907-1993
paintings: (L) $17; (H) $1,000

FORTI, Edouardo
Italian 19th cent.
paintings: (H) $18,400

FORTI, Ettore
Italian ac. 1893-1897
paintings: (L) $7,188; (H) $20,700

FORTIN, Marc Aurele
Canadian 1888-1970
paintings: (L) $18,700; (H) $93,500
drawings: (L) $10,450; (H) $19,250

FORTINI, A**
Italian 20th cent.
paintings: (H) $825

FORTNER, Gaylene
drawings: (H) $1,200

FORTT, Frederick
British 19th cent.
paintings: (H) $6,900

FORTUNATI
Italian 19th cent.
drawings: (L) $660; (H) $715

FORTUNE, Euphemia Charlton
American 1885-1969
paintings: (L) $6,325; (H) $33,000
drawings: (L) $863; (H) $2,750

FORTUNEY
French 19th/20th cent.
drawings: (H) $3,450

FORTUNI, A.
Italian 19th cent.
paintings: (H) $495

FORTUNY
sculpture: (H) $825

FORTUNY Y CARBO, Mariano
Spanish 1838-1874
paintings: (H) $1,430
drawings: (L) $1,650; (H) $3,520

FORTUNY Y MARSAL, Mariano
Spanish 1838-1874
drawings: (L) $1,320; (H) $6,325

FOSBURGH, James
American 20th cent.
paintings: (H) $1,760

FOSCH, P.
sculpture: (H) $770

FOSCHI, Pier Francesco di Jacopo
Italian 1502-1567
paintings: (H) $7,700

FOSDICK, James William
1858-1937
paintings: (H) $1,380

FOSMIRE, Cyrus
American 19th/20th cent.
drawings: (H) $467

FOSS, Harald Frederick
Danish b. 1843
paintings: (H) $1,320

FOSS, Olivier
American b. 1920
paintings: (L) $201; (H) $880

FOSSI
paintings: (H) $660

FOSTER
19th cent.
paintings: (H) $1,430

FOSTER, Alan
American b. 1892
paintings: (H) $4,400

FOSTER, Alice C.
American b. 1873
paintings: (H) $1,540

FOSTER, Arthur Turner
American 1867-1947
paintings: (H) $468

FOSTER, B. and N.R. WHITE
paintings: (H) $575

FOSTER, Ben
American 1852-1926
paintings: (L) $220; (H) $9,200
drawings: (L) $303; (H) $358

FOSTER, Birket
drawings: (H) $1,375

FOSTER, Charles Murray
American b. 1919
paintings: (L) $688; (H) $3,190
drawings: (L) $260; (H) $300

FOSTER, E.
paintings: (L) $110; (H) $1,045

FOSTER, G.H.
19th cent.
paintings: (H) $1,430

FOSTER, George
Continental 19th cent.
paintings: (H) $907

FOSTER, Hal
American 1892-1982
drawings: (L) $660; (H) $20,700

FOSTER, J.G.
drawings: (H) $2,530

FOSTER, J.W.
paintings: (H) $1,265

FOSTER, Myles Birket
British 1825-1899
drawings: (L) $412; (H) $13,200

FOSTER, Robert W.
ac. c. 1855-1880
paintings: (L) $2,860; (H) $3,960

FOSTER, Samuel B.
b. 1833
paintings: (H) $1,045

FOSTER, Will
American 1882-1953
paintings: (L) $440; (H) $4,400
drawings: (H) $275

FOSTER, William Gilbert
English 1855-1906
paintings: (H) $907

FOSTER, William Harnden
American d. 1941
paintings: (L) $345; (H) $8,625

FOUACE, Guillaume Romain
French 1827-1895
paintings: (L) $7,475; (H) $8,800

FOUBERT, Emile Louis
French 1840-1910
paintings: (L) $1,495; (H) $2,200

FOUJITA, Tsuguharu
Japanese 1886-1968
paintings: (L) $23,000; (H) $1,265,000
drawings: (L) $1,540; (H) $176,000

FOUJITA, Tsuguharu & Candido
PORTINARI
late 19th/20th cent.
drawings: (H) $8,800

FOULD, Consuelo
French 1862-1927
paintings: (H) $15,400

FOULKES, Llyn
American b. 1934
paintings: (H) $5,175
sculpture: (H) $8,800

FOULLON, Lucille
1775-1865
paintings: (H) $7,150

FOULQUIER, K.
paintings: (L) $825; (H) $1,045

FOUQUES, Henri Amedee
French late 19th cent.
sculpture: (L) $1,100; (H) $2,640

FOUQUET, Charles
paintings: (H) $770

FOURIE, Albert Auguste
French b. 1854
paintings: (L) $2,300; (H) $6,050

FOURNIER
paintings: (H) $880

FOURNIER, Alexis Jean
American 1865-1948
paintings: (L) $575; (H) $41,800

FOURNIER, George
American 20th cent.
paintings: (H) $1,760

FOURNIER, Paul
paintings: (H) $2,200

FOUTS, Herbert
19th/20th cent.
paintings: (H) $605

FOWERAKER, A. Moulton
British 1873-1942
drawings: (H) $748

FOWLER, Evangeline
American 1885-1934
paintings: (H) $605

FOWLER, Frank
American 1852-1910
paintings: (L) $220; (H) $8,050

FOWLER, Gilbert
paintings: (H) $2,475

FOWLER, O.R.
paintings: (H) $3,680

FOWLER, Robert
British b. 1853
paintings: (L) $3,300; (H) $6,050

FOWLER, Walter
paintings: (H) $575

FOWLER, William
American
paintings: (H) $2,750

FOWLER, William
British 19th cent.
paintings: (L) $2,645; (H) $8,050

FOWLES, A.W.
British 1815-1878
paintings: (H) $978

FOX, Charles James
English b. 1860
paintings: (H) $715

FOX, Charles Lewis
American 1854-1927
paintings: (H) $880

FOX, Edwin M.
English ac. 1830-1870
paintings: (H) $4,675

FOX, Henry Charles
English b. c. 1860
paintings: (H) $330
drawings: (L) $550; (H) $2,090

FOX, J.
paintings: (H) $1,760

FOX, J.
French 19th cent.
paintings: (H) $770

FOX, J.C.
Continental 19th/20th cent.
paintings: (H) $770

FOX, John
Canadian b. 1927
paintings: (H) $687

FOX, John Shirley
British 19th cent.
paintings: (H) $17,250

FOX, Robert Atkinson
Canadian/American b. 1860
paintings: (L) $412; (H) $5,775

FOX, Terry
drawings: (H) $2,750

FRABOUE, Arnoh
paintings: (L) $98; (H) $460

FRACCHETTI, Lorenzo
b. 1948
paintings: (H) $1,320

FRADEL, Henry J.
paintings: (H) $1,210

FRAGIACOMO, Pietro
Italian 1856-1922
paintings: (L) $4,620; (H) $23,100

FRAGONARD, Alexandre Evariste
French 1780-1850
drawings: (H) $47,150

FRAGONARD, Jean Honore
French 1732-1806
paintings: (L) $35,200; (H) $233,500
drawings: (L) $2,750; (H) $343,500

FRAGONARD, Theophile Evariste
French 1806-1876
drawings: (H) $1,725

FRALLON, Paul
paintings: (H) $920

FRAME, Robert
American b. 1924
paintings: (L) $575; (H) $1,430

FRAMSCHI, M. de
paintings: (H) $3,300

FRANCAIS, Francois Louis
French 1814-1897
paintings: (L) $1,100; (H) $6,325

FRANCAVILLA, workshop of
sculpture: (H) $9,430

FRANCE, Eurilda Loomis
American 1865-1931
paintings: (L) $165; (H) $990
drawings: (H) $5,750

FRANCE, Jesse Leach
American 1862-after 1926
paintings: (L) $175; (H) $1,430
drawings: (L) $88; (H) $316

FRANCES, Charles
British ac. 1881-1892
drawings: (H) $29,900

FRANCES, Esteban
Spanish 1914-1976
paintings: (H) $12,650
drawings: (L) $4,620; (H) $5,750

FRANCESCHI, Jules
French 1825-1893
sculpture: (H) $3,450

FRANCESCHI, Mariano de
Italian 1849-1896
paintings: (L) $1,320; (H) $8,050
drawings: (L) $385; (H) $2,640

FRANCESCHINI, Baldassarre, Il
Volterrano
Italian 1611-1689
drawings: (H) $1,725

FRANCESCHINI, Marcantonio
Italian 1648-1729
paintings: (L) $33,000; (H) $121,000

FRANCESHI, Paolo dei, Pauwels
FRANCK
Flemish 1540-1596
paintings: (H) $21,850

FRANCHI, Pietro
Italian 19th cent.
sculpture: (L) $1,375; (H) $3,190

FRANCHI, T***
Italian 19th cent.
paintings: (H) $4,400

FRANCIA, Alexandre T.
French/Belgian c. 1815/20-1884
drawings: (H) $880

FRANCIA, Giacomo
Italian before 1486-1557
paintings: (H) $104,500

FRANCIABIGIO, Francesco di
Cristofano
Italian 1482-1525
drawings: (H) $96,250

FRANCINI, Mauro
Italian b. 1924
paintings: (L) $3,300; (H) $3,520

FRANCIS, John F.
American 1808-1886
paintings: (L) $605; (H) $76,750

FRANCIS, M.
paintings: (H) $3,960

FRANCIS, Sam
American 1923-1994
paintings: (L) $7,150; (H) $1,267,500
drawings: (L) $12,650; (H) $107,000
sculpture: (H) $99

FRANCISCO, John Bond
American 1863-1931
paintings: (L) $605; (H) $2,750

FRANCISI, Anthony de
1887-1964
sculpture: (H) $4,600

FRANCISQUE
French ac. after 1929
sculpture: (H) $863

FRANCK, Albert Jacques
Canadian 1899-1973
paintings: (L) $220; (H) $6,050

FRANCK, Hans Ulrich
German 1603-1680
paintings: (H) $3,450

FRANCK, Philipp
German c. 1786-1837
paintings: (H) $9,488

FRANCKEN, Frans, II
Flemish 1581-1642
paintings: (L) $12,100; (H) $68,500

FRANCKENBERG, H.
paintings: (H) $450

FRANCO, Giovanni Battista, Il Semolei
1510-1580
drawings: (H) $6,600

FRANCO, Joseph Napoleon
French b. 1811
paintings: (H) $8,050

FRANCO, Siron
b. Brazil 1947
paintings: (L) $9,200; (H) $17,250

FRANCOIS, C.
sculpture: (H) $880

FRANCOIS, Guy
French 1578-1650
paintings: (H) $38,500

FRANCOIS, Pierre
French 20th cent.
paintings: (H) $1,100

FRANCOIS, Roger
sculpture: (H) $1,045

FRANCOLINI, C.
Italian 19th cent.
paintings: (H) $1,495

FRANCOLINO, C.
French School 19th cent.
paintings: (H) $3,850

FRANCUCCI, Innocenzo di Pietro,
called Innocenza da IMOLA
Italian c. 1494-c.1550
paintings: (L) $27,600; (H) $81,700

FRANDZEN, Eugene M.
American 1893-1972
paintings: (L) $660; (H) $1,210
drawings: (L) $55; (H) $605

FRANGIAMORE, Salvatore
Italian 1853-1915
paintings: (L) $5,175; (H) $14,300
drawings: (H) $138

FRANK, Friedrich
paintings: (H) $550

FRANK, Gerald A.
American b. 1889
paintings: (L) $66; (H) $1,650

FRANK, Joseph
German 19th/20th cent.
paintings: (H) $1,100

FRANK, Leo E.
20th cent.
drawings: (L) $935; (H) $1,650

FRANK, Mary
Anglo/American b. 1933
drawings: (L) $350; (H) $1,495
sculpture: (L) $230; (H) $7,150

FRANK-WILL
French 1900-1951
paintings: (L) $220; (H) $8,050
drawings: (L) $345; (H) $3,575

FRANKE, Albert J.
German 1860-1924
paintings: (L) $3,630; (H) $6,600

FRANKE, Albert S.
German 1860-1924
paintings: (L) $4,840; (H) $5,500

FRANKEN, Frans and circle of Jan
BRUEGEL I, II
1581-1642
paintings: (H) $10,450

FRANKEN, Will
German b. 1920
paintings: (H) $495

FRANKENBURG, Arthur J.
19th/20th cent.
paintings: (H) $605

FRANKENSTEIN, Curt
American 20th cent.
paintings: (H) $575

FRANKENSTEIN, Godfrey N.
American 1820-1873
paintings: (H) $1,210

FRANKENTHALER, Helen
American b. 1928
paintings: (L) $6,325; (H) $244,500
drawings: (L) $1,650; (H) $9,900

FRANKFORT, Edward
Dutch 1864-1920
paintings: (H) $1,045

FRANKL, Franz
German b. 1881
paintings: (L) $523; (H) $2,200

FRANKL, Walter H.
20th cent.
paintings: (H) $825

FRANKLIN, John
paintings: (L) $605; (H) $3,960

FRANKLIN, Richard
drawings: (H) $1,265

FRANQUELIN, Jean Augustin
French 1798-1839
paintings: (L) $9,200; (H) $18,400

FRANQUINET, Eugene P.
American 1875-1940
paintings: (L) $104; (H) $2,875

FRANS, *Gm.
19th cent.
paintings: (H) $12,075

FRANSESCHINI, Baldassare, called Il
VOLTERRANO
1611-1689
paintings: (H) $4,888

FRANSIOLI, Thomas Adrian, Jr.
American b. 1906
paintings: (L) $55; (H) $4,400

FRANTZ, Samuel Marshall
b. 1890
paintings: (L) $715; (H) $1,725

FRANZ, Ettore R.
Italian 1845-1907
drawings: (H) $5,500

FRANZ, Fritz
German 19th cent.
paintings: (H) $805

FRANZ, Otto D.
German b. 1871
paintings: (H) $1,760

FRANZ, W.A.
Continental 20th cent.
paintings: (H) $605

FRANZEN, August
American 1863-1938
drawings: (H) $8,800

FRANZI, E.
Italian 19th cent.
drawings: (H) $1,045

FRAPPA, Jose
French 1854-1904
paintings: (L) $3,960; (H) $4,400

FRASCHINI, J.
paintings: (L) $275; (H) $2,415

FRASER, Alexander
British 19th/20th cent.
paintings: (L) $264; (H) $1,540

FRASER, Alexander, Sr.
British 1786-1865
paintings: (L) $5,463; (H) $10,350

FRASER, Charles
American 1782-1860
paintings: (H) $4,400
drawings: (L) $385; (H) $475

FRASER, Jack
English 19th cent.
paintings: (H) $900

FRASER, James Earle
American 1876-1953
sculpture: (L) $110; (H) $198,000

FRASER, John Arthur
paintings: (H) $3,080

FRASER, Laura Gardin
1889-1966
sculpture: (L) $1,100; (H) $5,980

FRASER, Thomas Douglass
American 1883-1955
paintings: (L) $1,045; (H) $2,475

FRATIN, Christophe
French c. 1800-1864
sculpture: (L) $715; (H) $16,100

FRAUZ, W.A.
German early 20th cent.
paintings: (H) $550

FRAYE, Andre
French 1888-1963
paintings: (L) $1,650; (H) $1,870

FRAZER
sculpture: (H) $605

FRAZER, Oliver
American 1808-1864
paintings: (H) $1,210

FRAZER, Samuel W.
American 20th cent.
paintings: (H) $495

FRAZER, William Miller
British b. 1864
paintings: (L) $413; (H) $1,650

FRAZETTA, Frank
American b. 1928
paintings: (L) $11,000; (H) $90,500
drawings: (L) $920; (H) $48,400

FRAZETTA, Frank and Al
WILLIAMSON
American
drawings: (H) $5,175

FRAZIER, C. James
American b. 1924
paintings: (L) $1,980; (H) $6,600

FRAZIER, John Robinson
American b. 1889
paintings: (H) $1,210

FRAZIER, Kenneth
French/American 1867-1949
paintings: (H) $1,725
drawings: (H) $575

FREAS, Kelly
paintings: (L) $3,450; (H) $4,312
drawings: (L) $460; (H) $1,150

FRECKLETON, Harry
British 1890-1979
paintings: (L) $467; (H) $1,380

FREDDIE, Frederik Wilhelm Carlsin
Danish b. 1909
paintings: (L) $9,350; (H) $10,450

FREDENTHAL, David
American 1914-1958
drawings: (L) $165; (H) $715

FREDERIC, Millie Bruhl
American 1878-1939
paintings: (H) $550

FREDERICK, E.
Continental 19th cent.
paintings: (H) $1,725

FREDERICK, Rod
American
paintings: (H) $9,900

FREDERICK(?), E.
paintings: (H) $550

FREDERICKS, Alfred
drawings: (H) $495

FREDERICKS, Ernest
American 1877-1927
paintings: (L) $46; (H) $1,265

FREDERICKS, Marshall M.
American b. 1908
sculpture: (L) $3,575; (H) $11,000

FREDERICO, Cavalier Michele
Italian b. 1884
paintings: (H) $495

FREDRICK, Edmund
American b. 1870
drawings: (H) $495

American Pietà

One of the most memorable statues of the American West is James Earle Fraser's *The End of the Trail*. Fraser (1876-1953) was born in Minnesota and grew up in the Dakotas in Indian country. The original concept for the sculpture, inspired by Fraser's Indian friends, was executed when he was only 18 and working in the studio of sculptor Richard Bock. When he was 20, Fraser traveled to Paris to study at the École des Beaux-Arts and at the Académie Julien. He also worked as an assistant to sculptor August Saint-Gaudens.

Fraser returned to the United States in 1902 and established a studio in New York City. His first important commission, in 1908, was a bust of Theodore Roosevelt. In 1913 he designed the United States "Buffalo Nickel." The Indian Chief on the nickel was a composite of three Indian chiefs; the buffalo was modeled after a bison in the New York zoo. Fraser designed the buffalo side of the coin in a manner that left no room for the inscription "In God We Trust."

For the 1915 Panama-Pacific Exposition in San Francisco, Fraser completed an 18-foot plaster version of *The End of the Trail*. It received much acclaim and won the gold medal. The original plaster version, on permanent exhibition at the National Cowboy Hall of Fame in Oklahoma City, is the first thing visitors see at the dramatic new entrance. Former director of museum Dean Krakel said, "If the (American) West has a Pietà, it's *The End of the Trail*."

The sculpture was cast in several sizes by the Roman Bronze Works and later reissued by the Modern Art Foundry. This version by the Roman Bronze Works is 33½ inches high and is signed © Fraser, 1918. It was originally acquired by Colemant Duport, who had first seen the heroic plaster at the Exposition in 1915. Consigned by the descendants of the original owner, it realized $198,000, a record price for the artist. (James Earle Fraser, *The End of the Trail*, Altermann & Morris, bronze, 33½ inches high, May 20, 1994, $198,000)

Michigan Artist

Marshall Fredericks (b. 1908) was born in Illinois and studied sculpture at the Cleveland School of Art. His postgraduate study was in Paris and Munich, and in Stockholm with sculptor Carl Milles. After his year abroad, Fredericks returned to the United States and taught art in Cleveland. In 1932, when Milles was appointed artist-in-residence at the Cranbrook Academy in Bloomfield Hills, Michigan, Fredericks joined him as his assistant. Two years later he became a member of the Cranbrook faculty, where he taught until 1942. During his years at Cranbrook many of his monumental sculptures were first created on a small-scale. These 1930s sculptures are the epitome of Art Deco design with their long elegant lines and curves, smooth surfaces and simplified forms. After his return from the army, Fredericks competed successfully for numerous government commissions. His outdoor sculptures are monumental and are designed to be an integral part of the surrounding architecture. The American Institute of Architects and the Architectural League of New York awarded him gold medals in 1952 and 1955. In 1963 his bronze and polished nickel fountain was placed in the South Court of the new State Department building in Washington. At age 88, Fredericks is still working on large commissions.

Much of his outdoor sculpture is in Michigan: the carved stone eagle and seven pylons for the Veterans building in Detroit, a monumental bronze *Spirit of Detroit* for the City-County Building, a 140-foot wrought and repoussé metal relief for the Ford Auditorium, the 55-foot crucifix for the Catholic Shrine in Indian River, and the 7-foot high *Boy and Bear* at the Northland Mall in Southfield.

The *Boy and Bear* at the Northland Mall was installed with a limestone bear and a bronze boy in 1954 before the mall was enclosed. Later in 1988 and 1994, two 7-foot castings were made and installed in the Marshall M. Fredericks Study Center at Saginaw Valley State University and at the Fred Meijer Gardens in Grand Rapids. The Marshall M. Fredericks Study Center and Sculpture Gallery in University City, Michigan, contains over two hundred works spanning the artist's career. The collection includes original plaster models, selected bronze casts, drawings, paintings, and photographs.

The *Boy and Bear*, 11½ inches high, offered at Boos in 1994, was a cast of the model for the Northland Mall. Two generations have grown up with this regional icon and bidding was spirited. The price realized was $11,000. A year later, in March 1994, another cast of this bronze realized $8,250. (Marshall Fredericks, *Boy and Bear*, bronze, 11½ inches high, Boos, March 25, 1993, $11,000)

FREDRICKS, Ernest
American b. 1877
paintings: (L) $385; (H) $2,150

FREDRIKS, Jan Hendrik
Dutch 1751-1822
paintings: (H) $88,000

FREEDLANDER, Arthur R.
American 1875-1940
paintings: (L) $55; (H) $1,495

FREEDMAN, Maurice
American b. 1904
paintings: (L) $66; (H) $1,760

FREEMAN, Augusta
American 19th cent.
sculpture: (H) $1,650

FREEMAN, Barbara C.
drawings: (H) $715

FREEMAN, Bradford
American 19th cent.
paintings: (H) $770

FREEMAN, Charles H.
American 1859-1918
paintings: (L) $805; (H) $1,495

FREEMAN, Don
American 1908-1978
paintings: (H) $6,600
drawings: (L) $165; (H) $660

FREEMAN, Fred
1906-1988
drawings: (L) $3,300; (H) $4,125

FREEMAN, George
1787-1868
paintings: (H) $1,210

FREEMAN, James Edward
American b. Canada 1808, d. 1884
paintings: (L) $110; (H) $1,870

FREEMAN, Leonard
American contemporary
sculpture: (H) $825

FREEMAN, Richard
American 1932-1991
paintings: (L) $1,815; (H) $2,970

FREEMAN(?), G.
paintings: (H) $1,650

FREER, Frederick Warren
American 1849-1908
paintings: (L) $247; (H) $5,175
drawings: (L) $633; (H) $1,000

FREIFELD, Eric
drawings: (H) $2,200

FREILICHER, Jane
American b. 1924
paintings: (H) $15,400

FREIMAN, Lillian
drawings: (H) $1,210

FREISZ, Achille Emile Othon
French 1879-1949
paintings: (H) $18,400

FREITAG, ***
German 19th/20th cent.
paintings: (H) $920

Abraham Lincoln

American historical figures were a specialty of sculptor Daniel Chester French (1850-1931). One of the most illustrious sculptors of his day, he executed the seated *Abraham Lincoln* for the Memorial in Washington, D.C., the *Minute Man* at the Old North Bridge in Concord, Massachusetts, *John Harvard* at Harvard University, and the standing *Abraham Lincoln* at the state capital building in Lincoln, Nebraska.

French matriculated at M.I.T. but dropped out after failing physics, chemistry, and algebra. He returned to his hometown of Concord and began modeling busts and reliefs of friends. His first important commission was the *Minute Man* statue for the town of Concord, a job for which he did not receive any pay, only his expenses. The statue was very well-received. Self-taught, French departed in 1874 for Italy, where he spent a year and a half working as an invited guest in the studio of sculptor Thomas Ball. The climate of the late 19th century fostered the development of sculptors. Monuments were being erected to commemorate the Civil War dead, and the U.S. Congress was remodeling the House of Representatives chamber with two statues from each state. French prospered, and in 1888 he married and moved to New York. His commission for the 1893 World's Columbian Exposition in Chicago, the 60-foot statue *Republic*, further established his reputation. By 1894 he was able to afford a second home and built Chesterwood, his summer house and studio in Stockbridge, Massachusetts. Chesterwood is now a museum property of the National Trust for Historic Preservation.

In 1909 French received one of his most important commissions, the 9-foot 4-in. statue of Abraham Lincoln for the capital city of Nebraska. The statue was unveiled and dedicated in Lincoln three years later. An entrepreneur, French frequently made reductions of his best works. A request to the Lincoln Centennial Memorial Association for the rights to reproduce full-size copies was refused. Archival correspondence reveals that French did have bronze casts made from the working model and that when the Committee found out, it was very displeased. A compromise was reached when French agreed to forgo a portion of the final payment in exchange for the rights to sell these copies. Records show that French authorized at least 12 bronzes cast after 1912.

The model that sold at Hindman's in May 1994 is inscribed "D.C.French Jan. 1911" and "Gorham Co. Founders QZG." The date 1911 is that of the plaster working model after which this bronze was cast. The letters "QZG" refer to the date and casting by Gorham. Gorham continued to cast the standing Abraham Lincoln for French up until the sculptor's death. This version was from the Collection of Arthur Rubloff, a Chicago real-estate magnate who, for over 25 years, had his large collection of American and European bronzes on display at the Evergreen Shopping Plaza. Major works by French are scarce to the market and this statue of Lincoln was very desirable. Estimated by Hindman's to sell for $30,000 to $40,000 it sold to a private collector for $74,800. (Daniel Chester French, *Abraham Lincoln*, bronze with brown patina, 37¾ inches high, Hindman's, May 22, 1994, $74,800)

FRELINGHUYSEN, Suzy
American 1911-1988
paintings: (L) $86,250; (H) $92,000

FREMIET, Emmanuel
French 1824-1910
sculpture: (L) $230; (H) $23,000

FREMOND, Andre
French 20th cent.
paintings: (H) $4,600

FREMY, Antoine Alexandre Auguste
French 1816-1885
drawings: (H) $1,650

FREMY, Jacques Noel Marie
1782-1867
drawings: (H) $2,970

FRENCH, Annie
Scottish ac. 1865-1924
drawings: (H) $3,080

FRENCH, Daniel Chester
American 1850-1931
sculpture: (L) $1,320; (H) $74,800

FRENCH, Frank
American 1850-1933
paintings: (L) $55; (H) $770
drawings: (H) $385

FRENCH, Jared
American b. 1905
drawings: (L) $2,530; (H) $2,860

FRENCH, Michael
paintings: (H) $2,750

FRENKEL, Itzhak
Israeli 1900-1981
paintings: (H) $495

FRERE, Charles Theodore
French 1814/15-1888
paintings: (L) $1,430; (H) $63,000

FRERE, Pierre Edouard
French 1819-1886
paintings: (L) $605; (H) $16,100
drawings: (L) $220; (H) $9,625

FRERES, Pugi
sculpture: (H) $770

FRERICHS, William Charles Anthony
Belgian/American 1829-1905
paintings: (L) $2,875; (H) $15,400

FREROT, E.
Continental School 19th cent.
paintings: (L) $2,300; (H) $2,760

FREUD, Lucian
British b. 1922
paintings: (L) $54,625; (H) $57,500

FREUND, Fritz
German 1859-1942
paintings: (H) $3,575

FREUND, Harry Louis
American 1905-1979
paintings: (H) $1,430

FREY
German 19th cent.
paintings: (H) $1,980

FREY, I*** M.
18th cent.
paintings: (H) $3,450

FREY, Johann Jakob
Swiss 1813-1865
paintings: (H) $24,200

FREY, Johann Wilheim
Austrian b. 1830
drawings: (H) $1,100

FREY, Joseph
American 1892-1977
paintings: (L) $193; (H) $2,200

FREY, Max
German 20th cent.
paintings: (H) $660

FREY, Viola
American b. 1933
paintings: (H) $495
sculpture: (L) $1,320; (H) $43,700

FREY-MOOCK, A.
German 1881-1954
paintings: (H) $1,495

FREYBERG, Conrad
German b. 1842
paintings: (L) $29,900; (H) $46,000

FRIAS, Gato
paintings: (H) $5,750

FRIBERG, Arnold
American b. 1913
paintings: (H) $3,300

FRICK, William
drawings: (H) $460

FRIED, Pal
Hungarian 1893-1976
paintings: (L) $288; (H) $3,850
drawings: (L) $176; (H) $4,125

FRIED, Theodore
Hungarian/American 1902-1980
paintings: (L) $165; (H) $7,475
drawings: (H) $159

FRIEDEBERG, Pedro
Italian b. 1937
paintings: (L) $605; (H) $1,540

FRIEDENSOHN, Elias
American b. 1924
paintings: (H) $468

FRIEDENSON, Arthur A.
British 1872-1955
paintings: (H) $935

FRIEDENTHAL, David
American 20th cent.
paintings: (L) $385; (H) $1,150

FRIEDLAENDER, Friedrich
German 1825-1901
paintings: (L) $935; (H) $10,450

FRIEDLANDER, August M.
German 1856-1897
paintings: (H) $660

FRIEDLANDER, Camilla
Austrian 1856-1928
paintings: (L) $863; (H) $1,980
drawings: (H) $88

FRIEDLANDER, Maurice
American b. 1899
paintings: (H) $575

FRIEDLINGEN, J.
paintings: (H) $1,210

FRIEDLINGER, John
Hungarian b. 1908
paintings: (H) $550

FRIEDMAN, Arnold
American 1879-1946
paintings: (L) $2,200; (H) $18,700
drawings: (H) $230

FRIEDMAN, Dan
contemporary
sculpture: (H) $1,840

FRIEDRICH, Caroline Friederike
German 1749-1815
paintings: (H) $68,500

FRIEDRICH, M.G.
German 19th/20th cent.
paintings: (L) $495; (H) $4,312

FRIEL, Don
contemporary
sculpture: (H) $575

FRIEND, William F.
drawings: (H) $518

FRIER, Harry
British c. 1849-1919
paintings: (H) $4,400

Last Name First

Pal Fried (1893-1976) was born in Budapest, Hungary. He studied in Paris and at the Hungarian Academie under Professor Hugo Pohl, a famous pastelist. Under Pohl's influence he executed many nude and Oriental scenes in pastel. After World War II, he emigrated to New York and began to paint portraits in oil. A 1948 ad for Gimbel's department store announced that Pal Fried, a well-known Continental artist, was available to paint your Christmas portrait, a $1,200 value for only $498! Fried became well-known for his paintings of famous movie personalities and numerous portraits of ballerinas. Prints of his ballerina portraits were very popular and adorned the bedrooms of many young girls in the 1950s. Fried's signature on his paintings was Fried Pal, last name first in the Hungarian manner, and he is sometimes listed in auction catalogues and reference books erroneously under P.

Each auction season 10-12 paintings by this prolific artist are sold. The highest price realized for an oil is $7,475, but most of his works sell for $300 to $1,000. This portrait of a ballerina with black gloves is typical of his style and realized $1,100 when it sold at the Louisiana Auction House in June 1995. (Pal Fried, *Black Gloves*, oil on canvas, 30 x 24 inches, Louisiana Auction, June 17, 1995, $1,100)

FRIES, Charles A.
American 1854-1940
paintings: (L) $330; (H) $3,850
drawings: (L) $413; (H) $440

FRIESEKE, Frederick Carl
American 1874-1939
paintings: (L) $4,025; (H) $937,500
drawings: (H) $4,950

FRIESZ, Achille Emile Othon
French 1879-1949
drawings: (L) $2,200; (H) $3,300

FRIGERIO, Raffaele
Italian 19th cent.
paintings: (L) $77; (H) $2,300

FRIIS, Frederick Trapp
Swedish/American 1865-1909
paintings: (L) $115; (H) $14,300
drawings: (L) $201; (H) $1,540

FRILED, Pal
Hungarian b. 1914
paintings: (H) $880

FRILLI, Antonio
Italian 19th/20th cent.
sculpture: (L) $1,980; (H) $354,500

FRIMKISS, Michael
contemporary
sculpture: (H) $24,150

FRINK, Elisabeth
British 1930-1993
drawings: (L) $660; (H) $1,100
sculpture: (L) $8,800; (H) $25,300

FRIPP, Thomas William
1864-1931
drawings: (H) $1,210

FRIS, Jan
Dutch c. 1627-c. 1672
paintings: (H) $21,850

FRISCH, H.
Continental 19th/20th cent.
paintings: (H) $1,495

FRISCH, J.C.
American School 19th cent.
paintings: (H) $9,500

FRISCH, Johannes Christoph
German 1738-1815
paintings: (L) $1,540; (H) $3,335

FRISCHE, Heirich Ludwig
German 1831-1901
paintings: (H) $825

FRISHMUTH, Harriet Whitney
American 1880-1979
paintings: (H) $22,000
sculpture: (L) $308; (H) $107,000

FRISINE, Louis
American
drawings: (H) $550

FRISON, Jehan
1882-1961
paintings: (H) $2,750

FRISTROM, Claes Edward
1864-1950
paintings: (H) $518

FRITH, William Powell
English 1819-1909
paintings: (L) $3,410; (H) $24,200

FRITSCH, Katarina
b. 1956
sculpture: (H) $18,400

FRITSCH, Willibald
German b. 1876
sculpture: (H) $18,400

FRITZ, Charles
paintings: (L) $2,600; (H) $4,180

FRITZ, Dennis
drawings: (H) $770

FRITZ, Max
German b. 1849
drawings: (H) $825

FRITZLER, Gerald J.
drawings: (H) $880

FROBENIUS
American 20th cent.
drawings: (H) $935

FROHLICH, Bernhard
German 1823-1885
paintings: (L) $3,575; (H) $5,750

FROM, Einer
Norwegian 1872-1972
paintings: (L) $248; (H) $605

FROMENT
paintings: (L) $330; (H) $495

FROMENTIN, Eugene
French 1820-1876
paintings: (L) $495; (H) $277,500
drawings: (L) $1,265; (H) $2,990

FROMKES, Maurice
Russian/American 1872-1931
paintings: (H) $825

FROMUTH, Charles
drawings: (H) $3,850

FROPP, Fred W.
paintings: (H) $1,150

FROSCHL, Carl
Austrian 1848-1934
paintings: (H) $5,750
drawings: (H) $5,225

FROST, A.B.
paintings: (H) $3,410
drawings: (L) $1,320; (H) $2,035

FROST, Arthur Burdett
American 1851-1928
paintings: (L) $193; (H) $15,525
drawings: (L) $467; (H) $25,300

FROST, Emily
20th cent.
paintings: (H) $935

FROST, Francis Shedd
American 1825-1902
paintings: (H) $2,475

FROST, George Albert
American b. 1843
paintings: (L) $165; (H) $4,025
drawings: (L) $110; (H) $110

FROST, Jack
American 20th cent.
paintings: (L) $385; (H) $495

FROST, John
American 1890-1937
paintings: (H) $17,600

FROST, John Orne Johnson
American 1852-1928
paintings: (L) $9,200; (H) $486,500

FROST, William Edward
English 1810-1877
paintings: (L) $1,760; (H) $1,760

FROTHINGHAM, John
American 1786-1864
paintings: (H) $1,725

FRUDAKIS, Anthony
sculpture: (L) $288; (H) $495

FRUEHA, G.
Continental 19th/20th cent.
paintings: (H) $1,495

FRUHMESSER, Joseph
German b. 1927
paintings: (H) $550

FRY, Georgia Timken
American 1864-1921
paintings: (L) $550; (H) $1,265

FRY, John H.
American 1861-1946
paintings: (L) $330; (H) $3,960

FRY, Loren
American b. 1924
paintings: (H) $3,630

FRY, Rowena
American 20th cent.
paintings: (H) $1,760

FRY, Sherry Edmondson
American 1879-1966
sculpture: (H) $13,750

FRYE, Thomas
1710-1762
paintings: (H) $2,750

FRYE, William
American 19th cent.
paintings: (H) $23,100

FU BAOSHI, Fu PAO-SHIH
Chinese 1904-1965
drawings: (H) $134,500

FUCHS, Bernard
American b. 1932
paintings: (L) $385; (H) $3,025
drawings: (L) $330; (H) $440

FUCHS, Ernest
American 20th cent.
sculpture: (H) $1,650

FUCHS, Karl
German 1836-1886
paintings: (L) $330; (H) $632

FUECHSEL, Hermann
German/American 1833-1915
paintings: (L) $880; (H) $8,800

FUERTES, Louis Agassiz
American 1874-1927
paintings: (H) $17,600
drawings: (L) $935; (H) $12,650

FUESSEL, H.A.
paintings: (H) $1,320

FUGER, Friedrich Heinrich
German 1751-1818
paintings: (L) $1,265; (H) $19,550
drawings: (L) $412; (H) $5,175

FUGER, L.
paintings: (H) $550

FUGERE, Henry
French 1872-1944
sculpture: (L) $1,375; (H) $2,070

FUHR, Franz Xaver
1898-1973
paintings: (H) $9,200

FUJINAGA, Kei
Japanese 20th cent.
paintings: (H) $550

FUJINO
contemporary
paintings: (H) $1,870

FUJITA, Kenji
b. 1955
sculpture: (L) $345; (H) $6,600

FULCONIS, Louis Guillaume
French 1817-1873
sculpture: (H) $3,575

FULLER, A.W.
paintings: (H) $2,310

FULLER, Arthur D.
American 1889-1966
paintings: (L) $165; (H) $9,000
drawings: (L) $165; (H) $495

FULLER, Charles B.
1821-1893
paintings: (H) $1,980

FULLER, George
American 1822-1884
paintings: (L) $330; (H) $1,760

FULLER, Justin
paintings: (H) $1,320

FULLER, Richard Henry
American 1822-1871
paintings: (L) $1,045; (H) $2,640

FULLER, Samuel W.
American 19th cent.
paintings: (H) $935

FULLEYLOVE, John
English 1845/47-1908
paintings: (L) $1,980; (H) $2,310
drawings: (L) $605; (H) $1,380

FULLHORN
German 19th cent.
sculpture: (H) $690

FULLONTON, Robert D.
American 1876-1933
paintings: (L) $330; (H) $550

FULLWOOD, Albert Henry
British 1864-1930
paintings: (L) $688; (H) $880

FULOP, E. Wober
American 20th cent.
paintings: (H) $550

FULOP, Karoly
American b. 1898
drawings: (H) $550
sculpture: (L) $6,050; (H) $17,250

FULTON, Cyrus J.
American 1873-1949
paintings: (L) $121; (H) $715

FULTON, David
British b. 1850
paintings: (H) $1,760

FULTON, Fitch Burt
American 1879-1955
paintings: (L) $935; (H) $2,475

FULTON, Hamish
English b. 1946
drawings: (L) $9,350; (H) $24,200

FULTON, John
American 20th cent.
paintings: (L) $605; (H) $770

FULTON, R.
paintings: (H) $1,650

FULWIDER, Edwin
American b. 1914
paintings: (H) $14,300
drawings: (H) $1,150

FUNGAI, Bernardino
Italian c. 1460-1516
paintings: (H) $77,000

FUNNO, Michele
Italian 19th cent.
drawings: (L) $825; (H) $2,090

FUQUA, Robert
20th cent.
drawings: (H) $14,300

FURINI, Francesco
Italian 1604-1646
paintings: (H) $46,000

FURLAIN, Cippo
French 20th cent.
paintings: (H) $467

FURLONG, Charles W.
paintings: (H) $1,650

FURMAN, David
contemporary
sculpture: (H) $1,035

FURSE, Charles Wellington
British 1868-1904
paintings: (H) $1,725

FURST, Else
sculpture: (L) $935; (H) $1,980

FURST, Emil
American School 19th cent.
paintings: (H) $3,850

FUSARO, Jean
French b. 1925
paintings: (L) $1,265; (H) $4,600

FUSCO, J.W.
paintings: (L) $345; (H) $2,750

FUSELI, Johann Heinrich, Henry
Swiss 1741-1825
paintings: (H) $761,500
drawings: (H) $22,000

FUSS, Adam
b. 1961
drawings: (L) $633; (H) $1,380

FUSSELL, Charles Louis
American 1840-1909
drawings: (L) $1,650; (H) $11,500

FUSTER, Alberto
Mexican 19th/20th cent.
paintings: (L) $935; (H) $990

FUTACHIKA(?),
sculpture: (H) $690

FUTURA 2000
American 20th cent.
paintings: (H) $1,100

FYT, Jan
Flemish 1611-1661
paintings: (L) $24,200; (H) $134,500

GAAL, Cornelis Jacobus
Dutch 1796-1858
paintings: (H) $4,600

GABA
American 20th cent.
drawings: (L) $575; (H) $1,380

GABALL, A.
American 20th cent.
paintings: (H) $770

GABANI
Italian 19th cent.
paintings: (H) $1,100

GABANI Giuseppe
Italian 1846-1899
drawings: (L) $522; (H) $2,860

GABBRIELLI, D.
sculpture: (H) $1,100

GABEBLICKY, E**
19th/20th cent.
paintings: (H) $605

GABEL, Kurt
American
drawings: (L) $660; (H) $1,200

GABINI
paintings: (H) $4,290

GABLE, John
drawings: (H) $3,680

GABO, Naum
American 1890-1977
sculpture: (L) $25,300; (H) $134,500

GABOR, J.
drawings: (H) $9,350

GABRIEL, Arthur Marie, Comte Du
Passage
French 1838-1909
sculpture: (L) $3,850; (H) $5,775

GABRIEL, Francois
French d. 1993
paintings: (L) $715; (H) $6,670

GABRIEL, Paul Joseph Constantin
Dutch 1828-1903
paintings: (H) $4,025

GABRIELLI, P.
Italian School 19th cent.
drawings: (H) $2,750

GABRINI, Pietro
Italian 1856-1926
paintings: (L) $330; (H) $17,050
drawings: (L) $330; (H) $3,850

GADAIX, Fa
c. 1840-1900
sculpture: (H) $2,090

GADBOIS, Louis
French d. 1826
drawings: (H) $1,320

GAEL, Barent
Dutch 1620-1687/1703
paintings: (L) $3,450; (H) $15,400

GAERTNER
paintings: (H) $825

GAERTNER, Carl Frederick
American 1898-1952
paintings: (L) $192; (H) $11,000

GAERTNER, Fritz, GARTNER
American 1882-1952
paintings: (L) $4,950; (H) $5,225
drawings: (H) $144

GAGE, George William
1887-1957
paintings: (L) $88; (H) $660

GAGE, Jane
American b. 1914
paintings: (H) $715

GAGLIARDINI, Julien Gustave
French 1846-1927
paintings: (L) $1,650; (H) $16,100

GAGLIARDO, Gino
paintings: (H) $5,175

GAGNI
paintings: (L) $605; (H) $2,860

GAGNI, P.
French 20th cent.
paintings: (L) $275; (H) $880

GAGNON, Clarence Alphonse
Canadian 1881-1942
paintings: (L) $3,080; (H) $110,000

GAIGHER, Horazio
Austrian b. 1870
paintings: (H) $1,725

GAINES, Charles
contemporary
drawings: (L) $2,310; (H) $3,850

GAINES, Emily M. Holly
drawings: (H) $3,500

GAINSBOROUGH, Sir Thomas
English 1727-1788
paintings: (L) $7,590; (H) $54,625
drawings: (H) $13,255

GAIPER, T.E.
Continental 19th cent.
paintings: (H) $5,610

GAIREAU, P.E.
sculpture: (H) $633

GAISER, J.
19th cent.
paintings: (H) $2,200

GAISSER, Jacob Emmanuel
German 1825-1899
paintings: (L) $1,430; (H) $10,350

GAISSER, Max
German 1857-1922
paintings: (L) $990; (H) $17,250

GALAMUNICH, Yucca
sculpture: (H) $8,050

GALAN, Julio
Mexican b. 1958
paintings: (L) $7,150; (H) $19,800
drawings: (L) $10,925; (H) $17,600

GALANTIERE, Nancy
French 20th cent.
paintings: (H) $1,760

GALARNEAU, Leopold
Canadian b. 1896
paintings: (H) $1,210

GALE, George Albert
American 1893-1951
paintings: (L) $275; (H) $467
drawings: (L) $495; (H) $1,430

GALE, William
British 1823-1909
paintings: (L) $825; (H) $3,850

GALEA, Luigi M.
Maltese 1847-1917
paintings: (H) $4,830

GALEAZZI, Giovanni
Italian b. c. 1870
paintings: (H) $3,300

GALER, Ethel Caroline Hughes
British 19th/20th cent.
paintings: (H) $3,850

GALGIANI, Oscar
American b. 1903
paintings: (L) $605; (H) $1,650

GALIEN-LALOUE, Eugene
French 1854-1941
paintings: (L) $1,035; (H) $13,800
drawings: (L) $460; (H) $21,850

GALIGOL(?)
second half 19th cent.
sculpture: (H) $1,980

GALINBERTI, Silvio
Italian b. 1878
paintings: (H) $468

GALL, Francois
French 1912-1945
paintings: (L) $440; (H) $18,700
drawings: (L) $403; (H) $3,575

GALL, L.
French 19th/20th cent.
paintings: (H) $523

GALLAGHER, Michael
American contemporary
paintings: (H) $5,500
drawings: (H) $518

GALLAGHER, Sears
American 1869-1955
drawings: (L) $110; (H) $1,610

GALLAGHER, Sherry
American
drawings: (H) $1,000

GALLAIT, Louis
French 1810-1887
paintings: (L) $1,760; (H) $6,050

GALLAND, Pierre Victor
French 1822-1892
paintings: (H) $4,400

GALLARD, Michel de
French b. 1921
paintings: (L) $1,150; (H) $2,875

GALLARD-LEPINAY, Paul Charles
Emmanuel
French 1842-1885
paintings: (H) $4,400

GALLATIN, Albert E.
American 1881-1952
paintings: (L) $2,860; (H) $10,925

GALLATIN, James Francis de
Swiss 19th cent.
sculpture: (H) $23,000

GALLE, Gino de
Continental 19th cent.
paintings: (H) $1,100

GALLEGOS Y ARNOSA, Jose
Spanish 1859-1917
paintings: (L) $27,600; (H) $107,000

GALLELLI, Massimiliano
Italian b. 1863
paintings: (H) $4,600

GALLES, Ari
drawings: (H) $660

GALLET, Judd
contemporary
paintings: (H) $2,875

GALLETTI, Lia
b. 1943
paintings: (H) $6,900

GALLI, Giuseppe
Italian 1866-1953
paintings: (L) $4,290; (H) $6,600
drawings: (H) $770

GALLI, Riccardo
Italian b. 1839
paintings: (L) $1,210; (H) $1,380

GALLIANI, Omar
Italian b. 1954
paintings: (H) $2,750

GALLIARI, Bernardino
1707-1794
drawings: (L) $1,150; (H) $2,300

GALLIARI, Gasparo
1760-1818
drawings: (H) $3,520

GALLIARI, Giuseppe
Italian d. 1817
drawings: (H) $495

GALLIS, Pieter
Dutch 1633-1697
paintings: (H) $18,700

GALLISON, Henry Hammond
1850-1910
paintings: (L) $1,650; (H) $3,738

GALLO, Frank
American b. 1933
drawings: (L) $66; (H) $253
sculpture: (L) $173; (H) $16,500

GALLO, Giuseppe
b. 1954
paintings: (L) $1,035; (H) $1,210

GALLO, Ignacio
Spanish 20th cent.
sculpture: (L) $575; (H) $1,265

GALLO, Vincent
American contemporary
paintings: (H) $1,500
drawings: (H) $2,200
sculpture: (H) $2,200

GALLON, Robert
British 1845-1925
paintings: (L) $1,150; (H) $10,350

GALLYAS
Continental 20th cent.
paintings: (H) $605

GALOFRE Y GIMENEZ, Baldomero
Spanish 1848/49-1902
paintings: (L) $6,600; (H) $35,200
drawings: (H) $1,430

GALVAN, J. Ernest
American 19th cent.
paintings: (H) $632

GALVAN, Joseph
1705-1766
paintings: (H) $90,500

GALVAO, Alfredo
  b. 1900
  paintings: (H) $5,175

GAMARRA, Gregorio
  b. Peru 17th cent.
  paintings: (L) $15,400; (H) $26,400

GAMARRA, Jose
  b. 1934 Brazil
  paintings: (L) $1,100; (H) $29,700

GAMBA, Enrico
  Italian 1831-1883
  paintings: (L) $863; (H) $4,180
  drawings: (L) $385; (H) $1,430

GAMBA, Francesco
  Italian 1818-1887
  paintings: (H) $605

GAMBARTES, Leonidas
  Argentinean b. 1909
  paintings: (L) $5,500; (H) $8,800
  drawings: (H) $3,680

GAMBERINI, Giovacchino
  Italian b. 1859
  paintings: (H) $2,875

GAMBERT
  French 19th cent.
  paintings: (H) $1,840

GAMBINO, Giuseppe
  paintings: (H) $518

GAMBLE, Edwin
  American b. 1876
  paintings: (L) $288; (H) $546

GAMBLE, John Marshall
  American 1863-1957
  paintings: (L) $1,540; (H) $22,000
  drawings: (H) $2,475

GAMBLE, Roy C.
  American 1887-1964
  paintings: (L) $71; (H) $1,320
  drawings: (H) $165

GAMBOGE
  sculpture: (H) $690

GAMILIGI, G.
  Italian 19th cent.
  sculpture: (H) $2,475

GAMMELL, R.H. Ives
  American 1893-1981
  paintings: (L) $201; (H) $35,200
  drawings: (L) $230; (H) $1,955

GAMMERITH, F.L.
  19th cent.
  paintings: (H) $1,210

GAMOTIS, Alphonse J.
  19th cent.
  drawings: (H) $660

GAMPENREIDER, Karl
  German b. 1860
  paintings: (H) $10,350

GAMPENRIEDER
  paintings: (H) $605

GANBAULT, Alfred Emile
  French 19th cent.
  paintings: (H) $7,700

GANDOLFI, Gaetano
  Italian 1734-1802
  paintings: (L) $11,500; (H) $495,000
  drawings: (L) $2,300; (H) $27,500

GANDOLFI, Mauro
  Italian 1764-1834
  drawings: (L) $6,600; (H) $39,600

GANDOLFI, Ubaldo
  Italian 1728-1781
  drawings: (H) $4,400

GANDY, Joseph Michael
  British 1771-1843
  drawings: (L) $5,462; (H) $8,050

GANIERE, George E.
  American b. 1865
  sculpture: (H) $550

GANINE, Peter
  American 1900-1974
  sculpture: (H) $2,200

GANNAN, John
  American 1907-1965
  drawings: (L) $45; (H) $625

GANNE, Yves
  French b. 1931
  paintings: (L) $110; (H) $1,540

GANOT, Mary
  Austrian 20th cent.
  paintings: (H) $495

GANSO, Emil
  German/American 1895-1941
  paintings: (L) $605; (H) $19,550
  drawings: (L) $94; (H) $1,760

GANT, L.
  paintings: (H) $550

GANTNER, Bernard
French b. 1928
paintings: (L) $2,588; (H) $12,100
drawings: (L) $1,380; (H) $4,125

GANTTNER, W.
European School
paintings: (H) $495

GANZ, Edwin
Swiss b. 1871
paintings: (H) $3,960

GAO JIANFU, Kao CHIEN-FU
Chinese 1879-1951
drawings: (H) $11,500

GARABEDIAN, Charles
American b. 1924
paintings: (L) $330; (H) $11,500
drawings: (H) $1,380

GARABEDIAN, Giragos der
American 1892-1980
paintings: (L) $110; (H) $523

GARATE Y CLAVERO, Juan Jose
Spanish 1870-1939
paintings: (H) $17,825

GARAUD, Gustave Cesar
French 1847-1914
paintings: (H) $6,900

GARAY, Marie de
French 19th cent.
paintings: (L) $1,760; (H) $3,450

GARBELL, Alexandre
Latvian 1903-1970
paintings: (L) $161; (H) $4,400
drawings: (H) $220

GARBER, Daniel
American 1880-1958
paintings: (L) $1,320; (H) $398,500
drawings: (L) $518; (H) $3,800

GARBET, H.
French 19th cent.
paintings: (H) $863

GARBIERI, Lorenzo
Italian 1580-1654
paintings: (H) $10,350

GARCEAU, Harry Joseph
1876-1954
paintings: (H) $880

GARCES, Luis
Spanish 20th cent.
paintings: (H) $550

GARCIA, David
French b. 1936?
paintings: (L) $1,100; (H) $1,210

GARCIA, Domingo
Puerto Rican b. 1930
paintings: (L) $15,400; (H) $31,900

GARCIA, Francisco
paintings: (H) $715

GARCIA, Joaquin Torres
Uraguayan 1874-1949
paintings: (L) $121,000; (H) $198,000

GARCIA, Jose
ac. 1930-1945
paintings: (H) $805

GARCIA, Juan Gil
Cuban 1879-1930
paintings: (L) $690; (H) $4,600

GARCIA, Mario
American b. 1927
paintings: (H) $1,430

GARCIA, Rupert
American b. 1941
drawings: (H) $920

GARCIA MATA, E.
20th cent.
paintings: (H) $517

GARCIA NUNEZ, Armando
1883-1965
paintings: (L) $1,380; (H) $5,750
drawings: (H) $1,725

GARCIA SANTA OLALLA, Francisco
d. Brazil 1895
paintings: (L) $31,050; (H) $55,000

GARCIA Y MENCIA, Antonio
Spanish 19th cent.
paintings: (L) $28,750; (H) $29,900

GARCIA Y RAMOS, Jose
Spanish b. 1852
paintings: (H) $8,050

GARCIA Y RODRIGUEZ, Manuel
Spanish 1863-1925
paintings: (L) $1,265; (H) $34,500
drawings: (L) $2,750; (H) $5,225

GARCIA Y VALDEMORO, Juan
Spanish 19th cent.
paintings: (L) $880; (H) $1,320

GARCIA-SEVILLA, Ferran
contemporary
paintings: (H) $5,500

GARDELLI, Augusto
paintings: (H) $2,310

GARDEN, William Fraser
English 1856-1921
paintings: (H) $2,200

GARDET, Georges
French 1863-1939
sculpture: (L) $440; (H) $68,500

GARDEUR, Charles
Belgian 19th cent.
paintings: (H) $1,100

GARDIN, Laura
American 1889-1949
sculpture: (H) $715

GARDINER, Alan
paintings: (H) $863

GARDINER, Frank Joseph Henry
English b. 1942
drawings: (L) $1,320; (H) $2,200

GARDINER, Vernon
American ac. 19th cent.
paintings: (H) $1,980

GARDNER, Chris
b. 1953
sculpture: (H) $575

GARDNER, Derek G.M.
British 20th cent.
paintings: (L) $3,740; (H) $10,925

GARDNER, Donald
paintings: (H) $1,760

GARDNER, Fred
American 1880-1952
paintings: (H) $1,840

GARDNER, Sarah
19th cent.
paintings: (H) $3,220

GARDNER, Walter
English/American b. 1902
paintings: (L) $135; (H) $1,350

GARELLA, A.
Continental 19th cent.
sculpture: (H) $4,675

GARET, Jedd
American b. 1955
paintings: (L) $11; (H) $5,750
drawings: (H) $1,610

GARF
paintings: (H) $1,320

GARF, Salomon
Dutch 1879-1943
paintings: (H) $605

GARGALLO, Pablo
Spanish 1881-1934
drawings: (H) $1,380
sculpture: (L) $31,050; (H) $297,000

GARGIOLLO, A.
Italian 19th cent.
drawings: (H) $2,860

GARGIULLO, A.
Italian 19th cent.
drawings: (H) $5,500

GARGIULO, Domenico, called Micco
Spadaro
Italian 1612-1675
paintings: (L) $18,700; (H) $33,000

GARIBALDI, Joseph
French b. 1863
paintings: (H) $26,450

GARIKOW, Iwan
Russian 1918-1982
paintings: (L) $220; (H) $2,200

GARIN, E.
paintings: (L) $1,495; (H) $2,013

GARIN, Eugene R.
American b. 1922
paintings: (H) $1,760

GARIN, M.
European 19th/20th cent.
paintings: (H) $523

GARINEI, Giuseppe
Italian b. 1846
paintings: (H) $962

GARINEI, Michele
Italian 1871-1960
paintings: (L) $770; (H) $3,220

GARINO, Angelo
Italian b. 1860
paintings: (H) $880

GARIOT, Paul Cesaire
French b. 1811
paintings: (H) $15,400

GARLAND, H.
sculpture: (H) $9,075

GARLAND, Henry
English ac. 1854-1892
paintings: (L) $2,300; (H) $3,450

GARLAND, Leon
American 1913-1941
paintings: (H) $1,035
drawings: (H) $33

GARLIEB, Louise
Danish 19th cent.
paintings: (L) $34,500; (H) $51,750

GARMAN, Ed
American b. 1914
paintings: (H) $4,400

GARNER, Edith Mary
English b. 1881
paintings: (H) $1,320

GARNER, Lionel
French b. 1931
paintings: (L) $550; (H) $2,070

GARNERAY, Ambroise Louis
French 1783-1857
paintings: (L) $3,737; (H) $18,700

GARNIER, A.
Continental School 19th/20th cent.
paintings: (H) $1,495

GARNIER, E.
French 19th cent.
sculpture: (H) $825

GARNIER, H.
French 19th cent.
paintings: (H) $1,495

GARNIER, Jean
French 1890-1905
paintings: (H) $110
sculpture: (L) $544; (H) $770

GARNIER, Jules Arsene
French 1847-1889
paintings: (L) $2,300; (H) $32,200

GARNIER, Pierre
French b. 1847
paintings: (H) $1,320

GAROSSA
Czechoslovakian b. 1924
paintings: (H) $880

GARRATT, Arthur Paine
British 19th cent.
paintings: (H) $660

GARREAU, Georges
French early 20th cent.
sculpture: (H) $1,725

GARRETT, Edmund H.
American 1853-1929
paintings: (L) $633; (H) $3,300
drawings: (L) $110; (H) $605

GARRETT, John
contemporary
sculpture: (H) $2,875

GARRICK, R.
drawings: (H) $575

GARRIDO, Eduardo Leon
Spanish 1856-1949
paintings: (L) $3,080; (H) $96,000

GARRIDO, G.
Spanish 19th/20th cent.
paintings: (H) $1,430

GARRIDO, Hector
paintings: (H) $935

GARRISON, Larry, called Vincent
American 20th cent.
paintings: (L) $303; (H) $550

GARSOIAN, Inna
paintings: (L) $495; (H) $1,210
drawings: (H) $605

GARTNER, L.
Dutch 19th cent.
paintings: (H) $2,070

GARVIN, Jules
Continental 19th cent.
paintings: (H) $805

GARZI, Luigi
Italian 1638-1721
drawings: (H) $1,430

GARZONI, Giovanna
Italian 1600-1670
paintings: (H) $25,300

GASCAR, Henri
French 1635-1701
paintings: (L) $9,900; (H) $22,000

GASCOYNE, George
British 1862-1953
paintings: (L) $4,950; (H) $7,475

GASKELL, George Arthur
British ac. 1871-1900
paintings: (H) $11,000

GASPARD, Leon
Russian/American 1882-1964
paintings: (L) $1,955; (H) $255,500
drawings: (H) $1,610

GASQ, Paul Jean Baptiste
French 1860-1944
sculpture: (L) $1,650; (H) $6,600

GASSER, Henry Martin
American 1909-1981
paintings: (L) $132; (H) $3,300
drawings: (L) $55; (H) $5,775

GASSER, Louis
American 1909-1981
drawings: (H) $1,045

GASSIES, Jean Bruno
French 1786-1832
paintings: (H) $4,180

GASSNER, George
paintings: (L) $1,495; (H) $2,420

GASSNER, L.
American 19th cent.
paintings: (H) $1,760

GAST, John
American ac. 1870s
paintings: (H) $77,000

GASTON, L.
Continental School 19th cent.
paintings: (H) $1,320

GATCH, Lee
American 1902/09-1968
paintings: (L) $495; (H) $5,060
drawings: (L) $1,320; (H) $5,500

GATES
paintings: (H) $770

GATES, A.
American
paintings: (H) $5,280

GATES, Francis E.
American
paintings: (H) $550

GATSCH
paintings: (H) $1,600

GATSKI, Gerald
American 20th cent.
paintings: (H) $747

GATTA, Saverio Xavier della
Italian 1777-1811
drawings: (L) $4,025; (H) $29,900

GATTI, Bernardino, called Il Sojaro
c. 1495-1575
drawings: (H) $4,313

GATTO, Victor Joseph
American 1893-1965
paintings: (L) $2,310; (H) $4,600

GATTORNO, Antonio
b. Cuba 1904-1980
drawings: (H) $3,960

GATTUSO, Giuseppe
Italian 20th cent.
sculpture: (H) $770

GAUBAULT, Alfred Emile
French d. 1895
paintings: (L) $1,870; (H) $2,070

GAUCHER, Yves
paintings: (L) $2,200; (H) $3,080

GAUDEFROY, Alphonse
French 1845-1936
paintings: (H) $2,300

GAUDELT, B.
French 19th cent.
paintings: (H) $1,980

GAUDEZ, Adrien Etienne
French 1845-1902
sculpture: (L) $357; (H) $21,850

GAUDEZ, Antoine
sculpture: (H) $5,500

GAUDFROY, Fernand
Belgian 1885-1964
paintings: (H) $4,400

GAUDIN, Jean
French 1802-1880
paintings: (H) $1,210

GAUDISSARD
French early 19th cent.
drawings: (H) $517

GAUERMANN, Friedrich
Austrian 1807-1862
paintings: (L) $1,320; (H) $104,500

GAUFFIER, Louis
French 1716-1801
drawings: (H) $2,420

GAUGENGIGL, Ignaz Marcel
German/American 1855/56-1932
paintings: (L) $1,150; (H) $15,620

GAUGLER, Joseph P.
American b. 1896
paintings: (H) $550

GAUGUIN, Paul
French 1848-1903
paintings: (L) $25,300; (H) $4,182,500
drawings: (L) $2,090; (H) $134,500
sculpture: (L) $8,050; (H) $55,200

GAUL, Arrah Lee
American ac. 1915-1933
paintings: (L) $75; (H) $880

GAUL, Gilbert
American 1855-1919
paintings: (L) $495; (H) $27,500
drawings: (L) $374; (H) $1,045

GAULEY, Robert David
American 1875-1943
paintings: (L) $660; (H) $1,980

GAULLI, Giovanni Battista, called Il
Baciccio
Italian 1639-1709
drawings: (L) $16,500; (H) $30,800

GAUME, Henri Rene
French b. 1834
paintings: (H) $2,090

GAUMEL, Jean Alexandre
French 19th cent.
paintings: (H) $575

GAUQUIE, H.
sculpture: (H) $660

GAUQUIE, Henri Desire
1858-1927
sculpture: (H) $2,475

GAUSE, Wilhelm
German b. 1853
drawings: (H) $1,150

GAUSS, Eugen
20th cent.
sculpture: (H) $1,725

GAUSSON, Leo
French 1860-1944
paintings: (L) $935; (H) $1,650

GAUTHERIN, Jean
French 1840-1890
sculpture: (L) $550; (H) $1,650

GAUTHIER, Joachim George
paintings: (H) $1,540

GAUTHIER-D'AGOTY, Jacques
Fabien
French 1710-1781
paintings: (H) $20,900

GAUTIER, G.
French early 20th cent.
paintings: (H) $1,760

GAUTIER, Jacques Louis
French 19th cent.
sculpture: (L) $1,210; (H) $3,450

GAUTIER, L.
paintings: (H) $1,210

GAUTIER, Leon
French 19th cent.
paintings: (H) $2,420

GAUTIER, Rene George
French b. 1887
paintings: (H) $1,320

GAUTURA, Gonzalo
Spanish 19th/20th cent.
drawings: (H) $550

GAVAGNI, A.
Italian 19th cent.
paintings: (H) $1,093

GAVARNI, Paul
French 1804-1866
drawings: (L) $522; (H) $4,400

GAVARNI, Paul Sulpice Guillaume
French 1804-1866
drawings: (H) $1,100

GAVARNI, Pierre
French b. 1846
paintings: (L) $9,775; (H) $79,500

GAVENCKY, Frank
paintings: (H) $1,980

GAVREL, Genevieve
French b. 1909
paintings: (H) $550

GAW, William A.
American 1891-1973
paintings: (L) $1,100; (H) $7,475
drawings: (H) $3,025

GAY, August
Franco/American 1890-1949
paintings: (L) $5,225; (H) $16,500
drawings: (H) $6,600

GAY, Edward
Irish/American 1837-1928
paintings: (L) $605; (H) $6,160
drawings: (L) $137; (H) $880

GAY, George Howell
American 1858-1931
paintings: (L) $220; (H) $2,970
drawings: (L) $55; (H) $3,850

GAY, Lathrop
sculpture: (H) $770

GAY, Walter
American 1856-1937
paintings: (L) $1,375; (H) $27,600
drawings: (L) $575; (H) $10,925

GAY, Winkworth Allan
American 1821-1910
paintings: (L) $297; (H) $6,050
drawings: (L) $55; (H) $440

GAYLOR, Samuel Wood
American b. 1883
drawings: (H) $1,380

GAYLORD, M.A.V.
European 19th cent.
paintings: (H) $660

GAYRARD, Paul
French 19th cent.
sculpture: (H) $1,210

GAZE, Harold
American 20th cent.
drawings: (L) $1,100; (H) $1,840

GAZONAS, Alexander
American 20th cent.
drawings: (H) $550

GAZZERA, Romano
paintings: (L) $1,980; (H) $3,575

GEAR, William
Scottish b. 1915
drawings: (H) $1,100

GEBHARD, Albert
1869-1937
paintings: (H) $2,070

GEBHARDT, Wolfgang Magnus
ac. 1730-50
paintings: (H) $8,250

GEBLER, W.
sculpture: (H) $935

GECHTER, C.
French 19th cent.
sculpture: (H) $2,300

GECHTER, Jean Francois Theodore
French 1796-1844
sculpture: (L) $990; (H) $7,700

GECHTOFF, L.
paintings: (L) $450; (H) $825

GECHTOFF, Leonid
Russian/American 19th/20th cent.
paintings: (L) $99; (H) $1,870
drawings: (L) $138; (H) $852

GECHTOFF, Sonia
American b. 1926
paintings: (H) $1,035
drawings: (H) $1,210

GEDDES, Andrew
English 1783-1844
paintings: (H) $1,650

GEDDES, Jean
paintings: (H) $500

GEDLEK, Ludwig
Polish/Austrian b. 1847
paintings: (L) $726; (H) $17,600

GEDRICH, Edith
English 19th cent.
paintings: (H) $8,800

GEEFS, Fanny
Belgian 1807-1883
paintings: (H) $1,725

GEEL, Joost van
Dutch 1631-1698
paintings: (H) $11,500

GEENS, Louis and G. COLSOULLS
Belgian 19th cent.
paintings: (H) $3,450

GEERAERTS, Jan
Flemish 1818-1890
paintings: (H) $5,175

GEERAERTS, Martinus Josephus
Flemish 1707-1791
paintings: (L) $5,750; (H) $12,075

GEERTS, Casey
American 20th cent.
paintings: (H) $575

GEERTZ, Julius
German 1837-1902
paintings: (L) $6,325; (H) $7,700

GEERY, Samuel Lancaster
American 1813-1891
paintings: (H) $3,300

GEEST, Wybrand Simonsz. de
Dutch 1592-1659
paintings: (H) $11,500

GEETERE, Georges Francois de
French 19th cent.
paintings: (H) $16,100

GEGERFELT, Wilhelm von
Swedish 1844-1920
paintings: (L) $2,990; (H) $44,000

GEHRIG, Jacob
German 1846-1922
paintings: (H) $495

GEIBEL, Casimir
German 1839-1896
paintings: (H) $6,050

GEIGER, E.
Swiss 19th/20th cent.
paintings: (H) $1,100

GEIGER, Karl Joseph
German 1822-1905
drawings: (H) $1,495

GEIGER, Max
paintings: (L) $2,090; (H) $2,200

GEIGER, Richard
Austrian 1870-1945
paintings: (L) $1,210; (H) $5,175
drawings: (H) $605

GEIRNAERT, Jozef
Belgian 1791-1859
paintings: (H) $2,970

GEISEL, Theodor, Dr. Seuss
American 1904-1991
drawings: (H) $8,800

GEISSER, Johann Josef
Swiss 1824-1894
paintings: (H) $1,150

GEIST, Del
American 20th cent.
sculpture: (H) $935

GEISZEL, Margaret Malpass
ac. 1930s
drawings: (H) $605

GELANTI, Onorato
Italian 20th cent.
drawings: (H) $1,045

GELAVE, J.
paintings: (H) $550

GELDER, Nicolaes van
Flemish 1636-1676
paintings: (H) $167,500

GELDORP, George
c. 1595-1665
paintings: (H) $31,050

GELENA, Giovanni
Italian 19th/20th cent.
drawings: (H) $715

GELHAAR, Emil
American 1862-1934
paintings: (H) $715
drawings: (H) $77

GELIBERT, Gaston
French 1850-after 1931
paintings: (H) $4,400

GELIBERT, Jules Bertrand
French 1834-1916
paintings: (L) $3,300; (H) $6,325
drawings: (H) $1,093

GELIBERT, Paul Pierre
1802-1882
paintings: (H) $1,443

GELLER, Johann Nepomuk
Austrian 1860-1954
paintings: (H) $19,800

GELLER, William Overend
British ac. 1834-1850
paintings: (H) $978

GEMIGNANI, Ulysse
French
sculpture: (H) $5,175

GEMITO, Vincenzo
Italian 1852-1929
paintings: (H) $4,950
drawings: (H) $4,620
sculpture: (L) $1,760; (H) $14,950

GEMPT, Bernard Te
Dutch 1826-1879
paintings: (H) $4,400

GEMY, P***
Continental 20th cent.
paintings: (H) $4,887

GEN PAUL
French 1895-1975
paintings: (L) $4,025; (H) $27,500
drawings: (L) $605; (H) $8,800

GEN'ICHIRO, Inokuma
drawings: (L) $1,265; (H) $3,738

GENAILLE, Felix Francois Barthelemy
French 1826-1880
paintings: (H) $3,450

GENCE, Robert
French 18th cent.
paintings: (H) $46,000

GENDALL, John
British 1790-1865
paintings: (H) $36,800

GENDROMEAU, Pierre
French 19th cent.
drawings: (H) $2,300

GENDROT, Felix Albert
American b. 1866
paintings: (L) $110; (H) $880

GENICHIRO, Inokuma
1902-1993
paintings: (H) $34,500
drawings: (L) $1,150; (H) $2,300

GENIN, John
American 1830-1895
paintings: (L) $1,650; (H) $6,325

GENIN, Lucien
French 1894-1958
paintings: (L) $2,070; (H) $8,250
drawings: (L) $437; (H) $2,860

GENIS, Rene
French b. 1922
paintings: (L) $165; (H) $3,575

GENISSON, Jules Victor
Belgian 1805-1860
paintings: (L) $3,105; (H) $5,060

GENN, Robert
paintings: (H) $3,960

GENNARELLI, A.
sculpture: (H) $920

GENNARELLI, Amedeo
French, b. Naples ac. 1913-1930
sculpture: (L) $920; (H) $5,750

GENNARI, Benedetto
Italian 1633-1715
paintings: (L) $54,625; (H) $74,250

GENNARO, Gaetan de
Italian/Brazilian b. 1890
drawings: (H) $1,035

GENOVES, Juan
b. 1930
paintings: (H) $1,650
drawings: (L) $1,760; (H) $2,200

GENTH, Lillian
American 1876-1953
paintings: (L) $253; (H) $11,550

GENTILESCHI, Artemisia
Italian 1597-c. 1651
paintings: (L) $23,000; (H) $32,200

GENTILINI, Franco
Italian b. 1909
paintings: (L) $130; (H) $9,350

GENTZ, Karl Wilhelm
German 1822-1890
paintings: (H) $31,050

GEOFFROY, Henry Jules Jean
French 1853-1924
paintings: (L) $9,350; (H) $12,100
drawings: (H) $3,220

GEORGE, Eric
British 19th cent.
drawings: (L) $770; (H) $880

GEORGE, Frances
19th cent.
paintings: (H) $1,320

GEORGE, Sir Ernest
English 1839-1922
drawings: (L) $302; (H) $660

GEORGE, Thomas
American b. 1918
drawings: (H) $1,210

GEORGES, Jean Louis
French d. 1893
paintings: (H) $30,800

GEORGES-BAREAU
sculpture: (H) $4,400

GEORGES-MICHEL, Michel
paintings: (H) $3,300

GEORGI, Edwin A.
American 1896-1964
drawings: (L) $39; (H) $1,320

GEORGI, Friedrich Otto
German 1819-1874
paintings: (H) $2,750

GERAIS, Minas
18th/19th cent.
sculpture: (L) $518; (H) $2,530

GERARD, Marguerite
French 1761-1837
paintings: (L) $7,700; (H) $143,000

GERARD, Theodore
Belgian 1829-1895
paintings: (L) $1,320; (H) $27,600

GERARD, Theodore and Cornelis van
LEEMPUTTEN
paintings: (H) $8,525

GERARDIA, Helen
American b. 1903
paintings: (L) $88; (H) $825

GERASCH, August
Austrian b. 1822
paintings: (H) $2,310

GERBAUD, Abel
French 1888-1954
paintings: (H) $605
drawings: (H) $138

GERBER, Manfred
German b. 1949
paintings: (H) $1,093

GERBIER, Georges
French 19th/20th cent.
paintings: (L) $115; (H) $467

GERDAGO
sculpture: (L) $825; (H) $11,500

GERDANGO
sculpture: (H) $3,163

GERHARDT, Karl
American 1853-1940
paintings: (H) $550

GERINI, Niccolo di Pietro
Italian ac. 1368; d. 1415
paintings: (H) $51,750

GERLACH, Georg
German 1874-1962
drawings: (H) $1,725

GERMAIN, Jean Baptiste
French 1841-1910
sculpture: (L) $1,725; (H) $6,050

GERMITO, Vincenzo
Italian 1852-1929
sculpture: (H) $6,600

GERNEZ, Paul Elie
French 1888-1948
paintings: (H) $8,050
drawings: (H) $10,925

GERO, Mark
contemporary
sculpture: (H) $3,025

GEROME, Francois
French 20th cent.
paintings: (L) $110; (H) $3,575

GEROME, H.
French 20th cent.
paintings: (H) $522

GEROME, Jean Leon
French 1824-1904
paintings: (L) $3,450; (H) $800,000
drawings: (L) $2,185; (H) $11,000
sculpture: (L) $1,320; (H) $132,000

GEROME, Jean Leon, studio of
paintings: (H) $46,000

GERRER, Robert Gregory
American b. 1867
paintings: (H) $742

GERRY, Samuel Lancaster
American 1813-1891
paintings: (L) $440; (H) $11,500
drawings: (L) $275; (H) $770

GERTENBACH
paintings: (H) $632

GERVAIS, Lise
paintings: (L) $2,200; (H) $3,520

GERVAIS, Paul Jean
French 1859-1936
paintings: (L) $4,600; (H) $31,050

GERVEX, Henri
French 1852-1929
paintings: (L) $2,640; (H) $6,670

GERVILLE, A. de
French 19th cent.
paintings: (H) $880

GERZSO, Gunther
Mexican b. 1916
paintings: (L) $4,125; (H) $151,000
drawings: (L) $8,625; (H) $43,700

GESELSCHAP, Frederich
German 1835-1898
paintings: (H) $6,900

GESLIN, Jean Charles
French 1816-1885
sculpture: (L) $17,250; (H) $17,250

GESMAR, Charles
1900-1928
drawings: (L) $990; (H) $2,200

GESSA Y ARIAS, Sebastian
Spanish b. 1840
paintings: (H) $2,760

GESSI, Francesco Giovanni
Italian 1588-1649
paintings: (H) $24,750

GESSNER, Conrad
Swiss 1764-1826
paintings: (H) $8,525

GESTEL, Leo
drawings: (L) $55; (H) $550

GEVERS, Rene
French 1869-1944
paintings: (L) $99; (H) $5,500

GEYER, Georg
Austrian 1823-1912
paintings: (H) $770

GEYER, Herman
American 19th cent.
paintings: (L) $880; (H) $1,840

GEYGER, Ernest Moritz
German 1861-1941
sculpture: (H) $5,500

GEYLING, Rudolf
Austrian 1838-1904
paintings: (H) $8,250

GEYP, Adriaan Marinus
Dutch 1855-1926
paintings: (H) $2,300

GEZA, Peska
Hungarian 1859-1934
paintings: (H) $1,760

GEZA, Vastagh
French 19th/20th cent.
paintings: (H) $4,888

GHEERAERTS, Marcus, the younger,
studio of
paintings: (H) $4,070

GHEERAERTS, Marcus, the younger,
workshop of
paintings: (H) $28,600

GHENT, Maurice de
sculpture: (H) $1,650

GHERARDINI, Alessandro
Italian 1655-1723/28
paintings: (H) $27,500

GHERARDINI, Giovanni
Italian 1654-1725?
paintings: (H) $8,800

GHEYN, Jocob de, II
Dutch 1565-1629
drawings: (L) $14,375; (H) $38,500

GHEZZI, Pier Leone
Italian 1674-1755
paintings: (L) $35,200; (H) $187,000
drawings: (L) $522; (H) $3,850

GHIGLIERI, Lorenzo E.
American b. 1931
sculpture: (L) $1,050; (H) $1,210

GHIGLION-GREEN, Maurice
b. 1913
paintings: (L) $1,035; (H) $2,970

GHINI, G.
Italian 20th cent.
paintings: (H) $1,980

GHIRLANDAIO, Davide BIGORDI
Italian 1452-1525
paintings: (H) $66,000

GHISOLFI, Giovanni
Italian 1632-1683
paintings: (L) $17,250; (H) $121,000

GIACHI, E.
Italian 19th cent.
paintings: (L) $8,050; (H) $23,000

GIACOMELLI, Vincenzo
Italian 1841-1890
paintings: (H) $7,480

GIACOMETTI, Alberto
Swiss 1901-1966
paintings: (L) $38,500; (H) $827,500
drawings: (L) $2,860; (H) $107,000
sculpture: (L) $7,700; (H) $3,960,000

GIACOMETTI, Diego
Swiss 1902-1985
sculpture: (L) $1,650; (H) $107,000

GIACOMETTI, Giovanni
Swiss 1868-1933
paintings: (L) $4,400; (H) $24,200

Furniture and Sculpture

The Giacometti brothers, Alberto (1901-1966) and Diego (1902-1985), born in Switzerland, came to Paris in the 1920s. Alberto, a painter and sculptor, was the more famous of the two; the two brothers collaborated, Diego supervising the casting and applying the patinas, until Alberto's death in 1966. The brothers' earliest furniture commission was from a Paris decorator in 1933, and Diego continued to design furniture after his brother's death. The furniture was sold as functional pieces, not works of art, and they are not numbered as required for bronze sculptures under French law (which limits an art edition to 12 pieces). A

memorial exhibition of Giacometti furniture was held at the Musée des Arts Décoratifs in Paris in 1986. In 1992, five French dealers were arrested and convicted for selling fake Giacometti pieces. Some of the fakes were cast from original molds, others from existing work (surmoulages) and still others were copied from photographs. The pair of chairs consigned to Christie's, however, had been purchased in 1981, before Diego's death. Designed in 1963, the bronze chairs each sold for $21,850. (Diego Giacometti, *Chaise*, bronze with green patina, wrought iron and leather seats, height 36¼ inches, Christie New York, May 11, 1995, $21,850)

GIACOMOTTI, Felix Henri
French 1828-1909
paintings: (H) $8,800

GIALLINA, Angelos
Greek b. 1857
paintings: (H) $1,725

GIAMBOLOGNA
sculpture: (L) $2,530; (H) $11,000

GIAMBOLOGNA, workshop of
16th/17th cent.
sculpture: (L) $18,400; (H) $77,000

**GIAMBOLOGNA/SUSINI
WORKSHOP**
sculpture: (H) $63,000

GIANBOLOGNA
sculpture: (H) $550

GIANCELLO, G.
Italian 19th/20th cent.
paintings: (H) $990

GIANI, Felice
Italian c. 1760-1823
paintings: (L) $9,200; (H) $17,050
drawings: (L) $863; (H) $6,900

GIANI, Hugo
Italian 19th/20th cent.
paintings: (H) $3,850

GIANI, Ugo
paintings: (H) $750

GIANLISI, Antonio, the younger
1677-1727
paintings: (H) $85,000

GIANNETTI, Raffaele
Italian 1837-1915
paintings: (L) $4,620; (H) $16,500

GIANNI
Italian 19th cent.
paintings: (L) $825; (H) $3,220
drawings: (L) $143; (H) $431

GIANNI
Italian 19th/20th cent.
paintings: (H) $275
drawings: (L) $55; (H) $1,540

GIANNI, G.
drawings: (H) $550

GIANNI, G.
Italian 1829-1885
paintings: (H) $7,920

GIANNI, G.
Italian 19th/20th cent.
drawings: (L) $412; (H) $1,495

GIANNI, Gerolamo
Italian b. 1837
paintings: (L) $3,300; (H) $7,700

GIANNI, Gian
Italian 19th/20th cent.
paintings: (H) $4,950
drawings: (L) $137; (H) $303

GIANNI, M.
Italian 19th cent.
drawings: (L) $220; (H) $1,210

GIANQUINTO, Albert
paintings: (H) $863

GIARDIELLO, Giovanni
Italian 19th cent.
paintings: (L) $1,093; (H) $2,750

GIARDIELLO, Giuseppe
Italian 19th/20th cent.
paintings: (L) $1,650; (H) $4,840

GIAUDRONE, Domingo
Spanish b. 1889
paintings: (H) $11,500

GIBB, Thomas H.
English ac. 1832-1885
paintings: (H) $880

GIBBISON, J.
paintings: (H) $6,875

GIBBONS, Arthur
b. 1947
sculpture: (L) $1,150; (H) $2,750

GIBBONS, Grinling
b. Rotterdam 1648 d. London 1721
sculpture: (H) $156,500

GIBBS, Charles
English ac. 1878-1899
paintings: (H) $1,265

GIBBS, George
American 1870-1942
paintings: (L) $220; (H) $272
drawings: (L) $77; (H) $2,200

GIBBS, Percy William
British ac. 1894-1937
paintings: (H) $46,000

GIBBS, T. Bunny
American 19th/20th cent.
paintings: (L) $220; (H) $1,265

GIBELIN, Esprit Antoine
1739-1814
drawings: (H) $2,645

GIBNEY, Luke
American 1894-1960
paintings: (H) $495

GIBRAN, Kahlil George
American b. Lebanon 1883, d. 1931
drawings: (L) $1,320; (H) $9,350
sculpture: (L) $440; (H) $2,750

GIBSON, C.S.
paintings: (H) $1,100

GIBSON, Charles Dana
American 1867-1944
paintings: (L) $345; (H) $2,070
drawings: (L) $77; (H) $6,600

GIBSON, George
American b. 1904
drawings: (L) $303; (H) $467

GIBSON, John
paintings: (H) $2,090

GIBSON, Thomas
c. 1680-1751
paintings: (L) $3,450; (H) $6,038

GIBSON, Walter Hamilton
American 1850-1896
paintings: (H) $825

GIBSON, William Alfred
English 1866-1931
paintings: (L) $805; (H) $805

GIBSON, William H.
19th cent.
drawings: (H) $550

GIDE, Francois Theophile
French 1822-1890
paintings: (L) $2,200; (H) $23,100

GIEROWSKI, Stefan
paintings: (H) $1,540

GIES, Joseph
American 1860-1935
paintings: (L) $29; (H) $2,990

GIESEN
19th/20th cent.
paintings: (H) $660

GIET, Alfred
Belgian early 20th cent.
paintings: (L) $742; (H) $770

GIETL, Josua von
German 1847-1922
paintings: (H) $4,125

GIFFINGER, R.
19th cent.
paintings: (H) $1,210

GIFFORD, Charles Henry
American 1839-1904
paintings: (L) $440; (H) $27,500
drawings: (L) $935; (H) $1,265

GIFFORD, John
British 19th cent.
paintings: (L) $1,650; (H) $6,600

GIFFORD, Robert Swain
American 1840-1905
paintings: (L) $303; (H) $18,700
drawings: (L) $220; (H) $1,210

GIFFORD, Sanford Robinson
American 1823-1880
paintings: (L) $650; (H) $550,000
drawings: (H) $605

GIGANTE, Giacinto
Italian 1806-1876
paintings: (L) $7,700; (H) $20,700

GIGLI, R.
Italian 19th cent.
drawings: (L) $137; (H) $1,760

GIGLI, Robert
drawings: (H) $605

GIGNON, Louis
paintings: (H) $3,575

GIGNOUS, Eugenio
Italian 1850-1906
paintings: (H) $6,900

GIGNOUX, Regis Francois
French 1816-1882
paintings: (L) $1,870; (H) $26,400
drawings: (L) $138; (H) $2,070

GIHON, Clarence M.
American 1871-1929
paintings: (L) $165; (H) $2,860

GIL, Sala Ignacio
Italian b. 1912
paintings: (H) $495

GILANY, Y.
paintings: (H) $460

GILBERS, A.
British 19th cent.
paintings: (H) $460

GILBERT
British 19th cent.
paintings: (L) $518; (H) $770

GILBERT
Continental 20th cent.
sculpture: (H) $990

GILBERT
English 19th cent.
paintings: (H) $550

GILBERT, A.
French ac. 1920s
sculpture: (L) $4,600; (H) $4,888

GILBERT, Alfred
English 1854-1934
sculpture: (L) $2,070; (H) $3,163

GILBERT, Andre
sculpture: (H) $2,530

GILBERT, Arthur
British 1815-1895
paintings: (L) $330; (H) $2,185

GILBERT, Arthur Hill
American 1893/94-1970?
paintings: (L) $357; (H) $8,800

GILBERT, C. Allan
1873-1929
paintings: (L) $55; (H) $70
drawings: (L) $522; (H) $2,640

GILBERT, C. Ivar
paintings: (L) $495; (H) $990

GILBERT, Henry
drawings: (L) $470; (H) $1,100

GILBERT, John Graham
1794-1866
paintings: (H) $2,070

GILBERT, Lucien
sculpture: (H) $1,430

GILBERT, Rene Joseph
French 1858-1914
paintings: (H) $16,100

GILBERT, Sir John
English 1817-1897
paintings: (L) $2,185; (H) $18,400
drawings: (H) $2,200

GILBERT, Thomas
British 19th cent.
paintings: (H) $1,495

GILBERT, Victor Gabriel
French 1847-1933
paintings: (L) $1,320; (H) $209,000
drawings: (L) $2,475; (H) $23,000

GILBERT, W.J.
English 19th cent.
paintings: (H) $1,210

GILBERT and GEORGE
b. 1940s
paintings: (L) $5,175; (H) $40,250
drawings: (L) $6,325; (H) $74,250
sculpture: (L) $6,900; (H) $10,450

GILCHRIST, William Wallace, Jr.
American 1879-1926
paintings: (L) $345; (H) $25,300
drawings: (H) $1,725

GILDOR, Jacob
Israeli 20th cent.
drawings: (L) $1,210; (H) $1,650

GILE, Selden Connor
American 1877-1947
paintings: (L) $660; (H) $7,700
drawings: (L) $1,100; (H) $5,175

GILES, ***
American 19th cent.
paintings: (H) $468

GILES, Horace P.
American b. 1876,ac. 1892-1906
paintings: (L) $220; (H) $522

GILES, Howard Everett
American 1876-1955
paintings: (L) $990; (H) $2,645

GILES, John Alfred
British d. 1862
paintings: (H) $1,210

GILHOOLY, David
b. America 1943 ac. Canada 1970s
drawings: (H) $495
sculpture: (L) $460; (H) $6,325

GILIOLI, Emile
French 1911-1977
sculpture: (L) $1,725; (H) $4,600

GILKERSON, William
American 20th cent.
drawings: (H) $1,265

GILL, Andre
French 1840-1885
paintings: (H) $4,025

GILL, Colin
drawings: (H) $518

GILL, DeLancey W.
American 1859-1940
paintings: (L) $52; (H) $522
drawings: (H) $467

GILL, Edmund "Waterfall"
English 1820-1894
paintings: (L) $413; (H) $3,450

GILL, Elizabeth Andrea
American b. 1948
sculpture: (L) $1,840; (H) $4,025

GILL, Eric
British 1882-1940
drawings: (L) $825; (H) $1,650

GILL, Frederick J.
American 1906-1974
paintings: (L) $220; (H) $907

GILL, Mariquita
19th cent.
paintings: (H) $577

GILL, William
English ac. 1826-1869
paintings: (H) $880

GILLEMANS, Jan Pauwel, the elder
Flemish 1618-1675
paintings: (H) $17,600

GILLEMANS, Jan Pauwel, the younger
Flemish 1651-1704
paintings: (L) $7,150; (H) $11,000

GILLEN, Albert P.
American 20th cent.
paintings: (L) $220; (H) $690

GILLESPIE, Gregory
American b. 1936
paintings: (H) $8,250
drawings: (H) $6,050

GILLESPIE, J.
American 20th cent.
paintings: (H) $715

GILLESPIE, J.H.
American ac. c. 1828-1838
drawings: (L) $4,025; (H) $4,675

GILLESPIE, Russell
American contemporary
sculpture: (H) $1,100

GILLESPIE, William
b. c. 1817
paintings: (H) $1,045

GILLET, Numa Francois
French b. 1868
paintings: (H) $2,970

GILLIAM, Sam
American b. 1933
paintings: (H) $1,375
drawings: (H) $1,650
sculpture: (H) $3,410

GILLIS, Marcel
paintings: (H) $5,500

GILLOT, Eugene Louis
French 1868-1925
paintings: (L) $1,210; (H) $5,750

GILMAN, Hannah P.
drawings: (H) $550

GILMORE, H.
paintings: (H) $1,320

GILOT, Francoise
French b. 1921
paintings: (L) $880; (H) $7,700
drawings: (L) $550; (H) $1,540

GILPIN, Sawrey
British 1733-1807
paintings: (L) $1,265; (H) $46,750
drawings: (H) $4,370

GILQUIN, Albert
Continental 1861-1936
paintings: (H) $1,760

GILSOUL, Victor Olivier
Belgian 1867-1939
paintings: (L) $880; (H) $10,450

GIMAT, Marc
paintings: (H) $660

GIMENEZ, F. Fernandez
Spanish 19th cent.
paintings: (H) $1,650

GIMIGNANI, Giacinto
Italian 1611-1681
paintings: (L) $22,000; (H) $110,000

GIMMI, Wilhelm
Swiss 1886-1965
paintings: (H) $1,320

GINA
American 20th cent.
drawings: (L) $247; (H) $715

GINA, A.
sculpture: (H) $1,870

GINE, ***
Russian 19th cent.
paintings: (H) $2,415

GINNEVER, Charles
American b. 1931
sculpture: (H) $4,400

GINNOIELLO, G****
Italian 20th cent.
paintings: (H) $1,495

GINSBURG, Varda
20th cent.
paintings: (H) $6,325

GINSBURG, Yankel
American b. 1945
paintings: (L) $550; (H) $660

GIOBBI, Edward
American b. 1926
paintings: (L) $83; (H) $1,100
drawings: (H) $1,760

GIOJA, Belisario
Italian 1829-1906
drawings: (L) $330; (H) $7,820

GIORDANO, studio of
Italian 17th/18th cent.
paintings: (H) $5,463

GIORDANO, Felice
Italian 1880-1964
paintings: (L) $605; (H) $6,600
drawings: (L) $115; (H) $748

GIORDANO, Luca, called Fa Presto
Italian 1632-1705
paintings: (L) $16,500; (H) $288,500
drawings: (H) $6,900

GIORDANO, Luca, studio of
Italian 17th cent.
paintings: (H) $25,300

GIORDANO, Luigi
Italian 19th cent.
drawings: (H) $24,150

GIOVANELLI, G.
Italian 20th cent.
paintings: (H) $575

GIOVANNI, Gian
Italian 1903-1989
paintings: (L) $1,430; (H) $1,980

GIOVANNI DA MILANO
Italian ac. 1345-1370
paintings: (H) $970,500

GIOVANNI DEL BIONDO
Italian ac. c. 1356-1398
paintings: (H) $34,500

GIOVANNI DI PAOLO DI GRAZIA,
called Giovanni del Poggio
Italian 1403-1483
paintings: (L) $87,750; (H) $475,500

GIOVANNI DI PIETRO
ac. 1432-before 1479
paintings: (H) $17,600

**GIOVANNI DI SER GIOVANNI DI
SIMONE,** called Lo Scheggia
1407-1486
paintings: (L) $34,500; (H) $2,202,500

GIOVANNINI, Vincenzo
Italian 1817-1868
paintings: (L) $3,450; (H) $19,800

GIR, Charles
French b. 1883
sculpture: (H) $690

GIRADET, F.
paintings: (H) $770

GIRADET, Leon
French 1857-1895
drawings: (H) $1,955

GIRADIN, E.J.
paintings: (H) $522

GIRADOT, Louis Auguste
French b. 1858
paintings: (L) $6,900; (H) $10,925

GIRALDEZ Y PENYLVER, Adolfo
Spanish ac. 1874-1882
paintings: (L) $770; (H) $1,980

GIRARD
paintings: (H) $55
sculpture: (H) $990

GIRARD, Eugene
1819-1892
drawings: (H) $6,555

GIRARD, M.
French 19th cent.
paintings: (H) $1,840

GIRARD, Paul Albert
French 1839-1920
paintings: (H) $18,400

GIRARDET, Eugene Alexis
French 1853-1907
paintings: (L) $1,760; (H) $33,350

GIRARDET, Jules
French b. 1856
paintings: (L) $13,800; (H) $40,250

GIRARDET, Karl
Swiss 1813-1871
paintings: (L) $6,600; (H) $10,350

GIRARDET, Leon
French 1857-1895
drawings: (L) $660; (H) $2,300

GIRARDIN
paintings: (H) $9,350

GIRARDIN, A.
paintings: (H) $825

GIRARDIN, Frank J.
American 1856-1945
paintings: (L) $154; (H) $2,090

GIRARDOT, Louis Auguste
French b. 1858
paintings: (H) $20,700

GIRATTO, Napolean
European 19th cent.
drawings: (H) $605

GIRAUD
French 19th cent.
paintings: (H) $28,750

GIRAUD, Henri Emile
French 1825-1892
paintings: (H) $17,250

GIRAUD, Pierre Francois Eugene
French 1806-1881
paintings: (L) $13,200; (H) $18,700
drawings: (H) $550

GIRAULT, Louis C.
ac. 1870-1892
paintings: (H) $715
drawings: (L) $302; (H) $440

GIRODET-TRIOSON, Anne Louis
French 1767-1824
paintings: (H) $68,500
drawings: (L) $10,350; (H) $44,850

GIRONA, Julio
paintings: (H) $6,325

GIRONELLA, Alberto
Mexican b. 1929
paintings: (H) $17,600

GIRONES, Ramon Antonio Pichot
Spanish 1872-1925
paintings: (H) $6,600

GIROUARD, Henriquetta
French 1819-1966
paintings: (H) $3,450

GIROUD, Henri Emile
French 1825-1892
paintings: (H) $1,495

GIROUD, P.
French 19th cent.
paintings: (H) $4,125

GIROUD, Paul
19th/20th cent.
paintings: (H) $575

GIROUST, Jean Antoine Theodore
1753-1817
paintings: (H) $4,025

GISBERT, Antonio
Spanish 1835-1901
paintings: (L) $2,310; (H) $35,200

GISSING, Roland
Canadian 1895-1967
paintings: (L) $330; (H) $4,180

GISSON, Andre
paintings: (L) $198; (H) $5,750

GIUFFRIDA, Nino
Italian b. 1924
paintings: (H) $715

GIULIANI, G.
Italian 19th/20th cent.
drawings: (H) $1,430

GIUSEPPE, Mose Bianchi di
Italian 1836-1890
drawings: (L) $2,750; (H) $6,600

GIUSTI, G.
Italian 19th/20th cent.
drawings: (H) $2,860

GIUSTI, Guglielmo
Italian 1824-1916
paintings: (H) $13,750

GIUTTI, G.
Italian 19th cent.
drawings: (H) $1,320

GIVLER, William H.
paintings: (H) $935

GLACK, Zeam van der
paintings: (H) $1,540

GLACKENS, William
American 1870-1938
paintings: (L) $3,300; (H) $330,000
drawings: (L) $288; (H) $25,300

GLADENBECK
sculpture: (L) $165; (H) $460

GLADENBECK, Aklien Gese Schaft
sculpture: (H) $25,300

GLADENBECK, H. and SOHN
sculpture: (H) $1,035

GLADENBECK, Oskar
German 20th cent.
sculpture: (H) $489

GLAIZE, Auguste Barthelemy
French 1807-1893
drawings: (H) $2,640

GLAIZE, Pierre Paul Leon
French 1842-1932 •
paintings: (H) $5,750

GLANCY, Michael M.
American b. 1950
sculpture: (L) $2,070; (H) $6,600

GLANDIN, Alexei
Russian 1922-1983
paintings: (H) $1,650

GLARNER, Fritz
American 1899-1972
paintings: (L) $1,093; (H) $264,000
drawings: (H) $2,875

GLASCO, Joseph
American b. 1925
paintings: (L) $1,210; (H) $4,370
drawings: (H) $517

GLASER, David
American 20th cent.
paintings: (H) $2,200

GLASGOW
American 20th cent.
paintings: (H) $633

GLASGOW, Bernard
19th/20th cent.
paintings: (H) $2,640

GLASNER, William and Laura
sculpture: (H) $805

GLASS, James William
American 1825-1857
paintings: (L) $12,100; (H) $71,250

GLASS, John Hamilton
paintings: (L) $350; (H) $2,310

GLASS, Jonathan
English 20th cent.
drawings: (H) $550

GLATZ, Oszkar
German b. 1872
paintings: (H) $4,600

GLAZUNOV, Ilya
drawings: (H) $467

GLEASON, Joe Duncan
American 1881-1959
paintings: (L) $880; (H) $4,125
drawings: (H) $88

GLEERUP, Knud
Danish b. 1884
paintings: (H) $770

GLEESON, W.
19th cent.
paintings: (H) $825

GLEHN, Jane Emmet von
English 20th cent.
paintings: (H) $605

GLEHN, Jane Erin de
British 1873-1961
paintings: (L) $23,000; (H) $26,450

GLEHN, Wilfred Gabriel de
British 1870-1951
paintings: (H) $29,700
drawings: (H) $1,610

GLEICH, John
German b. 1879
paintings: (H) $3,575

GLEITSMANN, Raphael
American b. 1910
paintings: (L) $110; (H) $2,970
drawings: (L) $99; (H) $550

GLEIZES, Albert
French 1881-1953
paintings: (L) $143,000; (H) $220,000
drawings: (L) $3,738; (H) $31,050

GLEN, Robert
American b. 1940
sculpture: (L) $880; (H) $1,540

GLENDENING, Alfred Augustus, Jr.
English ac. 1861, d. 1907
paintings: (L) $2,588; (H) $19,550

GLENDENING, Alfred Augustus, Sr.
British 19th cent.
paintings: (H) $5,750

GLEW, E.L.
American 1817-1870
paintings: (L) $385; (H) $1,980

GLICENSTEIN, Enoch Henryk
American 1870-1942
sculpture: (L) $2,415; (H) $3,737

GLICKMAN, Maurice
American b. 1906
sculpture: (H) $1,320

GLINDONI, Henry Gillard
English 1852-1912/13
paintings: (L) $3,300; (H) $11,000

GLINSKY, Vincent
1895-1975
sculpture: (H) $1,150

GLISENTI, Achille
Italian 1848-1906
paintings: (L) $9,200; (H) $11,500

GLOAG, Isobel Lilian
British 1865-1917
paintings: (H) $3,680

GLOLO, A. Hortunai
paintings: (H) $715

GLOMB, Skip
American 1935-1988
sculpture: (L) $1,495; (H) $2,750

GLORES, J.W., Jr.
paintings: (H) $770

GLOSE, D.C.
paintings: (H) $990

GLOSHMAN (?)
paintings: (H) $880

GLOUTCHENKO, Nicholai Petrovitch
Russian b. 1902
paintings: (H) $19,800

GLOVER, John
British 1767-1849
paintings: (H) $6,900
drawings: (L) $259; (H) $495

GLUCKLICH, Simon
German b. 1863
paintings: (H) $27,600

GLUCKMANN, Grigory
Russian/American b. 1898
paintings: (L) $1,380; (H) $13,200
drawings: (H) $1,980

GLURA, Maes
Continental 19th cent.
paintings: (H) $3,080

GLUSING, Francis
European 19th/20th cent.
paintings: (H) $825

GLYDE, Henry George
Canadian b. 1906
paintings: (L) $1,870; (H) $3,520

GLYNDON, F.
paintings: (H) $5,280
drawings: (L) $358; (H) $550

GNOLI, Domenico
Italian 1933-1970
drawings: (H) $8,580

GOBBI, Adriano
Italian 20th cent.
paintings: (H) $2,420

GOBBIS, Giuseppe de
b. 1730
paintings: (L) $3,450; (H) $90,500

GOBER, Robert
American b. 1954
paintings: (H) $11,000
drawings: (L) $3,300; (H) $29,700
sculpture: (L) $14,950; (H) $198,000

GOBERT, Pierre
French 1662-1744
paintings: (H) $19,800

GOBI, Alpenore
Italian 19th/20th cent.
paintings: (L) $1,725; (H) $4,600

GOBI, W.
paintings: (H) $2,875

GOBILLARD, Paule
French 1867-1964
drawings: (H) $880

GOBL, Camilla
Austrian 1871-1965
paintings: (H) $1,150

GOBLET, A.
French 19th cent.
paintings: (H) $690

GODARD, A.
sculpture: (L) $1,955; (H) $13,200

GODARD, Gabriel
French b. 1933
paintings: (L) $660; (H) $2,070

GODBOLD, Samuel Berry
British ac. 1842-1875
paintings: (H) $7,150

GODCHAUX
French 19th/20th cent.
paintings: (L) $7,475; (H) $7,475

GODCHAUX, A.
French 19th cent.
paintings: (H) $5,175

GODCHAUX, H.
French 19th cent.
paintings: (H) $495

GODCHAUX, Roger
French b. 1878
paintings: (H) $11,500
sculpture: (L) $5,500; (H) $26,450

GODDARD, George Bouverie
British 1832-1886
paintings: (H) $17,250

GODDARD, Rainald William Knightly
English 19th/20th cent.
drawings: (H) $605

GODEFROY, Felix
French d. 1848
paintings: (H) $7,700
drawings: (H) $605

GODET, Henri
French b. 1863
sculpture: (L) $220; (H) $7,700

GODET, Julius
British ac. 1844-1884
paintings: (H) $1,320

GODFREY, Winifred
American contemporary
paintings: (H) $2,990

GODIE, Lee
d. 1944
paintings: (H) $460
drawings: (L) $115; (H) $460

GODINEAU, Jean
French b. 1935
paintings: (L) $77; (H) $880

GODMAN, A.C.
American 19th/20th cent.
paintings: (H) $1,760

GODOT, F.
Continental 20th cent.
paintings: (H) $880

GODOY Y CASTRO, Federico
Spanish 1869-1939
paintings: (H) $43,875

GODWARD, John William
British 1861-1922
paintings: (L) $2,750; (H) $563,500

GODWIN, Frank
1889-1959
paintings: (L) $488; (H) $3,300
drawings: (L) $385; (H) $3,300

GOEBEL, Carl
Austrian 1824-1899
paintings: (H) $2,640

GOEBEL, Karl
Austrian 1824-1899
drawings: (H) $1,100

GOEBEL, Rod
American 1946-1993
paintings: (L) $660; (H) $15,400

GOEJE, Pieter de
Dutch 1779-1859
paintings: (H) $3,738

GOELLER, Emily Shotwell
1887-1965
paintings: (H) $990

GOERG, Edouard
French, b Australia 1893-1968/69
paintings: (L) $920; (H) $7,700

GOERG, Emma
German b. 1860
paintings: (H) $1,320

GOETEMANN, Gordon
paintings: (H) $550

GOETHALS, Charles
Belgian 1854-1886
paintings: (H) $660

GOETSCH, Gustaf
American 1877-1969
paintings: (L) $99; (H) $575
drawings: (H) $209

GOETSCHMANN, H.
Dutch 19th cent.
sculpture: (H) $1,320

GOETZ, Henri
French 1909-1989
paintings: (H) $1,100
drawings: (L) $259; (H) $308

GOETZ, Johannes
German late 19th cent.
sculpture: (H) $1,150

GOFF, Fred E.J.
English 1855-1931
drawings: (H) $1,430

GOFF, Lloyd Lozes
American 1917-1983
paintings: (L) $322; (H) $6,600

GOFFREDO
Italian 19th cent.
paintings: (H) $5,750

GOGH, Vincent van
Dutch 1853-1890
paintings: (L) $200,500; (H) $13,202,500
drawings: (L) $138,000; (H) $8,360,000

GOIJA, B.
Italian 19th cent.
paintings: (H) $1,380

GOINGS, Ralph
American b. 1928
paintings: (L) $61,600; (H) $66,000
drawings: (H) $5,462

GOITIA, Francisco
Mexican b. 1884
paintings: (L) $13,800; (H) $40,250

GOLDATE, T.
paintings: (H) $605

GOLDBECK, Walter Dean
American 1882-1925
paintings: (L) $330; (H) $3,575

GOLDBERG, B.H.
American 19th cent.
paintings: (H) $605

GOLDBERG, Fred F.
American 20th cent.
paintings: (H) $2,090

GOLDBERG, Michael
American b. 1924
paintings: (L) $330; (H) $18,700
drawings: (H) $1,760

GOLDBERG, R.
paintings: (H) $546

GOLDBERG, Rube
American 1883-1970
drawings: (L) $247; (H) $1,540
sculpture: (H) $690

GOLDEN, Rolland
American 20th cent.
paintings: (H) $330
drawings: (L) $137; (H) $770

GOLDIN, Leon
American b. 1923
paintings: (H) $715

GOLDING, Cecil
sculpture: (H) $690

GOLDSCHEIDER
sculpture: (L) $1,035; (H) $2,070

GOLDSTEIN, Jack
Canadian b. 1945
paintings: (L) $207; (H) $5,500

GOLDTHWAITE (?), Harold
British 19th cent.
paintings: (H) $962

GOLDWAITHE, Anne Wilson
American 1869-1944
paintings: (H) $330
drawings: (L) $110; (H) $880

GOLDYNE, Joseph
contemporary
drawings: (H) $770

GOLI, A.
Italian 19th cent.
paintings: (H) $522

GOLLINGS, William E., Bill
1878-1932
paintings: (L) $495; (H) $9,900
drawings: (L) $4,400; (H) $4,510

GOLOVIN, ***
drawings: (H) $920

GOLOVIN, Alexander
drawings: (H) $920

GOLTZ, Alexander Demetrius
Austrian 1857-1944
paintings: (H) $11,500

GOLTZIUS, Hendrick
Dutch 1558-1617
drawings: (H) $34,500

GOLUB, Leon
American b. 1922
paintings: (L) $3,300; (H) $49,500
drawings: (H) $2,300

GOLUBOV, Maurice
contemporary
paintings: (L) $550; (H) $660
drawings: (H) $230

GOLWIG, T.
contemporary
paintings: (H) $1,100

GOMER
sculpture: (H) $990

GOMEZ, I. Hernandez
Spanish 19th/20th cent.
drawings: (H) $2,090

GOMEZ, Paul Pierre
French 19th cent.
paintings: (H) $3,300

GOMEZ Y GIL, Guillermo
Spanish 19th cent.
paintings: (H) $4,400

GOMMISH, John
drawings: (H) $575

GONDOUIN, Emmanuel
French 1883-1934
paintings: (L) $1,610; (H) $2,070

GONGELET, J.
paintings: (H) $1,955

GONNE, Christian Friedrich
German 1813-1906
drawings: (H) $7,700

GONNELLA, G.
sculpture: (H) $29,700

GONSKE, Walt
American b. 1942
paintings: (L) $5,500; (H) $7,700

GONTARD, J.
Italian 19th cent.
paintings: (H) $1,045

GONTCHAROVA, Natalia
Russian 1881-1962
paintings: (L) $3,300; (H) $112,500
drawings: (L) $330; (H) $4,600

GONTIER, L.
paintings: (H) $990

GONTIER, Louis
French 19th/20th cent.
paintings: (H) $2,300

GONTIER, Pierre Camille
French 19th/20th cent.
paintings: (L) $3,300; (H) $19,550

GONZAGUE-PRIVAT
French b. 1843
paintings: (H) $632

GONZALES, Jeanne Guerard
French 1868-1908
paintings: (H) $6,600

GONZALEZ, Carmelo
American ac. c. 1970
paintings: (H) $4,950

GONZALEZ, Juan Antonio
Spanish b. 1842
paintings: (L) $4,600; (H) $17,600

GONZALEZ, Juan Francisco
1853-1933
paintings: (H) $1,955

GONZALEZ, Juanita
American 1903-1935
paintings: (H) $1,320

GONZALEZ, Julio
Spanish 1876-1942
drawings: (L) $2,588; (H) $27,500
sculpture: (L) $21,850; (H) $85,000

GONZALEZ, Maximiliano
Cuban b. 1926
paintings: (L) $1,380; (H) $7,150

GOOD, Bernard Stafford
American 1897-1963
paintings: (L) $385; (H) $7,150

GOOD, John Willis
English exhib. 1870-1878
sculpture: (L) $1,320; (H) $5,280

GOOD, Samuel S.
1808-1885
paintings: (H) $2,750

GOODACRE, Glenna
American b. 1939
sculpture: (L) $990; (H) $2,090

GOODALL, Edward Angelo
English 1819-1908
drawings: (L) $1,035; (H) $3,680

GOODALL, Frederick
English 1822-1904
paintings: (L) $1,035; (H) $36,800
drawings: (L) $1,485; (H) $3,680

GOODALL, John Edward
English ac. 1880-1911
paintings: (H) $1,320
drawings: (H) $880

GOODALL, John S.
British b. 1908
drawings: (H) $1,210

GOODALL, W.
19th cent.
drawings: (H) $660

GOODE, Joe
b. 1937
paintings: (L) $2,475; (H) $4,600
drawings: (H) $4,400

GOODE, John
British 19th/20th cent.
paintings: (H) $1,380

GOODELL, J.C.
paintings: (H) $2,035

GOODISON, John
American 1834-1892
paintings: (H) $14,300

GOODMAN, Bertram
American b. 1904
paintings: (H) $247
drawings: (L) $495; (H) $1,320

GOODMAN, Brenda
American b. 1943
paintings: (L) $1,045; (H) $1,375
drawings: (L) $440; (H) $1,100
sculpture: (H) $825

GOODMAN, George
paintings: (H) $625

GOODMAN, Maud
British ac. 1860-1938
paintings: (H) $7,475

GOODMAN, Robert Gwelo
1871-1939
paintings: (H) $4,887

GOODMAN, Sidney
American b. 1936
paintings: (L) $2,750; (H) $15,400

GOODNOUGH, Robert
American b. 1917
paintings: (L) $575; (H) $7,150
drawings: (L) $29; (H) $1,430

GOODPASTER, Denzil
b. 1908
sculpture: (H) $605

GOODRICH, William Wells
ac. c. 1890
paintings: (H) $750

GOODRIDGE, Elizabeth (Eliza)
1798-1882
drawings: (L) $2,875; (H) $9,775

GOODRIDGE, Sarah
American 1788-1853
drawings: (H) $495

GOODWIN, Albert
English 1845-1932
paintings: (H) $605
drawings: (L) $577; (H) $6,600

GOODWIN, Arthur Clifton
American 1866-1929
paintings: (L) $403; (H) $21,850
drawings: (L) $358; (H) $6,600

GOODWIN, Betty Roodish
contemporary
sculpture: (L) $1,100; (H) $3,300

GOODWIN, Philip Russell
American 1881/82-1935
paintings: (L) $1,760; (H) $25,875
drawings: (H) $1,650

GOODWIN, Richard La Barre
American 1840-1910
paintings: (L) $495; (H) $28,600
drawings: (L) $176; (H) $550

GOOKINS, James F.
American 1840-1904
paintings: (H) $1,540

GOOL, Jan van
Dutch 1685-1763
paintings: (H) $10,925

GOOR, Ilana
sculpture: (H) $1,980

GOOSSENS, Josse
German 1876-1929
paintings: (H) $4,675

GORBATOFF, Konstantin
Russian 1876-1945
paintings: (L) $330; (H) $2,530

GORBELY, Edward
American b. 1909
paintings: (H) $2,875

GORCHOV, Ron
American b. 1930
paintings: (L) $605; (H) $4,125

GORDER, Levon
American 19th/20th cent.
paintings: (H) $3,740

GORDER, Luther Emerson van
American 1861-1931
paintings: (L) $484; (H) $3,450

GORDIETS, Eugene
Russian contemporary
paintings: (L) $1,650; (H) $1,650

GORDIGIANI, Michele
Italian 1830-1909
paintings: (L) $4,400; (H) $34,500

GORDILLO, Omar
Colombian b. 1942
drawings: (H) $575

GORDIN, Sidney
American 20th cent.
drawings: (L) $880; (H) $1,495
sculpture: (H) $302

GORDON, Bernard
American 19th cent.
paintings: (L) $825; (H) $990

GORDON, Lady Rachel
British 19th cent.
drawings: (L) $1,150; (H) $2,645

GORDON, Leon
1889-1943
paintings: (H) $1,650

GORDON, Samstag
American 20th cent.
paintings: (H) $2,145

GORDON, Sir John Watson
English 1790-1864
paintings: (L) $173; (H) $17,250

GORDON, Witold
drawings: (H) $2,200

GORDY, Robert
American 1933-1986
paintings: (H) $1,210

GORE, Frederick
English b. 1913
paintings: (H) $2,875

GORE, Joshua
drawings: (H) $1,650

GORE, Ken
American 1911-1991
paintings: (L) $115; (H) $990

GORGUE, Jean E.
Haitian b. 1930
paintings: (L) $2,200; (H) $2,300

GORHAM-CLARK, Hope
20th cent.
paintings: (H) $863

GORI, A.
sculpture: (H) $3,960

GORI, A.
French ac. 1895-1930
sculpture: (L) $4,313; (H) $4,888

GORI, Affortunato
sculpture: (H) $2,530

GORI, Alessandro
Italian 17th cent.
paintings: (L) $9,488; (H) $18,700

GORI, G.
sculpture: (H) $2,640

GORKA, Paul
American 20th cent.
paintings: (L) $231; (H) $715
drawings: (H) $66

GORKY, Arshile
Armenian/American 1904-1948
paintings: (L) $4,950; (H) $3,852,500
drawings: (L) $3,080; (H) $308,000

GORMAN, Carl Nelson
Native American 1907-1966
paintings: (H) $1,760
drawings: (H) $2,860

GORMAN, R.C.
American b. 1933
paintings: (H) $6,600
drawings: (L) $1,610; (H) $7,475
sculpture: (L) $345; (H) $4,888

GORMLEY, Anthony
b. 1948
sculpture: (L) $22,000; (H) $44,000

GORNIK, April
American b. 1953
paintings: (H) $11,500
drawings: (L) $2,185; (H) $3,450

GORNIK, Friedrich
Austrian ac. 1895-1925
sculpture: (L) $1,925; (H) $5,775

GORO
Japanese 19th cent.
sculpture: (H) $522

GORSE, France
Slovenian b. 1897
sculpture: (H) $797

GORSON, Aaron Henry
American 1872-1933
paintings: (L) $550; (H) $26,400
drawings: (L) $550; (H) $550

GORSTKIN-WYWIORSKI, Michael
Polish 1861-1926
paintings: (H) $2,530

GORTER, Arnold Marc
Dutch 1866-1933
paintings: (L) $440; (H) $7,425

GORY, A.
sculpture: (L) $495; (H) $9,350

GOS, Albert
Swiss 1852-1942
paintings: (L) $825; (H) $2,200

GOSER, J.
paintings: (H) $977

GOSHORN, John Thomas
American b. 1870
paintings: (H) $550

GOSLING, William
British 1824-1883
paintings: (L) $2,750; (H) $5,175

GOSS, John
American 1886-1963/64
paintings: (L) $1,210; (H) $3,300

GOSSAERT, Jan, called MABUSE
Flemish c. 1478-c. 1536
paintings: (H) $1,157,500

GOSSE, Nicolas Louis Francois
French 1787-1878
paintings: (L) $11,500; (H) $23,000

GOSSELIN, Ferdinand Jules Albert
French b. 1862
paintings: (L) $3,680; (H) $6,600

GOSSET, Adolphe Francois
French 1815-1896
drawings: (H) $3,162

GOSSIN, Louis
ac. 19th/20th cent.
sculpture: (L) $990; (H) $8,250

GOTLIEB, Jules
b. 1897
paintings: (H) $2,310

GOTSCHKE
paintings: (H) $9,350

GOTSCHKE, Walter
American 20th cent.
drawings: (L) $1,100; (H) $12,100
sculpture: (H) $1,265

GOTT, Bruce
American
paintings: (H) $500

GOTT, Joseph
British 1785-1860
sculpture: (L) $3,850; (H) $9,900

GOTTFREDSON, Floyd
b. 1907
drawings: (L) $1,265; (H) $4,887

GOTTFRIED, Oswald
German b. 1869
paintings: (H) $1,100

GOTTI, A.
Italian 19th cent.
paintings: (H) $3,450

GOTTLIEB, Adolph
American 1903-1974
paintings: (L) $5,175; (H) $277,500
drawings: (L) $6,600; (H) $21,850
sculpture: (H) $1,320

GOTTLIEB, Harry
American 1895-1992
paintings: (L) $258; (H) $4,125
drawings: (L) $61; (H) $1,093

GOTTLIEB, Jules
b. 1897
paintings: (H) $1,650

GOTTLIEB, Leopold
Polish 1883-1933
drawings: (L) $660; (H) $2,310

GOTTLIEB, Maxim
American b. 1903
paintings: (L) $577; (H) $743

GOTTSCHALK, E.
paintings: (H) $900

GOTTSCHALL, Samuel
paintings: (L) $25,000; (H) $65,000

GOTTSELIG, H.
paintings: (H) $880

GOTTSHALL, Walter
20th cent.
sculpture: (H) $1,150

GOTTWALD, Frederick Carl
American 1860-1941
paintings: (L) $143; (H) $2,070

GOTUZZO, Leopoldo
1887-1983
paintings: (H) $5,500

GOTZ-RACHNITZ, Paul
German 1873-1949
paintings: (L) $750; (H) $1,100

GOTZLOFF, Carl
German 1799-1866
paintings: (H) $4,950

GOUBAUD, Innocent Louis
French 1780-1847
drawings: (H) $22,000

GOUBAUD, M.
Continental 19th cent.
paintings: (H) $2,420

GOUBIE, Jean Richard
French 1842-1899
paintings: (L) $9,900; (H) $28,750

GOUD, Laxma
Indian b. 1940
drawings: (L) $805; (H) $6,900

GOULD, Chester
American b. 1900
drawings: (L) $528; (H) $3,450

GOULD, John Howard
Canadian b. 1929
paintings: (H) $690

GOULD, W.W.
paintings: (H) $935

GOULD, William Buelow
drawings: (H) $9,200

GOULDSMITH, Edward
English 1852-1934
paintings: (H) $770

GOUNIN, Marguerite
French 20th cent.
paintings: (H) $1,100

GOUPIL, Frederic
French d. 1878
paintings: (H) $1,840

GOUPIL, Jules Adolphe
French 1839-1883
paintings: (H) $15,400

GOURDET, Pierre Eugene
French d. 1889
paintings: (H) $4,312

GOURDON, Rene
French 19th cent.
paintings: (H) $805

GOURFAIN, Peter
American
sculpture: (H) $2,760

GOURGES, L*** de
Continental 19th cent.
drawings: (H) $1,265

GOURGUE, Jacques Enguerrand
b. Haiti 1930
paintings: (L) $385; (H) $13,200

GOURLEY, W.M.
American 20th cent.
paintings: (H) $660

GOUTMAN, Dolya
American 20th cent.
paintings: (H) $632

GOUVIEN, L.
paintings: (H) $522

GOUVION SAINT CYR, Henri de
French b. 1888 .
paintings: (H) $17,600

GOUVRANT, Gerard
French b. 1946
paintings: (H) $16,500

GOVAERTS, Hendrik
Flemish 1669-1720
paintings: (H) $7,700

GOW, Andrew Carrick
British 1848-1920
paintings: (L) $8,050; (H) $8,800

GOWER, Lord Ronald Sutherland
English d. 1915
sculpture: (H) $1,870

GOYA Y LUCIENTES, Francisco de
Spanish 1746-1828
paintings: (L) $550,000; (H) $1,020,000

GOYA Y LUCIENTES, Francisco de,
studio of
1746-1828
paintings: (H) $6,875

GOYEN, Jan Josefsz van
Dutch 1596-1656
paintings: (L) $8,625; (H) $266,500
drawings: (L) $468; (H) $20,700

GOZZARD, J. William
British 19th cent.
paintings: (L) $880; (H) $990
drawings: (L) $385; (H) $385

GRABACH, John R.
American 1880/86-1981
paintings: (L) $330; (H) $18,400
drawings: (L) $165; (H) $1,430

GRABAR, Igor
Russian 1872-1960
paintings: (L) $2,750; (H) $8,800

GRABWINKLER, Paul
Austrian 1880-1943
paintings: (H) $2,310

GRACE, Gerald
American b. 1918
paintings: (H) $660

GRACE, James E.
British 1851-1908
paintings: (L) $1,045; (H) $1,380

GRACHEV
sculpture: (L) $2,185; (H) $3,335

GRACHEV, Vasiliy
Russian late 19th cent.
sculpture: (L) $1,870; (H) $4,180

GRAECEN, Edmund
American 1877-1949
paintings: (L) $9,900; (H) $22,000
drawings: (H) $920

GRAEFLE
Italian 19th cent.
paintings: (H) $660

GRAEME, Colin
British 19th cent.
paintings: (L) $1,150; (H) $3,080

GRAETZ, Fritz Georg Friedrich
German b. 1875
drawings: (H) $1,495

GRAF, Carl C.
American 1890-1947
paintings: (L) $1,150; (H) $2,415

GRAF, Franz
German b. 1840
paintings: (H) $11,500

GRAF, Paul
20th cent.
sculpture: (H) $935

GRAF, Paul
Swedish 1866-1903
paintings: (L) $1,725; (H) $60,250

GRAFF, Anton
German 1736-1813
paintings: (H) $2,200

GRAFFIONE, Giovanni di Michele
Scheggini da Larciano
Italian b. 1455
paintings: (H) $66,000

GRAFTON, R.
paintings: (H) $1,155

GRAFTON, Robert Wadsworth
American 1876-1936
paintings: (L) $412; (H) $18,700

GRAHAM, C.
British 19th/20th cent.
paintings: (H) $880

GRAHAM, Dan
b. 1942
drawings: (L) $1,430; (H) $3,680

GRAHAM, F. Frederic
Continental School 19th cent.
paintings: (H) $990

GRAHAM, Gordon
paintings: (L) $88; (H) $302
drawings: (L) $605; (H) $605

GRAHAM, John
American 1881-1961
paintings: (L) $3,300; (H) $44,000
drawings: (L) $550; (H) $805

GRAHAM, Kathleen M.
b. 1913
paintings: (H) $4,180

GRAHAM, Lex
American b. 1935
sculpture: (L) $2,200; (H) $3,740

GRAHAM, Robert
American b. 1938
paintings: (H) $1,210
drawings: (H) $2,070
sculpture: (L) $1,380; (H) $62,500

GRAHAM, Robert Alexander
American 1873-1946
paintings: (L) $605; (H) $8,800

GRAHAM, William
1841-1910
paintings: (L) $259; (H) $467

GRAHE, E.
contemporary
paintings: (H) $467

GRAHS, Carl H.
American 20th cent.
paintings: (H) $460

GRAILLY, Victor de
French 1804-1889
paintings: (L) $1,100; (H) $7,590

GRAIN, Peter, Sr.
paintings: (H) $900

GRAME, Colin
paintings: (H) $915

GRAMMATICA, Antiveduto
Spanish/Italian 1571-1626
paintings: (H) $46,000

GRAN, Daniel
Austrian 1694-1757
paintings: (H) $10,350

GRANBERY, Henrietta Augusta
American 1831-1921
paintings: (H) $825

GRANBERY, V.
paintings: (H) $1,200

GRANCI, C.
paintings: (H) $660

GRAND-CARTERET, Jean Albert
French b. 1901
drawings: (L) $1,540; (H) $8,800

GRANDEE, Joe Ruiz
American 1929-1976
paintings: (L) $1,595; (H) $2,875

GRANDIN, Eugene
French ac. 1851-1909
drawings: (L) $523; (H) $1,320

GRANDMAISON, Nickolas de
Canadian/Russian 19th/20th cent.
paintings: (H) $6,050
drawings: (L) $1,100; (H) $7,700

GRANDMAISON, Orestes N.
Canadian 1932-1985
paintings: (H) $825

GRANER, Rosa Rainold
1904-1962
paintings: (H) $467

GRANER Y ARRUFI, Luis
b. Spain 1867-1927
paintings: (L) $770; (H) $35,750

GRANET, Francois Marius
French 1775-1849
paintings: (L) $880; (H) $6,440
drawings: (H) $990

GRANGE, Henri
French 20th cent.
paintings: (H) $495

GRANGER, Charles Henry
American 1812-1893
paintings: (H) $2,530

GRANGER, Genevieve
sculpture: (H) $1,495

GRANIE, Joseph
French 1866-1912
paintings: (H) $4,600

GRANJEAN, Raymond
drawings: (H) $460

GRANT, Ariel
paintings: (H) $522

GRANT, Blanche Chloe
American 1874-1948
paintings: (H) $1,045

GRANT, Charles Henry
American 1866-1938
paintings: (L) $137; (H) $2,200

GRANT, Clement Rollins
American 1849-1893
paintings: (L) $385; (H) $19,550
drawings: (H) $1,100

GRANT, Duncan
American 1885-1978
paintings: (H) $13,200
drawings: (H) $2,750

GRANT, Dwinnell
American b. 1912
drawings: (L) $1,320; (H) $2,200

GRANT, Frederic M.
American 1886-1959
paintings: (L) $440; (H) $13,200
drawings: (H) $385

GRANT, G.A.
paintings: (H) $5,520

GRANT, Gordon Hope
American 1875-1962
paintings: (L) $715; (H) $7,188
drawings: (L) $110; (H) $4,888

GRANT, J. Jeffrey
American 1883-1960
paintings: (L) $127; (H) $2,310

GRANT, James
American b. 1924
drawings: (H) $920

GRANT, Mimi
American
drawings: (L) $500; (H) $800

GRANT, Sir Francis
British 1803-1878
paintings: (L) $2,475; (H) $195,000

GRANT, Vernon
drawings: (H) $4,950

GRANT?, Gordon
American 1875-1962
drawings: (H) $660

GRANVILLE-SMITH, Walter
American 1870-1938
paintings: (L) $385; (H) $9,350
drawings: (L) $66; (H) $5,280

GRAS, Francisco
Spanish 19th/20th cent.
drawings: (H) $9,350

GRASEGGER, Georg
sculpture: (H) $1,150

GRASS, Carl Gotthard
Baltic 1767-1814
paintings: (H) $24,200

GRASSET, Edmund
French 1852-1880
sculpture: (H) $6,900

GRASSET, Eugene
Swiss 1841-1917
drawings: (H) $880

GRASSI, Nicola
Italian 1662-1748
paintings: (H) $13,200

GRASSON, L.D.
18th cent.
paintings: (H) $743

GRATCHEB
sculpture: (H) $1,980

GRATCHEFF, Alexei
Russian c. 1780-after 1850
sculpture: (H) $3,220

GRATCHEFF, George Ivan
Russian ac. 1860-1893
sculpture: (H) $6,050

GRATCHEV, Alexei Petrovich
Russian 19th cent.
sculpture: (L) $1,540; (H) $2,420

GRATE, Eric
1896-1983
sculpture: (H) $4,025

GRATH, Anton
Austrian b. 1881
sculpture: (H) $9,200

GRAU, Enrique
Colombian b. 1920
paintings: (L) $17,250; (H) $34,500
drawings: (L) $6,600; (H) $46,750

GRAU SANTOS, Julian
Spanish b. 1937
paintings: (H) $2,300

GRAU-SALA, Emile
Spanish 1911-1975
paintings: (L) $3,450; (H) $41,800
drawings: (L) $2,090; (H) $8,625

GRAU-SALA, Paolo
Spanish 1911-1975
paintings: (H) $63,250

GRAUER, William C.
American b. 1896
paintings: (L) $220; (H) $550
drawings: (L) $193; (H) $357

GRAVE, Josua de
Dutch 1660-1712
drawings: (H) $1,093

GRAVELOT, Hubert Francois
French 1699-1773
drawings: (H) $14,300

GRAVES, Abbott Fuller
American 1859-1936
paintings: (L) $798; (H) $137,500
drawings: (H) $2,640

GRAVES, Maitland
paintings: (H) $2,100

GRAVES, Mary de B(erniere)
American ac. 1920s
paintings: (H) $825

GRAVES, Morris
American b. 1910
paintings: (L) $1,725; (H) $96,000
drawings: (L) $2,200; (H) $41,800

GRAVES, Nancy
American b. 1940
paintings: (L) $2,300; (H) $19,550
drawings: (L) $5,750; (H) $11,000
sculpture: (L) $14,950; (H) $107,000

GRAY, C.S.
American 19th/20th cent.
paintings: (H) $550

GRAY, Cleve
American b. 1918
paintings: (L) $385; (H) $3,300
drawings: (H) $1,100

GRAY, George
English 1880-1943
paintings: (H) $687

GRAY, Harold
drawings: (H) $1,150

GRAY, Henry Percy
American 1869-1952
paintings: (L) $3,575; (H) $30,250
drawings: (L) $825; (H) $24,750

GRAY, Jack Lorimer
Canadian 1927-1981
paintings: (L) $3,300; (H) $34,500
drawings: (H) $880

GRAY, Jessie D.
paintings: (H) $1,100

GRAY, John
British ac. 1885-1904
paintings: (L) $374; (H) $1,320

GRAY, Kate
English 19th cent.
paintings: (H) $1,265

GRAY, Kay
paintings: (H) $690

GRAY, Mary
American 1891-1964
paintings: (L) $66; (H) $1,100

GRAY, Percy
American 1869-1952
paintings: (H) $7,700
drawings: (L) $3,300; (H) $9,900

GRAY, William
paintings: (H) $9,900

GRAYSON, A.
American 19th cent.
paintings: (H) $489

GRAZIANI, Ercole
1651-1726
drawings: (H) $1,100

GRAZIANI, Ercole, the younger
Italian 1688-1765
paintings: (L) $3,850; (H) $18,700
drawings: (H) $1,210

GRAZIANO, F***
American 20th cent.
paintings: (H) $1,610

GREACEN, Edmund William
American 1877-1949
paintings: (L) $935; (H) $13,200
drawings: (H) $330

GREACEN, Nan
American b. 1909
paintings: (L) $660; (H) $3,080
drawings: (L) $330; (H) $1,100

GREASON, William
American b. 1884
paintings: (L) $55; (H) $1,100

GREATOREX, Eleanor Elizabeth
American b. 1854
paintings: (H) $715

GREATOREX, Eliza Pratt
American 1820-1897
paintings: (L) $1,210; (H) $2,185

GREATOREX, Kathleen Honora
American b. 1851
paintings: (H) $1,320

GREAVES, E.L.
drawings: (H) $1,100

GREAVES, Susan F.
paintings: (H) $500

GREAVES, Walter
British 1846-1930
paintings: (L) $1,610; (H) $4,180

GREB, Nam
Austrian
sculpture: (L) $990; (H) $1,760

GREBER, Henri Leon
French 1869-1937
sculpture: (H) $4,600

GRECHOV, Ivanovitch
sculpture: (H) $605

GRECO, Aldo
20th cent.
sculpture: (H) $770

GRECO, El, Domenikos
THEOTOKOPOULOS
Spanish 1541?-1614
paintings: (L) $118,000; (H) $2,312,500

GRECO, El, workshop of
paintings: (H) $28,600

GRECO, Emilio
Italian b. 1913
drawings: (H) $1,320
sculpture: (L) $3,850; (H) $198,000

GRECO, Gennero, called Il Mascacotta
Italian c. 1667-1714
paintings: (L) $17,600; (H) $77,000

GREEFF, Peter
German b. 1865
paintings: (H) $467

GREEN, Alfred H.
English 19th cent.
paintings: (L) $1,980; (H) $3,910

GREEN, Bernard I.
American 1887-1951
paintings: (L) $110; (H) $715

GREEN, Charles
British 1840-1898
paintings: (L) $1,155; (H) $2,200
drawings: (H) $34,500

GREEN, Charles Edwin Lewis
American 1844-1915
paintings: (L) $467; (H) $2,750

GREEN, E* F*****
British 19th cent.
paintings: (H) $3,850

GREEN, Elizabeth Shippen
American 1871-1954
drawings: (L) $3,300; (H) $7,150

GREEN, Frank Russell
American 1856/59-1940
paintings: (L) $165; (H) $11,000

GREEN, James
British 1771-1834
drawings: (H) $1,380

GREEN, Martin
American 1920-1980
drawings: (L) $467; (H) $495

GREEN, Richard
20th cent.
paintings: (H) $907

GREEN, Roland
English 1896-1971
drawings: (L) $605; (H) $5,500

GREEN, Townley
drawings: (H) $1,760

GREENAWAY, Kate
English 1846-1901
drawings: (L) $110; (H) $8,800

GREENBAUM, Joseph
American 1864-1940
paintings: (L) $770; (H) $3,850

GREENBERG, Maurice
American b. 1893
paintings: (L) $247; (H) $908

GREENBLAT, Rodney Alan
American b. 1960
drawings: (L) $575; (H) $2,420

GREENBLUM, Mark
paintings: (L) $575; (H) $1,840

GREENBURG, Samuel
American b. 1905
paintings: (L) $489; (H) $2,300
drawings: (H) $345

GREENE, Albert van Nesse
American b. 1887
paintings: (L) $40; (H) $3,500
drawings: (L) $110; (H) $650

GREENE, Art
20th cent.
drawings: (H) $4,370

GREENE, Balcomb
American b. 1904
paintings: (L) $825; (H) $4,600
drawings: (L) $715; (H) $6,325

GREENE, Daniel
drawings: (H) $550

GREENE, Gertrude
American 1911-1956
paintings: (L) $1,380; (H) $3,630
drawings: (L) $1,320; (H) $2,420

GREENE, J. Barry
American 1895-1966
paintings: (L) $770; (H) $935

GREENE, Stephen
American b. 1917
paintings: (H) $2,530

GREENE, Vernon
drawings: (L) $977; (H) $2,587

GREENE, Walter L.
19th/20th cent.
paintings: (L) $440; (H) $770

GREENFIELD, Emalie
American School 19th/20th cent.
paintings: (H) $825

GREENHALGH, Thomas
British 19th cent.
drawings: (H) $990

GREENLEAF, Benjamin
American 1796-1821
paintings: (L) $2,090; (H) $16,100

GREENLEAF, Jacob
American 1887-1968
paintings: (L) $137; (H) $1,870

GREENMAN, Frances
American 1890-1982
paintings: (L) $1,100; (H) $1,925

GREENOUGH, Richard Saltonstall
American 1819-1904
sculpture: (L) $2,970; (H) $49,450

GREENWOOD
American
paintings: (H) $2,310

GREENWOOD
British 20th cent.
paintings: (H) $467

GREENWOOD, Eric David
sculpture: (H) $2,587

GREENWOOD, Ethan Allen
American 1779-1856
paintings: (L) $2,750; (H) $8,050

GREENWOOD, G.P.
ac. 1881-1894
paintings: (L) $2,860; (H) $3,450

GREENWOOD, George Parker
English ac. 1860-1890
paintings: (H) $1,100

GREENWOOD, Joseph H.
American 1857-1927
paintings: (L) $275; (H) $3,575

GREENWOOD, Marion
American 1909-1970
paintings: (L) $605; (H) $1,430
drawings: (L) $100; (H) $1,380

GREER, J.T.
American 19th cent.
paintings: (H) $1,650

GREEVES, Richard
sculpture: (L) $385; (H) $550

GREGER, Harold
American b. 1929
paintings: (H) $605

GREGOIR, L.
sculpture: (H) $690

GREGOIRE, Alexandre
Haitian b. 1922
paintings: (L) $660; (H) $825

GREGOIRE, Jean Louis
French 1840-1890
sculpture: (L) $660; (H) $17,600

GREGOOR, G. Smak
Dutch 1770-1843
paintings: (H) $518

GREGOR, Harold
American b. 1929
paintings: (L) $550; (H) $3,220

GREGOR, J. A.
paintings: (H) $660

GREGORI (?)
American
paintings: (H) $1,980

GREGORY, Angela
American 1903-1990
drawings: (L) $357; (H) $770

GREGORY, Arthur V.
drawings: (H) $1,100

GREGORY, C.F.
Australian 1815-1885
drawings: (H) $3,850

GREGORY, Catherine
sculpture: (H) $2,300

GREGORY, Dorothy Lake
American b. 1893
paintings: (L) $55; (H) $990

GREGORY, George
English 1849-1938
drawings: (L) $880; (H) $1,320

GREGORY, George Frederick
Anglo-Australian b. 1815
drawings: (H) $770

GREGORY, John
English/American 1879-1958
sculpture: (L) $1,725; (H) $8,250

GREGORY, Luigi
Italian/American 1819-1883
paintings: (H) $1,595

GREIG, George M.
Scottish 19th cent.
paintings: (H) $908

GREIL, Alois
Austrian 1841-1902
paintings: (L) $495; (H) $495
drawings: (H) $2,640

GREINER, Otto
German 1869-1916
drawings: (H) $3,190

GREIVE, Johan Conrad
Dutch 1837-1891
paintings: (H) $1,150

GREL, Schmit
paintings: (H) $4,400

GRELL, Louis Frederick
American b. 1887
paintings: (L) $522; (H) $2,200
drawings: (H) $220

GRELLE, Martin
American b. 1954
paintings: (L) $3,630; (H) $18,700
drawings: (H) $330

GREMION, Charles
French 19th cent.
sculpture: (H) $528

GREMKE, Diedrich Henry
American 1860-1939
paintings: (L) $1,045; (H) $2,750

GRENDE, C.A.
paintings: (H) $825

GRENDE, C.A.
American
sculpture: (H) $900

GRENDE, Janene
drawings: (L) $330; (H) $1,900

GRENIE, B.
French 19th/20th cent.
paintings: (L) $2,420; (H) $11,500

GRENIER, Cassering
American 20th cent.
drawings: (H) $467

GRENIER, Henri
French 20th cent.
paintings: (H) $1,495
drawings: (H) $825

GRENIER DE SAINT-MARTIN,
Francisque Martin Francois
French 1793-1867
paintings: (H) $3,850

GRESLY, Gabriel
1712-1756
paintings: (L) $6,900; (H) $7,150

GRESSEL, M.
American 20th cent.
sculpture: (H) $920

GRETZNER, Harold
American 1902-1977
drawings: (L) $550; (H) $1,760

GREUZE, Jean Baptiste
French 1725-1805
paintings: (L) $4,290; (H) $286,000
drawings: (L) $522; (H) $253,000

GREUZE, Jean Baptiste, studio of
paintings: (H) $5,175

GREVENBROECK, Orazio
Dutch ac. 1670-1730
paintings: (L) $33,350; (H) $38,500

GREY
paintings: (H) $920

GREY, Elmer
American 1872-1963
paintings: (H) $605

GREY, J.
19th cent.
paintings: (H) $690

GREY, John
20th cent.
paintings: (H) $495

GREY, Steve
American 20th cent.
paintings: (L) $660; (H) $1,100

GREYER, Emil
paintings: (H) $460

GREYTAK, Don
American
drawings: (L) $1,100; (H) $1,550

GRIBBLE, Bernard Finegan
British 1873-1962
paintings: (L) $770; (H) $1,210

GRIDLAND, H.
Continental 19th cent.
paintings: (H) $5,500

GRIEN, Hans Baldung, studio of
16th cent.
drawings: (H) $9,200

GRIENT, Cornelius Outboter van der
b. 1797
paintings: (H) $1,210

GRIER, Sir Edmund Wyly
paintings: (L) $1,045; (H) $7,700

GRIERSON, Charles Melver
drawings: (H) $660

GRIFFANY, J.
British 19th cent.
paintings: (H) $8,800

GRIFFIER, Jan, the elder
1652-1718
paintings: (L) $14,950; (H) $71,500

GRIFFIER, Jan, the younger
d. c. 1750
paintings: (H) $25,300

GRIFFIN, Charles Gerald
American 1864-1945
paintings: (H) $1,100

GRIFFIN, David
American b. 1952
paintings: (L) $2,420; (H) $5,500

GRIFFIN, De Lacy
American 19th/20th cent.
paintings: (L) $750; (H) $1,705

GRIFFIN, G.J.
American
paintings: (H) $48,875

GRIFFIN, Rick
American 1944-1991
paintings: (H) $4,400
drawings: (L) $880; (H) $5,500

GRIFFIN, Thomas Bailey
American b. 1858
paintings: (L) $193; (H) $2,475

GRIFFIN, Walter
American 1861-1935
paintings: (L) $193; (H) $8,050
drawings: (L) $33; (H) $1,430

GRIFFIN, William Davenport
b. 1894
paintings: (H) $2,750

GRIFFITH, Bill
drawings: (H) $4,400

GRIFFITH, E.N.
American 19th/20th cent.
paintings: (L) $770; (H) $35,650

GRIFFITH, Grace Allison
American 1885-1955
drawings: (L) $1,840; (H) $2,090

GRIFFITH, Louis Oscar
American 1875-1956
paintings: (L) $115; (H) $3,410

GRIFFITH, William Alexander
American 1866-1940
paintings: (L) $880; (H) $4,950
drawings: (L) $1,320; (H) $1,540

GRIGGS, Samuel W.
American 1827-1898
paintings: (L) $467; (H) $2,420

GRIGORESCU, Nicolas
Romanian 1838-1907
paintings: (H) $4,370

GRIGORIEV, Boris
Russian 1886-1939
paintings: (L) $1,980; (H) $11,000
drawings: (H) $825

GRIJS, Hendricus Fredericus de
Dutch 1866-1933
paintings: (H) $660

GRILL, Oswald
Austrian 1878-1969
paintings: (H) $1,650

GRILLON, Roger
paintings: (L) $1,100; (H) $3,300

GRILO, Sarah
Argentinean b. 1921
paintings: (H) $1,380

GRIMALDI, Giovanni Francesco,
called Il Bolognese
Italian 1606-1680
paintings: (H) $15,400
drawings: (L) $1,380; (H) $11,500

GRIMEAU, Bryan de
American 20th cent.
drawings: (H) $1,980

GRIMELUND, Johannes Martin
Norwegian 1842-1917
paintings: (L) $1,540; (H) $9,350

GRIMES, Robert
British b. 1940
paintings: (H) $467

GRIMLEY, Oliver
American 20th cent.
drawings: (L) $523; (H) $550

GRIMM, C. De
drawings: (H) $1,210

GRIMM, P.
paintings: (H) $715

GRIMM, Paul
American 1892-1974
paintings: (L) $275; (H) $12,100

GRIMM, Pierre
Russian/French b. 1898
paintings: (L) $550; (H) $825

GRIMM, Samuel Hieronymous
Swiss 1733-1794
drawings: (H) $715

GRIMMER, Abel
Flemish 1570/73-1619/40
paintings: (H) $66,000

GRIMS, Alfred M.
drawings: (H) $2,875

GRIMSHAW, Arthur F.
British 1868-1913
paintings: (H) $2,750

GRIMSHAW, John Atkinson
English 1836-1893
paintings: (L) $16,100; (H) $217,000

GRINNELL, George Victor
American 1878-1946
paintings: (L) $110; (H) $518

GRINNELL, Roy
American 20th cent.
paintings: (H) $4,950

GRIPPO, Robert Lo
paintings: (H) $3,740

GRIPS, Charles Joseph
Belgian 1852-1920
paintings: (H) $8,250

GRIPS, Jean Charles
Belgian 19th cent.
paintings: (H) $12,650

GRIS, Juan
Spanish 1887-1927
paintings: (L) $32,200; (H) $3,300,000
drawings: (L) $6,050; (H) $365,500

GRISARD, D.
French 19th/20th cent.
sculpture: (L) $2,300; (H) $2,530

GRISMER, Dennis
paintings: (H) $1,450

GRISON, Francois Adolphe
French 1845-1914
paintings: (L) $1,650; (H) $4,600
drawings: (L) $440; (H) $1,725

GRISON, Francois Adolphe and
Gaston Gilbert Daniel SAVE
French
paintings: (L) $15,400; (H) $15,400

GRISWOLD, Casmir Clayton
American 1834-1918
paintings: (L) $605; (H) $2,035

GRITCHENKO, Alexis
Russian b. 1883
drawings: (L) $715; (H) $1,495

GRITTEN, Henry C.
British 1818-1873
paintings: (L) $748; (H) $2,300

GRITZNER, A.
paintings: (H) $990

GRIVAZ, Eugene
French/Swiss 1852-1915
drawings: (H) $1,320

GROBET, H.
19th cent.
paintings: (H) $3,025

GROEBER, Hermann
German 1865-1935
paintings: (H) $4,313

GROEBER, P.
19th/20th cent.
paintings: (H) $770

GROENEWEGEN, Adrianus Johannes
Dutch 1874-1963
paintings: (L) $770; (H) $1,650
drawings: (L) $990; (H) $1,980

GROENEWEGEN, Gerrit
Dutch 1754-1826
drawings: (L) $1,150; (H) $7,150

GROENEWEGEN, K.L.
Dutch 19th cent.
drawings: (H) $715

GROLL, Albert Lorey
American 1866-1952
paintings: (L) $288; (H) $2,300
drawings: (L) $55; (H) $440

GROLL, C.
N. European 19th cent.
paintings: (H) $770

GROLLERON, Paul Louis Narcisse
French 1848-1901
paintings: (L) $1,540; (H) $7,700
drawings: (H) $1,540

GROMAIRE, Marcel
French 1892-1971
paintings: (L) $13,800; (H) $52,250
drawings: (L) $440; (H) $9,900

GRONLAND, Nel
German 19th/20th cent.
paintings: (H) $575

GRONLAND, Rene
German b. 1849
paintings: (L) $2,200; (H) $2,300

GRONLAND, T.H., Theude
German
paintings: (H) $19,250

GROOME, Esther M.
American b. 1929
paintings: (L) $440; (H) $4,400

GROOME, William H.C.
British ac. 1881-1907
paintings: (H) $4,312

GROOMS, Red
American b. 1937
paintings: (L) $715; (H) $3,575
drawings: (L) $316; (H) $26,400
sculpture: (L) $2,750; (H) $35,200

GROOT, Frans Arnold Breuhaus de
Belgian 1824-1872
paintings: (H) $20,700

GROOT, Maurits de
Dutch
paintings: (L) $550; (H) $825

GROOTH, Georg Christoph
Russian 1716-1749
paintings: (H) $6,600

GROPEANU, Nicolae
drawings: (H) $1,840

GROPPER, William
American 1897-1977
paintings: (L) $863; (H) $26,450
drawings: (L) $55; (H) $4,025
sculpture: (H) $690

GROS, Baron Antoine Jean
French 1771-1835
paintings: (H) $222,500
drawings: (H) $2,200

GROS, Baron Jean Baptiste Louis
French 1793-1870
paintings: (H) $35,650

GROS, Ed
sculpture: (H) $880

GROS, Lucien Alphonse
French 1845-1913
paintings: (H) $20,700

GROSE, D.C.
American ac. 1860-1880
paintings: (L) $143; (H) $2,200

GROSE, Daniel Charles
English 1760-1838
paintings: (H) $4,400

GROSPERRIN, Claude
French b. 1939
paintings: (H) $1,100

GROSS, Chaim
Austrian/American 1904-1991
drawings: (L) $88; (H) $2,310
sculpture: (L) $633; (H) $66,000

GROSS, Daniel C.
19th cent.
paintings: (H) $880

GROSS, George
paintings: (H) $2,420
drawings: (H) $1,430

GROSS, Milt
drawings: (H) $3,105

GROSS, Peter Alfred
American 1849-1914
paintings: (L) $110; (H) $1,100

GROSSER, Maurice
American b. 1903
paintings: (L) $345; (H) $12,100

GROSSMAN, Edwin Booth
American 1887-1957
paintings: (L) $110; (H) $2,090
drawings: (L) $220; (H) $220

GROSSMAN, Joseph B.
American/Lith. b. 1889
paintings: (L) $303; (H) $880

GROSSMAN, Nancy
American b. 1940
drawings: (L) $220; (H) $4,888
sculpture: (L) $1,725; (H) $25,300

GROSVENOR, Richard
paintings: (H) $660

GROSVENOR, Robert
American b. 1937
sculpture: (L) $5,000; (H) $24,150

GROSZ, George
German/American 1893-1959
paintings: (L) $990; (H) $34,500
drawings: (L) $467; (H) $45,100

GROTH, Georg Vilhelm Arnold
Danish 1842-1899
paintings: (H) $660

GROTH, John
American b. 1908
drawings: (L) $330; (H) $687

GROVER, Dorothy
contemporary
paintings: (H) $550

GROVER, Oliver Dennett
American 1861-1927
paintings: (L) $440; (H) $11,500

GROVES, Hannah C.
American 1868-1952
paintings: (L) $302; (H) $770

GRUAU, Rene
French 20th cent.
paintings: (H) $880

GRUBACS, Carlo
German ac. early 19th cent.
paintings: (H) $17,600
drawings: (L) $6,613; (H) $8,050

GRUBAS, Marco
Italian 1839-1910
paintings: (H) $825

GRUBB, Virginia
drawings: (H) $690

GRUBER
German ac. 1900
sculpture: (L) $990; (H) $1,320

GRUBER, A.
German
sculpture: (H) $550

GRUBER, B.
paintings: (H) $660

GRUBERSKI, Ladislas
Polish 19th/20th cent.
sculpture: (H) $1,092

GRUDEN, Arcimede
Italian b. 1878
paintings: (H) $825

GRUELLE, R.B.
drawings: (H) $1,100

GRUET, Simone
French 20th cent.
paintings: (H) $770

GRUGER, Frederic R.
American 1871-1953
drawings: (L) $302; (H) $2,750

GRUGHEY, F.
Continental 19th cent.
paintings: (H) $7,475

GRUND, Norbert
1717-1767
paintings: (H) $1,150

GRUNDMANN, B.
sculpture: (L) $330; (H) $852

GRUNER, C.
German 19th cent.
paintings: (H) $1,045

GRUNEWALD, Isaac
Swedish 1889-1946
paintings: (H) $3,300

GRUNFELD, J.
German 19th cent.
paintings: (H) $3,520

GRUNWALD, Bela Ivanyi
paintings: (H) $2,300

GRUPPE, Charles Paul
Canadian/American 1860-1940
paintings: (L) $104; (H) $4,950
drawings: (L) $98; (H) $1,540

GRUPPE, Emile Albert
American 1896-1978
paintings: (L) $88; (H) $15,400
drawings: (L) $115; (H) $413

GRUPPE, Karl Heinrich
American 1893-1982
sculpture: (H) $7,700

GRUPPE, Robert C.
American 20th cent.
paintings: (L) $27; (H) $1,045

GRUPPE, Virginia
American b. 1907
paintings: (L) $144; (H) $805
drawings: (H) $88

GRUST, F.G.
Dutch 19th/20th cent.
paintings: (L) $1,045; (H) $3,300

GRUST, Theodor
German b. 1859
paintings: (H) $7,150

GRUTZNER, Eduard von
German 1846-1925
paintings: (L) $770; (H) $35,200

GRUYTER, Jacob Willem
Dutch 1856-1908
paintings: (H) $4,830

GRYEFF, Adriaen de
Flemish 1670-1715
paintings: (L) $2,990; (H) $9,200

GSCHOSMANN, Ludwig
German b. 1901
paintings: (L) $132; (H) $1,955

GUACCIMANNI, Alessandro
Italian 1864-1927
paintings: (H) $5,775
drawings: (L) $550; (H) $660

GUACCIMANNI, Alessandro
Italian 19th/20th cent.
drawings: (H) $660

GUACCIMANNI, Vittorio
Italian 1859-1938
paintings: (H) $660
drawings: (L) $467; (H) $3,300

GUAGNINI, Nicolas
b. 1966
paintings: (L) $2,300; (H) $4,025

GUANZHONG, Wu
Chinese b. 1919
drawings: (H) $23,000

GUARANA, F.
Italian 20th cent.
paintings: (H) $495

GUARDABASSI, Guerrino
Italian b. 1841
paintings: (L) $275; (H) $3,300
drawings: (L) $1,045; (H) $1,265

GUARDI, Antonio and Francesco
GUARDI
paintings: (H) $115,500

GUARDI, Francesco
Italian 1712-1793
paintings: (L) $1,430; (H) $1,265,000
drawings: (L) $9,900; (H) $143,000

GUARDI, Francesco, studio of
18th cent.
paintings: (H) $11,500

GUARDI, Giacomo
Italian 1764-1835
paintings: (L) $17,600; (H) $132,000
drawings: (L) $990; (H) $29,900

GUARDI, Giovanni Antonio
Italian 1698-1760
paintings: (L) $46,200; (H) $198,000
drawings: (H) $17,250

GUARDIA, Wenceslao de la
American b. 1861
paintings: (H) $20,700

GUARINA, Salvatore
paintings: (H) $2,530

GUARINO
Italian 19th/20th cent.
paintings: (H) $522

GUARNERIO, P.
1842-1881
sculpture: (H) $4,313

GUARNIARE
paintings: (H) $550

GUAYASAMIN, Oswaldo
Ecuadorian b. 1919
paintings: (L) $3,300; (H) $34,500
drawings: (L) $2,760; (H) $18,400
sculpture: (L) $7,700; (H) $26,450

GUBA, Rudolph
German 19th/20th cent.
paintings: (L) $2,300; (H) $2,750

GUBSKY, Igor
paintings: (H) $715

GUCCILLATO, V.
sculpture: (H) $4,888

GUCCIONE, Piero
Italian b. 1935
paintings: (H) $35,750

GUDE, Hans Frederick
Norwegian 1825-1903
paintings: (L) $3,960; (H) $10,350

GUDE, Nils
paintings: (H) $825

GUDERNA, Ladislav
paintings: (H) $1,980

GUDIN, H.
French 19th cent.
paintings: (H) $715

GUDIN, Jean Antoine Theodore
French 1802-1880
paintings: (L) $523; (H) $2,300

GUDONE
Italian 20th cent.
paintings: (H) $1,035

GUE, David John
American 1836-1917
paintings: (L) $330; (H) $990

GUELDRY, Ferdinand Joseph
French b. 1858
paintings: (L) $6,900; (H) $11,000

GUENARD, Hortaire J.
American 1827-1899
paintings: (L) $990; (H) $1,210

GUENOT, Auguste
French b. 1882
sculpture: (L) $1,375; (H) $2,875

GUERCINO, Giovanni Francesco
Barbieri, called Il Guercino
Italian 1591-1666
paintings: (L) $12,100; (H) $305,000
drawings: (L) $3,220; (H) $112,500

GUERCINO, Giovanni Francesco
Barbieri, called Il Guercino studio of
17th cent.
paintings: (L) $3,680; (H) $40,250

GUERIN, Armand
French b. 1913
paintings: (L) $110; (H) $1,100

GUERIN, Charles
1875-1939
paintings: (H) $3,220

GUERIN, Ernest
drawings: (H) $1,100

GUERIN, Jules
American 1866-1946
paintings: (L) $330; (H) $518
drawings: (L) $546; (H) $4,950

GUERIN, P.
paintings: (H) $2,090

GUERIN, Pierre Narcisse Baron
French 1774-1833
drawings: (H) $5,750

GUERIN, Therese
French 1861-1933
paintings: (L) $4,313; (H) $11,500

GUERIN, V.
paintings: (H) $2,875

GUERINO, E.
paintings: (H) $770

GUERMACHEFF, Michel
Russian/Canadian b. 1867
paintings: (H) $1,925

GUERRA, Giovanni
1540-1618
drawings: (H) $1,380

GUERRERO, Manuel Ruiz
Spanish 19th cent.
paintings: (H) $7,150

GUERRERO GALVAN, Jesus
Mexico 1910-1973
paintings: (L) $8,800; (H) $184,000
drawings: (L) $3,080; (H) $10,450

GUERRESCHI, Guiseppe
1929-1985
paintings: (L) $460; (H) $2,090
drawings: (H) $440

GUERTHZEZ, T.
paintings: (H) $2,420

GUERVAL
sculpture: (H) $2,420

GUERY, Armand
French 1850-1912
paintings: (H) $4,025

GUES, Alfred Francois
French b. 1837
paintings: (L) $990; (H) $2,640

GUES, K.
French School 19th cent.
paintings: (H) $605

GUEY, Fernand
French b. 1877
paintings: (H) $55,000

GUEYTON, G.
sculpture: (H) $2,420

GUEYTON, H.
French 19th cent.
sculpture: (L) $138; (H) $495

GUGLIELMI
20th cent.
paintings: (H) $468

GUGLIELMI, Gennaro
Italian b. 1804
paintings: (H) $6,325

GUGLIELMI, Luigi
Italian 1834-1907
sculpture: (L) $1,955; (H) $11,500

GUGLIELMI, O. Louis
American 1906-1956
paintings: (L) $3,300; (H) $46,000
drawings: (L) $1,540; (H) $16,500

GUIBARA, Albert
sculpture: (H) $6,600

GUICHARD
sculpture: (H) $5,290

GUIDA, Wm.
paintings: (H) $475

GUIDI, Giuseppe
Italian 1881/84-1931
paintings: (L) $3,450; (H) $4,125

GUIDI, J***
Continental 19th cent.
paintings: (H) $2,970

GUIDI, Virgilio
Italian b. 1891
paintings: (H) $1,100

GUIDO, Giuseppe
Italian 20th cent.
paintings: (H) $1,610

GUIDOBONO, Bartolomeo
Italian 1654-1709
paintings: (L) $3,520; (H) $11,000

GUIET, A.
French 19th cent.
sculpture: (L) $660; (H) $4,125

GUIGNARD, Alberto da Veiga
Brazilian 1896-1962
paintings: (H) $34,500

GUIGOU, Paul
French 1834-1871
paintings: (L) $440; (H) $66,000

GUILBERT, Narcisse
French 1876-1942
paintings: (H) $6,900

GUILD, James
American 1797-1841
drawings: (H) $10,925

GUILLAUME, Albert
French 1873-1942
paintings: (L) $2,750; (H) $34,500

GUILLAUME, Louis Mathieu Didier
American 1816-1892
paintings: (H) $1,430

GUILLAUMET, Gustave Achille
French 1840-1887
paintings: (L) $1,725; (H) $5,750
drawings: (H) $1,100

GUILLAUMIN, Armand
French 1841-1927
paintings: (L) $11,000; (H) $121,000
drawings: (L) $1,495; (H) $34,500

GUILLEMARD, Marcel
sculpture: (H) $5,500

GUILLEMER, Ernest
French b. 1839
paintings: (H) $1,610

GUILLEMET, Jean Baptiste Antoine
French 1843-1918
paintings: (L) $2,990; (H) $13,225

GUILLEMIN
French 18th cent.
sculpture: (H) $5,175

GUILLEMIN, Alexandre Marie
French 1817-1880
paintings: (L) $1,320; (H) $4,600

GUILLEMIN, Emile Coriolan
Hippolyte
French 1841-1907
sculpture: (L) $220; (H) $250,000

GUILLEMINET, Claude
French 1821-1866
paintings: (L) $660; (H) $3,575

GUILLEMOT, Alexandre Charles
French 1786-1831
paintings: (H) $51,750

GUILLERMO, Juan
Spanish 1916-1968
paintings: (H) $2,860

GUILLET-SAGUEZ, Mme. A.
French 19th cent.
paintings: (H) $10,450

GUILLMOT
French 18th/19th cent.
paintings: (H) $3,680

GUILLONNET, Octave Denis Victor
French 1872-1967
paintings: (L) $990; (H) $4,600

GUILLOT, J.
late 19th cent.
sculpture: (H) $770

GUILLOU, Alfred
French 1844-1926
paintings: (H) $8,800

GUINART, Francisco
Spanish 19th/20th cent.
paintings: (H) $9,350

GUINEA, Anselmo de
Italian 1855-1906
paintings: (H) $6,325

GUINO
sculpture: (H) $467

GUINZBURG, Frederic Victor
1897-1978
sculpture: (H) $9,200

GUION, Molly
American b. 1910
paintings: (H) $2,860

GUIPON, Leon
Franco/American 1872-1910
paintings: (H) $357
drawings: (H) $1,430

GUIRAMAND, Paul
French b. 1926
paintings: (L) $1,430; (H) $5,775
drawings: (H) $275
sculpture: (H) $920

GUIRAND DE SCEVOLA, Lucien
Victor
French 1871-1950
paintings: (L) $3,737; (H) $4,600

GUIRANDE, T.D.
French
sculpture: (L) $880; (H) $1,980

GUIRAUD-RIVIERE, Maurice
French b. 1881
sculpture: (L) $2,185; (H) $12,650

GUISE, Marie
French 19th/20th cent.
paintings: (L) $1,540; (H) $1,650

GUITET, James
French b. 1925
drawings: (H) $2,185

GUITTENS, Eugene
paintings: (H) $1,438

GUITTON, Gaston Victor Eduard
Gustave
French 1825-1891
sculpture: (H) $550

GULACY, Paul
paintings: (H) $4,950

GULAGER, Charles
American ac. 1860
paintings: (L) $6,325; (H) $17,250

GULATSI, L.J.
Italian 19th/20th cent.
sculpture: (H) $880

GULDAGER, Christian
Danish/American 1762-1826
paintings: (H) $1,725

GULISEVSKI
Continental 19th cent.
paintings: (H) $29,900

GULIUNY, E***
Continental 19th/20th cent.
paintings: (H) $6,900

GULLAGER, Christian
American 1759-1826
paintings: (H) $1,980

GULLEN, Van
19th cent.
paintings: (H) $1,430

GUMERY, Adolphe Ernest
French b. 1861
paintings: (L) $300; (H) $2,200

GUNDELACH, Matthaus
c. 1566-1654
paintings: (H) $5,500

GUNN, Archie
American 1863-1930
paintings: (L) $3,300; (H) $7,475
drawings: (L) $357; (H) $3,575

GUNSENHAUSER
Continental 19th/20th cent.
drawings: (H) $1,725

GUNTHER
German 20th cent.
paintings: (H) $460

GUNTHER, Erwin Carl Wilhelm
German b. 1864
paintings: (H) $920

GUNTHER, Julius
German b. 1830
paintings: (H) $1,650

GUNTHER, Matthaus
German 1705-1788
drawings: (H) $11,000

GUNTHER, Max
Swedish b. 1934
paintings: (L) $110; (H) $550

GUOSONG, Liu
Chinese b. 1932
drawings: (H) $6,900

GURR, Lena
American b. 1897
paintings: (L) $165; (H) $1,320

GURSCHNER, Gustav
Austrian b. 1873
sculpture: (H) $3,300

GURSKY, Andreas
b. 1955
drawings: (L) $1,760; (H) $9,775

GURVICH, Jose
Lithuanian 1927-1974
paintings: (L) $5,750; (H) $18,700

GUSSONI, Vittorio
Italian 1873-1968
paintings: (L) $633; (H) $1,540

GUSSOW, Bernard
Russian/American 1881-1957
paintings: (L) $209; (H) $2,500
drawings: (L) $55; (H) $412

GUSSOW, Carl
German 1843-1907
paintings: (L) $1,100; (H) $5,750

GUSTAFSON, Sven
paintings: (H) $9,350

GUSTIN, Alfred
drawings: (H) $805

GUSTON, Philip
Canadian/American 1913-1980
paintings: (L) $26,450; (H) $1,056,000
drawings: (L) $4,025; (H) $44,000

GUTE, Herbert Jacob
American 1908-1977
paintings: (H) $2,200
drawings: (L) $247; (H) $275

GUTERSLOH, Albert Paris
Austrian 1887-1973
drawings: (H) $2,760

GUTHERZ, Carl Guthers
American 1844-1907
paintings: (H) $1,320

GUTHRIE, W.D.
English exhib. 1881-1882
paintings: (L) $220; (H) $770

GUTIERREZ, Ernesto
Spanish 20th cent.
paintings: (H) $1,210

GUTIERREZ, Felipe
Columbian 1824-1904
paintings: (H) $34,500

GUTIERREZ, Jose L.
Mexican b. 1900
paintings: (H) $2,750

GUTIERREZ, Oswaldo
paintings: (H) $3,300
drawings: (H) $3,850

GUTIERREZ DE LA VEGA, Jose
Spanish 19th cent.
paintings: (H) $4,887

GUTMAN, Nachum
paintings: (H) $2,750

GUTMAN, Nathan
paintings: (H) $2,750

GUTMANN, Bernhard
American 1869-1936
paintings: (L) $440; (H) $3,850

GUTMEZ (?), N.
drawings: (H) $495

GUTTERO, Alfredo
Argentinean 1882-1932
paintings: (H) $87,750

GUTTUSO, Renato
Italian b. 1912
paintings: (L) $25,300; (H) $66,000
drawings: (L) $1,495; (H) $12,075

GUY, Beresford de
20th cent.
paintings: (H) $1,380

GUY, Francis
American 1760-1820
paintings: (H) $44,000

GUY, James
b. 1909
paintings: (L) $605; (H) $715

GUY, James M.
1910-1963
drawings: (H) $690

GUY, Seymour Joseph
Anglo/American 1824-1910
paintings: (L) $1,092; (H) $103,400

GUYARD, Eugene
French 19th/20th cent.
paintings: (H) $6,900

GUYEI, A.V.
paintings: (H) $495

Psychology

There is a psychology to bidding at auction, to writing a catalogue description, and to placing a reserve. One now-defunct auction house had three categories of condition for their works of art: outstanding, excellent, and good. Very rarely was a piece just ordinary or in poor condition. Many consignors want a strong reserve to protect their property, and estimates can reflect this reserve. (Reserves are suggested by the auction house and agreed upon by the consignor, a reserve is usually two-thirds to three-quarters of the estimate.) A high estimate can scare away bidders; a low estimate can encourage prospective buyers to think, "Oh, what a bargain! I could afford that. I think I'll go to the auction!"

When *Children Roasting Apples by Fireplace with Kitty* by Seymour Joseph Guy (1824-1910) was consigned to auction at Clearing House in Hartford, Connecticut, a very conservative estimate of $14,000 to $22,000 was set. Guy is listed in *Who Was Who in American Art* and Bénézit and was a member of the National Academy. His works, mostly children's portraits and genre scenes, have been exhibited widely. After bidding from the phone and floor, the final hammer price was $94,000 plus a 10 percent buyer's premium—$103,400. (Seymour Joseph Guy, *Children Roasting Apples by Fireplace with Kitty*, oil on canvas, 37 x 30½ inches, Clearing House, June 2, 1995, $103,400)

GUYOT, Antoine Patrice, called Guyot
Le Jeune
b. 1777
paintings: (H) $29,900

GUYOT, Georges Lucien
French 1885-1973
paintings: (L) $302; (H) $2,875
drawings: (H) $1,955

GUYOT, Julie
French ac. early 19th cent.
paintings: (H) $60,250

GUYOT, L.
French 19th/20th cent.
paintings: (H) $575

GUYOT, Louise
French 19th cent.
paintings: (H) $633

GUYS, Constantin
French 1802-1892
paintings: (L) $575; (H) $3,680
drawings: (L) $368; (H) $4,025

GUYS, Constantine
French 1802-1892
paintings: (H) $3,680

GUZMAN, M.
paintings: (H) $57,500

GUZZARDI, Giuseppe
Italian 1845-1914
paintings: (H) $2,090

GUZZARDI, Rudolph G.
Italian 1903-1962
paintings: (L) $49; (H) $770
drawings: (H) $198

GWATHMEY, Robert
American 1903-1988
paintings: (L) $2,530; (H) $33,350
drawings: (L) $1,650; (H) $5,175

GWILT-JOLLEY, Martin
English b. 1859
paintings: (H) $5,750

GWOZDECKI, Gustax
Polish 1880-1935
paintings: (H) $1,430

GYBERSON, Indiana
American 20th cent.
paintings: (H) $805

GYNGELL, Albert E.
English 19th/20th cent.
paintings: (H) $715

GYSBRECHTS, Cornelis Norbertus
Italian ac. late 17th cent.
paintings: (H) $41,250

GYSBRECHTS, Franciscus
Dutch ac. 1674-1677
paintings: (H) $7,150

GYSELAER, Nicolaes de
1590-1654
paintings: (H) $16,500

GYSELINCKX, Joseph
Belgian 19th cent.
paintings: (L) $1,100; (H) $3,520

GYSELMAN, Warner
Dutch 1827-1862
paintings: (H) $2,090

GYSIS, Nicholas
Greek 1842-1901
paintings: (L) $1,870; (H) $37,400
drawings: (L) $385; (H) $5,500

GYULA, Stetka
Hungarian 19th/20th cent.
paintings: (H) $460

HAACKE, Hans
German/American b. 1936
drawings: (H) $3,850

HAAG, Carl
German 1820-1915
drawings: (L) $805; (H) $11,000

HAAG, Charles
Swedish/American 1867-1933
sculpture: (L) $94; (H) $935

HAAG, Jean Paul
French a.c. 1870-1895
paintings: (L) $3,080; (H) $7,150

HAAKSMAN, P.
Dutch 19th cent.
paintings: (H) $690

HAALAND, Lars Laurits
Norwegian 1855-1938
paintings: (H) $6,900

HAANEN, Cecil van
Dutch b. 1844
paintings: (L) $4,887; (H) $21,850

HAANEN, George Gillis
Dutch 1807-1881
paintings: (H) $7,763

HAANEN, Remigius Adrianus van
Dutch 1812-1894
paintings: (L) $24,150; (H) $31,625

HAAPANEN, John Nichols
American b. 1891
paintings: (L) $66; (H) $1,210

HAAS, Johannes Hubertus Leonardus de
Belgian 1832-1908
paintings: (L) $1,035; (H) $5,500
drawings: (H) $275

HAAS, Richard
American b. 1936
drawings: (L) $2,200; (H) $2,475

HAAS, Siegfried
19th/20th cent.
paintings: (H) $1,485

HAASE, ***
19th cent.
drawings: (L) $2,070; (H) $3,105

HAAXMAN, Pieter
Dutch b. 1854
paintings: (H) $34,500

HABERGRITZ, George
American 20th cent.
drawings: (H) $880

HABERLE, John
American 1856-1933
drawings: (L) $83; (H) $825

HABLUTZEL, Karen
American
drawings: (L) $350; (H) $5,000

HACKER, Arthur
British 1858-1919
paintings: (L) $1,320; (H) $3,300

HACKER, Dieter
German b. 1942
paintings: (L) $575; (H) $10,925
drawings: (L) $403; (H) $2,200
sculpture: (L) $1,380; (H) $2,475

HACKER, Horst
German 1842-1906
paintings: (L) $880; (H) $11,000

HACKETT, Mary
American 20th. cent.
paintings: (L) $550; (H) $825

HACKSTOCK, K.
sculpture: (H) $660

HADDART, J.
paintings: (H) $550

HADDOCK, Arthur Earl
American 1895-1980
paintings: (H) $770
drawings: (H) $605

HADDON, Al.
paintings: (H) $450

HADDON, Arthur Trevor
British 1864-1941
paintings: (L) $495; (H) $8,625

HADDON, David W.
British 1884-1914
paintings: (L) $330; (H) $578

HADDON, T.
paintings: (H) $660

HADDON, Wilberforce
British ac. 1880's
paintings: (H) $518

HADE, Pierre
French 20th cent.
paintings: (L) $1,980; (H) $12,650

HADER, Elmer Stanley
American 1889-1973
paintings: (H) $5,500

HADFIELD, Scott
American
sculpture: (L) $825; (H) $1,210

HADJU, Etienne
b. 1907
sculpture: (L) $9,200; (H) $9,775

HADLEY, W.E.
19th/20th cent.
drawings: (H) $1,035

HAEN, V. de
sculpture: (H) $2,750

HAENE, T* de
Dutch 19th cent.
paintings: (H) $880

HAENSBERGEN, Jan van
Dutch 1642-1705
paintings: (L) $3,300; (H) $4,025

HAES, Carlos de
Spanish 1829-1898
paintings: (H) $6,380

HAESELICH, Johann Georg
German 1806-1894
paintings: (H) $2,070

HAFNER, Carl
German 1814-1873
paintings: (H) $3,850

HAFNER, Charles Andrew
American b. 1888
sculpture: (H) $22,000

HAGAN, Frederick
paintings: (H) $2,420

HAGBORG, August
Swedish 1852-1925
paintings: (L) $6,600; (H) $13,200

HAGEDORN, Winkler
paintings: (L) $962; (H) $1,320

HAGEL, Frank
paintings: (L) $990; (H) $2,970
drawings: (L) $770; (H) $1,100

HAGEMAN, Victor Charles
Belgian 19th cent.
paintings: (H) $3,300

HAGEMANN, Godefroy de
French 1820-1877
paintings: (L) $403; (H) $21,275

HAGEMANN, Johann Thomas
German 1771-1853
paintings: (H) $1,150

HAGEMANS, Paul
Belgian 1884-1959
paintings: (H) $2,300

HAGEN, Dingeman van der
Flemish 1610/20- before 1682
paintings: (H) $74,000

HAGEN, John
American 19th cent.
paintings: (H) $575

HAGEN, Van
German 19th/20th cent.
paintings: (H) $715

HAGENAUER, Franz
Austrian b. 1903
sculpture: (L) $1,650; (H) $2,588

HAGERUP, Nels
American 1864-1922
paintings: (L) $412; (H) $2,090
drawings: (H) $770

HAGEY, Henry
paintings: (H) $4,500

HAGG, Jakob
Swedish b. 1839
drawings: (H) $1,210

HAGHE, Louis
Belgian b. 1806, d. London 1885
paintings: (H) $2,200
drawings: (L) $121; (H) $518

HAGIO, Kunio
paintings: (H) $770

HAGN, Ludwig von
German 1819-1898
paintings: (H) $10,450

HAGNY, J.
American 19th cent.
paintings: (H) $1,870

HAGUE, Maurice Stewart
b. 1862
paintings: (H) $660

HAGUE, Michael
drawings: (H) $2,200

HAGUE, Raoul
American b. 1904
sculpture: (H) $16,100

HAGUETTE, Georges Jean Marie
French 1854-1906
drawings: (H) $605

HAHN, Kail William
German/American 1829-1887
paintings: (L) $495; (H) $19,550

HAHS, Philip B.
American 1853-1882
paintings: (L) $880; (H) $8,525
drawings: (H) $770

HAIG, Axel Herman
b.Sweden, ac.London 1835-1921
drawings: (H) $3,850

HAIGH-WOOD, Charles
British 1856-1927
paintings: (H) $3,850

HAILMAN, Johanna K. Woodwill
drawings: (H) $7,150

HAINES, Frederick Stanley
Canadian
paintings: (L) $1,430; (H) $3,300

HAINES, Richard
American b. 1906
paintings: (L) $358; (H) $825

HAINES, William
English 1778-1848
paintings: (H) $550

HAINZ, Johann Georg
German ac. 1660-1770
paintings: (H) $14,300

HAITE, George C.
British 1855-1924
paintings: (H) $1,210

HAITE, W.
English 19th cent.
paintings: (H) $1,100

HAJAMADI, Fariba
20th cent.
paintings: (L) $805; (H) $1,093

HAJDU, Etienne
French b. 1907
sculpture: (L) $550; (H) $14,300

HAKE, Otto Eugene
American b. 1876
paintings: (L) $4,510; (H) $16,500

HALBACH, David
American b. 1931
drawings: (L) $110; (H) $3,300

HALBERSTADT, Ernst
b. 1910
paintings: (H) $880

HALE, Ellen Day
American 1855-1940
paintings: (L) $302; (H) $13,800

HALE, Gardner
1894-1931
paintings: (H) $990

HALE, Hetten Day
drawings: (H) $805

HALE, Lilian Westcott
American 1881-1963
paintings: (L) $550; (H) $48,300
drawings: (L) $575; (H) $16,500

HALE, Philip Leslie
American 1865-1931
paintings: (L) $978; (H) $10,450
drawings: (L) $110; (H) $1,840

HALE, W.
paintings: (H) $1,650

HALE, William Matthew
British b. 1849
drawings: (H) $1,265

HALEY
paintings: (H) $2,420

HALICKA, Alice
Polish 1895-1975
paintings: (H) $1,540

HALIFAX
British 19th cent.
paintings: (H) $460

HALKO, Joe
American b. 1940
sculpture: (L) $1,600; (H) $2,400

HALL, E.W.
19th cent.
paintings: (H) $1,265

HALL, Edith Emma
American b. 1883
paintings: (L) $66; (H) $852

HALL, Frederick Garrison
American 1879-1946
paintings: (L) $83; (H) $2,070
drawings: (H) $690

HALL, G.S.R.
paintings: (H) $3,025

HALL, George Edward
American 19th cent.
paintings: (H) $770

HALL, George Henry
American 1825-1913
paintings: (L) $275; (H) $15,400
drawings: (H) $193

HALL, George Lothian
English 1825-1888
paintings: (H) $1,100

HALL, H. Tom
b. 1932
paintings: (L) $440; (H) $550

HALL, H.R.
English 19th cent.
paintings: (H) $825

HALL, Harold
paintings: (H) $770

HALL, Harry
British 1814-1882
paintings: (L) $1,320; (H) $40,250

HALL, Henry Bryan, Jr.
English/American 19th cent.
paintings: (H) $522

HALL, Henry R.
British 19th cent.
paintings: (L) $330; (H) $852

HALL, J.D.
paintings: (H) $9,350

HALL, Mary
American 20th cent.
paintings: (L) $495; (H) $880

HALL, Peter Adolphe
Swedish 1739-1793
paintings: (H) $880

HALL, R.
paintings: (L) $550; (H) $935

HALLBERG, J. Henry
American 19th cent.
paintings: (H) $495

HALLE, Charles Edward
paintings: (H) $632

HALLE, Noel
French 1711-1781
paintings: (L) $7,150; (H) $11,000

HALLE, Samuel Baruch
French 1824-1889
paintings: (H) $6,600

HALLER, G.
paintings: (H) $660

HALLETT, Hendricks A.
American 1847-1921
paintings: (L) $413; (H) $3,520
drawings: (L) $110; (H) $1,320

HALLEY, Peter
American b. 1953
paintings: (L) $34,500; (H) $134,500

HALLEZ, Paul
French 19th/20th cent.
paintings: (H) $605

HALLIDAY, Edward J.
British 19th/20th cent.
paintings: (H) $2,185

HALLOWELL, George Hawley
American 1871-1926
paintings: (L) $110; (H) $5,750
drawings: (L) $3,335; (H) $5,175

HALM, Christian
German 19th cent.
paintings: (H) $4,400

HALM, Pauline
Austrian b. 1842
paintings: (H) $23,000

HALNON, Frederick James
English 1881-1958
sculpture: (H) $1,980

HALOW (?)
paintings: (H) $1,100

HALPEN, Francis
British 19th cent.
paintings: (H) $4,830

HALPERT, Samuel
American 1884-1930
paintings: (L) $1,430; (H) $13,200
drawings: (L) $3,300; (H) $9,900

HALS, Dirck
Dutch 1591-1656
paintings: (L) $5,175; (H) $32,200

HALS, Frans
Dutch 1580-1666
paintings: (L) $5,720; (H) $264,000

HALSALL, William Formby
American 1841-1919
paintings: (L) $440; (H) $5,500
drawings: (L) $192; (H) $605

HALSWELLE, Keeley
British 1832-1891
paintings: (L) $1,870; (H) $8,250

HALVERSON, Jean
drawings: (L) $400; (H) $1,500

HAMADA, Shoji
Japanese 1894-1978
sculpture: (H) $4,600

HAMBLEN, Robert
American 20th cent.
paintings: (H) $489

HAMBLEN, Sturtevant
American ac. c. 1837-1856
paintings: (H) $189,500

HAMBLER, Richard
20th cent.
paintings: (H) $467

HAMBLETON, Richard
b. 1954
paintings: (L) $58; (H) $3,300

HAMBOURG, Andre
French b. 1909
paintings: (L) $1,150; (H) $24,200
drawings: (L) $715; (H) $3,450

HAMBUCH, Carl W.
b. Germany d. U.S. 1879
paintings: (H) $145,500

HAMBURGER, ***
British 19th/20th cent.
paintings: (H) $633

HAMEL, Jr.
English 19th cent.
paintings: (H) $990

HAMEL, Adolphe
German b. 1820
paintings: (H) $3,300

HAMELIN, Jacques Gustave
French b. 1809
drawings: (H) $1,100

HAMEN Y LEON, Juan van der
Spanish 1596-1632
paintings: (H) $497,500

HAMILL
19th/20th cent.
drawings: (H) $550

HAMILTON, Edward Wilbur Dean
American 1862/64-1943
paintings: (L) $805; (H) $16,100
drawings: (H) $4,888

HAMILTON, F.A.
American 19th/20th cent.
paintings: (L) $165; (H) $495

HAMILTON, Ferdinand Philipp von
German 1664-1750
paintings: (H) $3,025

HAMILTON, Gavin
English 1723-1798
paintings: (H) $40,250

HAMILTON, Gawen
English 1697-1773
paintings: (H) $5,750

HAMILTON, Hamilton
Anglo/American 1847-1928
paintings: (L) $495; (H) $30,800
drawings: (H) $110

HAMILTON, J.
paintings: (L) $275; (H) $690

HAMILTON, James
American 1819-1878
paintings: (L) $605; (H) $7,700
drawings: (L) $275; (H) $880

HAMILTON, James
American c. 1850
paintings: (L) $792; (H) $4,400

HAMILTON, James
British
drawings: (H) $1,980

HAMILTON, James
British 1645?-1705?
paintings: (L) $1,650; (H) $7,700
drawings: (H) $605

HAMILTON, James
Irish/American 1819-1878
paintings: (L) $605; (H) $4,400

HAMILTON, James Whitelaw
Scottish 1860-1932
paintings: (H) $770

HAMILTON, John McClure
American 1853-1939
paintings: (L) $402; (H) $39,600
drawings: (L) $385; (H) $1,760

HAMILTON, Juan
sculpture: (L) $5,175; (H) $7,475

HAMILTON, L.
American 20th cent.
paintings: (H) $825

HAMILTON, Phillipp Ferdinand de
Flemish 1664-1750
paintings: (H) $3,738

HAMILTON, Wilbur Dean
American 1862/64-1943
paintings: (H) $550

HAMILTON, William R.
1810-1865
paintings: (H) $2,415

HAMLIN, Edith
American b. 1902
paintings: (L) $577; (H) $1,725

HAMLIN-WATSON
paintings: (H) $550

HAMMAN, Edouard Michel Ferdinand
French 19th/20th cent.
paintings: (H) $4,400

HAMME, Alexis van
Belgian 1818-1875
paintings: (L) $4,600; (H) $12,100

HAMMER, Hans Jorgen
Danish 1815-1882
paintings: (H) $4,950

HAMMER, John J.
German/American 1842-1906
paintings: (L) $440; (H) $9,900

HAMMER, William
Danish 1821-1889
paintings: (L) $46,000; (H) $118,000

HAMMERAS, Ralph
American 20th cent.
paintings: (L) $550; (H) $660

HAMMERSEN, W***
19th/20th cent.
paintings: (H) $1,840

HAMMERSHOI, Vilhelm
Danish 1864-1916
paintings: (H) $101,500

HAMMERSLOUGH, Ruth Helprin
American b. 1883
drawings: (H) $690

HAMMERSTAD, Johann J.
American 1842-1906
paintings: (H) $2,200

HAMMERSTAD, John H.
paintings: (L) $247; (H) $1,550

HAMMERSTAD, John O.
b. Norway 1842 d. U.S. 1925
paintings: (L) $55; (H) $550

HAMMON
Continental 20th cent.
paintings: (H) $805

HAMMOND, Arthur J.
American 1875-1947
paintings: (L) $55; (H) $660
drawings: (L) $88; (H) $258

HAMMOND, Horace
British ac. 1902-1939
drawings: (H) $495

HAMMOND, Jane
American b. 1950
paintings: (L) $550; (H) $6,325

HAMMOND, John A.
Canadian 1843-1939
paintings: (L) $1,045; (H) $2,640

HAMMOND, Jonathan
drawings: (H) $3,450

HAMMOND, Robert John
British ac. 1882-1911
paintings: (L) $1,650; (H) $4,400

HAMMONS, David
American b. 1943
drawings: (L) $5,750; (H) $7,150

HAMON, Jean Louis
French 1821-1874
paintings: (H) $5,500

HAMPSON, Albert W.
1911-1990
paintings: (H) $3,300

HAMPTON, John
American b. 1918
paintings: (L) $2,200; (H) $4,180
drawings: (L) $460; (H) $2,750
sculpture: (L) $5,500; (H) $6,710

HAMSCOM, Trude
American 20th cent.
paintings: (H) $575

HAMZA, Johann
German 1850-1927
paintings: (L) $2,645; (H) $31,625

HAN, Raymond
b. 1931
paintings: (H) $5,175

HANAU, Jean
French b. 1899
paintings: (H) $748

HANCK, Sophie
19th/20th cent.
paintings: (H) $1,485

HANCOCK, Charles
British 1793-1855
paintings: (H) $8,050

HANCOCK, John
British 1808-1890
drawings: (H) $495

HANCOCK, Mildred L.
British ac. 1890-1893
paintings: (H) $9,200

HAND, Donald
American 20th cent.
sculpture: (H) $1,100

HAND, I.
English 19th cent.
paintings: (H) $7,700

HAND, Roch
20th cent.
paintings: (H) $460

HAND, Thomas
English d. c. 1804
paintings: (L) $1,430; (H) $4,125

HANDL, Milan
sculpture: (H) $880

HANDLEN
20th cent.
paintings: (H) $517

HANDLEY-READ, E.
British 1870-1935
drawings: (H) $3,300

HANDMANN, Emmanuel Jakob
1718-1781
paintings: (H) $1,380

HANE, Roger
1938-1974
paintings: (L) $330; (H) $660

HANET, Joan
paintings: (H) $805

HANGELL
paintings: (H) $1,100

HANGER, Max
German 1874-1955
paintings: (H) $715

HANISCH, Aloys
Austrian 1866-1937
paintings: (H) $1,495

HANISS, A.L.
French 19th/20th cent.
drawings: (H) $468

HANKE, August
Austrian early 20th cent.
drawings: (H) $3,300

HANKE-FORSTER, Ursula
20th cent.
sculpture: (H) $1,150

HANKEY, William Lee
English 1869-1952
paintings: (L) $3,738; (H) $15,950
drawings: (L) $660; (H) $11,500

HANKIN, Abraham
American 20th cent.
paintings: (H) $577

HANKINS, Abraham
Russian/American 1903-1963
paintings: (L) $165; (H) $880
drawings: (L) $176; (H) $495

HANKINS, Cornelius H.
American 1864-1946
paintings: (L) $575; (H) $2,475

HANKS, Jarvis F.
1799-c. 1852
paintings: (H) $1,980

HANLEY, F.
drawings: (H) $1,320

HANNA, David
American 1941-1981
drawings: (H) $1,100

HANNA, K.J.
paintings: (H) $550

HANNA, R.J.
American
paintings: (H) $450

HANNA, Thomas King
American 1872-1957
paintings: (L) $275; (H) $605

HANNAFORD, M.
paintings: (H) $550

HANNAH, Duncan
American b. 1952
paintings: (H) $2,415

HANNAUX, Emmanuel
French b. 1855
sculpture: (L) $990; (H) $17,250

HANNIG, Henry C.
American 19th/20th cent.
paintings: (L) $58; (H) $632

HANNINGTON
paintings: (H) $1,430

HANNIS
American 19th cent.
paintings: (H) $1,870

HANOTEAU, Hector
French 1823-1890
paintings: (L) $1,320; (H) $4,600

HANRIOT, Jacques
French 20th cent.
paintings: (H) $467

HANRIOT, Jules Armand
French b. 1857
paintings: (H) $3,300

HANSEN, Al
American b. 1924
paintings: (H) $550

HANSEN, Armin Carl
American 1886-1957
paintings: (L) $1,610; (H) $60,500
drawings: (L) $660; (H) $5,225

HANSEN, Ejnar
Danish/American 1884-1965
paintings: (L) $247; (H) $4,950
drawings: (H) $275

HANSEN, Gaylen
b. 1921
paintings: (H) $1,725

HANSEN, Gordon
American 20th cent.
paintings: (L) $385; (H) $1,980
drawings: (H) $165

HANSEN, H.
Continental 19th cent.
paintings: (H) $2,200

HANSEN, Hans
British b. 1870
drawings: (L) $460; (H) $1,035

HANSEN, Heinrich
Danish 1821-1880
paintings: (L) $3,450; (H) $34,500

HANSEN, Herman Wendelborg
German/American 1854-1924
paintings: (H) $2,750
drawings: (L) $3,737; (H) $41,250

HANSEN, J.F.
Danish/American early 20th cent.
paintings: (L) $99; (H) $550

HANSEN, Jan
American contemporary
paintings: (H) $550

HANSEN, John F.
Danish School ac. 1900-1920
paintings: (L) $220; (H) $5,500

HANSEN, Josef Theodor
Danish 1848-1912
paintings: (L) $3,335; (H) $21,850

HANSEN, Knut
Danish b. 1876
drawings: (H) $1,380

HANSEN, Niels Christian
Danish 1834-1922
paintings: (H) $4,025

HANSEN, Nils E.
American 20th cent.
paintings: (H) $770

HANSEN, Steve
sculpture: (H) $690

HANSON, Ann
drawings: (H) $2,300

HANSON, Duane
American b. 1925
sculpture: (L) $38,500; (H) $140,000

HANSON, James
American 20th cent.
paintings: (H) $1,650

HANSON, Mary
drawings: (H) $3,300

HANSON, Peter
American 1821-1887
paintings: (H) $4,950

HANSON, R.
Continental 19th/20th cent.
paintings: (H) $3,850

HANSON, W.
American 20th cent.
paintings: (H) $550

HANSTEEN, Nils Severin Lynge
Norwegian 1855-1912
paintings: (H) $1,760

HANTAI, Simon
b. Hungary 1922
paintings: (H) $36,300

HANTMAN, Carl
b. 1935
paintings: (L) $1,650; (H) $2,200

HANYA, G.
Continental 19th cent.
paintings: (H) $605

HAPPEL, Carl J.
German/American 1819-1914
paintings: (H) $5,750

HAQUETTE, Georges Jean Marie
French 1854-1906
paintings: (L) $1,045; (H) $7,425
drawings: (H) $1,380

HARCOURT, George
British 1868-1947
paintings: (H) $37,375

HARDAKER, Charles
paintings: (H) $660

HARDENBERGH, Gerard R.
19th cent.
drawings: (L) $578; (H) $2,750

HARDERS, H.
sculpture: (L) $257; (H) $1,380

HARDEY, Mrs. Richard
paintings: (H) $2,588

HARDIE, Robert Gordon
American 1854-1904
paintings: (H) $4,400

HARDIME, Pieter
Flemish 1677/78-c. 1758
paintings: (L) $15,400; (H) $38,500

HARDIN, Helen
Native American 1946-1984
paintings: (H) $1,980

HARDING, Chester
American 1792-1866
paintings: (L) $748; (H) $825

HARDING, Frederic
English
drawings: (H) $880

HARDING, Mary E.
English ac. 1880-1893
paintings: (H) $4,510

HARDMAN, John
English 19th cent.
paintings: (H) $2,640

HARDMAN, Thomas Hawthorn
paintings: (H) $1,210

HARDWICK, Melbourne H.
American 1857-1916
paintings: (L) $193; (H) $2,310
drawings: (L) $44; (H) $1,840

HARDY, Anna Elizabeth
American 1839-1934
paintings: (L) $1,045; (H) $5,060

HARDY, David
British ac. 1855-1870
paintings: (H) $1,092

HARDY, David A.
drawings: (L) $690; (H) $690

HARDY, DeWitt
American b. 1940
drawings: (L) $440; (H) $1,495

HARDY, Dudley
English c. 1866-1922
paintings: (L) $575; (H) $1,925
drawings: (L) $440; (H) $4,025

HARDY, Frederick Daniel
British 1826-1911
paintings: (L) $1,870; (H) $13,200
drawings: (H) $605

HARDY, Heywood
English 1843-1932
paintings: (L) $288; (H) $60,500

HARDY, Heywood and Frank
WALTON
paintings: (H) $13,200

HARDY, J.P.
paintings: (H) $1,840

HARDY, James, Jr.
English 1832-1889
paintings: (L) $3,575; (H) $60,250

HARDY, Jeremiah P.
1800-1887
paintings: (H) $3,300

HARDY, Pat
drawings: (L) $66; (H) $460

HARDY, T.
paintings: (H) $1,650

HARDY, T.B.
drawings: (H) $825

HARDY, Thomas
ac. late 18th cent.
paintings: (H) $4,400

HARDY, Thomas Bush
English 1842-1897
paintings: (L) $1,320; (H) $1,320
drawings: (L) $660; (H) $2,860

HARDY, W.F.
British 19th cent.
paintings: (H) $1,300

HARE, Channing
American 1899-1976
paintings: (L) $220; (H) $1,210

HARE, David
American b. 1917
drawings: (H) $1,980

HARE, John Knowles
American 1884-1947
paintings: (L) $110; (H) $1,430
drawings: (L) $49; (H) $1,210

HARE, Julius
English 1859-1932
paintings: (L) $825; (H) $8,250

HARE, William
American ac. 1842-1859
paintings: (H) $5,290

HARGAS,
paintings: (H) $660

HARGRAVE, H.S.
American 1871-1965
paintings: (H) $660

HARIA, Josef
20th cent.
paintings: (H) $1,210

HARING, Keith
American 1958-1990
paintings: (L) $2,300; (H) $104,500
drawings: (L) $165; (H) $46,200
sculpture: (L) $2,300; (H) $60,500

HARING, Keith and Martin ROY
20th cent.
drawings: (H) $3,520

HARING, Keith, and L.A. 2
paintings: (H) $20,900
drawings: (H) $10,350
sculpture: (L) $5,175; (H) $22,000

HARITONOFF, Nicolas B.
Russian 1880-1944
paintings: (L) $385; (H) $2,640

HARLE, Jacob
paintings: (H) $1,320

HARLES, Victor Joseph
American 1894-1975
paintings: (L) $77; (H) $2,588

HARLESTON, Edwin
American 1882-1931
paintings: (H) $550

HARLOR, Joseph
English 19th cent.
paintings: (H) $2,200

HARLOW, George Henry
English 1787-1819
paintings: (L) $2,200; (H) $43,700
drawings: (H) $2,300

HARLOW, Louis K.
American 1850-1930
drawings: (L) $11; (H) $719

HARMENON, Eugene Scipion d'
French b. 1825
paintings: (H) $2,860

HARMER, Alexander F.
American 1856-1925
paintings: (H) $7,700
drawings: (H) $633

HARMON, Annie Lyle
American 1855-1930
paintings: (L) $220; (H) $1,980

HARMON, James
sculpture: (H) $550

HARMON, Lily
paintings: (H) $605
drawings: (H) $385

HARNETT, William M.
American 1848/51-1892
paintings: (L) $34,500; (H) $123,500
drawings: (L) $1,380; (H) $1,650

HARNEY, Paul E.
American 1850-1915
paintings: (L) $132; (H) $990
drawings: (H) $288

HARNISCH, Albert E.
American 19th cent.
sculpture: (H) $460

HARPER, J.
Austrian 19th cent.
paintings: (H) $660

HARPER, William
American b. 1944
paintings: (H) $2,420

HARPIGNIES, Henri Joseph
French 1819-1916
paintings: (L) $1,320; (H) $35,200
drawings: (L) $978; (H) $25,300

HARPSAU
paintings: (L) $1,045; (H) $1,045

HARR, Julian
American contemporary
sculpture: (H) $880

HARRER, Hugo Paul
German 1836-1876
paintings: (H) $5,060

HARRILL, James
paintings: (H) $920

HARRINGTON, Addie A.
American
paintings: (H) $7,425

HARRINGTON, Charles
English 1865-1943
drawings: (H) $2,070

HARRINGTON, George W.
American 1833-1911
paintings: (L) $385; (H) $605

HARRINGTON, J.
British 19th cent.
paintings: (H) $2,990

HARRIS, Charles Gordon
American b. 1891
paintings: (L) $275; (H) $1,430
drawings: (H) $138

HARRIS, Charles X.
American b. 1856
paintings: (H) $47,150

HARRIS, Conley
paintings: (H) $3,190

HARRIS, Dan
American 20th cent.
drawings: (H) $690

HARRIS, Edwin
British 1855-1906
paintings: (L) $825; (H) $27,600

HARRIS, F. H. Howard
English School 19th cent.
paintings: (H) $1,980

HARRIS, George F.
American
paintings: (H) $3,410

HARRIS, H.J.
paintings: (H) $660
drawings: (L) $275; (H) $550

HARRIS, Henry
British 1805-1865
paintings: (H) $935

HARRIS, Lawren Stewart
Canadian 1885-1970
paintings: (L) $6,600; (H) $286,000

HARRIS, Marion D.
American b. 1904
paintings: (L) $165; (H) $880
drawings: (H) $550

HARRIS, Robert
paintings: (H) $3,300

HARRIS, Robert George
American b. 1911
paintings: (H) $880

HARRIS, Robert M.
American ac. 1930s
paintings: (L) $55; (H) $605

HARRIS, Sam Hyde
American 1889-1977
paintings: (L) $468; (H) $6,600

HARRIS, William E.
British ac. 1882-1931
paintings: (L) $715; (H) $2,530

HARRIS, William E.
English 19th cent.
paintings: (H) $2,300

HARRISON, Allen
paintings: (H) $1,760

HARRISON, George L.
British ac. 1878-1883
paintings: (H) $2,645

HARRISON, Henry
American 1844-1923
paintings: (H) $660

HARRISON, John C.
British 1898-1985
drawings: (L) $770; (H) $3,300

HARRISON, Lowell Birge
American 1854-1929
paintings: (L) $165; (H) $7,150

HARRISON, Mark Robert
1819-1894
paintings: (L) $2,200; (H) $4,125

HARRISON, Rex
b. England 1908 d. 1990
paintings: (L) $192; (H) $1,320
drawings: (L) $220; (H) $687

HARRISON, Ted
b. 1926
paintings: (L) $1,705; (H) $2,310

HARRISON, Thomas Alexander
American 1853-1930
paintings: (L) $330; (H) $5,175

HARRISON, William H.
19th/20th cent.
paintings: (L) $605; (H) $935

HARROWING, Waller
British 19th cent.
paintings: (H) $467

HARROWING, Walter
English ac. 1877-1904
paintings: (L) $2,070; (H) $4,400

HARSH, Fred Dana
American
paintings: (H) $1,100

HARSHE, Robert Bartholow
American b. 1879
paintings: (L) $173; (H) $4,180

HARSING, Wilhelm
German b. 1861
paintings: (H) $2,200

HART, Claudia
b. 1955
drawings: (L) $115; (H) $3,850
sculpture: (H) $58

HART, Frederick
American 20th cent.
sculpture: (H) $1,150

HART, George Overbury, called Pop
American 1868-1933
paintings: (H) $805
drawings: (L) $550; (H) $1,870

HART, Henrietta
paintings: (H) $805

HART, James McDougal
American 1828-1901
paintings: (L) $660; (H) $28,750
drawings: (L) $115; (H) $1,380

HART, Joel Tanner
American 1810-1877
sculpture: (H) $9,075

HART, Marie Theresa Gorsuch
American 1829-1921
paintings: (H) $4,830

HART, Mary Theresa
American b. 1872
paintings: (H) $460

HART, Mrs. Robert
French c. 1680-1733/40
paintings: (H) $770

HART, S.
American/European 20th cent.
sculpture: (H) $770

HART, W.
British 19th cent.
drawings: (H) $880

HART, W.H.
American 19th cent.
paintings: (H) $450

HART, William
paintings: (L) $1,540; (H) $8,690
drawings: (H) $192

HART, William
British 1882-1901
paintings: (L) $1,375; (H) $1,870

HART, William M.
American 1823-1894
paintings: (L) $770; (H) $13,800
drawings: (L) $132; (H) $690

HART, William Matthew
British 1830-1908
drawings: (H) $2,530

HARTER, Thomas John
American 1905-1981
paintings: (H) $715

HARTIG, Hans
German b. 1873
paintings: (L) $220; (H) $1,540

HARTIGAN, Grace
American b. 1922
paintings: (L) $575; (H) $20,700
drawings: (L) $2,875; (H) $3,680

HARTINGER, Anton
Austrian 1806-1890
paintings: (L) $23,100; (H) $55,000

HARTLAND, Henry Albert
British 1840-1893
drawings: (H) $690

HARTLEY
sculpture: (H) $660

HARTLEY, George
English 19th cent.
paintings: (H) $605

HARTLEY, Jonathan Scott
American 1845-1912
sculpture: (L) $977; (H) $8,050

HARTLEY, Marsden
American 1877-1943
paintings: (L) $10,450; (H) $1,155,000
drawings: (L) $1,210; (H) $43,125

HARTLEY, Rachel V.
American b. 1884
paintings: (L) $1,210; (H) $2,090
drawings: (L) $38; (H) $1,650

HARTMAN, ***
German 19th/20th cent.
paintings: (H) $12,650

HARTMAN, Bertram
American 1882-1960
paintings: (L) $528; (H) $1,610
drawings: (L) $83; (H) $1,760

HARTMAN, George
American d. 1934
paintings: (H) $825

HARTMAN, K.
American 20th cent.
paintings: (H) $518

HARTMAN, Melvin
paintings: (H) $660

HARTMANN, C.
German 19th cent.
paintings: (H) $1,430

HARTMANN, Ludwig
German 1835-1902
paintings: (L) $16,500; (H) $71,250

HARTMANN, Mathias Christoph
German 1791-1839
drawings: (H) $990

HARTSELL, P.
paintings: (L) $440; (H) $990

HARTSON, Walter C.
American b. 1866
paintings: (L) $193; (H) $2,310
drawings: (L) $275; (H) $345

HARTUNG, Hans
German 1904-1989
paintings: (L) $19,800; (H) $104,500
drawings: (L) $4,400; (H) $38,500

HARTUNG, J.
German 19th/20th cent.
paintings: (L) $275; (H) $8,050

HARTUNG, Johann
German ac. 1846-1854
paintings: (L) $1,870; (H) $4,025
drawings: (H) $1,650

HARTWELL, George
American 1891-1949
paintings: (H) $16,500

HARTWELL, George G.
American 1815-1901
paintings: (L) $1,540; (H) $37,950

HARTWICH, Herman
American 1853-1926
paintings: (L) $220; (H) $60,500

HARTWIG, Cleo
1918-1988
sculpture: (L) $1,035; (H) $1,265

HARTWIG, Heinie
American b. 1937
paintings: (L) $247; (H) $3,300

HARVARD, James
b. 1937
drawings: (H) $4,830

HARVEY, Bessie
b. 1929
paintings: (H) $1,760

HARVEY, Eli
American 1860-1957
sculpture: (L) $1,760; (H) $2,875

HARVEY, G.
American b. 1933
paintings: (L) $3,190; (H) $82,500
sculpture: (L) $2,640; (H) $4,950

HARVEY, George
1799-1878
paintings: (H) $550

HARVEY, George
19th/20th cent.
paintings: (H) $575

HARVEY, George
American 19th cent.
paintings: (H) $13,200

HARVEY, George
American c. 1800-1878
paintings: (L) $385; (H) $30,800
drawings: (L) $440; (H) $13,800

HARVEY, George W.
American 1835-1920
paintings: (L) $1,430; (H) $1,980
drawings: (L) $88; (H) $440

HARVEY, George Wainwright
American b. 1855
paintings: (L) $660; (H) $2,420

HARVEY, Gerald
American b. 1933
paintings: (H) $23,000

HARVEY, H.J.
English 19th cent.
paintings: (H) $3,080

HARVEY, Henry T.
American
paintings: (L) $137; (H) $518

HARVEY, Sir George
British 1806-1876
paintings: (L) $1,725; (H) $5,175

HARWAY, J.
British 19th cent.
paintings: (H) $4,600

HARWEY, J.
British 19th/20th cent.
paintings: (H) $880

HARWOOD, Burt S.
American 1897-1924
paintings: (H) $660

HARWOOD, Francis
British ac. 1748-1783
sculpture: (H) $57,500

HAS, H.
ac. 1517-1548
paintings: (H) $46,200

HASCH, Carl
Austrian 1834/35-1897
paintings: (L) $1,100; (H) $5,225

HASELTINE, Charles Field
American b. 1840
paintings: (H) $825

HASELTINE, Herbert
American 1877-1962
sculpture: (L) $1,610; (H) $178,500

HASELTINE, William Stanley
American 1835-1900
paintings: (L) $660; (H) $29,700
drawings: (L) $302; (H) $2,750

HASEN, Irwin
American
drawings: (L) $747; (H) $1,150

HASENFUS, Richard C.
paintings: (L) $2,420; (H) $3,300

HASHAGEN, Antonio
American 19th cent.
paintings: (H) $5,775

HASILOWSKI, C.Z.
paintings: (H) $1,650

HASLAM, Ron
paintings: (H) $1,100

HASLEHUST, Ernest William
English 1866-1949
drawings: (L) $632; (H) $825

HASLENO, S.
Continental School 19th cent.
paintings: (H) $660

HASSALL, John
English 1868-1948
drawings: (H) $550

HASSAM, Frederick Childe
American 1859-1935
paintings: (L) $4,312; (H) $5,502,500
drawings: (L) $522; (H) $825,000
sculpture: (H) $6,600

HASSAN, E.
paintings: (H) $550

HASSE, Jeanne
sculpture: (H) $935

HASSELBACH, Wilhelm
German b. 1846
paintings: (H) $6,325

HASSELL, Hilton MacDonald
paintings: (H) $1,210

HASSELT, Willem van
Dutch 1882-1963
paintings: (L) $1,610; (H) $7,700

HASSLER, Carl von
American 1887-1962
paintings: (H) $2,310

HASTINGS, Howard L.
paintings: (L) $275; (H) $935

HASTINGS, T. Mitchell
American 20th cent.
paintings: (H) $1,045

HATFIELD, Joseph Henry
American 1863-1928
paintings: (L) $523; (H) $4,125

HATHAWAY, George M.
American c. 1852-1903
paintings: (L) $165; (H) $5,720
drawings: (L) $220; (H) $1,210

HATHAWAY, James S.
paintings: (H) $990

HATHAWAY, Rufus
American 1770-1822
paintings: (L) $23,100; (H) $59,700

HATTON, W.S.
drawings: (H) $661

HATVANY, Baron de Ferencz
Hungarian b. 1881
paintings: (H) $4,830

HATVANY, Christa Winsloe
sculpture: (L) $863; (H) $4,600

HAUBTMANN, Michael
Czechoslovakian 1843-1921
paintings: (L) $660; (H) $2,090

HAUDEBOURT, Antoinette Cecile
Hortense, Antoinette LESCOT
French 1784-1845
paintings: (H) $42,550

HAUGH, George
British ac. 1777-1818
paintings: (H) $880

HAUGHTON, Moses
British 1734-1804
paintings: (H) $10,450

HAUMONT, Emile Richard
French 19th cent.
paintings: (H) $5,500

HAUNOLD, Karl Franz Emanuel
Austrian 1832-1911
paintings: (H) $4,600

HAUPTMANN, Karl
German 1880-1947
paintings: (L) $575; (H) $1,210

HAUSDORF, George
paintings: (H) $770

HAUSER, John
American 1858/59-1913/18
paintings: (L) $935; (H) $8,800
drawings: (L) $330; (H) $8,800

HAUSER, K. Rex
German 19th cent.
paintings: (H) $1,650

HAUSHALTER, George M.
American b. 1862
paintings: (H) $495
drawings: (L) $110; (H) $495

HAUSHOFER, Maximilian
German 1811-1866
paintings: (H) $32,200

HAUSLEIGHTER, Rudolph
Austrian 19th/20th cent.
paintings: (H) $2,750

HAUSMANN, Gustav
German 1827-1899
paintings: (H) $3,300

HAUSMANN, W.
paintings: (H) $550

HAUSROF, George
paintings: (H) $1,100

HAVALL, Alfred Charles
1855-1928
paintings: (H) $935

HAVARD, James
American b. 1937
paintings: (L) $1,093; (H) $19,800
drawings: (L) $308; (H) $3,850

HAVELL, Edmund, Jr.
English 1819-after 1895
paintings: (H) $11,500

HAVELL, G***
Continental 19th cent.
paintings: (H) $3,565

HAVELL, Robert, Jr.
English 1793-1878
paintings: (H) $2,200

HAVEMEYER, Frederick C., II
paintings: (H) $3,850

HAVEN, B.J. von
paintings: (H) $6,325

HAVENER, J.J.
Continental 19th/20th cent.
paintings: (H) $2,640

HAVENITH, Hugo
English b. 1853
paintings: (H) $2,640

HAVENS, James D.
American 1900-1960
paintings: (L) $440; (H) $523

HAVERKAMP, Wilhelm
German b. 1864
sculpture: (H) $1,955

HAVRE, Antoine Roux
French 1765-1835
drawings: (H) $2,200

HAVRET, Pierre
20th cent.
paintings: (H) $825

HAWEIS, Stephen
1878-1969
paintings: (L) $1,380; (H) $1,380
drawings: (H) $110

HAWES, Charles "Bud"
drawings: (H) $1,430

HAWK, William
American contemporary
drawings: (L) $58; (H) $863

HAWKINS, Louis Welden
British 1849-1910
paintings: (H) $880

HAWKINS, P.R.
20th cent.
paintings: (H) $825

HAWKINS, Rocky L.
paintings: (H) $1,705
drawings: (H) $1,000

HAWKINS, William L.
American 1895-1990
paintings: (L) $3,300; (H) $33,350

HAWKS, Rachel Marshall
American b. 1879
sculpture: (H) $30,800

HAWKSLEY, Dorothy
American 19th/20th cent.
drawings: (H) $2,200

HAWLEY, Hughson
Anglo/American 1850-1936
drawings: (L) $495; (H) $4,400

HAWORTH, Bobs Coghill
paintings: (L) $1,045; (H) $3,025

HAWORTH, Edith E.
American 20th cent.
paintings: (H) $467

HAWORTH, Peter
drawings: (L) $770; (H) $2,420

HAWTHORNE, Charles W.
American 1872-1930
paintings: (L) $1,430; (H) $26,450

HAWTHORNE, Marion C.
American 1870-1945
paintings: (H) $660
drawings: (L) $1,100; (H) $1,650

HAXTON, Elaine Alys
Australian b. 1909
drawings: (H) $1,320

HAY, Bernard
English b. 1864
paintings: (L) $990; (H) $7,475

HAY, Jane Benham
English 1820-1870
paintings: (H) $15,950

HAY, Peter Alexander
Scottish 1866-1952
drawings: (H) $2,475

HAY, Sir George
English 1831-1912
paintings: (H) $1,430

HAYAKAWA, Miki
1904-1953
paintings: (L) $2,185; (H) $3,450

HAYDEN, C.H.
paintings: (H) $1,650

HAYDEN, Carl
20th cent.
paintings: (H) $880

HAYDEN, Ch.
paintings: (H) $1,400

HAYDEN, Edward Parker
American b. 1922
paintings: (L) $660; (H) $2,200

HAYDEN, Henri
French 1883-1970
paintings: (L) $5,500; (H) $29,700
drawings: (H) $1,980

HAYDEN, J.P.
American 19th cent.
paintings: (H) $1,100

HAYDEN, Palmer
drawings: (H) $1,100

HAYDEN, Vanda
paintings: (H) $523

HAYEK, Hans von
Austrian 1869-1940
paintings: (H) $1,320

HAYES, Claude
Irish 1852-1922
drawings: (L) $201; (H) $715

HAYES, David
sculpture: (H) $1,955

HAYES, Edd
b. 1945
sculpture: (H) $2,970

HAYES, Edwin
Irish 1819/20-1904
paintings: (L) $1,320; (H) $2,587

HAYES, J.W.
British 19th cent.
paintings: (H) $6,900

HAYES, John
British 19th cent.
paintings: (H) $8,050

HAYES, W.
paintings: (H) $1,035

HAYET, Louis
French 1864-1940
paintings: (H) $10,350

HAYLLAR, James
English 1829-1920
paintings: (L) $357; (H) $11,825
drawings: (H) $12,100

HAYLLAR, Jessica
British 1858-1940
paintings: (L) $6,900; (H) $22,000

HAYMAN, Francis
English 1708-1776
paintings: (H) $39,600

HAYNES, G.
British 19th/20th cent
paintings: (H) $2,760

HAYNES, John William
English 1834-1908
paintings: (L) $990; (H) $2,750

HAYNES, Ron
American
paintings: (H) $1,600

HAYS, Barton S.
American 1826-1914
paintings: (L) $522; (H) $8,580

HAYS, George A.
American b. 1854
paintings: (L) $138; (H) $4,950
drawings: (L) $193; (H) $880

HAYS, Lee
American 1854-1946
paintings: (H) $605

HAYS, William Jacob
American 1830-1875
paintings: (L) $440; (H) $1,320

HAYTER, Stanley William
English 1901-1988
paintings: (L) $1,725; (H) $16,500
drawings: (L) $715; (H) $3,080

HAYWARD, Alfred Frederick William
British 1856-1939
paintings: (H) $522

HAYWARD, E.M.
paintings: (H) $605

HAYWARD, Joshua Henshaw
American 19th cent.
paintings: (H) $1,980

HAYWARD, Peter
American b. 1905
paintings: (L) $137; (H) $460
sculpture: (H) $176

HAZARD, Arthur Merton
American 1872-1930
paintings: (L) $385; (H) $3,025
drawings: (L) $55; (H) $220

HAZARD, James
English 1748-1987
paintings: (H) $3,025

HAZELTON, Mary Brewster
American 1868-1953
paintings: (L) $403; (H) $6,050
drawings: (H) $1,150

HE, An
Chinese b. 1957
paintings: (H) $660

HEAD, Don
American 20th cent.
paintings: (H) $825

HEAD, John Loren
paintings: (L) $192; (H) $935

HEADE, Martin Johnson
American 1819-1904
paintings: (L) $12,100; (H) $717,500
drawings: (L) $27,600; (H) $41,250

HEADERMAN, N.
paintings: (L) $248; (H) $700

HEALD
drawings: (H) $575

HEALY, B.C.
American 19th/20th cent.
paintings: (L) $104; (H) $467

HEALY, George Peter Alexander
American 1808/13-1894
paintings: (L) $805; (H) $1,430

HEAPHY, Thomas Frank
British 1813-1873
paintings: (H) $460

HEARD, Joseph
English 1799-1859
paintings: (L) $1,725; (H) $7,188

HEATH, F.L.
19th cent.
paintings: (L) $550; (H) $770

HEATH, Howard
b. 1879
paintings: (H) $1,705
drawings: (H) $550

HEATH, Susan
American b. 1798
drawings: (H) $20,700

HEATHCOCK, Walter
b. 1903
paintings: (H) $2,300

HEATON, E.
English 19th cent.
paintings: (H) $522

HEATON, Maurice
American b. 1900
sculpture: (H) $1,430

HEBALD, Milton
American b. 1917
drawings: (H) $230
sculpture: (L) $825; (H) $3,737

HEBERER, Charles
American 19th cent.
paintings: (L) $880; (H) $1,035

HEBERT, Antoine
French 1817-1908
paintings: (L) $3,850; (H) $77,000

HEBERT, Emile
1828-1893
sculpture: (L) $719; (H) $1,380

HEBERT, J.K.
paintings: (H) $978

HEBERT, Jules
French 1812-1897
paintings: (H) $715

HEBERT, Pierre Eugene Emile
French 1828-1893
sculpture: (L) $1,365; (H) $26,450

HEBERT, Theodore
French 1829-1913
sculpture: (H) $632

HECHT, Victor David
American b. 1873
paintings: (L) $546; (H) $19,550

HECK, Don
drawings: (H) $1,210

HECK, Robert Wilhelm Emil
German 1831-1889
paintings: (H) $2,875

HECKEL, August von
German 1824-1883
paintings: (H) $18,975

HECKEL, Erich
German 1883-1970
paintings: (H) $101,500
drawings: (L) $6,600; (H) $12,650

HECKEN, Samuel van den
c. 1595-1637
paintings: (H) $3,450

HECKENDORF, Franz
German 1888-1962
drawings: (H) $2,970

HECKLEMANS, M V****
Dutch 18th/19th cent.
paintings: (H) $1,100

HECTOR, J.
Danish 19th cent.
paintings: (H) $770

HEDA, Willem Claesz.
Dutch 1594-c.1680
paintings: (L) $63,000; (H) $1,430,000

HEDELIN, C.
Continental School 20th cent.
paintings: (H) $633

HEDGES, Robert Danforth
American b. 1878
paintings: (H) $1,430

HEDLEY, G***
British 19th cent.
paintings: (H) $1,150

HEDLEY, Ralph
British 1851-1913
paintings: (H) $10,350

HEEKS, Willy
paintings: (H) $6,325

HEEM, Jan Davidsz. de
Dutch 1606-1684
paintings: (L) $51,750; (H) $1,542,500

HEEM, Jan Davidsz. de, studio of
17th cent.
paintings: (H) $297,000

HEEMSKERCK, Egbert van
Dutch c. 1634-1704
paintings: (L) $3,450; (H) $5,750

HEER, Margaretha de
German ac. 1650
drawings: (H) $3,737

HEERE, Lukas de
Flemish 1534-1584
paintings: (H) $19,800

HEEREMANS, Thomas
Dutch c. 1640-1697
paintings: (L) $8,800; (H) $35,200

HEERICH, Erwin
contemporary
drawings: (H) $550

HEES, Gerrit van
Flemish 1629-before 1702
paintings: (L) $5,750; (H) $32,200

HEES, Gustav Adolf van
German 1862-1918
paintings: (H) $880

HEESAKKERS, Thomas
Dutch 19th cent.
paintings: (H) $880

HEFFER, Edward A.
British 19th cent.
paintings: (H) $805
drawings: (H) $220

HEFFERICH, Franciscus Wilhelm
Dutch 19th/20th cent.
paintings: (H) $550

HEFFNER, Karl
German 1849-1925
paintings: (L) $605; (H) $34,500

HEGENBART, Fritz
German b. 1864
paintings: (H) $1,100

HEICKE, Joseph
Austrian 1811-1861
paintings: (H) $11,000

HEIDE, F.J. van der
Dutch 20th cent.
paintings: (H) $935

HEIDE, H. van der
paintings: (H) $525

HEIDNER, Heinrich
paintings: (L) $660; (H) $1,430

HEIKKA, Earle E.
American 1910-1941
drawings: (H) $2,600
sculpture: (L) $440; (H) $11,000

HEIL, Charles Emile
American 1870-1953
paintings: (L) $138; (H) $1,495
drawings: (L) $137; (H) $230

HEIL, Daniel van
1604-1662
paintings: (H) $14,950

HEILAND, Maximillian
German b. 1855
paintings: (H) $1,980

HEILBUTH, Ferdinand
French 1826-1889
paintings: (L) $11,000; (H) $71,500
drawings: (H) $2,200

HEILMAN, Mary
contemporary
paintings: (H) $10,350

HEILMAYER, Karl
German 1829-1908
paintings: (L) $467; (H) $3,220

HEIM
German/Aus. 19th cent.
paintings: (H) $990

HEIM, Harry
American 20th cent.
paintings: (H) $550

HEIMBACH, E.
late 19th cent.
paintings: (H) $633

HEIMBACH, F.
paintings: (H) $1,760

HEIMBACH, Wolfgang
German 1613-c. 1678
paintings: (H) $132,000

HEIMER, C.
German 19th cent.
paintings: (H) $1,100

HEIN, Allois Raimond
Austrian 1852-1936
paintings: (H) $1,320

HEIN, Einar
Danish b. 1875
paintings: (H) $1,150

HEIN, Hendrik Jan
Dutch 1822-1866
paintings: (H) $23,000

HEINE, Frederick W.
German/American 1845-1921
paintings: (H) $935

HEINE, Johann Adalbert
German 19th cent.
paintings: (L) $688; (H) $2,750

HEINE, W.
German 19th cent.
paintings: (H) $13,200

HEINEFETTER, Johann
German 1815-1902
paintings: (L) $3,080; (H) $9,775

HEINEN, Hans
German b. 1860
paintings: (H) $660

HEINISCH, Karl Adam
German 1847-1927
paintings: (L) $3,450; (H) $13,200

HEINRICH
20th cent.
sculpture: (H) $690

HEINRICH, Franz
Austrian 1802-1890
drawings: (L) $690; (H) $1,955

HEINRICI, John H.
19th/20th cent.
paintings: (H) $1,380

HEINS
paintings: (H) $825

HEINS, D***
1730-1780
paintings: (H) $4,675

HEINZ, F***
German 19th/20th cent.
paintings: (H) $5,500

HEINZE, Adolph
American 1887-1958
paintings: (L) $115; (H) $880
drawings: (H) $110

HEINZMAN, Louis
American 1905-1982
paintings: (H) $1,045

HEISE, Wilhelm
paintings: (H) $4,400

HEISS, Johann
German 1640-1704
paintings: (L) $2,990; (H) $25,300

HEIT, R.
German 18th cent.
paintings: (H) $2,420

HEITER, Michael
b. 1883
drawings: (H) $633

HEITLAND, W. Emerton
American 1893-1969
drawings: (L) $138; (H) $495

HEITMULLER, Louis
American b. 1863
paintings: (L) $88; (H) $1,540
drawings: (L) $77; (H) $165

HEIZER, Michael
American b. 1944
paintings: (L) $1,650; (H) $14,950
drawings: (L) $770; (H) $3,450
sculpture: (L) $6,600; (H) $44,000

HEKKING, Joseph Antonio
German/American ac. 1859-1885
paintings: (L) $770; (H) $5,175

HEKKING, Willem
Dutch 1796-1862
paintings: (L) $110; (H) $770
drawings: (L) $55; (H) $3,300

HELBERGER, Alfred
paintings: (H) $660

HELBIG, Bud
American b. 1915
paintings: (H) $660
drawings: (H) $385

HELCK, Clarence Peter
American b. 1893/97
paintings: (L) $467; (H) $2,420
drawings: (L) $192; (H) $12,100

HELD, Al
American b. 1928
paintings: (L) $9,200; (H) $70,700
drawings: (L) $3,220; (H) $11,000

HELD, D.
American 20th cent.
paintings: (H) $2,990

HELD, John, Jr.
American 1889-1958
drawings: (L) $550; (H) $2,530

HELDER, Johannes
Dutch 1842-1913
paintings: (L) $1,380; (H) $2,990

HELDNER, Colette Pope
American ac. 1930-1980s
paintings: (L) $165; (H) $1,980
drawings: (H) $374

HELDNER, Knute
Swedish/American 1877-1952
paintings: (L) $165; (H) $8,800
drawings: (H) $220

HELFERT, L.
paintings: (H) $825

HELFFERICH, Franciscus Willem
Franz
Dutch 1871-1941
paintings: (L) $1,045; (H) $1,650

HELIKER, John
American b. 1909/10
paintings: (L) $688; (H) $8,337

HELION, Jean
French 1904-1987
paintings: (L) $3,850; (H) $165,000
drawings: (L) $495; (H) $12,650

HELKE, Peter
American 20th cent.
drawings: (H) $2,860

HELLEN,
20th cent.
drawings: (H) $2,860

HELLEU, Jean
French b. 1894
paintings: (L) $825; (H) $949

HELLEU, Paul Cesar
French 1859-1927
paintings: (L) $1,210; (H) $51,750
drawings: (L) $460; (H) $38,500

HELLEU, Paulette
paintings: (H) $880

HELLWAG, Rudolf
German 1867-1942
paintings: (L) $550; (H) $990

HELMBERGER, Adolf
German 19th/20th cent.
paintings: (L) $575; (H) $700

HELMICK, Howard
American 1845-1907
paintings: (L) $770; (H) $1,430
drawings: (L) $150; (H) $385

HELMICK, Ralph
American 20th cent.
sculpture: (H) $2,200

HELMONT, Mattheus van
Flemish 1623-1674/79
paintings: (H) $70,700

HELOUIS
French 19th cent.
paintings: (H) $1,265

HELSBY, Alfredo
Chilean ac. c. 1889-1931
paintings: (L) $3,300; (H) $8,250

HELST, Bartholomeus van der
Dutch 1613-1670
paintings: (H) $68,500

HEM, Louise de
Belgian 1866-1922
paintings: (H) $17,250

HEM, Piet van der
Dutch 1885-1961
paintings: (H) $4,600

HEMERKA, Katharina
Continental 19th cent.
paintings: (H) $1,155

HEMINSON, R.
paintings: (H) $1,320

HEMON, Jean Marie
French 18th cent.
paintings: (H) $8,625

HEMPFING, Wilhelm
German 1886-1951
paintings: (L) $1,760; (H) $2,990

HEMSLEY, William
English b. 1819; ac. 1848-1893
paintings: (L) $3,575; (H) $7,700

HEMSTEDT, H.
German 19th cent.
paintings: (H) $1,610

HEMY, Bernard Benedict
English ac. 1875-1910; d. 1913
paintings: (H) $489

HENDERSEN, Edward
American contemporary
drawings: (H) $1,840

HENDERSON, Betty
American
paintings: (H) $500

HENDERSON, Charles Cooper
British 1803-1877
paintings: (L) $1,210; (H) $2,760
drawings: (H) $467

HENDERSON, Elyot
1908-1975
paintings: (L) $88; (H) $935

HENDERSON, G.
paintings: (H) $805
drawings: (H) $495

HENDERSON, James
Canadian 1871-1951
paintings: (L) $1,320; (H) $3,520

HENDERSON, W.
English 20th cent.
paintings: (H) $467

HENDERSON, W.
Scottish
paintings: (H) $550

HENDERSON, W.S.P.
English exhib. 1836-1874
paintings: (L) $550; (H) $2,200

HENDERSON, William Penhallow
American 1877-1943
paintings: (L) $1,840; (H) $1,980
drawings: (L) $495; (H) $2,640

HENDON, Cham
b. 1936
paintings: (L) $460; (H) $1,495

HENDRIKS, Willem
Dutch 1828-1891
paintings: (L) $575; (H) $2,860

HENDRIKS, Wybrand
Dutch 1744-1831
paintings: (L) $1,150; (H) $2,530

HENDRIX, Jimi
American 1942-1970
drawings: (H) $5,142

HENDRY, Frank
American School 20th cent.
paintings: (H) $546

HENG, Lee
Chinese
paintings: (H) $5,060

HENKE, B.
Dutch 19th cent.
paintings: (H) $2,185

HENKES, Gerke
Dutch 1844-1927
paintings: (H) $259
drawings: (L) $357; (H) $1,100

HENLEY, Jacob
drawings: (H) $10,925

HENLEY, W.B.
British 19th cent.
paintings: (H) $2,070

HENNECY, G.
paintings: (H) $467

HENNER, Georg
Austrian ac. c. 1788
drawings: (H) $5,175

HENNER, Jean Jacques
French 1829-1905
paintings: (L) $990; (H) $33,000
drawings: (L) $302; (H) $605

HENNESSEY, Frank Charles
1894-1941
drawings: (L) $440; (H) $3,080

HENNESSY, J.
American 20th cent.
paintings: (H) $908

HENNESSY, Patrick
paintings: (H) $1,760

HENNESSY, William John
Irish/American 1839/40-1917
paintings: (L) $110; (H) $23,000

HENNINGS, Ernest Martin
American 1886-1956
paintings: (L) $8,625; (H) $176,000
drawings: (H) $1,265

HENNINGSEN, Hans
Danish b. 1889
paintings: (H) $990

HENOCQUE, Narcisse
19th/20th cent.
paintings: (L) $1,380; (H) $2,530

HENRI, Michel
French b. 1928
paintings: (H) $2,420

HENRI, Paolo
drawings: (H) $1,840

HENRI, Robert
American 1865-1929
paintings: (L) $1,035; (H) $346,500
drawings: (L) $58; (H) $5,500

HENRICHSEN, Carsten
Danish 1824-1897
paintings: (H) $1,725

HENRICI, John H.
American b. 1839
paintings: (L) $302; (H) $1,840

HENRIKSEN, William
Danish 19th/20th cent.
paintings: (H) $5,750

HENRION, Armand Francois Joseph
French b. 1875
paintings: (L) $770; (H) $4,887

HENRY, D.M.
British 19th cent.
paintings: (H) $8,800

HENRY, Edward Lamson
American 1841-1919
paintings: (L) $2,090; (H) $93,500
drawings: (L) $2,860; (H) $26,400

HENRY, Edwin
b. 1900
paintings: (L) $660; (H) $1,320

HENRY, George
English 1858-1943
paintings: (H) $3,080

HENRY, Harry Raymond
American 1882-1974
paintings: (L) $1,650; (H) $8,250

HENRY, J.
paintings: (H) $495

HENRY, John
b. 1943
sculpture: (H) $2,300

HENRY, Michel
French b. 1928
paintings: (L) $275; (H) $3,696

HENRY, Paul
Irish 1877-1958
paintings: (L) $10,725; (H) $25,300

HENRY, Pierre
French b. 1924
paintings: (H) $777

HENSCHE, Henry
American b. 1901
paintings: (L) $192; (H) $3,300
drawings: (H) $27

HENSEL
paintings: (H) $495

HENSEL, Stephen Hopkins
American ac. 1945-1952
paintings: (L) $440; (H) $3,575

HENSELER, Ernst
German b. 1852
paintings: (H) $20,350

HENSEN, Ole Peter
Norwegian 1823-1906
paintings: (H) $1,100

HENSHAW, G.C.
drawings: (H) $990

HENSHAW, Glen Cooper
American 1881/85-1946
paintings: (L) $115; (H) $690
drawings: (L) $110; (H) $825

HENSLEY, Jackson
American 20th cent.
paintings: (H) $5,500

HENSTENBURG, Anton
1695-1781
drawings: (L) $13,200; (H) $15,400

HENSTENBURGH, Herman
Dutch 1667-1726
drawings: (L) $5,175; (H) $6,900

HENTER
British 19th cent.
paintings: (H) $4,675

HENTON, George Moore
British 1861-1924
paintings: (H) $1,495

HENZE, Ingfried, called Morro
paintings: (H) $2,750

HENZELL, Isaac
ac. 1854-1875
paintings: (H) $4,485

HEPBURN, Tony
contemporary
sculpture: (H) $1,725

HEPBURN, William
1817-1891
paintings: (H) $495

HEPPER, G.
British 19th cent.
paintings: (L) $660; (H) $1,375

HEPWORTH, Barbara
English 1903-1975
paintings: (H) $93,500
drawings: (H) $13,225
sculpture: (L) $6,600; (H) $275,000

HERALD, W.F.
Scottish 1868-1922
drawings: (H) $990

HERBE, A.(?)
French 20th cent.
paintings: (H) $468

HERBERT, Emile
sculpture: (H) $2,200

HERBERT, G.
British 20th cent.
paintings: (H) $863

HERBERT, J.G.S.
British School 19th cent.
paintings: (H) $6,325

HERBERT, John Rogers
British 1810-1980
paintings: (H) $2,530

HERBERT, Pierre Eugene Emile
French 1828-1893
sculpture: (H) $4,950

HERBERT, Sidney
British 1854-1914
paintings: (L) $518; (H) $1,045

HERBERT, Wilfrid Vincent
British 19th cent.
paintings: (H) $16,100

HERBERTE, Edward Benjamin
English ac. 1870-1880
paintings: (L) $1,100; (H) $34,100

HERBERTS, Charles
English 19th cent.
paintings: (H) $468

HERBIG, G.A.
European 19th cent.
paintings: (H) $825

HERBIN, Auguste
French 1882-1960
paintings: (L) $11,500; (H) $60,500
drawings: (L) $3,680; (H) $17,600

HERBO, Fernand
French b. 1905
paintings: (L) $523; (H) $3,450

HERBO, Leon
Belgian 1850-1907
paintings: (L) $1,320; (H) $8,050

HERBST, Adolf
paintings: (H) $2,300

HERBST, Frank C.
American 20th cent.
paintings: (L) $357; (H) $2,090

HERBST, Thomas
German 1848-1915
paintings: (L) $1,320; (H) $2,530

HERBSTOFFER, P.R.K.
Austrian 1821-1876
paintings: (H) $4,125

HERDMAN, Robert
British 1829-1888
drawings: (H) $825

HEREAU, Jules
French 1830/39-1879
paintings: (L) $748; (H) $2,760

HERFORD, Oliver
American 1863-1935
drawings: (H) $522

HERGENROEDER, Georg Heinrich
1736-1794
paintings: (H) $5,750

HERGESHEIMER, Ella Sophonisba
American b. 1943
paintings: (L) $550; (H) $2,300

HERGET, Herbert
American 1885-1950
paintings: (L) $605; (H) $7,475

HERHEL
paintings: (H) $7,920

HERING, George Edwards
English 1805-1879
paintings: (H) $1,210

HERINK, Francois
British 19th cent.
paintings: (L) $605; (H) $605

HERISSON, Louis Francois
French 1811-1859
paintings: (H) $7,475

HERKOMER, Sir Hubert von
German/English 1849-1914
paintings: (L) $978; (H) $5,500

HERMAN, Roger
American 20th cent.
paintings: (L) $863; (H) $2,300

HERMAN, Sali
Swiss b. 1898
paintings: (H) $8,140

HERMANN, Curt
paintings: (H) $10,925

HERMANN, H.
Austrian 20th cent.
paintings: (H) $1,210

HERMANN, Leo
French 1853-1927
paintings: (L) $2,420; (H) $3,450
drawings: (H) $880

HERMANN, Ludwig
German 1812-1881
paintings: (L) $6,325; (H) $8,800

HERMANN-PAUL
French 1874-1940
drawings: (H) $495

HERMANOVSKY, A.F.
American 20th cent.
paintings: (H) $489

HERMANS, Charles
Belgian 1839-1924
paintings: (H) $715,000

HERMANSEN, Olaf August
Danish 1849-1897
paintings: (L) $1,320; (H) $22,000

HERMS, George
b. 1935
paintings: (H) $2,530

HERNANDEZ, Daniel
Peruvian 1856-1932
paintings: (L) $1,045; (H) $19,550
drawings: (H) $5,500

HERNANDEZ, E.
Spanish 19th cent.
paintings: (H) $825

HERNANDEZ, J.
Mexican contemporary
paintings: (L) $77; (H) $1,760

HERNANDEZ, Sergio
b. Mexico 1957
paintings: (L) $17,600; (H) $31,625
drawings: (H) $13,800

HERNDORFF, Michael
American contemporary
paintings: (H) $1,540

HEROLD, Georg
b. Germany 1947
paintings: (L) $690; (H) $12,100
drawings: (L) $1,093; (H) $8,250
sculpture: (L) $3,450; (H) $17,600

HERON, Patrick
English b. 1920
drawings: (H) $2,875

HEROULT, Antoine Desire
French 1802-1853
drawings: (H) $605

HERP, Willem van
1614-1677
paintings: (L) $29,900; (H) $32,200

HERPFER, Carl
German 1836-1897
paintings: (L) $5,500; (H) $79,500

HERPIN, Leon Pierre
French 1841-1880
paintings: (H) $1,980

HERRAN, Saturnino
b. Mexico 1887 d. 1918
paintings: (H) $14,300
drawings: (H) $10,350

HERRERA, Fray Miguel de
Mexico ac. 1725-1752
paintings: (H) $12,650

HERRERA, Honorio
paintings: (H) $12,100

HERRERA, Velino Shije, Ma Pe Wi,
Oriole
Native American b. 1902
paintings: (H) $468
drawings: (L) $1,100; (H) $2,420

HERRERA, Velino Shije, Ma Pe Wi,
Red Bird
Native American b. 1902
drawings: (L) $2,200; (H) $2,420

HERRERA TORO, Antonio
Venezuelan 1857-1914
paintings: (H) $17,250

HERREYNS, Jacob, the elder
Flemish 1643-1732
drawings: (H) $715

HERRFELDT, Herman
paintings: (H) $4,600

HERRICK, Arthur R.
American 1897-1970
paintings: (L) $193; (H) $468

HERRIMAN, George
American 1880-1944
drawings: (L) $825; (H) $10,350

HERRING, Benjamin, Jr.
English 1830-1871
paintings: (L) $1,210; (H) $2,420

HERRING, Benjamin, Sr.
British 1806-1830
paintings: (L) $1,100; (H) $2,875

HERRING, James
English 1794-1867
paintings: (L) $2,750; (H) $11,500

HERRING, John Frederick, Jr.
British 1815-1907
paintings: (L) $1,320; (H) $57,500
drawings: (H) $1,100

HERRING, John Frederick, Jr. studio of
paintings: (L) $5,775; (H) $8,050

HERRING, John Frederick, Sr.
British 1795-1865
paintings: (L) $6,600; (H) $230,000
drawings: (H) $440

HERRING, John Frederick, Sr.
studio of
paintings: (H) $5,500

HERRING, John Frederick and James
Edwin MEADOWS, Jr.
British 19th/20th cent.
paintings: (H) $13,800

HERRING, Lee
American
paintings: (L) $358; (H) $4,400

HERRMAN, W.
19th cent.
paintings: (H) $1,320

HERRMANN, Frank S.
American 1866-1942
paintings: (H) $605
drawings: (L) $413; (H) $880

HERRMANN, Hans
German 1858-1942
paintings: (L) $1,100; (H) $16,100

HERRMANN, L.
German 19th cent.
paintings: (H) $1,320

HERRMANN, Leo
French 1853-1927
paintings: (L) $770; (H) $4,400
drawings: (H) $1,725

HERRMANN, Ludwig
German 1812-1881
paintings: (H) $5,750

HERRMANN, Willy
German b. 1895
paintings: (H) $2,300

HERRMANN-LEON, Charles
paintings: (H) $4,400

HERSCHEL, E.
British 19th/20th cent.
paintings: (H) $467

HERSCHEL, Otto
German b. 1871
paintings: (L) $121; (H) $550

HERSCHEL, Philip
paintings: (H) $475

HERSENT, Louis
French 1777-1860
paintings: (H) $40,250

HERSET, H.
American early 20th cent.
paintings: (H) $1,840

HERSHEY, Samuel Franklin
American b. 1904
paintings: (L) $625; (H) $1,540

HERSON, Emile Antoine Francois and
DIAZ DE LA PENA
French 19th cent.
paintings: (H) $5,750

HERSTYS, S.D.R.
American School late 19th cent.
drawings: (H) $880

HERTEL, Carl Konrad Julius
German 1837-1895
paintings: (H) $3,450

HERTER, Adele
American 1869-1946
paintings: (L) $748; (H) $8,050
drawings: (L) $550; (H) $2,530

HERTER, Albert
American 1871-1950
paintings: (L) $99; (H) $15,400
drawings: (L) $1,870; (H) $11,500

HERTER, Ernst Gustav
German 1846-1917
sculpture: (H) $4,840

HERVE, Jules Rene
French 1887-1981
paintings: (L) $575; (H) $13,200

HERVIER, Adolphe
Dutch 1871-1891
drawings: (H) $1,760

HERVIER, Louis Adolphe
French 1818-1879
paintings: (H) $1,650

HERWAARBEN, P. van
paintings: (H) $805

HERZOG, G.
paintings: (H) $500

HERZOG, Hermann
German/American 1832-1932
paintings: (L) $518; (H) $71,500
drawings: (L) $440; (H) $2,750

HESCOX, Richard
paintings: (H) $4,887

HESELTINE, Jane
American 20th cent.
paintings: (H) $4,400

HESS, ***
19th cent.
drawings: (H) $5,463

HESS, B.
paintings: (L) $110; (H) $3,300

HESS, Jaro J.
drawings: (H) $550

HESS, Marcel
Belgian b. 1878
paintings: (H) $4,620

HESS, Sara
American b. 1880
paintings: (L) $715; (H) $715

HESSE, Eva
American 1936-1970
paintings: (L) $11,500; (H) $14,300
drawings: (L) $16,100; (H) $63,000
sculpture: (L) $79,500; (H) $475,500

HESSELBERG, Abraham
drawings: (H) $3,740

HESSING, Valjean McCarty
Native American b. 1934
drawings: (L) $748; (H) $1,210

HETHERINGTON, Charles
British/American b. 1857
paintings: (L) $44; (H) $577

HETHERINGTON, John
British 20th cent.
sculpture: (H) $7,700

HETTNAR(?), Otto
paintings: (H) $1,100

HETZ, Carl
German 1828-1899
paintings: (H) $2,760

HETZ, William
paintings: (H) $550

HETZEL, George
French/American 1826-1906
paintings: (L) $935; (H) $12,100

HETZEL, Lila B.
American 20th cent.
paintings: (H) $550

HEUBACH, Walter
German b. 1865
paintings: (H) $14,950

HEUBLER, Douglas
contemporary
drawings: (H) $8,800

HEUGLER, A.
German 20th cent.
paintings: (L) $385; (H) $1,100

HEUGNER, D.
paintings: (H) $6,900

HEUKIN, John H.
American School
paintings: (H) $660

HEULLANT, Felix Armand
French b. 1834
paintings: (H) $9,200

HEURLIN, Colcord, "Rusty"
paintings: (H) $935

HEURS
paintings: (H) $1,430

HEUSER, Carl
German 19th cent.
paintings: (L) $1,760; (H) $2,875

HEUVEL, Theodore Bernard de
Flemish 1817-1906
paintings: (H) $2,750

HEWES, Horace G.
paintings: (L) $220; (H) $550

HEWES, Madeline
French 20th cent.
paintings: (H) $495

HEWIL, N.
19th/20th cent.
drawings: (H) $1,320

HEWINS, Amasa
American 1795-1855
paintings: (L) $6,050; (H) $19,550

HEWINS, Philip
American 1806-1850
paintings: (L) $137; (H) $1,650

HEWITT, Charles
b. 1946
paintings: (L) $220; (H) $880

HEWTON, Randolph Stanley
Canadian 1888-1960
paintings: (H) $1,925

HEY, Paul
German 1867-1952
paintings: (H) $1,540
drawings: (L) $2,420; (H) $4,950

HEYBOER, Anton
contemporary
drawings: (H) $660

HEYDE, Charles Louis
American c. 1820-1892
paintings: (H) $4,025

HEYDEN, **
German b. 1907
paintings: (L) $440; (H) $1,540

HEYDEN, Jan van der
Dutch 1637-1712
paintings: (H) $28,600

HEYDENDAHL, Friederich Joseph
Nicolai
German 1844-1906
paintings: (H) $3,575

HEYER, Arthur
German b. 1872
paintings: (L) $880; (H) $5,225

HEYL, G.
paintings: (H) $2,750

HEYL, Marinus
Dutch 1836-1931
paintings: (L) $330; (H) $1,760

HEYLIGERS, Gustaaf A.F.
Dutch 19th cent.
paintings: (L) $1,100; (H) $24,200

HEYLIGERS, Hendrik
Dutch b. 1877
paintings: (L) $1,035; (H) $5,500

HEYMANN, Paul
German 19th/20th cent.
paintings: (H) $23,000

HEYRAULT, Louis Robert
French 19th cent.
paintings: (H) $11,500

HEYTMAN, W.
Dutch 20th cent.
paintings: (H) $1,045

HEYWOOD, Tom
British ac. 1882-1913
paintings: (H) $4,400

HIBBARD, Aldro Thompson
American 1886-1972
paintings: (L) $440; (H) $37,375

HIBBERT, E.
German 19th cent.
paintings: (H) $2,420

HIBEL, Edna
American b. 1917
paintings: (L) $165; (H) $10,010
drawings: (L) $192; (H) $605

HICKEL, Joseph
Austrian 1736-1807
paintings: (H) $13,800

HICKEY, John
Irish late 18th cent.
sculpture: (H) $32,200

HICKMAN, N.
English 19th cent.
paintings: (H) $715

HICKMAN, Pat
contemporary
sculpture: (H) $2,013

HICKS
paintings: (H) $1,650

HICKS, David
American contemporary
paintings: (L) $805; (H) $1,045

HICKS, Edward
American 1780-1849
paintings: (L) $486,500; (H) $1,210,000

HICKS, G.
British 19th cent.
paintings: (H) $468

HICKS, George Edgar
English 1824-1914
paintings: (L) $7,475; (H) $34,500

HICKS, Thomas
American 1823-1890
paintings: (L) $467; (H) $8,000

HICKS, Thomas and John F. KENSETT
American 18th cent.
paintings: (H) $4,600

HIDALGO DE CAVIEDES, Hipolito
b. 1902
paintings: (H) $1,650

HIDDEMANN, J.
German 19th cent.
paintings: (H) $19,250

HIDDLESTON, Kate
sculpture: (H) $990

HIDER, Frank
British 19th cent.
paintings: (L) $250; (H) $495

HIDERMITSU
sculpture: (H) $1,980

HIDLEY, Joseph
American 1830-1872
paintings: (L) $1,100; (H) $4,620

HIENE, Adelbert
paintings: (H) $1,725

HIENEMAN, T.V.
Dutch 19th/20th cent.
paintings: (H) $2,860

HIEPES, Tomas
Spanish d. 1674
paintings: (L) $442,500; (H) $783,500

HIER, Joachim van
Austrian b. 1834
paintings: (H) $1,430

HIERHOLTZ, G.
20th cent.
sculpture: (H) $460

HIERLE, Louis
French 19th cent.
paintings: (L) $468; (H) $13,200

HIFTER, M.
Austrian 19th cent.
paintings: (L) $990; (H) $2,090

HIGBY, Wayne
American b. 1943
sculpture: (L) $220; (H) $3,960

HIGGINS, Esther
American 1831-1888
paintings: (L) $6,325; (H) $7,475

HIGGINS, Eugene
American 1874-1958
paintings: (L) $413; (H) $5,280
drawings: (L) $55; (H) $4,400

HIGGINS, George
American 19th/20th cent.
paintings: (H) $451

HIGGINS, George F.
American ac. 1850-1884
paintings: (L) $110; (H) $1,870

HIGGINS, J. Thomas R.
paintings: (L) $259; (H) $1,840

HIGGINS, Victor
American 1884-1949
paintings: (H) $770
drawings: (L) $1,980; (H) $18,400

HIGGINSON, Joseph
paintings: (H) $7,700

HIGHMORE, Joseph
English 1692-1780
paintings: (H) $2,750

HIGHSTEIN, Jene
b. 1942
drawings: (H) $2,070

HIGHWOOD, Charles
American ac. 1850's
paintings: (H) $660

HIKOYAMA, T.
American 20th cent.
paintings: (H) $460

HILAER, R.
Continental 19th cent.
paintings: (H) $5,500

HILAIRE, Camille
French 1916-1988
paintings: (L) $1,035; (H) $19,800
drawings: (H) $770

HILAIRE, Jean Baptiste
French 1753-1822
drawings: (L) $7,700; (H) $17,600

HILAIRE, Jean Baptiste
French 1753-1822
drawings: (H) $7,700

HILBERT, Robert
drawings: (L) $605; (H) $1,320

HILDEBRAND, Claire
French ac. 1873-1898
paintings: (H) $1,650

HILDEBRAND, Ernest
German b. 1833
paintings: (L) $920; (H) $1,650

HILDEBRANDT, A.
German 19th cent.
paintings: (H) $2,990

HILDEBRANDT, Aldro T.
1866-1972
paintings: (H) $1,870

HILDEBRANDT, Eduard
German 1818-1869
paintings: (H) $3,680

HILDEBRANDT, Ernst
paintings: (H) $1,980

HILDEBRANDT, F.
German 19th cent.
paintings: (H) $4,180

HILDEBRANDT, Howard Logan
American 1872-1958
paintings: (L) $259; (H) $1,375

HILDEBRANDT BROTHERS
paintings: (L) $862; (H) $9,200
drawings: (H) $3,162

HILDER, Richard
English exhib. 1830-1851
paintings: (H) $2,640

HILDRETH, Alison
drawings: (L) $604; (H) $863

HILDYARD, H.J.
19th cent.
paintings: (H) $1,265

HILER, Hilaire
American 1898-1966
drawings: (L) $220; (H) $550

HILGART, V.
paintings: (H) $1,000

HILGERS, Carl
German 1818-1890
paintings: (L) $2,640; (H) $8,338

HILL
American 19th cent.
paintings: (H) $12,650

HILL, Adrian
English b. 1896
paintings: (H) $1,320

HILL, Andrew P.
American 1853-1922
paintings: (H) $605

HILL, Arthur Turnbull
American 1868-1929
paintings: (L) $500; (H) $1,650

HILL, Carl G.
American 1884-1973
paintings: (L) $500; (H) $1,650

HILL, David Octavius
British 1802-1870
paintings: (H) $1,100

HILL, Derek
British b. 1916
paintings: (H) $1,430

HILL, Edward
American 1843-1923
paintings: (L) $660; (H) $4,950

HILL, Edward Rufus
American 1851-1908
paintings: (L) $605; (H) $1,650

HILL, F.J.
American 19th cent.
paintings: (H) $748

HILL, Henry
paintings: (H) $633

HILL, Howard
American ac. 1860-1870
paintings: (L) $495; (H) $5,750

HILL, J.
British 19th cent.
paintings: (H) $1,210

HILL, James John
British 1811-1882
paintings: (L) $2,090; (H) $7,475

HILL, John Henry
American 1839-1922
paintings: (H) $2,420
drawings: (L) $165; (H) $2,530

HILL, John Henry
British ac. 1865-1879
paintings: (H) $633

HILL, John William
Anglo/American 1812-1879
paintings: (H) $440
drawings: (L) $577; (H) $16,500

HILL, L.
19th/20th cent.
paintings: (H) $1,760

HILL, Mabel B.
b. 1877
drawings: (H) $825

HILL, Michael John
British contemporary
paintings: (H) $920

HILL, Pearl L.
b. 1884
drawings: (H) $2,640

HILL, Roswell S.
American 1861-1907
paintings: (H) $1,100

HILL, T.
paintings: (L) $302; (H) $1,540

HILL, T.W.
American 19th cent.
paintings: (H) $3,300

HILL, Thomas
American, b.England 1829-1908
paintings: (L) $605; (H) $98,750
drawings: (H) $1,045

HILL, Tom
20th cent.
drawings: (L) $978; (H) $1,093

HILL, W.F.
19th cent.
paintings: (H) $1,380

HILLAIRET, Anatole
French c. 1880-1928
paintings: (H) $633

HILLARD, William H.
American 1888-1951
paintings: (H) $2,420

HILLEN
American 19th cent.
paintings: (H) $880

HILLER, Heinrich
German 19th cent.
paintings: (H) $825

HILLIARD, William Henry
American 1836-1905
paintings: (L) $165; (H) $2,420

HILLIER, H.B.
British 19th cent.
paintings: (H) $1,320

HILLIER, H.D.
paintings: (L) $440; (H) $1,925

HILLIER, H.D.
Scottish 19th cent.
paintings: (H) $1,495

HILLINGFORD, Robert
English 1828-1893
paintings: (H) $1,320

HILLINGFORD, Robert Alexander
English 1825-1904
paintings: (L) $1,093; (H) $9,900

HILLS, Anna A.
American 1882-1930
paintings: (L) $385; (H) $5,225
drawings: (L) $385; (H) $1,045

HILLS, Laura Coombs
American 1859-1952
paintings: (L) $518; (H) $1,750
drawings: (L) $92; (H) $13,800

HILLSMITH, F.
European 19th cent.
paintings: (H) $550

HILLYER, William
ac. 1832-1864
paintings: (L) $2,530; (H) $4,950

HILTON, John W.
American b. 1904
paintings: (L) $1,045; (H) $3,300

HILTON, T.
20th cent.
paintings: (H) $715

HILVERDINK, Eduard Alexander
Dutch 1846-1891
paintings: (L) $1,320; (H) $3,850

HILZ, Sepp
German 1906-1967
paintings: (H) $2,013

HIMMEL, Joseph
paintings: (L) $248; (H) $1,760

HINCKLEY, Thomas Hewes
American 1813-1896
paintings: (L) $2,760; (H) $9,200

HINCKS-PLAUCHE, Leda
1887-1980
drawings: (H) $605

HINDS, Patrick Swazo, Gray Squirrel
Native American b. 1929
paintings: (H) $2,200

HINE, Charles
American 1827-1871
paintings: (H) $605

HINES, Frederick
English ac. 1875-1897
paintings: (H) $1,089

HINES, Jack
drawings: (L) $500; (H) $4,510

HINES, Richard
paintings: (H) $1,500

HINES, Theodore •
British ac. 1876-1889
paintings: (L) $275; (H) $3,080

HING, Lee
paintings: (H) $7,150

HINGQUA
Chinese 19th cent.
paintings: (H) $26,400

HINGRE, Louis Theophile
French d. 1911
paintings: (H) $7,475
sculpture: (L) $316; (H) $2,420

HINKLE, Clarence
American 1880-1960
paintings: (L) $1,100; (H) $22,000
drawings: (L) $357; (H) $1,210

HINMAN, Charles
American b. 1932
paintings: (H) $2,750

HINTERREITER, Hans
Swiss b. 1902
drawings: (H) $3,080

HINTON, Charles Louis
American 1869-1950
sculpture: (H) $4,950

HINTON, Walter Haskell
paintings: (H) $2,970

HIOLIN, Louis Auguste
French 1846-1910
sculpture: (L) $1,265; (H) $5,175

HIPPOLYTE-LUCAS, Marie Felix
French 1854-1925
paintings: (L) $2,185; (H) $8,337

HIQUILY, Philippe
French b. 1925
sculpture: (L) $1,610; (H) $18,700

HIRAGA, Kamesuke
Japanese 1890-1971
paintings: (L) $1,760; (H) $3,300

HIRCH, J.B.
American
drawings: (H) $550

HIROBOT, A.
19th/20th cent.
paintings: (H) $853

HIROI, Tsutomi
b. 1925
sculpture: (H) $1,210

HIROTA, Susumu
American b. 1898
paintings: (L) $345; (H) $605

HIRSCH, Alice
American 1888-1935
paintings: (H) $1,870

HIRSCH, Joseph
American 1910-1981
paintings: (L) $115; (H) $17,250
drawings: (L) $23; (H) $1,100

HIRSCH, Stefan
American 1899-1964
paintings: (L) $58; (H) $1,093

HIRSCHBERG, Alice
American b. 1856
drawings: (L) $220; (H) $460

HIRSCHBERG, Carl
American 1854-1923
paintings: (L) $633; (H) $6,600
drawings: (H) $1,650

HIRSCHE, H. Lee
American 20th cent.
sculpture: (H) $1,210

HIRSCHFELD, Al
American b. 1903
paintings: (L) $805; (H) $1,760
drawings: (L) $605; (H) $4,400

HIRSCHFIELD, Morris
1872-1946
paintings: (H) $1,265

HIRSCHMANN, Johann Baptist
German 1770-c. 1829
drawings: (H) $1,035

HIRSHFELD, Emile Bebedicktoff
Russian 1892-1910
paintings: (H) $1,540

HIRST, Claude Raguet
American 1855-1942
paintings: (L) $1,100; (H) $30,800
drawings: (L) $10,350; (H) $14,300

HIRTH DU FRENES, Rudolf
German 1846-1916
paintings: (L) $1,760; (H) $3,520

HIS, Rene Charles Edmond
French 1877-1960
paintings: (L) $77; (H) $5,500

HITCHCOCK, D. Howard
b. 1861
paintings: (H) $2,750

HITCHCOCK, George
American 1850-1913
paintings: (L) $4,620; (H) $34,500
drawings: (L) $330; (H) $1,035

HITCHCOCK, Lucius W.
American 1868-1942
paintings: (L) $330; (H) $4,400
drawings: (H) $192

HITCHINGS, Henry
American d. 1902
drawings: (L) $110; (H) $825

HITTELL, Charles Joseph
American 1861-1938
paintings: (L) $1,540; (H) $4,400

HLAVA, Pavel
Czechoslovakian c. 1924
sculpture: (L) $1,725; (H) $11,500

HLITO, Alfredo
1923-1993
paintings: (L) $4,025; (H) $21,850

HOAR, Steve
ac. 1975
sculpture: (H) $2,860

HOARE, William
1706-1792
paintings: (H) $4,313

HOBART, Clark
American c. 1868-1948
paintings: (L) $1,100; (H) $11,000

HOBBEMA, Meindert
Dutch 1638-1709
paintings: (H) $13,200

HOBBS, George Thompson
American b. 1846
paintings: (L) $460; (H) $3,850

HOBBS, John
paintings: (H) $578

HOBBS, Louise Allen
American ac. c. 1916
sculpture: (H) $1,100

HOBBS, Morris Henry
American 1892-1967
paintings: (L) $22; (H) $440
drawings: (L) $825; (H) $935

HOBBS, R.
British 19th cent.
paintings: (H) $920

HOBBY, Jess
20th cent.
paintings: (L) $176; (H) $495

HOBERT, A.
Continental 19th cent.
paintings: (H) $935

HOBSON, Henry E.
English ac. 1857-1866
drawings: (H) $660

HOCH, Franz Xaver
German 1869-1916
paintings: (H) $1,760

HOCH, Hannah
German 1889-1979
drawings: (L) $1,100; (H) $34,100

HOCH, Johann Jacob
1750-1829
drawings: (H) $9,200

HOCHSTEIN, A.
paintings: (H) $2,000

HOCK, Daniel
Austrian 1858-1934
paintings: (L) $303; (H) $4,400

HOCKER, P.
German 19th cent.
paintings: (H) $880

HOCKNEY, David
English b. 1937
paintings: (L) $13,200; (H) $1,100,000
drawings: (L) $1,955; (H) $321,500
sculpture: (H) $14,300

HODDER, Stephen
contemporary
sculpture: (L) $1,650; (H) $2,185

HODE, Pierre
French 1889-1942
paintings: (L) $24,200; (H) $49,500

HODEBERT, Leon Auguste Cesar
French 1852-1914
paintings: (H) $13,200

HODEL, Ernst
Swiss 1881-1955
paintings: (L) $1,430; (H) $1,540

HODGDON, Sylvester Phelps
American 1830-1906
paintings: (L) $345; (H) $5,463

HODGES, David
American 20th cent.
sculpture: (L) $440; (H) $880

HODGES, F.
British 19th cent.
paintings: (H) $770

HODGES, Merrell
British 19th/20th cent.
paintings: (H) $4,312

HODGES, William Merrett
British 1896-1938
paintings: (H) $770

HODGKIN, Eliot
paintings: (H) $3,410
drawings: (L) $81; (H) $2,310

HODGKIN, Howard
English b. 1932
paintings: (L) $9,200; (H) $332,500
drawings: (H) $8,050

HODGSON, John Evan
British 1831-1895
paintings: (L) $920; (H) $11,500

HODGSON, Thomas Sherlock
paintings: (L) $1,045; (H) $3,575

HODLER, Ferdinand
Swiss 1853-1918
paintings: (H) $2,070

HODSON, Samuel John
British 1836-1908
drawings: (H) $1,320

HOEBER, Arthur
American 1854-1915
paintings: (L) $357; (H) $7,150

HOECKE, Gaspar van den
c. 1575-c. 1648
paintings: (H) $156,500

HOECKE, Jan van den
Flemish 1611-1651
paintings: (H) $90,500

HOECKNER, Carl
American b. 1883
paintings: (H) $1,150

HOEDT, Ella Boocock
paintings: (L) $165; (H) $1,100

HOEF, Abraham van der
Dutch ac. 1642-1659
paintings: (L) $4,025; (H) $8,625

HOEFFLER, Adolf
German 1826-1898
paintings: (H) $3,850

HOEGER, Josef
Austrian 1801-1877
drawings: (H) $495

HOEGER, Rudolf A.
1876-1928
paintings: (H) $1,320

HOERMAN, Carl
American 1885-1955
paintings: (L) $220; (H) $495

HOESEN, Beth van
contemporary
drawings: (H) $715

HOESSLIN, George von
German 1851-1923
paintings: (H) $13,200

HOET, Gerard
Dutch 1648-1733
paintings: (L) $2,860; (H) $41,800

HOEUSSLER, H.
American 19th cent.
paintings: (H) $1,760

HOEVEN, Anton van den
Dutch b. 1940
paintings: (L) $460; (H) $460

HOEVENAAR, Jozef
Dutch 19th cent.
paintings: (H) $550

HOEYDONCK, Paul
sculpture: (H) $2,300

HOFER, Carl
German 1878-1956
paintings: (L) $1,100; (H) $39,600
drawings: (L) $2,990; (H) $7,700

HOFER, Karl
German 1878-1956
paintings: (H) $26,450
drawings: (H) $7,700

HOFER, Schmidt
German ac. 1900-1925
sculpture: (H) $495

HOFF, Carl Heinrich
German 1838-1890
paintings: (L) $13,800; (H) $14,950

HOFF, Guy
American 1889-1962
paintings: (L) $3,300; (H) $9,900
drawings: (H) $1,045

HOFF, Jakob
paintings: (H) $1,430

HOFF, Margo
American b. 1912
paintings: (H) $1,870
drawings: (L) $143; (H) $187

HOFFBAUER, Charles
French/American 1875-1957
paintings: (L) $138; (H) $11,500
drawings: (L) $33; (H) $863

HOFFLER, Othmar
American
paintings: (L) $550; (H) $605

HOFFLER, Othmar
German 20th cent.
paintings: (H) $605

HOFFMAN, Arnold
Russian/American 1886-1966
paintings: (L) $413; (H) $1,045

HOFFMAN, Frank B.
American 1888-1958
paintings: (L) $990; (H) $1,870
drawings: (L) $110; (H) $7,150

HOFFMAN, Gary
American b. 1947
paintings: (L) $715; (H) $2,415

HOFFMAN, Gustave Adolph
German/American 1869-1945
paintings: (L) $115; (H) $1,540

HOFFMAN, Hans
American 20th cent.
drawings: (H) $1,100

HOFFMAN, Harry Leslie
American 1874-1966
paintings: (L) $165; (H) $3,025

HOFFMAN, Irwin D.
American 1901-1989
paintings: (L) $330; (H) $825

HOFFMAN, John
American 20th cent.
paintings: (H) $9,900

HOFFMAN, Malvina
American 1887-1966
drawings: (L) $632; (H) $770
sculpture: (L) $299; (H) $33,000

HOFFMAN, Murray
American ac. 1900-1945
paintings: (L) $825; (H) $1,760

HOFFMAN, Ronald
American 20th cent.
drawings: (H) $605

HOFFMAN, William
paintings: (L) $77; (H) $633

HOFFMAN(?), P.
paintings: (H) $1,100

HOFFMANN, Clara
American 19th/20th cent.
paintings: (H) $8,050

HOFFMANN, Joseph
Austrian 1831-1904
paintings: (H) $1,375

HOFKER, Willem Gerard
Dutch b. 1902
paintings: (H) $880

. **HOFMAN, Hans O.**
American b. 1893
paintings: (H) $2,860

HOFMANN, Anton
German 1863-1938
paintings: (L) $2,750; (H) $23,000

HOFMANN, E. Anson
19th/20th cent.
paintings: (H) $467

HOFMANN, Earl Francis
20th cent.
paintings: (H) $770

HOFMANN, Hans
German/American 1880-1966
paintings: (L) $2,300; (H) $550,000
drawings: (L) $660; (H) $36,800

HOFMANN, Ludwig von
German 1861-1945
paintings: (H) $12,650
drawings: (L) $880; (H) $1,100

HOFNER, J.
German 19th cent.
paintings: (H) $1,760

HOFSTADTER, Theodore
late 19th cent.
drawings: (H) $1,380

HOFSTEIN, Hugo O. von
Swedish/American b. 1865
drawings: (H) $489

HOGAN, Jean, Virginia M.
b. 1909
paintings: (L) $138; (H) $880

HOGARTH, Burne
American b. 1911
drawings: (L) $3,162; (H) $9,350

HOGENBYL, Jan
paintings: (H) $880

HOGER, Rudolf A.
Austrian 1876-1928
paintings: (L) $1,650; (H) $3,450

HOGG, George
American
paintings: (H) $900

HOGHFIFELD, W.
Continental 19th cent.
paintings: (H) $920

HOGNER, Nils
American b. 1893
paintings: (L) $357; (H) $2,310

HOGUET, Charles
French 1821-1870
paintings: (L) $2,640; (H) $11,000

HOHENBERG, Josef Wagner
German b. 1870
paintings: (H) $6,160

HOHENBERG, Rosa
German b. 1852
paintings: (H) $5,175

HOHENBERG, Wagner
Austrian 19th cent.
paintings: (H) $4,125

HOHNBERG, Josef Wagner
Continental b. 1811
paintings: (H) $6,600

HOHNSTEDT, Peter L.
American 1872-1957
paintings: (L) $165; (H) $863

HOIN, Claude Jean Baptiste
1750-1817
drawings: (H) $9,200

HOKUSAI, Katsushika
Japanese 1760-1849
paintings: (H) $522

HOLBERG, Richard A.
American 1889-1942
paintings: (H) $605

HOLBERTON, Wakeman
1839-1898
paintings: (H) $1,100

HOLBROOK, Hollis
American b. 1909
paintings: (L) $110; (H) $3,575

HOLD, A.
British 19th cent.
drawings: (H) $990

HOLD, Ben
British 19th cent.
paintings: (H) $1,045

HOLD, F.
paintings: (H) $2,200

HOLDEN, James A.
American 1881-1956
paintings: (L) $247; (H) $770

HOLDER, E.H.
British 20th cent.
paintings: (H) $3,410

HOLDER, Edward Henry
British ac. 1864-1917
paintings: (L) $330; (H) $4,400

HOLDING, Henry James
British 1833-1872
paintings: (L) $1,320; (H) $2,860

HOLDREDGE, Ransom G.
American 1836-1899
paintings: (L) $1,495; (H) $4,888

HOLEGET
paintings: (H) $575

HOLFELD, Hippolyte Dominique
French 1804-1872
paintings: (H) $22,550

HOLGATE, Edwin Headley
Canadian 1892-1977
paintings: (L) $5,060; (H) $22,000

HOLK
paintings: (H) $518

HOLLAMS, F. Mabel
British 1877-1963
paintings: (L) $1,650; (H) $8,625

HOLLAND, James
British 1799-1870
paintings: (L) $1,320; (H) $4,400
drawings: (L) $302; (H) $9,775

HOLLAND, John
British 19th cent.
paintings: (H) $2,640

HOLLAND, John
British ac. 1831-1879
paintings: (L) $1,650; (H) $2,587

HOLLAND, John, Sr.
English 1805-1880
paintings: (H) $1,650

HOLLAND, Tom
American b. 1936
paintings: (L) $1,610; (H) $3,300
drawings: (L) $920; (H) $5,750
sculpture: (L) $880; (H) $10,450

HOLLANDINE OF THE PALATINE,
Louise
1622-1709
paintings: (H) $167,500

HOLLANDS, Una
paintings: (L) $137; (H) $467

HOLLERN, Mike
sculpture: (L) $550; (H) $2,200

HOLLIDAY, Frank
20th cent.
paintings: (H) $880

HOLLOWAY, Edward Stratton
American d. 1939
paintings: (L) $1,155; (H) $1,725

HOLLYER, Eva
British ac. 1891-1898
paintings: (L) $2,860; (H) $20,700

HOLLYER, Gregory
British 19th/20th cent.
paintings: (H) $2,530

HOLLYER, Maud
Scottish exhib. 1902-1903
paintings: (H) $1,430
drawings: (L) $385; (H) $575

HOLLYER, W.P.
English 19th cent.
paintings: (L) $495; (H) $2,475

HOLM, A.
19th cent.
paintings: (H) $1,430

HOLM, Ebba
Danish b. 1889
paintings: (H) $1,495

HOLMAG, V.
British 20th cent.
paintings: (H) $523

HOLMAN, Frank
American b. 1865
paintings: (H) $57,500

HOLMAN, Jonas
1805-1873
paintings: (H) $28,750

HOLMAN, M.V.
Dutch 17th cent.
paintings: (H) $2,420

HOLME, Lucy D.
American b. 1882
paintings: (L) $330; (H) $1,650

HOLMES, A.C.
British 19th/20th cent.
drawings: (H) $3,300

HOLMES, Basil
English ac. 1844-1850
paintings: (H) $1,100

HOLMES, Frank Graham, Jr.
American b. 1908
paintings: (L) $160; (H) $800

HOLMES, George Augustus
British d. 1911
paintings: (L) $4,025; (H) $10,350

HOLMES, Lucy
paintings: (H) $550

HOLMES, Philip H.
ac. 1873-1877
paintings: (H) $605

HOLMES, Ralph
American 1876-1963
paintings: (L) $220; (H) $3,450

HOLMES, William Henry
American 1846-1933
drawings: (L) $165; (H) $7,700

HOLMES(?), W.H.
paintings: (H) $460

HOLMGREN, John
1897-1963
drawings: (L) $247; (H) $1,430

HOLMSTEDT, J.
Scandinavian 20th cent.
paintings: (H) $2,475

HOLOR
English 19th cent.
paintings: (H) $990

HOLSOE, Carl Vilhelm
Danish 1863-1935
paintings: (L) $16,100; (H) $55,000

HOLSOE, Eilsa
Danish 19th cent.
paintings: (H) $3,575

HOLSON, B.
American 19th/20th cent.
paintings: (H) $550

HOLST, Laurits
Danish 1848-1934
paintings: (L) $1,320; (H) $2,420

HOLST, Theodor M. von
British 1810-1844
drawings: (H) $575

HOLSTAYN, Josef
German 20th cent.
paintings: (H) $5,500

HOLSTEYN, Pieter, II
1614-1687
drawings: (H) $825

HOLT, Edwin Frederick
British ac. 1864-1897
paintings: (L) $690; (H) $1,980

HOLT, Geoffrey
American 1882-1977
paintings: (L) $413; (H) $1,430

HOLT, Roger
American 20th cent.
paintings: (H) $550

HOLTY, Carl
American 1900-1973
paintings: (L) $230; (H) $2,875
drawings: (L) $110; (H) $5,463

HOLTZ (?)
paintings: (H) $605

HOLTZMAN, Chuck
paintings: (H) $660
drawings: (L) $385; (H) $660
sculpture: (H) $605

HOLYOAKE, Rowland
English exhib. 1880-1911
paintings: (L) $863; (H) $2,200

HOLYOAKE, William
British 1834-1894
paintings: (H) $7,700

HOLZER, Brigitte
German 20th cent.
paintings: (L) $2,200; (H) $3,850

HOLZER, Jenny
American b. 1950
paintings: (L) $2,185; (H) $6,600
sculpture: (L) $1,320; (H) $66,000

HOLZHAUER, Emil Eugen
American b. 1887
paintings: (H) $1,380

HOLZLHUBER, Franz
American ac. mid-19th cent.
drawings: (L) $2,860; (H) $7,150

HOLZTZMAN, Harry
b. 1912
paintings: (H) $3,450

HOMA, R.
Italian 19th cent.
paintings: (H) $1,430

HOMAN, Gertrude
British 19th cent.
paintings: (L) $6,900; (H) $10,350

HOMER, Winslow
American 1836-1910
paintings: (L) $244,500; (H) $1,210,000
drawings: (L) $1,320; (H) $1,817,500

HONDECOETER, Gillis Claesz. de
Dutch 1604-1653
paintings: (H) $22,000

HONDECOETER, Gysbert de and Jan
van BIJLERT
Dutch 17th cent.
paintings: (H) $27,600

HONDECOETER, Melchior de
Dutch 1636-1695
paintings: (L) $5,775; (H) $354,500

HONDECOETER, Melchior de,
studio of
17th cent.
paintings: (L) $13,800; (H) $18,400

HONDIUS, Abraham Danielsz.
1625-1693
paintings: (H) $2,990

HONDIUS, Gerrit
Dutch/American 1891-1970
paintings: (L) $303; (H) $1,430
drawings: (L) $220; (H) $522

HONE, Nathaniel
1718-1784
paintings: (H) $4,400

HONEGGER, Gottfried
paintings: (H) $4,400
drawings: (H) $4,370

HONTHORST, Gerrit van
Dutch 1590-1656
paintings: (H) $8,800

HOOCH, Pieter de
Dutch 1629-1681
paintings: (L) $55,200; (H) $103,700
drawings: (L) $632; (H) $715

HOOD, Dorothy
American b. 1918
paintings: (L) $1,980; (H) $2,145

HOOG, Bernard de
Dutch 1867-1943
paintings: (L) $688; (H) $15,400

HOOGLAND, WM. C.
19th cent.
drawings: (H) $805

HOOGLAND, William C.
drawings: (H) $1,760

HOOGSTRATEN, Samuel van
Flemish 1627-1678
paintings: (H) $22,000

HOOK, Bryan
English ac. 1880-1923
paintings: (H) $3,850

HOOK, James Clarke
British 1819-1907
paintings: (H) $1,380

HOOK, Julian
English 19th cent.
paintings: (H) $460

HOOK, Richard
drawings: (L) $385; (H) $825

HOOK, William C.
b. 1948
paintings: (L) $1,650; (H) $8,800

HOOKS, Mitchell
b. 1923
paintings: (H) $1,210
drawings: (H) $550

HOOLEN, F.
British 20th cent.
paintings: (L) $440; (H) $688

HOONSTRO, John
paintings: (H) $660

HOOPER, John Horace
English ac. 1870-1899
paintings: (L) $660; (H) $3,520

HOORDE, Ernest van
Belgian b. 1922
paintings: (H) $1,100

HOORDE, Louis van der
Dutch 20th cent.
paintings: (H) $489

HOPE
paintings: (H) $700

HOPE, James
American 1818/19-1892
paintings: (L) $412; (H) $8,250

HOPE, Robert
British 19th cent.
paintings: (H) $3,300

HOPKIN, Robert
Scottish/American 1832-1909
paintings: (L) $259; (H) $6,050
drawings: (L) $60; (H) $2,640

HOPKINGS, W.H.
paintings: (H) $450

HOPKINS, Arthur
English 1848-1930
drawings: (H) $7,150

HOPKINS, Budd
American b. 1931
paintings: (L) $220; (H) $1,650

HOPKINS, Eric
drawings: (L) $1,064; (H) $2,185

HOPKINS, Frances Anne
paintings: (H) $6,600

HOPKINS, James R.
American 1877-1969
paintings: (L) $6,050; (H) $6,100

HOPKINS, Kendal
American 1908-1991
paintings: (L) $330; (H) $1,045

HOPKINS, M.W.
American 1789-1844
paintings: (H) $41,800

HOPKINS, Peter
American b. 1911
paintings: (L) $2,310; (H) $6,325

HOPKINS, Robert
American b. 1934
paintings: (L) $143; (H) $1,650

HOPKINSON, Charles S.
American 1869-1962
paintings: (L) $192; (H) $29,700
drawings: (L) $467; (H) $2,310

HOPKINSON, Glen S.
American
paintings: (H) $4,000

HOPKINSON-SMITH, F.
American 1838-1915
drawings: (H) $1,870

HOPKYNS, W.H.
British 19th cent.
paintings: (H) $1,725

HOPPE, Emiel
American 19th cent.
paintings: (H) $1,705

HOPPER, David
sculpture: (H) $2,750

HOPPER, Edward
American 1882-1967
paintings: (L) $23,000; (H) $2,420,000
drawings: (L) $2,200; (H) $220,000

HOPPER, Jo N., Edward Hopper's wife
American 20th cent.
paintings: (H) $715

HOPPIN, T.
paintings: (H) $550

HOPPMANN, Arnold
paintings: (H) $920

HOPPNER, Sir John
British 1758-1810
paintings: (L) $1,650; (H) $79,750

HOPWOOD, Henry Silkstone
English 1860-1914
drawings: (H) $2,760

HORACIO
Mexican 1912-1972
paintings: (L) $1,150; (H) $9,350

HOREAU, Hector
1801-1872
drawings: (H) $1,265

HOREMANS, Jan Josef, the elder
Flemish 1682-1759
paintings: (H) $32,200

HOREMANS, Jan Josef, the elder
studio of
18th cent.
paintings: (L) $12,075; (H) $13,800

HOREMANS, Jan Josef, the younger
Flemish 1714-c. 1790
paintings: (L) $4,600; (H) $14,950

HORLOR, George W.
British ac. 1849-1890
paintings: (L) $2,750; (H) $14,300

HORLOR, Joseph
British 19th cent.
paintings: (L) $440; (H) $1,840

HORMANN, Theodor von
Austrian 1840-1895
paintings: (H) $148,500

HORN, **
drawings: (H) $1,840

HORN, Julius, Josef Kamenitzky
STEINER
Austrian 1910-1981
paintings: (H) $1,155

HORN, Rebecca
German b. 1944
paintings: (H) $6,900
drawings: (H) $4,025
sculpture: (L) $4,025; (H) $43,700

HORN, Roni
American b. 1955
paintings: (H) $4,600
drawings: (L) $2,530; (H) $6,038
sculpture: (L) $18,400; (H) $20,700

HORNAK, Ian
paintings: (H) $660

HORNBROOK, Richard Lyde
English 1783-1865
drawings: (H) $990

HORNEL, Edward Atkinson
British 1864-1933
paintings: (L) $9,240; (H) $11,500

HORNEMANN, Adolph
German 1813-1890
paintings: (H) $2,200

HORNING, William
20th cent.
paintings: (H) $518

HORNY, Franz
German 1798-1824
drawings: (H) $27,600

HORNYAK, Jennifer
Canadian b. 1940
paintings: (H) $1,155

HOROWITZ, Leopold
Hungarian 1838-1917
paintings: (H) $2,860

HORSLEY, John Calcott
British 1817-1903
paintings: (H) $3,575

HORSSEN, Winand Bastien van
Dutch b. 1863
paintings: (H) $4,675

HORST, Franz
Austrian 1862-1950
paintings: (H) $4,950

HORST, Gerrit Willemsz.
c. 1612-1652
paintings: (L) $7,700; (H) $15,400

HORTER, Earl
American 1881-1940
paintings: (L) $2,860; (H) $7,700
drawings: (L) $82; (H) $7,150

HORTON, C.
paintings: (H) $2,300

HORTON, E.
Scottish 20th cent.
paintings: (L) $350; (H) $825

HORTON, John M.
b. 1935
paintings: (L) $1,925; (H) $3,300

HORTON, M.C.
American School 19th cent.
paintings: (H) $1,870

HORTON, William S.
American 1865-1936
paintings: (L) $207; (H) $10,350
drawings: (L) $454; (H) $1,495

HORVATH, G.A.
Hungarian 19th cent.
paintings: (H) $907

HORWOOD, John
English 20th cent.
paintings: (L) $275; (H) $880

HORY, Elmyr de
Hungarian 1906-1979
paintings: (L) $920; (H) $3,300

HOSEMANN, Theodore
German 1807-1875
paintings: (H) $11,000

Over the Door

Paintings have traditionally been hung one above the other, sometimes as many as four, reaching up to the ceiling. It is only in modern times that works of art have been hung in a linear fashion. The Barnes Collection in Merion, Pennsylvania, and Gallery #223 in the American Wing of the Metropolitan Museum of Art have their paintings hung in the traditional manner.

Cupid and Psyche and *Flora and Zephyr* are *dessus-de-porte*, a French term meaning "over the door" applied to "paintings designed to fill a space between the top of the door frame and ceiling." The mythological scenes evoke the playfulness characteristic of French Rococo and were painted by 18th-century artist Michel-Ange Houasse (1680-1730), a French painter, who worked in the Spanish court of Philip V. When the large pair of paintings were offered at Butterfield's in the fall of 1995, they realized $28,750. (Michel-Ange Houasse, *Flora and Zephyr* and *Cupid and Psyche*, oil on canvas, 63 x 65¾ inches, Butterfield's, November 22, 1995, $28,750)

HOSIASSON, Philippe
  French b. 1898
  paintings: (L) $3,300; (H) $11,000

HOSKINS, Gayle Porter
  American 1887-1962
  paintings: (L) $715; (H) $25,300

HOSMA, T.
  German 19th cent.
  paintings: (H) $1,150

HOSMER, Billy Price
  American 20th cent.
  paintings: (H) $990

HOSMER, Florence A.
  19th/20th cent.
  paintings: (H) $468

HOSMER, Harriet
  American 1830-1908
  sculpture: (L) $715; (H) $1,870

HOSNER, Bill
  drawings: (H) $1,430

HOTTOT, Louis
  French 1834-1905
  sculpture: (L) $935; (H) $6,050

HOUASSE, Michel Ange
  French 1680-1730
  paintings: (H) $28,750

HOUBEN, Henri
  Belgian 20th cent.
  paintings: (L) $1,208; (H) $4,400

HOUBRAKEN, Arnold
  1660-1719
  paintings: (H) $4,950

HOUBRAKEN, Nicola van
  c. 1660-1723
  paintings: (H) $49,500

HOUBRON, Frederic Anatole
French 1851-1908
paintings: (H) $1,380

HOUCKGEEST, Gerard
1600-1661
paintings: (H) $27,600

HOUDON, Jean Antoine
French 1741-1828
sculpture: (L) $467; (H) $4,025

HOUDON, Jean Antoine, workshop of
sculpture: (H) $32,200

HOUGH, William
English 19th cent.
drawings: (H) $715

HOURY, Charles Borromee Antoine
French 1823-1898
paintings: (H) $1,150

HOUSER, Allan C., Haozous, Pulling
Roots
Native American b. 1915
drawings: (H) $3,410

HOUSER, G.
Continental 19th cent.
paintings: (H) $16,100

HOUSEZ, Charles Gustave
French 1822-1880
paintings: (H) $1,760

HOUSSER, Yvonne McKague
paintings: (H) $8,250

HOUSSIN, Edouard Charles Marie
French 1847-1917
sculpture: (L) $550; (H) $1,150

HOUSTON, A. C.
19th/20th cent.
drawings: (H) $575

HOUSTON, Cody
sculpture: (H) $2,420

HOUSTON, Frances C.
American 1867-1906
paintings: (H) $2,875

HOUSTON, Georges
British 1869-1947
paintings: (L) $660; (H) $6,875

HOUTEN, Justine Marie van
Dutch b. 1908
paintings: (H) $575

HOUTEN, Willem van
ac. c. 1632
paintings: (H) $8,050

HOVE, Edmond Theodor van
Belgian 1853-1913
paintings: (H) $12,650

HOVE, Hubertus van
Dutch 1814-1865
paintings: (L) $1,495; (H) $4,600

HOVEN, Gottfried von
19th/20th cent.
paintings: (H) $862

HOVEN, Van
Dutch 19th cent.
paintings: (H) $1,320

HOVENDEN, Thomas
Irish/American 1840-1895
paintings: (L) $1,320; (H) $24,200
drawings: (L) $11; (H) $358

HOVENER, J.J.
c. 1900 ?
paintings: (H) $1,320

HOVEY, Charles Mason
American
drawings: (H) $10,350

HOW, Kenneth
American b. 1883
paintings: (L) $330; (H) $1,100

HOWANIETZ, Franz Joseph
European 1897-1972
paintings: (H) $550

HOWARD, B.K.
American b. 1872
paintings: (L) $1,100; (H) $3,025

HOWARD, Cecil de Blaquiere
American 1888-1956
sculpture: (L) $990; (H) $17,250

HOWARD, George James
British 1843-1911
paintings: (H) $3,450

HOWARD, Humbert
American d. 1992
paintings: (L) $550; (H) $578
drawings: (L) $110; (H) $440

HOWARD, Joe
American
paintings: (H) $1,800

HOWARD, John Langley
American b. 1902
paintings: (L) $440; (H) $8,250
drawings: (L) $192; (H) $2,875

HOWARD, Josephine
paintings: (H) $715

HOWARD, M. Maitland
British 20th cent.
paintings: (H) $2,090

HOWARD, Marion P.
American b. 1883
paintings: (H) $3,163
drawings: (H) $165

HOWARD, S.
American 19th/20th cent.
paintings: (H) $2,090

HOWARTH, Glenn
paintings: (H) $2,420

HOWE, J.
paintings: (H) $1,760

HOWE, W.A., Jr.
American 19th cent.
paintings: (H) $5,500

HOWE, William Henry
American 1846-1929
paintings: (L) $165; (H) $2,530

HOWELL, E.A.
paintings: (H) $3,300

HOWELL, Felicie Waldo
American 1897-1968
paintings: (L) $550; (H) $2,530
drawings: (H) $1,650

HOWELL, Henry
ac. 1660-1720
paintings: (H) $17,250

HOWELL, Peter
American 20th cent.
paintings: (L) $2,070; (H) $3,738

HOWES, Edgar Allan
English b. 1888
sculpture: (H) $1,540

HOWES, Edith
19th/20th cent.
paintings: (H) $3,080

HOWES, Kenneth
English b. 1924
paintings: (L) $660; (H) $2,530

HOWES, Royce
paintings: (H) $1,265

HOWES, S.A.
American
paintings: (H) $15,400

HOWES, Samuel P.
American ac. c. 1829-1860
paintings: (H) $20,700

HOWITT, John Newton
American 1885-1958
paintings: (L) $173; (H) $1,760
drawings: (H) $2,640

HOWITT, William Samuel
British 1765-1822
paintings: (H) $4,290
drawings: (L) $96; (H) $12,100

HOWLAND, Alfred Cornelius
American 1838-1909
paintings: (L) $220; (H) $21,850

HOWLAND, Frank
American ac. c. 1854-1868
paintings: (H) $660

HOWLAND, George
American 1865-1928
paintings: (L) $468; (H) $1,650

HOWLAND, John Dare
American 1843-1914
paintings: (H) $4,400

HOWS, John Augustus
d. 1874
paintings: (H) $605

HOXIE, B. Davidson
19th/20th cent.
paintings: (H) $660

HOXIE, Mrs. Lathrop
paintings: (H) $825

HOYER, Edward
British 19th cent.
paintings: (H) $32,200

HOYLAND, John
English b. 1934
paintings: (L) $110; (H) $4,950

HOYLAND, Thomas R.
British 19th cent.
paintings: (H) $825

HOYNE, Tom
American 20th cent.
paintings: (L) $230; (H) $805
drawings: (L) $144; (H) $770

HOYOLL, Phillipp
German ac. 1836-1875
paintings: (L) $330; (H) $1,320

HOYOS, Ana Mercedes
b. Colombia 1942
paintings: (L) $9,775; (H) $55,200

HOYT, Vivian Church
American b. 1880
paintings: (L) $275; (H) $467

HOZENDORF, Johann Samuel
1694-1742
paintings: (H) $14,300

HRADECNY, B.
paintings: (H) $550

HSIA, Yan
Chinese/American b. 1937
paintings: (H) $6,900

HSIUNG, Dora
sculpture: (H) $523

HSU, Ti Shan
b. 1951
paintings: (H) $3,300
sculpture: (H) $8,250

HUANG BINHONG, Huang PIN-
HUNG
Chinese 1864-1955
drawings: (L) $5,750; (H) $20,700

HUBACEK, William
American 1866-1958
paintings: (L) $460; (H) $1,610

HUBARD, William James
American 1807-1862
paintings: (H) $7,700
drawings: (H) $3,220

HUBBARD, Celia
20th cent.
drawings: (H) $805

HUBBARD, Charles
American 1801-1864
paintings: (H) $2,530

HUBBARD, Charles
English 19th cent.
paintings: (H) $2,750

HUBBARD, Charles Daniel
American 1876-1951
paintings: (L) $33; (H) $880

HUBBARD, Harlan
paintings: (L) $605; (H) $2,200

HUBBARD, Lydia M.B.
19th/20th cent.
paintings: (H) $825
drawings: (H) $275

HUBBARD, R.
American 1817-1888
paintings: (H) $6,000

HUBBARD, Whitney Myron
American 1875-1965
paintings: (L) $110; (H) $4,887
drawings: (H) $165

HUBBELL, Henry Salem
American 1870-1949
paintings: (L) $990; (H) $7,475

HUBER
Continental 19th/20th cent.
drawings: (H) $1,725

HUBER, E.
Aus. 19th cent.
paintings: (H) $1,540

HUBER, Ernst
Austrian 1895-1960
paintings: (H) $330
drawings: (H) $3,450

HUBER, Leon Charles
French 1858-1928
paintings: (L) $1,100; (H) $9,200

HUBER, Urs
Swiss b. 1946
paintings: (H) $1,100

HUBERT, Leah
French 20th cent.
paintings: (H) $1,100

HUBERT, Louise Stephanie
French 19th/20th cent.
paintings: (H) $1,610

HUBERT, R.
19th/20th cent.
paintings: (H) $518

HUBERT, W.
Polish b. 1925
paintings: (H) $495

HUBERTI, Antonio
French 1898-1980
paintings: (L) $1,045; (H) $1,045

HUBNER, Anton
German 1818-1892
paintings: (H) $2,760

HUBNER, Carl Wilhelm
German 1814-1879
paintings: (L) $1,760; (H) $10,638

HUBNER, Heinrich
German b. 1869
paintings: (H) $2,530

HUBNER, Ulrich
German 1872-1932
paintings: (H) $4,888

HUCHTENBERG, Jan van
Dutch 1647-1733
paintings: (L) $2,970; (H) $19,550
drawings: (H) $920

HUCHTHAUSEN, David
American b. 1951
sculpture: (L) $1,840; (H) $4,950

HUCTENBURGH, Jan von
Dutch 1646-1753
paintings: (H) $2,970
drawings: (H) $920

HUDON, Norman
b. 1929
drawings: (H) $1,870

HUDSON, Charles Bradford
American 1865-1938/39
paintings: (H) $5,500
drawings: (H) $88

HUDSON, Eric
American 1864-1932
paintings: (L) $805; (H) $5,775

HUDSON, Grace Carpenter
American 1865-1937
paintings: (L) $550; (H) $26,400

HUDSON, Hanna Maria
Canadian School 19th cent.
paintings: (H) $3,850

HUDSON, John Bradley
American 1832-1903
paintings: (L) $719; (H) $1,760
drawings: (L) $99; (H) $880

HUDSON, Muriel
American 1890-1959
paintings: (H) $770

HUDSON, Robert
American b. 1938
drawings: (L) $805; (H) $2,750

HUDSON, Thomas
English 1701-1779
paintings: (L) $633; (H) $27,600

HUE, Charles Desire
French 19th cent.
paintings: (H) $3,680

HUE, Jean Francois
French 1751-1823
paintings: (H) $41,400

HUEBLER, Douglas
American b. 1924
drawings: (L) $4,025; (H) $4,950

HUEHL, Bob
American 20th cent.
paintings: (H) $1,100

HUENS, Jean L.
b. 1921
paintings: (H) $770

HUET, Christophe
French d. 1759
paintings: (L) $71,500; (H) $165,000

HUET, Frederick
1838-1916
paintings: (H) $715

HUET, Jean Baptiste
French 1745-1811
paintings: (L) $7,475; (H) $211,500
drawings: (L) $1,035; (H) $18,700

HUET, Paul
French 1803-1869
paintings: (L) $9,200; (H) $27,600
drawings: (L) $1,760; (H) $1,840

HUET, Rene Paul
French b. 1844
drawings: (L) $920; (H) $920

HUETER, Simon and Haveri
German 17th cent.
drawings: (H) $550

HUGE, Jurgan Frederick
American 1809-1878
drawings: (L) $5,500; (H) $25,300

HUGGINS, William
British 1820-1884
paintings: (L) $2,300; (H) $24,150

HUGGINS, William John
English 1781-1845
paintings: (L) $2,185; (H) $18,400

HUGGLER, Willi
sculpture: (H) $880

HUGHES, Edward
English 1832-1908
paintings: (H) $3,850

HUGHES, Edward John
Canadian b. 1913
paintings: (L) $19,800; (H) $39,600
drawings: (L) $5,500; (H) $7,150

HUGHES, Edward Robert
English 1851-1914
paintings: (H) $12,100
drawings: (H) $464,500

HUGHES, Edwin
British 1851-1904
paintings: (H) $3,025

HUGHES, George
American 1907-1990
paintings: (L) $154; (H) $16,500
drawings: (H) $550

HUGHES, J.
paintings: (H) $4,600

HUGHES, J.T.
paintings: (L) $155; (H) $990

HUGHES, John Joseph
British ac. 1838-1867
paintings: (L) $357; (H) $880

HUGHES, Marilyn Beth
American
drawings: (H) $700

HUGHES, Stanley C.
drawings: (L) $990; (H) $2,500

HUGHES, Talbot
English 1869-1942
paintings: (H) $11,000
drawings: (H) $230

HUGHES, William
British 1842-1901
paintings: (L) $920; (H) $7,975

HUGHES-STANTON, Sir Herbert
English 1870-1937
paintings: (H) $825

HUGHTO, Daryl
American b. 1943
paintings: (L) $770; (H) $3,450

HUGO, F.
American 19th cent.
paintings: (H) $3,300

HUGO, Jean
French 1894-1984
paintings: (L) $1,650; (H) $14,300
drawings: (L) $805; (H) $6,900

HUGO, Victor
French 1802-1885
drawings: (L) $880; (H) $1,610

HUGO, Victor and attrib. Charles
HUGO
French 19th cent.
drawings: (H) $18,400

HUGUE, Manolo
Spanish 20th cent.
sculpture: (L) $4,888; (H) $7,150

HUGUENIN-DUMITRAN, Andre
sculpture: (H) $2,530

HUGUET, Victor Pierre
French 1835-1902
paintings: (L) $6,900; (H) $41,400

HUILLIOT, Pierre Nicolas
French 1674-1751
paintings: (L) $6,900; (H) $30,800

HULBERT, Katherine Allmond
American d. 1937
paintings: (L) $220; (H) $1,540

HULDAH
American ac. 1940s-50s
paintings: (L) $138; (H) $4,950

HULETT, Ralph
American 1915-1974
drawings: (H) $495

HULINGS, Clark
American b. 1922
paintings: (L) $5,775; (H) $214,500
drawings: (L) $1,870; (H) $1,925

HULK, Abraham, Jr.
British ac. 1876-1898
paintings: (L) $440; (H) $4,600
drawings: (H) $110

HULK, Abraham, Sr.
British 1813-1897
paintings: (L) $2,200; (H) $18,700

HULK, Hendrik
Dutch 1842-1937
paintings: (L) $605; (H) $660

HULK, John Frederick, II
Dutch 1855-1913
paintings: (H) $3,450

HULK, John Frederik, Sr.
Dutch 1829-1911
paintings: (L) $4,370; (H) $11,500

HULK, William F.
English b. 1852; ac. 1875-1906
paintings: (L) $690; (H) $805

HULL, C.
American School 19th/20th cent.
paintings: (H) $690

HULL, Marie Atkinson
American 1890-1980
paintings: (L) $345; (H) $1,430
drawings: (H) $275

HULL, Richard
b. 1955
paintings: (L) $1,150; (H) $14,950

HULLEGARDEN, Carel van
Dutch ac. 1647-1669
paintings: (H) $24,200

HULME, Frederick William
English 1816-1884
paintings: (L) $1,400; (H) $2,300

HULSE, John
American
drawings: (L) $133; (H) $605

HULSMAN, Johann
17th cent.
paintings: (H) $4,600

HULSMANN, H.
paintings: (H) $577

HULST, Frans de
Flemish 1610-1661
paintings: (L) $3,575; (H) $20,700

HULTBERG, John
American b. 1922
paintings: (L) $920; (H) $2,860

HUMBERT, Jacques Frenand and H.
CONTOUR
French 19th cent.
paintings: (H) $13,800

HUMBLOT, George
French 20th cent.
paintings: (H) $2,530

HUMBLOT, Robert
1907-1962
paintings: (L) $2,013; (H) $3,680

HUMBORG, Adolf
Austrian b. 1847
paintings: (L) $1,380; (H) $38,500

HUMMEL, F.
sculpture: (H) $1,045

HUMPHREY, David
b. 1955
paintings: (L) $345; (H) $2,200
drawings: (H) $715

HUMPHREY, Jack Weldon
paintings: (H) $2,420

HUMPHREY, Ozias
British 1742-1810
drawings: (H) $770

HUMPHREY, Ralph
American 1932-1990
paintings: (L) $1,320; (H) $13,200
drawings: (L) $460; (H) $1,100
sculpture: (L) $16,500; (H) $16,500

HUMPHREY, Walter Beach
American 1892-1966
paintings: (L) $880; (H) $2,640
drawings: (H) $495

HUMPHREYS, ***
British 19th cent.
paintings: (H) $1,380

HUMPHREYS, Charles P.
paintings: (H) $1,750

HUMPHREYS, Malcolm
American b. 1894
paintings: (L) $110; (H) $2,300

HUMPHRIES, Jacqueline
American b. 1960
paintings: (L) $1,380; (H) $2,875

HUMPHRISS, Charles H.
b. England 1867 d. 1934/40
sculpture: (L) $1,980; (H) $31,050

HUMPHRY, K.
paintings: (H) $495

HUNDERTWASSER, Friedensreich
Austrian b. 1928
drawings: (L) $7,475; (H) $74,250

HUNDSTEDT, H.
German 19th cent.
paintings: (H) $1,380

HUNLA, J.
paintings: (H) $6,500

HUNSINGER, A.
Dutch 19th/20th cent.
drawings: (H) $776

HUNT, Bryan
American b. 1947
drawings: (L) $299; (H) $44,000
sculpture: (L) $4,600; (H) $51,750

HUNT, Charles
British 1803-1877
paintings: (L) $2,145; (H) $27,500

HUNT, Charles
British 1829-1900
paintings: (L) $7,475; (H) $14,950

HUNT, Charles
British 19th cent.
paintings: (L) $3,575; (H) $7,150

HUNT, Charles D.
American 1840-1914
paintings: (L) $275; (H) $1,725
drawings: (L) $330; (H) $373

HUNT, Edgar
English 1876-1953
paintings: (L) $3,300; (H) $26,450

HUNT, Edward Aubrey
British 1855-1922
paintings: (L) $374; (H) $7,150
drawings: (L) $575; (H) $1,093

HUNT, Esther A.
American 1885-1951
paintings: (L) $1,480; (H) $3,575
drawings: (L) $33; (H) $2,588
sculpture: (L) $770; (H) $1,840

HUNT, Henry
British 19th cent.
paintings: (H) $1,100

HUNT, Howard M.
English 19th cent.
paintings: (L) $1,320; (H) $2,310

HUNT, Joe
paintings: (L) $345; (H) $2,070

HUNT, Lynn Bogue
American 1878-1960
paintings: (L) $715; (H) $19,250
drawings: (L) $660; (H) $19,800

HUNT, Richard
American b. 1933
sculpture: (L) $1,100; (H) $4,125

HUNT, Thomas L.
b. Canada 1882 d. U.S. 1938
paintings: (L) $302; (H) $18,700

HUNT, W.
19th cent.
drawings: (H) $1,650

HUNT, W.S.
American 19th cent.
drawings: (L) $88; (H) $495

HUNT, Walter
British 1861-1941
paintings: (L) $1,430; (H) $41,400

HUNT, William
English exhib. 1880-1911
paintings: (H) $550

HUNT, William Henry
British 1790-1864
paintings: (H) $1,100
drawings: (L) $550; (H) $2,200

HUNT, William Morris
American 1824-1879
paintings: (L) $248; (H) $19,800
drawings: (L) $22; (H) $1,320

HUNTEN, Emil
German 1827-1902
paintings: (L) $99; (H) $6,600

HUNTEN, Franz
paintings: (H) $550

HUNTER, Clementine
American 1887-1988
paintings: (L) $303; (H) $9,200
drawings: (L) $880; (H) $3,080

HUNTER, Colin
Scottish, d. London 1841-1904
paintings: (L) $550; (H) $2,200

HUNTER, E.
drawings: (L) $302; (H) $550

HUNTER, Frederick Leo
American 1858-1943
paintings: (L) $165; (H) $1,100
drawings: (L) $110; (H) $161

HUNTER, George Leslie
British 1877-1931
paintings: (H) $11,000

HUNTER, Isabel
American 1878-1941
paintings: (L) $550; (H) $3,575

HUNTER, Jack D.
American 20th cent.
drawings: (L) $220; (H) $550

HUNTER, Leslie
British 1879-1934
paintings: (H) $8,625

HUNTER, Robert Douglas
American b. 1928
paintings: (L) $345; (H) $2,750

HUNTER, Sid
sculpture: (H) $690

HUNTINGTON
American early 20th cent.
drawings: (H) $4,400

HUNTINGTON, Anna Hyatt Vaughn
American 1876-1973
sculpture: (L) $1,760; (H) $25,300

HUNTINGTON, Chris
20th cent.
paintings: (H) $963

HUNTINGTON, D.W.
drawings: (L) $303; (H) $700

HUNTINGTON, Daniel
American 1816-1906
paintings: (L) $440; (H) $26,400
drawings: (L) $550; (H) $1,760

HUNTINGTON, Dwight
1860-1906
drawings: (H) $2,300

HUNTINGTON, Susan Terpning
American b. 1953
paintings: (H) $1,320
drawings: (H) $2,750

HUODON, Jean Antoine, workshop of
18th cent.
sculpture: (H) $23,000

HUPENDEN, Ernest
late 19th cent.
paintings: (H) $11,500

HURD, Michael
American 20th cent.
paintings: (H) $2,750

HURD, Peter
American 1904-1984
paintings: (L) $2,090; (H) $46,200
drawings: (L) $137; (H) $11,000

HURDMAN, J.
paintings: (H) $3,575

HUREL, Suzanne
French 1876-1956
paintings: (H) $690

HURK, Jan van den
paintings: (H) $475

HURLEY, Edward Timothy
American 1869-1950
paintings: (H) $2,310
drawings: (H) $3,200

HURLEY, Wilson
American b. 1924
paintings: (L) $303; (H) $68,500

HURST, Earl Oliver
1895-1958
drawings: (H) $550

HURST, Hal
English 1865-1938
drawings: (H) $2,750

HURT, Louis Bosworth
English 1856-1929
paintings: (L) $690; (H) $21,850

HURTADO, C.
British 19th cent.
paintings: (H) $920

HURTADO, Manuel Prieto
Spanish 19th cent.
paintings: (H) $2,645

HUSAIN, Maqbool Fida
Indian b. 1915
paintings: (L) $3,450; (H) $48,875
drawings: (L) $2,070; (H) $11,500

HUSAIN, Shamshad
paintings: (L) $1,150; (H) $1,725

HUSEIN
paintings: (L) $60; (H) $165
drawings: (H) $2,300

HUSSMAN, Albert Heinrich
German b. 1874
sculpture: (H) $2,860

HUSSMANN, A.
sculpture: (H) $1,320

HUSTEN, H.
paintings: (H) $523

HUSTON, A.
drawings: (H) $1,320

HUSTON, William
American 19th cent.
paintings: (L) $1,320; (H) $3,575
drawings: (H) $110

HUSZAR, Vilmos
paintings: (H) $3,025

HUTCHENS, Frank Townsend
American 1869-1937
paintings: (L) $385; (H) $11,000
drawings: (H) $165

HUTCHINSON, Allen
sculpture: (H) $880

HUTCHINSON, Donald C.
1869-1954
paintings: (H) $523

HUTCHINSON, Frederick W.
American 1871-1953
paintings: (L) $330; (H) $1,760

HUTCHINSON, Peter
b. 1930
paintings: (H) $220
drawings: (L) $58; (H) $2,645

HUTCHISON, Robert Gemmill
British 1855-1936
paintings: (L) $4,950; (H) $23,100
drawings: (H) $660

HUTHER, Julius
German 1881-1954
drawings: (H) $660

HUTSMANN, A.
German 20th cent.
sculpture: (H) $2,420

HUTT, Henry
American 1875-1950
drawings: (L) $275; (H) $3,300

HUTTER, Sydney
contemporary
sculpture: (H) $1,840

HUTTY, Alfred Heber
American 1877/78-1954
paintings: (L) $275; (H) $3,190
drawings: (L) $1,210; (H) $5,390

HUYGENS, Francois Joseph
Belgian 1820-1908
paintings: (L) $2,300; (H) $3,300

HUYGENS, Johannes
Dutch 1833-1910
paintings: (H) $2,310

HUYS, Modeste
Belgian 1875-1932
paintings: (L) $24,200; (H) $35,750

HUYSMANS, Jan Baptist
Belgian 1654-1716
paintings: (H) $20,900

HUYSMANS, Jan Baptist
Belgian b. 1826
paintings: (L) $1,150; (H) $79,500

HUYSMANS, P.J.
Flemish ac. c. 1790
paintings: (H) $5,750

HUYSUM, Jan van
Dutch 1682-1749
paintings: (L) $20,700; (H) $3,520,000
drawings: (H) $862

HUYSUM, Justus van
Dutch 1659-1716
paintings: (L) $31,050; (H) $38,500

HUYSUM, Van
Dutch 18th cent.
drawings: (H) $1,495

HUYSUMS, Cornelis
1648-1727
paintings: (H) $4,313

HYAMS, William
b. 1878
drawings: (H) $715

HYATT, Anna D.
sculpture: (H) $1,540

HYDE, Doug
Native American b. 1946
sculpture: (H) $2,750

HYDE, George
British 19th cent.
paintings: (H) $770

HYDE, Helen
American 1868-1919
paintings: (L) $1,072; (H) $1,210
drawings: (H) $440

HYDE, R.T.
American b. 1886
paintings: (H) $495

HYDE, Thomas
drawings: (H) $605

HYDE, William Henry
American 1858-1943
paintings: (H) $275
drawings: (H) $2,860

HYETT, Will J.
American b. 1876
paintings: (L) $165; (H) $605

HYMAN?, George
19th/20th cent.
paintings: (H) $770

HYND, Frederick S.
American b. 1905
paintings: (L) $220; (H) $880
drawings: (L) $275; (H) $660

HYNEMAN, Herman N.
American 1859-1907
paintings: (L) $220; (H) $6,875

HYNTERMEISTER, Henry
American b. 1897
paintings: (L) $550; (H) $13,800
drawings: (H) $143

HYON, George Louis
French b. 1855
paintings: (H) $935

HYPPOLITE, Hector
Haitian 1894-1948
paintings: (L) $9,200; (H) $74,800
drawings: (H) $6,600

HYUDEL, R.
18th cent.
paintings: (H) $715

IACCARINO, Ralph
American contemporary
drawings: (L) $715; (H) $1,430

IACOVLEFF, Alexandre
French 1887-1938
paintings: (H) $10,450
drawings: (L) $920; (H) $5,500

IANELLI, Arcangelo
Brazilian b. 1922
paintings: (L) $4,600; (H) $6,050

IBARRA, Jose de
Mexican 1688-1756
paintings: (H) $11,500

IBBETSON, Julius Caesar
English 1759-1817
paintings: (L) $2,070; (H) $12,100
drawings: (L) $1,100; (H) $4,600

ICART, Louis
French 1888-1950
paintings: (L) $2,310; (H) $385,000
drawings: (L) $770; (H) $3,960
sculpture: (H) $1,320

ICAZA, Ernesto
Mexican 1866-1935
paintings: (L) $16,100; (H) $552,500
drawings: (H) $2,300

ICON, Green
18th cent.
paintings: (H) $1,210

IFFLAND, Franz
German 20th cent.
sculpture: (L) $385; (H) $2,990

IGLER, Gustav
German 1842-1908
paintings: (L) $20,900; (H) $34,100
drawings: (H) $55

IGNATIEV, Alex
Russian/American b. 1913
paintings: (H) $522
drawings: (L) $330; (H) $1,650

IHLY, Daniel
Swiss 1854-1910
paintings: (H) $825

IL NOGE
paintings: (H) $2,475

ILLES, Aladar Edvi
Hungarian 1870-1911
paintings: (H) $468
drawings: (H) $825

ILLIAN, George
drawings: (L) $357; (H) $660

ILLIERS, Gaston d'
French b. 1876
sculpture: (L) $1,100; (H) $1,955

ILLIERS, Geo.
sculpture: (H) $500

ILLIES, Arthur
German 1870-1952
paintings: (H) $11,000

ILSLEY, Frederick J.
American 1855-1933
paintings: (L) $150; (H) $1,265

IMAI, Toshimitsu
Japanese/French b. 1926
paintings: (H) $20,900

IMHOF, Joseph A.
American 1871-1955
paintings: (L) $468; (H) $55,000
drawings: (L) $920; (H) $2,200

IMMENDORF, Jorg
German b. 1945
paintings: (L) $15,400; (H) $28,600
drawings: (H) $660

IMPARATO, Girolamo
Italian ac. 1573-1621
paintings: (L) $4,400; (H) $24,150

IMPENS, Josse
Belgian 1840-1905
paintings: (H) $863

INDELLI, M.
Italian 20th cent.
paintings: (H) $550

INDIANA, Robert
American b. 1928
paintings: (L) $11,500; (H) $277,500
sculpture: (L) $2,640; (H) $3,025

INDONI, Filippo
Italian 19th cent.
paintings: (L) $2,875; (H) $13,200
drawings: (L) $523; (H) $10,925

INDUNO, D.
paintings: (H) $1,150

INDUNO, Domenico
Italian 1815-1878
paintings: (H) $46,000

INDUNO, Girolamo
Italian 1827-1890
paintings: (H) $77,000

INGELRANS, Paul Leon Henri
French ac. 1893-1920
paintings: (H) $13,200

INGELS, Graham
paintings: (H) $2,300
drawings: (L) $747; (H) $1,610

INGERLE, Rudolf
American 1879-1950
paintings: (L) $550; (H) $3,300

INGERMANN, Keith
American 20th cent.
paintings: (L) $104; (H) $605

INGERSOLL, Sandy
paintings: (H) $2,750

INGHAM, Charles Cromwell
Irish/American 1796-1863
paintings: (L) $1,150; (H) $3,850

INGHAM, Elizabeth H.
American 19th/20th cent.
drawings: (L) $550; (H) $1,100

INGLE, Ella B.
American 1895-1981
paintings: (H) $715

INGLE, John S.
American b. 1933
drawings: (H) $42,900

INGLIS, John J.
Irish/American 1867-1946
paintings: (L) $633; (H) $7,188

INGRES, Jean Auguste Dominique
French 1780-1867
paintings: (L) $55,000; (H) $497,500
drawings: (L) $8,800; (H) $387,500

INJALBERT, Jean Antoine
French 1845-1933
sculpture: (H) $2,090

INMAN, George
American 1825-1894
paintings: (H) $935

INMAN, Henry
American 1801-1846
paintings: (L) $275; (H) $12,075

INMAN, Jerry
paintings: (H) $660
drawings: (H) $500

INMAN, John O'Brien
American 1828-1896
paintings: (L) $605; (H) $3,300

INNERST, Mark
American b. 1957
paintings: (L) $6,900; (H) $27,500
drawings: (L) $6,600; (H) $17,600

INNES, John
1863-1941
paintings: (L) $4,840; (H) $5,060

INNESS, George
American 1825-1894
paintings: (L) $2,090; (H) $184,000

INNESS, George, Jr.
American 1853-1926
paintings: (L) $495; (H) $6,875
drawings: (L) $220; (H) $2,185

INNOCENT, Franck
French b. 1912
paintings: (H) $2,200

INNOCENTI, Camillo
Italian 1871-1961
paintings: (L) $460; (H) $1,093

INNOCENTI, Gaetano
Italian 19th cent.
drawings: (H) $4,025

INNOCENTI, Guglielmo
Italian 19th cent.
paintings: (H) $1,540

INSLEY, Albert
American 1842-1937
paintings: (L) $193; (H) $3,960
drawings: (H) $94

INUKAI, Kyohei
American b. 1913, ac. 1920's
paintings: (L) $550; (H) $12,100

IOMMI, Enio
Argentina b. 1926
sculpture: (L) $3,300; (H) $9,200

IOVINE, Nello
paintings: (L) $259; (H) $460

IPCAR, Dahlov
American b. 1917
paintings: (L) $341; (H) $3,105

IPOUSTEGUY, Jean
French b. 1920
paintings: (H) $1,650
sculpture: (L) $2,990; (H) $7,150

IPSEN, Ernest Ludwig
American 1869-1951
paintings: (L) $165; (H) $6,600

IPSEN, Kent
American b. 1933
sculpture: (L) $288; (H) $1,380

IRIZARRY, Epifanio
Puerto Rican
paintings: (H) $1,650

IROLLI, Vincenzo
Italian 1860-c. 1937/42
paintings: (L) $2,990; (H) $110,000
drawings: (L) $9,350; (H) $11,000

IRVINE, Sarah, Sadie
American 1887-1970
drawings: (L) $357; (H) $550

IRVINE, Wilson Henry
American 1869-1936
paintings: (L) $467; (H) $20,700
drawings: (L) $357; (H) $825

IRWIN, Robert
American b. 1928
paintings: (L) $41,250; (H) $222,500
sculpture: (H) $51,750

ISAACS, Jessie M.
American 19th cent.
sculpture: (H) $978

ISABEY, Jean Baptiste
French 1767-1855
drawings: (L) $517; (H) $2,300

ISABEY, Louis Gabriel Eugene
French 1803-1886
paintings: (L) $1,035; (H) $26,400
drawings: (L) $275; (H) $2,970

ISENBART, Marie Victor Emile
French 1846-1921
paintings: (L) $2,530; (H) $4,620

ISENDIECK, Suzanne
paintings: (H) $1,495

ISHAM, Samuel
American 1855-1914
paintings: (L) $1,320; (H) $1,430

ISHIKAWA, K.M.
Japanese 19th/20th cent.
sculpture: (H) $1,430

ISHIKAWA, Shigeniko
paintings: (H) $1,380

ISKOWITZ, Gershon
Canadian 1921-1988
paintings: (L) $5,280; (H) $20,900

ISLAS, Andreas de
paintings: (H) $12,650

ISOLDA
Brazilian b. 1924
paintings: (H) $2,420

ISPEN, Kent
American b. 1933
sculpture: (H) $1,380

ISRAEL, Daniel
Austrian 1859-1901
paintings: (L) $4,620; (H) $44,000

ISRAELS, Isaac
Dutch 1865-1934
paintings: (L) $880; (H) $19,550
drawings: (H) $460

ISRAELS, Josef
Dutch 1824-1911
paintings: (L) $522; (H) $44,000
drawings: (L) $770; (H) $14,950

ISRAELS, R.
American 20th cent.
paintings: (H) $1,100

ISSUPOFF, Alessio
Russian 1889-1957
paintings: (L) $2,970; (H) $36,800

ISTRATI, Alexandre
French b. 1915
paintings: (H) $1,320

ITAYA, Foussa
Japanese/French b. 1919
paintings: (L) $440; (H) $2,750

ITO, Yoshihiko
1867-1942
drawings: (L) $66; (H) $1,955

ITTER, Diane
contemporary
sculpture: (H) $5,463

ITURRIA, Ignacio
b. Uruguay 1949
paintings: (L) $3,450; (H) $57,500

IVANOWSKI, Sigismund de
Russian/American 1875-1944
paintings: (L) $440; (H) $4,950

IVANYI
Hungarian 19th/20th cent.
paintings: (H) $1,650

IVERD, Eugene
American 1893-1938
paintings: (H) $3,190

IVES, Chauncey Bradley
American 1810/12-1894
sculpture: (L) $1,850; (H) $19,800

IVES, H.S.
20th cent.
drawings: (L) $220; (H) $578

IVES, Louis Thomas
paintings: (H) $550

IVES, Norman
sculpture: (H) $805

IVES, Percy
American 1864-1928
paintings: (L) $110; (H) $8,800

IWILL, Joseph
French 1850-1923
paintings: (L) $825; (H) $1,980

IWILL, Marie Joseph Clavel
French 1850-1923
paintings: (H) $825

IZQUIERDO, Maria
Mexican 1908-1950
paintings: (L) $40,250; (H) $140,000
drawings: (L) $16,100; (H) $22,000

IZZARD, Daniel
Canadian b. 1923
paintings: (L) $1,000; (H) $1,650

JAAR, Alfredo
b. 1956
drawings: (L) $3,450; (H) $5,500
sculpture: (L) $9,775; (H) $11,000

JACK, Kenneth
Austrian b. 1924
paintings: (H) $660

JACK, Richard
Canadian 1866-1959
paintings: (H) $935

JACKEL, R.H.
Continental 19th/20th cent.
paintings: (H) $2,875

JACKMAN, Oscar Theodore
American 1878-1940
paintings: (H) $1,320

JACKMAN, Theodore
American 20th cent.
paintings: (H) $1,650

JACKSON, Alexander Young
Canadian 1882-1974
paintings: (L) $3,740; (H) $220,000
drawings: (H) $7,700

JACKSON, B.
paintings: (H) $715

JACKSON, Elbert McGran
American 1896-1962
paintings: (L) $748; (H) $3,850

JACKSON, Everett Gee
American 1901/03-1995
paintings: (L) $1,955; (H) $12,100

JACKSON, Frederick William
English 1859-1918
drawings: (H) $1,380

JACKSON, G.
early 19th cent.
drawings: (H) $935

JACKSON, George
paintings: (H) $2,420

JACKSON, Harry
American b. 1924
paintings: (H) $3,850
drawings: (H) $110
sculpture: (L) $690; (H) $187,000

JACKSON, Hazel Brill
American b. 1894
sculpture: (L) $440; (H) $1,980

JACKSON, J.
American 19th/20th cent.
paintings: (H) $605

JACKSON, James Randolph
Australian 1886-1975
paintings: (H) $1,540

JACKSON, Jean Jones
paintings: (H) $935
drawings: (H) $495

JACKSON, John
1778-1831
paintings: (H) $2,475

JACKSON, Lee
American b. 1909
paintings: (L) $357; (H) $2,200

JACKSON, Lesley
1867-1958
drawings: (H) $577

JACKSON, M.
English 19th cent.
paintings: (H) $550

JACKSON, Martin Jacob
American 1871-1955
paintings: (L) $330; (H) $880

JACKSON, Michael
paintings: (H) $99
drawings: (H) $2,310

JACKSON, Oliver
American b. 1935
drawings: (H) $2,750

JACKSON, Robert Scott
American 20th cent.
drawings: (H) $1,018

JACKSON, Ronald
paintings: (L) $962; (H) $1,320

JACKSON, Samuel Phillips
British 1830-1904
drawings: (H) $550

JACKSON, William Franklin
American 1850-1936
paintings: (L) $385; (H) $8,250

JACKSON, William Henry
American 1843-1942
paintings: (L) $2,588; (H) $9,350
drawings: (L) $187; (H) $825

JACOB, Alexandre
French b. 1876
paintings: (L) $1,760; (H) $3,575

JACOB, Max
French 1876-1944
drawings: (L) $1,430; (H) $1,725

JACOB, Ned
American b. 1938
paintings: (L) $10,450; (H) $18,150
drawings: (H) $1,870

JACOBBER, Moise
French 1786-1863
paintings: (H) $145,500
drawings: (H) $1,320

JACOBI, F.C.
Italian (?) 18th cent.
paintings: (H) $16,500

JACOBI, M.M.
English 19th cent.
paintings: (L) $440; (H) $770

JACOBI, Otto Reinhold
Canadian 1812-1901
paintings: (L) $3,740; (H) $6,875

JACOBI, Rudolph
American b. 1889
paintings: (L) $173; (H) $805

JACOBS, Franz
paintings: (H) $6,050

JACOBS, Hobart B.
American 20th cent.
paintings: (H) $1,100

JACOBS, Jacob Emmanuel
British 19th cent.
paintings: (L) $715; (H) $6,325

JACOBS, Louis Adolphe
Belgian 19th cent.
paintings: (H) $3,220

JACOBS, Paul Emil
German 1802-1866
paintings: (H) $33,350

Western Artist

Western painter, sculptor, and muralist Harry Jackson was born in Chicago in 1924. Although he was a city boy, his mother ran a lunchroom near the stockyards and he grew up with stables and stockyards. As a child his primary interests were horses and drawing. When he was 14 he ran away to Wyoming and worked as a ranch hand. In 1942 he joined the marines and served in the Pacific. After being wounded, he served the remainder of the war as a combat artist. The years after the war were spent in New York studying with Rufino Tamayo and Hans Hoffman. Jackson's first one-man show was of Abstract Expressionist paintings, but by 1956 he had begun working as a Realist. A fellowship allowed him to travel in Europe in 1957. Courbet's *Burial at Ormans* at the Louvre proved inspirational, and he proposed to Robert Coe, a trustee of the Whitney Gallery of Art in Cody, Wyoming, that he paint two murals: a *Range Burial* and a *Stampede*, where the cowboy had been killed. He received a commission to paint two 10 x 21 foot murals; the fee was to be $10,000 for each. Almost as an afterthought, he also suggested two sculptures to act as studies for the paintings; the fee for the sculptures was to be $3,125 each. Jackson retreated into the hills north of Florence, Italy, and began to work at a foundry, learning the lost-wax process of casting bronzes. This was a time of experimentation and learning. *Range Burial* was cast in bronze and completed in time for the opening of the Whitney Gallery in April 1959; the bronze of *Stampede* was completed later the same year. Busy with his sculpture, Jackson did not complete the paintings until 1966. The two large murals hang at opposite ends of the Whitney Gallery of the Buffalo Bill Historical Center in Cody, Wyoming, in a room devoted to the works of Harry Jackson. In 1963 Jackson began to paint his bronzes in realistic colors. There are seven patinated versions and five painted versions of *Stampede*. The bronze offered at Selkirk's in St. Louis was a painted bronze, signed © Harry Jackson 1958-59, #1p. s. © Harry Jackson 1970. The price realized was $187,000, a record price for a Jackson sculpture. (Harry Jackson, *Stampede Painted*, © Harry Jackson, 1967, bronze, 60 inches in length, Selkirk, May 2, 1994, $187,000)

JACOBSEN, A.
paintings: (H) $4,125

JACOBSEN, A.
Danish 1858-1930
paintings: (H) $1,100

JACOBSEN, Antonio
American 1850-1921
paintings: (L) $1,650; (H) $43,125

JACOBSEN, Carl
Danish 19th/20th cent.
paintings: (L) $660; (H) $770

JACOBSEN, O.
paintings: (H) $650

JACOBSEN, Robert
Danish b. 1912
drawings: (H) $2,090
sculpture: (H) $63,250

JACOBSEN, Sophus
Norwegian 1833-1912
paintings: (L) $1,495; (H) $2,750

JACOBSHAGEN, Keith
American b. 1943
paintings: (H) $880

JACOBSON, F.
Danish 19th/20th cent.
paintings: (H) $880

JACOBSON, O.
American 19th cent.
paintings: (H) $825

JACOBSON, Oscar Brousse
American b. 1882
paintings: (L) $3,450; (H) $3,738

JACOBSZ, Lambert
Dutch c. 1598-1636
paintings: (H) $13,200

JACOMIN, Alfred Louis Vigny
French 1842-c. 1913
paintings: (H) $6,900

JACOMIN, Marie Ferdinand
French 1843-1902
paintings: (H) $1,540

JACOPO DI SANDRO, called Jacone
Italian d. 1553
paintings: (H) $18,700

JACOT, Don
American b. 1949
drawings: (L) $1,100; (H) $1,210

JACOUET, Gustave Jean
French 1846-1909
paintings: (H) $1,760

JACOUVLEFF, Vassily
contemporary
paintings: (H) $1,430

JACOVACCI, Francesco
Italian 1838-1908
paintings: (H) $13,200

JACOVLEFF, Alexandre
French 1887-1938
paintings: (H) $4,675

JACQUAND, Louis
French 19th cent.
paintings: (H) $2,530

JACQUART, Lucie
French 1882-1956
paintings: (L) $863; (H) $1,438

JACQUE, Charles Emile
French 1813-1894
paintings: (L) $605; (H) $103,700
drawings: (L) $575; (H) $3,960

JACQUE, Emile
French 1848-1912
paintings: (L) $1,100; (H) $1,980

JACQUELINE
sculpture: (H) $550

JACQUEMAIN, P.L.
French 19th cent.
paintings: (H) $2,185

JACQUEMART, Andre
sculpture: (H) $1,760

JACQUEMART, Henri Alfred
French 1824-1896
sculpture: (L) $805; (H) $3,680

JACQUES, C.H.
drawings: (H) $660

JACQUES, Charles Emile
French 1813-1894
paintings: (L) $1,100; (H) $20,700

JACQUES, F.L.
paintings: (H) $9,020

JACQUES, N.
sculpture: (H) $1,035

JACQUET, Alain
French b. 1939
paintings: (H) $20,700

Thomas Moran (1837–1926) was internationally famous for his panoramic landscapes of the American West. Moran made eight trips to the American West between 1871 and 1892, but most of his paintings were executed in his studio in Philadelphia or Newark. Moran painted five versions of this view of the buttes above the Green River; the location of one painting is unknown. When *The Cliffs of Green River, Wyoming* sold at Christie's American paintings sale in November 1994 for $2.752 million, it was a record price for the artist. (Thomas Moran, *The Cliffs of Green River, Wyoming*, oil on canvas, 25 x 65 inches, Christie New York, November 30, 1994, $2,752,000)

The paintings of Charles Deas (1818–1867) are valued as important historical documents. Deas settled in St. Louis in 1840 and spent eight years making trips into the wilderness recording the lives of Indians, traders, and trappers. Most of his works are drawings or watercolors. The estimate for this long-lost oil of an *Indian Warrior* was $100,000 to $150,000. The price realized at Christie's was $310,500. (Charles Deas, *Indian Warrior on the Edge of a Precipice*, oil on canvas, 36½ x 27½ inches, Christie New York, September 22, 1993, $310,500)

In his day, William Joseph McCloskey (1859–1941) was a well-known portrait painter and in the early 1920s was appointed the official portrait painter of the Los Angeles American Legion. His still lifes are rare and are mostly *trompe l'oeil* paintings of oranges wrapped in meticulously rendered tissue paper. When this version of his oranges was offered at Butterfield's, it reached a record price for the artist at $464,500. (William Joseph McCloskey, *Oranges and Wrappers*, oil on canvas, 8 x 18 inches, Butterfield's, December 13, 1994, $464,500)

Frenchman Henri Weigele (1858–1927) executed life-size busts of young women, often in a combination of marble and bronze. This work, almost six-feet-high excluding base, is exceptionally large and rare. Estimated by Sotheby's at $150,000 to $250,000, the sculpture set an artist record when it sold for $288,500. (Henri Weigele, *Deux Femmes Dansant*, marble on a 23-inch gilt bronze base, height 71 inches, Sotheby New York, May 24, 1995, $288,500)

The *oeuvre* (body of work) of Mexican artist Diego Rivera (1886–1957) includes murals, oil paintings, drawings, and watercolors. Peasants and calla lilies, the flower of sorrow, are two symbols that appear frequently in his paintings. *Vendedora de Alcatraces*, commissioned in 1938 from the artist by the consignor to Christie's, set a record for a Rivera watercolor when it sold for $1,102,500. (Diego Rivera, *Vendedora de Alcatraces*, watercolor, gouache, and charcoal on heavy paper, 53 x 75 inches, Christie New York, November 16, 1994, $1,102,500)

John Sloan (1871–1951) was a member of The Eight (or Ashcan School), a group of artists who painted realistic scenes of everyday city life. This large oil of Greenwich Village in the early 1900s, deaccessioned from the IBM Collection, had been widely exhibited: the list in the catalogue was more than 12 inches long! A record price was achieved when this painting sold for $855,000 at Sotheby's. (John Sloan, *Bleecker Street, Saturday Night*, oil on canvas, 26½ x 66⁷⁄₁₀ inches, Sotheby New York, May 22, 1995, $855,000)

German/American folk artist Wilhelm Schimmel (1817–1890) exchanged drink, room, and board for his carvings of toys and animals. His wood birds and farm animals decorated many homes and local bars in rural Pennsylvania. This small carved figure of a grinning tiger broke all records for the artist when it fetched $55,200 at Christie's. (Wilhelm Schimmel, *Painted Grinning Tiger*, 6 inches high, 11½ inches long, wood painted red, white, and black, Christie New York, June 3, 1995, $55,200)

The catalogue cover lot for Skinner's June 1995 Americana sale brought a record price, $167,500, for artist Zedekiah Belknap (1781–1858). The child on the right is a boy, George Frederick Farley, born in 1838, and the child on the left is a girl, Mary Adams Farley, born in 1833. The double portrait was consigned to Skinner's by a descendant of Mary Farley. (Zedekiah Belknap, *Portrait of the Farley Children*, oil on canvas, 26¼ x 32¼ inches, Skinner's, June 13, 1995, $167,500)

Most of the works of Italian painter and sculptor Amedeo Modigliani (1884–1920) are portraits or female nudes. *Nu Assis au Collier (Seated Nude with a Necklace)*, painted in 1917, is an erotic depiction of a woman posed like Botticelli's *Venus*. The oil had been purchased in 1947 by Ralph Colin, founder of the Art Dealers Association, and was fresh to the market when it was offered at Christie's in 1995. After spirited bidding, the final price was $12,432,500, a record for the artist. (Amedeo Modigliani, *Nu Assis au Collier*, oil on canvas, 36 x 23½ inches, Christie New York, May 10, 1995, $12,432,500)

Cape Cod artist Ralph Cahoon painted landscapes with mermaids, sailors, and balloons. This large oil of Boston Harbor had it all, and a record price for the artist was set when *Bon Voyage from Boston Harbor* sold for $80,500. (Ralph Cahoon, *Bon Voyage from Boston Harbor*, oil on masonite, 33 x 43 inches, Northeast, November 5, 1994, $80,500)

Doyle's catalogue cover lot for their November 1994 paintings sale was an idyllic summer scene of two young women having tea. Painted by Irving Ramsay Wiles, (1861–1948), a second-generation American Impressionist, the oil far exceeded the house's conservative estimate of $20,000 to $30,000 when it sold for $184,000. (Irving Ramsay Wiles, *Afternoon Tea*, oil on canvas, 26 x 36 inches, Doyle, November 9, 1994, $184,000)

Le Seize Septembre (The Sixteenth of September) depicts a moon in a tree, an irrational hallucinatory painting with a lyrical meaningless title. One of two versions painted by Surrealist painter René Magritte (1898–1967), the other is in the Menil Collection in Houston, Texas, the painting was the cover lot of Christie's November 1994 sale of Impressionist and Modern paintings. Consigned from the estate of philanthropist Alice Tully, the oil realized $1,102,500, a record auction price for the artist. (René Magritte, *Le Seize Septembre*, oil on canvas, 23⅝ x 19¾ inches, Christie New York, November 10, 1994, $1,102,500)

Austrian painter Gustav Klimt (1862–1918) began his career by painting decorative murals with his brother Ernst. In the 1900s he was the leading Austrian painter of Art Nouveau, but controversy surrounded his work and he turned to painting society portraits. The model for *Dame mit Facher (Lady with a Fan)* is not known, but Klimt lavished as much attention on her as he did on wealthy socialites. Painted in 1918, this stylized portrait with its Japanese-inspired patterned background broke all records when it realized $11,662,500. (Gustav Klimt, *Dame mit Facher*, oil on canvas, 39⅜ x 39½ inches, Sotheby New York, May 11, 1994, $11,662,500)

*U*ntitled by Post-Minimalist sculptor Joel Shapiro (b. 1941) is a life-size figure, one from an edition of four. Most of Shapiro's works have been left untitled, allowing the form and feeling of the piece to speak for itself. This 1986 bronze figurative work, delicately balanced on one leg, brought a record auction price for the artist at $288,500. (Joel Shapiro, *Untitled*, bronze, 63¾ x 45½ x 26 inches, Christie New York, May 3, 1995, $288,500)

Edward Robert Hughes, (1851–1914) worked mainly in watercolor but is also known to have executed portraits in chalk. His painting *Midsummer Eve* shows the influence of his first teacher and uncle, the Pre-Raphaelite Arthur Hughes. Edward Hughes painted subjects of a symbolist nature and on obscure literary themes. Lighthearted and playful, *Midsummer Eve* set a record for the artist when it sold for $464,500. (Edward Robert Hughes, *Midsummer Eve*, watercolor heightened with gouache on paper, 45 x 30 inches, Christie New York, February 15, 1995, $464,500)

Gerbrand van den Eeckhout (1621–1674) was apprenticed to Rembrandt at the age of 14. His apprenticeship ended in 1640, but he remained close friends with his teacher. Eeckhout's drawing of a contemplative boy shows Rembrandt's influence in the use of a softly diffused light. Drawn with ink framing lines and a brown wash, this small drawing fetched $365,000, a record for the artist. (Gerbrand van den Eeckhout, *A Seated Young Boy in a Hat, His Chin Cupped in his Hand*, brush and brown wash, brown ink on light brown paper, 5½ x 4½ inches, Christie New York, January 11, 1995, $365,000)

JACQUET, Gustave Jean
French 1846-1909
paintings: (L) $1,100; (H) $19,800
drawings: (L) $880; (H) $1,380

JACQUETTE, Yvonne
American b. 1934
drawings: (H) $1,380

JACUS, Jean Theobald
French 20th cent.
paintings: (H) $550

JAECKEL, Henry
German 19th cent.
paintings: (H) $3,520

JAECKEL, Henry
German 19th cent.
paintings: (L) $3,520; (H) $12,100

JAECKEL, Herman
German 19th cent.
paintings: (H) $6,050

JAEGER, G.
sculpture: (H) $880

JAENISCH, Hans
German b. 1907
drawings: (H) $1,100

JAFFEE, Al
drawings: (H) $1,870

JAGER, J.
sculpture: (H) $1,035

JAHRTHENKE, G.
sculpture: (H) $495

JAKOBIDES, Georgios
Greek 1852-1932
paintings: (H) $46,000

JAKOULOFF, Georges, or
YAKOULOV
Russian 1884-1928
paintings: (H) $1,320
drawings: (H) $385

JALZE, A.T.
Russian late 19th/20th cent.
sculpture: (H) $605

JAMAR, Armand
Belgian 1870-1946
paintings: (L) $2,860; (H) $3,190

JAMBOR, Louis
Hungarian/American 1884-1955
paintings: (L) $460; (H) $3,410
drawings: (H) $385

JAMES
British School c. 1900
paintings: (H) $1,045

JAMES, Alexander
1890-1946
paintings: (H) $880

JAMES, Charles
contemporary
drawings: (L) $660; (H) $2,200

JAMES, David
British ac. 1881-1898
paintings: (L) $1,210; (H) $24,200

JAMES, E.
British 19th/20th cent.
paintings: (H) $1,380

JAMES, Ezra
American 1768-1836
paintings: (H) $1,100

JAMES, Frederick
American 1845-1907
paintings: (L) $990; (H) $2,200
drawings: (L) $286; (H) $633

JAMES, John W.
American b. 1873
paintings: (L) $220; (H) $1,870

JAMES, M.
paintings: (H) $550

JAMES, Richard S.
English 19th cent.
paintings: (H) $2,750

JAMES, Roy Walter
American b. 1897
paintings: (L) $385; (H) $605

JAMES, Stewart Ross
American 20th cent.
drawings: (H) $550

JAMES, Will
American 1892-1942
drawings: (H) $715

JAMES, William
British ac. 1761-1771
paintings: (L) $32,200; (H) $79,500

JAMES, Willy
b. 1920
drawings: (H) $4,025

JAMESON, Middleton
British d. 1918
paintings: (L) $11,000; (H) $18,400

JAMIN, Paul Joseph
French 1853-1903
paintings: (H) $978

JAMISON, Lee
American b. 1957
paintings: (L) $1,100; (H) $4,950

JAMISON, Philip
American b. 1925
paintings: (L) $137; (H) $1,375
drawings: (L) $275; (H) $1,320

JAMISON, Phillip
b. 1929
drawings: (H) $990

JAMSEN, Jean
French b. 1920
paintings: (H) $1,760

JANCE, Paul Claude
French b. 1840
paintings: (L) $5,500; (H) $7,700

JANCK, Angelo
German 1868-1956
paintings: (H) $770

JANCO, Marcel
Israeli 1895-1984
paintings: (L) $6,600; (H) $18,400
drawings: (L) $385; (H) $3,850

JANDA, Hermine von
Austrian b. 1854
paintings: (H) $4,888

JANENSCH, Professor Gerhard Adolf
German b. 1860
sculpture: (L) $800; (H) $1,925

JANET, Adele
French d. 1877
drawings: (H) $6,325

JANIN, Jean
French 1838-1970
paintings: (L) $605; (H) $1,980

JANK, Angelo
German 1868-1956
paintings: (L) $1,725; (H) $2,200

JANKAY, Tibor
1899-1994
paintings: (L) $2,300; (H) $8,050

JANKOWSKI, J. Wilhelm
Austrian ac. 1825-1861
paintings: (L) $2,420; (H) $3,335

JANNSON, Alfred
American 1863-1931
paintings: (H) $3,163

JANOSZ, Moldvai Krajna
Hungarian 1875-1945
paintings: (H) $2,640

JANOWITZ, Joel
paintings: (H) $495
drawings: (L) $440; (H) $1,650

JANS, Edouard de
Belgian b. 1855
paintings: (H) $4,025

JANSEM, Jean
French b. Armenia 1920
paintings: (L) $1,870; (H) $115,500
drawings: (L) $330; (H) $8,250

JANSEN, Alfred J.
Belgian 19th/20th cent.
paintings: (H) $1,980

JANSEN, Joseph
German 1829-1905
paintings: (L) $2,420; (H) $20,700

JANSEN, W.S.T.
drawings: (H) $460

JANSEN, Willem George Frederick
Dutch 1871-1949
paintings: (L) $2,200; (H) $3,450

JANSON, Johannes
Dutch 1729-1784
paintings: (H) $660

JANSSENS, Abraham van Nuyssen
Flemish 1575-1632
paintings: (L) $11,000; (H) $71,500

JANSSENS, Hieronymous
Flemish 1624-1693
paintings: (H) $32,200

JANSSENS, Pieter
Belgian 19th cent.
paintings: (H) $11,000

JANSSENS, V.
Belgian 19th cent.
paintings: (H) $4,675

JANSSENS, Victor
German b. 1807
paintings: (H) $3,960

JANSSENS, Victor Honore
1658-1736
paintings: (H) $4,950

JANSSON, Alfred
Swedish/American 1863-1931
paintings: (L) $247; (H) $3,300

JANSSON, Eugene
Swedish 1862-1915
paintings: (H) $55,000

JAPY, Louis Aime
French 1840-1916
paintings: (L) $1,760; (H) $16,100

JAQUEMIN
sculpture: (H) $3,300

JARA, Jose
French ac. 1889
paintings: (L) $6,900; (H) $10,925
drawings: (L) $18,400; (H) $18,400

JARDET, Florence M.
American ac. 1911-1924
drawings: (H) $605

JARDINES, Jose Maria
Spanish b. 1862
paintings: (L) $1,210; (H) $7,475

JARL, Otto
AUstrian 19th cent.
sculpture: (H) $2,200

JARM, William
American 20th cent.
paintings: (L) $1,050; (H) $1,870

JARVIS, Donald
b. 1923
paintings: (H) $248
drawings: (H) $575

JARVIS, Georgia
1944-1990
paintings: (H) $2,530

JARVIS, Gina
American 20th cent.
paintings: (H) $605

JARVIS, Henry C.
English 1867-1955
paintings: (H) $1,540

JARVIS, John
American 20th cent.
drawings: (H) $1,760

JARVIS, John Wesley
American 1780-1839/40
paintings: (H) $1,650

JARVIS, W. Frederick
American b. 1868
paintings: (L) $770; (H) $1,380
drawings: (H) $220

JASMIN, Paul
paintings: (L) $460; (H) $483

JAUDON, Valerie
American b. 1945
paintings: (L) $2,300; (H) $24,200
drawings: (L) $1,100; (H) $1,150

JAUGEY, Daniel
b. 1929
paintings: (H) $805

JAULMES, Gustave Louis
paintings: (H) $9,350

JAVIER, Maximino
paintings: (L) $4,400; (H) $4,400

JAWLENSKY, Alexej
German 1864-1941
paintings: (L) $14,950; (H) $200,500
drawings: (L) $7,475; (H) $154,000

JAWLENSKY, Andreas
German 1902-1984
paintings: (H) $7,762

JAY, Cecil
American b. 1884
paintings: (H) $36,800

JAY, William Samuel
British 1843-1933
paintings: (L) $632; (H) $2,990

JAYET, Clement
1731-1804
sculpture: (H) $40,250

JAYNE, DeWitt W.
drawings: (H) $523

JAZET, Paul Leon
French b. 1848
paintings: (L) $3,450; (H) $48,875
drawings: (H) $2,875

JEAN, Nehemy
paintings: (H) $1,760

JEAN-BAPTISTE, Edger
b. 1917
paintings: (H) $2,760

JEANMOUGIN, Alfred Pierre Joseph
French 19th cent.
paintings: (H) $1,980

JEANNIN, Georges
French 1841-1925
paintings: (L) $9,200; (H) $59,700

JEANNIOT, Pierre Georges
French 1848-1934
paintings: (H) $6,325

JEANNOT, Joseph C.M.
French b. 1859
drawings: (H) $805

JEANRON, Philippe Auguste
French 1809-1877
drawings: (H) $2,587

JEAURAT, Etienne
French 1699-1789
paintings: (L) $1,100; (H) $46,000

JECT-KEY, David Wu
American 1890-1968
paintings: (L) $1,100; (H) $1,150

JEFFERSON, Joseph
1829-1905
paintings: (H) $935

JEFFERSON, P.
American 20th cent.
paintings: (H) $660

JEFFREYS, Charles William
drawings: (H) $1,320

JEGOROV, A.
Estonian b. 1878
paintings: (L) $935; (H) $1,035

JELENIK, R.
Austrian 19th/20th cent.
paintings: (H) $2,750

JELINEK, Fr** A.
Czechoslovakian 19th/20th cent.
paintings: (H) $468

JELINEK, R.E.
European 20th cent.
paintings: (H) $770

JELINEK, Rudolf
Austrian b. 1880
paintings: (L) $303; (H) $1,320

JELINEK, Vladimir
Czechoslovakian b. 1934
sculpture: (H) $1,725

JENKINS, F. Lynn
American 1870-1927
sculpture: (L) $990; (H) $2,420

JENKINS, George Henry
British 19th cent.
paintings: (L) $605; (H) $1,725

JENKINS, George Washington
American 1816-1907
paintings: (L) $1,840; (H) $15,400

JENKINS, John Eliot
American b. 1868
paintings: (L) $403; (H) $660

JENKINS, L.
paintings: (L) $330; (H) $907

JENKINS, Lynn
sculpture: (H) $1,045

JENKINS, Michael
sculpture: (H) $2,300

JENKINS, Paul
American b. 1923
paintings: (L) $690; (H) $46,000
drawings: (L) $440; (H) $5,060

JENKINS, Wilfred
English 19th cent.
paintings: (L) $770; (H) $2,640

JENNENS, Bettridge and
English 19th cent.
paintings: (H) $1,320

JENNEWEIN, Carl Paul
American 1890-1978
sculpture: (L) $4,400; (H) $9,775

JENNEY, Neil
American b. 1945
paintings: (L) $35,750; (H) $231,000
sculpture: (H) $57,500

JENNEY, U.D.
paintings: (H) $495

JENNINGS, William Robert
British 20th cent.
paintings: (H) $880

JENNYS, William
American ac. 1795-1810
paintings: (H) $14,950

JENSEN, Bill
American b. 1945
paintings: (H) $13,200

JENSEN, Alfred
1859-1935
drawings: (H) $5,462

JENSEN, Alfred
American 1903-1981
paintings: (L) $4,400; (H) $88,000
drawings: (L) $4,950; (H) $8,800

JENSEN, Bill
American b. 1945
paintings: (L) $403; (H) $44,000
drawings: (L) $550; (H) $9,200

JENSEN, Carl Milton
Danish b. 1855
paintings: (H) $7,700

JENSEN, Carlo Horning
Danish 20th cent.
paintings: (H) $770

JENSEN, George
paintings: (H) $990

JENSEN, George
American b. 1878
paintings: (L) $1,650; (H) $2,750
drawings: (L) $247; (H) $440

JENSEN, Horst
German 20th cent.
drawings: (H) $661

JENSEN, Johan Laurents
Danish 1800-1856
paintings: (L) $2,200; (H) $30,800
drawings: (L) $440; (H) $2,310

JENSEN, Judy Bally
American b. 1953
sculpture: (L) $3,450; (H) $4,370

JENSEN, Oluf Simony
Danish 1864-1923
paintings: (H) $2,750

JENSEN, R.
English 19th/20th cent.
paintings: (L) $303; (H) $1,100

JENSEN, Robert
American b. 1922
drawings: (L) $350; (H) $550

JENSEN, Thomas M.
1831-1916
paintings: (L) $495; (H) $3,737

JENSEN, Wilhem G.F.
paintings: (H) $1,150

JEPPSEN, Julie
paintings: (L) $700; (H) $990

JEREMENKO, Ted
American b. Yugoslavia 1938
paintings: (L) $2,090; (H) $3,740

JEREZAK, Lucas
20th cent.
paintings: (H) $880

JERNBERG, August
Swedish 1826-1896
paintings: (H) $4,025

JERNBERG, Olof
Swedish 1855-1935
paintings: (H) $483

JERRES, Antony
Italian 19th cent.
paintings: (H) $2,200

JERRY, Sylvester
American b. 1904
paintings: (H) $605

JERZY, Richard
American 20th cent.
paintings: (L) $110; (H) $1,760
drawings: (L) $66; (H) $1,150

JESPERS, Oscar
1887-1970
sculpture: (H) $2,860

JESPERSEN, Henrik Gamst
Danish 1853-1936
paintings: (H) $1,540

JESS
American b. 1923
paintings: (L) $11,500; (H) $96,000
drawings: (L) $29,900; (H) $57,500

JESSUP, Fred
American b. 1920
paintings: (L) $330; (H) $935

JESSUP, Robert
American 20th cent.
paintings: (H) $1,320

JETTEL, Eugen
Austrian 1845-1901
paintings: (H) $17,600

JETTMAR, Rudolf
Polish 1869-1939
paintings: (H) $8,800

JEURGENS, Alfred
American b. 1866
paintings: (H) $1,100

JEWELL, Elizabeth G.
American 1874-1956
paintings: (L) $88; (H) $467

JEWETT, Maude Sherwood
American 1873-1953
paintings: (H) $6,050
sculpture: (L) $1,380; (H) $31,900

JEWETT, William
American 1795-1873
drawings: (H) $495

JEWETT, William Smith
American 1812-1873
paintings: (H) $550

JEX, Garnet W.
American b. 1895
paintings: (L) $302; (H) $550

JIG, Fritz
Norwegian 19th cent.
paintings: (H) $1,320

JIMENEZ, Alonzo
American b. 1949
sculpture: (H) $1,725

JIMENEZ Y ARANDA, Jose
Spanish 1832-1903
paintings: (L) $4,600; (H) $23,000

JIMENEZ Y ARANDA, Luis
Spanish 1845-1928
paintings: (L) $1,840; (H) $159,500

JIMENEZ Y FERNANDEZ, Federico
Spanish b. 1841
paintings: (L) $5,463; (H) $8,800
drawings: (H) $460

JIMINEZ Y ARANDA, Jose
Spanish 1837-1903
paintings: (H) $60,250

JIMINEZ Y MARTIN, Juan
Spanish b. 1858
paintings: (L) $7,975; (H) $23,000

JIRO, Yoshihara
1905-1972
drawings: (H) $36,800

JIROUCH, Frank L.
American b. 1878
paintings: (L) $17; (H) $907
sculpture: (H) $1,540

JOANOVITCH, Paul
Austrian b. 1859
paintings: (H) $60,800

JOBERT, Fernand
French 19th cent.
paintings: (H) $1,650

JOCELYN, Nathaniel
American 1796-1881
paintings: (L) $715; (H) $1,430

JOCKER, C.
Dutch 20th cent.
paintings: (H) $522

JODE, Pieter de, I
Flemish 1570-1634
drawings: (H) $5,280

JOE, Oreland
b. 1958
sculpture: (H) $3,300

JOHANNENSON
Swedish 19th/20th cent.
paintings: (H) $990

JOHANNESEN, N.A.
Swedish 20th cent.
paintings: (L) $385; (H) $550

JOHANNESSEN, J.
Norwegian b. 1934
paintings: (H) $990

JOHANSEN, Anders D.
Danish/American ac. early 20th cent.
paintings: (L) $440; (H) $7,475

JOHANSEN, Axel
Danish 1872-1938
paintings: (L) $550; (H) $1,380

JOHANSSON, Stefan
Swedish 1876-1955
drawings: (L) $55,000; (H) $77,000

JOHFRA
paintings: (H) $2,640

JOHN, Augustus Edwin
British 1878-1961
paintings: (L) $1,840; (H) $8,800
drawings: (L) $412; (H) $14,850

JOHN, David C.
19th/20th cent.
paintings: (H) $550

JOHNS, C.M.
American 1843-1925
paintings: (H) $726

JOHNS, Jasper
American b. 1930
paintings: (L) $79,500; (H) $4,950,000
drawings: (L) $126,500; (H) $1,432,500
sculpture: (L) $9,900; (H) $266,500

JOHNSEN
20th cent.
paintings: (H) $1,380

JOHNSON, Ambrose
paintings: (H) $715

JOHNSON, Arthur Clark
American b. 1897
paintings: (L) $230; (H) $495
drawings: (L) $55; (H) $748

JOHNSON, C. Everett
20th cent.
paintings: (H) $2,875

JOHNSON, C.H.
American 1874-after 1940
paintings: (H) $8,338

JOHNSON, Charles Edward
English 1832-1913
paintings: (L) $990; (H) $1,100

JOHNSON, Clarence R.
American 1894-1981
paintings: (L) $1,320; (H) $71,250

JOHNSON, Cletus
b. 1941
sculpture: (H) $1,840

JOHNSON, Clovis N., Jr.
ac. 1920s
paintings: (H) $660

JOHNSON, David
American 1827-1908
paintings: (L) $880; (H) $209,000
drawings: (L) $385; (H) $5,225

JOHNSON, David Claypoole
American 1799-1865
drawings: (H) $460

JOHNSON, Eastman
American 1824-1906
paintings: (L) $2,420; (H) $145,500
drawings: (L) $440; (H) $11,500

JOHNSON, Edward
American b. 1911
paintings: (H) $3,025

JOHNSON, Eldred Clark
American b. 1926
paintings: (L) $880; (H) $990

JOHNSON, Francis Norton
1878-1931
paintings: (H) $4,600

JOHNSON, Frank Tenney
American 1874-1939
paintings: (L) $2,200; (H) $101,500
drawings: (L) $1,100; (H) $9,200

JOHNSON, G.
English 19th cent.
paintings: (H) $1,100

JOHNSON, Gordon
1924-1989
paintings: (H) $2,200
drawings: (H) $193

JOHNSON, Grace Mott
American 1882-1967
sculpture: (H) $2,420

JOHNSON, Guy
American b. 1927
paintings: (H) $935

JOHNSON, H.
British 18th cent.
paintings: (H) $8,250

JOHNSON, Harry
English 19th/20th cent.
paintings: (H) $550

JOHNSON, Harvey
American b. 1920/21
paintings: (L) $935; (H) $5,830

JOHNSON, Horace Chauncey
American 1820-1890
paintings: (L) $423; (H) $1,150

JOHNSON, J.W.
American 19th/20th cent.
paintings: (H) $1,725

JOHNSON, James Ralph
20th cent.
paintings: (H) $715

JOHNSON, Jan
American
drawings: (L) $400; (H) $550

JOHNSON, Jeremiah
paintings: (H) $1,210

JOHNSON, John
paintings: (L) $690; (H) $805

JOHNSON, Jonathan Eastman
American 1824-1906
paintings: (L) $8,800; (H) $66,000

JOHNSON, Joshua
American c. 1769-1824
paintings: (L) $10,450; (H) $55,200

JOHNSON, Larry
American 20th cent.
drawings: (H) $1,610
sculpture: (H) $1,100

JOHNSON, Lester
American b. 1919
paintings: (L) $1,725; (H) $16,100
drawings: (L) $690; (H) $4,888

JOHNSON, Marshall
American 1846/50-1915/21
paintings: (L) $495; (H) $11,550
drawings: (L) $230; (H) $880

JOHNSON, Martin
American contemporary
paintings: (H) $1,093

JOHNSON, Ray
b. 1927
paintings: (L) $2,300; (H) $3,910
drawings: (L) $1,725; (H) $2,300

JOHNSON, Robert
Australian 1890-1964
paintings: (L) $2,200; (H) $5,500

JOHNSON, Robert
British 1770-1896
paintings: (H) $660

JOHNSON, S.U.
American 19th/20th cent.
paintings: (H) $660

JOHNSON, Sidney Yates
English 19th/20th cent.
paintings: (L) $137; (H) $1,540

JOHNSON, Stanley Q.
American b. 1939
sculpture: (L) $825; (H) $8,050

JOHNSON, Theo
American 19th cent.
drawings: (H) $660

JOHNSON, Wesley
American contemporary
paintings: (H) $550

JOHNSON, Yvonne
paintings: (L) $385; (H) $700

JOHNSTON
paintings: (H) $3,190

JOHNSTON, Alexander
British 1815-1891
paintings: (L) $2,640; (H) $14,950

JOHNSTON, Frank Hans
Canadian 1888-1949
paintings: (L) $1,210; (H) $17,600
drawings: (L) $880; (H) $3,520

JOHNSTON, John
American 1753-1818
paintings: (L) $1,045; (H) $2,750

JOHNSTON, John B.
American 1847-1866
paintings: (L) $550; (H) $1,150

JOHNSTON, John Humphreys
French 1857-1941
paintings: (H) $770

JOHNSTON, John R.
American b. 1820s, ac. to 1872
paintings: (L) $330; (H) $4,400

JOHNSTON, Reuben Le Grand
American b. 1850
paintings: (L) $495; (H) $3,450
drawings: (L) $248; (H) $990

JOHNSTON, Walter R.
American 19th cent.
paintings: (H) $4,400

JOHNSTON, Ynez
American b. 1920
paintings: (H) $165
drawings: (L) $1,320; (H) $2,300

JOHNSTONE, George Whitton
paintings: (H) $1,870

JOHNSTONE, Henry J.
British 19th cent.
paintings: (H) $2,070

JOHNSTONE, John Young
Canadian 1887-1930
paintings: (L) $1,430; (H) $2,300

JOHS, Pieter Josselin de
Dutch 1861-1906
paintings: (H) $1,540

JOINER, Harvey
American 1852-1932
paintings: (L) $495; (H) $1,870

JOLI, Antonio
Venetian 1700?-1777
paintings: (L) $54,625; (H) $638,000

JOLIVARD, Andre
French 1787-1851
paintings: (H) $3,080

JOLLY, Bon
Belgian 19th cent.
paintings: (H) $1,870

JOLYET, Philippe
French 1832-1908
paintings: (H) $7,150

JONAS, E***
Continental 19th/20th cent.
paintings: (H) $2,185

JONAS, Louis Paul
1894-1971
sculpture: (H) $2,530

JONAS, Lucien
French 1880-1940
paintings: (L) $275; (H) $9,775

JONCHERIE, Gabriel Germain
French b. 1824
paintings: (H) $1,610

JONCHERY, Charles
French b. 1873
sculpture: (H) $805

JONCHERY, P.
French 19th/20th cent.
sculpture: (H) $1,150

JONCIERES, Leonce J.V. de
French b. 1871
paintings: (H) $52,250

JONES, Allan D., Jr.
American b. 1915
drawings: (H) $880

JONES, Allen
British b. 1937
drawings: (H) $3,300
sculpture: (L) $1,265; (H) $17,600

JONES, Amy
American b. 1899
paintings: (H) $1,045

JONES, Barry Leighton
English 20th cent.
paintings: (H) $920

JONES, Bob
drawings: (H) $5,720

JONES, Bradley
American 1944-1989
paintings: (L) $137; (H) $1,100
drawings: (H) $143
sculpture: (H) $330

JONES, C.S.
American 19th cent.
drawings: (H) $1,210

JONES, Carroll
American 20th cent.
paintings: (H) $1,100

JONES, Charles
English 1836-1892
paintings: (L) $7,150; (H) $7,700

JONES, Darryl
paintings: (H) $1,980

JONES, David
Canadian ac. 1823-1835
sculpture: (H) $1,925

JONES, E.B.
American 20th cent.
paintings: (H) $748

JONES, Edmund Roscoe
American 1886-1976
paintings: (H) $660

JONES, Elizabeth Sparhawk
American 20th cent.
paintings: (H) $3,000

JONES, Eugene Arthur
American 1881-1965
paintings: (H) $552

JONES, Francis Coates
American 1857-1932
paintings: (L) $2,185; (H) $49,500
drawings: (H) $13,800

JONES, Frank Eastman
American 19th cent.
paintings: (L) $1,840; (H) $2,200

JONES, Fred
American 20th cent.
paintings: (H) $550

JONES, Herbert H.
British 19th/20th cent.
paintings: (H) $1,320

JONES, Hugh Bolton
American 1848-1927
paintings: (L) $575; (H) $51,750
drawings: (L) $825; (H) $1,150

JONES, Hugh Bolton and Francis
Coates JONES
American 19th/20th cent.
paintings: (H) $8,800

JONES, J.
English 17th/18th cent.
paintings: (H) $880

JONES, Jeff
American b. 1944
paintings: (L) $805; (H) $1,495
drawings: (L) $550; (H) $3,850

JONES, Joe
American 1909-1963
paintings: (L) $345; (H) $66,000
drawings: (L) $330; (H) $2,070

JONES, John
American
paintings: (H) $700

JONES, John Paul
contemporary
drawings: (H) $825

JONES, Leighton
English 20th cent.
paintings: (H) $1,210

JONES, Murray
paintings: (H) $440
drawings: (H) $935

JONES, Nell Choate
American 1879-1981
paintings: (L) $920; (H) $6,600

JONES, Paul
American b. 1860
paintings: (L) $385; (H) $4,950
drawings: (H) $137

JONES, Robert
b. 1926
drawings: (H) $825

JONES, Robinson
paintings: (L) $605; (H) $2,200

JONES, Samuel John Egbert
English ac. 1820-1845
paintings: (H) $7,425

JONES, Shields Landon (S.L.)
American b. 1901
sculpture: (H) $18,400

JONES, Thomas Benedict
b. 1893
paintings: (H) $2,875

JONES, William
19th/20th cent.
paintings: (H) $715

JONES, William
British ac. mid 18th cent.
paintings: (H) $15,400

JONES, William F.
American b. 1815
paintings: (H) $770

JONG, Betty de
French 1881-1916
paintings: (H) $1,100

JONG, Germ de
Dutch b. 1886
paintings: (H) $1,210

JONG, J. de
Dutch School 20th cent.
paintings: (H) $660

JONGE, H. de
Dutch 19th/20th cent.
paintings: (H) $990

JONGE, L.V.D.
drawings: (H) $2,310

JONGH, Claude de
Dutch d. 1663
paintings: (H) $10,925

JONGH, Oene Romkes de
Dutch 1812-1896
paintings: (L) $1,840; (H) $6,325

JONGH, Tinus de
Dutch 1885-1942
paintings: (H) $550

JONGH, Tinus di
S. African 19th/20th cent.
paintings: (L) $770; (H) $1,430

JONGHE, Gustave Leonhard de
Belgian 1828/29-1893
paintings: (L) $2,760; (H) $23,100

JONGKIND, Johan Barthold
Dutch 1819-1891
paintings: (L) $2,310; (H) $71,500
drawings: (L) $1,840; (H) $6,050

JONNEVOLD, Carl Henrik
American 1856-1930
paintings: (L) $316; (H) $2,588

JONNIAUX, Alfred
Belgian/American b. 1882
paintings: (H) $550

JONSON, Raymond
American 1891-1982
paintings: (L) $2,990; (H) $88,000
drawings: (L) $4,400; (H) $8,800

JONZEN, Basil
paintings: (H) $460

JOPLING, Louise
British 1843-1933
paintings: (L) $5,500; (H) $20,700

JOPLING, Louise
British b. 1843
paintings: (H) $5,500

JORDAENS, Hans, called Potlepel
Dutch 1616-1680
paintings: (H) $14,300

JORDAENS, Jacob
Flemish 1593-1678
paintings: (L) $4,025; (H) $11,000
drawings: (L) $3,520; (H) $55,000

JORDAENS, Jacob, and Studio
1593-1678
paintings: (H) $24,200

JORDAN, Jack
paintings: (L) $230; (H) $1,150

JORDAN, Jerry
American b. 1944
paintings: (L) $3,740; (H) $6,600

JORDAN, Monique
French 20th cent.
paintings: (H) $880

JORDAN, Rudolf
German 1810-1887
paintings: (H) $9,900

JORGENSEN, Aksel Karl
Danish 1883-1957
paintings: (H) $935

JORGENSEN, Borge
Danish b. 1926
sculpture: (L) $330; (H) $1,760

JORGENSEN, Christian
Norwegian/American 1860-1935
paintings: (L) $1,760; (H) $4,400
drawings: (L) $247; (H) $4,675

JORGENSEN, Sven
Norwegian 1861-1940
paintings: (H) $700

JORIS, Pio
Italian 1843-1921
paintings: (L) $14,300; (H) $25,300
drawings: (L) $165; (H) $550

JORISSEN, W.
Belgian 19th/20th cent.
paintings: (H) $690

JORISSEN, Willem
Dutch 1871-1910
paintings: (L) $2,200; (H) $2,420

JORN, Asger
Danish 1914-1973
paintings: (L) $8,580; (H) $23,000
drawings: (L) $330; (H) $15,400

JOS, Julian
European 19th cent.
paintings: (L) $2,070; (H) $4,675

JOSAKU, Maeda
b. 1926
paintings: (H) $7,475

JOSEPH, A.M.
sculpture: (H) $2,750

JOSEPH, Albert
French 1868-1952
paintings: (L) $2,200; (H) $3,300

JOSEPH, George Francis
1764-1846
paintings: (H) $2,200

JOSEPH, Jasmin
Haitian b. 1923
paintings: (L) $3,220; (H) $3,520

JOSEPH, Julien
American 1882-1964
paintings: (H) $770

JOSEPHIN, ***
drawings: (H) $4,600

JOST, Charles A.
French 19th cent.
paintings: (H) $1,380

JOST, Josef
German 1875-1948
paintings: (L) $468; (H) $605

JOUANT, Jules
French ac. 1885-1913
sculpture: (H) $2,875

JOUAS, Charles
French 1866-1942
drawings: (H) $5,500

JOUBERT, Ferdinand Jean
French 1810-1884
drawings: (H) $748

JOUBERT, R.
19th/20th cent.
paintings: (H) $770

JOUDERVILLE, Isaac de
Dutch c. 1613-1645/8
paintings: (H) $14,300

JOUFFROY, Jean P.
French b. 1933
paintings: (L) $55; (H) $605

JOULLAIN, Francois
1697-1778
drawings: (H) $1,610

JOULLIN, Amedee
American 1862-1917
paintings: (L) $1,430; (H) $5,500

JOURDAIN, Henri
French 1864-1931
drawings: (H) $935

JOURDAIN, Roger Joseph
French 1845-1918
paintings: (L) $20,700; (H) $143,000
drawings: (H) $2,200

JOURDAN, Adolphe
French 1825-1889
paintings: (H) $35,200

JOURDAN, Felix Desire Joseph
paintings: (H) $770

JOURDAN, Jacques Jean Raoul
French 1880-1916
paintings: (H) $11,500

JOURDANS, H.
paintings: (L) $467; (H) $550

JOURDEUIL, Louis Marie Adrien
French 1849-1907
paintings: (H) $2,860

JOURNEAY, Helen
ac. early 20th cent.
sculpture: (H) $3,520

JOURNOD, M***
paintings: (H) $990

JOUSSET, Claude
French b. 1935
paintings: (L) $880; (H) $2,200

JOUVE, Auguste
French b. 1846
paintings: (H) $10,350

JOUVE, Louis
French 1829-1903
paintings: (H) $1,650

JOUVE, Maurice
French 19th cent.
paintings: (H) $12,650

JOUVE, Paul
French 1880-1973
paintings: (H) $2,875
drawings: (L) $1,100; (H) $1,840
sculpture: (H) $13,200

JOUVENET, Jean
French 1649-1674
paintings: (H) $33,000
drawings: (H) $747

JOY, George Williams
English 1844-1925
paintings: (H) $5,500

JOY, Thomas Musgrave
British 1812-1866
paintings: (L) $4,600; (H) $17,250

JOYANT, Jules Romain
French 1803-1854
paintings: (H) $2,990

JOYNER, Jacob
American ac. 1920s-1940s
sculpture: (L) $1,155; (H) $1,210

JOZON, Jeanne
French late 19th cent.
sculpture: (L) $288; (H) $2,750

JUAN, Ronaldo de
Argentinean 1933-1989
drawings: (H) $5,175

JUAN DE BORGONA
French c. 1470-v.1535
paintings: (H) $21,850

JUAREZ, Roberto
American b. 1952?
paintings: (L) $3,450; (H) $3,850

JUDD, Donald
American 1928-1994
drawings: (L) $4,370; (H) $66,000
sculpture: (L) $908; (H) $288,500

JUDSON, Alice
American d. 1948
paintings: (L) $275; (H) $2,640

JUDSON, William Lees
Anglo/American 1842-1928
paintings: (L) $748; (H) $17,600
drawings: (L) $220; (H) $715

JUEL, Jens
Dutch 1745-1802
paintings: (H) $16,500

JUENGLING, Frederick
American 1848-1889
paintings: (H) $8,625

JUERGENS, Alfred
American 1866-1934
paintings: (L) $230; (H) $4,400
drawings: (H) $345

JUETTE, P.
19th/20th cent.
paintings: (H) $575

JULES, Mervin
American b. 1912
paintings: (L) $275; (H) $1,650

JULIAN, Paul
American b. 1914
paintings: (L) $495; (H) $4,313

JULIANA Y ALBERT, Jose
Spanish 1840-1890
paintings: (H) $2,070

JULIEN, Joseph
Belgian 19th cent.
paintings: (H) $3,025

JULIO, A.
Italian 19th/20th cent.
paintings: (H) $5,500

JULLIAN
French 20th cent.
drawings: (H) $715

JUNCKER, Justus
German 1703-1767
paintings: (H) $14,950

JUNDT, Gustave
French 1830-1884
paintings: (L) $1,650; (H) $12,100

JUNG, Charles Jacob
American 1880-1940
paintings: (L) $1,100; (H) $8,800

JUNG, Tom
drawings: (H) $660

JUNGBLUT, Johann
German 1860-1912
paintings: (L) $550; (H) $5,750

JUNGE (?), Hors
Dutch 19th cent.
paintings: (H) $575

JUNGLING, J.F.
German 19th cent.
drawings: (H) $3,105

JURRES, Johannes Hendricus
Dutch b. 1875
paintings: (L) $660; (H) $1,150

JURUTKA, Josef
Continental 1880-1945
paintings: (H) $1,045

JUSKO, Joe
drawings: (L) $1,150; (H) $4,025

JUSZKO, Piroska
Hungarian 19th/20th cent.
paintings: (H) $688

JUTSUM, Henry
English 1816-1869
paintings: (L) $550; (H) $3,575

JUTZ, Carl, Sr.
German 1838-1916
paintings: (L) $13,200; (H) $51,750

JUVIN, Juliette
French b. 1896
paintings: (H) $16,500

KABELL, Ludwig
Danish 1853-1902
paintings: (H) $3,450

KABER, G. Frederick
American 20th cent.
drawings: (L) $165; (H) $990

KABOTIE, Fred
American
drawings: (H) $6,600

KABOTIE, Fred, Nakayoma, Day After Day
Native American 1900-1985
drawings: (H) $16,500

KABOTIE, Michael, Lomawywesa
Native American b. 1946
drawings: (H) $1,210

KACERE, John
American b. 1920
paintings: (L) $275; (H) $14,300

KADANOV, ***
paintings: (H) $7,475

KADAR, Bela
Hungarian 1877-1955
paintings: (L) $3,450; (H) $9,460
drawings: (L) $165; (H) $8,800

KADISHMAN, Menashe
Israeli b. 1932
paintings: (H) $1,870

KADLACSIK, Laszlo
Hungarian 1925-1989
paintings: (L) $5,500; (H) $13,200

KAELIN, Charles B.
American 20th cent.
drawings: (H) $1,100

KAELIN, Charles Salis
American 1858-1929
paintings: (L) $550; (H) $6,710
drawings: (L) $440; (H) $3,850

KAELIN, Martin
American b. 1926
paintings: (L) $495; (H) $1,650
drawings: (L) $110; (H) $225

KAEMMERER, Frederik Hendrik
Dutch 1839-1902
paintings: (L) $1,320; (H) $827,500
drawings: (L) $330; (H) $2,200

KAERCHER, Amalie
American 19th cent.
paintings: (L) $7,150; (H) $20,700

KAESBACH, Rudolph
German b. 1873
sculpture: (L) $550; (H) $1,210

KAESELAU, Charles
paintings: (H) $990
drawings: (L) $192; (H) $440

KAHCKREUTH, Stanislaus von
German 1821-1894
paintings: (H) $5,175

KAHLER, Carl
Austrian/American b. 1855
paintings: (L) $1,320; (H) $79,500
drawings: (L) $550; (H) $2,300

KAHLO, Frida
Mexican 1910-1954
paintings: (L) $935,000; (H) $3,192,500
drawings: (L) $19,800; (H) $38,500

KAHN, Max
American b. 1903
paintings: (L) $288; (H) $467

KAHN, Wolf
German/American b. 1927
paintings: (L) $1,320; (H) $18,400
drawings: (L) $220; (H) $1,495

KAILEY, T.
paintings: (H) $500

KAIROLY, Rosenthal
20th cent.
paintings: (H) $900

KAISER, August
American b. 1899
paintings: (H) $1,045

KAISER, Eduard
Austrian 1820-1895
drawings: (H) $3,738

KAKABADZE, David
Russian 1889-1952
sculpture: (H) $31,050

KAKAMONA
drawings: (L) $55; (H) $550

KALEKA, Ranbir Singh
Indian b. 1953
paintings: (H) $12,650
drawings: (H) $747

KALINOWSKI, Horst Egon
b. 1924
sculpture: (H) $2,990

KALISH, Lionel
American 20th cent.
paintings: (H) $2,415

KALISH, Max
Polish/American 1891-1945
sculpture: (L) $550; (H) $9,487

KALLA-PRIECHENFRIED, J.
German 19th cent.
paintings: (L) $1,760; (H) $3,300

KALLEM, Herb
paintings: (L) $253; (H) $1,725
sculpture: (L) $322; (H) $990

KALLMORGEN, Friedrich
German 1856-1924
paintings: (H) $5,225

KALLOS, A.
paintings: (H) $1,150

KALLOS, Arpad
Hungarian/American b. 1882
paintings: (L) $115; (H) $661

KALLOS, Paul
paintings: (H) $1,380

KALMAKOFF, Nikolai
Russian 1873-1955
drawings: (H) $1,035

KALRAET, Abraham
Dutch 1642-1722
paintings: (H) $17,250

KALRAET, Barent
1649-1737
paintings: (H) $4,600

KALTENMOSEM, C.
paintings: (H) $12,500

KALUTA, Michael
drawings: (H) $2,090

KALVACH, S.
German late 19th cent.
paintings: (H) $660

KALVAK, Helen
Native American b. 1901
drawings: (H) $495

KAMEKE, Otto von
paintings: (H) $825

KAMENEFF, Lieff Livovitch
Russian 1836-1886
paintings: (H) $863

KAMICH, J.
paintings: (H) $495

KAMITAKI, Gerald
20th cent.
sculpture: (H) $3,300

KAMMERER, Frederik Hendrik
Dutch 1839-1902
paintings: (H) $7,260

KAMP, Louise M.
American 1867-1959
paintings: (L) $138; (H) $1,035

KANDINSKY, Wassily
Russian 1866-1944
paintings: (L) $148,500; (H) $2,752,500
drawings: (L) $25,300; (H) $550,000

KANDLER, Ludwig
paintings: (H) $2,500

KANE, Bob
American b. 1937
drawings: (L) $374; (H) $29,900

KANE, Elisha Kent
drawings: (H) $1,980

KANE, John
American 1860-1934
paintings: (H) $19,800

KANE, Morgan
b. 1916
paintings: (H) $715
drawings: (L) $1,100; (H) $1,320

KANEKO, Jun
contemporary
sculpture: (H) $2,013

KANELBA
drawings: (H) $550

KANEMITSU, Matsumi
Japanese b. 1922
drawings: (L) $100; (H) $935

KANN, Frederick I.
American 1886-1965
paintings: (H) $9,900

KANOVITZ, Howard
b. 1929
paintings: (H) $5,750
drawings: (H) $55

KANTOR, Morris
American 1896-1974
paintings: (L) $138; (H) $6,600
drawings: (L) $715; (H) $1,150

KANTOR, Tadeusz
Polish b. 1915
paintings: (L) $2,200; (H) $2,750

KANTOROV, Dimitri
Russian contemporary
paintings: (H) $1,100

KAPOOR, Anish
Indian/American b. 1954
drawings: (H) $2,070
sculpture: (L) $6,900; (H) $31,625

KAPOOR, Bhagwan
Indian 20th cent.
drawings: (H) $770

KAPOS, June
American contemporary
sculpture: (H) $880

KAPOSTA, Eric
American b. 1951
sculpture: (H) $3,300

KAPP, Charles W.
American 1822-1900
paintings: (H) $825

KAPP, Gary
American b. 1942
paintings: (L) $3,850; (H) $10,450

KAPPES, Alfred
1850-1894
paintings: (H) $1,840

KAPPIS, Albert
German 1836-1914
paintings: (H) $25,300
drawings: (H) $55

KARATSONYI, Andrew F.
American early 20th cent.
paintings: (L) $440; (H) $1,100

KARBERG, L***
Continental 19th cent.
paintings: (H) $862

KARBOWSKY, Adrien
French b. 1855
paintings: (H) $9,900

KARDIN, Alexander
Austrian b. 1917
paintings: (H) $1,320

KARELLA, Marina
b. 1940
paintings: (H) $2,530

KARFIOL, Bernard
Hungarian/American 1866/86-1955
paintings: (L) $88; (H) $9,350
drawings: (L) $137; (H) $920

KARFUNKLE, David
paintings: (H) $550

KARLOVSZKY Bertalan
Hungarian b. 1858
paintings: (H) $29,900

KARLOVSZKY-BERCI,
Hungarian 19th cent.
paintings: (H) $4,400

KARLOWSKI, Bartolome de
paintings: (H) $660

KARMANSKI, Joseph von
Polish 1865-1904
paintings: (H) $7,475

KAROLY, A. and L. SZANTO
American 20th cent.
paintings: (L) $288; (H) $690

KAROLY, Cserna
paintings: (H) $500

KARPATHY, Jeno
Hungarian 1870-1950
paintings: (L) $302; (H) $770

KARPEL, Eli
sculpture: (H) $880

KARPOFF, Ivan
paintings: (H) $2,475

KARPOVA
Russian
sculpture: (H) $2,300

KARRAS, Spiros John
American 1897-1941
paintings: (H) $522

KARS, George
1882-1945
paintings: (H) $4,600

KARSON, Nat
American 20th cent.
drawings: (L) $403; (H) $1,840

KARSSEN, Anton
Dutch 20th cent.
paintings: (L) $605; (H) $1,540

KASIMIR, Luigi
Aus./American 1881-1962
paintings: (H) $1,150

KASPARIDES, Edouard
German 1858-1926
paintings: (H) $8,250

KASPROWICZ, J.M.
Polish b. 1920
paintings: (H) $550

KASS, Deborah
20th cent.
paintings: (H) $1,035

KASSO, Wende
paintings: (H) $1,650

KASTEN, Karl
American b. 1916
paintings: (H) $575

KASYN, John
Canadian b. 1926
paintings: (L) $1,540; (H) $4,620
drawings: (L) $1,100; (H) $1,870

KATE, Herman Ten
Dutch 1822-1890
paintings: (L) $1,650; (H) $7,700
drawings: (L) $605; (H) $1,725

KATE, Johan Mari Ten
Dutch 1831-1910
drawings: (L) $4,025; (H) $4,950

KATO, Kentaro
American 1889-1926
paintings: (H) $1,540

KATZ, Alex
American b. 1927
paintings: (L) $1,650; (H) $129,000
sculpture: (H) $9,680

KATZEN, Lila
b. 1932
sculpture: (L) $412; (H) $805

KAUB-CASALONGA, Alice
French b. 1875
paintings: (H) $10,450

KAUBA, Carl
Austrian 1865-1922
sculpture: (L) $187; (H) $20,700

KAUFFMAN
Continental 19th cent.
paintings: (H) $10,450

KAUFFMAN, Angelica
Swiss 1740-1807
paintings: (H) $2,185
drawings: (L) $990; (H) $1,210

KAUFFMAN, Craig
b. 1932
paintings: (H) $2,200
sculpture: (H) $3,450

KAUFFMAN, J.F.
paintings: (H) $1,760

KAUFFMANN, Hugo Wilhelm
German 1844-1915
paintings: (L) $6,600; (H) $85,000

KAUFMAN, Stuart
American 20th cent.
paintings: (H) $770

KAUFMANN, A. or R.
Continental 19th/20th cent.
paintings: (H) $687

KAUFMANN, Adolf
Austrian 1848-1916
paintings: (L) $880; (H) $15,400

KAUFMANN, Ferdinand
German/American 1864-after 1934
paintings: (L) $770; (H) $4,400

KAUFMANN, Isidor
Austrian 1853-1921
paintings: (L) $11,500; (H) $176,000
drawings: (H) $8,625

KAUFMANN, Karl
Austrian 1843-1901
paintings: (L) $1,035; (H) $11,500

KAUFMANN, Phillip
German 19th/20th cent.
paintings: (H) $770

KAUFMANN, Wilhelm
Austrian 1895-1945
paintings: (L) $330; (H) $605

KAULA, Lee Lufkin
American 1865-1957
paintings: (L) $385; (H) $2,200
drawings: (L) $880; (H) $1,320

KAULA, William Jurian
American 1871-1953
paintings: (L) $55; (H) $14,300
drawings: (L) $154; (H) $1,870

KAULBACH, Friedrich August von
German 1850-1920
paintings: (L) $3,738; (H) $16,100
drawings: (H) $2,300

KAULBACH, Hermann
German 1846-1909
paintings: (L) $4,840; (H) $66,000

KAUMEYER, George F.
American 1856-1951
paintings: (H) $605

KAUS, Max
German 1891-1977
paintings: (L) $16,675; (H) $35,200
drawings: (L) $1,610; (H) $7,475

KAUTEN, Mat
paintings: (L) $1,210; (H) $1,650

KAUTZKY, Ted
American d. 1953
paintings: (L) $1,320; (H) $1,980
drawings: (H) $357

KAVANAGH, Joseph M.
Irish 1856-1918/19
paintings: (L) $110; (H) $880

KAWAI, Shinzo
Japanese late 19th cent.
drawings: (H) $633

KAWAKUBO, Masana
Japanese 20th cent.
drawings: (L) $121; (H) $1,100

KAWARA, On
Japanese/American b. 1933
paintings: (L) $24,200; (H) $35,750
drawings: (L) $12,100; (H) $20,700
sculpture: (L) $16,500; (H) $24,150

KAWASHIMA, Takeshi
Japanese b. 1930
paintings: (L) $1,540; (H) $6,038

KAY, Bernard
American 20th cent.
paintings: (H) $770

KAY, Hermann
German 1839-1902
paintings: (H) $990

KAYANOWK, J.
Continental 19th/20th cent.
paintings: (H) $3,300

KAYE, Joseph
American
paintings: (H) $770

KAYE, Otis
American 1885-1974
paintings: (L) $13,200; (H) $112,500
drawings: (L) $2,750; (H) $2,760

KAYN, Hilde B.
American 1906-1950
paintings: (L) $418; (H) $1,540

KBLAT, Felix E.
Continental 19th cent.
paintings: (H) $805

KEAHBONE, George Compell, Asaute
b. 1916
drawings: (H) $633

KEARFOTT, Robert
American b. 1890
paintings: (H) $4,025

KEARNEY, John
sculpture: (L) $403; (H) $632

KEARNS, Bruce
American 20th cent.
paintings: (H) $805

KECK, Charles
American 1875-1951
sculpture: (L) $495; (H) $14,300

KECK, H.
German 19th cent.
sculpture: (H) $1,320

KEEHN, Evan
American 20th cent.
paintings: (H) $495

KEELHOFF, Frans and Eugene
VERBOECKHOVEN
Belgian 19th cent.
paintings: (H) $8,250

KEENE, E.E.
English 19th cent.
paintings: (H) $742

KEENER, Anna
American b. 1895
paintings: (H) $4,400

KEENS, A.W.
English 19th cent.
paintings: (H) $990

KEFLIX
paintings: (H) $1,155

KEHOE, Patrice
American b. 1952
paintings: (H) $770

KEIL, Bernhardt, called Monsu
Bernardo
Danish 1624-1687
paintings: (L) $5,500; (H) $29,700

KEIME, Jean
French 20th cent.
paintings: (H) $688

KEINHOLZ, Ed
drawings: (L) $1,265; (H) $2,420
sculpture: (H) $4,675

KEIRINCX, Alexander
Flemish 1600-1652
paintings: (H) $13,800

Art Deco Sculpture

The Art Deco movement of the 1920s and 1930s emphasized fine workmanship and the use of costly materials such as ivory, jade, and lacquer. The leading Art Deco sculptor, Demetre Chiparus (1888-1950) used bronze and ivory. The Hungarian sculptor Alexandre Kelety (ac. 1918-1940), known for the quality of his design, specialized in damascening, the inlaying of precious metals in a decorative pattern. This 18-inch bronze exotic dancer, with various patinas silvered and gilded, realized $13,800 at Skinner's January sale of Art Nouveau and Art Deco in Boston. (Alexandre Kelety, *Exotic Dancer*, bronze, 18½ inches on a black stone plinth, Skinner, January 21, 1995, $13,800)

KEIRSBILCK, Jules van
Belgian 1833-1896
paintings: (H) $4,400

KEITH, Castle William
American 1864-1927
paintings: (L) $440; (H) $1,495

KEITH, L.E.
Continental 19th cent.
paintings: (H) $2,200

KEITH, William
American 1838-1911
paintings: (L) $275; (H) $19,550
drawings: (H) $1,380

KELBE(?), Julia A.
19th/20th cent.
paintings: (H) $1,430

KELDERMAN, Jan
Dutch 1741-1820
paintings: (L) $192; (H) $310,500

KELETY, Alexandre
Hungarian ac. 1918-1940
sculpture: (L) $440; (H) $13,800

KELIAM, S.
sculpture: (H) $1,540

KELLER, Albert von
Swiss 1844-1920
paintings: (L) $2,587; (H) $5,750

KELLER, Arthur Ignatius
American 1866/67-1924
paintings: (H) $440
drawings: (L) $22; (H) $3,850

KELLER, Charles Frederick
1852-1928
paintings: (L) $440; (H) $797

KELLER, Clyde Leon
American 1872-1941
paintings: (L) $110; (H) $1,045

KELLER, Deane
American b. 1901
drawings: (L) $35; (H) $633

KELLER, Edgar M.
American 1868-1932
paintings: (L) $440; (H) $770

KELLER, F.
paintings: (H) $523

KELLER, Ferdinand
German 1842-1922
paintings: (L) $1,210; (H) $25,300

KELLER, Friederich von
German 1840-1914
paintings: (H) $13,800

KELLER, Henry George
American 1870-1949
paintings: (L) $33; (H) $2,090
drawings: (L) $44; (H) $825

KELLER, L.
American late 19th cent.
paintings: (H) $880

KELLER-REUTLINGEN, Paul Wilhelm
German 1854-1920
paintings: (L) $7,150; (H) $12,650

KELLEY, Gary
b. 1945
drawings: (H) $605

KELLEY, Mike
American b. 1964
paintings: (L) $1,150; (H) $12,650
drawings: (L) $4,025; (H) $5,280

KELLEY, Ramon
American b. 1939
paintings: (L) $900; (H) $1,400
drawings: (L) $1,100; (H) $3,850

KELLNER, Charles H.
American b. 1890
paintings: (H) $1,006

KELLOGG, Harry
19th/20th cent.
paintings: (H) $880
drawings: (H) $605

KELLY, Ellsworth
American b. 1923
paintings: (L) $55,000; (H) $805,500
drawings: (L) $2,530; (H) $16,500
sculpture: (L) $23,100; (H) $145,500

KELLY, Emmett
American 20th cent.
drawings: (H) $550

KELLY, Felix
British b. 1916
paintings: (L) $1,380; (H) $1,725

KELLY, James P.
American 1854-1893
paintings: (H) $3,850

KELLY, Ken
b. 1946
paintings: (L) $770; (H) $3,575

KELLY, Leon
Franco/American b. 1901
paintings: (L) $66; (H) $3,520
drawings: (L) $80; (H) $2,990

KELLY, Lloyd
American 20th cent.
paintings: (H) $2,070

KELLY, Mike
sculpture: (H) $13,800

KELLY, Mike
b. 1954
drawings: (H) $16,100

KELLY, Robert George
English 1822-1910
paintings: (L) $880; (H) $1,430

KELLY, Robert George Talbot
English 1861-1934
paintings: (L) $863; (H) $2,640
drawings: (L) $58; (H) $5,462

KELLY, Walt
American 1913-1973
drawings: (L) $1,870; (H) $11,500

KELPE, Paul
American 1902-1985
paintings: (L) $25,300; (H) $25,300
drawings: (H) $17,250

KELSEY, Richmond
American b. 1905
paintings: (H) $495

KELSEY, T.D.
American 20th cent.
sculpture: (L) $440; (H) $605

KEMBLE, Edward Windsor
American 1861-1933
paintings: (H) $110
drawings: (L) $302; (H) $4,675

KEMENY, Nandor
Hungarian b. 1885
paintings: (H) $2,750

KEMENY, Zoltan
1907-1965
sculpture: (L) $13,800; (H) $14,300

KEMEYS, Edward
American 1843-1907
sculpture: (L) $440; (H) $5,463

KEMM, Robert
English ac. 1874-1891
paintings: (L) $687; (H) $37,375

KEMP, Louise
American 20th cent.
paintings: (L) $460; (H) $460

KEMP, Oliver
American 1887-1934
paintings: (H) $880

KEMP-WELCH, Lucy
English 1869-1958
drawings: (H) $805

KENARD, G***
British 19th cent.
paintings: (H) $2,300

KENDALL, Margarida
Portuguese 20th cent.
paintings: (H) $1,100

KENDALL, Marie B.
American 1885-1953
paintings: (L) $193; (H) $523

KENDALL, William Sergeant
American 1869-1938
paintings: (L) $1,035; (H) $4,888
drawings: (H) $2,090

KENDAM, Frances
paintings: (H) $805

KENDE, Geza
American 1889-1952
paintings: (L) $248; (H) $3,450

KENDERDINE, Augustus Fredrick
1870-1947
paintings: (H) $880

KENDRICK, Mel
American b. 1949
sculpture: (L) $550; (H) $25,300

KENDRICK, Sydney
English 1874-1955
paintings: (L) $1,760; (H) $4,950

KENDZRIERSKI, Apolonius
Polish 19th cent.
paintings: (H) $1,100

KENEMY
drawings: (H) $468

KENINGH, S. de
Dutch 19th cent.
paintings: (H) $825

KENNEDY, A.
20th cent.
paintings: (H) $575

KENNEDY, Cecil
British b. 1905
paintings: (H) $3,300

KENNEDY, Charles Anthony
drawings: (H) $4,370

KENNEDY, Charles Napier
British 1852-1898
paintings: (H) $39,100

KENNEDY, David Johnston
1816/17-1898
drawings: (H) $2,750

KENNEDY, E. Sherand
English ac. 1863-1890
paintings: (H) $4,600

KENNEDY, John William
American b. 1903
paintings: (H) $2,200

KENNEDY, Joseph
English 19th cent.
paintings: (H) $7,975

KENNEDY, Margaret
paintings: (L) $1,000; (H) $1,500

KENNEDY, William
1818-1870
paintings: (H) $1,980

KENNEDY, William
American
paintings: (H) $3,300

KENNEDY, William
British 1860-1918
paintings: (L) $2,760; (H) $5,175

KENNEDY, William W.
American b. c. 1817
paintings: (L) $5,175; (H) $7,475

KENNEY, Charles F.
paintings: (H) $990

KENNEY, John T.
British 20th cent.
paintings: (H) $1,265

KENNEYS, Edward
American 1843-1907
sculpture: (L) $2,530; (H) $2,990

KENNICOTT, Robert
American 1892-1983
drawings: (H) $825

KENNINGTON, Thomas Benjamin
British 1856-1916
paintings: (H) $8,050

KENNY, A.J.
American 19th cent.
paintings: (H) $1,980

KENSETT, John F.
American 1816/18-1872
paintings: (L) $2,090; (H) $286,000
drawings: (L) $192; (H) $3,080

KENSETT, John Frederick and Jasper
Francis CROPSEY
American 19th cent.
paintings: (H) $79,500

KENSINGTON, C.
drawings: (H) $770

KENT, Augustus
English School
paintings: (L) $357; (H) $660

KENT, Frank Ward
1912-1977
paintings: (H) $978

KENT, Rockwell
American 1882-1971
paintings: (L) $1,100; (H) $112,500
drawings: (L) $165; (H) $5,940

KENT, Ron
contemporary
sculpture: (L) $1,150; (H) $1,495

KENT, W.
American 20th cent.
sculpture: (H) $990

KENWAY, James
paintings: (H) $1,210

KENYON, Henry R.
American d. 1926
paintings: (L) $303; (H) $2,310

KEOKKEOK, Johannes Hermanus
Barend
Dutch 1840-1912
paintings: (L) $4,400; (H) $5,225

KEPES, Gyorgy
American b. Hungary 1906
paintings: (L) $1,320; (H) $2,070
drawings: (H) $575

KERCHER, Bob
American
drawings: (L) $500; (H) $850

KERCKHOFF, Frans
ac. 1661
paintings: (H) $10,120

KERG, Theo
b. 1909
paintings: (H) $550

KERKAM, Earl
American c. 1890-1965
paintings: (L) $110; (H) $440
drawings: (L) $110; (H) $2,070

KERLING, Anne E.
Dutch 1862-1931
paintings: (H) $797

KERN, Albin
American 1884-1975
paintings: (H) $715

KERN, Edward Meyer
American 1823-1863
paintings: (H) $825

KERN, Hermann
Hungarian 1839-1912
paintings: (L) $1,320; (H) $11,550

KERNAN, Joseph F.
American 1878-1958
paintings: (L) $880; (H) $6,490

KERR, Charles Henry Malcolm
British 1858-1907
paintings: (H) $28,750

KERR, Illingworth Holey
Canadian 1905-1988
paintings: (L) $1,650; (H) $9,350

KERR, Vernon
American d. 1982
paintings: (L) $110; (H) $880

KERTESZ, Istvan
Hungarian 20th cent.
paintings: (H) $1,100

KESK
German 19th cent.
sculpture: (H) $546

KESSEL, Jan van, I
Flemish 1626-1679
paintings: (L) $21,850; (H) $495,000

KESSEL, Jan van, III
Dutch 1641/42-1680
paintings: (L) $17,250; (H) $40,250
drawings: (H) $23,100

KESSLER, Jon
b. 1957
sculpture: (H) $2,300

KESSLER, Michael
paintings: (L) $385; (H) $495

KESSLERE, G. Maillard
paintings: (H) $552

KESZTHELYI, Alexander S.
paintings: (H) $1,210

KETCHUM, Abijah E.
American 19th cent.
paintings: (L) $230; (H) $800

KETTEMANN, Erwin
German 1897-1971
paintings: (L) $137; (H) $1,430

KETTLE, Tilly
English 1735-1786
paintings: (L) $1,650; (H) $4,675

KEULEMANS, Johannes Gerardus
Dutch 19th cent.
drawings: (L) $3,575; (H) $6,050

KEVER, Jacob Simon Hendrik
Dutch 1854-1922
paintings: (L) $935; (H) $11,500
drawings: (L) $605; (H) $1,265

KEVORKIAN, Jean
American b. 1933
paintings: (L) $2,090; (H) $3,080

KEY, Adriaen Thomas
Flemish c. 1544-c.1590
paintings: (L) $19,500; (H) $66,000

KEY, John Ross
American 1832-1920
paintings: (L) $605; (H) $19,800
drawings: (L) $330; (H) $4,400

KEY, Mabel
American 1874-1926
drawings: (L) $357; (H) $2,200

KEY, Sato
1906-1978
paintings: (H) $34,500

KEY, Willem
Flemish c. 1515-1568
paintings: (H) $19,800

KEYSE, Thomas
1722-1800
paintings: (H) $7,700

KEYSER, Frederick Rudolph
19th/20th cent.
paintings: (H) $2,640

KEYSER, Hendrick de
Netherlandish 1565-1621
sculpture: (H) $9,775

KEYSER, Thomas de
Dutch 1596-1667
paintings: (H) $10,725

KEYT, George
Indian b. Ceylon 1901
paintings: (H) $4,830
drawings: (H) $4,887

KEZDI, E. Kovacs
Hungarian 19th/20th cent.
paintings: (H) $550

KHAKHAR, Bhupen
drawings: (L) $920; (H) $1,495

KHNOPFF, Fernand
Belgian 1858-1912
paintings: (H) $880,000

KIAERSKOU, Frederik
Danish 1805-1891
paintings: (H) $690

KICK, Cornelius
Dutch 1635-1681
paintings: (H) $23,000

KIDANETE, P.L. Koicalazeras
sculpture: (H) $2,300

KIDD, Joseph Bartholemew
Scottish 1808-1889
paintings: (H) $15,400

KIDDER, Harvey
b. 1918
paintings: (H) $2,200

KIECOL, Hubert
b. 1950
sculpture: (H) $1,380

KIEFER, Anselm
German b. 1945
paintings: (L) $27,500; (H) $638,000
drawings: (L) $13,800; (H) $181,500
sculpture: (L) $17,250; (H) $596,500

KIEFF
Spanish b. 1936
sculpture: (L) $187; (H) $2,070

KIELDRUP, Anton Edvard
Danish 1826-1869
paintings: (H) $1,150

KIEMIT (?), M.A.
Dutch 19th cent.
paintings: (H) $550

KIENBUSCH, William
American b. 1914
paintings: (H) $2,200
drawings: (L) $83; (H) $990

KIENHOLZ, Edward
American b. 1927
drawings: (H) $2,200
sculpture: (L) $4,950; (H) $49,500

KIENHOLZ, Edward and Nancy
American 20th cent.
sculpture: (L) $10,000; (H) $40,250

KIESEL, Conrad
German 1846-1921
paintings: (L) $3,450; (H) $14,850

KIESEWETTER, Johann Christian
German 19th cent.
paintings: (H) $550

KIESSLING, Johann Paul Adolf
German 1836-1919
paintings: (H) $36,800

KIFF, Ken
paintings: (H) $920

KIHN, Wilfred Langdon
American 1898-1957
paintings: (L) $220; (H) $495
drawings: (H) $2,420

KIJNO, Ladislas
French School b. 1921
drawings: (H) $5,550

KIKI, John
20th cent.
paintings: (H) $920

KIKOINE, Michel
French 1892-1968
paintings: (L) $220; (H) $23,000
drawings: (H) $1,955

KIKUCHI, Atsushi
Japanese/American 20th cent.
drawings: (L) $104; (H) $518

KILBERT, Robert P.
American 20th cent.
paintings: (H) $920

KILBOURNE, Samuel A.
American 1836-1881
paintings: (L) $1,100; (H) $2,475

KILBURNE, George Goodwin
British 1839-1924
paintings: (L) $1,210; (H) $4,950
drawings: (L) $440; (H) $7,188

KILGOUR, Scott
American contemporary
paintings: (L) $202; (H) $517

KILIMNICK, Karen
b. 1962
drawings: (H) $748

KILLAM, Walter H.
drawings: (H) $920

KILLEN, Susan
American
sculpture: (H) $518

KILLGORE, Charles
American 20th cent.
paintings: (L) $264; (H) $825

KILPATRICK, Aaron Edward
American 1872-1953
paintings: (L) $805; (H) $3,300

KIMBALL, Alonzo Myron
American 1874-1923
paintings: (H) $1,980
drawings: (L) $55; (H) $575

KIMBALL, Charles Frederick
American 1835/36-1907
paintings: (L) $748; (H) $18,700

KIMBALL, Henry
19th cent.
drawings: (H) $1,320

KIMBEL, Richard
American 1865-1942
paintings: (L) $805; (H) $4,840

KIMLER, Wesley
American b. 1953
paintings: (H) $2,750

KIMPO, R.
paintings: (H) $18,400

KIMURA
Japanese 19th/20th cent.
paintings: (H) $726

KINDERDINE, Augustine Frederick
1870-1947
paintings: (H) $4,600

KINDLEBERGER, David
American ac. 1900-1905
paintings: (H) $1,430

KINDON, Mary Eliva
British ac. 1881-1919
paintings: (H) $495

KING, Albert F.
American 1854-1945
paintings: (L) $248; (H) $8,913

KING, Baragwanath
British 1864-1939
drawings: (L) $192; (H) $488

KING, Charles Bird
American 1785-1862
paintings: (H) $14,950
drawings: (L) $2,420; (H) $5,463

KING, Francis Scott
American b. 1850
paintings: (H) $3,300

KING, Frank
drawings: (L) $690; (H) $2,875

KING, George W.
American 1836-1922
paintings: (L) $275; (H) $3,520

KING, H.F.
paintings: (H) $1,980

KING, Haynes
British 1831-1904
paintings: (H) $3,850

KING, Henry John Yeend
British 1855-1924
paintings: (L) $1,760; (H) $9,900
drawings: (L) $440; (H) $2,070

KING, James S.
American 1852-1925
paintings: (H) $17,250

KING, Jessie Marion
English 1875-1949
drawings: (L) $495; (H) $1,320

KING, M.E.
American 19th cent.
paintings: (L) $220; (H) $495

KING, Mark
American 20th cent.
paintings: (H) $1,320

KING, Paul
American 1867-1947
paintings: (L) $172; (H) $10,450
drawings: (H) $192

KING, William
American b. 1925
drawings: (H) $121
sculpture: (L) $1,760; (H) $4,400

KING, William Joseph
British b. 1857
paintings: (H) $550
drawings: (L) $35; (H) $137

KING FEATURES STUDIO
drawings: (H) $805

KINGAL, J.
German/Austrian 19th cent.
paintings: (H) $2,750

KINGLADDE
British 20th cent.
paintings: (H) $990

KINGMAN, Dong
American b. 1911
paintings: (L) $83; (H) $2,200
drawings: (L) $495; (H) $14,300

KINGMAN, Eduardo
Ecuador b. 1913
paintings: (L) $3,450; (H) $13,800

KINGMAN, Eugene
American 1909-1975
paintings: (H) $660

KINGMAN, Rioforio Eduardo
Ecuadorian b. 1913
drawings: (L) $165; (H) $990

KINGSBURY, Edward R.
American d. 1940
paintings: (L) $88; (H) $880

KINKADE, Thomas
American b. 1947
paintings: (H) $3,025

KINLEY, Peter
paintings: (H) $8,800

KINNAIRD, Frederick Gerald
British ac. 1864-1881
paintings: (L) $1,955; (H) $3,300

KINNAIRD, Henry John
English ac. 1880-c. 1920
paintings: (L) $550; (H) $4,600
drawings: (L) $460; (H) $1,980

KINNAIRD, J.G.
paintings: (H) $1,650
KINNELL, K*
American 20th cent.
paintings: (H) $920
KINNEY, Charles, Charley
1906-1991
drawings: (H) $2,090
KINNEY, Margaret West
American b. 1872
paintings: (H) $2,875
KINSBURGER, Sylvain
French b. 1855
sculpture: (H) $4,025
KINSEY, Alberta
American 1875-1955
paintings: (L) $200; (H) $1,430
drawings: (L) $330; (H) $330
KINSON, Francois Joseph
Flemish 1771-1839
paintings: (H) $7,700
KINZEL, Josef
Austrian 1852-1925
paintings: (H) $19,550
KIOERBOE, Carl Fredrik
Swedish 1799-1876
paintings: (H) $2,750
KIPNISS, Robert
American b. 1931
paintings: (L) $358; (H) $2,200
KIPPENBERGER, Martin
contemporary
paintings: (H) $7,150
KIPRENSKY, Orest Adamovitch
Russian 1778-1836
drawings: (H) $688
KIRAFLY, Verona Arnold
American b. 1893
paintings: (L) $385; (H) $660
KIRBERG, Otto Karl
German 1850-1926
paintings: (L) $2,200; (H) $14,950
KIRBY, Glo
Canadian b. 1911
paintings: (L) $38; (H) $495
KIRBY, J.
American 20th cent.
paintings: (H) $522

KIRBY, J.K.
English 20th cent.
paintings: (H) $605
KIRBY, Jack
drawings: (L) $1,100; (H) $4,312
KIRBY, Jack and Bill EVERETT
drawings: (H) $880
KIRBY, Jack and Dick AYERS
drawings: (H) $3,300
KIRBY, Jack and Joe SINNOTT
drawings: (H) $4,125
KIRBY, Jack and Vince COLLETTA
drawings: (H) $990
KIRBY, Rollin
b. 1875
drawings: (L) $55; (H) $880
KIRCHBACH, Franck
German 1859-1912
paintings: (L) $2,200; (H) $34,500
KIRCHMER, Paul J.
ac. in Italy c. 1945-60
sculpture: (H) $1,320
KIRCHNEN, Otto
paintings: (H) $863
KIRCHNER
sculpture: (H) $660
KIRCHNER, Albert Emil
German 1813-1885
drawings: (H) $2,750
KIRCHNER, Ernst Ludwig
German 1880-1938
paintings: (L) $244,500; (H) $1,540,000
drawings: (L) $2,185; (H) $71,250
KIRCHNER, Eugen
German b. 1865
paintings: (H) $1,100
KIRCHNER, Otto
German b. 1887
paintings: (L) $440; (H) $2,090
KIRILI, Alain
French b. 1946
sculpture: (H) $24,200
KIRISCHKE, Franz
Austrian 19th/20th cent.
paintings: (H) $1,320
KIRK, Eve
British 1900-?
paintings: (H) $500

KIRK, Frank C.
American 1889-1963
paintings: (L) $165; (H) $1,380

KIRK, Maria
b. 1860
drawings: (H) $1,210

KIRK, R.
English 19th cent.
paintings: (H) $880

KIRK, W.B.
English 19th cent.
sculpture: (H) $2,750

KIRKBY, Kenneth
paintings: (L) $1,045; (H) $1,045

KIRKEBY, Per
Danish b. 1938
paintings: (L) $10,350; (H) $34,500
drawings: (H) $5,500

KIRKMAN, Jay
British 20th cent.
paintings: (H) $1,760

KIRKPATRICK, J.L.
British 19th cent.
paintings: (H) $660

KIRKPATRICK, Joey and Flora MACE
sculpture: (H) $2,090

KIRKPATRICK, Joseph
English b. 1872, ac. 1891-1928
drawings: (L) $715; (H) $1,150

KIRMSE, Marguerite
Anglo/American 1885-1954
paintings: (H) $660
drawings: (L) $264; (H) $605
sculpture: (L) $715; (H) $1,210

KIRNBOCK, R.
Continental 19th cent.
paintings: (H) $4,125

KIROUAC, Louise
paintings: (H) $1,320

KIRSCH, Max E.
paintings: (H) $1,320

KIRSHENBAUM, Jules
American 20th cent.
paintings: (H) $6,900

KIRSHNER, Otto
paintings: (H) $1,045

KIRSTEN (?), L.E.
paintings: (H) $450

KISCHKA, Isis
French 1908-1974
paintings: (L) $230; (H) $1,210

KISELEV, Alexander Alexandrovich,
KISSELJOFF
Russian 1838-1911
paintings: (H) $1,430

KISILIOV, Alexander
Russian 19th cent.
paintings: (H) $8,250

KISLING, Moise
Polish/French 1891-1953
paintings: (L) $14,300; (H) $319,000
drawings: (L) $3,450; (H) $132,000

KISS, August
sculpture: (H) $6,900

KISSONERGIS, Ioannis
Greek d. 1963
drawings: (H) $1,725

KISTER, Roy C.
American b. 1886
paintings: (H) $495

KITAJ, R.B.
American b. 1933
paintings: (L) $51,750; (H) $330,000
drawings: (L) $9,200; (H) $25,300

KITAJIMA, Asaichi
Japanese 1877-1947
paintings: (H) $6,050

KITCHELL, Hudson Mindell
American 1862-1944
paintings: (L) $165; (H) $2,200

KITCHELL, M.M.
English 19th cent.
paintings: (H) $575

KITCHEN, Dennis
drawings: (H) $1,760

KITCHEN, Tella
paintings: (L) $1,900; (H) $2,600

KITCHME
paintings: (H) $605

KITE, Joseph Milner
English 1862-1946
paintings: (H) $2,200

KITSON, Samuel James
American 1848-1906
sculpture: (H) $11,500

KITTELL, Nicholas Biddle
American 1822-1894
paintings: (H) $3,850

KITTELSEN, Theodor
Norwegian 1857-1914
drawings: (L) $88; (H) $2,860

KIVETORUK, James, Kivetoruk, Bark
Dye
Eskimo b. 1901
drawings: (H) $1,210

KIYOMITSU SAKU
late 19th cent.
sculpture: (H) $2,875

KJARGOORD, O.A.
Dutch 20th cent.
paintings: (H) $660

KLAR, Mary Shepard
American b. 1882
paintings: (H) $1,725

KLASEN, Peter
German b. 1935
paintings: (L) $440; (H) $605

KLASS, Joseph
Belgian 20th cent.
paintings: (H) $6,900

KLAY, Jacob
Dutch 1848-1886
paintings: (H) $2,587

KLECZYNSKI, Bohdan von
Polish 1851-1916.
paintings: (L) $8,050; (H) $17,250

KLEE, Paul
Swiss 1879-1940
paintings: (L) $27,600; (H) $1,980,000
drawings: (L) $6,900; (H) $717,500

KLEEHAAS, Theodor
German b. 1854
paintings: (H) $4,370

KLEEMANN, Ronald
American b. 1937
paintings: (L) $1,100; (H) $36,800

KLEIBER, Hans
American 1887-1967
drawings: (L) $345; (H) $1,800

KLEIJN, Lodewyk Johannes
Dutch 1817-1897
paintings: (L) $3,300; (H) $16,675

KLEIN, Dan
American 20th cent.
paintings: (H) $550

KLEIN, G.
drawings: (L) $110; (H) $660

KLEIN, Pat
American 20th cent.
drawings: (H) $1,265

KLEIN, Wilhelm
German 1821-1897
paintings: (L) $330; (H) $1,760

KLEIN, Yves
French 1928-1962
paintings: (H) $18,400
drawings: (H) $662,500
sculpture: (L) $17,250; (H) $31,900

KLEINENBROICH, Wilhelm
German 1814-1893
paintings: (L) $1,760; (H) $2,875

KLEINSCHMIDT, Paul
German 1883-1949
paintings: (L) $90,500; (H) $118,000

KLEINSMIEDE, S.A.
Austrian 19th cent.
paintings: (H) $1,210

KLEIST, R.
American 19th cent.
drawings: (H) $7,425

KLEITSCH, Joseph
Hungarian/American 1885-1931
paintings: (L) $935; (H) $10,450

KLEMM, E.
Austrian 19th cent.
paintings: (L) $935; (H) $990

KLEMPNER, Ernest
Austrian/American b. 1867
paintings: (L) $357; (H) $3,575

KLERK, Willem de
Dutch b. 1800
paintings: (L) $1,035; (H) $1,380

KLEVER, Julius Sergius von
Russian 1850-1924
paintings: (L) $1,980; (H) $13,200

KLEY, Heinrich
German 1863-1945
drawings: (L) $132; (H) $7,150

KLIBAN, Bernard
1935-1990
drawings: (H) $550

KLIENSCHMIDT, Paul
1883-1949
paintings: (H) $4,600

KLIMLEY, Stan
drawings: (L) $357; (H) $990

KLIMSCH, Eugen Johann Georg
German 1839-1896
paintings: (H) $12,650

KLIMT, Gustav
Austrian 1862-1918
paintings: (H) $11,662,500
drawings: (L) $440; (H) $40,250

KLINE, Franz
American 1910-1962
paintings: (L) $5,500; (H) $2,640,000
drawings: (L) $460; (H) $85,000

KLING, Wendell
drawings: (L) $358; (H) $1,430

KLING, Wendell and Robert
JOHNSON
drawings: (H) $1,210

KLINGELHOFER, Fritz
German 1832-1903
paintings: (H) $3,850

KLINGENDER, Louis Henry Weston
British b. 1861
paintings: (H) $22,000

KLINGER
paintings: (H) $2,530

KLINGER, Karl
German 19th cent.
paintings: (H) $825

KLINGER, Max
German 1857-1920
sculpture: (L) $8,050; (H) $16,100

KLINGER, R.
paintings: (L) $522; (H) $880

KLINKENBERG, Johannes Christiaan
Karel
Dutch 1852-1924
paintings: (L) $1,200; (H) $13,200

KLINKER, Orpha
American 1891-1964
paintings: (L) $302; (H) $577
drawings: (H) $550

KLIPPERT, Howard
paintings: (L) $1,045; (H) $2,750

KLIUN, Ivan Vassilievich
Russian 1873-1942
drawings: (H) $5,750

KLOD, C.
drawings: (H) $550

KLOPPER, Zan D.
Russian/American 1870
paintings: (H) $1,540

KLOSS, Gene
American b. 1903
paintings: (L) $3,960; (H) $8,250
drawings: (L) $660; (H) $3,450

KLOTON
paintings: (H) $633

KLUGE, Constantine
French b. Russia 1912
paintings: (L) $467; (H) $8,250

KLUMPKE, Anna Elisabeth
American 1856-1942
paintings: (L) $2,750; (H) $6,900
drawings: (H) $1,430

KLUMPP, Gustav
American 1902-1980
paintings: (H) $3,450

KLUTH, Robert
American 1854-1921
paintings: (H) $10,350

KLUYVER, Pieter Lodewyk Francisco
Dutch 1816-1900
paintings: (L) $9,900; (H) $10,450

KLYN, J.
paintings: (H) $605

KLYSNER, J.
drawings: (H) $575

KMETTY, Janos
Hungarian b. 1889
paintings: (H) $770

KNAP, Joseph Day
b. 1875
paintings: (H) $138
drawings: (L) $302; (H) $1,210

KNAPP, Charles W.
American 1822-1900
paintings: (L) $825; (H) $13,200
drawings: (L) $55; (H) $330

KNAPP, G.A.
paintings: (H) $850

KNAPP, Stefan
Polish/American b. 1921
paintings: (H) $1,045

KNAPP, Tom
American b. 1925
sculpture: (H) $880

KNATHS, Karl
American 1891-1971
paintings: (L) $690; (H) $4,950
drawings: (L) $55; (H) $2,090

KNAU
19th cent.
paintings: (H) $715

KNAUBER, Alma Jordan
American b. 1893
drawings: (L) $110; (H) $825

KNAUS, Ludwig
German 1829-1910
paintings: (L) $138; (H) $41,250

KNEBEL, Franz, the younger
Swiss 1809-1877
paintings: (L) $23,100; (H) $33,000

KNELL, William Adolphus
English c. 1805-1875
paintings: (L) $990; (H) $8,250
drawings: (H) $863

KNELL, William Calcott
British 19th cent.
paintings: (H) $2,200

KNELLER, Johann Zacharias
1644-1702
paintings: (H) $10,450

KNELLER, Sir Godfrey
German/English 1646-1723
paintings: (L) $2,100; (H) $10,925

KNELLER, Sir Godfrey, studio of
paintings: (L) $1,980; (H) $7,700

KNIGHT, A. Roland
British b. 1900
paintings: (L) $1,495; (H) $3,163

KNIGHT, Adah
British 19th/20th cent.
paintings: (H) $1,035

KNIGHT, Avel de
American b. 1933
paintings: (H) $880
drawings: (H) $523

KNIGHT, Charles Robert
American 1874-1953
paintings: (L) $220; (H) $5,500

KNIGHT, Clayton
1891-1969
paintings: (H) $143
drawings: (H) $495

KNIGHT, Dame Laura
English 1877-1970
drawings: (H) $1,650

KNIGHT, Daniel Ridgway
American 1839-1924
paintings: (L) $633; (H) $96,000
drawings: (L) $632; (H) $14,950

KNIGHT, George
British 20th cent.
paintings: (L) $275; (H) $495

KNIGHT, Hilary
drawings: (H) $1,495

KNIGHT, Jacob
b. 1941
paintings: (H) $660

KNIGHT, John Buxton
British 1843-1908
paintings: (H) $715

KNIGHT, John Prescott
British 1803-1881
paintings: (H) $863

KNIGHT, Louis Aston
American 1873-1948
paintings: (L) $231; (H) $18,700
drawings: (L) $258; (H) $9,775

KNIGHT, William Henry
British 1823-1863
paintings: (H) $1,980

KNIKKER, Jan
Dutch b. 1911
paintings: (L) $275; (H) $990

KNIP, August
Dutch 1819-1852
paintings: (H) $1,375

KNIP, Hendrik Johannes
1819-after 1869
drawings: (H) $2,588

KNIP, Joseph August
1777-1847
drawings: (H) $1,380

KNIP, Nicolaas Frederik
Dutch 1742-c. 1809
paintings: (H) $8,250

KNIP, Willem
Dutch 1883-1967
paintings: (L) $825; (H) $1,760

KNOBLOCH, Josef Rolf
German 1891-1964
paintings: (H) $1,210

KNOCHEL, Hans
Czechoslovakian b. 1850
paintings: (H) $1,650

KNOCKE, W.C.
American 19th cent.
paintings: (H) $1,320

KNOEBEL, Imi
German b. 1940
paintings: (L) $4,313; (H) $38,500
drawings: (L) $1,870; (H) $13,200
sculpture: (L) $3,850; (H) $22,000

KNOGH, P.
drawings: (H) $1,980

KNOOP, August
German 1856-1900
paintings: (L) $1,045; (H) $3,300

KNOOP, J.H.
Dutch 1769-1834
paintings: (H) $770

KNOPF, Herman
Austrian b. 1870
paintings: (H) $1,210

KNOPF, Nellie A.
American 1875-1962
paintings: (H) $990

KNOPP, Imre
Hungarian 19th/20th cent.
paintings: (H) $4,620

KNOTT, Arthur Harold
American 1883-1977
paintings: (H) $550

KNOWLES, Davidson
English ac. 1879-1896
paintings: (L) $1,265; (H) $5,750

KNOWLES, Dorothy
Canadian b. 1927
drawings: (L) $1,375; (H) $1,650

KNOWLES, Farquhar McGillivray
American 1859-1932
paintings: (L) $632; (H) $1,495

KNOWLES, Frederick J.
English b. 1874
paintings: (H) $2,420

KNOWLES, George Sheridan
English 1863-1931
paintings: (L) $863; (H) $10,450

KNOWLES, W.L.
American 19th cent.
paintings: (L) $1,430; (H) $1,540

KNOWLTON, Win
American b. 1953
drawings: (H) $288
sculpture: (H) $1,265

KNOX, James
American b. 1866
paintings: (L) $660; (H) $1,320

KNOX, John
1778-1845
paintings: (H) $28,600

KNOX, L. Rebecca
American 19th/20th cent.
paintings: (L) $275; (H) $1,430

KNOX, Susan Ricker
American 1875-1959
paintings: (L) $192; (H) $4,600
drawings: (L) $110; (H) $303

KNOX, Wilfred
British 19th cent.
drawings: (H) $1,870

KNOX, William
British 20th cent.
paintings: (H) $1,840

KNUDSEN, Peder
Danish 1868-1944
paintings: (H) $1,430

KNUDSON, Robert
American b. 1929
paintings: (L) $440; (H) $2,300

KOBAYASHI, Milton
American b. 1950
drawings: (L) $3,335; (H) $4,950

KOBAYASHI, Tokusaburo
Japanese 1884-1949
drawings: (H) $1,540

KOBBE, Marie Olga
American b. 1870
drawings: (H) $460

KOBELL, Hendrik
Dutch 1751-1779
drawings: (H) $1,955

KOBELL, Jan, II
Dutch 1778-1814
paintings: (L) $1,870; (H) $9,200

KOBELL, Jan, III
Dutch 1800-1838
paintings: (H) $4,125

KOBELL, Jan Baptist
Dutch 1778-1814
paintings: (H) $9,200

KOBELL, Wilhelm Alexander
Wolfgang von
German 1766-1855
drawings: (H) $49,500

KOBERLING, Bernd
b. 1938
paintings: (L) $2,200; (H) $8,625

KOBIYASHI, T.
Japanese 19th/20th cent.
drawings: (H) $1,650

KOBOLD, Werner
German 1740-1803
paintings: (H) $1,150

KOCH, Charles Louis Phillip
American b. 1863
paintings: (H) $715

KOCH, Georg
German 1819-1889
paintings: (H) $4,025

KOCH, Henry
1846-1906
paintings: (H) $1,265

KOCH, Jakob
ac. 1900-1920
paintings: (H) $9,200
drawings: (H) $2,300

KOCH, John
American 1909/10-1978
paintings: (L) $1,100; (H) $308,000
drawings: (L) $110; (H) $2,420

KOCH, Ludwig
Austrian 1866-1934
drawings: (H) $4,025

KOCH, Samuel
American b. 1887
paintings: (H) $468

KOCHENDORFER
German 19th cent.
sculpture: (H) $690

KOCHER, Fritz
German/American 1904-1973
paintings: (L) $302; (H) $523
drawings: (H) $412

KOCKE, Hugo
German b. 1874
paintings: (H) $10,925

KOCKERT, Julius
German 1827-1918
paintings: (L) $5,225; (H) $9,350

KOEHLER, Henry
American b. 1927
paintings: (L) $2,587; (H) $17,250
drawings: (L) $880; (H) $3,850

KOEHLER, Paul R.
American 1875-1909
drawings: (L) $220; (H) $1,210

KOEHLER, Robert
American 19th cent.
paintings: (H) $1,100

KOEKKOEK, Barend Cornelis
Dutch 1803-1862
paintings: (L) $15,950; (H) $261,000
drawings: (H) $747

KOEKKOEK, Hendrik Barend
Dutch 1849-1909
paintings: (L) $3,025; (H) $3,190

KOEKKOEK, Hendrik Pieter
Dutch 1843-1890
paintings: (L) $2,420; (H) $6,050

KOEKKOEK, Hermanus, I
Dutch 1815-1882
paintings: (L) $4,400; (H) $66,000

KOEKKOEK, Hermanus, II Jan van
Couver
Dutch 1836-1929
paintings: (L) $1,210; (H) $9,350

KOEKKOEK, Hermanus Willem
Dutch 1867-1929
paintings: (L) $1,650; (H) $12,100

KOEKKOEK, Johannes
Dutch 1811-1831
paintings: (H) $5,290

KOEKKOEK, Johannes Hermanus
Dutch 1778-1851
paintings: (L) $2,875; (H) $25,300

KOEKKOEK, Johannes Hermanus
Barend
Dutch 1840-1912
paintings: (L) $2,750; (H) $7,150

KOEKKOEK, Marianus Adrianus and
Eugene Joseph VERBOECKHOVEN
Dutch 1807-1870
paintings: (H) $11,000

KOEKKOEK, Marinus Andrianus
Dutch 1807-1870
paintings: (L) $1,650; (H) $6,050

KOEKKOEK, Willem
Dutch 1839-1895
paintings: (L) $12,650; (H) $90,500
drawings: (H) $550

KOELMAN, Jan
Dutch 19th cent.
drawings: (H) $495

KOELMAN, Johan
Dutch 19th cent.
drawings: (H) $1,955

KOEMELBERG, M.
American early 20th cent.
paintings: (H) $825

KOEN, Irma Renee
American d. 1974
paintings: (L) $187; (H) $990

KOENE, Isaac
Dutch 1640-1713
paintings: (H) $4,313

KOENIG, Fritz
German b. 1924
sculpture: (L) $690; (H) $8,050

KOENIGER, Walter
German/American 1881-1943
paintings: (L) $110; (H) $12,100

KOEPPE, S.
European 19th/20th cent.
paintings: (H) $467

KOERNER, Henry
American b. 1915
paintings: (L) $550; (H) $52,250
drawings: (L) $460; (H) $2,587

KOERNER, William Henry Dethlef
German/American 1878-1938
paintings: (L) $288; (H) $28,600

KOESTER, Alexander Max
German 1864-1932
paintings: (L) $49,450; (H) $198,000

KOGAN, Moisey
b. 1924
paintings: (H) $2,090

KOGANOWSKY, Jakob
Austrian 1874-1926
paintings: (L) $528; (H) $2,200

KOGL, Benedict
German 1892-1969
paintings: (L) $3,400; (H) $6,210

KOHL, W.
Continental School 20th cent.
paintings: (H) $880

KOHLER, Christian
French 1809-1861
paintings: (H) $5,750

KOHLER, Gustave
German b. 1859
paintings: (H) $2,760

KOHLIE, John
American contemporary
sculpture: (L) $288; (H) $660

KOHLMEYER, Ida
American b. 1912
paintings: (H) $715

KOHN, Gabriel
contemporary
drawings: (H) $517
sculpture: (H) $6,600

KOHN, Irma
American 20th cent.
paintings: (H) $2,200

KOHOUT, Melissa
American
drawings: (H) $1,650

KOHRL, Anton
German 19th/20th cent.
paintings: (L) $385; (H) $715

KOHRL, Ludwig
German b. 1858
paintings: (L) $550; (H) $1,705

KOKEI, Kobayashi
1883-1957
drawings: (H) $27,600

KOKEN, Gustav
German 1850-1910
paintings: (H) $9,350

KOKINES, George
American b. 1930
paintings: (H) $489

KOKKEN, Henry
Belgian b. 1860
paintings: (H) $5,000

KOKOSCHKA, Oskar
Austrian 1886-1980
paintings: (H) $68,200
drawings: (L) $880; (H) $39,600

KOLAR, Jiri
Czechoslovakian b. 1914
paintings: (L) $770; (H) $8,800
drawings: (L) $402; (H) $5,750
sculpture: (L) $3,740; (H) $5,225

KOLARSKY, Maurice
Continental School 19th/20th cent.
paintings: (H) $2,300

KOLBE, Ernst
German 1876-1945
paintings: (L) $440; (H) $3,190

KOLBE, Georg
German 1877-1947
paintings: (H) $8,800
drawings: (L) $1,540; (H) $1,610
sculpture: (L) $6,050; (H) $40,250

KOLESNIKOFF, Sergei
Russian b. 1889
paintings: (L) $110; (H) $6,900
drawings: (H) $690

KOLLACK, Mary
American b. 1840
paintings: (L) $715; (H) $880

KOLLER, Guillaume
Austrian 1829-1884
drawings: (H) $1,320

KOLLER, John R.
Swiss 1828-1905
paintings: (H) $1,380

KOLLER, Wilhelm
Austrian 1829-1884
paintings: (H) $27,500

KOLLMAN, Carl, Karl Ivanovich
1788-1846
drawings: (H) $1,725

KOLLNER, Augustus
American b. 1813
drawings: (L) $345; (H) $3,850

KOLLWITZ, Kathe
German 1867-1945
drawings: (L) $6,613; (H) $38,500
sculpture: (L) $2,310; (H) $39,600

KOMAR & MELAMID
contemporary
paintings: (H) $4,600

KOMAR and MELAMID
b. 1940s
paintings: (L) $16,100; (H) $19,800

KOMLOSSY, Ferenc
Austrian 1817-1892
paintings: (H) $1,725

KOMOSKI, Bill
20th Cent.
paintings: (H) $1,100

KONDRATIENKO, Gavrul Pavlovitch
Russian b. 1854
paintings: (H) $1,320

KONIG, Hein
Austrian 20th cent.
paintings: (H) $495

KONINCK, Philips
Dutch 1619-1688
drawings: (H) $13,200

KONINCK, Salomon
Dutch 1609-1656
paintings: (H) $26,450

KONING, Roeland
Dutch 19th cent.
paintings: (H) $9,900

KONRAD, Adolf
paintings: (H) $1,150

KONTI, I.
sculpture: (H) $1,553

KONTI, Isidore
Austrian/American 1862-1938
sculpture: (L) $460; (H) $5,175

KONTNY, Pawel A.
Hungarian 20th cent.
paintings: (L) $220; (H) $578

KONTOPOULOS, Alex
paintings: (H) $12,650

KOOL, Benedict
paintings: (H) $880

KOOL, Spike
Dutch 1836-1902
paintings: (L) $632; (H) $825

KOONS, Jeff
American b. 1955
paintings: (L) $9,200; (H) $112,500
drawings: (L) $12,100; (H) $46,000
sculpture: (L) $17,600; (H) $233,500

KOOP, August
German 1856-1900
paintings: (H) $460

KOOPMAN, Augustus
American 1869-1914
paintings: (L) $220; (H) $3,960

KOOPS, Harmen C.
American 1898-1957
paintings: (L) $325; (H) $715

KOPETZKY, Jan
Czech 1666/67-1740
paintings: (H) $20,900

KOPF, Joseph von
German 1827-1903
sculpture: (H) $460

KOPMAN, Benjamin
Russian/American 1887-1965
paintings: (L) $110; (H) $2,640
drawings: (L) $55; (H) $517

KOPPAY
paintings: (H) $500

KOPPEL, Gustave
Austrian 1839-1905
paintings: (H) $2,200

KOPPENOL, Cornelis
Dutch 1865-1946
paintings: (L) $935; (H) $3,080
drawings: (H) $550

KOPPIEN, I.
German 19th cent.
paintings: (H) $990

KOPRIVA, Ena
sculpture: (H) $2,070

KOPTA, Emry
19th/20th cent.
sculpture: (H) $1,430

KORAB, Karl
German b. 1937
paintings: (H) $9,350

KORBEL, Mario Joseph
b. Czechoslovakia 1882-1954
sculpture: (L) $800; (H) $19,550

KORECKI, Wiktor
20th cent.
paintings: (H) $880

KORELL, Phil
paintings: (H) $550
drawings: (H) $800

KORELOV, Nikolai
Russian b. 1963
paintings: (L) $2,200; (H) $2,915

KORETSKY
European 19th cent.
paintings: (H) $550

KORNBECK, Peter
Danish 1837-1894
paintings: (L) $5,520; (H) $6,050

KORNHAUSER, David E.
American ac. 1930-50
paintings: (H) $550

KOROLYOV, B.
drawings: (H) $1,093

KOROVINE, Constantin Alexeievitch
Russian 1861-1939
paintings: (L) $440; (H) $6,875
drawings: (L) $288; (H) $1,210

KORSCHANN, Charles
Czechoslovakian b. 1872
sculpture: (L) $660; (H) $4,950

KORT
paintings: (H) $605

KORTE, Henricus Gerardus de
Dutch b. 1941
paintings: (L) $880; (H) $3,220

KORVER, John
American 20th cent.
drawings: (H) $467

KOSA, Emil, Jr.
American 1903-1968
paintings: (L) $303; (H) $11,000
drawings: (L) $275; (H) $4,313

KOSA, Emil, Jr.
American 1903-1968
paintings: (H) $15,400

KOSA, Emil, Sr.
American 1876-1955
paintings: (L) $1,320; (H) $5,500

KOSCIANSKI, Leonard
b. 1952
paintings: (H) $4,400

KOSICE, Gyula
Argentinian b. 1924
sculpture: (H) $605

KOSOROK, Michael J.
American
paintings: (L) $1,200; (H) $1,200

KOSSAK, Carol
Hungarian 19th/20th cent.
paintings: (H) $715

KOSSAK, Jerzy
Polish 1890-1963
paintings: (H) $1,210

KOSSAK, Woiciech von
French 1857-1942
paintings: (L) $5,750; (H) $8,250

KOSSOFF, Leon
British b. 1926
paintings: (L) $13,800; (H) $82,500

KOSSOWSKI
19th cent.
sculpture: (H) $1,100

KOSSOWSKI, Henryk
Polish 20th cent.
sculpture: (L) $550; (H) $990

KOSSUTH, Egon Josef
Czechoslovakian b. 1874
paintings: (H) $3,575

KOST, Frederick W.
American 1865-1923
paintings: (L) $688; (H) $2,990

KOST, H.R.
paintings: (H) $1,430

KOSTA, Alex
sculpture: (L) $3,025; (H) $4,600

KOSTABI, Mark
American b. 1960
paintings: (L) $460; (H) $13,750

KOSTABI, Mark and Still
ROCKEFELLER
contemporary
paintings: (H) $5,500

KOSTER, Carl Georg
German 1812-1893
paintings: (H) $2,070

KOSTER, Henny
Danish b. 1863
paintings: (H) $11,500

KOSUTH, Joseph
Hungarian/American b. 1945
paintings: (H) $13,800
drawings: (L) $1,840; (H) $33,000
sculpture: (L) $17,250; (H) $55,000

KOSZKOL, Jeno
Hungarian b. 1868
drawings: (L) $385; (H) $489

KOTARBINSKI, Milosz
Polish b. 1854
paintings: (H) $990

KOTARBINSKI, Vasili Aleksandrovich
Russian 1849-1921
paintings: (H) $2,990

KOTASZ, Karoly, called Charles
Hungarian 1872-1941
paintings: (L) $935; (H) $1,210

KOTKER, David
American contemporary
sculpture: (H) $1,610

KOTLAREVSKY, Paul
paintings: (L) $6,900; (H) $12,075

KOTSCHENREITER, Hugo
German 1854-1908
paintings: (L) $1,870; (H) $6,900

KOTSCHMIESTER, G.
German 19th/20th cent.
paintings: (H) $2,860

KOTTLER, Howard
American b. 1930
sculpture: (L) $33; (H) $2,200

KOUBA, Les
drawings: (H) $770

KOUDPIKE, J.
paintings: (H) $495

KOUNELLIS, Jannis
Greek/Italian b. 1936
paintings: (L) $18,400; (H) $63,000
drawings: (L) $2,760; (H) $15,400
sculpture: (L) $34,500; (H) $242,000

KOUTTS, Gordon
American 20th cent.
paintings: (H) $1,320

KOVALEVSKY, ***
Russian 19th cent.
paintings: (H) $2,070

KOVNER, Saul
American b. 1904
paintings: (L) $770; (H) $1,210

KOWALCZEWSKI, Karl
German b. 1876
sculpture: (H) $748

KOWALCZEWSKI, P. Ludwig
Polish b. 1876
sculpture: (L) $920; (H) $2,300

KOWALCZEWSKI, Paul
German 1865-1910
sculpture: (H) $1,100

KOWALSKI, A.
Polish b. 1926
paintings: (L) $247; (H) $633

KOWALSKI, Ivan Ivanovitch
Russian 20th cent.
paintings: (L) $550; (H) $880

KOWALSKI, Leopold F.
French b. 1856
paintings: (L) $1,100; (H) $15,525

KOWALSKI-WIERUSZ, Alfred von
Polish 1849-1915
paintings: (L) $2,200; (H) $30,250
drawings: (H) $660

KOZAKIEWICZ, Anton
Polish b. 1841
paintings: (H) $7,700

KOZLOW, Richard
American b. 1926
paintings: (L) $88; (H) $660

KRAEMER, Peter
German 1823-1907
drawings: (L) $1,150; (H) $1,955

KRAEN, van
Continental 19th cent.
paintings: (H) $3,850

KRAEWEL, V.
Italian 19th cent.
paintings: (H) $935

KRAFAEL
contemporary
paintings: (H) $660

KRAFFT, Carl R.
American 1884-1930
paintings: (L) $460; (H) $6,050

KRAFTS, Michel
German? 19th cent.
paintings: (H) $1,210

KRAIKE, Jane
American 20th cent.
paintings: (H) $2,300

KRAMER, Johann Victor
Austrian b. 1864
paintings: (H) $22,000

KRAMER, Konrad
American b. 1888
paintings: (H) $3,300

KRAMER, Peter
German/American 1828-1907
paintings: (L) $825; (H) $1,035
drawings: (H) $528

KRAMER, Stefan
20th cent.
drawings: (H) $550

KRAMSTYK, Roman
Polish 1885-1942
paintings: (L) $4,600; (H) $8,050

KRANTZ, E.
Continental 19th cent.
paintings: (H) $2,640

KRANTZ, F***
French 19th cent.
paintings: (H) $2,070

KRANTZ, F.
French 19th cent.
paintings: (H) $2,200

KRASNER, Lee
American 1912-1984
paintings: (L) $27,500; (H) $173,000
drawings: (L) $5,750; (H) $5,750

KRASNICAN, Susie
sculpture: (H) $1,840

KRASNY, Gretchen
American contemporary
paintings: (H) $880

KRASNYANSKY, Anatol
Russian b. 1930
drawings: (L) $209; (H) $440
sculpture: (H) $495

KRATINA, Joseph M.
American early 20th cent.
sculpture: (H) $1,610

KRATKE, Charles Louis
French 1848-1921
paintings: (L) $747; (H) $6,900

KRATKE, Marthe
French b. 1884
paintings: (H) $550

KRATOCHVIL, Stephen
American b. 1876
paintings: (H) $1,650

KRAUS, Friederich
German 1826-1894
paintings: (H) $1,725

KRAUS, Max
German b. 1891
paintings: (H) $715

KRAUSE, Emil A.
English exhib. 1891-1914
paintings: (L) $220; (H) $440
drawings: (L) $165; (H) $715

KRAUSE, Franz Emil
German 1836-1900
paintings: (H) $1,035

KRAUSE, Hans
German b. 1864
paintings: (H) $1,925

KRAUSE, Henry
German c. 1820-1860
paintings: (H) $1,430

KRAUSE, Lina
German b. 1857
paintings: (L) $935; (H) $5,280

KRAUSE, S.
German 19th cent.
paintings: (H) $1,650

KRAUSKOPF, Bruno
German 1892-1962
paintings: (L) $2,300; (H) $6,900
drawings: (H) $2,200

KRAUSS, Fritz Holberg
German 1874-1951
paintings: (H) $1,955

KRAWIEC, Harriet
American 1894-1968
paintings: (L) $110; (H) $715

KRAWIEC, Walter
American b. 1889
paintings: (L) $209; (H) $2,750

KRAY, Wilhelm
German 1828-1889
paintings: (L) $3,850; (H) $12,650

KREAPIN, Alexander
drawings: (H) $2,200

KREBS, Adolf
Swiss b. 1849
paintings: (H) $1,430

KREGTEN, Fedor van
Dutch 1871-1937
paintings: (L) $660; (H) $880

KREHBIEL, Albert H.
American 1875-1945
drawings: (L) $412; (H) $825

KREHM, William P.
American 1901-1968
paintings: (L) $110; (H) $468

KREIGHOFF, C.
American? 19th cent.
paintings: (H) $2,310

KREINS, Otto
Dutch 1873-1930
paintings: (H) $990

KREMEGNE, Pinchus
Russian b. 1890
paintings: (L) $2,530; (H) $15,400
drawings: (H) $460

KREMELBERG, Mary
American 19th/20th cent.
paintings: (L) $302; (H) $550

KREMER, Hans Peter
German
sculpture: (H) $978

KREMER, Michael
drawings: (H) $577

KREMER, Petrus
Flemish 1801-1888
paintings: (H) $3,850

KRENKEL, Roy G.
drawings: (L) $1,380; (H) $2,185

KRENN, Edmund Frederic Arthur
Austrian 1846-1902
paintings: (H) $2,640

KRESSLER, Barbara Reitze
American 20th cent.
paintings: (H) $467

KRETCHMER, Richard
American contemporary
paintings: (L) $121; (H) $495

KRETSCHMAR, Howard
American 19th cent.
sculpture: (H) $605

KRETSCHMER, Peter
German b. 1818
drawings: (H) $605

KRETSCHMER, V.
German 19th cent.
paintings: (H) $1,210

KRETZSCHMER, Johann Hermann
German 1811-1890
paintings: (L) $2,750; (H) $3,300

KREUTZER, B.
German 19th cent.
paintings: (L) $1,540; (H) $2,875

KREUZER, Adolf
Swiss 20th cent.
paintings: (H) $1,265

KREYDER, Alexis J.
French 1839-1912
paintings: (L) $770; (H) $57,500

KRICHELDORF, Carl
German b. 1863
paintings: (L) $1,045; (H) $3,740

KRIEGER, C.
American late 19th cent.
paintings: (H) $454

KRIEGHOFF, Cornelius
Canadian 1815-1872
paintings: (L) $7,480; (H) $170,500
drawings: (L) $1,210; (H) $3,300

KRIEHUBER, Fritz
Austrian 1836-1871
drawings: (H) $3,025

KRIEHUBER, Josef
Austrian 1800-1876
drawings: (L) $115; (H) $518

KRIENS, Otto
Dutch 1873-1930
paintings: (H) $550

KRIESMANN, Eduard Wilhelm
German 20th cent.
drawings: (H) $770

KRISCHKE, Franz
Austrian 1885-1960
paintings: (L) $880; (H) $2,420

KRISHNA HEBBAR, Kattingeri
Indian b. 1911
paintings: (H) $5,750

KROHG, Christian
Norwegian 1852-1925
paintings: (H) $68,750

KROLL, Leon
American 1884-1974
paintings: (L) $230; (H) $132,000
drawings: (L) $220; (H) $3,025

KROLL, Oskar
German 19th cent.
paintings: (H) $880

KRONBERG, Julius Johan Ferdinand
Swedish 1850-1921
paintings: (H) $1,265
drawings: (H) $1,980

KRONBERG, Louis
American 1872-1965
paintings: (L) $165; (H) $9,900
drawings: (L) $11; (H) $7,820

KRONBERGER, Carl
Austrian 1841-1921
paintings: (L) $2,070; (H) $24,200

KRONENBERG
Continental 20th cent.
paintings: (H) $825

KRONENGOLD, Adolph
American 1900-1986
paintings: (H) $3,190
drawings: (L) $198; (H) $330

KRONER, Johann Christian
German 1838-1911
paintings: (H) $4,888

KRONKE
Spanish 20th cent.
paintings: (H) $1,380

KROO, Sabina
American 20th cent.
drawings: (H) $460

KROTTER, Joseph
Austrian b. 1892
paintings: (L) $230; (H) $660

KROULIS, F.
paintings: (H) $990

KROYER, Peder Severin
Danish 1851-1909
paintings: (L) $20,700; (H) $82,500

KRUCEMANN, Jan
Dutch 19th cent.
paintings: (H) $1,100

KRUEGER, Gustav
paintings: (H) $1,320

KRUGER, Barbara
American b. 1945
drawings: (L) $2,530; (H) $38,500

KRUGER, Franz
German 1797-1857
paintings: (H) $1,650

KRUGER, Richard
American b. 1880
paintings: (L) $29; (H) $1,320

KRUSEMAN, Frederik Marianus
Dutch 1816-1882
paintings: (L) $20,700; (H) $55,000

KRUSEMAN, Frederik Marianus and
Eugene VERBOECKHOVEN
19th cent.
paintings: (H) $85,000

KRUSEMAN, J*** R***
Dutch 19th cent.
paintings: (H) $1,100

KRUSEMAN VAN ELTEN, Hendrik
Dirk
Dutch/American 1829-1904
paintings: (L) $345; (H) $18,400

KRUSHENICK, Nicholas
American b. 1929
paintings: (L) $115; (H) $1,150

KRUYPER, Cornelis
Dutch 1864-1932
paintings: (L) $302; (H) $825

KRUYS, Cornelis
Dutch d. 1660?
paintings: (H) $46,000

KRYZANOWSKI, Ramon
Russian/American 1885-1929
paintings: (L) $495; (H) $825

KRZYZANOWSKI, Konrad
paintings: (H) $1,650

KUBERT, Joe
drawings: (L) $495; (H) $1,495

KUBEYOR
19th cent.
paintings: (H) $3,450

KUCHLER, Rudolf
Austrian b. 1867
sculpture: (L) $220; (H) $1,380

KUDRIASHEV, Ivan
1896-1972
drawings: (H) $3,960

KUEHL, Gotthardt Johann
German 1850-1915
paintings: (L) $3,450; (H) $19,550

KUEHNE, Max
American 1880-1968
paintings: (L) $220; (H) $19,800
drawings: (L) $1,265; (H) $8,050

KUGELMAYR, M.
German
paintings: (H) $880

KUGHLER, Francis William Vandeveer
American b. 1901
paintings: (H) $1,150

KUGLER, Rudolph
20th cent.
paintings: (H) $862

KUHLER, Otto
American 1894-1977
drawings: (L) $1,320; (H) $3,680

KUHLING, Wilhelm
German 1823-1886
paintings: (H) $467

KUHLMANN, Edward
American 1882-1973
paintings: (L) $110; (H) $1,540

KUHLMANN-REHER, Emil
German b. 1886
paintings: (H) $660

KUHN, John
American b. 1949
sculpture: (L) $440; (H) $12,650

KUHN, Jon
contemporary
sculpture: (L) $440; (H) $7,475

KUHN, Justus Engelhardt
American ac. 1708-1717
paintings: (L) $17,250; (H) $32,200

KUHN, Max
paintings: (H) $1,320

KUHN, Robert (Bob)
American b. 1920
paintings: (L) $550; (H) $23,000
drawings: (L) $385; (H) $6,270

KUHN, Walt
American 1877/80-1949
paintings: (L) $990; (H) $308,000
drawings: (L) $110; (H) $32,200

KUHNEN, Pieter Lodewyk
Belgian 1812-1877
paintings: (H) $3,190

KUHNERT, Wilhelm
German 1865-1926
paintings: (L) $28,600; (H) $376,500

KUITCA, Guillermo
b. Argentina 1961
paintings: (L) $5,750; (H) $74,000
sculpture: (H) $16,100

KUKALIS, Romas
b. 1956
paintings: (H) $660

KULB, B.
German 19th cent.
paintings: (H) $1,100

KULHMANN, E.
paintings: (H) $880

KULICKE, Robert M.
American b. 1924
paintings: (L) $440; (H) $1,760
drawings: (L) $83; (H) $1,980

KULKOFF, A.
paintings: (H) $550

KULMALA, George Arthur
1896-1940
paintings: (H) $2,475

KULZ, Fred
drawings: (H) $522

KUMAR, Ram
Indian b. 1924
paintings: (L) $5,462; (H) $6,325
drawings: (H) $4,025

KUMMER, Julius Hermann
German 1817-1869
paintings: (L) $770; (H) $880

KUMPEL, William
English 19th cent.
paintings: (H) $825

KUNA, Henri
sculpture: (H) $3,300

KUNC, Milan
Czechoslovakian b. 1944
paintings: (L) $3,220; (H) $15,400

KUNIYOSHI, Yasuo
American 1893-1953
paintings: (L) $6,325; (H) $286,000
drawings: (L) $121; (H) $68,750

KUNSTLER, Mort
American b. 1931
paintings: (L) $1,650; (H) $4,400

KUNTZ, Roger E.
American 1926-1975
paintings: (L) $770; (H) $5,463
sculpture: (H) $2,300

KUNZ, Ludwig Adam
Austrian 1857-1929
paintings: (H) $3,450

KUNZE, William Luther
American 20th cent.
paintings: (H) $1,265

KUPCZYNSKI, Stanley
paintings: (H) $770

KUPER, Yuri
b. 1941
paintings: (L) $6,325; (H) $10,925
sculpture: (H) $16,500

KUPKA, Frantisek
Czechoslovakian 1871-1957
paintings: (H) $59,700
drawings: (L) $2,185; (H) $26,450

KURCHISHVILI, Zurab
Russian b. 1955
paintings: (L) $770; (H) $770

KURELEK, William
Canadian 1927-1977
paintings: (L) $4,180; (H) $28,600
drawings: (L) $3,300; (H) $44,000

KURO, Vladimir
Russian 20th cent.
paintings: (H) $920

KURTZ, Elaine
American b. 1928
paintings: (H) $660

KURTZ, Wilbur S.
1882-1967
drawings: (L) $440; (H) $550

KURTZMAN, Harvey
American b. 1924
drawings: (L) $1,100; (H) $11,500

KURTZMAN, Harvey and Will ELDER
drawings: (H) $9,900

KURZ, Glenna
paintings: (H) $690

KURZ, L.O.
German 19th cent.
paintings: (H) $575

KURZWEIL, Maximilian
Austrian 1867-1916
paintings: (H) $715

KURZWELLY, M.
American 20th cent.
paintings: (H) $715

KUSAMA
drawings: (H) $467
sculpture: (L) $55; (H) $55

KUSAMA, Yayoi
b. Japan 1929
paintings: (L) $11,000; (H) $59,700
drawings: (L) $2,070; (H) $6,325
sculpture: (H) $5,175

KUSHNER, Robert
American b. 1949
paintings: (L) $978; (H) $2,070
drawings: (L) $1,265; (H) $6,600

KUSS, Ferdinand
Austrian 1800-1886
paintings: (L) $8,800; (H) $8,800

KUTSCHA, Paul
Czechoslovakian b. 1872
paintings: (L) $173; (H) $1,045

KUWASSAGE and Fils
French
paintings: (H) $14,300

KUWASSEG, Charles Euphrasie
French 1838-1904
paintings: (L) $825; (H) $21,275
drawings: (H) $950

KUWASSEG, Karl Joseph
French 1802-1877
paintings: (L) $5,500; (H) $27,600

KUWAYAMA, Tadaaki
Japanese b. 1931
paintings: (L) $660; (H) $40,250
drawings: (H) $935

KUYPERS, Cornelis
Dutch b. 1864
paintings: (H) $1,650

KVAPIL, Charles
Belgian 1884-1958
paintings: (L) $605; (H) $6,900
drawings: (H) $440

KYNAST, A.
German 19th cent.
paintings: (H) $1,155

L'ENGLE, Lucy
American b. 1899
paintings: (L) $1,495; (H) $3,850
drawings: (L) $110; (H) $770

L'ENGLE, William
American 1884-1957
paintings: (L) $412; (H) $715
drawings: (L) $165; (H) $193

LA ABADIA, Juan de
Spanish ac. 1473-1496
paintings: (L) $3,740; (H) $165,000

LA BASQUE, Jean
French b. 1902
paintings: (H) $495

LA BASTIDA, Jose Marie de
c. 1783
paintings: (H) $7,150

LA BRUNIE, M.
drawings: (H) $660

LA CHANCE, Georges
American b. 1888
paintings: (L) $1,045; (H) $3,740

LA COUR, Janus
Danish 1837-1909
paintings: (L) $3,410; (H) $15,400

LA FAETTA
sculpture: (H) $1,100

LA FARGE, John
American 1835-1910
paintings: (L) $3,300; (H) $28,600
drawings: (L) $770; (H) $42,900

LA FARGUE, Paulus Constantine
Dutch 1732-1782
drawings: (H) $1,650

LA FONTAINE, Bruce
sculpture: (H) $1,650

LA FONTAINE, L.
French 19th cent.
paintings: (H) $4,600

LA FONTAINE, Thomas Sherwood
English b. 1915
paintings: (H) $4,600

LA FOREST, Wesner
b. Haiti 1965
paintings: (H) $7,700

LA FOSSE, Charles de
French 1636-1716
paintings: (H) $16,500
drawings: (H) $3,220

LA FRESNAYE, Roger de
French 1885-1925
paintings: (L) $16,100; (H) $176,000
drawings: (L) $357; (H) $43,700
sculpture: (L) $20,900; (H) $27,600

LA FUENTE, Manuel de
b. 1932
sculpture: (L) $6,325; (H) $6,900

LA HAYE, Renier de
Dutch 1640-1684
paintings: (H) $2,860

LA HOESE, Jean de
Belgian 1846-1917
paintings: (H) $12,190

LA HYRE, Laurent de
French 1606-1656
paintings: (L) $112,500; (H) $415,000

LA PATELLIERE, Amedee Marie
1890-1932
paintings: (H) $2,760

LA PIRA
Italian 19th cent.
drawings: (L) $1,150; (H) $8,050

LA PIRA
Italian ac. 1920-1931
drawings: (L) $825; (H) $9,350

LA RAIGUE, G. de
French 19th cent.
paintings: (L) $3,162; (H) $4,312

LA ROCHE, Armand
French 1826-1903
paintings: (H) $1,540

LA RUE, Philibert Benoit de
French 1716-1780
drawings: (H) $1,650

LA SALLE, Charles Louis
American 1894-1958
paintings: (L) $1,610; (H) $3,450

LA SERNA, Ismael de
Spanish 1900-1968
paintings: (L) $1,540; (H) $42,550
drawings: (H) $3,450

LA THANGUE, Henry Herbert
British 1859-1929
paintings: (L) $27,600; (H) $154,000

LA TORESTERIE
French
sculpture: (H) $13,200

LA TOUCHE, Gaston
French 1854-1913
paintings: (L) $16,100; (H) $43,700

LA VALLEY, Jonas Joseph
American 1858-1930
paintings: (L) $144; (H) $3,630

LA VILLEON, Emmanuel de
French 1859-1944
paintings: (L) $3,300; (H) $17,250

LA VOLPE, Alessandro
Italian 1820-1887/93
paintings: (L) $6,900; (H) $11,550

LAANEN, Jasper van der
Dutch c. 1592-after 1626
paintings: (L) $10,350; (H) $13,800

LAAR, Bartol Wilhelm van
Dutch 1818-1901
paintings: (H) $1,155

LABINO, Dominick
American b. 1910
sculpture: (L) $550; (H) $9,200

LABISSE, Felix
French 1905-1982
drawings: (H) $1,980

LABITTE, Eugene Leon
French b. 1858
paintings: (L) $330; (H) $16,500

Still-Life Painter

Some paintings are a hard sell—dead game, sinking ships, and Indians being massacred—but well-executed still lifes of fruits and flowers have a universal appeal.

Jonas Joseph LaValley (1858-1930) was the pride of turn-of-the-century Springfield, Massachusetts. His early years were spent as a laborer on his father's farm and in the cotton mills. After his marriage in 1880 he apprenticed as a barber and also began to draw. His teachers were local Springfield artists, Willis Adams, Edmund E. Case, and George Bowers, who had studied in New York and abroad. His trade allowed him free time to draw and study art, and by 1888 he was so well established as a painter and teacher that he sold his barbershop. LaValley was active in his community and cofounded the Springfield Art League with artist Harriet Lumis. *The Birth of Springfield*, his most important historical work, has had a place of honor in the Springfield mayor's office for the last 86 years. LaValley painted still lifes, figures, and landscapes but is known mainly for his still-life paintings of flowers and fruits. Raspberries were his favorite subject, and when an oil of raspberries in a bowl was offered at Jim Bakker's in Cambridge, Massachusetts, it sold for $1,760. (Jonas Joseph LaValley, *Still Life with Raspberries*, oil on canvas mounted on masonite, 14¼ x 20¼ inches, Bakker, March 12, 1995, $1,760)

LABORD
French 19th cent.
paintings: (H) $2,760

LABORDE, Charles
drawings: (H) $1,320

LABORNE, Edme Emile
French 1837-1913
paintings: (L) $11,000; (H) $29,700
drawings: (H) $3,220

LABROUCHE, Pierre
French 19th cent.
paintings: (H) $805

LABROUE, E. de
French 19th cent.
sculpture: (L) $109; (H) $1,650

LABRUZZI, Carlo
1748-1817
drawings: (H) $1,980

LACARREARI, S. Limma
Spanish 19th/20th cent.
paintings: (H) $575

LACASSE, Joseph
paintings: (H) $6,900

LACCETTI, Valerico
Italian 1836-1909
paintings: (H) $1,100

LACEUR, Nicole
German b. 1943
paintings: (H) $1,610

LACH, Andreas K.
Austrian 1817-1882
paintings: (L) $1,320; (H) $16,500
drawings: (H) $2,420

LACH, Ursula van
b. 1949
paintings: (H) $3,300

LACHAISE, Gaston
French/American 1882-1935
drawings: (L) $770; (H) $11,000
sculpture: (L) $192; (H) $121,000

LACHENWITZ, F. Sigmund
German 1820-1868
paintings: (H) $2,640

LACHMAN, Harry B.
American 1886-1975
paintings: (L) $165; (H) $13,200

LACK, Stephen
American b. 1946
paintings: (H) $2,200

LACOMBE, Georges
French 1868-1916
drawings: (H) $3,680
sculpture: (H) $20,900

LACOMBE, Laure
French 1834-1923
paintings: (H) $805

LACOMBI, L.
Italian
paintings: (H) $1,045

LACROIX, Charles Francois Grenier
de, called Lacroix de Marseille
French 1700-1782
paintings: (L) $5,750; (H) $123,600

LACROIX, Eugene
American 19th cent.
paintings: (H) $2,200

LACROIX, H.
Continental 19th cent.
paintings: (L) $1,210; (H) $1,430

LACROIX, H.
French 19th/20th cent.
paintings: (H) $1,430

LACROIX, Paul
American ac. 1858-1869
paintings: (L) $495; (H) $25,300

LADBROOKE, John Berney
British 1803-1879
paintings: (L) $715; (H) $12,650

LADD, Anna Coleman
American 1878-1939
sculpture: (L) $230; (H) $4,400

LADELL, Edward
British 1821-1886
paintings: (L) $1,210; (H) $41,250

LAER, Alexander T. van
American 1857-1920
paintings: (L) $275; (H) $1,540
drawings: (H) $935

LAER, J. H. van der
Dutch 19th cent.
paintings: (H) $3,910

LAER, Pieter van
Dutch 1582-1642
paintings: (H) $2,200

LAESSLE, Albert
paintings: (H) $578
sculpture: (H) $3,300

LAESSLE, Paul
American 1908-1988
drawings: (H) $3,220

LAEZZA, Giuseppe
ac. 1877-1903
paintings: (H) $13,225

LAFITTE, Louis
French 1770-1828
drawings: (H) $1,210

LAFON, Francois
French ac. 1875-1890
paintings: (L) $1,725; (H) $4,370

LAFON, Henri
French 19th c.
paintings: (H) $5,500

LAFORCE, Henri-Charles Albert de
French b. 1839
paintings: (H) $575

LAFOREST, Wesner
paintings: (H) $3,220

LAFORET, Alessandro
Italian 1863-1937
sculpture: (H) $37,375

LAFORET, Eugene
French 19th/20th cent.
paintings: (L) $1,650; (H) $1,650

LAFRENSEN, Niklas, called
LAVREINCE the younger
Swedish 1737-1807
paintings: (H) $11,000

LAGAGE, Pierre Cesar
paintings: (L) $7,700; (H) $8,800

LAGAR, Celso
1891-1966
paintings: (L) $4,620; (H) $7,700
drawings: (L) $4,400; (H) $7,700

LAGARDE, A.G.
Continental 19th cent.
paintings: (H) $2,970

LAGATTA, John
Italian/American 1894-1976
paintings: (L) $1,760; (H) $3,025
drawings: (L) $1,210; (H) $1,540

LAGLENNE, Jean Francis
French b. 1899
paintings: (H) $1,210

LAGNEAU
ac. c. 1590-1610
drawings: (L) $2,750; (H) $11,550

LAGONI, Luigi
Italian 19th/20th cent.
paintings: (H) $1,485

LAGOOR, Jan
ac. mid-17th cent.
paintings: (H) $7,475

LAGORIO, Liev Felixovitch
Russian 1826-1905
paintings: (L) $1,100; (H) $1,100

LAGRANGE, Jacques
French b. 1917
paintings: (H) $2,750

LAGRANGE, d'
sculpture: (H) $1,430

LAGRENEE
paintings: (H) $5,175

LAGRENEE, Anthelme Francois
French 1774-1832
paintings: (H) $49,450

LAGRENEE, Jean Jacques, the younger
French 1739-1821
paintings: (L) $3,740; (H) $154,000

LAGRENEE, Louis Jean Francois
French 1725-1805
paintings: (L) $7,150; (H) $184,000

LAGUNA, B.
Dutch 20th cent.
paintings: (L) $385; (H) $660

LAGYE, Victor
Belgian 1825-1896
paintings: (L) $4,313; (H) $6,900

LAHNER, Emile
paintings: (H) $880

LAI, C. Thomas
paintings: (H) $460

LAIB, Wolfgang
German b. 1950
sculpture: (L) $7,700; (H) $33,000

LAING, Gerald
b. 1936
paintings: (L) $575; (H) $2,185

LAING, Jamson
British 19th cent.
paintings: (H) $935

LAING, Tomson
British d. 1904
paintings: (H) $495

LAIRESSE, Gerard de
Flemish 1641-1711
paintings: (L) $14,300; (H) $126,500
drawings: (H) $690

LAISSEMENT, Henri Adolphe
French c. 1854-1921
paintings: (L) $2,310; (H) $20,700

LAITTRE, Eleanor de
b. 1911
paintings: (H) $4,600

LAJOS, Brucke Ludwig
Hungarian 1846-1910
paintings: (H) $522

LAJOS, K.
paintings: (H) $2,475

LAJOUE, Jacques de
French 1687-1761
paintings: (H) $21,850
drawings: (H) $1,265

LAKAREV, Victor
Russian/French 20th cent.
paintings: (H) $920

LAKHOVSKY, Arnold
Russian b. 1885
paintings: (L) $412; (H) $1,210

LALAISSE, Francois Hippolyte
French 19th cent.
paintings: (H) $1,045

LALANNE, Claude
French
sculpture: (H) $162,000

LALANNE, Claude and Francois
Xavier
contemporary
sculpture: (H) $24,200

LALAUZE, Alphonse
French b. 1872
paintings: (H) $1,430

LALIQUE, Rene
French 1860-1945
sculpture: (L) $4,025; (H) $55,200

LALIQUE, Suzanne
French b. 1899
paintings: (L) $1,840; (H) $24,150

LALLEMAND, Jean Baptiste
French c. 1710-c. 1803/1805
paintings: (H) $7,475

LALLICH, Giuseppe
Italian b. 1867
paintings: (H) $1,045

LAM, Wifredo
Cuban 1902-1982
paintings: (L) $4,025; (H) $965,000
drawings: (L) $2,750; (H) $145,500
sculpture: (L) $2,860; (H) $19,800

LAMA, Giulia
Italian 1681-1747
paintings: (L) $8,250; (H) $27,500

LAMAR, Howard
paintings: (H) $800

LAMARRA, Francesco
c. 1710-1780
drawings: (H) $660

LAMASURE, Edwin C.
American 1886-1916
drawings: (L) $110; (H) $1,150

LAMAY, Art
drawings: (H) $715

LAMB
19th cent.
paintings: (H) $935

LAMB, Aimee
American b. 1893, exhib. 1939
paintings: (L) $825; (H) $1,265
drawings: (H) $110

LAMB, Frederick Mortimer
American 1861-1936
paintings: (L) $110; (H) $1,870

LAMB, Frederick S.
American 1863-1928
paintings: (H) $1,100

LAMB, Matt
American contemporary
paintings: (H) $3,740

LAMBDIN, George Cochran
American 1830-1896
paintings: (L) $990; (H) $13,200

LAMBDIN, James Reid
American 1807-1889
paintings: (L) $209; (H) $24,150

LAMBDIN, Robert
1886-1981
paintings: (H) $495

LAMBEAUX, Jef, Joseph Marie Thomas
Belgian 1852-1908
sculpture: (L) $605; (H) $9,775

LAMBERT
20th cent.
paintings: (H) $495

LAMBERT, B.
German 19th cent.
paintings: (L) $105; (H) $990

LAMBERT, Ch.
Dutch 19th/20th cent.
paintings: (L) $660; (H) $1,320

LAMBERT, Edouard
French 20th cent.
paintings: (H) $660

LAMBERT, George
British 1710-1765
paintings: (H) $71,500

LAMBERT, George
English 19th century
paintings: (H) $468

LAMBERT, Georges
French b. 1919
paintings: (L) $402; (H) $1,980
drawings: (H) $660

LAMBERT, Louis Eugene
French 1825-1900
paintings: (L) $467; (H) $9,775
drawings: (H) $3,450

LAMBERT, Theodore Roosevelt
American 1905-1960
paintings: (L) $4,025; (H) $12,650
drawings: (H) $1,210

LAMBERT, Walter
20th cent.
paintings: (H) $805

LAMBERT-RUCKI, Jean
French 1888-1967
paintings: (L) $3,300; (H) $19,550
drawings: (L) $1,760; (H) $3,520
sculpture: (L) $3,575; (H) $39,600

LAMBERTON, Joseph
French 1867-1943
paintings: (H) $550

LAMBILLOTTE, George
Belgium b. 1915
paintings: (H) $825

LAMBINET, Emile Charles
French 1815-1877
paintings: (L) $1,760; (H) $9,075

LAMBRECHTS, Jan Baptist
Flemish 1680-after 1731
paintings: (L) $7,150; (H) $14,300

LAMBRON
paintings: (H) $1,980

LAMBSON, Hayden
American
paintings: (H) $2,700

LAMBUSSETI, ***
Italian 19th cent.
drawings: (H) $880

LAMEN, Christoph Jacobsz. van der
Flemish c. 1606-c. 1652
paintings: (H) $46,200

LAMESI
Italian 19th cent.
drawings: (H) $1,430

LAMI, Eugene Louis
French 1800-1890
paintings: (H) $32,200
drawings: (L) $1,495; (H) $5,520

LAMME, Arie Johannes
Dutch 1812-1900
paintings: (H) $2,420

LAMMONT, Degratious
ac. 1837-1851
paintings: (H) $7,475

LAMOND, William B.
American 20th cent.
paintings: (H) $1,045

LAMORE, Chet Harmon
American b. 1908
paintings: (H) $2,090
sculpture: (H) $288

LAMORINIERE, Jean Pierre Francoise
Belgian 1828-1911
paintings: (L) $920; (H) $4,600

LAMOTTE, Bernard
French b. 1903
paintings: (L) $220; (H) $1,955
drawings: (H) $99

LAMOTTE, Daniel
American 1898-1980
paintings: (H) $1,320

LAMOURD, Raoul
sculpture: (H) $660

LAMPE, Jean
French 1853-1919
paintings: (H) $1,980

LAMPERT, Emma E.
drawings: (H) $605

LAMPLOUGH, Augustus Osborne
English 1877-1930
drawings: (L) $132; (H) $4,830

LAMPURE, G.
Italian 19th cent.
paintings: (H) $633

LAMSON, Temperance D.
drawings: (H) $690

LAMY, Pierre Desire Eugene Franc
French 1855-1919
paintings: (H) $6,900

LANCASTER, Richard Hume
British 1773-1853
paintings: (H) $1,150

LANCE, George
English 1802-1864
paintings: (L) $660; (H) $935
drawings: (H) $1,840

LANCERAY, Eugene Alexandrovitch
Russian 1848-1886
sculpture: (L) $440; (H) $13,200

LANCEROTTI, P.
Italian 19th/20th cent.
paintings: (H) $5,750

LANCEROTTO, Egisto
Italian 1848-1916
paintings: (L) $8,800; (H) $19,250

LANCKOW, Ludwig
German 19th cent.
paintings: (H) $1,980

LANCRET, Nicolas
French 1690-1743
paintings: (L) $37,375; (H) $242,000
drawings: (L) $1,100; (H) $38,500

LANDALUZE, Victor Patricio
Cuban 1828-1889
paintings: (L) $8,050; (H) $48,875
drawings: (L) $3,450; (H) $26,450

LANDEAU, J***
French 19th cent.
paintings: (H) $1,725

LANDEAU, Sandor
French b. 1864
paintings: (H) $4,675

LANDELLE, Charles Zacharie
French 1821-1908
paintings: (L) $4,675; (H) $46,000

LANDESIO, Eugenio
Italian 1810-1879
paintings: (H) $74,000

LANDI
Italian 19th cent.
paintings: (H) $1,150

LANDINI, Andrea
Italian b. 1847
paintings: (L) $26,400; (H) $74,000

LANDIS, John
ac. 1830-1851
paintings: (H) $8,050

LANDIS, John
American b. 1805
paintings: (H) $1,595

LANDOWSKI, Paul Maximilien
French 1875-1961
sculpture: (L) $1,495; (H) $7,150

LANDSDALE
British 19th cent.
paintings: (H) $522

LANDSEER
British 19th cent.
paintings: (H) $1,265

LANDSEER, Sir Edwin Henry
English 1802-1873
paintings: (L) $38,500; (H) $525,000

LANE, Fitz Hugh
American 1804-1865
paintings: (L) $1,265; (H) $910,000

LANE, H.
Continental 19th cent.
paintings: (H) $1,100

LANE, Jack
drawings: (L) $259; (H) $1,380

LANE, Katherine Ward
American 1899-1989
sculpture: (L) $825; (H) $3,410

LANE, Leonard C.
Canadian d. 1978
paintings: (L) $660; (H) $2,530

LANE, Lois
American b. 1948
paintings: (L) $288; (H) $483

LANE, Susan Minot
American 1832-1893
paintings: (H) $1,100

LANEKOW, L.
paintings: (H) $1,320

LANEUVILLE, Jean Louis
French 1748?-1826
paintings: (H) $39,100

LANFAIR, Harold E.
American b. 1898
drawings: (L) $303; (H) $467

LANFANT DE METZ, Francois Louis
French 1814-1892
paintings: (L) $165; (H) $25,300

LANFRANCHI, Alessandro
1662-1730
paintings: (H) $4,675

LANFRANCO, Giovanni
Italian 1582-1647
paintings: (H) $33,000

LANG, Annie Traquair
American 1885-1918
paintings: (H) $1,430

LANG, Gary
20th cent.
paintings: (L) $110; (H) $2,875

LANG, Heinrich
German 1838-1891
paintings: (H) $660

LANG, Jean
Continental 19th cent.
paintings: (H) $2,090

LANG, Louis
German/American 1814/24-1893
paintings: (L) $385; (H) $8,800

LANG, Richard
German 19th cent.
paintings: (H) $4,888

LANGASKENS, Maurice
Belgian 1884-1946
paintings: (H) $1,380

LANGE, Edward
1846-1912
paintings: (H) $9,460

LANGE, Frederick
Danish 1870-1941
paintings: (H) $577

LANGE, Julius
German 1817-1878
paintings: (H) $1,870

LANGE, Rich W.
sculpture: (H) $880

LANGENBERG, Gustave C.
American d. 1915
paintings: (H) $28,750

LANGENDYK, Jan Anthonie
1780-1818
drawings: (L) $4,180; (H) $4,620

LANGER, Olaf Viggo Peter
Danish 1860-1942
paintings: (H) $4,400

LANGEROCK, Henri
Belgian 1830-1885
drawings: (H) $880

LANGEROCK, Henri
Belgian d. 1915
paintings: (H) $1,760

LANGEROCK, J.
drawings: (H) $1,017

LANGEVELD, Frans A.
Dutch 1877-1939
paintings: (L) $385; (H) $5,500

LANGEVIN, B.
19th/20th cent.
paintings: (H) $550

LANGEVIN, Claude
Canadian b. 1942
paintings: (L) $1,650; (H) $2,200

LANGHART, A.
Swiss 19th/20th cent.
paintings: (H) $3,450

LANGHAUS, I.
paintings: (H) $495

LANGLADE, Pierre
French 19th cent.
paintings: (H) $5,750

LANGLAIS, Bernard
American 1921-1977
sculpture: (L) $880; (H) $7,150

LANGLEY, Edward
British ac. 1904-1908
paintings: (L) $288; (H) $577

LANGLEY, Walter
English 1852-1922
paintings: (H) $34,500
drawings: (H) $7,475

LANGLEY, William
British 19th cent.
paintings: (L) $330; (H) $1,610
drawings: (H) $115

LANGLOIS, C.
British 19th cent.
paintings: (H) $2,587

LANGLOIS, J(?)
French 19th cent.
paintings: (H) $660

LANGLOIS, Mark W.
British 19th cent.
paintings: (L) $495; (H) $2,750

LANGWORTHY, William H.
American 19th cent.
paintings: (L) $220; (H) $1,100

LANIER, Fanita
American b. 1903
paintings: (H) $715

LANING, Edward
American 20th cent.
paintings: (H) $605

LANKES, Julius J.
American 1884-1960
paintings: (H) $715

LANKFORD, Kenneth
American 20th cent.
paintings: (H) $1,323

LANMAN, Charles
American 1819-1895
paintings: (H) $990
drawings: (H) $1,430

LANOY, Jules
Dutch 19th cent.
paintings: (H) $4,125

LANSDOWNE, F.
drawings: (H) $1,210

LANSDOWNE, James Fenwick
b. 1940
drawings: (L) $1,210; (H) $4,400

LANSIL, Walter Franklin
American 1846-1925
paintings: (L) $303; (H) $7,920

LANSING, A.L.
sculpture: (H) $2,750

LANSKOY, Andre
Russian/French 1902-1976
paintings: (L) $1,650; (H) $57,500
drawings: (L) $1,760; (H) $11,000

LANSON
sculpture: (H) $990

LANSON, Alfred Desire
1851-1898
sculpture: (H) $1,150

LANSONSEPT
sculpture: (H) $1,320

LANTIER, Lucien Louis Bernard
French b. 1879
paintings: (H) $37,375

LANTZ, Paul
American b. 1908
paintings: (L) $1,100; (H) $3,575

LANTZ, Walter
paintings: (L) $2,875; (H) $3,680
drawings: (H) $115

LANYON, Ellen
American 20th cent.
paintings: (L) $522; (H) $1,100

LANZA, Giovanni
Italian b. 1827
drawings: (H) $2,475

LANZA, Luigi
Italian 19th cent.
paintings: (L) $1,320; (H) $7,188
drawings: (H) $193

LANZIROTTI, A.C.
French
sculpture: (H) $3,190

LAPCHINE, G.
Russian 1885-1951
paintings: (H) $489

LAPCHINE, Georges
Russian 20th cent.
paintings: (H) $1,650

LAPICQUE, Charles
French b. 1898
sculpture: (H) $2,860

LAPINE, Andreas Christian Gottfried
paintings: (L) $1,980; (H) $2,420

LAPINI, Cesare
Italian b. 1848
sculpture: (L) $1,430; (H) $19,500

LAPINI, Gall F.
sculpture: (H) $14,000

LAPIQUE, Charles
1898-1988
paintings: (H) $2,990

LAPIRA
Italian 19th/20th cent.
paintings: (H) $4,370

LAPIRA, ***
Italian 19th/20th cent.
drawings: (L) $4,600; (H) $19,800

LAPORTE, Emile
French 1858-1907
sculpture: (L) $1,320; (H) $8,050

LAPORTE, George Henry
German/English 1799-1873
paintings: (L) $3,300; (H) $3,300

LAPORTE, Georges
French b. 1926
paintings: (L) $385; (H) $1,380

LAPORTE, John
British 1761-1839
paintings: (H) $9,200

LAPORTE, Marcellin
French b. 1839
paintings: (H) $11,500

LAPORTE-BLAIRSY, Leo
French 1865-1923
sculpture: (L) $8,800; (H) $32,200

LAPOSTOLET, Charles
French 1824-1890
paintings: (L) $2,860; (H) $3,520

LAPP, Henry
drawings: (H) $1,150

LAPPARENT-DELAZ
French 20th cent.
drawings: (H) $605

LAPRADE, Pierre
French 1875-1932
paintings: (L) $230; (H) $1,610

LAPRESLE, John
drawings: (H) $550

LARA, Edward
paintings: (H) $1,540

LARA, Georgina
British ac. 1862-1871
paintings: (L) $302; (H) $2,750

LARA, Magali
Mexican b. 1956
paintings: (H) $24,150

LARA, P. Leslie
British 19th cent.
paintings: (H) $920

LARCHE, Francois Raoul
French 1860-1912
paintings: (H) $3,850
sculpture: (L) $990; (H) $68,500

LARGILLIERE, Nicolas de
French c. 1656-1746
paintings: (L) $49,500; (H) $431,500

LARGILLIERE, Nicolas de, studio of
17th/18th cent.
paintings: (L) $6,555; (H) $8,050

LARIONOV, Mikhail
Russian/French 1881-1964
paintings: (L) $1,650; (H) $21,850
drawings: (L) $550; (H) $11,550

LARMON, Kevin
b. 1955
paintings: (L) $403; (H) $1,150

LAROCHE, C.A.
French 19th cent.
paintings: (H) $523

LAROON, Marcellus, the younger
1679-1774
paintings: (H) $1,650

LARPENTEUR, J.D.
French 19th cent.
paintings: (H) $2,200

LARRAZ, Julio
Cuban/American b. 1944
paintings: (L) $14,300; (H) $96,000
drawings: (L) $11,500; (H) $13,800

LARRINAGA, Mario
American 1895-1979
paintings: (H) $1,495

LARRIVE, Jean
sculpture: (H) $990

LARROUX, Antonin
French late 19th cent.
sculpture: (L) $330; (H) $1,100

LARSEN, Adolf Alfred
Danish 1856-1942
paintings: (H) $13,200

LARSEN, Johannes
paintings: (H) $495

LARSEN, Karl
American 20th cent.
paintings: (L) $220; (H) $460

LARSEN, Oskar
Austrian 1882-1972
paintings: (L) $66; (H) $935
drawings: (L) $1,045; (H) $1,495

LARSEN, Otto
German b. 1889
paintings: (L) $575; (H) $990

LARSON, Cecil
American b. 1908
paintings: (L) $550; (H) $1,100

LARSON, Edward
American contemporary
sculpture: (H) $605

LARSSON, Carl
Swedish 1853-1919
paintings: (H) $34,500
drawings: (L) $132,000; (H) $189,500

LARSSON, Virginia
Scandinavian 1844-1893
paintings: (H) $825

LARTIGUE, Jacques Henri
1894-1988
paintings: (L) $115; (H) $5,500

LARVIE, Calvin
Native American b. 1920
drawings: (H) $715

LARWIN, Hans
Austrian 1873-1938
paintings: (L) $302; (H) $7,700
drawings: (H) $880

LARY, Roland
Dutch 1855-1932
paintings: (H) $2,185

LASCANO, Juan
Argentinian b. 1947
paintings: (L) $29,900; (H) $35,200

LASCARI, Hilda Kristina
American 1886-1937
sculpture: (L) $440; (H) $825

LASCARI, Salvatore
American 1884-1967
paintings: (L) $192; (H) $1,650

LASCAUX, Elie
paintings: (L) $1,650; (H) $1,760

LASCELLES, L.
Scottish 19th cent.
paintings: (H) $770

LASCH, Carl Johann
German 1822-1888
paintings: (H) $9,900

LASELLAZ, Gustave Francois
French 1848-1910
paintings: (H) $7,700

LASH, Lee
American 20th cent.
paintings: (L) $385; (H) $2,640

LASKE, Oskar
Austrian 1874-1951
drawings: (L) $3,080; (H) $6,050

LASKER, Jonathan
American b. 1948
paintings: (L) $9,350; (H) $33,000
drawings: (L) $1,495; (H) $2,875

LASKY, Leslie
20th cent.
drawings: (H) $633

LASSAW, Ibram
American b. 1913
drawings: (H) $1,320
sculpture: (L) $1,980; (H) $7,150

LASSEN, Hans August
German b. 1857
paintings: (L) $412; (H) $2,310

LASSONDE, Omer T.
American 1903-1980
paintings: (L) $110; (H) $880

LASZLO, Barta
Hungarian b. 1927
paintings: (L) $605; (H) $660

LASZLO, Neogrady
Hungarian 1861-1942
paintings: (H) $690

LASZLO DE LOMBOS, Philip Alexius
de
English 1869-1937
paintings: (L) $575; (H) $14,950

LATAPIE, Louis
French 1891-1972
paintings: (H) $2,750

LATASTER, Ger
Dutch b. 1920
paintings: (H) $22,000
drawings: (L) $431; (H) $483

LATHAM, Barbara
American 1896-1976
paintings: (H) $3,575

LATHROP, Francis Augustus
American 1849-1909
paintings: (H) $3,080

LATHROP, Gertrude Katherine
American b. 1896
sculpture: (H) $1,320

LATHROP, Ida Pulis
American 1859-1937
paintings: (L) $66; (H) $14,950

LATHROP, William Langson
American 1859-1938
paintings: (L) $575; (H) $8,800

LATIMER, Lorenzo Palmer
American 1857-1941
paintings: (H) $2,185
drawings: (L) $880; (H) $3,738

LATORTUE, Franklin
paintings: (H) $4,950

LATORTUE, Phillipe
paintings: (H) $1,650

LATOUCHE, Claude Gaston
French 20th cent.
drawings: (H) $1,955

LATOUCHE, Gaston
French 1854-1913
paintings: (H) $17,250

LATOUCHE, Gaston de
French 1854-1913
paintings: (L) $1,265; (H) $121,000
drawings: (H) $1,380

LATOUCHE, Louis
French 1829-1884
paintings: (H) $715

LATOUR, Adrian
American 20th cent.
paintings: (H) $550

LATOUR, D.
French late 19th cent.
paintings: (H) $550

LATTARD, Phillip
American 19th/20th cent.
paintings: (L) $220; (H) $2,200

LATTE, Frank
American 20th cent.
paintings: (H) $715

LAU, Rex
paintings: (H) $2,200

LAUBIES, Rene
contemporary
paintings: (H) $1,210

LAUDER
American 20th cent.
drawings: (H) $715

LAUDRONE, G.
Continental 20th cent.
paintings: (H) $3,850

LAUDY, Jean
Dutch 1877-1956
paintings: (H) $5,500

LAUER, Josef
Austrian 1818-1881
paintings: (H) $24,150

LAUFMAN, Sidney
American b. 1891
paintings: (L) $1,035; (H) $1,870

LAUGE, Achille
French 1861-1944
paintings: (L) $3,910; (H) $17,250

LAUGEE, Georges
French b. 1853
paintings: (L) $633; (H) $40,250

LAUGHABAUGH, C.O.
drawings: (L) $880; (H) $990

LAUGIER, L.
French 19th cent.
paintings: (H) $2,970

LAUNAY, Fernand de
French 19th cent.
paintings: (H) $46,000

LAUR, Marie Yvonne
French b. 1879
paintings: (L) $1,540; (H) $5,225

LAURANT, G.H.
sculpture: (H) $880

LAURANT (?)
paintings: (H) $467

LAUREL, Pierre
sculpture: (L) $805; (H) $1,650

LAURENCE, Sydney
American 1860/65-1940
paintings: (L) $1,100; (H) $23,100
drawings: (L) $825; (H) $1,320

LAURENCIN, Marie
French 1883-1956
paintings: (L) $2,750; (H) $495,000
drawings: (L) $632; (H) $82,500
sculpture: (H) $2,875

LAURENS, Henri
French 1885-1954
drawings: (L) $1,320; (H) $154,000
sculpture: (L) $9,200; (H) $154,000

LAURENS, Jean Paul
French 1838-1921
paintings: (L) $1,320; (H) $16,100
drawings: (L) $1,150; (H) $1,150

LAURENS, Jules Joseph Augustin
French 1825-1901
paintings: (H) $16,500

LAURENS, Paul Albert
French 1870-1934
paintings: (H) $3,450

LAURENT, Ernest Joseph
French 1859-1929
paintings: (L) $770; (H) $34,500
drawings: (H) $18,400

LAURENT, Eugene
sculpture: (L) $325; (H) $1,525

LAURENT, Georges
French early 20th cent.
sculpture: (L) $1,840; (H) $2,640

LAURENT, Jean
French b. 1906
paintings: (L) $275; (H) $1,540

LAURENT, Jean Baptiste
French 18th cent.
paintings: (H) $4,950

LAURENT, John
American b. 1921
paintings: (L) $66; (H) $660

LAURENT, Robert
American 1890-1970
paintings: (H) $1,870
drawings: (L) $55; (H) $165
sculpture: (L) $143; (H) $5,500

LAURENTI, Cesare
Italian 1854-1936
paintings: (H) $66,000

LAURENTY, L.
French 19th cent.
paintings: (L) $1,650; (H) $2,200

LAURET, Francois
French 1820-1868
paintings: (H) $8,525

LAUREYS, Armand
Belgian
paintings: (H) $935

LAURITZ, Jack
American 20th cent.
paintings: (H) $605

LAURITZ, Paul
Norwegian/American 1889-1975
paintings: (L) $303; (H) $14,300
drawings: (L) $715; (H) $1,265

LAUSSUCQ, Henri L.
b. 1882
paintings: (L) $110; (H) $625

LAUTER, Richard
drawings: (H) $495

LAUTERS, Paul J.
Belgian 1806-1876
paintings: (H) $1,650

LAUTERS, Paul and Franz van SVERDONCK
Belgian 19th cent.
paintings: (H) $2,530

LAUTIER, Henri
French early 20th cent.
sculpture: (H) $1,870

LAUVERNAY-PETITJEAN, Jeanne
French b. 1875
paintings: (H) $1,540

LAUVRAY, Louis Alphonse Abel
French 1870-1950
paintings: (H) $1,650

LAUX, August
American 1847/53-1921
paintings: (L) $220; (H) $7,700

LAUYOT, E.
Continental 19th cent.
paintings: (H) $3,795

LAVAGNA, Francesco
ac. 2nd half 18th cent.
paintings: (L) $18,700; (H) $41,400

LAVALLE, John
American b. 1896
paintings: (L) $248; (H) $2,200
drawings: (L) $127; (H) $1,430

LAVALLEE, Geex de
Flemish 17th cent.
paintings: (H) $5,750

LAVALLEE-POUSSIN, Etienne de
French c. 1733-1793
drawings: (L) $462; (H) $1,430

LAVALLEY, William
19th/20th cent.
paintings: (L) $121; (H) $495

LAVASEUR, Henri
French 20th cent.
paintings: (H) $825

LAVATELLI, Carla
Italian 20th cent.
sculpture: (L) $1,035; (H) $2,090

LAVERY, Sir John
Irish 1856-1941
paintings: (L) $4,400; (H) $121,000

LAVIELLE, Eugene Antoine Samuel
French 1820-1889
paintings: (H) $5,500

LAVIGERIE, Samuel Marie Cledat de
French 19th cent.
paintings: (H) $3,080

LAVIGNE
sculpture: (H) $495

LAVILLE, Joy
b. England 1923
paintings: (L) $3,300; (H) $15,400
drawings: (L) $1,610; (H) $3,680

LAVIN, Robert
American b. 1919
paintings: (L) $440; (H) $880

LAVORO, E., studio
sculpture: (H) $1,050

LAVROFF, Georges
Russian/French b. 1895
sculpture: (L) $3,450; (H) $6,050

LAW, Anthony
Canadian 20th cent.
paintings: (H) $1,540

LAW, Margaret M.
20th cent.
paintings: (H) $1,320

LAWES, Harold
British ac. 1890s
drawings: (L) $330; (H) $800

LAWLER, Louise
b. 1947
drawings: (L) $3,450; (H) $7,475

LAWLESS, C.E.
paintings: (H) $1,430

LAWLESS, Carl
American 1894-1964
paintings: (L) $330; (H) $7,260

LAWLEY, Lisa
20th cent.
paintings: (L) $55; (H) $825

LAWLOR, F.A.
sculpture: (H) $467

LAWLOR, George W.
American b. 1878
paintings: (L) $345; (H) $825

LAWLOWSKI, L.
French 20th cent.
sculpture: (H) $3,080

LAWMAN, Jasper Holman
American 1825-1906
paintings: (L) $6,900; (H) $9,350

LAWRENCE, Edna W.
American b. 1898
paintings: (L) $110; (H) $550

LAWRENCE, Jacob
American b. 1917
paintings: (L) $60,250; (H) $68,750
drawings: (L) $5,225; (H) $107,000

LAWRENCE, John C.
English 19th cent.
paintings: (H) $748

LAWRENCE, Sir Thomas
English 1769-1830
paintings: (L) $990; (H) $277,500
drawings: (L) $1,540; (H) $3,575

LAWRENCE, Sir Thomas, studio of
British 18th/19th cent.
paintings: (L) $805; (H) $15,400

LAWRENCE, William Goadby
American 20th cent.
paintings: (L) $138; (H) $4,313

LAWS, Arthur J.
American 1894-1960
paintings: (L) $137; (H) $10,450

LAWS, Robin J.
American
sculpture: (H) $1,100

LAWSHE, Hank
American b. 1935
paintings: (L) $850; (H) $1,200

LAWSON, Cecil Gordon
Scottish 1851-1882
paintings: (H) $1,380

LAWSON, Constance B.
English 19th cent.
paintings: (H) $550

LAWSON, Ernest
American 1873-1939
paintings: (L) $1,045; (H) $374,000
drawings: (H) $46

LAWSON, Mehl
b. 1942
sculpture: (H) $2,420

LAWSON, Thomas
b. 1951
paintings: (H) $2,860

LAYCOCK, Brent R.
Canadian b. 1947
paintings: (H) $1,540

LAYNG, G.W.
19th/20th cent.
paintings: (H) $1,725

LAYTON
American 20th cent.
drawings: (H) $715

LAZAREV, Vladimir
European 20th cent.
paintings: (L) $220; (H) $632

LAZERGES, Jean Baptiste Paul
French 1845-1902
paintings: (L) $1,035; (H) $14,950

LAZERGES, Jean Raymond Hippolyte
French 1817-1887
paintings: (L) $4,830; (H) $8,338

LAZZARI, Pietro
Italian/American 1898-1979
paintings: (H) $495
drawings: (L) $137; (H) $550

LAZZELL, Blanche
American 1878-1956
paintings: (L) $605; (H) $10,450
drawings: (L) $110; (H) $2,640

LAZZERINI, Giuseppe
Italian 1831-1895
sculpture: (H) $2,875

LE BRETON, Constant
French 1895-1985
paintings: (L) $715; (H) $1,380

LE BROCQUY, Louis
British b. 1916
paintings: (L) $5,225; (H) $13,200
drawings: (L) $660; (H) $990

LE BRUN, Charles
French 1619-1690
drawings: (H) $1,540

LE CLEAR, Thomas
American 1818-1882
paintings: (H) $167,500

LE COEUR, Jules
French 1832-1882
paintings: (H) $29,900

LE COMPTE, Etienne
French 20th cent.
paintings: (H) $550

LE COMPTE DU PASSAGE, Arthur-
Marie-Gabriel
French 1838-1909
sculpture: (H) $1,100

LE CORBUSIER, Charles Edouard
JEANNERET
Swiss/French 1887-1965
paintings: (L) $275,000; (H) $319,000
drawings: (L) $1,725; (H) $17,600
sculpture: (L) $15,750; (H) $20,700

LE FAGUAYS, Pierre
French b. 1892
sculpture: (L) $275; (H) $20,700

LE GILLON, Jean Francois
Belgian 1739-1797
paintings: (H) $6,600

LE GUILLEMIN, E.
sculpture: (H) $3,163

LE HARVE, Montardier
French ac. 1812-1848
drawings: (H) $4,620

LE JEUNE, Henry
British 1819-1904
paintings: (H) $2,860

LE MOLT, Phillipe
French b. 1895
paintings: (H) $522

LE MORE
French School 19th cent.
paintings: (H) $1,540

LE MOYNE, F.
French ac. 1900-1910
sculpture: (H) $1,840

LE MOYNE, Francois
French 1688-1737
paintings: (H) $451,000
drawings: (L) $3,080; (H) $18,700

LE PARC, Julio
Argentinean b. 1928
sculpture: (H) $6,900

LE PAS DUBUISSON, Claude Nicolas,
I
1663-1733
drawings: (H) $2,300

LE PAUTRE, Jean
French 1618-1682
drawings: (H) $1,955

LE PHO
Vietnamese/French b. 1907
paintings: (L) $165; (H) $3,300

LE POITTEVIN, Eugene Modeste
Edmond
French 1806-1870
paintings: (H) $3,850

LE RAU, R.
paintings: (H) $770

LE ROY
American School 19th cent.
paintings: (H) $880

LE SENECHAL DE KERDROUET,
Gustave Edouard
French b. 1902
paintings: (H) $3,300

LE SEYEUX, Jean
drawings: (H) $990

LE SIDANER, Henri
French 1862-1939
paintings: (L) $5,000; (H) $385,000
drawings: (L) $990; (H) $15,400

LE SUEUR, Eustache
French 1617-1655
drawings: (L) $1,650; (H) $16,500

LE SUEUR, Hubert
French c. 1585-1660
sculpture: (H) $134,500

LE VA, Barry
American b. 1941
drawings: (L) $2,750; (H) $8,800

LE VASSEUR
sculpture: (H) $977

LE VERRIER
sculpture: (H) $3,680

LEA, Tom
American b. 1907
paintings: (H) $770
drawings: (H) $660

LEA, Wesley
American b. 1914
paintings: (H) $575
drawings: (L) $460; (H) $1,045

LEADER, Benjamin Williams
English 1831-1923
paintings: (L) $1,760; (H) $29,700

LEADER, Charles
British 19th cent.
paintings: (L) $633; (H) $1,955

LEADER, E.
English 19th/20th cent.
paintings: (H) $467

LEAKE, Eugene
20th cent.
paintings: (H) $1,495

LEAKE, Gerald
American 1885-1975
paintings: (L) $633; (H) $1,100

LEAR, Edward
English 1812-1888
drawings: (L) $660; (H) $21,850

LEAR, John
American 20th cent.
paintings: (L) $330; (H) $385
drawings: (L) $60; (H) $1,045

LEARNED, Harry
American b. 1842
paintings: (L) $518; (H) $4,025

LEAVER, Noel Harry
English 1889-1951
drawings: (L) $440; (H) $6,900

LEAVERS, Lucy Ann
British 19th cent.
paintings: (L) $8,800; (H) $8,800

LEAVITT, Edward Chalmers
American 1842-1904
paintings: (L) $220; (H) $14,300

LEAVITT, John Faunce
American 1905-1974
paintings: (H) $303
drawings: (L) $1,265; (H) $1,430

LEAVITT, Joseph Warren
American 1804-1833
drawings: (H) $101,500

LEAVITT, Sheldon
19th cent.
paintings: (H) $522

LEBADANG
Vietnamese/French b. 1922
paintings: (L) $412; (H) $1,210

LEBAS, Leonie
French 19th/20th cent.
paintings: (H) $495

LEBASQUE, Henri
French 1865-1937
paintings: (L) $4,313; (H) $134,500
drawings: (L) $600; (H) $82,500

LEBASQUE, Henri
French 1865-1937
paintings: (H) $880
drawings: (H) $248

LEBDUSKA, Lawrence H.
American 1894-1966
paintings: (L) $460; (H) $5,500

LEBEDEV, Klavdi Vasilievich
Russian 1852-1916
paintings: (H) $16,100

LEBEDEV, Vladimir
Russian 1891-1967
paintings: (L) $110; (H) $550

LEBEDEV, Vladimir W.
Russian 1875-1946
paintings: (H) $1,495

LEBEL, Edmond
French 1834-1909
paintings: (H) $1,430

LEBENSTEIN, Jan
b. 1930
paintings: (L) $138; (H) $2,475

LEBEUZE, C.
French 20th cent.
paintings: (H) $1,430

LEBIER, Daniel
French b. 1941
paintings: (H) $880

LEBLANC, Emilie Marie De Hoa
1870-1954
drawings: (H) $506

LEBLANC, M.
sculpture: (H) $825

LEBON, Charles
Belgian b. 1906
paintings: (H) $1,320

LEBOURG
French 19th cent.
paintings: (H) $2,070

LEBOURG, Albert
French 1849-1928
paintings: (L) $1,980; (H) $36,800
drawings: (L) $489; (H) $4,025

LEBRET, Frans
Dutch 1820-1909
paintings: (L) $990; (H) $5,175

LEBRET, Frans and Jon Frederik Pieter
PORTIELJE
19th cent.
paintings: (L) $3,738; (H) $5,500

LEBROC, Jean Baptiste
French 1825-1870
sculpture: (L) $2,475; (H) $6,600

LEBRUN, A.
French c. 1900
paintings: (L) $605; (H) $1,320

LEBRUN, Christopher
British contemporary
paintings: (L) $5,280; (H) $17,600

LEBRUN, Frederico
1900-1964
drawings: (L) $115; (H) $935

LEBRUN, Guillaume Charles
French 1825-1908
paintings: (L) $34,500; (H) $34,500

LEBRUN, Marcel
early 20th cent.
paintings: (H) $22,000

LEBRUN, Rico
Italian/American 1900-1964
paintings: (H) $4,125
drawings: (L) $440; (H) $1,840

LEBRUN, V.
Dutch School 19th cent.
paintings: (H) $468

LECHAT, Albert Eugene
drawings: (H) $575

LECHAY, Myron
American b. 1898
paintings: (L) $230; (H) $605

LECLAIR, Victor
French 1830-1885
paintings: (H) $9,775

LECLERC, Sebastien Jacques, called
LeClerc des Gobelins
French 1734-1785
paintings: (L) $6,325; (H) $132,000

LECLERE, Theodore
French 19th cent.
paintings: (H) $3,450

LECOLA, A.
French 19th/20th cent.
paintings: (H) $2,860

LECOMTE
sculpture: (H) $825

LECOMTE, E.
Dutch 20th cent.
paintings: (H) $1,430

LECOMTE, Hippolyte
French 1781-1857
paintings: (H) $4,830

LECOMTE, Louis
French 19th/20th cent.
paintings: (H) $1,725

LECOMTE, Paul
French 1842-1920
paintings: (L) $5,175; (H) $8,050

LECOMTE, Paul Emile
French 1877-1956
paintings: (L) $770; (H) $14,300
drawings: (H) $1,980

LECOMTE, Valentine
French b. 1872
paintings: (H) $30,250

LECOMTE, Victor
French 1856-1920
paintings: (L) $3,163; (H) $6,875

LECOMTE DU NOUY, Jean Jules
Antoine
French 1842-1923
paintings: (H) $13,800
drawings: (H) $2,475

LECOMTE-VERNET, Charles Emile
French 1821-1900
paintings: (H) $27,500

LECONTE, ***
18th/19th cent.
drawings: (H) $2,310

LECOQUE, Alois
Czech/American 1891-1981
paintings: (L) $483; (H) $5,500
drawings: (L) $403; (H) $1,150

LECOURTIER, Prosper
French 1855-1924
sculpture: (L) $550; (H) $5,175

LECOURTILE, H.F. Moreau
sculpture: (H) $1,035

LECREUX, Gaston Alfred
French 1846-1914
paintings: (H) $2,300

LEDESMA, Blas de
Spanish c. 1546-c. 1600
paintings: (H) $134,500

LEDI, V.
paintings: (H) $935

LEDIEU, Philippe
French 19th cent.
paintings: (H) $1,650

LEDOUX, Jeanne Philiberte
1767-1840
paintings: (H) $6,600

LEDRU, August
French 1860-1902
sculpture: (H) $1,725

LEDUC, Arthur Jacques
French 1848-1918
sculpture: (H) $5,175

LEE, Arthur
Norwegian/American 1881-1961
sculpture: (H) $1,760

LEE, Bertha Stringer
American 1873-1934/37
paintings: (L) $248; (H) $4,400

LEE, Catherine
b. 1950
paintings: (L) $2,860; (H) $3,450

LEE, Charlie, Hushka Yelhayah
Warrior Who Came Out
Navajo b. 1926
paintings: (H) $1,150
drawings: (H) $440

LEE, Doris
American 1905-1983
paintings: (L) $357; (H) $9,625
drawings: (L) $467; (H) $2,420

LEE, F.R.
English 19th/20th cent.
paintings: (H) $825

LEE, Frances
American 20th cent.
paintings: (H) $550

LEE, Frederick Richard
British 1798-1879
paintings: (L) $1,540; (H) $8,050

LEE, Henry Charles
American 1864-1930
paintings: (L) $165; (H) $660

LEE, Jim
American 20th cent.
drawings: (L) $1,100; (H) $44,000

LEE, Joseph
American 1827-1880
paintings: (L) $24,750; (H) $50,600

LEE, Laura
American b. 1867
paintings: (H) $1,017

LEE, Leslie W.
paintings: (H) $550

LEE, Sydney
British 1866-1949
paintings: (L) $143; (H) $605

LEE-HANKEY, William
British 1869-1952
paintings: (L) $5,175; (H) $8,625
drawings: (H) $1,320

LEE-SMITH, Hughie
American b. 1915
paintings: (L) $880; (H) $8,250
drawings: (H) $1,540

LEECH, Conrad
American 20th cent.
paintings: (H) $495

LEECH, John William
British 1881-1968
paintings: (H) $550

LEEDY, J. Harvey
American 1869-1947
paintings: (L) $358; (H) $743
drawings: (H) $72

LEEDY, Jim
American b. 1935
sculpture: (H) $4,400

LEEKE, Ferdinand
German b. 1859
paintings: (L) $2,200; (H) $2,530

LEEMPOELS, Jef
Belgian 1867-1935
paintings: (H) $8,625

LEEMPUTTEN, Cornelis van
Belgian 1841-1902
paintings: (L) $920; (H) $19,800

LEEMPUTTEN, Cornelis van and
Hendrick Pieter KOEKKOEK
paintings: (H) $4,840

LEEMPUTTEN, Frans van
Belgian 1850-1914
paintings: (L) $1,540; (H) $4,025

LEEMPUTTEN, Jef Louis van
Belgian 19th/20th cent.
paintings: (L) $577; (H) $6,600

LEEN, Willem van
Dutch 1753-1825
paintings: (H) $17,600

LEES, John
American b. 1943
paintings: (H) $1,650

LEETEG, Edgar
American 20th cent.
paintings: (L) $546; (H) $3,575

LEEUW, Alexis de
Belgian ac. 1864
paintings: (L) $1,430; (H) $4,888

LEEUW, Pieter van der
Dutch 1647-1679
paintings: (H) $1,610

LEEUWEN, Hendrik van
Dutch b. 1890
paintings: (L) $605; (H) $770

LEEUWEN, Henk van
Dutch 1866-1918
paintings: (H) $2,420

LEEUWEN, J.J. van
Dutch 20th cent.
paintings: (H) $1,870

LEFEBVRE, Jules Joseph
French 1834/36-1912
paintings: (L) $1,980; (H) $16,500

LEFEVRE, Adolphe Rene
French b. 1834
paintings: (H) $4,620

LEFEVRE, Jean
French b. 1916
paintings: (H) $2,200

LEFEVRE, Valentin
c. 1642-1682
drawings: (L) $2,185; (H) $3,220

LEFFEL, David
American b. 1931
paintings: (L) $575; (H) $11,000

LEFLER, Franz
Czechoslovakian 1831-1898
paintings: (L) $2,750; (H) $22,000

LEFONT, E.
French 19th cent.
paintings: (H) $825

LEFORT, Jean Louis
French b. 1875
paintings: (L) $440; (H) $17,600

LEFTWICH-DODGE, William de
American 1867-1935
paintings: (H) $1,100

LEFUEL, Hector
French 1810-1880
drawings: (H) $2,530

LEGACHEFF, Anton
Russian 1798-1865
paintings: (H) $3,025

LEGANGER, Nicolay Tysland
American 1832-1905
paintings: (L) $303; (H) $3,080

LEGAT, Leon
French b. 1829
paintings: (L) $11,000; (H) $35,200

LEGEAY, Jean Laurent
1710-1786
drawings: (H) $4,400

LEGENDRE, L.N.
French ac. early 20th cent.
paintings: (L) $247; (H) $483

LEGENDRE-HERAL, Jean Francoise
French 1796-1851
sculpture: (H) $4,715

LEGER, Fernand
French 1881-1955
paintings: (L) $25,300; (H) $9,900,000
drawings: (L) $1,870; (H) $308,000
sculpture: (L) $4,125; (H) $40,700

LEGER, H.
French 19th c.
paintings: (H) $1,980

LEGERE, John S.
paintings: (H) $1,100

LEGGE, Russell
drawings: (L) $165; (H) $1,100

LEGGETT, Alexander
Scottish ac. 1860-1870
paintings: (L) $935; (H) $4,950

LEGGETT, Rawley
English 20th cent.
paintings: (L) $330; (H) $1,705

LEGILLON, Jean Francois
1739-1797
drawings: (H) $1,650

LEGLER, Wilhelm
Italian 1875-1951
paintings: (H) $3,450

LEGOUT-GERARD, Fernand Marie
Eugene
French 1856-1924
paintings: (L) $1,320; (H) $26,450

LEGRAND
19th cent.
paintings: (H) $990

LEGRAND, Alexandre
French 1822-1901
paintings: (L) $633; (H) $17,600

LEGRAND, Louis
French 1863-1951
drawings: (L) $690; (H) $1,650

LEGRAND, Pierre
Dutch b. 1950
paintings: (L) $303; (H) $935

LEGROS, Alphonse
French 1837-1911
paintings: (L) $2,300; (H) $2,760
drawings: (H) $2,200

LEGUEULT, Raymond Jean
drawings: (H) $3,450

LEHMAN, Harold
American b. 1913
drawings: (H) $605

LEHMANN, Karl Ernest Rodolphe
Heinrich Salem
French 1814-1882
drawings: (H) $4,025

LEHMANN, Rudolph Wilhelm August
German 1819-1905
paintings: (H) $4,125

LEHMBRUCK, Wilhelm
German 1881-1919
drawings: (H) $11,000
sculpture: (L) $87,750; (H) $1,212,500

LEHNER, Joseph
Austrian b. 1909
paintings: (H) $495

LEHNERT, A.
German 19th/20th cent.
paintings: (H) $935

LEHOMAY
French 19th cent.
paintings: (H) $550

LEHR, Adam
American 1853-1910?
paintings: (L) $201; (H) $1,955

LEHR, Paul
b. 1930
drawings: (H) $1,100

LEIBER, Tom
American 20th cent.
paintings: (H) $2,588

LEIBLER, T.A.
German 19th cent.
drawings: (H) $990

LEICHMAN, Seymour
paintings: (H) $605

LEICKERT, Charles Henri Joseph
Belgian 1816/18-1907
paintings: (L) $2,200; (H) $60,500
drawings: (H) $1,840

LEICSER, N.B.
paintings: (H) $2,100

LEIGH, William Robinson
American 1866-1955
paintings: (L) $1,035; (H) $178,500
drawings: (L) $460; (H) $31,900

LEIGHTON, Alfred Crocker
Canadian 1901-1965
paintings: (H) $6,600
drawings: (L) $115; (H) $1,870

LEIGHTON, Edmund Blair
British 1853-1922
paintings: (L) $403; (H) $29,700

LEIGHTON, Frederic, Lord
English 1830-1896
paintings: (L) $90,500; (H) $277,500
drawings: (L) $345; (H) $17,600
sculpture: (L) $34,500; (H) $37,400

LEIGHTON, J.C.
English 19th cent.
paintings: (H) $3,080

LEIGHTON, Kathryn Woodman
American 1876-1952
paintings: (L) $1,210; (H) $3,850

LEIGHTON, Scott
American 1849-1898
paintings: (L) $330; (H) $35,200

LEIGHTON-JONES, Barry
English 20th cent.
paintings: (H) $687

LEIN
drawings: (H) $3,162

LEISSER, Martin B.
American 1846-1940
paintings: (L) $330; (H) $3,100

LEISTEN, Jacobus
German 1844-1918
paintings: (L) $770; (H) $1,980

LEISTIKOW, Walter
Russian 1865-1908
drawings: (H) $7,150

LEITH-ROSS, Harry
American 1886-1973
paintings: (L) $250; (H) $6,875
drawings: (L) $100; (H) $1,980

LEITZ, Otto
paintings: (H) $920

LEIVA, Nicolas
b. 1958
paintings: (L) $6,325; (H) $8,625

LEJEUNE, A.A.
18th cent.
drawings: (H) $5,500

LEJEUNE, Eugene
French 1818-1894
paintings: (H) $7,150

LEJEUNE, Ginette Bingguely
sculpture: (L) $920; (H) $3,575

LEJOUTEUX, Jules Gontran
French d. 1916
paintings: (H) $50,600

LELEUX, Adolphe Pierre
French 1812-1891
paintings: (H) $15,400

LELIEVRE, Eugene
French b. 1856
paintings: (L) $1,375; (H) $2,645

LELOIR, Alexandre Louis
French 1843-1884
paintings: (L) $1,870; (H) $46,000
drawings: (H) $2,200

LELOIR, Maurice
French 1853-1940
paintings: (L) $5,280; (H) $6,050
drawings: (L) $110; (H) $6,600

LELOIR, Maurice and Ch. Edouard
DELORT
French 19th cent.
drawings: (H) $1,760

LELONG, Rene
French 19th/20th cent.
paintings: (L) $6,900; (H) $8,800

LELTERRA, Caloni
sculpture: (H) $1,100

LELY, Sir Peter, studio of
British 17th cent.
paintings: (L) $1,100; (H) $14,300

LEMAIRE, Casimir
French 19th cent.
paintings: (H) $3,450

LEMAIRE, Jean
1598-1659
paintings: (H) $6,325

LEMAIRE, Madeleine
French 1845-1928
paintings: (L) $4,600; (H) $46,000
drawings: (L) $1,430; (H) $55,000

LEMAIRE, Marie Therese
French b. 1861
paintings: (H) $8,800

LEMAITRE, Hernando
Colombia b. 1925
drawings: (H) $5,500

LEMAITRE, Maurice
French b. 1929
paintings: (L) $440; (H) $2,875

LEMAN, Jacques Edmond
French 1829-1889
paintings: (H) $7,975

LEMBECK, Jack
American b. 1942
paintings: (L) $1,150; (H) $6,380

LEMEUNIER, Basile
French b. 1852
paintings: (H) $8,050

LEMIEUX, Annette
American b. 1957
paintings: (H) $1,300
drawings: (L) $1,840; (H) $6,600

LEMIEUX, Jean Paul
Canadian 1904-1990
paintings: (L) $15,400; (H) $72,600
drawings: (H) $7,150

LEMMEN, Georges
Belgian 1865-1916
paintings: (L) $4,675; (H) $88,000
drawings: (L) $825; (H) $17,250

LEMMENS, Theophile Victor Emile
French 1821-1867
paintings: (L) $990; (H) $4,180

LEMMI, Angeola
American 20th cent.
paintings: (H) $7,700

LEMMI, Angiolo
Italian 19th cent.
paintings: (H) $22,000

LEMO, Armond
French early 20th cent.
sculpture: (H) $1,725

LEMOGNIER, Jean
French 19th cent.
paintings: (H) $825

LEMOINE, Jacques Antoine Marie
1751-1824
drawings: (H) $6,600

LEMOINE, Marie Victoire
French 1753/54-1820
paintings: (H) $40,250

LEMORE, Paul
French ac. 1863-1883
paintings: (H) $22,000
drawings: (L) $385; (H) $920

LEMOYNE, Francois
1688-1737
drawings: (L) $6,050; (H) $6,900

LEMPICKA, Tamara de
Polish 1898-1980
paintings: (L) $1,320; (H) $1,982,500
drawings: (L) $880; (H) $4,620

LEMUS
paintings: (H) $522

LENBACH, Franz Seraph von
German 1836-1904
paintings: (L) $1,380; (H) $24,750
drawings: (L) $719; (H) $2,310

LENEPVEU, Jules Eugene
French 1819-1898
paintings: (H) $7,150
drawings: (H) $1,760

LENFESTEY, Giffard Hocart
English b. 1872
paintings: (H) $4,950
drawings: (H) $115

LENGO Y MARTINEZ, Horacio
Spanish 1840-1890
paintings: (L) $5,500; (H) $25,300

LENGYEL-RHEINFUSS, Ede
Hungarian b. 1873
paintings: (H) $2,185

LENNON, John
British 1940-1980
drawings: (L) $920; (H) $7,187

LENNON, John and Yoko ONO
20th cent.
drawings: (L) $9,775; (H) $12,650

LENOIR, Alfred Charles
French late 19th/20th cent.
sculpture: (H) $2,420

LENOIR, Andre Alfred Alexandre
French 1850-1920
sculpture: (H) $1,725

LENOIR, Charles Amable
French b. 1861
paintings: (L) $9,350; (H) $123,500

LENOIR, J. or T.
French 19th cent.
drawings: (H) $770

LENOIR, Paul Marie
French d. 1881
paintings: (L) $4,600; (H) $7,150

LENOIR, Simon Bernard
1729-1791
drawings: (H) $3,410

LENORDEZ, Pierre
French ac. 1855-1877
sculpture: (L) $1,900; (H) $6,050

LENPEN, A.
Continental 19th/20th cent.
paintings: (H) $5,500

LENS, Cornelis
ac. c. 1738
paintings: (H) $8,800

LENTELLI, Leo
American 1879-1962
sculpture: (L) $1,840; (H) $7,700

LENTZ, A.
19th cent.
paintings: (H) $1,870

LENTZ, Johannes Frans
Flemish ac. 1825-1831
paintings: (H) $3,450

LENZ, Alfred David
American 1872-1926
sculpture: (H) $1,045

LENZ, Norbert
American 20th cent.
paintings: (L) $83; (H) $467
drawings: (L) $28; (H) $55

LEON, Angel Acosto
1930-1963
drawings: (H) $4,600

LEON, Ernesto
contemporary
paintings: (H) $2,200

LEON, Jean
French 20th cent.
paintings: (H) $468

LEON, Omar de
Nicaraguan 20th cent.
paintings: (H) $1,100

LEON Y ESCOSURA, Ignacio de
Spanish 1834-1901
paintings: (L) $2,530; (H) $46,200

LEON-WILLETTE, Adolphe
French 1857-1926
drawings: (H) $2,420

LEONARD A***
British 19th cent.
paintings: (H) $1,980

LEONARD, Agathon
French b. 1841
sculpture: (L) $495; (H) $20,700

LEONARD, Hy
paintings: (H) $495

LEONARD, Jack de Coudres
American b. 1903
paintings: (H) $3,850

LEONARD, John Henry
English 1834-1904
paintings: (H) $1,870

LEONARD, Ruth
American b. 1955
paintings: (L) $1,045; (H) $1,100

LEONARD, S.M.
drawings: (H) $650

LEONARDI,
Italian 19th cent.
paintings: (H) $5,500

LEONARDI, Achille
Italian 19th cent.
paintings: (H) $5,175

LEONARDO DA VINCI,
Italian 1452-1519
sculpture: (H) $12,100

LEONCINI, Luca
paintings: (H) $880

LEONE, Andrea di
Italian 1610-1685
paintings: (L) $14,950; (H) $60,500

LEONE, Calle
Italian 19th cent.
paintings: (H) $8,250

LEONE, John
American b. 1929
paintings: (L) $2,530; (H) $5,500

LEONE, R.
French 19th/20th cent.
paintings: (H) $550

LEONE, Romolo
French 19th cent.
paintings: (L) $322; (H) $1,045

LEONI, Ottavio Maria
Italian 1587-1630
drawings: (H) $3,520

LEONORI, R.G.L.
American ac. mid-19th cent.
paintings: (H) $3,850

LEONTUS, Adam
Haitian 20th cent.
paintings: (H) $4,950

LEOPOLD-LEVY
French 1886-1966
paintings: (H) $1,100

LEOPOLDT, Johannes
Dutch 1877-1948
paintings: (H) $1,430

LEPAGE, Celine
French 1882-1928
sculpture: (L) $2,640; (H) $9,350

LEPAGE, J.
French School 19th cent.
paintings: (H) $1,540

LEPAPE, George
French 1887-1971
paintings: (H) $1,980

LEPERE, Auguste Louis
French 1849-1918
paintings: (H) $4,600

LEPERE, Jean Baptiste
French 1761-1844
drawings: (H) $550

LEPICIE, Nicolas Bernard
French 1735-1784
paintings: (L) $3,300; (H) $93,500
drawings: (H) $11,000

LEPINAY, E. Gallaid
paintings: (H) $1,100

LEPIND, Henri
French ac. 1880
paintings: (H) $5,750

LEPINE, Joseph
paintings: (H) $8,800

LEPINE, Stanislas
French 1835-1892
paintings: (L) $880; (H) $54,625
drawings: (L) $1,760; (H) $8,250

LEPOITTEVIN, Eugene Modeste
Edmond
French 1806-1870
paintings: (L) $1,100; (H) $11,500

LEPRI, Stanislas
paintings: (L) $1,320; (H) $4,400

LEPRIN, M.
paintings: (H) $3,080

LEPRIN, Marcel
French 1891-1933
paintings: (H) $5,225

LEPRINCE, Jean Baptiste
French 1734-1781
paintings: (L) $20,900; (H) $57,500
drawings: (L) $6,600; (H) $10,450

LEPROU
French 19th cent.
paintings: (H) $1,870

LEQUIER, William
contemporary
sculpture: (H) $10,350

LERAY, Prudent Louis
French 1820-1879
paintings: (L) $2,475; (H) $3,080

LERICHE, J.
French 19th/20th cent.
paintings: (H) $660

LERIN, Giralt
Spanish b. 1906
paintings: (L) $110; (H) $770

LERIUS, Joseph Henry Francois van
Belgian 1823-1876
drawings: (H) $687

LERNER, Leslie
American b. 1949
paintings: (H) $460

LEROLLE, Henri
French 1848-1929
paintings: (H) $6,900

LEROUX, Auguste
French 1871-1954
paintings: (H) $21,850

LEROUX, Colon
sculpture: (H) $7,700

LEROUX, Gaston Veuvenot
French 1854-1942
paintings: (L) $6,600; (H) $11,000
sculpture: (L) $1,100; (H) $9,775

LEROUX, Georges
French 1877-1957
paintings: (H) $715

LEROUX, Jean Robert
French 1823-1898
paintings: (H) $6,600

LEROUX, Laura Revault
European 19th cent.
paintings: (H) $935

LEROUX, Louis Hector
French 1829-1900
paintings: (L) $8,050; (H) $9,200

LEROUX, Marie Guillaume Charles
French 1814-1895
paintings: (H) $1,650

LEROY, Charles
French d. 1898
paintings: (H) $2,070

LEROY, Etienne
French b. 1828
paintings: (H) $8,050

LEROY, Gustave Jules
French 1833-1865
paintings: (H) $16,500

LEROY, James
paintings: (H) $525

LEROY, Jules
French 1833-1865
paintings: (L) $770; (H) $19,550

LEROY, P.
French 19th cent.
paintings: (H) $4,400

LERSY, Roger
French b. 1920
paintings: (H) $495

LESDEMA, Blas de
paintings: (H) $2,200

LESIEUR, Pierre
French b. 1922
paintings: (L) $1,955; (H) $5,500

LESLIE, Alfred
American b. 1927
paintings: (L) $880; (H) $44,000
drawings: (L) $575; (H) $23,000

LESLIE, Charles
British b. 1840
paintings: (L) $413; (H) $1,540

LESLIE, Charles Robert
English 1794-1859
paintings: (L) $605; (H) $7,475

LESLIE, Edward
American 1891-1960
paintings: (H) $1,840

LESLIE, George Dunlop
English 1835-1921
paintings: (H) $1,725
drawings: (H) $962

LESNE, Camille
French b. 1908
paintings: (L) $460; (H) $633

LESOURD-BEAUREGARD, Ange
Louis Guillaume
French b. 1800
paintings: (H) $9,200

LESREL, Adolphe Alexandre
French 1839-1921
paintings: (L) $2,200; (H) $173,000

LESSER-URY
German 1861-1931
paintings: (L) $2,070; (H) $74,000
drawings: (L) $920; (H) $48,875

LESSHAFFT, Franz
American b. 1862
paintings: (H) $550

LESSI, Giovanni
Italian 1852-1922
paintings: (H) $7,475

LESSI, Tito
drawings: (L) $460; (H) $770

LESSING, Karl Friedrich
German 1808-1880
paintings: (H) $4,620

LESSORE, Jules
French/British 1849-1892
drawings: (L) $460; (H) $8,250

LESTER, Leonard
b. 1876
paintings: (L) $1,380; (H) $3,737

LESTER, William Lewis
American b. 1910
paintings: (H) $2,300

LESUEUR, Louis
b. 1746
drawings: (H) $1,540

LESUR, Henri Victor
French b. 1863
paintings: (L) $4,600; (H) $19,800

LETELLIER, Pierre
contemporary
paintings: (H) $880

LETHBRIDGE, Julian
b. 1947
paintings: (L) $978; (H) $29,900
drawings: (L) $1,760; (H) $2,860

LETHIERE, Guillaume Guillon
1760-1832
drawings: (H) $9,900

LETO, A.
Continental 20th cent.
paintings: (H) $3,740

LETO, Antonino
Italian 1844-1913
paintings: (L) $4,600; (H) $53,900

LETOUR (?), A.J.
sculpture: (H) $3,850

LETOURNEAU, Edouard
French 1851-1907
sculpture: (L) $3,300; (H) $4,830

LETUAIRE, Pierre
French 1799-1884
drawings: (H) $4,125

LEU, August Wilhelm
German 1819-1897
paintings: (L) $1,925; (H) $5,500

LEULLIER, Felix Louis
French 1811-1882
paintings: (H) $27,500

LEURAT, R.
19th cent.
paintings: (H) $605

LEURS, Johannes Karel
Dutch 1865-1938
paintings: (H) $1,650

LEUTZE, Emanuel
German 1816-1868
paintings: (L) $3,025; (H) $13,800
drawings: (L) $1,725; (H) $6,600

LEUUS, Jesus
Mexican 20th cent.
paintings: (L) $220; (H) $4,313
drawings: (L) $1,045; (H) $1,980

LEVA, Barry
b. 1941
sculpture: (H) $4,620

LEVASSEUR, A.
French 19th cent.
sculpture: (H) $2,090

LEVASSEUR, Henri Louis
French b. 1853
sculpture: (L) $1,320; (H) $4,370

LEVEE, John Harrison
American b. 1924
paintings: (L) $302; (H) $1,320

LEVEILLE, Andre
French 1880-1963
paintings: (H) $3,300

LEVELT, Heinrich Jacob
b. 1808
paintings: (H) $4,600

LEVEQUE, Gabriel
Haitian b. 1923
paintings: (H) $3,680

LEVER, Richard Hayley
American 1876-1958
paintings: (L) $303; (H) $71,250
drawings: (L) $110; (H) $9,900

LEVERD, Rene
French 1872-1938
paintings: (H) $2,750

LEVERRIER, Max
Belgian 19th/20th cent.
sculpture: (H) $2,970

LEVI, Julian E.
American 1900-after 1940
paintings: (H) $1,045

LEVI, Luigi
Italian 1860-1939
paintings: (L) $3,162; (H) $8,050
drawings: (H) $4,025

LEVIER
paintings: (H) $127
drawings: (H) $690

LEVIER, Charles
American (?) b. 1920
paintings: (L) $66; (H) $4,675
drawings: (L) $247; (H) $1,210

LEVINE, David
American b. 1926
paintings: (H) $715
drawings: (L) $275; (H) $4,950

LEVINE, David Phillip
American b. 1910
paintings: (L) $345; (H) $605
drawings: (L) $715; (H) $1,045

LEVINE, Jack
American b. 1915
paintings: (L) $259; (H) $59,400
drawings: (L) $126; (H) $28,750

LEVINE, Marilyn
Canadian b. 1935
sculpture: (H) $23,000

LEVINE, Sherrie
American b. 1947
paintings: (L) $8,800; (H) $15,525
drawings: (L) $990; (H) $7,150
sculpture: (L) $16,100; (H) $57,500

LEVINSEN, Sophus Teobald
French 1869-1943
paintings: (H) $2,185

LEVIS, Maurice
French 1860-after 1927
paintings: (L) $1,100; (H) $17,600
drawings: (H) $440

LEVISON, Nanna
Scandinavian 19th/20th cent.
paintings: (H) $6,325

LEVITAN, Isaac Ilyitch
Lithuanian 1860-1900
paintings: (L) $4,600; (H) $19,800

LEVITT, Joel
American 20th cent.
paintings: (H) $748

LEVOLGER, A.
19th cent.
paintings: (H) $5,750

LEVOW, Irving
American b. 1902
paintings: (H) $1,265

LEVUS, Jesus
Mexican 20th cent.
paintings: (H) $2,310

LEVY, Alexander
American 1881-1947
paintings: (L) $247; (H) $3,080

LEVY, Beatrice S.
American 1892-1974
paintings: (L) $230; (H) $920

LEVY, Charles Octave
French d. 1899
sculpture: (L) $3,080; (H) $3,575

LEVY, Emile
French 1826-1890
paintings: (L) $4,600; (H) $43,125

LEVY, H.L.
19th cent.
paintings: (H) $1,100

LEVY, Henri Leopold
French 1840-1904
paintings: (H) $9,775

LEVY, Nat
American 1896-1984
drawings: (L) $1,650; (H) $2,475

LEVY-DHURMER, Lucien
French 1865-1953
paintings: (H) $112,500
drawings: (L) $1,100; (H) $3,450

LEWANDOWSKI, Edmund D.
American b. 1914
paintings: (H) $230
drawings: (H) $3,680

LEWESS (?), J.
paintings: (H) $990

LEWIN, Stephen
ac. 1890-1910
paintings: (L) $3,300; (H) $3,300

LEWIS, A.
paintings: (H) $1,150

LEWIS, Alonzo W.
American 1886-1946
paintings: (H) $1,210

LEWIS, Archie Henry
American 20th cent.
paintings: (H) $690

LEWIS, Charles James
British 1830-1892
paintings: (L) $575; (H) $2,750

LEWIS, E.
Continental School 19th/20th cent.
drawings: (H) $690

LEWIS, Edmonia
American 1843/45- after 1911
sculpture: (L) $9,775; (H) $87,750

LEWIS, Edmund Darch
American 1835-1910
paintings: (L) $495; (H) $25,300
drawings: (L) $77; (H) $3,850

LEWIS, Frederick
British 19th/20th cent.
paintings: (H) $4,140

LEWIS, Harry Emerson
American 1892-1958
paintings: (L) $110; (H) $2,875
drawings: (H) $522

LEWIS, Henry
English/German 1819-1904
paintings: (L) $715; (H) $2,530

LEWIS, Jeanette Maxfield
American 1894-1982
paintings: (H) $990

LEWIS, John
American b. 1942
sculpture: (L) $3,850; (H) $9,200

LEWIS, John Frederick
English 1805-1876
drawings: (H) $3,520

LEWIS, Laura Craven
American b. 1874
paintings: (H) $715

LEWIS, Martin
American 1881/83-1962
paintings: (H) $1,320
drawings: (L) $715; (H) $5,775

LEWIS, Phillips F.
American 1892-1930
paintings: (L) $1,495; (H) $17,250

LEWIS, Thomas L.
American b. 1907
paintings: (L) $100; (H) $500

LEWIS, William
drawings: (L) $93; (H) $1,093

LEWISOHN, Raphael
German 1863-1923
paintings: (L) $225; (H) $3,575

LEWITT, Sol
American b. 1928
paintings: (H) $3,300
drawings: (L) $1,100; (H) $82,500
sculpture: (L) $2,530; (H) $126,500

LEWY, James
American 19th cent.
paintings: (L) $467; (H) $880

LEXINGTON
paintings: (L) $660; (H) $3,300

LEY, Sophie
German 1859-1918
paintings: (H) $9,200

LEYDENFROST, Alexander
1888-1961
drawings: (L) $1,100; (H) $1,540

LEYENDECKER, Frank X.
American 1877/78-1924
paintings: (L) $1,650; (H) $11,000

LEYENDECKER, Joseph Christian
American 1874-1951
paintings: (L) $550; (H) $52,800
drawings: (H) $275

LEYENDECKER, Paul Joseph
French b. 1842
paintings: (L) $460; (H) $1,980

LEYS, Baron Hendrik
Belgian 1815-1869
paintings: (H) $17,250
drawings: (H) $403

LEYSTER, Judith
Dutch c. 1600-1660
paintings: (H) $115,500

**LEZAY-MARNESIA DE
NETTANCOURT,** Marie Claudine
Marquise de
French d. 1793
paintings: (H) $935

LHERMITTE, Leon Augustin
French 1844-1925
paintings: (L) $19,550; (H) $528,000
drawings: (L) $1,725; (H) $74,000

LHOEST, Eugene Leon
French 1874-1937
sculpture: (L) $1,840; (H) $1,840

LHOTE, Andre
French 1885-1962
paintings: (L) $3,850; (H) $244,500
drawings: (L) $605; (H) $11,000
sculpture: (H) $8,625

LHUILLIER, Jacques
French b. 1867
paintings: (H) $11,000

LI HUASHENG
Chinese b. 1944
drawings: (H) $2,875

LI RUIQING, Li Jui-ch'ing
1867-1920
drawings: (H) $1,955

LIANG, Yen Wan
Chinese
paintings: (H) $1,760

LIANI, Fernand
Italian 19th cent.
sculpture: (H) $2,587

LIAP, P.R.
paintings: (H) $489

LIAUTUD, Georges
sculpture: (H) $1,210

LIBBY, Francis Orville
American b. 1884
paintings: (L) $88; (H) $1,045

LIBENSKY, Stanislav
sculpture: (H) $1,430

LIBENSKY, Stanislav and Jaroslava
BRYCHTOVA
sculpture: (H) $6,900

LIBENSKY, Stanislav and Jaroslava
BRYCHTOVA-LIBENSKYA
Czechoslovakian both b. 1921
sculpture: (L) $7,475; (H) $14,950

LIBERI, Marco
1640-after 1725
paintings: (H) $18,400

LIBERI, Pietro, called Libertino
Italian 1614-1687
paintings: (L) $17,600; (H) $44,000

LIBERMAN, Alexander
Russian/American b. 1912
paintings: (L) $440; (H) $5,500
drawings: (L) $115; (H) $1,610
sculpture: (L) $990; (H) $66,000

LIBERMANN, Max
German 1847-1935
paintings: (H) $5,175

LIBERTE, Jean
American 1895-1965
paintings: (L) $110; (H) $550
drawings: (L) $137; (H) $247

LIBERTI, Carlos
paintings: (H) $7,700

LIBERTI, F.
18th cent.
paintings: (H) $7,700

LIBERTS, Ludolf
Latvian 1895-1945
paintings: (L) $863; (H) $5,500

LICHTENBERG, Manes
American b. 1920
paintings: (L) $1,955; (H) $4,025

LICHTENSTEIN, Roy
American b. 1923
paintings: (L) $1,610; (H) $2,532,500
drawings: (L) $1,430; (H) $244,500
sculpture: (L) $1,265; (H) $165,000

LICINIO, Bernardino
Italian c. 1489-after 1565
paintings: (L) $15,400; (H) $88,000

LIDDERDALE, Charles Sillem
English 1831-1895
paintings: (L) $1,650; (H) $12,650

LIDOV, Arthur Herschel
American b. 1917
paintings: (H) $1,150

LIE, Jonas
American 1880-1940
paintings: (L) $330; (H) $82,500
drawings: (L) $55; (H) $6,600

LIE, Robert
Danish/American 1899-1980
paintings: (L) $495; (H) $1,610

LIEBENWEIN, Maximilian
Austrian 1869-1926
paintings: (H) $3,850
drawings: (H) $220

LIEBER, Edvard
b. 1948
drawings: (H) $2,090

LIEBER, Tom
American b. 1949
paintings: (L) $1,035; (H) $1,840

LIEBERICH, Nicolai Ivanovich
Russian 19th cent.
sculpture: (L) $2,475; (H) $3,080

LIEBERMAN, Alexander
sculpture: (H) $3,300

LIEBERMAN, Harry
1876-1983
paintings: (H) $2,090

LIEBERMANN, Max
German 1847-1935
paintings: (L) $4,675; (H) $363,000
drawings: (L) $374; (H) $66,000

LIEBERS, A.
paintings: (H) $6,600

LIEBMAN, Aline Meyer
1879-1966
paintings: (H) $1,035

LIEBMANN, Gerhardt
American 20th cent.
paintings: (L) $1,045; (H) $1,650

LIEBOWITZ, Cary
b. 1963
sculpture: (H) $495

LIEFELD/GORDON, Robb
drawings: (H) $770

LIEGOIS, Paul
French 17th cent.
paintings: (H) $24,200

LIENDER, Paulus van
1727-1779
drawings: (H) $715

LIENZ, Egger Jules
Swiss 19th cent.
paintings: (H) $1,650

LIEPKE, Skip
b. 1933
paintings: (H) $5,225

LIETO, A. de
Italian 20th cent.
paintings: (H) $1,045

LIEVENS, Jan
Dutch 1607-1672/74
paintings: (H) $44,000

LIEVIN
French 20th cent.
paintings: (H) $1,320

LIEVRE, Lucien
French b. 1878
paintings: (H) $2,860

LIGARE, David
paintings: (L) $1,650; (H) $9,900

LIGORIO, Pirro
Italian c. 1500-1583
drawings: (H) $20,700

LIGOZZI, Bartolomeo
Italian 1630-1695
paintings: (H) $24,150

LIGOZZI, Jacopo, or Giacomo
Italian c. 1547-1627
paintings: (L) $104,500; (H) $308,000

LIGTELIJN, Evert Jan
Dutch 19th/20th cent.
paintings: (H) $990

LILDEFORS, Bruno
Swedish 1860-1939
paintings: (H) $13,200

LILES, Catherine
b. 1944
drawings: (H) $4,400

LILIO, Andrea
Italian c. 1570-c. 1631
drawings: (H) $14,950

LILJEFORS, Bruno
Swedish 1860-1939
paintings: (L) $29,900; (H) $79,500

LILJESTROM, Gustave
Swedish/American 1882-1958
paintings: (L) $1,150; (H) $5,750

LILLYWHITE, Raphael
1891-1980
paintings: (H) $1,955

LILS, Ivan
paintings: (H) $1,320

LIMA, H. Rosa van
Peruvian 19th cent.
sculpture: (H) $4,600

LIMBORCH, Hendrick van
Dutch 1681-1759
paintings: (H) $6,325

LIMOUSIN
sculpture: (L) $495; (H) $990

LIN, Hans
ac. late 17th cent.
paintings: (H) $11,000

LIN MEISHU, Lin MEI-SHU
Chinese 20th cent.
drawings: (H) $920

LINARD, Jacques
French c. 1600-1645
paintings: (L) $71,500; (H) $112,500

LINCOLN, Ephriam Frank
paintings: (L) $550; (H) $1,100

LINCOLN, James Sullivan
American 1811-1888
paintings: (L) $6,600; (H) $7,700

LINDAU, Dietrich Wilhelm
German 1799-1862
paintings: (H) $4,400

LINDBORG, Carl
American b. 1903
paintings: (L) $22; (H) $880

LINDE, Ossip L.
American 1871-1940
paintings: (L) $440; (H) $3,850

LINDEMANN, C.
Continental 19th cent.
paintings: (H) $935

LINDEMANN-FROMMEL, Karl
August
German 1819-1891
paintings: (H) $7,187

LINDENBERG, M.
sculpture: (L) $345; (H) $690

LINDENMUTH, Tod
American 1885-1976
paintings: (L) $160; (H) $2,420

LINDER, Harry
American 1886-1931
drawings: (L) $165; (H) $690

LINDER, Henry
American 1854-1910
sculpture: (H) $2,760

LINDER, Philippe Jacques
French ac. 1857-1880
paintings: (L) $1,430; (H) $25,300

LINDERUM, Richard
German b. 1851
paintings: (L) $3,850; (H) $14,950

LINDH, Bror
Swedish 1877-1941
paintings: (H) $46,750

LINDIN, Carl Olaf Eric
Swedish/American 1869-1942
paintings: (L) $330; (H) $1,540

LINDNER, Ernest
Canadian 1897-1988
drawings: (L) $1,650; (H) $3,410

LINDNER, Richard
German/American 1901-1978
paintings: (L) $51,750; (H) $319,000
drawings: (L) $1,955; (H) $47,150

LINDNEUX, Robert
1871-1970
paintings: (L) $77; (H) $2,070

LINDON
American 19th cent.
paintings: (H) $4,400

LINDQUIST, Carl Magnus
Swedish b. 1884
paintings: (H) $467

LINDSAY, H.
paintings: (H) $990

LINDSAY, Seymour
American 1848-1927
paintings: (L) $715; (H) $1,100

LINDSAY, Thomas Corwin
American 1845-1907
paintings: (L) $220; (H) $2,185

LINDSTROM, Arvid Mauritz
Swedish 1849-1923
paintings: (H) $2,588

LINDSTROM, Bengt
Swedish b. 1935
paintings: (L) $7,188; (H) $22,000

LINFORD, Charles
American 1846-1897
paintings: (L) $220; (H) $1,495

LINGELBACH, Johannes
Dutch c. 1622-1674
paintings: (H) $33,000

LINGENFELDER, Eugen
German b. 1862
paintings: (L) $660; (H) $2,875

LINGKE, Albert Muller
German b. 1844
paintings: (H) $5,775

LINGQUIST, A.
paintings: (H) $660

LINK, Carl
American b. 1887
drawings: (L) $440; (H) $880

LINKE, J. Conrad
paintings: (H) $2,420

LINKE, Simon
American b. 1958
paintings: (L) $1,380; (H) $11,000
drawings: (H) $13,200

LINLEY, Dora K.
American 20th cent.
paintings: (H) $522
drawings: (H) $5

LINNEL, John
paintings: (H) $6,600

LINNELL, John
English 1792-1882
paintings: (H) $1,650
drawings: (H) $2,475

LINNELL, William
British b. 1826
paintings: (H) $9,900

LINNIG, Egidius
Flemish 1821-1860
paintings: (L) $8,250; (H) $21,850

LINNIG, Willem, the elder
Belgian 1819-1885
paintings: (L) $2,760; (H) $3,738

LINO, Gustave
Italian b. 1893
paintings: (H) $2,990

LINO, Selvatico
paintings: (H) $880

LINS, Adolf
German 1856-1927
paintings: (L) $715; (H) $17,600

LINSON, Corwin Knapp
American 1864-1959
paintings: (L) $187; (H) $6,875

LINT, Hendrik Frans van, called
Monsu Studio
Flemish 1684-1763
paintings: (L) $20,700; (H) $107,000

LINTON, Frank Benton
American 1871-1943
paintings: (H) $1,430

LINTON, H.A.
British 19th cent.
drawings: (H) $880

LINTON, Sir James Dromgole
English 1840-1916
drawings: (H) $3,680

LINTON, William
British 1791-1876
paintings: (L) $1,000; (H) $1,760

LINTOTT, Edward Barnard
American 1875-1951
paintings: (L) $110; (H) $1,955
drawings: (L) $44; (H) $275

LINTZ, Frederik
Belgian 1824-1909
paintings: (H) $13,800

LINVILLE, Marlin
American b. 1950
paintings: (L) $4,400; (H) $4,400

LINZONI, P.
Italian 20th cent.
paintings: (H) $3,190

LIONELLI, *
Italian 19th cent.
paintings: (H) $660

LIONELLI, D.
Italian 19th/20th cent.
paintings: (H) $978

LIONNE, Enrico
Italian 1865-1921
paintings: (H) $48,300

LIONNI, Leo
sculpture: (H) $1,210

LIPCHITZ, Jacques
French/American 1891-1973
paintings: (H) $132,000
drawings: (L) $1,155; (H) $8,625
sculpture: (L) $1,610; (H) $530,500

LIPIND, Henri
French ac. 1880
paintings: (H) $16,100

LIPOFSKY, Marvin
American b. 1938
sculpture: (L) $82; (H) $8,800

LIPPI, Fillippino, workshop of
15th/16th cent.
paintings: (H) $34,500

LIPPINCOTT, William Henry
American 1849-1920
paintings: (L) $550; (H) $13,200
drawings: (L) $990; (H) $15,400

LIPPINE
American 19th cent.
paintings: (H) $4,070

LIPPOLD, Richard
20th cent.
drawings: (H) $1,610

LIPPS, Richard
German 1857-1926
paintings: (L) $14,300; (H) $16,500
drawings: (H) $770

LIPSKI, Donald
American b. 1947
sculpture: (L) $288; (H) $4,025

LIPSZYC, Samuel
French ac. 1918-1935
sculpture: (H) $4,600

LIPTON, Seymour
American b. 1903
drawings: (H) $715
sculpture: (L) $18,700; (H) $33,000

LIRA, Pedro
Chilean 19th cent.
paintings: (H) $12,650

LISIO, Arnaldo de
Italian b. 1869
paintings: (L) $1,045; (H) $1,100
drawings: (L) $330; (H) $2,420

LISIO, Michael de
sculpture: (H) $4,400

LISMER, Arthur
Canadian 1885-1969
paintings: (L) $2,200; (H) $26,400
drawings: (L) $770; (H) $1,650

LISSE, Dirck van der
Dutch d. 1669
paintings: (L) $4,950; (H) $17,600

LIST, Wilhelm
Austrian 1864-1918
drawings: (L) $550; (H) $825

LISZEWSKI, Christian Friedrich
Reinhold
German 1725-1794
paintings: (H) $20,700

LITTERMAN, Anne
b. 1956
paintings: (L) $7,150; (H) $8,250

LITTLE, John Geoffrey Carruthers
Canadian b. 1920
paintings: (L) $3,300; (H) $4,125

LITTLE, Philip
American 1857-1942
paintings: (L) $303; (H) $13,800
drawings: (L) $165; (H) $385

LITTLEJOHN, Cynthia Pugh
American d. 1959
drawings: (H) $2,200

LITTLEJOHN, Hugh Warwick
American 1892-1938
paintings: (H) $1,495

LITTLETON, Harvey K.
American b. 1922
sculpture: (L) $2,760; (H) $13,800

LITTROW, Leo von
Italian 1860-1914
paintings: (H) $880

LITZINGER, Dorothea M.
American 1889-1925
paintings: (L) $275; (H) $4,600
drawings: (L) $220; (H) $302

LIVEMONT, Privat
Belgian 1852/61-1936
paintings: (H) $9,900

LIVENS, Horace Mann
British b. 1862
paintings: (H) $467

LIVESAY, John
ac. 1799-1832
drawings: (H) $2,588

LIVINGSTON, Major Edward
1837-1898
paintings: (H) $880

LIVINIO DA ***
ac. 1596
paintings: (H) $16,500

LIZARD, Kate
Continental 19th cent.
sculpture: (H) $1,150

LIZCANO, A.
Continental 19th cent.
paintings: (L) $633; (H) $660

LIZCANO Y ESTEBAN, Angel
Spanish 1846-1929
paintings: (H) $7,475

LJUBA
paintings: (H) $6,050

LLANOS Y VALDES, Sebastian de
c. 1605-1677
paintings: (H) $19,550

LLASERA Y DIAZ, Jose
Spanish b. 1882
paintings: (H) $2,415

LLONA, Ramiro
b. Peru 1947
paintings: (L) $5,750; (H) $25,300

LLOPIS, Carlos Ruano
Spanish b. 1879
paintings: (L) $1,320; (H) $6,325

LLORENTE, Bernardo German
Spanish 1680-1759
paintings: (H) $3,960

LLOYD, Helen Sharpless
American 20th cent.
paintings: (H) $1,100

LLOYD, J.C.
British 19th cent.
paintings: (H) $8,800

LLOYD, James
British 1906-1974
drawings: (H) $1,540

LLOYD, Llewelyn
Italian 1879-1950
paintings: (H) $748

LLOYD, Marcia
paintings: (H) $3,300

LLOYD, Stuart
English ac. 1875-1929
paintings: (H) $2,200
drawings: (L) $198; (H) $1,760

LLOYD, Thomas Ivester
British 1873-1942
drawings: (L) $863; (H) $2,875

LLOYD, Thomas James
English 1849-1910
paintings: (L) $1,320; (H) $2,875

LLULL, Jose Pinello
Spanish 1861-1922
paintings: (L) $2,875; (H) $6,050

LLYOD, J**C**
English 19th/20th cent.
paintings: (H) $1,210

LOAGA, D.
Continental 19th cent.
paintings: (H) $2,875

LOAN, Dorothy van
American b. 1904
paintings: (L) $357; (H) $495

LOATES, Martin Glen
b. 1945
drawings: (L) $1,540; (H) $3,850

LOBBE, A. de
paintings: (H) $3,450

LOBBEDEZ, Charles Auguste Romain
French 1825-1882
paintings: (H) $8,800

LOBDELL, Frank
American b. 1921
paintings: (L) $3,025; (H) $4,675
drawings: (H) $1,380

LOBE, Robert
sculpture: (H) $3,738

LOBEJOGER, W.
paintings: (H) $825

LOBER, George John
American b. 1892
sculpture: (H) $23,000

LOBINGIER, Elizabeth Miller
American 1889-1973
paintings: (L) $467; (H) $715

LOBRE, Maurice
French 1862-1951
paintings: (H) $1,265

LOBRICHON, Timoleon Marie
French 1831-1914
paintings: (L) $4,370; (H) $8,250

LOCATELLI, Andrea
Italian 1693-1741
paintings: (L) $11,500; (H) $55,200

LOCCA, Albert
Swiss 1895-1966
paintings: (L) $550; (H) $690

LOCHER, Carl
Danish 1851-1915
paintings: (H) $4,400

LOCHER, Thomas
b. 1956
paintings: (L) $2,875; (H) $8,050
sculpture: (H) $6,600

LOCK(?), Cesar de
19th cent.
paintings: (H) $1,760

LOCKER, Edward Hawker
British 1777-1848
drawings: (H) $880

LOCKHART, David
drawings: (H) $825

LOCKHART, William Ewart
drawings: (H) $1,100

LOCKHEAD, John
English
paintings: (H) $550

LOCKMAN, Dewitt McClellan
American 1870-1957
paintings: (L) $58; (H) $4,400

LOCKWOOD, W.
19th cent.
drawings: (H) $798

LOCKWOOD, Ward
American 1894-1963
drawings: (H) $1,760

LOCKWOOD, Wilton Lyon
American 1862-1914
paintings: (H) $9,900

LODATO, Peter
American b. 1946
paintings: (H) $1,904
drawings: (L) $27; (H) $44

LODDER, Warren W.
American 19th/20th cent.
paintings: (H) $935

LODER, James
British 1784-1860
paintings: (L) $7,700; (H) $18,400

LODER, Matthaus
1781-1828
drawings: (H) $3,450

LODGE, George Edward
English 1860-1954
paintings: (L) $8,625; (H) $13,800
drawings: (L) $88; (H) $2,420

LODGE, Reginald
British ac. 1881-1892
paintings: (H) $6,600

LODI, Gaetano
Italian ac. c. 1850
paintings: (L) $550; (H) $6,050

LOEB, Dorothy
American b. 1887
paintings: (L) $165; (H) $523
drawings: (L) $55; (H) $660

LOEB, Louis
American 1866-1909
paintings: (L) $220; (H) $4,400

LOEBER, Lou
Dutch 1894-1983
paintings: (L) $3,300; (H) $6,050

LOEMANS, Alexander Francois
Canadian ac. 1882-1894
paintings: (L) $1,650; (H) $13,200

LOERR (?), C.
sculpture: (H) $990

LOESCH, Ernst
Austrian b. 1860
paintings: (H) $4,600

LOFFLER, Hugo
German b. 1859
paintings: (H) $1,430

LOFTUS, Peter
paintings: (H) $1,430

LOGAN, Erle
American b. 1905
drawings: (H) $1,840

LOGAN, Maurice
American 1886-1977
paintings: (L) $605; (H) $26,450
drawings: (L) $385; (H) $1,725

LOGAN, Robert Fulton
Canadian b. 1899
paintings: (L) $137; (H) $633

LOGAN, Robert Henry
American 1874-1942
paintings: (L) $83; (H) $550

LOGE, Daniel
paintings: (L) $99; (H) $990

LOGEROT, Louise
French 19th cent.
drawings: (H) $1,650

LOGIJUSTE, Joseph
sculpture: (H) $1,210

LOGRIPPO, Robert
b. 1947
paintings: (H) $2,530

LOGSDAIL, William
English 1859-1944
paintings: (H) $3,850

LOHMANN, C.
paintings: (L) $440; (H) $578

LOHR
German late 19th cent.
paintings: (H) $1,540

LOHR, Augusto
German/Mexican 1843-1919
paintings: (L) $23,000; (H) $55,200

LOIR, Luigi
French 1845-1916
paintings: (L) $2,420; (H) $123,500
drawings: (L) $4,950; (H) $85,000

LOIS, Jacob
Dutch 1620-1676
paintings: (H) $18,400

LOISEAU, Gustave
French 1865-1935
paintings: (L) $8,800; (H) $154,000
drawings: (H) $7,475

LOJACONO, Francesco
Italian 1841-1915
paintings: (L) $11,500; (H) $55,000

LOJACONO, Luigi
Italian 19th/20th cent.
paintings: (H) $9,200

LOKHORST, Dirk Pieter van
Dutch 1818-1893
paintings: (L) $605; (H) $1,610

LOMAX, John Arthur
British 1857-1923
paintings: (L) $1,540; (H) $1,870

LOMBARDI, Giovanni Battista
Italian 1823-1880
sculpture: (L) $7,150; (H) $50,600

LOMBARDI, Giovita
Italian 1837-1876
sculpture: (H) $3,300

LOMBARDO, Tullio, workshop of
Venetian c. 1500
sculpture: (H) $16,100

LOMBOG, Arthur Lasslow
American 19th cent.
paintings: (H) $770

LOMMEN, Wilhelm
German 1838-1895
paintings: (H) $2,300

LONA, J.
paintings: (H) $550

LONDER, J.A.
Dutch late 18th cent.
paintings: (H) $8,800

LONDONIO, Francesco
1723-1783
drawings: (H) $2,875

LONE WOLF
1882-1965
paintings: (H) $2,860

LONG, Christopher
b. 1946
paintings: (L) $20,900; (H) $31,900

LONG, Edwin
English 1829-1891
paintings: (L) $431; (H) $387,500

LONG, L.
Continental School 19th cent.
paintings: (H) $3,850

LONG, Richard
American b. 1945
paintings: (L) $6,050; (H) $38,500
drawings: (L) $3,738; (H) $29,700
sculpture: (L) $27,600; (H) $148,500

LONG, Steve
American 20th cent.
drawings: (H) $468

LONG, Ted
American 20th cent.
paintings: (H) $522

LONGBIS
paintings: (H) $770

LONGCHAMP, Henriette de
French 19th cent.
paintings: (H) $12,075

LONGENECKIR, Paul
American 20th cent.
paintings: (H) $805

LONGFELLOW, Ernest Wadsworth
American 1845-1921
paintings: (L) $275; (H) $2,750

LONGFELLOW, Mary K.
American 1852-1945
drawings: (L) $115; (H) $743

LONGHI, Alessandro
Italian 1733-1813
paintings: (H) $46,750

LONGHI, Barbara
Italian 1552-1638
paintings: (H) $11,000

LONGHI, Luca, called Raphael de
Ravenna
Italian 1507-1580
paintings: (L) $12,650; (H) $13,200

LONGHI, Pietro
Italian 1702-1785
paintings: (L) $30,800; (H) $330,000

LONGI
Italian 20th cent.
paintings: (H) $2,200

LONGMAN, Evelyn Beatrice
American 1874-1954
sculpture: (L) $880; (H) $3,910

LONGMORE, Ken
American
paintings: (H) $650

LONGO, Robert
American b. 1953
paintings: (L) $1,650; (H) $42,550
drawings: (L) $1,610; (H) $49,500
sculpture: (L) $2,990; (H) $38,500

LONGPRE, M. de
French 19th/20th cent.
drawings: (H) $1,610

LONGSTAFFE, Edgar
British 1849-1912
paintings: (H) $2,415

LONGSTREET, Stephen
American 20th cent.
paintings: (L) $345; (H) $690

LONGUET, Alexandre Marie
French 1805-1851
drawings: (H) $550

LONGUET, Frederic
paintings: (H) $1,725

LOO, Carle van
French 1705-1765
paintings: (L) $5,500; (H) $244,500

LOO, Jacob van
Dutch c. 1614-1670
paintings: (H) $22,000

LOO, Jules Cesar Denis van
French 1743-1821
paintings: (L) $8,250; (H) $25,875

LOO, Louis Michel van
Flemish/French 1707-1771
paintings: (L) $4,887; (H) $79,500

LOO, Pieter van
1731-1784
drawings: (L) $1,980; (H) $16,500

LOOK, Donna
contemporary
sculpture: (H) $1,265

LOOMIS, Andrew
American 1892-1959
paintings: (L) $1,100; (H) $6,600
drawings: (H) $4,400

LOOMIS, Charles Russell
American 1857-1936
paintings: (H) $1,380
drawings: (L) $55; (H) $440

LOOMIS, Chester
American 1854-1924
paintings: (L) $275; (H) $1,955
drawings: (H) $220

LOOMIS, Osbert Burr
American 1813-1886
paintings: (L) $546; (H) $3,300

LOOMIS, William Andrew
American 1892-1959
paintings: (L) $358; (H) $3,850

LOOP, H.B.
paintings: (H) $2,640

LOOP, Henry Augustus
American 1831-1895
paintings: (L) $440; (H) $1,210

LOOP, Jennette S.H.
1840-1909
paintings: (L) $632; (H) $1,650

LOOPER, Willem de
American b. 1932
paintings: (L) $99; (H) $863

LOOS, John
Belgian ac. 1871-1875
paintings: (L) $5,225; (H) $6,900

LOOSE, Basile de
Dutch 1809-1885
paintings: (L) $2,760; (H) $27,500

LOPER, Brock
American b. 1935
paintings: (L) $605; (H) $990
drawings: (H) $385

LOPER, Edward
American b. 1906
paintings: (L) $110; (H) $523

LOPEZ, Andres
paintings: (L) $3,737; (H) $20,700

LOPEZ, Gasparo, called Gasparo di
Fiori
Italian 1650-1732
paintings: (L) $13,200; (H) $43,700

LOPEZ, Gasparo and Paolo Di
MATTEIS
Italian 17th/18th cent.
paintings: (H) $28,600

LOPEZ CABRERA, Ricardo
Spanish b. 1866
paintings: (H) $41,400

LOPEZ DE VICTORIA, Jose
1898-1948
paintings: (H) $4,370

LOPEZ DIRUBE, Rolando
b. 1928
drawings: (H) $1,093

LOPEZ SAENZ, Antonio
paintings: (H) $10,450

LOPEZ Y PORTANA, Don Vincenti
Spanish 1772-1850
paintings: (L) $18,400; (H) $35,750

LOPEZ-REY,
paintings: (L) $1,840; (H) $2,860

LORAN, Erle
American b. 1905
paintings: (L) $1,320; (H) $3,850
drawings: (L) $748; (H) $4,025

LORBER, Stephen
20th cent.
paintings: (H) $4,312

LORD, Andrew
b. England 1950
drawings: (H) $2,645
sculpture: (H) $42,550

LORD, Caroline
American b. 1860
paintings: (H) $935

LORENZ, Richard
German/American 1858-1915
paintings: (L) $385; (H) $4,125

LORENZ, Willi
paintings: (H) $1,100

LORENZI, Francesco
Italian c. 1719-1787
paintings: (L) $22,000; (H) $33,350

LORENZINI, Sandro
Italian/American 20th cent.
sculpture: (H) $1,650

LORENZL, Joseph
sculpture: (L) $431; (H) $4,025

LORENZL, K.
French ac. 1910-1930
sculpture: (L) $1,430; (H) $13,200

LORIA, Vincenzo
Italian b. 1850
paintings: (L) $460; (H) $5,500
drawings: (L) $193; (H) $770

LORIMIER, Etienne Chevalier de
French 1759-1813
paintings: (H) $68,500

LORINCZ
Hungarian 20th cent.
paintings: (H) $1,210

LORING, David, Jr.
drawings: (H) $1,100

LORJOU, Bernard
French 1908-1986
paintings: (L) $1,500; (H) $14,300

LORMIER, J.
sculpture: (H) $2,760

LORRAIN, Claude, Claude GELLEE
French 1600-1682
paintings: (H) $310,500
drawings: (L) $26,400; (H) $203,500

LORY, Mathais Gabriel
Swiss 1784-1846
drawings: (H) $990

LOS, F.
19th cent.
paintings: (H) $1,760

LOSONCZY, John A.
paintings: (L) $150; (H) $500

LOSQUES, Daniel Thoroude de, called
Daniel THOROUDE
French 1880-1915
drawings: (H) $920

LOSSBERG, E.
German 19th cent.
paintings: (H) $1,650

LOSSI, T.
Italian 19th cent.
drawings: (H) $3,575

LOSSOW, Heinrich
German 1843-1897
paintings: (L) $863; (H) $3,850

LOSTUTTER, Robert
American contemporary
drawings: (H) $920

LOTH, Johann Karl
German 1632-1698
drawings: (H) $12,100

LOTIRON, Robert
paintings: (L) $715; (H) $2,530

LOTT, E.
Dutch 19th cent.
paintings: (L) $230; (H) $1,375

LOTTI, G.
Italian 17th/18th cent.
paintings: (H) $495

LOTTO, Lorenzo
Italian 1480-1556
drawings: (H) $44,000

LOTZ, Matilda
American 1858-1923
paintings: (L) $550; (H) $5,500

LOUCHET
sculpture: (L) $977; (H) $3,163

LOUCHET, Paul Francois
French 1854-1936
paintings: (H) $935

LOUCHET FRERES
French 19th/20th cent.
sculpture: (H) $5,500

LOUDERBACK, Walt
American 1887-1941
paintings: (L) $770; (H) $9,350
drawings: (H) $495

LOUGHEED, Robert Elmer
American 1910-1981
paintings: (L) $770; (H) $9,900
drawings: (L) $330; (H) $6,600

LOUIS, John F.
paintings: (H) $1,380

LOUIS, Morris
American 1912-1962
paintings: (L) $8,250; (H) $385,000

LOUIS, Paul
French 19th cent.
paintings: (H) $4,370

LOUPOT, Charles
French 1892-1962
drawings: (H) $9,900

LOURDES, Manuel Guillermo
b. Mexico 1898
paintings: (L) $6,600; (H) $8,800

LOUREIRO, Rita
Brazilian b. 1952
paintings: (H) $16,100

LOUSSAINT, Frank
Haitian 20th cent.
paintings: (H) $467

LOUSTAUNAU, Auguste Louis
Georges
French 1846-1898
paintings: (L) $8,338; (H) $32,200

LOUTERBURG, William
drawings: (H) $4,600

LOUTHERBOURG, Philippe Jacques
de
British 1740-1812
paintings: (H) $25,300
drawings: (H) $518

LOUVRIER, Maurice
1878-1954
paintings: (H) $3,850

LOUX, A.
French 19th/20th cent.
paintings: (H) $1,035

LOUYOT, Edmond
German 19th cent.
paintings: (L) $403; (H) $3,080

LOUYOT, Emile
French 19th cent.
paintings: (H) $12,650

LOVATTI, E. Augusto
Italian b. 1816
paintings: (L) $3,300; (H) $13,200

LOVE, John
paintings: (H) $660

LOVEJOY, Rupert Scott
American 1885-1975
paintings: (L) $110; (H) $770

LOVELING, J.
American 19th cent.
paintings: (H) $633

LOVELL, Katherine Adams
American ac. c. 1915-1923
paintings: (L) $110; (H) $690

LOVELL, Tom
American b. 1909
paintings: (L) $990; (H) $66,000
drawings: (L) $880; (H) $9,625

LOVELY, Candace Whittemore
American
paintings: (L) $220; (H) $2,750

LOVEN, Frank W.
American 1869-1941
paintings: (L) $220; (H) $3,220

LOVERIDGE, Clinton
American 1824-1902
paintings: (L) $247; (H) $3,850

LOVERIDGE, Rose
American 19th cent.
paintings: (H) $605

LOVET-LORSKI, Boris
Lithuanian/Am. 1894-1973
sculpture: (L) $935; (H) $151,000

LOVEWELL, R.
American 19th cent.
paintings: (H) $880

LOVING, Richard
American contemporary
paintings: (L) $330; (H) $770

LOVINS, Henry
American 1883-1960
paintings: (L) $413; (H) $1,320

LOVMAND, Christine Marie
Danish 1803-1872
paintings: (H) $2,300

LOW, Laurence G.
American b. 1912
paintings: (L) $303; (H) $550

LOW, Mary Fairchild
American 1858-1946
paintings: (L) $275; (H) $26,400

What's Her Name?

Researching a woman artist can sometimes be very difficult. Many women artists sign their works with their maiden name, their married name, or with Mrs. and their husband's name. Mary Fairchild (1858-1946) studied at the St. Louis Art Academy and at the Académie Julien in Paris. In 1888 she married the famous sculptor Frederick MacMonnies. When MacMonnies fell in love with one of his students, the couple divorced. In 1909 Mary married William Low, another artist, and they moved to New York. After her second marriage, Mary dropped the MacMonnies name. Auction records and reference books list her as Mary MacMonnies, Mary Low, Mary Fairchild, and Mary L. Fairchild. Petty's *Dictionary of Women Artists* is a reliable reference source for women artists and cross-indexes maiden and married names.

This light-filled painting of two women chatting was painted in 1887, a year before her first marriage. Catalogued as by Mary Fairchild, a record price was achieved when *Two Women Chatting in a Garden with a Mill in the Background* sold for $26,400. (Mary Fairchild Low, *Two Women Chatting in a Garden with a Mill in the Background*, oil on canvas, 70 x 56 inches, Dargate, June 10, 1995, $26,400)

LOW, Will Hicok
  American 1853-1932
  paintings: (L) $550; (H) $10,350
  drawings: (H) $1,980

LOW, William
  b. 1959
  paintings: (H) $495

LOWCOCK, Charles F.
  paintings: (L) $770; (H) $2,200

LOWE, Agatha
  Austrian 20th cent.
  paintings: (H) $4,180

LOWELL, Milton H.
  American 1848-1927
  paintings: (L) $275; (H) $2,310

LOWELL, Orson
  American 1871-1956
  paintings: (H) $5,775
  drawings: (L) $176; (H) $1,650

LOWES, Sadie H.
  American b. 1870
  paintings: (H) $770

LOWITH, Wilhelm
  Austrian b. 1861
  paintings: (L) $2,090; (H) $5,060

LOWMANS, B.
paintings: (H) $660

LOWNDES, Alan
1921-1978
paintings: (H) $880

LOWRIE, Alexander
American 1828-1917
paintings: (H) $990

LOWRY, Sarah
American 20th cent.
paintings: (H) $550

LOWVILLE, W.J. Allen
paintings: (H) $2,530

LOYEUX, Charles Antoine Joseph
French 1823-1893
paintings: (L) $1,870; (H) $26,400

LOYSEN, Arthur
American 20th cent.
paintings: (H) $715

LOZADA, T. Rodriguez
paintings: (H) $650

LOZANO, Margarita
b. France 1936
paintings: (L) $6,050; (H) $10,450

LOZOWICK, Louis
American 1892-1973
drawings: (L) $523; (H) $880

LUBBERS, Holger Peter Svane
Danish 1850-1929
paintings: (L) $1,760; (H) $10,925

LUBITCH, Ossip
French 1896-1986
paintings: (L) $605; (H) $920

LUCAS, Albert Durer
German 1828-1918
paintings: (L) $1,430; (H) $11,000

LUCAS, Albert Pike
American 1862-1945
paintings: (H) $518

LUCAS, August Georg Friedrich
German 1803-1863
paintings: (H) $134,500

LUCAS, Edward George Handel
British 1861-1936
paintings: (H) $1,725

LUCAS, Essie Leone Leavey
paintings: (H) $770

LUCAS, John Seymour
British 1849-1923
paintings: (L) $385; (H) $5,175

LUCAS, John Templeton
British 1836-1880
paintings: (H) $5,225

LUCAS VELASQUEZ, Eugenio
Spanish 1817-1870
paintings: (L) $8,250; (H) $14,300

LUCAS Y PADILLA, Eugenio
Spanish 1824-1870
paintings: (H) $4,620
drawings: (H) $1,265

LUCAS Y VILLAMIL, Eugenio
Spanish d. 1918
paintings: (L) $3,850; (H) $38,500

LUCAS-LUCAS, Henry Frederick
British d. 1943
paintings: (L) $1,760; (H) $20,700

LUCCA, Flaminio de
Italian 19th/20th cent.
sculpture: (H) $770

LUCCHA, U.
sculpture: (H) $2,200

LUCCHESI, Bruno
Italian/American b. 1926
sculpture: (L) $220; (H) $5,500

LUCCHESI, Giorgio
Italian 1855-1941
paintings: (L) $10,350; (H) $20,900

LUCCHESI, P.
Italian 19th cent.
paintings: (H) $1,650

LUCE, Maximilien
French 1858-1941
paintings: (L) $3,500; (H) $495,000
drawings: (L) $431; (H) $5,520

LUCEBERT, Jean
Dutch b. 1924
paintings: (H) $27,500
drawings: (L) $1,840; (H) $3,300

LUCERO, Michael
American b. 1953
sculpture: (L) $5,500; (H) $14,950

LUCHINI, Pietro
Italian 1800-1883
paintings: (H) $43,700

LUCIONI, Luigi
Italian/American 1900-1988?
paintings: (L) $248; (H) $37,375
drawings: (L) $863; (H) $8,050

LUCKX, Frans Josef
Belgian 1802-1849
paintings: (H) $16,500

LUCS(?), F. de
sculpture: (H) $1,650

LUCY, Charles
British 1814-1873
paintings: (H) $23,000
drawings: (H) $413

LUDECKE, A.
German b. 1868
paintings: (H) $1,430

LUDECKE-CLEVE, A.
19th/20th cent.
paintings: (H) $1,210

LUDEKENS, Fred
American 1900-1982
drawings: (L) $220; (H) $1,540

LUDINS, Eugene David
American b. 1904
paintings: (L) $220; (H) $690

LUDLOW, Mike
b. 1921
drawings: (L) $660; (H) $880

LUDOVICI, Albert
British 19th cent.
paintings: (H) $9,775

LUDOVICI, Albert, Jr.
English 1852-1932
paintings: (L) $770; (H) $2,970

LUDOVICI, Julius
American b. Germany 1837, d. 1906
drawings: (L) $66; (H) $2,875

LUDTKE, Larry
American b. 1929
sculpture: (L) $2,500; (H) $5,280

LUDWIG, *
19th/20th cent.
paintings: (H) $605

LUDWIG, Helen
American 20th cent.
paintings: (L) $275; (H) $935
drawings: (H) $110

LUEG, Konrad
contemporary
drawings: (H) $5,500

LUERZER, Friderick
German 1858-1917
paintings: (L) $660; (H) $1,980

LUFF
paintings: (H) $770

LUGERTH, Ferdinand
Austrian 19th/20th cent.
sculpture: (L) $385; (H) $2,090

LUGO, Amador
Mexican b. 1922
paintings: (H) $2,875

LUGO, Emil
German 1840-1902
paintings: (L) $1,840; (H) $4,125

LUIGI, Folli
Italian 19th cent.
paintings: (H) $2,640

LUIGI, Ludovico de
Italian b. 1933
paintings: (L) $1,380; (H) $2,420

LUIGINI, Ferdinand
French 1870-1943
paintings: (H) $770

LUINI, Aurelio
1530-1593
drawings: (H) $690

LUINI, Bernardino
Italian 1475-1532
paintings: (H) $10,925

LUINI, Bernardino, studio of
15th/16th cent.
paintings: (H) $18,400

LUIRE, Huin le
Continental 19th cent.
paintings: (H) $2,640

LUIS, Fernando
1932-1983
paintings: (L) $460; (H) $4,370
drawings: (H) $978

LUKE, Alexandra
paintings: (H) $1,760

LUKER
paintings: (H) $880

LUKER, William
English b. 1867
paintings: (H) $3,025

LUKER, William, Sr.
English ac. 1852-1889
paintings: (H) $13,800

LUKITS, Theodore N.
American b. 1897
paintings: (L) $660; (H) $3,850
drawings: (H) $1,045

LUKS
drawings: (H) $550

LUKS, George
American 1867-1933
paintings: (L) $1,265; (H) $103,700
drawings: (L) $138; (H) $19,550

LUMERMAN, Juana
1905-1982
paintings: (L) $6,900; (H) $8,050

LUMINAIS, Evariste Vital
French 1822-1896
paintings: (H) $1,380
drawings: (H) $518

LUMIS, Harriet Randall
American 1870-1953
paintings: (L) $715; (H) $5,610
drawings: (L) $55; (H) $330

LUMMEN MARCKE, Emile van de
French 1827-1890
paintings: (H) $2,750

LUMPKINS, William
American 20th cent.
paintings: (L) $1,540; (H) $2,420

LUMSDAINE, Leesa Sandys
British/American 20th cent.
paintings: (L) $1,650; (H) $2,200

LUNA, Justo Ruiz
Spanish 19th cent.
paintings: (H) $4,675

LUNARDI, W.
Italian late 19th/early 20th cent.
paintings: (H) $660

LUNDAHL, Amelie Helgh
Finnish 1850-1914
paintings: (H) $1,380

LUNDBERG, August Frederick
American 1878-1928
paintings: (L) $1,210; (H) $3,300

LUNDBOHM, Sixten
Swedish 1895-1982
paintings: (H) $715
drawings: (L) $385; (H) $605

LUNDE, Anders
Danish 1809-1886
paintings: (H) $805

LUNDE, Carl D. M.
Scandinavian 19th cent.
paintings: (H) $1,760

LUNDEBERG, Helen
American b. 1908
paintings: (L) $2,300; (H) $48,300

LUNDEEN, George W.
American b. 1948
sculpture: (H) $10,925

LUNDENS, Gerrit
Dutch 1622-1677
paintings: (L) $4,887; (H) $5,750

LUNDMARK
Swedish/American
paintings: (H) $880

LUNDMARK, Leon
American 1875-1942
paintings: (L) $173; (H) $1,980

LUNETTI, Tommaso di Stefano
c. 1490-1564
paintings: (H) $198,000

LUNGREN, Fernand
American 1859-1932
paintings: (H) $1,025
drawings: (L) $440; (H) $1,725

LUNOIS, Alexandre
1863-1916
drawings: (L) $440; (H) $1,430

LUNY, Thomas
English 1759-1837
paintings: (L) $1,320; (H) $46,000
drawings: (H) $2,475

LUONGO, Aldo
Argentinean b. 1940
paintings: (L) $1,100; (H) $4,950

LUPERTZ, Marcus
German b. 1941
paintings: (L) $14,300; (H) $28,750
drawings: (L) $4,620; (H) $5,175
sculpture: (L) $32,200; (H) $200,500

LUPO, Allesandro
paintings: (H) $1,725

LUPPEN, Gerard Josef Adrian van
Belgian 1834-1891
paintings: (L) $880; (H) $10,350

LURCAT, Jean
French 1892-1966
paintings: (L) $1,100; (H) $11,000
drawings: (L) $632; (H) $2,860

LURION, H.
British 19th cent.
paintings: (H) $1,380

LUSK, Marie Koupal
American b. 1862
paintings: (H) $1,150
drawings: (H) $1,430

LUSSIGNY, L.
French 18th/19th cent.
drawings: (H) $3,300

LUTI, Benedetto
Italian 1666-1724
paintings: (L) $3,162; (H) $8,625
drawings: (L) $2,640; (H) $19,550

LUTTEROTH, Ascan
German 1842-1923
paintings: (L) $2,300; (H) $13,800

LUTTICHUYS, Isaac
Dutch 1616-1673
paintings: (H) $8,250

LUTZ
contemporary
paintings: (H) $1,650
drawings: (H) $165

LUTZ, Dan
American 1906-1978
paintings: (L) $247; (H) $990
drawings: (H) $550

LUYKEN, Jan
drawings: (H) $2,860

LUYTEN, Jean Henri
Belgian 1859-1945
paintings: (H) $1,100

LUYTEN, Mark
b. 1955
sculpture: (H) $4,620

LUYTENS, Charles Augustus Henry
British 1829-1915
paintings: (H) $13,800

LUZ, Julius
Swiss 1868-1892
paintings: (H) $1,045

LUZI, Francesco
Italian 19th cent.
paintings: (H) $1,265

LUZRO, Antonio
Portuguese ac. 1815
drawings: (H) $3,163

LUZZI, Cleto
Italian 19th/20th cent.
paintings: (L) $1,100; (H) $4,125
drawings: (H) $805

LYBAERT, Theophile Marie Francoise
Belgium 1848-1927
paintings: (H) $805

LYFORD, Philip
American 1887-1950
paintings: (L) $330; (H) $715

LYMAN, Camille
paintings: (H) $605

LYMAN, Harry
1856-1933
drawings: (H) $550

LYMAN, John Goodwin
1886-1967
paintings: (H) $4,025

LYMAN, Joseph
1843-1913
paintings: (H) $935

LYNCH, Albert
Peruvian b. 1851, ac. Paris 1930
paintings: (L) $1,840; (H) $33,000
drawings: (L) $1,380; (H) $8,050

LYNCH, Anna
American 20th cent.
paintings: (L) $143; (H) $550

LYNE, Michael
English b. 1912
paintings: (L) $1,150; (H) $12,100
drawings: (L) $690; (H) $3,850
sculpture: (H) $495

LYNTON, Herbert S.
British ac. 1893
paintings: (H) $1,320
drawings: (H) $5,175

LYON, Hayes
American 20th cent.
paintings: (H) $2,090

LYON, Jeanette Agnew
American b. 1862
paintings: (L) $110; (H) $880

LYOUNS, Herbert F. Williams
English 1863-1939
paintings: (L) $403; (H) $577

LYRE, Adolphe la
French b. 1850
paintings: (H) $4,600

MAAR, Dora
French b. 1909
drawings: (L) $5,500; (H) $11,000

MAAREL, Marinus van der
Dutch 1857-1921
paintings: (H) $1,380

MAAS, Dirck
Dutch 1659-1717
paintings: (L) $9,200; (H) $18,400

MAAS, E.
paintings: (H) $550

MAAS, Paul
Belgian 1890-1962
paintings: (H) $2,200

MAASS, David
American 20th cent.
paintings: (L) $1,265; (H) $3,960

MABE, Manabu
Brazilian b. 1924 in Japan
paintings: (L) $2,200; (H) $18,700

MABERRY, Philip
American b. 1951
sculpture: (H) $1,380

MAC'AVOY, Edouard
b. 1905
paintings: (H) $2,200

MACAIS
Spanish contemporary
sculpture: (H) $660

MACALLUM, Hamilton
Scottish 1841/43-1896
paintings: (H) $660

MACARTNEY, Harry
b. 1870
paintings: (H) $460

MACARTNEY, Jack
American 1893-1976
paintings: (L) $412; (H) $770
drawings: (H) $495

MACBETH, Robert Walker
English 1848-1910
paintings: (H) $1,100

MACCARI, Mino
Italian 1898-1989
paintings: (L) $2,750; (H) $8,050

MACCARTER, Henry Bainbridge
American 1866-1942
paintings: (H) $2,200

MACCIO, Romulo
Argentinean b. 1931
paintings: (L) $3,450; (H) $20,900

MACCLOY, Samuel
British 1831-1904
drawings: (H) $2,200

MACCO, George
German 1863-1933
paintings: (L) $715; (H) $1,540

MACCONNEL, Kim
American b. 1946
paintings: (L) $5,750; (H) $6,325
drawings: (L) $1,150; (H) $1,760

MACCORD, Mary Nicholena
American 1864-1955
paintings: (H) $4,600
drawings: (L) $550; (H) $2,300

MACCOY, Guy
American b. 1904
paintings: (L) $302; (H) $660

MACDONALD, Christopher
American b. 1957
drawings: (H) $518
sculpture: (L) $518; (H) $1,540

MACDONALD, Grant
American b. 1944
paintings: (L) $2,200; (H) $14,300

MACDONALD, James Edward Hervey
Canadian 1873-1932
paintings: (L) $5,280; (H) $30,800
drawings: (H) $5,500

MACDONALD, James Williamson
Galloway
Canadian 1897-1961
paintings: (L) $2,640; (H) $16,500
drawings: (H) $4,400

MACDONALD, John Blake
English 1829-1901
paintings: (H) $605

MACDONALD, Kevin
American contemporary
drawings: (L) $184; (H) $880

MACDONALD, Manly Edward
paintings: (L) $1,100; (H) $12,100

MACDONALD-WRIGHT, Stanton
American 1890-1973/74
paintings: (L) $6,325; (H) $360,000
drawings: (L) $7,475; (H) $41,400

MACDOUGALL, Norman M.
British d. 1972
paintings: (H) $770

MACE, Flora
sculpture: (H) $2,530

MACEWEN, Walter
American 1860-1943
paintings: (L) $1,035; (H) $9,350
drawings: (L) $5,175; (H) $8,050

MACGEORGE, William Stewart
English 1861-1931
paintings: (H) $575

MACGILVARY, Norwood Hodge
American 1874-1950
paintings: (L) $880; (H) $1,320
drawings: (H) $550

MACGREGOR, David
British 19th cent.
paintings: (H) $920

MACGREGOR, Robert
English 1848-1922
paintings: (H) $935

MACGREGOR, Robert
Scottish b. 1896
paintings: (L) $495; (H) $1,668

MACHARD, Jules Louis
French 1839-1900
paintings: (H) $23,000

MACHELBACH
N. European 19th cent.
paintings: (H) $2,750

MACHELL, R.
British 19th cent.
paintings: (H) $9,200

MACHEN, William Henry
American 1832-1911
paintings: (L) $33; (H) $3,738

MACHETANZ, M.
paintings: (H) $550

MACINNES, Alex, poss. MCINNES
English 19th cent.
paintings: (H) $633

MACINTIRE, Kenneth S.
American 1891-1979
paintings: (L) $230; (H) $2,200
drawings: (H) $176

MACK, Bill
American contemporary
sculpture: (L) $633; (H) $1,045

MACKAY, Edwin Murray
American 1869-1926
paintings: (L) $935; (H) $11,000

MACKAY, Florence
British 19th cent.
drawings: (H) $2,200

MACKAY, J.C.
British 19th/20th cent.
paintings: (H) $1,610

MACKE, August
German 1887-1914
drawings: (H) $2,070

MACKELLAR, Duncan
British 1849-1908
paintings: (H) $1,045

MACKENNAL, Sir Edgar Bertram
Austrian 1863-1931
sculpture: (H) $10,925

MACKENZIE, Alexander
paintings: (H) $3,025

MACKENZIE, Frank J.
English/American 1865/67-1939
paintings: (L) $302; (H) $1,045

MACKENZIE, Frederick
Scottish c. 1787-1854
drawings: (L) $550; (H) $2,200

MACKENZIE, G.N.
Continental School 19th cent.
sculpture: (H) $1,840

MACKENZIE, Jim
paintings: (H) $1,100

MACKENZIE, Marie Henrie
Dutch 1878-1961
paintings: (L) $357; (H) $489

MACKENZIE, Roderick D.
English b. 1865
paintings: (H) $1,210

MACKEPRANG, Adolf
Danish 1833-1911
paintings: (H) $1,320

MACKINTOSH, Charles Rennie
Scottish 1868-1928
drawings: (H) $4,180

MACKINTOSH, Margaret Macdonald
1864-1933
paintings: (L) $71,500; (H) $132,000

MACKNIGHT, Dodge
American 1860-1950
drawings: (L) $385; (H) $3,190

MACLANE, Jean
American 1878-1964
paintings: (H) $6,600

MACLAUGHLAN, Donald Shaw
drawings: (H) $484

MACLEARY, Bonnie
American 1890-1971
sculpture: (L) $978; (H) $3,080

MACLELLAN, Charles A.
American b. 1885
paintings: (H) $8,525

MACLEOD, Pegi Nicol
paintings: (H) $3,300

MACLEOD, Yan
American 20th cent.
sculpture: (H) $2,070

MACLET, Elisee
French 1881-1962
paintings: (L) $1,840; (H) $25,300
drawings: (L) $1,100; (H) $3,080

MACLISE, Daniel
Irish 1806/11-1870
paintings: (L) $863; (H) $19,800
drawings: (H) $253

MACLOT, Armand Frans Karel
Belgian b. 1877
paintings: (H) $575

MACMONNIES, Frederick William
American 1863-1937
paintings: (L) $110; (H) $19,550
sculpture: (L) $660; (H) $101,500

MACNEIL, Ambrose, DeBarra
Scottish/American b. 1852
paintings: (H) $1,320

MACNEIL, Herman Atkins
American 1866-1947
sculpture: (L) $2,300; (H) $51,750

MACNEIR, L.
sculpture: (H) $9,200

MACOMBER, Mary Lizzie
American 1861-1916
paintings: (L) $880; (H) $6,160
drawings: (H) $1,840
sculpture: (H) $8,800

MACPHERSON, John Havard
American b. 1894
paintings: (L) $400; (H) $1,870

MACQUART, J.E.
French 20th cent.
drawings: (H) $489

MACRAE, Elmer Livingston
American 1875-1953
paintings: (L) $495; (H) $13,800
drawings: (L) $220; (H) $1,840

MACRAE, Emma Fordyce
American 1887-1974
paintings: (L) $110; (H) $9,350

MACRUM, George H.
American 19th/20th cent.
paintings: (L) $220; (H) $8,800

MACWHIRTER, John
English 1839-1911
paintings: (L) $495; (H) $990
drawings: (L) $330; (H) $5,290

MACY, Wendell
American 1845-1913
paintings: (L) $137; (H) $4,675

MACY, William Ferdinand
American 1852-1901
paintings: (L) $770; (H) $880

MACY, William Starbuck
American 1853-1916
paintings: (L) $288; (H) $3,300

MADALENA, Batiste
drawings: (L) $660; (H) $2,300

MADAN, Frederick
drawings: (H) $3,565

MADARASZ, Adelina Katona
Hungarian 1871-1962
paintings: (H) $990

MADDEN, J.E.
American 20th cent.
paintings: (H) $550

MADDEN, Jan
American 20th cent.
paintings: (L) $467; (H) $770

MADELAIN, Gustave
French 1867-1944
paintings: (L) $1,035; (H) $6,875

MADELINE, Paul
French 1863-1920
paintings: (L) $4,313; (H) $27,600

MADER, Georg
paintings: (H) $462

MADEWEISS, Hedwig von
German b. 1856
paintings: (H) $5,175

MADIOL, Adrien Jean
Dutch 1845-1892
paintings: (H) $2,185

MADIONO, Louis
Spanish 19th cent.
paintings: (H) $715

MADOU, Jean Baptiste
Belgian 1796-1877
paintings: (L) $1,650; (H) $11,500
drawings: (H) $550

MADRASSI
paintings: (H) $1,760

MADRASSI, Luca
Italian 19th/20th cent.
sculpture: (L) $575; (H) $5,520

MADRAZO Y GARRETA,
Raimundo de
Spanish 1841-1920
paintings: (L) $20,700; (H) $99,000
drawings: (L) $880; (H) $1,150

MADRAZO Y GARRETA, Ricardo de
Spanish 1852-1917
paintings: (L) $19,800; (H) $38,500

MAEDA SEISON
Japanese 1885-1977
drawings: (L) $9,200; (H) $321,500

MAELLA, Mariano Salvador
Spanish 1739-1819
paintings: (H) $16,500

MAENTEL, Jacob
American 1763-1863
drawings: (L) $3,080; (H) $31,050

MAES, A.
Dutch 18th/19th cent.
paintings: (H) $660

MAES, Eugene Remy
Belgian 1849-1912
paintings: (L) $2,860; (H) $12,650

MAES, Giacomo
Italian 19th cent.
paintings: (H) $31,900

MAES, Henri
Belgian 19th cent.
paintings: (H) $1,100

MAES, Nicolaes
Dutch 1632/34-1693
paintings: (L) $4,830; (H) $110,000

MAES, Nicolaes, studio of
paintings: (H) $1,870

MAESTOSI, F.
Italian 19th cent.
paintings: (L) $6,600; (H) $10,350

MAESTRI, Michelangelo
Italian d.c. 1812
paintings: (H) $440
drawings: (L) $770; (H) $10,925

MAESTRO DEL RIDOTTO
Italian 18th cent.
paintings: (L) $23,000; (H) $31,050

MAETERLINCK, Louis
Belgian 1846-1926
paintings: (H) $10,450

MAFFEI, L.
sculpture: (H) $1,955

MAFFIA, Daniel
paintings: (H) $3,300

MAGADA, Stephen
American 20th cent.
paintings: (H) $825

MAGAFAN, Ethel
American b. 1916
paintings: (L) $413; (H) $1,760

Catalog Cover Lot

Being featured on the cover of an auction catalog draws attention and bidders. When *A Cup of Tea* was consigned to Hanzel Galleries in Chicago, it was estimated to sell for $60,000. Raimundo de Madrazo y Garreta (1841-1920) was a well-known Spanish painter who had worked and studied in Paris. He exhibited at the Paris Exposition of 1878 and received the gold medal at the 1889 Exposition Universelle.

Paintings by Madrazo y Garreta appear fairly often at auction in the United States. *A Cup of Tea* was a very appealing picture and attracted numerous bidders. It sold after spirited bidding to a Spanish dealer, bidding on behalf of a client, who had flown to Chicago just for the sale. The final price with premium was $99,000. (Raimundo de Madrazo y Garreta, *A Cup of Tea*, oil on canvas, 34 x 26 inches, Hanzel, April 28, 1991, $99,000)

MAGAFAN, Jennie
  American 1916-c. 1950
  paintings: (H) $3,300

MAGANA, Enrique
  paintings: (H) $4,675

MAGANZA, Alessandro
  Italian 1556-1640
  drawings: (H) $13,800

MAGANZA, Giovanni Battista
  Italian c. 1513-1586
  drawings: (H) $8,250

MAGDICH, Dennis
  paintings: (H) $660

MAGEE, Alan
  American 20th cent.
  drawings: (H) $7,700

MAGEE, Guy
  paintings: (H) $770

MAGEE, James C.
  American 1846-1924
  paintings: (L) $192; (H) $1,955

MAGGI, Cesare
  Italian 1881-1961
  paintings: (H) $8,050

MAGHELLEN, Alfred de
  French b. 1871
  paintings: (H) $3,850

MAGILL, R.C.
paintings: (L) $1,350; (H) $1,800

MAGNASCO, Alessandro, Il
Lissandrino
Italian 1667-1749
paintings: (L) $18,400; (H) $45,100
drawings: (H) $12,650

MAGNASCO, Alessandro and Carlo
Antonio TAVELLA
17th/18th cent.
paintings: (H) $4,950

MAGNI
Italian
sculpture: (H) $10,450

MAGNI, Giuseppe
Italian 1869-1956
paintings: (L) $4,025; (H) $41,250

MAGNUS, Camille
French 19th cent.
paintings: (L) $1,840; (H) $7,700

MAGNUSSEN, Gustave A.
American 1868-1944
paintings: (L) $770; (H) $1,210

MAGONIGLE, Edith
American 20th cent.
paintings: (H) $880

MAGRATH, Georges Achilles de
French 19th cent.
drawings: (H) $1,320

MAGRATH, William
Irish 1838-1918
paintings: (L) $1,540; (H) $1,610

MAGRITTE, Rene
Belgian 1898-1967
paintings: (L) $123,500; (H) $2,200,000
drawings: (L) $920; (H) $374,000
sculpture: (L) $85,000; (H) $176,000

MAGROTTI, Ercole
Italian 19th/20th cent.
paintings: (H) $660

MAGUAVACCA, Ubaldo
Italian 20th cent.
paintings: (H) $467

MAGUIRE, Robert
paintings: (H) $935

MAGYAR-MANNHEIMER, Gustav
Hungarian b. 1859
paintings: (H) $605

MAHAFFEY, Merrill
American b. 1937
paintings: (H) $3,300

MAHELIN, Leon Lewis
French 19th cent.
paintings: (H) $1,100

MAHER, Kate Heath
American 1860-1946
paintings: (H) $1,980

MAHIEUX, Alfredo
paintings: (H) $5,462

MAHLKNECHT, Edmund
Austrian 1820-1903
paintings: (L) $5,520; (H) $14,300

MAHOKIAN, Wartan
19th/20th cent.
paintings: (L) $5,175; (H) $6,900

MAHONEY, James Owen
American 1907-1987
paintings: (L) $200; (H) $7,700
drawings: (H) $95

MAHONEY, M.
paintings: (H) $1,870

MAHONEY, Marion
American
drawings: (H) $19,800

MAHR, G.
20th cent.
sculpture: (H) $1,210

MAHU, Cornelis
Flemish 1613-1689
paintings: (H) $41,400

MAHU, Victor
d. 1700
paintings: (H) $4,025

MAIBACH
drawings: (H) $1,265

MAIER, Henry
German/American 1884-1949
drawings: (H) $1,045

MAIGNAN
Continental 19th cent.
sculpture: (H) $605

MAIGNAN, M.
sculpture: (H) $2,420

MAILLARD, Auguste
French b. 1864
sculpture: (H) $2,090

MAILLART, Diogene Ulysse Napoleon
French 1840-1926
paintings: (H) $9,200

MAILLAUD, Fernand
French 1862-1948
paintings: (L) $660; (H) $13,200

MAILLET, Auguste, called RIGON
French d. 1844
paintings: (L) $460; (H) $2,185

MAILLOL, Aristide
French 1861-1944
paintings: (H) $57,500
drawings: (L) $1,035; (H) $19,550
sculpture: (L) $12,650; (H) $2,200,000

MAINARDI, Sebastiano
Italian c. 1450-1513
paintings: (L) $25,300; (H) $115,500

MAINCENT, Gustave
French 1850-1887
paintings: (H) $8,625

MAINDRON, Etienne Hippolyte
French 1801-1884
sculpture: (L) $1,265; (H) $1,320

MAINE, Harry de
British/American 1880-1952
paintings: (L) $220; (H) $990
drawings: (H) $330

MAINELLA, Raffaele
Italian b. 1858
drawings: (L) $550; (H) $9,200

MAINERI, Giovanni Francesco
Italian ac. 1489-1506
paintings: (H) $51,750

MAIROVICH, Zvi
Israeli 1911-1973
paintings: (L) $550; (H) $1,265

MAISON, R.
sculpture: (H) $935

MAITLAND, Paul
British 1863-1909
paintings: (H) $2,415

MAITRE DES JEUX
17th cent.
paintings: (H) $52,250

MAJER, Gustave
German 1847-1900
paintings: (H) $6,325

MAJOR, B.
19th/20th cent.
paintings: (L) $50; (H) $605

MAJOR, Ernest Lee
American 1864-1950
paintings: (L) $192; (H) $26,450

MAK, Patrick
b. China, 1949
paintings: (H) $1,375

MAK, Paul
Russian 20th cent.
drawings: (L) $4,600; (H) $14,950

MAKART, Hans
Austrian 1840-1884/85
paintings: (L) $1,150; (H) $25,300

MAKIAN, Reuben
1897-1986
sculpture: (H) $2,530

MAKIELSKI, Leon A.
American b. 1885
paintings: (L) $88; (H) $3,520

MAKINS, James D.
American b. 1946
sculpture: (H) $4,025

MAKOVSKY, Vladimir
Russian 1846-1920
paintings: (H) $5,750
drawings: (H) $66

MAKOWSKY, Constantin Jegorovich
Russian 1839-1915
paintings: (L) $3,230; (H) $110,000

MALAINE, Joseph Laurent
French 1745-1809
paintings: (H) $44,000

MALANCA, Jose
b. Argentina 1897, d. 1967
paintings: (L) $5,750; (H) $6,900

MALAVOTTI, H.
sculpture: (H) $935

MALBON, William
British b. 1850
paintings: (H) $1,540

MALBRANCHE, Louis Claude
French 1790-1838
paintings: (L) $715; (H) $3,100

MALCZEWSKI, Jacek
1854-1929
drawings: (H) $1,840

Winter Landscape

French artist Louis Claude Malbranche (1790-1838), a member of the French Salon, specialized in painting autumn and winter landscapes. Landscape painting was an art form virtually nonexistent during the Middle Ages. The first landscapes appeared in the 15th-century *Book of Hours (Les Très Riches)* and portrayed each month's agricultural labors and outdoor festivals. Paintings during this period were executed in the studio; not until the late 19th century did artists begin to paint in the open air (*plein-air*). Malbranche's painting of a Dutch canal scene would have been very appealing to the prosperous Dutch bourgeois—a reminder of the country's prosperity and the reward of its industry. When this Dutch canal scene was offered at Willis Henry's auction in Massachusetts, it realized $3,100. (Louis Claude Malbranche, *Dutch Winter Landscape of House with People on a Horse and Sled, and Children Playing on a Sled*, oil on canvas, 18 x 24 inches, Willis Henry, August 5, 1995, $3,100)

MALDARELLI, Federico
Italian 1826-1893
paintings: (H) $20,700

MALDURA, Giovanni
Italian c. 1772-1849
paintings: (H) $4,400

MALEAS, Constantin
paintings: (H) $4,675

MALEMPRE, Leo
English ac. 1887-1901
paintings: (L) $748; (H) $1,265

MALESPINA, Louis Ferdinand
French b. 1874
paintings: (H) $32,200

MALET, Albert
French b. 1902
paintings: (L) $1,540; (H) $2,420

MALET, Harold
English 19th cent.
paintings: (H) $1,265

MALET, M.
paintings: (H) $660

MALEVICH, Kasimir
Russian 1878-1935
drawings: (H) $15,400

MALFROY, Charles
French 1862-1918
paintings: (L) $605; (H) $4,675

MALFROY, Henry
French b. 1895
paintings: (L) $1,380; (H) $2,915

MALHERBE, William
French 19th/20th cent.
paintings: (L) $523; (H) $6,600

MALI, Christian
German 1832-1906
paintings: (L) $26,450; (H) $28,600

MALIAVIN, Filippe Andreevich
paintings: (H) $3,520

MALICOAT, Philip Cecil
American b. 1908
paintings: (L) $165; (H) $1,100
drawings: (L) $935; (H) $1,760

MALKINE, Georges
French 1898-1970
paintings: (H) $7,700
sculpture: (L) $1,430; (H) $1,610

MALLERBRANCHE, Louis Claude
French 1790-1838
paintings: (L) $1,980; (H) $2,750

MALLET, Jean Baptiste
French 1759-1835
paintings: (L) $28,600; (H) $60,250
drawings: (L) $8,050; (H) $44,000

MALLEYN, Gerrit
Dutch 1753-1816
paintings: (L) $13,800; (H) $23,000

MALLINSON, Ethel. M.
British 20th cent.
drawings: (H) $460

MALLOY, Michael
American 20th cent.
paintings: (L) $467; (H) $825

MALNOVITZER, Zvi
b. 1945
paintings: (L) $12,650; (H) $17,250

MALOOF, Sam
American b. 1916
sculpture: (H) $17,250

MALTA, Edouardo
20th cent.
paintings: (H) $805

MALTZ
Continental School 19th cent.
paintings: (H) $1,495

MAN, Cornelis de
Dutch 1621-1706
paintings: (H) $55,000

MANABONI, Arthur
drawings: (H) $743

MANAGO, R.V.
19th cent.
paintings: (H) $495

MANAGO, Vincent
French 1880-1936
paintings: (L) $660; (H) $1,093

MANARESI, Ugo
Italian 1851-1917
paintings: (H) $18,400

MANBACH, A.
French 19th cent.
sculpture: (H) $2,750

MANCAZIO, E.
20th cent.
paintings: (H) $805

MANCHESTER, A.E.
paintings: (H) $550

MANCINI, Antonio
Italian 1852-1930
paintings: (L) $4,400; (H) $266,500
drawings: (L) $3,080; (H) $23,100

MANCINI, Bartolomeo
Italian ac. 17th/18th cent.
paintings: (H) $17,250

MANCINI, Francesco
paintings: (L) $1,800; (H) $4,025

MANCINI, Francesco
Italian 1679-1758
paintings: (H) $10,350

MANCINI, Frencesco Longo
Italian b. 1880
paintings: (L) $88; (H) $1,650

MANCINI, G.C.
Italian 19th/20th cent.
paintings: (H) $1,150

MANDEL, Howard
American b. 1917
paintings: (H) $825
drawings: (L) $137; (H) $198

MANDER, Karel van, III
Dutch 1610-1670
paintings: (L) $2,875; (H) $13,800

MANDER, William Henry
English 1850-1922
paintings: (L) $1,150; (H) $2,990

MANE-KATZ
French/Israeli 1894-1962
paintings: (L) $1,100; (H) $68,500
drawings: (L) $358; (H) $12,100
sculpture: (L) $1,955; (H) $5,520

MANEELY, Joe
drawings: (H) $3,910

MANELLA
Italian 19th cent.
paintings: (H) $550

MANESSIER, Alfred
French b. 1911
paintings: (H) $23,100
drawings: (L) $1,320; (H) $5,500

MANET, **
paintings: (H) $2,970

MANET, Edouard
French 1832-1883
paintings: (L) $310,500; (H) $4,400,000
drawings: (L) $66,000; (H) $365,000

MANGER, Henry K.
paintings: (H) $750

MANGILLI, Ada
Italian b. 1863
paintings: (L) $1,320; (H) $36,800

MANGINI
Italian 20th cent.
paintings: (H) $935

MANGLARD, Adrien
French 1695-1760
paintings: (L) $7,475; (H) $137,500

MANGOLD, Robert
American b. 1937
paintings: (L) $6,900; (H) $151,000
drawings: (L) $6,050; (H) $25,300

MANGOLD, Sylvia Plimack
American b. 1938
paintings: (L) $2,420; (H) $6,900
drawings: (L) $3,300; (H) $7,475

MANGRAVITE, Peppino
Italian/American 1896-1978
paintings: (L) $935; (H) $4,400
drawings: (H) $413

MANGUIN, Henri
French 1874-1943/49
paintings: (L) $11,500; (H) $440,000
drawings: (L) $275; (H) $1,540

MANHEIM, Erwin
American 20th cent.
paintings: (H) $4,600

MANHU
contemporary
paintings: (H) $495

MANIATTY, Stephen G.
American b. 1910
paintings: (L) $60; (H) $3,080

MANICCUL, Gustave
paintings: (H) $650

MANIGAULT, Edward Middleton
American 1877-1922
paintings: (L) $2,750; (H) $6,325

MANIGOT, A.
sculpture: (H) $1,430

MANINGAULT, Edward M.
American 1887-1922
paintings: (H) $8,800

MANINI, Gaetano
Italian 1730-1780
paintings: (H) $4,400

MANISER, Heinrich Matvejevitch
Russian 1847-1925
paintings: (H) $6,900

MANLEY, Thomas R.
American 1853-1938
paintings: (L) $825; (H) $1,870
drawings: (H) $66

MANN, Alexander
British 1853-1908
paintings: (L) $1,495; (H) $23,000

MANN, David
American b. 1948
paintings: (L) $2,640; (H) $15,400

MANN, Harrington
American 1865-1937
paintings: (H) $2,200

MANN, Joshua Hargrave Sams
British d. 1886
paintings: (H) $3,080

MANN, Wilhelm
German b. 1882
paintings: (H) $1,100

MANNERS, Paul
sculpture: (H) $2,420

MANNERS, W.
paintings: (H) $880

MANNERS, William
English ac. 1885-1910
paintings: (L) $1,100; (H) $3,080

MANNHEIM, Jean
German/American c. 1861/63-1945
paintings: (L) $550; (H) $11,000
drawings: (H) $385

MANNHEIMER, Gustav
Hungarian 1859-1937
paintings: (H) $1,035

MANNING, William
paintings: (L) $460; (H) $575
sculpture: (H) $1,035

MANNUCCI, Cipriano A.
Italian 1882-1970
paintings: (H) $1,210

MANOCHI, Giuseppe
1731-c. 1782
drawings: (H) $4,025

MANOIR, Irving K.
American 1891-1982
paintings: (L) $220; (H) $1,045

MANOLO, Manuel Martinez Hugue
Spanish 1872-1945
sculpture: (H) $6,050

MANQUIN, Henri Charles
French 1874-1949
drawings: (H) $990

MANS, Martha
drawings: (L) $440; (H) $1,000

MANSFELD, Josef
Austrian 1819-1894
paintings: (L) $4,675; (H) $4,950

MANSFELD, Moritz
Austrian 19th cent.
paintings: (H) $2,420

MANSFIELD, Joseph
Austrian 1819-1894
paintings: (L) $880; (H) $2,420

MANSHIP, Paul Howard
American 1885-1966
paintings: (H) $46,000
drawings: (L) $690; (H) $935
sculpture: (L) $276; (H) $244,500

MANSVELT-BECK, P.
Dutch School 20th cent.
paintings: (H) $1,980

MANTEGANI, Roger
b. Argentina 1957
paintings: (L) $8,625; (H) $14,300

MANTEGAZZA, Giacomo
Italian 1853-1920
paintings: (L) $5,500; (H) $22,000
drawings: (H) $1,760

MANTELET, Albert Goguet
French b. 1858
paintings: (L) $550; (H) $6,325

MANTOR, F.
Continental 19th/20th cent.
paintings: (H) $2,200

MANTOVANI, Alessandro
Italian 1814-1892
paintings: (H) $7,762

MANUEL, Jorge
paintings: (H) $3,300

MANUEL, Victor
Cuban 1867-1969
paintings: (L) $3,190; (H) $24,150
drawings: (L) $2,640; (H) $5,750

MANVILLE, Elsie
American 20th cent.
paintings: (L) $275; (H) $770

MANZONI, Ignazio
Italian 1799-1888
paintings: (H) $9,900

MANZONI, Paul
Continental 19th/20th cent.
paintings: (H) $460

MANZU, Giacomo
Italian 1908-1990
drawings: (L) $2,990; (H) $8,625
sculpture: (L) $17,600; (H) $407,000

MANZUOLI, Egisto
Italian 19th cent.
paintings: (H) $1,980

MANZUR, David
Columbian b. 1929
paintings: (H) $8,250
drawings: (L) $2,750; (H) $16,500

MANZZONI, F.
Italian 19th cent.
paintings: (H) $1,725

MAPPLETHORPE, Robert
American 1946-1989
drawings: (H) $24,750

MARA, Antonio, called Lo Scarpetta
Italian d.c. 1750
paintings: (L) $14,375; (H) $17,250

MARAFFI, Luigi
American b. 1891
sculpture: (H) $660

MARAGALL, Julio
Spain b. 1936
sculpture: (L) $2,750; (H) $7,700

MARAIS, Adolphe
French 1856-1940
paintings: (L) $1,870; (H) $16,500

MARAIS, C.
French 19th cent.
paintings: (H) $715

MARAIS-MILTON, Victor
French b. 1872
paintings: (L) $6,325; (H) $9,350

MARANTONIO
Italian 19th cent.
paintings: (H) $1,760

MARATTA, Carlo
Italian 1625-1713
paintings: (H) $11,500
drawings: (L) $1,840; (H) $57,500

MARBLE, Arthur D.
American 19th/20th cent.
drawings: (L) $4,025; (H) $5,463

MARC, Franz
German 1880-1916
drawings: (H) $26,400

MARCA-RELLI, Conrad
American b. 1913
paintings: (L) $935; (H) $57,200
drawings: (L) $127; (H) $12,650
sculpture: (L) $1,650; (H) $4,675

MARCEAUX, Rene St.
French late 19th cent.
sculpture: (H) $1,725

MARCEAUX, S.
sculpture: (H) $978

MARCEL, Louveau Roueryre
drawings: (H) $550

MARCEL-CLEMENT, Amedee Julien
French b. 1873
paintings: (H) $2,300

MARCELLIN, Jean Esprit
French 1821-1884
sculpture: (H) $1,540

MARCELLINI, U.
Italian 19th cent.
sculpture: (H) $1,265

MARCELLO, Duchesse Adele
Castiglione-Coloma nee d'Affry
Italian 1836-1879
sculpture: (H) $57,500

MARCELLO, D.
paintings: (H) $1,650

MARCH Y MARCO, Vicente
Spanish 1859-1914
paintings: (H) $40,700

MARCHAL, Charles Francois
French 1825-1877
paintings: (H) $3,450

MARCHAND
sculpture: (H) $825

MARCHAND, Andre
French
paintings: (L) $748; (H) $11,000
drawings: (L) $275; (H) $935

MARCHAND, Andre
French 1877-1951
paintings: (H) $1,650

MARCHAND, Andre
French b. 1907
paintings: (L) $880; (H) $4,620

MARCHAND, Charles
German b. 1843
paintings: (L) $468; (H) $3,300

MARCHAND, J.
French 19th/20th cent.
paintings: (H) $2,070

MARCHAND, Jean Hippolyte
French 1883-1940
paintings: (L) $1,760; (H) $3,960
drawings: (H) $1,035

MARCHAND, John
1875-1921
paintings: (L) $550; (H) $7,475

MARCHESINI, Alessandro
Italian 1664-1738
paintings: (H) $30,250

MARCHETTI, Ludovico
Italian 1853-1909
paintings: (L) $412; (H) $13,225
drawings: (H) $2,090

MARCHIG, Giannino
Italian 1897-1981
paintings: (H) $5,720

MARCHIONI, Elisabetta
Italian ac. c. 1700
paintings: (L) $8,050; (H) $88,000

MARCHISIO, Andrea
Italian 1850-1927
paintings: (L) $3,025; (H) $9,900

MARCHMENT, M.
English 19th cent.
paintings: (H) $550

MARCHOU, Georges
French 20th cent.
paintings: (H) $5,750

MARCILLO, Torres de
Spanish 19th cent.
paintings: (H) $770

MARCINI, Antonio
Italian 1852-1930
paintings: (H) $1,650

MARCIUS-SIMONS, Pinckney
American 1867-1909
paintings: (H) $20,900

MARCKE, Jean van
French 1875-1918
paintings: (H) $3,025

MARCKE DE LUMMEN, Emile van
French 1827-1890
paintings: (L) $1,150; (H) $11,000

MARCKE DE LUMMEN DIETERLE,
Marie van
French 1856-1935
paintings: (H) $9,200

MARCKS, Gerhard
German 1889-1981
drawings: (H) $550
sculpture: (L) $1,495; (H) $30,800

MARCLAY, Christian
b. 1955
sculpture: (L) $345; (H) $460

MARCOJONGE, A.
Spanish 20th cent.
paintings: (H) $578

MARCON, Charles
paintings: (H) $14,300

MARCONI, Tocco
Italian ac. c. 1504-1529
paintings: (H) $25,300

MARCOUSSIS, Louis
French 1883-1941
paintings: (L) $26,450; (H) $40,250
drawings: (L) $6,050; (H) $35,200
sculpture: (H) $58,300

MARCUCCI, F. Massimo
Italian 19th/20th cent.
drawings: (L) $220; (H) $715

MARCUS, Irving
American b. 1929
paintings: (H) $605

MARCUSE, Rudolf
German b. 1878
sculpture: (L) $1,980; (H) $3,410

MARDEN, Brice
American b. 1938
paintings: (L) $20,900; (H) $880,000
drawings: (L) $3,575; (H) $132,000

MAREC, Victor
French 1862-1920
paintings: (L) $8,250; (H) $9,900

MARECHAL, Jean Baptiste
French late 18th cent.
drawings: (L) $7,475; (H) $8,625

MAREL, A. van der
Dutch 19th/20th cent.
drawings: (H) $460

MARESA, U.
Italian 19th/20th cent.
paintings: (H) $522

MARESCA ⅰ
paintings: (H) $2,200

MARESCA, M.
Italian 19th/20th cent.
paintings: (L) $552; (H) $1,980

MARESCA, S.
Italian 19th cent.
paintings: (L) $412; (H) $1,430

MARESCALCO, Pietro, called Lo
SPADA
Italian c. 1503-1584
paintings: (H) $93,500

MARESOVA, Milada
paintings: (H) $6,600

MAREVNA
drawings: (H) $6,600

MAREVNA, Marie VOROBIEFF
Russian b. 1892
paintings: (H) $7,700

MARFAING, Andre
French b. 1925
paintings: (H) $1,870

MARGESON, George Tucker
American ac. 1910-1920
paintings: (H) $891

MARGESON, Gilbert Tucker
American 1852-1949
paintings: (L) $110; (H) $2,070
drawings: (H) $302

MARGETSON, William Henry
British 1861-1940
paintings: (H) $40,250

MARGILETH, Lynn
American 20th cent.
paintings: (L) $330; (H) $1,100

MARGITAY, Tihamer
Polish 1859-1922
paintings: (H) $1,980

MARGO, Boris
Russian/American b. 1902
drawings: (L) $880; (H) $3,520

MARGOLIS, Nathan
American 20th cent.
paintings: (H) $577

MARGOTTI, Anacleto
Italian 1895-1984
paintings: (L) $880; (H) $5,500

MARGOTTON, Rene
French b. 1915
paintings: (L) $138; (H) $1,045

MARGUET,
paintings: (H) $1,210

MARGULIES, Joseph
Austrian/American 1896-1984
paintings: (L) $110; (H) $2,200
drawings: (L) $38; (H) $1,430

MARHGOZZA(?), G.
Italian School 19th cent.
paintings: (H) $920

MARIA, A. de la
paintings: (H) $2,090

MARIA, D.
paintings: (H) $3,850

MARIA, Niccola de
Italian b. 1954
drawings: (H) $19,800

MARIANI
Italian 19th/20th cent.
paintings: (H) $660

MARIANI, Carlo Maria
Italian b. 1931
paintings: (L) $8,250; (H) $20,900
drawings: (L) $5,750; (H) $13,800

MARIANI, Pompeo
Italian 1857-1927
paintings: (L) $2,200; (H) $2,750

MARIBONA, Armando R.
Cuban 1894-1964
paintings: (H) $11,500

MARIE, Jacques
French 19th/20th cent.
paintings: (L) $165; (H) $605

MARIELLAC, De
French 20th cent.
drawings: (H) $1,045

MARIESCHI, Michele
Italian 1696-1743
paintings: (L) $93,500; (H) $1,375,000

MARIESCHI, Michele, and studio
Italian 18th cent.
paintings: (H) $28,600

MARIGINIARO, M.
paintings: (H) $550

MARIJNISSEN, Adrianus
Dutch b. 1899
paintings: (L) $385; (H) $990

MARIJS
Dutch 20th cent.
paintings: (H) $687

MARIK, A.
paintings: (H) $1,100

MARILHAT
Continental 19th cent.
paintings: (H) $550

MARILHAT, Prosper Georges Antoine
French 1811-1847
paintings: (L) $1,650; (H) $26,450

MARIN
Continental 19th/20th cent.
paintings: (L) $920; (H) $1,955

MARIN, Augusto
b. 1922
paintings: (H) $11,500

MARIN, John
American 1870-1953
paintings: (L) $7,700; (H) $44,000
drawings: (L) $550; (H) $198,000

MARINCIC, Donny
American
paintings: (H) $450

MARINELLI, V.
Italian 20th cent.
paintings: (H) $605

MARINI, Antonio
Italian 17th/18th cent.
paintings: (L) $12,650; (H) $77,000

MARINI, Marino
Italian 1901-1980
paintings: (L) $15,400; (H) $552,500
drawings: (L) $1,320; (H) $98,750
sculpture: (L) $9,775; (H) $1,102,500

MARINI, P.
Italian 19th/20th cent.
drawings: (H) $1,100

MARINKO, George
American 1908-1989
paintings: (L) $55; (H) $1,725
drawings: (L) $110; (H) $357

MARINO, Francesco di
Italian 19th c.
paintings: (H) $1,540

MARINO, Raffaele
Italian b. 1868
sculpture: (H) $31,900

MARINUS, Ancieto
Spanish late 19th cent.
sculpture: (H) $1,650

MARIO, Ugo
Italian 19th/20th cent.
paintings: (L) $220; (H) $528

MARIOTON, Eugene
French b. 1854
sculpture: (L) $1,100; (H) $3,850

MARIOTTO DE CRISTOFANO
Italian 1393-1457
paintings: (H) $27,500

MARIOTTO DI NARDO
Italian ac. 1394-1424
paintings: (H) $63,250

MARIS, Frits
Dutch 19th/20th cent.
paintings: (L) $165; (H) $1,650

MARIS, J**
Belgian 20th cent.
paintings: (H) $468

MARIS, Jacob Hendricus
Dutch 1837-1899
paintings: (L) $1,870; (H) $17,250

MARIS, Simon
Dutch 1873-1935
paintings: (H) $770

Modernist

John Marin (1870-1953), an early modernist, was a painter and an etcher. Marin was born in New Jersey and studied to become an architect. He studied at the Pennsylvania Academy of Fine Art from 1899 to 1901 with Thomas Anschutz and with William Merritt Chase at the Art Students League from 1901 to 1903. Marin spent a year abroad in 1905, and three-quarters of his print oeuvre (prints executed in his lifetime) were produced during this period. While in Paris, Marin met photographer Edward Steichen, who arranged for Marin to have an exhibition of his work at Alfred Stieglitz's Gallery 291 in New York. Marin's style shifted after 1912, becoming more Modernist and Cubist, as a result of his affiliation with Stieglitz. Marin began painting with bold brushstrokes, and his buildings were depicted as fragmented, frames painted within frames. Marin first went to Maine in 1914, and many of his paintings after this period are of the ocean. Marin also sketched and painted many scenes of circus life. Marin's works were widely exhibited and influential. He helped give Cubism and Futurism an American forum and an American shape. A retrospective of Marin's works was held at the National Gallery of Art in 1990. (John Marin, *Fishing Boat at Eastport, Maine*, watercolor and graphite on paper, Skinner, November 13, 1992, $24,200)

MARIS, Willem
Dutch 1844-1910
paintings: (L) $990; (H) $6,600

MARISOL
American b. France 1930
drawings: (L) $460; (H) $3,300
sculpture: (L) $11,500; (H) $66,000

MARK, D.
paintings: (H) $660

MARK, Lajos
paintings: (H) $2,070

MARKHAM, Charles Cole
American 1837-1907
paintings: (H) $8,800

MARKHAM, George
paintings: (H) $6,050

MARKHAM, Kyra
American 1891-1967
paintings: (L) $110; (H) $27,600

MARKINO, Yoshio
drawings: (H) $6,210

MARKO, Andreas
Austrian 1824-1895
paintings: (L) $4,950; (H) $18,700

MARKO, Henry
Italian 1855-1921
paintings: (H) $978

MARKO, Karl
Hungarian 19th cent.
paintings: (H) $2,750

MARKO, Karoly, Sr.
Hungarian 1791-1860
paintings: (H) $15,400

MARKOS, Frank
Romanian/American b. 1917
paintings: (H) $4,140

MARKOS, Lajos
American 1917-1993
paintings: (L) $880; (H) $11,000
drawings: (H) $385

MARKOWICZ, Arthur
Polish 1872-1934
drawings: (L) $880; (H) $1,320

MARKS, Claude
English 19th cent.
paintings: (L) $357; (H) $6,875

MARKS, George B.
American 1923-1983
paintings: (L) $4,620; (H) $4,620

MARKS, Henry Stacy
English 1829-1898
paintings: (H) $11,000

MARLATT, H. Irving
American d. 1929
paintings: (L) $495; (H) $2,860
drawings: (L) $385; (H) $633

MARLATT, W.
English 19th cent.
drawings: (L) $330; (H) $550

MARLIER, J.
20th cent.
paintings: (H) $990

MARLOW, William
English 1740-1813
drawings: (H) $880

MARMON (?)
drawings: (H) $690

MARNO, J.
Continental 19th cent.
paintings: (H) $3,025

MARNY, Paul
French 1829-1914
paintings: (H) $4,400
drawings: (L) $330; (H) $1,650

MAROCHETTI, Baron Charles
sculpture: (H) $4,025

MAROHN, Ferdinand
French 19th cent.
paintings: (L) $550; (H) $3,680
drawings: (H) $1,035

MARON, Anton von
Austrian 1733-1808
paintings: (H) $18,400

MARONIEZ, Georges Philibert Charles
French b. 1865
paintings: (L) $3,738; (H) $11,500

MAROT, Daniel
1663-1752
drawings: (L) $2,645; (H) $3,162

MAROT, Francois
1666-1719
paintings: (H) $8,800

MARPLE, William Lewis
1827-1910
paintings: (L) $363; (H) $4,600

MARQUEST, Laurent Honore
French 1848-1920
sculpture: (L) $1,725; (H) $1,870

MARQUET, Albert
French 1875-1947
paintings: (L) $15,950; (H) $255,500
drawings: (L) $880; (H) $12,650

MARQUET, Rene Paul
French b. 1875
sculpture: (L) $500; (H) $2,530

MARQUEZ, Esteban
d. 1696
paintings: (H) $1,150

MARQUEZ, Roberto
b. Mexico 1959
paintings: (H) $12,650

MARQUIS, James Richard
English ac. 1835-1885
paintings: (H) $2,500

MARQUIS, Richard
American b. 1945
sculpture: (L) $2,013; (H) $11,000

MARQULIES, Joseph
American 1896-1984
paintings: (H) $1,100

MARR, Carl von
American 1858-1936
paintings: (L) $8,250; (H) $13,200

MARR, Joseph Heinrich Ludwig
German 1807-1871
paintings: (H) $1,760

MARREL, Jacob
Dutch 1614-1681
paintings: (L) $189,500; (H) $376,500

MARRIOTT, Frederick
English ac. early 20th cent.
drawings: (H) $13,800

MARRON, Joan
American b. 1934
paintings: (L) $400; (H) $920

MARS, Peter Joseph Lawrence
American ac. 1893-1947
paintings: (L) $990; (H) $1,320
drawings: (L) $55; (H) $330

MARS-VALLETT, Marius
French b. 1867
sculpture: (H) $9,775

MARSANO, L.
Italian 19th cent.
paintings: (L) $10,925; (H) $13,200

MARSCHALK, Francis
drawings: (H) $920

MARSDEN
paintings: (H) $1,540

MARSDEN, Charles
American 1898-1980
paintings: (H) $770

MARSDEN, J.
English 19th cent.
paintings: (H) $1,265

MARSDEN, Theodore
American 19th cent.
paintings: (L) $330; (H) $2,420

MARSELLIS, E.
drawings: (H) $528

MARSEUS VAN SCHRIECK, Otto,
called Snuffelaer
Dutch 1619-1678
paintings: (L) $14,300; (H) $156,500

MARSH, J.P.
American b. 1910
paintings: (L) $935; (H) $990

MARSH, J.S.
paintings: (H) $770

MARSH, Lucille Patterson
American b. 1890
paintings: (H) $1,760

MARSH, Reginald
American 1898-1954
paintings: (L) $1,320; (H) $173,000
drawings: (L) $165; (H) $107,000

MARSHALL, Ben
English 1767-1835
paintings: (L) $19,550; (H) $96,000

MARSHALL, Bruce
American 20th cent.
paintings: (H) $633

MARSHALL, Charles
British 1806-1890
paintings: (L) $1,320; (H) $1,380

MARSHALL, Charles S.
American 19th/20th cent.
paintings: (L) $412; (H) $660

MARSHALL, Clark S.
American b. 1882
paintings: (L) $100; (H) $880

MARSHALL, Herbert M.
English 1841-1913
paintings: (H) $1,650

MARSHALL, J. Fitz
paintings: (H) $522

MARSHALL, J. Thurston
1908-1982
paintings: (L) $605; (H) $1,210

MARSHALL, K.
English 19th cent.
drawings: (H) $1,870

MARSHALL, Lambert
English 1809-1870
paintings: (H) $1,430

MARSHALL, R.
British 19th cent.
paintings: (H) $770

MARSHALL, Roberto
English 1849-1902
paintings: (H) $990

MARSHALL, Thomas Falcon
British 1818-1878
paintings: (H) $3,220

MARSHALL, Thomas William
American 1850-1874
paintings: (H) $2,875

MARSINI
Continental 19th/20th cent.
drawings: (H) $660

MARSTON, Brian
English 20th cent.
paintings: (H) $770

MARSTRAND, Wilhelm
Danish 1810-1873
paintings: (H) $5,980

MARTEL, Jan or Joel
French 1896-1966
sculpture: (L) $4,600; (H) $9,200

MARTEL, Jean Paul
American/Belgian 1879-1942
paintings: (H) $550

MARTENS, Conrad
British/Australian 1801-1878
drawings: (L) $6,050; (H) $6,600

MARTENS, Ernest Edouard
French b. 1865
paintings: (H) $12,100

MARTENS, Willy
Dutch 1856-1927
paintings: (H) $518

MARTIN
Continetal 19th cent.
paintings: (H) $9,075

MARTIN, A.
Swiss 19th/20th cent.
sculpture: (H) $518

MARTIN, Agnes
Canadian/American b. 1912
paintings: (L) $21,850; (H) $495,000
drawings: (L) $7,150; (H) $189,500

MARTIN, Andreas
ac. c. 1763
paintings: (H) $4,600

MARTIN, Catherine D.
drawings: (H) $688

MARTIN, Charles
British 1820-1906
paintings: (H) $977

MARTIN, David
1736-1798
paintings: (H) $5,500

MARTIN, Don
drawings: (L) $575; (H) $3,080

MARTIN, Eddie Owens
1908-1986
drawings: (H) $1,210
sculpture: (H) $1,540

MARTIN, Fletcher
American 1904-1979
paintings: (L) $798; (H) $14,950
drawings: (L) $110; (H) $4,600

MARTIN, Georg
German b. 1875
paintings: (H) $1,320

MARTIN, H.
paintings: (H) $550
drawings: (H) $1,760

MARTIN, H.
European 19th cent.
drawings: (H) $1,760

MARTIN, Henri
French 1860-1943
paintings: (L) $6,038; (H) $264,000

MARTIN, Homer Dodge
American 1836-1897
paintings: (L) $357; (H) $22,000
drawings: (H) $2,750

MARTIN, J. Hill
paintings: (L) $247; (H) $385
drawings: (H) $2,640

MARTIN, Jacques
French 1844-1919
paintings: (H) $2,475

MARTIN, James
American ac. c. 1794-1820
drawings: (H) $16,100

MARTIN, John
paintings: (L) $2,860; (H) $4,400

MARTIN, John
English 1789-1854
paintings: (H) $2,090
drawings: (L) $7,150; (H) $15,400

MARTIN, Keith
paintings: (H) $115
drawings: (L) $50; (H) $2,530

MARTIN, Knox
Colombian/Amer. b. 1923
paintings: (L) $2,185; (H) $4,888
drawings: (H) $1,980

MARTIN, L. Edna
paintings: (L) $1,210; (H) $5,500
drawings: (H) $165

MARTIN, S.
paintings: (L) $650; (H) $4,400

MARTIN, S.R.
Italian 19th cent.
drawings: (H) $3,080

MARTIN, Samuel
drawings: (H) $963

MARTIN, Sue Pettey
American b. 1896
paintings: (H) $990

MARTIN, Sylvester
English ac. 1870-1899
paintings: (L) $230; (H) $9,775

MARTIN, Thomas Mower
Canadian 1838-1934
paintings: (L) $413; (H) $880

MARTIN, W.
paintings: (L) $747; (H) $880

MARTIN, William A.K.
American 1817-1867
drawings: (L) $825; (H) $1,100

MARTIN-FERRIERES, Jac
French 1893-1972
paintings: (L) $2,990; (H) $34,500

MARTIN-KAVEL, Francois
French 1861-1931
paintings: (L) $1,000; (H) $18,700

MARTINE, Omar
Continental 19th cent.
paintings: (H) $3,300

MARTINETTI
Italian 19th/20th cent.
paintings: (H) $575

MARTINETTI, Angelo
Italian 19th cent.
paintings: (L) $9,900; (H) $11,000

MARTINETTI, Maria
Italian b. 1864
drawings: (L) $1,650; (H) $9,200

MARTINEZ
paintings: (L) $145; (H) $1,100
drawings: (H) $8,250

MARTINEZ, Ana Maria de
b. El Salvador 1937
paintings: (L) $11,500; (H) $16,100

MARTINEZ, F.E.
paintings: (L) $880; (H) $990

MARTINEZ, Gonzalo Bilbao
Spanish 1860-1938
paintings: (L) $9,350; (H) $15,400

MARTINEZ, Jaime
20th cent.
paintings: (H) $522

MARTINEZ, Julian, Pocano
Native American 1897-1943
drawings: (L) $248; (H) $2,200

MARTINEZ, Luis
ac. 1920-1930
paintings: (H) $129,000

MARTINEZ, Raymundo
Mexican b. 1945
paintings: (H) $2,875

MARTINEZ, Ricardo
Mexican b. 1918
paintings: (L) $935; (H) $79,500
drawings: (H) $660

MARTINEZ, Richard, Opa Mu Nu
Native American b. 1904
drawings: (H) $990

MARTINEZ, Xavier
Mexican/American 1869-1943
paintings: (L) $1,430; (H) $5,225
drawings: (H) $863

MARTINEZ BAEZ, Salvador
b. Mexico 1896-1987
paintings: (H) $13,200

MARTINEZ-PEDRO, Luis
Cuban b. 1910
paintings: (L) $4,025; (H) $11,500
drawings: (L) $5,750; (H) $10,350

MARTINI, Arturo
sculpture: (H) $9,200

MARTINI, Felix Lewis
American 1893-1965
paintings: (L) $1,100; (H) $1,760

MARTINI, Joseph de
American b. 1896
paintings: (L) $880; (H) $4,313

MARTINI, Simone
Italian 1284-1334
paintings: (H) $242,000

MARTINI, Simone, workshop of
Italian 13th/14th cent.
paintings: (H) $418,000

MARTINI, W.J.
Italian 19th cent.
paintings: (H) $4,400

MARTINO, Antonio P.
American 1902-1989
paintings: (L) $50; (H) $10,000
drawings: (L) $297; (H) $1,155

MARTINO, Giovanni
American b. 1908
paintings: (L) $100; (H) $3,850
drawings: (L) $253; (H) $900

MARTINS, Maria
Brazilian 1900-1973
sculpture: (H) $13,200

MARTINUS, Elsa
Dutch/American 20th cent.
sculpture: (L) $1,650; (H) $3,300

MARTINY, Philip
American 1856-1927
sculpture: (H) $3,850

MARTORI, Patty
20th cent.
drawings: (H) $575

MARTUNY, W.
drawings: (H) $550

MARTZ
paintings: (H) $748

MARUYAMA
drawings: (H) $4,070

MARVELLI, Edouard
French b. 1906
paintings: (H) $920

MARX, Ernest Bernhard
German b. 1864
paintings: (H) $10,725

MARX, Franz
German b. 1889
paintings: (H) $1,035

MARX, Samuel
American 20th cent.
drawings: (L) $110; (H) $1,380

MARZELLE, Jean
French b. 1916
paintings: (L) $550; (H) $1,955

MARZELLI, G.
Italian 19th cent.
paintings: (H) $6,500

MAS Y FONDEVILA, Arcadio
Spanish b. 1850
paintings: (H) $9,350

MASATSUNE CHU
late 19th cent.
sculpture: (L) $3,162; (H) $5,175

MASAYUKI, Nagare
b. 1923
sculpture: (L) $7,475; (H) $32,200

MASCAGNI, G.
sculpture: (H) $1,430

MASCART, Gustave
French 1834-1914
paintings: (L) $550; (H) $3,300

MASCART, Paul
French 1874-1958
paintings: (L) $690; (H) $7,187

MASCHERINI, Marcello
Italian b. 1906
sculpture: (H) $1,380

MASEREEL, Frans
Belgian 1889-1971
paintings: (L) $3,335; (H) $5,462
drawings: (H) $467

MASOLINO DA PANICALE,
Tommaso di Cristofano di Fino
Italian c. 1383/4-c. 1436
paintings: (H) $299,500

MASON, Barry
British b. 1947
paintings: (H) $5,500

MASON, Bateson
paintings: (H) $715

MASON, Benjamin Franklin
American 1804-1871
paintings: (H) $3,025

MASON, Concetta
American b. 1956
sculpture: (L) $3,850; (H) $4,180

MASON, Frank H.
English 1876-1975
paintings: (L) $110; (H) $1,760
drawings: (L) $127; (H) $825

MASON, Lewis G.
British 19th cent.
paintings: (H) $489

MASON, Mary Townsend
American 1882-1964
paintings: (L) $748; (H) $1,550

MASON, Max Wilson
American 20th cent.
paintings: (H) $978

MASON, Roy Martell
American 1886-1972
paintings: (L) $605; (H) $1,955
drawings: (L) $330; (H) $3,520

MASON, William Sanford
American 1824-1864
paintings: (L) $2,640; (H) $11,500

MASRIERA Y MANOVENS, Francisco
Spanish 1842-1902
paintings: (L) $7,425; (H) $41,250

MASSAD, G. Daniel
b. 1946
drawings: (L) $1,840; (H) $3,220

MASSANI, Pompeo
Italian 1850-1920
paintings: (L) $825; (H) $5,750

MASSE, Jules
French 1825-1897
paintings: (H) $43,700

MASSEAU, Fix
early 20th cent.
sculpture: (H) $715

MASSOLINI, S.
Italian 19th cent.
paintings: (H) $2,750

MASSON, Alexandre
French 19th cent.
paintings: (H) $2,300

MASSON, Andre
French 1896-1987
paintings: (L) $24,200; (H) $484,000
drawings: (L) $935; (H) $77,000

MASSON, Clovis Edmond
French 1838-1913
paintings: (H) $316
sculpture: (L) $330; (H) $660

MASSON, Henri Leopold
Canadian b. 1907
paintings: (L) $1,760; (H) $4,400
drawings: (H) $1,650

MASSON, Jules Edmond
French b. 1871
sculpture: (L) $604; (H) $7,700

MASSON, Paul le
French 19th/20th cent.
paintings: (L) $825; (H) $1,760

MASSONI, Egisto
drawings: (H) $825

MASSOY, S. Juan
sculpture: (H) $660

MASSYS, Quentin, studio of
15th/16th cent.
paintings: (H) $51,750

MASTENBROEK, Johann Hendrik van
Dutch 1875-1945
paintings: (H) $2,200
drawings: (L) $110; (H) $2,530

MASTER OF 1310
ac. 1310-c.1325
paintings: (H) $814,000

MASTER OF 1518
paintings: (L) $22,000; (H) $209,000

MASTER OF ALKMAAR
ac. 1490-1510
paintings: (H) $63,000

MASTER OF BOLOGNA
paintings: (H) $2,415

**MASTER OF BORGO ALLA
COLLINA**
ac. c. 1400
paintings: (H) $34,500

MASTER OF DORDRECHT
17th cent.
paintings: (H) $18,400

MASTER OF FRANKFURT
ac. 1493-1520
paintings: (H) $30,800

MASTER OF KRESS LANDSCAPES
ac. c. 1505-c. 1530
paintings: (H) $85,000

MASTER OF LONIGO
ac. 15th cent.
paintings: (H) $48,875

MASTER OF SAINT ANNA
ac. 15th cent.
paintings: (H) $442,500

MASTER OF SAINT IVO
ac. c. 1400
paintings: (L) $46,000; (H) $71,500

**MASTER OF SAN JACOPO A
MUCCIANA**
ac. c. 1400
paintings: (H) $255,500

**MASTER OF SAN MARTINO ALLA
PALMA**
ac. 1310-1335
paintings: (H) $937,500

MASTER OF SAN MINIATO
15th century,
paintings: (H) $55,000

MASTER OF STAFFOLO
15th cent.
paintings: (H) $52,250

MASTER OF THE 1540S,
ac. 1541-1551
paintings: (L) $60,500; (H) $85,000

**MASTER OF THE ANDRE
MADONNA**
ac. c. 1500
paintings: (H) $28,750

**MASTER OF THE APOLLO AND
DAPHNE LEGEND**
c. 1480-1510
paintings: (H) $38,500

**MASTER OF THE CASTELLO
NATIVITY,** 15th century
paintings: (H) $231,000

**MASTER OF THE CIRIE
POLYPTYCH,** PSEUDO GIUSEPPE
GIOVENONE
ac. first half 16th cent.
paintings: (H) $8,050

**MASTER OF THE EMBROIDERED
FOLIAGE**
ac. 1470-1500
paintings: (H) $195,000

**MASTER OF THE FEMALE HALF
LENGTHS,** 16th century
paintings: (L) $46,000; (H) $47,300

**MASTER OF THE FEMALE HALF-
LENGTHS,** studio of
ac. 1500-1550
paintings: (H) $17,250

**MASTER OF THE FIESOLE
EPIPHANY,** Filippo di Giuliano di
MATTEO?
ac. last qtr. 15th cent.
paintings: (H) $46,000

**MASTER OF THE FIESOLE
EPIPHANY,** poss. Filippo di
Guiliano deMATTEO
ac. turn of 15th cent.
paintings: (H) $123,500

**MASTER OF THE INCREDULITY OF
SAINT THOMAS**
ac. 1505/6-1525
paintings: (H) $16,500

**MASTER OF THE JOHNSON
ASSUMPTION OF THE
MAGDALEN**
ac. c. 1500
paintings: (H) $55,200

**MASTER OF THE KHANENKO
ADORATION (16TH CENTURY)**
paintings: (H) $22,000

**MASTER OF THE LATHROP
TONDO**
15th/16th cent.
paintings: (H) $16,500

**MASTER OF THE LEGEND OF ST.
URSULA**
ac. c. 1470-1500
paintings: (H) $77,000

**MASTER OF THE LEONARDESQUE
FEMALE PORTRAITS**
early 16th cent.
paintings: (H) $330,000

**MASTER OF THE LIVERPOOL
MADONNA**
ac. c. late 1490s
paintings: (H) $49,450

**MASTER OF THE MAGDALENE
LEGEND**
ac. late 15th cent.
paintings: (H) $24,200

**MASTER OF THE NAUMBERG
MADONNA,** FLORENCE
ac. c. 1485-1510
paintings: (H) $137,500

MASTER OF THE PARROT,
16th century
paintings: (H) $24,200

MASTER OF THE RUGS
17th cent.
paintings: (H) $38,500

**MASTER OF THE
SCHWARTZENBERG-PORTRAITS**
ac. mid. 17th cent.
paintings: (H) $10,925

**MASTER OF THE STORIES OF
HELEN**
early 1440s-c.1470
paintings: (H) $165,000

**MASTER OF THE TWELVE
APOSTLES**
ac. 1530-1542
paintings: (H) $16,100

MASTERS, Edwin
British 19th cent.
paintings: (L) $935; (H) $3,630

MASTERS, Thomas
English ac. 1870-1880
paintings: (H) $1,540

MASTROIANNI, Umberto
b. 1910
sculpture: (H) $3,450

MASUCCI, Agostino
1691-1758
paintings: (H) $10,350

MASULLO, Andrew
20th cent.
sculpture: (H) $460

MASUO, Ikeda
b. 1934
drawings: (L) $3,450; (H) $4,370

MATALUKA, J.
paintings: (H) $1,210

MATANIA, Fortunino
Italian 1881-1963
drawings: (L) $247; (H) $715

MATARE, Ewald
German 1887-1965
drawings: (H) $7,150
sculpture: (L) $4,025; (H) $12,650

MATAZO, Kayama
b. 1927
drawings: (L) $20,700; (H) $145,500

MATHEWS, Arthur F.
American 1860-1945
paintings: (L) $8,250; (H) $52,250

MATHEWS, J.
paintings: (H) $3,520

MATHEWS, John Chester
English ac. 1884-1900
paintings: (L) $2,760; (H) $3,080

MATHEWS, Lucia
American 1870-1955
drawings: (H) $12,100

MATHEWS, S.E.
American 19th/20th cent.
paintings: (H) $495

MATHEWS, W.T.
American 19th dent.
paintings: (H) $1,540

MATHEWSON, Frank Convers
American 1862-1941
paintings: (L) $130; (H) $2,310
drawings: (L) $110; (H) $440

MATHIEU, Gabriel
French 19th cent.
paintings: (L) $220; (H) $4,312

MATHIEU, Georges
French b. 1921
paintings: (L) $14,950; (H) $42,900
drawings: (L) $2,875; (H) $8,800

MATHIEU, Paul
Belgian 1872-1932
paintings: (L) $5,500; (H) $13,800

MATHONAT, A.
paintings: (H) $605

MATHURIN, Maurice
French 19th/20th cent.
paintings: (H) $550

MATIFAS, Louis Remy
Dutch 1847-1896
paintings: (H) $1,150

MATIK, Fiano
20th cent.
drawings: (H) $1,840

MATISSE, Camille
French 19/20th cent.
paintings: (H) $550

MATISSE, Henri
French 1869-1954
paintings: (L) $9,200; (H) $14,852,500
drawings: (L) $3,450; (H) $13,752,500
sculpture: (L) $17,600; (H) $420,500

MATISSE, Henri and Pablo PICASSO
19th/20th cent.
drawings: (H) $27,600

MATOUT, Louis
French 1811-1888
paintings: (H) $5,175

MATSON, Henry Ellis
1887-1971
paintings: (H) $798

MATSON, Victor
American 1898-1972
paintings: (L) $385; (H) $1,320

MATSUBARA, Kazuo
American b. 1895
paintings: (H) $1,430

MATTA
Chilean b. 1911
paintings: (L) $10,350; (H) $552,500
drawings: (L) $2,750; (H) $112,500
sculpture: (L) $2,310; (H) $29,900

MATTA-CLARK, Gordon
1945-1978
drawings: (L) $8,050; (H) $18,400

MATTEIS, Paolo de
Italian 1662-1728
paintings: (L) $3,850; (H) $132,000
drawings: (H) $1,980

MATTERN, Alice L.
American 1909-1945
paintings: (L) $825; (H) $1,210

MATTESON, Bartow V.
b. 1894
paintings: (L) $385; (H) $1,430

MATTESON, Tompkins H.
American 1813-1884
paintings: (H) $19,550

MATTHEWS, J.F.
Continental 19th cent.
paintings: (H) $2,185

MATTHEWS, James
British 19th cent.
drawings: (H) $1,725

MATTHEWS, Marmaduke
drawings: (L) $1,320; (H) $1,540

MATTHEWS, Michael
English b. 1933
paintings: (L) $403; (H) $1,210

MATTHEWS, William F.
American b. 1878
paintings: (L) $440; (H) $2,760
drawings: (H) $316

MATTHIESEN, Oscar Adam Otto
German 1861-1959
paintings: (H) $18,700

MATTHIEU, Cornelis
ac. 1637-1656
paintings: (H) $8,800

MATTO, Francisco
b. Uruguay 1911
paintings: (L) $3,850; (H) $15,400
sculpture: (H) $11,500

MATTONI DE LA FUENTE, Virgilio
Spanish b. 1842
paintings: (H) $71,500

MATTSON, Henry E.
American 1887-1971
paintings: (L) $385; (H) $4,180

MATULKA, Jan
Czech/American 1890-1972
paintings: (L) $770; (H) $9,200
drawings: (L) $440; (H) $5,225

MATURO, Joseph A.
1867-1938
paintings: (L) $825; (H) $2,970
drawings: (L) $1,650; (H) $9,200

MATYSEK, Petr.
paintings: (H) $770

MAUBOUCH, A.
French 19th cent.
sculpture: (H) $3,575

MAUCHIN, A.
Continental 20th cent.
drawings: (H) $605

MAUD, William T.
British 1865-1903
paintings: (H) $27,600

MAUER, Alfred Henry
American 1868-1932
paintings: (H) $10,925

MAUFRA, Maxime
French 1861/62-1918
paintings: (L) $9,350; (H) $60,500
drawings: (H) $2,300

MAUGSCH
sculpture: (H) $2,200

MAULIN, E.
sculpture: (H) $3,300

MAUNSBACH, George Eric
American 1890-1969?
paintings: (H) $1,320

MAUPERTEUS, L.
French ac. 1915-1925
sculpture: (H) $6,900

MAURER
American 1897-1961
paintings: (H) $468

MAURER, Alfred H.
American 1868-1932
paintings: (L) $2,185; (H) $800,000
drawings: (L) $3,300; (H) $29,700

MAURER, Hubert
1738-1810
paintings: (H) $2,420

MAURER, Jacob
German 1826-1887
paintings: (H) $1,870

MAURER, Louis
German/American 1832-1932
paintings: (H) $21,850

MAURICE-MARTIN
French 1894-1978
paintings: (L) $605; (H) $6,050

MAURIN, Charles
French 1856-1914
paintings: (H) $10,925
drawings: (L) $220; (H) $13,800

MAURY, Cornelia Field
American 19th cent.
paintings: (L) $50; (H) $770

MAURY, Francois
French 1861-1933
paintings: (L) $1,100; (H) $1,980

MAUVE, Anton
Dutch 1838-1888
paintings: (L) $748; (H) $34,100
drawings: (L) $715; (H) $11,000

MAX, Corneille
German 1875-1924
paintings: (H) $550

MAX, Gabriel von
Czechoslovakian 1840-1915
paintings: (L) $440; (H) $16,100

MAX, Peter
German/American b. 1937
paintings: (L) $1,320; (H) $7,975
drawings: (L) $660; (H) $2,090

MAXENCE, Edgard
French 1871-1954
paintings: (H) $19,550
drawings: (H) $8,050

MAXEY, Theobold
American 20th cent.
paintings: (H) $550

MAXFIELD, C.L.
drawings: (H) $1,540

MAXFIELD, Clara
American 1879-1959
drawings: (L) $247; (H) $1,100

MAXFIELD, James Emery
American b. 1848
paintings: (L) $770; (H) $2,310

MAXIM, David
contemporary
drawings: (H) $2,090

MAXWELL, J.
paintings: (H) $900

MAXWELL, Laura W.
American 1877-1967
paintings: (H) $660

MAXY
paintings: (H) $920

MAY, F.
poss. British 20th cent.
paintings: (L) $385; (H) $518

MAY, Henrietta Mabel
paintings: (L) $1,320; (H) $3,740

MAY, J.
European 19th cent.
paintings: (L) $143; (H) $825

MAY, Phil
English 1864-1903
paintings: (H) $1,100
drawings: (L) $330; (H) $330

MAY, Sibyl Huntington
1734/5-1798
paintings: (H) $145,500

MAY, Sibylle
French ac. 1925-1935
sculpture: (H) $4,025

MAY, Walter William
British 1831-1896
paintings: (H) $1,035

MAYBECK, Bernard
drawings: (L) $660; (H) $9,350

MAYDELL, Baron Ernst von
German 1888-1961
drawings: (L) $275; (H) $1,265

MAYER
sculpture: (L) $374; (H) $575

MAYER
American 19th cent.
paintings: (H) $880

MAYER, Alois
b. 1855
sculpture: (H) $660

MAYER, Auguste Etienne Francois
French 1805-1890
paintings: (L) $2,200; (H) $9,350

MAYER, C.
American 19th cent.
sculpture: (H) $11,000

MAYER, Christian
German 1805-1851
paintings: (H) $825

MAYER, Constant
French/American 1829/32-1911
paintings: (L) $5,980; (H) $43,125

MAYER, E.
German/Austrian 19th cent.
paintings: (H) $518

MAYER, Franz
19th cent.
paintings: (H) $1,100

MAYER, Hendrik de
drawings: (H) $805

MAYER, Henrik Martin
1908-1972
paintings: (L) $4,313; (H) $7,475

MAYER, Louis
American b. 1869
paintings: (H) $575
sculpture: (H) $9,900

MAYER, Lugi
ac. end of 18th cent.
paintings: (H) $2,530

MAYER, Nicolas
French 1852-1929
sculpture: (L) $2,640; (H) $8,050

MAYER, Peter Bela
American b. 1888
paintings: (L) $330; (H) $3,080

MAYER, Ralph
b. 1895
paintings: (H) $660

MAYER?
20th cent.
paintings: (H) $550

MAYERNIK, Ken
American
sculpture: (L) $650; (H) $650

MAYEUR, Jean le
Belgian 1890-1958
paintings: (H) $4,675

MAYFIELD, Robert Bledsoe
1869-1934
drawings: (L) $605; (H) $1,650

MAYHEW, Nell Brooker
American 1876-1940
paintings: (L) $88; (H) $1,430
drawings: (H) $575

MAYNARD, George Willoughby
American 1843-1923
paintings: (L) $2,420; (H) $8,250
drawings: (H) $880

MAYNARD, Richard Field
American b. 1875
paintings: (L) $165; (H) $3,960
sculpture: (H) $1,150

MAYO, Mary
American 20th cent.
drawings: (H) $550

MAYR, C.
Continental 19th cent.
paintings: (H) $978

MAYS, J.
Continental School 19th cent.
paintings: (H) $550

MAYS, Maxwell
American
paintings: (L) $2,310; (H) $7,150

MAYS, Victor
American 20th cent.
drawings: (L) $805; (H) $3,565

MAZA, Fernando
paintings: (H) $880

MAZE, Paul
French 1887-1979
paintings: (L) $575; (H) $2,300
drawings: (H) $575

MAZE, Paul
French b. 1928
paintings: (L) $1,320; (H) $8,800
drawings: (L) $550; (H) $10,450

MAZELLA, J.
French 19th cent.
paintings: (L) $935; (H) $1,595

MAZETTI, G.
paintings: (H) $460

MAZINI, Ciro
Italian 19th/20th cent.
drawings: (L) $165; (H) $825

MAZOLATI, L.
Italian 19th/20th cent.
drawings: (H) $825

MAZUR, Michael
American b. 1935
paintings: (L) $1,870; (H) $4,950
drawings: (L) $1,210; (H) $2,530

MAZZALO, Giuseppe
Italian 1748-1838
paintings: (H) $1,955

MAZZANOVICH, Laurence
American 1872-1946
paintings: (L) $990; (H) $7,700

MAZZETTA
Italian late 19th cent.
paintings: (H) $4,950

MAZZOLA-BEDOLI, Girolamo
c. 1500-1569
paintings: (H) $23,000

MAZZOLINI, G.
Italian 19th cent.
paintings: (H) $6,050

MAZZOLINI, G.***
19th cent.
paintings: (L) $4,400; (H) $6,325

MAZZOLINI, Giuseppe
Italian 1748-1838
paintings: (H) $1,495

MAZZOLINI, Giuseppe
Italian 1806-1876
paintings: (L) $1,495; (H) $7,150

MAZZOLINI, T.
paintings: (H) $1,485

MAZZOLINO, Ludovico
Italian c. 1480-1528?
paintings: (H) $178,500

MAZZONI, Emilo
Italian 1869-1935
paintings: (L) $1,045; (H) $1,540

MAZZONI, Sebastiano
Italian c. 1611-1678
paintings: (H) $40,250

MAZZOTTA, Federico
Italian 19th cent.
paintings: (L) $9,900; (H) $9,900

MAZZUCCHELLI
Italian 19th cent.
sculpture: (H) $1,540

MCAFEE, Ila
American b. 1900
paintings: (H) $2,200

MCALPINE, William
British 19th cent.
paintings: (H) $550

MCAULIFFE, James J.
American 1848-1921
paintings: (L) $330; (H) $12,650

MCBEY, James
English 1883-1959
paintings: (L) $2,750; (H) $4,370
drawings: (L) $79; (H) $1,265

MCBURNEY, James Edwin
American b. 1868
paintings: (L) $55; (H) $660

MCCAIN, Buck
American contemporary
paintings: (L) $880; (H) $3,105

MCCALL, Charles James
paintings: (H) $1,540

MCCALLION, P.
American 19th cent.
paintings: (L) $220; (H) $5,500

MCCARTEN, Edward
American 1879-1953
sculpture: (L) $4,600; (H) $7,480

MCCARTER, Henry
American 1866-1942
paintings: (L) $1,265; (H) $3,450
drawings: (L) $375; (H) $605

MCCARTHY, Doris Jean
paintings: (L) $1,650; (H) $2,200
drawings: (H) $1,210

MCCARTHY, Francis
American 20th cent.
drawings: (L) $55; (H) $748

MCCARTHY, Frank
American b. 1924
paintings: (L) $1,760; (H) $66,000

MCCARTHY, Justin
1892-1977
paintings: (L) $1,595; (H) $5,175
drawings: (H) $1,155

MCCAULIFFE, J.
American
paintings: (H) $4,888

MCCAW, Dan
American b. 1942
paintings: (L) $3,300; (H) $13,750
drawings: (H) $2,000

MCCAY, Winsor
American 1871-1934
drawings: (L) $1,980; (H) $24,200

MCCHESNEY, Clara
American 1860-1928
paintings: (L) $137; (H) $440
drawings: (H) $2,200

MCCHESNEY, Robert
American b. 1913
drawings: (L) $1,100; (H) $1,265

MCCLAIN, Helen Charlton
American b. 1887
paintings: (H) $3,220

MCCLAIRE, Gerald Armstrong
American b. 1897
drawings: (H) $495

MCCLEARY, Dan
American 20th cent.
paintings: (H) $863

MCCLELLAND, John
b. 1919
drawings: (H) $1,760

MCCLOORE
American contemporary
sculpture: (H) $460

MCCLOSKEY, Alberta Binford
American 1863-1911
paintings: (L) $46,000; (H) $68,500

MCCLOSKEY, Jim
American 20th cent.
paintings: (H) $1,540

MCCLOSKEY, William Joseph
American 1859-1941
paintings: (L) $2,300; (H) $464,500

MCCOLLUM, Allan
American b. 1944
paintings: (L) $3,738; (H) $11,000
drawings: (L) $2,875; (H) $12,650
sculpture: (L) $5,750; (H) $143,000

MCCOLVIN, John
British 19th cent.
paintings: (L) $220; (H) $1,100

MCCOMAS, Francis
American 1874-1938
paintings: (L) $2,475; (H) $9,200
drawings: (L) $138; (H) $7,475

MCCOMAS, Gene Francis
American 1886-1982
paintings: (H) $3,025
drawings: (L) $275; (H) $2,300

MCCONNELL, George
American 1852-1929
paintings: (L) $27; (H) $2,070

MCCORD, C.H.
drawings: (H) $550

MCCORD, George Herbert
American 1848-1909
paintings: (L) $330; (H) $16,100
drawings: (L) $86; (H) $440

MCCORMACK, Howard
American 1875-1943
paintings: (H) $1,320

MCCORMICK
American 20th cent.
paintings: (H) $1,380

MCCORMICK, Arthur David
British 1860-1943
paintings: (H) $4,600

MCCORMICK, Evelyn
American 1869-1948
paintings: (L) $3,575; (H) $5,225

MCCORMICK, Howard
American 1875-1943
paintings: (H) $1,430

MCCORMICK, Jyne
American 19th cent.
paintings: (H) $467

MCCOY, John W.
b. 1909
drawings: (H) $2,300

MCCOY, Raymond A.
b. 1893
paintings: (H) $1,650

MCCOY, Wilton
American 1902-1986
paintings: (L) $193; (H) $11,500
drawings: (H) $413

MCCRACKEN, John
American b. 1934
paintings: (L) $330; (H) $805
sculpture: (L) $4,600; (H) $17,600

MCCRADY, John
American 1911-1968
paintings: (L) $1,650; (H) $14,300

MCCREA, Harold Wellington
paintings: (H) $1,320

MCCROSSAN, Mary
English d. 1924
paintings: (H) $1,045

MCCRUM, Elizabeth
paintings: (H) $633

MCCULLOCH, Horatio
British 1805-1867
paintings: (L) $303; (H) $3,300

MCCULLOUGH, J.
paintings: (H) $3,575

MCCURDY, Allen
b. 1933
paintings: (H) $3,960

MCDERMITT, William T.
American 1884-1961
paintings: (L) $330; (H) $550

MCDERMOTT and MCGOUGH
Americans b. 1950s
paintings: (L) $1,150; (H) $8,250

MCDONALD, Mason
American 1880-1961
paintings: (H) $550

MCDONNELL, Charles E.
paintings: (H) $577

MCDORMAN, Donald
American 20th cent.
paintings: (H) $550

MCDOUGALL, G.F.
drawings: (H) $935

MCDOUGALL, John A.
American b. 1843
paintings: (H) $770

MCDOUGALL, John Alexander
1810-1894
paintings: (H) $2,090

MCDOUGALL, Walt H.
19th cent.
paintings: (H) $715

MCDOWELL, H.E.
paintings: (H) $825

MCDOWELL, William
British 1888-1950
drawings: (H) $2,070

MCDUFF, Frederick H.
American b. 1931
paintings: (L) $990; (H) $9,350

MCELROY, Mary
English 1870-1941
paintings: (H) $468

MCENTEE, Jervis
American 1828-1891
paintings: (L) $330; (H) $18,700
drawings: (L) $33; (H) $385

MCEVOY, Ambrose
English 1878-1927
drawings: (L) $1,320; (H) $4,125

MCEWAN, Thomas
British 1861-1914
paintings: (H) $2,200

MCEWAN, Tom
British 1846-1914
paintings: (H) $1,100

MCEWAN, Walter
19th cent.
paintings: (H) $1,320

MCFARLAND, Robert
paintings: (H) $1,760

MCFARLANE, David
English ac. 1840-1866
paintings: (H) $13,200

MCFARLANE, Duncan
British 1834-1871
paintings: (H) $14,850

MCFARLANE, Todd
drawings: (H) $747

MCFEE, Henry Lee
American 1886-1953
paintings: (L) $4,950; (H) $10,925
drawings: (H) $440

MCGARY, Dave
American b. 1958
sculpture: (L) $9,350; (H) $13,200

MCGEEHAN, Jessie M.
British ac. 1892-1913
drawings: (H) $467

MCGEORGE, Thomas
American
paintings: (H) $605

MCGHIE, John
Scottish b. 1867
paintings: (H) $3,850

MCGILL, Eloise Polk
American 1869-1939
paintings: (L) $489; (H) $1,650

MCGINNIS, Robert
b. 1926
paintings: (L) $1,650; (H) $7,700
drawings: (L) $1,650; (H) $3,080

MCGLYNN, Thomas
American 1876-1966
paintings: (L) $1,495; (H) $5,750

MCGRAITH, Marriet
drawings: (H) $1,035

MCGRATH, Clarence
American b. 1938
paintings: (L) $660; (H) $4,180

MCGREW, Ralph Brownell
American 1916-1994
paintings: (L) $715; (H) $66,000

MCGUINESS, Bingham
British ac. 1882-1892
drawings: (L) $345; (H) $2,475

MCHURON, Gregory I.
American
paintings: (H) $1,300

MCILHENNEY, C. Morgan
American b. 1858
paintings: (H) $33,000

MCINTIRE, Joseph Wrightson
English/American 19th cent.
paintings: (H) $550

MCINTOSH, Pleasant Ray
American b. 1897
paintings: (L) $412; (H) $550

MCINTYRE, J.
British 19th cent.
paintings: (L) $770; (H) $2,645

MCINTYRE, Joseph Wrightson
British 19th cent.
paintings: (H) $935

MCINTYRE, Robert Finlay
English ac. 1892-1897
paintings: (H) $1,870

MCKAIN, Bruce
American b. 1900
paintings: (L) $165; (H) $1,100

MCKAY, Edwin Murray
American 1869-1926
paintings: (H) $6,325

MCKAY, Thomas Hill
Scottish/American 1875-1941
paintings: (L) $1,150; (H) $1,430

MCKAY, William Darling
English 1844-1924
paintings: (H) $4,400

MCKEAN, Lance
American 20th cent.
sculpture: (H) $935

MCKEEVER, Ian
b. 1946
paintings: (H) $10,450
drawings: (L) $6,050; (H) $6,600

MCKELVEY, David
drawings: (H) $495

MCKENNA, T.G.
paintings: (H) $550

MCKENZIE, Robert Tait
Canadian/American 1867-1938
drawings: (H) $110
sculpture: (L) $770; (H) $40,700

MCKEWAN, David Hall
English 1816/17-1873
drawings: (H) $1,035

MCKIM, C.C.
paintings: (H) $468

MCKIMSON, Bob
drawings: (L) $920; (H) $1,610

MCKNIGHT, Dodge
American 1860-1950
drawings: (L) $1,045; (H) $1,870

MCKNIGHT, R.J.
American 1905-1989
sculpture: (H) $2,640

MCKNIGHT, Thomas
American b. 1941
paintings: (L) $1,320; (H) $3,190

MCLAUGHLIN, Charles J.
American b. 1888
paintings: (L) $230; (H) $1,265
drawings: (H) $110

MCLAUGHLIN, John
American 1898-1976
paintings: (L) $9,430; (H) $33,000

MCLAUGHLIN, Nancy
drawings: (H) $880

MCLEAN, A.M.
American 19th cent.
paintings: (H) $1,045

MCLEAN, Bruce
b. 1944
paintings: (L) $2,200; (H) $2,750

MCLEAN, Jack Lee
Canadian b. 1924
paintings: (L) $2,090; (H) $3,850

MCLEAN, Richard
American b. 1934
paintings: (H) $17,600

MCLEAN, Wilson
b. 1937
paintings: (H) $1,760

MCLEAY, M.
paintings: (H) $3,740

MCLEAY, McNeil Robert
British 1802-1878
paintings: (H) $2,530

MCLENNAN, Eunice
American 1886-1966
drawings: (H) $990

MCMAHAN, Gloria
American
paintings: (H) $3,300

MCMANUS, George
American 1884-1954
drawings: (L) $440; (H) $1,955

MCMANUS, James Goodwin
American 1882-1958
paintings: (L) $220; (H) $1,400

MCMASTER, William E.
American 1823-1860
paintings: (H) $1,610

MCMEIN, Neysa
American 1888-1949
drawings: (L) $880; (H) $1,430

MCMILLEN, Jack
b. 1910
paintings: (L) $6,325; (H) $6,900

MCMINN, W.K.
paintings: (H) $6,325

MCNAIR, William
paintings: (H) $2,420

MCNEIL, George
American b. 1908
paintings: (L) $715; (H) $17,600
drawings: (H) $4,830

MCNEILL, Lloyd G.
American 20th cent.
paintings: (H) $1,045

MCNOEL, A. and A. TAYLOR
British 19th cent.
paintings: (H) $719

MCNULTY, Marie
20th cent.
paintings: (L) $522; (H) $550

MCPHERSON-HAYE, J.
drawings: (H) $550

MCRAE, Roderick
drawings: (H) $1,210

MCSWINEY, Eugene
Irish b. 1866
paintings: (L) $219; (H) $2,420

MCVICKER, Charles
b. 1930
paintings: (H) $605

MCWHIRTER, John
British 1839-1911
drawings: (H) $1,650

MCWILLIAM, F.C.
British b. 1909
paintings: (H) $2,070

MEACCI, Ricciardo
Italian b. 1856
paintings: (H) $1,210
drawings: (H) $220

MEAD, Larkin Goldsmith
American 1835-1910
sculpture: (L) $1,495; (H) $12,000

MEAD, Ray John
paintings: (H) $2,200

MEADMORE, Clement
b.1929
sculpture: (L) $1,210; (H) $7,700

MEADOR, Joshua L.
American 1911-1965
paintings: (L) $275; (H) $550

MEADOWS, Arthur Joseph
English 1843-1907
paintings: (L) $1,100; (H) $5,500

MEADOWS, Bernard
American b. 1915
drawings: (L) $115; (H) $161
sculpture: (L) $275; (H) $2,990

MEADOWS, Edwin L.
English ac. 1854-1872
paintings: (L) $385; (H) $9,350

MEADOWS, J. Kenny
English 1790-1874
paintings: (H) $1,100

MEADOWS, James Edwin
British 1828-1888
paintings: (L) $825; (H) $12,075

MEADOWS, W.
paintings: (L) $715; (H) $990

MEADOWS, W.G.
English ac. 1874
paintings: (L) $1,725; (H) $2,300

MEADOWS, William
paintings: (H) $1,540

MEADOWS, William
British
paintings: (H) $880

MEADOWS, William
English 19th cent.
paintings: (H) $1,210

MEADOWS, William
English ac. 1870-1895
paintings: (H) $1,650

MEAGHER, Sister Patricia
contemporary
sculpture: (L) $247; (H) $770

MEAKIN, H.
British 19th cent.
paintings: (H) $1,045

MEAKIN, Louis Henry
American 1850-1917
paintings: (L) $2,070; (H) $2,530

MEARS, George
English ac. 1870-1896
paintings: (H) $1,870

MEARS, Henrietta Dunn
American b. 1877, ac. 1920s
paintings: (L) $357; (H) $1,540
drawings: (H) $412

MEASELLE, Clarence
American contemporary
paintings: (L) $633; (H) $690

MEAUX, Marie de
20th cent.
drawings: (H) $550

MECHAU, Frank Albert
American 1903-1946
paintings: (H) $17,050
drawings: (H) $3,737

MECRAY, John
American 20th cent.
paintings: (H) $1,495

MEDARD, Eugene
French 1847-1887
paintings: (L) $1,320; (H) $11,500

MEDARD, Jules Ferdinand
French 1855-1925
paintings: (H) $29,700

MEDLEY, Robert
paintings: (H) $880

MEEKER, Edwin James
1853-1936
drawings: (H) $605

MEEKER, Joseph Rusling
American 1827-1887/89
paintings: (L) $2,640; (H) $22,000

MEEKS, Eugene
American b. 1843
paintings: (L) $990; (H) $1,320

MEERHOUT, Jan
d. 1677
paintings: (H) $3,737

MEERMANN, Arnold
German 1829-1809
paintings: (H) $2,300

MEERT, Joseph
American b. 1905
paintings: (H) $2,200

MEERTS, Franz
paintings: (H) $2,200

MEGARGEE, Lawrence A., Lon
American 1883-1960
paintings: (L) $176; (H) $660

MEGE DU MALMONT, Rene
French 1859-1911
paintings: (H) $6,900

MEGNON, P.
Scottish 19th cent.
paintings: (H) $5,060

MEGRET, Marcel
French 1885-1956
paintings: (H) $1,265

MEGUAL
paintings: (H) $550

MEHRAN
Iranian b. 1960
paintings: (H) $1,495

MEHRING, Howard
American 1931-1978
paintings: (L) $605; (H) $1,870

MEHTA, Tyeb
Indian b. 1925
paintings: (L) $4,600; (H) $14,950

MEI, Bernardino
Italian c. 1615-1676
paintings: (H) $209,000

MEI, Paola
Italian 19th cent.
paintings: (H) $990

MEIDE, J.L. van der
Belgian 20th cent.
paintings: (L) $99; (H) $770

MEIDNER, Ludwig
German 1884-1966
paintings: (H) $14,950
drawings: (L) $1,100; (H) $7,475

MEIER-MICHEL, Johanna
Austrian b. 1880
sculpture: (H) $600

MEIERHAUS, Joseph
American 1890-1981
paintings: (L) $495; (H) $1,210

MEIFREN Y ROIG, Eliseo
Spanish 1859-1940
paintings: (L) $11,000; (H) $44,000

MEIGS, Walter
American b. 1918
paintings: (L) $29; (H) $605

MEIJER, Gerhardus
Dutch 1816-1875
paintings: (H) $16,500

MEINDL, Albert
Austrian 1891-1967
paintings: (H) $3,740

MEINERS, Piet
Dutch 1857-1903
paintings: (H) $633

MEIRELES DE LIMA, Victor
1832-1903
paintings: (H) $6,600

MEIREN, Jan Baptiste van der
Flemish 1664-1708
paintings: (L) $3,738; (H) $21,850

MEISSIER, Gregory F.
20th cent.
drawings: (H) $715

MEISSL, August von
German 1867-1921
paintings: (H) $4,600

MEISSNER, Adolf Ernst
German 1837-1902
paintings: (H) $13,200

MEISSNER, Leo
American b. 1895
paintings: (H) $935

MEISSONIER, Jean Charles
French 1848-1917
paintings: (L) $770; (H) $10,925
drawings: (H) $207

MEISSONIER, Jean Louis Ernest
French 1815-1891
paintings: (L) $11; (H) $34,500
drawings: (L) $863; (H) $321,500
sculpture: (H) $10,450

MEIXNER, Ludwig
German 1828-1885
paintings: (L) $748; (H) $2,990

MELBY, G.
American c. 1880
paintings: (H) $4,025

MELBYE, Daniel Hermann Anton
Danish 1818-1875
paintings: (H) $16,500

MELBYE, Wilhelm
Danish 1824-1882
paintings: (H) $12,650

MELCARTH, Edward
paintings: (H) $1,430
sculpture: (H) $3,575

MELCHER, George Henry
American 1881-1957
paintings: (L) $660; (H) $6,900

MELCHERS, Frantz
Belgian b. 1868
paintings: (H) $6,600

MELCHERS, Julius Gari
American 1860-1932
paintings: (L) $2,057; (H) $96,250
drawings: (L) $259; (H) $17,250

MELCHIOR, Wilhelm
German 1817-1860
paintings: (L) $2,200; (H) $4,370

MELE, Juan
Argentinean b. 1923
sculpture: (H) $24,150

MELENDES, Tiburcio
paintings: (H) $2,300

MELENDEZ, Luis
Spanish 1716-1780
paintings: (H) $660,000

MELINI, G**
Italian 19th/20th cent.
paintings: (H) $3,960

MELISSA
paintings: (H) $495

MELLEN, Mary Blood
American b. 1817
paintings: (L) $2,420; (H) $51,700

MELLENCAMP, John Cougar
American
paintings: (H) $2,541

MELLERY, Xavier
Belgian 1845-1921
drawings: (H) $2,070

MELLING, Antoine Ignace
French 1763-1831
drawings: (H) $151,000

MELLON, Eleanor
American 1894-1980
sculpture: (L) $1,150; (H) $2,750

MELLOR, J.
paintings: (L) $396; (H) $1,100

MELLOR, William
British 1851-1931
paintings: (L) $605; (H) $7,700

MELOHS, Charles
American 20th cent.
paintings: (L) $138; (H) $660
drawings: (H) $220

MELOTTI, Fausto
sculpture: (H) $9,350

MELROSE, Andrew W.
American 1836-1901
paintings: (L) $495; (H) $6,325

MELTON, Bruce
sculpture: (H) $1,000

MELTSNER, Paul
American 1905-1966
paintings: (L) $220; (H) $10,450
drawings: (H) $935

MELTZER, Anna E.
American 1896-1974
paintings: (L) $165; (H) $1,100

MELTZER, Arthur
American b. 1893
paintings: (L) $975; (H) $4,800
drawings: (L) $120; (H) $500

MELTZOFF, Stanley
b. 1917
paintings: (L) $660; (H) $1,320

MELVILLE, Alexander
British 19th cent.
paintings: (H) $2,530

MELVILLE, Arthur
British 1858-1904
drawings: (H) $5,750

MELVIN, Terry
American
drawings: (H) $750

MEMIN, S.
drawings: (L) $495; (H) $1,980

MEMLING, Hans
Flemish c. 1430/35-1494
paintings: (H) $90,500

MEMPES, Mortimer
English 19th cent.
drawings: (H) $518

MEMY
British 19th cent.
paintings: (H) $518

MENABONI, Athos
American 1895-1990.
paintings: (H) $880
drawings: (L) $880; (H) $3,300

MENAGEOT, Francois Guillaume
French 1744-1816
paintings: (L) $22,000; (H) $60,500

MENARD, Alfred
French 19th cent.
paintings: (H) $1,725

MENARD, Marie Auguste Emile Rene
French 1862-1930
paintings: (H) $2,588
drawings: (L) $1,430; (H) $5,463

MENASSIER, *A.***
16th cent.
paintings: (H) $6,050

MENCONI, D.
Italian 19th cent.
sculpture: (H) $4,730

MENDENHALL, Emma
American 1880-1963
paintings: (H) $154
drawings: (L) $66; (H) $468

MENDENHALL, Jack
American b. 1937
paintings: (L) $1,100; (H) $12,650

MENDEZ-GONZALES, Manuel
Spanish 19th cent.
paintings: (L) $5,750; (H) $15,400

MENDILAHARZU
Continental 19th cent.
paintings: (H) $3,575

MENDILAHARZU, Gratien
Argentinean 19th cent.
paintings: (L) $4,600; (H) $16,100

MENDIVE, Manuel
drawings: (H) $2,013

MENDJISKY, Serge
French b. 1929
paintings: (L) $660; (H) $5,175

MENDOZA
Spanish/Portuguese 19th cent.
paintings: (H) $3,850

MENDOZE, Robert
French 20th cent.
paintings: (H) $2,200

MENE, Pierre Jules
French 1810-1879
paintings: (H) $12,650
sculpture: (L) $110; (H) $16,100

MENEGAZZI, C.
Italian 19th/20th cent.
drawings: (L) $330; (H) $978

MENEGHELLI, Enrico
American 1853-after 1890
paintings: (H) $5,175

MENENDEZ-PIDAL, Luis
Spanish b. 1864
paintings: (H) $13,750

MENGARINI, Fausta Vittoria
1893-1952
sculpture: (H) $460

MENGIN, P.
sculpture: (H) $4,025

MENGORANCE
American 20th cent.
paintings: (L) $58; (H) $690

MENGS, Anton Raphael
German 1728-1779
drawings: (H) $12,100

MENGS, Anton Raphael, studio of
18th cent.
paintings: (H) $2,875

MENICUCCI, Pablo
Argentinean b. 1933
paintings: (H) $715

MENKER, F.
Continental 19th cent.
paintings: (H) $3,163

MENKES, Sigmund
Polish/American 1896-1986
paintings: (L) $220; (H) $10,450
drawings: (L) $1,760; (H) $1,760

MENKMAN, William
paintings: (H) $1,980

MENNEVILLE
sculpture: (H) $690

MENOTTI, V.A.
Italian 19th c.
paintings: (H) $4,950

MENTA, Edouard
French b. 1858
paintings: (L) $7,700; (H) $14,300

MENTOR, Blasco
Spanish b. 1918
paintings: (L) $330; (H) $4,830

MENTOR, Will
American b. 1958
paintings: (L) $2,750; (H) $4,400

MENTZEL, Otto
German 19th cent.
paintings: (H) $467

MENZEL, Adolph Friedrich Erdmann
German 1815-1905
drawings: (L) $5,500; (H) $29,900

MENZEL, Wilia
Belgian early 20th cent.
sculpture: (H) $7,700

MENZINGER
paintings: (L) $345; (H) $460

MENZL, Julie
Austrian b. 1863
paintings: (H) $5,750

MENZLER, Wilhelm
German b. 1846
paintings: (L) $440; (H) $25,300

MENZLER-PEYTON, Bertha
American 1871-1950
paintings: (L) $198; (H) $7,040
drawings: (H) $192

MERCHANT, Henry
British 19th/20th cent.
paintings: (H) $1,320

MERCHIE, D.
19th cent.
paintings: (H) $770

MERCIE
19th cent.
sculpture: (H) $3,300

MERCIE, Marius Jean Antonin
French 1845-1916
paintings: (L) $2,070; (H) $15,400
sculpture: (L) $633; (H) $31,900

MERCIER, Phillippe
French 1689-1760
paintings: (L) $907; (H) $55,000

MERCIER, Ruth
French 19th/20th cent.
paintings: (H) $2,090

MERCKER, Erich
German 1891-1973
paintings: (L) $495; (H) $880

MEREDITH, John
paintings: (H) $4,400
drawings: (L) $1,100; (H) $1,210

MEREILES DE LIMA, Vitor
Brazilian 1832-1903
paintings: (H) $41,800

MERELUS, Lusimond
paintings: (H) $1,760

MERFELD, Gerald
b. 1936
paintings: (L) $385; (H) $5,500

MERIAN, Matthaeus, I
1593-1650
drawings: (H) $4,400

MERICOURT, Felix
European 19th cent.
paintings: (H) $2,420

MERIDA, Carlos
b. Guatemala 1891, ac. Mexico, d.
1984
paintings: (L) $4,400; (H) $71,500
drawings: (L) $747; (H) $75,100

MERINO, Ignacio
Peruvian/French 1818-1876
paintings: (H) $27,600

MERKEL, Georg
Austrian 1881-1976
paintings: (H) $1,870

MERKEL, Otto
American 19th cent.
paintings: (H) $495

MERLE, Hugues
French 1823-1881
paintings: (L) $1,955; (H) $40,250

MERLIN, B.
French 19th cent.
paintings: (H) $3,450

MERLIN, Daniel
French 1861-1933
paintings: (L) $3,450; (H) $18,700

MERLINO, Silvio
b. 1952
drawings: (H) $7,700

MERODE, Karl Freiherr von
Austrian 1853-1909
paintings: (H) $8,913

MERRIAM, James Arthur
Canadian/American 1880-1951
paintings: (L) $165; (H) $3,850

MERRIAM, John J.
American 19th/20th cent.
paintings: (L) $230; (H) $1,035

MERRILD, Knud
American 1894-1954
sculpture: (H) $20,158

MERRILL, S.T.
American 19th/20th cent.
drawings: (H) $880

MERRITT, Anna Lea
American b. England 1844, d. 1930
paintings: (L) $825; (H) $13,800

MERRY, Godfrey
British 1883-1891
paintings: (H) $2,875

MERSFELDER, Jules
American 1865-1937
paintings: (L) $110; (H) $1,150

MERTENS, Stella
French 1896-1986
paintings: (L) $259; (H) $1,430
drawings: (L) $49; (H) $137

MERTENS, W.
Flemish ac. 1640-1660
paintings: (H) $118,000

MERTZ, Johann
Dutch 1819-1891
paintings: (H) $1,870

MERWART, Paul
Polish 1855-1902
paintings: (H) $17,250

MERY, Alfred Emile
French 1824-1896
drawings: (H) $825

MERZ, Gerhard ·
b. Germany 1947
paintings: (L) $16,500; (H) $23,000
sculpture: (L) $5,750; (H) $18,700

MERZ, Mario
Italian b. 1925
paintings: (L) $10,450; (H) $51,750
drawings: (L) $24,200; (H) $36,300
sculpture: (L) $46,000; (H) $143,000

MESCHERSKY, Arsenii Ivanovich
Russian 1834-1902
paintings: (H) $660

MESDAG, Hendrik Willem
Dutch 1831-1915
paintings: (L) $330; (H) $8,338
drawings: (L) $264; (H) $11,000

MESENS, E.L.T.
Belgian 1903-1971
drawings: (H) $1,840

MESGRIGNY, Claude Francois
Auguste
French 1836-1884
paintings: (L) $6,600; (H) $9,200

MESS, George J.
American 1898-1962
paintings: (L) $82; (H) $1,430

MESSAGER, Annette
French b. 1943
sculpture: (H) $12,650

MESSEL, Oliver
contemporary
drawings: (H) $1,100

MESSENGER, Ivan
American 1895-1983
paintings: (L) $165; (H) $2,310

MESSER, Edmund Clarence
American b. 1842
paintings: (L) $747; (H) $2,070

MESSICK, Ben
American 1901-1981
paintings: (L) $345; (H) $10,450
drawings: (L) $1,100; (H) $3,850

MESSIER, Gregory F.
20th cent.
drawings: (L) $220; (H) $550

MESSINA, A.
sculpture: (L) $805; (H) $863

MESSINA, Francesco
Italian b. 1900
sculpture: (L) $4,887; (H) $46,000

MESSNER, Rudolph Anton
Canadian 20th cent.
paintings: (L) $374; (H) $660

MESTRALLET, Andre Louis
paintings: (H) $920

MESTROVIC, Ivan
American 1883/84-1962
drawings: (H) $880
sculpture: (L) $1,650; (H) $3,300

METCALF, Arthur
American 20th cent.
paintings: (H) $1,870

METCALF, Conger
American b. 1914
paintings: (L) $357; (H) $605
drawings: (L) $165; (H) $2,090

METCALF, Willard Leroy
American 1858-1925
paintings: (L) $1,375; (H) $365,500
drawings: (L) $176; (H) $1,100

METEYARD, Sidney Harold
British 1868-1947
paintings: (L) $9,350; (H) $14,950

METEYARD, Thomas Buford
American 1865-1928
paintings: (H) $3,025

METHFESSEL, Adolfo
1836-1909
paintings: (H) $6,600

METSU, Gabriel
Dutch 1629-1667
paintings: (H) $19,550

METTLING, Louis
French 1847-1904
paintings: (L) $552; (H) $920

METZ, Alois
German b. 1869
paintings: (L) $440; (H) $920

METZ, Gerry Michael
American b. 1943
drawings: (L) $523; (H) $550

METZ, Mario
contemporary
paintings: (H) $46,750

METZGER, Edward
German b. 1807
paintings: (H) $1,100

METZINGER, Jean
French 1883-1956
paintings: (L) $8,050; (H) $209,000
drawings: (L) $6,900; (H) $9,900

METZLER, Karl
American 1909-1995
paintings: (L) $200; (H) $1,100
drawings: (H) $275

METZMACHER, Emile Pierre
French ac. 1863-1890
paintings: (L) $1,380; (H) $33,000
drawings: (H) $1,650

METZNER, F.
sculpture: (H) $2,588

METZNER, Franz
German 1870-1919
sculpture: (H) $1,955

MEUCCI, Michelangelo
Italian 19th cent.
paintings: (L) $330; (H) $10,350
drawings: (H) $275

MEUGNIER, J.
paintings: (L) $990; (H) $1,430

MEUHLENBERG
paintings: (H) $11,500

MEULEN, Edmond van der
Belgian 1841-1905
paintings: (L) $4,600; (H) $6,600

MEULENER, Pieter
Dutch 1602-1654
paintings: (L) $8,800; (H) $17,600

MEUNIER, Constantin Emile
Belgian 1831-1905
paintings: (H) $3,680
sculpture: (L) $3,680; (H) $10,925

MEUNIER, F.
paintings: (H) $495

MEUNIER, R.V.
French 19th cent.
paintings: (L) $1,210; (H) $1,430

MEURER, Charles Alfred
American 1865-1955
paintings: (L) $322; (H) $40,700

MEURIS, Emmanuel
Italian 1894-1969
drawings: (H) $6,325

MEURISSE-FRANCHOMME, H.J.
European 19th cent.
paintings: (H) $8,800

MEUSER
b. 1947
paintings: (H) $3,300

MEUSER
contemporary
sculpture: (H) $13,800

MEUTTMAN, William
American 20th cent.
paintings: (H) $460

MEWHINNEY, Ella
American b. 1891
paintings: (H) $605
drawings: (H) $66

MEYER, Emile
French 19th cent.
paintings: (L) $8,050; (H) $19,800

MEYER, Ernest
German/American b. 1863
paintings: (L) $110; (H) $2,090

MEYER, Frederick
1872-1960
sculpture: (H) $1,840

MEYER, G.K.
British 19th cent.
paintings: (H) $522

MEYER, Georges
French 19th cent.
paintings: (L) $330; (H) $7,150

MEYER, H.
British 19th cent.
paintings: (H) $4,950

MEYER, Hendrick de, the elder
Dutch c. 1600-before 1690
paintings: (L) $14,950; (H) $51,750

MEYER, Hendrick de, the younger
Dutch 1737-1793
paintings: (L) $18,700; (H) $65,200
drawings: (L) $1,650; (H) $11,000

MEYER, Herbert
American 1882-1960
paintings: (L) $275; (H) $2,750
drawings: (L) $165; (H) $550

MEYER, Johann Heinrich Louis
Dutch 1806-1866
paintings: (H) $3,080

MEYER, Louis
Dutch 1809-1886
paintings: (L) $1,375; (H) $2,530

MEYER, Sophie
German 19th cent.
paintings: (H) $550

MEYER DE HAAN, Jacob
Dutch 1852-1895
paintings: (H) $965,000

MEYER VON BREMEN, Johann Georg
German 1813-1886
paintings: (L) $7,475; (H) $140,000
drawings: (L) $3,850; (H) $4,025

MEYER VON BREMEN, Sophie
German 1813-1886
paintings: (H) $15,400

MEYER-WALDECK, Kunz
German 1859-1953
paintings: (H) $10,925

MEYER-WISMAR, Ferdinand
German 1833-1917
paintings: (H) $19,800

MEYERHEIM, E.
paintings: (H) $715

MEYERHEIM, Eduard Franz
German 1838-1880
paintings: (L) $11,500; (H) $25,300

MEYERHEIM, Friedrich Eduoard
German 1808-1879
paintings: (H) $6,600

MEYERHEIM, Hermann
German 19th cent.
paintings: (H) $13,200

MEYERHEIM, Paul Friedrich
German 1842-1915
paintings: (H) $9,200

MEYERHEIM, Robert
German/English 1847-1920
drawings: (L) $489; (H) $748

MEYERHEIM, Wilhelm Alexander
German 1814/15-1882
paintings: (L) $1,320; (H) $16,500

MEYERHEM, M.
Continental 19th cent.
paintings: (H) $4,125

MEYERINGH, Aelbert
1645-1714
paintings: (H) $10,350

MEYEROWITZ, William
Russian/American b.c. 1898, d. 1981
paintings: (L) $303; (H) $1,760
drawings: (H) $303

MEYERS, Harry Morse
American 1886-1961
paintings: (H) $412
drawings: (H) $1,650

MEYERS, Jerome
1867-1940
drawings: (L) $440; (H) $770

MEYERS, Ralph W.
American 19th/20th cent.
paintings: (H) $690

MEYERSAHM, Exene Reed
American 20th cent.
paintings: (L) $431; (H) $550

MEYNELL, Louis
American b. 1868
paintings: (L) $220; (H) $468

MEYNIER, Charles
French 1768-1832
paintings: (L) $6,050; (H) $486,500
drawings: (H) $7,188

MEYS, Marcel
French ac. 1880-1901
paintings: (H) $32,200

MEZA, Guillermo
Mexican b. 1917
paintings: (L) $467; (H) $19,800
drawings: (L) $1,725; (H) $2,760

MEZA, William de
American 19th cent.
paintings: (H) $2,200

MEZZETTI, L.
sculpture: (H) $550

MIAHLE, Federico
1800-1868
paintings: (H) $10,450

MICHAEL, H.H.
paintings: (H) $517

MICHAELIS, Heinrich H.J. von
South African b. 1912
paintings: (H) $1,840

MICHAELSON, Meyer
German 19th cent.
paintings: (H) $935

MICHALOWSKI, Herman V.
paintings: (L) $1,100; (H) $2,990

MICHALOWSKI, Norm
paintings: (H) $715

MICHALOWSKI, Piotr
Polish 1800-1855
paintings: (H) $2,760

MICHATOVSKI
sculpture: (H) $1,210

MICHAU, Theobald
Flemish 1676-1765
paintings: (L) $12,650; (H) $52,250

MICHAUD-MEUNIER
French 19th cent.
paintings: (H) $4,600

MICHAUX, Henri
Belgian b. 1899
paintings: (H) $55
drawings: (L) $77; (H) $1,320

MICHEALS
American 20th cent.
sculpture: (H) $460

MICHEL, A.
French 20th cent.
paintings: (L) $173; (H) $550

MICHEL, Alfonso
b. Mexico 1897-1957
paintings: (L) $38,500; (H) $48,875

MICHEL, Andree
French 20th cent.
paintings: (H) $550

MICHEL, G.
sculpture: (L) $1,430; (H) $2,310

MICHEL, Georges
French 1763-1843
paintings: (L) $863; (H) $19,800
drawings: (L) $385; (H) $9,775

MICHEL, Georges
French 19th cent.
paintings: (H) $2,750

MICHEL, Gustave Frederic
French 1851-1924
sculpture: (L) $4,125; (H) $14,300

MICHEL, Robert
drawings: (L) $4,185; (H) $13,200

MICHEL, William
Continental 19th cent.
paintings: (H) $4,400

MICHEL-HENRY
French b. 1928
paintings: (L) $575; (H) $633

MICHELET, G.C.
French 19th/20th cent.
paintings: (H) $16,500

MICHELLERIE, Francois Hubert
French 1802-1875
paintings: (H) $2,750

MICHELSON, Leo
American 1887-1978
paintings: (L) $330; (H) $550
drawings: (H) $550

MICHETTI, Francesco Paolo
Italian 1851/52-1929
paintings: (L) $2,875; (H) $38,500
drawings: (L) $575; (H) $35,650

MICHIELI, G.
sculpture: (H) $990

MICHIELSEN, Hendrik Evert
Dutch 1852-1929
paintings: (H) $2,875

MICHL, Ferdinand
Czechoslovakian b. 1877
paintings: (H) $550

MICHONZE, Gregoire
French 1902-1982
paintings: (H) $1,430
drawings: (H) $660

MICOTTA, J.
paintings: (L) $1,380; (H) $1,380

MIDDENDORF, Helmut
German b. 1953
paintings: (L) $7,475; (H) $17,600
drawings: (L) $2,200; (H) $2,640

MIDDLETON, Colin
British b. 1910, exhib. 1938-1940
paintings: (H) $6,875

MIDDLETON, J.
English 19th cent.
paintings: (H) $1,210

MIDDLETON, Stanley
American b. 1852
paintings: (L) $425; (H) $825

MIDJO, Christina M.S.
Norwegian/American 1880-1973
paintings: (H) $715

MIDWOOD, William Henry
British ac. 1867-1871
paintings: (L) $5,750; (H) $15,525

MIDY, Arthur
French 1887-1944
paintings: (H) $49,450

MIEDUCH, Dan
American b. 1947
paintings: (L) $2,970; (H) $6,820

MIEL, Jan
Flemish 1599-1663
paintings: (L) $30,800; (H) $36,800

MIELICH, Leopold Alphons
Austrian 1863-1929
paintings: (L) $4,400; (H) $14,850

MIENINGER, Ludwig
paintings: (H) $4,950

MIEREVELT, Michiel van
1567-1641
paintings: (L) $4,730; (H) $49,500

MIERIS, Frans van, the elder
Dutch 1635-1681
paintings: (H) $77,000

MIERIS, Willem van
Dutch 1662-1747
paintings: (L) $14,375; (H) $26,400

MIGLIARA, Giovanni
Italian 1785-1837
drawings: (H) $805

MIGLIARO, Vincenzo
Italian 1858-1938
paintings: (L) $2,200; (H) $10,063

MIGLIORETTI, Pasquale
Italian 1823-1881
sculpture: (H) $167,500

MIGNARD, Pierre
paintings: (H) $2,090

MIGNARD, Pierre
1612-1695
drawings: (H) $3,850

MIGNERY, Herb
American b. 1937
sculpture: (L) $1,980; (H) $6,600

MIGNON, Abraham
German 1640-1679
paintings: (H) $156,500

MIGNON, Leon
Belgian 1847-1898
sculpture: (H) $2,200

MIGNOT, Louis Remy
American 1831-1870
paintings: (L) $2,070; (H) $25,300

MIHALOVITIS, Miklos
Hungarian 1887-1960
paintings: (L) $137; (H) $1,760

MIJARES, Jose
Cuban b. 1921
paintings: (L) $1,430; (H) $14,300
drawings: (L) $2,750; (H) $3,680

MIJN, Francis van der
1719-1783
paintings: (L) $1,760; (H) $4,675

MIJN, Hieronymous van der
18th cent.
paintings: (H) $3,850

MIKESCH, Fritz
Austrian 1853-1891
paintings: (H) $25,300

MILANESI, Rocco
Italian 19th cent.
sculpture: (H) $4,400

MILANO
paintings: (H) $1,980

MILARSKY, A.
American 19th/20th cent.
paintings: (H) $5,500

MILBY, Frank
American 20th cent.
paintings: (H) $715

MILDER, Jay
American b. 1934
paintings: (L) $55; (H) $1,650
drawings: (H) $460

MILES, Donald E.
American b. 1912
paintings: (L) $165; (H) $990

MILES, Eugene
American 20th cent.
paintings: (L) $38; (H) $460

MILES, Helen Cabot
20th cent.
paintings: (H) $1,610

MILES, J.R.
Australian 19th cent.
paintings: (H) $1,430

MILES, Thomas Rose
English ac. 1869-1906
paintings: (L) $853; (H) $3,080

MILESI, Alessandro
Italian 1856-1945
paintings: (H) $25,300

MILIAN, Raul
b. Cuba 1914
drawings: (L) $209; (H) $518

MILICH, Abram Adolphe
paintings: (L) $1,650; (H) $1,980

MILIKEN, G.
Continental 19th cent.
paintings: (H) $880

MILLAIS, John Guille
British 1865-1931
drawings: (H) $1,650

MILLAIS, Sir J. Everett
English School 1829-1896
paintings: (H) $6,660

MILLAN
Spanish 19th/20th cent.
paintings: (H) $4,025

MILLAR, Addison Thomas
American 1860-1913
paintings: (L) $302; (H) $22,000
drawings: (L) $231; (H) $275

MILLAR, T.W.
19th cent.
paintings: (H) $518

MILLAR, William
Continental 19th cent.
paintings: (H) $1,760

MILLARD, Frederick
paintings: (H) $2,310

MILLARES, Manolo
Spanish 1926-1972
paintings: (H) $29,900

MILLEGON, Royal
Continental 20th cent.
paintings: (H) $633

MILLER, Alfred Jacob
American 1810-1874
paintings: (L) $1,320; (H) $189,500
drawings: (L) $440; (H) $65,750

MILLER, Alice
ac. 1881-1889
paintings: (H) $495

MILLER, Barse
American 1904-1973
paintings: (H) $825
drawings: (L) $357; (H) $1,725

MILLER, C.
paintings: (L) $302; (H) $450

MILLER, Carol
American b. 1933
sculpture: (L) $3,850; (H) $9,350

MILLER, Charles
American
paintings: (H) $4,400

MILLER, Charles Henry
American 1842-1922
paintings: (L) $5; (H) $1,100
drawings: (H) $121

MILLER, Charles Keith
British 19th cent.
paintings: (H) $7,700

MILLER, Charles W.
paintings: (H) $1,980

MILLER, David Humphreys
paintings: (H) $1,035

MILLER, Ernie Lee
paintings: (H) $660

MILLER, Evylena Nunn
American 1888-1966
paintings: (L) $247; (H) $1,045

MILLER, F.
American 19th cent.
drawings: (H) $605

MILLER, F.H.
American 19th cent.
paintings: (L) $2,145; (H) $2,530

MILLER, Frances
paintings: (H) $1,430

MILLER, George
British ac. 1827-1853
paintings: (H) $2,860

MILLER, George L.
American 19th cent.
paintings: (H) $495

MILLER, Gustaf
American 20th cent.
sculpture: (L) $690; (H) $1,150

MILLER, H.G.
19th cent.
paintings: (H) $1,150

MILLER, Henry
20th cent.
drawings: (L) $1,430; (H) $2,420

MILLER, Henry
American 1891-1975/80
drawings: (L) $880; (H) $1,320

MILLER, J.
English 19th cent.
paintings: (H) $1,760

MILLER, John Paul
American 20th cent.
drawings: (H) $880

MILLER, Josef
German 19th cent.
paintings: (H) $4,400

MILLER, Joseph
German 19th cent.
paintings: (H) $4,025

MILLER, Kenneth Hayes
American 1876-1952
paintings: (L) $605; (H) $23,000

MILLER, Lewis
American 1795-1882
drawings: (L) $1,980; (H) $2,530

MILLER, Melissa
b. 1951
paintings: (L) $2,760; (H) $3,450

MILLER, Melvin
American b. 1937
paintings: (L) $138; (H) $1,210

MILLER, Mildred Bunting
American 1892-1964
paintings: (L) $55; (H) $2,750

MILLER, Oscar
American 1867-1921
paintings: (L) $385; (H) $1,760

MILLER, R.
19th/20th cent.
drawings: (H) $467

MILLER, Ralph Davison
American 1858-1945
paintings: (L) $468; (H) $1,870

MILLER, Richard E.
American 1875-1943
paintings: (L) $275; (H) $662,500
drawings: (H) $2,530

MILLER, Robert A. Darrah
b. 1905
paintings: (H) $1,430

MILLER, Ron
b. 1947
drawings: (H) $1,870

MILLER, Ruth
sculpture: (H) $770

MILLER, William Rickarby
English/American 1818-1893
paintings: (L) $633; (H) $14,300
drawings: (L) $345; (H) $6,900

MILLER-CORNELIUS, L.
ac. 1800-1900
paintings: (H) $2,420

MILLES, Carl
Swedish 1875-1955
sculpture: (L) $2,300; (H) $154,000

MILLESON, Royal Hill
American 1849-1926
paintings: (L) $253; (H) $3,335
drawings: (L) $220; (H) $495

MILLET, Aime
French 19th cent.
sculpture: (H) $605

MILLET, Clarence
American 1897-1959
paintings: (L) $385; (H) $13,475

MILLET, Eugene Henri
French ac. 1861-1875
drawings: (H) $5,750

MILLET, Francis David (Frank)
American 1846-1912
paintings: (L) $660; (H) $17,600

MILLET, Francois
French 1851-1917
paintings: (H) $715
drawings: (L) $605; (H) $12,650

MILLET, Jean Baptiste
French 1831-1906
drawings: (H) $2,070

MILLET, Jean Francois
Flemish 1642-1679
paintings: (H) $15,400

MILLET, Jean Francois
French 1814-1875
paintings: (L) $11,000; (H) $2,145,000
drawings: (L) $1,265; (H) $882,500

MILLET, Jean Francois, called
Francisque II
French 1666-1723
paintings: (H) $13,225

MILLETT, George van
American b. 1864
paintings: (L) $440; (H) $7,700

MILLIER, Arthur Henry
American 1893-1975
drawings: (H) $715

MILLIERE, Maurice
French b. 1871
drawings: (L) $193; (H) $1,495

MILLIGAN, Gladys
American 1892-1973
paintings: (H) $605

MILLIKEN, Robert W.
British 19th/20th cent.
drawings: (L) $330; (H) $2,990

MILLION, J.
European 19th cent.
paintings: (H) $690

MILLNER, Karl
German 1825-1894
paintings: (L) $4,675; (H) $13,800

MILLOT, A.
French 19th cent.
paintings: (H) $863

MILLS, A.
British 19th cent.
paintings: (H) $2,200

MILLS, Clark
American 1815-1883
sculpture: (H) $7,700

MILLS, Edward
British 19th cent.
paintings: (H) $4,887

MILLS, John
British 19th cent.
paintings: (H) $6,900

MILLS, Wilfrid Taylor
American 20th cent.
paintings: (H) $468

MILMAN, F.
mid. 19th cent.
drawings: (H) $1,380

MILMORE, Martin
sculpture: (H) $1,210

MILNE, David Brown
Canadian 1882-1953
paintings: (L) $575; (H) $82,500
drawings: (L) $330; (H) $2,990

MILNE, John MacLaughlan
British 1885-1957
paintings: (H) $3,300

MILNE, Joseph
British d. 1911
paintings: (H) $3,450

MILON, A***
French 19th cent.
paintings: (H) $17,825

MILONE, Antonio
Italian 19th cent.
paintings: (L) $374; (H) $6,900

MILONE, Giuseppe
paintings: (L) $550; (H) $1,840

MILROY, Lisa
b. 1959
paintings: (L) $437; (H) $12,100

MILTON, V. Marais
French b. 1872
paintings: (H) $9,900

MIMNAUGH, Terry
American
paintings: (L) $1,450; (H) $3,300
sculpture: (H) $800

MINAMI, Keiko
b. 1911
paintings: (L) $231; (H) $852

MINAUX, Andre
French b. 1923
paintings: (L) $330; (H) $1,980

MINDERHOUT, Hendrik van
Dutch 1632-1696
paintings: (H) $49,500

MINER, Alita G.
paintings: (H) $825

MINER, Robert
paintings: (H) $880

MINET, Louis Emile
French d.c. 1920
paintings: (L) $9,200; (H) $27,600

MINETTI, P.
Italian School 20th cent.
paintings: (H) $2,200

MING, Ju
b. 1938
sculpture: (L) $17,250; (H) $28,750

MING HO ZU
Chinese b. 1949
paintings: (L) $880; (H) $1,100

MINGO, Norman
20th cent.
drawings: (L) $518; (H) $10,450

MINGRET, Jose
Spanish 20th cent.
paintings: (H) $528

MINGUZZI, Luciano
Italian b. 1911
sculpture: (L) $1,430; (H) $9,350

MINNE, George
Belgian 1866-1941
sculpture: (L) $8,050; (H) $37,375

MINNIGERODE, Ludwig
Austrian b. 1847
paintings: (H) $9,200

MINO, Augustus
American 20th cent.
paintings: (H) $880

MINOR, Anne Rogers
American b. 1864
paintings: (H) $770

MINOR, Ferdinand
German 1814-1883
paintings: (H) $27,600

MINOR, Robert Crannell
American 1840-1904
paintings: (L) $368; (H) $3,025

MINORU, Kawabata
b. 1911
paintings: (H) $27,600
drawings: (H) $13,800

MINOZZI, F***
paintings: (H) $1,980

MINTCHINE, Abraham
paintings: (L) $3,850; (H) $6,325

MINTER, Marilyn
American b. 1848
paintings: (L) $6,050; (H) $6,900

MIORI, Luciano
20th cent.
drawings: (H) $1,840

MIOTTE, Jean
b. 1926
paintings: (L) $1,150; (H) $4,620

MIRA, Alfred S.
American 20th cent.
paintings: (L) $1,650; (H) $8,525

MIRALLES, Enrique
Spanish 19th/20th cent.
paintings: (L) $3,300; (H) $5,175

MIRALLES, Francisco
Spanish b.c. 1850
paintings: (L) $4,600; (H) $60,250
drawings: (H) $12,650

MIRANDA, Juan de
ac. 17th cent.
paintings: (H) $66,000

MIRCOL
sculpture: (H) $1,980

MIRELLA
paintings: (H) $4,675

MIREN(?)
drawings: (H) $632

MIRKO, Mirko BASALDELLA
Italian 1910-1969
drawings: (H) $2,200
sculpture: (L) $192; (H) $9,200

MIRO, Joan
Spanish 1893-1983
paintings: (L) $2,200; (H) $7,150,000
drawings: (L) $2,200; (H) $4,732,500
sculpture: (L) $20,700; (H) $442,500

MIRO, Joan and Josep LLORENS
sculpture: (H) $50,600

MIROU, Anton
Flemish 1586-1661
paintings: (L) $33,000; (H) $40,250

MIRSKY, Samuel
American 20th cent.
paintings: (L) $412; (H) $2,300

MISCHELES, Margaret
English 1871-1924
paintings: (H) $935

MISSIRLIS, S.
Eastern Europe 19th/20th cent.
paintings: (H) $522

MITA, G.
French 20th cent.
paintings: (H) $9,200

MITCHELL, Alfred
American 1872-1953
paintings: (H) $7,700

MITCHELL, Alfred R.
American 1888-1972
paintings: (L) $220; (H) $18,700
drawings: (L) $412; (H) $495

MITCHELL, Arthur
1886-1977
paintings: (H) $2,310

MITCHELL, Charles D.
1887-1940
drawings: (L) $467; (H) $1,210

MITCHELL, E.
British 19th cent.
paintings: (H) $2,200

MITCHELL, George Bertrand
American 1872-1966
paintings: (L) $330; (H) $2,200
drawings: (L) $55; (H) $1,045

MITCHELL, Gladys Vinson
American b. 1894
paintings: (L) $88; (H) $1,950

MITCHELL, Henry
American 1915-1980
sculpture: (H) $1,100

MITCHELL, Janet
American b. 1915
paintings: (L) $250; (H) $1,430
drawings: (L) $1,155; (H) $1,650

MITCHELL, Joan
American 1926-1992
paintings: (L) $16,500; (H) $374,000
drawings: (L) $4,600; (H) $18,700

MITCHELL, John, of Aberdeen
Scottish 1838-1926
drawings: (H) $550

MITCHELL, John Campbell
American 1862-1922
paintings: (L) $550; (H) $1,430

MITCHELL, Marshall
sculpture: (L) $2,750; (H) $4,950

MITCHELL, Philip
British 1814-1896
drawings: (H) $990

MITCHELL, Thomas
British ac. 1763-1789
paintings: (H) $1,045

MITCHELL OF MARYPORT, William
British 19th cent.
paintings: (H) $3,737

MITCHNICK, Nancy
American 20th cent.
paintings: (L) $2,070; (H) $2,750

MITELLI, Agostino
1634-1718
drawings: (H) $2,990

MITRECEY, Maurice
French 1869-1894
paintings: (H) $1,610

MITSUTANE, Kunishiro
drawings: (L) $3,850; (H) $4,400

MITTERFELLNER, Andreas
German 1912-1972
paintings: (H) $715

MITURICH, Nicolai
drawings: (L) $920; (H) $4,888

MIXER, Orren
20th cent.
paintings: (H) $550

MIXTER, Felicia Howell
paintings: (H) $550

MIYAJIMA, Tatsuo
b. 1957
sculpture: (H) $4,950

MIYAKE, Katsumi
early 20th cent.
drawings: (H) $605

MIZEN, Frederick K.
1888-1965
paintings: (L) $770; (H) $2,860

MIZUNO, Mineo
sculpture: (H) $1,150

MJAANES, Otto
paintings: (H) $1,840

MOBIUS, Karl
sculpture: (H) $1,320

MODERSOHN, Otto
German 1865-1943
paintings: (H) $17,600

MODERSOHN-BECKER, Paula
1876-1907
drawings: (H) $7,700

MODIGLIANI, Amedeo
Italian 1884-1920
paintings: (L) $101,500; (H) $12,432,500
drawings: (L) $2,070; (H) $165,000
sculpture: (H) $1,047,500

MOEBIUS
drawings: (H) $1,870

MOELLER, E.D.
American 20th cent.
sculpture: (H) $825

MOELLER, Louis Charles
American 1855-1930
paintings: (L) $2,875; (H) $29,900
drawings: (H) $94

MOELLER, Robert
paintings: (H) $467

MOER, Jean Baptiste van
Belgian 1819-1884
paintings: (H) $2,200

MOERENHOUT, Joseph Jodocus
Flemish 1801-1874
paintings: (H) $1,045

MOERLIN, G.
sculpture: (H) $1,553

MOES, Wally
Dutch 1856-1918
paintings: (H) $1,430

MOEYAERT, Claes Cornelisz.
1590/91-1655
drawings: (H) $1,610

MOFFETT, Ross E.
American 1888-1971
paintings: (L) $192; (H) $5,225

MOGAN, John William
American 20th cent.
paintings: (L) $1,430; (H) $1,980

MOGFORD, John
English 1821-1885
drawings: (H) $1,100

MOHOKUHR, B.
sculpture: (H) $450

MOHOLY-NAGY, Laszlo
Hungarian 1895-1946
paintings: (L) $20,700; (H) $206,000
drawings: (L) $4,025; (H) $41,400

MOHR, Albert
French 20th cent.
paintings: (L) $460; (H) $1,980
drawings: (H) $77

MOHR, Karl
German b. 1922
paintings: (L) $330; (H) $770

MOHRMAN, Henry
American
paintings: (H) $2,750

MOHRMANN, John Henry
American 1857-1916
paintings: (L) $550; (H) $8,800

MOIGNIEZ, F.
sculpture: (H) $1,150

MOIGNIEZ, Jules
French 1835-1894
paintings: (L) $1,320; (H) $2,070
sculpture: (L) $138; (H) $8,250

MOISAND, Marcel Emmanuel
French 1874-1903
paintings: (H) $7,150

MOISE, Theodore Sidney
American 1808-1885
paintings: (L) $660; (H) $2,200

MOITTE, Jean Guillaume
French 1746-1810
drawings: (L) $4,675; (H) $8,250

MOJE, Klaus
German/Australian b. 1936
sculpture: (H) $8,050

MOKADY, Moshe
1902-1975
paintings: (H) $1,840

MOKUMA, Kikuhata
b. 1935
sculpture: (H) $90,500

MOLA, Pier Francesco
Italian 1612-1666
paintings: (L) $880; (H) $66,000
drawings: (L) $6,325; (H) $46,000

MOLARSKY, Abraham
Russian/American 1883-1951
paintings: (L) $1,540; (H) $1,760

MOLARSKY, Maurice
Russian/American 1885-1950
paintings: (L) $358; (H) $1,210

MOLDOVAN, Sacha
Russian/American b. 1901
paintings: (H) $605

MOLE, John Henry
English 1814-1886
paintings: (H) $2,750
drawings: (L) $220; (H) $275

MOLENAER, Jan Miense
Dutch c. 1610-1668
paintings: (L) $770; (H) $286,000

MOLENAER, Klaes
Dutch c. 1530-1676
paintings: (L) $2,530; (H) $20,700

MOLES, ***
19th/20th cent.
paintings: (H) $935

MOLESWORTH, Thomas
paintings: (H) $3,680

MOLIJN, Pieter
Dutch 1595-1661
paintings: (L) $12,100; (H) $23,000

MOLIN, Oreste da
Italian 1856-1912
paintings: (H) $6,380

MOLINA CAMPOS, Florencio
Argentinean 1891-1959
paintings: (L) $1,725; (H) $8,800
drawings: (L) $275; (H) $11,500

MOLINARI, Antonio
Italian 1665-1727
paintings: (L) $15,400; (H) $28,600

MOLINARY, Andres
1847-1915
paintings: (L) $990; (H) $6,600

MOLINS, A. de
French 19th cent.
paintings: (H) $28,750

MOLISE
sculpture: (H) $3,300

MOLITOR, Franz
German 1857-1929
paintings: (H) $10,350

MOLL, Carl
Austrian 1861-1945
paintings: (H) $74,000

MOLL, Evert
Dutch 1878-1955
paintings: (L) $4,600; (H) $6,050

MOLL, Margarete
b. 1884
sculpture: (H) $1,380

MOLLER, Carl Henrik Koch
Danish 1845-1920
paintings: (L) $550; (H) $1,380

MOLLER, F.
German 19th/20th cent.
paintings: (H) $3,520

MOLLER, Oscar
American 20th cent.
paintings: (L) $144; (H) $935

MOLLEY, Annie
drawings: (H) $1,035

MOLLICA, Achille
Italian 19th cent.
paintings: (L) $1,725; (H) $16,500

MOLLINA, F.
paintings: (H) $770

MOLLINS-BALLESTE, Enrique
Spanish b. 1893
sculpture: (H) $2,750

MOLNAR, Av
paintings: (H) $1,045

MOLNAR, Janos
1878-1924
paintings: (H) $544

MOLNARI, R.
paintings: (H) $1,430

MOLNE, Hector
Cuban b. 1935
paintings: (H) $12,650
drawings: (L) $330; (H) $385

MOLNE, Louis Vidal
Spanish 1907-1970
paintings: (L) $495; (H) $1,725

MOLSTED, Christian
Danish 1862-1930
paintings: (H) $4,400

MOLTINO, F.
paintings: (H) $690

MOLTINO, Francis
British 1818-1872
paintings: (H) $2,750

MOLTKE, Harald Viggo
Danish b. 1871
paintings: (H) $1,980

MOLYNEUX, Edward
b. England 1896
paintings: (H) $9,350

MOMADAY, Al
Native American b. 1913
paintings: (H) $1,650

MOMENT, Barbara C.
paintings: (H) $750

MOMMERS, Hendrik
Dutch c. 1623-1693
paintings: (L) $3,025; (H) $27,500

MOMPER, Frans de
Flemish 1603-1660
paintings: (H) $11,000

MOMPER, Frans de and Sebastian
VRANCX
16th/17th cent.
paintings: (H) $24,200

MOMPER, Joos de
Flemish 1564-1635
paintings: (L) $17,250; (H) $88,000
drawings: (H) $7,700

MOMPER, Joos de and Frans
FRANCKEN II
Flemish 16th/17th cent.
paintings: (H) $9,350

MOMPER, Philippe de
1598-1634
paintings: (H) $34,500

MOMPO, Manuel Hernandez
b. 1927
paintings: (L) $6,325; (H) $8,800

MONALDI, Paolo
Italian ac. c. 1760
paintings: (H) $2,090

MONAMY, Peter
English 1670/89-1749
paintings: (H) $675

MONCHABLON, Jean Ferdinand
French 1855-1904
paintings: (L) $6,900; (H) $57,750

MONCHOT, L.
French 1850-1920
paintings: (L) $1,100; (H) $1,870

MONDRIAAN, Frederic Hendrik, Frits
Dutch 1853-1932
paintings: (L) $1,540; (H) $2,300
drawings: (H) $1,430

MONDRIAN, Piet
Dutch 1872-1944
paintings: (L) $31,050; (H) $5,612,500
drawings: (L) $8,800; (H) $132,000

MONET, Claude
French 1840-1926
paintings: (L) $156,500; (H) $12,100,000
drawings: (L) $17,250; (H) $192,500

MONET, Jason
paintings: (L) $138; (H) $460
drawings: (L) $230; (H) $690

MONEY, Fred
French 1882-1956
paintings: (H) $1,650
drawings: (L) $440; (H) $1,100

MONFALLET, Adolphe Francois
French 1816-1900
paintings: (H) $2,970

MONFRIED, Georges Daniel de
French 1856-1929
paintings: (L) $2,875; (H) $15,950

MONGE, Jules
French b. 1855
paintings: (L) $2,200; (H) $2,750

MONGE, Luis
b. Ecuador 1920
paintings: (L) $9,200; (H) $14,300

MONGINOT, Charles
French 1825-1900
paintings: (L) $489; (H) $6,325

MONJE, Luis
b. Ecuador 1925
paintings: (L) $11,000; (H) $16,500

MONKS, John Austin Sands
American 1850-1917
paintings: (L) $330; (H) $1,430
drawings: (H) $302

MONNERET, Jean
French b. 1922
paintings: (L) $770; (H) $1,100

MONNICKENDAM, Martin
Dutch 1874-1930
paintings: (H) $990

MONNOYER, Antoine
French 1677-1735
paintings: (L) $19,800; (H) $33,000

MONNOYER, Jean Baptiste
French 1670-1747
paintings: (L) $3,220; (H) $255,500

MONNOYER, Jean Baptiste, studio of
17th cent.
paintings: (H) $28,750

MONOGRAMMIST G.S.,
16th cent.
drawings: (H) $2,070

MONOGRAMMIST I.K.,
ac. 1st ½ 16th cent.
drawings: (H) $35,200

MONOGRAMMIST IS,
paintings: (H) $1,650

MONREAL, Andres
20th cent.
paintings: (L) $575; (H) $1,725

MONROE, Albert F.
American 19th cent.
paintings: (H) $2,990

MONSIAU, Nicolas Andre
French 1755-1837
drawings: (H) $24,150

MONSON, Edith Dale
20th cent.
paintings: (L) $90; (H) $550

MONSTED, Peder Mork
Danish 1859-1941
paintings: (L) $825; (H) $29,900

MONT, Francois du
Belgian 19th cent.
paintings: (H) $2,420

MONTAGNE, Agricol Louis
French 1879-1960
drawings: (L) $1,045; (H) $1,650

MONTAGNE, Pierre Marius
French 19th cent.
sculpture: (H) $483

MONTAGNY, Elie Honore
French d. 1864
drawings: (H) $4,400

MONTAGU, Robert
paintings: (L) $805; (H) $2,070

MONTAGUE, A.
English 19th cent.
paintings: (H) $1,430

MONTAGUE, Alfred
British ac. 1832-1883
paintings: (L) $660; (H) $4,025

MONTAGUE, Clifford
British 19th cent.
paintings: (H) $2,860

MONTAGUE, R.
paintings: (H) $1,045

MONTALANT, I. O. de
French 19th cent.
paintings: (L) $2,090; (H) $27,500

MONTALANT, Julius O.
paintings: (H) $6,900

MONTALBA, Clara
British 1842-1929
paintings: (L) $523; (H) $1,100

MONTALBA, Ellen
English 19th cent.
paintings: (H) $1,430

MONTAN, Anders
Swedish 1846-1917
paintings: (H) $935

MONTANA
Italian b. 1890
sculpture: (H) $550

MONTARDIER
French ac. 1812-1848
drawings: (H) $4,600

MONTASSIER, Henri
French 1880-1946
paintings: (H) $880

MONTE, Ira
Spanish b. 1918
paintings: (L) $440; (H) $990

MONTEFIORE, A.
Italian 19th/20th cent.
drawings: (H) $660

MONTEFORTE, Eduardo
Italian 1849-1933
paintings: (H) $660

MONTELATICI, Francesco, called
Cecco BRAVO
Italian 1601-1661
paintings: (L) $1,495; (H) $71,500

MONTEMEZZO, Antonio
German 1841-1898
paintings: (L) $15,400; (H) $15,525

MONTENEGRO, Julio
Ecuadorian 1867-1932
paintings: (H) $11,500

MONTENEGRO, Roberto
Mexican 1885-1968
paintings: (L) $4,600; (H) $79,750
drawings: (L) $3,450; (H) $3,850

MONTERRO, Paulina
Spanish 19th cent.
paintings: (H) $825

MONTEZIN, Pierre Eugene
French 1874-1946
paintings: (L) $4,600; (H) $165,000
drawings: (H) $11,000

MONTFOORT, Anthonie Blocklandt
van
Dutch 1523-1583
paintings: (H) $9,350

MONTFORT, Charles de
French b. 1910
drawings: (H) $660

MONTGOMERY, Alfred
American 1857-1922
paintings: (L) $330; (H) $1,980

MONTGOMERY, Claude
American 20th cent.
drawings: (L) $908; (H) $1,870

MONTI, Francesco
Italian 1646-1712
paintings: (H) $18,700

MONTI, Francesco, Il Bolgnese
Italian 1685-1768
paintings: (H) $15,400

MONTI, Gaetano, of Ravenna
Italian 1776-1847
sculpture: (L) $1,150; (H) $7,700

MONTI, R.
American 19th cent.
paintings: (L) $440; (H) $495

MONTICELLI
Italian 19th cent.
drawings: (H) $825

MONTICELLI, Adolphe
French 1824-1886
paintings: (L) $440; (H) $55,000

MONTIGNY, J.
Belgian 20th cent.
paintings: (H) $1,045

MONTIGNY, Jenny
Belgian 1875-1937
paintings: (H) $8,800

MONTILLA TINOCO, Carmen
b. Venezuela 1936
paintings: (H) $7,700

MONTOYA, Gustavo
Mexican b. 1905
paintings: (L) $1,650; (H) $34,500

MONTPARNASSE, Kiki de, Alice
PRIN
1901-1953
paintings: (H) $3,283
drawings: (L) $1,277; (H) $2,736

MONTRICHARD, Raymond
American 1887-1937
paintings: (H) $1,540

MONTUFAR, Valdimir
b. 1956
sculpture: (H) $7,475

MONTULLO, J.
Italian 19th cent.
paintings: (H) $880

MONTULLO, S***
Italian 19th cent.
paintings: (H) $2,420

MONVOISIN, Raymond
French 1794-1870
paintings: (H) $7,700

MOODY, H.W.
paintings: (H) $1,150

MOON
drawings: (H) $523

MOON, Carl
American 1879-1948
paintings: (L) $1,380; (H) $3,630
drawings: (H) $220

MOON, J.T.
paintings: (H) $1,650

MOONELIS, Judy
American b. 1953
sculpture: (H) $1,320

MOOR, Carel de
1656-1738
paintings: (H) $4,620

MOOR, Christian de
Dutch 20th cent.
paintings: (L) $173; (H) $770

MOOR, Dimitri Straichevich
drawings: (H) $633

MOORE, Albert Joseph
British 1841-1893
paintings: (L) $121,000; (H) $220,000
drawings: (H) $25,300

MOORE, Arthur W.
British 1840-1913
paintings: (L) $715; (H) $1,210

MOORE, B. Robert
British 20th cent.
paintings: (H) $1,320

MOORE, Barlow
British 1834-1897
paintings: (L) $6,900; (H) $6,900

MOORE, Benson Bond
American 1882-1974
paintings: (L) $33; (H) $3,575
drawings: (L) $154; (H) $550

MOORE, Chris
drawings: (H) $2,587

MOORE, Claude
British 1853-1901
paintings: (L) $220; (H) $2,185

MOORE, Edwin A.
American 1858-1925
paintings: (L) $660; (H) $4,400

MOORE, Frank Montague
American 1877-1967
paintings: (L) $137; (H) $3,025
drawings: (H) $330

MOORE, Gerald C.
American 20th cent.
paintings: (H) $633

MOORE, Guernsey
1874-1925
drawings: (H) $3,300

MOORE, Harry Humphrey
American 1844-1926
paintings: (L) $1,150; (H) $1,380
drawings: (H) $6,900

MOORE, Henry
English 1898-1986
paintings: (H) $3,025
drawings: (L) $3,450; (H) $71,500
sculpture: (L) $3,850; (H) $2,037,500

MOORE, Henry Wadsworth
19th/20th cent.
paintings: (H) $715

MOORE, John
paintings: (H) $7,700

MOORE, John
English 1820-1902
paintings: (H) $770

MOORE, Martha
1907-1982
paintings: (L) $55; (H) $605

MOORE, Nelson Augustus
American 1824-1902
paintings: (L) $495; (H) $1,650

MOORE, Robert
paintings: (L) $330; (H) $1,045

MOORE, William
English 1790-1851
drawings: (H) $1,155

MOORE, William C.
British 19th cent.
paintings: (H) $935

MOORE(?), Benson
b. 1882
paintings: (L) $577; (H) $577

MOORMANS, Franz
Dutch 1831-1893
paintings: (L) $429; (H) $4,888

MOOTZKA, Waldo
Native American 1903-1940
paintings: (H) $193
drawings: (H) $770

MOOY, Cornelis Pietersz
Dutch 1656-1702
paintings: (H) $13,800

MOOY, Door T.
drawings: (H) $3,025

MOPOPE, Stephen, Qued Koi, Painted
Robe
Native American b. 1898
paintings: (H) $1,100

MORA, Francis Luis
Uruguayan/American 1874-1940
paintings: (L) $302; (H) $16,500
drawings: (L) $39; (H) $3,300

MORA, W.
paintings: (H) $805

MORADO, Jose Chavez
Mexican b. 1909
paintings: (L) $4,400; (H) $6,325

MORAGAS Y TORRAS, Tomas
Spanish 1837-1906
paintings: (H) $3,680

MORAHAN, Eugene
sculpture: (H) $5,775

MORALES, Armando
Nicaraguan/Amer. b. 1927
paintings: (L) $3,300; (H) $420,500
drawings: (L) $4,180; (H) $74,000

MORALES, Dario
Columbian b. 1944
paintings: (H) $51,750
drawings: (L) $5,175; (H) $60,500
sculpture: (L) $29,900; (H) $55,200

MORALES, Eduardo
b. Cuba 1890 d. 1938
paintings: (L) $2,875; (H) $10,175

MORALES, Francisco
late 19th cent.
paintings: (H) $10,350

MORALES, Juan Antonio
Spanish 19th/20th cent.
paintings: (L) $935; (H) $1,610

MORALES, Luis de, called EL DIVINO
1509?-1586
paintings: (H) $4,025

MORALES, Manuel Ruiz Sanchez
Spanish 1853-1922
paintings: (H) $935

MORALES, Rodolfo
Mexican b. 1925
paintings: (L) $5,500; (H) $74,000
drawings: (H) $518

MORALT, A.
German 19th cent.
paintings: (H) $935

MORAN, Edward
American 1819-1878
paintings: (L) $690; (H) $31,900
drawings: (H) $3,850

MORAN, Edward
American 1829-1901
paintings: (L) $550; (H) $156,500
drawings: (L) $83; (H) $3,450

MORAN, Edward
American 1901-1944
paintings: (H) $4,400

MORAN, Edward Percy
American 1862-1935
paintings: (L) $115; (H) $32,200
drawings: (L) $330; (H) $1,650

MORAN, J.
American 19th cent.
paintings: (H) $577

MORAN, John Leon
American 1864-1941
paintings: (L) $110; (H) $7,360
drawings: (L) $192; (H) $1,430

MORAN, Peter
American 1841-1914
paintings: (L) $715; (H) $4,125
drawings: (L) $138; (H) $805

MORAN, Thomas
American 1837-1926
paintings: (L) $1,760; (H) $2,752,500
drawings: (L) $770; (H) $264,000

MORANDI, Giorgio
Italian 1890-1964
paintings: (L) $140,000; (H) $605,000
drawings: (L) $3,450; (H) $38,500

MORANDINI, Francesco, Il Poppi
Italian 1544-1597
paintings: (H) $110,000

MORANE, C.
Continental School 19th c.
paintings: (H) $825

Nineteenth-century Paintings

Nineteenth-century auction catalogues at Christie's and Sotheby's can be quite hefty. With such large offerings, the buy-in rate can also be very large. A lot is bought-in when it is not sold, either because there was no bid or because the bidding did not reach the reserve. Not all auction houses have reserves, or they may offer some lots with a reserve and some without. Most auction houses will charge various fees if your consignment is not sold, but this may sometimes be waived if you have agreed to their estimate. Nineteenth-century artists were very prolific, and paintings from this period are sold in fancy New York showrooms as well as in country auctions. The works of many artists from this period are still undervalued. This sentimental 17th-century wedding scene by 19th-century French Romanticist Adrien Moreau (1843-1906) was sold at a country auction by Bider's in Andover, Massachusetts. Moreau was a painter of historical subjects, working in oils and watercolors. He made his debut in the French Salon in 1868 and won a second-class medal in 1876. He was also a book illustrator: Voltaire's *Candide* in 1893 and E. Moreau's *The Secret of Saint Louis* in 1899. *At the Wedding* realized $19,800. (Adrien Moreau, *At the Wedding*, oil on canvas, 38 x 24 inches, Bider's, September 28, 1994, $19,800)

MORANG, Alfred
  American 1901-1958
  drawings: (H) $1,380
MORANG, Dorothy
  American b. 1906
  paintings: (H) $2,750

MORAS, Walter
  German ac. 1876-1910
  paintings: (L) $1,540; (H) $3,025
MORBELLI, Angelo
  Italian 1853-1919
  paintings: (H) $2,202,500

MORCHAIN, Paul Bernard
paintings: (H) $1,380

MORCILLO, Gabriel
Spanish 19th/20th cent.
paintings: (H) $22,000

MORE, Paul le
French 19th/20th cent.
drawings: (L) $605; (H) $605

MORE, Ramon Aguilar
b. 1924
paintings: (H) $1,980

MOREAN, Aug.
sculpture: (H) $880

MOREAU
sculpture: (L) $302; (H) $7,150

MOREAU, A.
drawings: (H) $1,550

MOREAU, A.
19th cent.
paintings: (H) $2,090

MOREAU, Adrien
French 1843-1906
paintings: (L) $2,970; (H) $82,500
drawings: (H) $220

MOREAU, Auguste
French 1834-1917.
sculpture: (L) $880; (H) $12,650

MOREAU, Camille, nee NELATON
French 1840-1897
paintings: (H) $4,600

MOREAU, Charles
French b. 1830
paintings: (L) $2,750; (H) $13,800

MOREAU, Francois Hippolyte
French 19th cent.
sculpture: (L) $2,310; (H) $19,800

MOREAU, Gustave
French 1826-1898
paintings: (L) $4,600; (H) $33,000
drawings: (L) $156,500; (H) $550,000

MOREAU, H.
paintings: (H) $4,600

MOREAU, Henri
French 1869-1943
paintings: (H) $1,380

MOREAU, Hippolyte
French 1832-1917
sculpture: (L) $330; (H) $7,150

MOREAU, Jean Michel, the younger
French 1741-1814
drawings: (H) $13,225

MOREAU, Louis
French late 19th/20th cent.
sculpture: (H) $3,300

MOREAU, Louis Auguste
French 1855-1919
sculpture: (H) $5,750

MOREAU, Louis Gabriel, called
Moreau L'Aine
French 1740-1806
paintings: (H) $96,250
drawings: (L) $825; (H) $3,450

MOREAU, Louis and Francois
MOREAU
French ac. 19th cent.
sculpture: (H) $605

MOREAU, M***
20th cent.
paintings: (H) $2,300

MOREAU, Mathurin
French 1822-1912
sculpture: (L) $345; (H) $14,300

MOREAU-NELATON, Etienne
paintings: (H) $990

MOREAU-VAUTHIER, Paul Gabriel
Jean
French 1871-1936
sculpture: (L) $920; (H) $2,750

MOREAUX
paintings: (H) $715

MOREELSE, Paulus
Dutch 1571-1638
paintings: (L) $8,800; (H) $17,600

MOREL, J.E.
paintings: (H) $4,950

MOREL, Jan Baptiste
Flemish 1662-1732
paintings: (H) $28,750

MOREL, Jan Evert
Dutch 1777-1808
paintings: (H) $27,500

MOREL, Jan Evert, II
Dutch 1835-1905
paintings: (L) $460; (H) $14,300

MOREL, Jan Evert and Franz van
SEVERDONCK
Dutch/Belgian 1835-1905; 1809-1889
paintings: (H) $3,630

MOREL, Jan Evert and Franz van
SEVERDONCK, II
Dutch 19th cent.
paintings: (H) $2,640

MOREL-FATIO, Antonie Leon
French 1810-1871
paintings: (H) $800

MORELAND ?, George
paintings: (H) $725

MORELEY, James
Irish/American 19th cent.
paintings: (H) $605

MORELLI, A.
sculpture: (H) $4,400

MORELLI, Domenico
Italian 1826-1901
paintings: (H) $6,600
drawings: (L) $192; (H) $5,500

MORELLI, L.
Italian 20th cent.
sculpture: (L) $1,265; (H) $1,430

MORELLO, F.
Italian 20th cent.
paintings: (L) $605; (H) $605

MORELLO, Leonardo
Italian 19th/20th cent.
drawings: (H) $1,072

MORELY, Malcolm
American b. London 1931
paintings: (L) $7,700; (H) $231,000
drawings: (L) $3,450; (H) $6,600

MORENO, Miguel
Spanish contemporary
sculpture: (H) $715

MORENO, Servando Cabrera
1923-1981
paintings: (H) $4,025
drawings: (H) $4,025

MORENO TEJADA, J.
Spanish 19th cent.
paintings: (H) $17,600

MOREROD, A.
Swiss School b. 1902
paintings: (H) $798

MORET, Henri
French 1856-1913
paintings: (L) $16,500; (H) $48,300

MORETT, D.
European 20th cent.
paintings: (H) $550

MORETTI,
paintings: (H) $1,320

MORETTI, A.
paintings: (H) $935

MORETTI, Giovanni
Italian 19th cent.
paintings: (H) $2,200

MORETTI, Lucien Philippe
Italian b. 1922
paintings: (L) $863; (H) $4,600
drawings: (L) $1,980; (H) $3,300

MORETTI, R.
Italian 19th cent.
drawings: (L) $467; (H) $3,080

MORETTO DA BRESCIA, Alessandro
BONVICINO
1498-1554
paintings: (H) $28,600

MORETTO DA BRESCIA, Alessandro
Bonvicino
Italian 1498-1554
paintings: (H) $4,400

MOREY, Leo
d. 1965
drawings: (L) $4,400; (H) $9,775

MORGAN
paintings: (L) $27; (H) $1,210

MORGAN, Paris School
20th cent.
paintings: (L) $550; (H) $880

MORGAN, Evelyn de, nee Pickering
British 1855-1919
paintings: (H) $19,550

MORGAN, Frederick
English c. 1856-1927
paintings: (L) $2,200; (H) $88,000
drawings: (H) $12,100

MORGAN, Griffith
b.1819
paintings: (H) $2,640

MORGAN, Jim
b. 1947
paintings: (L) $138; (H) $3,300

MORGAN, John
British 1823-1897
paintings: (H) $27,600

MORGAN, John William
20th cent.
paintings: (H) $1,650

MORGAN, Lynn T.
American b. 1889
paintings: (H) $1,760

MORGAN, Mary De Neale
American 1868-1948
paintings: (L) $467; (H) $7,700
drawings: (L) $467; (H) $3,450

MORGAN, Mary Vernon
British ac. 1871-1927
paintings: (H) $990

MORGAN, Maud
American 20th cent.
paintings: (H) $2,415

MORGAN, Robert F.
paintings: (L) $1,100; (H) $2,700

MORGAN, Sister Gertrude
American 1900-1980
drawings: (L) $2,090; (H) $4,887

MORGAN, T.A.
19th/20th cent.
paintings: (H) $660

MORGAN, Wallace
American 1873-1948
drawings: (L) $55; (H) $825

MORGAN, William
American 1826-1900
paintings: (L) $920; (H) $4,887

MORGANTINI, Luigi
Italian 1867-1938
paintings: (H) $1,540

MORGENSTERN, Frederick Ernst
German 1853-1919
paintings: (L) $1,093; (H) $2,200

MORGENSTERN, Karl
German 1811-1893
paintings: (H) $19,550

MORGENSTERN, Karl Ernst
German 1847-1928
paintings: (H) $1,650

MORI
Japanese 19th/20th cent.
paintings: (H) $660

MORI, A.
Italian 19th/20th cent.
paintings: (H) $2,070

MORIARTY, David
b. 1957
paintings: (L) $403; (H) $1,840

MORICE, Leon
French b. 1868
sculpture: (H) $825

MORIMURA, Yasumasa
b. 1961
drawings: (L) $5,750; (H) $12,075

MORIN
late 19th/20th cent.
sculpture: (H) $1,610

MORIN, Emile
French 19th cent.
drawings: (H) $1,650

MORIN, Georges
French b. 1874
sculpture: (L) $1,100; (H) $3,450

MORIN, Willard
sculpture: (H) $1,045

MORINA, Giulio
Italian 1555/60-1609
drawings: (H) $5,175

MORINI, Fortunato
Italian 19th/20th cent.
paintings: (H) $825

MORISE, Louis Marie
French 19th cent.
sculpture: (L) $4,950; (H) $7,700

MORISE, Max
French 20th cent.
sculpture: (H) $3,575

MORISOT, Berthe
French 1841-1895
paintings: (L) $30,800; (H) $1,267,500
drawings: (L) $2,300; (H) $151,000

MORISOT, Henriette
French 19th cent.
paintings: (H) $4,600

MORISSET, Francois Henri
French b. 1870
paintings: (H) $6,050

MORITINI
sculpture: (H) $1,320

MORITZ, Louis
Dutch 1773-1850
paintings: (H) $1,100

MORITZ, William
Swiss 1816-1860
paintings: (H) $6,325

MORLAND, George
British 1763-1804
paintings: (L) $207; (H) $23,000
drawings: (L) $330; (H) $990

MORLAND, George, studio of
paintings: (H) $990

MORLEY, Eugene
b. 1909
paintings: (H) $11,500

MORLEY, G.H.
paintings: (H) $525

MORLEY, Malcolm
American b. 1931
paintings: (L) $1,725; (H) $627,000
drawings: (L) $550; (H) $54,625
sculpture: (H) $10,350

MORLEY, Robert
British 1857-1941
paintings: (L) $1,035; (H) $17,250

MORLEY, T.W.
British 1859-1925
drawings: (H) $495

MORLON, Alexandre
French b. 1878
sculpture: (L) $578; (H) $863

MORLON, Paul Emile Antony
French 19th cent.
paintings: (L) $3,220; (H) $11,000

MORMILE, Gaetano
Italian 1839-1890
paintings: (L) $825; (H) $4,620

MOROT, Aime Nicolas
French 1850-1913
paintings: (L) $3,025; (H) $11,500

MORPHESIS, Jim
contemporary
paintings: (H) $3,850
sculpture: (H) $2,200

MORRELL, Edith Whitcomb
American 20th cent.
drawings: (H) $495

MORRELL, Wayne B.
American b. 1923
paintings: (L) $92; (H) $907
drawings: (H) $137

MORREN, Georges
Belgian 1868-1941
paintings: (L) $16,500; (H) $57,500

MORRICE, James Wilson
Canadian 1865-1924
paintings: (L) $3,740; (H) $572,000

MORRILA, John
20th cent.
paintings: (L) $110; (H) $495

MORRILL, Rowena
paintings: (H) $1,265

MORRIS, C.
American 19th cent.
paintings: (L) $143; (H) $2,860

MORRIS, Carl
American b. 1911
paintings: (H) $2,090

MORRIS, Cedric
b. 1895
paintings: (H) $650

MORRIS, Charles Greville
British 1861-1922
paintings: (L) $660; (H) $1,760

MORRIS, E.
19th cent.
paintings: (H) $460

MORRIS, E. Butler
British 19th c.
paintings: (H) $1,210

MORRIS, Fred
English 20th cent.
drawings: (H) $460

MORRIS, George Ford
American 1873-1960
paintings: (L) $242; (H) $385
drawings: (L) $550; (H) $1,323

MORRIS, George L.K.
American 1905/06-1975
paintings: (L) $110; (H) $27,500
drawings: (L) $2,640; (H) $2,750

MORRIS, H.
British ac. 1840s
paintings: (L) $1,925; (H) $2,200

MORRIS, J.
British 19th cent.
paintings: (L) $1,320; (H) $5,750

MORRIS, J.W.
paintings: (L) $1,100; (H) $1,650

MORRIS, John
American 20th cent.
paintings: (L) $173; (H) $1,540

MORRIS, John
British? 19th cent.
paintings: (H) $770

MORRIS, John Floyd
20th cent.
paintings: (L) $880; (H) $1,650

MORRIS, Kathleen Moir
Canadian 1893-1986
paintings: (L) $5,500; (H) $10,450

MORRIS, Lee
20th cent.
paintings: (H) $518

MORRIS, P.
paintings: (H) $1,155

MORRIS, Robert
American b. 1931
paintings: (H) $7,475
drawings: (L) $1,380; (H) $12,100
sculpture: (L) $154; (H) $35,750

MORRIS, W.
British 19th cent.
paintings: (H) $2,640

MORRIS, Walter
paintings: (H) $650

MORRIS, William
sculpture: (H) $1,045

MORRIS, William
American b. 1957
sculpture: (L) $2,760; (H) $5,463

MORRIS, William
British 19th cent.
paintings: (H) $1,980

MORRIS, William Walker
1834-1896
paintings: (H) $3,300

MORRIS, William Walker
British 1834-1896
paintings: (L) $3,300; (H) $4,025

MORRISH, Sydney S.
British ac. 1855-1894
paintings: (H) $1,725

MORRISON, G.
19th cent.
paintings: (H) $660

MORRISON, Kenneth M.
British 19th/20th cent.
paintings: (H) $2,200

MORRISROE, Mark
b. 1959
drawings: (L) $660; (H) $715

MORRISSEAU, Norval
b. 1930
paintings: (L) $1,430; (H) $5,225

MORROW, Raymond
American 19th cent.
paintings: (H) $1,100

MORSE, Connie L.
American
paintings: (H) $500

MORSE, J.B.
American ac. 1875-1890
paintings: (L) $165; (H) $4,400

MORSE, Jay Vernon
American 1898-1965
paintings: (L) $660; (H) $1,980
drawings: (H) $1,540

MORSE, Jonathan Bradley
American 1834-1898
paintings: (L) $550; (H) $1,495

MORSE, Samuel Finley Breese
American 1791-1872
paintings: (L) $1,980; (H) $4,950

MORTEL, Jan
Dutch 1650-1719
paintings: (H) $99,000

MORTELMANS, Frans
Belgian 1865-1936
paintings: (H) $16,500

MORTLOCK
British 20th cent.
paintings: (H) $3,080

Canadian Artist

   Kathleen Moir Morris (1893-1986) painted picturesque scenes of city life. A Montreal native, she lived there most of her life, and the old city and its tram cars, market scenes, and old churches and people were her primary subjects. Morris began her studies at the Art Association of Montreal when she was 14 years old and studied there for seven years. Two summers were spent in sketching classes with Maurice Cullen, a Canadian artist who had studied abroad with the Impressionists. Morris's works of Old Montreal were first exhibited at the Ontario Society of Artists in 1921. As an invalid, her travels were limited, but her paintings were widely exhibited in both group and solo shows. During a seven year period while she was living in Ottawa, she painted *Harness Shop, York Street, Ottawa*. The painting, dated 1930, sold at Ritchie's in Toronto for $10,450 Canadian in 1994. The painting is almost identical to *Saddler's Shop, Ottawa 1928*, the painting used to illustrate her work in the 1975 *Women Painters in Canada* by Dorothy Farr and Natalie Luckyi. (Kathleen Moir Morris, *Harness Shop, York Street, Ottawa*, oil on panel, $10\frac{1}{8}$ x $13\frac{7}{8}$ inches, Ritchie's, November 29, 1994, $10,450)

MORTLOCK, Ethel
  French ac. 1878-1904
  paintings: (H) $1,495

MORTON, Geer
  American 20th cent.
  paintings: (L) $605; (H) $1,610

MORTON, Gustel
  American b. 1902
  sculpture: (L) $330; (H) $935

MORTON, Helen
  American 19th/20th cent.
  sculpture: (H) $770

MORTON, William E.
American 1843-1916
paintings: (H) $468

MORVILLER, Joseph
American ac. 1855-1870
paintings: (L) $247; (H) $43,700

MOSELEY, R.S.
British ac. 1862-1893
paintings: (L) $605; (H) $1,437

MOSELSIO, Simon
sculpture: (H) $605

MOSER, H.
paintings: (L) $88; (H) $550

MOSER, James Henry
American 1854-1913
paintings: (H) $110
drawings: (L) $165; (H) $546

MOSER, Kurt
German 20th cent.
paintings: (H) $460

MOSER, R.
German 19th/20th cent.
paintings: (H) $1,100

MOSER, Richard
Austrian b. 1874
drawings: (H) $2,420

MOSER, Wilfrid
paintings: (H) $4,400

MOSES, Anna Mary Robertson
("Grandma")
American 1860-1961
paintings: (L) $2,750; (H) $200,500

MOSES, B.& G.
ac. 1858-1869
paintings: (H) $3,850

MOSES, Ed
American b. 1926
paintings: (H) $27,500
drawings: (L) $1,725; (H) $3,300

MOSES, Forrest K.
American 1893-1974
paintings: (L) $345; (H) $1,430

MOSES, Mary Wade
American 19th cent.
paintings: (H) $522

MOSES, Thomas G.
English/American 1856-1934
paintings: (L) $58; (H) $1,320

MOSES, Thomas P.
American 1808-1881
paintings: (H) $211,500

MOSES, Walter Farrington
American 1874-1947
paintings: (L) $303; (H) $880

MOSGROVE, Fannie
American
paintings: (L) $1,100; (H) $1,870

MOSHER, Donald Allen
20th cent.
paintings: (H) $495

MOSKOWITZ, Robert
American b. 1935
paintings: (L) $22,000; (H) $33,000
drawings: (L) $2,200; (H) $44,000

MOSLER, Gustave Henry
American 1841-1920
paintings: (L) $920; (H) $12,650
drawings: (H) $1,870

MOSMAN, Warren T.
American b. 1908
sculpture: (H) $1,980

MOSS, Charles E.
Canadian 1860-1901
paintings: (H) $935

MOSS, L.V.
early 20th cent.
sculpture: (H) $2,750

MOSSA, Gustave Adolphe
French 1883-1971
paintings: (H) $34,500
drawings: (L) $7,475; (H) $13,225

MOSSET, Olivier
b. 1944
paintings: (L) $1,760; (H) $3,300

MOSSON, Georges
1851-1933
paintings: (H) $2,875

MOSTAERT, Gillis
Flemish ac. 1554-1598
paintings: (L) $8,050; (H) $22,000

MOSTYN, Thomas E., Tom
British 1864-1930
paintings: (L) $1,100; (H) $8,250

MOTE, George William
English 1832?-1909
paintings: (H) $1,430

MOTE, Marcus
American
paintings: (H) $2,750

MOTHERWELL, Robert
American 1915-1991
paintings: (L) $6,820; (H) $770,000
drawings: (L) $2,760; (H) $104,500

MOTHU, Morceau
sculpture: (H) $742

MOTLEY, D.
British 19th cent.
paintings: (H) $990

MOTTER, Anna May
American
drawings: (H) $42,550

MOTTET, Yvonne
French 1906-1968
paintings: (L) $990; (H) $2,090

MOUALLA, Fikret
1903-1967
drawings: (H) $3,220

MOUCHERON, Frederik de
1633-1686
paintings: (L) $4,370; (H) $9,350

MOUCHOT, Louis Claude
French 1830-1891
paintings: (H) $1,725

MOUCHOT, Louis Hippolyte
French 1846-1893
paintings: (L) $1,093; (H) $1,870

MOUCHOT, Ludwig
French 19th cent.
paintings: (H) $920

MOUGINS, Pierre de
paintings: (H) $6,900

MOUILLOT, Marcel
French b. 1889
paintings: (H) $1,870

MOULIN, Charles Lucien
French 19th cent.
paintings: (L) $8,800; (H) $8,800

MOULIN, Hippolyte Alexandre
French 1832-1884
sculpture: (L) $2,553; (H) $2,878

MOULINET, Antoine Edouard J.
French 1833-1891
paintings: (L) $1,380; (H) $4,600

MOULT, Christian le
French b. 1941
paintings: (H) $550

MOULTHROP, Ed
contemporary
sculpture: (H) $978

MOULTON, Frank
American 1847-1932
paintings: (L) $220; (H) $660

MOULY, Marcel
French b. 1918
paintings: (L) $460; (H) $1,100

MOUNT, Shepard Alonzo
American 1804-1868
paintings: (L) $2,875; (H) $8,800

MOUNT, Ward
American ac. 1898-1990
sculpture: (H) $1,760

MOUNT, William Sidney
American 1807-1868
paintings: (L) $1,955; (H) $33,350
drawings: (L) $633; (H) $16,500

MOUNTZ, Aaron
1873-1949
sculpture: (H) $8,625

MOWBRAY, Henry Siddons
English b. Egypt 1858, d. 1928
paintings: (L) $605; (H) $68,500

MOWER, Martin
American b. 1870
paintings: (H) $2,300
drawings: (H) $907

MOWERY, Geoff
paintings: (H) $550

MOY, Seong
b. 1921
paintings: (H) $862

MOYA, Federico
Italian 1802-1885
paintings: (H) $24,150

MOYER, Joseph
1883-1962
sculpture: (H) $748

MOYERS, John
American b. 1958
paintings: (L) $3,740; (H) $12,100

MOYERS, William (Bill)
American b. 1916
drawings: (H) $605
sculpture: (L) $660; (H) $990

MOYLAN, Lloyd
b. 1893
paintings: (L) $3,450; (H) $5,750
drawings: (H) $440

MOYNE, A***
British 19th/20th cent.
paintings: (H) $2,300

MOYS, Rolan de
ac. 1571-1592
paintings: (H) $13,800

MOZERT, Zoe
1904-1993
drawings: (L) $1,430; (H) $4,400

MOZIER, Joseph
American 1812-1870/90
sculpture: (L) $2,420; (H) $17,600

MUCHA, Alphonse
Czechoslovakian 1860-1939
paintings: (L) $9,200; (H) $63,000
drawings: (L) $990; (H) $34,500

MUCHEN, William Henry
American 1832-1911
paintings: (H) $1,430

MUCKE, Carl Emil
German 1847-1923
paintings: (L) $330; (H) $2,588

MUCKLEY, William Jabez
British 1837-1905
paintings: (L) $3,025; (H) $12,650

MUELEMANN
drawings: (H) $550

MUELLER, Alexander
American 1872-1935
paintings: (H) $495

MUELLER, Ned
American
drawings: (H) $450

MUELLER, Otto
German 1874-1930
drawings: (L) $5,175; (H) $88,000

MUELLER, Stephen
contemporary
paintings: (H) $4,950

MUELLER, W.
German 19th cent.
paintings: (H) $1,430

MUENCH, John
American 1914-1992
paintings: (H) $1,150

MUENDEL, George F.
American 1871-1948
paintings: (L) $1,380; (H) $2,420

MUENIER, Jules Alexis
French 1863-1934/42
paintings: (H) $12,075

MUHL, Roger
French b. 1929
paintings: (L) $460; (H) $8,912

MUHLENEN, Max von
Swiss 1903-1971
paintings: (H) $4,675

MUHLENFELD, Otto
American 1871-1907
paintings: (H) $1,150

MUHLFIELD, Joseph Molitor von
German 1856-1890
paintings: (H) $8,625

MUHLIG, Bernhard
German 1829-1910
paintings: (L) $2,200; (H) $6,325

MUHLIG, Hugo
German 1854-1929
paintings: (L) $11,000; (H) $32,200

MUHOKIAN, Wartan
19th cent.
paintings: (H) $4,312

MUIR, Emily
American b. 1904
paintings: (H) $825

MULARD, Francois Henri
French 1769-1850
paintings: (H) $165,000

MULDER, A.R.
American 1903-1971
paintings: (L) $715; (H) $825

MULDERS, Camille van
Continental 19th cent.
paintings: (H) $14,950

MULERTT, Carl Eugene
American 1869-1915
paintings: (L) $825; (H) $2,300

MULFORD, Stockton
b. 1886
paintings: (H) $880

MULHAUPT, Frederick
American 1871-1938
paintings: (L) $330; (H) $35,650

MULHERN, Mark
b. 1951
paintings: (L) $275; (H) $990

MULHOLLAND, S.A.
British 19th/20th cent.
drawings: (H) $489

MULIER, Pieter, the elder called
Tempesta
Dutch c. 1615-1670
paintings: (L) $12,650; (H) $36,800

MULIER, Pieter, the younger Il
Tempesta
Dutch 1637-1701
paintings: (L) $10,350; (H) $71,500

MULIERE, Claude
French b. 1940
paintings: (H) $660

MULLER, Professor
German early 20th cent.
sculpture: (H) $1,320

MULLER, Adolf and Wilhelm BAYRER
German 17th cent.
drawings: (H) $1,320

MULLER, C.
paintings: (L) $192; (H) $700

MULLER, C.
19th cent.
paintings: (L) $605; (H) $6,325

MULLER, Carl
German 19th/20th cent.
paintings: (H) $1,980

MULLER, Carl Leopold
German 1834-1892
paintings: (H) $16,100

MULLER, Charles
British 19th cent.
paintings: (H) $1,495

MULLER, Charles
German 19th cent.
paintings: (H) $1,150

MULLER, Charles Arthur
sculpture: (H) $6,325

MULLER, Charles Louis
French 1815-1892
paintings: (L) $935; (H) $10,925

MULLER, Daniel, Dan
American 1888-1977
drawings: (L) $330; (H) $468

MULLER, E.
paintings: (H) $1,045

MULLER, Erich
German 1888-1972
paintings: (L) $440; (H) $1,980

MULLER, Ernst
German 1823-1875
paintings: (L) $440; (H) $1,100

MULLER, Ernst
German 1844-1915
paintings: (H) $2,750

MULLER, Franz
German 1843-1929
paintings: (L) $2,200; (H) $22,000

MULLER, Fritz
b. 1814
paintings: (L) $450; (H) $4,887

MULLER, Fritz
German 1913-1972
paintings: (L) $374; (H) $978

MULLER, Fritz
German b. 1897
paintings: (L) $302; (H) $2,090

MULLER, G.
paintings: (H) $800

MULLER, Gustav Otto
German 1827-1922
drawings: (H) $1,210

MULLER, H.
late 19th cent.
sculpture: (H) $2,860

MULLER, Hans
Austrian b. 1873
sculpture: (L) $110; (H) $1,320

MULLER, Jan
1571-1628
drawings: (H) $12,650

MULLER, Jan
American 1922-1958
paintings: (H) $1,150
drawings: (H) $2,200

MULLER, Joseph
  German b. 1860
  paintings: (H) $2,970

MULLER, Karl
  German 1818-1893
  paintings: (H) $1,380
  sculpture: (L) $1,430; (H) $2,920

MULLER, Leopold Carl
  German 1834-1892
  paintings: (H) $51,750

MULLER, M.
  German 19th cent.
  paintings: (H) $1,375

MULLER, Moritz
  German 1841-1899
  paintings: (H) $6,050

MULLER, Peter Paul
  German b. 1843
  paintings: (H) $1,430

MULLER, Rosa
  English 19th cent.
  drawings: (H) $770

MULLER, Victor
  German 1829-1871
  paintings: (L) $5,500; (H) $6,325

MULLER, W.
  paintings: (H) $825

MULLER, William
  b. 1881
  paintings: (H) $750

MULLER, William
  British 19th cent.
  paintings: (H) $2,760

MULLER, William James
  British 1812-1845
  paintings: (L) $330; (H) $6,600

MULLER-BAUNGARTEN, Carl
  German b. 1879
  paintings: (H) $880

MULLER-CORNELIUS, Ludwig
  German 1864-1946
  paintings: (L) $1,495; (H) $3,680

MULLER-FELIX, Adolph
  American 1868-1947
  paintings: (H) $522

MULLER-GOSSENY, Franz
  German b. 1817
  paintings: (H) $523

MULLER-KURZWELLY, Konrad
  Alexander
  German 1855-1914
  paintings: (H) $1,045

MULLER-LINGKE, Albert
  German b. 1844
  paintings: (L) $550; (H) $770

MULLER-SAMERBERG, K.H.
  paintings: (H) $550

MULLER-SCHEESSEL, Ernst
  German
  paintings: (L) $385; (H) $805

MULLEY, Oskar
  Austrian b. 1891
  paintings: (H) $3,300

MULLHOLLAND, Saint John
  British 19th cent.
  paintings: (H) $7,150

MULLICAN, Lee
  American b. 1919
  paintings: (L) $1,610; (H) $3,450

MULLICAN, Matt
  American b. 1951
  paintings: (L) $2,300; (H) $11,550
  drawings: (L) $10,350; (H) $12,650

MULLIGAN, J.C.
  drawings: (H) $1,870

MULLIN, Willard
  1902-1978
  drawings: (H) $495

MULREADY, Augustus
  British d. 1886
  paintings: (H) $1,610

MULREADY, William
  Irish 1786-1863
  drawings: (H) $460

MULVANY, Thomas James
  Irish 1779-1845
  paintings: (H) $5,500

MUNAKATA, Shika
  Japanese 1903-1975
  drawings: (L) $14,950; (H) $32,200

MUNARI, Cristoforo
  Italian 1648-1730
  paintings: (L) $68,500; (H) $264,000

MUNCH, Edvard
  Norwegian 1863-1944
  paintings: (H) $55,000
  drawings: (H) $11,500

MUNDHENK, August
1848-1922
drawings: (H) $5,175

MUNDY, Rosemary
paintings: (L) $990; (H) $3,737

MUNGER, Gilbert
American 1836/37-1903
paintings: (L) $990; (H) $4,620

MUNIER, Emile
French 1810-1885
paintings: (L) $12,100; (H) $121,900
drawings: (H) $440

MUNIZ, Vik
b. 1961
drawings: (H) $4,025

MUNKACSY, Michel Lieb
Hungarian 1844-1900/09
paintings: (L) $3,575; (H) $49,450

MUNN, George Frederick
American 1852-1907
paintings: (L) $2,300; (H) $2,750

MUNNINGER, Ludwig
German 20th cent.
paintings: (L) $605; (H) $4,675

MUNNINGS, Sir Alfred J.
English 1878-1959
paintings: (L) $9,900; (H) $431,500
drawings: (L) $2,070; (H) $46,750

MUNOZ, Alberto
Spanish 20th cent.
paintings: (L) $58; (H) $546

MUNOZ, Godofredo Ortega
contemporary
paintings: (H) $8,800

MUNOZ, Juan
Spanish b. 1953
sculpture: (L) $4,600; (H) $27,600

MUNOZ, Lucio
Spanish b. 1929
sculpture: (H) $47,300

MUNOZ VERA, Guillermo
b. Chile 1949
paintings: (H) $29,700
drawings: (H) $7,700

MUNOZ Y CUESTA, Domingo
Spanish 1850-1912
paintings: (L) $2,645; (H) $26,450

MUNOZ-DEGRAIN, Antoine
French 1843-1927
paintings: (H) $4,025

MUNRO, Hugh
contemporary
paintings: (H) $8,250

MUNRO, Janet
American b. 1949
paintings: (H) $660

MUNSCH, Leopold
Austrian 1826-1888
paintings: (L) $1,650; (H) $5,520

MUNSELL, Albert H.
1858-1918
paintings: (H) $2,070

MUNSTERHJELM, Hjalmar
Finnish 1840-1905
paintings: (H) $11,500

MUNTER, Gabriele
German 1877-1962
paintings: (L) $5,750; (H) $236,500

MUNTHE, Gerhard Arij Ludvig
Morgenstjerne
Dutch b. 1875
paintings: (H) $798

MUNTHE, Gerhard Peter Franz
Vilhelm
Norwegian 1849-1929
paintings: (H) $2,760

MUNTHE, Ludvig
Norwegian 1841-1896
paintings: (L) $550; (H) $16,500

MUNTZ, Johann Heinrich
1727-1798
drawings: (H) $2,640

MUNZER, Adolf
1870-1952
paintings: (H) $3,450

MUNZIG, George Chickering
American 1859-1908
paintings: (H) $1,610

MURA, Angelo della
Italian 1867-1922
paintings: (H) $577
drawings: (L) $165; (H) $770

MURA, Francesco de
Italian 1696-1782
paintings: (L) $8,250; (H) $19,800

MURABITO, Rosario
Spanish 20th cent.
sculpture: (H) $1,320

MURAT, Jean Gilbert
French 1807-1863
paintings: (H) $13,225

MURATON, Euphemie, nee Duhanot
French b. 1840
paintings: (L) $7,188; (H) $17,600

MURATORI, Domenico Maria
Italian 1655-1742
paintings: (H) $6,900

MURCH, Frank J.
drawings: (H) $660

MURCH, Walter
American 1907-1967
paintings: (L) $1,100; (H) $29,900
drawings: (L) $1,100; (H) $3,740

MURER, Christoph
1558-1614
drawings: (H) $8,625

MURGATROYD, John
American School 20th cent.
sculpture: (H) $1,210

MURILLO, Bartolome Esteban
Spanish 1618-1682
paintings: (L) $770; (H) $277,500

MURILLO, Bartolome Esteban,
studio of
Spanish 17th cent.
paintings: (L) $2,420; (H) $104,500

MURILLO, Bartolome Esteban,
workshop of
17th cent.
paintings: (H) $12,100

MURPHY, Christopher, Jr.
American 1902-1969
paintings: (L) $575; (H) $1,100
drawings: (H) $110

MURPHY, Christopher, Jr.
American 1902-1973
paintings: (H) $575
drawings: (H) $110

MURPHY, Herman Dudley
American 1867-1945
paintings: (L) $357; (H) $21,850
drawings: (L) $165; (H) $1,380

MURPHY, John Cullen
American b. 1919
drawings: (L) $550; (H) $550

MURPHY, John Francis
American 1853-1921
paintings: (L) $990; (H) $10,350
drawings: (L) $220; (H) $4,950

MURPHY, Nelly Littlehale
American 1867-1941
paintings: (L) $138; (H) $138
drawings: (L) $55; (H) $1,100

MURRAY
British 19th cent.
paintings: (H) $6,820

MURRAY, Elisabeth Heaphy
English 1815-1882
drawings: (L) $825; (H) $1,265

MURRAY, Elizabeth
American b. 1940
paintings: (L) $8,050; (H) $126,500
drawings: (L) $7,700; (H) $20,900

MURRAY, Ellen
American 1908-1989
sculpture: (H) $748

MURRAY, H.
English ac. 1850-1860
drawings: (L) $440; (H) $4,600

MURRAY, J.R.
paintings: (H) $770

MURRAY, Samuel
American 1870-1941
sculpture: (L) $110; (H) $550

MURRAY, Sir David
British 1849-1933
paintings: (H) $1,380

MURRY, Jerre
American b. 1904
paintings: (H) $2,200

MURTEIRA, James
Portuguese 20th cent.
paintings: (H) $660

MUSCHAMP, F. Sydney
English ac. 1870-1903, d. 1929
paintings: (L) $577; (H) $28,750
drawings: (H) $1,265

MUSGRAVE, Arthur F.
paintings: (H) $550

MUSIC, Antonio Zoran
Italian 1909-1952
paintings: (L) $8,800; (H) $264,000
drawings: (L) $578; (H) $18,400

MUSICK, Archie Leroy
American b. 1902
paintings: (H) $578

MUSIN, Auguste Henri
Belgian 1852-1920
paintings: (L) $2,090; (H) $8,625

MUSIN, Francois Etienne
Belgian 1820-1888
paintings: (L) $4,025; (H) $24,150

MUSIN, Jean Francois
paintings: (H) $9,900

MUSLER, Jay
American b. 1949
sculpture: (L) $4,600; (H) $5,463

MUSS-ARNOLT, Gustav
American 1858-1927
paintings: (L) $2,090; (H) $4,125

MUSSCHER, Michiel van
Dutch 1645-1705
paintings: (H) $19,800

MUSSELMAN, Darwin B.
American b. 1916
paintings: (L) $880; (H) $1,650

MUSSILL, W.
Austrian 19th cent.
paintings: (H) $1,840

MUSSINI, Luigi
Italian 1813-1888
paintings: (H) $7,150
drawings: (H) $1,100

MUTER, Marie Mela
paintings: (H) $4,950

MUTRIE, Martha Darlay
British 1824-1885
paintings: (H) $3,450

MUTTICH, Kamil Vladislav
Czechoslovakian 1873-1924
drawings: (H) $2,990

MUTTONI, Pietro de, called Pietro
della Vecchia
Italian 1605-1678
paintings: (L) $5,500; (H) $46,200

MUYDEN, Ewert Louis van
Swiss 1853-1922
paintings: (L) $825; (H) $6,325
drawings: (H) $110

MUZZIOLI, Giovanni
Italian 1854-1894
paintings: (H) $14,300

MYERS, D.
19th/20th cent.
paintings: (H) $770

MYERS, Frank Harmon
American 1899-1956
paintings: (L) $715; (H) $6,600

MYERS, Harry
American 20th cent.
paintings: (L) $137; (H) $1,650

MYERS, Jerome
American 1867-1940/41
paintings: (L) $1,870; (H) $16,500
drawings: (L) $275; (H) $4,180

MYERS, Joel Philip
American b. 1934
sculpture: (L) $863; (H) $3,520

MYERS, Marie
American 20th cent.
paintings: (H) $550

MYERS, Walter
American early 20th cent.
paintings: (H) $690

MYGATT, Robertson
American d. 1919
paintings: (L) $165; (H) $3,960

MYLES, J.W.
paintings: (H) $1,540

MYLINDER, Anton
paintings: (H) $770

MYN, Frans van der
1719-1783
paintings: (H) $4,025

MYN, George van der
Dutch 1723-1763
paintings: (H) $101,500

MYN, Gerard van der
Dutch b. 1706
paintings: (H) $2,990

MYN, H. van der
Continental School late 18th cent.
paintings: (H) $3,850

MYN, Herman van der
Dutch 1684-1741
paintings: (H) $74,000

MYRAH, Newman
American
paintings: (H) $3,600

MYRICK, Burny
American contemporary
paintings: (H) $82
drawings: (L) $385; (H) $935

MYTENS, Daniel, the elder
Dutch c. 1590-before 1648
paintings: (H) $16,100

MYTENS, Jan
Dutch 1614-1670
paintings: (L) $6,900; (H) $46,000

MYTENS, Martin van, II
Swedish 1695-1770
paintings: (H) $14,300

MYTENS, Martin van, studio of
paintings: (H) $3,300

NAAGER, Franz
German b. 1870
paintings: (L) $495; (H) $550

NACHTMANN, F.
German
sculpture: (H) $1,093

NACHTMANN, Franz Xaver
German 1799-1846
drawings: (H) $9,350

NACHTRIEB, Michael Strieby
1835-1916
paintings: (H) $1,495

NADELMAN, Elie
American, b.Poland 1882-1946
drawings: (L) $1,150; (H) $9,075
sculpture: (L) $1,495; (H) $345,000

NADIN, Peter
b. 1954
paintings: (H) $138
drawings: (L) $132; (H) $1,100

NAEGELE, Charles Frederick
American 1857-1944
paintings: (H) $5,750

NAES(?), J.L.
Norwegian 19th cent.
paintings: (H) $1,980

NAFTEL, Paul Jacob
British 1817-1891
drawings: (H) $1,100

NAGARE, Masayuki
Japanese b. 1923
sculpture: (H) $25,300

NAGEL, Andres
b. 1947
drawings: (H) $12,650
sculpture: (H) $29,900

NAGEL, Patrick
drawings: (H) $1,100

NAGEL, Wilhelm
German b. 1866
paintings: (H) $660

NAGLE, Ron
American b. 1939
sculpture: (L) $3,520; (H) $6,325

NAGLER, Edith Kroger
American 1895-1978
paintings: (L) $495; (H) $518
drawings: (H) $192

NAGY, Peter
b. 1959
paintings: (L) $748; (H) $1,320

NAHA, Raymond
Native American b. 1933
drawings: (L) $495; (H) $4,070

NAHL, Charles C.
German/American 1818-1878
paintings: (L) $550; (H) $25,300
drawings: (H) $99

NAHL, Hugo Arthur
1833-1889
paintings: (H) $2,300

NAHL, Perham Wilhelm
American 1869-1935
paintings: (L) $1,100; (H) $6,050

NAILOR, Gerald A., Toy Yah, Walking
By The River
Native American 1917-1952
drawings: (L) $247; (H) $4,400

NAISH, John George
British 1824-1905
paintings: (H) $23,000

NAIVEU, Matthys
1647-1721
paintings: (L) $1,725; (H) $9,200

NAKAGAWA, Hachiro
Japanese 1877-1922
drawings: (L) $467; (H) $3,575

NAKAMURA, Kanzi
Japanese 19th/20th cent.
paintings: (H) $2,860

NAKAMURA, Kazuo
paintings: (L) $1,980; (H) $2,640

NAKAMURA, Naondo
paintings: (L) $1,380; (H) $2,185
drawings: (H) $3,680

NAKASHIMA, George
1905-1990
sculpture: (L) $2,200; (H) $7,700

NAKIAN, Reuben
American 1897-1986
drawings: (L) $258; (H) $1,380
sculpture: (L) $575; (H) $6,037

NAKKEN, Willem Carel
Dutch 1835-1926
drawings: (H) $719

NALDINI, Giovanni Battista, called
BATTISTA DEGLI INNOCENTI
studio of
16th cent.
paintings: (H) $51,750

NANKIVEL, John Frederick
American 1876-1950
paintings: (L) $302; (H) $2,185

NANKOKU, Hidai
b. 1912
drawings: (H) $4,600

NANNINI, Raphael
Italian early 20th cent.
sculpture: (L) $825; (H) $8,800

NANTES
French School
paintings: (H) $770

NANTEUIL, Charles Gaugiran
French b. 1811
paintings: (L) $3,960; (H) $9,900

NAPPI, Rudy
paintings: (L) $633; (H) $1,045

NARAHA, Takashi
sculpture: (H) $2,070

NARAY, Aurel
Hungarian b. 1883
paintings: (H) $748

NARAYAN, Badri
Indian b. 1929
paintings: (H) $1,150
drawings: (L) $805; (H) $1,035

NARDEUX, Henri
French 19th cent.
paintings: (L) $1,650; (H) $4,313

NARDI, Enrico
Italian b. 1864
drawings: (L) $1,100; (H) $2,750

NARDI, Francois
French 1861-1936
paintings: (L) $6,600; (H) $9,200
drawings: (L) $1,045; (H) $1,925

NARDINI, Mario
sculpture: (L) $330; (H) $1,150

NARDONE, Vincent Joseph
American b. 1937
paintings: (H) $605
drawings: (L) $413; (H) $2,970

NARJOT, Ernest E.
American 1827-1898
paintings: (H) $1,980

NARVAEZ, Francisco
Venezuelan b. 1905/08
paintings: (H) $4,950
sculpture: (L) $11,000; (H) $24,200

NASH
paintings: (L) $98; (H) $605

NASH, David
b. 1945
drawings: (H) $1,035
sculpture: (H) $16,500

NASH, Joseph
British 1808-1878
drawings: (L) $230; (H) $3,450

NASH, Manley K.
American 20th cent.
paintings: (L) $495; (H) $2,640

NASH, Thomas
American 20th cent.
paintings: (H) $1,430

NASH, Willard Ayer
American 1898-1943
paintings: (L) $4,400; (H) $11,000
drawings: (L) $715; (H) $3,575

NASMYTH, Alexander
Scottish 1758-1840
paintings: (H) $2,860

NASMYTH, P.
English 1787-1831
paintings: (H) $1,870

NASMYTH, Patrick
British 1787-1831
paintings: (L) $715; (H) $16,500

NASON, Gertrude
American 1890-1968
paintings: (L) $425; (H) $1,495
drawings: (L) $110; (H) $192

NASON, Pieter
Dutch c. 1612-1688/90
paintings: (L) $5,775; (H) $9,350

NAST, Thomas
American 1840-1902
drawings: (L) $275; (H) $4,180

NATALI, Renato
Italian 1883-1979
paintings: (L) $316; (H) $1,650

NATAPOFF, Flora
paintings: (L) $440; (H) $544

NATCHEZ
American contemporary
paintings: (H) $546

NATKIN, Robert
American b. 1930
paintings: (L) $115; (H) $12,100
drawings: (L) $115; (H) $1,840

NATOIRE, Charles Joseph
French 1700-1777
paintings: (L) $506,000; (H) $737,000
drawings: (L) $3,737; (H) $16,500

NATORP, Gustav
German b. 1836
sculpture: (H) $12,650

NATTIER, Jean Marc
French 1685-1766
paintings: (L) $10,450; (H) $35,200
drawings: (H) $297,000

NATTIER, Jean Marc, studio of
18th cent.
paintings: (L) $2,070; (H) $65,750
drawings: (H) $1,150

NATTINO, Girolamo
Italian 19th cent.
drawings: (H) $633

NATTONIER, C.
French 19th/20th cent.
paintings: (H) $2,200

NATZLER, Gertrud and Otto
b. Austria 20th cent.
sculpture: (L) $1,610; (H) $3,680

NATZLER, Otto
sculpture: (H) $1,100

NAUER, Ludwig
German b. 1888
paintings: (H) $2,750

NAUMAN, Bruce
American b. 1941
paintings: (L) $110,000; (H) $143,000
drawings: (L) $5,750; (H) $101,500
sculpture: (L) $17,600; (H) $1,925,000

NAUMANN, Johann Friedrich
drawings: (H) $2,750

NAVA, John
American b. 1947
drawings: (L) $1,725; (H) $2,588

NAVARRA, Douglas
sculpture: (L) $1,100; (H) $1,540

NAVARRA, Pietro
Italian ac. 17th/18th cent.
paintings: (H) $17,250

NAVARRO, Jose
Spanish 19th cent.
paintings: (L) $7,475; (H) $9,200

NAVARRO Y LLORENS, Jose
Spanish 1867-1923
paintings: (L) $9,200; (H) $25,300
drawings: (H) $5,500

NAVLET, Joseph
French 1821-1889
paintings: (H) $8,050

NAVONE, Eduardo
Italian 19th cent.
paintings: (H) $8,050
drawings: (H) $1,210

NAVRATIL, Joseph
Czechoslovakian 1798-1865
drawings: (H) $1,035

NAY, Ernst Wilhelm
German 1902-1968
drawings: (L) $28,750; (H) $33,350

NAY, W.
American 19th cent.
drawings: (H) $1,815

NEAGELE, Charles Frederick
American 1857-1944
paintings: (L) $4,950; (H) $8,250

NEAGLE, John
American 1796-1865
paintings: (L) $1,100; (H) $2,200

NEAL, Bill
paintings: (L) $303; (H) $2,310

NEALE, George Hall
British ac. 1883-1935
paintings: (H) $2,530

NEALE, John
British 20th cent.
paintings: (L) $165; (H) $3,850

NEAVES, Dorothy
American 20th cent.
drawings: (H) $550

NEAVES, Robert
paintings: (L) $500; (H) $880

NEBBIA, Cesare
1536-1614
drawings: (L) $1,320; (H) $3,300

NEBEKER, Bill
American b. 1942
sculpture: (L) $1,980; (H) $4,180

NEBEL, Berthold
American 1889-1964
sculpture: (H) $1,045

NEBEL, Otto
1892-1975
paintings: (L) $1,150; (H) $1,955
drawings: (L) $1,265; (H) $1,955

NECHVATAL, Joseph
paintings: (H) $1,650

NECK, Jan van
Dutch 1635-1714
paintings: (L) $8,625; (H) $10,350

NEDER, Johann Michael
paintings: (H) $6,050

NEDHAM, William
British ac. 1823-1849
paintings: (L) $16,500; (H) $23,000

NEEBE, Louis Alexander
American b. 1873
paintings: (H) $5,060

NEEBE, Minnie Harms
American b. 1873
paintings: (H) $550

NEEDHAM, Charles Austin
American 1844-1923
paintings: (H) $5,175

NEEFFS, Lodewijk
Flemish 1617-c. 1655
paintings: (H) $17,250

NEEFFS, Pieter, the elder
Flemish 1578-1656/1661
paintings: (L) $9,900; (H) $90,500

NEEFFS, Pieter, the younger
Flemish 1620-after 1675
paintings: (L) $2,990; (H) $33,000

NEEL, Alice
American 1900-1984
paintings: (L) $4,600; (H) $17,250
drawings: (H) $2,530
sculpture: (H) $6,050

NEER, Aert van der
Dutch 17th cent.
paintings: (H) $22,000

NEER, Eglon Hendrick van der
Dutch 1634-1703
paintings: (L) $1,980; (H) $825,000

NEERGARD, Hermania Sigvardine
Danish 1799-1874
paintings: (L) $4,125; (H) $55,000

NEES, Gerald L.
American 20th cent.
paintings: (L) $46; (H) $495

NEFF, Edith
American 20th cent.
paintings: (L) $3,080; (H) $3,300

NEFKENS, Martinus Jacobus
Dutch 1866-1941
paintings: (H) $1,100

NEGELY, Rudolph
Hungarian b. 1883
paintings: (H) $1,210

NEGRAE, Guy de
drawings: (L) $275; (H) $518

NEGRET, Edgar
Columbian b. 1920
sculpture: (L) $1,150; (H) $18,700

NEGRI, Mario
Italian b. 1916
sculpture: (L) $2,750; (H) $17,600

NEGULESCO, Jean
drawings: (L) $144; (H) $489

NEGUS, Caroline
American 1814-1867
drawings: (H) $2,530

NEHLIG, Victor
French/American 1830-1910
paintings: (L) $550; (H) $11,000

NEILL, John R.
American 19th/20th cent.
drawings: (L) $115; (H) $19,800

NEILLOT, Louis
French 1898-1973
paintings: (L) $2,420; (H) $8,250
drawings: (L) $259; (H) $1,350

NEILSON
paintings: (H) $1,870

NEILSON, Charles Peter
ac. 1890-1910
drawings: (L) $660; (H) $1,320

NEILSON, Raymond Perry Rodgers
American 1881-1964
paintings: (L) $165; (H) $18,700

NEIMAN, Leroy
American b. 1927
paintings: (L) $1,380; (H) $4,950
drawings: (L) $259; (H) $5,500
sculpture: (L) $1,760; (H) $3,080

NEIRA, Pedro Dominguez
Argentinean b. 1894
drawings: (H) $518

NEIXILLER, A.
19th/20th cent.
sculpture: (H) $495

NELLI, Pietro
ac. by 1360- d. 1419
paintings: (H) $96,000

NELSON, Carl G.
American b. 1898
paintings: (L) $330; (H) $990
drawings: (H) $110

NELSON, Ernest Bruce
American 1888-1952
paintings: (L) $1,430; (H) $2,750

NELSON, George Laurence
American 1887-1978
paintings: (L) $55; (H) $1,650
drawings: (H) $385

NELSON, Joan
American b. 1958
paintings: (L) $4,400; (H) $33,350

NELSON, Kay
drawings: (H) $660

NELSON, Martin H.
American
paintings: (H) $1,210

NELSON, Roger Laux
b. 1945
paintings: (H) $1,035

NELSON, William
American b. 1942
paintings: (L) $137; (H) $770
drawings: (L) $550; (H) $990

NEME, Clarel
b. Uruguay 1926
paintings: (H) $7,150

NEMETH, Gyorgy
Hungarian ac. c. 1900
paintings: (L) $451; (H) $495

NEMETHY, Albert S.
American 20th cent.
paintings: (L) $495; (H) $2,970

NEOGRADY, Antal
Hungarian 1861-1942
paintings: (L) $578; (H) $605
drawings: (H) $1,725

NEOGRADY, Laszlo
Hungarian 1861-1942
paintings: (L) $165; (H) $9,200
drawings: (H) $715

NEPOLSKY, Hermann
European 19th/20th cent.
paintings: (H) $1,320

NEPOTE, Alexander
American 1913-1986
paintings: (L) $770; (H) $1,100
drawings: (L) $600; (H) $1,100

NERI, Manuel
American b. 1930
drawings: (H) $1,955
sculpture: (L) $22,000; (H) $30,250

NERI DI BICCI
Italian 1419-1491
paintings: (L) $35,200; (H) $440,000

NERLY, Friedrich, the younger
Italian 1824-1919
paintings: (H) $48,875

NERMAN, Lenardo
Mexican b. 1932
paintings: (H) $3,300

NESBIT, Robert H.
American 1879-1961
paintings: (L) $247; (H) $990

NESBITT, Frances E.
British 20th cent.
paintings: (H) $4,600

NESBITT, Jackson Lee
American b. 1913
paintings: (H) $9,200

NESBITT, Lowell
American 1933-1994
paintings: (L) $403; (H) $12,100
drawings: (L) $546; (H) $920
sculpture: (H) $1,100

NESLET, Pollek S.
British 19th/20th cent.
paintings: (H) $460

NESS, Frank Lewis van
American b. 1866
paintings: (H) $715

NESSE, J. Paul
sculpture: (H) $8,250

NESSI, Marie Lucie
French b. 1910
paintings: (L) $690; (H) $5,500

NESTERUK, Ed
American
sculpture: (H) $690

NESTOROV, Mikhail Vasilievich
Russian 1862-1942
drawings: (H) $880

NETSCHER, Caspar
Dutch 1639-1684
paintings: (L) $4,180; (H) $60,250

NETSCHER, Caspar, and studio
17th cent.
paintings: (H) $13,800

NETSCHER, Constantin
Dutch 1668-1723
paintings: (H) $13,200

NETTER, Benjamin
French 1811-1881
paintings: (H) $1,650

NETTI, Francesco
paintings: (H) $935

NETTLETON, Walter
American 1861-1936
paintings: (L) $1,045; (H) $1,870

NEUBAUER, H.
paintings: (H) $3,300

NEUBER, Hermann
German ac. 1891-1895
paintings: (H) $19,550

NEUBERG, Carl
paintings: (L) $688; (H) $1,725

NEUBERGER, Klara
paintings: (H) $3,300

NEUBERT
German 19th cent.
paintings: (H) $550

NEUBERT, Ludwig
German 1846-1892
paintings: (H) $1,840

NEUFELD, Woldemar
Russian/American b. 1909
paintings: (L) $330; (H) $495
drawings: (L) $165; (H) $1,595

NEUHAUS, Karl Eugen
American 1879-1963
paintings: (L) $990; (H) $6,900

NEUHUYS, Albert
Dutch 1844-1914
paintings: (L) $1,540; (H) $19,800
drawings: (L) $2,875; (H) $3,740

NEUMAN, Carl
American 1858-1932
paintings: (H) $990

NEUMANN, A.
paintings: (H) $1,980

NEUMANN, Alexander
German b. 1831
paintings: (L) $6,325; (H) $8,625

NEUMANN, Carl
1833-1891
paintings: (L) $715; (H) $3,630

NEUMANN, Johan Carl
Danish 1883-1891
paintings: (L) $7,150; (H) $13,200

NEUQUELMAN, Lucien
French b. 1909
paintings: (L) $3,300; (H) $5,500

NEUSCHUL, Ernest
paintings: (H) $4,675

NEUVILLE, Alphonse Marie de
French 1835-1885
paintings: (L) $495; (H) $6,600
drawings: (H) $550

NEUVILLE, Brunel
French 19th/20th cent.
paintings: (L) $2,090; (H) $3,410

NEUVILLE, Bruno
French 19th/20th cent.
paintings: (L) $1,100; (H) $1,403

NEVAQUAYA, Joyce Lee Tate, Doc
Tate
Native American b. 1932
drawings: (L) $660; (H) $715

NEVELSON, Louise
Russian/American 1900-1988
paintings: (H) $4,830
drawings: (L) $1,210; (H) $16,500
sculpture: (L) $1,610; (H) $195,000

NEVIL, E**
English 19th/20th cent.
drawings: (L) $495; (H) $550

NEVIL, E.
British 19th cent.
paintings: (H) $550
drawings: (L) $523; (H) $2,013

NEVILLE, A.
paintings: (H) $1,980

NEVILLE, Ralf
19th/20th cent.
paintings: (H) $935

NEVINSON, Christopher Richard
Wynne
1889-1946
drawings: (L) $2,415; (H) $2,530

NEWCOMB, Marie Guise
paintings: (H) $1,127

NEWCOMBE, W.J.B.
Canadian 20th cent.
drawings: (L) $316; (H) $460

NEWCOMBE, Warren
American b. 1894
paintings: (H) $1,320

NEWELL, George Glenn
American 1870-1947
paintings: (L) $275; (H) $1,760
drawings: (H) $193

NEWELL, Henry C.
American ac. 1865-1885
paintings: (H) $3,520

NEWELL, Hugh
American 1830-1915
paintings: (L) $1,035; (H) $8,250
drawings: (H) $110

NEWELL, Peter
American 1862-1924
paintings: (L) $230; (H) $1,980
drawings: (L) $440; (H) $1,320

NEWHALL, T.M.
paintings: (H) $8,250

NEWMAN, Alan G.
American 1875-1940
sculpture: (L) $550; (H) $3,850

NEWMAN, George A.
paintings: (L) $55; (H) $1,200

NEWMAN, Henry Roderick
American c. 1833-1918
drawings: (L) $2,750; (H) $60,500

NEWMAN, Howard
American 20th cent.
sculpture: (L) $1,380; (H) $2,185

NEWMAN, John
American b. 1952
drawings: (L) $2,588; (H) $5,500
sculpture: (H) $6,900

NEWMAN, Joseph
1890-1979
paintings: (H) $1,092

NEWMAN, Robert Loftin
American 1827-1912
paintings: (L) $2,860; (H) $3,738
drawings: (H) $115

NEWMANN, A.
German 19th/20th cent.
paintings: (H) $1,035

NEWMANN, Vicky
b. 1963
drawings: (H) $2,500

NEWMARCH, Strafford
British ac. 1866-1874
paintings: (L) $467; (H) $825

NEWMARK, Marilyn
American b. 1928
sculpture: (L) $605; (H) $1,100

NEWNHAM, Margaret
English 19th cent.
paintings: (H) $467

NEWTON, Francis
American 1872-1944
paintings: (H) $660

NEWTON, Gilbert Stuart
b. Canada, d. Eng. c. 1794-1835
paintings: (L) $165; (H) $10,350

NEWTON, H.
American 20th cent.
paintings: (H) $523

NEWTON, Parker
American d. 1928
paintings: (L) $297; (H) $1,210

NEWTON, Richard
English 1777-1798
paintings: (L) $1,375; (H) $2,090

NEWTON, Richard
English 1777-1798
paintings: (H) $4,830

NEWTON, Richard, Jr.
American 20th cent.
paintings: (L) $990; (H) $10,350

NEY, Lloyd Raymond
American 1893-1964
drawings: (L) $517; (H) $2,200

NEYAC, Guy de
French 20th cent.
drawings: (L) $55; (H) $605

NEYLAND, Harry
American 1877-1958
paintings: (L) $605; (H) $3,025
drawings: (L) $935; (H) $935

NEYMARK, Gustave Mardoche
French b. 1850
paintings: (L) $1,760; (H) $4,675

NEYN, Pieter de
Dutch 1597-1639
paintings: (L) $13,800; (H) $31,900

NEYRAC, Guy de
French 20th cent.
drawings: (L) $83; (H) $2,850

NEYTS, Gillis
1623-1687
drawings: (H) $5,500

NEZZO, Luciano
Italian b. 1856
paintings: (H) $6,037

NIBBS, Richard Henry
English 1816-1893
paintings: (L) $413; (H) $7,475
drawings: (H) $935

NIBLETT, Gary
American b. 1943
paintings: (L) $2,750; (H) $12,650
drawings: (H) $230

NIBRIG, Ferdinand Hart
Dutch 1866-1915
paintings: (H) $5,500

NICCOLO DI PIETRO
Italian ac. 1394-1430
paintings: (H) $35,650

NICCOLO DI SEGNA
Italian ac. 1331-1345
paintings: (H) $46,000

NICE, Don
American b. 1923
paintings: (H) $413
drawings: (L) $920; (H) $3,080

NICHELSON, George Washington
American 1832-1911
paintings: (H) $1,155

NICHOLAS, Benvenueto
Italian 1848-1900
paintings: (H) $1,100

NICHOLAS, Lori
American
paintings: (H) $700

NICHOLAS, N.
paintings: (L) $231; (H) $522

NICHOLAS, T.M.
20th cent.
paintings: (H) $495

NICHOLAS, Thomas Andrew
American b. 1934
paintings: (L) $330; (H) $2,200
drawings: (L) $193; (H) $935

NICHOLL, Andrew
Irish 1804-1886
drawings: (L) $3,080; (H) $5,775

NICHOLLS, Burr H.
American 1848-1915
paintings: (L) $550; (H) $2,420
drawings: (H) $5,175

NICHOLLS, John E.
English ac. 1922-1955
paintings: (H) $2,200

NICHOLLS, Rhoda Holmes
Anglo/American 1854-1930
paintings: (H) $1,100
drawings: (L) $715; (H) $1,320

NICHOLS, Burr H.
American 1848-1915
paintings: (H) $825

NICHOLS, Carroll L.
American b. 1882
paintings: (L) $110; (H) $1,210

NICHOLS, Dale
American 1904-1989
paintings: (L) $121; (H) $20,700
drawings: (L) $137; (H) $3,910

NICHOLS, Edward W.
19th cent.
paintings: (H) $688

NICHOLS, Henry Hobart
American 1869-1962
paintings: (L) $468; (H) $9,200
drawings: (L) $220; (H) $1,150

NICHOLS, Perry
paintings: (H) $805

NICHOLS, William
b. 1942
paintings: (H) $7,500
drawings: (H) $1,500

NICHOLSEN, W.
English 19th cent.
paintings: (H) $770

NICHOLSON, Ben
British 1894-1982
paintings: (L) $32,200; (H) $1,540,000
drawings: (L) $11,000; (H) $37,375

NICHOLSON, Charles W.
American 1886-1965
paintings: (L) $165; (H) $1,100
drawings: (H) $1,870

NICHOLSON, Edward H.
American 1901-1966
paintings: (L) $193; (H) $611,050
drawings: (L) $193; (H) $413

NICHOLSON, G.W.
American 1901-1966
paintings: (L) $475; (H) $605

NICHOLSON, George W.
American 1832-1912
paintings: (L) $546; (H) $10,925
drawings: (L) $330; (H) $2,750

NICHOLSON, Lillie Mae
American 1884-1964
paintings: (L) $440; (H) $1,035

NICHOLSON, W.
paintings: (H) $500

NICKELE, Isaac
ac. 1660-1703
paintings: (L) $5,462; (H) $11,000

NICKERSON, R.E.
paintings: (L) $3,300; (H) $3,300

NICKERSON, Reginald E.
American b. 1915
paintings: (L) $853; (H) $13,800

NICKERSON, Robert E.
American b. 1915
paintings: (L) $1,595; (H) $2,420

NICLAUSSE, Paul Francois
sculpture: (H) $4,025

NICOL, Erskine
British 1825-1904
paintings: (L) $1,100; (H) $31,625

NICOLAIDES, Kimon
1892-1938
paintings: (H) $2,300

NICOLAUS, Martin
German 1870-1945
paintings: (H) $1,320

NICOLAY, Helen
American 1866-1954
drawings: (L) $690; (H) $2,990

NICOLET, Gabriel Emile
Swiss 1856-1921
paintings: (H) $770

NICOLETTI, Joseph
paintings: (L) $489; (H) $2,185

NICOLINA, A.
Italian 19th c.
paintings: (H) $2,200

NICOLINI, G.
sculpture: (L) $385; (H) $2,970

NICOLINI, Giovanni
Italian b. 1872
sculpture: (H) $770

NICOLL, James Craig
American 1846-1918
paintings: (L) $385; (H) $4,600
drawings: (L) $1,540; (H) $2,645

NICOLLE, Victor Jean
French 1754-1826
drawings: (L) $990; (H) $24,150

NICZKY, Edouard
German b. 1850
paintings: (H) $4,400

NIEBERGALL (?)
paintings: (H) $1,092

NIEDECKEN, George
drawings: (H) $2,530

NIEHOLSON, C.
American
paintings: (H) $715

NIEL, Robert
German/Austrian 19th/20th cent.
paintings: (H) $715

NIELSEN, Amaldus Clarin
Norwegian 1838-1932
paintings: (H) $2,200

NIELSEN, E.F.
American
drawings: (H) $990

NIELSEN, Jais
paintings: (H) $4,950

NIELSEN, Kai
Danish 20th cent.
paintings: (H) $605

NIELSEN, Kay
b. Denmark 1886-1957
drawings: (L) $8,050; (H) $20,700
sculpture: (H) $357

NIELSEN, Otto
Danish b. 1877
paintings: (H) $990

NIELSEN, Peter
American 1873-1965
paintings: (H) $660

NIELSEN, Th.
Scandinavian 19th/20th cent.
paintings: (H) $605

NIEMANN, Edmund John, Jr.
British 1813-1876
paintings: (L) $1,100; (H) $21,850

NIEMANN, Edward H., Jr.
British ac. 1863-1867
paintings: (L) $1,540; (H) $6,325

NIEMIRSKI, N.
Polish 20th cent.
paintings: (H) $1,650

NIEPOLD, Frank
American b. 1890
paintings: (H) $935

NIERMAN, Leonardo
Mexican b. 1932
paintings: (L) $287; (H) $3,850
drawings: (L) $220; (H) $1,760
sculpture: (H) $1,980

NIESEN, Charles
American ac. 1868
paintings: (H) $23,000

NIETO, John
b. 1936
paintings: (L) $8,800; (H) $8,800

NIETO, Rodolfo
b. Mexico 1936-1988
paintings: (L) $3,850; (H) $19,800
drawings: (L) $978; (H) $9,775

NIEULANDT, Adriaen van
Dutch 1587-1658
paintings: (H) $18,400

NIEULANDT, Willem van
Flemish 1584-1635/36
paintings: (H) $38,500

NIEUWENHOVEN, Willem van
Dutch 1879-1973
paintings: (L) $460; (H) $1,955

NIEUWERKERKE, Alfred Emile
O'Hara
French 1811-1892
sculpture: (H) $12,100

NIGHTINGALE, Basil
British 1864-1940
paintings: (H) $9,200
drawings: (L) $413; (H) $2,185

NIGHTINGALE, Robert
British 1815-1895
paintings: (H) $17,250

NIGNET, Georges
French b. 1926
paintings: (L) $1,210; (H) $5,500

NIGRO, Adolfo
b. 1942
paintings: (L) $2,300; (H) $6,900
drawings: (H) $1,725

NIKEL, Lea
b. 1918
paintings: (H) $6,900

NIKOKAY, C.
drawings: (H) $660

NIKOLAKI, Z.P.
paintings: (H) $2,090

NIKUTOWSKI, Arthur Johann Severin
German 1830-1888
paintings: (H) $16,100

NILES, G.S.
American School 19th cent.
paintings: (H) $1,650

NILSON
Continental 19th cent.
paintings: (H) $8,050

NILSON, Johann Esaias
German 1721-1788
drawings: (H) $4,950

NILSSON, Gladys
paintings: (H) $2,185

NILSSON, Willy
Danish 20th cent.
paintings: (H) $605

NIMMO, H.
French 19th cent.
paintings: (H) $1,650

NIMMO, Louise Everett
American
paintings: (H) $522

NINAS, Paul
American 1932-1964
paintings: (H) $3,025

NINERZE-RUIZ, E***
Spanish 19th/20th cent.
paintings: (H) $1,870

NINGUIK
sculpture: (H) $715

NINI, Jean Baptiste
sculpture: (H) $1,430

NINNES, Bernard
British b. 1899
paintings: (H) $3,080

NINO, Carmelo
Venezuela b. 1951
paintings: (H) $10,350

NISBET, Marc
American 20th cent.
paintings: (H) $495

NISBET, P.A.
20th cent.
paintings: (H) $2,300

NISBET, Pollok Sinclair
Scottish 1848-1922
paintings: (L) $165; (H) $863

NISBET, Robert Buchanan
British 1857-1952
drawings: (L) $715; (H) $805

NISBET, Robert Hogg
American 1879-1961
paintings: (L) $220; (H) $5,500

NISHIZAWA, Luis
Mexico b. 1926
paintings: (L) $4,950; (H) $59,700
drawings: (H) $9,900

NISS, Thorvald Simeon
Danish 1842-1905
paintings: (H) $8,050
drawings: (H) $1,320

NISSEN, Chris
American 20th cent.
paintings: (H) $1,045

NISSL, Rudolph
Austrian 1870-1955
paintings: (H) $1,540

NITSCH-WILLIM, H.
Dutch 19th cent.
paintings: (H) $1,100

NITSCHKE, W.
sculpture: (H) $1,035

NITSOH-WILLINER, *
19th cent.
paintings: (H) $920

NITTIS, Giuseppe de
Italian 1846-1884
paintings: (L) $12,100; (H) $715,000
drawings: (H) $178,500

NIVELT, Roger
French 1899-1962
paintings: (H) $660

NIVERT, Georgette
French 20th cent.
paintings: (L) $440; (H) $495

NIVET, A.
French 19th cent.
paintings: (H) $1,430

NIXON, David Sinclair
American 1904-1967
paintings: (L) $165; (H) $825
drawings: (L) $66; (H) $550

NOBELE, Henry de
Belgian 1820-1870
paintings: (H) $605

NOBLE, G.
American 19th/20th cent.
paintings: (H) $518

NOBLE, John A.
1874-1935
paintings: (H) $468
drawings: (H) $104

NOBLE, John Sargent
English 1848-1896
paintings: (L) $16,500; (H) $132,000

NOBLE, Raymond E.
American 1880-1947
paintings: (H) $825

NOBLE, Robert
British 1857-1917
paintings: (H) $2,090
drawings: (H) $288

NOBLE, Thomas S.
American 1835-1907
paintings: (L) $220; (H) $24,150

NODDER, R.P.
British ac. 1793-1820
paintings: (H) $1,725

NOE, Luis Felipe
Argentinean b. 1933
paintings: (L) $5,750; (H) $6,600
drawings: (H) $1,150

NOEGRADY, Laszlo
Hungarian b. 1900
paintings: (H) $1,540

NOEL, Alexandre Jean
French 1752-1834
paintings: (H) $32,200
drawings: (L) $3,450; (H) $30,800

NOEL, Edme Antony Paul
French 1845-1909
sculpture: (L) $4,370; (H) $9,200

NOEL, Georges
French b. 1924
paintings: (H) $4,950
drawings: (H) $5,500

NOEL, John Bates
British 19th/20th cent.
paintings: (L) $633; (H) $990

NOEL, Jules Achille
French 1813/15-1881
paintings: (L) $1,100; (H) $28,600
drawings: (L) $1,430; (H) $1,955

NOEL, Peter Paul Joseph
French 1789-1822
paintings: (H) $12,100

NOEL, R.
late 19th cent.
sculpture: (H) $605

NOEL (?), I.
paintings: (H) $2,185

NOELLE, Frederick
American ac. 1854-1857
paintings: (H) $3,850

NOELSMITH, Thomas
drawings: (H) $900

NOGUCHI, Isamu
American 1904-1988
drawings: (L) $1,980; (H) $9,200
sculpture: (L) $13,200; (H) $552,500

NOHEIMER, Mathias John
American b. 1909
paintings: (L) $165; (H) $575

NOIR, Ernest
French 1864-1931
paintings: (L) $550; (H) $1,210

NOLAND, Cady
b. 1956
paintings: (L) $3,450; (H) $8,625
sculpture: (L) $10,350; (H) $21,850

NOLAND, Kenneth
American b. 1924
paintings: (L) $4,950; (H) $220,000
drawings: (H) $1,725

NOLDE, Emil
German 1867-1956
paintings: (L) $189,500; (H) $638,000
drawings: (L) $8,050; (H) $181,500

NOLLE
19th/20th cent.
paintings: (H) $578

NOLLEKENS, Josef Frans
Flemish 1702-1748
paintings: (H) $13,200

NOLLEKENS, Joseph
English 1737-1823
drawings: (H) $460
sculpture: (H) $4,620

NOME, Francois de, called Monsu
Desiderio
French 1593-c. 1640
paintings: (L) $5,500; (H) $44,000

NONAS, Richard
American b. 1936
sculpture: (L) $2,300; (H) $10,450

NONETTI, A.
Italian 19th/20th cent.
paintings: (H) $1,760

NONNAST, Paul
b. 1918
drawings: (H) $1,760

NOOD, Roland
paintings: (H) $605

NOONSEN, M.
19th/20th cent.
paintings: (H) $1,540

NOORT, Adrianus Cornelis van
Dutch b. 1914
paintings: (L) $797; (H) $3,740

NOORT, Adrianus van
Dutch b. 1914
paintings: (L) $1,100; (H) $3,300
drawings: (H) $413

NOORT, Jan van
1620-1676
paintings: (H) $4,400

NOORT, Lambert van
c. 1520-1571
paintings: (H) $2,300

NOORTIG, Jan
mid-17th cent.
paintings: (H) $8,525

NORBLIN DE LA GOURDAINE, Jean
Pierre
French 1745-1830
drawings: (H) $1,870

NORDALM, Federico
b. Nicaragua 1949
paintings: (L) $6,600; (H) $12,650

NORDELL, Carl J.
American b. 1885
paintings: (L) $55; (H) $3,850
drawings: (H) $440

NORDELL, Polly
1876-1956
drawings: (L) $192; (H) $550

NORDENBERG, Carl Henrik
Swedish 1857-1928
paintings: (H) $19,800

NORDFELDT, Bror Julius Olsson
Swedish/American 1878-1955
paintings: (L) $1,980; (H) $33,000
drawings: (L) $66; (H) $5,225
sculpture: (L) $3,300; (H) $7,700

NORDHAUSEN, August Henry
American b. 1901
paintings: (L) $935; (H) $1,320

NORDSTROM, Carl Harold
American 1876-1965
paintings: (L) $660; (H) $920
drawings: (L) $110; (H) $303

NORDSTROM, Varl H.
American 1876-1934
paintings: (H) $880

NORIERI, August
American 1860-1898
paintings: (H) $660

NORMAN, Irving
contemporary
drawings: (L) $660; (H) $1,870

NORMAND, Ernest
French 1857-1923
paintings: (H) $550

NORMANN, Adelsteen
Norwegian 1848-1918
paintings: (L) $1,100; (H) $13,200

NORMIL, Andre
Haitian 20th cent.
paintings: (L) $275; (H) $4,620

NORREGAARD, Asta Carlsen
Norwegian 1868-1908
paintings: (H) $5,750

NORRETRANDERS, Johannes
Danish b. 1871
paintings: (H) $1,210

NORRIS, S. Walter
American b. 1868
paintings: (H) $3,410

NORRIS, Thomas Bowler
1866-1927
paintings: (H) $935

NORRIS, W. Walker
British ac. 1850-1860
paintings: (H) $4,400

NORTH, John William
British 1842-1924
paintings: (H) $17,600

NORTH, Noah
American 1809-1880
paintings: (H) $495

NORTH, T.E.
American 20th cent.
drawings: (H) $577

NORTHCOTE, H.B.
English 19th cent.
paintings: (H) $522

NORTHCOTE, James
American 1747-1831
paintings: (L) $2,530; (H) $6,325

NORTHCOTE, James
American 1822-1904
paintings: (L) $358; (H) $1,650
drawings: (H) $110

NORTON, Benjamin Cam
British 1835-1900
paintings: (L) $10,350; (H) $60,500

NORTON, Charles W.
American ac. 1870s-80s
drawings: (L) $1,210; (H) $1,980

NORTON, Crandall
American b. 1920
drawings: (H) $523

NORTON, Lewis D.
American 1868-1940
paintings: (L) $110; (H) $1,980
drawings: (L) $49; (H) $1,540

NORTON, William Edward
American 1843-1916
paintings: (L) $330; (H) $8,470
drawings: (L) $55; (H) $605

NORWELL, Graham Noble
Canadian 1901-1967
paintings: (L) $805; (H) $825
drawings: (L) $220; (H) $550

NOSON, E.
sculpture: (H) $1,150

NOSWORTHY, Florence E.
1872-1936
drawings: (H) $550

NOTER, David Emile Joseph de
Belgian 1818-1892
paintings: (L) $3,450; (H) $22,000

NOTER, David de
Belgian b. 1825
paintings: (H) $6,600

NOTERMAN, Zacharias
German 1820-1890
paintings: (L) $3,162; (H) $8,050

NOTT, Raymond
American 1888-1948
paintings: (L) $770; (H) $880
drawings: (L) $132; (H) $1,320

NOTTER, Louis de
Flemish 19th cent.
paintings: (H) $2,750

NOTTI, H. van
American 20th cent.
paintings: (H) $1,980

NOTZ, Johannes
Swiss 1802-1862
drawings: (H) $1,760

NOURSE, Elizabeth
American 1859/60-1938
paintings: (L) $3,850; (H) $35,200
drawings: (L) $715; (H) $13,200

NOUSVEAUX, Edouard Auguste
French 1811-1867
paintings: (H) $2,750

NOUVEAU, Henri
French 1901-1959
drawings: (L) $920; (H) $4,600

NOVAK, Bretislav
sculpture: (L) $660; (H) $660

NOVAK, Joseph
drawings: (H) $3,850

NOVAK, Louis
American 1903-1988
paintings: (L) $99; (H) $1,540
drawings: (H) $110

NOVANI, C.
19th/20th cent.
sculpture: (H) $660

NOVARO, Jean Claude
sculpture: (H) $935

NOVELLI
paintings: (H) $550

NOVELLI, Pietro, Il MONREALESE
1603-1648
paintings: (H) $16,100

NOVELLI, Pietro Antonio
1729-1804
drawings: (L) $5,750; (H) $5,750

NOVELLI, Sebastiano
Italian 1853-1916
paintings: (L) $10,925; (H) $14,950

NOVO, Stefano
Italian b. 1862
paintings: (L) $715; (H) $11,000
drawings: (L) $437; (H) $546

NOVOA, Gustavo
Chilean b. 1939
paintings: (L) $247; (H) $1,265
drawings: (H) $316

NOVOTNY, Elmer L.
American b. 1910
paintings: (L) $330; (H) $1,210

NOWAK, Ernst
American
paintings: (H) $1,870

NOWAK, Ernst
Austrian 1853-1919
paintings: (L) $1,265; (H) $3,850

NOWAK, Franz
Austrian 20th cent.
paintings: (L) $220; (H) $2,300

NOWAK, Leo
American 20th cent.
paintings: (L) $330; (H) $1,430

NOWAK, Otto
Austrian 1875-1947
paintings: (L) $550; (H) $1,980

NOWEY, Adolf
Continental School 19th cent.
paintings: (H) $1,840

NOYER, Denis Paul
French b. 1940
paintings: (L) $110; (H) $1,760

NOYER, Philippe
French 1917-1985
paintings: (L) $58; (H) $3,565
drawings: (L) $165; (H) $1,155

NOYES, Abbey
American early 19th cent.
drawings: (H) $3,520

NOYES, C.
Continental 20th cent.
paintings: (H) $935

NOYES, E.L.
American 20th cent.
paintings: (H) $1,365

NOYES, George Loftus
Canadian/American 1864-1951/54
paintings: (L) $302; (H) $25,300
drawings: (L) $330; (H) $440

NOZKOWSKI, Thomas
b. 1944
paintings: (L) $345; (H) $1,650

NOZKOWSKI, Tom
contemporary
paintings: (H) $2,750

NUDERSCHER, Frank B.
American 1880-1959
paintings: (L) $137; (H) $5,060
drawings: (L) $127; (H) $550
sculpture: (H) $518

NUMAN, Hermanus
1744-1820
paintings: (H) $21,850

NUNAMAKER, Kenneth R.
American 1890-1957
paintings: (L) $1,155; (H) $27,600

NUNE, William de
ac. 1729-1750
paintings: (H) $1,210

NUNES, J.A.
American 20th cent.
paintings: (H) $715

NUNES-VAIS, Italo
Italian 1860-1932
paintings: (H) $5,750

NUNEZ, Dulce Maria
b. Mexico 1950
paintings: (H) $6,900

NUNEZ, M.
Spanish 20th cent.
sculpture: (H) $1,320

NUNEZ DEL PRADO, Marina
Bolivian b. 1912
sculpture: (L) $880; (H) $5,750

NUNZIO
b. 1954
sculpture: (L) $4,620; (H) $7,150

NUSSBAUM, Ervin
20th cent.
paintings: (H) $920

NUSSIO, ***
Italian 20th cent.
paintings: (H) $2,300

NUTT, Jim
American b. 1938
paintings: (L) $14,300; (H) $17,250
drawings: (L) $316; (H) $5,520

NUVOLONE, Carlo Francesco
Italian 1608-1661/65
paintings: (H) $13,800

NUVOLONE, Carlo Francesco, called
Panfilo
Italian 1608-1661/65
paintings: (L) $13,800; (H) $123,500

NUVOLONE, Panfilo
Italian ac. 1608-1661
paintings: (H) $123,500

NUYSSEN, Abraham Janssens van, the
elder and studio
1575-1632
paintings: (H) $66,000

NUZZI, Mario, called Mario de'Fiori
paintings: (H) $5,225

NYBO, Povl Friis
Danish b. 1869
paintings: (H) $3,850

NYE, Edgar H.
1879-1943
paintings: (L) $220; (H) $4,025

NYE, M.
paintings: (H) $2,860

NYE, William
American 19th cent.
paintings: (H) $660

NYHOLM, Arvid Frederick
American 1866-1927
paintings: (L) $132; (H) $3,163

NYL-FROSCH, Marie
paintings: (H) $2,970

NYMEGEN, Dionys van
Dutch 1705-1789
paintings: (H) $4,950

NYROP, Borge Christoffer
Danish 1881-1948
paintings: (L) $852; (H) $935

NYS, Carl
Belgian b. 1858
paintings: (H) $880

O'BOTAMAN, S.
Continental 19th cent.
paintings: (H) $550

O'BRADY, Gertrude
drawings: (H) $1,100

O'BRIEN, Lucius Richard
Canadian 1832-1899
drawings: (L) $1,100; (H) $6,875

O'CONNELL, D.
sculpture: (H) $825

O'CONNER, Andrew
1874-1941
sculpture: (H) $3,450

O'CONNER, James
Irish 1790-1840
paintings: (H) $2,200

O'CONNOR, James Arthur
Irish 1792-1841
paintings: (L) $1,380; (H) $2,990

O'CONNOR, John
Irish 1830-1889
paintings: (L) $2,588; (H) $8,800

O'GORMAN, Juan
Mexican 1905-1982
paintings: (L) $30,800; (H) $440,000
drawings: (L) $2,300; (H) $22,000

O'HARA, Eliot
American 1890-1969
drawings: (L) $39; (H) $1,100

O'HARA, Frederick
American 1904-1981
paintings: (H) $770

O'HARA, Juan
sculpture: (H) $495

O'HIGGINS, Pablo
Mexican 1904-1983
paintings: (L) $3,025; (H) $10,350
drawings: (L) $1,840; (H) $8,625

O'KEEFFE, Georgia
American 1887-1986
paintings: (L) $110,000; (H) $1,210,000
drawings: (L) $77,000; (H) $288,500

O'KELLEY, Mattie Lou
American b. 1908
paintings: (L) $1,061; (H) $9,775
drawings: (H) $3,080

O'KELLY, Aloysius
Irish/American b. 1850/53
paintings: (L) $920; (H) $19,800

O'LOUGHLIN, Thomas
paintings: (H) $495

O'LYNCH VAN TOWN, Karl
Austrian b. 1869
paintings: (L) $2,500; (H) $3,190

O'MALLEY, Power
Irish b. 1870
paintings: (L) $330; (H) $1,320

O'NEIL, George Bernard
English 1828-1917
paintings: (H) $4,400

O'NEIL, Henry Nelson
British 1817-1880
paintings: (H) $43,700

O'NEIL, Thomas F.
ac. 1852-1922
paintings: (H) $550

O'NEILL, Daniel
Irish 20th cent.
paintings: (L) $1,540; (H) $7,150

O'NEILL, George Bernard
British 1828-1917
paintings: (L) $9,775; (H) $13,800

O'NEILL, James
American contemporary
paintings: (H) $467

O'NEILL, Raymond Edgar
American 1893-1962
paintings: (H) $18,700

O'NEILL, Rose
American 1875-1944
drawings: (L) $770; (H) $2,750

O'SHEA, John
American 1876-1956
paintings: (L) $575; (H) $12,100
drawings: (L) $193; (H) $1,725

O'SICKEY, Joseph B.
American 20th cent.
paintings: (L) $1,100; (H) $3,220

O'SULLIVAN, Daniel
paintings: (H) $1,100

O***, Marie
Dutch 19th cent.
paintings: (H) $6,900

OAKES, Minnie F.
American ac. 1891
paintings: (H) $2,200

OAKLEY, Thornton
American 1881-1953
paintings: (L) $440; (H) $55,000
drawings: (L) $55; (H) $4,025

OAKLEY, Violet
American 1874-1960
paintings: (L) $220; (H) $9,625
drawings: (L) $125; (H) $990

OBENICHE, D.
paintings: (H) $2,475

OBERG, Ralph E.
paintings: (L) $550; (H) $1,700
drawings: (H) $1,100

OBERHEIDE, Heide
b. 1957
paintings: (H) $1,980

OBERMAN, Antonis
Dutch 1781-1845
paintings: (L) $385; (H) $25,300

OBERMULLER, Franz
Austrian 1869-1917
paintings: (L) $220; (H) $990

OBERSTEINER, Ludwig
Austrian b. 1857
paintings: (H) $2,750

OBERTEUFFER, George
American 1878-1940
paintings: (L) $440; (H) $8,525

OBIN, Antoine
Haitian b. 1929
paintings: (L) $165; (H) $1,320

OBIN, Michael
Haitian 20th cent.
paintings: (H) $1,100

OBIN, Philome
Haitian 1892-1986
paintings: (L) $2,300; (H) $25,300
drawings: (L) $26,450; (H) $31,625

OBIN, Seneque
Haitian 1893-1977
paintings: (L) $90; (H) $14,950

OBIOLS, Gustave
Spanish 19th/20th cent.
sculpture: (L) $935; (H) $1,540

OBREGON, Alejandro
Spanish/Colombian b. 1920
paintings: (L) $3,850; (H) $167,500
drawings: (L) $5,225; (H) $17,250

OCAMPO, Isidro
Mexican b. 1902
drawings: (L) $330; (H) $2,185

OCHTERVERLT, Jacob
Dutch 1634-1682
paintings: (H) $178,500

OCHTMAN, Leonard
Dutch/American 1854-1934
paintings: (L) $385; (H) $13,200
drawings: (L) $110; (H) $4,400

OCKERT, Carl Frederick
German 1825-1899
paintings: (H) $825

ODDIE, Walter Mason
American 1808-1865
paintings: (L) $1,320; (H) $12,650

ODELL, Thomas Jefferson
American d. 1849
paintings: (H) $29,700

ODELMARK, Frans Wilhelm
Swedish b. 1849
paintings: (L) $2,300; (H) $4,025

ODIE, Walter M.
American 1808-1865
paintings: (L) $495; (H) $2,200

ODIERNA, Guido
Italian b. 1913
paintings: (L) $115; (H) $660

ODIO, Saturnino Portuondo, Pucho
b. 1928
sculpture: (L) $1,265; (H) $5,405

ODIOT, workshop of
French early 19th cent.
drawings: (H) $1,725

ODJIG, Daphne
paintings: (H) $4,675

ODOM, Mel
b. 1950
drawings: (H) $1,980

OECONOMO, George Aristide
Austrian 19th cent.
paintings: (H) $550

OEHLEN, Albert
German b. 1956
paintings: (L) $8,050; (H) $20,900
drawings: (L) $22,000; (H) $24,200

OEHMICHEN, Hugo
German 1843-1933
paintings: (H) $11,000

OEHRING, Hedwig
German b. 1855
paintings: (L) $825; (H) $4,950

OERDER, Frans D.
Dutch 1866-1944
paintings: (H) $1,760

OERTEL, Johannes Adam Simon
American 1823-1909
paintings: (H) $13,200

OERTEL, Wilhelm
German b. 1870
paintings: (L) $468; (H) $1,150

OEVER, Hendrick Ten
Dutch c. 1639-1716
paintings: (H) $11,500

OFFERMANS, Tony Lodewyk George
Dutch 1854-1911
drawings: (H) $5,463

OFNER, J.
sculpture: (H) $522

OFNER, Josef
German b. 1868
sculpture: (H) $2,588

OGDEN, Frederick D.
paintings: (L) $302; (H) $1,045

OGE, Pierre
sculpture: (H) $1,650

OGIER, Abraham
paintings: (H) $690

OGIER, Marie Louise
paintings: (H) $805

OGILVIE, Clinton
American 1838-1900
paintings: (L) $358; (H) $3,680

OGILVY, Charles
English 1832-1890
paintings: (L) $1,650; (H) $31,900

OGLE, Mark
paintings: (H) $1,650

OGLE, Mark
American
paintings: (H) $550

OGUISS, Takanori
Japanese 1901-1986
paintings: (L) $8,050; (H) $418,000

OHASHI, Yutaka
Japanese b. 1923
paintings: (L) $248; (H) $1,495

OHLSEN, Theodor
German b. 1855
paintings: (L) $660; (H) $798

OHLSON, Doug
b. 1936
paintings: (L) $330; (H) $1,100

OHLSON, Walter
American 20th cent.
paintings: (H) $460

OHLSSON, C.
paintings: (H) $1,430
drawings: (H) $22

OHRING, H.
paintings: (H) $862

OHRMANN
American 20th cent.
sculpture: (H) $920

OKADA, Kenzo
Japanese/American b. 1902
paintings: (L) $18,400; (H) $187,000

OKAMOTO, Yajiro
Japanese/American 1891-1963
paintings: (H) $495

OKAMURA, Arthur
American b. 1932
paintings: (L) $385; (H) $1,265
drawings: (H) $495

OKASHI, Avshalom
1916-1980
paintings: (H) $1,092

OKULICK, John
American b. 1947
sculpture: (L) $2,300; (H) $7,475

OLBRICH, W.
paintings: (L) $192; (H) $1,375

OLDENBURG, Claes
Swedish/American b. 1929
paintings: (L) $1,650; (H) $43,700
drawings: (L) $990; (H) $32,200
sculpture: (L) $2,070; (H) $409,500

OLDFIELD, John Edwin
English ac. 1825-1854
drawings: (H) $550

OLDFIELD, Otis
American 1890-1969
paintings: (L) $3,450; (H) $13,200

OLDS, Gary L.
sculpture: (L) $1,000; (H) $1,430

OLINSKY, Ivan G.
Russian/American 1878-1962
paintings: (L) $770; (H) $90,500
drawings: (L) $231; (H) $880

OLINSKY, Tosca
Italian/American b. 1909
paintings: (L) $220; (H) $2,310

OLIS, Jan
1610-1676
paintings: (H) $7,475

OLITSKI, Jules
Russian/American b. 1922
paintings: (L) $2,860; (H) $220,000

OLIVA, F.
paintings: (H) $5,500

OLIVA, F.
Italian 19th/20th cent.
paintings: (H) $1,495

OLIVA, F.
Spanish (?) 19th cent.
paintings: (H) $1,840

OLIVA, Francesco
Italian 19th/20th cent.
paintings: (L) $4,312; (H) $7,475

OLIVA, Pedro Pablo
b. Cuba 1949
paintings: (L) $7,475; (H) $27,600

OLIVE, Jean Baptiste
French 1848-1936
paintings: (H) $9,775

OLIVEIRA, Nathan
American b. 1928
paintings: (L) $4,888; (H) $38,500
drawings: (L) $770; (H) $37,375

OLIVER, Archer James
English 1774-1842
paintings: (L) $2,310; (H) $16,500

OLIVER, Cecelia E.
American ac. 1881-1897
paintings: (H) $1,725

OLIVER, Clark T.
American 19th cent.
paintings: (L) $200; (H) $2,640

OLIVER, E.
paintings: (L) $440; (H) $495

OLIVER, H.
British 19th cent.
paintings: (L) $1,200; (H) $10,350

OLIVER, Jean Nutting
American d. 1946
drawings: (H) $2,300

OLIVER, Myron
American 1891-1967
paintings: (H) $3,575

OLIVER, Sarah E.C.
drawings: (H) $575

OLIVER, T. Clark
American d. 1893
paintings: (L) $247; (H) $2,530

OLIVER, W.
English 19th cent.
paintings: (L) $2,310; (H) $3,795

OLIVER, William
British 1804-1853
paintings: (L) $3,520; (H) $6,900

OLIVER, William
British ac. 1865-1897
paintings: (H) $2,300

OLIVERA, Nathan
contemporary
paintings: (H) $17,600

OLIVERI, A.
Italian 19th/20th cent.
paintings: (H) $660

OLIVETTI, Luigi
Italian 19th/20th cent.
drawings: (L) $518; (H) $2,640

OLIVIER, E.
paintings: (H) $880

OLIVIER, Ferdinand
1873-1957
paintings: (H) $1,035

OLIVIER, Herbert Arnould
British 1861-1952
paintings: (H) $9,200

OLIVIERA, Nathan
American b. 1928
paintings: (H) $68,750
drawings: (L) $1,150; (H) $3,850

OLIVIERI, Camilla
Italian b. 1844
paintings: (H) $1,725

OLIVOS, T.
Italian 19th cent.
paintings: (H) $2,420

OLLEFAVRE
20th cent.
paintings: (H) $990

OLLEROS Y QUINTANA, Blas
Italian 1851-1919
paintings: (L) $7,150; (H) $8,250

OLLIVARY, Annette
French 20th cent.
paintings: (L) $275; (H) $575

OLLIVIER, Michel Barthelemy
French 1712-1784
paintings: (L) $36,800; (H) $57,200
drawings: (H) $9,350

OLMSTEAD, Frederick Law
American 1822-1903
drawings: (H) $468

OLSEN, Christian Benjamin
Danish 1873-1935
paintings: (L) $330; (H) $4,950

OLSEN, John
drawings: (L) $880; (H) $990

OLSON, George Wallace
American 19th/20th cent.
paintings: (L) $605; (H) $1,100

OLSON, J. Olaf
American 1894-1979
paintings: (L) $1,650; (H) $1,980
drawings: (H) $138

OLSSON, Julius
British 1864-1942
paintings: (H) $863

OLSSON, Nils J.
19th cent.
paintings: (H) $495

OLTEN, R. van
Dutch 19th/20th cent.
paintings: (L) $748; (H) $1,430

OMAN, Edwin
paintings: (H) $770
drawings: (H) $27

OMERTH
sculpture: (L) $605; (H) $3,300

OMERTH, Georges
French ac. 1895-1925
sculpture: (L) $3,450; (H) $5,500

OMMEGANCK, Balthasar Paul
Flemish 1755-1826
paintings: (L) $3,080; (H) $10,925

ONDERDONK, Julian
American 1882-1922
paintings: (L) $825; (H) $28,750
drawings: (H) $550

ONDERDONK, Robert Jenkins
American 1853-1917
paintings: (L) $440; (H) $29,700

ONGANIA, Umberto
Italian 19th cent.
drawings: (L) $220; (H) $1,980

ONGLY, W.
American 19th cent.
paintings: (L) $275; (H) $1,840

ONLEY, Norman Anthony (Toni)
Canadian b. 1928
paintings: (L) $880; (H) $11,000

ONO, Yoko
Japanese/American b. 1933
sculpture: (L) $978; (H) $10,350

ONOFRIO, Crescenzio
Italian 1632-1698
drawings: (L) $1,650; (H) $2,750

ONSLOW-FORD, Gordon
American b. 1912
paintings: (H) $2,750
drawings: (L) $1,150; (H) $6,325

OOLEN, Adriaen van
Dutch d. 1694
paintings: (H) $7,475

OOSTEN, Isaac van
Flemish 1613-1661
paintings: (L) $13,200; (H) $32,200

OPAZO, Rodolfo
Chile b. 1935
paintings: (L) $12,650; (H) $13,800

OPDENHOFF, George Willem
Dutch 1807-1873
paintings: (L) $2,310; (H) $7,150

OPELIC, Hans
Continental 19th cent.
paintings: (H) $18,400

OPERTI, Albert Jasper
Italian/American 1852-1927
paintings: (L) $412; (H) $3,630

OPFER, Gustav
German b. 1876
paintings: (H) $3,850

OPIE, John
English 1761-1807
paintings: (L) $2,300; (H) $25,300

OPIE, Julian
American b. 1936
paintings: (L) $4,600; (H) $12,100
sculpture: (L) $322; (H) $9,775

OPISSO, Alfredo
paintings: (H) $1,150

OPPENHEIM, Dennis
American b. 1938
drawings: (L) $58; (H) $13,200

OPPENHEIM, Meret
German 1913-1985
drawings: (H) $3,115

OPPENHEIM, Moritz Daniel
German 1800-1882
paintings: (H) $412
drawings: (L) $110; (H) $1,725

OPPENHEIMER, Charles
British 1875-1961
paintings: (H) $4,290

OPPENHEIMER, Josef
German 1876-1966
drawings: (H) $1,100

OPPENHEIMER, Max, MOPP
German 1885-1954
paintings: (H) $2,300

OPPENORT, Gilles
1672-1742
drawings: (L) $1,380; (H) $8,912

OPPER, Frederick B.
1857-1937
drawings: (H) $1,045

OPPER, John
American b. 1908
paintings: (H) $1,380

OPPLER, Ernst
German 1867-1929
paintings: (H) $6,270

OPSOMER, Isidore
paintings: (H) $3,520

ORANGE, Maurice Henri
French 1868-1916
paintings: (H) $4,400

ORANT, Marthe
French 1874-1957
paintings: (L) $1,265; (H) $2,875
drawings: (H) $440

ORBAN, Paul
drawings: (L) $165; (H) $747

ORCHARDSON, Sir William Quiller
British 1832-1910
paintings: (H) $22,000

ORD, Joseph Biays
American 1805-1865
paintings: (L) $1,650; (H) $29,700

ORDONEZ, Sylvia
Mexican b. 1956
paintings: (L) $18,400; (H) $19,550

ORDWAY, Alfred T.
American 1819-1897
paintings: (L) $165; (H) $2,200

ORELAND, Joe
American b. 1958
sculpture: (H) $2,750

ORFEI, Orfeo
Italian ac. 1862-1889
paintings: (L) $4,950; (H) $11,500

ORGAN, Marjorie, Mrs. Robert Henri
American 1886-1931/36
drawings: (L) $44; (H) $523

ORGNANI, O.
Italian 20th cent.
drawings: (H) $862

ORITZ MONASTERIO, Luis
b. Mexico 1906
paintings: (H) $7,700
sculpture: (H) $8,800

ORLANDO, Felipe
Cuban b. 1911
paintings: (L) $715; (H) $2,200

ORLEY, Barent van, studio of
16th cent.
paintings: (H) $17,600

ORLEY, Bernard van
Flemish c. 1492-1541/42
drawings: (L) $299,500; (H) $387,500

ORLEY, Hieronymus van, III
Flemish ac. c. 1652
paintings: (H) $16,500

ORLEY, Richard van
Flemish 1663-1732
drawings: (L) $825; (H) $5,500

ORLIK, Emil
German 1870-1932
paintings: (H) $9,200
drawings: (H) $440

ORLOFF, Chana
Russian/French 1888-1968
sculpture: (L) $8,050; (H) $29,900

ORLOVA, A.
Russian 19th/20th cent.
paintings: (H) $575

ORLOVSKY, Vladimr Donatovitch
Russian 1842-1914
paintings: (H) $13,200

Trusting Your Eye

At a small country auction in Vermont in the middle of the winter, a still-life painting signed and dated "J.B. Ord 1843" sold for $27,000. Auction records showed the previous high for an Ord still life, $13,750, had been realized in 1989 in New York at the height of the art market. Who was J.B. Ord? Was this painting worth $27,000? Research showed listings for Ord (1805-1865) in both Fieldings and Young and a brief description in Gerdts's *American Still-Life Paintings*. Gerdts cited Ord as an important link between the works of Raphaelle and James Peale and the profusion of still-life painters in the mid-19th century. Although he painted portraits and miniatures, Ord is most well-known for his still lifes. Further examination of auction records showed that the painting that sold in 1989 was an early 1823 Ord copy of a Raphaelle Peale still life. The Vermont painting, *Still Life with Vase, Fruit and Nuts,* was larger and painted in 1843; it was a refined example of a Philadelphia table top still-life painting with a sensual rendering of the draped fabric and an exquisitely painted porcelain vase. The painting, in impeccable condition with the original frame, was well worth $27,000. Nine months later after this book was sent to press, in November 1995, the painting was offered at Christie's; this time around *Still Life with Vase, Fruit and Nuts* fetched $79,500—a well-deserved profit for someone who trusted their eye. (Joseph Biays Ord, *Still Life with Vase, Fruit and Nuts*, oil on canvas, 18 x 24 inches, Nathan, February 11, 1995, $27,000)

OROZCO, E.R.
sculpture: (H) $550

OROZCO, J.C.
paintings: (H) $605

OROZCO, Jose Clemente
Mexican 1883-1949
paintings: (L) $8,050; (H) $374,000
drawings: (L) $2,750; (H) $66,000

OROZCO ROMERO, Carlos
Mexican 1898-1984
paintings: (L) $3,300; (H) $26,400
drawings: (L) $1,540; (H) $6,050

ORPEN, Sir William
Irish 1878-1931
paintings: (L) $460; (H) $4,312
drawings: (H) $440

ORR, Elliot
American b. 1904
paintings: (L) $110; (H) $550

ORR, Eric
contemporary
paintings: (L) $3,080; (H) $3,300
drawings: (H) $863

ORR, George P.
American
paintings: (H) $770

ORROCK, James
British 1829-1913
paintings: (H) $1,380
drawings: (H) $230

ORSAY, Alfred d'
French 1801-1852
sculpture: (H) $12,100

ORSELLI, Arturo
Italian 19th cent.
paintings: (H) $9,350

ORSI, Achille d'
Italian 1845-1929
sculpture: (H) $748

ORSI, Lelio
1511-1587
drawings: (H) $8,800

ORSINI, C.
Italian 19th cent.
paintings: (H) $1,320

ORSINI, Giustina
Italian 19th cent.
paintings: (H) $5,520

ORSINI, J.
paintings: (H) $550

ORTEGA, Carlos
paintings: (H) $468

ORTEGA, Charles
b. 1925
paintings: (H) $1,100

ORTH, John William
American b. 1889
paintings: (H) $660

ORTIZ, Jose Chavez
Spanish 1834-1903
paintings: (H) $4,477

ORTIZ-ECHAGUE, Antonio
Spanish 1883-1942
paintings: (H) $6,900

ORTLIEB, Friedrich
German 1839-1909
paintings: (L) $8,800; (H) $14,950

ORTLIP, Aimee E.
American b. 1888
paintings: (L) $715; (H) $1,430

ORTLIP, H. Willard
American b. 1886
paintings: (L) $200; (H) $1,452

ORTLIP, W. H.
American 19th/20th cent.
paintings: (H) $907

ORTMAN, George
20th cent.
paintings: (H) $805

ORTMANS, Francois Auguste
French 1827-1884
paintings: (L) $1,320; (H) $14,950

ORTNER, F.
Austrian 19th cent.
paintings: (H) $715

ORZE, Joseph
American b. 1932
sculpture: (H) $1,100

OS, Georgius Jacobus Johannes van
Dutch 1782-1861
paintings: (L) $7,475; (H) $233,500
drawings: (H) $1,840

OS, Jan van
Dutch 1744-1808
paintings: (L) $387,500; (H) $607,500

OS, Toon van
Belgian b. 1866
paintings: (H) $1,100

OSBAUER(?), Ch.
paintings: (H) $1,035

OSBORN, Emily Mary
English 1834-after 1913
paintings: (L) $4,312; (H) $17,250

OSBORNE, Emily May
British 1834-1893
drawings: (H) $770

OSBORNE, J.
American 19th cent.
paintings: (H) $14,300

OSBORNE, S.M.
19th cent.
paintings: (H) $1,650

OSCAR
paintings: (H) $1,870

OSGOOD, Phillips E.
American 20th cent.
paintings: (H) $715

OSHITA, Tojiro
Japanese 1870-1911
drawings: (H) $1,430

OSIR, Paulo
paintings: (H) $935

OSNAGHI, Josefine
Austrian ac. 1890-1920
paintings: (H) $1,380

OSSORIO, Alfonso
American b. 1916
drawings: (L) $4,180; (H) $14,300
sculpture: (L) $3,450; (H) $8,800

OSTADE, Adriaen van
Dutch 1610-1685
paintings: (L) $1,320; (H) $1,982,500
drawings: (H) $40,250

OSTADE, Adriaen van, studio of
Dutch 17th cent.
paintings: (H) $68,500

OSTADE, Isaac van
Dutch 1621-1649
drawings: (H) $41,800

OSTEN, E. van
German 18th/19th cent.
paintings: (H) $2,310

OSTERSETZER, Carl
German 19th/20th cent.
paintings: (L) $1,540; (H) $4,950

OSTHALL
paintings: (H) $495

OSTHAUS, Edmund Henry
German/American 1858-1928
paintings: (L) $3,575; (H) $41,400
drawings: (L) $165; (H) $11,000

OSTROUKHOV, Ilia Semionovich
Russian 1858-1929
paintings: (H) $9,775

OSTROUMOVA-LEBEDEVA, Anna
Petrovna
Russian 1871-1955
drawings: (L) $550; (H) $770

OSTROWSKY, Sam
American b. 1885
paintings: (L) $44; (H) $770

OSWALD, Charles W.
British
paintings: (H) $575

OTERO, Alejandro
Venezuelan b. 1921
paintings: (L) $33,000; (H) $40,250

OTIS, Bass
American 1784-1861
paintings: (L) $660; (H) $4,510

OTIS, George Demont
American 1877/79-1962
paintings: (L) $550; (H) $19,800

OTT, E.L.
drawings: (H) $3,300

OTT, Jerry
American b. 1947
paintings: (L) $770; (H) $1,650

OTT, Johann Nepomuk
Swiss 1804-1870
paintings: (H) $4,290

OTT, Philip A.
American 19th cent.
drawings: (H) $6,600

OTT, Sabina
American b. 1955
paintings: (L) $1,610; (H) $2,200

OTTE, Carol
British 20th cent.
paintings: (L) $412; (H) $687

OTTE, William Louis
American 1871-1957
paintings: (L) $1,650; (H) $13,200
drawings: (L) $495; (H) $3,738

OTTERNESS, Tom
American b. 1952
sculpture: (L) $5,175; (H) $26,400

OTTERSON, Joel
American b. 1859
sculpture: (L) $3,850; (H) $6,050

OTTESEN, Otto Didrik
Danish 1816-1892
paintings: (L) $2,070; (H) $13,200

OTTINGER, Ken
American b. 1945
paintings: (H) $2,090
sculpture: (L) $990; (H) $2,310

OTTINI, Pasquale
1580-1630
paintings: (H) $7,700

OTTMAN, H.
drawings: (H) $1,100

OTTMANN, Henry
paintings: (L) $797; (H) $3,300

OTTO, Carl
German 1830-1902
paintings: (L) $1,100; (H) $11,000

OUBRE, Hayward L.
American 20th cent.
paintings: (L) $880; (H) $6,600

OUDENDICK
Dutch School early 19th cent.
paintings: (H) $1,035

OUDENHOVEN, Joseph van
Flemish ac. 1845
paintings: (H) $1,650

OUDENROGGE, Johannes Dircksz.
van
1622-1653
paintings: (H) $8,050

OUDERRA, Pierre Jan van der
Belgian 1841-1915
paintings: (L) $21,000; (H) $24,200

OUDET, Roland
French 1897-1981
paintings: (H) $797

OUDINOT, Achille Francois
French 1820-1891
paintings: (L) $1,100; (H) $10,450

OUDOT, Roland
French 1897-1981
paintings: (L) $862; (H) $5,550
drawings: (L) $165; (H) $523

OUDRY, Jacques Charles
French 1720-1778
paintings: (H) $46,000

OUDRY, Jean Baptiste
French 1686-1755
drawings: (L) $7,475; (H) $18,400

OULINE, A.
French ac. 1918-1940
sculpture: (H) $1,980

OULTON, Therese
contemporary
paintings: (H) $5,500

OUREN, Karl
Norwegian/American 1882-1943
paintings: (L) $230; (H) $2,310

OUSLEY, William
American early 20th cent.
paintings: (H) $484

OUTCAULT, Richard F.
1863-1923
drawings: (L) $1,870; (H) $4,400

OUVET, Louis
French exhib. 1910-1920
sculpture: (H) $1,320

OUVRE, Justin
French 1806-1879
drawings: (H) $1,650

OVENS, Jurgen
Dutch 1623-1678
paintings: (H) $126,500

OVERBECK, Gijsbertus Johannes van
Dutch 1882-1947
paintings: (H) $1,210

OVERSTREET, Anne Aller
American
drawings: (H) $600

OVIATT
drawings: (L) $550; (H) $990

OVIEDO, Ramon
b. Dominican Repub b. 1927
paintings: (L) $2,750; (H) $7,150
drawings: (L) $4,400; (H) $6,600

OWEN, Albert Gallatin
American 1810-1888
paintings: (H) $2,750

OWEN, Bill
American b. 1942
paintings: (L) $6,600; (H) $18,150
sculpture: (L) $2,420; (H) $3,960

OWEN, C.B.
American 20th cent.
paintings: (H) $605

OWEN, Robert Emmett
American 1878-1957
paintings: (L) $181; (H) $5,175
drawings: (H) $230

OWEN, Samuel
British 1768-1857
drawings: (H) $715

OWEN, Vera Andrus
American 1896-1979
paintings: (H) $575

OWEN, William
British 1769-1825
paintings: (L) $1,650; (H) $11,500

OWENS, Edward
American ac. 1920's-1940's
paintings: (H) $935

OWS, William Alfred Delamotte
drawings: (H) $8,800

OZENFANT, Amedee
French 1886-1966
paintings: (L) $11,500; (H) $154,000
sculpture: (H) $8,800

OZOLS, Vilis
Russian b. 1929
paintings: (H) $990

PAALEN, Wolfgang
Mexican 1905/07-1959
paintings: (L) $9,900; (H) $20,700

PAAP, Hans
American 1894-1966
paintings: (L) $770; (H) $1,050

PACH, Walter
American 1883-1952
paintings: (L) $440; (H) $500

PACHAUBES
paintings: (H) $715

PACHECO, Dr. Ferdie
American contemporary
paintings: (H) $4,600

PACHECO, Fernando Castro
Mexican b. 1918
paintings: (H) $990

PACHECO, Maria Luisa
Bolivian b. 1919
paintings: (H) $2,200
drawings: (H) $2,990

PACHECO ALTAMIRANO, Arturo
Chilean b. 1903
paintings: (L) $1,100; (H) $4,400

PACHNER, William
20th cent.
paintings: (H) $660

PACKARD, Anne
American 20th cent.
paintings: (L) $275; (H) $550

PACKMAN, Harry
paintings: (H) $605

PACZKA, Ferencz
Hungarian 1856-1925
paintings: (H) $770

PADCETTI, Jose
1902-1958
paintings: (H) $57,500

PADDOCK, W.D.
sculpture: (H) $1,100

PADILLA, Antonio
paintings: (H) $28,750

PADILLA, J.
paintings: (H) $33,000

PADILLA, Rafael Maria
Spanish 20th cent.
paintings: (H) $1,100

PADOVANINO, Alessandro Varotari, Il
1588-1648
paintings: (H) $40,250

PADRIAND, Jules
19th cent.
paintings: (H) $467

PADURA, Miguel
b. Cuba 1975
paintings: (L) $8,625; (H) $10,450

PAEFF, Bashka
American early 20th cent.
sculpture: (H) $1,100

PAELINCK, Joseph
Belgian 1781-1839
paintings: (H) $118,000

PAEZ, Jose de
Mexican 18th cent.
paintings: (L) $1,870; (H) $36,800

PAGANI, Vincenzo
ac. 1786
drawings: (H) $2,300

PAGE, Celine le
sculpture: (H) $550

PAGE, Edward A.
American 1850/53-1928
paintings: (L) $165; (H) $1,980
drawings: (H) $385

PAGE, Marie Danforth
American 1869-1940
paintings: (H) $16,500

PAGE, Walter Gilman
American 1862-1934
paintings: (L) $770; (H) $3,025

PAGE, William
British 1794-1872
drawings: (L) $7,700; (H) $11,000

PAGELS, Herman J.
German ac. 1876-1935
paintings: (H) $6,050

PAGES, Irene
French 20th cent.
paintings: (L) $193; (H) $1,380

PAGES, Jules E.
b. France 1867 d. U.S. 1946
paintings: (L) $330; (H) $8,050
drawings: (H) $495

PAGES, Jules F.
American 1833-1910
paintings: (H) $1,540

PAGIN, R.
European 19th cent.
paintings: (H) $935

PAGLAPH, G.
sculpture: (H) $2,200

PAGLIACCI, Aldo
Italian b. 1913
paintings: (L) $358; (H) $4,312

PAGLIEI, Gioacchino
Italian d. 1896
paintings: (H) $1,870

PAGURAU, Gaston
paintings: (H) $3,300

PAHSETOPAH, Loren Louis, Shapa
Nazhi, Stands Brown
Native American b. 1934
drawings: (H) $546

PAICE, George
English 1854-1925
paintings: (L) $460; (H) $3,025

PAIER, Th.
19th cent.
paintings: (H) $650

PAIK, Nam June
Korean/American b. 1932
paintings: (L) $14,375; (H) $34,500
sculpture: (L) $40,250; (H) $65,750

PAIL, Edouard
French b. 1851
paintings: (L) $412; (H) $4,675

PAILES, Isaac
French b. 1895
paintings: (L) $1,870; (H) $2,300

PAILLET, Charles
French b. 1871
sculpture: (L) $805; (H) $2,415

PAIN, Robert Tucker
English ac. 1863-1877
paintings: (H) $2,475

PAIO
European 19th cent.
drawings: (H) $1,045

PAJETTA, Pietro
Italian 1845-1911
paintings: (H) $52,800

PAJOU, Augustin
French 1730-1809
drawings: (H) $4,675
sculpture: (H) $385

PALACEK, Ladislav
Czechoslovakia
sculpture: (H) $1,380

PALACIAS, Cinicio
paintings: (H) $575

PALACIOS, Alirio
Venezuelan b. 1944
drawings: (L) $9,900; (H) $20,900

PALADINO, Mimmo
Italian b. 1948
paintings: (L) $10,350; (H) $132,000
drawings: (L) $3,680; (H) $60,500
sculpture: (L) $8,800; (H) $47,150

PALAEZ, Amelia
drawings: (H) $46,000

PALAEZ, Amelia
1897-1968
drawings: (L) $2,300; (H) $3,450

PALAMEDES, Anthonie, called
Stevaerts
Dutch 1607-1673
paintings: (L) $600; (H) $40,250

PALANDRA, L.
sculpture: (H) $2,475

PALANQUINOS MASTER
late 15th cent.
paintings: (H) $34,100

PALANTI, Giuseppe
Italian 1881-1946
paintings: (H) $2,200

PALAU, Albertina
Spanish 19th cent.
paintings: (H) $21,850

PALENCIA, Benjamin
Spanish b. 1902
paintings: (L) $5,750; (H) $16,100
drawings: (L) $1,650; (H) $3,450

PALERMO, Blinky
German 1943-1977
drawings: (L) $8,250; (H) $24,200
sculpture: (H) $24,200

PALEY, Albert
American b. 1944
sculpture: (L) $5,500; (H) $19,800

PALEZIEUX, Gerard
Swiss b. 1919
paintings: (H) $1,265

PALIN, William Mainwaring
British 1862-1947
paintings: (H) $518

PALING, Johannes Jacobus
paintings: (H) $4,675

PALINGH, Isaac
1630-1719
paintings: (H) $101,500

PALIZZI, Filippo
Italian 1818-1899
paintings: (L) $27,500; (H) $68,500

PALIZZI, Giuseppe
Italian 1810/13-1887/89
paintings: (L) $4,600; (H) $19,800

PALLADINI
drawings: (H) $1,430

PALLANDT, Charlotte van
sculpture: (L) $1,840; (H) $4,370

PALLANDT, Charlotte van
Dutch b. 1898
sculpture: (H) $1,430

PALLARES Y ALLUSTANTE, Joaquin
Spanish 1853-1935
paintings: (L) $1,540; (H) $33,000

PALLAVERA, Giovanni
paintings: (H) $633

PALLENBERG, Josef
German 1882-1945
sculpture: (H) $2,090

PALLENTINE, A**
Italian 20th cent.
paintings: (H) $825

PALLIERE, Juan Leon
1823-1887
paintings: (H) $27,600

PALLISSAT, C.
French 19th cent.
drawings: (H) $3,300

PALLYA, Carolus
Hungarian b. 1875
paintings: (H) $495

PALLYA, Celesztin
Hungarian b. 1864
paintings: (H) $2,185

PALM, Anna Sofia
Norwegian 1859-1924
drawings: (H) $523

PALMA, Jacopo, Palma Il Giovane
1544-1628
paintings: (L) $3,300; (H) $33,000
drawings: (L) $1,320; (H) $15,400

PALMA, Jacopo, called Il Vecchio
Italian 1480-1528
drawings: (H) $3,163

PALMA, Jacopo, called Il Vecchio
workshop of
Italian 15th/16th cent.
paintings: (H) $132,000

PALMAROLI Y GONZALEZ, Vicente
Spanish 1834-1896
paintings: (L) $440; (H) $33,000

PALMEDEE (?), Jed
American
drawings: (H) $715

PALMEIRO, Jose
Spanish 1903-1984
paintings: (L) $1,150; (H) $4,180

PALMER, Adelaide
American 1851-1928
paintings: (H) $4,140

PALMER, E.V.
sculpture: (L) $165; (H) $467

PALMER, Erastus Dow
1817-1904
sculpture: (L) $2,875; (H) $20,700

PALMER, G.K.
paintings: (H) $1,320

PALMER, Harry Sutton
English 1854-1933
drawings: (L) $605; (H) $4,180

PALMER, Herbert Sidney
Canadian 1881-1970
paintings: (L) $299; (H) $3,080

PALMER, James Lynwood
British 1865-1941
paintings: (L) $2,300; (H) $28,750

PALMER, Pauline
American 1865-1938
paintings: (L) $110; (H) $12,100
drawings: (H) $275

PALMER, Walter Launt
American 1854-1932
paintings: (L) $3,410; (H) $36,800
drawings: (L) $1,100; (H) $17,250

PALMER, William C.
American b. 1906
paintings: (L) $1,072; (H) $2,200
drawings: (H) $165

PALMERIUS, G.
Italian 18th cent.
drawings: (H) $660

PALMERTON, Don
American 1899-1937
paintings: (H) $575

PALMERTON, Don F.
American 1899-1937
paintings: (L) $495; (H) $935

PALMEZZANO, Marco
Italian c. 1458-1539
paintings: (L) $18,700; (H) $110,000

PALMOROLI Y GONZALEZ, Vicente
Spanish 1834-1896
paintings: (H) $77,000

PALOMAR, T.
20th cent.
paintings: (H) $860

PALTRONIERI, Pietro, called Il
Mirandolese
Italian 1673-1741
paintings: (H) $51,750
drawings: (H) $4,025

PALTRONIERI (Il Mirandolese),
Pietro and Vittorio Maria BIGARI
17th/18th cent.
paintings: (L) $101,500; (H) $233,500

PALUMBO, Alphonse
American b. 1890
paintings: (L) $605; (H) $2,875

PALUMBO, L.
Italian 19th cent.
paintings: (H) $468

PALUSEN, Erich
German b. 1932
paintings: (H) $1,430

PALZER, Victor R.
paintings: (H) $4,370

PAN, Arthur
20th cent.
paintings: (H) $3,300

PANABAKER, Frank Shirley
paintings: (L) $1,540; (H) $2,420

PANAYOTOU, Angelos
Greek 20th cent.
paintings: (L) $920; (H) $1,093

PANCOAST, Henry Boller
American b. 1876
paintings: (L) $303; (H) $1,430

PANCOAST, Morris Hall
American 1877-1963
paintings: (L) $99; (H) $9,900
drawings: (L) $137; (H) $302

PANDIANI, Antonio
Italian 1820-1901
sculpture: (L) $660; (H) $1,430

PANEPINTO, Alfred
drawings: (L) $400; (H) $550

PANERAI, Gino
Italian 19th/20th cent.
drawings: (H) $880

PANERAI, Ruggero
Italian 1862-1923
paintings: (L) $1,210; (H) $7,700

PANICHI, Ugolini
Italian 19th cent.
sculpture: (H) $2,090

PANINI, Francesco
Italian 1720/25-c. 1794
paintings: (H) $44,000

PANINI, Gian Paolo
1691-1765
paintings: (H) $387,500

PANINI, Gian Paolo, studio of
paintings: (H) $17,250

PANITZSCH, Robert
b. 1879
paintings: (L) $1,980; (H) $2,420

PANKIEWICZ, Josef
Polish 1866-1943
paintings: (H) $1,610

PANNETT, R.
British 19th/20th cent.
paintings: (H) $1,610
drawings: (H) $1,380

PANNINI, Francesco
Italian 1745-1812
paintings: (L) $41,250; (H) $50,600

PANNINI, Giovanni Paolo
Italian 1691/92-1765
paintings: (L) $26,450; (H) $640,500

PANNINI, Giovanni Paolo, and studio
Italian 18th cent.
paintings: (L) $55,000; (H) $220,000

PANNINI, Giovanni Paolo, studio of
Italian 1691-1765
paintings: (L) $12,650; (H) $165,000

PANSING, Fred
American 1854-1912
paintings: (L) $418; (H) $19,800
drawings: (L) $495; (H) $1,650

PANTON, Lawrence Arthur Colley
drawings: (H) $3,080

PANTUHOFF, Igor
American 20th cent.
paintings: (H) $4,600

PANUNZI, Sebastiano
Italian 19th cent.
paintings: (L) $1,725; (H) $3,850

PANZA, Giovanni
Italian 19th cent.
paintings: (L) $2,760; (H) $4,950

PANZIRONI
20th cent.
paintings: (H) $1,100

PAOLETTI
Italian 20th cent.
paintings: (H) $935

PAOLETTI, Antonio
Italian 1834-1912
paintings: (L) $523; (H) $21,850

PAOLETTI, Rodolfo
Italian 1866-1940
paintings: (L) $825; (H) $1,870

PAOLETTI, Silvio D.
Italian 1864-1921
paintings: (L) $1,760; (H) $16,500

PAOLILLO, Luigi
Italian b. 1864
paintings: (L) $825; (H) $2,750
drawings: (H) $358

PAOLINI, Giulio
Italian b. 1940
drawings: (L) $19,550; (H) $33,000
sculpture: (L) $21,850; (H) $55,000

PAOLINI, Pietro
Italian 1603/05-1681/82
paintings: (H) $187,000

PAOLO, C.S.
Italian b. 1882
sculpture: (H) $550

PAOLO DI GIOVANNI FEI
Italian 14th/15th cent.
paintings: (H) $253,000

PAOLOZZI, Eduardo
Italian/British b. 1924
drawings: (H) $920
sculpture: (L) $1,035; (H) $28,750

PAONE, Peter
American b. 1936
paintings: (L) $287; (H) $605

PAP, Emil
Hungarian 19th/20th cent.
paintings: (H) $1,870

PAPA, L.
Italian 19th cent.
paintings: (H) $660

PAPALUCA, D***
Italian
paintings: (H) $575

PAPALUCA, Louis
Italian 20th cent.
paintings: (L) $210; (H) $1,870
drawings: (H) $489

PAPART, Max
French b. 1911
paintings: (L) $1,870; (H) $6,325
drawings: (L) $550; (H) $4,125

PAPAZOFF, Georges
Bulgarian 1894-1972
paintings: (L) $546; (H) $1,725

PAPE, Emile
Hungarian b. 1884
paintings: (H) $1,980

PAPE, Eric
American 1870-1938
paintings: (L) $385; (H) $15,400
drawings: (L) $403; (H) $9,200

PAPETY, Dominique Louis
French 1815-1849
paintings: (H) $1,980
drawings: (L) $1,150; (H) $4,370

PAPINI, Professor
Italian 19th/20th cent.
sculpture: (H) $28,600

PAPLUCA, L.
Italian 20th cent.
paintings: (H) $460

PAPPAS, John
Greek/American 1899-1976
paintings: (L) $17; (H) $690
drawings: (H) $17

PAPPERITZ, Fritz Georg
German 1846-1918
paintings: (H) $4,400

PAPSDORF, Richard
paintings: (H) $11,000

PAQUEAU, Gaston
French 19th cent.
paintings: (H) $16,100

PAQUIN, Pauline T.
Canadian b. 1952
paintings: (L) $1,760; (H) $1,815

PARADISE, John
American 1809-1862
paintings: (H) $1,320

PARADISE, Phil
American b. 1905
paintings: (H) $1,210
drawings: (L) $176; (H) $1,650

PARADISE, Phillip
American b. 1905
drawings: (H) $3,575

PARAMONOV, Vasilii
Russian b. 1923
paintings: (L) $110; (H) $715

PARCELL, Malcolm Stephens
American b. 1896
paintings: (H) $1,430

PARDI
paintings: (L) $58; (H) $495

PAREDES, Mariano
paintings: (H) $863

PAREDES, V. Se
paintings: (H) $1,320

PAREDES, Vicenta de
Spanish 1845-1900
paintings: (L) $1,200; (H) $24,200
drawings: (L) $4,400; (H) $8,250

PAREDES, Vincenta de
Spanish b. 1857
paintings: (H) $7,700

PARELLE, M.A.
ac. late 18th cent.
paintings: (H) $9,200

PARENT, Leon
paintings: (H) $1,955

PARESCE, Renato
drawings: (L) $1,380; (H) $6,900

PARIGI, Giulio
1570-1636
drawings: (H) $7,130

PARIS, Alfred Jean Marie
1846-1908
paintings: (H) $4,950

PARIS, Joseph Francois
paintings: (H) $1,265

PARIS, Rene
French b. 1881
sculpture: (H) $690

PARIS, Roland
German b. 1894
sculpture: (L) $198; (H) $10,350

PARIS, Walter
Anglo/American 1842-1906
drawings: (L) $275; (H) $3,575

PARISH, W.D.
American 19th/20th cent.
drawings: (L) $495; (H) $605

PARK, David
American 1911-1960
paintings: (L) $3,300; (H) $107,250
drawings: (L) $770; (H) $9,900

PARK, Henry
British 1816-1871
paintings: (H) $3,850

PARK, J.A.
British 1880-1962
paintings: (H) $1,705

PARK, John Anthony
British 1888-1962
paintings: (H) $3,850

PARK, Madeleine
American 1891-1960
sculpture: (H) $660

PARK, R.H.
late 19th cent.
sculpture: (H) $1,320

PARK, Robert Hamilton
American 19th cent.
sculpture: (H) $9,900

PARK, Stuart
British 1862-1933
paintings: (H) $935

PARKER, Al
1906-1985
drawings: (H) $660

PARKER, Agnes Miller
American 19th/20th cent.
paintings: (H) $3,960

PARKER, Al
1906-1985
drawings: (L) $1,045; (H) $1,870

PARKER, Alfred
American 1906-1985
drawings: (H) $575

PARKER, Cushman
1882-1940
paintings: (H) $1,760

PARKER, Cushman
American 1882-1940
paintings: (L) $770; (H) $3,025

PARKER, Eliza
American
drawings: (H) $880

PARKER, George Waller
American b. 1888
paintings: (L) $110; (H) $3,630

PARKER, Henry H.
British 1858-1930
paintings: (L) $1,035; (H) $19,550

PARKER, Henry Perle
British 1795-1873
paintings: (L) $1,265; (H) $1,840

PARKER, John
British 19th cent.
drawings: (H) $1,320

PARKER, John A.
b. 1827
paintings: (H) $632

PARKER, John F.
b. 1884
sculpture: (H) $1,100

PARKER, Lawton S.
American 1868-1954
paintings: (L) $330; (H) $31,900
drawings: (L) $110; (H) $1,100

PARKER, P.R.
paintings: (H) $2,750

PARKER, Ray
American 1922-1990
paintings: (L) $1,380; (H) $4,600

PARKER, S.
American 19th/20th cent.
paintings: (H) $825

PARKER, Susan
English 20th cent.
paintings: (H) $1,100

PARKHURST, Thomas
American 1853-1923
paintings: (L) $863; (H) $1,100

PARKS, Bob
American b. 1948
sculpture: (L) $1,265; (H) $3,680

PARKS, J.
American ac. c. 1830
paintings: (H) $2,750

PARMEGGIANINO, Michele ROCCA
studio of
Italian 18th cent.
paintings: (H) $5,750

PARMIGIANINO, Michele ROCCA
Italian 1670/75-1751
paintings: (L) $6,900; (H) $10,925

PARMIGIANINO, Il, Girolamo
Francesco Maria MAZZOLA
Italian 1503-1540
drawings: (L) $16,100; (H) $21,850

PARR, James Wingate
American 20th cent.
paintings: (H) $1,210

PARR, Lenton
sculpture: (H) $1,150

PARR, Nuna
b. 1949
sculpture: (H) $1,980

PARRA, Carmen
Mexican b. 1944
paintings: (H) $11,550

PARRA, Gines
Spanish 1895-1960
paintings: (H) $1,150

PARRA, Jose Felipe P.
Spanish ac. 1832-1858
paintings: (H) $4,600

PARRATT, Marthe
French 19th cent.
paintings: (H) $605

PARREIRAS, Antonio
Brasilian 1860-1937
paintings: (H) $4,313

PARRIS, Edmond Thomas
paintings: (H) $3,850

PARRISH, Maxfield
American 1870-1966
paintings: (L) $11,500; (H) $187,000
drawings: (L) $460; (H) $12,100

PARRISH, Stephen W.
American 1846-1938
paintings: (L) $880; (H) $4,400

PARROCEL, Etienne, called Le Romain
French 1696-1776
drawings: (H) $715

PARROT, Phillipe
French 1831-1894
paintings: (H) $9,200

PARROTT, F.W.
Scottish 19th cent.
drawings: (H) $495

PARROTT, William
British 1813-1869
paintings: (H) $19,800

PARROTT, William Samuel
American 1844-1915
paintings: (L) $880; (H) $7,150

PARSHALL, DeWitt
American 1864-1956
paintings: (L) $165; (H) $2,300

PARSHALL, Douglas Ewell
American b. 1899
paintings: (L) $302; (H) $3,025
drawings: (H) $1,870

PARSONS, Alfred
British 1847-1920
paintings: (L) $575; (H) $4,887
drawings: (L) $92; (H) $3,190

PARSONS, Beatrice
English 1870-1955
drawings: (L) $58; (H) $3,163

PARSONS, Betty
paintings: (L) $633; (H) $1,100
drawings: (H) $253
sculpture: (H) $1,320

PARSONS, Edith Baretto
American 1878-1956
sculpture: (L) $302; (H) $26,400

PARSONS, John F.
British 19th cent.
paintings: (H) $1,380

PARSONS, Marion Randall
American 1878-1953
paintings: (L) $1,650; (H) $3,300

PARSONS, Orrin Sheldon
American 1866/68-1943
paintings: (L) $1,045; (H) $6,613

PARSONS, Philip Brown
American 1896-1977
paintings: (H) $743
drawings: (L) $72; (H) $460

PARSONS, Sheldon
American 1866/68-1943
paintings: (L) $1,650; (H) $4,125

PARTHENIS, Constantine
Greek 1878-1967
paintings: (H) $21,850
drawings: (H) $9,775

PARTINGTON, John H. E.
British 1843-1899
drawings: (H) $978

PARTINGTON, Richard Langtry
American 1868-1929
paintings: (L) $220; (H) $7,150

PARTON
19th cent.
paintings: (H) $935

PARTON, Arthur
American 1842-1914
paintings: (L) $275; (H) $8,000

PARTON, Ernest
American 1845-1933
paintings: (L) $173; (H) $4,025

PARTRIDGE, Alfred A.
British 19th/20th cent.
paintings: (H) $1,980

PARTRIDGE, Ellen
British ac. 1844-1893
paintings: (H) $1,610

PARTRIDGE, John
1772-1837
paintings: (H) $1,100

PARTRIDGE, John
British 1790-1872
paintings: (H) $1,150

PARTRIDGE, William H.
American b. 1858
paintings: (L) $66; (H) $1,760

PARTRIDGE, William Ordway
American 1861-1930
sculpture: (L) $2,750; (H) $6,050

PARTURIER, Marcel
1901-1976
paintings: (H) $2,875

PASCAL, P.B.
Continental 19th cent.
paintings: (H) $8,050
drawings: (H) $770

PASCAL, Paul
French 1832-1903
paintings: (L) $248; (H) $5,750
drawings: (L) $110; (H) $5,175

PASCAL, Paul
French b. 1867
drawings: (L) $605; (H) $6,900

PASCAU
paintings: (H) $935

PASCHKE, Ed
American b. 1939
paintings: (L) $7,700; (H) $35,200

PASCIN, Jules
French/American 1885-1930
paintings: (L) $9,570; (H) $462,000
drawings: (L) $165; (H) $18,400

PASCUAL, Manolo
sculpture: (H) $1,725

PASCUTTI, Antonio
Austrian 19th cent.
paintings: (H) $6,600

PASHLEY, E.
English 19th cent.
paintings: (H) $742

PASINELLI, Lorenzo
1629-1700
paintings: (H) $8,250

PASINELLI, Lorenzo, studio of
Italian 17th cent.
paintings: (H) $14,950

PASINI
drawings: (H) $550

Orientalism

Orientalism was a popular movement of the late 19th century. It has always been a part of an artist's education to travel abroad, and Napoleon's Egyptian campaigns in the late 18th century, France's conquest of Algeria in 1830, and the opening of the Suez canal in 1869 introduced northern Europeans and Americans to the countries of North Africa and the Middle East. And an ever-expanding network of railroads made these distant lands accessible. The exotic quality of Orientalist paintings, with their dazzling colors and blinding light, commanded high prices at the turn of the century. The highly successful 1985 sale at Sotheby's of Orientalist paintings from the Coral Petroleum Collection once again proved the popularity of these works.

Alberto Pasini (1826-1899) was born in Italy. Known primarily as a painter of the Orient and Venice, he was also an honorary professor at the Academies of Parma and Turin. His works were exhibited in Paris and Vienna and won many awards. Bénézit, the French dictionary of artists, notes that Pasini had visited the Shah of Persia. When *Arabian Sentry on Horseback*, an oil on wood panel, was offered at Myers Auction Gallery in St. Petersburg, Florida, it fetched $14,850. (Alberto Pasini, *Arabian Sentry on Horseback*, oil on canvas, 8½ x 6½ inches, Myers, February 19, 1995, $14,850)

PASINI, Alberto
  Italian 1826-1899
  paintings: (L) $4,180; (H) $77,000
  drawings: (L) $517; (H) $18,400
PASINI, Lazzaro
  Italian 1861-1949
  paintings: (H) $1,045
PASINI, V***
  Italian 19th cent.
  drawings: (L) $715; (H) $880

PASKELL, William
  American 1866-1951
  paintings: (L) $25; (H) $1,650
  drawings: (L) $22; (H) $550
PASMORE, Daniël
  British 1829-1891
  paintings: (L) $2,530; (H) $3,300
PASMORE, John
  English ac. 1835-1845
  paintings: (H) $605

PASMORE, Victor
English b. 1908
paintings: (H) $25,300

PASQUALINO DA VENEZIA
Italian ac. 1496-1504
paintings: (H) $51,750

PASSANI, Juan
Argentinean early 20th cent.
sculpture: (H) $2,750

PASSANTE, Bartolomeo, Master of Annunciation to Shepherd
Italian 1618-1648
paintings: (L) $51,750; (H) $165,000

PASSANTINO, George
paintings: (H) $1,210

PASSAROTTI, Bartolomeo
Italian 1529-1592
drawings: (L) $3,450; (H) $41,400

PASSAVANT, Lucile
French b. 1910
sculpture: (H) $1,650

PASSE, Crispijn van de, II
1594/95-1670
drawings: (H) $6,900

PASSERI, Giuseppe
Italian 1654-1714
drawings: (H) $13,800

PASSET, Gerard
French b. 1936
paintings: (L) $230; (H) $1,210

PASSEY, Charles H.
British ac. 1883-1885
paintings: (L) $805; (H) $4,180

PASSIG, B.
German 19th cent.
paintings: (H) $20,700

PASSINI, Ludwig Johann
Austrian 1832-1903
drawings: (H) $518

PASSOT, Nicolas
French ac. 1521
paintings: (H) $33,000

PASTEGA, Luigi
Italian 1858-1927
paintings: (L) $1,150; (H) $17,250

PASTERNAK, Leonid Ossipovitch
Russian 1862-1945
drawings: (H) $3,300

PASTINA, Ed
Italian 19th cent.
paintings: (H) $8,800

PATAKY, Laszlo von Sospatak
Hungarian 1857-1912
paintings: (H) $1,100

PATEL, Antoine Pierre
French 1648-1707
drawings: (L) $2,645; (H) $7,475

PATEL, Gieve
Indian b. 1940
paintings: (L) $1,150; (H) $3,450

PATEL, Pierre Antoine, II
1605-1676
drawings: (H) $6,600

PATER, Jean Baptiste
French 1695-1736
paintings: (L) $387,500; (H) $577,500
drawings: (L) $17,600; (H) $35,200

PATERSON, Caroline
British ac. 1878-1892
drawings: (H) $4,950

PATERSON, James
1854-1932
paintings: (L) $259; (H) $1,650

PATINIER, Joachim
Flemish c. 1485-1524
paintings: (H) $33,000

PATINO, Virgilio
b. Colombia 1947
paintings: (L) $7,475; (H) $11,000

PATKIN, Izhar
b. 1955
paintings: (L) $5,500; (H) $6,600
drawings: (H) $15,400

PATKO, Karoly
b. 1895
drawings: (H) $517

PATON, Donald A.
English
drawings: (H) $550

PATON, Waller Hugh
English 1828-1895
drawings: (L) $633; (H) $1,210

PATRICK, James H.
American 1911-1944
paintings: (H) $467

PATROIS, Isidore
French 1815-1884
paintings: (H) $6,050

PATRONI, Jacobi
paintings: (H) $5,500

PATTARINO, Prof. E.
sculpture: (H) $990

PATTE, Fernand
French b. 1857
paintings: (H) $990

PATTEIN, Cesar
b. Norway ac. 1882-1914 Paris
paintings: (L) $5,500; (H) $18,975

PATTEN, James van
paintings: (L) $3,080; (H) $3,850

PATTERSON, Charles Robert
American 1875/78-1958
paintings: (L) $220; (H) $8,800

PATTERSON, Howard Ashman
American b. 1891
paintings: (H) $1,265

PATTERSON, Margaret Jordan
American 1867-1950
paintings: (L) $275; (H) $3,300
drawings: (L) $55; (H) $2,640

PATTERSON, Neil
b. 1947
paintings: (L) $1,100; (H) $1,430

PATTERSON, Russell
American 1896-1977
paintings: (H) $121
drawings: (L) $1,035; (H) $1,760

PATTI, Thomas
American b. 1943
sculpture: (L) $4,125; (H) $8,250

PATTISON, Abbott
American b. 1916
paintings: (L) $82; (H) $495
sculpture: (L) $121; (H) $230

PATTISON, James W.
American 1844-1915
paintings: (L) $495; (H) $1,375

PATTON, James
paintings: (H) $605

PATTON, Shirley
paintings: (H) $770

PATTY, Johnson
paintings: (H) $825

PATTY, William Arthur
American 1889-1961
paintings: (L) $110; (H) $935

PATWARDHAN, Sudhir
Indian b. 1949
paintings: (L) $1,495; (H) $2,185

PATY, Leon du
French 19th cent.
paintings: (H) $1,610

PAUL, Frank R.
paintings: (H) $6,900
drawings: (L) $920; (H) $10,350

PAUL, John
British 19th cent.
paintings: (L) $1,650; (H) $63,250

PAUL, Joseph
British 1804-1887
paintings: (L) $1,320; (H) $4,400

PAUL, Julian
drawings: (H) $660

PAULA
paintings: (L) $1,430; (H) $1,650

PAULEMILE-PISSARRO
French 1884-1972
paintings: (L) $920; (H) $4,675
drawings: (L) $418; (H) $12,100

PAULI, Richard
American 1855-1892
paintings: (L) $550; (H) $1,980

PAULIN, Paul
French late 19th cent.
sculpture: (L) $4,313; (H) $16,100

PAULMAN
paintings: (H) $900

PAULMAN, Joseph
English 19th/20th cent.
paintings: (L) $715; (H) $4,400

PAULSEN, Erich
German b. 1932
paintings: (L) $575; (H) $1,430

PAULSEN, N. Chr.
Danish 19th cent.
paintings: (H) $5,225

PAULUCCI, Enrico
paintings: (H) $3,300

PAULUS, Francis Petrus
American 1862-1933
paintings: (L) $40; (H) $2,090
drawings: (H) $88

PAULUS, Josef
German b. 1877
paintings: (H) $825

PAUS, Herbert
1880-1946
drawings: (L) $660; (H) $1,540

PAUSER, Sergius
paintings: (H) $7,475

PAUSINGER, Clemens von
Austrian 1855-1936
drawings: (L) $770; (H) $935

PAUTROT, Ferdinand
French 19th cent.
sculpture: (L) $138; (H) $4,025

PAUW, Victor de
American 1902-1971
drawings: (L) $978; (H) $1,725

PAUWELS, Henri J.
Belgian 1903-1987
paintings: (L) $431; (H) $523

PAVESI, Pietro
Italian 19th cent.
drawings: (L) $1,100; (H) $13,800

PAVIL, Elie Anatole
French 1873-1948
paintings: (L) $2,640; (H) $6,900

PAVLIK, Michael
b. Czech. 1901
sculpture: (L) $1,093; (H) $5,750

PAVY, Eugene
French 19th cent.
paintings: (L) $1,650; (H) $79,500

PAVY, Philippe
French ac. 1877-1887
paintings: (H) $3,162

PAWE, H.R.
paintings: (H) $770

PAWLA, Frederick A.
American 1876-1964
paintings: (H) $3,025

PAWLEY, James
British ac. 1854-1869
paintings: (L) $6,325; (H) $12,650

PAWLISZAK, Waclaw
Polish 1866-1905
paintings: (H) $11,000

PAXON, E.S.
paintings: (H) $8,910

PAXON, William McGregor
American 1869-1941
drawings: (H) $489

PAXSON, Edgar Samuel
American 1852-1919
paintings: (L) $5,750; (H) $23,000
drawings: (L) $275; (H) $15,400

PAXSON, Ethel
American 1885-1982
paintings: (L) $138; (H) $1,045
drawings: (L) $104; (H) $715

PAXTON, Elizabeth Okie
American 1877-1971
paintings: (L) $1,650; (H) $11,500

PAXTON, William McGregor
American 1869-1941
paintings: (L) $345; (H) $211,500
drawings: (L) $230; (H) $4,675

PAY, Michel
French 19th cent.
paintings: (H) $1,650

PAYNE, David
British 19th cent.
paintings: (L) $805; (H) $3,080
drawings: (H) $61

PAYNE, Edgar
American 1882-1947
paintings: (L) $193; (H) $74,250
drawings: (L) $495; (H) $10,350

PAYNE, Elsie Palmer
American 1884-1971
paintings: (L) $523; (H) $3,575
drawings: (L) $330; (H) $4,400
sculpture: (L) $550; (H) $990

PAYNE, Henry Arthur
British 1868-1940
paintings: (H) $167,500

PAYNE, Ken
American b. 1937
sculpture: (L) $770; (H) $2,200

PAYSAGE, A. du
sculpture: (H) $2,090

Atypical Paintings

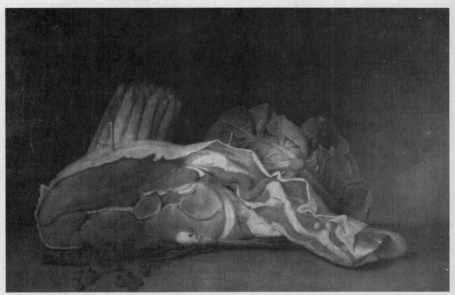

Charles Willson Peale (1741-1827), a naturalist and successful artist, taught his five sons, Raphaelle, Rembrandt, Rubens, Franklin, and Titian, as well as his brother James, to become artists. Rembrandt (1778-1860) became a successful portrait painter, but Raphaelle (1774-1825), the eldest son, is known for his still lifes. Portrait painting was considered to be the highest form of art in early 19th-century America. Still-life paintings were thought to be training exercises or for amateurs and still-life objects were used in portraits only to give a hint of the sitter's character or occupation.

Raphaelle was never as successful as his brother Rembrandt. The only time he made enough money to support himself was when he traveled with a physiognotrace, an English device that could produce silhouette portraits in vast numbers. Unsuccessful as a portrait painter and suffering from poor health (now thought to be arsenic poisoning from working as a taxidermist in his father's museum) he turned to painting still lifes. Most of his paintings are of fruits and vegetables atop a table, with accessories of fine china, silver, or glass; many are close in style and subject to 17th-century Flemish, Dutch, and Spanish still lifes. At the time of his death when only 51 years old, Raphaelle was working as a baker's assistant, writing rhymes and decorating cakes.

When a Raphaelle Peale painting of raw meat was consigned to Skinner's, it carried a conservative estimate of $5,000 to $7,000. Raphaelle had begun experimenting with painting raw meat in 1817, and there are very few known examples. (*Still Life with Steak* is in the Munson-William-Proctor Institute Museum of Art in Utica, New York.) Atypical works do not always sell well, and raw meat is not as appealing as cake. Previous auction records were for the more decorative cake, fruit, and vegetable paintings. The painting reached an unexpected high when it sold for $134,500. (Raphaelle Peale, *Still Life—Beef and Cabbage*, oil on board, 18 x 24½ inches, Skinner, November 11, 1994, $134,500)

Overcoming a Handicap

Painting lessons were the recommended therapy for a promising young pianist stricken with polio. Marguerite Stuber Pearson (1898-1978) was only 15 when she became ill. Her case was severe: her hands were partly paralyzed, and she spent the rest of her life in a wheelchair. Her art lessons, recommended by the family minister, helped her recover from a deep depression. Pearson's family lived in Somerville, Massachusetts, just outside Boston, and when she had mastered her lessons at home, she enrolled at the Museum of Fine Arts and the Fenway School of Illustration. She studied portraiture and figure painting with William James and Frederick Bosly and landscape painting with Aldro Thomas Hibbard and Harry Leith-Ross, and she had private lessons with Edmund Tarbell. Tarbell was "dean" of the Boston School of painters, and Pearson's attention to detail and rendering of texture are characteristic of this school. Her first works were illustrations for books, magazines, and newspapers. A versatile artist, she painted portraits, landscapes, still lifes and interior genre scenes. In 1930 she became a member of the Guild of Boston Artists, a prestigious guild that admitted only the most talented of artists. Her paintings were so popular, especially the interior genre scenes, that a print titled *Blue Danube* sold over 10,000 copies in 1938 and 1941. A success, she built a home/studio in Rockport, Massachusetts. In the entry there was a classic stairway that she used as a prop for her models, but it ended at the ceiling! Pearson was prolific and her paintings appear frequently at auction. Many of her landscapes are of the streets or harbor of Gloucester, and most of her still lifes are of flowers. The flower paintings were her warm-up exercise each day before she began her more serious paintings. None of Pearson's interiors have an open window, perhaps a symbol of her limited mobility. Most of her portraits include a piano or musical instrument. *The Repertoire*, a portrait of a refined, elegant young woman next to a spinet, is a classic Pearson portrait. The price realized for the oil at Boos in Bloomfield Hills, Michigan, was $7,475. (Marguerite Stuber Pearson, *The Repertoire*, oil on canvas, 25 x 30 inches, Boos, May 16, 1995, $7,475)

PAYSON, Emma
American ac. mid-19th cent.
paintings: (H) $483

PAYTON, Joseph
British 19th cent.
paintings: (H) $825

PAYZANT, Charles
American 1898-1980
drawings: (L) $495; (H) $1,100

PEACOCK, Clifton
American 20th cent.
paintings: (H) $805

PEAG, J. van
Dutch 19th cent.
paintings: (H) $1,265

PEAK, Bob
1928-1992
drawings: (L) $230; (H) $1,540

PEAKE, Channing
American 1910-1989
drawings: (H) $460

PEALE, Anna Claypoole
American 1791-1878
paintings: (H) $2,860

PEALE, Charles Willson
American 1741-1827
paintings: (L) $10,175; (H) $107,000

PEALE, Harriet Cary
American 1800-1869
paintings: (L) $550; (H) $3,520
drawings: (H) $83

PEALE, Henry W.
paintings: (H) $1,210

PEALE, James
American 1749-1831
paintings: (L) $14,300; (H) $49,500

PEALE, James
American 19th cent.
paintings: (H) $3,850

PEALE, Mary Jane
American 1827-1902
paintings: (L) $385; (H) $12,650

PEALE, Raphaelle
American 1774-1825
paintings: (L) $134,500; (H) $354,500

PEALE, Rembrandt
American 1778-1860
paintings: (L) $3,335; (H) $299,500
drawings: (H) $440

PEALE, Rubens
American 1784-1864/65
paintings: (L) $5,775; (H) $8,800

PEALE, Sarah Miriam
American 1800-1885
paintings: (L) $2,645; (H) $21,850

PEALE STUDIO,
American 18th/19th cen.
paintings: (H) $33,000

PEARCE, Charles Sprague
American 1851-1914
paintings: (L) $2,070; (H) $79,200

PEARCE, Waldo
paintings: (L) $1,320; (H) $1,650
drawings: (L) $55; (H) $105

PEARCE, William H.S.
19th/20th cent.
paintings: (L) $201; (H) $605

PEARLMUTTER, Stella
American 1911-1993
paintings: (L) $412; (H) $3,080

PEARLSTEIN, Philip
American b. 1924
paintings: (L) $4,400; (H) $46,200
drawings: (L) $1,045; (H) $10,350

PEARS, Charles
British 1873-1958
paintings: (H) $920

PEARS, Dion
British 20th cent.
paintings: (L) $115; (H) $1,760
drawings: (L) $220; (H) $495

PEARSON, Albert
drawings: (H) $2,200

PEARSON, Cornelius
Anglo/American 1805-1891
drawings: (L) $176; (H) $690

PEARSON, Cornelius and Thomas
Francis WAINWRIGHT
drawings: (H) $3,190

PEARSON, Henry
sculpture: (L) $550; (H) $880

PEARSON, Marguerite Stuber
American 1898-1978
paintings: (L) $110; (H) $22,000
drawings: (L) $303; (H) $495

PEASE, Alonzo
American 19th cent.
paintings: (H) $19,250

PEASE, Ray
American b. 1908
paintings: (L) $385; (H) $1,045

PEBBLES, Frank M.
American 1839-1928
paintings: (L) $110; (H) $4,070

PECAULT, C.E.
French 19th cent.
paintings: (H) $2,750

PECH, Gabriel Edouard Baptiste
French early 20th cent.
sculpture: (H) $5,500

PECHAUBES, Eugene
French 1890-1967
paintings: (L) $1,815; (H) $7,762

PECHE, Dale
American
paintings: (H) $1,265

PECHSTEIN, Max
German 1881-1955
paintings: (L) $57,200; (H) $77,000
drawings: (L) $1,210; (H) $51,750

PECK, Anne M.
b. 1884
paintings: (H) $550

PECK, Henry Jarvis
American 1880-1964?
paintings: (L) $220; (H) $747

PECK, Sheldon
American 1797-1868
paintings: (H) $8,525

PECKHAM, Robert
American 1785-1877
drawings: (H) $57,750

PECRUS, Charles F.
French 1826-1907
paintings: (L) $1,210; (H) $22,000

PEDERSEN, Carl Henning
Danish b. 1913
drawings: (H) $3,025

PEDERSEN, Finn
b. 1944
paintings: (L) $230; (H) $3,450

PEDERSEN, Viggo
Danish 1854-1926
paintings: (L) $495; (H) $4,370

PEDERSON, Carl Henning
paintings: (H) $805

PEDERSON, Hugo Vilfred
Danish 1854-1926
paintings: (H) $2,090

PEDEVILLA, F.
Continental 18th cent.
sculpture: (H) $4,125

PEDIASO, Manuel
paintings: (H) $4,600

PEDRO, Luis Martinez
drawings: (H) $2,970

PEDULLI, Federigo
Italian b. 1860
drawings: (L) $990; (H) $6,050

PEEL, James
English 1811-1906
paintings: (L) $165; (H) $4,675

PEEL, Paul
Canadian 1861-1892
paintings: (L) $16,500; (H) $104,500

PEELE, John Thomas
Anglo/American 1822-1897
paintings: (L) $1,265; (H) $3,080

PEELOR, Harold
American 1856-1940
paintings: (H) $2,200

PEER, G.
paintings: (H) $687

PEERS, Gordon Franklin
American b. 1909
paintings: (H) $6,038

PEETERS, Bonaventura, the elder
Flemish 1614-1652
paintings: (L) $2,070; (H) $46,000

PEETERS, E.
American 19th cent.
paintings: (H) $1,210

PEETERS, Gillis
Flemish 1612-1653
paintings: (H) $684,500

PEETERS, Jan
Flemish 1624-1680
paintings: (H) $22,000

PEGURIER, Auguste
French 1856-1936
paintings: (H) $2,090

PEIFFER, Auguste Joseph
French 1832-1886/79
sculpture: (L) $385; (H) $935

PEIGNE
ac. 1790-1815
drawings: (L) $690; (H) $2,530

PEIGNE, Madame
ac. 1790-1815
drawings: (L) $1,380; (H) $2,760

PEINTE, Henri
French 19th cent.
sculpture: (H) $3,740

PEIRANO
late 17th cent.
paintings: (H) $28,600

PEIRCE, H. Winthrop
American 1850-1935/36
paintings: (L) $247; (H) $1,760
drawings: (L) $165; (H) $165

PEIRCE, Waldo
American 1884-1970
paintings: (L) $440; (H) $5,520
drawings: (L) $55; (H) $1,430

PEISER, Mark
American b. 1938
sculpture: (L) $1,150; (H) $9,775

PEISLEY, W. John
paintings: (H) $605

PEIXOTTO, Ernest Clifford
American 1869-1940
paintings: (L) $550; (H) $3,850
drawings: (L) $88; (H) $495

PELAEZ, Amelia
Cuban 1897-1968
paintings: (L) $2,420; (H) $46,000
drawings: (L) $1,540; (H) $30,800
sculpture: (H) $1,495

PELESCHKA
sculpture: (L) $385; (H) $495

PELESKA,
sculpture: (H) $1,840

PELEVIN, Ivan Andreievitch
Russian b. 1840
paintings: (H) $4,600

PELKIN, E. van
Dutch 19th cent.
paintings: (H) $4,313

PELLAN, Alfred
Canadian 1906-1988
drawings: (H) $14,300

PELLEGRIN, Joseph Honore Maxime
French 1793-1869
drawings: (L) $770; (H) $5,175

PELLEGRINI
Italian 19th cent.
paintings: (H) $3,680

PELLEGRINI, Giovanni Antonio, and
studio
18th cent.
paintings: (H) $57,500

PELLEGRINI, Honore
1793-1869
drawings: (H) $8,625

PELLEGRINI, Riccardo
Italian 1863/66-1934
paintings: (L) $12,100; (H) $12,100

PELLEGRINO, J.
Italian 20th cent.
paintings: (L) $330; (H) $770

PELLETIER, Pierre Jacques
French 1869-1931
paintings: (L) $288; (H) $5,280

PELLEW, John C.
Anglo/American b. 1903
paintings: (L) $193; (H) $1,430
drawings: (L) $165; (H) $302

PELLICCIA, Ferdinando
Italian 1808-1892
sculpture: (H) $33,350

PELLICCIOTTI, Tito
Italian 1872-1943
paintings: (L) $523; (H) $9,350

PELLICEROTTI, Frederico
Italian 19th cent.
paintings: (H) $10,450

PELLIER, Jean
paintings: (H) $1,100

PELLIG, L. Axis
paintings: (H) $1,320

PELLON, Gina
b. Cuba 1925
paintings: (L) $575; (H) $6,325

PELLON, Jo Alice
paintings: (H) $522

PELOUSE, Leon Germain
French 1838-1891
paintings: (L) $1,840; (H) $74,000

PELS, Albert
American b. 1910
paintings: (L) $50; (H) $3,300

PELTIER, Leon
French 19th/20th cent.
paintings: (H) $770

PELTIER, Marcel
French 19th/20th cent.
paintings: (H) $550

PELTON, Agnes
German/American 1881-1961
paintings: (L) $275; (H) $11,000
drawings: (L) $495; (H) $2,860

PELUSO, E.
Italian 19th cent.
paintings: (H) $863

PELUSO, Francesco
Italian b. 1836
paintings: (L) $605; (H) $3,850

PEMBROKE, Theodore Kenyon
1865-1917
paintings: (H) $550

PENA, Angel
b. Venezuela 1949
paintings: (L) $13,200; (H) $15,400

PENA, Jose Encarnacion, Soqueen,
Frost on the Mountain
Native American b. 1902
drawings: (L) $330; (H) $1,430

PENA, Tonita, Quah Ah, White Coral
Beads
Native American 1895-1949
drawings: (L) $165; (H) $2,200

PENALBA, Alicia
Argentinean 1918-1982
sculpture: (L) $4,675; (H) $57,750

PENCK, A.R.
German b. 1939
paintings: (L) $5,750; (H) $137,500
drawings: (L) $1,150; (H) $13,800

PENCK, T.E.
French b. 1929
paintings: (L) $176; (H) $990

PENE DU BOIS, Guy
American 1884-1958
paintings: (H) $115,500
drawings: (L) $770; (H) $7,150

PENFIELD, Edward
American 1866-1925
drawings: (L) $230; (H) $3,850

PENFOLD, Frank C.
American 1849-1920
paintings: (L) $1,045; (H) $9,900
drawings: (H) $550

PENLEY, Edwin Aaron
English ac. 1844-1890
drawings: (L) $660; (H) $1,035

PENMAN, Edith
American d. 1929
paintings: (H) $715

PENNACHINI, Domenico
Italian b. 1860
paintings: (H) $8,800
drawings: (L) $2,420; (H) $3,300

PENNASILICO, Giuseppe
Italian b. 1860
paintings: (H) $50,600

PENNE, Charles Olivier de
French 1831-1897
paintings: (L) $1,725; (H) $12,650
drawings: (L) $633; (H) $1,725

PENNELL, Harry
British
paintings: (L) $1,725; (H) $1,760

PENNELL, Joseph
American 1860-1926
drawings: (L) $165; (H) $6,325

PENNIMAN, John Ritto
American 1783-1841
drawings: (L) $5,462; (H) $79,500

PENNINGTON, Harper
paintings: (H) $3,000

PENNOYER, Albert Sheldon
American 1888-1957
paintings: (L) $220; (H) $6,900
drawings: (L) $330; (H) $1,760

PENNY, Edwin
British 19th/20th cent.
drawings: (L) $1,760; (H) $4,313

PENONE, Giuseppe
b. 1947
drawings: (H) $2,530

PENOT, A.
French School 19th cent.
paintings: (H) $3,080

PENOT, Albert Joseph
French ac. 1910
paintings: (L) $2,090; (H) $16,100

PENSKE
20th cent.
paintings: (H) $715

PENTHER, Daniel
Polish 1837-1887
paintings: (H) $715

PEOLI, Juan Jorge
Spanish 19th cent.
paintings: (H) $6,600

PEPLOE, Samuel John
British 1871-1935
paintings: (L) $9,350; (H) $43,700

PEPPER, Beverly
American b. 1924
paintings: (H) $4,125
drawings: (H) $138
sculpture: (L) $1,495; (H) $29,900

PEPPER, Charles Hovey
American 1864-1950
paintings: (L) $1,265; (H) $2,860
drawings: (L) $825; (H) $1,540

PEPPERCORN, Arthur D.
British 1847-1926
paintings: (H) $825

PERAHIM, Jules
Israeli 19th cent.
paintings: (H) $1,320

PERAIRE, Paul Emanuel
French 1829-1893
paintings: (L) $6,325; (H) $15,950

PERALTA DEL CAMPO, Francisco
Spanish 1837-1897
paintings: (H) $17,250

PERBANDT, Carl von
American 1832-1911
paintings: (L) $605; (H) $10,450

PERBOYRE, Paul Emile Leon
French 1826-1907
paintings: (L) $550; (H) $12,650

PERCEVAL, Don
American 1908-1979
paintings: (H) $715
drawings: (H) $660

PERCIER, Charles
1764-1838
drawings: (L) $2,990; (H) $7,762

PERCY, R.
British 19th cent.
paintings: (H) $552

PERCY, Sidney Richard
English 1821-1886
paintings: (L) $2,200; (H) $50,600

PEREA MASTER
ac. 15th/16th cent.
paintings: (H) $55,000

PEREDA, Antonio
Spanish 1608-1678
paintings: (H) $40,250

PEREGO, Eugenio
Italian 1845-1923
drawings: (H) $1,265

PEREGOY, Walter
drawings: (H) $2,875

PEREHUDOFF, William
Canadian b. 1919
paintings: (L) $2,200; (H) $6,600

PEREIRA, Irene Rice
American 1907-1971
paintings: (L) $247; (H) $302
drawings: (L) $357; (H) $6,325

PERELLI, Achille
Italian/American 1822-1891
drawings: (L) $770; (H) $5,500

PERENY, Madelaine
American b. 1896
paintings: (H) $550

PERET, Jean Francois
French 19th cent.
paintings: (H) $1,540

PERETTI, Achille
Italian/American 1857/62-1923
paintings: (L) $605; (H) $3,520
drawings: (L) $440; (H) $7,700

PEREZ, Alonso
Spanish ac. 1893-1914
paintings: (L) $2,530; (H) $11,550
drawings: (L) $690; (H) $1,650

PEREZ, Augusto
b. 1929
sculpture: (H) $550

PEREZ, Cayetano
Spanish ac. c. 1760
paintings: (H) $82,250

PEREZ, Rafael Senet
Spanish 1856-1927
paintings: (L) $9,900; (H) $19,800

PEREZ DE HOLGUIN, Melchor
1665-c. 1724
paintings: (L) $3,737; (H) $8,050

PERFETTI, Giorgio
Italian 1932-1961
paintings: (L) $495; (H) $880

PERGOLA, Linnea
American 20th cent.
paintings: (H) $523

PERICONI, D.F.
American 20th cent.
paintings: (L) $715; (H) $990

PERIGAL, Arthur
British 1816-1884
paintings: (L) $1,238; (H) $2,875

PERIGNON, Alexis Nicolas
French 1726-1782
drawings: (H) $5,500

PERILLI, Achille
Italian b. 1927
paintings: (L) $8,800; (H) $30,800

PERILLO, Gregory
American b. 1929
paintings: (L) $413; (H) $1,650
sculpture: (H) $770

PERIS, V****
Spanish 20th cent.
paintings: (H) $1,840

PERKIN, Isabelle L.
British ac. c. 1888-1928
paintings: (H) $2,750

PERKINS, Granville
American 1830-1895
paintings: (L) $550; (H) $11,000
drawings: (L) $220; (H) $2,200

PERKINS, Mary Smyth
American 1875-1931
paintings: (H) $15,400
drawings: (H) $690

PERKINS, Parker
1875-1949
paintings: (L) $137; (H) $1,045

PERKINS, Parker S.
American b. 1862
paintings: (L) $247; (H) $605

PERL, Karl
Austrian b. 1876
sculpture: (L) $1,265; (H) $1,870

PERLASCA, Martino
Swiss 1860-1899
paintings: (H) $11,000

PERLBERG, Friedrich
German 1848-1921
drawings: (H) $920

PERLE, Edmund
Polish 19th/20th cent.
paintings: (H) $2,990

PERLET, Marion
paintings: (H) $1,320

PERLEY, Myron
1883-1939
drawings: (H) $575

PERLIN, Bernard
American b. 1918
paintings: (L) $413; (H) $24,200
drawings: (L) $55; (H) $385

PERLROTT-CSABA, Vilmos
1880-1955
drawings: (H) $660

PERMAN, Louis E.
French d. 1921
paintings: (H) $1,380

PERON, Guy
French b. 1931
paintings: (L) $275; (H) $990

PERONE, Jeff
American b. 1953
sculpture: (L) $1,725; (H) $2,640

PEROUX, A.
paintings: (H) $990

PEROWSKI, Richard
British 19th cent.
drawings: (H) $4,600

PERRATT, Marthe
French 19th/20th cent.
paintings: (H) $1,980

PERRAULT, Leon Jean Basile
French 1832-1908
paintings: (L) $2,070; (H) $107,000

PERRE, Henri
Canadian 1828-1890
paintings: (L) $1,650; (H) $1,980
drawings: (H) $27

PERRET, Aime
French 1847-1927
paintings: (L) $2,750; (H) $7,975

PERRETT, Galen Joseph
American 1875-1949
paintings: (L) $1,210; (H) $2,420

PERREY, Leon Auguste
French 1841-1900
paintings: (H) $8,800

PERRIE, Bertha E.
American 1868-1921
paintings: (H) $715
drawings: (L) $99; (H) $1,840

PERRIER, Emilio Sanchez
Spanish 1855-1907
paintings: (H) $9,900

PERRIER, Francois
French 1590-1650
drawings: (H) $2,990

PERRIER, H.F.
paintings: (H) $6,050

PERRIGARD, Hal Ross
Canadian 19th/20th cent.
paintings: (L) $440; (H) $1,210

PERRIN, A. Moncel Conte Alphonse
Emmanuel de Marcel de
French b. 1866
sculpture: (H) $7,150

PERRIN, Alfred Feyen
British d. 1918
paintings: (H) $1,725

PERRIN, Francois Nicolas Augustin
Feyen
French 1826-1888
paintings: (H) $6,050

PERRIN, Gabriel
French 19th cent.
paintings: (H) $29,900

PERRINE, Van Dearing
American 1869-1955
paintings: (H) $2,090

PERRON, C.
Spanish 20th cent
paintings: (H) $880

PERRON, Charles
contemporary
paintings: (L) $1,100; (H) $1,540

PERRONE, Jeff
American b. 1953
sculpture: (L) $1,380; (H) $1,725

PERROT, Ferdinand
French 1808-1841
paintings: (H) $1,380

PERRTTEN, E.
French 19th cent.
paintings: (H) $2,750

PERRY, Enoch Wood
American 1831-1915
paintings: (L) $413; (H) $18,400

PERRY, J.
American 20th cent.
paintings: (L) $220; (H) $1,430

PERRY, Lilla Cabot
American 1848-1933
paintings: (L) $88; (H) $35,200

PERRY, Roland Hinton
American 1870-1941
paintings: (L) $690; (H) $715
sculpture: (L) $990; (H) $6,050

PERSAN, Jean Raffy Le
b. 1920
paintings: (H) $1,760

PERTZ, Anne J.
English ac. 1880-1911
paintings: (H) $468

PERUGINO, Pietro Vannucci
workshop of
15th/16th cent.
paintings: (H) $104,500

PESARO, G.
paintings: (H) $1,540

PESCHAUBES, Eugene
French b. 1890
paintings: (H) $715

PESCHERET, Leon
American 1892-1961
drawings: (L) $330; (H) $1,018

PESINT, J.
19th cent.
paintings: (H) $1,955

PESKE, Geza
Hungarian 1859-1934
paintings: (L) $4,140; (H) $6,900

PESKE, Jean
paintings: (H) $12,100

PESKE, Jean
French 1870-1949
drawings: (H) $1,150

PESKOLLER, Johannes Matthias
Austrian b. 1873
paintings: (H) $1,725

PETER, Alexander
20th cent.
paintings: (H) $990

PETER, Johann Wenzel
1745-1829
paintings: (H) $16,100

PETERDI, Gabor
Hungarian/American b. 1915
paintings: (L) $880; (H) $1,650
drawings: (H) $302

PETERELLE, Adolphe
French 1874-1947
paintings: (H) $467

PETERIS, J.H.
American 20th cent.
paintings: (H) $550

PETERS, Anna
German 1843-1926
paintings: (L) $6,325; (H) $29,700

PETERS, Carl William
American 1897-1980
paintings: (L) $715; (H) $22,425

PETERS, Charles Rollo
American 1862-1928
paintings: (L) $220; (H) $8,800

PETERS, Les
American
paintings: (L) $660; (H) $950

PETERS, Matthew William
Irish 1742-1814
paintings: (L) $330; (H) $3,300

PETERS, Pieter Francis
Dutch 1818-1903
paintings: (H) $3,520
drawings: (H) $550

PETERSEN, Einar C.
American 1885-1986
paintings: (L) $1,210; (H) $1,980

PETERSEN, H.
German 19th cent.
paintings: (H) $6,050

PETERSEN, Jane
American 1876-1965/68
drawings: (L) $2,310; (H) $5,225

PETERSEN, John E.C.
1839-1874
paintings: (L) $2,640; (H) $3,190

PETERSEN, L.C.
American 19th/20th cent.
paintings: (H) $577

PETERSEN, Martin
Danish/American b. 1870
paintings: (L) $660; (H) $4,180
drawings: (H) $440

PETERSEN, Roland
American b. Denmark 1926
paintings: (L) $3,025; (H) $14,300

PETERSEN, Sophus
Danish 1837-1904
paintings: (H) $1,320

PETERSEN, W.
Dutch School 20th cent.
paintings: (L) $578; (H) $605

PETERSEN, William
Dutch 20th cent.
paintings: (H) $550

PETERSON, Heinrich A.
British 19th cent.
paintings: (L) $9,900; (H) $11,000

PETERSON, Jacob
Danish 1774-1854
drawings: (H) $6,613

PETERSON, Jane
American 1876-1965/68
paintings: (L) $110; (H) $48,875
drawings: (L) $55; (H) $18,700

PETERSON, Oswald
paintings: (H) $1,320

PETERSON, Roland
contemporary
paintings: (L) $7,150; (H) $7,700

PETERSON, Thomas
American 1861-1926
paintings: (H) $575

PETHAM, G***K***
paintings: (H) $4,025

PETHER, Abraham
English 1756-1812 ·
paintings: (L) $1,870; (H) $2,875

PETHER, Henry
English ac. 1828-1865
paintings: (H) $660

PETHER, Sebastian
British 1790-1844
paintings: (H) $825

PETIT, Alfred
French d. 1895
paintings: (H) $3,080

PETIT, Charles
French exhib. 1884-1896
paintings: (H) $3,850

PETIT, Corneille
Belgian 19th cent.
paintings: (H) $6,325

PETIT, E***
French 19th/20th cent.
paintings: (H) $1,725

PETIT, E.
paintings: (L) $1,430; (H) $2,420

PETIT, Eugene
French 1839-1886
paintings: (L) $2,310; (H) $5,500

PETIT, Jacques
French 20th cent.
paintings: (H) $1,064

PETIT, L.
French 19th/20th cent.
paintings: (H) $2,420

PETIT, Sylvain
French 19th cent.
drawings: (H) $1,035

PETIT, Wilfre S.
paintings: (H) $495

PETIT JEAN, O.
French 20th cent.
paintings: (H) $660

PETIT-GERARD, Pierre
French b. 1852
paintings: (H) $1,045

PETITI, Filiberto
Italian 1845-1924
paintings: (H) $6,050

PETITJEAN
French 19th cent.
paintings: (H) $2,530

PETITJEAN, Edmond Marie
French 1844-1925
paintings: (L) $2,990; (H) $22,000

PETITJEAN, Hippolyte
French 1854-1929
paintings: (L) $1,380; (H) $18,400
drawings: (L) $3,680; (H) $36,800

PETITOT, Ennemond Alexandre
1727-1801
drawings: (H) $1,840

PETIZYNSKI, Adam
Polish 20th cent.
paintings: (H) $715

PETKEVICH, Sergei
Russian b. 1936
paintings: (H) $660

PETO, John Frederick
American 1854-1907
paintings: (L) $2,310; (H) $107,000

PETRI, P.
Norwegian/American 20th cent.
paintings: (H) $3,105

PETRIDES, Konrad
Austrian 1863-1943
paintings: (H) $660

PETRILLI, Professor A.
Italian 19th cent.
sculpture: (L) $1,320; (H) $16,500

PETRINI, Giuseppe Antonio
Italian 1677-1759
paintings: (H) $16,500

PETRITTI, Professor A.
Italian 20th cent.
sculpture: (H) $770

PETROCELLI, **
Italian 19th cent.
paintings: (H) $935

PETROVITS, Milan
American 1892-1944
paintings: (H) $578

PETRUOLO, Salvatore
Italian b. 1857
paintings: (L) $6,050; (H) $10,925

PETTENKOFEN, August von
Austrian 1822-1889
paintings: (H) $1,380

PETTER, Franz Xaver
Austrian 1791-1866
paintings: (H) $16,100

PETTERSON, Margo
paintings: (L) $400; (H) $1,600

PETTI, Cesare Auguste
Italian 1847-1914
paintings: (H) $2,200

PETTIBONE, Richard
paintings: (L) $805; (H) $1,150

PETTIBONE, Robert
paintings: (L) $110; (H) $1,430

PETTIBONE, Shirley
paintings: (L) $1,380; (H) $3,080

PETTIE, John
Scottish/English 1839-1893
paintings: (L) $495; (H) $1,650

PETTORUTI, Emilio
Argentinean 1892-1971
paintings: (L) $16,500; (H) $264,000
drawings: (H) $12,100

PETTY, George
American 1894-1975
drawings: (L) $8,250; (H) $9,350

PEVILKIN, S.
paintings: (H) $690

PEVSNER, Antoine
French 1884-1962
paintings: (H) $63,250

PEW, Gertrude L.
American b. 1876
drawings: (H) $2,200

PEYFUSS, J. Karl
Austrian late 19th cent.
paintings: (H) $605

PEYNOT, Emile Edmond
French 1850-1932
sculpture: (L) $880; (H) $8,800

PEYRAUD, Frank Charles
American 1858-1928
paintings: (L) $358; (H) $4,600

PEYRE, R. Ch.
sculpture: (L) $2,300; (H) $4,025

PEYROL, Francois Auguste Hippolyte
French 1856-1929
sculpture: (L) $1,320; (H) $3,450

PEYROL, Rene
French 19th cent.
paintings: (H) $550

PEYROL-BONHEUR, Juliette
French 1830-1891
paintings: (L) $2,875; (H) $8,250

PEYTEL, Adrienne
French 19th cent.
paintings: (H) $10,925

PEYTON, Bertha
American 1871-1950
drawings: (H) $1,980

PEZANT, Aimard Alexandre
French b. 1846
paintings: (H) $6,325

PEZANT, Aymar
French 1846-after 1914
paintings: (L) $880; (H) $2,530

PEZZATO, Santo
Italian 20th cent.
paintings: (H) $825

PEZZUTI, P.
Italian 19th cent.
paintings: (H) $5,500

PFAFF, Judy
American b. 1946
drawings: (L) $805; (H) $4,888

PFALZ, Severin
Czechoslovakian b. 1796
paintings: (H) $467

PFEIFFER, August Joseph
French 19th cent.
sculpture: (H) $4,840

PFEIFFER, Friedrich Wilhelm
German 1822-1891
paintings: (H) $5,225

PFEIFFER, Fritz
American 1889-1960
paintings: (L) $192; (H) $440
drawings: (L) $165; (H) $825

PFLUEGER, Timothy L.
American contemporary
drawings: (L) $115; (H) $495

PFORR, Johann Georg
German 1745-1798
paintings: (H) $82,500

PHELAN, Charles T.
American b. 1840
paintings: (L) $220; (H) $1,725

PHELAN, Ellen
b. 1943
drawings: (H) $748

PHELPS, Edith C.
American 1875-1961
paintings: (L) $715; (H) $1,320

PHELPS, Emily
paintings: (H) $660

PHELPS, William Preston
American 1848-1923
paintings: (L) $468; (H) $7,700

PHIL, Daniel
American 20th cent.
sculpture: (L) $364; (H) $504

PHILBRICK, Otis
American 1888-1973
paintings: (H) $690
drawings: (H) $137

PHILIPP, Robert
American 1895-1981
paintings: (L) $385; (H) $11,500
drawings: (L) $165; (H) $2,750

PHILIPPE, Auguste Salnave
paintings: (H) $4,180

PHILIPPE, Louis
sculpture: (H) $7,475

PHILIPPE, M.
Belgian early 20th cent.
sculpture: (H) $462

PHILIPPE, Paul
Polish ac. 1900-1930
sculpture: (L) $550; (H) $12,100

PHILIPPE, R. Abel
French early 20th cent.
sculpture: (H) $16,100

PHILIPPEAU, Karel Frans
Dutch 1825-1897
paintings: (L) $2,990; (H) $7,700

PHILIPPOTEAUX, Henri Felix
Emmanuel
French 1815-1884
paintings: (L) $2,070; (H) $71,500

PHILIPPOTEAUX, Henri Felix
Emmanuel and Horace VERNET
French 19th cent.
paintings: (H) $28,750

PHILIPPOTEAUX, Paul Dominique
French b. 1846
paintings: (L) $431; (H) $11,500

PHILIPS, Hermann
paintings: (H) $11,000

PHILIPS, J.E.W.
British 19th cent.
paintings: (H) $1,650

PHILIPS, Marjorie Acker
American 1894-1985
paintings: (L) $385; (H) $495

PHILLIP, John
English 1817-1967
paintings: (L) $2,185; (H) $3,850

PHILLIP, Robert
American 1895-1981
paintings: (H) $2,300

PHILLIPE, A.
sculpture: (H) $2,990

PHILLIPE, P.
French ac. 1900-1930
sculpture: (L) $440; (H) $2,013

PHILLIPE-AUGUSTE, Salnave
paintings: (L) $1,870; (H) $3,080

PHILLIPP, Werner
1897-1982
paintings: (H) $1,495

PHILLIPPE, Paul
German ac. 1902-1914
sculpture: (L) $2,875; (H) $4,600

PHILLIPPOTEAUX, Paul D.
French b. 1846
paintings: (H) $990

PHILLIPS
American 19th cent.
drawings: (H) $460

PHILLIPS, Ammi
American 1788-1865
paintings: (L) $600; (H) $74,800

PHILLIPS, Barye
d. 1969
drawings: (H) $550

PHILLIPS, Bert Greer
American 1868-1956
paintings: (L) $3,575; (H) $18,700

PHILLIPS, C.L.G. or C.G.L.
paintings: (H) $650

PHILLIPS, Charles
1708-1747
paintings: (H) $24,200

PHILLIPS, Coles
American 1880-1927
drawings: (L) $9,350; (H) $15,400

PHILLIPS, Gordon
American b. 1927
paintings: (L) $2,750; (H) $18,700
sculpture: (H) $1,430

PHILLIPS, Joel
American b. 1960
paintings: (H) $1,870
drawings: (L) $2,750; (H) $3,300

PHILLIPS, John Campbell
paintings: (H) $715

PHILLIPS, Marjorie
American 1894-1985
paintings: (L) $121; (H) $935

PHILLIPS, Melville A.
American b. 1893
paintings: (L) $302; (H) $550

PHILLIPS, Peter
b. 1939
paintings: (H) $17,600

PHILLIPS, Robert J.
American b. 1946
drawings: (H) $460

PHILLIPS, S. George
American 20th cent.
paintings: (L) $500; (H) $26,000

PHILLIPS, Thomas
English 17701-1845
paintings: (L) $7,150; (H) $8,050

PHILLIPS, Walter Joseph
Canadian 1884-1963
drawings: (L) $3,300; (H) $5,225

PHILLIPS, Winifred E.
American b. 1881
paintings: (L) $44; (H) $495

PHILLOTT, Constance
English 1842-1931
drawings: (H) $660

PHILPOT, Glyn
English 1884-1937
paintings: (H) $10,450
drawings: (H) $4,600
sculpture: (H) $4,025

PHIPPEN, George
American 1916-1966
paintings: (L) $4,400; (H) $9,900
sculpture: (L) $1,495; (H) $25,300

PHYSICK, Robert
British 19th cent.
paintings: (H) $5,775

PI, Oqwa, Red Cloud, Abel Sanchez
Native American b. 1899
drawings: (H) $1,840

PIACENZA, Aldo
Italian/American b. 1888
paintings: (H) $605

PIACENZA, Armodio
Italian 20th cent.
paintings: (H) $1,430

PIANCHI, Ruis
Spanish 20th cent.
paintings: (L) $489; (H) $605

PIANELLO, F.
Italian 19th cent.
paintings: (H) $1,320

PIAZZA, A.
Italian 19th cent.
sculpture: (L) $575; (H) $2,750

PIAZZA, Calisto, called Calisto da Lodi
Italian c. 1500-1561
paintings: (H) $121,000

PIAZZA, Dino
Italian 20th cent.
paintings: (H) $550

PIAZZETTA, Giovanni Battista
Italian 1862-1754
drawings: (L) $12,100; (H) $132,000

PIAZZONI, Gottardo
American 1872-1945
paintings: (L) $935; (H) $5,463

PICABIA, Francis
French 1878-1953
paintings: (L) $6,600; (H) $330,000
drawings: (L) $2,185; (H) $48,875

PICARD, F.
sculpture: (H) $4,675

PICARD, Gustave
French 19th cent.
paintings: (H) $4,600

PICART, Bernard
French 1673-1733
drawings: (H) $6,050

PICART, Jean Michel
Flemish 1600-1682
paintings: (L) $43,700; (H) $70,700

PICART, O**
French 19th cent.
paintings: (H) $1,870

PICASSO, Pablo
b. Spain 1881 d. France 1973
paintings: (L) $19,550; (H) $29,152,500
drawings: (L) $1,150; (H) $6,272,500
sculpture: (L) $358; (H) $2,530,000

PICAULT, Claude E.
French 20th cent.
paintings: (H) $1,100

PICAULT, Emile Louis
French ac. 1863-1909
sculpture: (L) $495; (H) $7,700

PICCARDI, Sestiani
sculpture: (H) $2,750

PICCI, Pio
paintings: (H) $4,300

PICCILLO, Joseph
American 20th cent.
drawings: (H) $978

PICCIRILLI, Attilio
American 1866-1945
sculpture: (L) $1,540; (H) $40,250

PICCIRILLO,
sculpture: (H) $2,530

PICCOLI, Girolamo
Italian 1902-1971
sculpture: (L) $220; (H) $495

PICHETTE, James
French b. 1920
paintings: (L) $805; (H) $6,600

PICHON, G.
sculpture: (H) $4,312

PICHOT, Emile Jules
French b. 1857
paintings: (H) $3,410

PICHOT, Ramon
Spanish b. 1925
paintings: (L) $200; (H) $3,220

PICKEN, George Alexander
American b. 1898
paintings: (L) $172; (H) $1,093

PICKENOY, Nicolas Eliasz.
Dutch c. 1590/1-1654/6
paintings: (L) $33,000; (H) $112,500

PICKENS, Lucien Alton
b. 1917
paintings: (L) $1,760; (H) $7,475

PICKERING, Henry
English ac. 1740-1790
paintings: (H) $4,600

PICKERING, J.L.
American 19th cent.
paintings: (H) $3,300

PICKERSGILL, Frederick Richard
British 1820-1900
paintings: (L) $110; (H) $24,200

PICKERSGILL, Henry William
English 1728-1875
paintings: (H) $24,150

PICKETT, Joe
American 1848-1918
paintings: (H) $715

PICKHARDT, Carl E., Jr.
American b. 1908
paintings: (H) $2,750
drawings: (H) $275

PICKNELL, George W.
American 1864-1943
paintings: (L) $144; (H) $1,840
drawings: (L) $259; (H) $460

PICKNELL, William Lamb
American 1854-1897
paintings: (L) $3,450; (H) $27,500

PICOT, Jean Claude
French b. 1930
paintings: (L) $805; (H) $935
drawings: (L) $288; (H) $413

PICOU, Henri Pierre
French 1824-1895
paintings: (L) $3,025; (H) $162,000

PIELER, Franz Xaver
German 1879-1952
paintings: (L) $2,750; (H) $40,250

PIENOTTI
19th cent.
sculpture: (H) $2,475

PIERCE, C.F.
paintings: (L) $165; (H) $605

PIERCE, Charles Franklin
American 1844-1920
paintings: (L) $248; (H) $4,675
drawings: (L) $317; (H) $1,430

PIERCE, Elijah
American 1892-1982
paintings: (L) $7,475; (H) $8,912
sculpture: (L) $275; (H) $9,200

PIERCE, Joseph W.
American 19th cent.
paintings: (L) $412; (H) $3,300
drawings: (L) $2,750; (H) $2,875

PIERCE, Lucy
American 1887-1974
paintings: (H) $1,100

PIERCE, R.E.
American
paintings: (L) $1,000; (H) $1,430

PIERON, Henri
Belgian 19th/20th cent.
paintings: (H) $1,840

PIERPONT, Stanley
English ac. 1905-1925
paintings: (H) $1,650

PIERRE, Andre
Haitian b. 1916
paintings: (L) $1,760; (H) $5,175

PIERRE, Ferdinand
Haitian 20th cent.
paintings: (H) $770

PIERRE, Fernand
Haitian
paintings: (L) $550; (H) $770

PIERRE, Gustave Rene
French b. 1875
paintings: (L) $660; (H) $660

PIERRE, Jean Baptiste Marie
French 1713-1789
paintings: (L) $85,000; (H) $189,500

PIERRE, Laureus
Haitian 20th cent.
paintings: (H) $1,760

PIERSON, Christoffel
Dutch 1631-1714
paintings: (H) $36,800

PIERSON, John C.
paintings: (H) $578

PIETERS, Evert
Dutch 1856-1932
paintings: (L) $1,430; (H) $29,700

PIETERSZ, D.
19th cent.
paintings: (H) $575

PIETRI, Pietro Antonio dei
1663-1716
drawings: (L) $2,310; (H) $8,800

PIETRO DA CORTONA Pietro
BERRETTINI
Italian 1596-1669
drawings: (L) $6,600; (H) $61,600

PIETRO DI DOMENICO
Italian 1457-1506?
paintings: (H) $118,000

PIETRONI, A.
paintings: (L) $360; (H) $715

PIETZSCH, Richard
German b. 1872
paintings: (L) $82; (H) $550

PIGAL, Edme Jean
French 1798-1872
paintings: (L) $1,093; (H) $1,540

PIGNA, A.
European School 19th/20th cent.
paintings: (H) $8,050

PIGNON, Edouard
French 1905-1993
paintings: (L) $2,875; (H) $19,800
drawings: (L) $345; (H) $15,400

PIGNONI, Simone
Italian 1614-1698
paintings: (H) $19,550

PIGNOUX
French 19th cent.
paintings: (H) $7,150

PIGUET, Rodolphe
Swiss 1840-1915
paintings: (H) $2,990
drawings: (H) $28,600

PIHNNERO, H.
Italian 19th cent.
paintings: (H) $8,800

PIKE, Gordon B.
19th cent.
drawings: (H) $1,035

PIKE, John
American b. 1911
paintings: (L) $935; (H) $990
drawings: (L) $633; (H) $1,100

PIKE, William
British 1846-1908
drawings: (L) $220; (H) $825

PIKELNY, Robert
b. 1904
paintings: (H) $660

PILCH, Adahbert
European 19th cent.
paintings: (H) $1,430

PILET, Leon
French 1836-1916
sculpture: (L) $522; (H) $5,750

PILIEY, L.M. and Eugene
Alexandrovich LANCERAY
Russian 19th cent.
sculpture: (H) $7,150

PILLEMENT, Jean Baptiste
French 1728-1808
paintings: (L) $4,887; (H) $167,500
drawings: (L) $1,380; (H) $16,500

PILLET, Leon
French 1839-1916
sculpture: (L) $1,980; (H) $2,420

PILON
sculpture: (H) $632

PILOT, Robert Wakeham
Canadian 1898-1967/68
paintings: (L) $2,760; (H) $59,400

PILOTY, Carl Theodor von
German 1826-1886
paintings: (L) $825; (H) $57,750

PILS, Isidore
French 1813-1875
drawings: (L) $605; (H) $920

PILSBURY, Wilmot
English 1840-c. 1908
drawings: (H) $1,980

PILTERS, Joseph
German 1877-1957
paintings: (H) $14,950

PILTZ, Otto
German 1846-1910
paintings: (L) $4,888; (H) $25,300

PILZ, Otto
German b. 1976
sculpture: (H) $770

PIMENTEL, Rodrigo Ramirez
b. Mexico 1945
paintings: (L) $9,900; (H) $13,800

PINA, Alfredo
Italian 1883-1966
sculpture: (L) $2,200; (H) $31,625

PINAL, Ferdinand
French 1881-1958
paintings: (H) $15,400

PINCEMIN, Jean Pierre
French b. 1944
paintings: (H) $12,100

PINCHART, Emile Auguste
French 1842-after 1930
paintings: (L) $1,760; (H) $25,875

PINCHON, Jean Antoine
French 1772-1850
drawings: (H) $2,750

PINCHON, Robert Antoine
French 1886-1943
paintings: (L) $7,150; (H) $14,850

PINE, Robert Edge
English 1730-1788
drawings: (H) $1,045

PINE, Theodore E.
American 1828-1905
paintings: (L) $825; (H) $920

PINEDA, Jose
1837-1907
drawings: (H) $4,180

PINEDO, Emile
French late 19th/early 20th cent
sculpture: (L) $1,100; (H) $3,520

PINEL, M.L.
paintings: (H) $467

PINEL DE GRANDSCHAMP, Louis
Emile
French d. 1894
paintings: (H) $2,070

PINELLI, Bartolomeo
Italian 1781-1835
drawings: (L) $522; (H) $3,300

PINELO, Jose
Spanish 19th/20th cent.
paintings: (H) $1,870

PINGGERA, H.
Austrian 19th/20th cent.
paintings: (H) $1,210

PINGGERA, H.
Italian 19th cent.
paintings: (L) $1,650; (H) $7,700

PINGRET, Edouard Henri Theophile
French 1788-1875
paintings: (L) $85,000; (H) $167,500
drawings: (H) $5,750

PINI, Wendy
drawings: (H) $2,530

PINKSTON, M.W.
American 1898-1972
paintings: (H) $1,650

PINNEY, Eunice
American 1770-1849
drawings: (L) $4,600; (H) $17,250

PINNGERA, H.
paintings: (L) $460; (H) $1,320

PINO, Jose Moya del
1891-1969
paintings: (H) $3,450

PINQQERA, H.
Continental 19th cent.
paintings: (L) $4,313; (H) $25,300

PINTO, Alberto
Portuguese 19th cent.
paintings: (H) $2,860

PINTO, Angelo
American b. 1908
paintings: (L) $798; (H) $1,100

PINTO, Biagio
American b. 1911
paintings: (L) $990; (H) $8,250

PINTURICCHIO, Bernardino Betti,
called PINTORICCHIO
Italian c. 1454-1513
paintings: (H) $178,500

PINX, Franciscus Riedmaier
paintings: (H) $2,600

PINX, Kriege
drawings: (H) $600

PIO, Giacomo del
1652-1726
paintings: (H) $14,950

PIOLA, Domenico
Italian 1627-1703
paintings: (H) $132,000
drawings: (L) $5,175; (H) $5,175

PIOLA, Paolo Girolamo
Italian 1666-1724
drawings: (L) $4,025; (H) $6,900

PIOMANELLI, A.
sculpture: (H) $1,925

PIOSHUMO, H.
Italian 19th/20th cent.
paintings: (H) $660

PIOT, Adolphe Etienne, studio of
French 19th cent.
paintings: (H) $11,500

PIOT, Etienne Adolphe
French 1850-1910
paintings: (L) $1,725; (H) $40,250

PIOTROWSKI, Antoni
Polish 1853-1924
paintings: (H) $2,588

PIPER, Jane
American d. 1992
paintings: (H) $550

PIPER, John
English b. 1903
drawings: (L) $1,760; (H) $7,150

PIPO, Emanuel Ruiz
Spanish b. 1928
paintings: (L) $550; (H) $1,072

PIPO, Manolo Ruiz
Spanish b. 1929
paintings: (L) $977; (H) $9,350

PIPPEL, Otto
German 1878-1960
paintings: (L) $3,450; (H) $17,600

PIQUEMAL, Francois Alphonse
French ac. early 20th cent.
sculpture: (H) $1,610

PIRA, La
Italian 19th cent.
drawings: (L) $3,850; (H) $5,175

PIRANESI, Giovanni Battista
Italian 1720-1778
drawings: (L) $1,045; (H) $76,750

PIRNIE, Larry
American b. 1940
drawings: (H) $550

PIRON, Leo
Belgian 20th cent.
paintings: (H) $1,320

PISA, Alberto
Italian 1864-1936
paintings: (H) $1,725
drawings: (L) $1,540; (H) $3,740

PISANI, Gustavo
Italian b. 1877
paintings: (H) $1,320

PISANI, T.
paintings: (H) $1,610

PISCHINGER, Carl
Austrian 1823-1886
paintings: (H) $1,380

PISI, R.
Italian 19th cent.
paintings: (H) $14,950

PISIS, Filippo de
Italian 1896-1956
paintings: (L) $34,500; (H) $65,750
drawings: (L) $1,840; (H) $3,630

PISSARRO, Camille
French 1830-1903
paintings: (L) $22,000; (H) $6,820,000
drawings: (L) $797; (H) $882,500

PISSARRO, H. Claude
French b. 1935
paintings: (L) $1,380; (H) $15,400
drawings: (L) $1,100; (H) $6,600

PISSARRO, Ludovic Rodo
French 1878-1952
paintings: (H) $1,610

PISSARRO, P.
paintings: (H) $2,640

PISSIS, Amaro
drawings: (L) $2,090; (H) $2,420

PISTOLETTO, Michelangelo
Italian b. 1933
paintings: (H) $49,500
drawings: (L) $16,100; (H) $34,500
sculpture: (L) $1,725; (H) $2,300

PISTORI, G.
Italian 19th cent.
paintings: (H) $1,870

PITATI, Bonifazio de, called Bonifazio
Veronese studio of
16th cent.
paintings: (L) $22,000; (H) $23,100

PITCHER, Henrie
English 19th/20th cent.
paintings: (H) $990

PITT, William
English ac. 1853-1890
paintings: (L) $403; (H) $3,300

PITTARA, Carlo
Italian 1836-1890
paintings: (H) $1,650

PITTMAN, Hobson
American 1898-1972
paintings: (L) $1,760; (H) $6,325
drawings: (L) $198; (H) $1,870

PITTO, Giacomo
Italian b. 1872
paintings: (H) $1,600

PITTONI, Giovanni Battista
Italian 1687-1767
paintings: (L) $23,100; (H) $90,500

PITTS, Elizabeth McCord
American 1880-1963
paintings: (L) $57; (H) $1,035

PITZ, Henry Clarence
American 1895-1976
drawings: (L) $70; (H) $770

PITZNER, Max Joseph
German 1855-1912
paintings: (L) $1,210; (H) $1,320

PIVOT, Louis
French 19th cent.
paintings: (H) $1,980

PIZIZELLI
Italian School
paintings: (H) $770

PLA Y GALLARDO, Cecilio
Spanish b. 1860
paintings: (L) $16,500; (H) $17,600

PLA Y RUBIO, Alberto
Spanish b. 1867
paintings: (L) $3,220; (H) $8,800

PLAC, van der
Belgian 20th cent.
paintings: (H) $1,200

PLADINO, Mimmo
b. 1948
drawings: (H) $3,910

PLANCHER, A.
American 20th cent.
paintings: (H) $990

PLANQUETTE, Felix
French 1873-1964
paintings: (L) $1,380; (H) $1,980

PLANSON, Andre
drawings: (L) $1,320; (H) $2,640

PLANSON, Joseph Alphonse
French b. 1799
paintings: (H) $23,000

PLANT, Stafford
paintings: (H) $550

PLANTE, Daniel
b. 1958
paintings: (H) $2,420

PLANTEY, M.
paintings: (H) $2,090

PLAS, Nicholas van der
Dutch b. 1954
paintings: (L) $440; (H) $3,220

PLASCHKE, Moriz
German 1818-1888
paintings: (H) $2,415

PLASKETT, Joseph Francis
Canadian b. 1918
paintings: (L) $1,925; (H) $6,050

PLASSAN, Antoine Emile
French 1817-1903
paintings: (L) $3,080; (H) $6,038

PLATHNER, Hermann
German 1831-1902
paintings: (H) $4,950

PLATT, Charles Adams
American 1861-1933
paintings: (L) $3,850; (H) $9,200

PLATT, George W.
American 1839-1899
paintings: (L) $460; (H) $6,325

PLATTEEL, Jean
Belgian 1839-1867
paintings: (L) $1,430; (H) $5,750

PLATTENBURG, Matthieu van, called
Monsu Montagna
1608-1660
paintings: (L) $8,250; (H) $12,650

PLATZER, Johann Georg
Austrian 1704-1761
paintings: (H) $239,000

PLAUZEAU, Alfred
French 1875-1918
paintings: (H) $2,530

PLAYER, William H.
British ac. 1858-1884
paintings: (H) $3,300

PLAZA, N.
20th cent.
sculpture: (H) $1,430

PLAZOTTA, Enzo
Italian 1921-1981
sculpture: (L) $575; (H) $4,950

PLE, Henri Honore
French 1853-1922
sculpture: (L) $4,313; (H) $20,900

PLEHN, Alice
German 19th cent.
paintings: (H) $935

PLEISSNER, Ogden M.
American 1905-1983
paintings: (L) $2,415; (H) $41,400
drawings: (L) $264; (H) $29,900

PLIMPTON, William E.
American 20th cent.
paintings: (H) $518

PLISSON, Henri
French b. 1908
paintings: (L) $4,950; (H) $20,900

PLOCK, K.
19th/20th cent.
paintings: (H) $1,210

Sporting Paintings

   Public and private painting collections often have a focus: White Mountains, still lifes, beach scenes, photography, Abstract Expressionism, or a specific sport. There are many sporting museums that include within their specialized collections relevant paintings, drawings, and prints. The International Boxing Hall of Fame in Canastota, New York, the P.G.A. World Golf Hall of Fame in Pinehurst, North Carolina, and the National Bowling Hall of Fame and Museum in St. Louis, Missouri, all have some art. Private collectors may also collect paintings, prints, or sculpture that depict their favorite sport: horse racing, duck hunting, fishing and the like. Ducks Unlimited is an association that raises money to support the conservation of wetlands and migratory waterfowl. Among the most popular items at this group's fund raising auctions is always a print or painting of a duck hunter. Fishing is also a very popular sport. Ogden Minton Pleissner (1905-1983), a Brooklyn-born artist, studied in New York at the Art Students League. He was well-known for his watercolors but also worked in oils. This highly successful artist won many awards during his long career. Much of his time was spent in Wyoming, and he did numerous paintings of grouse shooting, quail hunting, and fishermen. *Landing a Heavy Salmon*, an oil on canvas dated 1931, sold at Mapes Auction Gallery in Vestal, New York, for $37,400. (Ogden M. Pleissner, *Landing a Heavy Salmon*, oil on canvas, 22 x 24 inches, Mapes, March 3, 1995, $37,400)

PLOLL, Victor
German 19th cent.
paintings: (L) $1,430; (H) $2,200

PLUMMER, Elmer G.
American 1910-1987
drawings: (L) $825; (H) $990

PLUMMER, W.H.
American ac. 1872-1876
paintings: (H) $4,675

PLUMMER, William
paintings: (L) $175; (H) $963

PLUMMER, William H.
American ac. 1872-1876
paintings: (L) $374; (H) $4,675

PLUMMER, William Henry
American b. 1839
paintings: (H) $1,100
drawings: (L) $165; (H) $330

PLUMOT, Andre
Belgian 1829-1906
paintings: (L) $2,860; (H) $12,075

PO, Giacomo del
Italian 1652-1726
paintings: (L) $3,300; (H) $35,200

PO-YE-GE
Native American 20th cent.
drawings: (H) $715

POBL, Josef
sculpture: (H) $660

POCCETTI, Bernardino Barbatelli,
called Il
1548-1612
drawings: (H) $8,625

POCOCK, Nicholas
English 1740-1821
drawings: (L) $468; (H) $825

PODCHERNIKOFF, Alexis
b. 1912
paintings: (L) $330; (H) $2,300

PODCHERNIKOFF, Alexis M.
Russian/American 1886-1931
paintings: (L) $522; (H) $7,700

PODOLAK, C.
20th cent.
sculpture: (H) $660

POEL, Egbert Lievensz. van der
Dutch 1621-1664
paintings: (L) $2,750; (H) $22,000

POEL, Theo van der
Belgian b. 1942
paintings: (L) $935; (H) $1,100

POELENBURGH, Cornelis van
Dutch 1586-1667
paintings: (L) $9,900; (H) $17,250

POERTZEL, Professor Otto
German b. 1876
sculpture: (L) $440; (H) $27,600

POGANY, Willy
Hungarian/American 1882-1955
paintings: (L) $920; (H) $1,150
drawings: (L) $28; (H) $990

POGGENBEEK, Goerge Jan Hendrik
Dutch 1852-1903
drawings: (H) $1,725

POGGETTO, Count Stanislas Grimaldi
del
Italian 19th cent.
sculpture: (H) $4,312

POGGIOLI, Marcel Dominique
French b. 1882
paintings: (H) $6,600

POGOLOTTI, Marcelo
Cuban 1902-1988
paintings: (H) $40,250

POGZEBA, Wolfgang
paintings: (H) $1,980

POHL, Adolf Josef
Austrian b. 1872
sculpture: (H) $468

POHL, Edward H.
American 1874-1956
paintings: (L) $374; (H) $1,093
drawings: (H) $467

POHLE, Hermann
German 1831-1901
paintings: (H) $3,738

POILPOT, Theophile and Leon du
PATY
French 19th cent.
paintings: (H) $7,150

POINT, Armand
French 1860/61-1932
paintings: (H) $34,500
drawings: (L) $9,200; (H) $28,750

POIRIER, Anne and Patrick
contemporary
drawings: (L) $687; (H) $4,125

POIRSON, Maurice
French 1850-1882
paintings: (H) $41,400

POISSON
paintings: (L) $660; (H) $2,875

POISSON, Louverture
Haitian 1914-1985
paintings: (L) $805; (H) $5,500

POITEVIN, J.
paintings: (H) $575

POITEVIN, Philippe
French 1831-1907
sculpture: (L) $575; (H) $4,888

POITEVIN, T**
French 19th/20th cent.
paintings: (H) $2,200

POITTEVIN, Eugene Modeste Le
French 1806-1870
paintings: (H) $2,860

POKITONOV, Ivan
Russian 1851-c. 1924
paintings: (L) $6,050; (H) $9,900

POKRASSO, Ron
contemporary
drawings: (H) $550

POL, Arend van de
Dutch 1886-1956
paintings: (H) $1,650

POL, Louis van der
Dutch 1896-1982
paintings: (L) $192; (H) $3,850
drawings: (L) $137; (H) $495

POLAHA, Stephen
1891-1977
sculpture: (L) $3,162; (H) $4,600

POLAR, H.
drawings: (H) $990

POLAR, J.
Dutch School 20th cent.
drawings: (H) $770

POLASEK, Albin
b. Czechoslovakia b. 1897
sculpture: (L) $935; (H) $4,600

POLAZZO, Francesco
Italian 1683-1753
paintings: (H) $6,600

POLDERMAN, W.
paintings: (H) $825

POLEDNE, Franz
Austrian b. 1873
drawings: (H) $1,265

POLELONEMA, Otis, Lomadamocvia,
Springtime
Native American b. 1902
drawings: (L) $2,530; (H) $3,520

POLENOFF, Vassili Dimitrievitch
Russian 1844-1927
paintings: (H) $9,775

POLEO, Hector
Venezuelan b. 1918
paintings: (L) $18,700; (H) $143,000
drawings: (H) $3,450
sculpture: (H) $8,800

POLESELLO, Rogelio
Argentinean b. 1939
paintings: (H) $1,650

POLI, Gherardo
Italian c. 1679-1739
paintings: (H) $16,100

POLI, Giuseppe
Italian 19th cent.
paintings: (H) $1,430

POLIAKOFF, Nicholas
Russian 1899-1976
paintings: (H) $6,900

POLIAKOFF, Serge
French 1900-1969
paintings: (L) $38,500; (H) $74,000
drawings: (L) $10,350; (H) $25,300

POLIDORI, C.
drawings: (H) $1,100

POLIDORI, C.
Italian 19th cent.
drawings: (L) $115; (H) $1,100

POLIDORI, Giancarlo
Italian 20th cent.
drawings: (H) $1,210

POLINI, A.
Italian 19th/20th cent.
paintings: (H) $2,475

POLK, Charles Peale
American 1767-1822
paintings: (H) $34,500

POLKE, Sigmar
German b. 1941
paintings: (L) $17,250; (H) $453,500
drawings: (L) $4,600; (H) $486,500
sculpture: (H) $9,200

POLL, Hugo
Hungarian 1867-1931
paintings: (H) $51,750

POLLAK, August
Austrian b. 1838
paintings: (H) $3,960

POLLENTINE, Alfred
English ac. 1861-1880
paintings: (L) $385; (H) $4,600

POLLET
sculpture: (H) $825

POLLET, Jean
French b. 1929
paintings: (H) $495

POLLET, Joseph Michel Ange
French 1814-1870
sculpture: (L) $4,600; (H) $140,000

POLLET, Victor Florence
French 1811-1882
drawings: (H) $2,860

POLLEY, Frederick
American 1875-1958
paintings: (H) $550

POLLINI, Cesare
c. 1560-c. 1630
drawings: (L) $2,300; (H) $2,640

POLLOCK, Charles
American 20th cent.
paintings: (H) $715

POLLOCK, Jackson
American 1912-1956
paintings: (L) $4,400; (H) $3,080,000
drawings: (L) $18,400; (H) $330,000
sculpture: (H) $9,020

POLO, Roberto
paintings: (H) $17,600

POMEROY, Florence W.
American b. 1899
paintings: (L) $330; (H) $550

POMEROY, Frederick Willam
1856-1924
sculpture: (H) $5,175

POMODORO, Arnaldo
Italian b. 1926
sculpture: (L) $1,650; (H) $90,500

POMODORO, Gio
Italian b. 1930
paintings: (H) $3,450
sculpture: (L) $1,725; (H) $17,600

POMPE, Gerrit
ac. 1687-1691
paintings: (H) $6,670

POMPON, Francois
French 1855-1933
sculpture: (L) $1,380; (H) $32,200

PONCE DE LEON, Fidelio
b. Cuba 1896-1957
paintings: (L) $3,450; (H) $104,500

PONCET, Antoine
Swiss b. 1928
sculpture: (L) $2,645; (H) $10,450

PONCHON, A.
French 19th cent.
paintings: (H) $3,910

PONCHON, Anthony
French/American ac. 1850s
paintings: (H) $690

POND, Charles Dana
American 1880-1962
paintings: (L) $121; (H) $2,185

PONDEL, Friedrich
German b. 1830
paintings: (H) $715

PONS, Fortune
paintings: (H) $525

PONSEN, Tunis
Dutch/American 1891-1968
paintings: (L) $77; (H) $3,105
drawings: (L) $173; (H) $220

PONSIN-ANDARASY, Charles
French 1835-1885
sculpture: (H) $3,850

PONSON, Aime
French 1825-1885
paintings: (H) $5,750

PONSON, Aime
French b. 1850
paintings: (H) $1,100

PONTECORVO, Raimondo
Italian 19th cent.
drawings: (H) $2,420

PONTHIER, E.
paintings: (H) $1,045

PONTOY, Henry Jean
French b. 1888
paintings: (H) $1,540

PONZA, Giovanni
Italian 1894-1989
paintings: (H) $990

POOKE, Marion Louise
American 1883-1975
paintings: (L) $248; (H) $22,000

POOLE, A.
British 20th cent.
paintings: (H) $550

POOLE, Burnell
British 20th cent.
paintings: (H) $3,450

POOLE, Eugene Alonzo
American 1841-1912
paintings: (L) $825; (H) $6,050

POOLE, Gail
American 20th cent.
paintings: (H) $715

POOLE, Horatio N.
American 1884-1949
paintings: (L) $1,045; (H) $3,300

POOLE, Leslie
paintings: (H) $800

POOLE, Paul Falconer
British 1807-1879
paintings: (L) $288; (H) $22,000
drawings: (L) $275; (H) $1,870

POOLE-SMITH, Leslie A.
British 20th cent.
drawings: (H) $518

POONS, Larry
American b. 1937
paintings: (L) $5,500; (H) $121,000
drawings: (L) $1,150; (H) $4,800

POOR, Henry Varnum
American 1888-1970
paintings: (L) $275; (H) $4,675
drawings: (L) $11; (H) $248

POORE, Henry Rankin
American 1859-1940
paintings: (L) $715; (H) $5,175

POORTEN, Hendrik Josef Franciscus
van der
Belgian 1789-1874
paintings: (H) $4,675

POORTER, Willem de
Dutch 1608-1648
paintings: (L) $16,500; (H) $20,700

POPE, Alexander
American 1849-1924
paintings: (L) $1,048; (H) $24,150
drawings: (L) $550; (H) $1,760
sculpture: (L) $1,100; (H) $29,700

POPE, Arthur and George COOK
American 19th/20th cent.
paintings: (H) $8,360

POPE, Frank L.
19th cent.
drawings: (H) $1,265

POPE, Thomas Benjamin
American d. 1891
paintings: (H) $935

POPHAM, M.
British 19th/20th cent.
paintings: (H) $4,025

POPLAVSKI, Ludwig Ludwigovitch
Russian 1852-1885
paintings: (H) $4,600

POPOVA, Liubov
Russian 1889-1924/1929
drawings: (L) $3,738; (H) $16,500

POPOVICH, Milosh
contemporary
paintings: (L) $288; (H) $550

POPPEL, Rudolph
German 1823-1889
paintings: (L) $1,100; (H) $1,210

PORAY, Stanislaus
American 1888-1948
paintings: (L) $330; (H) $1,980

PORCELLIS, Jan
Dutch c. 1584-1632
paintings: (H) $46,000

PORCELLIS, Julius
Dutch 1609-1645
paintings: (H) $11,500

PORCHAZKA, Joseph
b. 1909
paintings: (H) $1,045

PORCHER, Albert
French 1834-1895
drawings: (H) $522

PORISSE, Julien
French b. 1927
paintings: (L) $55; (H) $660

PORPORA, Paolo
Italian 1617-1673
paintings: (L) $20,700; (H) $33,000

PORRET, Jean Jacques
sculpture: (H) $880

PORTAELS, Jean Francois
Belgian 1818-1895
paintings: (L) $2,760; (H) $16,500

PORTAIL, Jacques Andre
French 1695-1759
drawings: (L) $715; (H) $29,700

PORTAL, B.B.
paintings: (H) $575

PORTALIS
sculpture: (H) $1,760

PORTER, Charles Ethen
American 1847-1923
paintings: (L) $632; (H) $3,410

PORTER, Fairfield
American 1907-1975
paintings: (L) $9,625; (H) $83,600
drawings: (L) $198; (H) $29,700

PORTER, John J.
American ac. mid-19th cent.
paintings: (L) $880; (H) $18,700

PORTER, Katherine
American b. 1941
paintings: (L) $660; (H) $6,325
drawings: (L) $173; (H) $2,200

PORTER, Maud
British ac. 1888-1908
paintings: (H) $3,850

PORTER, Rufus
American 1792-1884
paintings: (H) $38,500
drawings: (L) $1,093; (H) $6,900

PORTIELJE, Edward Antoon
Belgian 1861-1949
paintings: (L) $6,270; (H) $9,900

PORTIELJE, Gerard
Belgian 1856-1929
paintings: (L) $1,375; (H) $54,625

PORTIELJE, Jan Frederik Pieter
Belgian 1829-1895
paintings: (L) $3,738; (H) $29,900

PORTIELYE, Edward
Belgian 1861-1949
paintings: (H) $2,860

PORTINARI, Candido
Brazilian 1903-1962
paintings: (L) $8,800; (H) $167,500
drawings: (L) $2,310; (H) $19,550

PORTOCARRERO, Rene
Cuban 1912-1986
paintings: (L) $1,320; (H) $143,000
drawings: (L) $1,150; (H) $32,200

POSCHINGER, Richard von
German 1839-1915
paintings: (H) $2,415

POSE, Eduard Wilhelm
German 1812-1878
paintings: (H) $18,400

POSEN, Leonid Vladimirovich
Russian b. 1849
sculpture: (L) $1,380; (H) $7,150

POSILINO
Italian 19th/20th cent.
drawings: (H) $1,650

POSSART, Felix
German 1837-1928
paintings: (L) $2,860; (H) $3,300

POSSENTI, Antonio
paintings: (H) $920

POSSIN, Rudolph
European b. 1861
paintings: (H) $2,640

POST, Frans
Dutch 1612-1680
paintings: (H) $473,000

POST, Frans Jansz.
Dutch 1608-1669
paintings: (L) $233,500; (H) $3,577,500

POST, George
American b. 1906
paintings: (H) $990
drawings: (L) $330; (H) $1,210

POST, Phinehas
American late 18th cent.
drawings: (H) $3,300

POST, Pieter Jansz
Dutch 1608-1669
paintings: (H) $8,250

POST, William Merritt
American 1856-1935
paintings: (L) $467; (H) $6,820
drawings: (L) $275; (H) $1,870

POSTELLE, Germain
French 19th cent.
paintings: (H) $863

POSTIGLIONE, Luca
Italian 1876-1936
paintings: (L) $275; (H) $19,550

POSTIGLIONE, Salvatore
Italian 1861-1906
paintings: (H) $4,675

POT, Hendrick Gerritsz
Dutch c. 1585-1657
paintings: (H) $495

POTHAST, Bernard
Dutch 1882-1966
paintings: (L) $2,300; (H) $37,375
drawings: (H) $1,980

POTRONAT, L.
paintings: (L) $412; (H) $525

POTT, Laslett John
English 1837-1898
paintings: (L) $2,860; (H) $13,200

POTT, Lester T.
paintings: (H) $495

POTTER, Agnes
b. 1892
paintings: (H) $770

POTTER, Louis McClellan
American 1873-1912
sculpture: (L) $2,100; (H) $2,760

POTTER, M.N.
drawings: (H) $880

POTTER, Philip
American 19th cent.
paintings: (H) $1,870

POTTER, William J.
American 1883-1964
paintings: (L) $454; (H) $550

POTTHAST, Edward Henry
American 1857-1927
paintings: (L) $660; (H) $310,500
drawings: (L) $550; (H) $17,250

POTTS, J.
Continental 19th cent.
paintings: (H) $978

POTTS, William Sherman
American 1867-1927
paintings: (L) $138; (H) $1,650

POTUCEK, Eva
American 20th cent.
paintings: (H) $1,100

POUCETTE
French b. 1935
paintings: (L) $247; (H) $550

POUGET, Marcel
French b. 1923
paintings: (H) $880

POUGHEON, Eugene Robert
French b. 1886
paintings: (H) $2,070
drawings: (L) $2,070; (H) $3,850

POUGIALIS, Constantine
American b. Greece 1894
paintings: (L) $55; (H) $3,220
drawings: (L) $55; (H) $207

POUGNY, Jean
French 1894-1956
paintings: (L) $3,080; (H) $12,650

POULSEN, Charles
American 19th/20th cent.
paintings: (H) $978

POUPELET, Jane
sculpture: (H) $4,125

POURBUS, Frans, the younger
Flemish 1569/70-1622
paintings: (H) $5,750

POURBUS, Pieter Jansz.
Flemish ac. 1549-after 1575
paintings: (H) $79,500

POUSETTE-DART, Richard
American 1916-1992
paintings: (L) $8,250; (H) $49,500
drawings: (L) $1,045; (H) $16,500
sculpture: (H) $2,070

POUSSEAU, *J**J**
18th cent.
drawings: (H) $632

POUSSIN, Louverture
Haitian 20th cent.
paintings: (L) $550; (H) $907

POUTROUX, E.
French 19th cent.
drawings: (H) $1,380

POWELL, Ace
American 1912-1978
paintings: (L) $1,050; (H) $7,500
drawings: (L) $900; (H) $2,100
sculpture: (L) $600; (H) $1,700

POWELL, Arthur James Emery
American 1864-1956
paintings: (L) $27; (H) $3,163

POWELL, Charles Martin
British 1790(?)-1824
paintings: (H) $2,990

POWELL, Lucien Whiting
American 1846-1930
paintings: (L) $1,210; (H) $5,720
drawings: (L) $275; (H) $1,760

POWELL, William E.
British b. 1878
drawings: (L) $460; (H) $1,760

POWELL/SAUNDERS
drawings: (H) $920

POWERS, Asahel
American 1813-1843
paintings: (L) $34,500; (H) $51,750

POWERS, Hiram
American 1805-1873
sculpture: (L) $4,830; (H) $47,150

POWERS, Longworth
American c. 1835-1904
sculpture: (L) $302; (H) $2,200

POWERS, Ralph E.
paintings: (H) $550

POWERS, Richard
drawings: (L) $880; (H) $1,495

POWIS, Paul
paintings: (L) $385; (H) $1,210

POWLES, Lewis Charles
British 20th cent.
paintings: (H) $550

POWS, Anthony Vandyke Copley
Fielding
drawings: (H) $1,650

POYNTER, Sir Edward John
French/English 1836-1919
drawings: (L) $920; (H) $1,320

POZZO, Dal
Italian 19th cent.
paintings: (H) $660

POZZO, G. da
Italian 19th cent.
paintings: (H) $518

PRADES, Alfred F. de
British ac. 1844-1883
paintings: (L) $5,500; (H) $8,800

PRADIER
sculpture: (H) $920

PRADIER, J.
sculpture: (H) $650

PRADIER, Jean Jacques, James
French 1792-1852
paintings: (H) $2,990
drawings: (H) $1,100
sculpture: (L) $460; (H) $13,800

PRADILLA, M.
Spanish 19th cent.
paintings: (H) $3,850

PRADILLA Y ORTIZ, Francisco
Spanish 1848-1921
paintings: (L) $1,870; (H) $23,100

PRAMPOLINI, Enrico
Italian 1894-1956
drawings: (H) $16,500

PRANOLSKI, W.
Polish 19th cent.
paintings: (H) $2,530

PRASAD, Jaggo
drawings: (L) $193; (H) $1,540

PRASSINOS, Mario
Greek 1916-1965
drawings: (H) $550

PRATELLA, Attilio
Italian 1856-1949
paintings: (L) $2,090; (H) $38,500
drawings: (H) $3,520

PRATELLA, Fausto
Italian 1888-1964
paintings: (L) $1,495; (H) $1,650

PRATELLA, Paolo
Italian b. 1892
paintings: (H) $6,600

PRATERE, Edmond Joseph de
Belgian 1826-1888
paintings: (H) $5,500

PRATERE, Edmond Joseph de
Belgian 1826-1888
paintings: (L) $605; (H) $5,225

PRATERE, Henri de
Belgian 1815-1890
paintings: (H) $4,025

PRATS, Ramon
American 20th cent.
paintings: (H) $468

PRATT, Bela Lyon
American 1867-1917
sculpture: (L) $3,163; (H) $17,600

PRATT, Henry Cheever
American 1803-1880
paintings: (L) $863; (H) $12,650

PRATT, Jonathan
British 1835-1911
paintings: (L) $1,210; (H) $5,940

PRATT, William
British b. 1855
paintings: (L) $550; (H) $7,475

PRAX, Valentine
1899-1981
paintings: (L) $1,150; (H) $2,200

PREAULT, Antoine Augustin
French 1809-1879
sculpture: (H) $41,400

PREDEGER, H.
German b. 1886
paintings: (H) $715

PREISS, Johan Philipp Ferdinand, Fritz
German 1882-1943
sculpture: (L) $1,150; (H) $20,700

PREISS & KAESTNER
sculpture: (H) $1,265

PRELL, Walter
French b. 1857
paintings: (L) $4,400; (H) $4,675

PRELLWITZ, Henry
American 1865-1940
paintings: (H) $1,265

PREM, Heimrad
German 1934-1978
paintings: (H) $2,310

PRENDERGAST, Charles
American 1868-1948
paintings: (H) $519,500

PRENDERGAST, Maurice B.
American 1859-1924
paintings: (L) $5,500; (H) $1,432,500
drawings: (L) $690; (H) $836,000

PRENNER, Georg Casper von
1720-66
paintings: (H) $3,450

PRENTICE, Levi Wells
American 1851-1935
paintings: (L) $120; (H) $44,850

PRENTISS, Chuck
American 20th cent.
sculpture: (H) $690

PRESSER, Josef
Russian/American 1907-1967
paintings: (L) $264; (H) $577
drawings: (L) $77; (H) $220

PRESSLER, Gene
American 20th cent.
drawings: (H) $2,415

PRESSMANE, Joseph
1904-1967
paintings: (H) $2,300

PRESTINI, James
American b. 1908
sculpture: (H) $6,900

PRESTON, Alice Bolam
American 1888-1958
paintings: (L) $55; (H) $1,760
drawings: (L) $660; (H) $1,430

PRESTON, Bert
Native American b. 1930
drawings: (H) $468

PRESTON, James M.
American 1874-1962
paintings: (L) $550; (H) $1,035
drawings: (H) $385

PRESTON, May Wilson
American 1873-1949
paintings: (L) $468; (H) $17,250
drawings: (L) $88; (H) $770

Fresh to the Market

The Adirondacks were the birthplace of Levi Wells Prentice (1851-1935), and the forests and lakes of his childhood were the subject matter of his early paintings. The Prentice family moved frequently, from the Adirondacks to Syracuse, then to Buffalo, and finally to the borough of Brooklyn. A Brooklyn directory lists Prentice from 1883 til 1901, when he moved to Philadelphia. Very little else is known about Prentice's training or his artist friends.

After moving to Brooklyn, Prentice began to paint still lifes. His brilliantly colored oils of fruit spilling out of pails, boxes, or baskets are the works for which he is most well-known and command the highest prices. Only recently have Prentice's landscapes begun to sell in the same price range. *Panoramic View of a Lake in Autumn* was fresh to the market when it was consigned to Grogan's. Prentice had given the painting to a Mr. Clarke as repayment of a college loan, and this scenic view had been passed on within the family to the present consignor. When the large panorama realized $40,700, it was an auction record for a landscape by Prentice. (Levi Wells Prentice, *Panoramic View of a Lake in Autumn*, oil on canvas, 30 x 44 inches, Grogan's, March 24, 1993, $40,700)

PRESTON, W.F.
paintings: (H) $900

PRESTOPINO, Gregorio
American 1907-1984
paintings: (L) $1,035; (H) $4,025
drawings: (L) $660; (H) $747

PRETELLA, Fausto
Italian 19th/20th cent.
paintings: (L) $577; (H) $605

PRETI, Mattia, called Il Cavaliere
Calabrese
Italian 1613-1699
paintings: (L) $25,300; (H) $506,500

PREUSSER, Robert
American b. 1919
paintings: (L) $1,100; (H) $8,800

PREVAN, Christiane de
French b. 1876
paintings: (L) $345; (H) $1,840

PREVOST
French 19th cent.
paintings: (H) $935

PREVOST, Jean Louis
c. 1760-1810
drawings: (H) $5,750

PREVOST, Jean Louis, the younger
1760-1810
paintings: (H) $57,500

PREVOT-VALERI, Andre
contemporary
paintings: (H) $2,200

PREVOT-VALERI, Auguste
French 1857-1930
paintings: (L) $1,540; (H) $2,990

PREY, Ruth F.
paintings: (H) $633

PREYER, Emilie
German 1849-1930
paintings: (L) $16,500; (H) $44,000

PREYER, Johann W.
German 1803-1889
paintings: (H) $3,300

PREZIOSI, Amadeo
Italian 1816-1882
drawings: (L) $550; (H) $1,210

PREZZI, Wilma Maria
American 1915-1965?
paintings: (H) $2,200

PRICE, Clayton S.
American 1874-1950
paintings: (L) $3,850; (H) $14,950
drawings: (H) $1,210

PRICE, Edna Pattison
19th cent.
paintings: (H) $2,300

PRICE, Garrett
American 1986-1979
drawings: (L) $110; (H) $2,200

PRICE, Gary
b. 1955
sculpture: (L) $3,190; (H) $3,300

PRICE, George
b. 1901
drawings: (L) $660; (H) $715

PRICE, Janis L.
American b. 1933
paintings: (H) $468

PRICE, Kenneth
American b. 1935
sculpture: (L) $3,163; (H) $12,650

PRICE, Mary Elizabeth
American 1875-1960.
paintings: (L) $440; (H) $3,520
drawings: (H) $403

PRICE, Norman M.
American 1877-1951
drawings: (L) $220; (H) $2,420

PRICE, William Henry
American 1864-1940
paintings: (L) $357; (H) $1,150

PRICERT, Raphael
20th cent.
paintings: (H) $770

PRICHENFRIED, Alois
German 1867-1953
paintings: (H) $1,265

PRICHETT, Edward
British 19th cent.
paintings: (H) $24,200

PRIDA, Fernando Ramos
paintings: (H) $575

PRIEBE, Karl
American 1914-1976
paintings: (L) $546; (H) $546
drawings: (L) $184; (H) $605

PRIECHENFRIED, Alois
German 1867-1953
paintings: (L) $467; (H) $25,300

PRIESTLEY
British (?) 19th cent.
paintings: (H) $747

PRIESTLEY, Edward
British 19th cent.
paintings: (H) $1,320

PRIESTMAN, Bertram Walter
British 1868-1951
paintings: (L) $330; (H) $2,200

PRIEUR, Barthelemy
French d. 1611
sculpture: (H) $43,125

PRIEUR, Georges Etienne
French 19th/20th cent.
paintings: (H) $880

PRIKING, Frantz
German b. 1927
paintings: (L) $3,220; (H) $13,200

PRIMATICCIO, Francesco
French 1504-1570
drawings: (L) $1,760; (H) $112,500

PRINA, Stephen
b. 1954
drawings: (L) $690; (H) $1,380

PRINCE, Luke Rundy, Jr.
American 1815-1851
paintings: (H) $2,013

PRINCE, Richard
American b. 1925
paintings: (H) $6,600
drawings: (L) $4,400; (H) $18,700

PRINCE, Richard Edmund
American b. 1949
paintings: (L) $13,225; (H) $27,500
drawings: (L) $880; (H) $60,500
sculpture: (H) $8,625

PRINCE, William Meade
American 1893-1951
paintings: (L) $1,650; (H) $2,475

PRINET, Rene Francois Xavier
French 1861-1946
paintings: (H) $107,000

PRINGLE, James Fulton
British/American 1788-1847
paintings: (H) $18,700

PRINGLE, William
British ac. 1834-1858
paintings: (H) $9,900

PRINS, Benjamin
Dutch 1860-1934
paintings: (H) $4,950

PRINS, Johannes Huibert
1757-1806
paintings: (H) $9,200
drawings: (H) $4,400

PRINS, Pierre
French 1838-1913
paintings: (H) $4,125

PRINSEP, Lilian
French 19th cent.
paintings: (H) $1,430

PRINSEP, Valentine Cameron
English 1836-1904
paintings: (H) $22,000

PRINZ, A. Emil
American 19th cent.
paintings: (L) $358; (H) $1,650

PRIOR, Scott
American 20th cent.
paintings: (H) $715
drawings: (H) $137

PRIOR, William Matthew
American 1806-1873
paintings: (L) $920; (H) $97,100

PRIOR, William Matthew and
Sturtevant J. HAMBLEN
American 19th cent.
paintings: (H) $825

PRIOU, Louis
French b. 1845
paintings: (L) $5,175; (H) $11,500

PRIOUS, Marie C.
French 19th/20th cent.
paintings: (H) $990

PRITCHARD, Edward
British 1809-1905
paintings: (L) $275; (H) $2,300

PRITCHARD, George Thompson
American 1878-1962
paintings: (L) $220; (H) $3,025
drawings: (L) $137; (H) $550

PRITCHARD, J. Ambrose
American 1858-1905
paintings: (H) $330
drawings: (L) $110; (H) $805

PRITCHETT, Edward
British ac. 1828-1864
paintings: (L) $2,640; (H) $51,750

PRITCHETT, Samuel
English 1827-1907
paintings: (H) $5,775

PRIVAT Auguste Gilbert
French 1892-1970
sculpture: (H) $6,613

PRIVAT-LIVEMONT
Belgian 1861-1936
paintings: (H) $4,180

PROBIAS, W.
American
drawings: (L) $978; (H) $1,610

PROBST, Carl
Austrian 1854-1924
paintings: (L) $308; (H) $880

PROBST, Karl
Austrian 1854-1924
paintings: (L) $1,045; (H) $12,650

PROBST, Thorwald
American 1886-1948?
paintings: (L) $357; (H) $6,600

PROCACCINI, Ercole
1596-1676
drawings: (H) $4,600

PROCACCINI, Giulio Cesare
Italian 1570-1625
paintings: (H) $11,500
drawings: (H) $10,450

PROCHASKA
Czechoslovakian 20th cent.
paintings: (H) $935

PROCHAZKA, Iaro
Czechoslovakian 1886-1945/7
paintings: (H) $1,320

PROCTOR, Alexander P.
American 1862-1950
drawings: (H) $242
sculpture: (L) $650; (H) $50,600

PROCTOR, Burt
American 1901-1980
paintings: (L) $495; (H) $4,313

PROCTOR, R.
19th cent.
paintings: (H) $1,150

PROHASKA, Ray
American 1901-1981
paintings: (L) $440; (H) $935

PROHIAS, Antonio
Cuban/American 20th cent.
drawings: (L) $440; (H) $460

PROL, Rick
20th cent.
paintings: (L) $220; (H) $2,200

PROLSS, Fredrich Anton Otto
German b. 1855
paintings: (H) $2,860

PRONK, Cornelis
Dutch 1691-1759
drawings: (H) $8,050

PROOM, Al
American b. 1933
paintings: (H) $2,750

PROPHET, Nancy Elizabeth
American b. 1890
drawings: (H) $748

PROSALENTIS, Emilios
Greek 1859-1926
paintings: (H) $3,450

PROSCHWITZKY, Frank
British ac. 1883-1889
paintings: (H) $2,750

PROSDOCINI, Alberto
Italian b. 1852
drawings: (L) $183; (H) $2,875

PROSQUOCINI, A.
Italian 19th cent.
drawings: (H) $687

PROSSALENDI, Pavlo
Greek 1857-1894
paintings: (H) $34,500

PROSSNITZ, G.
paintings: (H) $518

PROST, Maurice
French b. 1894
sculpture: (H) $2,588

PROTAIS, Alexander
French 1826-1890
paintings: (H) $3,025

PROTICH, Bata
Yugoslavian b. 1922
paintings: (H) $3,080

PROUDFOOT, William
English 1822-1901
paintings: (L) $330; (H) $825

PROUT, Charles
paintings: (L) $605; (H) $632

PROUT, Samuel
English 1783-1852
paintings: (H) $1,155
drawings: (L) $247; (H) $9,200

PROUTY, Robert V.
American 20th cent.
paintings: (H) $633

PROUVE, Victor Emile
French 1858-1943
drawings: (H) $1,870
sculpture: (H) $483

PROVIS, Alfred
English 19th cent.
paintings: (H) $660

PROVOST, Jan
Dutch 1462/5-1529
paintings: (H) $123,500

PRUBER, A.
German 19th cent.
paintings: (H) $2,875

PRUCHA, Gustave
Austrian b. 1875
paintings: (L) $1,035; (H) $3,960

PRUD'HON, Pierre Paul
French 1758-1823
paintings: (H) $310,500
drawings: (L) $2,200; (H) $13,800

PRUITT-EARLY
b. 1960s
drawings: (L) $863; (H) $1,150

PRUNA, Pedro
Spanish 1904-1977
paintings: (L) $1,650; (H) $17,600
drawings: (L) $825; (H) $1,870

PRY, Lamont Alfred "Old Ironsides"
American 1921-1987
paintings: (L) $690; (H) $1,100

PRYN, Harald Julius Niels
Danish b. 1891
paintings: (H) $1,650

PRYNNE, Edward A.F.
English 1854-1921
paintings: (H) $1,870

PSEUDO-BOLTRAFFIO
early 16th cent.
paintings: (H) $25,300

PSEUDO-HENDRICK
paintings: (H) $9,775

PSEUDO-PIER FRANCESCO FIORENTINO
Italian ac. 1475-1500
paintings: (L) $43,700; (H) $63,800

PSEUDO-SONJE
ac. late 17th cent.
paintings: (H) $11,500

PUDOVKIN, Vsevolod
drawings: (H) $3,738

PUECH, Denys Pierre
French 1854-1942
sculpture: (H) $37,950

PUETT, Garnett
b. 1959
sculpture: (H) $1,265

PUGH, David
b. 1946
paintings: (H) $1,100

PUHL, Louis Francois Gerard van der
Dutch 1750-1824
paintings: (H) $1,980

PUIG, V.
Spanish 19th/20th cent.
paintings: (H) $2,420

PUIG-RODA, Gabriel
Spanish 1865-1919
paintings: (H) $18,700
drawings: (L) $4,887; (H) $14,850

PUIGAUDEAU, Fernand Loyen de
French 1866-1930
drawings: (H) $1,540

PUIGAUDEAU, Fernand du
French 1864/66-1930
paintings: (L) $6,037; (H) $19,550

PUJOL, Paul
French 19th cent.
paintings: (H) $12,100

PUJOL DE GUASTAVINO, Clement
French ac. late 19th cent.
paintings: (L) $24,150; (H) $29,900
drawings: (H) $13,800

PULINCKX, Louis
Belgian b. 1843
paintings: (H) $1,265

PULLER, John Anthony
British 19th cent.
paintings: (L) $2,300; (H) $2,875

PULLICINO, Alberto
Maltese 1719-1765
paintings: (H) $14,950

PULLIN, Edgar
British 20th cent.
paintings: (H) $605

PULLING, F. W.
19th cent.
paintings: (H) $2,420

PULZONE, Scipione, studio of
16th cent.
paintings: (H) $9,200

PUMMILL, Robert
American b. 1936
paintings: (L) $660; (H) $22,000

PUNCHATZ, Don Ivan
b. 1936
paintings: (H) $660

PUNT, Johannes
1711-1779
drawings: (H) $825

PURDOM, M.A.
American 20th cent.
paintings: (H) $1,650

PURNELL, Vernon
American 20th cent.
paintings: (H) $605
drawings: (L) $137; (H) $220

PURVIS, William G.
American 1870-1924
paintings: (L) $550; (H) $605

PURY, Edmond Jean de
Swiss 1845-1911
paintings: (H) $2,750

PURYEAR, Martin
American b. 1941
sculpture: (H) $36,300

PUSHMAN, Hovsep
American 1877-1966
paintings: (L) $1,100; (H) $43,125

PUSINELLI, Doris
Continental 20th cent.
drawings: (L) $1,265; (H) $1,610

PUSKAS, John
American
paintings: (H) $577

PUTHUFF, Hanson
American 1875-1972
paintings: (L) $412; (H) $24,750

PUTMAN, Arthur
American 1873-1930
sculpture: (H) $6,900

PUTMAN, Donald
American b. 1927
paintings: (H) $495

PUTNAM
paintings: (H) $575

PUTNAM, Arthur
American 1873-1930
sculpture: (L) $437; (H) $13,200

PUTNAM, B.
sculpture: (H) $5,750

PUTNAM, Brenda
American 1890-1975
sculpture: (L) $368; (H) $3,450

PUTNAM, Stephen Greely
b. 1852
paintings: (H) $7,763

PUTTI, Massimiliano
Italian 1809-1890
sculpture: (H) $1,650

PUTTNER, Walther
German 1872-1953
paintings: (H) $4,830

PUTZ, Leo
German 1869-1940
paintings: (H) $34,500

PUTZ, Michel Richard
Continental 19th cent.
paintings: (H) $11,500

PUVIS DE CHAVANNES, Pierre
French 1824-1898
paintings: (H) $418,000
drawings: (L) $690; (H) $2,875

PUY, Jean
French b. 1876
paintings: (L) $4,950; (H) $6,050

PUYT, A.
French
sculpture: (H) $1,438

PUYTLINCK, Christoffel
Dutch 1640-after 1670
paintings: (H) $11,000

PYCKE, Francois
Belgian 1890-1922
paintings: (H) $4,400

PYLE, Aaron G.
American
paintings: (H) $2,860

PYLE, Howard
American 1853-1911
paintings: (L) $4,675; (H) $66,000
drawings: (L) $935; (H) $14,300

PYLER, Boyard H.
American 20th cent.
paintings: (H) $770

PYNACKER, Adam
Dutch 1622-1673
paintings: (H) $55,000

PYNAS, Jacob
Dutch c. 1585-1648
paintings: (H) $51,750

PYNE, Ganesh
Indian b. 1937
paintings: (H) $20,700
drawings: (L) $1,725; (H) $20,700

PYNE, James Baker
British 1800-1870
paintings: (L) $495; (H) $4,675

PYNE, Robert Lorraine
American late 19th cent.
paintings: (L) $303; (H) $880

PYNE, Thomas
English 1843-1935
drawings: (L) $165; (H) $770

PYNENBURG, R.
Dutch 19th/20th cent.
paintings: (H) $550

QI BAISHI, Ch'i PAI-SHIH
Chinese 1864-1957
drawings: (H) $43,125

QI LIANGCHI, Ch'i LIANG-CH'IH
Chinese b. 1921
drawings: (L) $690; (H) $1,150

QUA, Lam
paintings: (H) $11,000

QUA, Sun
paintings: (H) $55,000

QUACKENBUSH, Ralph
b. 1933
paintings: (L) $920; (H) $1,265

QUADAL, Martin Ferdinand, known
as CHWATEL
German 1736-1808
paintings: (H) $2,640

QUADRONE, Giovanni Battista
Italian 1844-1898
paintings: (H) $14,300

QUAEDVLIEG, Carel Max Gerlach
Dutch 1823-1874
paintings: (L) $2,530; (H) $34,500

QUAGLIA, Carlo
contemporary
paintings: (L) $3,300; (H) $3,575

QUAGLIO, Franz
German 1844-1920
paintings: (L) $2,200; (H) $4,400

QUAINTANCE, Andrew
paintings: (H) $1,100

QUARENGHI, Giacomo
Italian 1744-1817
drawings: (L) $5,175; (H) $33,000

QUARTARARO, Riccardo
Italian ac. 1485-1501
paintings: (H) $44,000

QUARTERLY, Arthur P.
American 1839-1886
paintings: (H) $660

QUARTLEY, Arthur
American 1839-1886
paintings: (L) $259; (H) $10,780
drawings: (L) $55; (H) $193

QUAST, Pieter
Dutch 1605/06-1647
drawings: (H) $27,500

QUAY, John
19th cent.
paintings: (H) $5,280

QUAYTMAN, Harvey
American b. 1937
paintings: (L) $2,760; (H) $7,475
drawings: (H) $1,725

QUELLINUS, Erasmus, II
Flemish 1607-1678
paintings: (H) $38,500

QUENTEL, Holt
contemporary
paintings: (H) $3,300

QUERENA, Luigi
Italian 1860-1890
paintings: (H) $28,600

QUERFURT, August
German 1696-1761
paintings: (L) $2,200; (H) $23,100

QUESNEL, Francois
French 1543-1619
drawings: (H) $25,300

QUESNEL, Jacques
French d. 1629
drawings: (H) $43,700

QUESTA, Francesco della
Italian 1652-1723
paintings: (H) $7,700

QUEVERDO, Francois Marie Isidore
French 1748-1797
drawings: (H) $935

QUIDOR, John
American 1801-1881
paintings: (H) $398,500

QUIGLEY, Edward B. "Quig"
American 1895-1986
paintings: (L) $935; (H) $8,800
drawings: (H) $110
sculpture: (H) $1,045

QUIGNON, Fernand Just
French b. 1854
paintings: (H) $990

QUILP
paintings: (H) $1,610

QUIMBY, Fred G.
American 1863-1923
paintings: (L) $246; (H) $825

QUINAUX, Joseph
Belgian 1822-1895
paintings: (H) $1,100

QUINCHEY, Othon
French 19th cent.
drawings: (H) $2,300

QUINCY, Edmund
American b. 1903
paintings: (H) $1,045

QUINELL, Cecil
drawings: (H) $605

QUINN, Edmund Thomas
1867-1929
sculpture: (H) $4,025

QUINONES, Lee
b. 1960
paintings: (H) $1,100

QUINQUELA MARTIN, Benito
Argentinean 1890-1977
paintings: (L) $6,600; (H) $25,300

QUINSAC, Paul Francois
French b. 1858
paintings: (L) $24,150; (H) $79,500

QUINTANA, Ben, Ha A Tee
1923-1944
drawings: (H) $690

QUINTANILLA
Spanish 1918-
drawings: (H) $660

QUINTON, Alfred Robert
English 1853-after 1929
drawings: (H) $3,410

QUINTON, Clement
French b. 1851
paintings: (L) $715; (H) $2,530

QUINTON, H.
British 19th cent.
paintings: (H) $4,025

QUINTON, J.
English 19th cent.
paintings: (H) $990

QUIROZ, Cesareo Bernaldo de
b. Argentina 1881-1968
paintings: (L) $17,250; (H) $20,900

QUIROZ, Marco Augusto
paintings: (H) $2,200

QUISPE TITO, Diego
Cuzco School 17th cent.
paintings: (H) $18,700

QUIST, E.
American 20th cent.
paintings: (H) $770

QUITO
late 18th cent.
sculpture: (L) $1,380; (H) $2,070

QUITTON, Edouard
Belgian b. 1842
paintings: (H) $2,300

QUIZET, Alphonse
French 1885-1955
paintings: (L) $920; (H) $6,600
drawings: (H) $575

RAAB, George
American d. 1943
paintings: (H) $690

RAAPHORST, Cornelis
Dutch 1875-1954
paintings: (L) $1,870; (H) $9,680

RAAPHORST, Wilhelmus
Dutch 1870-1963
paintings: (L) $440; (H) $687

RABBIT, Bill
paintings: (L) $330; (H) $632

RABE, Edmund Friederich Theodor
German 1815-1902
paintings: (H) $7,475

RABE, Fredrick
paintings: (H) $5,175

RABEL, Roche
paintings: (H) $9,900

RABENDING, Fritz
German 1862-1929
drawings: (H) $770

RABES, Max
Austrian 1868-1944
paintings: (L) $412; (H) $1,380

RABILLON, Pierre Paul
French b. c. 1773
paintings: (H) $18,400

RABINOWITCH, David
b. 1943
sculpture: (L) $8,800; (H) $18,700

RABUS, Carl
German b. 1898
drawings: (L) $220; (H) $1,100

RABUT, Paul
American 1914-1983
paintings: (H) $1,100
drawings: (H) $605

RABUZIN, Ivan
b. 1919
paintings: (H) $2,640

RACHMIEL, Jean
American b. 1871
paintings: (H) $1,980

RACKHAM, Arthur
English 1867-1939
paintings: (H) $110,000
drawings: (L) $990; (H) $21,850

RACOFF, Ratislaw
Russian b. 1904
paintings: (L) $275; (H) $2,200

RADCLIFF, Paul
19th cent.
paintings: (H) $1,540

RADEMAKER, Abraham
Dutch 1675-1735
paintings: (H) $2,310
drawings: (L) $1,100; (H) $16,100

RADEN, Marinus van
paintings: (H) $1,650

RADOLPH, Daisy
drawings: (H) $742

RADTKE, C.L.
German 19th cent.
paintings: (H) $9,900

RADY, Elsa
contemporary
sculpture: (L) $330; (H) $2,300

RADZIWILL, Franz
1895-1983
drawings: (H) $3,680

RAE, Henriette R.
British 1859-1928
paintings: (H) $46,000

RAE, John
American b. 1882
paintings: (H) $3,300

RAEBURN, Sir Henry
Scottish 1756-1823
paintings: (L) $1,035; (H) $299,500

RAEMDONCK, Georges van
Dutch b. 1888
paintings: (H) $2,530

RAETZ, Markus
b. 1941
drawings: (H) $1,265

RAFFAEL, Joseph
American b. 1933
paintings: (L) $12,650; (H) $34,100
drawings: (L) $690; (H) $1,100

RAFFAELE, Ambrogio
Italian b. 1860
paintings: (H) $1,380

RAFFAELLI, Jean Francois
French 1850-1924
paintings: (L) $2,070; (H) $218,500
drawings: (L) $1,760; (H) $8,250

RAFFALT, Ignaz
Austrian 1800-1857
paintings: (L) $2,750; (H) $14,950

RAFFALT, John Gualbert
Austrian 1836-1865
paintings: (H) $4,950

RAFFEL, Alvin R.
American b. 1905
paintings: (H) $690

RAFFET, Auguste
French 1804-1860
drawings: (H) $660

RAFFY LE PERSAN
French b. 1919
paintings: (L) $1,540; (H) $4,950

RAGGI, Giovanni
Italian 1712-1792/94
paintings: (H) $66,000

RAGGIO, Giuseppe
Italian 1823-1916
paintings: (L) $4,180; (H) $13,800

RAGIONE, Raffaele
Italian 1851-1925
paintings: (L) $12,075; (H) $36,300

RAGON, Adolphe
English d. 1924
drawings: (H) $605

RAGOT, Frederick Emile Jean Baptiste
French b. 1872
paintings: (H) $495

RAGOT, Jules Felix
French ac. 1867-1882
paintings: (L) $660; (H) $2,310

RAGUSA, Giovanni
American 20th cent.
paintings: (L) $825; (H) $1,045

RAHON, Alice
b. France ac. 20th cent.
paintings: (L) $7,000; (H) $42,900

RAHOULT, Charles Diodore
French 1819-1874
paintings: (H) $27,600

RAIMONDI, Aldo
drawings: (H) $2,200

RAIMONDI, R.
Italian 19th cent.
drawings: (H) $660

RAIN, Charles
20th cent.
paintings: (H) $8,050

RAINER, Arnulf
German b. 1929
paintings: (L) $7,150; (H) $7,700
drawings: (L) $5,750; (H) $9,900

RAINEY, Clifford
English b. c. 1950
sculpture: (H) $4,313

RAJON, P.
British 19th cent.
paintings: (H) $825

RAKIA, David
b. 1928
paintings: (H) $2,875

RALEIGH, Charles Sidney
American 1831-1925
paintings: (L) $11,000; (H) $22,000

RALEIGH, Henry P.
American 1880-1945
drawings: (L) $201; (H) $1,430

RALSTON, J.K.
paintings: (H) $550

RAMANIA, C.
Italian 19th cent.
paintings: (H) $4,600

RAMANUJAM, K.G.
Indian 1941-1973
paintings: (H) $2,300
drawings: (L) $805; (H) $1,035

RAMBERT, Rene
French 20th cent.
paintings: (L) $660; (H) $1,650

RAME, E.
European 19th cent.
paintings: (H) $2,970

RAMENGHI, Bartolomeo, called Il
Bagnacavallo
Italian 1484?-1542?
paintings: (H) $18,700

RAMET, J.
French 19th/20th cent.
paintings: (H) $1,650

RAMIREZ IBANEZ, Manuel
Spanish 1856-1925
paintings: (H) $7,700

RAMON, A.A.
American ac. 1930's
paintings: (L) $357; (H) $1,210

RAMONDI, R.
Italian 19th cent.
drawings: (H) $935

RAMOS, Alvaro Delgado
b. 1922
paintings: (H) $2,200

RAMOS, Carlo
20th cent.
paintings: (H) $2,875

RAMOS, Domingo
Cuban 1894-1967
paintings: (L) $2,300; (H) $28,750

RAMOS, L.C.
continental 20th cent.
paintings: (H) $880

RAMOS, Mel
American b. 1935
paintings: (L) $5,500; (H) $96,000
drawings: (L) $1,610; (H) $20,900

RAMOS, Nelson
b. 1932
sculpture: (H) $13,800

RAMOS MARTINEZ, Alfredo
b. Mexico 1872-1946
paintings: (L) $1,725; (H) $71,500
drawings: (L) $1,725; (H) $79,500

RAMPAZO, Luciano
French b. 1936
paintings: (L) $805; (H) $5,775

RAMSAY, Allan
English 1713-1784
paintings: (L) $4,950; (H) $16,500

RAMSDELL, Frederick W.
American 1865-1915
paintings: (L) $165; (H) $825

RAMSEY, Milne
American 1847-1915
paintings: (L) $467; (H) $16,100

RANC, Jean
French 1674-1735
paintings: (L) $14,950; (H) $24,200

RANCOULET, Ernest
French 19th cent.
sculpture: (L) $247; (H) $13,800

RAND, Henry Asbury
American b. 1886
paintings: (L) $495; (H) $880

RAND, J.
American ac. c. 1820
paintings: (H) $633

RANDALL, Alfred
British 19th/20th cent.
drawings: (H) $1,840

RANDALL, Richard
British ac. 1895
drawings: (H) $1,100

RANDALL, Wallace
drawings: (H) $2,420

RANDOLPH, Lee Fritz
American 1880-1956
paintings: (L) $715; (H) $2,475

RANELBA
paintings: (H) $715

RANFT, Richard
Swiss 1862-1931
paintings: (H) $1,650

RANFTL, Johann Mathias
Austrian 1805-1854
paintings: (L) $1,320; (H) $17,250

RANGE, Andreas
German 1762-1828
paintings: (H) $605

RANGER, Henry Ward
American 1858-1916
paintings: (L) $165; (H) $16,100
drawings: (L) $138; (H) $825

RANIERI, L.
Italian 19th c.
drawings: (H) $1,430

RANN, Vollian Burr
American 1897-1956
paintings: (L) $358; (H) $550

RANNEY, William T. and Otto
SOMMER
late 19th cent.
paintings: (H) $35,650

RANNEY, William Tylee
American 1813-1857
paintings: (L) $40,250; (H) $431,500
drawings: (H) $1,955

RANSOM, Caroline L. Ormes.
American 1839-1910
paintings: (H) $1,100

RANSON
drawings: (H) $880

RANUCCI, Lucio
b. 1934
paintings: (H) $1,035

RANZONI, Gustav
Austrian 1826-1900
paintings: (H) $1,320

RAOUX, Jean
French 1677-1734
paintings: (H) $28,750

RAPHAEL, Raffaello SANZIO
Italian 1483-1520
paintings: (H) $1,650,000
drawings: (H) $39,600

RAPHAEL, Anna
American 19th cent.
paintings: (H) $770

RAPHAEL, Joseph
American 1869/72-1950
paintings: (L) $2,070; (H) $76,750
drawings: (L) $575; (H) $863

RAPHAEL, L.
French late 19th cent.
sculpture: (H) $1,210

RAPHAEL, Mary F.
British ac. 1896-1915
paintings: (H) $10,450

RAPHAEL, William
Prussian/Canadian 1833-1914
paintings: (L) $1,320; (H) $2,530

RAPHANEL, X.
sculpture: (L) $715; (H) $1,035

RAPOPORT, Nathan
Polish/American b. 1911
sculpture: (L) $1,610; (H) $2,185

RAPP, ***
paintings: (L) $1,265; (H) $1,980

RASCH, Heinrich
paintings: (L) $3,163; (H) $3,163

RASCH, Heinrich
German 1840-1913
paintings: (L) $2,200; (H) $3,163

RASCHEN, Henry
American 1856/57-1937/38
paintings: (L) $275; (H) $8,250
drawings: (H) $770

RASER, J. Heyl
American 1824-1901
paintings: (L) $3,300; (H) $10,450

RASINELLI, Roberto
Italian 19th cent.
paintings: (L) $1,650; (H) $5,500

RASKIN, Joseph
American 1897-1981
paintings: (L) $330; (H) $4,887

RASKIN, Saul
Russian/American b. 1878
drawings: (L) $159; (H) $690

RASKO, Maxmilian Aurel Reinitz
American/Hungarian 1883-1961
paintings: (H) $1,760

RASMUS, E.
Dutch School 20th cent.
paintings: (H) $770

RASMUSSEN, Georg Anton
Swedish, d. Germ. 1842-1914
paintings: (L) $3,520; (H) $3,565

RASMUSSEN, John
American 1828-1895
paintings: (H) $880

RASPI, Piero
paintings: (H) $605

RASPIS, Francesco
second half 18th cent.
paintings: (H) $11,000

RASSENFOSSE, Andre Louis Armand
Belgian 1862-1934
drawings: (H) $1,610

RATHBONE, John
English 1750-1807
paintings: (H) $5,775

RATHOUD, A.
German 19th cent.
paintings: (H) $550

RATLIFF, Margaret
20th cent.
paintings: (H) $715

RATTERMAN, Walter G.
American 1887-1944
paintings: (L) $175; (H) $1,430
drawings: (L) $77; (H) $121

RATTI, A.
19th cent.
paintings: (H) $3,450

RATTNER, Abraham
American 1895-1978
paintings: (L) $1,540; (H) $9,200
drawings: (L) $137; (H) $660

RAU, Emil
German b. 1858
paintings: (L) $8,250; (H) $16,500

RAU, William
American b. 1874
paintings: (L) $275; (H) $825

RAUCH, Johann Nepomuk
Austrian 1804-1847
paintings: (H) $6,050

RAUDNITZ, Albert
German 1814-1899
paintings: (L) $7,700; (H) $37,375

RAUGHT, John Willard
American 1857-1931
paintings: (L) $120; (H) $1,210

RAUL, Josephine G.
American 20th cent.
paintings: (L) $523; (H) $1,100

RAUMANN, Joseph
Hungarian b. 1908
paintings: (H) $517

RAUPP, Karl
German 1837-1918
paintings: (H) $7,700

RAUSCH
German 19th cent.
paintings: (H) $460

RAUSCHENBERG, Robert
American b. 1925
paintings: (L) $9,350; (H) $7,260,000
drawings: (L) $2,200; (H) $770,000
sculpture: (L) $1,725; (H) $242,000

RAUSCHER, Theo
German b. 1931
paintings: (L) $385; (H) $880

RAUTT, Gab
drawings: (H) $2,420

RAVANNE, Leon Gustave
French 1854-1904
paintings: (H) $2,990

RAVEN, Samuel
British 1775-1847
paintings: (L) $468; (H) $978

RAVENEL, Pamela Vinton
American b. 1888
drawings: (H) $575

RAVENSWAAY, Adriana van
Dutch 1816-1872
paintings: (H) $5,390

RAVESON, Sherman H.
American 1905-1974
paintings: (H) $660

RAVESTEYN, Jan Anthonisz. van
Dutch c. 1570-1657
paintings: (L) $2,200; (H) $170,500

RAVIER, Francois Auguste
French 1814-1895
paintings: (L) $550; (H) $1,870

RAVINOV, P.
Russian 19th/20th cent.
paintings: (H) $1,150

RAWSON, Carl W.
American 1884-1970
paintings: (L) $275; (H) $990

RAY, Man
American 1890-1976
paintings: (L) $3,680; (H) $839,787
drawings: (L) $547; (H) $115,778
sculpture: (L) $1,650; (H) $75,652

RAYMOND, Alex
American 1909-1956
drawings: (L) $275; (H) $4,675

RAYMOND, H***
19th cent.
paintings: (H) $2,990

RAYMONDS, E***
Continental 19th cent.
paintings: (H) $2,530

RAYNAUD, Auguste
French b. 1845
paintings: (H) $7,480

RAYNER, Louise
British 1832-1924
drawings: (L) $1,705; (H) $2,420

RAYNES, Sidney
American b. 1907
paintings: (L) $253; (H) $525

RAYNOLT, Antoine Marie
French b. 1874
paintings: (L) $2,300; (H) $3,162

RAYO, Omar
South American 20th cent.
paintings: (H) $3,300

RAYSSE, Martial
b. 1936
drawings: (L) $7,820; (H) $9,775
sculpture: (H) $4,600

RAZA, Syed Haider
Indian b. 1922
paintings: (L) $4,025; (H) $18,400
drawings: (L) $1,380; (H) $11,500

RE, Giovanni del
Italian 1829-1915
paintings: (H) $2,090

REA, Louis Edward
paintings: (H) $1,100

READ, Catherine
British 1723-1778
paintings: (H) $7,820

READ, Thomas Buchanan
American 1822-1872
paintings: (L) $357; (H) $9,350

READY, Leonard H.
American 1899-1956
drawings: (H) $633

READY, William James Durant
British 1823-1873
paintings: (H) $3,850

REALFONSO, Tommaso, called
Masillo
Italian 18th cent.
paintings: (L) $19,800; (H) $27,500

REAM, Carducius Plantagenet
American 1837-1917
paintings: (L) $440; (H) $7,150

REAM, Ethel
American 20th cent.
paintings: (H) $460

REAM, Morston C.
American 1840-1898
paintings: (L) $935; (H) $16,500

REASER, Wilbur Aaron
American 1860-1942
paintings: (H) $4,950
drawings: (H) $3,450

REBAY, Hilla
American 1890-1967
paintings: (L) $1,725; (H) $7,150
drawings: (L) $770; (H) $3,738

REBEK, Tom
drawings: (L) $247; (H) $660

REBELL, Joseph
Austrian 1787-1828
paintings: (H) $770

REBER, John
1857-1938
sculpture: (L) $4,830; (H) $6,325

REBEYROLLE, Paul
French b. 1926
paintings: (H) $25,300

REBOUR, F.
drawings: (H) $660

REBRY, Gaston
Canadian b. 1933
paintings: (L) $2,090; (H) $3,520

REBULL, Santiago
b. Mexico 1829 d. 1902
paintings: (H) $7,700

RECCHIA, Richard H.
American b. 1885
drawings: (H) $46
sculpture: (L) $137; (H) $9,350

RECCHIAN, Russell
American b. 1959
paintings: (H) $715

RECCO, Giuseppe
Italian 1634-1695
paintings: (H) $13,200

RECHEL, Carl
German 19th cent.
paintings: (H) $935

RECHNITZ, H.
Austrian 19th/20th cent.
paintings: (H) $1,150

RECIPON, Georges
French b. 1860
sculpture: (L) $770; (H) $990

RECKELBUS, Louis
Belgian 1864-1958
drawings: (H) $770

RECKLESS, Stanley L.
American b. 1892
paintings: (H) $41,250

RECKNAGEL, Otto
German 1845-1926
paintings: (H) $1,540

RED STAR, Kevin
Native American b. 1943
paintings: (L) $220; (H) $2,860
drawings: (H) $495

REDDIE, MacIver
paintings: (L) $330; (H) $880

REDELIUS, F.H.
American 20th cent.
paintings: (L) $495; (H) $1,155

REDER, Bernard
Romanian/American 1897-1963
drawings: (H) $13,800
sculpture: (H) $1,495

REDER-BROILI, Franz
German 1854-1918
paintings: (H) $1,100

REDERER, Franz
German 20th cent.
paintings: (H) $1,320

REDFIELD, Edward W.
American 1869-1965
paintings: (L) $2,700; (H) $107,000

REDIG, Laurent Herman
Belgian 1822-1861
paintings: (H) $18,700

REDIN, Carl
American, b. Switz 1892-1944
paintings: (L) $330; (H) $3,025

REDMOND, Granville
American 1871-1935
paintings: (L) $1,100; (H) $77,000
drawings: (H) $2,200

REDMORE, Edward King
English 1860-1941
paintings: (L) $385; (H) $1,650

REDMORE, Henry
English 1820-1887
paintings: (L) $3,850; (H) $18,400

REDON, Georges
French 1869-1943
drawings: (H) $1,430

REDON, Odilon
French 1840-1916
paintings: (L) $17,600; (H) $605,000
drawings: (L) $7,475; (H) $332,500

REDOUTE, Pierre Joseph
French 1759-1840
drawings: (L) $9,200; (H) $28,750

REDWINE
American contemporary
paintings: (H) $605

REECE, Maynard
paintings: (H) $880

REED, B.
British 19th/20th cent.
paintings: (H) $990

REED, D.C.
British 19th cent.
paintings: (H) $3,025

REED, David
American b. 1946
paintings: (L) $1,840; (H) $16,500

REED, F., Jr.
early 19th cent.
drawings: (H) $1,840

REED, Joseph Chacler
English 1822-1877
drawings: (H) $495

REED, Marjorie
American b. 1915
paintings: (L) $161; (H) $2,750

REED, T. Buchanon
American 19th cent.
paintings: (H) $800

REED, William Elford
British 19th cent.
paintings: (L) $575; (H) $688

REEDY, Leonard Howard
American 1899-1956
paintings: (H) $2,185
drawings: (L) $121; (H) $1,870

Pennsylvania Impressionist

Initially Impressionism in the United States was centered in New York and Boston, but there were regional "schools" of Impressionism in Pennsylvania, Indiana, California, and Connecticut. The major school of Impressionism in Pennsylvania flourished in the area around New Hope. The leader was Edward Willis Redfield (1869-1965) who had studied at the Pennsylvania Academy with Robert Henri and Hugh Breckenbridge. As a student in Paris Redfield had studied the works of Monet, Pissarro, and Frits Thaulow, the leading Norwegian Impressionist. After traveling abroad, Redfield settled in 1892 in Center Bridge, Pennsylvania. Daniel Garber, Walter Schofield, and Robert Spencer were other artists associated with the Pennsylvania Impressionists. Redfield painted numerous landscapes and specialized in snow scenes. When *Sleigh Heading for the Mill* was consigned to Alderfer's Auction Company in Hatfield, Pennsylvania, the original bill of sale was included. The painting was purchased for $1,200; its auction price in 1995 was $60,000. Alderfer's is one of the few remaining auction houses that does not charge a buyer's premium. (Edward W. Redfield, *Sleigh Heading for the Mill*, oil on canvas, 20 x 24 inches, Alderfer's, September 20, 1995, $60,000)

REEP, Edward
American b. 1918
drawings: (L) $605; (H) $715

REEVES, Richard Stone
American 20th cent.
paintings: (L) $3,575; (H) $8,800

REEVES, Walter
British 19th cent.
paintings: (H) $1,210

REGAGNON, Albert
paintings: (L) $440; (H) $3,300

REGAMEY, Frederic
French 1849-1925
paintings: (H) $10,925

REGGIANINI, Vittorio
Italian 1858-1924
paintings: (L) $2,475; (H) $118,000

REGIS, Pajou
sculpture: (H) $3,575

REGNARD, Jean
French 20th cent.
paintings: (H) $1,320

REGNAULT, Henri Alexandre Georges
French 1843-1871
paintings: (L) $660; (H) $3,220

REGNIER, Leopold
French 1897-1981
paintings: (H) $3,162

REGNIER, Nicolas, called Nicolo
RENIERI
Flemish 1591-1667
paintings: (L) $10,350; (H) $187,000

REGO MONTEIRO, Vicente do
b. Mexico 1872 d. 1946
drawings: (H) $18,400

REHBERGER, Gustave
b. 1910
paintings: (H) $2,990

REHDER, Julius Christian
German/American 1861-1955/66?
paintings: (L) $55; (H) $605
drawings: (L) $66; (H) $193

REHER, Emil Kuhlmann
German b. 1886
paintings: (H) $605

REHN, Frank K.M.
American 1848-1914
paintings: (L) $110; (H) $3,850
drawings: (H) $165

REHPENI, J.D.
American
sculpture: (H) $4,025

REICH
German 19th/20th cent.
paintings: (H) $3,080

REICH, Albert
German b. 1881
paintings: (L) $605; (H) $748

REICHARDT, Ferdinand
Austrian 1819-1895
paintings: (H) $15,400

REICHEL, C.
paintings: (H) $605

REICHEL, Hans
1892-1958
paintings: (H) $8,050
drawings: (L) $1,840; (H) $10,350

REICHELT, Augusta Wilhemine
German 1840-1907
paintings: (H) $3,850

REICHERT, Carl
Austrian 1836-1918
paintings: (L) $3,630; (H) $20,700

REICHMANN, George Friedrich
German 1798-1853
paintings: (H) $1,320

REICHMANN, Josephine Lemos
American 1864-1939
paintings: (H) $605

REID, Archibald David
British 1844-1908
paintings: (L) $55; (H) $863

REID, George Agnew
Canadian 1860-1947
paintings: (L) $990; (H) $3,025

REID, George Ogilvy
Scottish 1851-1918
paintings: (H) $8,250

REID, Jack
b. 1928
drawings: (L) $440; (H) $578

REID, John Robertson
British 1851-1926
paintings: (L) $115; (H) $660

REID, Patty
American
paintings: (H) $800
drawings: (L) $800; (H) $850

REID, Robert
American 1862-1929
paintings: (L) $1,540; (H) $44,000
drawings: (L) $302; (H) $28,750

REID, Robert O.
American
paintings: (H) $2,300
drawings: (L) $275; (H) $385

REID, Robert Payton
British b. 1859
paintings: (H) $19,800

REID, Tom
American 19th/20th cent.
paintings: (H) $660

REIDER, Marcel
French b. 1852
paintings: (H) $2,310

REIFFEL, Charles
American 1862-1942
paintings: (L) $550; (H) $19,550
drawings: (L) $1,650; (H) $2,875

REILLY, Frank
1906-1967
paintings: (H) $495
drawings: (H) $440

REIN, Eimerich Johan
Norwegian 1827-1900
paintings: (H) $2,860

REINAGLE, Philip
English 1749-1833
paintings: (L) $23,100; (H) $34,500

REINAGLE, Ramsay R.
British 18th/19th cent.
paintings: (H) $2,750

REINDEL, Edna
American 1900-1990
paintings: (L) $110; (H) $9,200
drawings: (L) $22; (H) $165
sculpture: (H) $220

REINES, Ira Bruce
contemporary
sculpture: (L) $316; (H) $460

REINHARDT
paintings: (H) $660

REINHARDT, Ad
American 1913-1967
paintings: (L) $23,000; (H) $495,000
drawings: (L) $24,150; (H) $55,200

REINHARDT, Louis
German d. 1870
paintings: (L) $605; (H) $4,600

REINHARDT, Siegfried
German/American 1925-1984
paintings: (L) $165; (H) $2,970
drawings: (L) $58; (H) $863

REINHART, Benjamin Franklin
American 1829-1885
paintings: (L) $715; (H) $1,100

REINHERZ, Conrad
German 1835-1892
paintings: (L) $4,025; (H) $5,750

REINHOLD, Bernhard ·
German 1824-1892
paintings: (H) $5,175

REINHOLD, F.
Austrian 19th cent.
paintings: (H) $605

REINIKE, Charles H.
American 1906-1983
paintings: (H) $2,200
drawings: (L) $110; (H) $825

REINMUTH, Kim
drawings: (L) $500; (H) $800

REINPRECHT, T.K.
Austrian 20th cent.
paintings: (L) $467; (H) $633

REISENBERG, Sidney
paintings: (H) $2,200

REISMAN, Philip
American b. 1904
paintings: (L) $1,495; (H) $3,220
drawings: (L) $302; (H) $1,760

REISNER, H.
19th cent.
paintings: (H) $715

REISNER, Martin Andreas
American 1798-1862
paintings: (H) $13,800

REISS, F.
German 19th cent.
paintings: (H) $550

REISS, Fritz Winold
German/American 1886-1953
drawings: (H) $1,380

REISTRUP, K. Hansen
Danish 19th/20th cent.
paintings: (H) $467

REITER, Carl
German ac. c. 1920-1940
sculpture: (H) $495

REITER, Johann Baptist
Austrian 1813-1890
paintings: (H) $7,187

REITZEL, Marquese
American 1896-1963
paintings: (L) $1,320; (H) $3,450

RELINGER, Jos.
paintings: (H) $1,200

RELLI, Conrad Marca
contemporary
sculpture: (H) $6,050

RELYEA, Charles M.
American b. 1863
paintings: (L) $138; (H) $770
drawings: (H) $275

REMBRANDT
Dutch 1606-1669
drawings: (H) $332,500

REMBRANDT, studio of
17th cent.
paintings: (H) $33,350

REMDE, Friedrich
German 1801-1878
paintings: (H) $1,210

REMENICK, Seymour
American b. 1923
paintings: (L) $176; (H) $1,155
drawings: (L) $38; (H) $192

REMFREY, David
contemporary
drawings: (H) $825

REMICK, Christian
b. 1726
drawings: (L) $3,680; (H) $3,680

REMIN
American
paintings: (H) $1,430

REMINGTON, Frederic Sackrider
American 1861-1909
paintings: (L) $37,400; (H) $992,500
drawings: (L) $1,430; (H) $82,500
sculpture: (L) $2,200; (H) $1,982,500

REMINGTON, S.J.
American 19th cent,
paintings: (H) $1,045

REMISOFF, Nicolai
Russian/American b. 1887
paintings: (L) $1,100; (H) $3,025
drawings: (L) $880; (H) $1,650

REMMEY, Paul
American 20th cent.
drawings: (H) $748

REMNICK, Seymour
American b. 1923
paintings: (H) $660

REMY, Jean
French b. 1893
paintings: (L) $316; (H) $920

REN, Chuck
American b. 1941
paintings: (L) $3,410; (H) $15,000

RENARD, Charles
French 19th cent.
paintings: (L) $288; (H) $805

RENARD, Emile
French 1850-1930
paintings: (H) $63,000

RENARD, Fernand
French? contemporary
paintings: (H) $1,870

RENARD, Marcel
sculpture: (H) $2,200

RENARD, Paul
French 1871-1920
paintings: (L) $495; (H) $3,520
drawings: (L) $1,100; (H) $2,475

RENARD, Pierre
French 1870-1914?
drawings: (H) $1,320

RENARD, Stephen J.
British 20th cent.
paintings: (H) $17,250

RENAUD, H.
French 19th cent.
paintings: (H) $495

RENAUDIN, Alfred
French b. 1866
paintings: (L) $5,500; (H) $8,250

RENAULT, Charles
French 1829-1905
paintings: (L) $660; (H) $825

RENAULT, L.
paintings: (H) $6,270

RENAULT, Lex de
French 19th/20th cent.
paintings: (H) $880

RENAULT, Luigi
Italian ac. 1850-1880
paintings: (L) $440; (H) $8,800

RENAULT, R.
paintings: (H) $9,900

RENDON, Manuel
Ecuadorian 1894-1980
paintings: (L) $12,650; (H) $18,400
drawings: (L) $605; (H) $4,600

RENE
paintings: (H) $66
sculpture: (H) $4,255

RENE
Austrian b. 1925
paintings: (H) $550

RENE, J. Emile
French 19th/20th cent.
paintings: (H) $1,980

RENESON, Chet
drawings: (L) $1,650; (H) $3,410

RENESSE, Constantijn Daniel van
1626-1680
drawings: (H) $3,738

RENGIFO, William
Peruvian b. 1958
paintings: (L) $173; (H) $495

RENI, Guido
Italian 1575-1642
paintings: (L) $220; (H) $618,500
drawings: (L) $7,150; (H) $19,550

RENNER, Adelaine
American 1869-1961
paintings: (L) $1,760; (H) $1,980

RENNER, Paul Friedrich August
German b. 1878
paintings: (H) $1,870

RENO, Jim
American b. 1929
paintings: (H) $5,500
sculpture: (L) $495; (H) $3,960

RENOIR, Pierre Auguste
French 1841-1919
paintings: (L) $11,000; (H) $18,150,000
drawings: (L) $6,050; (H) $990,000
sculpture: (L) $17,600; (H) $33,350

RENOIR, Pierre Auguste and Louis
MOREL
French 19th/20th cent.
sculpture: (H) $2,588

RENOIR, Pierre Auguste and Richard
GUINO
sculpture: (L) $11,500; (H) $55,000

RENOUARD, George
American 1885-1954
paintings: (L) $55; (H) $1,210

RENOUF, Edda
Mexican/American b. 1943
drawings: (H) $1,725

RENOUF, Emil
French 1845-1894
paintings: (H) $550

RENOUX, Andre
French b. 1939
paintings: (L) $345; (H) $2,990

RENTZELL, August von
German 1810-1891
paintings: (H) $1,650

REPIN, Ilya
Russian 1844-1930
paintings: (L) $10,350; (H) $39,100
drawings: (L) $825; (H) $1,650

RESCH, Walter Sebastian
German b. 1889
sculpture: (H) $1,495

RESCHI, Pandolfo
Polish 1634/43-1699
paintings: (L) $4,370; (H) $44,000

RESIO, R.
drawings: (L) $467; (H) $550

RESIO, Raffaele
Italian 19th cent.
paintings: (H) $1,650

RESNICK, Milton
American b. 1917
paintings: (L) $748; (H) $74,000
drawings: (H) $5,175

RESNIKOFF, I.
contemporary
paintings: (H) $6,600

RETER, V.
19th cent.
sculpture: (H) $825

RETH, Alfred
1884-1966
paintings: (L) $1,320; (H) $8,050

RETHEL, Alfred
German 1816-1859
paintings: (H) $2,530

RETTEGI, S.W.
European 20th cent.
paintings: (H) $4,730

RETTIG, Heinrich
German 1859-1921
paintings: (L) $3,300; (H) $5,750

RETTIG, John
American 1860-1932
paintings: (H) $1,495
drawings: (L) $193; (H) $1,100

RETZLAFF, E.C.W.
German 1898-1976
paintings: (H) $1,265

REULANDT, Le Grand de
Dutch ac. 1860
paintings: (H) $20,700

REUSSWIG, William
1902-1978
paintings: (L) $488; (H) $1,870
drawings: (L) $2,200; (H) $2,200

REUTER, Helmut
German b. 1913
paintings: (H) $460

REUTERDAHL, Henry
American 1871-1925
drawings: (L) $385; (H) $2,760

REUTLINGEN, Paul Wilhelm Keller
German 1854-1920
paintings: (H) $8,800

REVERCHON, Victor Bachereau
French b. 1842
paintings: (H) $715

REVERE, P.
paintings: (H) $862

REVERON, Armando
Venezuelan 1889/90-1954
paintings: (L) $35,200; (H) $165,000
drawings: (L) $13,800; (H) $77,000

REVESZ, Imre Emerich
Hungarian b. 1859
paintings: (H) $8,625

REVILLE, H. Whittaker
British ac. 1881-1903
paintings: (H) $9,200

REVIOLA, Maki
American 19th/20th cent.
paintings: (H) $2,185

REVOLG
drawings: (H) $1,100

REWICH, J.
18th/19th cent.
paintings: (H) $550

REYES, Jesus
Mexican 1882-1977
paintings: (L) $990; (H) $1,725
drawings: (H) $3,105

REYHER, Max
American 1862-1945
paintings: (H) $3,300

REYN, A.T.
paintings: (H) $990

REYNA, Antonio
Spanish 1859-1937
paintings: (L) $2,090; (H) $35,200
drawings: (L) $805; (H) $11,500

REYNAUD, F.
French 19th cent.
paintings: (L) $660; (H) $1,320

REYNOLDS, Alan
b. 1926
paintings: (H) $5,462

REYNOLDS, Charles H.
American 19th/20th cent.
paintings: (L) $220; (H) $1,870
drawings: (L) $1,540; (H) $2,475

REYNOLDS, D.K.
paintings: (L) $165; (H) $1,870

REYNOLDS, Frederick Thomas
American b. 1882
paintings: (H) $990

REYNOLDS, J.F.
American 19th/20th cent.
paintings: (L) $275; (H) $660

REYNOLDS, James E.
American b. 1926
paintings: (L) $440; (H) $27,500

REYNOLDS, Sir Joshua
English 1723-1792
paintings: (L) $7,188; (H) $772,500

REYNOLDS, Sir Joshua, and studio
1723-1792
paintings: (L) $3,740; (H) $6,900

REYNOLDS, W.S.
19th/20th cent.
paintings: (L) $4,125; (H) $5,462

REYNOLDS, Wade
contemporary
paintings: (L) $495; (H) $3,300

REYNOLDS, Wellington Jarrard
American b. 1869
paintings: (L) $412; (H) $1,035

REYNTJENS, Henrich Engelbert
Dutch 1817-1859
paintings: (L) $1,650; (H) $5,500

REZA, Jorge de la
Bolivian 20th cent.
paintings: (H) $1,265

REZIA, Felice A.
ac. 1866-1902
paintings: (L) $650; (H) $2,035

RHEAD, George Wooliscroft
British 1835-1920
paintings: (H) $57,500

RHEAD, Louis John
American 1857-1926
drawings: (H) $2,640

RHEAM, Henry Meynell
English 1859-1920/21
drawings: (H) $4,887

RHEES, Morgan
American 19th/20th cent.
paintings: (H) $715

RHIND, John Massey
Scottish/American 1860-1936
sculpture: (H) $6,900

RHINEHART, M. Charles
American contemporary
paintings: (L) $247; (H) $495

RHOADS, C.V.
paintings: (H) $4,500

RHODES, Charles Ward
d. 1905
paintings: (H) $1,210

RHODES, George F.
American/British 19th cent.
paintings: (H) $3,162

RHODES, John
English 1809-1842
paintings: (H) $2,530

RHOMBERG, Hanno
German 1820-1869
paintings: (L) $6,600; (H) $44,000

RHYS, Oliver
German ac. 1876, d. 1893
paintings: (L) $1,495; (H) $13,200

RIBA, Paul
American b. 1912
paintings: (L) $467; (H) $660
drawings: (H) $55

RIBA-ROVIRA, Francois
paintings: (L) $1,320; (H) $3,575

RIBAK, Louis
American 1902/03-1980
paintings: (L) $302; (H) $5,500

RIBARD, Jules
Continental 19th cent.
paintings: (H) $3,080

RIBAUD, Francois
French 19th cent.
paintings: (H) $1,610

RIBBS, Keke
contemporary
sculpture: (H) $4,370

RIBERA, Jusepe de, called Lo
Spagnoletto
Spanish c. 1588-1656
paintings: (H) $77,000
drawings: (H) $99,000

RIBERA, Jusepe de, called Lo
Spagnoletto studio of
Spanish 17th cent.
paintings: (L) $4,025; (H) $13,800

RIBERA, Pierre
French 1867-1932
paintings: (L) $4,370; (H) $37,375

RIBERA CIRERA, Roman
Spanish 1848-1935
paintings: (H) $31,625

RIBLOWSKY, D.
19th/20th cent.
paintings: (H) $467

RIBO-ROVIRA, Francisco
paintings: (H) $1,760

RIBOT, Germain Theodore
French 1823-1893
paintings: (L) $2,200; (H) $35,750

RIBOT, Theodule Augustin
French 1823-1891
paintings: (L) $748; (H) $110,000

RICA Y ORTEGA, Martin
Spanish 1833-1908
paintings: (H) $22,000

RICARD, Louis Gustave
French 1823-1873
paintings: (H) $1,100

RICARDI
Italian 19th cent.
paintings: (H) $1,045

RICARDI, Ernesto
Italian 19th cent.
paintings: (H) $6,900

RICARDI, G.
Italian 19th cent.
paintings: (H) $2,860

RICCA, Ignazio
Italian
paintings: (L) $825; (H) $2,310

RICCARDI, Caesar
American b. 1892
paintings: (L) $247; (H) $605

RICCARDI, L.
Italian 19th/20th cent.
paintings: (H) $5,500

RICCHI, Pietro, called Il LUCCHESE
1605/6-1675
paintings: (H) $13,200

RICCHIARDI, Giovanni
d. 1820
paintings: (H) $5,500

RICCI, A.
Italian 19th/20th cent.
paintings: (H) $1,150

RICCI, Alfredo
Italian 1864-1889
drawings: (L) $110; (H) $990

RICCI, Arturo
Italian b. 1854
paintings: (L) $368; (H) $35,650

RICCI, Dante
Italian 1879-1957
paintings: (H) $920
drawings: (L) $467; (H) $770

RICCI, F.
Italian 19th cent.
paintings: (H) $1,100

RICCI, Giovanni, called Giampedrini
Italian ac. c. 1520-1540
paintings: (L) $22,000; (H) $134,500

RICCI, Marco
Italian 1676-1729
paintings: (L) $29,700; (H) $52,900
drawings: (L) $8,800; (H) $46,000

RICCI, Pio
Italian d. 1919
paintings: (L) $2,990; (H) $19,000

RICCI, Sebastiano
Italian 1659-1734
paintings: (L) $18,700; (H) $200,500

RICCI, Sebastiano, studio of
Italian 17th/18th cent.
paintings: (H) $43,700

RICCI, T.S.
Italian early 20th cent.
paintings: (H) $522

RICCIARDE, Oscar
paintings: (H) $3,300

RICCIARDELLI, Gabriele
Italian ac. 1745-1777
paintings: (L) $26,400; (H) $86,100

RICCIARDI, Caesare
Italian/American b. 1892
paintings: (L) $10; (H) $880
drawings: (L) $132; (H) $253

RICCIARDI, Oscar
Italian 1864-1935
paintings: (L) $412; (H) $4,950
drawings: (H) $2,200

RICCIO, Andrea, workshop
Paduan early 16th cent.
sculpture: (L) $5,750; (H) $46,000

RICCIO, L.F.
Italian 19th cent.
paintings: (H) $1,650

RICCO, Wassmer
Swiss b. 1915
paintings: (L) $1,210; (H) $1,320

RICE, Anne Estelle
American b. 1879
paintings: (H) $4,125

RICE, G.S.
paintings: (H) $2,750

RICE, Jessica
20th cent.
paintings: (H) $5,462

RICE, William M.
1854-1922
paintings: (H) $1,955

RICE, William Seltzer
American 1873-1963
drawings: (L) $605; (H) $715

RICE-PEREIRA, Irene
American 1907-1971
drawings: (H) $1,150

RICH, John Hubbard
American 1876-1955?
paintings: (L) $495; (H) $6,050

RICHARD, Alexander Louis Marie
Theodore
French 1782-1859
paintings: (H) $460

RICHARD, Edna Vergon
American 1890-1985
paintings: (L) $1,540; (H) $2,090

RICHARD, Jacob
paintings: (H) $1,900

RICHARD, John H.
German/American b. c. 1807
paintings: (H) $1,760

RICHARD, P.
French 19th cent.
paintings: (H) $4,950

RICHARD, Rene Jean
Swiss/Canadian 1895-1982
paintings: (L) $165; (H) $4,950

RICHARD, Will
American 20th cent.
paintings: (L) $1,100; (H) $1,320

RICHARDS, A.M.
American 19th cent.
paintings: (H) $770

RICHARDS, Addison T.
paintings: (H) $3,220

RICHARDS, Ceri
British b. 1903
drawings: (H) $880

RICHARDS, Charles
American 1906-1992
paintings: (L) $22; (H) $1,760
drawings: (L) $125; (H) $130

RICHARDS, Frederick de Bourg
American 1822-1903
paintings: (L) $875; (H) $2,750

RICHARDS, Harriet Roosevelt
American d. 1932
paintings: (H) $1,705
drawings: (L) $302; (H) $440

RICHARDS, L.
British b. 1878
paintings: (H) $4,600

RICHARDS, Thomas Addison
Anglo/American 1820-1900
paintings: (L) $770; (H) $17,600
drawings: (H) $385

RICHARDS, W**
English 19th/20th cent.
paintings: (H) $550

RICHARDS, W.
English 19th cent.
paintings: (L) $137; (H) $863

RICHARDS, William Trost
American 1833-1905
paintings: (L) $863; (H) $93,500
drawings: (L) $375; (H) $32,200

RICHARDSON, A.J.
sculpture: (H) $605

RICHARDSON, Constance
paintings: (H) $1,237

RICHARDSON, Daniel
British 18th/19th cent.
paintings: (H) $10,560

RICHARDSON, Francis Henry
American 1859-1934
paintings: (L) $275; (H) $770
drawings: (H) $110

RICHARDSON, Gerard
American 20th cent.
paintings: (H) $550

RICHARDSON, Hollis
paintings: (L) $950; (H) $1,320

RICHARDSON, Jonathan
1665-1745
drawings: (H) $3,520

RICHARDSON, Louis H.
American 1853-1923
paintings: (L) $110; (H) $1,430

RICHARDSON, Mary Curtis
American 1848-1931
paintings: (L) $440; (H) $10,450
drawings: (H) $55

RICHARDSON, Mary Neal
American 1859-1937
paintings: (H) $1,100
drawings: (L) $330; (H) $770

RICHARDSON, Paul
British 20th cent.
paintings: (H) $632

RICHARDSON, Sam
American contemporary
paintings: (H) $825

RICHARDSON, Theodore J.
American 1855-1914
drawings: (L) $400; (H) $2,200

RICHARDSON, Thomas Miles, Jr.
English 1813-1890
drawings: (L) $575; (H) $2,185

RICHARDSON, Thomas Miles, Sr.
English 1784-1848
paintings: (L) $1,300; (H) $1,430

RICHARDSON, Volney A.
American b. 1880
paintings: (L) $303; (H) $6,900

RICHARDSON, W.G.
paintings: (H) $1,210

RICHARDSON, William
drawings: (H) $6,612

RICHARDT
Continental School 19th cent.
paintings: (H) $2,200

RICHARDT, Joachim Ferdinand
Danish 1819-1895
paintings: (L) $1,210; (H) $26,400

RICHE, Adele
French 1791-1878
paintings: (L) $920; (H) $13,800
drawings: (H) $1,650

RICHE, J.
paintings: (H) $550

RICHE, Louis
French b. 1887
sculpture: (L) $660; (H) $2,185

RICHEFEU, Charles Edward
French b. 1868
sculpture: (L) $247; (H) $2,860

RICHENBURG, Robert
American b. 1917
paintings: (L) $198; (H) $2,750

RICHER, Ira
20th cent.
drawings: (H) $1,650

RICHER, Paul M.L. Pierre
French 1849-1933
sculpture: (L) $495; (H) $3,300

RICHERT, Charles H.
American b. 1880
paintings: (L) $110; (H) $550
drawings: (L) $55; (H) $330

RICHET, Ch**
French 19th/20th cent.
paintings: (H) $605

RICHET, Leon
French 1847-1907
paintings: (L) $550; (H) $107,000

RICHEZ, Jean
French b. 1929
paintings: (H) $575

RICHIER, Germaine
French 1904-1959
sculpture: (L) $41,800; (H) $55,000

RICHIR, Hermann Jean Joseph
Belgian 1866-1942
paintings: (L) $3,850; (H) $17,600

RICHLEY, Rudolf
paintings: (H) $2,750

RICHMOND, Agnes M.
American c. 1870-1964
paintings: (L) $770; (H) $3,080

RICHMOND, Leonard
British d. 1965
paintings: (H) $1,320
drawings: (H) $288

RICHMOND, Thomas, Jr.
British 1802-1874
paintings: (H) $6,050

RICHTER, A.
German 19th cent.
drawings: (H) $1,430

RICHTER, Adrian Ludwig
German 1803-1884
paintings: (H) $2,750
drawings: (H) $880

RICHTER, Aurel
Hungarian b. 1870
paintings: (L) $2,875; (H) $2,875
drawings: (L) $1,210; (H) $1,760
sculpture: (H) $880

RICHTER, Edouard Frederic Wilhelm
French 1844-1913
paintings: (L) $7,150; (H) $23,100

RICHTER, Gerhard
German b. 1932
paintings: (L) $978; (H) $662,500
drawings: (L) $4,125; (H) $18,400

RICHTER, Gustav Karl Ludwig
German 1838-1884
paintings: (H) $26,450

RICHTER, Hans
German ac. 1597
drawings: (L) $28; (H) $1,100

RICHTER, Hans Rudolf
Austrian b. 1920
paintings: (L) $605; (H) $660

RICHTER, Henry L.
American 1871-1960
paintings: (L) $77; (H) $2,475

RICHTER, Herbert Davis
English 1874-1955
paintings: (H) $1,100

RICHTER, J.
German 19th cent.
paintings: (H) $977

RICHTER, Klaus
German b. 1887
paintings: (L) $605; (H) $2,420

RICHTER, M.J.
German 19th cent.
paintings: (H) $522

RICHTER, Robert E.
German b. 1860
paintings: (H) $1,650

RICHTER, Scott
b. 1933
sculpture: (H) $1,100

RICHTER, Wilhelm
Austrian 1824-1892
paintings: (H) $2,200

RICHTER-DAM, Hans
German b. 1881
paintings: (H) $978

RICK, Mary Ann
American
drawings: (H) $650

RICKARD, Jack
drawings: (L) $990; (H) $5,720

RICKATSON, Octavius
English ac. 1877-1893
paintings: (H) $4,830

RICKERT, Paul
American contemporary
paintings: (H) $1,045

RICKEY, George
American b. 1907
paintings: (H) $11,500
sculpture: (L) $1,610; (H) $110,000

RICKMAN, Philip
English b. 1891, exhib. 1936
drawings: (L) $1,155; (H) $1,980

RICKMAN, Thomas
British 1776-1841
drawings: (L) $1,100; (H) $1,100

RICKS, Douglas
American contemporary
paintings: (L) $1,980; (H) $5,720
drawings: (L) $715; (H) $825

RICO Y CEJUDO, Jose
Spanish b. 1864
paintings: (H) $21,850

RICO Y ORTEGA, Martin
Spanish 1833-1908
paintings: (L) $4,400; (H) $104,500
drawings: (L) $275; (H) $4,950

RICREAZIONE
sculpture: (H) $1,380

RIDDLES, Leonard, Black Moon
Native American b. 1910
drawings: (H) $1,100

RIDELL, Annette Irwin
American ac. 1920s-1930s
paintings: (H) $7,150

RIDEOUT, Phillip H.
British ac. 1897-1912
paintings: (H) $1,650

RIDER, Arthur Grover
American 1886-1975
paintings: (L)　$660; (H) $38,500
drawings: (L) $1,045; (H)　$6,325

RIDINGER, Johann Elias
German 1698-1767
drawings: (H) $770

RIDOUT, P.L.H.
paintings: (H) $920

RIE, Lucy
sculpture: (H) $2,530

RIECKE, George
American 1848-1924
paintings: (L) $920; (H) $2,310

RIECKE, Johann Georg Lodewyck
Dutch 1817-1898
paintings: (L) $660; (H) $3,410

RIEDEL, August
German 1799-1883
paintings: (H) $4,600

RIEDEL, Boris
American 20th cent.
drawings: (L) $115; (H) $2,415

RIEDEL, Helene
Belgian ac. 1930s
paintings: (L) $1,045; (H) $6,613

RIEDER, C.
paintings: (H) $825

RIEDER, F.
sculpture: (H) $1,380

RIEDER, Marcel
French b. 1852
paintings: (L) $2,090; (H) $6,600

RIEGEN, Nicolaas
Dutch 1827-1889
paintings: (L) $770; (H) $11,550

RIEGER, Albert
Austrian 1834-1905
paintings: (L) $2,420; (H) $3,960

RIEGER, Max
German 19th cent.
paintings: (H) $2,990

RIEMAN, Sheila A.
drawings: (H) $1,500

RIEMERSCHMIED, Richard
German 1868-1957
paintings: (H) $1,320

RIESBOROUGH
paintings: (H) $3,300

RIESENBERG, Sidney R.
American b. 1885
paintings: (L) $165; (H) $1,100

RIESENER, Leon Louis Antoine
French 1808-1878
drawings: (H) $550

RIESZ, Paul
German 1857-1933
paintings: (H) $1,045

RIETSCHOOF, Jan Claesz.
c. 1652-1719
paintings: (L) $5,500; (H) $9,350

RIETVELD, Antoine
Dutch 1789-1868
paintings: (L) $3,740; (H) $6,900

RIFFORD,
paintings: (H) $880

RIGAUD, F.
sculpture: (H) $7,475

RIGAUD, John Francis
English 1742-1810
paintings: (H) $4,600

RIGBY, W.
paintings: (H) $525

RIGGS, Robert
American 1896-1970
paintings: (L)　$115; (H) $275
drawings: (H) $1,380

RIGHETTI, Francesco
Italian b. Rome 1738-1819
sculpture: (L) $3,850; (H) $74,000

RIGNAND, Pierre G.
French b. 1874
paintings: (H) $715

RIGNANO, V.
Italian 19th cent.
paintings: (H) $1,320

RIGOLOT, Albert
French 1862-1932
paintings: (L) $2,185; (H) $20,900

RIGOT, Georges
sculpture: (H) $1,980

RIGUAL, P.
ac. c. 1900-1925
sculpture: (H) $2,530

RIHA, Don
American
drawings: (H) $5,175

RIJKELIJKHUISEN, J.
Dutch 1813-1883
paintings: (H) $577

RIJLAARSDAM, Jan
Dutch b. 1911
paintings: (L) $193; (H) $990

RIJN, G. von
paintings: (H) $605

RIJNENBURG, Nicolaas
Dutch 1716-1776
paintings: (H) $4,125

RIKET, Leon
European 19th cent.
paintings: (H) $1,650

RILEY, Arthur I., Art
American b. 1911
drawings: (L) $165; (H) $1,650

RILEY, Bridget
British b. 1931
paintings: (L) $20,700; (H) $57,750
drawings: (L) $1,430; (H) $15,400

RILEY, John
English 1646-1691
paintings: (L) $4,400; (H) $7,920

RILEY, Kenneth
American b. 1919
paintings: (L) $715; (H) $62,700
drawings: (H) $138

RILEY, Larry
b. 1947
paintings: (H) $3,520

RILEY, Nicholas F.
American 1900-1944
paintings: (H) $495
drawings: (H) $770

RIMER, William
British 19th cent.
drawings: (L) $715; (H) $990

RIMINALDI, Orazio
Italian 1594-1630
paintings: (H) $68,500

RIMMEL, P.H.
paintings: (H) $880

RIMMER, William
American 1816-1879
paintings: (H) $8,800

RIMSA, Juan
b. Lithuania 1903
paintings: (H) $3,738

RINALDI, Claudio
Italian 19th/20th cent.
paintings: (L) $797; (H) $3,450

RINALDI, S.
Italian 19th cent.
paintings: (H) $2,760

RINCK, Adolph D.
b.c. 1810-d.c. 1871
paintings: (L) $770; (H) $3,740

RINDIN, V.F.
drawings: (H) $1,100

RINDISBACHER, Peter
American 1806-1834
drawings: (L) $49,500; (H) $60,500

RINEHART, William H.
American 1825-1874
sculpture: (H) $10,500

RINES, Frank M.
b. 1892
paintings: (H) $467

RING, Alice Blair
American 1860-1947
paintings: (L) $770; (H) $6,050

RING, K.
paintings: (H) $550

RING, Ludger Tom, the younger
German 1522-1584
drawings: (H) $66,000

RING, Ole
Danish 1902-1972
paintings: (H) $3,300

RINGDAHL, Johan Julius
Swedish 1813-1882
paintings: (H) $26,450

RINGI, H. Sorensen
sculpture: (H) $495

RINGNESS, Charles
b. 1923
drawings: (H) $1,320

RINGOLD, Faith
American b. 1934
sculpture: (H) $24,150

RINK, ***
Continental 19th/20th cent.
paintings: (H) $1,210

RINKE, Klaus
German b. 1939
drawings: (H) $1,320

RINKOVSKY, Margaret
American 20th cent.
paintings: (H) $805

RINOVIANNA
paintings: (H) $467

RIOPELLE, Jean Paul
Canadian b. 1922/23
paintings: (L) $5,775; (H) $770,000
drawings: (L) $7,475; (H) $20,900

RIOS, Luigi da
Italian 1844-1892
paintings: (H) $3,740
drawings: (L) $523; (H) $12,100

RIOS, Miguel Angel
b. Argentina 1943
sculpture: (L) $6,900; (H) $18,400

RIOULT, Louis Edouard
French 1790-1855
paintings: (L) $935; (H) $19,800

RIP, Willem Cornelis
Dutch 1856-1922
paintings: (L) $2,090; (H) $4,400
drawings: (L) $440; (H) $1,540

RIPAMONTI, Carlos Pablo
Argentinean 1874-1968
paintings: (L) $5,280; (H) $8,525

RIPAMONTI, Guiliano
Italian 19th/20th cent.
paintings: (H) $660

RIPARI
paintings: (H) $990

RIPARI, Virgilio
Italian 1843/46-1902
paintings: (L) $137; (H) $1,870

RIPLEY, Aiden Lassell
American 1896-1969
paintings: (L) $247; (H) $27,500
drawings: (L) $110; (H) $20,700

RIPPEL, Morris
American b. 1930
drawings: (H) $8,800

RIPPER, Rudolph Charles von
Austrian b. 1905
paintings: (H) $633
drawings: (L) $440; (H) $4,887

RIPPON, Tom
contemporary
sculpture: (H) $2,875

RIPPS, Rodney
American 20th cent.
sculpture: (L) $115; (H) $7,151

RIS, Gunther
American
sculpture: (H) $2,070

RISDALE, Wendy
American
paintings: (H) $1,200

RISEBOROUGH
paintings: (H) $1,760

RISHER, Anna
American b. 1875
paintings: (L) $605; (H) $1,430

RISING, John
ac. 1756-1815
paintings: (H) $9,200

RISPOLI, G.
paintings: (L) $275; (H) $687

RISSANEN, Juho
Dutch 20th cent.
paintings: (H) $575

RITCHER, Aurel
Hungarian b. 1870
paintings: (L) $2,875; (H) $2,875

RITCHIE, Jane
paintings: (L) $495; (H) $605

RITCHIE, John
British ac. 1858-1875
paintings: (L) $2,090; (H) $13,800

RITCHIE, Muriel
paintings: (L) $523; (H) $990

RITMAN, Louis
American 1889-1963
paintings: (L) $275; (H) $266,500
drawings: (L) $880; (H) $1,650

RITSCHEL, William
German/American 1864-1949
paintings: (L) $853; (H) $82,500
drawings: (L) $1,840; (H) $7,475

RITTENBERG, Henry R.
Russian/American 1879-1969
paintings: (L) $138; (H) $1,540

RITTENBERG, Henry R. and William
Merritt CHASE
19th/20th cent.
paintings: (H) $1,035

RITTER, Lorenz
German 1820-1892
drawings: (H) $1,320

RITTER, Louis
American 1854-1892
paintings: (H) $19,550
drawings: (L) $1,650; (H) $3,220

RITTER, Louis Fernand
Swiss b. 1871
paintings: (H) $2,530

RITTER, Paul
American 1829-1907
paintings: (L) $550; (H) $8,800

RITTER, Richard
sculpture: (L) $1,035; (H) $6,325

RIUS, Ramon Ribas
Spanish 1903-1983
drawings: (H) $605

RIVA, Giuseppe
drawings: (L) $715; (H) $1,760

RIVAS, Antonio
Italian 19th/20th cent.
paintings: (L) $715; (H) $8,800

RIVATTA, Pietro
Italian 19th/20th cent.
drawings: (H) $1,485

RIVEIRO, J.D.
American 20th cent.
paintings: (H) $825

RIVELLI
Continental 19th/20th cent.
paintings: (H) $990

RIVER, David
British 19th cent.
paintings: (H) $2,860

RIVERA, Diego
Mexican 1886-1957
paintings: (L) $41,800; (H) $3,082,500
drawings: (L) $1,495; (H) $1,102,500

RIVERA, Elias
Mexican 20th cent.
paintings: (H) $550

RIVERA, Jose de
American b. 1904
sculpture: (L) $3,163; (H) $17,600

RIVERA, Manuel
b. Spain 1927
paintings: (H) $28,600

RIVERON, Enrique
b. 1902
drawings: (L) $230; (H) $1,150

RIVERS, Larry
American b. 1923
paintings: (L) $17,600; (H) $137,500
drawings: (L) $1,380; (H) $96,250
sculpture: (L) $2,760; (H) $6,325

RIVERS, Larry and Kenneth KOCH
20th cent.
paintings: (H) $51,750

RIVERS, Leopold
British 1850/52-1905
paintings: (L) $176; (H) $715
drawings: (H) $460

RIVIERE, Briton
British 1840-1920
paintings: (L) $2,300; (H) $76,750

RIVIERE, Henri
French 1864-1951
drawings: (L) $1,380; (H) $2,200

RIVIERE, Joseph
sculpture: (H) $2,415

RIVIERE, Joseph
French b. 1912
paintings: (L) $1,760; (H) $2,970

RIVIERE, Maurice Guiraud
French b. 1881
sculpture: (H) $2,090

RIVIERE, Theodore Louis August
French 1857-1912
sculpture: (L) $5,750; (H) $8,050

RIVIERE, William
British 1806-1876
paintings: (H) $8,050

RIVOIRE, Francois
French 1842-1919
drawings: (L) $2,860; (H) $4,950

RIVOLTA, Baudolino
Italian 19th cent.
drawings: (H) $605

RIX, Julian Walbridge
American 1850-1903
paintings: (L) $330; (H) $9,900
drawings: (L) $440; (H) $1,540

RIYNTJENS, H. E.
Dutch 19th cent.
paintings: (H) $2,200

RIZZI, James
American 20th cent.
paintings: (H) $495

RIZZONI, Alexandre A.
Russian 1836-1902
paintings: (H) $5,175

ROBAUDI, Alcide Theophile
French 19th cent.
paintings: (H) $2,200
drawings: (H) $575

ROBB, Elizabeth B.
19th/20th cent.
paintings: (H) $495

ROBB, Samuel
American 1851-1928
sculpture: (H) $33,350

ROBB, William George
British b. 1872
paintings: (L) $1,100; (H) $1,650

ROBBE, Joseph
Belgian 1862-1935
paintings: (L) $575; (H) $748

ROBBE, Louis
Belgian 1806-1887
paintings: (L) $1,045; (H) $5,500

ROBBE, Wolfgang
20th cent.
sculpture: (H) $805

ROBBECKE, Moritz Friedrich
German 1857-1916
paintings: (H) $5,500

ROBBINS, Ellen
American 1828-1905
paintings: (H) $3,575
drawings: (L) $330; (H) $3,850

ROBBINS, Horace Wolcott
American 1842-1904
paintings: (H) $4,400

ROBERT, Alexandre Nestor Nicolas
Belgian 1817-1890
paintings: (H) $13,800

ROBERT, Henri
French 1881-1961
drawings: (H) $825

ROBERT, Hubert
French 1733-1808
paintings: (L) $10,350; (H) $495,000
drawings: (L) $4,025; (H) $44,000

ROBERT, Leopold
Swiss 1794-1835
paintings: (H) $1,045

ROBERT, Marc
sculpture: (H) $1,840

ROBERT, Marius Hubert
French 19th/20th cent.
paintings: (L) $330; (H) $577

ROBERT, Nicolas
1614-1685
drawings: (H) $2,300

ROBERT, Paul Theophile
Swiss 1879-1954
paintings: (H) $990

ROBERT-FLEURY, Tony
French 1837-1912
paintings: (L) $1,870; (H) $2,200
drawings: (H) $1,495

ROBERTI
Italian 19th cent.
drawings: (H) $1,150

ROBERTI, Albert Pierre
Belgian 1811-1864
drawings: (L) $522; (H) $1,725

ROBERTI, R.M.
Italian 19th cent.
drawings: (L) $460; (H) $920

ROBERTI, Roberto
Italian 1786-1837
drawings: (H) $990

ROBERTO ROBERTI, Fernando di
Italian 1786-1837
drawings: (H) $8,050

ROBERTS, A.
paintings: (H) $747

ROBERTS, Alice T.
American 20th cent.
paintings: (L) $55; (H) $1,320

ROBERTS, Arthur
paintings: (H) $5,720

ROBERTS, David
b.Scotland, British 1796-1864
paintings: (L) $2,090; (H) $46,000
drawings: (L) $192; (H) $1,650

ROBERTS, Dr. F.E.
American 20th cent.
paintings: (H) $690

ROBERTS, Edwin
British 1840-1917
paintings: (L) $2,750; (H) $15,400

ROBERTS, Elizabeth W.
paintings: (H) $825

ROBERTS, Ella A.
American 1886-1930
paintings: (H) $990

ROBERTS, Gary Lynn
b. 1953
paintings: (L) $1,430; (H) $1,980

ROBERTS, Helen L.
American 20th cent.
paintings: (H) $825

ROBERTS, Herbert H.
British 19th cent.
paintings: (H) $495

ROBERTS, J.
paintings: (H) $495

ROBERTS, J.
English 19th cent.
paintings: (H) $1,210

ROBERTS, Joe Rader
American 1925-1982
paintings: (L) $2,070; (H) $2,070
drawings: (H) $330

ROBERTS, Nathan B.
American 19th cent.
paintings: (H) $3,520

ROBERTS, Priscilla Warren
b. 1916
paintings: (H) $1,840

ROBERTS, R.S.
British 19th cent.
paintings: (H) $935

ROBERTS, Thomas E.
English 1820-1901
paintings: (H) $3,300

ROBERTS, Thomas Keith, Tom
b. 1909
paintings: (L) $1,210; (H) $2,310

ROBERTS, Thomas William
Australian 1856-1931
paintings: (H) $2,750

ROBERTS, William
British 1895-1980
paintings: (L) $2,760; (H) $3,680

ROBERTS, William Goodridge
Canadian 1904-1974
paintings: (L) $2,200; (H) $33,000
drawings: (H) $1,045

ROBERTSON, Alexander
1772-1841
drawings: (H) $920

ROBERTSON, Charles
British d. 1891
drawings: (H) $575

ROBERTSON, Charles F.
b. 1891
drawings: (H) $1,955

ROBERTSON, G.A.
American School 19th/20th cent.
paintings: (H) $935

ROBERTSON, George E.
British ac. 1883-1926
paintings: (H) $1,840

ROBERTSON, George Edward
British b. 1864
paintings: (H) $34,500

ROBERTSON, Mary
contemporary
paintings: (H) $550

ROBERTSON, Percy
British 1868-1934
drawings: (H) $3,300

ROBERTSON, Tom
Scottish 1863-1910
paintings: (H) $518

ROBERTY, Andre Felix
French b. 1877
paintings: (H) $5,175

ROBESON, Eliza Ann
1798-1834
drawings: (L) $17,250; (H) $57,500

ROBIDA, Albert
French 1848-1926
paintings: (H) $1,150

ROBIE, Jean Baptiste
Belgian 1821-1910
paintings: (L) $5,225; (H) $90,500

ROBIN, Georges
French 19th/20th cent.
paintings: (L) $495; (H) $1,725

ROBIN, Michel
French b. 1930
paintings: (H) $2,310

ROBINS, D. Lee
American
drawings: (L) $650; (H) $1,150

ROBINSON, Albert Henry
Canadian 1881-1956
paintings: (L) $4,400; (H) $121,000

ROBINSON, Alexander C.
American 1867-1940
paintings: (H) $1,955
drawings: (L) $88; (H) $303

ROBINSON, Boardman
American 1876-1952
paintings: (L) $247; (H) $550
drawings: (L) $230; (H) $330

ROBINSON, Charles D.
American 1847-1933
paintings: (L) $192; (H) $9,900

ROBINSON, Florence Vincent
American 1874-1937
paintings: (H) $660
drawings: (L) $220; (H) $2,200

ROBINSON, H.W.
American 19th cent.
paintings: (H) $990

ROBINSON, Hal
American 1875-1933
paintings: (L) $440; (H) $2,420

ROBINSON, Irene
1891-1973
paintings: (H) $1,093

ROBINSON, J.M.
paintings: (L) $110; (H) $920

ROBINSON, M.
American 19th/20th cent.
paintings: (H) $935

ROBINSON, M.F.
20th cent.
paintings: (H) $1,840

ROBINSON, Robert
1886-1952
paintings: (H) $2,530

ROBINSON, Theodore
American 1852-1896
paintings: (L) $1,955; (H) $1,102,500
drawings: (L) $220; (H) $63,000

ROBINSON, Thomas
Canadian/American 1834-1888
paintings: (L) $138; (H) $2,860

ROBINSON, Walter
20th cent.
paintings: (H) $550

ROBINSON, William
British 1835-1895
drawings: (H) $805

ROBINSON, William Heath
British 1872-1944
drawings: (L) $1,045; (H) $2,420

ROBINSON, William S.
American 1861-1945
paintings: (L) $357; (H) $1,760
drawings: (L) $468; (H) $495

ROBINSON, William T.
American b. 1852
paintings: (L) $110; (H) $1,760

ROBUS, Hugo
American 1885-1964
paintings: (H) $11,000
drawings: (H) $220
sculpture: (L) $330; (H) $9,900

ROCCA, Giovanni della
Italian 1788-1858
paintings: (H) $9,775

ROCCA BRITO, Luis
b. Venezuela 1964
paintings: (H) $8,800

ROCCATAGLIATA, Niccolo
Venetian ac. 1593-1636
sculpture: (H) $63,000

ROCCATAGLIATA, Niccolo, studio of
Venetian School late 16th cent.
sculpture: (H) $27,600

ROCCATAGLIATA, Niccolo,
workshop of
Venetian c. 1600
sculpture: (H) $11,500

ROCCHI, F.
Italian 19th cent.
drawings: (H) $1,540

ROCH, Georg
sculpture: (H) $990

ROCHBURNE, Dorothea
drawings: (H) $2,090

ROCHE, A.
British 19th cent.
paintings: (H) $805

ROCHE, P.
American 20th cent.
sculpture: (H) $632

ROCHEGROSSE, Georges Antoine
French 1859-1938
paintings: (L) $22,000; (H) $40,250

ROCHENADE, G.
sculpture: (H) $552

ROCHER, Charles
French 1890-1962
paintings: (L) $220; (H) $1,650

ROCHER, M***
French 19th/20th cent.
paintings: (H) $2,310

ROCHUSSEN, Charles
Dutch 1814-1894
drawings: (L) $385; (H) $522

ROCK, Geoffrey Allan
b. 1923
paintings: (H) $1,320

ROCKBURNE, Dorothea
Canadian ac. 1970-1974
paintings: (H) $550
drawings: (L) $9,200; (H) $27,500
sculpture: (H) $15,400

ROCKENSCHAUB, Gerwald
Austrian b. 1952
paintings: (L) $1,100; (H) $1,760

ROCKEY, A.B.
American 1779-1834
paintings: (L) $1,045; (H) $1,540

ROCKMAN, Alexis
paintings: (L) $5,175; (H) $25,300

ROCKMORE, Noel
American 1928-1995
paintings: (L) $144; (H) $1,870
drawings: (L) $55; (H) $660

ROCKWELL, Augustus
American ac. 1855-after 1860
paintings: (L) $440; (H) $8,050
drawings: (H) $173

ROCKWELL, Cleveland
American 1837-1907
paintings: (L) $1,320; (H) $9,200
drawings: (L) $550; (H) $3,738

ROCKWELL, Evelyn
American b. 1887
paintings: (H) $1,320

ROCKWELL, Mary Chauplin
American early 20th cent.
paintings: (H) $1,320

ROCKWELL, Norman
American 1894-1978
paintings: (L) $2,200; (H) $800,000
drawings: (L) $1,089; (H) $85,000

ROCKWELL, Robert Henry
b. 1885
sculpture: (H) $1,495

ROCLE, Marius R.
American 1897-1967
paintings: (H) $8,250

RODA, Antonio
b. Spain 1921-1970
paintings: (H) $13,200

RODA, Leonardo
Italian 1868-1933
paintings: (H) $880

RODCHENKO, Alexander
Russian 1891-1956
drawings: (H) $26,450

RODDE, Michel
French b. 1913
paintings: (L) $230; (H) $747

RODE, Edmund A.
Dutch 1841-1909
paintings: (L) $4,950; (H) $11,000

California Painter

Marius Romain Rocle (1897-1967) was born in Belgium, and his early years were spent in Paris. He served in World War I in the U.S. Army, and in 1918 he met his future wife, Margaret King (Margot), an artist and dancer who was serving as a nurse for the Allied forces. Rocle worked in Paris after the war as a sales rep for an American company, but in 1921 the Rocles moved to Southern California, where they had purchased a lemon ranch. Margot had

studied art under William Merritt Chase and at the Art Students League under Robert Henri, and both Marius and Margot began to paint. The couple became active in the San Diego art community and still managed to supervise their successful ranch. After 1940 the Rocles sold the lemon ranch, stopped painting, and raised Arabian horses. John Moran Auctioneers, in Pasadena, California, is an auction house that specializes in California painters. This oil on canvas of *Shorty Shoeing Silver* brought $8,250. (Marius R. Rocle, *Shorty Shoeing Silver*, oil on canvas, 36 x 40 inches, Moran, February 16, 1993, $8,250)

RODE, Edmund Adler
German 1871-1965
paintings: (H) $6,875

RODEN, William Thomas
English School 1817-1892
paintings: (H) $770

RODETTI, A***
Italian 19th cent.
paintings: (H) $2,645

RODETTI, A.
Italian 19th cent.
paintings: (L) $165; (H) $880

RODEWALD, Fred
drawings: (H) $523

RODGERS, Raymond Perry
American 1881-1964
paintings: (H) $550

RODIN, Auguste
French 1840-1917
paintings: (L) $968; (H) $37,375
drawings: (L) $275; (H) $104,500
sculpture: (L) $2,200; (H) $1,322,500

RODMAN, E.
paintings: (H) $660

RODO BOULANGER, Graciela
b. Bolivia 1935
paintings: (L) $4,675; (H) $8,800
drawings: (H) $201

RODON, Francisco
b. Puerto Rico 1934
paintings: (L) $66,000; (H) $104,500

RODRIGUEZ, Arturo
Cuba b. 1956
paintings: (L) $3,680; (H) $14,950
drawings: (H) $115
sculpture: (H) $253

RODRIGUEZ, C.N.
paintings: (H) $2,200

RODRIGUEZ, M.
Continental 19th cent.
paintings: (H) $4,400

RODRIGUEZ, Mariano
Cuban 1912-1990
paintings: (L) $13,800; (H) $299,500
drawings: (L) $863; (H) $15,400

RODRIGUEZ DE GUZMAN, Manuel
Spanish 1818-1867
paintings: (H) $9,775

RODRIGUEZ JUAREZ, Juan
1675-c. 1728
paintings: (H) $25,300

RODRIGUEZ LOZANO, Manuel
Mexican 1896-1971
paintings: (L) $20,700; (H) $48,300

RODRIGUEZ LUNA, Antonio
b. Spain 1910
paintings: (H) $11,550

RODRIGUEZ MOREY, Antonio
Cuban 1874-1930
paintings: (H) $3,450

RODRIQUEZ SAN CLEMENT,
Francisco
Spanish 1861-1956
paintings: (H) $1,320

RODVOGIN, Harris
American 20th cent.
paintings: (L) $880; (H) $1,210

RODWITTIYA, Rekha
Indian b. 1958
paintings: (L) $2,070; (H) $3,105
drawings: (L) $690; (H) $805

ROE, Christopher
paintings: (H) $605

ROE, Clarence
English ac. 1870; d. 1909
paintings: (L) $275; (H) $1,380

ROE, Frederick Rushing
British 1864-1947
paintings: (L) $230; (H) $1,320

ROE, Robert Ernest
English 19th cent.
paintings: (H) $2,310

ROE, Robert Harvey
British 19th cent.
paintings: (H) $550

ROECKER, H.L.
American 1865-1941
paintings: (L) $220; (H) $880
drawings: (L) $88; (H) $154

ROEDIG, Johannes Christian
Dutch 1750-1802
paintings: (H) $28,600

ROEKENS, Paulette van
b. 1896
paintings: (L) $1,925; (H) $4,070

ROELOFS, Willem
Dutch 1822-1897
paintings: (L) $805; (H) $8,050

ROEPEL, Coenraet
Dutch 1678-1748
paintings: (H) $39,600

ROERICH, Nicholaj Konstantinov
Russian 1874-1947
paintings: (H) $2,475
drawings: (H) $550

ROERMOND, Joep Nicolas
paintings: (H) $3,300

ROESCH, Kurt
American b. 1905
paintings: (L) $1,035; (H) $1,980

ROESEN, Severin
German/American d. 1871
paintings: (L) $4,400; (H) $253,000
drawings: (H) $21,850

ROESLER-FRANZ, Ettore
Italian 1845-1907
drawings: (L) $5,750; (H) $18,700

ROESSLER, Walter
Russian 19th/20th cent.
paintings: (L) $460; (H) $1,760

ROFFIAEN, Jean Francois
Belgian 1820-1898
paintings: (L) $3,162; (H) $7,700

ROFFIAEN, Jean Francois and Eugene
VERBOECKHOVEN
Belgian 19th cent.
paintings: (H) $6,600

ROFFO, Sergio
drawings: (L) $385; (H) $935

ROGER, Augustin
French 19th cent.
paintings: (H) $2,750

ROGER, Biron
American 20th cent.
paintings: (H) $990

ROGER, J.
drawings: (L) $230; (H) $483

ROGER, Suzanne
French b. 1898
paintings: (H) $1,150

ROGER-BLOCHE
sculpture: (H) $468

ROGERS
British contemporary
paintings: (H) $2,420

ROGERS, Charles A.
American 1840-1913
paintings: (L) $385; (H) $990

ROGERS, Charles B.
American b. 1911
drawings: (L) $495; (H) $495

ROGERS, Claude
British b. 1907
paintings: (H) $770

ROGERS, D.F.
paintings: (H) $935

ROGERS, Franklin Whiting
American b. 1854
paintings: (L) $264; (H) $1,650
drawings: (H) $715

ROGERS, Howard
American
paintings: (H) $2,970

ROGERS, Hubert
American 20th cent.
paintings: (H) $715

ROGERS, John
1829-1904
sculpture: (L) $259; (H) $29,900

ROGERS, Louis
paintings: (H) $550

ROGERS, Margaret E.
American 1872-1961
paintings: (L) $110; (H) $523

ROGERS, Randolph
American 1825-1892
sculpture: (L) $2,090; (H) $20,900

ROGERS, W.
English 19th cent.
paintings: (L) $688; (H) $1,650
drawings: (L) $660; (H) $1,045

ROGERS, Wendell M.
American 20th cent.
paintings: (L) $110; (H) $550

ROGERS, William
English 19th cent.
paintings: (H) $3,025

ROGERS, William P.
British ac. 1842-1872
paintings: (L) $1,210; (H) $1,870

ROGNE, Bill D.
sculpture: (H) $1,430

ROHDE, H.
American 19th cent.
paintings: (L) $230; (H) $1,380

ROHLFS, Charles
American 1853-1936
drawings: (H) $550

ROHLFS, Christian
German 1849-1938
paintings: (L) $33,000; (H) $55,000
drawings: (L) $7,475; (H) $30,800

ROHNER, George
b. 1913
paintings: (H) $1,760

ROITER, Andrei
b. 1960
paintings: (H) $1,265

ROJAK, Efim Moissewitch
drawings: (L) $1,150; (H) $5,175

ROJAS, Elmar
Guatemalan b. 1938
paintings: (L) $4,950; (H) $33,000

ROJAY, G.
paintings: (H) $3,080

ROJE, Arsen
paintings: (H) $2,970

ROJKA, Fritz
Austrian b. 1878
paintings: (H) $2,300

ROLAND
Dutch 18th/19th cent.
paintings: (H) $1,210

ROLAND, Philippe Laurent
French 1746-1816
sculpture: (L) $11,000; (H) $23,000

ROLAND DE LA PORTE, Henri
Horace
French 1724-1793
paintings: (H) $231,000

ROLDAN, Enrique
Spanish 19th cent.
paintings: (L) $2,300; (H) $6,875

ROLDAN, Jose
Spanish 19th cent.
paintings: (L) $3,450; (H) $8,625

ROLFE, Alexander F.
British 1839-1873
paintings: (H) $39,600

ROLFE, Edmund
British ac. 1830-1847
paintings: (H) $5,225

ROLFE, Henry Leonidas
English ac. 1847-1881
paintings: (L) $605; (H) $9,775
drawings: (H) $1,320

ROLING, Gerard Victor Alphons
Dutch b. 1904
paintings: (L) $192; (H) $1,320

ROLLE, A.
French 19th cent.
sculpture: (H) $10,450

ROLLE, August H.O.
American 1875-1941
paintings: (L) $522; (H) $9,075

ROLLENTINE, V.
European 19th cent.
paintings: (H) $1,760

ROLLETON, J.
paintings: (H) $748

ROLLIN, J.
19th cent.
paintings: (L) $518; (H) $798

ROLLINS, J.
American 19th/20th cent.
paintings: (H) $990

ROLLINS, John
American 19th cent.
paintings: (H) $770

ROLLINS, Tim and K.O.S.
contemporary
paintings: (L) $8,800; (H) $33,000
drawings: (L) $770; (H) $11,000

ROLLINS, Warren E.
American 1861-1962
paintings: (L) $385; (H) $8,250

ROLPH, A.
paintings: (H) $2,640

ROLSHOVEN, Julius
American 1858-1930
paintings: (L) $55; (H) $11,550

ROMAGNOLI, Giovanni
1873-1933
paintings: (H) $9,200

ROMAGNOLI, Giovanni
Italian 1893-1976
paintings: (H) $14,300

ROMAGNOLI, R.
Italian 20th cent.
paintings: (H) $880

ROMAIN, E.
paintings: (H) $825

ROMAKO, Anton
Austrian 1832-1889
paintings: (H) $20,900

ROMANACH, Leopoldo
Cuban/American 1862-1951
paintings: (L) $2,990; (H) $33,000
drawings: (H) $920

ROMAND, M.
paintings: (H) $798

ROMANELLA, R.
sculpture: (H) $3,300

ROMANELLI
sculpture: (H) $748

ROMANELLI, Giovanni Francesco,
called Il Viterbese
Italian 1610-1662
paintings: (L) $2,090; (H) $96,000
drawings: (H) $2,875

ROMANELLI, P.
sculpture: (H) $467

ROMANELLI, Pasquale
Italian 1812-1887
sculpture: (L) $1,955; (H) $5,225

ROMANELLI, Raffaelo
Italian 1856-1928
sculpture: (L) $825; (H) $14,950

ROMANI, Juana
Italian 1869-1924
paintings: (H) $14,950

ROMANI, M.
Italian 19th/20th cent.
paintings: (H) $5,175

ROMANIE, H.
paintings: (H) $747

ROMANO, Giulio, Guilio PIPPI
1499-1546
drawings: (L) $412; (H) $14,950

ROMANO, Giulio, studio of
drawings: (H) $3,163

ROMANO, Umberto
American 1905-1984
paintings: (L) $28; (H) $8,800
drawings: (L) $110; (H) $440

ROMANO, V.
Italian 19th/20th cent.
paintings: (H) $460

ROMANOFF, Ouida
20th cent.
paintings: (H) $880

ROMBALD, J.
paintings: (H) $550

ROMBOUTS, Gillis
Dutch 1630-1678
paintings: (H) $5,500

ROMBOUTS, Salomon
Dutch ac. c. 1652; d. c. 1702
paintings: (H) $9,775

ROME, Albert de
American 1885-1959
paintings: (H) $1,760

ROMEK, Arpad
Hungarian b. 1883
paintings: (H) $550

ROMERO
Spanish 19th/20th cent.
paintings: (H) $550

ROMERO Y ESCALANTE, Juan de
Sevilla
1643-1695
paintings: (H) $2,860

ROMIEU, Leon Edouard
French 19th cent.
paintings: (H) $2,750

ROMITA, John
American b. 1930
drawings: (L) $605; (H) $14,950

ROMITI, Romano
Italian 1906-1951
paintings: (H) $3,080

ROMMEL, Lee
paintings: (H) $660
drawings: (L) $750; (H) $900

ROMNEY, George
English 1734-1802
paintings: (L) $825; (H) $44,000
drawings: (L) $632; (H) $6,050

ROMO, Jose Luis
Mexican b. 1953
paintings: (H) $2,750

RONALD, William Smith
paintings: (L) $1,210; (H) $3,300

RONAY, J.L.
Continental 19th cent.
paintings: (L) $1,100; (H) $2,860

RONCALLI, Cristofano, called Il
Pomarancio
1552-1626
drawings: (H) $13,200

RONCHI, Arnaldo
Italian 19th cent.
drawings: (H) $825

RONDAHL, Emmery
Danish 1858-1914
paintings: (H) $4,370

RONDEL, Frederick
American 1826-1892
paintings: (L) $495; (H) $15,400
drawings: (H) $880

RONDEL, Henri
French 1857-1919
paintings: (L) $1,430; (H) $5,280

RONEY, Z.L.
Hungarian
paintings: (H) $690

RONGET, Elisabeth
Polish 1896-1962
paintings: (L) $3,162; (H) $6,900

RONNER-KNIP, Henriette
Dutch 1821-1909
paintings: (L) $935; (H) $35,200

ROOIJEN, Carl van
Dutch b. 1945
paintings: (L) $1,925; (H) $2,750

ROOK, Edward
1870-1960
paintings: (H) $4,675

ROOKE, Thomas Matthews
English 1842-1942
drawings: (H) $7,475

ROOKER, Michael Angelo
English 1743-1801
paintings: (H) $63,000

ROONEY, Anne
American 20th cent.
sculpture: (H) $3,680

ROORBACH, A.S.
paintings: (L) $275; (H) $460

ROORE, Jacobus Ignatius de
Flemish 1686-1747
paintings: (H) $35,200

ROOS, Johann Heinrich
1631-1685
drawings: (H) $2,760

ROOS, Peter
Swedish/American b. 1850
paintings: (L) $715; (H) $3,163

ROOS, Philipp Peter, called Rosa da
Tivoli
German 1657-1706
paintings: (L) $2,530; (H) $46,000

ROOSDORP, Frederick
Dutch 1839-1865
paintings: (H) $880

ROOSE, Aage
paintings: (H) $550

ROOSE, Ch. van
Belgian 19th/20th cent.
paintings: (H) $7,700

ROOSENBOOM, Albert
Belgian 1845-1875
paintings: (L) $1,430; (H) $4,600

ROOSENBOOM, Albert and Hendrick
Pieter KOEKKOEK
Northern European 19th cent.
paintings: (H) $18,400

ROOSENBOOM, Margaretha Vogel
Dutch 1843-1896
paintings: (H) $6,600

ROOSENBOOM, Nicholas J.
Dutch 1805-1880
paintings: (L) $5,500; (H) $9,075

ROOSVAL, Gerda
Swedish 19th cent.
paintings: (H) $6,875

ROOT, Peggy
20th cent.
paintings: (H) $550

ROOT, Robert Marshall
American b. 1863
paintings: (H) $935
drawings: (L) $77; (H) $137

ROOTIUS, Jan Albertsz.
1615-1674
paintings: (H) $1,760

ROOY, Johannes Embrosius van de
Wetering de
Dutch b. 1877
paintings: (H) $715

ROOYEN, H. van
paintings: (H) $962

ROPER, Matilda
American 1886-1958
paintings: (H) $1,380

ROPER, Richard
English 18th century
paintings: (H) $8,337

ROPES, George
American 1788-1819
drawings: (L) $220; (H) $6,325

ROPP, Roy M.
American b. 1888
paintings: (H) $990

ROPS, Felicien
Belgian 1833-1898
drawings: (H) $1,100

ROQUE, C. La
paintings: (H) $3,300

ROQUEPLAN, Camille
French 1803-1855
paintings: (L) $528; (H) $1,093
drawings: (L) $259; (H) $522

RORKE, Edward A.
1856-1905
paintings: (H) $1,955

ROSA, Don
drawings: (L) $633; (H) $2,750

ROSA, Francesco de, called Pacecco de
Rosa
Italian c. 1600-1654
paintings: (L) $1,870; (H) $60,500

ROSA, Louis
French 19th/20th cent.
paintings: (H) $550

ROSA, Pacecco de, aka Francesco de
Rosa
Italian ac. 1600-1654
paintings: (L) $1,870; (H) $7,475

ROSA, Salvator
Italian 1615-1673
drawings: (L) $990; (H) $24,150

ROSALBIN DE BUNCEY, Marie
Abraham
French d. c. 1876
paintings: (H) $748

ROSAM, Walter Alfred
German 1883-1916
paintings: (H) $5,500

ROSANJIN, Kitaoji
1883-1959
drawings: (H) $14,950

ROSAS, Benito
sculpture: (H) $4,950

ROSASPINA, Antonio
Italian 1830-1871
paintings: (H) $3,850

ROSATI, E.
Italian 19th/20th cent.
paintings: (H) $1,210

ROSATI, Giulio
Italian 1858-1917
paintings: (L) $12,650; (H) $33,000
drawings: (L) $3,080; (H) $23,000

ROSATI, James
American b. 1912
drawings: (L) $715; (H) $990
sculpture: (L) $3,300; (H) $3,575

ROSCH, Ludwig
Austrian 1865-1908
paintings: (H) $3,080

ROSE, A.
Italian 19th cent.
paintings: (L) $165; (H) $2,530

ROSE, Anthony Lewis de
American 1803-1886
paintings: (H) $2,640

ROSE, Antonio Julius Karl
German 1828-1911
paintings: (H) $1,650

ROSE, Guy
American 1867-1925
paintings: (L) $48,875; (H) $110,000
drawings: (H) $4,950

ROSE, Iver
American 1899-1972
paintings: (L) $385; (H) $1,870

ROSE, J.
19th cent.
paintings: (H) $1,650

ROSE, Julius
German 1828-1911
paintings: (L) $248; (H) $16,500

ROSE, Manuel
b. Uruguay 1887-1961
paintings: (L) $7,700; (H) $46,000

ROSE, Robin
American contemporary
paintings: (L) $357; (H) $825
drawings: (H) $275

ROSE, Samuel
American b. 1941
paintings: (H) $1,760

ROSE, W.
American 19th cent.
paintings: (H) $660

ROSE, William S., Sr.
British 1810-1873
paintings: (L) $1,375; (H) $1,540

ROSEBEE
20th cent.
paintings: (L) $88; (H) $715

ROSEBOOM, A.
Dutch 19th cent.
paintings: (H) $2,760

ROSELAND, Harry
American 1868-1950
paintings: (L) $303; (H) $253,000
drawings: (L) $1,150; (H) $3,575

ROSELL, Alexander
British 19th cent.
paintings: (L) $2,200; (H) $7,150

ROSEN, A.
paintings: (H) $1,760

ROSEN, Charles
American 1878-1950
paintings: (L) $2,200; (H) $30,800
drawings: (H) $126

ROSEN, George
20th cent.
paintings: (H) $660

ROSEN, Jan
Polish b. 1854
paintings: (H) $805

ROSENAU, T.
20th cent.
paintings: (H) $1,035

ROSENBAUER, William Wallace
American b. 1900
paintings: (H) $275
sculpture: (L) $275; (H) $2,090

ROSENBAUM, Richard
Austrian b. 1864
drawings: (L) $220; (H) $1,540

ROSENBERG, Henry M.
Canadian 1858-1947
paintings: (H) $800
drawings: (H) $108

ROSENBOOM, Albert
Belgian 1845-1875
paintings: (H) $14,950

ROSENKRANZ, Carl C.
American 19th/20th cent.
paintings: (H) $550

ROSENQUIST, James
American 1933-1991
paintings: (L) $23,100; (H) $319,000
drawings: (L) $1,650; (H) $36,800
sculpture: (L) $1,725; (H) $83,600

ROSENSTOCK, Isadore
German 1880-1956
drawings: (H) $633

ROSENTHAL
paintings: (H) $825

ROSENTHAL, Albert
American 1863-1939
paintings: (L) $1,210; (H) $15,400
drawings: (H) $200

ROSENTHAL, Bernard
contemporary
sculpture: (H) $7,700

ROSENTHAL, Doris
American 1895-1971
paintings: (H) $880
drawings: (L) $83; (H) $690

ROSENTHAL, Toby Edward
American 1848-1917
paintings: (H) $33,000

ROSENTHAL, Tony
American b. 1914
sculpture: (H) $4,140

ROSENTHALIS, Moshe
paintings: (L) $3,575; (H) $6,600

ROSHARDT, Walter
1897-1966
drawings: (H) $978

ROSIER, Amedee
French b. 1831
paintings: (L) $5,175; (H) $17,825

ROSIER, Henri
French 19th cent.
paintings: (H) $1,265

ROSIER, Jean Guillaume
Belgian 1858-1931
paintings: (H) $10,350

ROSIERSE, Johannes
Dutch 1818-1901
paintings: (L) $1,760; (H) $26,450

ROSLER, Franz
Austrian 1864-1941
paintings: (H) $2,530

ROSLIN, Alexandre
Swedish 1718-1793
paintings: (H) $5,500

ROSLIN, Alexandre, studio of
18th cent.
paintings: (H) $12,650

ROSNER, Charles
German/American 1894-after 1975
paintings: (L) $770; (H) $770
drawings: (L) $330; (H) $633

ROSOFSKY, Seymour
American 1925-1981
paintings: (L) $460; (H) $3,520
drawings: (L) $230; (H) $660

ROSPINI, G.
Italian 19th/20th cent.
paintings: (H) $1,210

ROSS, Alex
American 1909-1990
paintings: (L) $3,300; (H) $3,450
drawings: (L) $83; (H) $1,430

ROSS, Alvin
American 20th cent.
paintings: (H) $1,320

ROSS, Christian Meyer
Norwegian 1843-1904
paintings: (H) $21,850
drawings: (H) $575

ROSS, Frederick Joseph
paintings: (H) $2,420

ROSS, Harry Leith
American 1886-1973
drawings: (L) $357; (H) $770

ROSS, Isabel
American 20th cent.
paintings: (H) $575

ROSS, J. McPherson
paintings: (H) $1,540

ROSS, James
American 20th cent.
paintings: (L) $165; (H) $357
drawings: (L) $198; (H) $1,265

ROSS, Johnny
drawings: (H) $575

ROSS, Joseph Halford
British b. 1866
drawings: (H) $880

ROSS, Robert Thorburn
Scottish 1816-1876
paintings: (L) $1,870; (H) $7,700

ROSS, Sir William Charles
English 1794-1860
paintings: (H) $2,645

ROSS, Stuart
paintings: (L) $403; (H) $990

ROSS, Victoria
paintings: (L) $220; (H) $467

ROSSANO, Federico
Italian 1835-1912
paintings: (H) $29,900

ROSSATI(?), G.
Italian(?) 19th cent.
paintings: (H) $2,200

ROSSBACH, Ed
contemporary
sculpture: (L) $920; (H) $1,725

ROSSE?
sculpture: (H) $1,760

ROSSEAU, J.J.
European 18th/19th cent.
drawings: (L) $3,850; (H) $4,400

ROSSEAU, Percival Leonard
American 1859/69-1937
paintings: (L) $978; (H) $26,450

ROSSELETTI, Rosso
Italian 18th-19th cent.
paintings: (H) $797

ROSSELLI, Bernardo
Italian 1450-1526
paintings: (L) $44,000; (H) $473,000

ROSSELLI, Matteo
Italian 1578-1650
paintings: (H) $46,000

ROSSERT, Paul
French 19th cent.
paintings: (H) $10,063
drawings: (H) $770

ROSSET, Joseph, called Dupont
sculpture: (H) $8,800

ROSSETTI, Luigi
Italian 1881-1912
drawings: (H) $2,090

ROSSETTO, A.
sculpture: (H) $660

ROSSI
Continental School 19th cent.
paintings: (H) $770

ROSSI, Alberto
Italian 1858-1936
paintings: (H) $1,210

ROSSI, Alexander M.
English ac. 1870-1903
paintings: (L) $6,900; (H) $16,500

ROSSI, C.
paintings: (H) $1,100

ROSSI, Enrico
Italian 1856-1916
paintings: (L) $1,980; (H) $3,220

ROSSI, Francesco del, IL SALVIATI
Italian 1510-1563
paintings: (H) $25,875
drawings: (L) $16,100; (H) $74,000

ROSSI, G***
Italian 19th cent.
paintings: (L) $3,025; (H) $4,025

ROSSI, Gaeta
sculpture: (H) $550

ROSSI, Lucius
French 1846-1913
paintings: (L) $3,850; (H) $31,050
drawings: (L) $715; (H) $3,300

ROSSI, Luigi
Italian 1853-1923
paintings: (L) $5,463; (H) $60,500
drawings: (L) $475; (H) $2,200

ROSSI, Nicola Maria
Italian 1699-1755
paintings: (H) $3,300

ROSSI, Pasqualino
1641-1725
paintings: (H) $5,500

ROSSI, Prof.
sculpture: (H) $2,200

ROSSI, S.L.
French 1853-1913
drawings: (H) $715

ROSSIGNOL, Lily
French 19th/20th cent.
paintings: (H) $9,350

ROSSIN, Geo. H.
paintings: (H) $1,540

ROSSITER, Louis
British 1837-1901
paintings: (H) $715

ROSSITER, Thomas P.
American 1818-1871
paintings: (L) $546; (H) $79,500

ROSSLER, Rudolf
Austrian b. 1864
paintings: (H) $2,750

ROSSO
paintings: (H) $1,650

ROSSO, Medardo
Italian 1858-1928
sculpture: (L) $12,650; (H) $418,000

ROSZAK, Theodore
contemporary
sculpture: (H) $15,400

ROSZEZEWSKI, Henri Dominique
French 19th cent.
paintings: (H) $2,875

ROTA, G.
Italian 19th cent.
paintings: (H) $3,575

ROTARI, Pietro Antonio
Italian 1707-1762
paintings: (L) $4,180; (H) $46,750
drawings: (L) $28,750; (H) $51,750

ROTELLA, Mimmo
Italian b. 1918
paintings: (H) $5,280
drawings: (L) $2,300; (H) $7,150
sculpture: (H) $12,100

ROTENBERG, Harold
American b. 1905
paintings: (L) $165; (H) $523

ROTERMUNOT, J.
German
sculpture: (H) $523

ROTH, Andreas
American 20th cent.
paintings: (L) $44; (H) $2,200

ROTH, Dieter
German b. 1930
paintings: (L) $1,495; (H) $7,475
drawings: (H) $5,980

ROTH, Ernest D.
American 1879-1964
paintings: (L) $523; (H) $1,760
drawings: (H) $605

ROTH, Frederick George Richard
American 1872-1944
sculpture: (L) $550; (H) $3,080

ROTH, Philipp
German 1841-1921
paintings: (L) $8,800; (H) $9,775

ROTHAUG, Alexander
Austrian 1870-1946
paintings: (L) $7,425; (H) $9,350

ROTHAUG, Leopold
Austrian b. 1868
paintings: (L) $880; (H) $2,860

ROTHBORT, Samuel
American 1882-1971
paintings: (L) $825; (H) $3,575
sculpture: (H) $437

ROTHE, G.H.
paintings: (L) $440; (H) $1,320

ROTHENBERG, Susan
American b. 1945
paintings: (L) $6,600; (H) $506,000
drawings: (L) $2,475; (H) $19,550

ROTHENSTEIN, Sir William
drawings: (H) $2,013

ROTHERMEL, Peter Fred
American b. 1817
paintings: (L) $1,150; (H) $3,450

ROTHERY, R. Cadogan
19th cent.
drawings: (H) $825

ROTHKO, Mark
Russian/American 1903-1970
paintings: (L) $8,625; (H) $3,190,000
drawings: (L) $8,337; (H) $48,300

ROTHMAN, Jerry
American b. 1933
sculpture: (L) $1,150; (H) $2,300

ROTHSTEIN, Charlotte
American b. 1912
drawings: (H) $460

ROTIER, Peter
American 1887-1963
paintings: (H) $1,100
drawings: (H) $550

ROTIG, Georges Frederic
French 1873-1961
paintings: (L) $2,420; (H) $3,300

ROTTA, Antonio
Italian 1828-1903
paintings: (L) $14,375; (H) $43,700

ROTTENHAMMER, Johann
German 1564-1625
drawings: (H) $5,750

ROTTENHAMMER, Johann (or Hans),
the elder
German 1564-1625
paintings: (H) $60,500
drawings: (H) $5,750

ROTTMANN, Mozart
Hungarian b. 1874
paintings: (L) $1,155; (H) $5,750

ROTTMANNER, Alfred
German 20th cent.
paintings: (H) $660

ROTTMAYR, Johann Franz Michael
Austrian 1654-1730
paintings: (H) $33,000

ROUAN, Francois
b. 1943
paintings: (H) $57,200

ROUARGUE, S***
French 19th cent.
drawings: (H) $990

ROUART, Ernest
French 1874-1942
paintings: (H) $25,300

ROUAULT, Georges
French 1871-1958
paintings: (L) $27,600; (H) $1,760,000
drawings: (L) $660; (H) $385,000
sculpture: (H) $12,075

ROUAULT, Georges Dominique
French b. 1904
drawings: (H) $715

ROUBAUD, F.F.
sculpture: (H) $770

ROUBAUD, Franz
Russian 1856-1928
paintings: (L) $1,380; (H) $6,600

ROUBICKOVA, Miluse Kytova
Czechoslovakian b. 1922
sculpture: (H) $1,725

ROUBY, Alfred
French b. 1849
paintings: (H) $2,875

ROUGELET, Benedict
French 1834-1894
sculpture: (L) $403; (H) $5,175

ROUGERON, Jules James
French 1841-1880
paintings: (L) $2,300; (H) $8,913

ROULAND, Orlando
American 1871-1945
paintings: (L) $154; (H) $7,370

ROULLAUD, F.
German School 19th/20th cent.
paintings: (H) $460

ROULLET, Gaston
French 1847-1925
paintings: (H) $4,400

ROUMEGOUS, Auguste Francois
French 19th cent.
paintings: (L) $1,840; (H) $6,600

ROUND, Cecil M.
English d. 1898
paintings: (H) $500

ROUSE, G.
sculpture: (H) $550

ROUSE, Robert William Arthur
British 19th/20th cent.
paintings: (L) $715; (H) $6,050

ROUSEFF, W. Vladimir
American 20th cent.
paintings: (H) $6,900

ROUSSE, Frank
British ac. 1897-1915
drawings: (H) $660

ROUSSE, Robert W. Arthur
English 19th cent.
paintings: (H) $2,200

ROUSSEAU
sculpture: (H) $2,875

ROUSSEAU, Adrien
French 19th cent.
paintings: (H) $1,045

ROUSSEAU, Alain
French b. 1926
paintings: (L) $1,100; (H) $2,530

ROUSSEAU, Etienne Pierre Theodore
French 1812-1867
paintings: (L) $4,950; (H) $55,000

ROUSSEAU, Helen Hoffman
American b. 1898
paintings: (L) $1,320; (H) $5,500

ROUSSEAU, Henri
paintings: (H) $16,500

ROUSSEAU, Henri, called Le Douanier
French 1844-1910
paintings: (H) $90,500
drawings: (H) $13,800

ROUSSEAU, Henri Emilien
French 1875-1933
paintings: (L) $2,530; (H) $19,550
drawings: (L) $259; (H) $1,430

ROUSSEAU, Jeanne Rij
French 1870-1956
paintings: (H) $5,500

ROUSSEAU, Marguerite, Anne Marie
DE SAEGER
Belgian b. 1888
paintings: (L) $1,320; (H) $35,200

ROUSSEAU, Maurice
Continental 19th cent.
paintings: (H) $1,925

ROUSSEAU, Percival
American 1859/69-1937
paintings: (H) $6,600

ROUSSEAU, Philippe
French 1816-1887
paintings: (L) $880; (H) $29,700

ROUSSEAU, Theodore
French 1812-1867
paintings: (L) $1,100; (H) $123,500
drawings: (L) $920; (H) $24,150

ROUSSEAU, Victor
Belgian b. 1865
sculpture: (H) $2,475

ROUSSEAU-DECELLE, Rene
French 1881-1964
paintings: (H) $10,350

ROUSSEAUX, Jacques des
Dutch 1600-1638
paintings: (H) $46,000

ROUSSEL, Georges
French 19th/20th cent.
sculpture: (H) $19,800

ROUSSEL, Ker Xavier
French 1867-1944
paintings: (L) $7,975; (H) $9,350
drawings: (L) $193; (H) $34,500

ROUSSEL, Pierre
French b. 1927
paintings: (L) $330; (H) $8,250

ROUSSELIN, Joseph Auguste
French 19th cent.
paintings: (H) $40,250

ROUSSET, Jules
French b. 1840
paintings: (H) $3,025

ROUSSIN, Georges
French b. 1854
drawings: (H) $4,600

ROUSSSEAU, Etienne Pierre Theodore
French 1812-1867
paintings: (H) $12,650

ROUVIERE
French 1905-1989
paintings: (H) $1,650

ROUX, Antoine
drawings: (L) $3,025; (H) $4,140

ROUX, Antoine, the elder
French 1765-1835
drawings: (L) $302; (H) $8,250

ROUX, Antoine, the younger
French 1799-1872
drawings: (L) $4,125; (H) $17,600

ROUX, Constant Ambroise
French 19th/20th cent.
sculpture: (L) $1,430; (H) $7,150

ROUX, Frederick
drawings: (L) $632; (H) $5,520

ROUX, Joseph Antoine
French 1765-1835
drawings: (H) $3,025

ROUX, Paul
French 1840-1918
paintings: (H) $4,950
drawings: (H) $176

ROUX FAMILY
French 19th cent.
drawings: (H) $3,300

ROUX-CHAMPION, Joseph Victor
French 1871-1953
drawings: (L) $460; (H) $1,840

ROUZEE, M.
paintings: (L) $825; (H) $1,100

ROVEL, Henri
French 19th cent.
paintings: (L) $3,450; (H) $3,450

ROVELLO, E.
paintings: (H) $660

ROVELLO, G.
Italian 19th cent.
paintings: (L) $440; (H) $1,725

ROVERE, Giovanni Mauro della, called
Il Fiammenghino
Italian 1575-1640
paintings: (H) $19,800

ROVERS, Jos.
Continental 19th/20th cent.
paintings: (H) $2,750

ROWBOTHAM, Charles
English ac. 1877-1913
drawings: (L) $605; (H) $1,320

ROWBOTHAM, Thomas Charles
Leeson
English 1823-1875
drawings: (L) $345; (H) $4,950

ROWDEN, Thomas
British 1842-1926
drawings: (L) $220; (H) $825

ROWE, Clarence
British ac. 1870-1909
paintings: (L) $605; (H) $715

ROWE, E. Arthur
British 1885-1893
drawings: (H) $920

ROWE, Ernest Arthur
British 1863-1922
drawings: (L) $2,530; (H) $3,025

ROWE, Nellie Mae
1900-1982
drawings: (L) $1,610; (H) $2,070

ROWLAND
American
paintings: (H) $660

ROWLAND, Benjamin, Jr.
American b. 1904
paintings: (H) $1,210

ROWLAND, Edith
British ac. 1901-1940
paintings: (L) $660; (H) $805

ROWLAND, William
British 20th cent.
paintings: (L) $88; (H) $2,420

ROWLANDSON, George Derville
British b. 1861
paintings: (L) $825; (H) $20,900

ROWLANDSON, Thomas
English 1756-1827
paintings: (L) $1,430; (H) $2,530
drawings: (L) $330; (H) $16,100

ROWLEY, Reuben
American 19th cent.
paintings: (L) $1,495; (H) $1,610

ROWORTH, Edward
British 1880-1964
paintings: (H) $518

ROY, Alix
paintings: (L) $1,265; (H) $3,960

ROY, Dolf van
Belgian 1858-1943
paintings: (H) $880

ROY, Jamini
Indian 1887-1972
drawings: (L) $2,990; (H) $25,300

ROY, Jules le
French 1833-1865
paintings: (L) $4,600; (H) $5,225

ROY, Lyn Aus
American
drawings: (L) $250; (H) $500

ROY, Marius
French b. 1833
paintings: (L) $748; (H) $5,175

ROY, Pierre
paintings: (L) $10,350; (H) $35,750

ROYAL, Thomas
English 18th cent.
paintings: (H) $550

ROYBAL, Alfonso, Awa Tsireh, Cattail
Bird
1898-1955
drawings: (L) $110; (H) $2,875

ROYBAL, Jose D., J.D. Roybal, Oquwa,
Rain God
1922-1978
paintings: (L) $55; (H) $198
drawings: (L) $605; (H) $5,175

ROYBET, Ferdinand
French 1840-1920
paintings: (L) $770; (H) $27,600
drawings: (H) $440

ROYE, Jozef van de
Belgian b. 1861
paintings: (H) $2,090

ROYEN, Willem Frederik van
German c. 1654-1723
paintings: (H) $66,000

ROYER, L.
paintings: (H) $247
sculpture: (H) $800

ROYER, Lionel Noel
French 1852-1926
drawings: (H) $1,725

ROYLE, Herbert
English 1870-1958
paintings: (H) $2,200

ROYLE, Stanley
Canadian 1888-1961
paintings: (L) $1,045; (H) $4,600

ROYSET, L.
European 19th cent.
drawings: (H) $577

ROZAIRE, Arthur D.
Canadian 1879-1922
paintings: (L) $935; (H) $4,400

ROZEN, George
paintings: (L) $2,970; (H) $3,575

ROZEN, Jerome G.
American ac. c. 1933
paintings: (L) $1,430; (H) $2,310

ROZET, Fanny
French b. 1881
sculpture: (L) $2,420; (H) $4,025

ROZIER, A.
French 19th cent.
paintings: (H) $2,200

ROZIER, Jules Charles
French 1821-1882
paintings: (L) $1,320; (H) $4,025

ROZMAINSKY, Vladimir
Polish
paintings: (H) $3,450

RUBALCAVA, Cristina
b. 1943
paintings: (H) $13,800

RUBBIANI, Felice
Italian 1677-1752
paintings: (H) $77,000

RUBBIANI, Felice and Francesco
VELLANI
17th/18th cent.
paintings: (H) $37,400

RUBENS, Peter Paul, studio of
17th cent.
paintings: (L) $5,775; (H) $79,750

RUBENS, S.S.
American 19th cent.
paintings: (H) $770

RUBENS, Sir Peter Paul
Flemish 1577-1640
paintings: (L) $71,500; (H) $1,652,500
drawings: (H) $5,750

RUBIN, Michael
American
paintings: (H) $7,150

RUBIN, Reuven
Israeli 1893-1974
paintings: (L) $7,150; (H) $90,200
drawings: (L) $880; (H) $10,350
sculpture: (H) $2,475

RUBIO, Gabriel Silva
b. 1955
drawings: (H) $9,200

RUCKER, Harrison Campbell
American 20th cent.
paintings: (H) $825

RUCKRIEM, Ulrich
German b. 1938
drawings: (H) $2,200
sculpture: (L) $220; (H) $32,200

RUDDER, De
Continental School 19th cent.
paintings: (H) $1,100

RUDE, Francois
French 1784-1855
paintings: (H) $1,840

RUDE, Sophie, nee FREMIET
French 1797-1867
paintings: (H) $156,500

RUDINSKI, M.
paintings: (H) $650

RUDNAY, Gyula
Hungarian 1878-1957
paintings: (H) $1,430

RUDOLPH, G.J.
Continental 19th cent.
paintings: (H) $23,000

RUDOLPH, Harold
1850-1884
paintings: (H) $715

RUDOLPH, Paul
drawings: (L) $2,860; (H) $3,850

RUDY, Charles
sculpture: (L) $450; (H) $725

RUE, Louis Felix de la
1731-1765
drawings: (H) $1,840

RUEDIGER
paintings: (H) $460

RUEL, Pierre Lion Horace
French 19th cent.
paintings: (H) $1,540

RUEL, William H.
drawings: (H) $1,540

RUELLAN, Andree
American b. 1905
paintings: (L) $660; (H) $1,100
drawings: (L) $39; (H) $303

RUELLAND, L.
American
paintings: (H) $4,400

RUELLES, P. von
German 19th/20th cent.
paintings: (H) $1,100

RUFF, Andor
Hungarian b. 1885
sculpture: (L) $275; (H) $1,210

RUFF, Thomas
German b. 1958
drawings: (L) $2,200; (H) $13,800

RUFFIER, Noel
sculpture: (H) $770

RUFFNER, Ginny
contemporary
sculpture: (L) $5,750; (H) $6,900

RUFFOLO, Gaspar J.
paintings: (L) $55; (H) $550

RUGENDAS, Georg Philipp, I
1666-1742
paintings: (H) $16,100
drawings: (H) $1,150

RUGENDAS, Johann Moritz
German 1802-1858
paintings: (L) $18,400; (H) $57,750
drawings: (H) $41,250

RUGG, Charlotte A.
drawings: (H) $12,100

RUGGERI, C.
paintings: (H) $600

RUGGIERO, Pasquale
Italian 19th cent.
paintings: (L) $137; (H) $495

RUGGLES, Edward
paintings: (H) $1,430

RUHTENBERG, Cornelis
American b. 1923
paintings: (L) $173; (H) $633

RUIPEREZ, Luis
Spanish 1832-1867
paintings: (H) $8,050

RUISDAEL, Isaack van
Dutch 1599-1677
paintings: (H) $63,000

RUISDAEL, Salomon Jacobsz. van
Dutch 1629/30-1681
paintings: (L) $16,100; (H) $552,500

RUIZ, Antonio
drawings: (H) $8,800

RUIZ, Gilberto
b. 1950
paintings: (H) $4,025

RUIZ, Guillermo Varges
Spanish 20th cent.
paintings: (H) $1,100

RUIZ, Juan Patricio Morlete
1715-c. 1780
paintings: (H) $48,300

RUIZ, Tommaso
18th cent.
paintings: (L) $7,700; (H) $33,000

RUIZ, Yamero
American ac. 1890-1910/
paintings: (H) $2,090

RUIZ Y PICASSO, Pablo
Spanish 1881-1973
drawings: (H) $27,500

RUIZ-PIPO, Manolo
Spanish b. 1929
paintings: (L) $2,750; (H) $3,300

RULE, Nicholas
b. 1956
paintings: (L) $173; (H) $2,300
drawings: (H) $1,093

RULLO, Germano
Italian 20th cent.
paintings: (H) $825

RULON, Bart
paintings: (L) $385; (H) $1,100
drawings: (H) $750

RUMLEY, J.
English 19th cent.
paintings: (H) $3,850

RUMSEY, Charles Cary
American 1879-1922
sculpture: (L) $550; (H) $1,980

RUMSEY, Daniel Lockwood
American 1900-1956
sculpture: (H) $12,100

RUNACRES, Frank
British b. 1904
paintings: (H) $550

RUNDLE, Kirk
American 20th cent.
drawings: (H) $1,320

RUNDT, Hans Hinrich
c. 1660-c. 1750
paintings: (H) $7,700

RUNGE, John
drawings: (H) $880

RUNGIUS, Carl
American 1869-1959
paintings: (L) $1,210; (H) $71,250

RUNGOIPIO, J**
German 20th cent.
paintings: (H) $550

RUNZE, Wilhelm
German 1887-1972
paintings: (L) $248; (H) $495

RUPERTI, Madja
drawings: (H) $880

RUPPERSBERG, Allen
b. 1944
drawings: (L) $2,070; (H) $23,000
sculpture: (H) $4,600

RUPPERT, Otto von
German b. 1841
paintings: (H) $805

RUPPRECHT, H.
paintings: (H) $495

RUSCHA, Ed
American b. 1937
paintings: (L) $11,500; (H) $187,000
drawings: (L) $2,420; (H) $24,200

RUSCHA, Edward
American b. 1937
paintings: (L) $8,625; (H) $112,500
drawings: (L) $5,750; (H) $23,100
sculpture: (L) $9,350; (H) $12,100

RUSCHI, Francesco
Italian ac. 1643-1656
paintings: (H) $18,700

RUSHOLN, J.
English 19th cent.
paintings: (H) $1,540

RUSHTON, George
paintings: (H) $2,420

RUSINOL, Santiago
Spanish 1861-1931
paintings: (H) $25,300

RUSK, L.S.
American 20th cent.
paintings: (H) $1,100

RUSKIN, John
English 1819-1900
drawings: (L) $2,475; (H) $4,370

RUSLING, Joseph
American 1827-1889
paintings: (H) $1,210

RUSS, C.B.
American ac. 1880-1920
paintings: (L) $302; (H) $3,738
drawings: (H) $357

RUSS, Robert
Austrian 1847-1922
drawings: (H) $17,250

RUSSELL, Benjamin
American 1804-1885
drawings: (L) $2,200; (H) $5,500

RUSSELL, Charles
British 1852-1910
paintings: (H) $1,725

RUSSELL, Charles Marion
American 1864-1926
paintings: (L) $2,875; (H) $192,500
drawings: (L) $935; (H) $222,500
sculpture: (L) $600; (H) $32,000

RUSSELL, Edward J.
Canadian/American 1832/35-1906
drawings: (L) $77; (H) $3,190

RUSSELL, G.D.
paintings: (H) $1,980

RUSSELL, George Horne
Canadian 1860-1933
paintings: (L) $412; (H) $2,640

RUSSELL, Gyrth
Canadian 1892-1970
paintings: (L) $715; (H) $1,540

RUSSELL, John
1745-1806
paintings: (L) $1,840; (H) $36,800

RUSSELL, John
British 19th cent.
paintings: (L) $880; (H) $11,550

RUSSELL, John Wentworth
Canadian b. 1879
paintings: (H) $3,850

RUSSELL, Joseph Shoemaker
1795-1860
drawings: (L) $6,325; (H) $123,500

RUSSELL, Morgan
American 1886-1953
paintings: (L) $192; (H) $31,050
drawings: (L) $138; (H) $1,210

RUSSELL, Moses B.
American c. 1810-1884
paintings: (H) $1,380

RUSSELL, R.
19th/20th cent.
paintings: (H) $935

RUSSELL, Shirley
b. 1886
paintings: (H) $605

RUSSELL, Sir Walter Westley
British 1867-1949
paintings: (L) $1,430; (H) $34,500

RUSSELL, Walter
American 1871-1963
paintings: (L) $1,650; (H) $77,000
drawings: (H) $577

RUSSELLE, E.N.
paintings: (H) $550

RUSSO, Germano
Italian b. 1935
paintings: (L) $517; (H) $715

RUSSO, Mario
Italian b. 1925
paintings: (H) $1,650

RUST, Johan Adolph
Dutch 1828-1915
paintings: (L) $1,210; (H) $3,080
drawings: (H) $58

RUTH, Horace van
British 19th/20th cent.
drawings: (H) $3,450

RUTH, Jan de
Czech/American 1922-1991
paintings: (L) $91; (H) $495
drawings: (L) $82; (H) $247

RUTHENBECH, Reiner
contemporary
drawings: (H) $1,100

RUTHLING, Ford
b. 1933
paintings: (H) $770

RUTHVEN, Jerry
American b. 1947
paintings: (L) $2,090; (H) $5,720

RUTLEDGE, Jane
American 20th cent.
paintings: (H) $605

RUTVIN, J.
paintings: (H) $825

RUTYEN, Jan Michael
Belgian 1813-1881
paintings: (H) $4,025

RUVOLO, Felix
American b. 1912
paintings: (L) $468; (H) $1,210
drawings: (H) $99

RUYERS, W.
Dutch 19th/20th cent.
paintings: (H) $605

RUYSCH, Anna Elisabeth
ac. 1680-1741
paintings: (H) $28,750

RUYSCH, Rachel
Dutch 1664-1750
paintings: (H) $96,000

RUYTEN, Jean Michel
Belgian 1813-1881
paintings: (L) $5,750; (H) $33,000

RUYTINX, Alfred
Belgian b. 1871
paintings: (H) $4,400

RYAN, Anne
American 1889-1954
paintings: (H) $8,050
drawings: (L) $2,875; (H) $7,475

RYAN, Frank
20th cent.
paintings: (H) $4,887

RYAN, Tom
American b. 1922
drawings: (L) $8,800; (H) $15,950

RYBACK, Issachar
Russian b. 1897
paintings: (L) $6,050; (H) $10,450
drawings: (L) $2,200; (H) $4,125
sculpture: (H) $1,725

RYBKOVSKI, Thadeusz
Polish 1848-1926
paintings: (L) $1,760; (H) $1,840

RYCKAERT, David, III
1612-1661
paintings: (H) $7,150

RYCKAERT, Marten
Flemish 1587/91-1631/38
paintings: (H) $79,500

RYCKHOF, J***
18th cent.
drawings: (H) $1,540

RYDER, Chauncey Foster
American 1868-1949
paintings: (L) $88; (H) $19,550
drawings: (L) $55; (H) $2,860

RYDER, Jack van
American 1898-1968
paintings: (L) $412; (H) $2,310

RYDER, Platt P.
American 1821-1896
paintings: (L) $345; (H) $5,390
drawings: (H) $110

RYDINGSVARD, Ursula von
sculpture: (H) $3,450

RYKAERT, Marten
Flemish 1587/91-1631/38
paintings: (H) $825

RYLAARSDAM, Jan
Dutch 20th cent.
paintings: (H) $605

RYLAND, Henry
English 1856/59-1924
paintings: (H) $7,150
drawings: (L) $2,530; (H) $4,370

RYLAND, Robert Knight
American 1873-1951
paintings: (L) $138; (H) $4,600

RYMAN, Herbert D.
American ac. 1930s
paintings: (H) $770

RYMAN, Robert
American b. 1930
paintings: (L) $18,700; (H) $330,000
sculpture: (H) $132,000

RYNECKI, Moses
drawings: (H) $1,955

RYOHEI, Koiso
1903-1988
drawings: (H) $23,000

RYOTT, J.R.
British ac. 1810-1860
paintings: (H) $13,200

RYSBRACK, Michael
Flemish 1694-1770
drawings: (H) $1,210
sculpture: (L) $17,050; (H) $46,000

RYSSELBERGHE, Theo van
Belgian 1862-1926
paintings: (L) $9,350; (H) $550,000
drawings: (H) $2,640

RYSWYCK, Edward van
Belgian 19th cent.
paintings: (L) $2,640; (H) $8,800

RYUKO
Japanese 20th cent.
drawings: (H) $660

RYUSHO, Kobayashi
20th cent.
drawings: (H) $1,725

SAAKOE, Del Nero
sculpture: (H) $2,805

SAAL, Georg Otto
German 1818-1870
paintings: (H) $9,350

SAALBURG, Allen R.
American b. 1899
paintings: (H) $1,092
drawings: (H) $230

SAARI, Peter
American b. 1951
drawings: (H) $6,325
sculpture: (L) $110; (H) $5,225

SABATINI, I.
Italian 19th cent.
paintings: (H) $20,700

SABATINI, Luigi
Italian 19th cent.
paintings: (H) $8,050

SABATINI, Raphael
American b. 1898
paintings: (H) $935

SABATTIER, Louis Anet
French ac. 1880-1898
paintings: (H) $1,495

SABBAGH, Georges H.
French 1887-1925
paintings: (H) $747

SABBATINI, Lorenzo
Italian c. 1530-1576
paintings: (H) $16,500

SABBET, Francois Jean
paintings: (H) $3,163

SABINA
19th cent.
paintings: (H) $1,000

SABLET, Jean Francois
1745-1819
paintings: (H) $12,650

SABLICKY, L.
sculpture: (H) $1,200

SABOIA, Jose
paintings: (H) $3,105

SABOURAUD, Emile
French b. 1900
paintings: (L) $413; (H) $2,200
drawings: (H) $575

SACCAGGI, Cesare
Italian b. 1868
drawings: (H) $660

SACCARDI, A.
Italian 19th/20th cent.
sculpture: (H) $2,875

SACCARO, John
American 1913-1981
paintings: (L) $863; (H) $12,100

SACCURDY, A.
sculpture: (H) $3,850

SACHAROFF, Olga
Russian 1889-1967
paintings: (H) $1,725
drawings: (H) $1,100

SACHS, Lambert
American ac. 1899-1906
paintings: (H) $25,300

SACHS, R.
German 19th cent.
paintings: (H) $1,540

SACKLARIAN, Stephen
Bulgarian/American b. 1899
paintings: (H) $605

SACKS, B.
British 19th cent.
drawings: (H) $1,650

SACKS, Joseph
American 1887-1974
paintings: (L) $220; (H) $3,575
drawings: (H) $286

SADEE, Philippe Lodowyck Jacob Fred
Dutch 1837-1904
paintings: (L) $1,265; (H) $19,550

SADEK, K.C.
European 19th cent.
sculpture: (H) $1,760

SADLER, Walter Dendy
English 1854-1923
paintings: (L) $2,310; (H) $25,300

SADOVNIKOV, Vasili Semionovich
1800-1879
drawings: (H) $2,990

SAEYENS, Ant.
sculpture: (H) $550

SAEYS, Jacob Ferdinand
c. 1658-1725/26
paintings: (L) $16,100; (H) $57,500

SAFFORD, Arthur R.
American b. 1900
paintings: (H) $715

SAFTLEVEN, Cornelis
Dutch 1607-1681
paintings: (L) $6,900; (H) $134,500
drawings: (L) $6,900; (H) $35,200

SAFTLEVEN, Herman
Dutch 1609-1685
paintings: (L) $9,900; (H) $32,200
drawings: (L) $863; (H) $10,450

SAGATES
drawings: (H) $550

SAGRESTANI, Giovanni Camillo
c. 1660-1730
paintings: (L) $4,600; (H) $12,100

SAILMAKER, Isaac
English c. 1633-1721
paintings: (H) $22,000

SAIN, Edouard Alexandre
French 1830-1910
paintings: (L) $4,400; (H) $27,500

SAINT
paintings: (H) $577

SAINTIN, Henri
French 1846-1899
paintings: (L) $1,150; (H) $4,180

SAINTIN, Jules Emile
French 1829-1894
paintings: (L) $8,050; (H) $32,200

SAITO, Yoshishige
Japanese b. 1904
paintings: (L) $167,500; (H) $376,500

SAKAI, Kazuya
Argentinean b. 1927/31
paintings: (L) $495; (H) $5,500

SALA, Eliseo
Italian 1813-1879
paintings: (H) $4,125

SALA, Ignacio Gil
Spanish b. 1912
paintings: (H) $5,520

SALA, Jean
Spanish b. 1895
paintings: (H) $34,500

SALA, Juan
Spanish 1867-1918
paintings: (H) $11,000

SALA, Kurt
American contemporary
drawings: (L) $1,380; (H) $2,530

SALA, Paolo
Italian 1859-1924
paintings: (L) $19,800; (H) $34,500
drawings: (L) $908; (H) $5,520

SALA Y FRANCES, Emilio
Spanish 1850-1910
paintings: (L) $1,150; (H) $14,300

SALABET, Jean
French 20th cent.
paintings: (L) $192; (H) $2,640

SALANSON, Eugene Marie
French 19th cent.
paintings: (H) $11,550

SALANTINE, ***
German 19th cent.
paintings: (H) $3,850

SALAS, Antonio
paintings: (H) $5,175

SALAS, M.
Spanish 19th/20th cent.
paintings: (H) $8,050

SALAS, Manuel
paintings: (H) $605

SALAZAR, Carlos
Colombian b. 1956
paintings: (L) $3,300; (H) $3,520

SALBET, Jean
French 20th cent.
paintings: (H) $770

SALEC, de
paintings: (H) $5,060

SALEH, Radeaa Sarief Bastaman
Javanese 1814-1880
paintings: (H) $55,000

SALEMME, Antonio
American b. 1892
sculpture: (L) $2,300; (H) $4,620

SALEMME, Attilio
American 1911-1955
paintings: (L) $2,640; (H) $17,600
drawings: (H) $4,025

SALENTIN, Hubert
German 1822-1910
paintings: (L) $1,100; (H) $23,100

SALES, Francesco
paintings: (H) $1,610

SALGUERO, A.
Peruvian early 20th cent.
drawings: (H) $1,100

SALIERES, Paul Narcisse
French 19th cent.
paintings: (H) $22,000

SALIMBENI, Ventura
paintings: (H) $9,200

SALINAS, Baruj
Cuban/American b. 1935
paintings: (L) $5,750; (H) $9,200

SALINAS, Porfirio
American 1910-1972
paintings: (L) $633; (H) $15,950

SALINAS Y TERUEL, Augustin
Spanish b. 1862
paintings: (L) $2,200; (H) $7,150

SALINAS Y TERUEL, Juan Pablo
Spanish 1871-1946
paintings: (L) $4,125; (H) $79,500

SALINI, Tommaso, called Mao
Italian c. 1575-c.1625
paintings: (H) $55,000

SALISBURY, Frank O.
British 1874-1962
paintings: (H) $1,870

SALKIN, Ferdinand
paintings: (H) $1,650

SALLE, David
American b. 1952
paintings: (L) $5,750; (H) $143,000
drawings: (L) $1,100; (H) $143,000

SALLES, Jules Wagner
French 1814-1898
paintings: (H) $3,300

SALM, Abraham van
Dutch 1660-1720
paintings: (H) $107,000

SALM, Wilhelmus Antonie
paintings: (L) $605; (H) $633

SALM, Wilhelmus Vander
paintings: (H) $1,210

SALMON, Emile Frederic
French 1840-1913
sculpture: (H) $1,925

SALMON, Helen R.
paintings: (H) $805

SALMON, John Cuthbert
English 1844-1917
drawings: (L) $231; (H) $495

SALMON, Robert
Anglo/American 1775-c. 1842/44
paintings: (L) $2,970; (H) $165,000

SALMONES, Victor
Mexican b. 1937
sculpture: (L) $143; (H) $8,250

SALMSON
sculpture: (H) $1,430

SALMSON, Hugo Frederik
Swedish 1844-1894
paintings: (L) $2,475; (H) $13,800

SALMSON, Hugo Frederik and S.
SCHOENFELS
19th cent.
paintings: (H) $6,600

SALMSON, J.
sculpture: (H) $2,070

SALMSON, Jean Jules
French 1823-1902
sculpture: (L) $1,840; (H) $2,530

SALOM, Germain B.
sculpture: (H) $1,925

SALOME
b. 1954
paintings: (L) $5,500; (H) $9,775

SALOME and CASTELLI
paintings: (H) $17,250

SALT, James
British 19th cent.
paintings: (H) $1,700

SALT, John
American b. 1937
paintings: (L) $11,000; (H) $19,800

SALTER, William
British 1804-1875
paintings: (H) $719

SALTINI, Pietro
Italian 1839-1908
paintings: (H) $1,650

SALTMER, Florence A.
British ac. 1882-1900
paintings: (L) $1,650; (H) $1,870

SALTZMAN, William
American b. 1916
drawings: (H) $518

SALUCCI, Alessandro
Italian c. 1590-1660
paintings: (H) $51,750

SALVADOR Y GOMEZ, Vicente
1637-1680
drawings: (H) $4,025

SALVAT, Francois Martin
French 1892-1976
paintings: (H) $633
drawings: (H) $247

SALVATI, G.
Italian 20th cent.
paintings: (L) $220; (H) $605

SALVEA, J.
American 19th cent.
paintings: (H) $468

SALVETTI, Antonio
Italian 1854-1931
paintings: (H) $1,210

SALVI, Giovanni Battista, called Il
Sassoferrato
Italian 1609-1685
paintings: (L) $12,075; (H) $40,700

SALVIN, M. de
French 19th/20th cent.
paintings: (H) $1,610

SALVIN, M.A. de
Italian 19th cent.
paintings: (H) $4,950

SALVO
b. 1947
paintings: (H) $3,520

SALZER, Friedrich
German 1827-1876
paintings: (H) $6,325

SAMACCHINI, Orazio
1532-1577
drawings: (H) $13,800

SAMANT, Monmohan
paintings: (H) $2,530

SAMARA, Helga
German b. 1941
paintings: (L) $385; (H) $660
sculpture: (H) $495

SAMARAS, Lucas
Greek/American b. 1936
paintings: (L) $3,850; (H) $6,900
drawings: (L) $575; (H) $35,200
sculpture: (L) $3,850; (H) $88,000

SAMBARI, Nicola
Italian b. 1927
paintings: (H) $8,050

SAMBROOK, Russell
American 20th cent.
paintings: (L) $357; (H) $2,860

SAMBUSETTI
Italian 19th cent.
drawings: (H) $1,760

SAMEL
British 20th cent.
paintings: (H) $1,870

SAMMONS, Carl
1886-1968
paintings: (H) $770

SAMMONS, Carl
American 1853-1917
paintings: (L) $517; (H) $748

SAMMONS, Carl
American 1857-1938
paintings: (H) $4,125

SAMMONS, Carl
American 1886-1968
paintings: (L) $275; (H) $4,675
drawings: (H) $605

SAMOKICH, Nicolai Semionovitch
Russian b. 1860
drawings: (H) $1,100

SAMPLE, Paul Starrett
American 1896-1974
paintings: (L) $412; (H) $9,200
drawings: (L) $33; (H) $2,588

SAMPSON, Alden
American b. 1853
paintings: (L) $220; (H) $1,210

SAMPSON, James Henry
English ac. 1869-1879
paintings: (H) $4,125

SAMSON, M.
sculpture: (H) $550

SAMUELS, Daniel
British b. 1917
paintings: (H) $578

SAMUELSON, Bruce
American b. 1946
paintings: (L) $110; (H) $550
drawings: (L) $110; (H) $650

SAMUELSON, Peter
British b. 1912
paintings: (H) $1,320

SAN MARZANO, Pasquale Ruggiero
di
Italian 1851-1916
paintings: (H) $7,150

SANBORN, Percy A.
American 1849-1929
paintings: (L) $3,410; (H) $6,325
drawings: (L) $66; (H) $88

SANCHEZ
Spanish 19th cent.
paintings: (L) $288; (H) $1,100

SANCHEZ, A. Cortellini
Spanish 19th cent.
paintings: (H) $770

SANCHEZ, Adolfo
contemporary
paintings: (H) $495

SANCHEZ, E.
Spanish School 19th cent.
paintings: (H) $935

SANCHEZ, Edgar
Venezuelan b. 1940
paintings: (L) $6,900; (H) $10,450
drawings: (H) $1,980

SANCHEZ, Eduardo Sola
Spanish 19th cent.
paintings: (H) $2,990

SANCHEZ, Edward
Spanish 19th cent.
paintings: (H) $3,300

SANCHEZ, Emilio
Cuban b. 1921
paintings: (L) $27; (H) $12,650
drawings: (H) $825

SANCHEZ, Enrique
Latin b. 1938
paintings: (H) $1,375

SANCHEZ, J*
18th cent.
paintings: (H) $6,037

SANCHEZ, Tomas
b. Cuba 1948
paintings: (L) $7,475; (H) $79,500
drawings: (L) $5,280; (H) $25,300

SANCHEZ DE GUADALUPE,
Anton, II
Spanish ac. c. 1510-1561
paintings: (H) $57,500

SANCHEZ-BARBUDO, Salvador
Spanish 1857-1917
paintings: (L) $990; (H) $63,000

SANCHEZ-PERRIER, Emilio
Spanish 1855-1907
paintings: (L) $3,080; (H) $33,000

SAND, George
French 1804-1876
drawings: (H) $1,375

SAND, Maximilen E.
American 19th cent.
paintings: (H) $2,070
drawings: (H) $522

SANDBACK, Fred
American b. 1943
sculpture: (L) $1,650; (H) $8,250

SANDBY, Paul
English 1725-1809
drawings: (H) $660

SANDER, A.H.
b. 1892
sculpture: (H) $825

SANDER, Ludwig
American 1906-1975
paintings: (L) $1,380; (H) $4,313
drawings: (H) $57

SANDER, Sherry
American b. 1941
sculpture: (L) $950; (H) $4,290

SANDER, Tom
paintings: (L) $1,100; (H) $2,750
drawings: (L) $825; (H) $1,900

SANDERS, Christopher
English b. 1905
paintings: (H) $523

SANDERS, David
American b. 1933
paintings: (L) $5,500; (H) $14,580
drawings: (L) $2,750; (H) $6,325

SANDERS, G.E.
Continental 19th cent.
drawings: (H) $2,090

SANDERS, Gail
American contemporary
paintings: (H) $605

SANDERS, Robert
English/American 20th cent.
paintings: (L) $484; (H) $935

SANDERSON, Robert
British ac.c. 1895
paintings: (H) $546

SANDERSON-WELLS, John
British 1872-1955
paintings: (L) $2,185; (H) $15,400

SANDHAM, Henry
Canadian/American 1842-1912
paintings: (H) $1,100

SANDHOLT, Marie
Danish b. 1872
paintings: (H) $1,045

SANDHURST, G.
British 19th c.
paintings: (H) $4,675

SANDOR, Mathias
American 1857-1920
paintings: (L) $825; (H) $935
drawings: (H) $201

SANDOZ, Edouard Marcel
Swiss 1881-1971
paintings: (H) $863
sculpture: (L) $935; (H) $4,950

SANDRECZKI, Otto
American 20th cent.
drawings: (H) $550

SANDRUCCI, Giovanni
Italian 19th cent.
paintings: (L) $5,225; (H) $5,750

SANDY, Percy Tsisete, Kai Sa, Red
Moon
Zuni b. 1918
drawings: (L) $144; (H) $1,150

SANDZEN, Birger
American 1871-1954
paintings: (L) $3,080; (H) $10,925
drawings: (L) $990; (H) $1,760

SANETY, Gide
Continental 20th cent.
paintings: (H) $1,375

SANFORD, Edward Field
American b. 1867
sculpture: (H) $690

SANFORD, Marion
American 1904-1988
sculpture: (L) $575; (H) $3,850

SANFORD, Thomas D.
drawings: (H) $4,830

SANGER, Grace H.C.
American b. 1881
paintings: (L) $55; (H) $1,100
drawings: (H) $220

SANGER, I.M.
19th/20th cent.
paintings: (H) $880

SANGER, Ricard
German 20th cent.
paintings: (H) $2,530

SANGIOVANNI, A.
18th cent.
paintings: (H) $15,400

SANGSTER, Alfred
British 19th/20th cent.
paintings: (H) $12,650

SANI, Alessandro
Italian 19th cent.
paintings: (L) $330; (H) $44,850

SANI, B.
Italian 19th cent.
paintings: (H) $1,100

SANI, David
Italian 19th cent.
paintings: (L) $935; (H) $9,200

SANKUHL, Herman
German b. 1872
paintings: (H) $1,100

SANO DI PIETRO
Italian 1406-1481
paintings: (L) $52,800; (H) $167,500

SANQUIRICO, Alessandro
1780-1849
drawings: (L) $1,725; (H) $2,070

SANSON
paintings: (H) $1,155

SANSON, J.
sculpture: (H) $2,090

SANSON, Justin Chrysostome
French 1833-1910
sculpture: (H) $1,955

SANSONE
Italian 20th cent.
paintings: (H) $633

SANSOVINO, Jacopo, workshop of
Venetian 16th cent.
sculpture: (H) $103,700

SANSUGUET
paintings: (H) $1,150

SANT, James
English 1820-1916
paintings: (L) $6,600; (H) $6,900
drawings: (H) $660

SANTA MARIA, Andres de
b. Colombia 1860 d. 1945
paintings: (H) $18,150

SANTACROCE, Girolamo da
Italian ac. 1503-1556
paintings: (H) $20,700

SANTENS, James
American contemporary
sculpture: (H) $633

SANTERRE, Jean Baptiste
French 1651/58-1771
paintings: (L) $39,100; (H) $66,300

SANTINI, G.
Italian 19th/20th cent.
paintings: (H) $522

SANTINI, M.
19th/20th cent.
paintings: (H) $920

SANTINI, Pio
Italian b. 1908
paintings: (H) $1,540

SANTOMASO, Giuseppe
Italian 1907-1990
paintings: (H) $6,820
drawings: (L) $990; (H) $8,625

SANTORO, Francesco Raffaello
Italian b. 1844
paintings: (L) $302; (H) $3,850

SANTORO, Rubens
Italian 1843/59-1942
paintings: (L) $2,300; (H) $85,000

SANTOS, M. Gonzalez
paintings: (H) $4,550

SANTOS, Sebastian Tiao
Brazilian
paintings: (H) $495

SANTOSH, Gulam Rasool
Indian b. 1929
paintings: (L) $805; (H) $3,162

SANTRY, Daniel
American 1867-1915
paintings: (L) $144; (H) $1,540

SANTVOORT, Dirck Dircksz van
Dutch 1610-1680
paintings: (L) $7,150; (H) $10,925

SANVITALE, Giovanni
Italian b. 1935
paintings: (L) $660; (H) $3,850

SANZ, Bernhard Lukas
c. 1650-after 1710
paintings: (H) $6,600

SANZ CARTA, Valentin
Cuban 1850-1898
paintings: (H) $5,462

SANZEL, Felix
French 19th cent.
sculpture: (H) $2,750

SAPIA, Mariano
b. 1964
paintings: (L) $2,875; (H) $4,485

SAPORETTI, Edgardo
Italian 1865-1909
drawings: (H) $489

SAPP, Allen
Canadian b. 1929
paintings: (L) $460; (H) $7,260

SAPPEL, Marta
German b. 1914
paintings: (L) $605; (H) $605

SARDO, S.
paintings: (H) $1,650

SARET, Alan
American b. 1944
drawings: (L) $1,320; (H) $1,650
sculpture: (L) $1,265; (H) $8,800

SARG, Tony
American 1882-1942
drawings: (L) $412; (H) $9,900

SARGEANT, Geneve Rixford
American 1868-1957
paintings: (L) $1,540; (H) $1,955

SARGENT, Dick
1911-1978
paintings: (H) $3,575
drawings: (L) $193; (H) $8,800

SARGENT, John Singer
American 1856-1925
paintings: (L) $2,255; (H) $7,592,500
drawings: (L) $440; (H) $90,500

SARGENT, Margarett McKean
American 20th cent.
paintings: (H) $1,495

SARGENT, Margarett W.
American 1892-1978
paintings: (H) $550
drawings: (H) $192
sculpture: (H) $1,045

SARGENT, Paul Turner
American 1880-1946
paintings: (L) $187; (H) $1,610

SARGENT, Walter
American 1868-1927
paintings: (H) $1,540

SARIAN, Martiros Segveevitch
Armenian 1880-1956
drawings: (H) $2,530

SARKA, Charles N.
American 1879-1960
paintings: (L) $192; (H) $908
drawings: (L) $385; (H) $715

SARKISIAN, Paul
American b. 1928
drawings: (L) $2,200; (H) $2,200

SARKISIAN, Sarkis
American 1909-1977
paintings: (L) $137; (H) $3,025
drawings: (L) $110; (H) $1,320

SARLUIS, Leonard
1874-1949
paintings: (L) $2,300; (H) $5,750

SARNOFF, Arthur
American b. 1912
paintings: (L) $220; (H) $1,980
drawings: (H) $715

SARNOFF, Lolo
American b. 1916
sculpture: (H) $460

SARNOFF ?, Ivan
20th cent.
paintings: (H) $700

SARRE, Carmen
American early 20th cent.
paintings: (L) $165; (H) $605

SARRI, Egisto
Italian 1837-1901
paintings: (L) $2,860; (H) $16,100

SARROCCHI, Tito
Italian 1824-1900
sculpture: (H) $825

SARROFF
sculpture: (H) $880

SARSONY, Robert
American b. 1938
paintings: (H) $770

SARTAIN, William
American 1843-1924
paintings: (L) $460; (H) $3,630

SARTELLE, Herbert
American 1885-1955
paintings: (H) $1,540

SARTER, Armin
German b. 1937
paintings: (H) $880

SARTHOU, Maurice Elie
French b. 1911
paintings: (L) $173; (H) $880

SARTO, Andrea del
Italian 1486/88-1530/31
drawings: (H) $4,830

SARTO, Lucia
Italian b. 1950
paintings: (L) $1,610; (H) $1,980

SARTORE, Hugo
b. Uruguay 1935
paintings: (H) $5,750
sculpture: (L) $5,750; (H) $6,600

SARTORIO, Giulio Aristide
Italian 1860-1932
paintings: (L) $1,650; (H) $12,075
drawings: (L) $1,100; (H) $6,050

SARTORIUS, Francis
English 1734-1804
paintings: (L) $4,600; (H) $48,875

SARTORIUS, John Francis
English c. 1775-1831
paintings: (H) $24,200

SARTORIUS, John Nost
English 1759-1828
paintings: (L) $2,640; (H) $40,250
drawings: (L) $288; (H) $550

SASSI, Pietro
Italian 1834-1905
paintings: (H) $495

SASSO, Antonio
Italian 19th cent.
paintings: (L) $825; (H) $920

SATALINO, V.
20th cent.
paintings: (H) $605

SATO, Key
Japanese 1906-1978
paintings: (L) $1,100; (H) $6,050

SATO, Tadashi
American b. 1923
paintings: (H) $1,320

SATTERLEE, Walter
American 1844-1908
paintings: (L) $303; (H) $495
drawings: (L) $66; (H) $1,430

SATTLER, Hubert
Austrian 1817-1904
paintings: (H) $20,900

SAUBERT, Tom
paintings: (L) $950; (H) $990
drawings: (L) $440; (H) $440

SAUERFELT, Leonard
French 19th cent.
paintings: (L) $863; (H) $1,100

SAUERWEID, Alexandre Ivanovitch
Russian 1783-1844
drawings: (H) $13,800

SAUERWEIN, C.D.
American 1839-1918
paintings: (H) $550

SAUERWEIN, Frank Peters
American 1871-1910
paintings: (L) $308; (H) $10,450
drawings: (L) $468; (H) $863

SAUL, F.
sculpture: (H) $1,320

SAUL, Peter
American b. 1934
paintings: (L) $9,200; (H) $13,800
drawings: (L) $1,955; (H) $8,050

SAUNDERS, Charles L.
English ac. 1881-1885
paintings: (H) $1,650
drawings: (H) $385

SAUNDERS, Norman
1908-1986
paintings: (L) $1,430; (H) $9,900
drawings: (L) $935; (H) $1,150

SAUNDERS, Raymond
American b. 1934
paintings: (H) $1,540
drawings: (H) $6,050

SAUNIER, Noel
French 1847-1890
paintings: (L) $3,300; (H) $11,000

SAURA, Antonio
Spanish b. 1930
paintings: (L) $15,400; (H) $79,200
drawings: (L) $8,050; (H) $16,500

SAURFELT, Leonard
French 19th cent.
paintings: (L) $660; (H) $4,400

SAUSSY, Hattie
American 1890-1978
drawings: (H) $880

SAUTER, Williard J.
American b. 1912
paintings: (H) $550

SAUTEUR, Claude le
Canadian b. 1926
paintings: (H) $2,200

SAUTNER, Franz Adolph
German ac. 1890-1915
sculpture: (L) $1,100; (H) $2,875

SAUTNER, Johann
Austrian 1747-1823
sculpture: (H) $25,300

SAUVAGE, Arsene Symphorien
French 19th cent.
paintings: (H) $1,650

SAUVAGE, Georges
French
· *paintings:* (H) $7,700

SAUVAGE, Philippe Francois
French ac. 1863
paintings: (H) $2,875

SAUVAGE, R-tion
sculpture: (H) $880

SAUVAGEAU, Louis
French b. 1822
sculpture: (H) $28,750

SAUVAGEOT, Charles Theodore
French 1826-1883
paintings: (H) $3,520

SAUWIN, P***
American 19th cent.
paintings: (H) $1,955

SAUZAY, Adrien Jacques
French 1841-1928
paintings: (L) $2,300; (H) $3,300

SAVAGE, Anne Douglas
paintings: (L) $1,100; (H) $3,300

SAVAGE, Edward
American 1761-1817
paintings: (H) $10,925

SAVAGE, Eugene Francis
American 1883-1978
paintings: (L) $1,870; (H) $44,000
drawings: (H) $1,320

SAVELIEVA, Valentina
Russian 20th cent.
paintings: (H) $13,200

SAVERY, Roelandt
Flemish 1576-1639
paintings: (L) $35,200; (H) $99,000

SAVIAN, Petion
Haitian 20th cent.
paintings: (L) $231; (H) $1,485

SAVIGNAC, Raymond P.G.
b. 1907
drawings: (H) $770

SAVIN, Maurice
French 1894-1973
paintings: (L) $1,100; (H) $5,175

SAVINE, Leopold
French b. 1861
sculpture: (L) $247; (H) $1,100

SAVINI, Alfonso
Italian 1836-1908
paintings: (L) $2,760; (H) $17,250

SAVINIO, Alberto
Italian 1891-1952
paintings: (H) $275,000

SAVITSKY, Jack
American 1910-1991
paintings: (L) $900; (H) $1,500
drawings: (L) $45; (H) $575

SAVOLDO, Giovanni Girolamo
Italian ac. 1508-1548
paintings: (H) $1,542,500

SAVRASOV, Alexei
Russian 1830-1897
paintings: (H) $3,163

SAVRY, Hendrick
Dutch 1823-1907
paintings: (L) $2,860; (H) $12,650

SAWYER, Clifton Howard
American 1896-1966
paintings: (H) $1,540

SAWYER, Helen Alton
American b. 1900
paintings: (L) $165; (H) $3,300
drawings: (L) $218; (H) $413

SAWYER, Paul
American 19th cent.
paintings: (H) $9,350

SAWYER, Warren
American 1904/14-1977
paintings: (L) $247; (H) $522
drawings: (L) $110; (H) $385

SAWYER, Wells M.
American 1863-c. 1960
paintings: (L) $330; (H) $1,760

SAWYIER, Paul
American 1865-1917
drawings: (L) $330; (H) $8,800

SAXE, Ad.
French(?) 19th cent.
paintings: (H) $605

SAXE, Adrian
American b. 1943
sculpture: (L) $6,325; (H) $9,200

SAYRE, F. Grayson
American 1879-1938/39
paintings: (L) $248; (H) $9,350
drawings: (H) $1,100

SCAFFAI, Luigi
Italian b. 1837
paintings: (L) $3,300; (H) $4,290

SCAHRY, Saul
b. 1904
paintings: (H) $660

SCALA, Vincenzo
Italian 19th cent.
paintings: (H) $6,050

SCALBERT, Jules
French b. 1851, ac 1876-1891
paintings: (L) $517; (H) $19,800
drawings: (H) $3,100

SCALELLA, Jules
American b. 1895
paintings: (L) $1,320; (H) $2,640
drawings: (L) $70; (H) $99

SCAMANDA, ***
paintings: (L) $550; (H) $660

SCANGA, Italo
American b. 1932
drawings: (H) $880
sculpture: (L) $1,320; (H) $5,462

SCANLAN, Robert Richard
British d. 1876
paintings: (H) $10,450

SCARBOROUGH, Frederick W.
British ac. 1896-1939
drawings: (H) $3,450

SCARF, S. Thomas
American contemporary
sculpture: (L) $247; (H) $546

SCARLETT, Rolph
American 1889-1984
paintings: (L) $1,600; (H) $8,800
drawings: (L) $350; (H) $3,575

SCARLETT, Samuel
American
paintings: (H) $7,150

SCARPA
sculpture: (H) $990

SCARPA, Gino
paintings: (H) $1,650

SCARPITTA, Salvatore
American b. 1919
paintings: (H) $26,450

SCARSBOROUGH (CONANT), Lucy
American 1867-1921
drawings: (H) $920

SCARSELLA, Ippolito, called LO
SCARSELLINO
Italian 1551-1620
paintings: (L) $5,462; (H) $123,500

SCARVELLI
Italian 19th/20th cent.
drawings: (H) $13,800

SCARVELLI, S.
Greek 19th/20th cent.
drawings: (H) $1,430

SCATIZZI, Sergio
Italian b. 1918
paintings: (H) $880

SCHAAN, Paul
French 19th/20th cent.
paintings: (L) $990; (H) $7,475

SCHACHNER, Therese
Austrian b. 1869
paintings: (H) $6,038

SCHACHT, Rudolph
German 19th/20th cent.
paintings: (L) $330; (H) $489

SCHADOW, Johan Gottfried
German 1764-1850
sculpture: (H) $8,250

SCHADOW, Wilhelm von
German 1788-1862
paintings: (H) $920

SCHAEFELS, Hendrik Frans
Belgian 1827-1904
paintings: (L) $920; (H) $29,900

SCHAEFELS, Lucas
Belgian 1824-1885
paintings: (L) $3,850; (H) $17,600

SCHAEFER, Carl Fellman
Canadian b. 1903
drawings: (L) $1,035; (H) $1,430

SCHAEFFER, August
Austrian 1833-1916
drawings: (H) $460

SCHAEFFER, Frederick Ferdinand
American 1839-1927
paintings: (H) $460

SCHAEFFER, H.
paintings: (L) $577; (H) $742
drawings: (H) $715

SCHAEFFER, Henri
French 1900-1975
paintings: (H) $2,310

SCHAEFFER, Henry Thomas
British b. 1854
paintings: (H) $1,380

SCHAEFFER, J.
20th cent.
paintings: (H) $605

SCHAEFFER, Mead
American 1898-1980
paintings: (L) $248; (H) $14,300
drawings: (H) $138

SCHAEFFING, Jim
paintings: (H) $880

SCHAEP, Henri Adolphe
Dutch 1826-1870
paintings: (H) $8,050

SCHAETTLE, Louis
American d. 1917
paintings: (H) $1,045

SCHAFER, Frederick
German/American 1839-1927
paintings: (L) $440; (H) $4,888
drawings: (H) $187

SCHAFER, H.
paintings: (L) $1,760; (H) $1,760
drawings: (L) $440; (H) $825

SCHAFER, H. Thomas
British ac. 1873-1915
paintings: (H) $6,600

SCHAFER, Henry
British 19th cent.
paintings: (L) $770; (H) $4,620
drawings: (H) $2,750

SCHAFER, Henry
British/French 19th cent.
paintings: (L) $935; (H) $17,250
drawings: (L) $330; (H) $1,760

SCHAFER, Henry Thomas
English ac. 1873-1915
paintings: (L) $920; (H) $20,700
drawings: (L) $660; (H) $3,300

SCHAFER, Joseph
paintings: (H) $1,840

SCHAFFER, H.
German 19th cent.
paintings: (H) $4,400

SCHAFFNER, Barbara
drawings: (H) $1,045

SCHAFFNER, W.
paintings: (H) $743

SCHAGGIE, Cesare
Italian 19th cent.
sculpture: (H) $40,250

SCHAKEWITS, Josef
Belgian 1848-1913
paintings: (H) $9,200

SCHALCH, Johann Jacob
Swiss 1723-1789
paintings: (H) $23,000

SCHALCKEN, Godfried
Dutch 1643-1706
paintings: (H) $6,600

SCHALL, Jean Frederic
French 1752-1825
paintings: (L) $3,220; (H) $52,250

SCHALTER, Jakob E.
drawings: (H) $460

SCHAMBERG, Morton Livingston
American 1881-1918
paintings: (H) $1,100
drawings: (H) $14,300

SCHANKER, Louis
American b. 1903
paintings: (L) $2,310; (H) $5,463
drawings: (L) $825; (H) $4,370

SCHANTZ, Amos
paintings: (L) $125; (H) $800

SCHARF, Kenny
American b. 1958
paintings: (L) $4,370; (H) $41,400
drawings: (H) $16,100
sculpture: (L) $6,900; (H) $6,900

SCHARFF, S.F.
paintings: (H) $1,650

SCHARFF, William
Danish 1866-1959
paintings: (H) $660

SCHARL, Josef
German 1896-1958
paintings: (H) $3,300
drawings: (H) $1,650

SCHARP, Henri
Continental 19th cent.
paintings: (H) $3,410

SCHARY, Saul
American 1904-1978
paintings: (L) $100; (H) $19,800
drawings: (L) $60; (H) $110

SCHATTENSTEIN, Nikol
American 1877-1954
paintings: (L) $575; (H) $8,800

SCHATZ, Daniel Leon
American b. 1908
paintings: (H) $1,540

SCHATZ, Lincoln
American b. 1963
sculpture: (L) $1,045; (H) $1,320

SCHAUMBURG, Jules
Belgian 19th cent.
paintings: (H) $2,070

SCHAUSS, Ferdinand
German 1832-1916
paintings: (H) $22,000

SCHAWINSKY, Xanti
Swiss, b. 1904 d. 1979
paintings: (L) $1,380; (H) $10,725

SCHEAKMAN, Anna Weatherby Parry
American d. 1937
paintings: (H) $660

SCHEDONE, Bartolomeo
Italian c. 1570-1615
paintings: (H) $97,900

SCHEELE, Kurt
German b. 1905
paintings: (H) $1,840

SCHEERBOOM, Andries
Dutch 1832-1880
paintings: (L) $3,080; (H) $3,450

SCHEERES, Henricus J.
Dutch 1829-1864
paintings: (H) $1,210

SCHEFFER, Ary
Dutch/French 1795-1858
paintings: (L) $978; (H) $13,200

SCHEFFER, Robert
Austrian b. 1859
paintings: (H) $6,600

SCHEFFERS, Glen C.
American 19th/20th cent.
paintings: (L) $330; (H) $748

SCHEFFLER, Rudolph
American 1884-1973
paintings: (L) $5,610; (H) $19,800

SCHEGGI, Paolo
Italian 20th cent.
paintings: (H) $1,210

SCHEIBE, Richard
sculpture: (H) $2,875

SCHEIBER, Hugo
Hungarian 1873-1950
paintings: (L) $1,495; (H) $2,200
drawings: (L) $303; (H) $2,640

SCHEIBL, Hubert
b. 1951
paintings: (H) $7,150

SCHEIDEL, Franz Anton von
Austrian 1731-1801
drawings: (L) $690; (H) $2,420

SCHEIDER, Gold
sculpture: (H) $770

SCHELFHOUT, Andreas
Dutch 1787-1870
paintings: (L) $6,900; (H) $27,500
drawings: (H) $495

SCHELL, Francis H.
1834-1909
drawings: (L) $330; (H) $1,430

SCHELL, Susan Gertrude
American 1891-1970
paintings: (L) $192; (H) $1,320

SCHELLIN, Robert
American 20th cent.
paintings: (H) $575

SCHELLINKS, Willem
1627-1678
paintings: (H) $9,200

SCHENAU, Johann Eleazer
German 1737-1806
paintings: (L) $2,475; (H) $6,600

SCHENCK, August Friedrich Albrecht
Danish 1828-1901
paintings: (L) $825; (H) $5,500

SCHENCK, W.H.
American late 19th cent.
paintings: (H) $16,500

SCHENCK, William
c. 1947
paintings: (L) $4,312; (H) $4,313

SCHENDEL, A. van
Dutch 19th cent.
paintings: (H) $1,100

SCHENDEL, Petrus van
Belgian 1806-1870
paintings: (L) $1,650; (H) $138,000

SCHENER
French
sculpture: (H) $1,045

SCHENK, A.F.A.
German 1828-1901
sculpture: (H) $3,300

SCHEPANSKY, Adolf
American ac. early 20th cent.
paintings: (L) $460; (H) $1,610

SCHERER, Fred
paintings: (H) $604

SCHERER, Joseph
German 1814-1891
paintings: (H) $5,500

SCHERFIG, Hans
paintings: (H) $690

SCHERMAN, Tony
b. 1950
paintings: (L) $978; (H) $17,250

SCHERMERS, Florent
Continental 19th cent.
paintings: (H) $719

SCHERRES, Carl
German 1833-1923
paintings: (H) $2,860

SCHERREWITZ, Johan
Dutch 1868-1951
paintings: (L) $1,320; (H) $13,800

SCHEUERER, Frengen von Frelius
paintings: (H) $715

SCHEUERER, Julius
German 1859-1913
paintings: (L) $2,750; (H) $9,200

SCHEUERER, Otto
German 1862-1934
paintings: (L) $863; (H) $5,750

SCHEYERER, Franz
Austrian 1770-1839
paintings: (L) $6,325; (H) $20,700

SCHGOER, Julius
German 1847-1885
paintings: (H) $1,430

SCHIAVO, Paolo
Italian 1397-1478
paintings: (H) $77,000

SCHIAVONE, Andrea, Andrea
MELDOLLA
Italian c. 1501-1563
paintings: (L) $5,175; (H) $23,000

SCHIAVONI, Natale
Italian 1777-1858
paintings: (L) $2,070; (H) $28,600

SCHICK, R.
paintings: (H) $2,640

SCHICKTANT?
drawings: (H) $660

SCHIEDGES, Peter Paulus
Dutch 1812-1876
paintings: (H) $3,450

SCHIEFER, Johannes
20th cent.
paintings: (L) $275; (H) $880
drawings: (L) $275; (H) $1,430

SCHIELE, Egon
German 1890-1918
paintings: (L) $37,400; (H) $4,677,500
drawings: (L) $23,000; (H) $412,500

SCHIELENS
Dutch 19th cent.
paintings: (H) $2,990

SCHIER, Franz
German 1852-1922
paintings: (H) $3,850

SCHIERTZ, August Ferdinand
German 1804-1878
paintings: (H) $3,300

SCHIFFEREL, Lou
paintings: (H) $770

SCHILCHER, Frederich
Austrian 1811-1881
paintings: (H) $1,265

SCHILDT, Gary
American
paintings: (L) $1,400; (H) $2,640
drawings: (H) $1,320
sculpture: (L) $550; (H) $1,000

SCHILDT, N.M.
Dutch 20th cent.
drawings: (H) $495

SCHILLE, Alice
American 1869-1955
paintings: (L) $3,520; (H) $4,675
drawings: (L) $1,980; (H) $6,600

SCHIMMEL, John
sculpture: (H) $1,320

SCHIMMEL, Wilhelm
German/American 1817-1890
sculpture: (L) $977; (H) $55,200

SCHIMPF, Georg
German 1898-1938
drawings: (H) $9,200

SCHINDLER, A. Zeno
American 1813-1880
paintings: (H) $2,200

SCHINDLER, Albert
Austrian 1805-1861
paintings: (H) $5,175

SCHINDLER, Emil Jakob
Austrian 1842-1892
paintings: (L) $6,600; (H) $7,150

SCHINDLER, Thomas
German b. 1959
paintings: (H) $2,875

SCHIODTE, Harald
Danish 1852-1924
paintings: (H) $12,650

SCHIPPERS, Joseph
Belgian 1868-1950
paintings: (H) $1,650

SCHIRFEN, Johannes
German 20th cent.
paintings: (H) $770

SCHIRM, Carl C.
German 1852-1928
paintings: (H) $1,980

SCHISSLER, Janeen A.
American
drawings: (L) $950; (H) $990

SCHIVERT, Victor
Romanian b. 1863
paintings: (L) $308; (H) $2,640

SCHIWETZ, Berthold "Tex"
American 1909-1971
sculpture: (L) $357; (H) $11,000

SCHIWETZ, E.M. "Buck"
1898-1984
drawings: (L) $660; (H) $2,200

SCHJELDERUP, Leis
Norwegian 19th cent.
paintings: (H) $14,300

SCHLEDORN
German 19th cent.
paintings: (H) $6,325

SCHLEGELL, William von
20th cent.
paintings: (H) $1,210

SCHLEICH, Robert
German 1845-1934
paintings: (L) $4,140; (H) $22,000

SCHLEICHER, Carl
Austrian 1830-1888
paintings: (L) $715; (H) $1,725

SCHLEISNER, Christian Andreas
Danish 1810-1882
paintings: (H) $2,185

SCHLESER, F.
paintings: (H) $1,210

SCHLESINGER, C.
paintings: (H) $1,650

SCHLESINGER, Felix
German 1833-1910
paintings: (L) $2,300; (H) $129,000

SCHLESINGER, Georg
German ac. 1816-1827
paintings: (H) $605

SCHLESINGER, Henri Guillaume
French 1814-1893
paintings: (L) $1,210; (H) $14,950

SCHLESINGER, Karl
Swiss 1825/26-1893
paintings: (H) $2,200

SCHLESINGER, Leon
drawings: (H) $1,150

SCHLICHTING-CARLSEN, Carl
Danish 1852-1903
paintings: (H) $605

SCHLICK, Benjamin
French ac. 19th/20th cent.
drawings: (L) $715; (H) $715

SCHLICKUM, Carl
German 19th cent.
paintings: (H) $825

SCHLIEPSTEIN, Gerhard
German b. 1886
sculpture: (H) $1,955

SCHLIMARSKI, Heinrich Hans
Austrian b. 1859
paintings: (H) $1,045

SCHLIPF, E.
sculpture: (H) $1,265

SCHLIPPE, Alexis von
20th cent.
paintings: (L) $83; (H) $770

SCHLITT, Heinrich
German b. 1849
paintings: (H) $5,463

SCHLOESSER, Carl
German 1832-1914
paintings: (L) $3,220; (H) $5,775

SCHLUTER, August
German d. 1928
paintings: (L) $220; (H) $518

SCHMEDTGEN, William Herman
American
paintings: (H) $908
drawings: (L) $55; (H) $110

SCHMID, Erich
19th/20th cent.
paintings: (H) $715

SCHMID, Richard
American b. 1934
paintings: (L) $460; (H) $40,700
drawings: (H) $10,780

SCHMID, Rudolf
American b. 1896
paintings: (H) $1,430

SCHMID, Rudolf and V** BING
paintings: (H) $1,018

SCHMIDHAMMER, Arpad
German 1857-1921
paintings: (H) $6,990

SCHMIDLIN, Adolf
German b. 1868
paintings: (H) $575

SCHMIDT
Continental 19th cent.
paintings: (H) $9,625

SCHMIDT, Albert H.
American 1885-1957
paintings: (H) $770

SCHMIDT, Alwin
1900-1984
drawings: (H) $770

SCHMIDT, Bill
American 20th cent.
paintings: (H) $495

SCHMIDT, Carl
American 1885-1969
paintings: (L) $275; (H) $9,900
drawings: (L) $121; (H) $176

SCHMIDT, Carl
American b. 1889
paintings: (L) $193; (H) $1,210

SCHMIDT, Carl
American b. 1909
paintings: (L) $690; (H) $5,225

SCHMIDT, E. Allan
German 19th cent.
paintings: (H) $2,475

SCHMIDT, E. Trier
British ac. 1879-1903
paintings: (H) $7,700

SCHMIDT, Hans W.
German b. 1859
paintings: (L) $10,350; (H) $17,050

SCHMIDT, Harold von
American 1893-1982
paintings: (L) $1,650; (H) $15,400
drawings: (H) $880

SCHMIDT, Henrich
German 1740-1821
paintings: (H) $23,000

SCHMIDT, Johann Martin, called
Kremser-Schmidt
1718-1801
paintings: (H) $18,400
drawings: (H) $3,850

SCHMIDT, Karl
American 1890-1962
paintings: (L) $357; (H) $8,250
drawings: (L) $805; (H) $1,430

SCHMIDT, Katherine
American 1898-1978
paintings: (L) $115; (H) $920
drawings: (L) $184; (H) $437

SCHMIDT, Leonhard
German 1892-1978
paintings: (H) $1,870

SCHMIDT, Thomas Lanagan
American 20th cent.
drawings: (H) $805

SCHMIDT FELLY
sculpture: (H) $700

SCHMIDT-CASSEL, Otto
German b. 1876
sculpture: (L) $3,025; (H) $6,050

SCHMIDT-HOFER, Otto
German 19th/20th cent.
sculpture: (L) $220; (H) $605

SCHMIDT-KASSEL, Gustav
German ac. 1925
sculpture: (H) $1,725

SCHMIDT-ROTTLUFF, Karl
German 1884-1976
paintings: (H) $440,000
drawings: (L) $7,700; (H) $14,950

SCHMILA, J.
paintings: (H) $750

SCHMIS, Richard
paintings: (H) $3,575

SCHMITSON, Teutwart
German 1830-1863
paintings: (H) $3,163

SCHMITT, Albert Felix
American b. 1873
paintings: (H) $550

SCHMITZ, Carl Ludwig
American 1900-1967
paintings: (H) $1,100
sculpture: (H) $4,675

SCHMITZ, Ernst
German 1859-1917
paintings: (L) $1,100; (H) $6,325

SCHMITZBERGER, Josef
German b. 1851
paintings: (L) $3,850; (H) $8,050

SCHMUD, M.
German or Austrian 18th cent.
paintings: (H) $2,200

SCHMUTZER, Jakob Mathias
German 1733-1811
drawings: (L) $308; (H) $605

SCHMUTZHARDT, Berthold
sculpture: (H) $575

SCHMUTZLER, Leopold
German 1864-1941
paintings: (L) $2,090; (H) $11,000

SCHNABEL, Julian
American b. 1951
paintings: (L) $5,462; (H) $319,000
drawings: (L) $690; (H) $189,500
sculpture: (L) $34,500; (H) $319,000

SCHNAKENBERG, Henry
American 1892-1970
paintings: (L) $55; (H) $1,150
drawings: (L) $220; (H) $1,210

SCHNARS-ALQUIST, Hugo
German b. 1855
paintings: (L) $550; (H) $1,650

SCHNAUDER, Reinhard
German 19th cent.
sculpture: (H) $4,600

SCHNECTENBERG
sculpture: (H) $575

SCHNEE, Hermann
German 1840-1926
paintings: (H) $660
drawings: (H) $2,185

SCHNEIDAU, Christian von
American 1893-1976
paintings: (L) $605; (H) $6,325
drawings: (H) $468

SCHNEIDER
paintings: (H) $8,140
sculpture: (L) $55; (H) $825

SCHNEIDER, ***
Continental School 19th cent.
paintings: (H) $3,450

SCHNEIDER, Arthur
American 1866-1942 (?)
paintings: (L) $605; (H) $747
drawings: (H) $209

SCHNEIDER, Charlotte
ac. 1910-1925
paintings: (H) $605

SCHNEIDER, Christian
American 20th cent.
sculpture: (H) $1,725

SCHNEIDER, Felicie
French 1831-1888
paintings: (H) $5,750

SCHNEIDER, Frank
American ac. early 20th cent.
paintings: (L) $358; (H) $550

SCHNEIDER, G.
German 19th cent.
paintings: (L) $2,530; (H) $5,520

SCHNEIDER, Gerard Ernest
French 1896-1948
drawings: (H) $805

SCHNEIDER, Hermann
German 1847-1918
paintings: (H) $8,625

SCHNEIDER, Otto
American 1865-1950
paintings: (L) $165; (H) $1,320

SCHNEIDER, Susan Hayward
American b. 1876
paintings: (H) $880

SCHNEIDER, Theophile
German/American b. 1872
paintings: (L) $275; (H) $825

SCHNEIDER-BLUMBERG, Bernhard
German b.1881
paintings: (H) $990

SCHNEIDER-BLUMBERG, Ernst
American 20th cent.
paintings: (H) $715

SCHNEIR, Jacques
American 1898-1988
drawings: (H) $978

SCHNELLE, William G.
American b. 1897
paintings: (H) $2,760

SCHNETZ, Jean Victor
French 1787-1870
drawings: (H) $4,400

SCHOCK, Elmer
American
paintings: (H) $700

SCHODL, Max
Austrian 1834-1921
paintings: (H) $8,050

SCHOELLHORN, Hans Karl
Swiss b. 1892
paintings: (H) $523
drawings: (H) $165

SCHOENBAUER, Henry
American b. 1895
sculpture: (H) $2,300

SCHOENEWERK, Alexandre
French 1820-1885
sculpture: (L) $460; (H) $880

SCHOENZEIT, Ben
b. 1942
paintings: (H) $8,050

SCHOETTLE, L.
Austrian 19th cent.
paintings: (H) $2,420

SCHOEVAERTS, Mathys
Flemish c. 1665-after 1694
paintings: (L) $39,100; (H) $40,250

SCHOFIELD, Flora
American 20th cent.
paintings: (H) $3,910

SCHOFIELD, Kershaw
British 19th/20th cent.
paintings: (L) $374; (H) $805
drawings: (H) $55

SCHOFIELD, Walter Elmer
American 1867-1944
paintings: (L) $525; (H) $43,700
drawings: (H) $600

SCHOLDER, Fritz
American b. 1937
paintings: (L) $2,588; (H) $18,400

SCHOLL, J.
German 19th/20th cent.
paintings: (H) $1,870

SCHOLTEN, Hendrik Jacobus
Dutch 1824-1907
paintings: (L) $3,080; (H) $7,150

SCHOLZ, Max
German b. 1855
paintings: (L) $1,100; (H) $9,775

SCHOMBURG, Alex
paintings: (H) $3,450
drawings: (L) $2,420; (H) $6,900

SCHOMMER, Francois
French 1850-1935
paintings: (H) $1,210

SCHON, Andreas
paintings: (L) $1,380; (H) $11,500

SCHONBERG, J.
Austrian 19th cent.
paintings: (H) $1,540

SCHONBORN, Anton
American d. 1871
drawings: (L) $16,500; (H) $22,000

SCHONBRUNNER, Ignaz
German 1835-1921
paintings: (L) $550; (H) $1,650

SCHONDEL, Ludwig Otto
Danish 1837-1905
paintings: (H) $1,375

SCHONEACHER, J.
German 20th cent.
paintings: (H) $863

SCHONEBERG, S.C.
20th cent.
drawings: (L) $345; (H) $460

SCHONFELDT, Johann Heinrich
German 1609-1683
paintings: (H) $46,000

SCHOONOVER, Frank Earle
American 1877-1972
paintings: (L) $880; (H) $38,500

SCHOOPALLY, E.H.
Continental 19th/20th cent.
paintings: (H) $1,320

SCHOOTEN, Floris Gerritsz van
Dutch ac. 1605-1655
paintings: (L) $25,300; (H) $33,350

SCHOOTEN, Floris van, studio of
17th cent.
paintings: (H) $35,200

SCHOPPE, Julius
German 1795-1868
paintings: (H) $4,400

SCHOR, Ilya
paintings: (H) $1,870

SCHOTANUS, Petrus
second half 17th cent.
paintings: (H) $5,175

SCHOTEL, Jan Christianus
Dutch 1787-1838
paintings: (L) $1,100; (H) $4,180

SCHOTT, Max
Continental 19th cent.
paintings: (H) $2,090

SCHOTT, Walter
German 1861-1938
sculpture: (L) $990; (H) $6,050

SCHOUMAN, Aert
Dutch 1710-1792
paintings: (H) $16,100

SCHOUTEN
20th cent.
paintings: (L) $2,090; (H) $2,200

SCHOUTEN, Henri
Belgian 1864-1927
paintings: (L) $3,300; (H) $4,675

SCHOUTEN, Henry
Dutch 1791-1835
paintings: (H) $2,300

SCHOUTEN, Henry and Paul
paintings: (H) $1,210

SCHOUTEN, Pieter Hubert
Dutch 1747-1822
paintings: (H) $2,588

SCHOYERER, Josef
German 1844-1923
paintings: (L) $1,840; (H) $12,650

SCHRADER, Julius Friedrich Anton
German 1815-1900
paintings: (H) $11,000

SCHRADER, Rudolf
German b. 1853
paintings: (H) $1,725

SCHRAG, Julius
German 1864-1948
paintings: (L) $825; (H) $1,100

SCHRAG, Karl
American b. Germany 1912
drawings: (L) $44; (H) $550

SCHRAM, Alois Hans
Austrian 1864-1919
paintings: (L) $2,070; (H) $11,550

SCHRAMM, Viktor
Romanian 1865-1929
paintings: (H) $5,500

SCHRAUDOLPH, John
paintings: (H) $825

SCHRECKENGOST, Victor
American b. 1906
drawings: (L) $412; (H) $467

SCHREIBER, Charles Baptiste
French d. 1903
paintings: (L) $1,320; (H) $8,625

SCHREIBER, Georges
Belgian/American 1904-1977
paintings: (L) $440; (H) $11,500
drawings: (L) $201; (H) $1,380

SCHREIBER, Paul
Austrian 19th cent.
paintings: (H) $1,725

SCHREUER
German 19th/20th cent.
paintings: (H) $1,980

SCHREYER, Adolf
German 1828-1899
paintings: (L) $330; (H) $134,500

SCHREYER, Claudius W.
American 1864-1902
paintings: (L) $140; (H) $3,080

SCHREYVOGEL, Charles
American 1861-1912
paintings: (L) $2,990; (H) $255,500
drawings: (L) $747; (H) $1,320
sculpture: (L) $19,800; (H) $37,950

SCHRIMPF, Georg
German 1889-1938
paintings: (L) $32,200; (H) $78,200
drawings: (L) $1,265; (H) $10,350

SCHRODER, Albert Friedrich
German b. 1854
paintings: (L) $1,925; (H) $6,325

SCHRODER, Justin
German 20th cent.
paintings: (H) $1,430

SCHRODER, T.
drawings: (H) $550

SCHRODER-SONNESTERN, Friedrich
drawings: (H) $2,645

SCHRODL, Anton
Austrian 1823-1906
paintings: (H) $1,870

SCHROEDER, A.
German 19th cent.
paintings: (H) $4,025

SCHROFF, Alfred Hermann
American 1863-1939
paintings: (L) $403; (H) $1,980

SCHROTTER, Alfred von
Austrian 1856-1935
paintings: (L) $3,630; (H) $8,250

SCHRYVER, Louis Marie de
French 1862-1942
paintings: (L) $3,680; (H) $165,000

SCHUBAUER, Fredrich Leopold
German
paintings: (H) $23,000

SCHUBERT, Heinrich Carl
German 1827-1897
paintings: (H) $495

SCHUCH, Carl
Austrian 1846-1903
paintings: (H) $6,900

SCHUCHARDT, F., Jr.
German 1835-1902
paintings: (H) $2,760

SCHUCK
paintings: (H) $935

SCHUESSLER, C.
British 19th cent.
paintings: (H) $1,760

SCHUFFENECKER, Claude Emile
French 1851-1934
paintings: (L) $18,400; (H) $22,000
drawings: (L) $357; (H) $15,400

SCHUFRIED, Dominik
Austrian b. 1810
paintings: (H) $1,100

SCHULTE, Antoinette
American 1897-1981
paintings: (L) $275; (H) $605

SCHULTHEISS, Karl Max
German b. 1885
paintings: (H) $4,600

SCHULTHEISS, Nathalie
Austrian 1865-1952
paintings: (H) $4,600

SCHULTZ, A.
German 19th cent.
paintings: (H) $1,155

SCHULTZ, Carl
German 19th cent.
paintings: (H) $550

SCHULTZ, Erdmann
German b. 1810
paintings: (H) $8,800

SCHULTZ, George F.
American b. 1869
paintings: (L) $110; (H) $1,610
drawings: (L) $220; (H) $3,450

SCHULTZ, Gottfried
German b. 1842
paintings: (H) $2,200

SCHULTZ, Hart "Lone Wolf"
paintings: (H) $660

SCHULTZ, Robert
American Contemporary
paintings: (H) $1,150

SCHULTZBERG, Anshelm Leonhard
Swedish 1862-1942
paintings: (L) $2,475; (H) $17,600

SCHULTZE, Andreas
b. 1955
paintings: (H) $4,600

SCHULTZE, Robert
German b. 1828
paintings: (H) $3,450

SCHULYER, C.
19th/20th cent.
paintings: (L) $303; (H) $550

SCHULZ, Ada Walter
American 1870-1928
paintings: (L) $7,700; (H) $17,600

SCHULZ, Adolph Robert
American 1869-1963
paintings: (H) $3,300

SCHULZ, Adrien
French 1851-1931
paintings: (L) $690; (H) $14,300

SCHULZ, Carl
German 19th cent.
paintings: (H) $920

SCHULZ, Charles
American b. 1922
drawings: (L) $330; (H) $6,325

SCHULZ, Robert
American 20th cent.
paintings: (H) $920

SCHULZ, Robert E.
1928-1978
drawings: (H) $770

SCHULZ-STRADTMANN, Otto
German 20th cent.
paintings: (L) $1,100; (H) $1,650

SCHULZE, Andreas
German b. 1955
paintings: (L) $440; (H) $7,700

SCHUMACHER, C.J.
paintings: (H) $2,530

SCHUMACHER, Mathias
German 20th cent.
sculpture: (H) $1,870

SCHUMAN, ***
German 19th cent.
paintings: (H) $1,540

SCHUMPERT, William
drawings: (H) $1,045

SCHURCHARDT, F.
paintings: (H) $1,760

SCHURJIN, Raul
1907-1983
paintings: (H) $747

SCHURR, Claude
French b. 1921
paintings: (L) $625; (H) $8,800

SCHUSSELE, Christian
French/American 1824/26-1879
paintings: (H) $2,990

SCHUSTER, Donna
American 1883-1953
paintings: (L) $440; (H) $10,350
drawings: (L) $275; (H) $3,163

SCHUSTER, Josef
Austrian 1812-1890
paintings: (L) $935; (H) $3,450

SCHUSTER, Joseph
Austrian 1873-1945
paintings: (H) $3,520

SCHUSTER, Karl Maria
Austrian 1871-1953
paintings: (L) $5,225; (H) $5,500

SCHUSTER, Ludwig
Austrian b. 1820
paintings: (L) $4,125; (H) $6,600

SCHUSTER, Rudolf Heinrich
German 1848-1902
paintings: (H) $2,875

SCHUTTE, Thomas
b. 1954
paintings: (H) $2,070

SCHUTZ, Christian Georg
German 1718-1791
paintings: (L) $19,800; (H) $60,500

SCHUTZ, Heinrich
German b. 1875
paintings: (H) $1,210

SCHUTZ, Johan Frederick
1817-1888
paintings: (H) $1,980

SCHUTZE, August
German 1805-1847
paintings: (H) $13,800

SCHUTZE, Wilhelm
German 1840-1898
paintings: (L) $25,300; (H) $71,500

SCHUTZENBERGER, Paul Rene
French 1860-1916
paintings: (H) $5,500

SCHUYFF, Peter
Dutch b. 1958
paintings: (L) $920; (H) $12,100
drawings: (H) $3,450

SCHUYLER, Remington
American 1884/87-1955
paintings: (L) $330; (H) $5,060

SCHUZ, Theodor
German 1830-1900
paintings: (L) $1,045; (H) $1,380

SCHWABE, Carlos
Swiss 1866-1926
paintings: (H) $17,250

SCHWABE, Emil
German 1856-1887
paintings: (H) $1,150

SCHWABE, Heinrich
German 1847-after 1907
sculpture: (H) $2,300

SCHWABE, Heinrich August
American 1843-1916
paintings: (L) $110; (H) $4,400

SCHWABE, R.
sculpture: (H) $1,495

SCHWACHA, George
b. 1908
paintings: (L) $110; (H) $467

SCHWANFELDER, Charles Henry
English 1774-1837
paintings: (H) $4,400

SCHWAR, Wilhelm
German b. 1869
paintings: (H) $1,323

SCHWARCZ, June
American b. 1918
sculpture: (H) $1,925

SCHWARTZ, Alvin Howard
American b. 1916
paintings: (H) $770

SCHWARTZ, Andrew Thomas
American 1867-1942
paintings: (L) $91; (H) $19,550

SCHWARTZ, C.A.
drawings: (H) $825

SCHWARTZ, Davis F.
American 1879-1969
paintings: (L) $495; (H) $1,045
drawings: (H) $330

SCHWARTZ, Karl
American 19th/20th cent.
paintings: (H) $1,035

SCHWARTZ, Lew
American
drawings: (H) $5,175

SCHWARTZ, Manfred
American 1909-1970
paintings: (L) $880; (H) $1,540
drawings: (H) $220

SCHWARTZ, Raphael
French
sculpture: (H) $8,050

SCHWARTZ, Robert
American 20th cent.
drawings: (H) $2,090

SCHWARTZ, Theresa
Dutch 1851-1918
paintings: (H) $2,760

SCHWARTZ, William S.
Russian/American 1896-1977
paintings: (L) $1,150; (H) $39,100
drawings: (L) $403; (H) $1,650

SCHWARTZKOPF, Earl
American b. 1888
paintings: (H) $990

SCHWARZ, Alfred
German b. 1833
paintings: (H) $8,800

SCHWEIZER, J. Otto
American ac. 1863-1955
sculpture: (H) $11,550

SCHWENINGER, Carl, Jr.
Austrian 1854-1903
paintings: (L) $8,250; (H) $13,750

SCHWENINGER, Karl, Sr.
Austrian 1818-1887
paintings: (L) $7,150; (H) $18,400

SCHWENK, F.
19th/20th cent.
paintings: (H) $805

SCHWIERING, Conrad
American b. 1916
paintings: (L) $715; (H) $15,950

SCHWIMER, Rika
20th cent.
paintings: (H) $1,725

SCHWIND, Moritz von
Austrian 1804-1871
drawings: (H) $4,400

SCHWINGER, Laurence
b. 1941
paintings: (H) $192
drawings: (H) $605

SCHWITTERS, Kurt
German 1887-1948
paintings: (L) $1,870; (H) $2,185
drawings: (L) $11,500; (H) $244,500
sculpture: (H) $77,000

SCIALOJA, Toti
b. 1914
paintings: (H) $2,090

SCIFONI, Anatolio
Italian 1841-1884
paintings: (H) $8,800

SCILLA, Agostino
Italian 1639-1700
paintings: (L) $1,870; (H) $2,200

SCIPIONI
drawings: (L) $468; (H) $1,150

SCMUTZLER, Leopold
Austrian 1864-1941
paintings: (H) $27,500

SCOGNAMIGLIO, Cavalier Antonio
Italian 19th cent.
paintings: (L) $2,875; (H) $3,850

SCOGNAMIGLIO, E.
Italian 19th cent.
paintings: (L) $440; (H) $3,300

SCOMPI, Joe de
sculpture: (H) $2,200

SCOPPETTA, Pietro
Italian 1863-1920
paintings: (L) $4,400; (H) $13,750

SCORRANO, Luigi
Italian 1842-1924
paintings: (L) $600; (H) $3,300

SCOTT Anna Page
American d. 1925
paintings: (L) $715; (H) $990

SCOTT, C.W. and J.W.A. SCOTT
paintings: (H) $3,850

SCOTT, Campbell
Scottish/American b. 1930
paintings: (L) $275; (H) $2,145

SCOTT, Charles II
paintings: (H) $1,210

SCOTT, Clyde
American 1884-1959
paintings: (H) $2,475

SCOTT, David
paintings: (H) $1,320

SCOTT, Edwin
paintings: (L) $345; (H) $715

SCOTT, Flavia B.
American
paintings: (L) $400; (H) $650

SCOTT, Frank Edwin
American 1862-1929
paintings: (L) $935; (H) $2,750

SCOTT, Henry
British ac. 1930-1966
paintings: (H) $2,300

SCOTT, Henry
English b. 1911
paintings: (H) $13,200

SCOTT, Howard
1902-1983
drawings: (H) $880

SCOTT, Janet Laura
American ac. c. 1919
drawings: (H) $2,013

SCOTT, John
American 1907-1987
paintings: (L) $1,210; (H) $11,000
drawings: (H) $880

SCOTT, John Martin
paintings: (H) $1,045

SCOTT, John White Allen
American 1815-1907
paintings: (L) $935; (H) $2,530

SCOTT, Julian
American 1846-1901
paintings: (L) $805; (H) $3,520

SCOTT, Katherine
American b. 1871
paintings: (L) $330; (H) $1,320

SCOTT, Michael
b. 1958
paintings: (L) $920; (H) $1,725

SCOTT, Peter
British 20th cent.
paintings: (H) $4,950

SCOTT, Punkie
paintings: (H) $1,100

SCOTT, Randall
20th cent.
sculpture: (H) $1,610

SCOTT, Robert Bagge
English ac. 1886-1896
paintings: (H) $633

SCOTT, Sir Peter
paintings: (L) $1,045; (H) $11,275
drawings: (H) $330

SCOTT, W.
paintings: (H) $2,300

SCOTT, Walt
American 20th cent.
drawings: (H) $1,320

SCOTT, William
b. 1884
paintings: (H) $990
drawings: (H) $55

SCOTT, William
contemporary
paintings: (L) $13,800; (H) $22,000

SCOTT, William George
British 1913-1989
paintings: (H) $18,700
drawings: (L) $1,035; (H) $8,625

SCRIVER, Robert M., Bob
American b. 1914
sculpture: (L) $193; (H) $5,500

SCROTS, William
ac. 1537-1554
paintings: (H) $5,500

SCUDDER, Janet
American 1875-1940
paintings: (L) $1,650; (H) $5,225
sculpture: (L) $3,850; (H) $46,000

SCULL, Nina W.
American 20th cent.
paintings: (H) $742

SCULLY, Sean
Irish b. 1945
paintings: (L) $6,600; (H) $264,000
drawings: (L) $2,970; (H) $20,900

SEABOURN, Bert Dail
American b. 1931
paintings: (H) $495
drawings: (H) $495

SEABY, Allan William
British b. 1867
paintings: (H) $1,870

SEAGER, Edward
American 1809-1886
paintings: (H) $39
drawings: (L) $33; (H) $1,150

SEAGO, Edward Brian
English 1910-1974
paintings: (L) $9,350; (H) $34,500

SEALY, Allen C.
British ac. 1873-1886
paintings: (L) $8,338; (H) $83,600

SEARLE, Helen R.
American 1830-1889
paintings: (H) $10,925

SEARLE, Ronald
British b. 1920
drawings: (L) $316; (H) $2,200

SEARS, Benjamin Willard
American 1846-1905
paintings: (H) $1,760

SEARS, Francis
British 20th cent.
paintings: (H) $770

SEARS, Olga
American 1906-1990
paintings: (L) $82; (H) $1,980

SEARS, Philip Shelton
American 1867-1953
sculpture: (L) $192; (H) $4,400

SEARS, Sarah Choate
American 1858-1935
drawings: (L) $220; (H) $1,100

SEARS, Taber
American 1870-1950
paintings: (L) $358; (H) $770
drawings: (L) $330; (H) $330

SEAVER, Elizabeth A.
American ac. 1939-1940
sculpture: (L) $660; (H) $4,290

SEAVEY, E.L.
American 19th cent.
paintings: (L) $225; (H) $1,093

SEAVEY, George W.
American 1841-1916
paintings: (L) $440; (H) $1,380

SEAWRIGHT, J.
American 20th cent.
sculpture: (H) $550

SEBASTIANO DEL PIOMBO
Italian 1485-1547
paintings: (H) $1,980

SEBEN, Henri van
Belgian 1825-1913
paintings: (L) $1,650; (H) $8,050
drawings: (H) $115

SEBES, Pieter Willem
Dutch b. 1830
paintings: (H) $2,200

SEBIRE, Gaston
French b. c. 1920/25
paintings: (L) $173; (H) $7,150

SEBOROVSKI, Carole
drawings: (H) $6,613

SEBRON, Hippolyte Victor Valentin
French 1901-1879
paintings: (H) $3,738

SECOLA, A.
Continental School 19th cent.
paintings: (L) $550; (H) $4,620

SEDELMAYER, Ferdinand von
German 19th cent.
paintings: (H) $2,200

SEDGLEY, Peter
paintings: (L) $2,200; (H) $2,200

SEDLACEK, Franz
1891-1944
paintings: (H) $31,050

SEDLACEK, Stephan
German 19th/20th cent.
paintings: (L) $825; (H) $2,750

SEEBACH, Lothar von
German 1853-1930
paintings: (H) $546

SEEBOLD, Marie Madeleine
American 1866-1948
paintings: (H) $3,740

SEEGER, Hermann
German 1857-1920
paintings: (L) $16,100; (H) $26,450

SEEKATZ, Joseph Conrad
German 1719-1768
paintings: (L) $26,450; (H) $60,250

SEEMAN, Ed
American 20th cent.
paintings: (H) $467

SEEMAN, Enoch
Polish c. 1694-1744
paintings: (L) $4,400; (H) $6,900

SEERY, John
American b. 1914
paintings: (L) $715; (H) $3,410

SEETH, Frederick
1845-1929
paintings: (L) $2,070; (H) $4,025

SEFFNERFER
sculpture: (H) $990

SEGAL, Arthur
Romanian 1875-1944
paintings: (L) $825; (H) $935

SEGAL, George
American b. 1924
paintings: (H) $3,025
drawings: (L) $1,840; (H) $3,163
sculpture: (L) $660; (H) $211,500

SEGANTINI, Giovanni
Italian 1858-1899
drawings: (H) $19,800

SEGAR, E.C.
drawings: (L) $1,870; (H) $8,625

SEGAR, Elzie Crisler
American 1894-1938
paintings: (H) $1,650

SEGE, Alexandre
French 1818-1885
paintings: (H) $5,500

SEGER, Ernst
German 1868-1939
sculpture: (H) $2,300

SEGHERS, Daniel
Flemish 1590-1661
paintings: (L) $2,750; (H) $28,750

SEGNA DI BONAVENTURA
Italian ac. 1298-1327
paintings: (L) $118,000; (H) $528,000

SEGNER, E.B.
paintings: (H) $1,430

SEGOVIA, Andres
Spanish b. 1929
paintings: (L) $385; (H) $2,860

SEGRE, Sergio
b. 1932
paintings: (H) $920

SEGUI, Antonio
Argentinean b. 1934
paintings: (L) $6,600; (H) $26,400
drawings: (L) $5,750; (H) $46,000
sculpture: (H) $8,800

SEGUIN, Jocelyne
French 20th cent.
paintings: (H) $460

SEGUIN-BERTAULT, Paul
1869-1964
paintings: (H) $1,760

SEGUINO, F.J.
Continental 19th cent.
drawings: (H) $715

SEGUSO, Armando
paintings: (H) $770

SEGUSO, Livio
Italian b. 1930
sculpture: (H) $1,150

SEHRING, Adolf
Russian/American b. 1930
paintings: (L) $230; (H) $3,300

SEIBELS, Carl
German 1844-1877
paintings: (H) $2,640

SEICKETT, Charles
Flemish School 19th cent.
paintings: (H) $605

SEIDE, Paul
American b. 1949
sculpture: (L) $5,175; (H) $6,900

SEIDEL, Emory P.
American ac. 1925-1935
sculpture: (L) $1,100; (H) $2,875

SEIFERT, Alfred
Czechoslovakian 1850-1901
paintings: (L) $800; (H) $5,462

SEIFERT, Franz
Austrian b. 1866
sculpture: (H) $550

SEIFERT, Paul
American 1840-1921
drawings: (H) $24,200

SEIFERT, Victor Heinrich
German 1870-1953
sculpture: (L) $460; (H) $4,600

SEIFFERT, Paul
French b. 1874
paintings: (H) $5,520

SEIGNAC, Guillaume
French 1870-1924
paintings: (L) $3,740; (H) $110,000

SEIGNAC, Paul
French 1826-1904
paintings: (L) $3,300; (H) $46,000

SEIGNEURGENS, Ernest Louis
Augustin
French d. 1904
paintings: (H) $715

SEIHO, Takeuchi
1864-1942
drawings: (H) $6,900

SEIKA
late 19th cent.
sculpture: (H) $4,312

SEILER, Carl William Anton
German b. 1846
paintings: (L) $1,485; (H) $3,680

SEILER, Joseph Albert
Austrian ac. 1848
paintings: (H) $9,900

SEILERN, Imre
Austrian b. 1907
paintings: (H) $715

SEIROKU, Noma
1902-1966
drawings: (H) $1,380

SEITZ, Anton
German 1829-1900
paintings: (H) $1,760

SEITZ, John
American
drawings: (H) $1,150

SEJOURNE, Bernard
paintings: (H) $7,700

SEKINE, Yoshio
b. 1922
paintings: (L) $3,162; (H) $4,950

SEKOTO, Gerard
South African 1913-1933
paintings: (H) $2,760

SEKULA, Sonja
Swiss 1918-1963
paintings: (L) $1,430; (H) $1,760

SEL, Jean-Baptiste
1780/90-1832
paintings: (H) $1,870

SELBY, Joe
American 1893-1960
paintings: (L) $935; (H) $1,045
drawings: (L) $248; (H) $495

SELDEN, Henry Bill
American 1886-1934
paintings: (H) $468

SELDON, Charles
1889-1961
drawings: (H) $825

SELER, Carl
German 1846-1921
paintings: (H) $4,840

SELEY, Jason
sculpture: (H) $880

SELIGER, Charles
  paintings: (H) $1,495
  drawings: (H) $138

SELIGMANN, Kurt
  Swiss 1900-1962
  paintings: (L) $550; (H) $96,000
  drawings: (L) $690; (H) $18,400
  sculpture: (H) $36,800

SELINGER, Emily
  American 1848-1927
  paintings: (L) $220; (H) $743

SELINGER, Jean Paul
  American 1850-1909
  paintings: (L) $137; (H) $5,463

SELL, Christian
  German 1831-1883
  paintings: (L) $1,650; (H) $3,850

SELLAER, Vincent
  Flemish ac. 1538-after 1544
  paintings: (H) $31,900

SELLAIO, Jacopo del
  Italian 1441/42-1493
  paintings: (H) $82,500

SELLARS, David R.
  English 19th cent.
  drawings: (H) $522

SELLERS, Anna Peale
  American 1824-1905
  paintings: (L) $247; (H) $1,650

SELLIN, Joachim
  drawings: (H) $1,045

SELLMAYR, Ludwig
  German 1834-1901
  paintings: (H) $2,530

SELMERSHEIM-DESGRANGE,
  Jeanne
  French 1879-1958
  paintings: (H) $5,500

SELOUS, Henry Courtney
  British 1811-1890
  paintings: (H) $14,850

SELTZER, Olaf Carl
  American 1877-1957
  paintings: (L) $1,540; (H) $46,000
  drawings: (L) $3,025; (H) $36,800

SELTZER, W. Steve
  American
  paintings: (L) $2,600; (H) $3,500

SELTZER, W.W.
  drawings: (H) $2,750

SELVA, E.
  paintings: (H) $495

SELZER, F.
  paintings: (H) $935

SEM
  drawings: (L) $605; (H) $660

SEMENOWSKY, Emile Eisman
  Polish d. 1911
  paintings: (L) $1,925; (H) $14,950

SEMINO, Andrea
  Italian 1525-1595
  paintings: (H) $2,860

SEMON, John
  American d. 1917
  paintings: (L) $220; (H) $550

SEMPLE, J.
  German (?) ac. 1868
  paintings: (L) $3,850; (H) $5,500

SEN, Sarbani
  Indian 20th cent.
  paintings: (H) $1,650

SENAPE, Antonio
  ac. 19th cent.
  drawings: (L) $715; (H) $920

SENAT, Prosper Louis
  American 1852-1925
  paintings: (L) $688; (H) $3,520
  drawings: (L) $358; (H) $1,320

SENDAK, Maurice
  American b. 1928
  drawings: (L) $198; (H) $825

SENET, Rafael
  Spanish b. 1856
  paintings: (L) $11,000; (H) $43,125
  drawings: (H) $1,955

SENETT, Michael and Coburn
  MORGAN
  paintings: (H) $1,210

SENIOR, Abraham Hulk
  British 19th cent.
  paintings: (H) $1,840

SENISE, Daniel
  Brazil b. 1955
  paintings: (H) $9,200

SENNA, Pietro
Italian 1831-1904
paintings: (H) $2,860

SENNHAUSER, John
Swiss/American 1907-1978
paintings: (L) $431; (H) $6,600
drawings: (L) $110; (H) $1,265

SENTINIS, Rene
European 20th cent.
sculpture: (H) $1,210

SENTIS, Juan Alfonso Carro
paintings: (H) $863

SEOANE, Luis
b. Argentina 1910
paintings: (H) $10,350

SEPESHY, Zoltan
Hungarian/American 1898-1974
paintings: (L) $192; (H) $5,500
drawings: (L) $220; (H) $1,650

SEPHTON, George Harcourt
British 19th cent.
paintings: (H) $1,540

SEPP, George
American 1880-1956
paintings: (L) $412; (H) $935

SERANNO, Andres
American b. 1950
drawings: (H) $3,450

SERANVOER, T.
paintings: (H) $8,250

SERAUX, A.A.
French 19th cent.
drawings: (H) $1,320

SERGENT, Lucien Pierre
French 1849-1904
paintings: (H) $5,060

SERISAWA, Sueo
Japanese/American b. 1910
paintings: (L) $99; (H) $2,750
drawings: (H) $805

SERL, Jon
b. 1894
paintings: (L) $1,320; (H) $3,162

SERPA, Fernando Claudio
ac. 1880s
paintings: (L) $5,175; (H) $5,750

SERPAN, Iaroslav
1922-1976
paintings: (H) $3,850

SERPIONI, Alberro
drawings: (H) $990

SERPOTTA, Giacomo
Italian 1656-1723
sculpture: (H) $68,500

SERRA, Ernesto
Italian b. 1860
paintings: (L) $1,150; (H) $22,000

SERRA, Richard
American b. 1939
paintings: (L) $13,800; (H) $49,500
drawings: (L) $550; (H) $44,000
sculpture: (L) $33,000; (H) $231,000

SERRA BADUE, Daniel
b. 1914
paintings: (H) $5,520

SERRA Y AUQUE, Enrique
Spanish 1859-1918
paintings: (L) $1,610; (H) $8,050

SERRANO, Andres
American b. 1950
drawings: (L) $7,150; (H) $8,625
sculpture: (H) $6,325

SERRANO, Manuel
Mexican 1814-1883
paintings: (H) $79,500

SERRANO, Manuel Gonzalez
Mexican b. 1916
paintings: (L) $1,210; (H) $4,400

SERRES, Dominic
British 1722-1793
drawings: (H) $1,320

SERRES, John Thomas
English 1759-1825
paintings: (L) $1,610; (H) $11,550
drawings: (H) $1,430

SERRI, Alfredo
Italian 1898-1972
paintings: (L) $259; (H) $2,640

SERRITELLI, Giovanni
Italian 18th cent.
paintings: (H) $2,310

SERRURE, Auguste
Flemish 1825-1903
paintings: (H) $3,450

SERRURE, Berthe
Belgian 19th/20th cent.
drawings: (H) $2,300

SERSEN, Fred M.
American 1890-1962
paintings: (H) $715

SERUSIER, Louis Paul Henri
French 1863-1927
paintings: (H) $233,500
drawings: (H) $605

SERVIERES, Eugenie Marguerite
Honoree Lethiere
French b. 1786
paintings: (H) $16,100

SERVIN, Jose Maria
sculpture: (H) $633

SERVULO, Esmeraldo
b. Brazil 1929
sculpture: (H) $1,320

SESSIONS, James M.
American 1882-1962
drawings: (L) $138; (H) $2,760

SEST (?), H. Carp
paintings: (H) $935

SETHER, Gulbrand
Norwegian 1869-1910
paintings: (L) $150; (H) $1,380
drawings: (L) $44; (H) $330

SETKOWIN, H.
paintings: (H) $1,100

SETON, John Thomas
ac. 1758-1806
paintings: (L) $1,210; (H) $4,140

SETTANNI, Luigi
American b. Italy 1908
paintings: (L) $1,815; (H) $8,250

SETTERBERG, Carl
American b. 1897
paintings: (L) $138; (H) $605
drawings: (H) $880

SEUL, Laurent del
paintings: (H) $5,500

SEUPLHOR, Michael
drawings: (H) $978

SEURAT, Georges
French 1859-1891
paintings: (H) $1,375,000
drawings: (L) $9,200; (H) $486,500

SEVERDONCK, Francois van and Jan
Evert MOREL, Jr.
19th cent.
paintings: (H) $8,050

SEVERDONCK, Franz van
Belgian 1809-1889
paintings: (L) $1,100; (H) $6,900

SEVERDONCK, Joseph van
Belgian 1819-1905
paintings: (L) $495; (H) $1,760

SEVERENI, Louis
c. 20th cent.
paintings: (H) $715

SEVERIN, John
drawings: (L) $575; (H) $690

SEVERINI, Gino
Italian 1883-1966
paintings: (L) $3,080; (H) $77,000
drawings: (L) $2,875; (H) $110,000

SEVERINUS, A. de
Italian 19th cent.
paintings: (H) $1,320

SEVERO DA RAVENNA,
workshop of
Paduan c. 1500
sculpture: (L) $10,350; (H) $18,700

SEVERO DE RAVENNA
Italian ac. late 1400s
sculpture: (H) $96,000

SEVILLA, Ferran Garcia
b. 1949
paintings: (L) $4,400; (H) $7,150

SEVIN, Pierre Paul
1650-1710 or 1720
drawings: (H) $1,150

SEWELL, Amos
American 1901-1983
paintings: (L) $880; (H) $6,050
drawings: (L) $110; (H) $1,100

SEWELL, Robert van Vorst
American 1860-1924
paintings: (L) $413; (H) $9,350

SEXTON, Frederick Lester
American b. 1889
paintings: (L) $165; (H) $2,200

SEYDEL, Eduard Gustav
German 1822-1881
paintings: (H) $5,225

SEYFFERT, Leopold Gould
American 1887-1956
paintings: (L) $225; (H) $4,600
drawings: (H) $358

SEYFRIED, A.
Continental 19th/20th cent.
paintings: (H) $2,200

SEYLER, Julius
German 1873-1958
drawings: (H) $1,380

SEYMOUR, Edouard
Austrian b. 1894
paintings: (H) $825

SEYMOUR, George L.
English ac. 1876-1888
paintings: (L) $2,420; (H) $4,600

SEYMOUR, James
English 1702-1752
paintings: (L) $36,300; (H) $68,500

SEYMOUR, Samuel
American 1797-1882
paintings: (H) $17,250
drawings: (H) $13,200

SEYPPEL, Carl Maria
German 1847-1913
paintings: (H) $1,725

SEYSSAUD, Rene
French 1867-1952
paintings: (L) $4,180; (H) $14,300

SHABUNIN, H.A.
Russian 19th cent.
paintings: (H) $5,390

SHADBOLT, Jack
English b. 1909
paintings: (L) $6,050; (H) $11,000
drawings: (L) $2,090; (H) $6,050

SHADDIX, Bill
b. 1931
paintings: (H) $2,200

SHADE, William A.
1848-1890
paintings: (H) $578

SHAFER, Catherine
American early 19th cent.
drawings: (L) $660; (H) $1,760

SHAFER, L.E. Gus
American b. 1907
sculpture: (L) $605; (H) $3,680

SHAFER, S.P.
American 19th cent.
paintings: (L) $605; (H) $990

SHAHN, Abby
drawings: (H) $460

SHAHN, Ben
Russian/American 1898-1969
paintings: (L) $2,875; (H) $93,250
drawings: (L) $150; (H) $21,850

SHANKER, Louis
20th cent.
paintings: (H) $660

SHANKS, Nelson
American b. 1937
paintings: (L) $489; (H) $1,380

SHANKS, William Somerville
English 1864-1951
paintings: (H) $660

SHANNON, Charles Haslewood
English 1863-1937
paintings: (H) $2,750
drawings: (H) $550

SHANNON, Sir James Jebusa
British 1862-1923
paintings: (L) $23,100; (H) $118,000

SHAO KUANG TING
Chinese 20th cent.
sculpture: (H) $1,595

SHAPIRO, David
b. 1916
paintings: (H) $880

SHAPIRO, Joel
American b. 1941
paintings: (L) $1,100; (H) $15,400
drawings: (L) $5,500; (H) $42,900
sculpture: (L) $13,200; (H) $288,500

SHAPLAND, John
British 1901-1929
paintings: (L) $489; (H) $1,650
drawings: (L) $288; (H) $690

SHAPLEIGH, Frank Henry
American 1842-1906
paintings: (L) $330; (H) $8,800
drawings: (L) $137; (H) $1,955

SHARE, Henry Pruett
American 1853-1905
paintings: (L) $495; (H) $770
drawings: (H) $1,540

SHARER, W.E.
b. 1935
paintings: (H) $550

SHARER, William
b. 1934
paintings: (H) $770

SHARMA, Mahan
Indian contemporary
paintings: (H) $495

SHARON, Mary Bruce
American 1878-1961
drawings: (L) $1,320; (H) $2,090

SHARP, Albert
American b. 1925
paintings: (H) $1,540

SHARP, J.H.
paintings: (L) $2,185; (H) $11,000
drawings: (H) $4,950

SHARP, John
paintings: (H) $1,200

SHARP, Joseph Henry
American 1859-1953
paintings: (L) $523; (H) $148,500
drawings: (H) $770

SHARP, Louis Hovey
American 1875-1946
paintings: (L) $518; (H) $4,950

SHARP, William
American 1900-1961
paintings: (L) $460; (H) $715

SHARPE, David
American 20th cent.
paintings: (L) $920; (H) $1,495

SHARPE, Dorothea
English 1874-1955
paintings: (L) $1,725; (H) $12,650

SHARPE, H. Alvin
American late 20th cent.
paintings: (L) $242; (H) $550

SHARPE, James
American b. 1936
drawings: (H) $3,025

SHARPLES, Ellen Wallace, or James
SHARPLES, Jr.
American 1769-1849
drawings: (H) $1,650

SHARPLES, James
English 1751-1811
drawings: (H) $31,050

SHARYLEN, Maria
American 20th cent.
paintings: (H) $550

SHATTUCK, Aaron Draper
American 1832-1928
paintings: (L) $880; (H) $4,950
drawings: (L) $110; (H) $2,200

SHAULOR, H.W.
paintings: (H) $798

SHAVER, Samuel
American 1816-1878
paintings: (H) $25,875

SHAW, A. Winter
British 19th cent.
paintings: (H) $2,875

SHAW, Annie Cornelia
American 1852-1887
paintings: (L) $467; (H) $1,100

SHAW, Arthur Winter
British 1869-1948
paintings: (H) $1,100

SHAW, Austin
19th cent.
paintings: (H) $880

SHAW, Charles Green
American 1892-1974
paintings: (L) $138; (H) $15,400

SHAW, Charles L.
British 19th cent.
paintings: (H) $1,320

SHAW, Charles S.
British 19th cent.
paintings: (H) $1,300

SHAW, Frederick A.
American 1855-1912
paintings: (H) $935

SHAW, George
American 20th cent.
paintings: (L) $880; (H) $1,650

SHAW, Jim
b. 1952
paintings: (L) $1,380; (H) $3,220
drawings: (L) $1,150; (H) $2,200

SHAW, John Liston Byam
British 1872-1919
paintings: (H) $2,750

SHAW, Joshua
American 1776-1860
paintings: (L) $3,850; (H) $129,000

SHAW, Richard
American b. 1941
sculpture: (L) $575; (H) $4,313

SHAW, Stuart Clifford
1896-1970
paintings: (L) $303; (H) $495

SHAW, Sydney Dale
American 1879-1946
paintings: (L) $413; (H) $880
drawings: (H) $220

SHAW, W.R.B.
American 19th cent.
paintings: (H) $935

SHAWE, George
b. 1915
paintings: (L) $770; (H) $1,760

SHAWHAN, Ada Romer
American 1865-1947
paintings: (H) $1,430

SHAYER, Charles Waller
British ac. 1860-1880
paintings: (H) $13,225

SHAYER, H. and C.
English 19th cent.
paintings: (H) $4,400

SHAYER, Henry and Charles SHAYER
British 19th cent.
paintings: (H) $4,400

SHAYER, William
British 19th cent.
paintings: (L) $1,955; (H) $3,300

SHAYER, William J., Sr.
English 1788-1879
paintings: (L) $2,310; (H) $55,000

SHAYER, William Joseph
English 1811-1892
paintings: (L) $3,300; (H) $31,050

SHAYER, William Joseph and John
Frederick HERRING, Jr.
British 18th/19th cent.
paintings: (H) $14,950

SHCHUKIN, Stepan Semionovich
Russian 1754-1828
paintings: (H) $43,125

SHEAHAN, D.B.
American c. 1900
sculpture: (H) $550

SHEARER, Christopher H.
American 1840-1926
paintings: (L) $264; (H) $4,500
drawings: (H) $350

SHEARER, E.L.
paintings: (H) $2,070

SHEARER, James Elliot
British b. 1858
paintings: (H) $550

SHEARER, Victor
paintings: (L) $140; (H) $500

SHED, Charles Dyer
American 1818-1893
paintings: (L) $748; (H) $2,875

SHEE, Sir Martin Archer
b. Ireland 1769 d. England 1850
paintings: (L) $4,400; (H) $28,600

SHEELER, Charles
American 1883-1965
paintings: (L) $1,980; (H) $220,000
drawings: (L) $11,000; (H) $11,000

SHEERBOOM, Andrew
British 1832-1880
paintings: (H) $3,025

SHEETS, Millard
American 1907-1989
paintings: (L) $4,600; (H) $33,000
drawings: (L) $345; (H) $11,500

SHEETS, Nan Jane, Mrs. Fred C.
American b. 1885/89
paintings: (L) $104; (H) $1,035

SHEFFER, Glen
American 1881-1948
paintings: (L) $143; (H) $3,335

SHEFFIELD, Isaac
American 1798/1806-1845
paintings: (H) $6,325

SHEILDS, Emma B.
paintings: (H) $577

SHELDON, Charles
1889-1961
drawings: (L) $715; (H) $715

SHELTON, Gilbert
drawings: (H) $1,100

SHENTAN, Annie F.
British 20th cent.
paintings: (H) $5,175

SHEPANDES, Henry Lerolle
French 1848-1929
paintings: (H) $633

SHEPARD, Ernest H.
English b. 1879
drawings: (H) $605

SHEPARD, Warren J.
American 1859-1937
paintings: (H) $1,760

SHEPERD, J. Clinton
American b. 1888
paintings: (H) $880

SHEPHERD, David
British 20th cent.
paintings: (L) $8,625; (H) $51,750

SHEPHERD, J. Clinton
American 1888-1963
paintings: (L) $1,100; (H) $1,925

SHEPHERD, Joy Clinton
b. 1888
sculpture: (L) $2,200; (H) $4,888

SHEPPARD, Peter Chapman
paintings: (H) $1,045

SHEPPARD, Warren
American 1858-1937
paintings: (L) $920; (H) $4,400

SHEPPARD, Warren W.
American 1858-1937
paintings: (L) $726; (H) $10,230

SHERBELL, Rhoda
sculpture: (H) $632

SHERINGHAM, George
British b. 1884
paintings: (H) $2,200

SHERLINGH, Michael
American 19th/20th cent.
paintings: (H) $1,100

SHERLOCK, W.
British 19th cent.
paintings: (H) $2,415

SHERMAN, Al
American 20th cent.
drawings: (H) $920

SHERMAN, Cindy
American b. 1954
drawings: (L) $2,310; (H) $40,250

SHERMAN, G.
paintings: (L) $192; (H) $742

SHERMAN, G.
American 20th cent.
paintings: (H) $6,600

SHERMAN, Gail Corbett
American 1871-1953
paintings: (H) $2,640

SHERMAN, Gwen
American 20th cent.
paintings: (H) $1,650

SHERMAN, Heyman
American 19th/20th cent.
paintings: (H) $467

SHERMAN, Pamela
American ac. 1860
drawings: (L) $1,870; (H) $1,980

SHERRIN, David
English b. 1868; ac. 1898-1900
paintings: (L) $302; (H) $5,500

SHERRIN, John
English 1819-1896
drawings: (L) $220; (H) $2,760

SHERWOOD, Franklin Paul
American 1864-1952
paintings: (H) $825

SHERWOOD, Mary Clare
American 1868-1943
paintings: (L) $1,210; (H) $1,540
drawings: (H) $115

SHERWOOD, Rosina Emmet
American b. 1854
paintings: (H) $9,350
drawings: (L) $690; (H) $3,450

SHERWOOD, Walter J.
American b. 1865
paintings: (L) $935; (H) $1,380
drawings: (H) $1,045

SHERWOOD, William
American 1875-1951
paintings: (L) $264; (H) $495
drawings: (H) $110

SHIE, Susan
contemporary
sculpture: (H) $6,900

SHIELDS, Alan
American b. 1944
paintings: (H) $110
drawings: (H) $825
sculpture: (H) $5,463

SHIELDS, Carrie B.
American 19th cent.
paintings: (H) $546

SHIELDS, Emma Barber
American 1863-1912
paintings: (H) $605

SHIELDS, Irion
American 1895-1983
paintings: (H) $1,650

SHIELS, William
British 1785-1857
paintings: (H) $3,450

SHIFFER, Glen
paintings: (H) $495

SHIGERU, Izumi
b. 1922
drawings: (H) $5,750

SHIKI, Eiki
Japanese 20th cent.
sculpture: (H) $1,100

SHIKLER, Aaron
American b. 1922
paintings: (L) $322; (H) $3,300

SHILLING, Arthur
paintings: (L) $1,250; (H) $5,750
drawings: (H) $385

SHIMITU, Ninato
Japanese contemporary
paintings: (L) $431; (H) $489

SHINN, Everett
American 1876-1953
paintings: (L) $1,100; (H) $176,000
drawings: (L) $23; (H) $88,000

SHINODA, Ryusen
drawings: (H) $863

SHINODA, Toko
b. 1913
drawings: (H) $2,200

SHINZEL, W.
drawings: (H) $1,100

SHIPLEY
paintings: (H) $660

SHIPLEY
British 20th cent.
paintings: (H) $605

SHIRE, Peter
American b. 1947
sculpture: (L) $644; (H) $5,175

SHIREY, Sally
American b. 1939
drawings: (L) $135; (H) $660

SHIRLAW, Walter
Scottish/American 1838-1909
paintings: (L) $715; (H) $14,850
drawings: (L) $193; (H) $2,300

SHIRVERT, Victor
German 19th cent.
paintings: (H) $4,025

SHISHKIN, Ivan
Russian 1832-1898
paintings: (L) $1,100; (H) $68,500

SHLAPAIKON, A.M.
paintings: (L) $546; (H) $633

SHMIED, Th.
Dutch 19th cent.
paintings: (H) $770

SHMITZ, Ernst
German 1859-1917
paintings: (H) $18,700

SHOEMAKER, Vaughn
American 1902-1991
drawings: (L) $138; (H) $578

SHOKLER, Harry
American 1896-1978
paintings: (L) $165; (H) $8,250

SHONNARD, Eugenie F.
1886-1978
sculpture: (L) $110; (H) $8,050

SHONTZ, Amos
paintings: (L) $375; (H) $525

SHOOP
sculpture: (H) $748

SHOOP, Wally
American b. 1941
sculpture: (L) $138; (H) $660

SHOPEN, Kenneth
American b. 1902
paintings: (H) $633
drawings: (H) $81

SHORT, John T.
19th cent.
drawings: (H) $2,875

SHORT, W.
European 19th cent.
paintings: (H) $1,100

SHOSEI
late 19th cent.
sculpture: (H) $5,462

SHOTWELL, Margaret Harvey
American 1873-1965
paintings: (H) $605

SHOUP, Charles
American 20th cent.
paintings: (H) $715

SHRADY, Henry Mervin
American 1871-1922
sculpture: (L) $3,575; (H) $23,000

SHREVE, Carl
paintings: (H) $1,320

SHREYER, Adolf
German 1828-1899
paintings: (H) $32,200

SHRYOCK, John
American b. 1969
paintings: (H) $605

SHUFNAGEL, A.
paintings: (H) $977

SHUGRIN, Anatoly
Russian 20th cent.
paintings: (L) $5,750; (H) $31,050

SHUKHAEV, Vasilii Ivanovich
Russian 1887-1972
paintings: (H) $1,980

SHULL, Delia
American ac. 1920's-30's
paintings: (L) $330; (H) $880

SHULMAN, Morris
1912-1978
paintings: (H) $2,300

SHULZ, Ada Walter
American 1870-1928
paintings: (L) $5,060; (H) $18,700

SHULZ, Adolph R.
American 1869-1963
paintings: (L) $880; (H) $4,950

SHUNKAI, Bundo, Keichu
1877-1970
drawings: (H) $2,875

SHURTLEFF, R.G.
paintings: (H) $880

SHURTLEFF, Roswell Morse
American 1838-1915
paintings: (L) $115; (H) $7,150
drawings: (L) $303; (H) $330

SHUSTER, Joe
20th cent.
drawings: (L) $880; (H) $8,250

SHUSTER, William Howard
American 1893-1969
paintings: (L) $3,575; (H) $11,500

SHUTE, Mrs. R.W.
American ac. 1834-1836
paintings: (H) $3,450

SHUTE, R.W. and S.A.
American 19th cent.
drawings: (H) $18,400

SHUTE, Ruth
paintings: (H) $6,900

SHUTE, Samuel Addison
American ac. c. 1834-1836
drawings: (L) $20,700; (H) $42,550

SHUTER, W.
British 18th cent.
paintings: (H) $1,210

SIBERECHTS, Jan
Flemish 1627-1700
paintings: (L) $11,000; (H) $782,000

SICARD, Francois Leon
French 1862-1934
sculpture: (L) $3,850; (H) $8,250

SICARD, Pierre
French 1900-1980
paintings: (H) $2,300

SICHEL, Harold M.
American 1881-1948
paintings: (L) $605; (H) $3,575
drawings: (H) $275

SICHEL, Nathaniel
German 1843-1907
paintings: (H) $4,313

SICILIA, Jose Maria
b. Spain 1954
paintings: (L) $11,500; (H) $55,000

Which Estate?

The Flemish painter Jan Siberechts (1627-1700), a landscape painter, studied in Italy and worked in Belgium. In 1672 the Duke of Buckingham, passing through Flanders, saw his paintings and was impressed with his work. Siberechts traveled with the duke to London and began to paint fox hunt scenes and panoramic views. His specialty was portraits of country estates and houses. *View of Nannau Hall, Cardiganshire, Wales* had been in a New York private collection since the 1920s; the estate had been identified as Nannau Hall in a 1931 catalogue of Siberechts's works. When the painting was consigned to Doyle's in New York, the modest estimate, $50,000 to $70,000, was based on previous sales of portraits of less-well-known British country houses. Savvy London dealers immediately recognized a distant view of London in the background and realized that the house was "*The Grove at Highgate*," a country house that still stands today just off Hampstead Heath. Ten London dealers bid for the painting, it was knocked down at $782,000. (Jan Siberechts, *View of Nannau Hall, Cardiganshire, Wales*, oil on canvas, 42½ x 54¾ inches, Doyle, January 26, 1994, $782,000)

SICILIANO, Marie Dominique
French b. 1879
paintings: (H) $4,830

SICKERT, Walter Richard
English 1860-1942
paintings: (H) $1,210
drawings: (H) $4,400

SICKLES, Noel
American 1911-1982
drawings: (L) $412; (H) $1,540

SIDEBOTTOM, A.
British ac. c. 1851
drawings: (H) $770

SIDERIS, S.
American 20th cent.
paintings: (L) $207; (H) $1,610

SIEBERT, Edward
American 1856-1944
paintings: (L) $247; (H) $1,045
drawings: (L) $66; (H) $468

SIEBURGER, Gustave
Continental 19th/20th cent.
paintings: (H) $3,680

SIEFEHLE, Franz
sculpture: (H) $3,080

SIEFERT, Alfred
Czech 1850-1901
paintings: (H) $8,050

SIEFERT, Paul
American 1840-1921
drawings: (H) $16,500

SIEFFERT, Paul
French b. 1874
paintings: (L) $1,045; (H) $3,738

SIEGEL, C.
sculpture: (H) $880

SIEGEL, Jerry and Joe SHUSTER
drawings: (H) $4,125

SIEGEN, August
German 1820-1883
paintings: (L) $1,725; (H) $6,900

SIEGER, Rudolph
German 1867-1925
paintings: (H) $8,800

SIEGERT, August
German 1786-1869
paintings: (H) $4,125

SIEGERT, August Friedrich
German 1820-1883
paintings: (L) $2,310; (H) $16,500

SIEGFRIED, Edwin C.
American 1889-1955
drawings: (L) $220; (H) $2,475

SIEGRIEST, Louis
American 1899-1989
paintings: (L) $1,760; (H) $8,800
drawings: (L) $550; (H) $1,380

SIEGRIEST, Lundy
American 1925-1985
paintings: (L) $357; (H) $4,600
drawings: (H) $1,650

SIEMER, Christian
American 1874-1940
paintings: (L) $935; (H) $990

SIEMIRADZKI, Hendrik
Russian 1843-1902
paintings: (L) $19,550; (H) $29,900
drawings: (H) $1,725

SIERRA, Paul
paintings: (H) $4,950

SIEURAC, Henry
French 1823-1863
paintings: (H) $1,540

SIEVAN, Maurice
Russian/American b. 1898
paintings: (L) $110; (H) $550

SIEVERS, Gregory
American
paintings: (L) $1,930; (H) $2,600

SIEVERS, Rein
Dutch b. 1929
paintings: (L) $3,850; (H) $4,950

SIEVERT, August Wilhelm
German d. 1751
paintings: (H) $34,500

SIFFERT
Continental 18th/19th cent.
paintings: (H) $990

SIGALL, J.
paintings: (H) $577

SIGARI, Y.
Italian 19th cent.
drawings: (H) $990

SIGFUSSON, Sigfus
American 20th cent.
paintings: (H) $690

SIGHIERI
sculpture: (H) $4,025

SIGLER, Hollis
American b. 1948
paintings: (H) $1,725

SIGMUND, Benjamin D.
English ac. 1879-1904
drawings: (H) $1,430

SIGNAC, Paul
French 1863-1935
paintings: (L) $11,500; (H) $1,817,500
drawings: (L) $1,380; (H) $40,250

SIGNORET, Charles Louis Eugene
French 1867-1932
paintings: (L) $2,530; (H) $13,200

SIGNORET-LEDIEU, Lucie
1858-1904
sculpture: (H) $11,500

SIGNORINI, Giuseppe
Italian 1857-1932
paintings: (H) $5,750
drawings: (L) $403; (H) $24,200

SIGNORINI, Telemaco
Italian 1835-1901
paintings: (H) $23,000

SIGRISTE, Guido
Swiss 1864-1915
paintings: (L) $1,840; (H) $23,000

SIHVONEN, Oli
b. 1921
paintings: (H) $467

SIJTHOFF, Gijsbertus Jan
Dutch 1867-1949
paintings: (H) $1,725

SIKES, Charles
sculpture: (H) $468

SILAR, Patrick
American b. 1939
sculpture: (H) $2,300

SILBERBERG, Gustave
German/American b. 1867
paintings: (H) $990

SILBERHORN, Tibor
American 20th cent.
paintings: (H) $460

SILBERT, Max
French b. 1871
paintings: (L) $1,610; (H) $3,300

SILIS, Antoine
Belgian 19th cent.
paintings: (H) $6,050

SILLEN, Herman Gustaf Af
Swedish 1857-1908
paintings: (L) $2,090; (H) $2,750

SILMAN, Susan
contemporary
paintings: (H) $495

SILSBY, Wilson
American 1883-1952
paintings: (L) $880; (H) $3,163

SILVA, Benjamin
South American 20th cent.
paintings: (L) $3,025; (H) $6,600

SILVA, Francis Augustus
American 1835-1886
paintings: (L) $6,050; (H) $255,500
drawings: (L) $330; (H) $17,250

SILVA, William P.
American 1859-1948
paintings: (L) $385; (H) $7,150

SILVANI, Ferdinando
Italian 1823-1899
paintings: (H) $2,530

SILVERCRUYS, Suzanne
American 1898-1973
sculpture: (H) $1,495

SILVERMAN, Burton
American b. 1928
paintings: (H) $3,850
drawings: (L) $264; (H) $3,850

SILVERMAN, Martin
American b. 1951
sculpture: (L) $288; (H) $2,200

SILVERSMITH, Mark
drawings: (H) $715

SILVESTRE
sculpture: (L) $176; (H) $2,200

SILVESTRE, Israel, the younger
1621-1691
drawings: (L) $523; (H) $1,760

SILVESTRE, Louis, II
French 1675-1760
paintings: (H) $46,200

SILVESTRE, Paul
French b. 1884
sculpture: (H) $4,950

SIM, Dave
drawings: (H) $805

SIMARD, Claude A.
b. 1943
paintings: (H) $1,980

SIMARD, Marie Louise
sculpture: (H) $920

SIMBARI, Nicola
Italian b. 1927
paintings: (L) $385; (H) $13,800
drawings: (L) $1,035; (H) $1,650

SIMBOLI, Raymond
American 1894-1964
paintings: (H) $5,500

SIMCOCK, Jack
paintings: (H) $690

SIME, Sidney Herbert
English 1867-1944
drawings: (H) $1,980

SIMENSEN, Sigvald
Norwegian d. 1920
paintings: (L) $330; (H) $1,495

SIMKHOVITCH, Simka
American b. 1893
paintings: (H) $30,800

SIMMERS, Henry
Belgian 19th cent.
paintings: (H) $2,875

SIMMLER, Wilhelm
German 1840-1914
paintings: (H) $2,420

SIMMONDS, Julius
1843-1924
drawings: (H) $2,415

SIMMONS
American 19th/20th cent.
paintings: (L) $468; (H) $715

SIMMONS, Edward Emerson
American 1852-1931
paintings: (L) $1,955; (H) $34,500
drawings: (L) $1,150; (H) $2,365

SIMMONS, Freeman Willis
American d. 1926
paintings: (L) $385; (H) $1,650

SIMMONS, Laurie
b. 1949
drawings: (L) $6,600; (H) $8,800

SIMMONS, Schtockschnitzler
American ac. c. 1885-1910
sculpture: (H) $4,370

SIMON, A***
paintings: (H) $2,200

SIMON, Ernest Constant
French d. 1895
paintings: (H) $8,050

SIMON, Hermann Gustave
American 1846-1895
drawings: (H) $1,495

SIMON, Joe and Jack KIRBY
drawings: (H) $2,875

SIMON, John
American d. 1917
paintings: (H) $660

SIMON, Lucien J.
French 1861-1945
paintings: (L) $6,325; (H) $17,250

SIMON, Pincus Marcius
American 19th cent.
paintings: (H) $2,530

SIMON, Tavik Frantisek
Czechoslovakian 1877-1942
paintings: (L) $2,420; (H) $8,625

SIMON, Yochanan
Israeli 1905-1976
paintings: (L) $1,725; (H) $5,462

SIMONDS, Charles
contemporary
sculpture: (H) $10,450

SIMONE, A. J. de
Italian 19th cent.
paintings: (H) $550

SIMONE, Antoino de
Italian 1851-1907
drawings: (H) $2,300

SIMONE, Medgard
sculpture: (H) $1,980

SIMONE, Roberto de
ac. 1903
drawings: (H) $2,300

SIMONE, Tommaso de
Italian ac. 1852-1857
paintings: (H) $8,050
drawings: (L) $303; (H) $2,860

SIMONELLI, Giuseppe
c. 1650-1710
paintings: (H) $12,100

SIMONETTI, A.
paintings: (L) $575; (H) $990
drawings: (H) $303

SIMONETTI, Amedeo
Italian 1874-1922
paintings: (H) $1,650
drawings: (L) $1,870; (H) $24,150

SIMONETTI, Andres
Italian 19th/20th cent.
drawings: (H) $5,500

SIMONETTI, Attilio
Italian 1843-1925
paintings: (H) $6,900
drawings: (L) $8,625; (H) $13,225

SIMONETTI, Ettore
Italian 19th cent.
paintings: (L) $6,900; (H) $26,400
drawings: (L) $1,610; (H) $22,000

SIMONI, Alfredo de
Italian 19th cent.
drawings: (H) $880

SIMONI, Cesare
Italian 19th cent.
paintings: (H) $4,950

SIMONI, Gustavo
Italian b. 1846
paintings: (L) $2,415; (H) $21,850
drawings: (L) $330; (H) $26,450

SIMONI, Paolo
Italian 1882-1960
drawings: (H) $1,380

SIMONI, Scipione
Italian ac. 1891-1898
paintings: (L) $4,400; (H) $4,950
drawings: (L) $863; (H) $6,050

SIMONIDY, Michel
Romanian 1870-1933
paintings: (L) $460; (H) $9,350

SIMONIN, Victor
Belgian 1877-1946
paintings: (L) $880; (H) $1,650

SIMONINI, Francesco
Italian 1686-1753
paintings: (L) $7,360; (H) $18,700

SIMONNET, Lucien
French 1849-1926
paintings: (L) $1,320; (H) $1,840

SIMONS, George
1834-1917
paintings: (H) $770

SIMONS, Michiel
Dutch d. 1673
paintings: (L) $25,300; (H) $57,500

SIMONSEN, Niels
Danish 1807-1885
paintings: (L) $4,313; (H) $9,775

SIMONSEN, Simon
Danish 1841-1928
paintings: (H) $1,320

SIMONSEN, Soren
Danish 1834-1900
paintings: (H) $1,650

SIMONSON-CASTELLI, Ernst Oskar
German 1831-1896
paintings: (H) $1,100

SIMONY, Stefan
Austrian b. 1860
paintings: (H) $8,800

SIMPKINS, Henry John
b. Canada 1906
paintings: (H) $1,540
drawings: (H) $220

SIMPSON, David
contemporary
paintings: (L) $23; (H) $1,760

SIMPSON, Frank H.
paintings: (H) $880

SIMPSON, Lorna
b. 1960
drawings: (L) $6,900; (H) $8,050

SIMPSON, Maxwell Stewart
American b. 1896
paintings: (L) $66; (H) $2,310

SIMPSON, W***H***
British 1866-1886
paintings: (H) $4,313

SIMS, Agnes
American b. 1910
drawings: (H) $805

SIMS, Charles
British 1873-1928
paintings: (L) $880; (H) $1,840

SINCLAIR, Alfredo
paintings: (H) $7,700

SINCLAIR, Gerrit V.
American 1890-1955
paintings: (L) $385; (H) $660

SINCLAIR, Irving
American 1895-1969
paintings: (L) $1,495; (H) $7,700

SINCLAIR, Max
British 19th cent.
paintings: (L) $577; (H) $2,530

SINCLAIR, Olga
paintings: (H) $4,400

SINDELAR, Charles
19th/20th cent.
paintings: (H) $484

SINDING, Otto Ludvig
Norwegian 1842-1909
paintings: (H) $6,900

SINDING, Paul
Danish 20th cent.
paintings: (H) $4,312

SINDING, Stephen Abel
1846-1922
sculpture: (H) $5,225

SINET, Louis Andre
French b. 1867
paintings: (H) $1,610
drawings: (H) $14,300

SINGDAHLSON, Andreas
Norwegian b. 1855
paintings: (H) $1,955

SINGER, Burr
American b. 1912
paintings: (L) $715; (H) $1,870
drawings: (L) $358; (H) $1,650

SINGER, Clyde
American b. 1908
paintings: (L) $77; (H) $9,680
drawings: (L) $66; (H) $880

SINGER, Michael
b. 1945
drawings: (L) $2,185; (H) $2,990

SINGER, William H., Jr.
American 1868-1943
paintings: (H) $2,875

SINGH, Arpita
Indian b. 1937
paintings: (L) $1,725; (H) $7,475
drawings: (L) $1,150; (H) $2,760

SINGH, Gurcharan
Indian b. 1949
drawings: (L) $460; (H) $1,035

SINGIER, Gustave
French 1909-1984
paintings: (H) $30,800

SINGLETARY, Michael
American b. 1950
paintings: (H) $1,210

SINGLETON, Henry
English 1766-1839
paintings: (L) $2,200; (H) $2,420

SINIBALDI, Jean Paul
French 1857-1909
paintings: (L) $6,050; (H) $6,900

SINIBALDO
Italian 20th cent.
paintings: (H) $10,925

SINIBALDO, Toroi
Italian 19th cent.
paintings: (L) $715; (H) $2,090

SINICKI, Rene
French 20th cent.
paintings: (L) $230; (H) $2,090

SINNATOG, Henry
paintings: (H) $2,588

SINTENIS, Renee
German 1888-1965
sculpture: (L) $2,640; (H) $12,650

SINTSOV, N.
Russian 19th cent.
paintings: (H) $1,925

SIQUEIROS, David Alfaro
Mexican 1896/98-1974
paintings: (L) $4,400; (H) $178,500
drawings: (L) $1,150; (H) $33,350
sculpture: (H) $2,860

SIRANI, Elisabetta
Italian 1638-1665
paintings: (L) $43,125; (H) $46,000

SIRONI, Mario
Italian 1885-1961
paintings: (L) $3,450; (H) $35,200
drawings: (L) $2,300; (H) $36,300

SIRVENT
Continental 19th/20th cent.
paintings: (H) $1,840

SISLEY, Alfred
French 1839-1899
paintings: (L) $222,500; (H) $1,652,500

SISLEY, S**
English 19th cent.
paintings: (H) $495

SISSON, Frederick Rhodes
American 1893-1962
paintings: (L) $605; (H) $1,035

SISSON, Laurence P.
American b. 1928
paintings: (L) $220; (H) $5,500
drawings: (L) $193; (H) $575

SISSON, Richard
Irish d. 1767
paintings: (H) $1,100

SISTERE, A. de
French 19th cent.
paintings: (H) $3,450

SITZINGER
paintings: (H) $4,025

SITZMAN, Edward R.
American b. 1874
paintings: (L) $412; (H) $2,310
drawings: (L) $38; (H) $150

SIVARD, Robert
French 20th cent.
paintings: (L) $110; (H) $1,045

SIVERS, Clara von
German b. 1854
paintings: (H) $14,950

SIVILLA, E.
Continental 19th/20th cent.
paintings: (H) $5,750

SIX, Michael
Austrian late 19th/20th cent.
sculpture: (L) $660; (H) $715

SJAMAAR, Pieter Geerard
Dutch 1819-1876
paintings: (L) $1,650; (H) $4,400

SJOSTROM, G.J.
paintings: (H) $18,700

SKAAR, Jane
American
drawings: (L) $385; (H) $700

SKARBINA, Franz
German 1849-1910
paintings: (H) $19,800

SKEAPING, John Rattenbury
English b. 1901
paintings: (L) $715; (H) $6,600
drawings: (L) $1,155; (H) $4,950

SKELTON, Leslie James
Canadian 1848-1929
paintings: (L) $575; (H) $605

SKELTON, Red
American b. 1913
paintings: (L) $220; (H) $2,750

SKEMP, Robert Oliver
American 1907-1979
paintings: (H) $633

SKILLIN, Simeon, III
American ac. c. 1789-1830
sculpture: (H) $8,625

SKILLING
American contemporary
paintings: (H) $990

SKILLING, William
British/American 20th cent.
paintings: (L) $1,100; (H) $3,575

SKILLINGS, A.L.P.
19th cent.
paintings: (H) $825

SKIPWORTH, Frank Markham
British 1854-1929
paintings: (H) $17,600

SKLAR, Dorothy
American 20th cent.
paintings: (L) $467; (H) $1,045
drawings: (L) $220; (H) $1,100

SKOGLUND, Sandy
b. 1946
sculpture: (L) $3,163; (H) $3,163

SKOOG, Karl Frederick
Swedish/American 1878-1934
sculpture: (H) $6,600

SKOU, Sigurd
Norwegian/American 1878-1929
paintings: (L) $220; (H) $8,625
drawings: (H) $110

SKOVGAARD, Johan Thomas
Danish b. 1888
paintings: (H) $2,090

SKRAMSTAD, Ludwig
Norwegian 1855-1912
paintings: (H) $4,950

SKREDSWIG, Christian Eriksen
Danish 1854-1924
paintings: (H) $14,300

SKRETA, Karel Sotnovski
1610-1674
drawings: (H) $6,325

SLABBINCK
Belgian 20th cent.
paintings: (H) $605

SLACK, L.
paintings: (H) $550

SLADE, Caleb Arnold
American 1882-1961
paintings: (L) $165; (H) $2,090

SLADE, Cora
d. 1938
paintings: (L) $825; (H) $1,650

SLADEN, T.
19th cent.
paintings: (H) $467

SLAFTER, A.R.
paintings: (H) $770

SLATER, John Folconar
British 1857-1937
paintings: (L) $440; (H) $2,970

SLAUGHTER, W.A.
b. 1923
paintings: (L) $220; (H) $11,000

SLAVIN, John
American 20th cent.
paintings: (L) $137; (H) $522

SLENDZINSKI, Ludomir
Polish b. 1889
paintings: (H) $3,737

SLEVOGT, Max
German 1868-1932
paintings: (H) $13,800

SLINGELANDT, Pieter van
Dutch 1640-1691
paintings: (L) $7,700; (H) $8,800

SLINGENEYER, Ernest
Belgian 1820-1894
paintings: (H) $1,380

SLIVKA, David
sculpture: (H) $1,150

SLOAN, C.
American 20th cent.
paintings: (H) $550

SLOAN, James Blanding
American b. 1886
paintings: (L) $660; (H) $1,045

SLOAN, John
American 1871-1951
paintings: (L) $440; (H) $855,000
drawings: (L) $138; (H) $3,738

SLOAN, Junius R.
American 1827-1900
paintings: (L) $440; (H) $3,450
drawings: (L) $28; (H) $230

SLOAN, Marianna
American 1875-1954
paintings: (H) $1,100
drawings: (H) $1,045

SLOAN, Peter
American 20th cent.
paintings: (H) $935

SLOANE, Eric
American 1905-1985
paintings: (L) $577; (H) $36,800
drawings: (L) $138; (H) $1,650

SLOANE, George
American 19th/20th cent.
paintings: (L) $853; (H) $3,410

SLOANE, Marian Parkhurst
American d. 1955
paintings: (L) $330; (H) $1,485

SLOBODKINA, Esphyr
American b. 1914
paintings: (L) $4,600; (H) $7,700
drawings: (H) $6,037

SLOMAN, Joseph
American b. 1883
paintings: (L) $110; (H) $990

Auction Action in Cyberspace

Although more and more auction houses have home pages and provide sale results online, Young Fine Arts Auctions, Inc. in Portsmouth, New Hampshire, was the first auction house to put their entire catalogue online. Three to four weeks before an auction date, the Young's home page (http://www.maine.com/yfa) has the complete catalogue text and an image for each lot. Sale results are posted one week after the auction. George Young, says, "Many new customers have viewed our catalogues on the Internet and left bids. Some lots have been sold to new customers as far away as Australia and Sweden."

Eric Sloane (1905-1985) was a pseudonym for Everard Jean Henrichs. Born in New York, Henrichs was bitten at an early age by the "art bug" and spent his early twenties working as an itinerant sign painter. In Pennsylvania Amish country he supplemented his income by painting portraits of farmers' barns. His travels took him as far as Santa Fe, where he met the famous Taos Eight: Walter Ufer, E.I. Course, Joseph Sharp, Victor Higgins, Burt Phillips, Oscar Berninghaus, W.H. Dunton, and Ernest Blumenschein. On his return to the East Coast, he began to paint cloudscapes. Delving into the subject, he studied meteorology at M.I.T. and wrote a book, *Clouds, Air, and Wind*, one of forty books he wrote and illustrated on the weather and on tools. (Sloane's tool collection was donated to the state of Connecticut and is now the Sloane-Stanley Museum in Kent.) Sloane also instigated and designed the Hall of Atmosphere for the Museum of Natural History in New York. He studied art at the Yale School of Fine Arts and the Art Students League. It was while Sloane was at the ASL in 1930 that he began using a *nom de plume*. John Sloan and George Luks, teachers at the ASL and well-known artists, recommended that he use a pseudonym until he had achieved a "satisfaction level" with his art. He choose Sloane after John Sloan but spelled it with an E to distinguish himself; Eric came from the middle letters of "America." He never changed his name back, and in the last 15 years of his life, recalling the reason for his pseudonym, he made a practice of buying his old paintings and destroying them. Sloane was well-known for his murals, and in 1975 he was asked to be one of two artists to paint a mural for the entrance of the new Air and Space Museum. His mural was "air" and he painted a monumental cloudscape, 58½ feet high (about the height of a six-story building) and 68 feet wide. Cloudscapes and rural landscapes with barns and covered bridges were the subjects of most of his paintings. When *The Red Bridge, Montgomery, Vermont* was offered at Young's in April 1994, the sale price was $9,900. (Eric Sloane, *The Red Bridge, Montgomery, Vermont*, oil on board, 24 x 36 inches, Young, April 16, 1994, $9,900)

SLONE, Sandi
  American contemporary
  paintings: (L) $385; (H) $467

SLOTT-MOLLER, Harald
  Danish 1864-1937
  paintings: (L) $3,450; (H) $11,000

SLOUN, Frank van
  American 1879-1938
  paintings: (L) $3,450; (H) $4,125

SLOUT-VALMINGON, A. van der
  Continental 19th/20th cent.
  paintings: (H) $4,400

SLUSSER, Jean Paul
  American b. 1886
  paintings: (L) $247; (H) $3,740
  drawings: (L) $248; (H) $330

SLUYS, Theo van
  Belgian 1849-1931
  paintings: (L) $2,475; (H) $4,510

SMAITH, Wuanita
  American b. 1866
  paintings: (H) $2,640

SMALL, David
  drawings: (H) $715

SMALL, Frank O.
  American b. 1960
  paintings: (L) $247; (H) $550
  drawings: (H) $3,300

SMALLFIELD, Frederick
  British 1829-1915
  paintings: (H) $6,612

SMALLWOOD, Kenneth
  paintings: (H) $495

SMALLWOOD, William Frome
  English 1806-1834
  drawings: (H) $467

SMART, Jeffrey
  Australian b. 1921
  paintings: (H) $18,700

SMART, John
  British 1838-1899
  paintings: (H) $1,650

SMEDLEY, William Thomas
  American 1858-1920
  drawings: (L) $275; (H) $10,450

SMEERS, Frans
  Belgian b. 1873
  paintings: (H) $13,200

SMEETON, Burn
  British 19th cent.
  paintings: (H) $880

SMET, Leon de
  Belgian b. 1881
  paintings: (H) $71,250

SMETH (OR SMET), Henri de
  Belgian 1865-1940
  paintings: (H) $2,970

SMETS, Albert
  Belgian 19th cent.
  paintings: (L) $1,035; (H) $1,540

SMETS, Louis
  Dutch 19th cent.
  paintings: (L) $1,760; (H) $4,950

SMIBERT, John
  American 1688-1751
  paintings: (H) $11,000

Monographs

Publication of a monograph on an artist can bring greater recognition of an artist and serve as a validation of the monetary value of their works. In 1993 a monograph on Alice Ravenel Huger Smith (1876-1958) *Alice Ravenel Huger Smith: An Artist, a Place, and a Time*, by Martha R. Severens, was published by the Carolina Art Association/Gibbes Museum of Art.

Alice Ravenel Huger Smith was born to an old Charleston, South Carolina, family. In the late 1800s Charleston was still recovering economically from the Civil War, and the Smith family was unable to send Alice off to school. Her education was through fellow Charleston artists (some of whom had traveled north to attend art school), visiting artists, and her cousin's collection. Smith's cousin, a former Harvard professor, had a major collection of Japanese prints, from early black and white examples to color masterpieces by Hiroshige. Smith helped catalogue the collection and was able to experiment with the actual woodblocks by pulling her own impressions.

Visiting artist Lovell Birge Harrison, a Woodstock, New York, artist, traveled to Charleston in 1908 to paint its harbor, streets, and buildings. Although he was not Smith's teacher, they were acquainted and she saw his paintings and read his philosophical book *Landscape Painting*. Harrison espoused Tonalism, blurred edges and muted colors, and his influence is seen in Smith's later watercolors. The two corresponded, and when she began to exhibit in New York 10 years later, Harrison wrote her a congratulatory note. American artists Helen Hyde and Bertha Jaques were another source of inspiration. Printmakers who worked in the Japanese manner, they traveled to Charleston in 1916 and 1917. The two helped Smith by giving her encouragement and sources for paper and cherry wood for her blocks. Jaques, president of the Chicago Society of Etchers, arranged for Smith's work to be exhibited in Chicago, which was the first time her works were exhibited outside Charleston

In 1914 Smith collaborated with her father on a book on the historical Pringle House, and the two worked together for the next 20 years, writing and illustrating books. By 1927 Smith had stopped her printmaking and was concentrating on her watercolors. The last book she and her father wrote, *A Carolina Rice Plantation of the Fifties*, was her father's boyhood recollection of the family's plantation. The book was published in 1936, shortly after her father's death, and reviewers made special note of the illustrations based on her watercolors. Smith became nationally known for her realistic, detailed book illustrations, but her large Tonalist watercolors of local scenery are some of her most exciting works. In 1937 she was awarded an honorary degree of Doctor of Letters from Mount Holyoke College. There was a sharp jump in Smith's auction prices after the publication of Severens' monograph, and her watercolor *Early Spring* realized $30,800 at Goldberg's in New Orleans. (Alice Ravenel Huger Smith, *Early Spring*, watercolor on paper, 31 x 21¾ inches, Goldberg, January 21, 1994, $30,800)

SMILIE, James David
American 1833-1909
drawings: (H) $3,575

SMILLIE, George Henry
American 1840-1921
paintings: (L) $300; (H) $14,300
drawings: (L) $300; (H) $4,400

SMILLIE, James
1807-1885
paintings: (H) $8,140

SMILLIE, James David
American 1833-1909
paintings: (L) $920; (H) $14,300

SMITH
20th cent.
paintings: (H) $550

SMITH, Albert E.
American 1862-1940
paintings: (L) $247; (H) $990

SMITH, Alexis
American b. 1949
drawings: (L) $7,700; (H) $10,350

SMITH, Alice Ravenel Huger
American 1876-1958
drawings: (L) $132; (H) $30,800

SMITH, Andre
American 1880-1959
paintings: (H) $880

SMITH, Archibald Cary
American 1837-1911
paintings: (L) $193; (H) $6,325

SMITH, B.S.
paintings: (H) $2,750

SMITH, Bissell Phelps
American b. 1892
paintings: (L) $55; (H) $660

SMITH, Carlton A.
English 1853-1946
paintings: (H) $5,500
drawings: (H) $12,100

SMITH, Catterson
Irish 19th cent.
paintings: (H) $1,610

SMITH, Charles
British 1857-1908
paintings: (L) $99; (H) $1,320

SMITH, Charles L.A.
American 1871-1937
paintings: (L) $550; (H) $1,430
drawings: (L) $660; (H) $3,850

SMITH, Christopher Webb
drawings: (H) $23,000

SMITH, D.W.
American 19th cent.
drawings: (H) $805

SMITH, Dan
American 1865-1934
paintings: (H) $2,300
drawings: (L) $1,430; (H) $1,955

SMITH, David
American 1906-1965
paintings: (L) $5,500; (H) $145,500
drawings: (L) $863; (H) $9,775
sculpture: (L) $28,600; (H) $4,072,500

SMITH, De Cost
American 1864-1939
paintings: (L) $3,520; (H) $18,700

SMITH, Denzil
British 19th cent.
paintings: (L) $880; (H) $2,970

SMITH, E. Boyd
American 1860-1943
paintings: (H) $495
drawings: (H) $110

SMITH, Elde
American b. c. 1900
paintings: (H) $1,150

SMITH, Elmer Boyd
American 1860-1943
paintings: (H) $10,450

SMITH, Ernest Browning
American 1866-1951
paintings: (L) $110; (H) $1,430

SMITH, F. Carl
American 1868-1955
paintings: (L) $242; (H) $1,870

SMITH, Firthjof
German d. 1910
paintings: (H) $1,980

SMITH, Francis Drexel
American 1874-1956
paintings: (H) $1,870

SMITH, Francis Hopkinson
American 1838-1915
paintings: (L) $2,860; (H) $3,575
drawings: (L) $220; (H) $16,500

SMITH, Frank Anthony
American b. 1939
paintings: (H) $522

SMITH, Frank Vining
American 1879-1967
paintings: (L) $220; (H) $6,900
drawings: (L) $165; (H) $440

SMITH, Fred W.
American
drawings: (H) $6,325

SMITH, Frederick Carl
American 1868-1955
paintings: (L) $220; (H) $1,320

SMITH, Frederick Marlette Bell
Canadian 1846-1923
drawings: (L) $330; (H) $605

SMITH, Gean
American 1851-1928
paintings: (L) $137; (H) $2,875

SMITH, George
British 1714-1776
paintings: (L) $1,760; (H) $15,950

SMITH, George Melville
American b. 1879
paintings: (L) $2,750; (H) $3,300

SMITH, Gerard
20th cent.
paintings: (H) $550

SMITH, Gord
Canadian b. 1937
paintings: (H) $1,540

SMITH, Gordon Appelbe
Canadian b. 1919
paintings: (L) $1,650; (H) $4,125

SMITH, Gorham P.
American 19th cent.
drawings: (H) $920

SMITH, Graham
drawings: (H) $2,200

SMITH, H.
German 19th cent.
paintings: (H) $770

SMITH, Hassel
American b. 1915
paintings: (L) $1,100; (H) $5,750
drawings: (H) $1,100

SMITH, Henry Pember
American 1854-1907
paintings: (L) $330; (H) $10,350
drawings: (L) $605; (H) $3,450

SMITH, Hope
American b. 1879
paintings: (L) $374; (H) $3,575

SMITH, Houghton Cranford
paintings: (H) $1,540

SMITH, Howard E.
American b. 1885
paintings: (L) $173; (H) $1,840
drawings: (H) $880

SMITH, Hughie Lee
American b. 1915
paintings: (L) $660; (H) $8,800
drawings: (H) $605

SMITH, J. Andre
American 1880-1959
paintings: (H) $2,860
drawings: (L) $138; (H) $495

SMITH, J. Christopher
1891-1943
paintings: (H) $2,300

SMITH, J. Wells
British 19th cent.
paintings: (H) $660

SMITH, J.H.
American 1861-1941
paintings: (L) $288; (H) $403
drawings: (H) $4,140

SMITH, J.R.
British 18th/19th cent.
paintings: (H) $1,760

SMITH, Jack
American b. 1928
paintings: (H) $495

SMITH, Jack Martin
American 20th cent.
drawings: (L) $550; (H) $4,400

SMITH, Jack Wilkinson
American 1873-1949
paintings: (L) $440; (H) $63,000
drawings: (H) $303

SMITH, James Burrell
English 1822-1897
paintings: (H) $2,200
drawings: (H) $963

SMITH, Jerome Howard
American 1861-1941
paintings: (L) $495; (H) $1,540

SMITH, Jessie Wilcox
American 1863-1935
paintings: (L) $1,430; (H) $5,980
drawings: (L) $413; (H) $18,400

SMITH, Joelle
American
paintings: (H) $3,000
drawings: (L) $1,320; (H) $2,800

SMITH, John Brandon
British 1848-1884
paintings: (L) $2,200; (H) $7,150

SMITH, John Christopher
American 1891-1943
paintings: (L) $495; (H) $1,540

SMITH, John Raphael
English 1752-1812
drawings: (L) $322; (H) $3,520

SMITH, John Rowson
1810-1864
paintings: (H) $660

SMITH, John Rubens
1775-1849
paintings: (H) $2,090

SMITH, Jon
paintings: (L) $357; (H) $467

SMITH, Jori
paintings: (H) $1,045

SMITH, Joseph B.
American 1798-1876
drawings: (H) $3,300

SMITH, Joseph Lindon
American 1863-1950
paintings: (L) $230; (H) $16,500
drawings: (L) $345; (H) $2,860

SMITH, Keith C.
b. 1924
paintings: (H) $1,650

SMITH, Kiki
b. 1954
drawings: (H) $2,860

SMITH, Langdon
American 1870-1959
paintings: (L) $99; (H) $1,430
drawings: (L) $247; (H) $440

SMITH, Lawrence Beall
American b. 1909
paintings: (H) $35,200
drawings: (H) $495

SMITH, Leon Polk
American b. 1906
paintings: (L) $4,950; (H) $20,700
drawings: (L) $1,265; (H) $5,750

SMITH, Lowell Ellsworth
American b. 1924
paintings: (H) $1,430
drawings: (L) $575; (H) $1,760

SMITH, M.
20th cent.
paintings: (L) $259; (H) $660

SMITH, Marshall Joseph, Jr.
American 1854-1923
paintings: (L) $2,640; (H) $82,500

SMITH, Mary
American 1842-1878
paintings: (L) $1,430; (H) $9,075

SMITH, Mary T.
b. 1904
paintings: (H) $990

SMITH, Miriam Tindall
American 20th cent.
paintings: (H) $1,150

SMITH, Mortimer L.
American 1840-1896
paintings: (L) $605; (H) $9,900
drawings: (L) $110; (H) $440

SMITH, Noel
British 19th/20th cent.
drawings: (H) $495

SMITH, Ray
American b. 1959
paintings: (L) $2,530; (H) $32,200

SMITH, Richard
contemporary
paintings: (H) $8,800
drawings: (H) $2,200

SMITH, Richard
British b. 1931
sculpture: (L) $1,045; (H) $1,100

SMITH, Rufus Way
American ac. 1800
paintings: (L) $460; (H) $3,080

SMITH, Rupert Jasen
contemporary
paintings: (H) $1,980

SMITH, Russell
American 1812-1896
paintings: (L) $170; (H) $7,700

SMITH, S. Catterson
1806-1872
paintings: (H) $495

SMITH, Sarah Katharine
b. c. 1877
drawings: (H) $4,675

SMITH, Sir Matthew
English 1879-1959
drawings: (H) $880

SMITH, Stephen Catterson
British 1806-1872
paintings: (L) $1,100; (H) $2,070

SMITH, Theodore J.
American
sculpture: (H) $600

SMITH, Thomas Lochlan
American 1835-1884
paintings: (L) $575; (H) $2,860

SMITH, Tony
American 1912-1980
sculpture: (L) $7,700; (H) $85,000

SMITH, Vernon B.
American b. 1894
paintings: (L) $173; (H) $546

SMITH, W.T. Russell
1812-1896
paintings: (H) $1,725

SMITH, Wallace H.
American b. 1901
paintings: (L) $690; (H) $4,888

SMITH, Wallace Herndon
American b. 1901
paintings: (L) $440; (H) $4,400

SMITH, William A.
American 1918-1982
paintings: (H) $55
drawings: (L) $385; (H) $715

SMITH, William H.
paintings: (H) $1,045
drawings: (H) $110

SMITH, William Thompson Russell
American 1812-1896
paintings: (L) $880; (H) $7,700
drawings: (H) $385

SMITH, Wuanita
American 1866-1959
paintings: (L) $88; (H) $770

SMITH, Xanthus Russell
American 1838/39-1929
paintings: (L) $440; (H) $12,100
drawings: (L) $165; (H) $3,025

SMITH-HALD, Frithjof
Norwegian 1846-1903
paintings: (L) $3,300; (H) $8,050

SMITHBURN, Florence Bartley
ac. 1930
paintings: (H) $2,760

SMITHERS, Collier
British 19th/20th cent.
paintings: (H) $18,700

SMITHSON, Robert
American 1938-1972/73
paintings: (H) $2,530
drawings: (L) $1,380; (H) $15,400
sculpture: (L) $3,300; (H) $93,500

SMITS, Jakob
Belgian 1856-1928
paintings: (L) $3,300; (H) $35,200

SMITS, Johann Gerard
Dutch 1823-1910
paintings: (L) $1,380; (H) $5,750
drawings: (H) $880

SMOUT, Lucas, the younger
1671-1713
paintings: (H) $3,450

SMYTH, Edward Robert
English 1810-1899
drawings: (H) $3,025

SMYTH, Eugene L.
paintings: (L) $330; (H) $550

SMYTH, Ned
b. 1948
drawings: (H) $978

SMYTHE, Edward Robert
English 1810-1899
paintings: (L) $1,100; (H) $3,300

SMYTHE, Edwin
English 19th cent.
paintings: (H) $605

SMYTHE, Emily R.
English ac. 1850-1874
paintings: (H) $1,035

SMYTHE, Eugene Leslie
American 1857-1932
paintings: (L) $288; (H) $1,150

SMYTHE, Lionel Percy
Scottish/English 1839/40-1918
paintings: (L) $1,595; (H) $3,740
drawings: (H) $1,100

SMYTHE, Minnie
English 1839-1913
drawings: (H) $4,620

SMYTHE, Thomas
English 1825-1906/07
paintings: (L) $5,500; (H) $8,250

SNAYERS, Peeter
Flemish 1592-1667
paintings: (L) $23,000; (H) $184,000

SNEAD, Louise W.
American 19th/20th cent.
drawings: (H) $605

SNEEP, Jan van
Dutch 19th/20th cent.
paintings: (H) $1,100

SNELGROVE, Walter
American b. 1924
paintings: (H) $3,025

SNELL, Florence Francis
drawings: (H) $650

SNELL, Henry B.
American 1858-1943
paintings: (L) $110; (H) $38,500
drawings: (H) $1,045

SNELL, James Herbert
English 1861-1935
paintings: (L) $880; (H) $1,650

SNELLER, Sir Godfrey, and Studio
1646-1723
paintings: (H) $3,450

SNELSON, Kenneth
American b. 1927
drawings: (H) $322
sculpture: (L) $2,860; (H) $66,000

SNIDER, Dan L.
American
sculpture: (H) $1,100

SNIDOW, Gordon
American b. 1936
drawings: (L) $600; (H) $22,000

SNITKOVSKY, Janet and Emmanuil
20th cent.
paintings: (H) $11,500

SNODGRASS, Jerry L.
sculpture: (H) $2,750

SNOEYERBOSCH, Cornelius Johannes
Dutch 1891-1955
paintings: (L) $1,760; (H) $1,760

SNOW, Dora Donaldson
paintings: (H) $1,430

SNOW, Francis W.
paintings: (H) $2,200

SNOW, J.A.
American 19th cent.
drawings: (H) $550

SNOWMAN, Isaac
Israeli b. 1874
paintings: (L) $3,080; (H) $7,700

SNYDER, A.
paintings: (L) $495; (H) $3,500

SNYDER, Joan
American b. 1940
paintings: (H) $5,280
drawings: (L) $748; (H) $3,680

SNYDER, Peter Etril
paintings: (H) $1,980

SNYDER, William Henry
American 1829-1910
paintings: (L) $431; (H) $1,870

SNYDER, William McKinley
American 19th/20th cent.
paintings: (L) $660; (H) $935

SNYDERS, Frans
Flemish 1579-1657
paintings: (L) $110,000; (H) $222,500

SNYDERS, Frans, studio of
Flemish 17th cent.
paintings: (H) $16,100

SNYDERS, Frans, workshop of
17th cent.
paintings: (H) $57,500

SNYERS, Pieter
Flemish 1681-1752
paintings: (L) $57,500; (H) $63,000

SOARE, William F.
1896-1940
paintings: (L) $2,860; (H) $2,970

SOBRINO, Carmelo
b. 1948
paintings: (H) $6,900

SOCKWELL, Carroll
American contemporary
paintings: (H) $1,540
drawings: (L) $165; (H) $825

SODERBERG, Yvngue E.
American 1896-1971
drawings: (L) $110; (H) $633

SODERSTON, Herman
Swedish/American 1862-1926
paintings: (H) $990

SOELEN, Theodore van
American 1890-1964
paintings: (H) $2,750
drawings: (H) $385

SOEN, Charles
paintings: (H) $550

SOGGI, Niccolo
Italian 1474/80-1552
paintings: (H) $159,500

SOGLIARA, Giovanni Antonio
Italian 1492-1544
paintings: (H) $107,000

SOHIER, Alice Ruggles
American b. 1880
paintings: (L) $3,520; (H) $7,425

SOHN, August Wilhelm
German 1830-1899
paintings: (H) $2,640

SOHN, Eric
American 1905/10-1985
paintings: (H) $460

SOHN., H. Cladenbok
sculpture: (H) $880

SOILEAU, Hodges D.
b. 1943
paintings: (L) $522; (H) $660

SOKOLOFF, Anatolio
Russian 1891-1971
paintings: (L) $104; (H) $5,750

SOKOLOV, Sergei
Russian b. 1936
paintings: (H) $1,150

SOLANO, Susana
b. 1943
sculpture: (L) $3,575; (H) $14,950

SOLAR, Xul
b. Argentina 1887-1963
paintings: (H) $35,200
drawings: (H) $16,100

SOLARIO, Andrea
Italian 1460-1522
paintings: (H) $222,500

SOLARIO, Andrea, studio of
paintings: (H) $11,500

SOLARIO, Antonio, studio of
Italian 16th cent.
paintings: (H) $3,850

SOLBRIG, H.
paintings: (H) $1,210

SOLDANI-BENZI, Massimiliano
Italian 17th/18th cent.
sculpture: (L) $27,600; (H) $55,000

SOLDATENKOV, Eugely
Russian 20th cent.
paintings: (H) $575

SOLDI, Antenore
Italian 1844-1877
paintings: (H) $3,575

SOLDI, Raul
b. Argentina 1905
paintings: (H) $10,925
drawings: (L) $12,100; (H) $17,250

SOLDI-COLBERT, Emile Arthur
French 1846-1906
sculpture: (H) $1,150

SOLDNER, Paul
American b. 1921
sculpture: (L) $2,070; (H) $2,200

SOLDY, O.
paintings: (H) $495

SOLE, Giovanni Gioseffo dal
Italian 1654-1719
paintings: (H) $220,000

SOLER, Antonio
paintings: (H) $6,600

SOLER, Jean
French 19th/20th cent.
paintings: (H) $1,320

SOLIDAY, Tim
American 20th cent.
paintings: (H) $2,750

SOLIMENA, Francesco
Italian 1657-1747
paintings: (L) $16,500; (H) $497,500

SOLIMENA, Francesco, studio of
Italian 17th/18th cent.
paintings: (H) $7,150

SOLMAN, Joseph
Russian/American b. 1909
paintings: (L) $220; (H) $1,610
drawings: (H) $2,300

SOLNECK, Franz
18th/19th cent.
drawings: (H) $6,050

SOLOMON, Abraham
English 1823/24-1862
paintings: (H) $6,600

SOLOMON, Simeon
British 1840-1905
drawings: (L) $990; (H) $4,025

SOLOMON, Solomon Joseph
British 1860-1927
paintings: (H) $57,500

SOLOMON, Stan
American 20th cent.
paintings: (H) $1,008

SOLOMON, Syd
American b. 1917
paintings: (L) $220; (H) $495

SOLOTAIRE, Robert
paintings: (L) $460; (H) $1,006

SOLOTAREFF, Boris
Russian 1889-1966
paintings: (H) $220
drawings: (L) $165; (H) $1,100

SOLOWEY, Ben
Polish/American 1900/01-1978
drawings: (H) $850

SOLTAU, Pauline, nee SUHRLANDT
German 1833-1902
paintings: (H) $8,800

SOMAINI, Francesco
sculpture: (H) $1,760

SOMER, Hendrik van
Dutch 1615-1685
paintings: (L) $4,025; (H) $19,550

SOMERS
sculpture: (H) $1,870

SOMERS, H.
Franco/American b. 1922
paintings: (L) $715; (H) $4,125

SOMERSET, Richard Gay
British 1848-1928
paintings: (L) $431; (H) $2,200

SOMME, Theophile Francois
French b. 1871
sculpture: (L) $935; (H) $4,400

SOMMER
German 19th cent.
sculpture: (H) $2,860

SOMMER
Italian Late 19th/20th cent.
sculpture: (H) $6,600

SOMMER, A.
German 19th cent.
paintings: (H) $1,092

SOMMER, Carl August
German b. 1829
paintings: (H) $3,410

SOMMER, Charles A.
1829-1894
paintings: (L) $1,650; (H) $7,150

SOMMER, Giorgio
Italian 20th cent.
sculpture: (H) $495

SOMMER, Otto
American ac. 1860-1870s
paintings: (L) $1,650; (H) $17,600

SOMMER, William
American 1867-1949
paintings: (L) $2,200; (H) $7,040
drawings: (L) $22; (H) $5,060

SOMOV, Konstantin
Russian 1869-1939
paintings: (H) $2,200

SON, Johannes
French b. 1859
paintings: (L) $288; (H) $3,850

SON, Joris van
Flemish 1623-1667
paintings: (L) $15,400; (H) $23,000

SONDERLAND, Fritz
German 1836-1896
paintings: (L) $4,675; (H) $7,150

SONDERMANN, Hermann
German 1832-1901
paintings: (H) $24,150

SONN, Albert H.
American 1867-1936
drawings: (L) $50; (H) $467

SONNIER, Keith
American b. 1941
drawings: (H) $550
sculpture: (H) $17,600

SONNTAG, William Louis, Jr.
American 1869-1898
paintings: (L) $1,650; (H) $4,125
drawings: (L) $2,760; (H) $9,200

SONNTAG, William Louis, Sr.
American 1822-1916
paintings: (L) $1,210; (H) $33,000

SONREL, Elizabeth
French 1874-1953
paintings: (H) $550
drawings: (L) $330; (H) $10,350

SONTAG, W.L.
paintings: (H) $715

SOOLMAKER, Jan Frans
ac. 1654-1665
paintings: (H) $7,700

SOONIUS, Louis
Dutch 1883-1956
paintings: (H) $467

SOPER, J.
paintings: (H) $2,200

SORBI, Raffaelo
Italian 1844-1931
paintings: (L) $57,750; (H) $107,000

SOREAU, Isaac
1604-after 1638
paintings: (H) $88,000

SOREL, Edward
b. 1929
drawings: (H) $522

SORENSEN, Carl Eiler
Danish 1869-1953
paintings: (H) $935

SORENSON, Don
American 20th cent.
paintings: (H) $1,725

SORENSON-RINGI, Harold
Swedish 1872-1912
sculpture: (H) $6,900

SORGH, Hendrik Maertensz.
Dutch 1611-1670
paintings: (L) $2,475; (H) $629,500

SORIA, Martin de
Spanish ac. 1475
paintings: (H) $28,600

SORIANO, Juan
Mexican b. 1919/20
paintings: (L) $7,150; (H) $79,500
drawings: (L) $1,150; (H) $19,800
sculpture: (H) $11,000

SORIANO, Rafael
b. Mexico 1920
paintings: (L) $13,800; (H) $20,700

SORKAU, Albert
French b. 1874
paintings: (H) $660

SOROLLA Y BASTIDA, Joaquin
Spanish 1863-1923
paintings: (L) $19,800; (H) $2,640,000
drawings: (L) $4,600; (H) $4,600

SORRAM, J.
Continental early 20th cent.
sculpture: (H) $1,380

SORRENTI, G.
Italian 19th cent.
drawings: (H) $880

SOSPATAK, Laszlo Pataky von
Hungarian 1857-1912
paintings: (H) $1,725

SOSSON, L.
sculpture: (H) $1,210

SOTO, Jesus Rafael
Venezuelan b. 1923
paintings: (L) $27,600; (H) $93,500
drawings: (L) $29,900; (H) $39,100
sculpture: (L) $6,900; (H) $66,000

SOTOMAYOR Y ZARAGOZA,
Fernando
Spanish 1875-1960
paintings: (L) $27,500; (H) $44,000

SOTTER, George W.
American 1879-1953
paintings: (L) $650; (H) $38,000

SOTTSASS, Ettore
contemporary
sculpture: (L) $863; (H) $8,800

SOUBRE, Charles
Belgian 1821-1895
paintings: (H) $5,750

SOUCCIOL
paintings: (L) $440; (H) $495

SOUCEK, Karel
Czechoslovakian b. 1915
paintings: (H) $687
drawings: (L) $385; (H) $990

SOUDEIKINE, Sergei
Russian/American 1883/86-1946
paintings: (L) $120; (H) $4,675
drawings: (L) $523; (H) $920

SOULACROIX, Joseph Frederic
Charles
French 1825-1877
paintings: (L) $6,325; (H) $145,500

SOULAGES, Pierre
French b. 1919
paintings: (L) $37,375; (H) $129,000
drawings: (L) $11,000; (H) $25,300

SOULE, Clara
American 19th cent.
paintings: (H) $805

SOULEN, H.
paintings: (H) $1,300

SOULEN, Henry James
American 1888-1965
paintings: (L) $440; (H) $6,325

SOULIES, Paul
ac. 1850's
drawings: (H) $2,970

SOUTER, John Bulloch
British 1890-1972
paintings: (H) $7,150

SOUTHWELL, C. Elmer
British 19th cent.
paintings: (H) $2,070
drawings: (H) $3,220

SOUTINE, Chaim
Russian 1894-1943
paintings: (L) $71,250; (H) $638,000

SOUTNER, Theodore
French 19th cent.
paintings: (H) $57,750

SOUTO
Spanish 19th/20th cent.
paintings: (H) $1,380
drawings: (H) $2,640

SOUVERBIE, Jean
French b. 1891
paintings: (L) $4,830; (H) $9,350

SOUZA-PINTO, Jose Guilio
Portuguese b. 1855
paintings: (H) $19,800

SOVETSKI, Bunn
American contemporary
sculpture: (H) $522

SOWERS, Robert
paintings: (L) $1,650; (H) $1,725

SOYA-JENSEN, Carl
Danish 1860-1912
paintings: (H) $2,640

SOYER, Isaac
Russian/American 1907-1981
paintings: (L) $2,530; (H) $18,400
drawings: (L) $550; (H) $748

WPA Artist

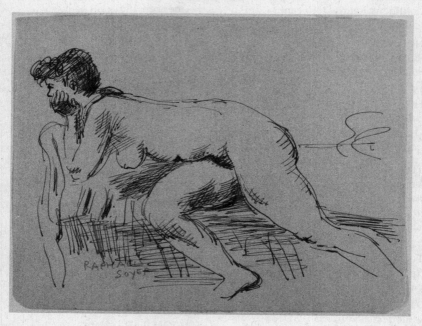

The Works Progress Administration, a program to give work to the unemployed under Roosevelt's New Deal, was established in 1935. Most of the jobs were in construction, building bridges, parks, dams, roads, and fairgrounds. Artists of all kinds had been especially hard-hit by the Depression, and the Federal Writers Project, the Federal Theater Project, the Federal Music Project, and the Federal Art Project (collectively called the Federal Arts Project) was the WPA program to employ artists. At its peak, the WPA employed 5,000 musicians, writers, actors, and artists. The original focus of the Federal Art Project was to decorate public buildings with murals and sculpture, but the program expanded to include artists who made prints, posters, and crafts. Very little of this art was "great," but the goals of the program were to give employment to artists and to fulfill Roosevelt's commitment to a "cultural democracy." Prints and posters from this period are distinct: most are in the Social Realist manner and depict urban genre scenes and the suffering of the poor. Paintings, drawings, and prints by WPA artists are the focus of many collections.

Raphael Soyer (1899-1987) and his twin Moses (1899-1974) were well-known artists who worked for the WPA. Most of the murals commissioned by the WPA have been lost, but the Soyers' mural at the old Kingsessing Station Post Office in Philadelphia has been preserved and relocated to the post office at 6th and Chestnut. The Soyer family had emigrated from Tsarist Russia to the United States in 1912. Twin brothers Raphael and Moses and their brother Isaac (1907-1981) all had distinguished careers as artists. Raphael worked at factory jobs and sold newspapers while he studied in night classes at Cooper Union from 1914 to 1917, at the National Academy of Design from 1918 to 1922, and intermittently at the Arts Students League. During the 1920s and 1930s

Raphael Soyer's favorite themes were urban views of working girls, shoppers, dancers, and Bowery bums. His lithographs from this period were very popular. After the 1940s he began to draw and paint studies of women at work or posing in the nude. *Reclining Nude on a Sofa*, a drawing dated circa 1945, sold for $747 at Swann's in December 1994. (Raphael Soyer, *Reclining Nude on a Sofa*, pen on paper, 7½ x 9½ inches, Swann, December 1, 1994, $747)

SOYER, Moses
Russian/American 1899-1974
paintings: (L) $368; (H) $13,800
drawings: (L) $110; (H) $1,980

SOYER, Raphael
Russian/American 1899-1987
paintings: (L) $22; (H) $55,000
drawings: (L) $83; (H) $3,850

SPACEK, Dr. Jaromir
Czechoslovakian b. 1911
sculpture: (H) $2,875

SPADER, William E.
American b. 1875
paintings: (L) $690; (H) $825
drawings: (H) $633

SPADINO, Giovanni Paolo
Italian 1659-1738
paintings: (L) $24,150; (H) $24,200

SPAENDONCK, Gerard van
French 1746-1822
paintings: (L) $363,000; (H) $1,047,500

SPAGNA, Lo, Giovanni di PIETRO
c. 1450-1528
paintings: (H) $43,125

SPAGNOLETTO, Il, Bartolomeo
GAGLIARDO
Italian 1555-c.1626
drawings: (H) $2,200

SPALATIN, Marco
Yugoslavian contemporary
paintings: (H) $880

SPALDING, C.B.
British 1801-1873
paintings: (H) $3,575

SPAMPINATO, Clemente
American b. 1912
sculpture: (L) $1,045; (H) $2,185

SPANG, F.
paintings: (H) $4,400

SPANG, T. Neville
European 19th cent.
paintings: (H) $770

SPANGENBERG, Frederick T.
paintings: (H) $4,675

SPANGENBURG, George
American 1907-1964
paintings: (L) $935; (H) $1,760

SPANISH FORGER
paintings: (H) $1,100

SPARE, Austin Osmond
British 1888-1956
drawings: (H) $978

SPARKS, H. Blande
British ac. 1892-1893
drawings: (L) $207; (H) $460

SPARKS, Will
American 1862-1937
paintings: (L) $715; (H) $13,800

SPAT, Gabriel
American 1890-1967
paintings: (L) $247; (H) $3,575
drawings: (L) $1,100; (H) $1,540

SPAULDING, Florence
b. 1899
paintings: (H) $1,430

SPAULDING, Henry Plympton
American b. 1868
paintings: (L) $192; (H) $742
drawings: (L) $99; (H) $2,860

SPAULDING, P.B.
English 19th cent.
paintings: (H) $2,530

SPAUN, P.V.
Continental 20th cent.
paintings: (H) $935

SPAVENTA, George
1918-1978
sculpture: (H) $1,150

SPAZZALI, Luciano
20th cent.
paintings: (H) $462

SPEAR, Arthur P.
American 1879-1959
paintings: (L) $825; (H) $2,310
drawings: (L) $385; (H) $468

SPEAR, Thomas Truman
American 1803-1882
paintings: (L) $522; (H) $578

SPEAR, W.H.
British 19th cent.
paintings: (H) $3,300

SPECK, Loran
American b. 1944
paintings: (L) $3,410; (H) $5,500

SPECK, Walter
20th cent.
paintings: (L) $690; (H) $1,840

SPECKAERT, Hans
Flemish d. c. 1577
paintings: (H) $77,000

SPEED, Grant
American b. 1930
sculpture: (L) $2,310; (H) $7,700

SPEER, J.A.
paintings: (L) $110; (H) $1,210

SPEICHER, Eugene
American 1883-1962
paintings: (L) $575; (H) $4,180
drawings: (L) $44; (H) $1,430

SPEIGELMAN, Art
drawings: (H) $2,750

SPEIGHT, Francis
American 1896-1989
paintings: (L) $715; (H) $3,410

SPEISER
19th cent.
paintings: (H) $1,150

SPELCE, Fannie Lou
American b. 1908
paintings: (L) $1,650; (H) $5,500

SPELMAN, John A.
American b. 1880
paintings: (L) $115; (H) $3,300

SPELT, Adriaen van der
1630-1673
paintings: (H) $6,325

SPENCE, Andrew
b. 1947
paintings: (L) $1,380; (H) $4,140

SPENCE, Harry
English b. c. 1870
paintings: (H) $1,380

SPENCE, Thomas Ralph
English b. 1855
paintings: (H) $4,675

SPENCELAYH, Charles
English 1865-1958
paintings: (L) $8,800; (H) $69,000

SPENCER, Emma Sonneoecker
paintings: (H) $1,100

SPENCER, Frederick R.
American 1806-1875
paintings: (L) $200; (H) $1,035

SPENCER, H.
19th cent.
paintings: (H) $1,650

SPENCER, Howard Bonnell
American 1871-1967
paintings: (H) $825

SPENCER, J.C.
American 19th/20th cent.
paintings: (L) $248; (H) $2,310
drawings: (H) $220

SPENCER, J.R.
paintings: (H) $1,980

SPENCER, John C.
American 1861-1919
paintings: (L) $770; (H) $1,540
drawings: (H) $192

SPENCER, Lilly Martin
American 1822/27-1902
paintings: (L) $786; (H) $40,250
drawings: (L) $55; (H) $605

SPENCER, Niles
American 1893-1952
paintings: (H) $18,700
drawings: (L) $220; (H) $690

SPENCER, Richard B.
British 19th cent.
paintings: (H) $990

SPENCER, Robert
American 1879-1931
paintings: (L) $990; (H) $50,600

SPENCER, Stanley
1891-1959
drawings: (L) $1,320; (H) $2,640

SPENCER, Thomas
British c. 1700-1767
paintings: (H) $2,875

SPENCER, William B.
British ac. 1863-1884
paintings: (H) $3,300

SPERLICH, Sophie
German 19th cent.
paintings: (H) $990

SPERLING, Heinrich
German 1844-1924
paintings: (H) $3,850

SPERLING, Johann Christian
German 1690/91-1746
paintings: (H) $30,800

SPERMAN, L.
American 19th/20th cent.
paintings: (H) $3,080

SPERO, Nancy
b. 1928
paintings: (H) $440
drawings: (L) $1,045; (H) $4,312

SPERRY, Reginald T.
American b. 1845
paintings: (L) $495; (H) $550

SPEY, Martinus
Flemish b. 1777
paintings: (H) $28,600

SPICUZZA, Francesco J.
Italian/American 1883-1962
paintings: (L) $110; (H) $495
drawings: (L) $82; (H) $403

SPIELER, J.P.
drawings: (H) $1,320

SPIELMANN, Vicktor
Swiss 1769-1848
drawings: (H) $660

SPIERS, Harry
English/American 1869-after 1934
paintings: (H) $2,300
drawings: (L) $88; (H) $770

SPILIMBERGO, Lino Eneas
Argentinean 1896-1964
paintings: (H) $134,500

SPINDLER, Joshua
American
drawings: (L) $2,750; (H) $3,575

SPINETTI, Mario
Italian 19th/20th cent.
paintings: (L) $6,440; (H) $6,900
drawings: (L) $165; (H) $330

SPINKS, Thomas
British ac. 1872-1907
paintings: (H) $2,200

SPINNY, Guillaume Jean Joseph de
1721-1785
paintings: (H) $1,650

SPINSKI, Victor
contemporary
sculpture: (H) $1,725

SPIRIDON, Ignace
Italian ac. 1889-1900
paintings: (L) $990; (H) $5,500

SPIRO, Georges
French 1909-1948
paintings: (L) $550; (H) $2,760

SPITLER, W.W.
American
drawings: (L) $220; (H) $495

SPITZER, Emmanuel
German 1844-1919
paintings: (H) $6,325

SPITZER, Walter
Polish b. 1927
paintings: (L) $1,210; (H) $5,225

SPITZWEG, Carl
German 1808-1885
paintings: (L) $34,500; (H) $123,500
drawings: (L) $1,320; (H) $2,640

SPIZZIRI, Luigi
American b. 1894
paintings: (H) $1,150
drawings: (H) $77

SPODE, Sam
British ac. 1825-1858
paintings: (L) $5,750; (H) $11,500

SPOERRI, Daniel
European b. 1930
sculpture: (L) $2,875; (H) $17,600

SPOHLER, J.F.
paintings: (H) $2,090

SPOHLER, J.J. or J.F.
paintings: (H) $4,500

SPOHLER, Jan Jacob Coenraad
Dutch 1837-1923
paintings: (L) $1,320; (H) $4,025

SPOHLER, Johannes Franciscus
Dutch 1853-1894
paintings: (L) $5,280; (H) $39,100

SPOHN, Clay
contemporary
paintings: (H) $2,090

SPOLDI, A.
drawings: (H) $1,045

SPOLVERINI, Ilario, called Il
MERCANTI
Italian 1657-1734
paintings: (H) $8,250

SPRAGUE, C.A.
American School 19th/20th cent.
paintings: (H) $715

SPRAGUE, Howard F.
American ac. 1871-1899
paintings: (L) $6,600; (H) $14,300

SPRATLING, William P.
American 20th cent.
drawings: (H) $770

SPRECKELS, R.C.
Dutch 19th cent.
paintings: (H) $1,045

SPREEUWEN, Jacob van
Dutch b. 1611
paintings: (H) $46,000

SPRETER, Roy
b. 1899
paintings: (L) $1,980; (H) $2,090

SPRICK, Daniel
American 20th cent.
paintings: (L) $495; (H) $7,700

SPRINCHORN, Carl
American 1887-1971
paintings: (L) $523; (H) $13,200
drawings: (L) $330; (H) $1,320

SPRING, Alphons
German 1843-1908
paintings: (L) $6,600; (H) $9,775

SPRINGER, Cornelis
Dutch 1817-1891
paintings: (L) $22,000; (H) $159,500

SPRUANCE, Benton
American 1904-1967
paintings: (L) $1,980; (H) $7,762
drawings: (L) $55; (H) $1,650

SPRUCE, Everett
American b. 1907
paintings: (L) $550; (H) $1,485

SPUEHLER, Ernst A.
American 1900-1973
paintings: (H) $467

SPURLING, Jack
English 1871-1933
drawings: (H) $495

SPURR-CUTTS, Gertrude
paintings: (H) $660

SQUIRE, Maud
drawings: (H) $1,320

SQUIRES, C. Clyde
American 1883-1970
paintings: (L) $770; (H) $1,540

ST. ALERIE
drawings: (H) $1,035

ST. ANDRE, Berthome
French 1905-1977
paintings: (L) $2,415; (H) $3,850

ST. AUBERT, Charles Leroy
French 1852-1907
paintings: (H) $607,500

ST. AUBIN, Augustin de
French 1736-1807
drawings: (L) $770; (H) $5,500

ST. AUBIN, Gabriel Jacques de
French 1724-1780
drawings: (L) $2,200; (H) $154,000

ST. BRICE, Robert
Haitian 1898-1973
paintings: (L) $2,090; (H) $9,350

ST. CLAIR, Norman
American 1863-1912
drawings: (H) $825

ST. CROIX, Robert
American 20th cent.
sculpture: (H) $990

ST. GAUDENS, Annetta Johnson
1869-1943
sculpture: (H) $1,093

Making a Living as an Artist

Benton Spruance (1904-1967) was orphaned as a child and raised in Philadelphia by his stepfather. Benton loved drawing, but his stepfather thought that the life of an artist was not practical and insisted that his stepson follow a more conventional career. After high school Benton worked in an architect's office and studied architecture at the University of Pennsylvania. Suffering a nervous breakdown in 1921, he decided to follow his dream of becoming an artist and attended the Pennsylvania Academy of Art on a scholarship. A traveling scholarship allowed him to study in Europe, where he executed his first lithograph. In 1928 Spruance married and began teaching at Beaver College in Glenside, Pennsylvania, and at the School of Industrial Art of the Philadelphia Museum. He taught studio art, lectured on art history, worked in his own studio, and was active in the Philadelphia art community. Spruance exhibited widely and received many awards. He was chairman of the Fine Arts Department at Beaver College when he died suddenly in 1967.

Spruance produced hundreds of paintings and drawings and completed several architectural commissions, but he is known primarily as a printmaker. During the Depression years his themes were the cityscape, still life, imaginative symbolic pieces, and portraits. His oeuvre includes few landscapes, but the 1940s were a time of change and experimentation for Spruance. Influenced by Cubism, and drawing upon his architectural background, he made several lithographs of landscapes that had stylized abstract forms. His oil *American Pattern* was most likely painted about the same time.

Atypical works do not always sell well, but *American Pattern* (est. $2,500-3,500) sold for $7,762, an auction record for a painting by Spruance. It is interesting to note that his lithograph *American Pattern, Barn* has sold for as much as $12,650. (Benton Spruance, *American Pattern*, oil on board, 22 x 30 inches, Doyle, November 9, 1994, $7,762)

ST. GAUDENS, Augustus
American 1848-1907
paintings: (H) $3,450
sculpture: (L) $3,030; (H) $242,000

ST. GAUDENS, Augustus
American 1848-1907
sculpture: (L) $11,500; (H) $165,000

ST. JEAN, Simon
French 1808-1860
paintings: (H) $20,900

ST. JOHN, David
paintings: (H) $2,200

ST. JOHN, J. Allen
American b. 1872
paintings: (H) $2,310
drawings: (H) $25,300

ST. JOHN, S.H.
paintings: (H) $1,760

ST. JOHN, Terry
contemporary
paintings: (L) $748; (H) $2,750

ST. MARCEAUX, Charles Rene de
French 19th/20th cent.
sculpture: (H) $1,980

ST. MARCEL, Emile Normand
French b. 1840
drawings: (H) $605

ST. MEMIN, Charles Balthazar Fevret de
American 1770-1852
drawings: (H) $3,300

ST. MEMIN, Charles Balthazar Julien Fevret de
French 1770-1852
drawings: (L) $403; (H) $8,800

ST. PHALLE, Niki de
French b. 1930
drawings: (L) $4,370; (H) $8,050
sculpture: (L) $4,600; (H) $34,500

ST. PHALLE, Niki de and Jean TINGUELY
contemporary
sculpture: (H) $49,500

ST. RUBLE, Clair
American 20th cent.
sculpture: (H) $935

ST. VIDAL, Francis de
French 1840-1900
sculpture: (H) $74,000

STACEY, Anna Lee
American 1871-1943
paintings: (L) $220; (H) $4,675

STACEY, John F.
American 1859-1941
paintings: (L) $495; (H) $2,750

STACEY, Walter S.
British 1846-1929
paintings: (H) $4,400
drawings: (H) $275

STACHIEWICZ, Piotr
Polish 19th/20th cent.
paintings: (H) $1,320

STACHOUWER, Jacobus Nicolaas Tjarda van Starkenborgh
Dutch 1822-1895
paintings: (H) $7,763

STACK, Michael
American b. 1947
paintings: (L) $4,620; (H) $9,020

STACKHOUSE, Robert
American 20th cent.
drawings: (H) $2,310

STACKMANN, A.
paintings: (H) $550

STACKPOLE, Ralph W.
1885-1973
drawings: (H) $1,150

STADELHOFER, H.
paintings: (H) $495

STADEMANN, Adolf
German 1824-1895
paintings: (L) $4,290; (H) $7,700

STADLER, Toni von
Austrian 1850-1917
paintings: (H) $2,200

STAEBLER, Stephen de
contemporary
sculpture: (H) $19,800

STAEHR-NIELSEN, Olaf Christian
Danish b. 1896
sculpture: (H) $460

STAEL, Nicolas de
French 1914-1955
paintings: (L) $43,700; (H) $682,000
drawings: (L) $18,150; (H) $23,000

STAFFANONI, Luigi
French 1905-1984
paintings: (H) $1,100

STAFFEL, Rudolf
American b. 1911
drawings: (H) $77
sculpture: (L) $1,840; (H) $4,888

STAFFORD, George
Australian 1827-188?
paintings: (H) $1,150

STAHL, Ben
American 1910-1987
paintings: (L) $184; (H) $4,675
drawings: (L) $44; (H) $220

STAHL, Fried
paintings: (H) $2,200

STAHR, Paul C.
American b. 1883
paintings: (L) $357; (H) $3,850
drawings: (H) $1,100

STAINFORTH, Martin
paintings: (H) $1,980

STAINTON, George
British 19th cent.
paintings: (L) $1,540; (H) $2,090

STALLAERT, Joseph
Belgian 1825-1903
paintings: (H) $21,850

STALLER, Gerard
Dutch 1880-1956
paintings: (H) $990

STAMICK, A.
German 19th cent.
paintings: (H) $2,070

STAMMEL, Eberhard
German 1832/33-1906
paintings: (H) $2,750

STAMOS, Theodoros
American b. 1922
paintings: (L) $1,265; (H) $33,000
drawings: (L) $1,610; (H) $5,225

STAN, Walter
American b. 1917
paintings: (H) $1,595

STANCLIFF, J.W.
American 1814-1891
paintings: (H) $3,850

STANCZAK, Julian
American b. 1928
paintings: (L) $55; (H) $5,462

STANDING, Guy
paintings: (H) $633

STANDING, H.W.
English 19th/20th cent.
drawings: (L) $495; (H) $935

STANDING, William
paintings: (L) $1,760; (H) $3,410
drawings: (L) $500; (H) $800

STANFIELD, Charles
British 19th/20th cent.
paintings: (H) $715

STANFIELD, George Clarkson
English 1828-1878
paintings: (L) $1,650; (H) $15,400

STANFIELD, William Clarkson
English 1793-1867
paintings: (L) $3,025; (H) $4,950
drawings: (L) $440; (H) $3,520

STANIER,
sculpture: (H) $805

STANIER, Henry
British ac. 1855-1864
drawings: (L) $121; (H) $1,320

STANKIEWICZ, Richard
American b. 1922
sculpture: (L) $2,300; (H) $27,600

STANLAWS, Penrhyn, Penrhyn
Stanley Adamson
American 1877-1957
paintings: (H) $825
drawings: (L) $345; (H) $2,200

STANLEY, Herbert
British 19th cent.
paintings: (H) $1,150

STANLEY, John
drawings: (H) $3,300

STANLEY, John Mix
American 1814-1872
paintings: (H) $57,500
drawings: (L) $35,650; (H) $37,950

STANLEY, Robert
American 20th cent.
paintings: (H) $660

STANNARD, Emilly
British 1803-1885
paintings: (H) $6,325

STANNARD, Eva
paintings: (H) $1,045

STANNARD, Henry Sylvester
English 1870-1951
drawings: (L) $248; (H) $3,738

STANNARD, Lilian
British 1877/84-1944
drawings: (L) $935; (H) $4,400

STANNARD, Theresa
British 1898-1947
paintings: (H) $1,870
drawings: (L) $2,750; (H) $3,850

STANTON, Gideon T.
American 1885-1964
paintings: (L) $132; (H) $500

STANTON, Horace Hughes
British 1843-1914
paintings: (H) $575

STANTON, Penrhyn
American 20th cent.
drawings: (H) $1,375

STANWOOD, Atkinson
Continental School 19th cent.
drawings: (H) $1,210

STANWOOD, Franklin
American 1856-1888
paintings: (L) $303; (H) $8,250
drawings: (L) $99; (H) $688

STANZANI, E.
Italian 20th cent.
sculpture: (H) $2,860

STANZIONE, Massimo
Italian c. 1585-1656
paintings: (L) $27,500; (H) $154,000

STAPLES, Sir Robert Ponsonby
British 1853-1943
paintings: (H) $1,495

STAPPEN, Pierre Charles van der
Belgian 1843-1910
sculpture: (L) $2,475; (H) $3,300

STAPPERS, Y.
paintings: (H) $1,320

STARK, Arthur James
British 1831-1902
paintings: (L) $660; (H) $2,760

STARK, Jack Gage
1882-1950
paintings: (H) $1,265

STARK, James
British 1794-1859
paintings: (H) $2,200

STARK, Karl
drawings: (H) $920

STARK, Melville F.
American b. 1904
paintings: (L) $165; (H) $1,200

STARK, Otto
American 1859-1926
paintings: (H) $4,950
drawings: (L) $825; (H) $2,200

STARKENBORGH, Jacobus Nicolas,
Baron Tjarda van
German/Dutch 1822-1895
paintings: (H) $1,955

STARKWEATHER, William E.B.
American 1879-1969
paintings: (L) $440; (H) $6,600
drawings: (L) $247; (H) $2,200

STARN TWINS
American b. 1961
drawings: (L) $880; (H) $55,000
sculpture: (L) $4,000; (H) $15,400

STAROSEL'SKAYA, Tatiana N.
Russian b. 1916
paintings: (H) $1,100

STASIAK, Ludwik
Polish 1858-1924
paintings: (L) $1,725; (H) $2,875

STAURT, Gilbert
American 1755-1828
paintings: (H) $28,600

STAVROWSKY, Oleg
American b. 1927
paintings: (L) $1,870; (H) $16,500

STAYTON, Bob
sculpture: (L) $800; (H) $3,080

STEA, Cesare
drawings: (H) $1,320

STEACY, Ken
paintings: (L) $3,025; (H) $3,220
drawings: (L) $1,725; (H) $3,737

STEAD, Fred
British 1863-1940
paintings: (L) $4,887; (H) $6,050

STEADMAN, Ralph
b. 1936
drawings: (H) $1,210

STEARNS, Junius Brutus
American 1810-1885
paintings: (H) $8,050

STEARNS, Robert L.
drawings: (H) $467

STEARNS, Sally
American School 19th cent.
drawings: (H) $825

STEBBINS, Emma
sculpture: (H) $1,600

STEBBINS, Roland
American 1883-1974
paintings: (H) $715

STECHER, R***
American 20th cent.
paintings: (L) $489; (H) $1,495
drawings: (H) $920

STEEL, Adolf
German 1829-1907
drawings: (H) $4,600

STEELE, Daniel
American 19th cent.
paintings: (H) $1,100

STEELE, Edwin
British 19th cent.
paintings: (L) $357; (H) $8,800

STEELE, Georgia
American 19th/20th cent.
paintings: (H) $460

STEELE, J.
American 19th cent.
paintings: (H) $660

STEELE, Juliette
American 1909-1980
paintings: (L) $3,025; (H) $3,025

STEELE, Marian Williams
American b. 1916
paintings: (L) $99; (H) $715

STEELE, T.C.
paintings: (H) $17,050

STEELE, Theodore Clement
American 1847-1926
paintings: (L) $3,850; (H) $9,790

STEELE, Thomas Sedgwick
American 1845-1903
paintings: (L) $275; (H) $2,530

STEELE, Tim
drawings: (H) $825

STEELE, Zulma
American 1881-1979
paintings: (L) $50; (H) $550
drawings: (H) $523

STEELINK, Willem
Dutch 1826-1913
drawings: (H) $880

STEELINK, Willem, the younger
Dutch 1856-1928
paintings: (L) $2,300; (H) $6,325

STEELINK, William
paintings: (H) $2,530

STEELL, David George
British 1856-1930
paintings: (L) $1,035; (H) $6,050

STEELL, Gourlay
Scottish 1819-1894
paintings: (L) $3,960; (H) $9,200

STEEN, Jan
Dutch 1625-1679
paintings: (L) $181,500; (H) $200,500

STEEN, Jan
Dutch 1626-1679
paintings: (H) $181,500

STEENBERGEN, Albertus
Dutch b. 1814
paintings: (L) $4,600; (H) $17,250

STEENE, William
American 1888-1965
paintings: (L) $302; (H) $660

STEENKS, Gerard L.
American 1847-1926
paintings: (L) $978; (H) $16,100

STEENWYCK, Hendrik van, the younger
Flemish 1580-c. 1649
paintings: (L) $34,500; (H) $66,000

STEER, Philip Wilson
English 1860-1942
paintings: (L) $4,400; (H) $27,500

STEFAN, Ross
American b. 1934
paintings: (L) $385; (H) $2,588
drawings: (H) $385

STEFFANI, Luigi
Italian 1827-1898
paintings: (L) $3,300; (H) $13,800

STEFFELAAR, Nicolaas
Dutch 1852-1918
paintings: (H) $1,650

STEFFENS, L.
Continental School 19th/20th cent.
paintings: (H) $1,610

STEHLIN, Caroline
American 1879-1954
paintings: (L) $2,530; (H) $8,050

STEIDMAN, Eugene M.
American 20th cent.
paintings: (H) $522

STEIN, Daniel
paintings: (H) $460

STEIN, Georges
French 20th cent.
paintings: (L) $4,600; (H) $18,400
drawings: (L) $1,320; (H) $3,737

STEIN, K.
paintings: (L) $220; (H) $550

STEIN, L.
drawings: (H) $1,380

STEIN, Modest
drawings: (L) $715; (H) $880

STEINACH, Anton
Swiss 1819-1891
paintings: (H) $2,200

STEINBACH, Haim
Israeli/American b. 1944
sculpture: (L) $3,220; (H) $23,100

STEINBERG, Saul
Romanian/American b. 1914
paintings: (L) $8,050; (H) $36,800
drawings: (L) $1,100; (H) $222,500
sculpture: (L) $2,750; (H) $66,000

STEINER
20th cent.
paintings: (H) $570

STEINER
late 19th cent.
sculpture: (H) $4,675

STEINER
German early 20th cent.
paintings: (H) $1,980

STEINER, Clement Leopold
French 1853-1899
sculpture: (L) $4,140; (H) $10,450

STEINER, Emmanuel
Swiss 1778-1831
paintings: (H) $1,650

STEINER, Johann Nepomuk
1725-1793
paintings: (H) $4,400

STEINER, John
1796-187?
drawings: (H) $9,200

STEINER, Lilly
1884-1954
drawings: (H) $733

STEINER, Michael
b. 1945
sculpture: (H) $1,320

STEINER, Michael
Austrian c. 1684-1764
sculpture: (L) $2,200; (H) $4,400

STEINFURTH, Hermann
German 1823-1880
paintings: (H) $1,035

STEINHARDT, Therese
American 1896-1948
paintings: (H) $1,840

STEINKOPF, Johann Friedrich
German 1737-1825
paintings: (H) $2,588

STEINLEN, Christian Gottlieb
1779-1847
drawings: (H) $2,415

STEINLEN, Theophile Alexandre
Swiss/French 1859-1923
paintings: (L) $6,875; (H) $6,900
drawings: (L) $220; (H) $8,800
sculpture: (L) $660; (H) $4,600

STEINMETZ, Noris Fritz
German b. 1860
paintings: (H) $2,090

STEINMETZ-NORIS, Fritz
German b. 1860
paintings: (H) $4,400

STEINSBERG, Eugene
Continental 19th cent.
paintings: (H) $43,125

STEIR, Pat
American b. 1938
paintings: (L) $8,250; (H) $20,900
drawings: (H) $10,450

STELLA, Etienne Alexandre
French 19th cent.
sculpture: (H) $2,300

STELLA, Frank
American b. 1936
paintings: (L) $11,500; (H) $662,500
drawings: (L) $1,035; (H) $363,000
sculpture: (L) $16,100; (H) $385,000

STELLA, Joseph
American, b. Italy 1880-1946
paintings: (L) $1,150; (H) $38,500
drawings: (L) $209; (H) $18,400

STELLMACHER, Ed.
sculpture: (H) $550

STELLWAG, F.
Dutch ac. 1880
paintings: (H) $1,320

STELZER, F.
German 19th cent.
paintings: (L) $550; (H) $550

STELZNER, Heinrich
German 1833-1910
paintings: (L) $1,540; (H) $2,200

STEMATSKY, Avigdor
1908-1989
drawings: (H) $2,760

STEMKOWSKI, Gerald
American 20th cent.
paintings: (H) $660

STENBERG, Vladimir
drawings: (L) $2,875; (H) $3,738

STENEBERG, Alami
drawings: (H) $575

STEPHAN, Gary
American b. 1942
paintings: (L) $330; (H) $10,450

STEPHAN, M.J.
American
drawings: (H) $605

STEPHANE, Micius
Haitian b. 1912
paintings: (L) $110; (H) $2,420

STEPHANOFF, Francis Philip
British 1788-1860
paintings: (H) $1,840

STEPHENS, Alice Barber
American 1858-1932
paintings: (L) $1,760; (H) $6,600
drawings: (L) $660; (H) $1,430

STEPHENS, James
American b. 1961
paintings: (L) $715; (H) $1,210

STEPHENS, M.
Continental 20th cent.
paintings: (H) $495

STEPHENSON, J.G.
American 20th cent.
paintings: (H) $935

STEPHENSON, Peter
American 1823-c. 1860
sculpture: (H) $1,650

STEPHENSON, Quinton J.
b. 1920
drawings: (H) $815

STEPHENSON, Susanne
contemporary
sculpture: (H) $805

STEPHON, A.
paintings: (H) $660

STEPPE, Romain
Belgian 1859-1927
paintings: (H) $4,400

STERN, Anton Alois
Austrian 1827-1924
drawings: (H) $3,220

STERN, Bernard
French b. 1920
paintings: (L) $2,070; (H) $9,350

STERN, Ignaz, called Stella
German 1679-1748
paintings: (H) $14,375

STERN, Max
German 1872-1943
paintings: (H) $4,675

STERN (?), F.
paintings: (H) $1,540

STERNE, Hedda
Romanian/American b. 1916
drawings: (H) $467

STERNE, Maurice
American 1877-1957
paintings: (L) $220; (H) $7,475
drawings: (L) $121; (H) $1,100

STERNER, Albert
American 1863-1946
paintings: (L) $550; (H) $7,700
drawings: (L) $22; (H) $467

STERNER, Albert Edward
American 1863-1946
paintings: (H) $920
drawings: (L) $633; (H) $2,420

STERNER, Harold
American 20th cent.
paintings: (H) $690
drawings: (H) $805

STERONI
Italian 19th cent.
drawings: (H) $495

STERRE DE JONG, Jacobus
Dutch 1866-1920
paintings: (H) $1,495
drawings: (H) $1,380

STERRE DE JONG, Jacobus S.
Dutch 1863-1901
paintings: (H) $1,320

STERRER, Franz
Austrian 1818-1901
paintings: (H) $605

STERRER, Karl
Austrian 1844-1918
paintings: (H) $8,625

STETSON, Charles Walter
American 1858-1911
paintings: (L) $220; (H) $3,025
drawings: (L) $173; (H) $302

STETSON, J.B.
American 19th cent.
paintings: (H) $1,121

STETSON, William D.
American 19th cent.
drawings: (L) $300; (H) $1,980

STETTHEIMER, Florine
American 1871-1944
paintings: (L) $66,000; (H) $110,000

STEVANS, A.
paintings: (H) $1,495

STEVELS, Marie van Waning
Dutch 1874-1943
paintings: (H) $550

STEVENS
Dutch/Belgian 19th cent.
paintings: (H) $4,950

STEVENS, Agapit
Belgian 19th cent.
paintings: (L) $220; (H) $8,800

STEVENS, Alfred
Belgian 1823-1906
paintings: (L) $1,725; (H) $266,500
drawings: (L) $259; (H) $345

STEVENS, Brad
American 20th cent.
paintings: (H) $880

STEVENS, Craig Alan
sculpture: (L) $316; (H) $661

STEVENS, Dalton
American 1878-1939
paintings: (H) $2,200

STEVENS, Dorothy
paintings: (H) $5,500

STEVENS, Edith Briscoe
American 1896-1931
sculpture: (H) $990

STEVENS, G.
American 20th cent.
paintings: (H) $460

STEVENS, George
British 19th cent.
paintings: (H) $3,080

STEVENS, J** A**
American 19th/20th cent.
paintings: (H) $605

STEVENS, John
British 1793-1868
paintings: (L) $660; (H) $4,950

STEVENS, John Calvin
American 1855-1940
paintings: (L) $550; (H) $4,400

STEVENS, Lester
American b. 1888
paintings: (H) $1,035

STEVENS, Will Henry
American 1881-1949
paintings: (L) $1,210; (H) $2,750
drawings: (L) $264; (H) $1,760

STEVENS, William Dodge
American b. 1870
paintings: (L) $3,575; (H) $5,500

STEVENS, William Lester
American 1888-1969
paintings: (L) $137; (H) $9,900
drawings: (L) $220; (H) $1,870

STEVENSON, Amy L.
paintings: (H) $575

STEVENSON, Beulah
b. 1965
paintings: (H) $1,380

STEVENSON, Gordon
American b. 1892
paintings: (L) $275; (H) $495

STEVENSON, J.
British 19th cent.
paintings: (H) $3,300

STEVENSON, William Lewy Leroy
1905-1966
paintings: (L) $92; (H) $1,100

STEWARD, Joseph
American 1753-1822
paintings: (H) $57,500

STEWARD, Seth
1844-after 1927
paintings: (H) $2,860

STEWART, F.A.
British 19th cent.
drawings: (H) $1,150

STEWART, Frances De Forest
paintings: (H) $770

STEWART, James Lawson
British ac. 1883-1889
drawings: (L) $69; (H) $633

STEWART, John A.
British 19th cent.
drawings: (H) $3,163

STEWART, Julius Leblanc
American 1855-1919
paintings: (L) $5,500; (H) $847,000

STEWART, Mark
American b. 1951
drawings: (L) $2,420; (H) $3,410

STEWART, Mary R.
American 19th/20th cent.
paintings: (H) $715

STEWART, Robert W.
paintings: (H) $715

STEWART, Ron
paintings: (L) $220; (H) $4,200
drawings: (L) $154; (H) $2,200

STEWART, Sir David
drawings: (H) $920

STEZAKER, John
drawings: (H) $2,300

STICK, Frank
paintings: (H) $3,850

STICK, Frank
American 1884-1966
paintings: (H) $550
drawings: (H) $374

STICKS, George Blackie
British 1843-1938
paintings: (L) $660; (H) $770

STICKS, Harry
English ac. 1894-1911
paintings: (H) $1,300

STIEPEVICH, Vincent B.
Russian 1841-1910
paintings: (L) $1,210; (H) $20,700
drawings: (H) $6,325

STIFTER, F.
paintings: (H) $4,950

STIFTER, Ferdinand
Austrian 19th cent.
paintings: (H) $467

STIFTER, Moritz
Austrian 1857-1905
paintings: (L) $2,990; (H) $10,450

STIGLMAYER, Johann Babtist
German 1791-1844
paintings: (H) $1,760

STIHA, Vladan
b. 1910
paintings: (L) $2,070; (H) $2,875

STILLMAN, Effie
Anglo/American 19th/20th cent.
sculpture: (H) $880

STILLMAN, Marie Spartali
British b. 1844
drawings: (H) $2,090

STILLWELL, B.W.
American 19th cent.
paintings: (H) $575

STILWELL-WEBER, Sarah S.
1878-1939
paintings: (H) $4,290

STINE, Van der
Dutch 19th cent.
paintings: (H) $798

STIRLING, Dave
American 1889-1971
paintings: (L) $27; (H) $660

STITES, John Randolphe
American ac. 1870-1887
paintings: (H) $550

STITT, Hobart D.
American b. 1880
paintings: (L) $1,870; (H) $2,200

STIVERS, Don
American contemporary
paintings: (H) $3,520

STIVERS, Harley E.
b. 1891
drawings: (H) $467

STOBBE, Marie
American b. 1912
paintings: (L) $1,870; (H) $6,050

STOCK, C.
sculpture: (H) $605

STOCK, Francis R.
British ac. 1875-1884
paintings: (H) $770

STOCK, Ignatius van der
Dutch ac. c. 1660
paintings: (H) $13,200

STOCK, Joseph Whiting
American 1815-1855
paintings: (L) $1,650; (H) $85,000

STOCK, W***
British 19th cent.
paintings: (H) $1,840

STOCKBRIDGE, D.
American 19th cent.
paintings: (H) $715

STOCKFLETH, J.
paintings: (H) $2,185

STOCKLIN, Christian
Swiss 1741-1795
paintings: (H) $66,000

STOCKS, Arthur
British 1846-1889
paintings: (H) $1,380

STOCKS, Minna
German 1846-1928
paintings: (H) $2,530

STOCKWELL, John B.
drawings: (L) $440; (H) $990

STODDARD, Alice Kent, Pearson
American 1884-1976
paintings: (L) $143; (H) $10,450

STOENESCO, Eustatin Grigorie
French 1885-1956
paintings: (L) $412; (H) $1,725

STOFFE, Jan Jacobsz. van der
Dutch 1611-1682
paintings: (H) $19,800

STOILOFF, Constantin
Russian 1850-1924
paintings: (L) $460; (H) $5,500
drawings: (H) $935

STOITZNER, Constantin
Austrian 1863-1934
paintings: (L) $165; (H) $5,750

STOITZNER, Josef
Austrian 1884-1951
paintings: (H) $4,675

STOJANOW, C.
Russian 19th cent.
paintings: (L) $1,380; (H) $4,600

STOJANOW, C. Pjotr
Russian 19th cent.
paintings: (L) $2,420; (H) $7,475

STOJANOW, O.
Continental 19th/20th cent.
paintings: (H) $2,860

STOK, Jacobus van der
Dutch 1794-1864
paintings: (H) $1,870

STOKES, Adrian
English 1854-1935
paintings: (L) $550; (H) $3,190

STOKES, Frank Wilbert
American b. 1858
paintings: (L) $138; (H) $1,650
drawings: (H) $99

STOKES, Marianne, nee
PREINDLSBERGER
British 1855-1927
paintings: (H) $140,000

STOKES, Rhoda Brady
American 1902-1988
paintings: (L) $330; (H) $1,760

STOKES, Susan Murray
drawings: (L) $330; (H) $495

STOLKER, Jan
1724-1785
paintings: (L) $1,320; (H) $5,280

STOLL, Leopold von
German ac. 1828-1869
paintings: (H) $11,500

STOLL, Rolf
German/American b. 1892
paintings: (L) $220; (H) $1,980

STOLLZ (?), J.
paintings: (H) $495

STOLTENBERG, Hans J.
American 1880-1963
paintings: (L) $495; (H) $1,725

STOLTZ, David
b. 1943
sculpture: (L) $1,265; (H) $3,680

STOM, Antonio
ac. Early 18th cent.
paintings: (H) $27,600

STOMER, Matthias
Flemish c. 1600-after 1650
paintings: (L) $49,500; (H) $123,500

STOMER, Matthias, studio of
17th cent.
paintings: (H) $28,750

STONE, Don
American b. 1929
paintings: (L) $440; (H) $1,955

STONE, Horatio
American 1808-1875
sculpture: (H) $2,750

STONE, Jacob
British 19th cent.
paintings: (H) $1,265

STONE, Marcus C.
English 1840-1921
paintings: (L) $11,000; (H) $41,400

STONE, Marland
drawings: (H) $1,760

STONE, Molly
sculpture: (H) $880

STONE, Reynolds A.
English b. 1909
drawings: (H) $660

STONE, Robert
British 20th cent.
paintings: (L) $2,300; (H) $11,000

STONE, Sarah
English 18th/19th cent.
drawings: (L) $1,650; (H) $1,840

STONE, Seymour Millais
American b. 1877
paintings: (L) $345; (H) $4,600

STONE, W.
British 19th cent.
paintings: (L) $467; (H) $1,320

STONE, Walter King
American 1875-1949
paintings: (L) $220; (H) $495

STONEHAM, G.
paintings: (H) $3,100

STONEHOUSE, Fred
American contemporary
paintings: (H) $1,380

STONELAKE, Frank
British d. 1910
paintings: (H) $935

STONER
paintings: (H) $14,950

STOOP, Dirk
Dutch 1610/18-1681/86
paintings: (H) $3,450

STOOPENDAAL, Mosse
Swedish 1901-1948
paintings: (H) $16,500

STOOPS, Herbert Morton
American 1888-1948
paintings: (L) $275; (H) $4,950
drawings: (L) $303; (H) $1,210

STORCH, Frederick
Danish 1805-1883
paintings: (L) $990; (H) $1,210

STORCK, Abraham Jansz.
Dutch 1644-1708
paintings: (L) $20,700; (H) $310,500

STORCK, Adolf Eduard
German b. 1854
paintings: (L) $770; (H) $1,380

STORCK, Jacobus
Dutch ac. 1610-1686
paintings: (L) $9,200; (H) $24,200

STORER, Charles
American 1817-1907
paintings: (L) $330; (H) $1,375
drawings: (L) $248; (H) $330

STORER, Inez
contemporary
drawings: (H) $1,100

STOREY, H.L.
American 19th/20th cent.
paintings: (H) $7,820

STORIE, Jose
paintings: (H) $6,050

STORKE,
German 19th/20th cent.
paintings: (H) $2,310

STORM, Juan
Uruguayan b. 1927
paintings: (L) $4,887; (H) $10,925

STORMANZ, C.
Continental 19th cent.
paintings: (H) $605

STORRS, Immi C.
b. 1945
sculpture: (H) $14,950

STORRS, John
American 1885-1956
sculpture: (H) $33,350

STORRS, John Henry Bradley
American 1885-1956
paintings: (H) $7,700
drawings: (H) $4,950

STORTENBECKER, Peter
Dutch 1828-1898
paintings: (H) $935

STORY, George Henry
American 1835-1923
paintings: (L) $1,320; (H) $22,000

STORY, Julian Russel
American 1850-1919
paintings: (L) $330; (H) $962

STORY, William Wetmore
American 1819-1895
sculpture: (H) $51,750

STOTHARD, Thomas
British 1755-1834
paintings: (L) $230; (H) $28,750
drawings: (H) $517

STOTT, Edward
British 1859-1918
paintings: (L) $575; (H) $5,750

STOUT, Myron
American 1908-1987
paintings: (H) $74,800
drawings: (L) $17,250; (H) $27,600

STOUT, William
drawings: (H) $3,575

STOVER, Allan James
American b. 1887
paintings: (H) $2,860

STOWITTS, Hubert
paintings: (L) $660; (H) $660

STRACHAN, Arthur Claude
English b. 1865, ac. 1885-1929
drawings: (L) $1,650; (H) $4,070

STRACK, E.W.
American 19th/20th cent.
paintings: (H) $467

STRACKE, Louis
paintings: (H) $6,050

STRAET, Jan van der, called Stradanus
Flemish 1523-1605
paintings: (H) $8,625
drawings: (L) $16,500; (H) $48,400

STRAETEN, Georges van der
Belgian b. 1865
sculpture: (L) $303; (H) $3,300

STRAETEN, J. van der
French 19th cent.
sculpture: (H) $747

STRAETEN, Vander
sculpture: (H) $1,100

STRAETER, S. von der
sculpture: (H) $550

STRAGLIATI, Carlo
Italian 1868-1925
paintings: (H) $8,800

STRAHALM, Franz
American/Austrian 1879-1935
paintings: (H) $468

STRAHOLM, Franz S.
Austrian/American 1879-1935
paintings: (L) $230; (H) $605

STRAIN, Daniel J.
American d. 1925
paintings: (L) $605; (H) $2,475

STRAIN, John Paul
American b. 1955
paintings: (H) $2,640
drawings: (L) $3,740; (H) $6,050

STRALSER, A.
sculpture: (H) $4,000

STRANG, Ray
American 1893-1954/57
paintings: (L) $1,650; (H) $6,050

STRANOVER, Tobias
Czechoslovakian 1684-after 1724
paintings: (L) $11,000; (H) $17,600

STRANOVER, Tobias, studio of
17th/18th cent.
paintings: (H) $44,000

STRASS, van
Dutch/Belgian 19th cent.
paintings: (H) $1,045

STRASSER, Arthur
Austrian 1854-1927
sculpture: (L) $3,025; (H) $8,050

STRASSER, Jacob
German 19th cent.
paintings: (H) $2,070

STRATEN, Georges van der
French b. 1856
sculpture: (H) $1,375

STRAUS, Meyer
American 1831-1905
paintings: (L) $805; (H) $6,600
drawings: (H) $99

STRAUTIN, Wally
American b. 1898
paintings: (L) $173; (H) $460

STRAWN, Mel
American 1885-1952
paintings: (H) $550

STRAYER, Paul
American 1885-1981
paintings: (L) $99; (H) $4,675
drawings: (H) $3,300

STREAN, Maria Judson
American 20th cent.
drawings: (H) $1,725

STREATOR, Harold
American 1861-1926
paintings: (H) $2,530

STREBELLE, Jean Marie
Belgian 20th cent.
drawings: (H) $495

STRECKENBACH, Max Thomas
German 1865-1936
paintings: (L) $192; (H) $3,575

STREECK, Juriaan van
Dutch c. 1632-1687
paintings: (H) $330,000

STREET, Frank
American 1893-1944
paintings: (L) $275; (H) $2,035
drawings: (H) $302

STREET, Robert
American 1796-1865, ac. 1840
paintings: (L) $115; (H) $16,100

STREHL, Johann
Austrian d. 1862
paintings: (H) $8,625

STREICEK, Werner
sculpture: (H) $600

STREIGHT, Howard A.
1836-1912
paintings: (H) $715

STREITT, Franciszek
Polish 1839-1890
paintings: (L) $4,950; (H) $6,613

STRELERS, O
paintings: (H) $715

STRETTON, Philip Eustace
British ac. 1884-1915
paintings: (L) $2,750; (H) $12,650

STREVENS, John
b. 1902
paintings: (L) $247; (H) $1,210

STREVENS, John
British b. 1902
paintings: (H) $605

STRIEWSKI, W.
paintings: (H) $4,025

STRIJ, Abraham van
German b. 1753
paintings: (L) $1,150; (H) $1,870

STRINDBERG, August
Swedish 1849-1912
paintings: (H) $1,072,500

STRINGER, Francis
British ac. 1760-1772
paintings: (L) $28,600; (H) $39,100

STRISIK, Paul
American b. 1918
paintings: (L) $575; (H) $3,105
drawings: (H) $805

STRNAD, Oskar
Austrian 1879-1935
sculpture: (H) $10,350

STROBL, Zsofia
Hungarian b. 1866
paintings: (H) $2,300

STROEBEL, Johann Anthonie Balthasar
Dutch 1821-1905
paintings: (L) $6,325; (H) $8,800

STROMBOTNE, James
contemporary
paintings: (H) $3,575

STRONG, Elizabeth
American 1855-1941
paintings: (L) $330; (H) $2,750

STRONG, Ray
American b. 1905
paintings: (L) $550; (H) $7,475

STROOBANT, Francois
Belgian 1819-1916
paintings: (H) $3,738

STROZZI, Bernardo
Italian 1581-1644
paintings: (H) $376,500
drawings: (L) $8,050; (H) $39,600

STROZZI, Bernardo, Il CAPPUCINO
1581-1641/44
paintings: (H) $8,625

STRUCK, Herman G.
American 1876-1954
paintings: (L) $1,725; (H) $1,760

STRUDWICK, John Melhuish
British 1849-1935
paintings: (H) $134,500

STRUM, Pierre Henri
French 1785-1869
paintings: (H) $4,510

STRUTH, Thomas
American b. 1954
drawings: (L) $1,150; (H) $4,180

STRUTT, Alfred William
English 1856-1924
paintings: (L) $357; (H) $10,063
drawings: (L) $209; (H) $1,150

STRUTT, W.
paintings: (H) $8,250

STRUTZEL, Leopold Otto
German 1855-1930
paintings: (L) $605; (H) $12,650

STRY, Abraham van, the elder
Dutch 1753-1826
paintings: (H) $12,650
drawings: (H) $4,180

STRY, Jacob van
1756-1815
paintings: (L) $2,860; (H) $5,225
drawings: (H) $1,980

STRYJENSKA, Sophie
Polish 1894-1976
paintings: (L) $2,090; (H) $2,475

STUART
English 19th cent.
paintings: (H) $578

STUART, Alexander Charles
drawings: (H) $3,410

STUART, Charles
British ac. 1880-1904
paintings: (L) $1,045; (H) $6,050

STUART, Douglas Edward Algernon
paintings: (H) $8,250

STUART, Gilbert
American 1755-1828
paintings: (L) $3,630; (H) $310,500

STUART, James Everett
American 1852-1941
paintings: (L) $110; (H) $1,760

STUART, James Reeve
American 1834-1915
paintings: (H) $8,250

STUART, Raymond J.
paintings: (L) $605; (H) $4,675

STUART, T.H.
American 19th cent.
paintings: (H) $770

STUART, William
British 19th cent.
paintings: (H) $42,550

STUBBS, George
British 1724-1806
paintings: (L) $23,000; (H) $990,000

STUBBS, Ralph
British 19th cent.
paintings: (H) $2,090

STUBBS, W.B.
paintings: (H) $3,520

STUBBS, W.F.
paintings: (H) $1,870

STUBBS, W.P.
American 1842-1909
paintings: (L) $460; (H) $5,060

STUBBS, W.T.
paintings: (H) $2,310

STUBBS, William Pierce
American 1842-1909
paintings: (L) $1,045; (H) $20,700

STUBER, Dedrick B.
American 1878-1954
paintings: (L) $715; (H) $10,450

STUCK, Franz von
German 1863-1928
paintings: (L) $9,200; (H) $242,000
drawings: (H) $2,760
sculpture: (L) $7,700; (H) $20,900

STUEMPFIG, Walter
American 1914-1970
paintings: (L) $575; (H) $5,463

STUHLMULLER, Karl
German 1858-1930
paintings: (L) $9,625; (H) $37,400
drawings: (H) $14,950

STULL, Henry
American 1851-1913
paintings: (L) $1,540; (H) $28,750
drawings: (L) $193; (H) $1,045

STULL, John DeForest
American 1910-1972
paintings: (L) $330; (H) $2,970

STUMP, Pamela
American b. 1928
sculpture: (H) $495

STURGESS, John
British ac. 1875-1884
paintings: (H) $1,980

STURGIS, Frank E.
American 20th cent.
paintings: (H) $605

STURGIS, M.R.
paintings: (H) $660

STURM, Gustav
Austrian 19th cent.
drawings: (H) $715

STURSA, Jan
sculpture: (H) $4,675

STURTEVANT, Elaine
American b. 1926
paintings: (L) $4,400; (H) $18,700
sculpture: (H) $3,450

STUVEN, Ernst
German 1657/60-1712
paintings: (L) $33,000; (H) $110,000

STYKA, Adam
French 1890-1959
paintings: (L) $1,430; (H) $10,350

STYKA, Jan
Polish/French 1858-1925
paintings: (L) $1,100; (H) $1,540

STYKA, Tade
French 1889-1954
paintings: (L) $1,430; (H) $3,680
drawings: (H) $1,495

SU RENSHAN, Su JEN-SHAN
Chinese 1814-1849?
drawings: (H) $920

SUBRAMANYAN, K.G.
paintings: (H) $1,610

SUCRY, Armand
1879-1943
paintings: (H) $1,870

SUDKOVSKI, Rufin Gavrilovich
Russian 1850-1885
paintings: (H) $16,100

SUDRE, Raymond
sculpture: (H) $1,320

SUE, Louis
French 1875-1968
paintings: (H) $747

SUGAI, Kumi
Japanese b. 1919
paintings: (L) $4,600; (H) $374,000
drawings: (H) $7,700

SUGAR, Zsuzsanna
Hungarian b. 1939
paintings: (L) $288; (H) $518

SUGHI, Alberto
Italian b. 1928
paintings: (H) $1,610

SUHRLANDT, Carl
German 1828-1919
paintings: (H) $7,700

SUKER, Arthur
English b. 1857, ac. 1886
drawings: (L) $165; (H) $1,650

SUKER, W.
British 19th cent.
paintings: (H) $14,950

SULHAUS, Leghe
paintings: (H) $4,400

SULLIVAN, Charles
1794-1867
paintings: (H) $6,037

SULLIVAN, Edmund
paintings: (H) $605

SULLIVAN, Tim
American
sculpture: (H) $750

SULLIVAN, William Holmes
British d. 1908
paintings: (H) $4,312

SULLIVANT, Thomas S.
American b. 1854-after 1926
drawings: (L) $660; (H) $2,420

SULLY, Alfred
English 1820-1879
paintings: (H) $990

SULLY, General Alfred
American 1820-1879
drawings: (H) $605

SULLY, George Washington
American 19th cent.
drawings: (L) $66; (H) $578

SULLY, Jane Cooper
American 1807-1877
paintings: (H) $715

SULLY, Robert Matthew
American 1803-1855
drawings: (L) $468; (H) $4,290

SULLY, Thomas
American 1783-1872
paintings: (L) $825; (H) $121,000
drawings: (L) $632; (H) $17,600

SULLY, Thomas Wilcocks
American 1811-1847
paintings: (H) $17,250

SULTAN, Altoon
b. 1948
paintings: (H) $2,200

SULTAN, Donald
American b. 1951
paintings: (L) $2,300; (H) $85,000
drawings: (L) $690; (H) $90,500
sculpture: (L) $978; (H) $29,900

SULTZER, Fletcher
paintings: (H) $605

SULYON PAPP, J.
20th cent.
paintings: (H) $605

SUMERY, A.
French 19th/20th cent.
paintings: (H) $2,300

SUMMER, A.
Austrian 19th/20th cent.
paintings: (H) $1,650

SUMMERFIELD, Frazier
English 20th cent.
paintings: (H) $550

SUMMERS, Alick D.
British 1864-1938
paintings: (L) $719; (H) $1,210

SUMMERS, Charles
British 1825-1878
paintings: (H) $33,350

SUMMERS, Ivan F.
American 20th cent.
paintings: (L) $303; (H) $1,650

SUMMERS, P**H**
American 19th cent.
paintings: (H) $1,870

SUMMERS, Robert
American b. 1940
paintings: (L) $2,640; (H) $8,250
sculpture: (L) $1,650; (H) $11,825

SUN, R. van
paintings: (H) $467

SUNDBLOM, Haddon H.
American 1899-1976
paintings: (L) $825; (H) $27,500
drawings: (L) $1,210; (H) $2,860

SUNDERLAND, Nita
American b. 1927
sculpture: (H) $550

SUNG, Lai
1850-1855
paintings: (H) $20,700

SUNQUA
drawings: (H) $880

SUNQUA
Chinese School ac. 1830-1870
paintings: (H) $24,200

SUNYER, Joaquin
Spanish 1875-1956
paintings: (H) $7,475
drawings: (H) $5,500

SUPPANTSCHITSCH, Max
Austrian 1865-1954?
paintings: (H) $1,725

SURAND, Gustave
French b. 1860
paintings: (L) $4,370; (H) $36,800
drawings: (H) $1,840

SURBER, Paul
drawings: (L) $220; (H) $715

SURDI, Luigi
Italian 1897-1959
paintings: (H) $2,200

SUREAU
French 19th/20th cent.
paintings: (H) $495

SURIKOV, Vasilii Ivanovich
Russian 1848-1916
paintings: (H) $1,725

SURLS, James
American b. 1943
sculpture: (H) $6,440

SURTEES, John
English 1817-1915
paintings: (H) $825

SURVAGE, Leopold
French 1879-1968
paintings: (L) $3,850; (H) $28,600
drawings: (L) $990; (H) $4,125

SUSEMIHL, Johann Theodor
German b. 1772
paintings: (H) $8,050

SUSENIER, Abraham
Dutch ac. 1640-1666
paintings: (H) $110,000

SUSINI, workshop of
sculpture: (H) $43,700

SUSS, Johan, or SIESS
Austrian 19th cent.
paintings: (H) $1,300

SUSS, Josef
Austrian 19th cent.
paintings: (H) $920

SUSTERMANS, Justus, studio of
paintings: (L) $3,450; (H) $43,700

SUSTERMANS, Justus, workshop of
17th cent.
paintings: (H) $25,300

SUSTRIS, Friedrich
Flemish c. 1540-1599
paintings: (H) $66,000
drawings: (H) $13,225

SUSTRIS, Lambert
German 1515/20-1658
paintings: (H) $66,000

SUTCLIFFE, Lester
British 19th cent.
paintings: (L) $700; (H) $825

SUTHERLAND, Graham
English 1903-1980
drawings: (L) $2,070; (H) $46,200

SUTHERLAND, Ross
sculpture: (H) $550

SUTTON, Harry, Jr.
American b. 1897
paintings: (L) $55; (H) $660
drawings: (L) $88; (H) $247

SUTTON, Pat Lipsky
20th cent.
paintings: (H) $550

SUYCKER, Reyer Claesz.
Dutch 1590-1653
paintings: (H) $23,000

SUZOR-COTE, Marc Aurele de Foy
Canadian 1869-1937
paintings: (L) $1,540; (H) $27,600
drawings: (L) $6,050; (H) $38,500
sculpture: (L) $1,980; (H) $2,750

SUZUHIKO, Kawasaki
b. 1925
drawings: (H) $1,725

SVABINSKY, Max
Czechoslovakian 1873-1962
paintings: (H) $1,100

SVENDSEN, Svend
Norwegian/American 1864-1930
paintings: (L) $132; (H) $2,475
drawings: (L) $193; (H) $660

SVENDSON, Charles C.
American 1871-1959
paintings: (H) $935

SVERDONCK, Franz van
Belgian 1809-1889
paintings: (H) $4,830

SVERTSCHKOFF, Nicolas
Gregorovitch
Russian 1817-1889
paintings: (H) $8,050

SVERTSCHKOFF, Nicolas
Gregorovitch
Russian 1817-1898
paintings: (H) $2,530
drawings: (L) $412; (H) $495

SWAGERS, Frans
1756-1836
paintings: (H) $2,420

SWAIN, William
American 1803-1847
paintings: (H) $935

SWAN, Curt
drawings: (H) $920

SWAN, Cuthbert Edmund
Irish 1870/73-1931
paintings: (H) $10,350
drawings: (L) $403; (H) $4,370

SWAN, Emma L.
American 1853-1927
paintings: (H) $1,955

SWANE, Sigurd
Danish b. 1879
paintings: (H) $6,050

SWANENBURG, Isaac Claesz. van
1537-1614
paintings: (H) $9,075

SWANEVELT, Herman
c. 1600-1655
paintings: (H) $17,250
drawings: (H) $4,950

SWANK, Grace G.
paintings: (L) $495; (H) $522

SWANSON, Gary
American b. 1941
paintings: (H) $7,920

SWANSON, Mark
American b. 1941
paintings: (L) $550; (H) $7,425

SWANSON, Ray
American b. 1937
paintings: (L) $825; (H) $14,300

SWANWICK, Harold
British 1866-1929
drawings: (H) $5,750

SWAR, Fred
American
paintings: (H) $550

SWARZ, Sahl
contemporary
sculpture: (H) $935

SWEBACH, Jacques Francois Jose,
called Swebach-Desfontaines
1769-1823
paintings: (H) $5,060
drawings: (H) $6,050

SWEBACH-DEFONTAINES, Jacques
Francois Joseeph
1769-1823
paintings: (H) $7,150

SWEERTS, Michael
Dutch 1624-1664
paintings: (L) $2,035; (H) $308,000

SWEET, Walter H.
British 19th cent.
drawings: (H) $495

SWEETMAN, Arch W.
drawings: (L) $633; (H) $1,208

SWENGEL, Faye
paintings: (H) $2,500

SWERINGEN, Ron van
American b. 1936
paintings: (L) $228; (H) $577

SWIESZEWSKI, Alexander
Polish 1839-1895
paintings: (H) $3,850

SWIFT, Clement
American 1846-1918
paintings: (L) $495; (H) $880

SWIGGETT, Jean
American b. 1910
drawings: (H) $1,320

SWINNERTON, James
American 1875-1974
paintings: (L) $385; (H) $18,400

SWINSTEAD, George Hillyard
British 1860-1926
paintings: (H) $4,950

SWITTE?, Arnold E.
American 20th cent.
paintings: (H) $2,185

SWOBODA, Edward
Austrian 1814-1902
paintings: (H) $8,050

SWOBODA, Josefine
drawings: (H) $1,100

SWOBODA, Rudolph, Jr.
Austrian 1859-1914
paintings: (L) $3,450; (H) $19,550

SWOPE, H. Vance
1879-1926
paintings: (L) $138; (H) $715

SWOPE, Kate Francis
American b. 1872
paintings: (H) $3,300

SWOPE, Vance H.
American 1879-1926
paintings: (H) $1,430

SWORD, James Brade
American 1839-1915
paintings: (L) $440; (H) $18,975
drawings: (L) $80; (H) $385

SWORDS, Cramer
American 20th cent.
paintings: (H) $2,310

SYBORCK, R.
French 19th/20th cent.
paintings: (H) $1,485

SYCHKOV, Th.
Russian 19th/20th cent.
paintings: (H) $6,600

SYER, John
British 1815-1885
paintings: (L) $138; (H) $2,588
drawings: (H) $467

SYKES, Charles
American 1875-1950
sculpture: (L) $1,320; (H) $4,070

SYKES, S.D. Gilchrist
19th/20th cent.
paintings: (L) $55; (H) $880
drawings: (H) $50

SYKORA, G.
Hungarian 20th cent.
paintings: (H) $2,860

SYLLUFF, G.D.
paintings: (H) $1,375

SYLVESTER, Frederick Oakes
American 1869-1915
paintings: (L) $350; (H) $11,000

SYLVESTER, Joseph Noel
French 1847-1926
paintings: (H) $1,100

SYLVESTRE, Paul
French b. 1884
sculpture: (H) $2,875

SYLVIA, Louis
20th cent.
paintings: (L) $275; (H) $880

SYME, John
Scottish 1795-1861
paintings: (H) $2,530

SYMONS, George Gardner
American 1863-1930
paintings: (L) $247; (H) $44,000
drawings: (H) $1,760

SYMONS, William Christian
British 1845-1911
paintings: (H) $10,925

SYNAVE, Tancrede
French b. 1860
paintings: (L) $550; (H) $17,250

SYSMANN, W.S.
American 20th cent.
, *paintings:* (H) $1,150

SYVERSON, Judy
American
paintings: (L) $1,700; (H) $3,000

SZABO, Endre
ac. 1960s
paintings: (H) $550

SZAFRAN, Sam
French b. 1930
paintings: (H) $633
drawings: (H) $550

SZANKOWSKI, Boleslaw von
Polish b. 1873
paintings: (H) $2,860

SZANTHO, Maria
Hungarian 1898-1984
paintings: (L) $192; (H) $770

SZANTO, Louis
Hungarian b. 1889
paintings: (L) $522; (H) $1,650

SZASZ, Paul
paintings: (H) $3,575

SZCZEBLEWSKI, V.
Polish ac. 1875-1900
sculpture: (L) $715; (H) $1,980

SZEKELY, Bertalan
Hungarian 1835-1910
paintings: (H) $935
drawings: (H) $55

SZEMEREI, Bela M.
Hungarian 20th cent.
paintings: (H) $522

SZOBEL, Geza
paintings: (H) $1,760

SZTRIHA, S.
European 19th/20th cent.
paintings: (H) $605

SZULE, Peter
Hungarian 1886-1944
paintings: (L) $192; (H) $3,738

SZYK, Arthur
Polish/American 1894-1951
drawings: (L) $460; (H) $5,463

SZYMANOWSKI, Wenceslas
Polish 1859-1930
sculpture: (H) $14,300

SZYSZLO, Fernando de
Peruvian b. 1925
paintings: (L) $2,875; (H) $28,600
drawings: (L) $2,200; (H) $18,400

TAAFFE, Philip
b. 1955
paintings: (L) $1,540; (H) $93,500
drawings: (L) $1,320; (H) $41,800

TABARY, E****
Continental 19th cent.
paintings: (H) $2,875

TABER, Isaac Walton
1830-1916
drawings: (H) $660

TABER, Lincoln
English 20th cent.
paintings: (H) $1,045

TABER, Sarah A.
American 1844-1928
paintings: (H) $1,320

TABUENA, Romeo
Mexico b. 1921
paintings: (H) $7,475

TACCA, Pietro, workshop of
sculpture: (H) $27,500

TACK, Augustus Vincent
American 1870-1949
paintings: (L) $1,870; (H) $37,375
drawings: (L) $330; (H) $7,150

TACKETT, William
American ac. 1950-1970
paintings: (H) $1,100

TACLA, Jorge
b. 1958
paintings: (L) $20,700; (H) $20,700

TADAMA, Fokko
American 1871-1937
paintings: (H) $468

TADOLINI, Scipione
Italian late 19th cent.
sculpture: (H) $39,100

TAFURI, Raffaele
Italian 1857-1929
paintings: (L) $28,750; (H) $31,900

TAG, Willy
German b. 1886
paintings: (H) $3,520

Animal Portraits

Portraits of horses, bulls, cows, and dogs—especially recorded champions— were very popular during the 19th century. Dog shows and the status of owning a pure bred dog, a new concept, had originated in England, and Queen Victoria, who bred chows and Pekingese, had popularized the commissioning and collecting of dog portraits.

Arthur Fitzwilliam Tait (1819-1905), an Englishman who emigrated to New York in 1850, was the leading sporting painter of 19th-century America. His specialty was animals and sporting scenes, and many of his most popular paintings were made into lithographs by Currier and Ives. The top price for a Tait painting is the $605,000 paid at Christie's in 1992 for a large oil of *Trappers Following the Trail.* Most of Tait's animal paintings of dogs, chickens, ducks, rabbits, grouse, sheep, buffalo, stags, and doe sell in the range of $1,100 to $21,000. Tait's mountain guide in the Adirondacks, for over two decades, was former military scout Calvin Parker. When *Man's Best Friend* was consigned to Barridoff Auction Galleries in Portland, Maine, the inscription on the back of the frame read "?Parker/May 1869 (98)." The lot was accompanied by a 19th-century engraving of the painting. Captain Parker's hunter, one of a pair framed in period Victorian frames, realized $4,840 in August 1994. (Arthur Fitzwilliam Tait, *Man's Best Friend II, Portrait of a Hunter*, oil on canvas, 19 x 25 inches, Barridoff, August 3, 1994, $4,840)

TAHOMA, Quincy, Tahoma, Water Edge
Native American 1921-1956
paintings: (H) $2,530
drawings: (L) $920; (H) $2,875

TAILROY, L.
paintings: (H) $920

TAIT, A.F. and J.M. HART
paintings: (H) $10,120

TAIT, Arthur Fitzwilliam
American 1819-1905
paintings: (L) $1,955; (H) $605,000

TAIT, John Robinson
1834-1909
paintings: (L) $935; (H) $4,370

TAKACH, Bein de
19th/20th cent.
paintings: (H) $495

TAKACS
Hungarian b. 1935
paintings: (L) $330; (H) $550

TAKAEZU, Toshiko
b. Hawaii 1922
sculpture: (L) $715; (H) $1,725

TAKAMATSU, J.
paintings: (H) $880

TAKASHIMA, Y.
Japanese/American 20th cent.
paintings: (H) $1,650

TAKIS
Greek/American b. 1925
drawings: (H) $330
sculpture: (L) $8,050; (H) $28,750

TAKIS, Nicholas
American 1903-1965
paintings: (L) $121; (H) $577

TAKIS, Vassilakis
b. 1925
sculpture: (H) $747

TAL-COAT, Pierre Jacob
French b. 1905
paintings: (H) $24,150

TALBOT, Grace Helen
American b. 1901
sculpture: (L) $1,210; (H) $5,225

TALBOT, Jesse
American 1806-1879
paintings: (H) $11,500

TALBOYS, Agnes A.
English 19th cent.
paintings: (H) $1,430

TALCONNET
sculpture: (H) $605

TALCOTT, Allen Butler
American 1867-1908
paintings: (L) $920; (H) $4,125

TALIAFERRO, Al
American 1905-1969
drawings: (L) $2,300; (H) $5,175

TALLANT, Richard H.
American 1853-1934
paintings: (L) $193; (H) $1,870

TALLENBERG, Jose
sculpture: (H) $2,860

TALON
paintings: (H) $3,080

TALWINSKI, Igor
Polish b. 1907
paintings: (L) $385; (H) $880

TAM, Reuben
American b. 1916
paintings: (H) $3,220
drawings: (H) $358

TAMARIZ, Eduardo
b. Mexico 1945
paintings: (L) $121; (H) $805

TAMAYO, Rufino
Mexican 1899-1991
paintings: (L) $24,150; (H) $2,587,500
drawings: (L) $3,680; (H) $68,500
sculpture: (L) $90,500; (H) $530,500

TAMBURINI, Arnaldo
Italian b. 1843
paintings: (L) $605; (H) $7,187
drawings: (L) $192; (H) $1,610

TAMM, Franz Werner von
German 1658-1724
paintings: (L) $31,625; (H) $93,500

TAMOTZU, Chuzo
1891-1975
paintings: (H) $220
drawings: (H) $550

TAMPLOUGH, A.
English 1877-1930
drawings: (H) $1,650

TAMSON, George M.
German 1873-1939
paintings: (H) $523

TANABE, Takao
Canadian b. 1926
paintings: (L) $550; (H) $2,475

TANAKA, Akira
Japanese b. 1918
paintings: (L) $1,955; (H) $15,525

TANAKA, Chiyoko
contemporary
sculpture: (H) $1,725

TANAKA, Shu
paintings: (H) $1,320

TANAKA, Yasushi
1886-1941
paintings: (H) $460

TANGUY, Yves
French/American 1900-1955
paintings: (L) $96,000; (H) $387,500
drawings: (L) $2,750; (H) $99,000

TANNAHILL, Mary H.
20th cent.
paintings: (H) $1,320

TANNARD, J*C*
English 19th cent.
paintings: (H) $963

TANNER, H.D.
American 20th cent.
paintings: (H) $770

TANNER, Henry Ossawa
American 1859-1937
paintings: (L) $5,500; (H) $18,500
drawings: (H) $9,200

TANNER, Jean
American
drawings: (L) $400; (H) $500

TANNER, O.
paintings: (H) $632

TANNERT, Louis
German 19th cent.
paintings: (H) $13,200

TANNERT, Volker
contemporary
paintings: (H) $4,950

TANNEUR, Philip
French 1795-1878
paintings: (H) $8,625

TANNING, Dorothea
American b. 1912
paintings: (L) $1,380; (H) $6,900
drawings: (L) $916; (H) $4,000

TANNOR, Harold Drake
American 20th cent.
paintings: (H) $605

TANOUX, Adrien Henri
French 1865-1923
paintings: (L) $1,150; (H) $23,000
drawings: (H) $6,325

TANSEY, Mark
American b. 1949
paintings: (L) $15,400; (H) $242,000
drawings: (H) $29,700

TANWAR, Viren
Indian b. 1952
paintings: (L) $2,875; (H) $4,600

TANZI, Leon
French 1846-1913
paintings: (H) $3,450

TANZIO, Antonio d'Enrico
Italian 1575-1635
drawings: (H) $4,400

TAPIES, Antoni
Spanish b. 1923
paintings: (L) $10,925; (H) $176,000
drawings: (L) $5,463; (H) $66,000

TAPIRO Y BARO, Jose
Spanish 1830-1913
paintings: (L) $1,092; (H) $1,320
drawings: (L) $3,080; (H) $34,500

TAPPERT, Georg
German 1880-1957
paintings: (L) $140,000; (H) $222,500

TAQUE, Robert Bruce
American b. 1912
drawings: (H) $605

TARALLO, Jorge
20th cent.
paintings: (H) $660

TARAVAL, Hugues
French 1728/29-1785
paintings: (L) $8,250; (H) $25,300

TARBELL, Edmund C.
American 1862-1938
paintings: (L) $12,100; (H) $442,500
drawings: (L) $825; (H) $3,080

TARENGHI, Enrico
Italian b. 1848
paintings: (H) $4,887
drawings: (L) $385; (H) $6,900

TARINI, G***
Italian 19th cent.
paintings: (H) $2,875

TARKAY, Itzchak
Yugoslavia/Israeli b. 1935
paintings: (L) $6,325; (H) $7,475

TARKHANOV, Mikhail
drawings: (H) $2,990

TARLOWSKY, Vladimir
Polish 1886-1942
sculpture: (H) $9,900

TARNOWSKI, Glen P.
American
paintings: (H) $900

TARTAS, Augustus A.
drawings: (H) $825

TASKER, N.
American 19th cent.
paintings: (H) $805

TASSEL, Jean
French 1608-1667
paintings: (H) $4,400

TASSET, Tony
b. 1960
paintings: (H) $495
drawings: (H) $825

TASSO Y NADAL
Spanish 19th cent.
sculpture: (H) $2,300

TATE, Gayle Blair
American b. 1944
paintings: (L) $345; (H) $8,625

TATE, W.K.
English early 19th cent.
sculpture: (H) $880

TATIN, Robert
French b. 1902
paintings: (H) $920

TATOSSIAN, Armand
paintings: (L) $2,090; (H) $2,090

TAUBER-ARP, Sophie
Swiss 1889-1943
drawings: (H) $39,600

TAUBERT, Bertoldo
French b. 1915
paintings: (L) $196; (H) $1,100

TAUBES, Frederick
American 1900-1981
paintings: (L) $55; (H) $5,225
drawings: (H) $207

TAUNAY, Adrien A.
French 1803-1828
drawings: (L) $77; (H) $715

TAUNAY, Nicolas Antoine
French 1755-1830
paintings: (H) $33,000
drawings: (L) $201; (H) $440

TAURELLE, Bernard
French 20th cent.
paintings: (L) $403; (H) $1,265

TAUSZKY, David Anthony
American 1878-1972
paintings: (L) $605; (H) $1,650
sculpture: (H) $2,875

TAUZIN, Louis
French ac. 1867-1914
paintings: (L) $2,588; (H) $38,500

TAVELLA, Carlo Antonio
1668-1738
drawings: (H) $3,520

TAVERA, F.P. de
sculpture: (H) $550

TAVERNIER, Jules
French/American 1844-1889/99
paintings: (L) $4,950; (H) $40,250
drawings: (L) $302; (H) $2,300

TAVERNIER, Paul
French b. 1852
paintings: (L) $1,150; (H) $57,500

TAWNEY, Leonore
contemporary
sculpture: (H) $2,588

TAYLER, Albert Chevallier
British 1862-1925
paintings: (H) $1,760

TAYLER, Edward
English 1828-1906
drawings: (H) $660

TAYLOR, Annie
19th cent.
paintings: (H) $1,430

TAYLOR, Arthur
drawings: (H) $880

TAYLOR, Charles
English 19th cent.
paintings: (H) $330
drawings: (H) $852

TAYLOR, Charles Jay
American 1855-1929
paintings: (L) $237; (H) $1,760
drawings: (L) $110; (H) $302

TAYLOR, D.
paintings: (L) $523; (H) $935

TAYLOR, Dr. Robert
American contemporary
sculpture: (H) $690

TAYLOR, E.A.
drawings: (H) $3,300

TAYLOR, Edgar J.
American b. 1862
paintings: (H) $1,320

TAYLOR, Edward
British 1828-1906
drawings: (H) $605

TAYLOR, Edward Dewitt
American 1871-1962
paintings: (H) $660

TAYLOR, Frank Walter
American 1874-1921
paintings: (H) $3,300

TAYLOR, G.T.
paintings: (H) $467

TAYLOR, Grace Martin Frame
American b. 1903
paintings: (L) $880; (H) $2,750
drawings: (L) $770; (H) $1,320

TAYLOR, Henry Fitch
American 1853-1925
drawings: (H) $990

TAYLOR, Henry King
British ac. 1857-1869
paintings: (H) $9,900

TAYLOR, Jay C.
American
paintings: (L) $247; (H) $632

TAYLOR, John C.E.
American b. 1902
paintings: (L) $495; (H) $550

TAYLOR, John W.
American 20th cent.
drawings: (L) $495; (H) $550

TAYLOR, Leonard Campbell
English 1874-1963
paintings: (L) $990; (H) $13,800

TAYLOR, Norman
English ac. 1863-1915
paintings: (H) $1,320

TAYLOR, Philip Meadows
British 1808-1876
paintings: (H) $2,990

TAYLOR, Richard
American 1902-1970
drawings: (L) $440; (H) $715

TAYLOR, Samuel
paintings: (H) $23,000

TAYLOR, W.F.
paintings: (L) $600; (H) $2,100

TAYLOR, Will
b. 1882
paintings: (H) $1,100

TAYLOR, William
contemporary
sculpture: (H) $770

TAYLOR, William F.
American b. 1883
paintings: (L) $1,320; (H) $6,000

TCHAKALIAN, Sam
contemporary
paintings: (H) $605

TCHELITCHEW, Pavel
Russian/American 1898-1957
paintings: (L) $1,150; (H) $17,600
drawings: (L) $248; (H) $11,500

TCHERNTZKYI, A.
Russian 19th cent.
paintings: (H) $460

TCHETCHET, Victor
1891-1974
drawings: (H) $660

TCHOUMAKOFF, Theodore
Russian 1823-1911
paintings: (H) $2,090

TEAD, Arthur
British 19th cent.
paintings: (H) $4,887

TEAGUE, Donald
American b. 1897
paintings: (L) $1,155; (H) $8,800
drawings: (L) $920; (H) $12,100

TEAL, William P.
American 20th cent.
paintings: (H) $605

TEDESCHI, Carlo
Italian 20th cent.
paintings: (H) $550

TEDESCHI, Petrus
c. 1750-after 1805
paintings: (H) $2,860

TEED, Douglas Arthur
American 1864-1929
paintings: (L) $518; (H) $19,800

TEEL, Raymond
American ac. 1940's
drawings: (H) $1,980

TEERLINK, Abraham
Dutch 1776-1857
paintings: (H) $16,100

TEFFT, Charles
American 1874-c. 1950
sculpture: (H) $1,430

TEGNER, Rudolf Christopher Puggard
Danish 1873-1950
sculpture: (L) $23,000; (H) $55,000

TEICHEL, Franz
German 19th cent.
paintings: (H) $522

TEIXEIRA, Oswaldo
1905-1974
paintings: (L) $1,650; (H) $17,250

TEIXEIRA DE MATTOS, Henri
Dutch 1856-1908
paintings: (H) $660

TELEKI, Ralf
Hungarian b. 1890
paintings: (H) $715

TELETY, A.H.
sculpture: (H) $990

TELKESSY, Valeria
Hungarian 1870-1950
paintings: (L) $1,725; (H) $2,750

TELLANDER, A. Frederic
American b. 1878
paintings: (L) $230; (H) $6,900
drawings: (H) $176

TELLER, Grif
20th cent.
paintings: (L) $83; (H) $3,450

TELLING, Smidt
sculpture: (H) $825

TELSER, A.
paintings: (L) $330; (H) $1,725

TEMPESTA, Antonio
Italian 1555-1630
drawings: (H) $17,600

TEMPLE, Reginald
paintings: (H) $1,955

TEMPLE, T.
British ac. 1865-1871
paintings: (H) $34,100

TEN COMPE, Jan
Dutch 1713-1761
paintings: (H) $34,100

TEN EYCK, John
American 1893-1932
paintings: (H) $605

TEN KATE, Herman Frederik Carel
Dutch 1822-1891
paintings: (L) $7,425; (H) $20,700
drawings: (H) $2,185

TEN KATE, Johan Mari
Dutch 1831-1910
paintings: (L) $20,900; (H) $63,800

TEN KATE, Johannes Marinus
Dutch 1859-1896
paintings: (H) $11,000

TENCY, Jean Baptiste
Flemish 1755-1808
paintings: (H) $7,187

TENDUCCI, M.
paintings: (H) $1,400

TENERANI, Pietro
Italian
sculpture: (H) $16,100

TENGELER, Johannes Willem
Dutch 1746-1811
paintings: (H) $11,500

TENIERS, Abraham
Flemish baptized 1629, d. 1670
paintings: (H) $9,350

TENIERS, David, the younger
Flemish 1610-1690
paintings: (L) $6,600; (H) $211,500
drawings: (L) $385; (H) $2,860

TENIERS, David, the younger
studio of
Flemish 17th cent.
paintings: (H) $18,400

TENISWOOD, George F.
British ac. 1856-1876
paintings: (H) $4,675

TENNANT, Allie Victoria
American d. 1971
sculpture: (H) $805

TENNANT, Craig
b. 1946
paintings: (H) $3,850

TENNANT, John F.
British 1796-1872
paintings: (L) $2,875; (H) $18,400

TENNANT, Thomas R.
English 19th cent.
paintings: (H) $1,045

TENRE, Charles Henry
French 1864-1926
drawings: (H) $1,265

TEOLECKI, Alfred
paintings: (H) $518

TEPPER, Saul
American 1899-1987
paintings: (L) $1,100; (H) $5,500

TEPTMEIER, K.
German 19th/20th cent.
paintings: (H) $660

TER MEULEN, Frans Pieter
Dutch 1843-1927
paintings: (L) $1,320; (H) $2,300
drawings: (H) $3,300

TER-ARUTUNIAN, Rouben
1920-1922
drawings: (L) $460; (H) $1,725

TERATT (?), G.
paintings: (H) $660

TERAUCHI
Japanese early 20th cent.
drawings: (H) $935

TERBORCH, Gerard
Dutch 1617-1681
paintings: (L) $40,700; (H) $321,500

TERBORCH, Gerard and Gesina
TERBORCH
17th cent.
paintings: (H) $343,500

TERBORGH, H.
19th cent.
paintings: (H) $825

TERBRUGGHEN, Hendrick
Dutch 1588-1629
paintings: (H) $220,000

TERECHKOVITCH, Constantin
Russian/French 1902-1978
paintings: (L) $1,380; (H) $45,100
drawings: (L) $1,840; (H) $26,400

TERELAK, John C.
American b. 1942
paintings: (L) $374; (H) $3,850

TERESZCZUK, Paul
early 20th cent.
sculpture: (L) $300; (H) $5,500

TERLOUW, Kees
Dutch 1890-1948
paintings: (H) $1,540

TERMAHLEN, Karl E.
American b. 1863
paintings: (L) $77; (H) $660

TERMOHLEN, Karl
American b. 1863
paintings: (L) $173; (H) $715

TERNEU, Albert
paintings: (H) $2,185

TERNI, A.L.
Italian 19th cent.
paintings: (L) $300; (H) $2,750

TERPENING, Sonya
American
drawings: (L) $800; (H) $3,960

TERPNING, Howard
American b. 1927
paintings: (L) $2,200; (H) $170,500
drawings: (L) $1,980; (H) $93,500

TERRAIRE, Clovis Frederick
French 1858-1931
paintings: (L) $660; (H) $8,800

TERRELL, Richard
paintings: (H) $1,870

TERRINI, Alberto
Italian 20th cent.(?)
paintings: (L) $1,320; (H) $1,380

TERRIS, John
Scottish 1865-1914
drawings: (H) $935

TERRY, Jack
American b. 1952
paintings: (L) $3,300; (H) $13,200

TERSZUK, P.
Austrian 20th cent.
paintings: (H) $1,210

TERWESTEN, Augustinus
1649-1711
drawings: (H) $7,475

TERWESTEN, Matthaus
Dutch 1670-1757
paintings: (L) $5,750; (H) $11,000

TESHIGAHARA, Sofu
Japanese b. 1900
paintings: (H) $10,450
sculpture: (H) $14,300

TESI, Mauro
1730-1766
drawings: (L) $1,540; (H) $1,840

TESSARI, Romolo
Italian b. 1868
paintings: (L) $5,500; (H) $9,350
drawings: (L) $176; (H) $440

TESSARI, Vittorio
Italian b. 1860
paintings: (L) $276; (H) $660
drawings: (H) $1,150

TESTA, Pietro
Italian 1617-1650
paintings: (H) $55,000
drawings: (H) $1,320

TESTER, Jefferson
American b. 1900
paintings: (H) $575

TESTI, A.
Italian 19th/20th cent.
sculpture: (L) $825; (H) $26,450

TESTI, Paolo
Italian 19th/20th cent.
sculpture: (L) $1,725; (H) $2,760

TETAR VAN ELVEN, Pierre Henri
Theodore
Dutch 1831-1908
paintings: (L) $2,090; (H) $6,600
drawings: (L) $88; (H) $1,210

TETE, Maurice Louis
French 1881-1948
paintings: (L) $2,300; (H) $4,600

TETENS, C.H.
Danish 19th cent.
paintings: (L) $770; (H) $1,210

TETHEROW, Michael
drawings: (H) $978

TEUTRE, P. du
paintings: (H) $1,100

TEWARI, Vasundhara
Indian b. 1955
drawings: (L) $1,035; (H) $1,840

TEYE
drawings: (H) $7,700

THACKERAY, William Makepeace
English 1811-1863
drawings: (L) $467; (H) $3,575

THALINGER, E. Oscar
American b. 1885
paintings: (L) $110; (H) $2,415

THAMER, Otto
German b. 1892
paintings: (H) $880

THAMES, Emmitt Eugene
American b. 1933
drawings: (L) $385; (H) $1,430

THAREL, Leon
sculpture: (H) $1,840

THARFI
sculpture: (H) $518

THARRATS, Juan Jose
Spanish b. 1918
paintings: (L) $825; (H) $1,650

THAULOW, Frits
Norwegian 1847-1906
paintings: (L) $1,035; (H) $60,250
drawings: (L) $1,980; (H) $33,000

THAYER, Abbott Handerson
American 1849-1921
paintings: (L) $253; (H) $107,000
drawings: (L) $1,650; (H) $4,600

THAYER, Ethel Randolph
American b. 1904
paintings: (L) $522; (H) $825

THAYER, Karen
paintings: (L) $1,400; (H) $2,200

THAYER, Polly
American b. 1904
paintings: (H) $715

THAYER, William J.
19th c.
paintings: (H) $1,100

THECLA, Julia
American 20th cent.
drawings: (L) $115; (H) $978

THEIL, Johann Gottfried
1745-1797
drawings: (H) $3,163

THEISS, John W.
American b. 1863
drawings: (H) $660

THEK, Paul
drawings: (H) $1,380
sculpture: (H) $9,200

THELWALL, John Augustus
British ac. 1883-1896
paintings: (H) $9,200

THEMMEN, Charles
American ac. c. 1856
paintings: (H) $3,738

THENN, K.
Austrian
sculpture: (H) $805

THEOBALD
French b. 1926
paintings: (H) $1,980

THEOLSEGOUX
American 19th cent.
drawings: (H) $825

THERBUSCH, Anna Dorothea, nee LIZIEWSKI
German 1721-1782
paintings: (H) $74,000

THERIAT, Charles James
American b. 1860
paintings: (L) $468; (H) $14,950

THERKILDSEN, Michael
Danish 1850-1925
paintings: (H) $8,913

THEROUX, Carol
drawings: (L) $650; (H) $660

THERRIEN, Robert
American b. 1947
paintings: (L) $12,650; (H) $40,250
drawings: (H) $2,200
sculpture: (L) $2,420; (H) $40,250

THEUERKAUFF, Carl Rudolph
1875-1926
paintings: (H) $605

THEUVENOT, A.
French 19th cent.
paintings: (H) $6,600

THEVENET, Jacques
French b. 1891
paintings: (H) $1,100

THEVENET, Louis
Belgian 1874-1930
paintings: (L) $440; (H) $8,800

THEVENIN, A.H.
Continental School 19th cent.
paintings: (H) $4,620

THEVENIN, Al.
French 19th cent.
paintings: (H) $1,100

THIAUCOURT, P.
Continental 19th cent.
paintings: (H) $1,650

THIBESART, Raymond
French 1874-1968
paintings: (L) $575; (H) $2,420

THIBODEAU, V. Durbin
paintings: (H) $546

THIBODEAUX, Michael
drawings: (H) $1,540

THIEBAUD, Wayne
American b. 1920
paintings: (L) $66,000; (H) $220,000
drawings: (L) $990; (H) $51,750

THIEBLIN, Reine Josephine
French 19th/20th cent.
paintings: (H) $8,800

THIELE, Alexander
German b. 1924
paintings: (L) $330; (H) $990

THIELE, Johann Alexander
German 1685-1752
paintings: (H) $21,850

THIELEMANN, Alfred
German b. 1883
paintings: (L) $275; (H) $770

THIELEMANN, Alfred Rudolph
Danish 1851-1927
paintings: (H) $770

THIELEN, Jan Philips van
Flemish 1618-1667
paintings: (H) $48,875

THIEME, Anthony
Dutch/American 1888-1954
paintings: (L) $212; (H) $43,700
drawings: (L) $275; (H) $3,740

THIERMANN, F.
German 20th cent.
sculpture: (H) $3,450

THIERRIAT, Augustin Alexandre
French 1789-1870
paintings: (L) $6,600; (H) $29,700

THIERRY, Jean Alexandre
French 19th cent.
drawings: (H) $10,350

THIRION, Charles Victor
French 1833-1878
paintings: (H) $13,200

THIVET, Antoine Auguste
French ac. c. 1880
paintings: (H) $880

THOLEN, Willem Bastiaan
Dutch 1860-1931
paintings: (L) $715; (H) $16,500
drawings: (L) $2,090; (H) $2,200

THOLER, Raymond
French b. 1859
paintings: (H) $1,100

THOM, James Crawford
American 1838/42-1898
paintings: (L) $550; (H) $4,140
drawings: (L) $275; (H) $1,650

THOM, Robert
American contemporary
paintings: (L) $259; (H) $3,850

THOMA, Hans
German 1839-1924
drawings: (H) $1,955

THOMA, Josef
Austrian 1828-1899
paintings: (L) $3,450; (H) $13,800

THOMAS, A.
19th cent.
paintings: (H) $1,045

THOMAS, Alma W.
American 1891-1978
paintings: (L) $825; (H) $1,760
drawings: (L) $330; (H) $330

THOMAS, Barry
American b. 1961
paintings: (L) $1,760; (H) $6,600

THOMAS, Carol
American b. 1958
paintings: (H) $4,840

THOMAS, Charles
Belgian 1827-1892
paintings: (H) $2,300

THOMAS, Collins
paintings: (L) $175; (H) $625

THOMAS, Emily
19th/20th cent.
paintings: (H) $1,430

THOMAS, Gerard
1663-1720
paintings: (H) $4,370

THOMAS, Henri Joseph
Belgian 1878-1972
paintings: (H) $1,955

THOMAS, Howard
American b. 1899
paintings: (H) $1,430

THOMAS, Karl
American b. 1948
paintings: (L) $2,750; (H) $9,350

THOMAS, Margaret
British 19th/20th cent.
paintings: (H) $1,650
sculpture: (H) $6,037

THOMAS, Mark
Belgian late 19th/20th cent.
sculpture: (H) $1,540

THOMAS, Mathilde
French b. 1860
sculpture: (H) $4,125

THOMAS, Melina
French exhib. 1837-1840
paintings: (H) $3,520

THOMAS, Paul
French b. 1859
paintings: (L) $385; (H) $4,950

THOMAS, Richard
b. 1940
paintings: (L) $2,200; (H) $11,000

THOMAS, Stephen Seymour
American 1868-1956
paintings: (L) $165; (H) $2,420
drawings: (L) $99; (H) $1,265

THOMASON, Jim
drawings: (H) $880

THOMASSIN, D.
paintings: (H) $5,000

THOMASSIN, Desire
German 1858-1933
paintings: (L) $4,140; (H) $9,200

THOMASSON, E.
sculpture: (H) $4,830

THOMIRE, Pierre Phillipe
French 1751-1843
drawings: (H) $990

THOMOPOULOS, Epaminondas A.
Greek 1878-1974
paintings: (L) $192; (H) $3,450

THOMPSON
paintings: (H) $605

THOMPSON
American 19th cent.
paintings: (L) $550; (H) $800

THOMPSON, Albert
American b. 1853
paintings: (H) $715

THOMPSON, Alfred Wordsworth
American 1840-1896
paintings: (L) $1,650; (H) $17,250
drawings: (H) $2,640

THOMPSON, Bob
American 1937-1966
paintings: (L) $3,300; (H) $4,400
drawings: (L) $2,640; (H) $4,400

THOMPSON, Cephas Giovanni
American 1809-1888
paintings: (L) $715; (H) $6,600

THOMPSON, E.
American 19th cent.
drawings: (H) $550

THOMPSON, E.
American 20th cent.
paintings: (H) $1,045

THOMPSON, Ernest Thorne
Canadian b. 1897
paintings: (L) $230; (H) $550

THOMPSON, Frank Wildes
1836-1905
paintings: (H) $2,185

THOMPSON, Frederic Louis
American b. 1868
paintings: (H) $1,150

THOMPSON, G.
British 19th cent.
paintings: (L) $303; (H) $517

THOMPSON, George A.
American 1868-1938
paintings: (L) $495; (H) $1,980

THOMPSON, H.
paintings: (H) $460

THOMPSON, H.
19th/20th cent.
paintings: (H) $550

THOMPSON, Henry Grinell
American 1850-1939
paintings: (H) $2,070

THOMPSON, J.
British 19th cent.
paintings: (H) $920

THOMPSON, J. Arthur
American early 20th cent.
paintings: (L) $660; (H) $1,760

THOMPSON, Jerome
American 1814-1886
paintings: (L) $9,200; (H) $18,400

THOMPSON, John
British 19th c.
paintings: (H) $990

THOMPSON, Leslie P.
American 1880-1963
paintings: (L) $2,200; (H) $3,300

THOMPSON, Robert
American 1937-1966
paintings: (L) $2,875; (H) $13,800

THOMPSON, Robert
American b. 1936
paintings: (H) $23,000

THOMPSON, Sydney Lough
English 1877-1973
paintings: (H) $20,700

THOMPSON, Taylor
British 20th cent.
drawings: (L) $495; (H) $715

THOMPSON, Walter Whitcomb
American 1881/82-1948
paintings: (L) $250; (H) $1,045

THOMPSON, Wilfred H.
British ac. 1884-1893
paintings: (H) $977
drawings: (H) $33

THOMPSON, Wordsworth
American 1840-1896
paintings: (L) $4,370; (H) $4,830

THOMPSON-BUTTLER, H.
British 19th cent.
paintings: (H) $1,100

THOMPSON-PRITCHARD, George
American 1878-1962
paintings: (L) $715; (H) $1,595

THOMSEN, August Carl Vilhelm
Danish 1813-1886
paintings: (L) $2,310; (H) $7,700

THOMSEN, Henry Grinnell
American b. 1850
paintings: (H) $3,850

THOMSEN, Pauline
Danish 1858-1931
paintings: (H) $22,000

THOMSON, E. W.
British 1770-1847
drawings: (H) $1,495

THOMSON, G.F.
British 19th cent.
paintings: (H) $3,410

THOMSON, George
b. 1868
paintings: (L) $400; (H) $990

THOMSON, Henry Grinnell
American 1850-1939
paintings: (L) $440; (H) $1,925
drawings: (H) $495

THOMSON, Hugh
British 1860-1920
drawings: (H) $3,960

THOMSON, Rev. John
paintings: (H) $522

THOMSON, Tom
Canadian 1877-1917
paintings: (L) $77,000; (H) $209,000

THON, William
American b. 1906
paintings: (L) $230; (H) $990
drawings: (L) $2,090; (H) $3,080

THONNARD, F.
paintings: (H) $1,430

THONTIMAN, T.
drawings: (H) $660

THONY, Wilhelm
Austrian 1888-1949
paintings: (H) $16,100

THORBURN, Archibald
Scottish 1860-1935
drawings: (L) $770; (H) $12,100

THOREN, Otto Karl Kasimir von
Austrian 1828-1889
paintings: (L) $3,450; (H) $5,750
drawings: (H) $825

THORENFELD, Anton Erik Christian
Danish 1839-1907
paintings: (H) $8,250

THORN, Diana
Canadian b. 1894
paintings: (L) $330; (H) $2,090

THORNBERY, William A.
British 19th/20th cent.
paintings: (H) $1,980

THORNBURN, Archibald
British 1860-1935
drawings: (L) $3,220; (H) $14,300

THORNDIKE, Charles Hall
American b. 1875
paintings: (H) $633

THORNDIKE, George Quincy
American 1827-1886
paintings: (H) $4,888

THORNE, William
American b. 1884
paintings: (H) $1,540

THORNELY, Charles
British d. 1898
paintings: (H) $1,705

THORNLEY, William
British 19th/20th cent.
paintings: (H) $2,300

THORNLEY, William
French b. 1857
paintings: (L) $880; (H) $4,400

THORNSON, Lars
American/Norwegian 1880-1952
drawings: (H) $460

THORNTON, Alfred Henry Robinson
British 1863-1939
drawings: (H) $1,035

THORNYCROFT, Mary
British 1841-1895
sculpture: (H) $4,400

THORNYCROFT, Thomas
British 1815-1885
sculpture: (H) $7,150

THOROLD, A.J.
paintings: (H) $2,090

THORP, J.
19th/20th cent.
paintings: (H) $1,320

THORPE, Freeman
American 1844-1922
paintings: (H) $900

THORPE, John Hall
English b. 1874
drawings: (L) $220; (H) $467

THORPE, William
English b. 1901
drawings: (H) $578

THORRESTRUP, Jens Christian
Danish 1823-1892
paintings: (H) $1,320

THORS, Joseph
English exhib. 1883-1898
paintings: (L) $440; (H) $6,050

THORSEN, Lars
Norwegian/American 1876-1952
paintings: (L) $345; (H) $7,763
drawings: (H) $165

THOURON, Henry Joseph
American 1851-1915
paintings: (L) $633; (H) $715

THRASHER, Leslie
American 1889-1936
paintings: (L) $1,045; (H) $3,960

THRONER, T.
American
paintings: (H) $660

THU, Mai
drawings: (L) $460; (H) $863

THULDEN, Theodor van
Dutch 1606-1669
paintings: (L) $9,775; (H) $40,250

THULSTRUP, Thure de
American 1848-1930
paintings: (L) $1,150; (H) $7,475
drawings: (L) $110; (H) $1,150

THUMA, Marilyn
American 20th cent.
drawings: (H) $2,200

THUMANN, Paul
German 1834-1908
paintings: (H) $1,100

THUN, Matteo
sculpture: (H) $690

THURAU, Friedrich
paintings: (H) $3,300

THURBER, James
American 1894-1961
drawings: (L) $220; (H) $6,325

THURMANN, Peder
Scandinavian 1839-1919
paintings: (H) $660

THUSS
sculpture: (H) $1,430

THYLLMANI
sculpture: (H) $3,300

THYLLMANI
Italian 19th cent.
sculpture: (H) $4,950

TIBALDI, Pellegrino
Italian 1527-1596
drawings: (H) $27,500

TIE-FENG, Jiang
Chinese b. 1938
drawings: (H) $4,180

TIELENS, Alexandre
Belgian 1868-1959
paintings: (H) $1,540

TIEPOLO, Giovanni Battista
Italian 1696-1770
paintings: (L) $200,500; (H) $506,000
drawings: (L) $4,600; (H) $118,000

TIEPOLO, Giovanni Domenico
Italian 1727-1804
paintings: (L) $19,800; (H) $222,500
drawings: (L) $1,650; (H) $206,000

TIEPOLO, Lorenzo Baldissera
Italian 1736-1776
paintings: (L) $11,000; (H) $28,600
drawings: (L) $7,150; (H) $717,500

TIFFANY, Lee Wilson
American contemporary
sculpture: (L) $253; (H) $633

TIFFANY, Louis Comfort
American 1848-1933
paintings: (L) $660; (H) $60,500
drawings: (L) $920; (H) $55,000

TIFFANY, Louis Comfort, studio of
American 19th/20th cent.
paintings: (H) $1,045

TIFFANY, P.D.
paintings: (H) $1,650

TILBORCH, Gillis van, the younger
Flemish c. 1625-1678
paintings: (H) $63,000

TILCHE, O.
Continental 19th cent.
drawings: (L) $55; (H) $1,100

TILGNER, F.
Continental 19th cent.
paintings: (L) $330; (H) $1,495

TILIUS, Jan
Dutch 1660-1719
paintings: (H) $18,400

TILL, Jean Claude
Austrian 1827-1894
paintings: (H) $495

TILL, Johann, the younger
Austrian 1827-1894
paintings: (H) $6,900

TILLEMANS, P.J.
Flemish 17th cent.
paintings: (H) $1,650

TILLEMANS, Peter
Flemish, b. Antwerp 1684-1734, d.
England
paintings: (H) $36,800

TILLYER, William
20th cent.
drawings: (H) $517

TILNEY, Fred Colin
1870-1952
paintings: (H) $467

TILTON, John Rollin
American 1833-1888
paintings: (L) $275; (H) $21,850

TIMLIN, William M.
Anglo/American 1893-1943
paintings: (H) $4,312

TIMM, Richard
American 20th cent.
paintings: (H) $495

TIMMERMANS, A.
paintings: (L) $690; (H) $825

TIMMERMANS, Henri
Belgian 1858-1942
paintings: (H) $4,255

TIMMERMANS, Louis
French 1846-1910
paintings: (H) $3,850
drawings: (H) $330

TIMMINS, William
American 20th cent.
paintings: (H) $1,650

TIMOTEO Y OROZCO MARTINEZ,
Xavier
American 1869-1943
paintings: (H) $1,265

TIMPSON, Lillian
19th/20th cent.
paintings: (H) $495

TING, Wallasse
paintings: (L) $1,840; (H) $4,950
drawings: (L) $935; (H) $2,090

TINGLE, Minnie
American 1875-1926
paintings: (L) $330; (H) $523

TINGUELY, Jean
Swiss 1925-1991
drawings: (L) $920; (H) $14,300
sculpture: (L) $11,000; (H) $104,500

TINKER, H.L.
American 20th cent.
paintings: (H) $660

TINNEY, Adna
paintings: (H) $550

TINTORE, Simone del
Italian 17th cent.
paintings: (H) $12,650

TINTORETTO, Jacopo ROBUSTI
1518-1594
paintings: (L) $41,800; (H) $910,000
drawings: (H) $41,400

TINTORETTO, Domenico Robusti
Italian 1560-1635
paintings: (L) $55,000; (H) $57,750

TINTORETTO, Domenico Robusti,
studio of
Italian 1560-1635
paintings: (H) $4,400

TINTORETTO, Jacopo Robusti,
workshop of
16th cent.
paintings: (H) $33,000

TIPPET, W.V.
British 19th cent.
paintings: (H) $715

TIPPETTS, Linda
American
paintings: (L) $650; (H) $4,100

TIPPING, William J.
British ac. c.1810-1897
drawings: (H) $920

TIRATELLI, Aurelio
Italian 1842-1900
paintings: (H) $5,060

TIRIBACCO,
Italian 19th/20th cent.
paintings: (H) $990

TIRONI, Francesco
Italian 18th/19th cent.
paintings: (H) $79,500
drawings: (H) $16,500

TISCHBEIN, Johann Heinrich, the
elder
German 1722-1789
paintings: (L) $7,475; (H) $57,750

TISCHBEIN, Johann Heinrich Wilhelm
German 1751-1829
drawings: (L) $275; (H) $935

TISCHLER, Tom
American b. 1948
sculpture: (H) $2,200

TISIO, Benvenuto di Garafalo
Italian c. 1481-1519
paintings: (L) $15,400; (H) $59,700

TISSOT, James Jacques Joseph
French 1836-1902
paintings: (L) $51,750; (H) $5,282,500
drawings: (L) $4,290; (H) $101,500

TITCOMB, Mary Bradish
American 1856-1927
paintings: (L) $4,675; (H) $20,900
drawings: (H) $660

TITCOMB, William Henry
American 1824-1888
paintings: (L) $990; (H) $1,650

TITIAN, Tiziano Vecelli
Italian 1487/90-1576
paintings: (H) $1,100,000

TITIAN, studio of
16th cent.
paintings: (H) $46,200

TITIAN, studio of
16th cent.
paintings: (L) $46,000; (H) $46,200

TITO,
Italian School 19th/20th cent.
paintings: (H) $1,045

TITO, Diego Quispe, workshop
17th cent.
paintings: (H) $13,800

TITO, Ettore
Italian 1859-1941
paintings: (L) $9,775; (H) $20,700

TITO, Santi di
Italian 1536-1603
paintings: (L) $41,400; (H) $74,000

TITTLE, Walter Ernest
American 1880/83-1960
paintings: (L) $83; (H) $1,955

TITUS, Earle A.
20th cent.
paintings: (H) $1,210

TITZE
sculpture: (L) $275; (H) $2,475

TIZIANO, S**
Italian 19th cent.
paintings: (H) $523

TNDONI
drawings: (H) $2,600

TOBAR, Alonso Miguel de
Spanish 1678-1758
paintings: (H) $9,200

TOBERENTZ, Robert
ac. late 19th cent.
sculpture: (H) $3,850

TOBEY, Mark
American 1890-1976
paintings: (L) $1,840; (H) $66,000
drawings: (L) $165; (H) $60,500

TOBIASSE, Theo
Israeli/French b. 1927
paintings: (L) $1,760; (H) $31,080
drawings: (L) $1,540; (H) $24,200
sculpture: (H) $154

TOBURG, O.
paintings: (H) $4,675

TOCQUE, Louis
French 1696-1772
paintings: (L) $33,000; (H) $189,500

TODD, Ralph
drawings: (H) $2,200

TODDY, Jimmy, Beatien Yazz, Little
No Shirt
Native American b. 1928
paintings: (H) $413
drawings: (L) $22; (H) $1,210

TODHUNTER, Francis Augustus
American 1884-1963
paintings: (L) $550; (H) $7,475
drawings: (L) $1,100; (H) $1,540

TODT, Max
German 1847-1890
paintings: (H) $2,640

TOEPUT, Lodewijk, IL
POZZOSERRATO
1550-1603
drawings: (H) $3,450

TOESCHI, G.
Italian 19th cent.
paintings: (H) $14,300

TOFANO, Eduardo
Italian 1838-1920
paintings: (L) $1,870; (H) $5,500
drawings: (L) $4,950; (H) $8,800

TOFEL, Louis
French 20th cent.
paintings: (H) $715
drawings: (H) $192

TOFFOLI, Louis
French b. 1907
paintings: (L) $8,250; (H) $15,400
drawings: (H) $4,830

TOFT, Peter Petersen
b. Denmark 1825-1901
drawings: (L) $303; (H) $14,300

TOJETTI, Domenico
Italian/American ac. 1871-1892
paintings: (H) $770

TOJETTI, Virgilio
Italian/American 1849-1901
paintings: (L) $2,300; (H) $20,900

TOKO, Shinoda
b. 1913
drawings: (L) $2,530; (H) $24,150

TOL, Claes Nicolas Jacobsz
Dutch ac. Utrecht 1634-1636
paintings: (H) $24,200

TOLEDO, Francisco
Mexican b. 1940
paintings: (L) $5,750; (H) $387,500
drawings: (L) $1,100; (H) $134,500
sculpture: (L) $4,400; (H) $8,800

TOLEDO, Jose Rey, Shobah Woonhon,
Morning Star
b. 1915
drawings: (H) $518

TOLEGIAN, Manuel
paintings: (H) $500

TOLFORD, Joshua
American 20th cent.
paintings: (H) $550

TOLLANT, R.H.
American early 20th cent.
paintings: (H) $1,595

TOLLIVER, Mose
American b. 1919
paintings: (L) $99; (H) $1,150

TOLMAN, Stacy
American 1860-1935
paintings: (L) $165; (H) $550
drawings: (L) $27; (H) $220

TOLSON, Edgar
American 1904-1984/86
sculpture: (L) $8,360; (H) $10,925

TOM OF FINLAND
drawings: (H) $1,430

TOMANEK, Joseph
Czech/American b. 1889
paintings: (L) $440; (H) $12,650

TOMASELLO, Luis
Argentinean b. 1915
sculpture: (L) $385; (H) $1,610

TOMASO, Rico
American 1898-1985
paintings: (L) $770; (H) $4,950

TOMBA, Aldini Casimiro
Italian 1857-1929
paintings: (H) $2,415

TOMBA, Casimiro
Italian 1857-1929
paintings: (H) $5,500
drawings: (L) $632; (H) $2,750

TOMEC, Heinrich, Juidrich
Austrian 1863-1928
drawings: (H) $825

TOMGUINETTI, G.
sculpture: (H) $5,500

TOMINZ, Alfredo
Italian 1854-1936
paintings: (L) $3,850; (H) $5,500

TOMKPKINS, Alan
American b. 1907
paintings: (H) $7,475

TOMLIN, Bradley Walker
American 1899-1953
paintings: (L) $13,200; (H) $16,500
drawings: (L) $110; (H) $770

TOMLINSON, Anna C.
American 20th cent.
paintings: (H) $193
drawings: (H) $990

TOMLINSON, E.L.
paintings: (H) $495

TOMLINSON, Henry Welling
American b. 1875
paintings: (H) $825

TOMLINSON, Lorena
drawings: (H) $1,045

TOMMASI, Adolfo
Italian 1851-1933
paintings: (H) $3,410

TOMMASI, Angiolo
Italian 1858-1923
drawings: (H) $7,700

TOMMASI, Paolo
20th cent.
paintings: (H) $467

TOMMASINI, V.
paintings: (H) $750

TOMMASO
15th/16th cent.
paintings: (H) $159,500

TOMME, Luca di
Italian 1330-after 1389
paintings: (H) $35,200

TOMMEY, Bob
b. 1928
paintings: (L) $1,100; (H) $1,100

TOMPKINS, A.F.
American 19th cent.
paintings: (H) $17,250

TOMPKINS, Frank H.
American 1847-1922
paintings: (L) $302; (H) $3,960

TOMSER, H.
Continental 20th cent.
paintings: (H) $633

TOMSON, Clifton
English 1775-1835
paintings: (H) $4,025

TONER, Thomas M.
American 20th cent.
paintings: (L) $161; (H) $605
drawings: (H) $86

TONES, Lillian C.
American 20th cent.
paintings: (H) $605

TONEY, Anthony
American b. 1913
paintings: (L) $88; (H) $1,045

TONEY, Don
b. 1954
sculpture: (H) $1,100

TONGE, Lammert van der
Dutch 1871-1937
paintings: (H) $2,300

TONGEN, Louis van de
Dutch 1871-1937
paintings: (H) $1,870

TONNANCOUR, Jacques Godefroy de
Canadian b. 1917
paintings: (L) $18,700; (H) $26,400

TONNEAU, J.
English 19th cent.
paintings: (H) $2,200

TONSBERG, Gertrude Martin
American 1903-1973
paintings: (L) $110; (H) $1,100

TOOK, William
British 1857-1892
paintings: (H) $3,335

TOOKER, George
American b. 1920
paintings: (L) $60,500; (H) $176,000

TOOMEY & VOLLAND
early 20th cent.
drawings: (L) $892; (H) $1,438

TOORENBURGH, Gerrit
Dutch 1732-1785
paintings: (H) $19,550

TOORENVLIET, Jacob
Dutch c. 1635-1719
paintings: (L) $7,700; (H) $17,600

TOORENVLIET, Jacob
Dutch c. 1635/41-1719
paintings: (L) $7,700; (H) $13,800

TOOROP, Jan Theodor
drawings: (H) $605

TOPFFER, Adam
Swiss 1766-1847
drawings: (H) $605

TOPHAM, Frank William Warwick
British 1838-1924
paintings: (L) $2,300; (H) $68,500

TOPOLSKI, Feliks
Polish 1907-1989
drawings: (L) $165; (H) $1,380

TOPPI, Mario
Italian 20th cent.
drawings: (H) $1,100

TOPPING, James
American 1879-1949
paintings: (L) $259; (H) $4,070

TORAN, Alfonso T.
American b. 1898
paintings: (L) $248; (H) $1,045

TORDI, Sinibaldo
Italian 1876-1955
paintings: (L) $1,100; (H) $24,150

TORDIA, Radish
Russian b. 1936
paintings: (L) $3,080; (H) $3,080

TORETTI, P.
Italian School 19th cent.
paintings: (H) $1,540

TORGENSEN, Alex
20th cent.
paintings: (H) $518

TORGERSON, William
American ac. 1912-1937
paintings: (H) $1,035

TORINANA, F.
paintings: (H) $1,210

TORLAKSON, James
American b. 1951
drawings: (H) $1,725

TORNAI, Gyula
Hungarian 1861-1928
paintings: (L) $18,400; (H) $26,450

TORO, Jean Bernard
1661-1731
drawings: (L) $6,325; (H) $6,900

TORO, Luigi
Italian 1836-1950
paintings: (H) $990

TOROKIN, V.
sculpture: (H) $2,200

TORR, Helen
American 1886-1967
paintings: (L) $3,080; (H) $17,600
drawings: (L) $220; (H) $7,475

TORRALBA MASTER
15th cent.
paintings: (H) $93,500

TORRE, Flaminio
1621-1661
paintings: (H) $8,050

TORRE, Giulio del
Italian 1856-1932
paintings: (L) $3,520; (H) $26,450

TORRE, Nicolas Andre
ac. mid 17th cent.
paintings: (H) $7,150

TORREANO, John
American b. 1941
sculpture: (L) $345; (H) $2,475

TORRENTO, J.
20th cent.
drawings: (H) $495

TORRES, Antonio
Spanish b. 1851
paintings: (H) $1,210

TORRES, Antonio de
Spanish
paintings: (H) $38,500

TORRES, Augusto
Spanish ac. mid 17th cent.
paintings: (L) $4,600; (H) $8,800
sculpture: (H) $9,200

TORRES, Francisco
paintings: (H) $24,150

TORRES, Horacio
American 1924-1976
paintings: (H) $13,800

TORRES, Jose Samano
paintings: (H) $6,600

TORRES, Julio Romero de
Spanish 1879-1930
paintings: (L) $17,250; (H) $26,450

TORRES, R.
Mexican 20th cent.
paintings: (H) $522

TORRES GARCIA, Joaqin
b. Mexico 1899
paintings: (H) $33,000

TORRES-GARCIA, Joaquin
Uruguayan 1874-1949
paintings: (L) $9,900; (H) $937,500
drawings: (L) $2,760; (H) $77,000
sculpture: (L) $35,650; (H) $110,000

TORRES-GARCIA, Taller
20th cent.
sculpture: (H) $11,500

TORREY, Elliot Bouton
American 1867-1949
paintings: (L) $605; (H) $8,050

TORREY, George Burroughs
American 1863-1942
paintings: (L) $184; (H) $1,540

TORRI, Flaminio, called Dagli
Ancinelli
Italian 1621-1661
paintings: (L) $4,400; (H) $39,600

TORRICELLI, Giovanni Antonio
Italian 1716-1781
drawings: (H) $1,100

TORRIGLIA, Giovanni Battista
Italian 1858-1937
paintings: (L) $4,675; (H) $17,250

TORRINI, E.
Italian 19th cent.
paintings: (L) $1,210; (H) $7,700
drawings: (H) $605

TORRINI, Pietro
Italian b. 1852
paintings: (L) $1,650; (H) $8,800
drawings: (H) $920

TORSKY, D.J.
American ac. 1930-1950
paintings: (H) $990

TOSCANO, Dee
b. 1932
drawings: (H) $3,850

TOSHINOBU, Onosato
1912-1986
paintings: (L) $63,000; (H) $107,000

TOSINI, Michele, called Ghirlandaio
1503-1577
paintings: (L) $11,500; (H) $32,200

TOSO, Gianni
American contemporary
sculpture: (H) $3,025

TOSSEY, Verne
paintings: (H) $3,520
drawings: (H) $500

TOTH, Alex
drawings: (H) $2,750

TOTIN, V.
paintings: (H) $715

TOUCHEMOLIN, Alfred
French 1829-1907
paintings: (H) $880

TOULMOUCHE, Auguste
French 1829-1890
paintings: (L) $3,850; (H) $36,800

TOULOUSE-LAUTREC, Henri de
French 1864-1901
paintings: (L) $51,750; (H) $4,787,500
drawings: (L) $1,150; (H) $1,980,000
sculpture: (L) $50,600; (H) $82,250

TOUPIN, Fernand
Canadian b. 1930
drawings: (H) $2,970

TOURGUENEFF, Pierre Nicolas
Russian late 19th/20th cent.
sculpture: (L) $1,650; (H) $2,640

TOURNEMINE, Charles Emile de
French 1812-1872
paintings: (H) $17,250

TOURNY, Leon Auguste
French b. 1835
paintings: (H) $990

TOURRIER, G.L.
French 20th cent.
paintings: (H) $2,090

TOURTE, Frederick Pierre Marc
French 1873-1960
sculpture: (H) $633

TOUSSAINT, Armand
French 1806-1862
paintings: (H) $28,750
sculpture: (L) $2,875; (H) $12,650

TOUSSAINT, Fernand
Belgian 1873-1955
paintings: (L) $9,900; (H) $43,700

TOUSSAINT, Louis
German 1826-1879
paintings: (L) $2,420; (H) $7,975

TOUSSAINT, Pierre
French b. 1825
paintings: (L) $1,430; (H) $5,750

TOVAR, Ivan
Czechoslovakian 20th cent.
paintings: (H) $32,200

TOVISH, Harold
American b. 1921
sculpture: (L) $550; (H) $847

TOWLE, H. Ledyard
American b. 1890
paintings: (H) $1,320
drawings: (L) $1,495; (H) $3,300

TOWN, Harold Barling
Canadian b. 1924
paintings: (H) $3,850
drawings: (L) $1,540; (H) $17,600

TOWNE
American 20th cent.
paintings: (L) $330; (H) $660

TOWNE, Charles
British 1763-1840
paintings: (L) $3,680; (H) $79,750

TOWNE, Charles
British 1781-1854
paintings: (H) $9,240

TOWNER, Xaripa Hamilton
American 20th cent.
drawings: (L) $110; (H) $935

TOWNLEY, Charles
British 1746-1800
paintings: (H) $27,500

TOWNSEND, Arthur Louis
British ac. 1880-1912
paintings: (H) $1,035
drawings: (H) $748

TOWNSEND, Frances B.
American d. 1916
paintings: (L) $770; (H) $1,430

TOWNSEND, Richard Laird
paintings: (H) $660

TOWNSLEY, Channel Pickering
American 1867-1921
paintings: (L) $172; (H) $880

TOYA, Patricio
Native American 20th cent.
drawings: (H) $550

TOYOSAKU, Saito
1880-1951
sculpture: (H) $21,850

TOZER, Henry Spernon
English ac. 1889-1892
paintings: (L) $715; (H) $5,463
drawings: (H) $1,650

TOZO
American 20th cent.
paintings: (H) $550

TRACEY, John Michael
1843-1893
paintings: (H) $6,050

TRACY
19th/20th cent.
paintings: (H) $990

TRACY, Charles
19th/20th cent.
paintings: (H) $748

TRACY, Glen
b. 1883
paintings: (H) $2,875

TRACY, John Martin
American 1844-1893
paintings: (L) $604; (H) $18,400

TRACY, Michael
b. 1943
sculpture: (L) $575; (H) $2,185

TRAPPES, Francis M.
British ac. 1868-1885
paintings: (L) $550; (H) $990

TRAQUAIR, Phoebe Anna
Irish 1852-1936
paintings: (H) $11,000

TRAUTSCHOLD, Carl Friedrich
Wilhelm
German 1815-1877
paintings: (H) $46,000
drawings: (H) $1,760

TRAVELI, M.
late 19th cent.
sculpture: (L) $6,050; (H) $8,250

TRAVERS, H.H.
British 19th cent.
paintings: (H) $1,320

TRAVERSE, Pierre
French b. 1892
sculpture: (H) $1,610

TRAVIS, L.
paintings: (L) $550; (H) $715

TRAVIS, Olin
American 1888-1974
paintings: (L) $550; (H) $2,310

TRAVIS, Paul
American 1891-1975
paintings: (L) $165; (H) $605
drawings: (L) $28; (H) $880

TRAVIS, Wanina
American
drawings: (H) $500

TRAYER, Jules
French 1824-1908
paintings: (H) $20,700
drawings: (H) $3,737

TRAYLOR, Bill
American 1854-1947
paintings: (L) $8,800; (H) $14,950
drawings: (L) $7,150; (H) $14,950

TRAZZINI, Angelo
Italian 19th cent.
paintings: (H) $3,300

TREBILOCK, Paul
American b. 1902
paintings: (L) $248; (H) $6,600

TREBUTIEN, Etienne Leon
French 1823-1871
paintings: (H) $24,150

TREE, Michael
American 20th cent.
drawings: (H) $1,430

TREFONIDES, Steven
American b. 1926
drawings: (L) $165; (H) $1,210

TREFORTI
American 20th cent.
paintings: (H) $1,100

TREGANZA, Ruth C. Robinson
American b. 1877
paintings: (H) $1,870

TREIMAN, Joyce Wahl
American 1922-1991
paintings: (H) $660
drawings: (H) $403

TRELLES, Rafael
Puerto Rico b. 1957
paintings: (L) $6,325; (H) $11,500

TREMLETT, David
b. 1945
drawings: (H) $2,300

TRENTANOVE, Raimondo
Italian 1792-1832
sculpture: (H) $3,740

TREVES, Andre
paintings: (H) $550

TREVISAN, A.
Italian 19th/20th cent.
drawings: (L) $137; (H) $880

TREVISANI, Francesco
Italian 1656-1746
paintings: (H) $22,000

TREVISO, Girolamo da, the elder
Italian c. 1450-1496?
paintings: (H) $40,250

TREVOR, Jean Pierre
French 20th cent.
paintings: (H) $605

TRIBB, C.
19th cent.
paintings: (H) $1,045

TRICCA, Marco Aurelio
American 1880-1969
paintings: (L) $483; (H) $690

TRICKETT, W. Wasdell
American 20th cent.
paintings: (H) $2,090

TRIEBEL, Carl and August von
RENTZELL
German 19th cent.
paintings: (H) $4,125

TRIEBEL, Frederick Ernst
American 1865-1944
sculpture: (H) $4,715

TRINIDAD, Jose
paintings: (L) $798; (H) $1,925

TRINKA, Randi
American contemporary
paintings: (H) $1,650

TRINQUESSE, Louis R.
French 1746-c. 1800
paintings: (H) $37,400

TRIP, Victor
American 20th cent.
paintings: (H) $467

TRIPP, Wilson B. Evan
American b. 1896
paintings: (H) $1,705

TRIQUET, Jules Octave
French 1867-1914
paintings: (H) $3,450

TRIRUM, Johannes Wouterus van
Dutch b. 1924
paintings: (H) $495

TRISCOTT, Samuel Peter Rolt
American 1846-1925
paintings: (H) $660
drawings: (L) $110; (H) $2,200

TRIVAS, Irene
drawings: (H) $8,800

TROCCOLI, Giovanni
1882-1940
paintings: (H) $1,320

TROCKEL, Rosemarie
German b. 1952
drawings: (L) $1,150; (H) $23,000
sculpture: (L) $14,950; (H) $17,820

TRODOUX
French 19th cent.
sculpture: (H) $660

TRODOUX, Henri Emile Adrien
French late 19th cent.
sculpture: (L) $220; (H) $605

TROFONDIES, Steven
drawings: (H) $990

TROGER, Paul
Austrian 1698-1762
paintings: (L) $5,520; (H) $11,000
drawings: (L) $3,450; (H) $4,400

TROIANI, Troiano
sculpture: (L) $1,380; (H) $2,990

TROMBADORI, Francesco
Italian 1886-1961
paintings: (H) $1,610

TROMP, Jan Zoetelief
Dutch 1872-1947
paintings: (L) $5,225; (H) $17,600

TROMPIZ, Virgilio
Venezuelan b. 1927
paintings: (H) $5,500

TROOD, William Henry Hamilton
English 1848/60-1899
paintings: (H) $1,045

TROON, Einar
19th/20th cent.
paintings: (H) $660

TROOST, Cornelis
Dutch 1697-1750
paintings: (H) $9,200
drawings: (H) $28,600

TROTTER, Newbold Hough
American 1827-1898
paintings: (L) $495; (H) $6,325

TROUBETZKOY, Prince Paul
Russian/American 1866-1933/38
paintings: (H) $495
sculpture: (L) $4,400; (H) $90,500

TROUILLARD, Gustave
French 19th cent.
sculpture: (L) $605; (H) $1,980

TROUILLEBERT, Paul Desire
French 1829-1900
paintings: (L) $605; (H) $63,000
drawings: (H) $660

TROUTOVSKY, Konstantin A.
Russian 1826-1893
paintings: (H) $3,105

TROVA, Ernest
American b. 1927
paintings: (L) $259; (H) $4,600
drawings: (L) $880; (H) $1,438
sculpture: (L) $550; (H) $23,000

TROY, Francois de
French 1645-1730
paintings: (L) $2,200; (H) $360,000

TROY, Jean Francois de
French 1697-1752
paintings: (H) $43,125

TROYE, Edward
American 1808-1874
paintings: (L) $825; (H) $18,700

TROYEN, Rombout van
1605-1650
paintings: (L) $4,600; (H) $9,200

TROYER, F.F.
Austrian 19th cent.
paintings: (H) $715

TROYON, Constant
French 1810-1865
paintings: (L) $345; (H) $497,500
drawings: (L) $1,045; (H) $4,620

TRUBNER, Wilhelm
German 1851-1917
paintings: (H) $1,210

TRUE, Allen Tupper
1881-1955
paintings: (H) $2,200

TRUE, David
American b. 1942
paintings: (L) $575; (H) $3,300
drawings: (L) $690; (H) $1,980

TRUE, Grace Hopkins
American b. 1870
paintings: (H) $488

TRUE, Virginia
ac. 1926-1939
paintings: (H) $880

TRUESDELL, Gaylord Sangston
American 1850-1899
paintings: (L) $550; (H) $5,060

TRUJILLO, Guillermo
Panamanian b. 1927
paintings: (H) $4,400

TRUMAN, Timothy
paintings: (H) $748

TRUMBULL, Edward
American 20th cent.
paintings: (L) $115; (H) $1,150

TRUMBULL, Gordon
1841-1903
paintings: (L) $7,475; (H) $8,050

TRUMBULL, John
American 1756-1843
paintings: (L) $20,700; (H) $39,600

TRUPHEMUS, Jacques
paintings: (L) $6,600; (H) $7,150

TRUTH, Dan
20th cent.
paintings: (L) $165; (H) $495

TRYON, Benjamin F.
American b. 1824
paintings: (L) $330; (H) $690

TRYON, Dwight William
American 1849-1925
paintings: (L) $605; (H) $44,000
drawings: (L) $1,430; (H) $3,300

TSCHACBASOV, Nahum
American b. 1899
paintings: (L) $77; (H) $1,320
drawings: (H) $880

TSCHAGGENY, Edmond Jean Baptiste
Belgian 1818-1973
paintings: (H) $7,700

TSELMARDINOS, Dimitrios
paintings: (H) $920

TSIKHELASHVILI, Nicolas
Russian b. 1953
paintings: (L) $660; (H) $770

TSINGOS, Thanos
1914-1965
paintings: (L) $2,640; (H) $3,737

TSIREH, Awa, Alfonso Roybal, Cattail
Bird
Native American 1895-1955
drawings: (L) $330; (H) $2,420

TSUJI, H.
Japanese 20th cent.
paintings: (H) $1,100

TUAILLON, Louis
German 1862-1919
sculpture: (L) $1,540; (H) $9,200

TUBACH, Allan K.
American 20th cent.
paintings: (H) $770

TUCEK, Karl
Austrian b. 1889
paintings: (H) $1,650

TUCKER, Allen
American 1866-1939
paintings: (L) $308; (H) $20,900
drawings: (L) $110; (H) $1,150

TUCKER, John Wallace
British 1808-1869
paintings: (H) $1,760

TUCKERMAN, Stephen Salisbury
American 1830-1904
paintings: (L) $247; (H) $825

TUDGAY, F.
paintings: (H) $24,200

TUDGAY, F.J.
British 19th cent.
paintings: (H) $5,500

TUDGAY, I.
British 19th cent.
paintings: (H) $5,500

TUDGAY, J. K. E.
British 19th cent.
paintings: (H) $7,700

TUDGAY, J. and R.
American 19th cent.
paintings: (H) $38,500

TUDOR, Robert M.
American 20th cent.
paintings: (H) $523

TUFTS, Florence Inglesbee
American early 20th cent.
paintings: (L) $220; (H) $1,320

TUKE, Henry Scott
English 1858-1929
paintings: (L) $7,475; (H) $11,500
drawings: (H) $577

TULLAT, Luc
French b. 1895
paintings: (H) $1,540

TULLOCH, William Alexander
American b. 1887
paintings: (L) $412; (H) $2,530

TULLY, Sydney Strickland
paintings: (H) $4,400

TUNAY, J.
paintings: (H) $467

TUNNILLIE, Tayaraq
b. 1918
sculpture: (H) $1,122

TUPNELL, E.
British 20th cent.
drawings: (H) $495

TURANO, Don
American b. 1930
sculpture: (H) $550

TURAS, Jules
American 19th/20th cent.
paintings: (H) $715

TURCATO, Giulio
Italian b. 1912
paintings: (H) $6,875
drawings: (H) $632

TURCHI, Alessandro, called L'Orbetto
Italian 1578-1649
paintings: (L) $10,350; (H) $74,000

TURNBULL
b. 1880
paintings: (H) $495

TURNBULL, Gale
b. 1889
paintings: (H) $770

TURNBULL, James
1909-1976
paintings: (L) $275; (H) $450

TURNBULL, William
b. 1922
sculpture: (L) $2,640; (H) $7,187

TURNER, A.D.
paintings: (L) $330; (H) $1,210

TURNER, Alan
b. 1943
paintings: (H) $667

TURNER, Alfred M.
American 1851/52-1932
paintings: (H) $2,310
drawings: (H) $1,100

TURNER, August D.
American d. 1919
paintings: (H) $577

TURNER, C.E.
British 20th cent.
paintings: (H) $3,300

TURNER, Charles Henry
American 1848-1908
paintings: (L) $66; (H) $2,530
drawings: (L) $99; (H) $3,740

TURNER, Charles Yardley
American 1850-1919
paintings: (L) $770; (H) $6,600
drawings: (L) $248; (H) $385

TURNER, Francis Calcraft
British ac. 1782-1846
paintings: (L) $1,725; (H) $145,500

TURNER, Frank James
English ac. 1863-1875
paintings: (L) $605; (H) $2,090

TURNER, George
British 1843-1910
paintings: (L) $2,530; (H) $6,050

TURNER, George
British 19th cent.
paintings: (H) $2,750

TURNER, H.W.
19th cent.
paintings: (H) $605
drawings: (H) $165

TURNER, Helen M.
American 1858-1958
paintings: (L) $550; (H) $38,500

TURNER, J.M.W.
English 1775-1851
paintings: (H) $302
drawings: (L) $137; (H) $3,740

TURNER, Janet
American 20th cent.
drawings: (H) $605

TURNER, Joseph Mallord William
English 1775-1851
paintings: (H) $2,145
drawings: (L) $715; (H) $409,500

TURNER, Kenneth
paintings: (L) $2,990; (H) $8,360

TURNER, M.
American 20th cent.
sculpture: (H) $550

TURNER, Michael
American 20th cent.
drawings: (H) $1,100

TURNER, Raymond
American 1903-1986
sculpture: (H) $935

TURNER, Robert
American b. 1913
sculpture: (L) $1,870; (H) $6,670

TURNER, Ross Sterling
American 1847-1915
paintings: (L) $440; (H) $1,265
drawings: (L) $165; (H) $10,350

TURNER, Terrence
paintings: (H) $715

TURNER, W.
British 19th cent.
paintings: (H) $2,420

TURNER, W.H.
American 20th cent.
paintings: (H) $633

TURNER, W.L.
paintings: (H) $2,300

TURNER, William, called William
Turner of Oxford
British 1789-1862
paintings: (H) $63,000
drawings: (H) $3,025

TURNER, William L.
English 1867-1936
paintings: (H) $605

TURNEY, E.H.
paintings: (H) $575

TURNEY, Winthrop
1884-1965
paintings: (L) $880; (H) $4,125
drawings: (H) $88

TURPIN, P***
19th/20th cent.
paintings: (H) $1,380

TURRELL, James
American b. 1943
paintings: (L) $7,475; (H) $10,350
drawings: (L) $3,450; (H) $9,200

TUSQUETSY MAIGNON, Ramon
Italian d. 1904
drawings: (H) $8,800

TUTHILL, Abraham G.D.
American 1776-1843
paintings: (H) $3,850

TUTTLE, Macowin
American 1861-1935
paintings: (H) $660

TUTTLE, Richard
American b. 1941
paintings: (L) $3,300; (H) $121,000
drawings: (L) $1,955; (H) $28,600
sculpture: (L) $1,045; (H) $88,000

TUTTLEY
American 19th cent.
paintings: (H) $748

TUTUNDJIAN, Leon
French 1906-1968
drawings: (H) $1,100

TUXEN, Laurits
American 1853-1927
paintings: (H) $1,725

TVETEN, Connie
sculpture: (L) $770; (H) $1,100

TWACHTMAN, John Henry
American 1853-1902
paintings: (L) $6,050; (H) $517,000
drawings: (L) $2,530; (H) $20,700

TWELVETREES, Charles
drawings: (L) $440; (H) $2,475

TWITTY, James Watson
American b. 1916
paintings: (L) $88; (H) $660

TWOMBLY, Cy
American b. 1929
paintings: (L) $63,000; (H) $4,840,000
drawings: (L) $4,840; (H) $2,145,000

TWORKOV, Jack
Polish/American 1900-1982
paintings: (L) $2,070; (H) $88,300

TYING, Griswold
American 20th cent.
paintings: (H) $495

TYLER, Bayard Henry
American 1855-1931
paintings: (L) $220; (H) $4,675
drawings: (H) $460

TYLER, George Washington
American 1803/5-1833
paintings: (H) $1,210

TYLER, James Gale
American 1855-1931
paintings: (L) $220; (H) $19,550
drawings: (L) $275; (H) $1,045

TYLER, Timmothy Carrol
paintings: (H) $4,000

TYLER, W.R.
American 1825-1896
paintings: (L) $220; (H) $1,485

TYLER, William
English d. 1801
sculpture: (H) $14,950

TYLER, William R.
American 1825-1896
paintings: (L) $460; (H) $3,850

TYNDALE, Thomas Nicholson
British 19th/20th cent.
drawings: (L) $550; (H) $805

TYNDALE, Walter
British 1855-1943
paintings: (H) $863
drawings: (L) $275; (H) $660

TYNER, William P.
American 20th cent.
drawings: (L) $440; (H) $550

TYNG, Griswold
b. 1883
paintings: (L) $990; (H) $1,650
drawings: (H) $2,640

TYNG, Margaret Fuller
American 20th cent.
paintings: (H) $2,640

TYPAGSNE
Russian 19th cent.
sculpture: (H) $1,610

TYSCHLER, Alexander
contemporary
drawings: (H) $660

TYSON, Carroll
American 1878-1956
paintings: (L) $550; (H) $6,600
drawings: (L) $550; (H) $1,540

TZEYTLINE, Leon
Russian 19th/20th cent.
paintings: (H) $605
drawings: (L) $247; (H) $467

UBEDA, Augustin
Spanish b. 1925
paintings: (L) $660; (H) $9,900

UDALTSOVA, N.
Russian 19th/20th cent.
drawings: (H) $1,035

UDEN, Lucas van
Flemish 1595-1672/1673
paintings: (L) $6,900; (H) $68,500

UDVARY, Paul
paintings: (H) $748

UECKER, Gunther
German b. 1930
paintings: (H) $37,375
drawings: (H) $35,650
sculpture: (L) $22,000; (H) $38,500

UFER, Walter
American 1876-1936
paintings: (L) $5,175; (H) $332,500

UGALDE, Manuel
b. Peru 1819 d. 1881
paintings: (H) $14,300

UGO, Antonio
Italian b. 1870
sculpture: (H) $3,335

UGUCCIONE, Irene
French/Italian 19th cent.
paintings: (H) $2,750

UHL, S. Jerome
American 1842-1916
paintings: (H) $632

UHLE, Albert Bernard
American 1847-1930
paintings: (L) $468; (H) $687

ULFT, Jacob van der
Dutch 1627-1689
drawings: (H) $13,800

ULI, Julius
German b. 1897
sculpture: (H) $3,025

ULIANOFF, Vsevolod
American 1880-1940
paintings: (H) $1,210

ULLMAN, Eugene Paul
American 1877-1953
paintings: (H) $7,150

ULLMAN, Max
paintings: (H) $495

ULLMAN, Raoul Andre
French b. 1867
paintings: (H) $550

ULLMANN, Charles
Scandinavian 19th cent.
paintings: (L) $2,200; (H) $5,280

ULLOA, Victor
paintings: (H) $3,850

ULMANN, Charles
German/Swedish 19th cent.
paintings: (L) $1,380; (H) $3,300

ULMANN, Raoul Andre
French 1867-1907
paintings: (H) $690

ULP, Clifford
paintings: (H) $1,980

ULRICH, Friedrich
German 1750?-1808
paintings: (H) $3,025

ULTHUES, T.
sculpture: (H) $1,840

UMBRICHT, Honore Louis
French b. 1860
paintings: (H) $23,000

UMLAUF, Charles
American b. 1911
drawings: (L) $193; (H) $220
sculpture: (H) $2,200

UNBEREIT, Paul
German/Austrian 1884-1937
paintings: (L) $330; (H) $2,990

UNDERHILL
American 20th cent.
paintings: (H) $633

UNDERHILL, William
English 19th cent.
paintings: (H) $2,300

UNDERWOOD, Clarence Frederick
American 1871-1929
paintings: (H) $1,035
drawings: (H) $1,380

UNDERWOOD, Leon
English b. 1890
paintings: (H) $2,310
sculpture: (H) $2,530

UNG NO, Lee
1905-1989
drawings: (H) $36,800

UNGER, Max
German 1854-1918
sculpture: (H) $1,210

UNGERER, Tomi
b. 1931
drawings: (L) $715; (H) $880

UNTERBERGER, Fr.
German 19th/20th cent.
paintings: (H) $660

UNTERBERGER, Franz Richard
Belgian 1838-1902
paintings: (L) $8,800; (H) $60,250

UNTERBERGER, J.B.
German 19th cent.
paintings: (H) $605

UPHUES, Josef
German 1850-1911
sculpture: (L) $330; (H) $2,645

UPHUES, T.
French 19th/20th cent.
sculpture: (H) $1,093

UPJOHN, Anna Milo
American d. 1951
paintings: (L) $127; (H) $6,600
drawings: (L) $743; (H) $880

UPPINK, Willem
Dutch 1757-1849
paintings: (L) $35,650; (H) $35,650

URBAN, Hermann
German 1866-1946
paintings: (H) $1,150

URBAN, L.
German/Austrian 19th/20th cent.
paintings: (H) $1,045

URBANI, Marin
ac. late 18th cent.
drawings: (H) $920

URBIETA, Jesus
b. 1959
paintings: (L) $9,200; (H) $9,200

URBINO, W.
19th cent.
paintings: (H) $3,163

URIA Y URIA, Jose
Spanish 19th cent.
paintings: (H) $23,575

URIANO
sculpture: (H) $1,150

URIBURU, Nicolas Garcia
paintings: (H) $2,415

URLAUB, Henrietta
18th/19th cent.
drawings: (H) $5,175

URSELINCX, Johannes
Dutch 1598/9-1664
paintings: (H) $23,575

URUETA, Cordelia
Mexican b. 1908
paintings: (L) $16,500; (H) $27,500
drawings: (H) $4,025

URY, Adolph Muller
American 1868-1947
paintings: (H) $495

UTRECHT, Adriaen van
Flemish 1599-1652
paintings: (L) $68,500; (H) $134,500

UTRECHT, Adriaen van and Jan COSSIERS
paintings: (H) $37,950

UTRILLO, Lucie Valore
paintings: (H) $3,025

UTRILLO, Maurice
French 1883-1955
paintings: (L) $8,625; (H) $880,000
drawings: (L) $275; (H) $132,000

UTZ, Thornton
b. 1914
paintings: (H) $1,650
drawings: (H) $605

VAARBERG, H.
Dutch 19th cent.
paintings: (H) $5,280

VAARBERG, Johannes Christoffel
Dutch 1825-1871
paintings: (H) $2,530

VAARBERGH, H.
Continental 19th/20th cent.
paintings: (L) $633; (H) $770

VAARDT, Jan van der
Dutch 1647-1721
paintings: (H) $8,250

VABACCI, O.
sculpture: (H) $825

VACANO, L.
19th cent.
paintings: (H) $1,265

VACATKO, Ludvig
Austrian 19th/20th cent.
paintings: (H) $6,900

VACCARO, Andrea
Italian 1598(?)-1670
paintings: (L) $7,150; (H) $38,500

VACCARO, Nicola
Italian 1637-1717
paintings: (H) $41,250

VACHA, Rudolf
Czechoslovakian b. 1860
paintings: (H) $880
drawings: (H) $275

VADAHC
American early 20th cent.
paintings: (H) $2,530

VADDER, L. de
paintings: (H) $2,640

VADENBERGE, Peter
contemporary
sculpture: (H) $6,325

VAEA
Tahitian b. 1929
sculpture: (H) $858

VAERENBERGH, G.V.
European 19th/20th cent.
sculpture: (H) $2,420

VAGANO, L.
Italian 19th/20th cent.
paintings: (H) $605

VAGO, Sandor
Hungarian/American b. 1887
paintings: (L) $495; (H) $660
drawings: (L) $11; (H) $33

VAIL, Eugene Lawrence
American 1857-1934
paintings: (L) $440; (H) $3,220
drawings: (H) $127

VAIL, Pegeen
d. 1966
paintings: (H) $632
drawings: (L) $373; (H) $632

VAILLANT, Wallerand
Dutch 1623-1677
paintings: (L) $41,400; (H) $41,800

VAISMAN, Meyer
b. Venezuela 1960
paintings: (L) $5,750; (H) $44,000
sculpture: (L) $7,475; (H) $34,500

VALADE, J***
French 19th cent.
paintings: (H) $2,070

VALADIER, Giuseppe
1762-1834
drawings: (H) $9,200

VALADON, Suzanne
French 1865-1938
paintings: (L) $17,250; (H) $110,000
drawings: (L) $6,875; (H) $28,750

VALAPERTA, Francesco
Italian 1836-1908
paintings: (H) $2,640

VALCIN, Gerard
Haitian b. 1923
paintings: (L) $825; (H) $16,500

VALCKENBORCH, Lucas van
Dutch 1535-1597
paintings: (H) $321,500

VALDEN, D. van der
Dutch 20th cent.
paintings: (L) $440; (H) $467

VALDENUIT, Thomas Bluget de
French 1763-1846
drawings: (L) $4,950; (H) $16,100

VALDES LEAL, Juan de
Spanish 1622-1690
paintings: (L) $6,600; (H) $70,700

VALDIVIESO, Raul
Chilean b. 1931
sculpture: (H) $1,150

VALENCIA, Manuel
American 1856-1935/36
paintings: (L) $330; (H) $6,050

VALENKAMPH, Theodore V.C.
American 1868-1924
paintings: (L) $261; (H) $4,125
drawings: (L) $192; (H) $413

VALENTE, P.
paintings: (H) $1,100

VALENTIEN, Albert R.
1862-1925
drawings: (H) $5,750

VALENTIN, L*** di
sculpture: (L) $633; (H) $1,265

VALENTIN DE BOULOGNE
French 1591-1632
paintings: (H) $88,000

VALENTINE, Francis Barker
American b. 1897
paintings: (H) $522

VALENTINI, Valentino
Italian b. 1858
paintings: (H) $880

VALENTINO, Giovanni Domencio
Roman ac. late 17th cent.
paintings: (H) $1,980

VALENZI, ***von
19th cent.
paintings: (H) $1,320

VALERI, Prevot
Continental 19th cent.
paintings: (L) $550; (H) $1,650

VALERI, Silvestro
Italian 1814-1902
drawings: (H) $2,640

VALERIO, F.F.
American 20th cent.
paintings: (H) $990

VALERIO, Ruth
American contemporary
paintings: (H) $1,064

VALERIO, Theodore
French 1819-1879
paintings: (L) $288; (H) $4,400
drawings: (L) $286; (H) $605

VALERO, Ricardo
French 19th cent.
paintings: (H) $2,875

VALETTA, Swan Malinowski
drawings: (H) $920

VALETTE, Rene
drawings: (H) $660

VALHANTONES, Anthony
American 20th cent.
sculpture: (H) $546

VALK, Hendrik de
Dutch 17th cent.
paintings: (L) $4,025; (H) $30,800

VALK, J.M. Vander
paintings: (H) $1,540

VALKENBURG, Hendrik
Dutch 1826-1896
drawings: (L) $550; (H) $1,840

VALLA, G.
Continental School 19th cent.
paintings: (H) $1,380

VALLAYER-COSTER, Anne
French 1744-1818
paintings: (H) $57,750

VALLE, Pietro della
Italian 19th cent.
paintings: (H) $4,400

VALLE, Rosina Becker Do
paintings: (H) $1,650

VALLEE, Etienne Maxime
French ac. 1873-1881
paintings: (L) $1,495; (H) $3,450

VALLEE, Ludovic
paintings: (L) $4,600; (H) $5,500

VALLEJO, Boris
20th cent.
paintings: (L) $1,430; (H) $8,250
drawings: (L) $220; (H) $2,185

VALLEJO, Don Francisco Antonio
Mexican ac. 1752-1784
paintings: (H) $33,000

VALLEPERAS, Eusebio
Spanish b. 1827
paintings: (H) $1,980

VALLET, Jean Emile
French d. 1899
paintings: (L) $4,400; (H) $4,400

VALLET-BISSON, Frederique
French b. 1865
paintings: (H) $1,610
drawings: (H) $1,265

VALLEZ, E.
French School 19th cent.
paintings: (H) $1,210

VALLIEN, Bertil
b. Sweden 1938
sculpture: (L) $1,035; (H) $3,300

VALLIN, Jacques Antoine
French 1760-1831
paintings: (H) $10,925

VALLOIS, Paul Felix
French 19th cent.
paintings: (L) $1,610; (H) $3,850

VALLON, Alexis
paintings: (H) $725

VALLORZ, Paolo
Italian b. 1931
paintings: (L) $230; (H) $10,925

VALLS, Ernesto
Spanish 19th/20th cent.
paintings: (L) $9,900; (H) $27,500

VALMER, Charles H.
paintings: (H) $770

VALMIER, Georges
French 1885-1937
paintings: (L) $31,050; (H) $57,500
drawings: (L) $2,200; (H) $7,700

VALMINCK, Maurice de
French 1876-1958
drawings: (H) $12,100

VALMONT, P.
French 19th/20th cent.
paintings: (H) $3,450

VALTAT, Louis
Frènch 1869-1952
paintings: (L) $1,150; (H) $181,500
drawings: (L) $247; (H) $4,312
sculpture: (L) $5,750; (H) $22,000

VALTIER, Gerard
French 20th cent.
paintings: (L) $2,090; (H) $3,190

VALTON
sculpture: (L) $467; (H) $2,750

VALTON
French 20th cent.
sculpture: (H) $550

VALTON, Charles
French 1851-1918
sculpture: (L) $550; (H) $6,050

VAN BOSKERCK, Robert Ward
American 1855-1932
paintings: (H) $1,430

VAN DER VAN, A.
Dutch 19th cent.
paintings: (H) $605

VAN DER VEER, Mary
American b. 1865
paintings: (H) $1,380

VAN DER WEYDEN, Harry
American/British b. 1868
paintings: (L) $880; (H) $990
drawings: (H) $403

VAN EVEREN, Jay
American 1875-1947
drawings: (H) $1,100

VAN GANA
20th cent.
drawings: (H) $500

VAN LAER, Alexander T.
American 1857-1920
paintings: (L) $165; (H) $770

VAN ROEKENS, Paulette, Mrs. Arthur
Meltzer
American b. 1896
paintings: (H) $5,300

VAN RYDER, Jack
American 1898-1968
paintings: (H) $550

VAN SINCLAIR, Gerrit
American 1890-1955
paintings: (H) $605

VAN TYNE, Peter
American b. 1857
paintings: (L) $358; (H) $1,100

VAN VLECK, Natalie
paintings: (L) $55; (H) $2,200
drawings: (L) $49; (H) $627

VAN ZANDT, William
American 19th/20th cent.
paintings: (H) $3,575

VANBERGER, Rubin
20th cent.
paintings: (H) $4,400

VANCE, Fredrick Nelson
paintings: (H) $4,400

VANDENBERGE, Peter
American b. Holland 1935
paintings: (H) $575
sculpture: (H) $4,888

VANDERBANCK, John
English c. 1694-1739
paintings: (L) $825; (H) $12,100

VANDERBANK, M.
British 18th c.
paintings: (H) $2,200

VANDERBILT, Gloria
American 20th cent.
paintings: (H) $660

VANDERHOOF, Mabell
paintings: (L) $660; (H) $825

VANDERLYN, John
American 1776-1852
paintings: (L) $1,000; (H) $1,100
drawings: (H) $7,150

Vargas

Luscious, tantalizing, scantily clad, perfectly shaped, fictional females are the primary subjects of Alberto Vargas's (1896-1983) oeuvre. Vargas was born in Peru, the son of a successful photographer and trained briefly as his father's assistant. When he was 15 he was sent to Europe to study, and in 1916 amidst World War I, he traveled to New York. Vargas worked briefly at Butterick Patterns where he drew hats and heads. Soon he was freelancing watercolors of the saucy sexy beauties he had seen in Paris and New York at the Ziegfeld Follies. The Depression years were difficult. He did some advertising art: hairstyle illustrations for *Harper's Bazaar* and a series of full-length movie-star portraits for Hellman's mayonnaise. In 1934 he began working in the art departments of Hollywood studios, painting set designs and portraits, but in 1939, when he participated in a union walkout he was blackballed. Vargas left California to look for work. At the time *Esquire* magazine was having contract disputes with their cartoonist and chief artist George Petty and was looking for a replacement. Vargas was hired on a "work for hire" basis. He was to be paid a salary, and the artwork belonged to *Esquire*. Just before the first femme fatale appeared in print, the publisher called Vargas and said he thought that "Varga girl" sounded more euphonious than "Vargas girl." The signature was changed, and almost all Vargas's *Esquire* artwork had the type slug Varga. His freelance work during this period was hand-signed Varga. The Varga Girl was an instantaneous hit; two months later the first Varga calendar sold 320,000 copies. Six years later sales of the calendar had reached 3 million copies! A 1944 contract that Vargas signed, without legal advice, gave *Esquire* all rights to the name "Varga, Varga Girls, or

Varga, Esquire." By April 1946 *Esquire* and Vargas were in an acrimonious lawsuit. *Esquire* won the rights to the name Varga and then changed the name of the Varga Girl to the *Esquire* Girl. Alberto Vargas was out of a job and the rights to the Varga name. His career had a second life when *Playboy* magazine did a feature on Vargas in 1957, and by 1960 he had become a regular contributor. Vargas worked for *Playboy* until he was 80 years old, contributing 152 watercolors. The *Playboy* girls Vargas painted were a variation of the Varga girl but younger (19 vs. 25 years) and more scantily clad, and just as popular. The signature on the *Playboy* paintings is Vargas, with the "s" reinstated. The eroticism of Vargas's paintings have a strong appeal, and private sale prices have been reported as high as $100,000. This undated watercolor and pencil drawing sold for $5,175 at Skinner's in Bolton, Massachusetts. (Alberto Vargas, *Reverie*, watercolor and graphite on paper board, 27½ x 10½ inches, Skinner, September 9, 1994, $5,175)

VANDERVELDE, Hanny
  paintings: (H) $990
VANDEVERDONCK, Franz
  Belgian 19th cent.
  paintings: (L) $1,500; (H) $3,163
VANETTEN, Sheldon
  American
  paintings: (H) $750
VANETTI
  Italian 19th cent.
  paintings: (H) $632
VANHAGENDOREN, H.
  Dutch 19th cent.
  paintings: (H) $9,488
VANLAER, Alexander Theobald
  1857-1920
  paintings: (H) $990
VANNINI, Ottavio
  Italian 1585-1643
  paintings: (H) $55,000
VANNUTELLI, Scipione
  Italian 1834-1894
  paintings: (L) $4,950; (H) $6,325
VANTER, Wilhelm Vander
  Dutch 19th cent.
  paintings: (H) $5,280
VANTONGERLOO, Georges
  Belgian 1886-1965
  paintings: (H) $2,200
VANTORE, Erik Mogens Christian
  Danish b. 1895
  paintings: (H) $20,900

VARADY, Frederic
  American b. 1908
  drawings: (L) $330; (H) $880
VARELA, Abigail
  Venezuelan b. 1948
  sculpture: (L) $7,700; (H) $55,000
VARENNE, Henry Frederic
  French 1860-1933
  sculpture: (H) $9,775
VARESE, Edgard
  French 1888-1965
  paintings: (L) $660; (H) $1,210
  drawings: (L) $413; (H) $660
VARGAS, Alberto
  American 1896-1983
  paintings: (H) $770
  drawings: (L) $2,750; (H) $35,750
VARGAS, Ismael
  Mexican b. 1945
  paintings: (L) $9,775; (H) $14,950
VARIAN, Dorothy
  American b. 1895
  paintings: (L) $110; (H) $880
VARIAN, George Edmund
  American 1865-1923
  paintings: (H) $4,370
VARLEY, Edgar John
  English ac. 1861-1887, d. 1888
  drawings: (H) $935
VARLEY, Frederick Horsman
  Canadian 1881-1969
  paintings: (L) $8,250; (H) $18,700
  drawings: (L) $1,760; (H) $8,800

VARLEY, John
drawings: (L) $467; (H) $2,100

VARLEY, John, Jr.
English ac. 1870-1896; d. c. 1899
paintings: (L) $715; (H) $4,600
drawings: (H) $275

VARLEY, John, Sr.
British 1778-1842
paintings: (H) $5,175
drawings: (L) $220; (H) $1,610

VARMIER, Pierre H.L.
sculpture: (H) $2,475

VARNIER
sculpture: (H) $1,725

VARO, Remedios
Mexican, b. Spain 1908-1963
paintings: (L) $60,500; (H) $605,000
drawings: (L) $21,850; (H) $48,400

VARONI, Giovanni
Austrian 1832-1910
paintings: (H) $3,220

VARRIALE, W. Stella
American b. 1927
paintings: (H) $1,760

VASA
Yugoslav/American b. 1933
sculpture: (L) $230; (H) $1,495

VASARELY, Victor
French b. Hungary 1908
paintings: (L) $248; (H) $46,750
drawings: (L) $132; (H) $27,500
sculpture: (L) $6,050; (H) $7,700

VASARI, Antone
paintings: (H) $1,200

VASARRI, Emilio
Italian ac. 1900-1904
paintings: (H) $34,100

VASIDIV, N.
paintings: (H) $1,430

VASQUEZ SAEZ, Raul
b. 1954
paintings: (H) $9,775

VASQUEZ Y UBEDA, Carlos
Spanish ac. 1889-1907
paintings: (H) $9,625

VASSALO, Philip
drawings: (H) $5,500

VASSANT, G.
French 20th cent.
paintings: (H) $495

VASSE, Louis Claude
French 1716-1772
sculpture: (H) $22,000

VASSILIEFF, Marie
Russian 1884-1957
paintings: (L) $483; (H) $920
drawings: (H) $920

VASSILIEFF, Nicolai
Russian/American 1892-1970
paintings: (H) $1,840

VASSILIEV, Oleg
Russian b. 1931
paintings: (H) $7,150

VASSOS, John
American b. 1898
paintings: (H) $2,760
drawings: (L) $1,725; (H) $2,645

VASUDEVAN
Indian contemporary
paintings: (L) $1,610; (H) $1,610

VASZARY, Janos
paintings: (H) $1,150

VASZARY, Jean
drawings: (H) $920

VATIN, E.
drawings: (H) $3,300

VAUCHELET, Theophile Auguste
French 1802-1873
paintings: (H) $19,800

VAUCORBEIL, Maurice Romberg de
French 19th cent.
drawings: (L) $990; (H) $5,750

VAUGHAN, Keith
English b. 1912
paintings: (L) $4,025; (H) $6,900

VAUQUELIN, Alphonse de
French 19th cent.
paintings: (H) $2,760

VAUQUELIN, Rene
French 19th cent.
paintings: (H) $6,875

VAUTHIER, Pierre Louis Leger
French 1845-1916
paintings: (L) $7,475; (H) $17,250

VAUTIER, B.
German 1829-1898
paintings: (H) $16,500

VAUTIER, J.C.
19th/20th cent.
paintings: (L) $715; (H) $1,100

VAVAK, Joseph
American b. 1899
paintings: (H) $2,300

VAVRA, Frank
American 1898-1967
paintings: (H) $2,200

VAVRINA
paintings: (L) $1,760; (H) $3,740

VAVRINA, Charles
American b. 1928
paintings: (H) $3,850

VAWTER, William John
American b. 1871
paintings: (H) $935

VAYANA, Nunzio
b. Italy d. U.S. 1960
paintings: (L) $110; (H) $605

VAZQUEZ, Pedro Ramirez
sculpture: (H) $1,093

VEAUX CLEMENTS, Gabrielle de
paintings: (H) $1,210

VECSEY
East European 20th cent.
paintings: (H) $550

VEDDER, Elihu
American 1836-1923
paintings: (L) $605; (H) $35,650
drawings: (L) $88; (H) $2,860

VEEDER, Susan C. Austin
drawings: (H) $10,780

VEEN, Otto van, and studio
1556-1625
paintings: (H) $9,775

VEEN, Pieter van
Flemish 1563-1629
paintings: (L) $660; (H) $30,800

VEEN, Stuyvesant van
American b. 1910
paintings: (H) $825
drawings: (L) $345; (H) $633

VEGA, Jorge de la
b. Argentina 1930 d. 1971
paintings: (L) $15,400; (H) $17,600
drawings: (H) $2,875

VEGA Y MUNOZ, Pedro
Spanish 19th cent.
paintings: (H) $2,300

VEIT, H.
German 19th cent.
paintings: (H) $825

VEITH, Edouard
Austrian 1856-1925
paintings: (L) $2,530; (H) $13,200

VELA, Alberto R.
Mexican b. 1920
paintings: (L) $935; (H) $1,705

VELARDE, Pablita, Tse Tsan, Golden Dawn
Santa Clara Pueblo b. 1918
drawings: (L) $1,093; (H) $2,990

VELASCO, Jose Maria
Mexican 1840-1912
paintings: (L) $20,900; (H) $2,420,000
drawings: (L) $3,450; (H) $25,300

VELASQUEZ, Eugenio Lucas
Spanish 1824-1870
paintings: (L) $1,150; (H) $8,338

VELASQUEZ, Jose Antonio
Honduran 1906-1985
paintings: (L) $2,300; (H) $4,830

VELDE, Adriaen van de
Dutch 1636-1672
paintings: (L) $6,900; (H) $96,000

VELDE, Bram van
Dutch 1895-1981
drawings: (L) $57,500; (H) $74,000

VELDE, Esaias van de, the elder
Dutch 1590/91-1630
paintings: (H) $68,500
drawings: (L) $3,738; (H) $5,750

VELDE, Geer van
Dutch b. 1898
paintings: (H) $22,000
drawings: (H) $5,500

VELDE, Hanny van der
American b. 1868
paintings: (L) $345; (H) $2,875

VELDE, Pieter van de
1634-1687
paintings: (L) $1,725; (H) $14,950

VELDE, Willem van de, the elder
Dutch 1611-1693
drawings: (H) $1,925

VELDE, Willem van de, the younger
Dutch 1633-1707
paintings: (L) $112,500; (H) $200,500
drawings: (L) $990; (H) $15,400

VELDE, Willem van de, the younger
studio of
Dutch 17th cent.
paintings: (H) $14,300

VELICKOVIC, Vladimir
b. Yugoslavia 1935
paintings: (H) $1,540

VELIER, E.
French 19th cent.
paintings: (H) $7,700

VELLAY
drawings: (H) $1,265

VELTEN, Wilhelm
Russian 1847-1929
paintings: (L) $1,980; (H) $23,100

VELY, Anatole
French 1838-1882
paintings: (H) $1,210

VENARD, C.
paintings: (H) $1,150

VENARD, Claude
French b. 1913
paintings: (L) $13; (H) $14,300
sculpture: (H) $4,400

VENDITTI, Jerry
American b. 1942
paintings: (L) $660; (H) $5,500

VENET, Bernar
French b. 1941
drawings: (L) $345; (H) $4,312

VENET, F.E.
19th cent.
paintings: (H) $920

VENITIEN
paintings: (H) $715

VENNE, Adolf van der
Austrian 1828-1911
paintings: (L) $805; (H) $10,450

VENNE, Adriaen van de
Dutch 1589-1662
paintings: (L) $3,850; (H) $44,000

VENNE, Fritz van der
German c. 1900
paintings: (L) $825; (H) $3,450

VENNE, Pseudo Adriaen van de
17th cent.
paintings: (H) $4,400

VENNEMAN, Charles, Karel
Ferdinand
Flemish 1802-1875
paintings: (L) $440; (H) $8,050

VENTNOR, Arthur
British 19th/20th cent.
paintings: (H) $2,750

VERA Y CALVO, Juan Antonio
Spanish 19th cent.
paintings: (L) $805; (H) $1,430

VERAGE, F.
paintings: (L) $460; (H) $522

VERBEECK, Francois Xavier Henri
1686-1755
paintings: (H) $2,420

VERBEECK, Pieter Cornelisz.
c. 1610/15-c. 1652/4
paintings: (H) $8,250

VERBEET, Gijsberta
Dutch 1838-1916
paintings: (H) $8,250

VERBOCKHOVEN, Eugene and
Augustus ORTMANS
paintings: (H) $5,500

VERBOECKHOVEN, Charles Louis, I
Belgian 1802-1889
paintings: (H) $4,370

VERBOECKHOVEN, Eugene Joseph
Belgian 1798/99-1881
paintings: (L) $220; (H) $60,250
drawings: (L) $1,210; (H) $1,430

VERBOECKHOVEN, Eugene Joseph
and Alexander Joseph DAIWAILLE
19th cent.
paintings: (H) $9,200

VERBOECKHOVEN, Eugene Joseph
and Frans KEELHOFF
18th/19th cent.
paintings: (H) $5,225

VERBOECKHOVEN, Eugene and
Edouard de VIGNE
Belgian 19th cent.
paintings: (H) $28,750

VERBOECKHOVEN, Eugene and
Frans KEELHOFF
Belgian 19th cent.
paintings: (H) $20,900

VERBOECKHOVEN, Eugene and
Willem ROELOFS
Belgian/Dutch ac. 19th cent.
paintings: (H) $35,200

VERBOECKHOVEN, Louis
Belgian 1802-1889
paintings: (L) $2,990; (H) $17,250

VERBOOM, Adriaen Hendriksz.
Dutch c. 1628-1670
paintings: (L) $6,325; (H) $18,400
drawings: (H) $30,800

VERBRUGGEN, Gaspar Pieter, the
elder
Flemish 1635-1687
paintings: (L) $7,150; (H) $17,250

VERBRUGGEN, Gaspar Pieter, the
younger
Flemish 1664-1730
paintings: (L) $8,800; (H) $68,500

VERBRUGGEN, Henri
Continental 19th cent.
paintings: (H) $2,530

VERBRUGGEN, Jan
Dutch 1712-c. 1780
paintings: (H) $17,250

VERBUECKEN, J.
Continental 19th cent.
paintings: (H) $8,800

VERBURGH, Dionys
Dutch 1655-1722
paintings: (L) $14,300; (H) $17,600

VERBURGH, J.C.
Dutch 19th/20th cent.
paintings: (H) $550

VERBUYS, Arnold
1645-1729
paintings: (H) $862

VERDI, S.
paintings: (H) $880

VERDIER, Francois
French 1651-1730
drawings: (L) $660; (H) $1,320

VERDIER, H.
French 19th cent.
paintings: (L) $1,705; (H) $2,640

VERDIER, Jean
French 1889-1976
paintings: (L) $132; (H) $1,380

VERDIER, Jules Victor
French b. 1862
paintings: (L) $440; (H) $1,760

VERDILHAN, Mathieu
French 1875-1928
drawings: (L) $143; (H) $550

VERDOEL, Adriaen
Dutch c. 1620-after 1695
paintings: (H) $8,050

VERDUN, Raymond Jean
French 19th cent.
paintings: (H) $2,200

VERDUSSEN, Jan Peeter
Flemish c. 1700-1763
paintings: (H) $23,000

VERDUSSEN, Paul
Continental 19th cent.
paintings: (H) $5,500

VERELST, John
ac. 1698-1734
paintings: (H) $3,520

VERELST, Pieter
Dutch 1618-after 1671
paintings: (L) $14,950; (H) $220,000

VERELST, Simon Pietersz.
Dutch 1644-1721
paintings: (L) $17,250; (H) $28,600

VERETSHCHAGIN, Vassily Petrovich
Russian 19th cent.
paintings: (L) $1,725; (H) $9,775

VERGEZ, Eugene
French 19th cent.
paintings: (H) $2,588

VERGNE, Jean Louis
French b. 1929
paintings: (L) $660; (H) $990

VERHAECHT, Tobias
Flemish 1561-1631
paintings: (H) $85,000

VERHAS, Frans
Belgian 1827-1897
paintings: (L) $8,050; (H) $13,200

VERHAS, Jan Francois
Belgian 1834-1896
paintings: (H) $17,250

VERHEYDEN, Francois
Belgian 1806-1890(?)
paintings: (L) $357; (H) $15,400

VERHEYDEN, Francois Isidore
Belgian/American b. 1880
paintings: (H) $1,380

VERHEYEN, Jan Hendrick
1778-1846
paintings: (H) $13,800

VERHEYEN, L.
Belgian(?) 20th cent.
paintings: (H) $522

VERHOESEN, Albertus
Dutch 1806-1881
paintings: (L) $1,380; (H) $9,488

VERHOEVEN-BALL, Adrien Joseph
Belgian 1824-1882
paintings: (L) $1,380; (H) $17,250

VERITY, Colin
British 20th cent.
paintings: (L) $2,530; (H) $3,910

VERKADE, Kies
Dutch 20th cent.
sculpture: (L) $1,320; (H) $16,500

VERKOLJE, Nicolaes
Dutch 1673-1746
paintings: (H) $28,750

VERLOT, O.
French 19th/20th cent.
paintings: (H) $2,200

VERMEER, Jan van der Meer the younger
Dutch 1656-1705
paintings: (H) $14,375

VERMEER, Jan van Haarlem, the elder
Dutch 1628-1691
paintings: (H) $7,150

VERMEER VAN HAARLEM,
Johannes, the elder
1628-1691
paintings: (H) $4,950

VERMEHREN, Johan Frederick Nikolai
Danish 1823-1910
paintings: (H) $14,950

VERMEHREN, Sophus
Danish b. 1866
paintings: (H) $715

VERMEULEN, Andries
Dutch 1763-1814
paintings: (L) $1,650; (H) $63,800
drawings: (H) $990

VERMEULEN, Jan
Dutch ac. 1638-1674
paintings: (H) $55,200

VERMEULEN, M.
Dutch 19th/20th cent.
paintings: (L) $3,575; (H) $9,200

VERMOND, G.
Continental School 19th cent.
paintings: (H) $6,900

VERMONT, Henri
French b. 1879
paintings: (H) $3,737

VERMORCKEN, Berthe
Belgian 19th cent.
paintings: (H) $1,100

VERMORCKEN, Frederic Marie
Belgian b. 1860
paintings: (H) $4,180

VERNE, Alfred
American 1850-1910
paintings: (H) $2,860

VERNER, Elizabeth O'Neill
American 1883/84-1979
paintings: (H) $8,250
drawings: (L) $3,575; (H) $18,700

VERNER, Frederick Arthur
Canadian 1836-1928
paintings: (L) $4,620; (H) $30,800
drawings: (L) $275; (H) $9,350

VERNET, Antoine Charles Horace
French 1758-1836
paintings: (H) $3,025
drawings: (H) $825

VERNET, Carle, studio of
French 19th cent.
drawings: (H) $550

VERNET, Claude Joseph
French 1712/14-1789
paintings: (L) $2,420; (H) $1,540,000
drawings: (H) $16,500

VERNET, Horace
French 1789-1863
paintings: (L) $3,300; (H) $495,000

VERNIER, Emile Louis
French 1829-1887
paintings: (L) $1,430; (H) $13,800

VERNIER, J.
paintings: (L) $880; (H) $4,125

VERNON, A.
Continental School 19th cent.
paintings: (H) $2,990

VERNON, Alexandre Rene
French 1826-1897
paintings: (H) $6,900

VERNON, Arthur Longley
British ac. 1871-1922
paintings: (L) $1,210; (H) $4,600

VERNON, C.H.
19th cent.
paintings: (H) $2,070

VERNON, Della
American 1876-1962
paintings: (H) $2,090

VERNON, Emile
British ac. 1904
paintings: (L) $220; (H) $60,250

VERNON, Paul
French 19th cent.
paintings: (L) $770; (H) $1,100

VERNON, W.H.
British 1820-1909
paintings: (H) $1,650

VERON, A.L.
French 19th cent.
paintings: (H) $4,025

VERON, Alexandre Rene
French 1826-1897
paintings: (L) $4,025; (H) $20,900
drawings: (H) $207

VERON, P.
French School 19th/20th cent.
drawings: (H) $825

VERONESE, Paolo CALIARI
Italian 1528-1588
paintings: (L) $176,000; (H) $1,045,000
drawings: (L) $22,000; (H) $42,900

VERONESE, Paolo CALIARI studio of
Italian 16th cent.
paintings: (H) $46,000

VERONESE, Zenone
1484-1552/54
paintings: (H) $51,750

VERPILLEUX, Emile Antoine
British b. 1888
paintings: (H) $3,105

VERRIER, M. Le
French ac. 1918-1930
sculpture: (L) $192; (H) $3,575

VERROCHIO
sculpture: (H) $3,575

VERSCHNEIDER, Jean
French 1872-1943
sculpture: (L) $1,210; (H) $7,188

VERSCHURING, Hendrik
Dutch 1627-1690
paintings: (L) $4,312; (H) $15,400

VERSCHURR, Cornelius
paintings: (H) $3,300

VERSCHUUR, Wouterus
Dutch 1812-1874
paintings: (L) $3,080; (H) $178,500

VERSPRONCK, Johannes Cornelisz
Dutch 1597-1662
paintings: (H) $25,300

VERSTEEGH, Miachiel
1756-1843
paintings: (H) $3,450

VERTANGEN, Daniel
Dutch c. 1598-before 1684
paintings: (L) $5,750; (H) $6,325

VERTES, Marcel
French 1895-1961
paintings: (L) $1,430; (H) $6,050
drawings: (L) $187; (H) $1,650

VERTIN, Pieter Gerardus
Dutch 1819-1893
paintings: (L) $743; (H) $4,290

VERTUNNI, Achille
Italian 1826-1897
paintings: (L) $990; (H) $12,650

VERVEER, Elchanon
Dutch 1826-1900
paintings: (L) $440; (H) $3,300

VERWEE, Alfred
Belgian b. 1895
paintings: (H) $1,210

VERWEE, Charles Louis
Belgian 19th cent.
paintings: (L) $5,175; (H) $14,950

VERWEE, Louis Pierre
Belgian 1807-1877
paintings: (L) $3,025; (H) $13,200

VERWEE, Louis Pierre and Eugene
VERBOECKHOVEN
Belgian 17th cent.
paintings: (L) $8,510; (H) $16,500

VERWEY, Klees
Dutch b. 1900
drawings: (H) $2,200

VERWORNER, Enrico Ludolf
German 1867-1927
paintings: (H) $4,600

VESCOVI, A.
Italian 19th cent.
paintings: (H) $825

VESIN, Jaroslav Fr. Julius
Bulgarian d. 1915
paintings: (L) $1,100; (H) $11,500

VESPIGNIANI, Renzo
Italian b. 1924
paintings: (H) $8,800
drawings: (H) $1,610

VESS, Charles
drawings: (H) $3,575

VESTER, Gesina and Jean RUYTEN
paintings: (H) $2,185

VESTER, Willem
Dutch 1824-1871
paintings: (L) $13,800; (H) $16,100

VESTIER, Antoine
French 1740-1824
paintings: (H) $2,800

VEUIER-ALEXANDER, A.
paintings: (H) $770

VEYRASSAT, Jules Jacques
French 1828-1893
paintings: (L) $1,045; (H) $27,600
drawings: (H) $825

VEZIN, Charles
American 1858-1942
paintings: (L) $1,380; (H) $5,500

VIALLAT, Claude
French b. 1936
paintings: (H) $4,600

VIANELLI, Achille
Italian 1803-1894
paintings: (H) $6,600
drawings: (H) $575

VIANELLI, Alberto
Italian 1841-1927
paintings: (H) $25,300

VIANELLI, P.
Italian 19th cent.
paintings: (H) $2,300

VIANELLO, Cesare
Italian ac. 1902-1908
paintings: (L) $2,090; (H) $6,670

VIANI, Alberto
Italian b. 1906
sculpture: (H) $18,400

VIANI, Domenico Maria
Italian 1668-1711
paintings: (H) $40,250

VIAVANT, George Louis
American 1872-1925
paintings: (H) $1,650
drawings: (L) $880; (H) $7,700

VIAVANT, Ruby
American 1904-1925
drawings: (L) $1,430; (H) $1,650

VIBERT, Claude
French 19th/20th cent.
sculpture: (H) $2,200

VIBERT, Jehan Georges, or Jean
French 1840-1902
paintings: (L) $2,970; (H) $46,000
drawings: (L) $1,265; (H) $17,250

VICAT-COLE, Rex
English 1870-1940
paintings: (H) $1,100

VICENTE, Esteban
Spanish/American b. 1904/06
paintings: (L) $2,750; (H) $18,700
drawings: (L) $805; (H) $3,738

VICHI, F.
Italian late 19th cent.
sculpture: (L) $770; (H) $24,150

VICKERS, Alfred
British 19th cent.
paintings: (L) $275; (H) $4,620

VICKERS, Alfred
English 19th cent.
paintings: (H) $825

VICKERS, Alfred, Sr.
British 1786-1868
paintings: (L) $550; (H) $10,350

VICKERS, Alfred H.
British ac. 1853-1907
paintings: (L) $660; (H) $2,750

VICKERS, Charles
American
paintings: (H) $1,320

VICKERS, Henry Harold
paintings: (L) $748; (H) $1,320

VICKERS, Russ
b. 1923
paintings: (L) $715; (H) $6,600

VICKERY, Charles Bridgeman
American b. 1913
paintings: (L) $302; (H) $2,310
drawings: (H) $522

VICKERY, William
20th cent.
paintings: (H) $750

VICKNAIRS, Alfred
20th cent.
paintings: (H) $522

VICKREY, Robert
American b. 1926
paintings: (L) $3,960; (H) $12,100
drawings: (H) $1,380

VICTOR
drawings: (H) $5
sculpture: (L) $825; (H) $1,210

VICTORS, Jacobus
Dutch 1640-1705
paintings: (L) $5,750; (H) $7,700

VICTORS, Jan
Dutch 1620-1676
paintings: (L) $8,050; (H) $101,500

VIDAL
paintings: (L) $110; (H) $2,200

VIDAL, A.
Italian 19th/20th cent.
paintings: (H) $797

VIDAL, Eugene Vincent
French 19th/20th cent.
paintings: (H) $26,450

VIDAL, Georges
French b. 1895
paintings: (H) $825

VIDAL, Hahn
20th cent.
paintings: (H) $660

VIDAL, L.
c. 1754-after 1805
paintings: (L) $7,425; (H) $17,600

VIDAL, Louis
French 1831-1892
paintings: (H) $2,070
sculpture: (L) $440; (H) $3,450

VIDAL, Louis L'Aveugle Navatel
1831-1892
sculpture: (H) $1,760

VIDAL, Margarita Hahn
American 20th cent.
paintings: (L) $440; (H) $575

VIEGERS, Bernard
Dutch 1886-1947
paintings: (L) $412; (H) $7,700

VIEIRA DA SILVA, Maria Elena
French 1908-1992
paintings: (L) $8,800; (H) $93,500
drawings: (L) $3,680; (H) $110,000

VIEN, Joseph Marie
1716-1809
drawings: (H) $1,100

VIENER, Louis
paintings: (H) $605

VIERA DE MATTOS, Francisco, II
Italian 1599-1678
drawings: (H) $1,045

VIERIN, Emmanuel
Belgian b. 1869
paintings: (H) $1,380

VIERREINK, T.W.
Continental 20th cent.
paintings: (H) $1,430

VIGAL, G.
paintings: (H) $975

VIGAS, Oswaldo
Venezuelan b. 1926
paintings: (H) $5,175

VIGEE, Louis
French 1715 or 1720/27-1767
drawings: (L) $3,450; (H) $14,950

VIGEE-LEBRUN, Marie Louise
Elisabeth
French 1755-1842
paintings: (L) $41,400; (H) $781,000

VIGHI, Coriolano
Italian 1846-1905
drawings: (H) $2,860

VIGIL, Romando, Tse Ye Mu, Falling
In Winter
Native American b. 1902
drawings: (L) $518; (H) $3,565

VIGIL, Thomas, Pan Yo Pin, Summer
Mountain
Native American 1889-1960
drawings: (H) $990

VIGIL, Veloy
American b. 1931
paintings: (L) $412; (H) $1,100

VIGNALI, Jacopo, studio of
17th cent.
paintings: (H) $4,675

VIGNAUD
French 19th cent.
paintings: (H) $5,750

VIGNAUD, Jean
1775-1826
paintings: (H) $4,600

VIGNE, Edouard de
Belgian 1806-1866
paintings: (H) $9,775

VIGNET, Henri
French 1857-1920
paintings: (L) $1,610; (H) $2,310

VIGNEUX, A.
French ac. 1799-1814
drawings: (H) $605

VIGNOLES, Andre
French b. 1920
paintings: (L) $345; (H) $3,850

VIGNON, Charles
paintings: (H) $715

VIGNON, Claude
French c. 1590-1670
paintings: (L) $16,500; (H) $17,600

VIGNON, Victor
French 1847-1909
paintings: (L) $193; (H) $11,000

VIGNONE, J.
American 20th cent.
paintings: (H) $825

VIGNY, Andre
drawings: (H) $6,050

VIGON, Louis Jacques
1897-1985
paintings: (H) $825

VIGOR, Charles
British ac. 1882-1917
paintings: (H) $14,375

VIGOUREUX-DUPLESSIS, Jacques
before 1680-1732
paintings: (H) $16,100

VIKOS, K.
paintings: (H) $1,265

VILA Y PRADES, Julio
Spanish 1873-1930
paintings: (L) $650; (H) $16,500

VILALLONGA, Jesus Carlos de
Canadian b. 1927
paintings: (L) $550; (H) $660

VILARO, Carlos Peaz
Latin American 20th cent.
paintings: (H) $1,650

VILATO, Javier
Spanish b. 1921
paintings: (L) $550; (H) $2,200

VILLA, Carlos
American b. 1936
drawings: (H) $770

VILLA, E.
paintings: (H) $2,750

VILLA, Emile
French 19th cent.
paintings: (H) $2,200

VILLA, Hernando
American 1881-1952
paintings: (L) $495; (H) $5,175
drawings: (L) $358; (H) $2,475

VILLACRES, A.
French School 19th cent.
paintings: (H) $690

VILLACRES, Cesar
Ecuadorian b. 1880
paintings: (L) $138; (H) $1,725

VILLALOBOS, J.
ac. c. 1910
paintings: (H) $10,350

VILLALOBOS MASTER
ac. mid-15th cent.
paintings: (H) $21,450

VILLALPANDO, Cristobal de
Mexican 1875-1964
paintings: (L) $16,100; (H) $36,300

VILLANIS, E.
sculpture: (L) $935; (H) $1,210

VILLANIS, Emmanuele
French ac. 1880-1920
sculpture: (L) $193; (H) $9,200

VILLANUEVA, Leoncio
b. Peru 1936
paintings: (H) $8,800

VILLARD, H.
French 20th cent.
sculpture: (H) $577

VILLARREAL, Victor Manuel
Mexican b. 1944
sculpture: (L) $578; (H) $1,650

VILLEGAS, Armando
b. Peru 1928
paintings: (H) $16,500
sculpture: (H) $18,700

VILLEGAS Y CORDERO, Jose
Spanish 1848-1922
paintings: (L) $2,475; (H) $332,500
drawings: (L) $1,150; (H) $7,700

VILLEGOS, F.
Spanish 19th cent.
paintings: (H) $1,430

VILLENEUVE, Arthur
paintings: (H) $1,100

VILLENEUVE, Boulard de
French 1884-1971
paintings: (H) $880

VILLEVALDE, Bogdan Pavlovich
Russian 1818-1903
paintings: (H) $18,400

VILLEZ, Eugen Ransonnet
paintings: (H) $690

VILLON, Eugene
French b. 1879
paintings: (H) $605

VILLON, Jacques
French 1875-1963
paintings: (L) $460; (H) $33,000
drawings: (L) $552; (H) $15,400

VIN, Paul van der
Belgian 1823-1887
paintings: (H) $2,420

VINALL, Joseph Williams Topham
British b. 1873
paintings: (H) $2,200

VINAY, Jean
French 1907-1978
paintings: (L) $173; (H) $660
drawings: (H) $110

VINCENT, Alexander
paintings: (H) $11,500

VINCENT, Francois Andre
French 1746-1816
drawings: (L) $440; (H) $6,325

VINCENT, George
English 1796-1831
paintings: (H) $12,100

VINCENT, Harry Aiken
American 1864-1931
paintings: (L) $403; (H) $9,200
drawings: (L) $357; (H) $1,540

VINCENTE, Esteban
Spanish/American b. 1904/06
drawings: (H) $2,990

VINCIATA
paintings: (L) $357; (H) $550

VINCK, Franz Kaspar Hulbrecht
Belgian 1827-1903
paintings: (H) $6,600

VINCKEBONS, David
Flemish 1576-1629
paintings: (L) $4,400; (H) $363,000

VINEA, Francesco
Italian 1845/46-1902/04
paintings: (L) $3,575; (H) $33,000

VINES, Roberto
Spanish 19th/20th cent.
paintings: (H) $10,450

VINES SOTO, Hernando
Spanish 1904-1993
paintings: (H) $2,070

VINGTRI, Bayard de la
Belgian late 19th cent.
sculpture: (H) $3,738

VINOGRADOFF, M.
paintings: (H) $1,210

VINTON, Frederic Porter
American 1846-1911
paintings: (L) $797; (H) $7,700

VINTON, John Rogers
American 1801-1847
paintings: (L) $550; (H) $16,500

VINTON, P.
paintings: (H) $880

VIOLLET-LE-DUC, Adolphe Etienne
French 1817-1878
drawings: (H) $1,210

VIOLLET-LE-DUC, Victor
French 1848-1901
paintings: (H) $3,300

VIOLLIER, Jean
paintings: (H) $1,840

VION, A.
paintings: (H) $1,092

VIRACI, L.
Italian 19th cent.
paintings: (H) $3,520

VIRANO, A.J.
Italian 19th cent.
paintings: (H) $770

VIRBICKY
English 19th cent.
paintings: (H) $550

VIRNOLDES, F.
Continental School 19th Cent.
paintings: (H) $37,375

VIRY, Paul Alphonse
French 1861-1881
paintings: (L) $9,900; (H) $44,850

VISENTINI, Antonio
Italian 1688-1782
drawings: (H) $7,475

VISSER, Adrian Nicholaas
Dutch 1887-1933
paintings: (H) $1,430

VITAL, Not
b. 1948
paintings: (H) $7,475
sculpture: (L) $2,750; (H) $5,500

VITAL, Pauleus
b. 1918
paintings: (L) $1,540; (H) $4,025

VITAL-CORNU, Charles
French late 19th cent.
sculpture: (H) $1,980

VITALI, E.
Italian 19th cent.
drawings: (L) $165; (H) $2,200

VITERBO, Andrea di Niccolo da
ac. by 1465
paintings: (H) $9,200

VITERI, Alicia
drawings: (H) $2,750

VITO, Camillo da
Italian 19th/20th cent.
drawings: (L) $1,650; (H) $4,312

VITO, Michele de
Italian 19th cent.
drawings: (L) $220; (H) $770

VITOLLO, C.
paintings: (H) $850

VITRI, Giusto
sculpture: (H) $1,380

VITRINGA, Wigerus
Dutch 1657-1721
drawings: (H) $920

VITTEL, Gaspar van
Italian 1653-1736
drawings: (H) $33,000

VITTORIA, Alessandro, workshop of
Venetian 1525-1608
sculpture: (H) $23,000

VITTURI, I.
Italian 19th cent.
paintings: (L) $550; (H) $550

VITY, Antonio de
Italian b. 1901
paintings: (H) $825

VIUDES, Vicente
b. 1916
paintings: (L) $110; (H) $1,100

VIVANT-DENON, Baron Dominique
French 1747-1825
drawings: (L) $467; (H) $1,210

VIVES-ATSARA, Jose
American b. 1919
paintings: (L) $8,030; (H) $8,030

VIVES-ATSARA, Jose
Mexican 1919-1988
paintings: (L) $880; (H) $8,030

VIVIAN, Calthea Campbell
American 1857-1943
paintings: (H) $935

VIVIAN, George
British 1798-1873
paintings: (H) $10,350

VIVIANI, Professor
sculpture: (H) $2,200

VIVIN, Louis
French 1861-1936
paintings: (L) $165; (H) $9,775

VIVOLO, John
sculpture: (L) $770; (H) $880

VIZKELATI, W.E.
Hungarian 1819-1895
paintings: (L) $100; (H) $1,760

VIZKELETI, W. E.
Hungarian 1819-1895
paintings: (L) $660; (H) $1,210

VIZZINI, Andrea
drawings: (L) $1,380; (H) $2,300

VKHUTEMAS
Russian 19th/20th cent.
drawings: (H) $1,150

VLAMINCK, Maurice de
French 1876-1958
paintings: (L) $4,180; (H) $6,822,500
drawings: (L) $2,875; (H) $49,500
sculpture: (H) $4,290

VLETTER, Samuel de
Dutch 1816-1844
drawings: (H) $1,210

VLEUGHELS, Nicolas
French 1668-1737
paintings: (L) $5,750; (H) $16,100

VLIET, Hendrick Cornelisz. van
Dutch 1611-1675
paintings: (L) $2,200; (H) $48,300

VLIST, Leendert van der
Dutch b. 1894
paintings: (L) $468; (H) $3,850

VOELCKER, Gottfried Wilhelm
German 1775-1849
paintings: (H) $15,400

VOELKERS, J.
German 19th cent.
paintings: (H) $2,530

VOET, Jacob Ferdinand
Flemish 1639-c. 1700
paintings: (H) $11,500

VOGEL, Valentine
American 1906-1965
paintings: (L) $176; (H) $770

VOGELAER, Karel van, called Carlo
dei FIORI DISTELBLOOM
Dutch 1653-1695
paintings: (L) $10,925; (H) $20,900

VOGLER, F.
Continental 19th cent.
paintings: (H) $1,320

VOGLER, F.
French(?)
paintings: (H) $2,200

VOGLER, Hermann
German b. 1859
paintings: (L) $4,025; (H) $11,000

VOGLER, P.
Continental 19th/20th cent.
paintings: (H) $2,300

VOGT, Fritz
American 1842-1900
drawings: (L) $2,090; (H) $11,500

VOGT, Louis Charles
American b. 1864
paintings: (L) $605; (H) $1,540
drawings: (H) $1,540

VOILLE, Jean Louis
French 1744-after 1801
paintings: (L) $11,500; (H) $34,500

VOINIER, Antoine
French ac. 1795-1810
drawings: (H) $11,500

VOIRIN, Leon Joseph
French 1833-1887
paintings: (L) $9,200; (H) $20,700
drawings: (H) $2,300

VOIS, Arie de
Flemish c.1632-1680
paintings: (L) $2,300; (H) $43,700

VOITL
Austrian 19th cent.
paintings: (H) $4,600

VOJNITS, Richard
Hungarian b. 1942
paintings: (L) $412; (H) $550

VOKERT, Edward
paintings: (H) $2,640

VOLAIRE, Pierre Jacques
French 1729-1802
paintings: (L) $99,000; (H) $214,500

VOLANEK, Raimund
Austrian 20th cent.
paintings: (H) $1,540

VOLGER, H.
19th cent.
paintings: (H) $2,640

VOLK, Douglas Stephen A.
American 1856-1935
paintings: (L) $467; (H) $17,250

VOLK, Leonard Wells
American 1828-1895
sculpture: (L) $1,100; (H) $7,475

VOLK, Leonard Wells and Augustus
SAINT-GAUDENS
19th cent.
sculpture: (H) $1,650

VOLKERS, Adrianus
Dutch 19th cent.
paintings: (H) $935

VOLKERS, Emil
German 1831-1905
paintings: (L) $1,045; (H) $3,680

VOLKERT, Edward Charles
American 1871-1935
paintings: (L) $230; (H) $3,300
drawings: (L) $165; (H) $1,650

VOLKHART, Max
German 1848-1924/35
paintings: (H) $6,050

VOLKMANN, Hans Richard von
German 1860-1927
paintings: (H) $4,950

VOLKMAR, Charles
American 1841-1914
paintings: (L) $247; (H) $2,750
drawings: (L) $413; (H) $440

VOLL, Frederick Usher de
American b. 1873
paintings: (H) $4,400
drawings: (H) $460

VOLLERDT, Johann Christian
German 1708/09-1769
paintings: (L) $8,050; (H) $41,400

VOLLET, Henry Emile
paintings: (H) $1,430

VOLLET, Jean
French 20th cent.
paintings: (H) $550

VOLLMAR, Ludwig
German 1842-1884
paintings: (L) $8,050; (H) $41,400

VOLLMER, Adolph F.
German 19th cent.
paintings: (H) $3,080

VOLLMER, Grace L.
American 1884-1977
paintings: (L) $330; (H) $2,200

VOLLMER, Ruth
1903-1982
sculpture: (L) $220; (H) $2,420

VOLLMERING, Joseph
American 1810-1887
paintings: (L) $1,650; (H) $2,300

VOLLON, A.
French 19th cent.
paintings: (L) $467; (H) $605
drawings: (H) $1,540

VOLLON, Alexis
French b. 1865
paintings: (L) $1,725; (H) $90,200
drawings: (H) $1,380

VOLLON, Antoine
French 1833-1900
paintings: (L) $1,725; (H) $92,000

VOLLRATH, Kelly
American
drawings: (L) $550; (H) $650

VOLLWEIDER, Johann Jakob
German 1834-1891
paintings: (H) $2,070

VOLPEDO, Giuseppe Pellizza da
Italian 1868-1907
paintings: (H) $5,750

VOLTAIRE, Pierre Jacques Antoine,
called Chevalier Voltare
1729-after 1802
drawings: (H) $16,500

VOLTI, Antoniucci
Italian/French b. 1915
drawings: (H) $1,540
sculpture: (L) $13,200; (H) $22,000

VOLTZ, Friedrich Johann
German 1817-1886
paintings: (L) $1,045; (H) $32,200
drawings: (H) $575

VOLZ, Hermann
German 1814-1894
paintings: (L) $3,738; (H) $7,360

VOLZ, Robert
drawings: (H) $500

VON EICKEN, Elisabeth
German b. 1862
paintings: (L) $546; (H) $633

VON HERWIG, William Henry
American 1901-1947
paintings: (H) $495

VON SCHMIDT, Harold
American 1893-1982
paintings: (L) $16,500; (H) $18,700

VON SCHNEIDAU, Christian
American 1893-1976
paintings: (L) $440; (H) $2,090

VONCK, Elias
1605-1652
paintings: (H) $5,750

VONCK, Jan
1630-after 1660
paintings: (H) $12,100

VONNOH, Bessie Potter
American 1872-1955
sculpture: (L) $2,750; (H) $66,000

VONNOH, Robert William
American 1858-1933
paintings: (L) $805; (H) $60,500

VONNOT-VIOLLET, Yvonne
Belgian 1883-1936
paintings: (H) $460

VONSCHNEIDAU, Christian
American 1893-1976
paintings: (L) $187; (H) $3,575

VOORDE, Georges van de
sculpture: (H) $690

VOORHEES, Clark Greenwood
American 1871-1933
paintings: (L) $192; (H) $9,900

VOORHOUT, Johannes, I
1647-before 1773
paintings: (H) $3,850

VOORT, Van der
Dutch
paintings: (H) $2,200

VORCE, Caroline Bwin
paintings: (H) $495

VORDERMAUER, Ludwig
German 19th/20th cent.
sculpture: (L) $468; (H) $1,150

VOROSHILOV
Russian 19th cent.
paintings: (H) $19,800

VOS, Cornelis de, studio of
Flemish 17th cent.
paintings: (H) $37,950

VOS, Florence Marie de
American b. 1892
drawings: (H) $4,620

VOS, Georges van den
Belgian 1853-1911
paintings: (H) $1,840

VOS, Hubert
Dutch/American 1855-1935
paintings: (L) $825; (H) $13,200
drawings: (H) $467

VOS, J. de
Belgian 19th cent.
paintings: (H) $467

VOS, Maerten de
1532-1603
paintings: (H) $15,400
drawings: (L) $4,370; (H) $4,950

VOS, Paul de, studio of
Flemish 17th cent.
paintings: (H) $46,200

VOS, Simon de
Flemish 1603-1676
paintings: (H) $9,900

VOS, Vincent de
Belgian 1829-1875
paintings: (L) $1,210; (H) $7,700

VOSS, Franklin Brook
American 1880-1953
paintings: (L) $1,840; (H) $4,313

VOSS, William
American 20th cent.
paintings: (H) $578

VOSTELL, Wolf
contemporary
drawings: (H) $8,250

VOTOIX, L.
French 20th cent.
paintings: (L) $577; (H) $1,017

VOUET, Simon
French 1590-1641/49
paintings: (H) $354,500
drawings: (L) $4,180; (H) $28,600

VOULKOS, Peter
American b. 1924
sculpture: (L) $1,725; (H) $25,300

VOYET, Jacques
French b. 1927
paintings: (L) $495; (H) $4,070

VRANCX, Sebastian
Flemish 1573/78-1647
paintings: (L) $2,090; (H) $695,500

VRANESH, George
American 20th cent.
paintings: (H) $550

VRBOUA, Miloslava
Czechoslovakian 20th cent.
paintings: (H) $1,725

VREEDENBURGH, Cornelis
Dutch 1880-1946
paintings: (L) $4,400; (H) $9,488

VREELAND, E. van
Dutch 19th cent.
drawings: (L) $825; (H) $825

VREELAND, Francis van
American 1879-1954
drawings: (L) $165; (H) $863

VRIENDT, Albrecht de
Belgian 1843-1900
paintings: (H) $24,200

VRIES, Dirck de
Dutch ac. 1590-1592
paintings: (H) $55,000

VRIES, Emanuel de
German 1812-1875
paintings: (H) $1,540

VRIES, Roelof van
Dutch c. 1631-after 1681
paintings: (L) $8,800; (H) $34,100

VROLYK, Adrianus Jacobus
Dutch 1834-1862
paintings: (L) $1,320; (H) $6,900

VROOM, Cornelis
Dutch c. 1591-1661
paintings: (H) $61,900

VROOM, Hendrik Cornelisz
Dutch 1566-1640
paintings: (H) $3,850

VU, Michel
French b. 1941
paintings: (H) $605

VUCHT, Gerrit van
Dutch ac. 1658-1697
paintings: (H) $11,000

VUILLARD, Edouard
French 1868-1940
paintings: (L) $2,300; (H) $1,927,500
drawings: (L) $863; (H) $220,000

VUILLEFROY, Felix Dominique de
French b. 1841
paintings: (H) $2,530

VUILLEFROY, George Jean Eugene de
French 19th cent.
paintings: (H) $1,045

VUKOVIC, Marko
American b. 1892
paintings: (L) $83; (H) $770

VYSEKAL, Edouard
American 1890-1939
paintings: (L) $440; (H) $12,100
drawings: (L) $220; (H) $1,980

VYSEKAL, Luvena
American 1873-1954
paintings: (L) $605; (H) $3,025

VYTLACIL, Vaclav
American 1892-1984
paintings: (L) $193; (H) $3,080
drawings: (L) $440; (H) $16,100

WAAGEN
German 19th cent.
sculpture: (L) $165; (H) $14,300

WAAGEN, Adalbert
German 1867-1952
paintings: (H) $2,860

WAAGEN, Arthur
German 1833-1898
sculpture: (L) $17,250; (H) $18,700

WABE
20th cent.
paintings: (H) $1,540

WACHTEL, Elmer
American 1864-1929
paintings: (L) $690; (H) $33,000
drawings: (L) $523; (H) $3,575

WACHTEL, Julie
b. 1956
paintings: (H) $2,185

WACHTEL, Marion Kavanaugh
American 1876-1954
paintings: (L) $1,650; (H) $30,250
drawings: (L) $440; (H) $18,700

WACKER, K.
20th cent.
paintings: (H) $495

WACTAWIAK?, L.
19th/20th cent.
paintings: (H) $1,320

WADDELL, Lillian
American early 20th cent.
paintings: (L) $40; (H) $633

WADDINGHAM, John
American b. 1915
drawings: (L) $193; (H) $523

WADERE, Heinrich
German 19th/20th cent.
sculpture: (H) $4,830

WADSWORTH, Adelaide E.
American 1844-1928
paintings: (L) $275; (H) $935

WADSWORTH, Wedworth
American 1846-1927
drawings: (L) $39; (H) $660

WAEL, Cornelis de
Flemish 1592-1667
paintings: (H) $27,500

WAERING, R.
paintings: (H) $990

WAGEMANS, P.G.A.
Continental 19th cent.
paintings: (H) $1,320

WAGEMANS, Pieter Johannes
Alexander
Dutch 1879-1955
paintings: (H) $977

WAGNER, A.
paintings: (H) $935

WAGNER, Eugene
sculpture: (L) $385; (H) $660

WAGNER, Ferdinand
German 1847-1927
paintings: (L) $330; (H) $28,600

WAGNER, Ferdinand, Sr.
German 1819-1881
paintings: (H) $37,950

WAGNER, Franz
German b. 1810
paintings: (H) $5,175

WAGNER, Fred
American 1864-1940
paintings: (L) $165; (H) $10,175
drawings: (L) $115; (H) $935

WAGNER, Fritz
German 1896-1939
paintings: (L) $165; (H) $1,430

WAGNER, Fritz
Swiss b. 1872
paintings: (H) $715

WAGNER, George
German b. 1823
paintings: (H) $1,650

WAGNER, Hans
Swiss b. 1805
paintings: (L) $99; (H) $467
drawings: (L) $99; (H) $121

WAGNER, I***
German 19th cent.
paintings: (H) $920

WAGNER, Jacob
American 1852-1898
paintings: (L) $7,260; (H) $11,000
drawings: (L) $440; (H) $495

WAGNER, Jas. D.L. van
American 19th cent.
drawings: (H) $1,980

WAGNER, Jorg
German 20th cent.
paintings: (H) $1,760

WAGNER, L.
German 19th cent.
paintings: (H) $467

WAGNER, Morgan
American 1917-1950
paintings: (H) $489

WAGNER, Paul Hermann
German b. 1852
paintings: (H) $21,850

WAGNER, Robert L., Rob
American 1872-1942
paintings: (H) $825
drawings: (H) $99

WAGNER, T.
paintings: (H) $920

WAGNER, V.
paintings: (H) $1,045

WAGNER, Wilhelm
Austrian b. 1887
paintings: (H) $1,100

WAGNER, Wilhelm Georg
Dutch b. 1814
paintings: (H) $2,200

WAGONER, Harry B.
American 1889-1950
paintings: (L) $825; (H) $3,163
drawings: (L) $110; (H) $193

WAGREZ, Jacques
French 1846-1908
paintings: (L) $25,300; (H) $27,600

WAGREZ, Jacques Alice
French ac. 1877-1880
paintings: (H) $28,750

WAGREZ, Jacques Clement
French 1846-1908
paintings: (L) $17,250; (H) $101,500

WAHLBERG, Alfred
Swedish 1834-1906
paintings: (H) $6,900

WAHLBERG, Ulf
Swedish b. 1938
drawings: (L) $605; (H) $1,100

WAHLQVIST, Ehrnfried
Swedish 1815-1895
paintings: (H) $10,925

WAICHI, Tsutaka
b. 1911
paintings: (H) $13,800

WAIDMAN, Pierre
French 1860-1937
paintings: (H) $1,650

WAILLY, Charles de
French 1730-1798
drawings: (H) $24,200

WAIN, Louis
English 1860-1939
drawings: (H) $1,045
sculpture: (H) $880

WAINEWRIGHT, Thomas Francis
French 19th cent.
paintings: (H) $5,500
drawings: (L) $242; (H) $303

WAINWRIGHT, Christine H.
American
paintings: (H) $550

WAINWRIGHT, I.
British 19th cent.
paintings: (H) $1,430

WAINWRIGHT, John
British ac. 1859-1869
paintings: (L) $2,070; (H) $3,025

WAINWRIGHT, Thomas Francis
English 19th cent.
drawings: (H) $633

WAINWRIGHT, William John
English 1855-1931
paintings: (H) $1,320

WAIT, J.C.
English School 19th cent.
paintings: (H) $495

WAIT, Lizzie F.
American ac. 1887
drawings: (H) $460

WAITE, Edward Wilkins
British ac. 1880-1920
paintings: (H) $3,450

Department Store Art Gallery

Jacques Wagrez (1846-1908) was a Frenchman who painted scenes of mythology, history, the lives of saints, and idealized representations of medieval romance. Wagrez was a respected and prolific artist and is listed in several reference sources. Bénézit, the French dictionary of artists, states that Wagrez first exhibited at the Sociétaire des Artistes Francais in 1884 and that his painting *The First Meeting*, a scene of Florence in the 15th century, established his reputation. Wagrez is also listed in *Public 19th Century Paintings* and in *Artists of the 19th Century*. He exhibited widely in France and the U.S. An 1895 exhibition catalog from the Jordan Marsh Department Store art gallery in Boston includes Wagrez as one of

the exhibiting artists. A Jordan Marsh circular says that 40,000-50,000 visitors a week attended the exhibition of 240 paintings! When Garth's Auction Gallery in Granville, Ohio, was consigned *Prince Choosing His Bride* from the Carstensen Collection, it was listed in the catalog with no estimate, as is customary with this auction house. The painting, which had also been reproduced as an engraving, was illustrated on the cover of the catalog. The price realized was $26,400. (Jacques Wagrez, *Prince Choosing His Bride*, oil on canvas, 62 x 34 inches, Garth, January 27, 1995, $26,400)

WAITE, James Clarke
  Australian/English ac. 1863-1885
  paintings: (H) $39,100
WAITE, Robert Thorne
  British 1842-1935
  drawings: (H) $1,265
WAITT, Marion Parkhurst
  American b. 1875
  paintings: (H) $495

WAKELIN, R.
  paintings: (H) $750

WAKHEVITCH, Georges
  paintings: (H) $3,025
  drawings: (L) $1,430; (H) $2,310

WALBOURN, Ernest
  British ac. 1895-1920
  paintings: (L) $990; (H) $6,050

WALCUTT, H.B.
American 19th cent.
paintings: (H) $2,200

WALDAU, A.
19th cent.
paintings: (H) $3,025

WALDEK, H.
paintings: (H) $4,125

WALDEN, Lionel
American 1861-1933
paintings: (L) $330; (H) $17,250

WALDER, Louise
American 19th/20th cent.
paintings: (H) $468

WALDERSEE, L. van
drawings: (L) $248; (H) $460

WALDMULLER, Ferdinand Georg
Austrian 1793-1865
paintings: (L) $4,950; (H) $629,500

WALDO, Frank
American ac. 1910-1930
paintings: (H) $2,750
drawings: (H) $1,870

WALDO, J. Frank
American 1832-c. 1914
paintings: (L) $440; (H) $29,900
drawings: (H) $55

WALDO, Samuel Lovett and William
JEWETT
18th/19th cent.
paintings: (L) $805; (H) $3,680

WALDORP, Antonie
Dutch 1803-1866
paintings: (L) $1,380; (H) $18,400

WALDRON, Charles J.
British ac. 1867-1883
paintings: (H) $15,400

WALENTYNOWICZ, Janusz Andrzej
Danish b. 1956
sculpture: (H) $2,415

WALES, H.
paintings: (H) $467

WALES, Orlando G.
American 20th cent.
paintings: (L) $193; (H) $935

WALES, Susan Makepeace Larkin
American 1839-1927
paintings: (H) $489
drawings: (L) $173; (H) $1,430

WALKER, Addison
American 20th cent.
paintings: (H) $550

WALKER, Arthur
paintings: (H) $825

WALKER, Chuck
American contemporary
paintings: (H) $1,210

WALKER, D.B.
paintings: (H) $522

WALKER, F.G.
paintings: (H) $1,430

WALKER, Frederick
English 1840/41-1874/75
paintings: (H) $1,650

WALKER, Frederick R.
19th/20th cent.
paintings: (H) $2,860

WALKER, Henry Oliver
American 1843-1929
paintings: (L) $853; (H) $2,090

WALKER, Horatio
Canadian 1858-1938
paintings: (H) $15,400
drawings: (H) $110

WALKER, Inez Nathaniel
American 1910-1990
drawings: (L) $440; (H) $1,540

WALKER, J.B.
English 19th cent.
paintings: (H) $990

WALKER, J.G.
English 19th cent.
paintings: (H) $605

WALKER, James
American 1819-1889
paintings: (L) $247; (H) $4,400

WALKER, James Alexander
British 1841-1898
paintings: (L) $978; (H) $3,575

WALKER, James William
British 1831-1898
paintings: (L) $605; (H) $715

WALKER, Jeff
paintings: (L) $715; (H) $2,200

WALKER, John
contemporary
paintings: (L) $13,200; (H) $14,300

WALKER, John Law
American b. 1899
paintings: (L) $110; (H) $2,200
drawings: (L) $165; (H) $412

WALKER, Lucy
British 19th/20th cent.
paintings: (H) $42,550

WALKER, Myrtle
American 20th cent.
paintings: (H) $3,080

WALKER, Robert Hollands
British 19th/20th cent.
drawings: (H) $523

WALKER, Stuart
20th cent.
paintings: (H) $990

WALKER, T.E.
19th/20th cent.
paintings: (H) $800

WALKER, William Aiken
American c. 1838-1921
paintings: (L) $1,250; (H) $99,000
drawings: (L) $748; (H) $13,800

WALKER and WEEKS
paintings: (H) $2,750
drawings: (L) $440; (H) $880

WALKLEY, David B.
American 1849-1934
paintings: (L) $110; (H) $2,970

WALKOWITZ, Abraham
American 1880-1965
paintings: (L) $192; (H) $6,600
drawings: (L) $99; (H) $6,900

WALL, A. Bryan
American d.c. 1938
paintings: (L) $125; (H) $8,500

WALL, Alfred S.
American 1825-1896
paintings: (H) $8,800
drawings: (H) $550

WALL, H.A.
British 19th cent.
paintings: (H) $4,830

WALL, Jeff
contemporary
drawings: (H) $36,800
sculpture: (H) $24,150

WALL, Sue
American 20th cent.
paintings: (H) $660

WALL, W.C.
American 19th cent.
paintings: (L) $4,400; (H) $6,600

WALL, William Allen
American 1801-1885
paintings: (L) $2,970; (H) $15,400
drawings: (L) $935; (H) $1,610

WALL, William Coventry
English/American 1810-1886
paintings: (H) $15,400

WALL, William Guy
American 1792-after 1864
paintings: (H) $2,145
drawings: (L) $575; (H) $2,070

WALLACE, Frederick E.
American 1893-1958
paintings: (H) $2,310

WALLACE, Harold Frank
British 1881-1962
drawings: (H) $1,320

WALLACE, J.
British 19th cent.
paintings: (H) $550

WALLACE, James
British 1872-1911
paintings: (H) $1,210

WALLACE, John
British 1841-1905
paintings: (L) $748; (H) $1,656

WALLACE, Lucy
American b. 1884
paintings: (H) $495

WALLACE, Robin
British b. 1897
paintings: (H) $825

WALLASEY, Grant
British 19th cent.
paintings: (H) $1,150

WALLENN, Frederick D.
British ac. 1880-1920
drawings: (H) $2,760

WALLER, F.
Continental 19th cent.
paintings: (H) $3,300

WALLER, Frank
American 1842-1923
paintings: (L) $137; (H) $1,035

WALLERS, B.
Anglo/American 19th cent.
paintings: (H) $575

WALLIS, Hugh
English 1894-1922
drawings: (H) $2,475

WALLIS, Joseph Haythorn
British 19th/20th cent.
paintings: (H) $1,760

WALORGIST, R. de
drawings: (H) $495

WALRAVEN, Jan
Dutch 1827-after 1874
paintings: (L) $4,400; (H) $22,000

WALSCAPELLE, Jacob van
Dutch 1644-1727
paintings: (L) $39,100; (H) $255,500

WALSETH, Niels
Danish 20th cent.
paintings: (L) $495; (H) $550

WALSH, John Stanley
paintings: (H) $825

WALSH, Richard M.L.
American 1848-1908
drawings: (L) $193; (H) $575

WALT DISNEY STUDIOS
drawings: (L) $69; (H) $8,050

WALTENSPERGER, Charles
American 1871-1931
paintings: (L) $110; (H) $4,510
drawings: (H) $275

WALTER, Almeric
sculpture: (H) $1,610

WALTER, Christian
American 1872-1938
paintings: (L) $58; (H) $2,070

WALTER, F.
British 19th cent.
paintings: (H) $660

WALTER, Franz Erhard
contemporary
drawings: (H) $550

WALTER, Joseph
British 19th cent.
paintings: (H) $605

WALTER, Martha
American 1875-1976
paintings: (L) $935; (H) $63,250
drawings: (H) $2,090

WALTER, Otto
Austrian 19th cent.
paintings: (H) $3,190

WALTER, Valerie Harrisse
b. 1892
sculpture: (L) $357; (H) $1,150

WALTERS, Curt
b. 1958
paintings: (L) $4,400; (H) $10,725

WALTERS, Emile
American b. 1893
paintings: (L) $489; (H) $1,980

WALTERS, George Stanfield
British 1838-1924
paintings: (L) $715; (H) $6,600
drawings: (L) $302; (H) $1,265

WALTERS, Samuel
British 1811-1882
paintings: (L) $6,900; (H) $33,000

WALTHER, Charles H.
American 1879-1937
paintings: (L) $275; (H) $3,410

WALTHER, Ludwig
sculpture: (H) $3,680

WALTMANN, Harry F.
1871-1951
paintings: (L) $412; (H) $495

WALTON, Edward Arthur
British 1860-1922
paintings: (H) $2,420

WALTON, Frank
English 1840-1928
paintings: (H) $2,750

WALTON, Henry
American 1804-1865
paintings: (H) $54,625
drawings: (L) $7,150; (H) $9,775

WALTON, Henry
British 19th/20th cent.
paintings: (H) $880

WALTON, Henry and Sawrey GILPIN
British 18th/19th cent.
paintings: (H) $14,950

WALTON, John Whitehead
British 19th cent.
paintings: (H) $1,760

WALTON, Tony
drawings: (H) $550

WALTZ, Carl B.
Continental 19th cent.
paintings: (H) $3,680

WALWORTH, Heldegarde
American 20th cent.
paintings: (H) $715

WANDESFORDE, Juan Buckingham
1817-1902
paintings: (L) $2,070; (H) $8,625

WANDSCHNEIDER, Wilhelm
German 1866-1942
sculpture: (H) $2,200

WANG SU
Chinese 1794-1877
drawings: (H) $16,100

WANG ZHEN, Wang CHEN
Chinese 1866-1938
drawings: (H) $12,650

WANING, Cornelis Antoine van
Dutch 1861-1929
paintings: (H) $1,540

WANING, R.
Dutch 19th/20th cent.
sculpture: (H) $546

WANLASS, Stanley
sculpture: (H) $12,100

WANTE, Ernest
French b. 1872
sculpture: (L) $2,475; (H) $6,050

WAPPERS, Baron Gustave
Belgian 1803-1874
paintings: (H) $14,300

WARASHINA, Patti
contemporary
sculpture: (L) $2,013; (H) $14,950

WARD, Alfred
British ac. 1880-1929
paintings: (H) $561

WARD, C.
ac. c. 1850
paintings: (H) $11,500

WARD, Charles, I
British ac. 1826-1969
paintings: (H) $1,980

WARD, Charles Caleb
Canadian/American c. 1831-1896
paintings: (L) $880; (H) $1,980

WARD, Charles S.
American 1850-1937
paintings: (L) $151; (H) $495

WARD, Edgar Melville
American 1849-1915
paintings: (L) $660; (H) $3,795

WARD, Edmund F.
American 1892-1991
paintings: (L) $99; (H) $9,900
drawings: (L) $550; (H) $575

WARD, Edward Matthew
English 1816-1879
paintings: (L) $4,400; (H) $12,650
drawings: (H) $1,430

WARD, Edwin Arthur
British ac. 1883
paintings: (H) $489

WARD, Enoch
British 1859-1922
paintings: (H) $1,035

WARD, Hilda
American 20th cent.
drawings: (H) $575

WARD, J. Stephen
American 1876-1941
paintings: (L) $275; (H) $1,100

WARD, Jacob C.
1809-1891
paintings: (H) $825

WARD, James
English 1769-1859
paintings: (H) $17,250

WARD, James Charles
British ac. 1830-1859
paintings: (H) $4,600

WARD, John Quincy Adams
American 1830-1910
paintings: (H) $37,375
sculpture: (L) $550; (H) $34,500

WARD, Keith
1882-1953
drawings: (H) $3,300

WARD, Martin Theodore
English 1799-1874
paintings: (H) $1,955

WARD, S.
paintings: (H) $1,045

WARD, Vernon de Beauvoir
British b. 1905
paintings: (L) $1,320; (H) $1,725

WARD, William
American 19th/20th cent.
paintings: (H) $495

WARD, William, Jr.
American d. 1935
paintings: (L) $220; (H) $1,045

WARD OF HULL, John
1798-1849
paintings: (H) $2,300

WARDLE, Arthur
English 1864-1949
paintings: (L) $1,210; (H) $85,000
drawings: (L) $1,375; (H) $4,950

WARDLEWORTH, J.L.
British 19th cent.
paintings: (L) $1,380; (H) $2,200

WARE, Harry Fabian
Scottish ac. 1932-1942
paintings: (H) $12,650

WARE, Thomas
American ac. c. 1820
paintings: (H) $4,888

WARFEL, Floretta Emma
American b. 1916
paintings: (L) $440; (H) $1,540
drawings: (L) $27; (H) $330

WARHOL, Andy
American 1928-1987
paintings: (L) $880; (H) $3,632,500
drawings: (L) $690; (H) $577,500
sculpture: (L) $467; (H) $43,700

WARING, Henry Franks
English exhib. 1900-1928
drawings: (H) $467

WARMAN
Continental 19th cent.
drawings: (H) $29,900

WARMINGTON, E.
Anglo/American 19th cent.
drawings: (H) $550

WARNEKE, Heinrich
German/American b. 1895
sculpture: (H) $2,875

WARNER, Everett Longley
American 1877-1963
paintings: (L) $358; (H) $11,000

WARNER, G.
English 19th cent.
paintings: (H) $550

WARNER, Mary Loring
American b. 1860
paintings: (L) $247; (H) $6,380
drawings: (H) $137

WARNER, Nell Walker
American 1891-1970
paintings: (L) $550; (H) $5,750
drawings: (L) $110; (H) $1,320

WARNER, Olin Levi
American 1844-1896
sculpture: (L) $275; (H) $2,860

WARNER BROS. STUDIO
paintings: (H) $1,725
drawings: (L) $345; (H) $1,782

WARNER(?), Albert
20th cent.
paintings: (H) $468

WAROQUIER, Henry de
French 1881-1970
paintings: (H) $3,850
drawings: (H) $605

WARREN, Bonomi
British 19th/20th cent.
drawings: (H) $805

WARREN, Constance Whitney
American 1888-1948
sculpture: (H) $4,025

WARREN, Ferdinand E.
American b. 1899
paintings: (L) $220; (H) $495

WARREN, Harold B.
American 1859-1934
drawings: (L) $82; (H) $2,750

WARREN, Joseph
20th cent.
paintings: (H) $2,990

WARREN, Melvin C.
American b. 1920
paintings: (L) $2,070; (H) $85,250
drawings: (L) $137; (H) $7,700
sculpture: (L) $330; (H) $4,950

WARREN, Rand
drawings: (H) $715

WARSHAW, Howard
American 1920-1977
paintings: (L) $660; (H) $1,320
drawings: (H) $690

WARSHAWSKY, Abel George
American 1883-1962
paintings: (L) $385; (H) $6,325

WARSHAWSKY, Alexander
American b. 1887
paintings: (L) $660; (H) $2,530

WARTHEN, Ferol
paintings: (H) $880

WASEV, J.
20th cent.
sculpture: (H) $605

WASHBURN, Cadwallader Lincoln
American 1866-1965
paintings: (L) $880; (H) $1,150
drawings: (H) $660

WASHBURN, Mary Nightingale
American 1861-1932
paintings: (L) $50; (H) $1,320

WASHINGTON, A.C.
paintings: (H) $880

WASHINGTON, Elizabeth A.
paintings: (H) $990

WASHINGTON, Elizabeth Fisher
American 20th cent.
paintings: (L) $1,100; (H) $1,870
drawings: (L) $83; (H) $248

WASHINGTON, Georges
French 1827-1910
paintings: (L) $8,250; (H) $52,900
drawings: (L) $55; (H) $9,200

WASHINGTON, James W., Jr.
contemporary
sculpture: (H) $468

WASHINGTON, William De Hartburn
American 1834-1870
paintings: (H) $3,163

WASILEWSKI, Czeslaw
Polish 1875-1946
paintings: (H) $2,070

WASMULLER, J.H.
paintings: (H) $1,650

WASSENAAR, W.A.
Dutch 1873-1956
drawings: (H) $1,150

WASSON, George Savary
American 1855-1926
paintings: (L) $770; (H) $1,815

WATANABE, H.
Japanese 19th cent.
drawings: (L) $544; (H) $660

WATANABE, Torajiro
b. 1866
paintings: (H) $660
drawings: (H) $99

WATANABE SAKU
late 19th cent.
sculpture: (H) $9,200

WATELET, Charles Joseph
Belgian 1867-1954
paintings: (H) $6,600

WATELET, Louis Etienne
French 1780-1866
paintings: (H) $9,900

WATELIN, Louis
French 1838-1905
paintings: (H) $3,410

WATERHOUSE, John William
British 1849-1917
paintings: (L) $1,650; (H) $137,500
drawings: (L) $2,070; (H) $18,700

WATERLOO, Anthonie
Dutch 1609/10-1690
drawings: (H) $41,800

WATERLOW, Sir Ernest Albert
English 1850-1919
paintings: (L) $460; (H) $3,220
drawings: (H) $495

WATERMAN, Marcus
American 1834-1914
paintings: (L) $330; (H) $3,850

WATERS, George Stanfield
English 1838-1924
drawings: (H) $1,375

WATERS, George W.
American 1832-1912
paintings: (L) $176; (H) $4,620
drawings: (L) $523; (H) $605

WATERS, Susan C.
American 1823-1900
paintings: (L) $1,725; (H) $15,400

WATKINS, Francis
drawings: (L) $220; (H) $1,210

WATKINS, Franklin Chenault
American 1894-1972
paintings: (L) $220; (H) $1,980
drawings: (L) $50; (H) $770

WATKINS, J.
Continental 19th cent.
paintings: (H) $1,760

WATKINS, Susan
American 1875-1913
paintings: (H) $76,750

WATKINS, William Reginald
American b. 1890
paintings: (L) $132; (H) $550
drawings: (H) $412

WATRIN, D.
sculpture: (H) $1,320

WATRIN, Etienne
French ac. 1890-1915
sculpture: (H) $4,025

WATROUS, E.
American 1858-1921
paintings: (H) $577

WATROUS, Harry Willson
American 1857-1940
paintings: (L) $412; (H) $14,300

WATSON, A.H.
drawings: (H) $660

WATSON, Adele
American 1873-1947
paintings: (L) $303; (H) $935

WATSON, C.
British 19th cent.
paintings: (H) $5,500

WATSON, Charles
British 19th cent.
paintings: (H) $1,150

WATSON, Charles A.
American 1857-1923
paintings: (L) $88; (H) $1,650

WATSON, Charles H.R.
Irish 19th/20th cent.
paintings: (H) $1,760

WATSON, Edward Facon
British 19th cent.
drawings: (H) $4,675

WATSON, Elizabeth H.
American b. 1875
drawings: (H) $495

WATSON, George
English 1767-1837
paintings: (H) $605

WATSON, George Spencer
British 1869-1933
paintings: (H) $10,925

WATSON, Henry S.
paintings: (H) $825

WATSON, Homer Ransford
paintings: (L) $3,300; (H) $4,400

WATSON, Hy S.
paintings: (H) $935

WATSON, Jessie N.
American 1870-1963
paintings: (H) $990
drawings: (H) $440

WATSON, John Dawson
English 1832-1892
paintings: (L) $2,090; (H) $5,175
drawings: (L) $220; (H) $1,100

WATSON, P.
19th cent.
paintings: (L) $605; (H) $825

WATSON, P. Fletcher
English 1842-1907
drawings: (H) $1,100

WATSON, R.
20th cent.
paintings: (H) $660

WATSON, R.
British 19th/20th cent.
paintings: (H) $4,950

WATSON, Robert
American b. 1923
paintings: (L) $192; (H) $550

WATSON, Robert
English 19th/20th cent.
paintings: (L) $1,210; (H) $3,080

WATSON, Ross
20th cent.
paintings: (H) $575

WATSON, Syd
English/Scottish? 19th/20th cent.
paintings: (H) $1,600

WATSON, W.R.C., Jr.
British 19th cent.
paintings: (H) $7,475

WATSON, Walter J.
British b. 1879
paintings: (L) $1,980; (H) $13,800

WATSON, William
British 19th/20th cent.
paintings: (L) $2,000; (H) $20,900

WATSON, William
British ac. 1883, d. 1921
paintings: (L) $3,450; (H) $16,500

WATSON, William H.
English 19th cent.
paintings: (H) $1,100

WATTEAU, Francois Louis Joseph,
called Watteau de LILLE
French 1758-1823
paintings: (L) $25,300; (H) $26,450
drawings: (H) $3,220

WATTEAU, Jean Antoine, or Antoine
French 1684-1721
paintings: (H) $1,760
drawings: (L) $38,500; (H) $242,000

WATTEAU, Louis Joseph, called
Watteau de Lille
French 1731-1798
drawings: (H) $1,100

WATTER, Joseph
German 1838-1913
paintings: (H) $8,050

WATTIER, Charles Emile
French 1800-1868
drawings: (L) $352; (H) $575

WATTS, D.
Scottish 19th/20th cent.
paintings: (H) $990

WATTS, Frederick Waters
English 1800-1862
paintings: (L) $1,650; (H) $63,000

WATTS, George Frederick
British 1817-1904
paintings: (L) $11,500; (H) $198,000
drawings: (H) $220

WATTS, James Thomas
English 1853-1930
drawings: (H) $1,725

WATTS, Leonard
British 19th cent.
paintings: (H) $6,325

WATTS, Nicholas
paintings: (H) $2,200
drawings: (L) $2,200; (H) $3,300

WATTS, Robert
sculpture: (H) $2,320

WATTS, William Clothier
American 1869-1961
paintings: (H) $2,875
drawings: (L) $275; (H) $770

WAUD, Alfred R.
American 1828-1891
drawings: (L) $483; (H) $7,150

WAUD, H.A.
19th cent.
paintings: (H) $1,760

WAUGH, Coulton
American 1896-1973
paintings: (L) $110; (H) $825

WAUGH, Frederick Judd
American 1861-1940
paintings: (L) $550; (H) $41,400
drawings: (L) $275; (H) $7,700

WAUGH, Ida
American d. 1919
paintings: (H) $4,125
drawings: (H) $633

WAUGH, Samuel Bell
American 1814-1884
paintings: (L) $275; (H) $495

WAUTER, Camille
Belgian 1856-1919
paintings: (H) $9,350

WAUTERS, Constant
Belgian 1826-1853
paintings: (L) $1,495; (H) $4,888

WAY, Andrew John Henry
American 1826-1888
paintings: (L) $1,155; (H) $20,700

WEARY, Allen M.
American ac. 1930-1940
drawings: (H) $719

WEATHERBEE, George Faulkner
American 1851-1920
paintings: (H) $2,070

WEATHERFORD, Mary
20th cent.
drawings: (L) $230; (H) $460

WEATHERHEAD, William Harris
English 1843-c. 1903
drawings: (H) $1,870

WEATHERHILL, George
British 19th cent.
paintings: (H) $2,090

WEAVER, Arthur
American 20th cent.
paintings: (L) $99; (H) $2,200

WEAVER, John Barney
Canadian b. 1920
sculpture: (H) $2,200

WEAVER, Thomas
English 1774-1844
paintings: (H) $5,500

WEAVER, William H.
American 19th cent.
paintings: (H) $880

WEBB, Boyd
drawings: (H) $5,175

WEBB, Byron
British ac. 1846-1866
paintings: (H) $5,500

WEBB, Charles Meer
British 1830-1895
paintings: (L) $825; (H) $9,900

WEBB, E.
British 1805-1854
paintings: (H) $1,150

WEBB, James
English 1825-1895
paintings: (L) $825; (H) $19,800
drawings: (H) $467

WEBB, Matthew W.
British 20th cent.
paintings: (H) $990

WEBB, Thomas
American 20th cent.
paintings: (H) $1,430

WEBB, W.
Canadian ac. 1869-70
paintings: (H) $3,960

WEBB, W.G.
19th/20th cent.
paintings: (H) $575

WEBB, William
British 19th cent.
paintings: (H) $36,800

WEBB, William Edward
British ac. 1881 d. 1903
paintings: (L) $4,180; (H) $6,600

WEBBE, William J.
British ac. 1853-1878
paintings: (H) $5,750

WEBBER, Carl
American 1850-1921
drawings: (H) $1,760

WEBBER, Charles T.
American 1825-1911
paintings: (L) $247; (H) $5,720

WEBBER, Elbridge Wesley
American 1839-1914
paintings: (H) $1,150

WEBBER, J.
drawings: (H) $1,430

WEBBER, K.
drawings: (H) $468

WEBBER, Paul
German 1823-1916
paintings: (H) $21,850

WEBBER, W.B.
paintings: (H) $2,750

WEBBER, Wesley
American 1839/41-1914
paintings: (L) $110; (H) $13,800

WEBER, Alfred
Swiss b. 1859
paintings: (H) $2,200

WEBER, Alfred Charles
French 1862-1922
paintings: (L) $2,145; (H) $9,200
drawings: (H) $880

WEBER, C. Phillip
American b. Germany 1849
paintings: (L) $325; (H) $10,450
drawings: (H) $240

WEBER, F.W.
paintings: (L) $175; (H) $550

WEBER, Gottlieb Daniel Paul
1823-1916
paintings: (H) $5,750

WEBER, Idele
contemporary
paintings: (H) $715

WEBER, M***
German 19th cent.
paintings: (H) $3,300

WEBER, Maria
German ac c. 1876
paintings: (H) $2,420

WEBER, Max
American 1881-1961
paintings: (L) $460; (H) $99,000
drawings: (L) $264; (H) $26,400

WEBER, Otis S.
American 19th cent.
paintings: (L) $330; (H) $7,810
drawings: (L) $20; (H) $220

WEBER, Otto
German 1832-1888
paintings: (L) $1,150; (H) $17,600

WEBER, P.
paintings: (H) $825

WEBER, Paul
German/American 1823-1916
paintings: (L) $1,150; (H) $9,900
drawings: (H) $248

WEBER, Philip
American b. 1849
paintings: (H) $1,100

WEBER, R.
paintings: (H) $495

WEBER, Rudolf
Austrian b. 1872
paintings: (L) $825; (H) $2,541

WEBER, Sarah S. Stilwell
American 1878-1939
paintings: (H) $5,225

WEBER, Theodore
German 1838-1907
paintings: (L) $3,080; (H) $10,350

WEBER, Walter A.
American 20th cent.
drawings: (L) $325; (H) $450

WEBER-FULOP, Elizabeth
American 20th cent.
paintings: (H) $1,870

WEBSTER, Alfred George
paintings: (H) $978

WEBSTER, C.
British 19th cent.
paintings: (H) $1,150

WEBSTER, Edwin Ambrose
American 1869-1935
paintings: (L) $110; (H) $7,700

WEBSTER, Harold T.
1885-1953
drawings: (L) $330; (H) $468

WEBSTER, J.
English 19th cent.
paintings: (H) $1,210

WEBSTER, Meg
sculpture: (H) $4,400

WEBSTER, Thomas
British 1800-1886
paintings: (L) $605; (H) $4,125

WEBSTER, Walter Ernest
British 1878-1959
paintings: (H) $3,680

WEDEMEIER, Dietrich
ac. early 17th cent.
paintings: (H) $4,600

WEDIG, Gottfried von
German 1583-1641
paintings: (H) $55,000

WEDIN, Elof
1901-1983
paintings: (H) $6,325

WEEDON, A.W.
drawings: (H) $468

WEEDON, Augustus Walford
English 1838-1908
drawings: (L) $138; (H) $770

WEEGEE, William
American 20th cent.
drawings: (L) $385; (H) $1,045

WEEKES, Henry
British ac. 1851-1888
paintings: (L) $3,105; (H) $4,675
sculpture: (H) $46,000

WEEKES, Herbert William
British ac. 1856-1909
paintings: (L) $1,760; (H) $11,500

WEEKES, W.
English 19th cent.
paintings: (H) $770

WEEKES, William
British ac. 1864-1904
paintings: (H) $1,955

WEEKS, Charlotte
British ac. 1876-1890
paintings: (L) $9,200; (H) $25,300

WEEKS, Edwin Lord
b. U.S. 1849 d. Paris 1903
paintings: (L) $523; (H) $134,500

WEEKS, James
American b. 1922
paintings: (L) $2,750; (H) $23,000
drawings: (L) $935; (H) $3,575

WEELE, Herman Johannes van der
Dutch 1852-1930
paintings: (L) $2,750; (H) $3,575

WEENIX, Jan
Dutch c. 1642-1719
paintings: (L) $17,250; (H) $40,250

WEENIX, Jan Baptiste
Dutch 1621-1660/61
paintings: (L) $17,600; (H) $332,500

WEERTS, Jan Joseph
French 1847-1927
paintings: (H) $1,320

WEGENER, Gerda
Danish 1889-1940
paintings: (L) $4,025; (H) $107,000
drawings: (L) $990; (H) $4,950

WEGER, Marie
American 1882-1980
paintings: (L) $220; (H) $1,100

WEGMAN, William
American b. 1943
paintings: (L) $920; (H) $8,800
drawings: (L) $880; (H) $9,350

WEGNER, Erich
German b. 1899
paintings: (H) $3,850

WEGUELIN, John Reinhard
British 1849-1927
paintings: (H) $1,980

WEHN, Randolf
paintings: (H) $633

WEIBLING, John
American ac. c. 1832-1833
drawings: (H) $3,680

WEIDENAAR, Clair A.
paintings: (H) $450

WEIDENBACH, Augustus
American ac. 1853-1869
paintings: (H) $4,125

WEIDNER, Carl A.
American 19th cent.
paintings: (H) $605

WEIDNER, Roswell
American 20th cent.
paintings: (H) $990

WEIGAND, Gustave A.
American 1870-1957
paintings: (L) $358; (H) $935

WEIGELE, Henri
French 1858-1927
sculpture: (H) $288,500

WEIGHT, H.A.
British 19th cent.
paintings: (H) $2,090

WEIKERT, Marcia J.
American 20th cent.
drawings: (H) $460

WEILAND, James
American b. 1872
paintings: (L) $83; (H) $3,025

WEILAND, Johannes
Dutch 1856-1909
paintings: (L) $1,150; (H) $9,900

WEILER, Casper
American 19th cent.
paintings: (H) $550

WEILER, J.
American 20th cent.
paintings: (H) $715

WEILER, Milt
drawings: (H) $2,200

WEILER, Milton
drawings: (H) $3,000

WEIN, Albert W.
b. 1915
sculpture: (H) $3,738

WEINBERG, Emilie
1882-1958
paintings: (L) $374; (H) $3,738

WEINBERG, Steven
American b. 1954
sculpture: (L) $1,870; (H) $5,500

WEINDORF, Arthur
American b. 1885
paintings: (L) $230; (H) $1,210

WEINDORF, Paul F.
American 1887-1965
paintings: (L) $137; (H) $770

WEINER, Lawrence
b. 1942
paintings: (L) $9,775; (H) $19,550
drawings: (L) $2,990; (H) $16,500

WEINGART, Joachim
Polish 1896-1942
paintings: (H) $1,100

WEINLES, F.
paintings: (H) $11,000

WEINMAN, Adolph Alexander
German/American 1870-1952
sculpture: (L) $2,300; (H) $44,000

WEINMANN, P.
American 20th cent.
paintings: (H) $1,093

WEINRIB, David
contemporary
sculpture: (H) $1,150

WEINRICH, Agnes
American 1873-1946
paintings: (L) $523; (H) $1,320
drawings: (L) $110; (H) $935

WEINSTEIN, Matthew
b. 1964
paintings: (L) $1,610; (H) $4,025

WEIR, J.
paintings: (H) $935

WEIR, John Ferguson
American 1841-1926
paintings: (L) $552; (H) $52,800
drawings: (L) $55; (H) $358

WEIR, Julian Alden
American 1852-1919
paintings: (L) $715; (H) $74,000
drawings: (L) $1,210; (H) $8,800

WEIR, Julien Alden and Robert
WALTER
19th/20th cent.
drawings: (H) $1,980

WEIR, Robert Walter
American 1803-1899
paintings: (L) $385; (H) $18,400
drawings: (L) $55; (H) $825

WEIROTTER, Franz Edmund
Austrian 1730-1771
drawings: (H) $935

WEIS, John Ellsworth
American b. 1892
paintings: (L) $440; (H) $1,650

WEISBUCH, Claude
French b. 1928
paintings: (L) $1,870; (H) $8,250

WEISE, Alex
b. 1883
paintings: (H) $1,375

WEISE, Alexander
Russian b. 1883
paintings: (L) $605; (H) $660

WEISENBORN, Rudolph
American b. 1881
paintings: (L) $495; (H) $2,200
drawings: (L) $460; (H) $3,960

WEISER, B.
paintings: (H) $1,000

WEISMAN, Joseph
American 1906-1977
paintings: (H) $715
drawings: (L) $248; (H) $660

WEISMAN, William H.
American 1840-1922
paintings: (L) $88; (H) $743

WEISMANN, Jacques
French b. 1878
drawings: (H) $1,610

WEISS, Emil Rudolf
German 1875-1942
paintings: (L) $690; (H) $2,070

WEISS, Emile Georges
French b. 1861
paintings: (L) $770; (H) $7,975

WEISS, Johann Baptist
German 1812-1879
paintings: (H) $2,200

WEISS, Jose
British 1859-1929
paintings: (L) $578; (H) $5,520

WEISS, Milton
American 20th cent.
paintings: (H) $770

WEISS, Rudolf Johannes
Swiss b. 1846
paintings: (H) $2,860

WEISS, Rudolph
Czechoslovakian b. 1869
paintings: (H) $1,725

WEISSBERG, Leon
1894-1943
paintings: (H) $805

WEISSE
sculpture: (H) $1,760

WEISSE, Rudolf
Swiss b. 1846
paintings: (L) $8,800; (H) $55,000

WEISSENBRUCH, Johannes Hendrik
Dutch 1824-1903
paintings: (L) $2,200; (H) $13,800
drawings: (L) $5,175; (H) $7,475

WEISSENBRUCH, Willem Johannes
Dutch 1864-1941
paintings: (L) $2,185; (H) $2,750

WEISZ, Adolphe
French b. 1868; ac. 1875-1900
paintings: (L) $4,180; (H) $18,400

WEISZ, Karl
German 1839-1914
paintings: (H) $4,675

WEIXLGARTNER, Julius Richard
Austrian 1849-1912
drawings: (H) $1,320

WELCH, E.R.
American
paintings: (H) $3,575

WELCH, Ludmilla P.
American 1867-1925
paintings: (L) $1,380; (H) $2,588

WELCH, Ray
American
paintings: (H) $1,430

WELCH, Thaddeus
American 1844-1919
paintings: (L) $880; (H) $25,875
drawings: (H) $880

WELDON, Charles Dater
American 1855-1935
paintings: (H) $4,125
drawings: (L) $316; (H) $1,650

WELDON, Felix de
b. 1907
paintings: (H) $110
sculpture: (L) $55; (H) $578

WELIE, Antoon van
Continental 19th cent.
paintings: (H) $550

WELLER, Frank
American 19th cent.
paintings: (H) $468

WELLING, James
b. 1951
paintings: (L) $1,380; (H) $4,600
drawings: (L) $1,725; (H) $5,280

WELLINGTON, C.H.
drawings: (H) $575

WELLIVER, Neil
American b. 1929
paintings: (L) $1,610; (H) $36,800

WELLS, John Sanderson
British 1872-1955
paintings: (L) $3,162; (H) $5,610
drawings: (H) $220

WELLS, Lynton
American b. 1940
paintings: (H) $880

WELLS, William
paintings: (H) $1,650

WELSCH, Karl Friedrich Christian
German 1828-1904
paintings: (H) $6,670

WELSH, Horace Devitt
1888-1942
paintings: (H) $1,100

WENCKER, Joseph
French 1848-1919
paintings: (H) $11,500

WENDEL, Theodore
American 1857-1932
paintings: (L) $412; (H) $37,375
drawings: (L) $990; (H) $5,500

WENDELBERGER, W.H.
German 19th/20th cent.
paintings: (H) $550

California Impressionist

Chicago-trained and German-born, William Wendt (1865-1946) has been called the dean of California painters. An immigrant to the United States when only 15, he lived with an uncle in Chicago. His only formal training was in evening classes at the Art Institute of Chicago. During the day he worked in a commercial art shop painting display scenery; in his free time he worked at an easel. In 1893, after winning second place at a Chicago Society of Artists exhibition, he devoted himself full-time to his own work. George Gardner Symons was a close friend, and the two made several trips to Southern California, spending several winters there from 1894 until Wendt's marriage in 1906. After his marriage, Wendt and his wife, the sculptor Julia Bracken, moved to Los Angeles. They began to exhibit jointly and very successfully, in both Los Angeles and Chicago. Wendt was very active in the Los Angeles art community and was a cofounder and first president of the California Art Club in 1911. Before 1915, Wendt's work is characterized by light, short brushstrokes; his later works, landscapes of the rolling hills and arroyos of Southern California, have broader, bolder brushstrokes with a palette primarily of greens and browns. *Snow Cloud Heights,* an early work painted in 1913, brought $24,750 at Moran's auction in Pasadena, California. (William Wendt, *Snow Cloud Heights,* oil on canvas, 30 x 45 inches, Moran, June 13, 1995, $24,750)

WENDEROTH, Frederick August
  American 1819-1884
  paintings: (H) $1,320
WENDLING, Gustave
  German b. 1862
  paintings: (H) $660

WENDT, Julia Bracken
  1871-1942
  sculpture: (H) $2,875
WENDT, William
  American 1865-1946
  paintings: (L) $990; (H) $74,000

WENGENROTH, Stow
American 1906-1976
drawings: (L) $460; (H) $1,380

WENGER, John
American 1887-1976
paintings: (L) $577; (H) $1,495
drawings: (L) $99; (H) $880

WENGLEIN, Joseph
German 1845-1919
paintings: (L) $7,150; (H) $36,800

WENNERWALD, Emil
Danish 1859-1934
paintings: (L) $316; (H) $518

WENNING, Ype Heerke
Dutch b. 1879
paintings: (H) $825

WENTWORTH, Daniel F.
American 1850-1934
paintings: (L) $302; (H) $3,190
drawings: (L) $55; (H) $413

WENTWORTH, David
1850-1934
paintings: (H) $6,050

WENTWORTH, Richard
b. 1947
sculpture: (L) $880; (H) $5,750

WENTZ, Henry Frederick
American 20th cent.
paintings: (H) $1,100

WENTZEL, Nils Gustav
Norwegian 1859-1927
paintings: (H) $1,870

WENZEL, David
drawings: (L) $1,093; (H) $1,093

WENZELL, Albert Beck
American 1864-1917
paintings: (L) $1,265; (H) $2,875
drawings: (L) $440; (H) $10,450

WERCOLLIER, Lucien
sculpture: (H) $2,200

WERENSKIOLD, Erik Theodor
Norwegian 1855-1936
paintings: (H) $55,000

WERFF, Adriaen van der
Dutch 1659-1722
paintings: (H) $8,800

WERFF, Adriaen van der, studio of
Dutch 17th/18th cent.
paintings: (H) $30,800

WERFF, Pieter van der
Dutch 1655-1722
paintings: (L) $2,587; (H) $13,200

WERNER, Anton Alexander von
German 1843-1915
drawings: (L) $880; (H) $990

WERNER, Carl Friedrich Heinrich
German 1808-1894
paintings: (L) $5,750; (H) $23,000
drawings: (H) $1,430

WERNER, Fritz
b. 1898
paintings: (H) $2,300

WERNER, Fritz Carl, and Eugene Joseph VERBOECKHOVEN
paintings: (H) $10,450

WERNER, Hermann
German 1816-1905
paintings: (H) $8,913

WERNER, Joseph, the younger
Swiss 1637-1710
paintings: (H) $22,000
drawings: (H) $2,875

WERNER, Nat
American b. 1910
sculpture: (L) $460; (H) $2,200

WERTHEIM, Heinrich J.
drawings: (H) $2,090

WERTHEIMER, Mrs.
American 19th cent.
paintings: (H) $605

WERTHEIMER, Gustave
Austrian 1847-1904
paintings: (L) $7,425; (H) $13,800

WERTMULLER, Adolf Ulrich
Swedish 1751-1811
paintings: (H) $29,900

WESCHLER, Anita
American ac. 1951-1982
sculpture: (H) $460

WESCOTT, Paul
paintings: (H) $1,750

WESCOTT, Paul
American 1904-1970
paintings: (L) $1,320; (H) $1,750

WESLEY, John
American b. 1928
paintings: (L) $2,760; (H) $4,830

WESSELMANN, Tom
American b. 1931
paintings: (L) $3,000; (H) $244,500
drawings: (L) $358; (H) $27,600
sculpture: (L) $798; (H) $107,000

WESSELS, Glenn
American 1895-1982
drawings: (H) $1,540

WESSOLOWSKI, Hans, Wesso
b. 1894
drawings: (H) $660

WESSON, Robert Shaw
American 1902-1967
paintings: (L) $55; (H) $990

WEST, Benjamin
American 1738-1820
paintings: (L) $5,175; (H) $60,250
drawings: (L) $385; (H) $19,800

WEST, Benjamin F.
American 1818-1854
paintings: (H) $12,100

WEST, Edgar E.
English ac. 1857-1889
drawings: (L) $385; (H) $935

WEST, Edith
paintings: (H) $6,325

WEST, Francis
American/Canadian 19th/20th cent.
sculpture: (H) $880

WEST, Francis J.
American 20th cent.
paintings: (H) $660

WEST, Franz
contemporary
sculpture: (H) $4,400

WEST, J.H.
American
sculpture: (H) $825

WEST, Levon
American 1900-1968
drawings: (H) $522

WEST, Louise
paintings: (H) $1,300

WEST, Michael
paintings: (H) $1,725

WEST, Peter B.
British/American 1837-1913
paintings: (L) $259; (H) $460

WEST, Raphael Lamar
British 1769-1850
drawings: (L) $110; (H) $1,210

WEST, Reginald
British ac. 1900-1910
drawings: (H) $522

WEST, Richard Whatley
Irish 1848-1905
paintings: (H) $2,875

WEST, Samuel
Irish 1810-1867
paintings: (H) $13,800

WEST, W.
paintings: (H) $1,100

WEST, W.
British 19th cent.
paintings: (H) $550

WEST, William
British 1801-1861
paintings: (H) $8,625

WESTALL, Richard
English 1765-1836
paintings: (L) $2,090; (H) $8,625
drawings: (H) $550

WESTCHILOFF, C.
paintings: (H) $633

WESTCHILOFF, Constantin
b. Russia 1880 d. N.Y.C. 1945
paintings: (L) $88; (H) $6,600
drawings: (L) $330; (H) $935

WESTENHOLME, Charles Dean
British 1798-1883
paintings: (H) $5,750

WESTERBEEK, Cornelis
Dutch 1844-1903
paintings: (L) $1,320; (H) $5,500

WESTERMANN, H.C.
American b. 1922
drawings: (L) $1,100; (H) $10,925
sculpture: (L) $4,620; (H) $54,050

WESTEROH
Continental 19th cent.
paintings: (H) $1,495

WESTEROP, Wilhelm
19th cent.
paintings: (H) $977

WESTHOFF, D.
Austrian 19th cent.
paintings: (H) $3,450

WESTHOVEN, Huybert van
Dutch c. 1643-before 1687
paintings: (H) $63,000

WESTIN, Frederik
Swedish 1782-1862
paintings: (H) $4,313

WESTMACOTT
American 19th cent.
paintings: (H) $1,430

WESTMACOTT, Stuart
Canadian 1818-1862?
paintings: (H) $34,500

WESTON, Harry Alan
American 1885-1931
paintings: (H) $2,070
drawings: (L) $173; (H) $201

WESTON, William Percival
Canadian 1897-1967
paintings: (L) $25,300; (H) $44,000

WET, Gerrit de
1616-1674
paintings: (H) $2,875

WET, Jacob Willemsz. de
Dutch 1610-1671
paintings: (L) $3,738; (H) $27,600

WETERING-DE ROOY, Johan van de
Dutch 1877-1972
paintings: (H) $990

WETHERBY, Isaac Augustus
American 1819-1904
paintings: (L) $770; (H) $2,750

WETHERILL, Elisha Kent Kane
American 1874-1929
paintings: (L) $1,100; (H) $1,870

WETMORE, Mary M.
American 19th/20th cent.
paintings: (H) $715

WETMORE, T.
American 20th cent.
paintings: (L) $460; (H) $489

WETTSCHER
paintings: (H) $1,760

WEX, Willibald
German 1831-1892
paintings: (L) $1,870; (H) $2,760

WEYDE, Van Der, Jr.
American ac. mid 19th cent.
drawings: (H) $4,180

WEYDEN, Harry van der
American/English 1868-after 1935
paintings: (L) $495; (H) $1,870

WEYL, Max
American 1837-1914
paintings: (L) $357; (H) $6,050

WEYTS, Petrus Cornelius
Belgian 1799-1855
paintings: (H) $12,100

WHAITE, T.
British 19th cent.
paintings: (H) $2,070

WHALLEY, J.K.
British 19th cent.
paintings: (H) $4,400

WHARTON, Margaret
b. 1943
paintings: (H) $2,185
sculpture: (L) $935; (H) $6,900

WHARTON, Philip Fishbourne
American 1841-1880
paintings: (H) $990

WHATLEY, Henry
British 1841-1901
drawings: (H) $2,530

WHEATLEY, Francis
English 1747-1801
paintings: (L) $1,870; (H) $110,000
drawings: (H) $3,680

WHEATLEY, G.H.
American 20th cent.
paintings: (L) $308; (H) $495

WHEATLEY, Warik
b. 1928
paintings: (L) $82; (H) $550

WHEATON, Francis
American b. 1849
paintings: (L) $132; (H) $2,530
drawings: (H) $185

WHEELER, Alfred
British 1851-1932
paintings: (L) $3,025; (H) $17,250

WHEELER, Charles "Shang"
paintings: (H) $1,650

WHEELER, Clifton
paintings: (H) $475
drawings: (H) $30

WHEELER, Hughlette, Tex
American 1900-1955
sculpture: (L) $825; (H) $2,420

WHEELER, James
English 1820-1885
paintings: (L) $440; (H) $3,850

WHEELER, John Alfred, of Bath
British 1821-1903
paintings: (L) $1,955; (H) $11,550

WHEELER, John Arnold, Jr.
English ac. 1889
paintings: (L) $1,045; (H) $1,980

WHEELER, Kathleen
English b. 1884
sculpture: (H) $880

WHEELER, Shang
paintings: (L) $440; (H) $5,500
drawings: (L) $330; (H) $1,870

WHEELER, William R.
American 1832-1894
paintings: (H) $4,400

WHEELOCK, M.G.
drawings: (H) $863

WHEELWRIGHT, N.H.
British 19th cent.
drawings: (H) $715

WHEELWRIGHT, Rowland
Australian 1870-1955
paintings: (H) $8,250

WHEELWRIGHT, W.H.
British 1857-1897
paintings: (H) $5,175

WHEELWRIGHT, W.H.
British ac. 1857-1897
drawings: (H) $1,100

WHELAN, Michael
paintings: (H) $12,100

WHELAN, Sylvester J.
American 19th/20th cent.
paintings: (H) $605

WHICHELO, A.G.
English 19th cent.
paintings: (H) $1,100

WHIPPLE, J.
British 1880-1919
paintings: (H) $522

WHISTLER, James Abbott McNeill
American 1834-1903
paintings: (L) $33,000; (H) $231,000
drawings: (L) $451; (H) $145,500

WHITAKER, Frederic
American b. 1891
drawings: (L) $121; (H) $715

WHITAKER, George William
American 1841-1916
paintings: (L) $110; (H) $2,310
drawings: (H) $110

WHITAKER, William
American b. 1943
paintings: (L) $1,320; (H) $11,000
drawings: (L) $660; (H) $1,760

WHITCOMB, Jon
American 1906-1988
paintings: (L) $259; (H) $3,300
drawings: (L) $220; (H) $2,420

WHITCOMBE, Thomas
English c. 1760-c. 1824
paintings: (L) $7,700; (H) $22,000

WHITE, Charles
African/American 1918-1979
paintings: (L) $3,680; (H) $10,925
drawings: (H) $1,840

WHITE, Edith
American 1855-1946
paintings: (L) $385; (H) $4,025
drawings: (H) $990

WHITE, Fritz
American b. 1930
sculpture: (H) $1,320

WHITE, Gabriella Antoinette
American ac. 1880-1915
paintings: (H) $1,320

WHITE, George
American 1826-1872
paintings: (H) $2,200

WHITE, Gilbert
American 19th/20th cent.
paintings: (H) $1,430

WHITE, H.M.
19th cent.
sculpture: (H) $1,980

WHITE, Henry
1819-1896
paintings: (H) $978

WHITE, Henry Cooke
1861-1952
paintings: (H) $1,210
drawings: (H) $660

WHITE, J.W.
drawings: (H) $1,925

WHITE, Janet
American 20th cent.
paintings: (H) $935

WHITE, Joe
American contemporary
paintings: (H) $1,210

WHITE, John
British 1851-1933
paintings: (L) $3,630; (H) $21,850

WHITE, John
English 1851-1933
drawings: (H) $2,420

WHITE, Juliet
American 19th/20th cent.
drawings: (H) $2,750

WHITE, Laura
drawings: (H) $1,035

WHITE, Mary Bayard
American b. 1947
sculpture: (H) $1,380

WHITE, Orrin A.
American 1883-1969
paintings: (L) $495; (H) $18,700
drawings: (L) $220; (H) $1,540

WHITE, R. Lee
American 20th cent.
paintings: (H) $1,955
drawings: (L) $578; (H) $3,738

WHITE, Robert
American 20th cent.
paintings: (L) $220; (H) $1,320

WHITE, Thomas Gilbert
American 1877-1939
paintings: (H) $5,175
drawings: (H) $495

WHITE, Wade
American b. 1909
paintings: (H) $3,850

WHITEFIELD, Edwin
British 1816-1892
paintings: (H) $1,980
drawings: (L) $1,035; (H) $4,400

WHITEHEAD, Margaret van Cortland
paintings: (H) $500

WHITEHEAD, R*** H***
British 1855-1889
paintings: (H) $14,950

WHITELEY, T.J.
American 19th cent.
paintings: (H) $907

WHITEMAN, M.H.
British 19th cent.
paintings: (H) $1,150

WHITESIDE, Brian
American 19th/20th cent.
paintings: (L) $1,840; (H) $2,475

WHITESIDE, Brian
British b. 1934
paintings: (L) $2,070; (H) $2,875

WHITESIDE, Frank Reed
American 1866-1929
paintings: (L) $715; (H) $3,575
drawings: (H) $825

WHITFIELD, E.
paintings: (H) $550

WHITFORD, Richard
British 1854-1887
paintings: (L) $1,045; (H) $21,850

WHITING, Henry W.
American 19th cent.
paintings: (L) $1,760; (H) $3,300

WHITLEY, B.
paintings: (H) $550

WHITLEY, Harold C.
paintings: (H) $1,100

WHITLEY, William T.
English 1885-1902
paintings: (H) $495

WHITMORE, M. Coburn (Coby)
American b. 1913
paintings: (L) $770; (H) $1,980
drawings: (H) $1,210

WHITNEY, Gertrude Vanderbilt
American 1878-1942
sculpture: (L) $1,725; (H) $9,200

WHITNEY, Ogden
drawings: (H) $770

WHITTAKER, George W.
paintings: (H) $935

WHITTAKER, John Barnard
American 1836-1926
paintings: (L) $1,100; (H) $2,300

WHITTEMORE, William John
American 1860-1955
paintings: (L) $550; (H) $1,430
drawings: (L) $2,475; (H) $3,450

WHITTLE, Thomas, Jr.
British ac. 1865-1885
paintings: (H) $1,035

WHITTREDGE, Worthington
American 1820-1910
paintings: (L) $1,650; (H) $266,500

WHITWRIGHT, W.H.
paintings: (H) $1,650

WHORF, John
American 1903-1959
paintings: (L) $633; (H) $26,400
drawings: (L) $104; (H) $9,900

WHORF, Richard
American 20th cent.
paintings: (L) $489; (H) $935

WICAR, Jean Baptiste
1762-1834
paintings: (H) $17,250

WICART, Nicolas
1748-1815
drawings: (H) $1,430

WICHBERG, H.
Danish 19th cent.
paintings: (H) $1,320

WICHERA, Raimund von
Austrian 1862-1925
paintings: (H) $2,090

WICHT, John von
paintings: (H) $935

WICHT, John von
American 1888-1970
paintings: (L) $302; (H) $2,420

WICHT, John von
American 1888-1970
paintings: (L) $302; (H) $2,420
drawings: (H) $5,175

WICKENDEN, Robert J.
Canadian 1861-1931
paintings: (H) $5,720

WICKES, Ethel Marian
American 1872-1940
drawings: (H) $495

WICKSTAAD, R.
paintings: (H) $5,500

WIDERBERG, Frans
paintings: (L) $2,415; (H) $6,440

WIDFORSS, Gunnar
Swedish/American 1879-1934
paintings: (L) $8,625; (H) $14,950
drawings: (L) $330; (H) $21,850

WIDGERY, F. John
British 1861-1899
drawings: (L) $302; (H) $660

WIDMANN, Bruno
Uruguayan b. 1930
paintings: (H) $8,625

WIDMAR, G.
20th cent.
paintings: (H) $550

WIECK, J.
European 20th cent.
paintings: (H) $715

WIECZOREK, Max
American 1863-1955
drawings: (H) $3,300

WIEGAND, Albert
sculpture: (H) $1,035

WIEGAND, Bernhardt
German 19th cent.
paintings: (H) $880

WIEGAND, Charmion von
American b. 1899/1900
paintings: (H) $12,100
drawings: (L) $2,300; (H) $4,950

WIEGAND, Don
American contemporary
sculpture: (L) $115; (H) $4,180

WIEGAND, Gustave Adolph
German/American 1870-1957
paintings: (L) $225; (H) $6,050
drawings: (H) $192

WIEGANDT, Bernhard
German 1851-1918
drawings: (L) $6,900; (H) $13,800

WIEGANDT, Charles
Continental 19th/20th cent.
paintings: (H) $3,450

WIEGHORST, Olaf
American 1899-1988
paintings: (L) $747; (H) $66,000
drawings: (L) $1,320; (H) $7,700
sculpture: (H) $5,000

WIELAND, Hans Beat
Swiss 1867-1945
drawings: (H) $858

WIERTZ, C.
Dutch 19th cent.
paintings: (L) $385; (H) $1,320

WIESELTHIER, Vally
sculpture: (L) $4,400; (H) $6,325

WIESENDANGER, Dan
American b. 1915
paintings: (H) $935

WIESENTHAL, Franz
Hungarian b. 1856
paintings: (L) $247; (H) $11,000

WIGAND, Balthasar
Austrian 1771-1846
drawings: (L) $2,530; (H) $5,750

WIGAND, Otto Charles
1856-1944
paintings: (H) $2,760

WIGGERS, Dirk
Dutch 1866-1933
paintings: (H) $1,495

WIGGIN, Alfred J.
American 1823-1883
paintings: (H) $546

WIGGINS, Carleton
American 1848-1932
paintings: (L) $385; (H) $6,600
drawings: (L) $110; (H) $413

WIGGINS, Guy Carleton
American 1883-1962
paintings: (L) $7,700; (H) $184,000
drawings: (L) $357; (H) $2,530

WIGGINS, John Carleton
American 1848-1932
paintings: (L) $605; (H) $7,700
drawings: (H) $920

WIGGINS, K. Douglas
American b. 1960
paintings: (L) $1,430; (H) $19,525

WIGHLAN, William
British 19th cent.
paintings: (H) $605

WIGHT, Frederick S.
American 1902-1986
paintings: (H) $1,840

WIGMANA, Gerard
1673-1741
paintings: (H) $10,638

WIKSTROM, Bror Anders
Swedish c. 1840-1909
paintings: (L) $1,320; (H) $7,150
drawings: (L) $330; (H) $2,090

WILBER, Lawrence N.
b. 1897
paintings: (H) $2,070

WILBERT, Robert
American b. 1929
paintings: (H) $3,795
drawings: (H) $978

WILBUR, Theodore E.
19th cent.
paintings: (H) $1,089

WILCKENS, August
German 1870-1939
paintings: (H) $575

WILCOX, Frank
American 1887-1964
paintings: (L) $385; (H) $467
drawings: (L) $71; (H) $1,100

WILCOX, I.R.
ac. 19th/20th cent.
drawings: (L) $550; (H) $550

WILCOX, John
paintings: (H) $3,300

WILCOX, Louis
paintings: (H) $577

WILCOX, R.D.
American 20th cent.
paintings: (L) $110; (H) $990

WILCOX, W.H.
American b. 1831
paintings: (H) $935

WILCOX, W.S.
late 19th cent.
paintings: (L) $935; (H) $4,025

WILCOX, William H.
American
paintings: (H) $4,070

WILD, Hamilton Gibbs
paintings: (H) $1,320

WILD, Michael
British 19th cent.
paintings: (H) $2,185

WILDA, Charles
Austrian 1854-1907
paintings: (L) $6,325; (H) $51,750

WILDE, Frans de
Belgian 1840-1918
paintings: (L) $8,625; (H) $14,850

WILDE, H.
paintings: (H) $2,420

WILDE, John
American b. 1919
paintings: (L) $3,850; (H) $4,400

WILDENS, Jan
Flemish 1586-1653
paintings: (L) $40,250; (H) $74,000

WILDER
Continental
paintings: (H) $1,760
drawings: (L) $1,100; (H) $1,430

WILDER, Andre
French 1871-1965
paintings: (H) $1,840

WILDER, Arthur B.
American 1857-1945
paintings: (L) $575; (H) $2,200

WILDER, Tom
paintings: (L) $138; (H) $2,200

WILES, Irving Ramsay
American 1861-1948
paintings: (L) $110; (H) $184,000
drawings: (L) $110; (H) $11,500

WILES, Irving and Lemuel WILES
paintings: (H) $3,300

WILES, Lemuel Maynard
American 1826-1905
paintings: (L) $715; (H) $14,950
drawings: (H) $633

WILES, Walter G.
S. African 20th cent.
paintings: (H) $825

WILEY, William
sculpture: (H) $1,980

WILEY, William T.
American b. 1937
drawings: (L) $770; (H) $18,400
sculpture: (L) $1,320; (H) $3,450

WILFORD, Loran F.
American b. 1892
paintings: (L) $220; (H) $990
drawings: (H) $240

WILHELM, A. Wayne
b. 1901
paintings: (H) $1,725

WILHELM, J.
paintings: (L) $385; (H) $770

WILHELM, Joseph
American contemporary
paintings: (H) $935

WILHELM, Rudolph
German b. 1889
paintings: (H) $825

WILHELMSOM, Carl Wilhelm
Swedish 1866-1928
paintings: (H) $19,550

WILK, Harry Nils
paintings: (H) $550

WILKIE
paintings: (L) $88; (H) $880

WILKIE, Robert D.
American 1828-1903
paintings: (L) $192; (H) $3,300

WILKIE, Sir David
English 1785-1841
paintings: (L) $1,100; (H) $2,420

WILKIE-KILGOUR, A.
British 20th cent.
paintings: (H) $578

WILKINSON, Arthur
British 19th/20th cent.
paintings: (L) $1,380; (H) $4,400
drawings: (L) $715; (H) $880

WILKINSON, Henry
paintings: (H) $605

WILKINSON, Norman
English 1878-1971
paintings: (H) $825

WILKS, Maurice C.
British 1911-1983
paintings: (L) $522; (H) $1,760

WILKS, R.
American 19th cent.
paintings: (H) $550

WILL, G.
Continental School 19th cent.
paintings: (H) $1,540

WILLAERT, Fega
Belgian 20th cent.
paintings: (H) $4,600

WILLAERT, Ferdenand
Belgian 1823-1905
paintings: (H) $2,750

WILLAERTS, Adam
Flemish 1577-1664
paintings: (L) $21,850; (H) $66,000

WILLARD, Archibald
American 1836-1918
paintings: (L) $605; (H) $8,625
drawings: (H) $385

WILLBRIGHT, Monroe
American 20th cent.
paintings: (H) $550

WILLCOCK, George Barrell
British 1811-1852
paintings: (L) $660; (H) $2,420

WILLE, Johann Georg
1715-1808
drawings: (L) $2,640; (H) $3,300

WILLE, Pierre Alexandre, called Wille
fils
French 1748-1821
drawings: (L) $1,320; (H) $2,750

WILLEBOIRTS, Thomas, called
Willeboirts Bosschaert
Flemish 1614-1654
paintings: (H) $76,750

WILLEMART, Louise
French b. 1863
paintings: (H) $2,420

WILLEMS, Florent
Belgian 1823-1905
paintings: (L) $1,650; (H) $17,600

WILLEMS, J.
Belgian 19th cent.
paintings: (H) $770

WILLEMS, L.
Dutch 19th cent.
paintings: (L) $550; (H) $770

WILLEMS, S.
Belgian 19th cent.
paintings: (H) $2,990

WILLEMSENS, Abraham
Flemish ac. 1627-1672
paintings: (L) $23,000; (H) $33,000

WILLENECH, Michel, WILLENIGH
French c. 1891
paintings: (H) $797

WILLET, G.
American 19th cent.
paintings: (H) $605

WILLIA
Scottish 19th cent.
paintings: (L) $660; (H) $3,080

WILLIAM
Hungarian
paintings: (H) $825

WILLIAMS, A. Sheldon
British d. 1880
paintings: (H) $11,500

WILLIAMS, Adele
American ac. c. 1947
paintings: (H) $1,725

WILLIAMS, Albert Henry
British 20th cent.
paintings: (L) $770; (H) $1,100

WILLIAMS, Alexander
British
paintings: (H) $1,925

WILLIAMS, Charles
English b. 1823
paintings: (H) $1,760

WILLIAMS, Dwight
American 1856-1932
paintings: (H) $2,530

WILLIAMS, E.C.
English 19th cent.
paintings: (H) $962

WILLIAMS, Edward, Jr.
British 1782-1855
paintings: (H) $2,300

WILLIAMS, Edward B.
paintings: (L) $450; (H) $575

WILLIAMS, Edward Charles
English ac. 1839-1845
paintings: (L) $302; (H) $5,390

WILLIAMS, Edward K.
paintings: (L) $825; (H) $1,100

WILLIAMS, F.
paintings: (H) $770

WILLIAMS, F.D.
American 1829-1915
paintings: (H) $863

WILLIAMS, Florence White
American d. 1953
paintings: (L) $66; (H) $1,430
drawings: (H) $33

WILLIAMS, Florent
Belgian 1823-1905
paintings: (H) $9,350

WILLIAMS, Fred
drawings: (H) $880

WILLIAMS, Frederick Ballard
American 1871-1956
paintings: (L) $165; (H) $4,400

WILLIAMS, Frederick Dickinson
American 1829-1915
paintings: (L) $220; (H) $15,400
drawings: (L) $413; (H) $978

WILLIAMS, George
b. 1910
sculpture: (L) $1,045; (H) $1,540

WILLIAMS, George Augustus
British 1814-1901
paintings: (L) $1,265; (H) $4,125

WILLIAMS, Gluyas
American 1888-1982
drawings: (H) $660

WILLIAMS, Graham
British 19th cent.
paintings: (L) $403; (H) $1,840

WILLIAMS, H.
English/Scottish 19th cent.
paintings: (H) $1,320

WILLIAMS, H.D.
English 19th cent.
paintings: (H) $1,650

WILLIAMS, Harry
British ac. 1854-1877
paintings: (H) $6,037

WILLIAMS, Helen
American 20th cent.
paintings: (H) $1,725
drawings: (H) $28

WILLIAMS, John Haynes
British 19th cent.
paintings: (H) $4,400

WILLIAMS, John L. Scott
1897-1976
paintings: (H) $247
drawings: (L) $468; (H) $825

WILLIAMS, M.
20th cent.
paintings: (L) $66; (H) $518

WILLIAMS, Mary Belle
American 1873-1943
paintings: (L) $165; (H) $1,210

WILLIAMS, Micah
American 1782/83-1837
paintings: (H) $5,175

WILLIAMS, Neil
20th cent.
paintings: (H) $2,860

WILLIAMS, O.
drawings: (H) $546

WILLIAMS, Paul A.
American b. 1934
paintings: (L) $660; (H) $2,640

WILLIAMS, Pauline Bliss
American b. 1888
paintings: (L) $550; (H) $660

WILLIAMS, Penry
English, d. Rome 1798-1885
paintings: (L) $1,610; (H) $6,600

WILLIAMS, Peter
American 20th cent.
paintings: (H) $1,035

WILLIAMS, Rene
American 20th cent.
sculpture: (L) $605; (H) $935

WILLIAMS, Richard
drawings: (L) $3,850; (H) $4,950

WILLIAMS, Terrick
English 1860-1936
paintings: (L) $2,530; (H) $7,700

WILLIAMS, Virgil
American 1830-1886
paintings: (L) $880; (H) $8,800

WILLIAMS, W.
paintings: (H) $1,320

WILLIAMS, W.
British 19th cent.
paintings: (H) $1,540

WILLIAMS, Walter
paintings: (H) $1,870

WILLIAMS, Walter
British 1835-1906
paintings: (L) $1,430; (H) $6,900

WILLIAMS, Walter Heath
British 19th cent.
paintings: (L) $1,980; (H) $3,450

WILLIAMS, Wheeler
American 1897-1972
sculpture: (L) $1,210; (H) $79,500

WILLIAMS, William
British 1727-1791
paintings: (H) $3,450

WILLIAMSON, A.
paintings: (H) $1,100
drawings: (H) $412

WILLIAMSON, Al
drawings: (L) $253; (H) $715

WILLIAMSON, Al and Frank
FRAZETTA
drawings: (H) $7,700

WILLIAMSON, Frederick
British 19th cent.
paintings: (H) $770

WILLIAMSON, H.
paintings: (H) $633

WILLIAMSON, John
American 1826-1885
paintings: (L) $523; (H) $35,200

WILLIAMSON, Skip
drawings: (H) $2,200

WILLIAMSON, William Henry
British 1820-1883
paintings: (L) $880; (H) $6,325

WILLIFORD, Hollis
b. 1940
sculpture: (L) $4,400; (H) $6,050

WILLIGEN, Claes Jansz. van der
c. 1630-1676
paintings: (H) $8,800

WILLING, John Thompson
b. 1860
paintings: (H) $715

WILLIOT, P.
Belgian 19th cent.
paintings: (H) $1,650

WILLIS, A.V.
British 19th cent.
paintings: (L) $115; (H) $4,950

WILLIS, Edmund
American 1808-1899
paintings: (L) $220; (H) $2,200

WILLIS, Fritz
paintings: (L) $2,090; (H) $2,750

WILLIS, Henry Brittan
English 1810-1884
paintings: (H) $4,400

WILLIS, J.V.
19th cent.
paintings: (H) $495

WILLIS, T.
American 1850-1912
paintings: (L) $250; (H) $1,980

WILLIS, Thomas
American 1850-1912
paintings: (L) $385; (H) $6,600
drawings: (L) $330; (H) $770

WILLISON, T.J.
American 20th cent.
paintings: (L) $110; (H) $770

WILLLIAMSON, W.H.
English 1820-1883
paintings: (H) $935

WILLMANN, Michael Lucas Leopold
1630-1706
paintings: (H) $8,913
drawings: (H) $3,080

WILLMS, Arnold
British 19th cent.
paintings: (H) $6,325

WILLROIDER, Josef
German 1838-1915
paintings: (H) $3,630

WILLROIDER, Ludwig
German 1845-1910
paintings: (L) $3,575; (H) $20,700

WILLS, G.
Continental 19th cent.
paintings: (H) $748

WILLSON, Robert
contemporary
sculpture: (H) $1,725

WILLUMS, Olaf
European 20th cent.
paintings: (H) $523

WILMARTH, Christopher
American b. 1943
drawings: (L) $2,200; (H) $10,925
sculpture: (L) $7,700; (H) $57,500

WILMOT, James
Australian 20th cent.
paintings: (L) $275; (H) $495

WILMS, Peter Joseph
German 1814-1892
paintings: (H) $2,970

WILNER, Marie
American b. 1910
paintings: (H) $1,320

WILSON
paintings: (L) $55; (H) $275
drawings: (H) $88
sculpture: (H) $1,320

WILSON, Anna
American 19th cent.
paintings: (H) $7,975

WILSON, Ashton
b. 1880
paintings: (H) $825

WILSON, C.J.A.
American 1880-1965
drawings: (H) $805

WILSON, Charles Theller
American 1855-1920
paintings: (H) $825

WILSON, David Forrester
British b. 1873
paintings: (H) $2,970

WILSON, Donald Roller
American 20th cent.
paintings: (L) $2,588; (H) $17,250

WILSON, Edward A.
British/American 1886-1970
paintings: (H) $3,105
drawings: (L) $66; (H) $1,430

WILSON, Edward N.
American c. 1900
sculpture: (H) $2,090

WILSON, F.
paintings: (H) $4,125

WILSON, Francis Vaux
1874-1938
drawings: (H) $1,210

WILSON, Hart
drawings: (H) $1,045

WILSON, Helen
b. 1884
paintings: (H) $880

WILSON, James Perry
American 1889-1976
paintings: (L) $302; (H) $1,100

WILSON, Jane
American b. 1924
paintings: (L) $715; (H) $1,840
drawings: (H) $165

WILSON, John
British 1774-1855
paintings: (L) $880; (H) $4,025

WILSON, John James
British 1818-1875
paintings: (H) $5,750

WILSON, M.B.
American late 19th cent.
paintings: (H) $1,650

WILSON, Martha S.
paintings: (H) $1,210

WILSON, Mary Loomis
1898-1954
paintings: (H) $7,475

WILSON, Mortimer
American b. 1906
drawings: (H) $1,980

WILSON, Nick
drawings: (H) $1,100

WILSON, P. MacGregor
English d. 1928
drawings: (H) $495

WILSON, Raymond C.
American 1906-1972
paintings: (H) $4,400
drawings: (L) $110; (H) $1,870

WILSON, Richard
British 1714-1782
paintings: (L) $1,035; (H) $22,000
drawings: (H) $1,093

WILSON, Richard, studio of
18th cent.
paintings: (H) $9,200

WILSON, S. Chester
American 19th cent.
paintings: (H) $990

WILSON, S. Clay
drawings: (H) $2,475

WILSON, Sol
Polish/American 1894/96-1974
paintings: (L) $110; (H) $3,080
drawings: (L) $132; (H) $385

WILSON, Thomas Walter
British b. 1851
paintings: (H) $2,200

WILSON, W.
paintings: (H) $660

WILSON, W.
English 19th cent.
paintings: (H) $605

WILSON, W. Reynolds, Jr.
American 1899-1934.
paintings: (H) $1,017

WILSON, William
American 19th cent.
paintings: (H) $825

WILSON, William Heath
Scottish 1849-1927
paintings: (H) $4,600

WILTZ, Arnold
1889-1937
paintings: (L) $2,640; (H) $3,737

WILTZ, E. Madeline Shiff
American 20th cent.
paintings: (H) $110
drawings: (H) $495

WILWERDING, William J.
b. 1891
paintings: (H) $1,320

WIMAR, Carl
American 1828-1862
paintings: (H) $57,500

WIMAR, Carl
American 1828-1862
paintings: (H) $222,500

WIMBUSH, Henry B.
English 19th/20th cent.
drawings: (H) $660

WIMMER, Konrad
German 1844-1905
paintings: (L) $5,500; (H) $8,250

WIMPERIS, Edmund Morison
English 1835-1900
paintings: (L) $2,750; (H) $13,800

WINANS, Walter
English 1852-1920
sculpture: (L) $990; (H) $34,500

WINCHELL, Paul
American 20th cent.
paintings: (L) $33; (H) $3,300

WINCK, Johann Amandus
German c. 1748-1817
paintings: (L) $9,775; (H) $165,000

WINCKLEMANN, Gustavo
Langenberg
ac. c. 1896
paintings: (H) $17,250

WINDER, Daniel H.
British ac. 1880-1920
paintings: (H) $805

WINDER, Rud.
sculpture: (H) $880

WINDHAGER, Franz
Austrian 1879-1959
paintings: (L) $660; (H) $2,200

WINDMAIER, Anton
German 1840-1896
paintings: (L) $2,200; (H) $4,370

WINE, J.
French 18th/19th cent.
drawings: (H) $495

WINFIELD, Rodney
American contemporary
drawings: (H) $2,970
sculpture: (H) $230

WING, J.A.E.
Scottish 19th cent.
sculpture: (H) $604

WINGERT, Edward Oswald
American 1846-1924
paintings: (L) $220; (H) $1,045

WINGFIELD, James Digman
British d. 1872
paintings: (L) $2,185; (H) $10,450

WINGREN, Dan
contemporary
paintings: (L) $523; (H) $660

WINHART, A.
German 19th/20th cent.
paintings: (L) $715; (H) $825

WINK, Johann Amandus
German c. 1748-1817
paintings: (L) $46,000; (H) $93,500

WINKLER, Ferdinand
Austrian b. 1879
sculpture: (H) $1,150

WINKLEY, J.
American 19th cent.
paintings: (H) $920

WINNER, William E.
American c. 1815-1883
paintings: (H) $28,600
drawings: (H) $275

**WINSLOW, WETHERELL AND
BIGELOW,** Architects
American 19th/20th cent.
drawings: (H) $2,875

WINSOR, Jackie
Canadian/American b. 1941
sculpture: (L) $2,185; (H) $19,800

WINSTANLEY, H.
British 19th cent.
paintings: (H) $633

WINSTANLEY, William H.
paintings: (H) $4,950

WINSTON, Harold
British 19th/20th cent.
paintings: (H) $605

WINTER, Abraham Hendrik
Dutch 1800-1861
paintings: (H) $5,750

WINTER, Alice Beach
American 1877-1970
paintings: (L) $230; (H) $2,640

WINTER, Andrew
American 1893-1958
paintings: (L) $302; (H) $6,900

WINTER, Bernhard
German 1871-1964
paintings: (H) $660

WINTER, Charles Allan
American 1869-1942
paintings: (L) $165; (H) $8,050

WINTER, Ezra Augustus
American 1886-1949
paintings: (H) $1,430
drawings: (H) $55

WINTER, Fritz
German 1905-1978
paintings: (L) $37,400; (H) $112,500

WINTER, J. Greenwood
British ac. 1891-1914
paintings: (H) $880

WINTER, William Arthur
b. 1909
paintings: (L) $1,210; (H) $1,650

WINTERHALTER, Franz Xavier
1805-1973
paintings: (H) $5,500

WINTERHALTER, Hermann
German 1808-1891
paintings: (H) $33,350

WINTERS, Robin
American b. 1950
paintings: (H) $4,400

WINTERS, Terry
American b. 1949
paintings: (L) $29,900; (H) $148,500
drawings: (L) $1,955; (H) $66,000

WINTHER, Borge
Scandinavian 20th cent.
paintings: (H) $550

WINTHER, Frederik
Danish 1853-1916
paintings: (H) $1,650

WINTZ, Guillaume
French 1823-1899
paintings: (L) $1,955; (H) $2,990

WINTZ, Raymond
French b. 1884
paintings: (L) $880; (H) $1,650

WIREMAN, Eugenie
paintings: (L) $1,870; (H) $2,200

WIRGMAN, C.A.
19th/20th cent.
drawings: (H) $770

WIRGMAN, Theodore Blake
British 1848-1925
paintings: (H) $13,800

WIRSINO, Johann Christian, Jr.
drawings: (H) $1,610

WIRSUM, Karl
American b. 1939
paintings: (L) $690; (H) $1,150
drawings: (L) $220; (H) $460

WIRTZ, Johan
1640-c. 1709
paintings: (H) $5,750

WISBY, Jack
American 1856-1888
paintings: (H) $1,320

WISBY, Jack
American 1870-1940
paintings: (L) $1,035; (H) $4,950

WISE, Jack M.
b. 1928
paintings: (H) $500

WISE, Louise Waterman
paintings: (H) $770

WISELBERG, Rose
paintings: (H) $1,870

WISINGER FLORIAN, Olga
Austrian 1844-1926
paintings: (L) $6,325; (H) $63,000

WISNIEWSKI, Bronislaw
Polish 19th cent.
paintings: (H) $1,650

WISSING, Willem
Dutch 1653/56-1687
paintings: (L) $1,430; (H) $4,950

WISTEHUFF, Revere F.
American 1900-1971
paintings: (L) $605; (H) $2,860
drawings: (H) $1,980

WIT, Jacob de
Dutch 1695-1754
paintings: (L) $27,600; (H) $27,600
drawings: (L) $2,300; (H) $3,850

WIT, Jacob de and Isaac de
MOUCHERON
17th/18th cent.
paintings: (H) $21,850

WITHAM, J.
American
paintings: (H) $1,430

WITHERIDGE, W.
paintings: (H) $660

WITHERINGTON, William Frederick
British 1785-1865
paintings: (H) $920

WITHOLM, K.
Austrian 19th/20th cent.
paintings: (H) $467

WITHOOS, Matthias
Dutch 1627-1703
paintings: (L) $3,960; (H) $16,110

WITHOOS, Peter
1654-1693
drawings: (H) $6,613

WITHROW, Eva Almond
American 1858-1928
paintings: (L) $220; (H) $1,380
drawings: (H) $385

WITKIN, Isaac
b. 1936
sculpture: (L) $2,300; (H) $8,250

WITKOWSKI, H.
American 19th/20th cent.
paintings: (H) $1,210

WITKOWSKI, Karl
American 1860-1910
paintings: (L) $3,300; (H) $26,450
drawings: (H) $1,840

WITMAN, C.F.
American 19th cent.
paintings: (H) $2,760

WITSEN, W.A.
paintings: (H) $715

WITT, Jan Le
paintings: (H) $715

WITT, John Henry
1840-1901
paintings: (H) $3,575

WITTE, Emanuel de
Dutch 1617/18-1692
paintings: (H) $7,700

WITTE, Gaspar de
1624-1681
paintings: (H) $3,520

WITTEL, Gaspar van, called Gaspare
VANVITELLI
Dutch 1653-1736
paintings: (L) $5,500; (H) $827,500
drawings: (L) $19,550; (H) $27,600

WITTERS, Nell
American 20th cent.
paintings: (L) $660; (H) $660

WITTERWULGHE, J.
Belgian 1883-1967
sculpture: (H) $2,070

WITTKE, Carl
German 1849-1927
paintings: (H) $880

WITTLE, H.A.
British 19th cent.
paintings: (H) $633

WITTMACK, Edgar
1894-1956
drawings: (H) $1,650

WIWEL, Niels
Danish 1855-1914
paintings: (H) $1,265

WIZON, Tod
20th cent.
paintings: (H) $1,320

WOELFFER, Emerson
American b. 1914
paintings: (L) $1,150; (H) $5,750
drawings: (H) $173

WOELFLE, Arthur W.
American 1873-1936
paintings: (L) $1,725; (H) $3,737

WOENSEL, Petronella van
Dutch 1785-1839
paintings: (H) $25,300

WOGENSKY, Robert
French b. 1919
paintings: (H) $1,430

WOGUN, F.
Dutch
paintings: (H) $460

WOHNER, Louis
German b. 1888
paintings: (H) $4,125

WOJNAROWICZ, David
1954-1992
paintings: (L) $2,750; (H) $6,050
drawings: (L) $7,700; (H) $11,000

WOLBERS, Hermanus Gerhardus
Dutch 1856-1926
paintings: (H) $577

WOLCHONOK, Louis
1898-1973
drawings: (L) $920; (H) $2,760

WOLCOTT, Harold C.
American 20th cent.
paintings: (L) $110; (H) $660

WOLCOTT, James
American 19th cent.
paintings: (H) $1,430

WOLF
paintings: (H) $990

WOLF, Augusto
Italian 19th cent.
paintings: (H) $6,325

WOLF, Franz Xavier, Professor
German 19th/20th cent.
paintings: (L) $440; (H) $8,050

WOLF, G.
German 19th/20th cent.
paintings: (H) $3,300

WOLF, Hamilton
American 1883-1967
paintings: (L) $330; (H) $2,750

WOLF, Joseph
British 1820-1899
paintings: (H) $71,500

WOLF, Lone
1882-1965
paintings: (H) $2,415

WOLF, Raimund Anton
Austrian 1865-1924
paintings: (H) $2,070

WOLF, Toni
paintings: (H) $489

WOLFE, Ada
American 20th cent.
paintings: (H) $748

WOLFE, Edward
British 20th cent.
paintings: (H) $575

WOLFE, Karl
b. 1904
paintings: (H) $715

WOLFE, M.
Russian 19th cent.
sculpture: (H) $770

WOLFE, Wayne
American contemporary
paintings: (L) $2,530; (H) $3,300

WOLFERS, Philippe
Belgian 1858-1929
sculpture: (H) $5,750

WOLFF, E.
sculpture: (H) $7,975

WOLFF, Franz Alexander Friedrich
Wilhelm
German 1816-1887
sculpture: (H) $2,090

WOLFF, Gustave
German/American 1863-1935
paintings: (L) $275; (H) $550

WOLFF, Henrik
Danish 19th cent.
paintings: (H) $6,600

WOLFF, Robert Jay
American b. 1905
drawings: (H) $1,870

WOLFFORT, Artus
Flemish 1581-1641
paintings: (H) $35,200

WOLFLE, Franz Xavier
Austrian 1887-1989
paintings: (L) $690; (H) $5,750

WOLFSON, Irving
American b. 1899
drawings: (L) $165; (H) $605

WOLFSON, William
b. 1894
paintings: (H) $1,100

WOLLASTON, John, I
English c. 1672-after 1741
paintings: (L) $550; (H) $4,400

WOLLASTON, John, II
ac. 1738-1775
paintings: (L) $2,300; (H) $8,800

WOLLHEIM, Gert
1894-1974
paintings: (H) $1,495

WOLLON, William Barnes
British 1857-1936
paintings: (H) $990

WOLMARK, Alfred Aaron
British 1877-1961
paintings: (L) $880; (H) $3,850

WOLS, Alfred Otto Wolfgang
SCHULZE
German 1913-1951
drawings: (H) $39,600

WOLSKY, Milton
drawings: (H) $1,210

WOLSTENHOLME, Dean, Jr.
English 1798-1882
paintings: (L) $3,450; (H) $27,500

WOLSTENHOLME, Dean, Sr.
English 1757-1837
paintings: (L) $1,980; (H) $70,700

WOLTRECK, Franz
German 1800-1847
sculpture: (H) $2,645

WOLTZE, Berthold
German 1829-1896
paintings: (L) $4,025; (H) $13,200

WONG, Tyrus Y.
American b. 1910
drawings: (H) $550

WONNER, Paul
American b. 1920
paintings: (L) $1,430; (H) $43,125
drawings: (L) $880; (H) $5,175

WONTNER, William Clarke
English ac. 1879-1912
paintings: (L) $43,700; (H) $74,000

WOO, Jade Fon
American 1911-1983
paintings: (H) $1,760
drawings: (L) $468; (H) $2,090

WOO, Pun
ac. 1860-1880
paintings: (H) $4,370

Washington and the Cherry Tree

Grant Wood (1891-1942) grew up on a farm in Iowa. His father died when he was just a boy, and he supplemented the family income with odd jobs, farming, and working as a silversmith. Wood attended the Minneapolis School of Design and Handicraft and Normal Art for two summers in 1910 and 1911 and studied briefly at the Académie Julian in the 1920s. After World War I, Wood made four trips to Europe. His 1928 trip to Germany was a turning point in his career, for the German and Flemish primitive paintings from the High Renaissance (16th century) transformed his style and content. Prior to 1928, his work can be described as oil sketches of European scenery, landscapes of Cedar Rapids, and Impressionist sketchy paintings with impasto (thickly applied paint). Wood began to paint ordinary people and everyday life in a meticulous, sharply detailed manner. His painting *American Gothic*, 1930, a depiction of a long-faced farmer and his stern wife in front of their farmhouse, is his most famous painting and an icon of American Regionalism.

Parson Weems' Fable, painted in 1939, tells the story of George Washington and the cherry tree, a tale fabricated by the late 18th century clergyman Mason Locke Weems in his biography of George Washington. In a 1940 interview, Wood explained that he grew up thinking the story was true. "It is of course good that we are wiser today and recognize historical fact from historical fiction. Still, when we began to ridicule the story of George and the cherry tree and quit teaching it to our children, something of color and imagination departed from American life. It is this something that I am interested in helping to preserve."

The painting, *Parson Weems' Fable*, is in the Amon Carter Museum in Houston, Texas. The cartoon for the oil, a full-scale preparatory drawing, was consigned to Christie's in January 1995. Ten years earlier the cartoon had sold for $297,000; this time around the price was $508,500. (Grant Wood, *Parson Weems' Fable*, charcoal, pencil, and chalk on paper, 38¼ x 50 inches, Christie New York, January 28, 1995, $508,500)

WOOD, Beatrice
American b. 1893
sculpture: (L) $690; (H) $8,625

WOOD, Carlos C.
1792-1856
drawings: (H) $27,600

WOOD, Catherine M.
British 19th/20th cent.
paintings: (L) $138; (H) $10,350

WOOD, Charles Haigh
British 1856-1927
paintings: (L) $1,610; (H) $10,350

WOOD, Edith
American 1885-1967
paintings: (L) $110; (H) $2,860

WOOD, Edmond
paintings: (H) $770

WOOD, Francis Derwent
1871-1926
sculpture: (H) $880

WOOD, Frank W.
drawings: (H) $1,320

WOOD, George
British 18th cent.
drawings: (H) $863

WOOD, George Albert
American 1845-1910
paintings: (L) $2,310; (H) $3,600

WOOD, George Bacon, Jr.
American 1832-1910
paintings: (H) $15,400
drawings: (H) $605

WOOD, Grant
American 1891-1942
paintings: (L) $467; (H) $20,700
drawings: (L) $825; (H) $508,500

WOOD, H.
British 19th cent.
paintings: (H) $550

WOOD, H. S.
19th/20th cent.
drawings: (H) $748

WOOD, J. Ogden
Franco/American 1851-1912
paintings: (L) $495; (H) $770

WOOD, John T.
1845-1919
paintings: (L) $550; (H) $1,495

WOOD, Lewis John
British 1813-1901
paintings: (L) $1,840; (H) $5,060

WOOD, Mary
American ac. 1907-1931
paintings: (H) $1,093
drawings: (H) $577

WOOD, Michael
English 20th cent.
paintings: (L) $770; (H) $770

WOOD, Ogden
American 1851-1912
paintings: (H) $4,950

WOOD, Peter
British b. 1914
paintings: (H) $660

WOOD, Robert
paintings: (L) $1,320; (H) $1,870

WOOD, Robert
American 1889-1979
paintings: (L) $495; (H) $16,500
drawings: (H) $1,210

WOOD, Robert
American 1926-1979
paintings: (L) $495; (H) $8,800
drawings: (H) $495

WOOD, Robert
American 20th cent.
paintings: (L) $2,475; (H) $2,750

WOOD, Robert E.
American 20th cent.
paintings: (H) $550

WOOD, Shakespere
Irish 19th cent.
sculpture: (H) $5,500

WOOD, Stanley
American b. 1894
drawings: (L) $275; (H) $550

WOOD, Stanley L.
English 1866-1928
paintings: (H) $2,420
drawings: (H) $437

WOOD, Thomas Waterman
American 1823-1903
paintings: (L) $517; (H) $121,000
drawings: (H) $25,300

WOOD, William Thomas
British 1877-1958
paintings: (H) $1,100
drawings: (H) $121

WOOD, Worden G.
American 20th cent.
drawings: (L) $88; (H) $1,650

WOOD(?), D.A.
paintings: (H) $1,650

WOOD-THOMAS, A.
American 20th cent.
paintings: (H) $467

WOODARD, Ellsworth
1861-1939
drawings: (H) $880

WOODBRIDGE, George
drawings: (L) $770; (H) $770

WOODBURY, Charles H.
American 1864-1940
paintings: (L) $275; (H) $32,200
drawings: (L) $88; (H) $6,600

WOODBURY, Lloyd
American b. 1917
sculpture: (L) $825; (H) $2,185

WOODBURY, Marcia Oakes
American 1865-1913
drawings: (H) $1,430

WOODBURY, Susan Marcia Oakes
drawings: (H) $825

WOODCOCK, Hartwell Leon
American 1853-1929
paintings: (L) $165; (H) $935
drawings: (L) $55; (H) $798

WOODHOUSE, H.J.
British 19th cent.
paintings: (H) $6,600

WOODHOUSE, William
English 1857-1939
paintings: (L) $1,045; (H) $5,500

WOODLOCK, David
Irish 1842-1929
drawings: (H) $4,675

WOODMAN, Betty
American b. 1930
sculpture: (L) $1,650; (H) $11,000

WOODMAN, F.
British 19th cent.
paintings: (H) $468

WOODMAN, Timothy
b. 1953
sculpture: (H) $2,750

WOODROOFE, L.
19th/20th cent.
paintings: (H) $880

WOODROW, Bill
American
sculpture: (L) $4,950; (H) $16,500

WOODS, Edith Longstreth
American 19th cent.
paintings: (H) $495

WOODS, G.D.
British 19th cent.
drawings: (H) $518

WOODS, Henry
English 1846-1921
paintings: (L) $1,650; (H) $28,750

WOODSIDE, John Archibald, Sr.
American 1781-1852
paintings: (L) $2,200; (H) $32,200

WOODVILLE, Richard Caton
British 1856-1927
paintings: (H) $13,800

WOODWARD, Cleveland
American contemporary
paintings: (H) $605

WOODWARD, Ellsworth
American 1861-1939
paintings: (H) $2,860
drawings: (L) $220; (H) $1,760

WOODWARD, Helen M.
American 1902-1986
paintings: (L) $110; (H) $880

WOODWARD, Kavch H.
American 20th cent.
paintings: (H) $605

WOODWARD, Louise
American ac. 1888-1913
paintings: (H) $825

WOODWARD, Mabel
American 1877-1945
paintings: (L) $220; (H) $27,500
drawings: (L) $357; (H) $27,500

WOODWARD, Robert Strong
American b. 1885
paintings: (L) $660; (H) $3,575
drawings: (L) $275; (H) $1,045

WOODWARD, Stanley Wingate
American 1890-1970
paintings: (L) $220; (H) $2,475
drawings: (L) $165; (H) $1,870

WOODWARD, Thomas
British 1801-1852
paintings: (H) $23,000

WOODWARD, William
American 1859-1939
paintings: (L) $550; (H) $4,950

WOODWELL, J.R.
paintings: (L) $1,400; (H) $1,550

WOOG, Raymond
French b. 1875
paintings: (H) $1,870

WOOL, Christopher
American b. 1955
paintings: (L) $1,955; (H) $55,000
drawings: (L) $4,370; (H) $23,000
sculpture: (H) $21,850

WOOL, Lewis Martin
American 20th cent.
paintings: (H) $6,038

WOOLF, Samuel Johnson
American 1880-1948
paintings: (L) $29; (H) $60,500
drawings: (L) $29; (H) $660

WOOLLETT, H.
paintings: (H) $1,980

WOOLLETT, Henry A.
British ac. 1857-1873
paintings: (H) $990

WOOLLETT, Henry Charles
British 19th cent.
paintings: (H) $920

WOOLNER, Thomas
English 1825-1892
sculpture: (H) $27,600

WOOLRIDGE, Thomas
British 19th cent.
drawings: (H) $489

WOOLRYCH, Bertha Hewit
American b. 1868
drawings: (L) $550; (H) $715

WOOLSEY, Carl
American b. 1902
paintings: (H) $5,500

WOOSTER
20th cent.
paintings: (H) $1,320

WOOSTER, Austin C.
American ac. 1910
paintings: (L) $1,485; (H) $5,750

WOOSTER, Austin L.
American 19th cent.
paintings: (H) $1,650

WOPFNER, Joseph
Austrian 1843-1927
paintings: (L) $9,350; (H) $36,300

WORES, Theodore
American 1859/60-1939
paintings: (L) $1,100; (H) $60,250
drawings: (L) $935; (H) $7,150

WORKS, Katherine Swann
American b. 1904
paintings: (L) $3,738; (H) $4,313

WORMS, Jules
French 1832-1924
paintings: (L) $880; (H) $57,500
drawings: (L) $1,045; (H) $1,100

WORRAL, A.R.
French 19th cent.
paintings: (H) $550

WORSTER
19th cent.
paintings: (H) $660

WORTH, Thomas
American 1834-1917
paintings: (L) $578; (H) $990
drawings: (L) $104; (H) $1,100

WORTH-HAUGH, Maria
paintings: (H) $690

WORTHINGTON, W.G.
paintings: (H) $550

WOSE, E.G.
European 19th/20th cent.
paintings: (H) $660

WOSTRY, Carlo
Italian 1865-1943
paintings: (L) $18,700; (H) $20,700

WOUTERS, Frans
Flemish 1612/14-1659/60
paintings: (L) $7,150; (H) $9,200

WOUW, A. Vin
sculpture: (H) $1,700

Soup Kitchen

Katherine Swan Works (b. 1904) studied art in New York at the Art Students League with Thomas Hart Benton and Walter Kuhn. She met her husband while in New York and the couple moved to San Francisco in 1929. Works was active in the local San Francisco art scene until 1933, when she moved to Marin County and raised a family. In 1949 she began working and exhibiting again and won many local awards. *Soup Kitchen*, dated 1932, is a typical Social Realist painting. Offered at Butterfield's in San Francisco, the painting realized $3,738. (Katherine Works, *Soup Kitchen*, oil on canvas, 24 x 21 inches, Butterfield, June 15, 1995, $3,738)

WOUW, Anton van
South African 1862-1945
sculpture: (L) $10,925; (H) $19,800

WOUWERMAN, Philips
Dutch 1619-1668
drawings: (H) $3,080

WOUWERMANS, Philips
Dutch 1619-1668
paintings: (L) $4,370; (H) $467,500

WOUWERMANS, Pieter
Dutch 1623-1682
paintings: (H) $77,000

WRIGHT, Alice Morgan
American 1881-1975
sculpture: (H) $1,495

WRIGHT, Charles Lennox, II
1876-after 1955
paintings: (L) $460; (H) $517

WRIGHT, David
American contemporary
drawings: (H) $2,200

WRIGHT, E.G.
paintings: (H) $23,100

WRIGHT, Ethel
British ac. 1893-1898
paintings: (H) $11,000

WRIGHT, Frank Lloyd
American 1869-1959
drawings: (L) $3,575; (H) $34,500

WRIGHT, G.T.
paintings: (H) $8,800

WRIGHT, George
paintings: (H) $11,550
drawings: (L) $35; (H) $55

WRIGHT, George
American 1828-1881
paintings: (H) $24,750

WRIGHT, George
British 1860-1942
paintings: (L) $2,860; (H) $17,600
drawings: (H) $440

WRIGHT, George Hand
American 1872-1951
paintings: (H) $10,350
drawings: (L) $302; (H) $2,310

WRIGHT, Gilbert S.
British ac. 1896-1900
paintings: (L) $8,800; (H) $18,400

WRIGHT, Gilbert Scott
British 1880-1958
paintings: (L) $3,738; (H) $5,225

WRIGHT, James C.
American 1906-1969
drawings: (L) $66; (H) $1,955

WRIGHT, John
American ac. 1860's
paintings: (H) $1,540

WRIGHT, Joseph
American 1756-1793
paintings: (H) $55,000

WRIGHT, Michael
drawings: (L) $1,320; (H) $1,430

WRIGHT, R. Stephens
American b. 1903
paintings: (L) $1,210; (H) $2,200

WRIGHT, Rufus
American 1827/32-1895
paintings: (H) $3,575

WRIGHT, W. Spencer
American 20th cent.
paintings: (H) $715

WRIGHT, Walter
English 1866-1933
paintings: (H) $550

WRIGHTSON, Bernie
drawings: (L) $1,035; (H) $6,900

WRINCH, Mary Evelyn
Canadian 1877-1969
paintings: (L) $1,210; (H) $2,420

WTEWAEL, Joachim, studio of
paintings: (H) $19,800

WTEWAEL, Joachim Antonisz.
Dutch c. 1566-1638
paintings: (L) $607,500; (H) $772,500
drawings: (H) $28,600

WTEWAEL, Pieter, or UYTEWAEL
1596-1660
paintings: (L) $5,175; (H) $20,700

WU ZUOREN, Wu TSO-JEN
Chinese b. 1908
drawings: (H) $9,775

WUCHTERS, Abraham
Danish c. 1610-1682
paintings: (H) $18,700

WUERMER, Carl
American 1900-1983
paintings: (L) $1,540; (H) $19,550

WULFFAERT, Adrien
Belgian 1804-1873
paintings: (H) $990

WUNDER, Wilhelm Ernst
1713-1787
paintings: (H) $12,100

WUNDERLICH, Herman
German 1839-1915
drawings: (H) $1,155

WUNDERLICH, Paul
German b. 1927
paintings: (H) $5,500
drawings: (H) $3,450
sculpture: (H) $805

WUNNENBERG, Carl
German 1850-1929
paintings: (H) $8,800

WUNNENBERG, Walther
German 1818-1900
paintings: (H) $990

WUNSCH, Mizzi
German 1862-1898
paintings: (H) $18,400

WUNSCHE
German 19th cent.
sculpture: (H) $4,312

WUNSCHE
German School 20th cent.
sculpture: (H) $1,725

WURBEL, Franz
Austrian 1822-1900
paintings: (H) $16,100

WUST
Continental 19th cent.
paintings: (H) $3,850

WUST, Alexander
American 1837-1876
paintings: (H) $1,540
drawings: (L) $110; (H) $165

WUZER, Johann Matthias
Austrian 1760-1839
paintings: (H) $3,738

WYANT, Alexander H.
American 1836-1892
paintings: (L) $460; (H) $35,650
drawings: (L) $83; (H) $2,750

WYANT, Arabella L.
American d. 1919
paintings: (H) $468

WYATT, A*C*
American d. 1933
drawings: (H) $575

WYATVILLE, Sir Jeffrey
English 1766-1840
drawings: (H) $522

WYBURD, Francis John
English 1826-1893
paintings: (H) $9,200

WYCK, Jan
Dutch 1640-1700
drawings: (H) $935

WYDEVELD, Arnoud
American ac. 1855-1862
paintings: (L) $880; (H) $15,400

WYETH, Andrew
American b. 1917
drawings: (L) $2,750; (H) $176,000

WYETH, Caroline
American b. 1909
paintings: (H) $6,600

WYETH, Henriette
American b. 1907
paintings: (L) $5,500; (H) $46,200

WYETH, Jamie
American b. 1946
paintings: (L) $34,100; (H) $40,250
drawings: (L) $275; (H) $52,900

WYETH, N.C. and Andrew and Jamie
WYETH et al.
American 19th/20th cent.
drawings: (H) $10,925

WYETH, Newell Convers (N.C.)
American 1882-1945
paintings: (L) $3,738; (H) $99,000
drawings: (L) $2,750; (H) $33,000

WYGANT, Bob
American b. 1927
paintings: (L) $6,600; (H) $26,400

WYGRZYWALSKI, Feliks H.
b. 1875
paintings: (L) $1,540; (H) $1,980

WYJNGAERDT, Piet van
Dutch 1873-1964
paintings: (H) $3,520

WYK, Charles van
Dutch 1875-1917
sculpture: (H) $1,045

WYK, Henri van
Dutch b. 1833
paintings: (H) $1,955

WYLAND, A.
paintings: (H) $770

WYLAND, H.
American 19th cent.
paintings: (H) $1,035

WYLD, William
English 1806-1889
paintings: (L) $1,155; (H) $18,400
drawings: (L) $1,100; (H) $2,860

WYLIE, Robert
American 1839-1877
paintings: (L) $8,800; (H) $46,000
sculpture: (H) $1,100

WYLLIE, Charles William
English 1853-1923
paintings: (L) $3,080; (H) $3,450

WYLLIE, Charlotte Major
British ac. 1872-1888
paintings: (H) $7,700

WYLLIE, William Lionel
British 1851-1931
paintings: (H) $2,300
drawings: (H) $2,475

WYMAN, Dorothy Churchill
American 1899-1993
paintings: (L) $110; (H) $1,840

WYMAN, M.A.
American 20th cent.
paintings: (L) $450; (H) $1,980

WYNANTS, Jan
Dutch 1631/2-1684
paintings: (H) $35,650

WYNEN, Oswald
Dutch 1736-1790
drawings: (H) $3,025

American Illustrator

Newell Convers Wyeth (1882-1945), known as N.C. Wyeth, was the leading artist of America's Golden Age of Illustration. Born on a farm in Needham, Massachusetts, he studied at Howard Pyle's school of art in Wilmington, Delaware. Other students were W.H.D. Koerner, Stanley Arthurs, Harvey Dunn, and Frank Schoonover. Pyle was an influential and gifted teacher, who taught that drama and emotional content were vital to successful illustration. Wyeth's first illustration was a *Saturday Evening Post* cover of a bucking bronco with rider. After his marriage in 1906 he settled in Chadds Ford, Pennsylvania, home to many illustrators. A gifted artist and a fast, tireless worker, he completed more than 3,000 illustrations, including 25 books for Scribner's juvenile classics: *Treasure Island*, *Robin Hood*, and *The Last of the Mohicans*. His book illustrations were timeless classics and are still being used today. Wyeth also did advertising art, much to his distaste. A success as an illustrator and financially secure, he decided in 1925 to become a "real artist." During this period of exploration he painted in various styles—Modernist, Expressionist, Folk—but his work was not well-received so in 1935, with a family to support, he returned to illustration. Some of his best works were created after 1935. Wyeth encouraged his children to paint, and Andrew, Henriette, and Caroline became professional artists. Andrew's son Jamie has continued the dynasty.

Both illustration art and advertising art have often been denigrated and undervalued, in part because the art's direction and scope was dictated by an art director, and in part because the public viewed illustrators as second-class artists for hire. The book illustrations Wyeth did for Scribner's were done on a work-for-hire basis, and the artwork belonged to the publishing house. Thirty to forty years ago, many of Wyeth's wonderful canvases were propped up on books and used as tables for stacking books and coffee cups. It is only recently that these works have been properly valued. Illustration House, in New York, is a gallery and auction house that specializes in the art of illustrators. *Indian in Canoe*, from *Scribner's Magazine* of October 1906, was an oil on canvas in brown tones. The auction price realized was $99,000. (Newell Convers Wyeth, *Indian in Canoe*, oil on canvas, 27 x 19 inches, Illustration House, May 7, 1994, $99,000)

WYNFIELD, David Wilkie
British 1837-1887
paintings: (H) $12,100

WYNGAARD, A.J.
Dutch 20th cent.
paintings: (H) $1,320

WYNGAERDT, Anthonie Jacobus van
Dutch 1808-1887
paintings: (L) $1,725; (H) $8,338

WYNGAERDT, Petrus Theodorus van
Dutch 1816-1893
paintings: (L) $3,300; (H) $6,050

WYNGAERDT, Piet van
Dutch 1875-1964
paintings: (L) $550; (H) $1,045

WYNGARDT, A.V.
Dutch 19th cent.
drawings: (H) $605

WYNN
paintings: (H) $805

WYON, Edward William
English 19th cent.
sculpture: (L) $38; (H) $748

WYSMULLER, Jan Hillebrand
Dutch 1855-1925
paintings: (L) $1,150; (H) $1,540

WYSOCKI, Charles
American 20th cent.
paintings: (H) $11,000

WYSOCKI, M.
Austrian 20th cent.
paintings: (L) $385; (H) $495

WYWIORSKI, Michael G.
Polish 1861-1926
paintings: (H) $3,450

XAVERY, Jacob
Dutch 1736-after 1769
paintings: (H) $8,250

XCERON, Jean
Greek/American 1890-1967
drawings: (L) $495; (H) $1,200

XIMENES, Ettore
Italian 1855-1926
paintings: (L) $3,300; (H) $3,850

XIMENES, G.
Italian 19th cent.
paintings: (H) $2,420

XOCHITIONTZIN, Desiderio
Hernandez
b. 1922
paintings: (H) $11,500

XU BEIHONG, Hsu PEI-HUNG
Chinese 1895-1953
drawings: (H) $43,125

XU GU, Hsu KU
Chinese 1824-1896
drawings: (H) $3,450

XUL SOLAR, Alejandro
b. Argentina 1887-1963
drawings: (L) $11,000; (H) $55,000

YAEGER, Edgar
American b. 1904
paintings: (L) $440; (H) $1,760
drawings: (H) $575

YAGER, Rick
drawings: (H) $1,092

YALE, Lilla
American 1855-1929
paintings: (H) $523

YAMAMOTO, Taro
American b. 1919
paintings: (L) $330; (H) $660
drawings: (L) $82; (H) $1,650

YANDELL, Enid
American 20th cent.
sculpture: (H) $935

YANKEL, Jacques
French b. 1920
paintings: (L) $1,035; (H) $2,860
drawings: (H) $173

YANKOVITZ, Nina
contemporary
sculpture: (H) $3,450

YAOUAC, Alain le
French c. 1940
paintings: (H) $1,650
drawings: (H) $1,380

YARBER, Robert
American b. 1948
paintings: (L) $5,500; (H) $12,650
drawings: (H) $3,080

YARD, Sydney Janis
American 1855-1909
drawings: (L) $275; (H) $2,200

YARNELL, Agness
American b. 1904
sculpture: (L) $402; (H) $1,155

YARNOLD, George B.
British 19th cent.
paintings: (H) $825

YART?, Wm.
paintings: (H) $500

YARZ, Edmond
French 19th/20th cent.
paintings: (H) $2,200

YASUO, Kazuki
1911-1974
paintings: (H) $101,500
drawings: (H) $36,800

YATES, Cullen
American 1866-1945
paintings: (L) $400; (H) $7,425

YATES, Ruth
American b. 1896
sculpture: (H) $13,200

YATES, W.
paintings: (H) $550

YATES, W., Jr.
paintings: (H) $1,210

YATES, W.H.
American 1848-1934
paintings: (H) $1,035

YATES, William
British 19th cent.
paintings: (L) $2,990; (H) $4,312

YATRIDES, Georges
Greek b. 1931
paintings: (L) $403; (H) $7,150

YAZAKI, C.
paintings: (H) $4,025

YEAGER, Edgar
American b. 1904
paintings: (H) $1,320

YEANIES, William Frederick
British 1835-1918
paintings: (H) $770

YEARSLEY, Merritt W.
American 20th cent.
paintings: (H) $518

YECKLEY, Norman H.
American b. 1914
paintings: (L) $357; (H) $1,045

YEKROSAZ, M.
paintings: (H) $550

YELLY
European early 20th cent.
sculpture: (H) $6,600

YERNAULT, E. Hiernault
ac. late 18th cent.
paintings: (H) $129,000

YESTEBAN, Angel Lizcano
Spanish 1846-1929
paintings: (H) $8,525

YETO, Genjiro
American b. Japan 1867
drawings: (H) $770

YEWELL, George Henry
American 1830-1923
paintings: (L) $275; (H) $1,650

YEYDEN, Jan van
Dutch 19th cent.
paintings: (H) $1,320

YGLESIAS, Vincent Philip
English 1845-1911
paintings: (H) $880

YIP, Richard
American 1919-1981
drawings: (L) $715; (H) $1,430

YIRSA, Brenda Hermundstad
drawings: (H) $495

YKENS, Frans
1601-1683/93
paintings: (H) $66,300

YOAKUM, Joseph E.
American 1886-1973
drawings: (L) $935; (H) $5,463

YOCKNEY, A.
American ac. 1873-1889
drawings: (H) $805

YOHN, Frederick C.
American 1875-1933
paintings: (L) $467; (H) $550
drawings: (L) $193; (H) $1,540

YON, Edmond
French 1836-1897
paintings: (L) $1,495; (H) $16,100

YONG, Joe de
1849-1975
paintings: (H) $4,313

YORK, C.E.
paintings: (L) $489; (H) $660

YORK, Star Liana
American
sculpture: (H) $660

YORK, William G.
ac. 1872-1881
paintings: (L) $5,500; (H) $14,850

YORKE, William Hoard
British ac. 1858-1903
paintings: (L) $5,390; (H) $36,300

YOSHIDA, H.
drawings: (H) $4,400

YOSHIDA, Hiroshi
Japanese 1876-1950
paintings: (H) $9,350
drawings: (L) $1,980; (H) $2,750

YOSHIDA, R.
Japanese 19th/20th cent.
paintings: (L) $748; (H) $1,320

YOSHIMITSU
sculpture: (H) $1,553

YOUNG, A.
English 19th cent.
paintings: (L) $522; (H) $1,265

YOUNG, August
American 1837-1913
paintings: (H) $2,750

YOUNG, Charles Morris
American 1869-1964
paintings: (L) $303; (H) $5,500

YOUNG, Florence Upson
American b. 1872
paintings: (L) $358; (H) $605
drawings: (H) $275

YOUNG, Gordan
American School 20th cent.
paintings: (H) $1,210

YOUNG, H.B.
British 19th cent.
drawings: (H) $825

YOUNG, Harvey
American 1840-1901
paintings: (L) $248; (H) $3,520
drawings: (L) $248; (H) $715

YOUNG, Henry
American
drawings: (H) $3,300

YOUNG, James Harvey
American 1830-1918
paintings: (H) $460

YOUNG, Mahonri Mackintosh
American 1877-1957
drawings: (L) $770; (H) $1,540
sculpture: (L) $2,420; (H) $49,500

YOUNG, Michael
b. 1952
paintings: (L) $863; (H) $7,700

YOUNG, Murat "Chic"
1901-1973
drawings: (L) $137; (H) $5,500

YOUNG, Oscar van
b. 1906
paintings: (H) $1,320

YOUNG, S. Lee
paintings: (H) $550

YOUNG, W.
paintings: (H) $1,430

YOUNG, W.
19th cent.
paintings: (H) $460

YOUNG, William
American 19th cent.
paintings: (H) $2,860

YOUNG, William S.
American ac. 1850-1870
paintings: (L) $2,475; (H) $2,530

YOUNG-HUNTER, John
American 1874-1955
paintings: (L) $633; (H) $9,200
drawings: (L) $690; (H) $920

YOUNGERMAN, Jack
American b. 1926
paintings: (L) $633; (H) $11,500
drawings: (L) $440; (H) $1,430
sculpture: (H) $990

YOURIEVITCH, Serge
20th cent.
sculpture: (H) $1,840

YOVITS, E.
American
paintings: (H) $550

YUAN, S.C.
American 1912-1974
paintings: (L) $1,100; (H) $5,225

YUKI, Katsura
b. 1913
drawings: (H) $4,830

YUNKERS, Adja
American 1900-1983
drawings: (L) $121; (H) $495

YUZBASIYAN, Arto
paintings: (L) $935; (H) $2,090

YVON, Adolphe
French 1817-1893
paintings: (H) $1,650
drawings: (H) $88

ZABALETA, Wladimir
b. Venezuela 1944
paintings: (H) $8,250

ZABAROV, Boris
b. 1935
paintings: (H) $20,700

ZABEL, Larry V.
American
paintings: (H) $2,200
drawings: (H) $6,250

ZACH, Bruno
Austrian early 20th cent.
sculpture: (L) $660; (H) $14,950

ZACHO, Christian
Danish 1843-1913
paintings: (L) $4,600; (H) $20,700

ZACK, Bruno
Austrian early 20th cent.
sculpture: (L) $2,200; (H) $6,600

ZACK, Leon
French 1892-1980
paintings: (H) $4,070

ZADKINE, Ossip
Russian/French 1890-1967
drawings: (L) $880; (H) $12,100
sculpture: (L) $2,300; (H) $211,500

ZAGANELLI DI BOSIO, Francesco, called Francesco Da COTIGNOLA
c. 1470-1532
paintings: (L) $55,000; (H) $57,500

ZAGANELLI DI COTIGNOLA, Francesco
Italian c. 1460/70-1532
paintings: (H) $39,600

ZAGO, Erman
paintings: (L) $330; (H) $1,100

ZAHND, Johann
Swiss 1854-1934
paintings: (H) $9,200

ZAHRTMANN, P.H. Kristian
Danish 1843-1917
paintings: (H) $7,475

ZAIS, Giuseppe
Italian 1709-1784
paintings: (L) $30,800; (H) $181,500
drawings: (L) $6,050; (H) $17,250

ZAJAC, Jack
American b. 1929
sculpture: (L) $880; (H) $4,675

ZAJICEK, Carl Wenzel
Austrian 1860-1923
drawings: (H) $5,520

ZAJICEK, Karl Josef Richard
drawings: (H) $1,380

ZAK, Eugene
Polish 1884-1926
paintings: (L) $2,860; (H) $48,300

ZAKANITCH, Robert
American b. 1935
paintings: (L) $1,725; (H) $4,830
drawings: (H) $825

ZALCE, Alfredo
b. Mexico 1908
paintings: (L) $6,050; (H) $44,000

ZALIOUK, Sacha
drawings: (H) $1,610

ZALOPANY, Michele
contemporary
drawings: (L) $3,850; (H) $6,050

ZAMACOIS Y ZABALA, Eduardo
Spanish 1842-1871
paintings: (L) $6,325; (H) $134,500
drawings: (H) $5,280

ZAMECNIKOVA, Dana
sculpture: (L) $1,100; (H) $2,750

ZAMORA, Gimenez
Italian 19th cent.
paintings: (H) $1,320

ZAMORA, Jesus Maria
Colombian 1875-1949
paintings: (L) $2,875; (H) $2,875

ZAMORA, Jose de
drawings: (L) $330; (H) $1,980

ZAMPIGHI, E.
Italian 20th cent.
paintings: (H) $690

ZAMPIGHI, Emiliano
Italian 19th cent.
paintings: (H) $3,850

ZAMPIGHI, Eugenio
Italian 1859-1944
paintings: (L) $3,300; (H) $49,500
drawings: (L) $2,185; (H) $6,600

ZANCHI, Antonio
Italian 1631-1722
paintings: (L) $13,800; (H) $38,500

ZANDINI
Italian 19th cent.
paintings: (H) $8,800

ZANDOMENEGHI, Federico
Italian 1841-1917
paintings: (L) $189,500; (H) $907,500
drawings: (L) $357; (H) $22,000

ZANDT, Thomas Kirby van
American 1814-1886
paintings: (L) $1,650; (H) $2,070

ZANDT, William Thompson van
paintings: (L) $220; (H) $4,400

ZANETTI-ZILLA, Vettore
Italian b. 1864
drawings: (H) $1,980

ZANG, John J.
American ac. 1883
paintings: (L) $633; (H) $3,025

ZANIERI, Arturo
Italian b. 1870
paintings: (L) $431; (H) $1,100

ZANIN, Francesco
Italian 19th cent.
paintings: (H) $23,000

ZANINI, Luigi
Italian b. 1893
paintings: (H) $550

ZANNONI, Giuseppe
Italian 1849-1903
paintings: (H) $5,390

ZANO, Lameck
Zimbabwian 20th cent.
sculpture: (H) $495

ZAO-WOU-KI
Chinese/French b. 1921
paintings: (L) $3,300; (H) $79,750
drawings: (L) $2,420; (H) $6,050

ZAPKUS, Kes
contemporary
paintings: (H) $2,200

ZARATE
paintings: (H) $33,000

ZARDO, Alberto
Italian 1876-1959
paintings: (L) $550; (H) $2,420

ZARINI, L.
Continental 19th/20th cent.
paintings: (H) $575

ZARRAGA, Angel
Mexican 1886-1946
paintings: (L) $13,200; (H) $211,500
drawings: (L) $2,875; (H) $8,050

ZATZKA, Hans
Austrian 1859-1951
paintings: (L) $1,610; (H) $15,950

ZAWISKI, Edward
Continental 19th/20th cent.
paintings: (H) $17,825

ZAYAC
drawings: (H) $550

ZBISKO, B.
Hungarian
paintings: (H) $863

ZEEBROECK, van
Dutch School 19th cent.
paintings: (H) $1,100

ZEEMAN, Joost
c. 1776-1845
drawings: (H) $7,475

ZEEMAN, Regnier Nooms
Dutch 1623-1668
drawings: (H) $1,210

ZEEMAN, Reinier
Dutch 1623-1664
paintings: (H) $3,850

ZEFADA (?)
paintings: (H) $1,100

ZEFERINO DA COSTA, J.
b. Brazil 1840-1915
paintings: (H) $13,200

ZEIGLER, Lee Woodward
American 1868-1952
paintings: (L) $220; (H) $770

ZEISLER, Claire B.
1903-1991
sculpture: (H) $6,875

ZELAZNY, Mary Lou
American contemporary
paintings: (H) $825

ZELIKSON, S.
sculpture: (H) $1,210

ZELLINSKY, Charles L.
American ac. 1886-1905
paintings: (L) $1,495; (H) $20,700

ZELONI, R.
Italian 19th/20th cent.
paintings: (H) $1,150

ZEMSKY, Illya
American 1892-1961
paintings: (H) $3,300
drawings: (L) $2,475; (H) $3,300

ZEMSKY, Jessica
American
drawings: (L) $700; (H) $1,900

ZENDA, Pat
American b. 1930
paintings: (L) $165; (H) $805

ZENDEL, Gabriel
French b. 1906
paintings: (L) $403; (H) $748
drawings: (H) $935

ZENIL, Nahum
b. Mexico 1947
drawings: (L) $5,500; (H) $7,150

ZENISEK, Franz
Austrian 1849-1916
paintings: (H) $1,980

ZENNARO, Giorgio
sculpture: (H) $605

ZENO, E.
Italian School 19th/20th cent.
paintings: (H) $1,725

ZENO, Jorge
b. U.S. 1956
paintings: (L) $4,125; (H) $19,550
drawings: (H) $6,050

ZENOBIO DI JACOPO, called Zanobi
MACHIAVELLI
Italian 1418-1479
paintings: (H) $242,000

ZERBE, Karl
German/American 1903-1972
paintings: (L) $110; (H) $3,300
drawings: (L) $33; (H) $345
sculpture: (H) $2,070

ZEREGA, Andrea Pietro de
contemporary
paintings: (H) $550

ZERILLO, Francesco
French d. 1837
drawings: (H) $10,925

ZERMATI, Jules
Italian 19th/20th cent.
paintings: (L) $863; (H) $2,875

ZERMETT, J.
Italian 19th/20th cent.
paintings: (L) $605; (H) $1,320

ZERPA, Carlos
b. 1950
drawings: (H) $3,737

ZETSCHE, Eduard
German 1844-1927
drawings: (H) $935

ZETTLER, Emil Robert
American 1878-1946
sculpture: (H) $2,200

ZEWY, Karl
Austrian 1855-1929
paintings: (L) $1,320; (H) $6,900

ZEZZOS, Alessandro
Italian 1848-1913
drawings: (H) $4,400

ZHANG DAQIAN and ZHU YIFAN,
Chang TA-CHIEN and Chu YI-FAN
Chinese 19th cent.
drawings: (H) $3,738

ZHAO SHAO'ANG, Chao SHAO-
ANG
Chinese b. 1905
drawings: (H) $3,738

ZHAO ZHIQIAN, Chao CHIH-
CH'IEN
Chinese 1829-1884
drawings: (H) $3,163

ZHITENEV, V.
drawings: (H) $1,150

ZIACHAROFF, A.
19th cent.
paintings: (H) $990

ZICK, Januarius
1730-1797
paintings: (L) $13,200; (H) $79,200

ZIE
paintings: (H) $495

ZIEGLAR
paintings: (H) $2,145

ZIEGLER, Eustace Paul
American 1881-1969
paintings: (L) $165; (H) $11,500
drawings: (L) $1,150; (H) $2,875

ZIEGLER, Nellie E.
American 1874-1948
paintings: (L) $385; (H) $3,575

ZIEGLER, S.P.
1882-1967
paintings: (H) $495

ZIEITTI, A.F.
sculpture: (H) $3,575

ZIEM
French 20th cent.
paintings: (H) $1,100

ZIEM, Felix
French 1821-1911
paintings: (L) $605; (H) $74,000
drawings: (L) $3,738; (H) $6,050

ZIER, Francois Edouard
French 1856-1924
paintings: (L) $1,210; (H) $23,000

ZIESENIS, Johann Georg
Danish 1716-1776
paintings: (H) $3,630

ZIG
drawings: (L) $550; (H) $1,210

ZIG, Louis GAUDIN
French d. 1936
paintings: (H) $5,750
drawings: (H) $1,430

ZILLE, Heinrich
German 1858/64-1929
drawings: (L) $2,200; (H) $3,738

ZILLINGER
German School 19th cent.
paintings: (H) $1,540

ZILOTTI, Domenico Battisha
Italian b. 1887
paintings: (L) $1,155; (H) $1,540

ZIM, Marco
American b. 1880
paintings: (H) $1,980

ZIMMER, Bernd
German b. 1948
paintings: (L) $2,420; (H) $7,475

ZIMMER, Hans Peter
German 1936-1992
paintings: (H) $605

ZIMMERMAN, Carl
American b. 1900
paintings: (H) $1,430
drawings: (H) $275

ZIMMERMAN, Ernst
German 1852-1901
drawings: (H) $1,980

ZIMMERMAN, Eugene
American 1878-1935
paintings: (H) $467

ZIMMERMAN, Frederick
paintings: (H) $715
drawings: (H) $58

ZIMMERMAN, Frederick Almond
American 1886-1974
paintings: (L) $3,575; (H) $4,025

ZIMMERMAN, Friedrich August
German 1805-1876
paintings: (H) $1,320

ZIMMERMAN, Jame
drawings: (H) $450

ZIMMERMAN, John von
Continental 20th cent.
paintings: (H) $978

ZIMMERMAN, Reinhard Sebastian
German 1815-1893
paintings: (H) $1,540

ZIMMERMANN, Alfred
German 1854-1910
paintings: (H) $715

ZIMMERMANN, August Albert
German 1808-1888
paintings: (L) $4,125; (H) $7,475 •

ZIMMERMANN, Ernest Karl Georg
  German 1852-1901
  paintings: (L) $990; (H) $2,530

ZIMMERMANN, Jan Wendel
  Gerstenhauer
  Dutch 1816-1887
  paintings: (H) $7,700

ZIMMERMANN, Julius
  German 1824-1906
  paintings: (H) $12,100

ZIMMERMANN, Reinhard Sebastian
  German 1815-1893
  paintings: (L) $4,950; (H) $24,200

ZINFORNITI, E.
  paintings: (H) $1,210

ZINGG, Jules Emile
  French 1882-1942
  paintings: (H) $3,300

ZINGONI, Aurelio
  Italian 1853-1922
  paintings: (L) $5,720; (H) $9,200

ZINK, Joseph
  German 1838-1907
  paintings: (H) $2,640

ZINKEISEN, Doris Clare
  British b. 1898
  paintings: (H) $3,450

ZINNOGGER, Leopold
  Austrian 1811-1872
  paintings: (L) $9,350; (H) $76,750

ZINSKY
  sculpture: (H) $805

ZITMAN, Cornelius
  b. Holland 1926
  sculpture: (L) $9,200; (H) $19,800

ZOARCH, William
  1887-1966
  drawings: (H) $2,070

ZOBEL, Benjamin
  Swabian 1762-1831
  paintings: (L) $2,090; (H) $2,090

ZOBEL, Curtis
  American 20th cent.
  sculpture: (L) $460; (H) $978

ZOBOLI, Jacopo
  1681-1767
  drawings: (H) $2,640

ZOCCHI, Guglielmo
  Italian b. 1874
  paintings: (L) $1,650; (H) $21,275

ZOFFOLI, A.
  Italian 20th cent.
  paintings: (H) $10,350

ZOFFOLI, Andrea
  Italian 19th cent.
  drawings: (H) $550

ZOGBAUM, Rufus Fairchild
  1849-1925
  paintings: (L) $220; (H) $2,750
  drawings: (L) $138; (H) $1,265

ZOGBAUM, Wilfrid
  American 1915-1965
  paintings: (H) $88
  drawings: (H) $57
  sculpture: (L) $920; (H) $3,910

ZOI, D.
  Italian 19th cent.
  sculpture: (L) $2,070; (H) $20,900

ZOIR, Emil
  Swedish 1867-1936
  paintings: (H) $5,500

ZOMBORY, Lajos
  Hungarian 1867-1933
  paintings: (H) $690

ZONA, Antonio
  Italian 1813-1892
  paintings: (L) $8,800; (H) $16,500

ZONARO, Fausto
  Italian 1854-1929
  paintings: (H) $2,300

ZOPPI, Antonio
  Italian 1860-1926
  paintings: (L) $4,830; (H) $12,650

ZORACH, Marguerite
  American 1887-1968
  paintings: (L) $4,600; (H) $38,500
  drawings: (L) $1,705; (H) $8,625

ZORACH, William
  Lithuanian/Am. 1887-1966
  paintings: (L) $550; (H) $44,000
  drawings: (L) $220; (H) $9,200
  sculpture: (L) $275; (H) $121,000

ZORACH, Marguerite and William
  ZORACH
  paintings: (H) $33,350

Pioneer Fauvist

Marguerite Thompson Zorach (1887-1968) was a pioneering artist, one of the first to introduce Fauvist and Cubist styles to America. Born to a genteel California family, she was a brilliant student and one of a few women admitted to Stanford in 1908. An unexpected letter from an aunt in Paris, with a check enclosed, invited her to come to Paris and study art. Her first day in Paris was spent viewing the 1908 Salon d'Automne, an exhibition that included the works of Henri Matisse and André Derain. Matisse and Derain were leaders of the Fauves (wild beasts), a group of painters who used vivid, often non-naturalist colors. Marguerite did not enter the Academy as her aunt had expected, but studied at an avant-garde school, La Palette, run by Scottish Fauve painter John Duncan Fergusson. In her painting classes she met and fell in love with William Zorach, a poor first-generation Lithuanian Jew from Cleveland, Ohio. Alarmed at her romance, her aunt took her on an extended tour of the Orient, inspiration for many of Marguerite's later works. Back in California in 1912, Marguerite painted and waited for Zorach to save enough money to send for her. A series of Fauvist paintings of the High Sierras, made in the summer of 1912 while camping with her family, were exhibited in Los Angeles in the fall, and later that year Marguerite moved to New York City and married Zorach. The two lived in Brooklyn for the rest of their lives. Their first child was born in 1915, the second in 1917. Although both Zorachs exhibited in 1916, William's career as a sculptor began to overshadow his wife's. Finding it difficult to concentrate on her paintings with two young children, Marguerite began to work with needlepoint and eventually began to work on large tapestries, a major source of income for many years. Marguerite had many important patrons, but her work was considered a craft, not an art, and the Museum of Modern Art in New York turned down a gift of her tapestries because it did not fit into any of their categories. In her 40s, Marguerite was a painter and printmaker and a designer of rugs, batiks, and tapestries. Both Zorachs exhibited extensively and were teachers at the Skowhegan School of Art in Maine, but it is only recently that Marguerite's work, both as a painter and tapestry designer, has been appreciated. The painting of *Golden Harvest/Hunters* was consigned to Skinner's in Bolton, Massachusetts, from the family of the artist and sold for $28,750. (Marguerite Zorach, *Golden Harvest/Hunters*, oil on canvas mounted on masonite, 17¾ x 23 inches, Skinner, November 11, 1994, $28,750)

ZORN, Anders
  Swedish 1860-1920
  paintings: (L) $11,500; (H) $550,000
  drawings: (L) $5,175; (H) $82,500

ZORN, John
  20th cent.
  paintings: (H) $460

ZORNES, Jane Milford
  American b. 1907
  paintings: (H) $1,320
  drawings: (L) $495; (H) $3,850

ZORTHIAN, Jirayr Hamparzoom
  American b. 1912
  paintings: (H) $880
  drawings: (H) $880

ZOTTMAN, H.
  drawings: (H) $770

ZOX, Larry
  b. 1937
  paintings: (L) $575; (H) $1,650

ZSCHIMMER, Emil
  German 1842-1917
  paintings: (H) $34,500

ZU, Ming Ho
  Chinese b. 1949
  paintings: (H) $578

ZU MING HO
  Chinese b. 1949
  paintings: (H) $578

ZUBER-BUHLER, Fritz
  Swiss 1822-1896
  paintings: (L) $5,280; (H) $25,300

ZUBIAURRE, Ramon de
  Spanish 1882-1969
  paintings: (L) $2,000; (H) $2,500

ZUBIAURRE, Valentin de
  Spanish 1879-1963
  paintings: (H) $24,200

ZUCCA, Edward
  American b. 1946
  sculpture: (H) $7,475

ZUCCARELLI, Francesco
  Italian 1701/02-1788
  paintings: (L) $33,000; (H) $104,500
  drawings: (L) $4,125; (H) $9,200

ZUCCARO, Federico
  Italian 1542/43-1609
  drawings: (L) $2,970; (H) $19,550

ZUCCARO, Taddeo
  Italian 1529-1566
  drawings: (H) $28,750

ZUCCHI, Antonio
  1726-1795
  drawings: (H) $2,990

ZUCCHI, Antonio Pietro Francesco
  1726-1795
  drawings: (H) $4,888

ZUCKER, J.
  paintings: (H) $475

ZUCKER, Jacques
  Polish/American b. 1900
  paintings: (L) $431; (H) $880

ZUCKER, Joe
  American b. 1941
  paintings: (L) $1,265; (H) $2,750
  drawings: (L) $220; (H) $1,840
  sculpture: (L) $990; (H) $1,430

ZUCKERBERG
  American 20th cent.
  paintings: (H) $522

ZUCKERBERG, Stanley
b. 1919
drawings: (H) $1,320

ZUGEL, Heinrich Johann von
German 1850-1941
paintings: (L) $3,025; (H) $104,500

ZUGNO, Francesco
1709-1787
paintings: (L) $5,280; (H) $55,000

ZUILL, Abbie Luella
1856-1921
paintings: (L) $825; (H) $3,025

ZULIANI
Italian 19th cent.
paintings: (H) $880

ZULOAGA Y ZABALETA, Ignacio
Spanish 1870-1945
paintings: (L) $1,265; (H) $242,000
drawings: (H) $495

ZUNIGA, Francisco
Mexican b. Costa Rica 1913
paintings: (L) $3,105; (H) $6,900
drawings: (L) $770; (H) $46,200
sculpture: (L) $3,300; (H) $178,500

ZURAWSKI, Stanislaw
paintings: (H) $1,150

ZURBARAN, Francisco de
Spanish 1598-1664
paintings: (L) $110,000; (H) $825,000

ZURBARAN, Francisco de, studio of
Italian
paintings: (H) $19,800

ZUSI, A.
paintings: (H) $3,190

ZWAAN, Cornelisz C.
Dutch/American 1882-1964
paintings: (L) $44; (H) $4,125

ZWACK, Michael
b. 1949
drawings: (L) $805; (H) $1,265

ZWAHLEN, Abraham Andre
Swiss 1830-1903
paintings: (L) $2,090; (H) $4,730

ZWARA, John
American b. 1880
paintings: (H) $660
drawings: (H) $440

ZWART, Willem de
Dutch 1862-1931
paintings: (L) $1,320; (H) $7,475
drawings: (H) $1,650

ZWARTT, Andreas
20th cent.
paintings: (H) $770

ZWENGAUER, Anton
German 1810-1884
paintings: (H) $2,530

ZWICK, W.
sculpture: (H) $3,080

ZWILLINGER, Rhonda
b. 1950
paintings: (H) $1,100

ZYNSKY, Mary Ann "Toots"
American b. 1951
sculpture: (L) $1,725; (H) $5,463

Appendix A: Museums

ALABAMA

Birmingham
Birmingham Museum of Art

Huntsville
Huntsville Museum of Art

Montgomery
Montgomery Museum of Fine Arts

Tuscaloosa
The Warner Collection at Gulf States
  Paper Corporation

ALASKA

Anchorage
Anchorage Museum of History and Art

Fairbanks
University of Alaska Museum

Juneau
Alaska State Museum

ARIZONA

Phoenix
Heard Art Museum
Phoenix Art Museum

Tempe
Arizona State University Art Museum

Tucson
Tucson Museum of Art
University of Arizona Museum of Art

ARKANSAS

Jonesboro
Arkansas State University Museum

Little Rock
Arkansas Arts Center

CALIFORNIA

Bakersfield
Bakersfield Museum of Art

Berkeley
University Art Museum, University of
  California, Berkeley

Escondido
California Center for the Arts Museum

Fresno
Fresno Art Museum

Long Beach
Long Beach Museum of Art

Los Angeles
Craft and Folk Art Museum
Los Angeles County Museum of Art
UCLA at the Armand Hammer
  Museum of Art and Cultural Center

Malibu
J. Paul Getty Museum

Monterey
Monterey Peninsula Museum of Art

Newport Beach
Newport Harbor Art Museum

Oakland
Oakland Museum of California

Palo Alto
Stanford University Museum of Art
  (closed till 1998)

Pasadena
Norton Simon Museum of Art

Sacramento
Crocker Art Museum

San Diego
Museum of Contemporary Art,
  San Diego
San Diego Museum of Art
Timken Museum of Art

San Francisco
Asian Art Museum of San Francisco
California Palace of the Legion of
  Honor
Cartoon Art Museum
M.H. de Young Memorial Museum
The Mexican Museum
San Francisco Museum of Modern Art

San Marino
Huntington Library, Art Collection and
  Botanical Gardens

898

Santa Barbara
Santa Barbara Museum of Art

Stockton
The Haggin Museum

COLORADO

Colorado Springs
Colorado Springs Fine Arts Center

Denver
Denver Art Museum
Museum of Western Art

CONNECTICUT

Bridgeport
Housatonic Museum of Art

Farmington
Hill-Stead Museum

Hartford
Wadsworth Atheneum

Mystic
Mystic Seaport Museum

New Britain
New Britain Museum of American Art

New Haven
Yale Center for British Art
Yale University Art Gallery

New London
Lyman Allyn Museum

Old Lyme
Florence Griswold House of the Lyme
  Historical Society

Storrs
William Benton Museum of Art,
  University of Connecticut

DELAWARE

Wilmington
Delaware Art Museum

Winterthur
Winterthur Museum and Gardens

DISTRICT OF COLUMBIA

Washington
Corcoran Gallery of Art
Hirshhorn Museum and Sculpture
  Garden
National Museum of American Art
National Gallery of Art

National Portrait Gallery
The Phillips Collection

FLORIDA

Boca Raton
International Museum of Cartoon Art

Coral Gables
Lowe Art Museum, University of
  Miami
Metropolitan Museum and Art Centers

Fort Lauderdale
Museum of Art

Jacksonville
Cummer Gallery of Art
Jacksonville Art Museum

Miami Beach
Bass Museum of Art
The Wolfsonian

North Miami
Museum of Modern Art

Orlando
Orlando Museum of Art

Pensacola
Pensacola Museum of Art

Palm Beach
Henry Morrison Flagler Museum
Society for the Four Arts Museum

Rollins
Cornell Fine Arts Center

St. Petersburg
Museum of Fine Arts

Sarasota
The John and Mable Ringling Museum
  of Art

West Palm Beach
Norton Gallery and School of Art

GEORGIA

Albany
Museum of Art

Athens
Georgia Museum of Art, University of
  Georgia

Atlanta
High Museum of Art

Savannah
Telfair Academy of Arts and Sciences,
  Inc.

HAWAII

Honolulu
The Contemporary Museum
Honolulu Academy of Arts

IDAHO

Boise
Boise Art Museum

ILLINOIS

Champaign
Krannert Art Museum, University of
  Illinois

Chicago
Art Institute of Chicago
Museum of Contemporary Art
Museum of Contemporary
  Photography, Columbia College
Terra Museum of American Art

INDIANA

Bloomington
Indiana University Art Museum

Evansville
Evansville Museum of Arts and Science

Fort Wayne
Fort Wayne Museum of Art

Indianapolis
Indianapolis Museum of Art

Lafayette
Greater Lafayette Museum of Art

South Bend
Smite Museum of Art, University of
  Notre Dame

Terre Haute
Sheldon Swope Art Gallery

IOWA

Cedar Falls
University of Northern Iowa Museum

Cedar Rapids
Cedar Rapids Museum of Art

Davenport
Davenport Museum of Art

Des Moines
Des Moines Art Center

Fort Dodge
Blanden Memorial Art Museum

Iowa City
University of Iowa Museum of Art

Mason City
Charles H. MacNider Museum

Muscatine
Muscatine Art Center

Sioux City
Sioux City Art Center

KANSAS

Lawrence
Spencer Museum of Art, University of
  Kansas

Topeka
Mulvane Art Center

Wichita
Edwin A. Ulrich Museum of Art,
  Wichita State University
Wichita Art Museum

KENTUCKY

Lexington
University of Kentucky Art Museum

Louisville
J.B. Speed Art Museum

Owensboro
Owensboro Museum of Fine Art

LOUISIANA

Alexandria
Alexandria Museum of Art, Visual Art
  Center

Jennings
Zigler Museum

New Orleans
Louisiana State Museum
New Orleans Museum of Art

Shreveport
The R.W. Norton Art Gallery

MAINE

Brunswick
Bowdoin College Museum of Art

Portland
Portland Museum of Art

Rockland
William A. Farnsworth Library and Art
  Museum

Waterville
Colby College Museum of Art

MARYLAND

Baltimore
American Visionary Art Museum
Baltimore Museum of Art
Walters Art Gallery

Hagerstown
Washington County Museum of Fine
  Arts

MASSACHUSETTS

Amherst
Mead Art Museum

Andover
Addison Gallery of American Art

Boston
The Institute of Contemporary Art
Isabella Stewart Gardener Museum
Museum of Fine Arts

Brockton
Fuller Museum of Art

Cambridge
Arthur M. Sackler Art Museum
Busch-Reisinger Museum
Fogg Art Museum
M.I.T.—List Visual Arts Center

Chestnut Hill
The Boston College Museum of Art

Framingham
Danforth Museum

Lincoln
DeCordova and Dana Museum and
  Sculpture Park

Northhampton
Smith College Museum of Art

Salem
Peabody Essex Museum

Springfield
Museum of Fine Art

Stockbridge
Chesterwood

Waltham
Rose Art Museum, Brandeis University

Wellesley
Wellesley College Museum, Jewett Art
  Center

Williamstown
Sterling and Francine Clark Art
  Institute
Williams College Museum of Art

Worcester
Worcester Art Museum

MICHIGAN

Ann Arbor
University of Michigan Museum of Art

Detroit
Detroit Institute of Arts

Flint
Flint Institute of Arts

Grand Rapids
Grand Rapids Art Museum

Kalamazoo
Kalamazoo Institute of Arts

Muskegon
Muskegon Museum of Art

Saginaw
Saginaw Art Museum

University Center
The Marshall M. Fredericks Sculpture
  Gallery

MINNESOTA

Duluth
Tweed Museum of Art, University of
  Minnesota

Minneapolis
Frederick R. Weisman Art Museum,
  University of Minnesota
Minneapolis Institute of Arts
Walker Art Center

St. Paul
Minnesota Museum of Art

MISSISSIPPI

Laurel
Lauren Rogers Museum of Art

MISSOURI

Kansas City
Nelson-Atkins Museum of Art

St. Joseph
Albrecht-Kemper Museum of Art

St. Louis
Laumeier Sculpture Park and Museum
St. Louis Art Museum
Washington University Gallery of Art

MONTANA

Billings
Yellowstone Art Center

Great Falls
C.M. Russell Museum

Missoula
The Art Museum of Missoula

NEBRASKA

Lincoln
Sheldon Memorial Art Gallery,
  University of Nebraska Art Gallery

Omaha
Joslyn Art Museum

NEVADA

Las Vegas
Las Vegas Art Museum

Reno
Nevada Museum of Art

NEW HAMPSHIRE

Hanover
Hood Museum of Art, Dartmouth
  College

Manchester
Currier Gallery of Art

NEW JERSEY

Montclair
Montclair Art Museum

Newark
Newark Museum

New Brunswick
Jane Voorhees Zimmerli Art Museum
  of Rutgers University

Princeton
The Art Museum, Princeton University

Trenton
New Jersey State Museum

NEW MEXICO

Albuquerque
Albuquerque Museum
Jonson Gallery, University of New
  Mexico

Santa Fe
Museum of New Mexico

NEW YORK

Brookville
Hillwood Art Museum

Buffalo
Albright-Knox Art Gallery

Canajoharie
Canajoharie Library and Art Gallery

Corning
The Rockwell Museum

Elmira
Arnot Art Museum

Glens Falls
Hyde Collection

Hamilton
Picker Art Gallery, Colgate University

Hempstead
Hofstra Museum, Hofstra University

Hudson
Olana State Historic Site

Huntington
Heckscher Museum

Ithaca
Herbert F. Johnson Museum of Art,
  Cornell University

Mountainville
Storm King Art Center

New York City
The Bronx Museum of the Arts
The Brooklyn Museum
Cooper-Hewitt Museum
Dahesh Museum
The Frick Collection
International Center of Photography
Jewish Museum
Metropolitan Museum of Art
Museum of American Folk Art
Museum of Modern Art
New Museum of Contemporary Art
New York Historical Society
Solomon R. Guggenheim Museum
Whitney Museum of American Art

Ogdensburg
Frederic Remington Art Museum

Poughkeepsie
Frances Lehman Loeb Art Center at
Vassar

Rochester
Memorial Art Gallery of the University
of Rochester

Southampton
Parrish Art Museum

Syracuse
Everson Museum of Art of Syracuse
and Onondaga County

Utica
Munson-Williams-Proctor Institute,
Museum of Art

Yonkers
Hudson River Museum

NORTH CAROLINA

Chapel Hill
Ackland Art Museum, University of
North Carolina

Charlotte
Mint Museum of Art

Durham
Duke University

Greensboro
Weatherspoon Art Gallery

Greenville
Greenville Museum of Art

Raleigh
North Carolina Museum of Art

Wilmington
St. John's Museum of Art

Winston-Salem
Southeastern Center for Contemporary
Art

OHIO

Akron
Akron Art Museum

Canton
Canton Art Institute

Cincinnati
Cincinnati Art Museum
Taft Museum

Cleveland
Cleveland Museum of Art

Columbus
Columbus Museum of Art
Wexner Center for the Arts, Ohio State
University

Dayton
Dayton Art Institute

Oberlin
Allen Memorial Art Museum, Oberlin
College

Oxford
Miami University Art Museum

Toledo
Toledo Museum of Art

Youngstown
Butler Institute of American Art

OKLAHOMA

Norman
The Fred Jones Jr. Museum of Art,
University of Oklahoma

Oklahoma City
National Cowboy Hall of Fame and
Western Heritage Center
Oklahoma City Art Museum

Tulsa
Philbrook Museum of Art
Thomas Gilcrease Institute of American
History and Art

OREGON

Eugene
Museum of Art, University of Oregon

Portland
Portland Art Museum

PENNSYLVANIA

Allentown
Allentown Art Museum

Bethlehem
Lehigh University Art Galleries

Chadds Ford
Brandywine River Museum

Greensburg
Westmoreland Museum of Art

Philadelphia
Barnes Foundation
Pennsylvania Academy of the Fine Arts

Philadelphia Museum of Art and the
 Rodin Museum
Woodmere Art Museum

Pittsburgh
Andy Warhol Museum
Museum of Art, Carnegie Institute

Reading
Reading Public Museum and Art
 Gallery

RHODE ISLAND

Providence
Museum of Art, Rhode Island School of
 Design

SOUTH CAROLINA

Charleston
Gibbes Museum of Art

Columbia
Columbia Museum of Art

Greenville
Greenville County Museum of Art

Murrells Inlet
Brookgreen Gardens

SOUTH DAKOTA

Brookings
South Dakota Art Museum

TENNESSEE

Chattanooga
Hunter Museum of Art

Knoxville
Knoxville Museum of Art

Memphis
Dixon Gallery and Gardens
Memphis Brooks Museum of Art

Nashville
Carl Van Vechten Gallery of Fine Arts,
 Fisk University
Cheekwood Botanical Gardens and
 Fine Arts Center
Vanderbilt Art Gallery

TEXAS

Austin
Archer M. Huntington Art Gallery,
 University of Texas at Austin

Beaumont
Art Museum of Southeast Texas

Corpus Christi
Art Museum of South Texas

Dallas
Dallas Museum of Art

El Paso
El Paso Museum of Art

Fort Worth
Amon Carter Museum
Kimbell Art Museum
Modern Art Museum of Fort Worth

Houston
Contemporary Arts Museum
Museum of Fine Arts, Houston

UTAH

Provo
Museum of Art at Brigham Young
 University

Salt Lake City
Utah Museum of Fine Arts, University
 of Utah

Springville
Springville Museum of Art

VERMONT

Bennington
Bennington Museum

Middlebury
Middlebury College Museum of Art

Shelburne
Shelburne Museum

VIRGINIA

Charlottesville
Bayly Art Museum of the University of
 Virginia

Newport News
Mariners Museum

Norfolk
Chrysler Museum

Richmond
Virginia Museum of Fine Arts

Williamsburg
Abby Aldrich Rockefeller Folk Art
 Center

Muscarella Museum of Art, College of William and Mary

WASHINGTON

Pullman
Museum of Art, Washington State University

Seattle
Henry Art Gallery, University of Washington
Seattle Art Museum

Tacoma
Tacoma Art Museum

WEST VIRGINIA

Huntington
Huntington Museum of Art

WISCONSIN

Madison
Elvehjem Museum of Art, University of Wisconsin-Madison
Madison Art Center

Manitowoc
Rahr-West Art Museum

Milwaukee
Milwaukee Art Museum

WYOMING

Cody
Whitney Gallery of Western Art in the Buffalo Bill Historical Center

Laramie
Art Museum, University of Wyoming

Rock Springs
Community Fine Arts Center

Appendix B: Publications[1]

AFTERIMAGE (M)
Visual Studies Workshop
31 Prince Street
Rochester, NY 14607

AMERICAN ART (M)
National Museum of American Art
8th and G Streets, N.W.
Washington, D.C. 20001

AMERICAN ART JOURNAL (J)
Kennedy Galleries
40 West 57th Street, 5th floor
New York, NY 10019

AMERICAN ARTIST (M)
1515 Broadway
New York, NY 10036

ANTIQUE GAZETTE (T)
6949 Charlotte Pike, Suite 106
Nashville, TN 37209

ANTIQUE PRESS (T)
12403 North Florida Avenue
Tampa, FL 33612

ANTIQUE REVIEW (T)
P. O. Box 538
12 East Stafford Avenue
Worthington, OH 43085

ANTIQUE TRADER WEEKLY (T)
P.O. Box 1050
100 Bryant Street
Dubuque, IA 52004

ANTIQUE WEEK (T)
P.O. Box 90
27 North Jefferson Street
Knightstown, IN 46148

**ANTIQUES AND THE ARTS
WEEKLY/THE NEWTOWN BEE** (T)
5 Church Hill Road
Newtown, CT 06470-5503
http://www.thebee.com/aweb/aa.htm

ANTIQUES AND AUCTION NEWS
(T)
P.O. Box 500
Mount Joy, PA 17552

ANTIQUES WEST (T)
3315 Sacramento Street, Suite 618
San Francisco, CA 94118

APOLLO MAGAZINE (M)
29 Chesham Place
London Sw1X 8HB
England

**ARCHIVES OF AMERICAN ART
JOURNAL** (J)
Smithsonian Institution
8th and G Streets, N.W.
Washington, DC 20560

ART & ANTIQUES (M)
3 East 54th Street
New York, NY 10022

ART & AUCTION (M)
440 Park Avenue South
New York, NY 10016

**THE ART/ANTIQUES INVESTMENT
REPORT** (N)
99 Wall Street
New York, NY 10005

ART BULLETIN (M)
College Art Association
Getty Center for the History of Art and
  the Humanities
401 Wilshire Boulevard, Suite 400
Santa Monica, CA 90401

ARTFORUM (M)
65 Bleecker Street
New York, NY 10012

ART HISTORY (J)
Association of Art Historians
108 Cowley Road
Oxford 0X41Jf
England

ART IN AMERICA (M)
575 Broadway, 5th Floor
New York, NY 10012

---

[1] *Key:* (J)—Journal, (M)—Magazine, (N)—Newsletter, (T)—Tabloid.

ART JOURNAL (J)
College Art Association
275 Seventh Avenue
New York, NY 10001

ART MONTHLY (M)
26 Charing Cross Road, Suite 17
London WC2H ODG
England

ARTNEWS (N)
48 West 38th Street
New York, NY 10018

THE ARTNEWSLETTER (N)
48 West 38th Street
New York, NY 10018

ARTWEEK (T)
12 South First Street, Suite 520
San Jose, CA 95113

BURLINGTON MAGAZINE (M)
14-16 Duke's Road
London WC1 H9AD
England

COLLECTOR (T)
436 West 4th Street, Suite 222
Pomona, CA 91765

**COLLECTOR'S NEWS & THE
ANTIQUE REPORTER** (T)
P.O. Box 156
506 Second Street
Grundy Center, IA 50638

DRAWING (N)
Drawing Society
15 Penn Plaza, Box 66
415 7th Avenue
New York, NY 10001

FLASH ART (M)
68 Via Carlo Farini
20159 Milan
Italy

FMR (M)
Via Montecucconi 32
Milan, Italy

**INTERNATIONAL REVIEW OF
AFRICAN AMERICAN ART**
Hampton University Museum
Hampton, VA 23668

**LATIN AMERICAN ART
MAGAZINE** (M)
7824 East Lewis Avenue
Scottsdale, AZ 85257

THE MAGAZINE ANTIQUES (M)
575 Broadway, 5th Floor
New York, NY 10012

**MAINE ANTIQUE DIGEST
(M.A.D.)** (T)
P.O. Box 1429
911 Main Street
Waldoboro, ME 04572
http://www.maine.com/mad

MASS BAY ANTIQUES (T)
P.O. Box 192
2 Washington Street
Ipswich, MA 01938

**THE MIDATLANTIC ANTIQUES
MAGAZINE** (T)
P.O. Box 908
309 South Chestnut Street
Henderson, NC 27536

MODERN PAINTERS (M)
Universal House
10 Barley Mow Passage
Cheswick, London W4 4PH
England

NEW ART EXAMINER (M)
314 West Institute Place
Chicago, IL 60610

**NEW ENGLAND ANTIQUES
JOURNAL** (T)
4 Church Street
Ware, MA 01082

**THE NEW YORK ANTIQUE
ALMANAC** (T)
P.O. Box 335
Lawrence, NY 11559

**THE NEW YORK-PENNSYLVANIA
COLLECTOR** (T)
P. O. Box C
Fishers, NY 14453

OCTOBER (J)
M.I.T. Press
55 Hayward Street
Cambridge, MA 02142

OXFORD ART JOURNAL (J)
Oxford University Press, Walton St.
Oxford OX2 6DP, UK
England

RENNINGER'S ANTIQUE GUIDE (T)
P.O. Box 495
Lafayette Hill, PA 19444

SCULPTURE (M)
International Sculpture Center
1050 17th Street, Suite 250
Washington, D.C. 20036

SCULPTURE REVIEW (J)
National Sculpture Society
301 East 57th Street
New York, NY 10022

SOUTHWEST ART (M)
5444 Westheimer, Suite 1440
Houston, TX 77056

TODAY'S COLLECTOR (T)
700 East State Street
Iola, WI 54990

WEST COAST PEDDLER (T)
P.O. Box 5134
Whittier, CA 90607

WOMEN'S ART JOURNAL (J)
1711 Harris Road
Laverock, PA 19118

Appendix C: Auction Houses

ALDERFER AUCTION COMPANY
501 Fairgrounds Road
Hatfield, Pennsylvania 19440
(215) 368-5477

ALTERMANN & MORRIS GALLERIES
3461 West Alabama
Houston, Texas 77027
(713) 840-1922

JAMES R. BAKKER ANTIQUES, INC.
236 Newbury Street
Boston, Massachusetts 02116
(617) 262-8020

BARRIDOFF GALLERIES
Post Office Box 9715
Portland, Maine 04104
(207) 772-5011
http://www.biddeford.com/barridoff

BIDER'S AUCTION HOUSE
241 South Union Street
Lawrence, Massachusetts 01843
(508) 688-4347

FRANK H. BOOS GALLERY, INC.
420 Enterprise Court
Bloomfield Hills, Michigan 48302
(313) 332-1500

WILLIAM BUNCH AUCTION
11 North Brandywine Street
Westchester, Pennsylvania 19380
(610) 696-1530

JEFFREY BURCHARD GALLERIES
2528 30th Avenue North
St. Petersburg, Florida 33713
(813) 823-4156

BURLINGAME'S
182 Old Route 9
Fishkill, New York 12524
(914) 896-0566

BUTTERFIELD & BUTTERFIELD
220 San Bruno Avenue
San Francisco, California 94103
(415) 861-7500

CADDIGAN AUCTIONEERS & APPRAISERS
1130 Washington Street
Hanover, Massachusetts 02339
(617) 826-8648

CHAMBERLIN'S AUCTIONEERS & APPRAISERS
18727 Ventura Boulevard
Tarzana, California 91356
(818) 774-2855

CHRISTIE'S
502 Park Avenue
New York, New York 10022
(212) 546-1000
http://www.christies.com

CHRISTIE'S EAST
219 East 67th Street
New York, New York 10021
(212) 606-0400

CLEARING HOUSE AUCTION GALLERIES, INC.
207 Church Street
Wethersfield, Connecticut 06019
(203) 529-3344

CLEVELAND PRINT AUCTION
12803 Larchmere Boulevard
Shaker Heights, Ohio 44120
(216) 791-6663

COLLINS GALLERIES
35 Western Avenue
Kennebunk, Maine 04043
(207) 967-5004

CONCORD AUCTION STUDIO
2350 Willow Pass Road
Concord, California 94520
(510) 689-4884

CYR AUCTION COMPANY
Post Office Box 1238
Gray, Maine 04039
(207) 657-5253

DARGATE AUCTION GALLERIES
5607 Baum Boulevard
Pittsburgh, Pennsylvania 15206
(412) 362-3558
http://www.dargate.com

DOUGLAS AUCTIONEERS
Route 5
South Deerfield, Massachusetts 01373
(413) 665-2877

WILLIAM DOYLE GALLERIES
175 East 87th Street
New York, New York 10128
(212) 427-2730
http://www.doylegalleries.com

DU MOUCHELLE ART GALLERIES
409 East Jefferson Avenue
Detroit, Michigan 48226
(313) 963-0248

DUNNING'S AUCTION SERVICE, INC.
P.O. Box 866
Elgin, Illinois 60123
(847) 741-3483

ROBERT C. ELDRED CO., Inc.
1483 Route 6A
East Dennis, Massachusetts 02641-0796
(508) 385-3116

ROBERT L. FOSTER, JR. AUCTIONEER & APPRAISER
Route 1, P. O. Box 203
Newcastle, Maine 04553
(207) 563-8110

FREEMAN/FINE ARTS OF PHILADELPHIA, INC.
1808 Chestnut Street
Philadelphia, Pennsylvania 19103
(215) 563-9275

GARTH'S AUCTIONS, INC.
2690 Stratford Road
Delaware, Ohio 43015
(614) 362-4771

MORTON M. GOLDBERG AUCTION GALLERIES, INC.
547 Baronne Street
New Orleans, Louisiana 70113
(504) 592-2300

GROGAN & COMPANY
268 Newbury Street
Boston, Massachusetts 02116
(617) 437-9550

GARY GUYETTE/FRANK SCHMIDT, INC.
Post Office Box 522
West Farmington, Maine 04992
(207) 778-6256

HANZEL GALLERIES, INC.
1120 South Michigan Avenue
Chicago, Illinois 60605
(312) 922-6234

HART GALLERIES
2311 Westheimer
Houston, Texas 77098
(713) 266-3500

WILLIS HENRY AUCTIONS
22 Main Street
Marshfield, Massachusetts 02050
(617) 834-7774

LESLIE HINDMAN AUCTIONEERS
215 West Ohio Street
Chicago, Illinois 60610
(312) 670-0010

HODGINS ART AUCTIONS LTD.
#100, 437-36th Avenue S.E.
Calgary, Alberta T2G 1W5
Canada
(403) 243-0866

ILLUSTRATION HOUSE, INC.
96 Spring Street
New York, New York 10012
(212) 966-9444

JACKSON'S AUCTION GALLERY
5330 Pendleton Avenue
Anderson, Indiana 46013
(317) 255-7563

ARTHUR JAMES GALLERIES
615 East Atlantic Avenue
Delray Beach, Florida 33483
(407) 278-2373

JOYNER AUCTIONEERS & APPRAISERS
222 Gerrard Street East
Toronto, Ontario M5A 2E8
Canada
(416) 323-0909

JAMES D. JULIA, INC.
Post Box 830
Route 201, Skowhegan Road
Fairfield, Maine 04937
(207) 453-7125

KAMINSKI AUCTIONS
193 Franklin Street
Stoneham, Massachusetts 02180
(617) 438-7595

LOUISIANA AUCTION EXCHANGE
2031 Government Street
Baton Rouge, Louisiana 70806
(504) 387-9777

LUBIN GALLERIES
30 West 26th Street
New York, New York 10010
(212) 924-3777

**JOY LUKE FINE ART BROKERS,
AUCTIONEERS & APPRAISERS**
The Gallery
300 East Grove Street
Bloomington, Illinois 61701
(309) 828-5533

MAPES
1600 Vestal Parkway West
Vestal, New York 13850
(607) 754-9193

**MAYNARDS ANTIQUES & FINE
ART**
415 West 2nd Avenue
Vancouver, British Columbia V5Y 1E3
Canada
(604) 876-6787

PAUL MCINNIS
356 Exeter Road
Hampton Falls, New Hampshire 03844
(603) 778-8989

**JOHN MORAN AUCTIONEERS,
INC.**
3202 East Foothill Boulevard
Pasadena, California 91107
(818) 793-1833

**MYERS ANTIQUE & AUCTION
GALLERY**
1600 4th Street N.
St. Petersburg, Florida 33704
(813) 823-3249

MYSTIC FINE ARTS
47 Holmes Street
Mystic, Connecticut 06355-2623
(860) 572-8873

NADEAU'S AUCTION GALLERY
184 Windsor Avenue
Windsor, Connecticut 06095
(203) 246-2444

**ERIC NATHAN AUCTION
COMPANY, INC.**
Post Office Box 36, West Road
Manchester, Vermont 05254
(802) 362-3194

NEAL AUCTION COMPANY
4038 Magazine Street
New Orleans, Louisiana 70115
(504) 899-5329

**NEW ORLEANS AUCTION
GALLERIES, INC.**
801 Magazine Street
New Orleans, Louisiana 70130
(504) 566-1849

CARL NORDBLOM
Post Office Box 167
Harvard Square
Cambridge, Massachusetts 02238
(617) 491-1196

**NORTHEAST AUCTIONS
RONALD BOURGEAULT,
AUCTIONEER**
694 Lafayette Road, P.O. Box 363
Hampton, New Hampshire 03842
(603) 926-9800

O'GALLERIE, INC.
228 Northeast Seventh Avenue
Portland, Oregon 97232
(503) 238-0202

**RAFAEL OSONA AUCTIONEERS &
APPRAISER**
Post Office Box 2607
Nantucket, Massachusetts 02584
(508) 228-3942

J.W. PAUL AUCTION CO.
23 C.P.E. Penny Drive
Wallkill, New York 12589
(914) 895-8104

**PENNYPACKER-ANDREWS
AUCTION CENTRE, INC.**
Post Office Box 558
Shillington, Pennsylvania 19607
(215) 777-6121

PETTIGREW AUCTION COMPANY
405 South Nevada Avenue
Colorado Springs, Colorado 80903
(719) 633-7963

PIONEER AUCTION HOUSE
Post Office Box 593
Jct. Rt. 116 and 63
N. Amherst, Massachusetts 01595
(413) 253-9914

POOK & POOK INC.
Post Office Box 268
Downington, Pennsylvania 19335
(610) 269-0695

D & L RITCHIE INC.
288 King Street East
Toronto, Ontario M5A 1KA
Canada
(416) 364-1864

ROYAL YORK AUCTION GALLERY
5925 Baum Boulevard
Pittsburgh, Pennsylvania 15206
(412) 661-1171

SANDERS & MOCK ASSOCIATES
Box 37
Tamworth, New Hampshire 03886
(603) 323-8749

SELKIRK'S
4166 Olive Street
St. Louis, Missouri 63108
(314) 533-1700

SKINNER'S INC., AUCTIONEERS
357 Main Street
Bolton, Massachusetts 01740
(617) 779-6241

C.G. SLOAN & COMPANY, INC.
4920 Wyaconda Road
North Bethesda, Maryland 20852
(301) 468-4911

SOTHEBY'S, INC.
1334 York Avenue
New York, New York 10021
(212) 606-7000
http://www.sothebys.com

SOTHEBY'S ARCADE AUCTIONS
1334 York Avenue
New York, New York 10021
(212) 606-7409

SOUTH BAY AUCTIONS
485 Montauk Highway
Post Office Box 330
East Moriches, L.I., New York 11940
(516) 878-2909

CARL W. STINSON, INC.
293 Haverhill Street
Reading, Massachusetts 01867
(617) 944-6488

SWANN GALLERIES, INC.
104 East 25th Street
New York, New York 10010
(212) 254-4710

KENNETH VAN BLARCOM
63 Eliot Street
South Natick, Massachusetts 01760
(508) 653-7017

WESCHLER'S
909 E Street, N.W.
Washington, D.C. 20004
(202) 628-1281

**GUSTAVE J.S. WHITE
AUCTIONEERS**
37 Bellevue Avenue
Newport, Rhode Island 02840
(401) 841-5780

JOHN WHITE
57 South Main Street
Middleboro, Massachusetts 02346
(508) 947-9281

WINTER ASSOCIATES
Box 823
21 Cooke Street
Plainville, Connecticut 06062-0288
(203) 793-0288

RICHARD W. WITHINGTON, INC.
Auctioneer & Appraiser
R.R. 2, Box 440
Hillsboro, New Hampshire 03244
(603) 464-3232

WOLF'S AUCTION GALLERY
1239 West 6th Street
Cleveland, Ohio 44113
(216) 575-9653

YOUNG FINE ARTS AUCTIONS, INC.
Post Office Box 313
North Berwick, Maine 03906
(207) 676-3104
http://www.maine.com/yfa

Appendix D: Indexing Guidelines ———————————

Guidelines for Listing Artists' Last Names

These fundamental rules are based on the *Anglo-American Cataloging Rules* revised in 1979 and published by the American Library Association.*

Try to ascertain how the artist signed his name, or the most common listing of the name, before turning to the general rules.

> *Ex.* The famous American cartoonist Al Capp is listed "CAPP, Al," and not by his given name, Alfred Gerald Caplin.

English — Names are listed under the prefix.

> *Ex.* DECAMP, Joseph Rodefer

Dutch — The listing is under the part of the name that follows the prefix unless the prefix is "ver."

> *Ex.* GOGH, Vincent van

French — Look under the prefix if it is an article (le, la, les) or a contraction of an article and a preposition (du, des, de le, del).

> *Ex.* LE SIDANER, Henri

> If the article and preposition are separate words, look under the part of the name following the preposition.

> *Ex.* LA PAGE, Raymond de

German — If the prefix is an article or a contraction of an article and a preposition, look under the prefix (Am, Aus'm, Von, Zum, Zur). Otherwise, look under the name following the prefix.

> *Ex.* SCHWIND, Moritz Ludwig von

Italian — Modern names are cataloged under the prefix.

> *Ex.* DEL LUNGO, Isidoro

> Medieval names are listed under the name that follows the prefix.

> *Ex.* ROBBIA, Luca della

Spanish — If the prefix is an article only, look under the article.

> *Ex.* LAS HERAS, Manuel Antonio

> Look for other Spanish names under the part following the prefix (de, del, de las).

Exceptions — There are exceptions to every rule. If you can't find a name where you think it should be, look under the variants.

> *Ex.* MEYER VON BREMEN, George

* Indexes of names in books published prior to 1979 may not conform to these rules.

Appendix E: Classification Index ────────

For the purpose of this price guide, it was necessary to divide all works of art into one of three categories—paintings, drawings, and sculpture. When defining categories, the media *and* the support were considered. Examples of the media by category are listed below.

PAINTINGS

acrylic on canvas
acrylic on paper
acrylic, oil, India ink, and graphite on canvas
aquatec
casein
en grisaille on board
distemper
dry-brush
enamel
encaustic
epoxy
etched and painted
fresco
gesso
gold ground, oil on panel
leimfarbe
mirrored glass
monoprint
oil on canvas
oil on board
oil on copper
oil on masonite
oil on paper
oil on panel
oil on wood
oil on paper laid down
oil and sand
polyvinyl emulsion
poster acrylic
sand painting
tempera on paper
tempera on canvas
tempera on panel
tempera on artistboard
tempera on canvas board
velum
Verre eglomise

DRAWINGS

acrylic and charcoal on paper
assemblage
bistre
body color on vellum
brush and ink
casein on paper
chalk
charcoal
collage
colored graphite
conte crayon
crayon
drawing
gouache on canvas
gouache on paper
gouache on vellum
gouache on panel/ artist board/canvas board
mixed media
mixed media on paper
oil and pencil
oil stick on paper
oil crayon on paper
pastel
pen and ink
photography collage
pochoir
sanguine
sepia ink
tissue collage on paper
wash
watercolor
watercolor on canvas

SCULPTURE

anything 2- or 3-dimensional
anything listed as "cast from a model by"
bas relief
bronze
construction
Cornell boxes
Earthworks
ivory relief
lacquered wood
marble
mosaic tile
plaster
polyester resin
steatite
steel
terracotta
wood

Appendix F: List of Illustrations*

---

* Italicized page numbers refer to artwork in the color insert.

Permissions

The author would like to thank the following for use of photographs (works are listed in the order in which they appear in the book):

Photograph of the Brimfield flea market, courtesy of Susan Theran; Photograph of the Atlantic City Convention Center flea market, courtesy "Atlantique City"; *Full Length Portrait of Young Woman in White Dress*, courtesy of Gustave White Auctioneers; A. Neleson portraits, courtesy of Peter Williams Museum Services; *Shot Red Marilyn*, courtesy of Christie's New York; *Man Seated with Pipe*, courtesy Butterfield & Butterfield; *Age of Sputnik*, courtesy Butterfield & Butterfield; *Portrait of Alison Davison*, courtesy Christie's New York; *Sortie du Conservatoire*, courtesy William Doyle Galleries; *Willow Tree*, courtesy Freeman/Fine Arts Company; *Unstringing Tobacco Leaves*, courtesy Christie's New York; *Relief Bronze*, copyright © 1994 Sotheby's, Inc.; *Portrait of a Young Girl with Flowers*, courtesy Royal York Auction Gallery; *Ship in Harbor*, courtesy Frank C. Kaminski Co.; *Le Baiser*, courtesy Christie'sNew York; *Two Black Women on the Road to Covington*, courtesy Neal Auction Company, Inc.; *Peasants Traveling the Hills Above Rome*, courtesy William Bunch Auction; *Essex Shipyard*, courtesy Skinner, Inc.; *Cape Mudge Totem Poles*, courtesy Weschler's; *Ikebana*, copyright © 1995 Sotheby's, Inc.; *Among the Hollyhocks*, courtesy James D. Julia Inc.; *Portrait of William B. Chamberlain*, courtesy Caddigan Auctioneers; *Portrait of a Young Girl*, courtesy Bakker's; *Monumental Woman*, copyright © 1994 Sotheby's, Inc., *Violets in a Glass Vase*, courtesy Butterfield & Butterfield; *Young Girl with Life Preserver*, courtesy Illustration House, Inc.; *Madame Butterfly*, courtesy O'Gallerie, Inc.; *The Basilica*, courtesy Kenneth W. Van Blarcom; *The End of the Trail*, courtesy Altermann & Morris Galleries; *Boy and Bear*, courtesy Frank H. Boos Gallery; *Abraham Lincoln*, courtesy Leslie Hindman Auctioneers; *Black Gloves*, courtesy Louisiana Auction Exchange, Inc.; *Chaise*, courtesy Christie's New York; *Children Roasting Apples by Fireplace with Kitty*, courtesy Clearing House Auction Galleries; *Flora and Zephyr* and *Cupid and Psyche*, courtesy Butterfield & Butterfield; *Stampede*, courtesy Selkirk's; *Exotic Dancer*, courtesy Skinner, Inc.; *Still Life with Raspberries*, courtesy Bakker's; *Two Women Chatting in a Garden with a Mill in the Background*, courtesy Dargate Auction Galleries; *A Cup of Tea*, courtesy Hanzel Galleries, Inc.; *Dutch Winter Landscape of House with People*, courtesy Willis Henry Auctions; *Fishing Boat at Eastport, Maine*, courtesy Skinner, Inc.; *At the Wedding*, courtesy Bider's; *Harness Shop, York Street, Ottawa*, courtesy D & J Ritchie Inc.; *Still Life with Vase, Fruit and Nuts* courtesy Eric Nathan Auction Co., Inc.; *Arabian Sentry on Horseback*, courtesy Myers; *Still Life—Beef and Cabbage*, courtesy Skinner, Inc.; *The Repertoire*, courtesy Frank H. Boos Gallery; *Landing a Heavy Salmon*, courtesy Mapes; *Panoramic View of a Lake in Autumn*, courtesy Grogan & Company; *Sleigh Heading for the Mill*, courtesy Alderfer's; *Shorty Shoeing Silver*, courtesy John Moran Auctioneers, Inc.; *View of Nannau Hall, Cardiganshire, Wales*, courtesy William Doyle Galleries; *The Red Bridge, Montgomery*, Vermont, courtesy Young Fine Arts Auctions, Inc.; *Early Spring*, courtesy Morton M. Goldberg; *Reclining Nude on a Sofa*, courtesy Swann Galleries, Inc.; *American Pattern*, courtesy William Doyle Galleries; *Man's Best Friend II, Portrait of a Hunter*, courtesy Barridoff Galleries; *Reverie*, courtesy Skinner, Inc.; *Prince Choosing His Bride*, courtesy Garth's Auctions; *Snow Cloud Heights*, courtesy John Moran Auctioneers, Inc.;

917